THE
SPIRITUAL
LIFE

April 15, 2001

THE SPIRITUAL LIFE

A TREATISE ON
ASCETICAL AND MYSTICAL THEOLOGY

By

The Very Reverend
ADOLPHE TANQUEREY, S.S., D.D.
(1854-1932)

Translated by
THE REV. HERMAN BRANDERIS, S.S., A.M.
(1893-1963)

SECOND AND REVISED EDITION

TAN BOOKS AND PUBLISHERS, INC.
Rockford, Illinois 61105

Nihil Obstat: A. Vieban, S.S.
              Censor Deputatus

Imprimatur: ✠ Michael J. Curley
             Archbishop of Baltimore
             Baltimore
             May 24, 1930

Published in approximately 1930 by Desclee & Co., Tournai. Also published in 1930 by St. Mary's Seminary, Baltimore. Re-published by photographic reproduction in 2000 by TAN Books and Publishers, Inc. by arrangement with Gedit Editions S.A.

ISBN 0-89555-659-6

Library of Congress Control No.: 00-131540

Printed and bound in the United States of America.

TAN BOOKS AND PUBLISHERS, INC.
P.O. Box 424
Rockford, Illinois 61105
2000

The author humbly dedicates this book
to the Word Incarnate
and to His Blessed Mother, Seat of Wisdom,
happy indeed to contribute in some way
to the glory of the
Most Holy and Adorable Trinity.

*Ut in omnibus honorificetur Deus
per Jesum Christum.*

— AD. TANQUEREY
Issy, France
Feast of the Annunciation, 1923

FOREWORD

BY HIS EXCELLENCY

THE MOST REVEREND MICHAEL J. CURLEY, D. D.

ARCHBISHOP OF BALTIMORE.

The many American priests who studied under Father Tanquerey at St. Mary's Seminary, Baltimore, will welcome this English translation of his treatise on Ascetical and Mystical Theology. After the lapse of more than a quarter of a century they take pride in recalling that Father Tanquerey published the first volumes of his Dogmatic Theology while he was their teacher. Always perfectly clear, and eminently practical, he had in a marked degree the gift of arousing interest and obtaining the co-operation of his students. These qualities have made his text-books of Dogma and Moral popular in seminaries and among the clergy all over the world. In this field Father Tanquerey had many models; the general outline, the questions treated and the method of procedure had been determined long before. Among our many excellent text-books there can be now but accidental differences.

It is quite otherwise with Asceticism, the science of the spiritual life. There are indeed innumerable books, ancient and modern, on spirituality, but most of them were written less for instruction than for edification. Very few of them can be looked upon as text-books covering the whole field and in a methodical way. As a theological science, Asceticism is far behind either Dogma or Moral. Father Tanquerey then appears as one of the pioneers. In his treatise of 800 pages he has a complete and orderly summary of all the questions of the spiritual life. Nearly one fourth of the work is devoted to the fundamental doctrines of the elevation and the fall of man and his redemption through the grace merited by Christ. These first pages constitute a brief review of Dogma from a pratical, devotional point of view, and lay a solid foundation for the study of Christian perfection.

Father Tanquerey's book can be used and is indeed being used as a text-book; but it can be made to serve as well as a devotional treatise for spiritual reading, since it avoids in great measure the stiffness and dryness of the text-book style. In this work as in his other writings Father Tan-

querey is what he was in his class-room at St. Mary's
Seminary: clear, lively, and practical, careful to avoid
extreme views and to reduce controversies to their proper
place.

A mere glance at the table of contents and the alphabetical index will convince priests that they can find in this
book an outline for sermons on many important subjects as
well as material for their own meditations or for conferences
or even a complete retreat to Religious.

Although the treatise was composed chiefly for priests
and seminarians, it has also obtained wide circulation in
religious communities and among the faithful who are
striving to live a devout life in the world and are looking
for a guide to point the way to an enlightened and well-
balanced piety.

✠ MICHAEL J. CURLEY
Archbishop of Baltimore

AUTHOR'S PREFACE

This is not an exhaustive treatise on the spiritual life, but rather an outline which may serve as the basis for deeper study. However, in order to avoid the dryness of a mere outline it was deemed necessary to develop the most important points of the spiritual life, such as, the indwelling of the Holy Ghost in the soul, our incorporation into Christ, the rôle of the Blessed Virgin in our sanctification, the nature of Christian perfection and the duty of striving after it. For the same reason the essential characteristics of the Three Ways are stressed in the Second Part of this treatise.

It is the writer's conviction that Dogma is the foundation of Ascetical Theology and that an exposition of what God has done and still does for us is the most efficacious motive of true devotion. Hence, care has been taken to recall briefly the truths of faith on which the spiritual life rests. This treatise then is first of all doctrinal in character and aims at bringing out the fact that Christian perfection is the logical outcome of dogma, especially of the central dogma of the Incarnation. The work however is also practical, for a vivid realization of the truths of faith is the strongest incentive to earnest and steady efforts towards the correction of faults and the practice of virtues. Consequently in the first part of this treatise the practical conclusions that naturally flow from revealed truths and the general means of perfection are developed. The second part contains a more detailed exposition of the special means of advancing along the Three Ways towards the heights of perfection.

This book has been written chiefly for seminarians and priests. It is the writer's hope however that it may also prove useful to Religious and even to such of the laity as are seeking to live a thoroughly Christian life and thus fit themselves for the lay-apostolate.

The author has developed first and foremost the teachings commonly received in the Church and has given but little space to disputed questions. There are of course various Schools of spirituality, but the more discriminating writers in all of them are of one mind on all that is of real importance for the direction of souls. It is such teachings as these that the author has tried to expose in logical and psychological order.

If at times the writer shows a certain preference for the spirituality of the French School of the seventeenth century, a spirituality based on the writings of St. Paul and St. John and in complete accord with the doctrines of St. Thomas, he professes nevertheless a sincere esteem for all the other Schools, borrows largely from them and strives to stress the points of agreement rather than the points of difference.

The author humbly dedicates this book to the Word Incarnate and to His Blessed Mother, Seat of Wisdom, happy indeed to contribute in some way to the glory of the Most Holy and Adorable Trinity.

Ut in omnibus honorificetur Deus
per Jesum Christum

AD. TANQUEREY

Issy, France, the Feast of the Annunciation, 1923.

TABLE OF CONTENTS.

Bibliography.

Introduction.

PART FIRST : Principles.

PART SECOND : The three ways

PRELIMINARY REMARKS

BOOK TWO : Progress in Christian virtues, or, the illuminative way.

Introduction.

APPENDICES

BIBLIOGRAPHY

The authors consulted are listed in their *chronological* instead of alphabetical order. They are further arranged methodically and, beginning with the Middle Ages, grouped according to schools of mysticism. This was thought of greater service for the reader. Only the most important authors are mentioned. For a complete survey of the field see Rev. P. POURRAT : *Christian Spirituality*, E. tr. Mitchell and Jacques, 4 vols. New York, 1922-1930. Works of non-Catholics should only be read with required permission and due caution.

I. — THE PATRISTIC AGE

During the age of the Fathers the elements of a theory of spiritual life come progressively to light and mature into a valuable body of teaching with the work of *Cassian* in the West and that of *St. John Climacus* in the East.

1. THE FIRST THREE CENTURIES.

St. Clement of Rome, *Epistle to the Corinthians*, written c. 95 to restore peace in the church of Corinth. Gr.-Lat. : *P. G.* i [1]; Gebhardt and Harnack : *Patr. Apost.* i, Leipzig, 1876, edit. min. 1877; Funk : *Patr. Ap.* i. Tübingen, 1890. Gr.-Eng : J. B. Lightfoot : *St. Clement of Rome*, 2 vols. 2d edit. London, 1890, the best text and discussion; K. Lake : *Apostolic Fathers*, i (in Loeb Clas. Lib.) New York : Putnam. Eng. tr. A. C. Coxe in *ANF*. i; A. Menzies in *ANF*. ix [2]; H. E. Hall in *Christian Classics*, Lond. R. T. S.; J. A. F. Gregg in *Early Church Classics*, Lond. S. P. C. K.; W. Burton in *Ancient and Modern Library of Theological Literature*, London : Griffith.

Hermas, *The Shepherd* (140-155), in which are described at length the conditions for true penance. Gr.-Lat. *PG.* ii. 891-1012; Gebhardt, Harnack and Zahn : *Patr. Apost.*, iii. 1-272; Funk : *Patr. Apost.*, i. 334-563; a more recent edition of the Greek text according to the Cod. Petropolit. was given out by K. Lake, Oxford, 1911. Gr.-Eng. K. Lake : *Apostolic Fathers* ii, in Loeb Clas. Lib. Eng. tr. F. Crombie in *ANF.*, ii; W. Burton : *Apost. Fathers*, pt. I, in *Anc. and Mod. Lib. of Theo. lit.*, London : Griffith; C. Taylor : *The Shepherd of Hermas*, 2 vols. in *Early Church Classics*, London : S. P. C. K.

Clement of Alexandria, *The Instructor (Pædagogus)*, written after 195, describes the spiritual progress of a true gnostic. The best Greek text is that of O. Stählin : *Clemens Alexandrinus*, i. 89-292, Leipzig, 1903. Gr.-Lat. *PG.* ix. 247-794, reproduces with additions the Oxford edition of 1715. Eng. tr. W. Wilson in *ANF*. ii. 209-298; P. M. Barnard in *Early Church Classics*, London : S. P. C. K., 1901; R. Ornsby (selections) in *The Month*, xix 1873; cf. E. G. Sihler : *From Augustus to Augustine*, Cambridge, 1923.

St. Cyprian, (200-258), *De habitu virginum*, *De dominica oratione*, *De opere et eleemosynis*, *De bono patientiæ*, *De zelo et livore*, *De lapsis*. PL. iv [3];

---

[1] Migne, edr., *Patrologiæ Cursus Completus, Series Græca*, 161 quarto volumes, Paris, 1857-1866. The *Series græca prior* contains the works of the Fathers and Ecclesiastical writers down to Photius (c. 867). The *Series posterior*, down to Cardinal Bessarion (d. 1472.)

[2] *Ante-Nicene Fathers*, the Edinburgh Edition text edited by Drs. Roberts and Donaldson, Chronologically arranged with Notes and Historical Prefaces, by Rt. Rev. A. Cleveland Coxe, D. D., Supplemented with General Index and Bibliographical Synopsis, and a new volume containing manuscripts discovered since the completion of the Ante Nicene Library. Edited by A. Menzies. 10 vols., New York : Scribners, 1926.

[3] Migne, edr., *Patrologiæ Cursus Completus, Series Latina*, 221 quarto vols., Paris, 1844-55, and 1865-66 for the last four volumes containing the index tables. The *Series prior* goes as far as St. Gregory the Great (d. 604). The *Series posterior*, as far as Pope Innocent III (d. 1216).

Hurter : *SS. Pat. Opusc. select.*, i; the best text is that of W. Hartel : *S. Thasci Cæcilii Cypriani opera omnia*, 3 vols., Vienna, 1868-71. Eng. tr. J. H. Newman, Oxford, 1839 in *LF.* [1]; E. Wallis in *ANF.*, v; T. N. Bindley : *St. Cyprian on the Lord's Prayer*, London : S. P. C. K.

2. — THE FOURTH TO THE SEVENTH CENTURY

A) *In the West :*

St. Ambrose, (333-397), *De officiis ministrorum, De virginibus, De viduis, De virginitate. PL.* xvi. 25-302, reprints the editions of J. du Frische and N. Le Nourry, first issued, Paris, 1686-90; J. G. Krabinger has edited separately the *De officiis ministrorum*, Tübingen, 1857. Eng. tr. Rev. H. De Romestin : *Some of the principal works of St. Ambrose*, in *NPNF.* 2d series vol. x, New York, 1896 [2].

St. Augustine, (354-430), *Confessiones, Soliloquia, De doctrina christiana, De civitate Dei, Epistola ccxi*, etc. St. Augustine's works contain the elements of a complete theology of asceticism and mysticism. His teaching supplements and corrects that of Cassian. For an exposition of it see Pourrat, *op. cit.* I, c. viii. The Latin text of the works listed above is found in *PL.* xxxii, xxiv, xli, reprinting the Maurists Blampin and Constant. A better text is given by the *Corpus Script. Eccles. Latin.*, Vienna : *Confessionum libri xiii* ed. P. Knöll, 1896; *Epistolæ* xxxi-cxxxiii, ed. A. Goldbacher, 1898 ; *De civitate Dei*, ed. E. Hoffmann, 1900. Also, *The Confessions of St. Augustine* ed. J. Gibb and W. Montgomery, *(Cambridge Patristic Texts)* 1908, 2d edit. 1927; *De civitate Dei*, ed. J. E. C. Welldon, 2 vols., London : Macmillan, 1924; *De doctrina christiana*, St. Louis : Concordia Publish. House; *Soliloquiorum libri ii*, ed. P. E. Tourscher, Phila : Reilly, 1922. *Confessions* ed. and tr. by W. Watts (Loeb Clas. Lib.) New York : Putnam, 1912; Eng. tr. in *NPNF.* 1st Series : *Confessions* by J. G. Pilkington and *Letters* by J. G. Cunningham, vol. i, *City of God* and *Christian Doctrine* by M. Dods and J. F. Shaw, vol. ii, *Soliloquies* by C. C. Starbuck, vol. vii, 219-593. Also, *Confessions* tr. W. Hutchings, London : Longmans, 1883; C. Bigg *(Library of Devotion)* London : Methuen; J. Healy *(Temple Classics)* New York : Dutton, 1903; E. B. Pusey (in *LF.* i, and *Everyman's Lib.*) New York : Dutton, 1907; Tobie Matthew revised by Dom R. Huddleston, New York : Benziger; *City of God*, tr. Healy *(Temple Classics)* 1903; F. R. M. Hitchcock *(Early Church Classics)* London : S. P. C. K.; M. Dods, New York, Benziger; *Letters*, tr. W. J. Sparrow Simpson *(Handbooks of Christian Lit.)* London : Macmillan, 1920; sel. and tr. Mary H. Allies, London : Burns and Oates, 1890. cf. also, Mary H. Allies : *Leaves from St. Augustine*, London : Washbourne, 1900; E. L. Cutts : *St. Augustine (Fathers for English Readers)* London : S. P. C. K. cf. Hewitt : *Studies in St. Augustine*, New York, 1868; E. C. Butler : *Western Mysticism*, New York; Dutton, 1923; A. Hatzfeld : *St. Augustine* (tr.) 3d ed. London : Burns Oates and Washbourne, 1924.

Cassian, (360-435), *Collationes xxiii* recens. M. Petschenig, Vienna, 1886; *De institutis cœnobiorum et de octo principalium vitiorum remediis libri xii. — De Incarnatione Domini contra Nestorium libri vii* recens. M. Petschenig, Vienna, 1888. The older and less critical edition by Gazet is found in *PL.* xlix-l. The works of John Cassian tr. by E. S. S. Gibson in *NPNF.* 2d Series vol. xi. Cassian's Conferences sum up the spiritual doctrine of the first four centuries as practiced in monasteries, and they became a storehouse from which all subsequent writers on spiritual life have drawn.

---

[1] Pusey, Keble, Newman et al., *A Library of the Fathers of the Holy Catholic Church*, 47 vols., Oxford : Parker, 1838-1880.

[2] *Nicene and Post-Nicene Fathers of the Christian Church*, 28 vols. New York : Scribners 1886-1898. First Series edited by the late Philip Schaff. Second Series edited by the late Philip Schaff and Henry Wave.

Dominican Contemplatives, by a Dominican of Carisbrooke, with Preface by V. Rev. BEDE JARRETT, O. P., London : Burns Oates and Washbourne.

St. Leo I, the Great, Pope 440-461, *Sermones.* The discourses of St. Leo for the principal feasts of the year are full of piety. The Church has borrowed from them for her liturgy; 96 of the *sermones* current under his name are genuine. Quesnel's edition, Paris, 1675, improved by P. and G. Ballerini, Venice, 1753-57, is reprinted in *PL.* liv. 158-458. Hurter : *SS. Pat. opusc. sel.* xiv, xxv, xxvi. Eng. tr. by Charles L. Feltoe in *NPNF.* 2d Ser. xii. cf. C. Gore ; *Leo the Great (Fathers for English Readers)* London : S. P. C. K.

St. Benedict of Nursia, (480-543). His rule, brought from 66 to 73 chapters in its 2d edition, has become that of almost all the monks in the West from the 8th to the 13th century. It can be easily adapted to the conditions of any country and time and this is the key to its great success. The text of the Regula is available in *L.* lxvi, 215-932; better editions are those of E. Wölfflin : *Benedicti regula monachorum,* Leipzig, 1895; Dom O. Hunter Blair (with tr. and notes) London : Sands, 1906, 2d ed. St. Louis : Herder, 1907; Abbot C. Butler, London : Herder, 1912. Eng. tr. London, 1886 and 1896 in Thatcher and McNeal, *Source Book,* pp. 432-485; in Henderson, *Documents,* pp. 274-313; by D. O. H. Blair, cf. above; Rt. Rev. Paul Delatte, *The Rule of St. Benedict : A Commentary,* London : Burns Oates and Washbourne. New York : Benziger, 1921; *The Rule of St. Benedict* translated with an introduction by Cardinal Gasquet, Oxford, 1925. Rt. Rev. Ildephonsus Herwegen, O. S. B. : *St. Benedict, A character study,* translated by Dom Peter Nugent, O. S. B. London : Sands and Co., 1924.

St. Gregory I, the Great, Pope, (540-604), *Expositio in Librum Job, sive Moralium libri xxxv, Liber regulæ pastoralis curæ, Dialogorum libri IV.* The edition of the Maurist Sainte-Marthe, Paris 1705, reprinted with additions by J. B. Gallicioli, Venice, 1768-76 is reprinted in *PL.* lxxv-lxxvii. The Dialogues have been often separately edited, particularly the 2nd Book on the Life and Miracles of St. Benedict. The Pastoral Rule also, cf. ed. Westhoff, Münster, 1860; Hurter S. J. in *SS. Pat. opusc. sel.* xx; A. M. Michelletti, Tournai, 1904; B. Sauter, Freiburg, 1904; Rt. Rev. J. C. Hedley : *Lex Levitarum,* New York : Benziger, 1905, St. Louis : Herder, with the *Regula pastoralis* of St. Gregory the Great. Bishop Hedley's work is a set of lectures adapting the work of St. Gregory to the needs of our time. Eng. tr. *The Morals of the Books of Job* in three volumes in *LF.* Oxford, 1844-50. King Alfred's West Saxon version of Gregory's Pastoral Care ed. H. Sweet, London, 1871 ; *The Book of Pastoral Care* tr. J. Barmby in *NPNF.* 2d Series xii. An old English tr. of the *Dialogues* by J. W., Paris, 1608, was reprinted by H. Coleridge, S. J., London, 1874, and more recently reedited by E. G. Gardner with annotations by G. F. Hill, London : Macmillan, 1911. cf. Rt. Rev. Abbot Snow, O. S. B., *St. Gregory the Great : His Work and His Spirit,* 2d edition, London : Burns Oates and Washbourne, 1926.

B) *In the East :*

St. Athanasius, (297-373), *Life of St. Anthony* gives an account of the spiritual doctrine of the great organizer of Egyptian monasticism. *PG.* xxvii. 838-976 reprints the edition of N. A. Giustiniani, Padua, 1777, based on that of the Maurists J. Lepin and B. de Montfaucon, Paris, 1627. Handy edition of the Greek by Maunoury, Paris, 1887 and 1890. The credibility of the work attacked by Weingarten : *Der Ursprung des Monachtums im nachconstantinischen Zeitalter,* Gotha, 1877 was defended by A. Eichhorn : *Athanasii de vita ascetica testimonia collecta* (inaug.-diss.) Halle, 1886; Mayer in *Der Katholik,* 1886, I. 495-516, 619-636, II. 72-86; Dom C. Butler : *The Lausiac History of Palladius* I, Text and Studies, Cambridge, 1898. Eng. tr. T. W. Allies in *Monastic Life* (vol. vii of *Formation of Christendom*) London, 1869-96; H. Ellershaw in *NPNF.* 2d Series iv. 188-221 ; J. B. McLaughlin : *St. Anthony the Hermit,* London : Burns, Oates and Washbourne, New York, Benziger, 1924.

St. Cyril of Jerusalem, (315-386), in his *Catechetical Lectures* portrays the life of a true Christian. *PG.* xxxiii reprints the ed. of the Maurist A. A. Touttée, Paris, 1720. A better edition is that of W. K. Reischl and J. Rupp 2 vols., Munich, 1848 and 1860. Eng. tr. J. H. Newman in *LF.* ii, Oxford,

1838; H. de Romestin : *Mysteries and other Sacramental Lectures* (the five catecheses on the Sacraments); E. H. Gifford in *NPNF*. 2d Series vii. 1-157. •

St. **Basil** the Great, (330-379), describes in his book *On the Holy Ghost* the workings of the Holy Spirit in a regenerated soul, and in his two works on the rules of monastic life, the fundamentals of asceticism. The 55 longer rules, *Rules at length* (Horoi kata platos) set forth the principles. The 313 shorter rules, *Rules in abridgement* (Horoi kat' epitomen), their application to the daily life of a monk. These rules were universally received in the East and have survived to this day in the Greek Church. The best ed. of the works of St. Basil is still that of the Maurist J. Garnier, Paris, 1721 and 1730 in three vols., the last of them issued after the editor's death by his colleague P. Maran. An excellent critical ed. of the treatise *On the Holy Ghost* is that of C. F. H. Johnston, Oxford : Parker, 1892. A Latin version of the work is found in Hurter : *SS. Pat. opusc. sel.* xxxi. Eng. tr. G. Lewis : *Treatise on the Holy Spirit*, London, 1888; B. Jackson : *The Book on the Holy Spirit* in *NPNF*. 2d Series viii. 1-50; E. F. Morison : *St. Basil and his Rule*, Oxford, 1913; W. K. L. Clarke : *St. Basil's Ascetical Works*, London : Macmillan, 1925.

St. **John Chrysostom**, (344-407), has left in his *Homilies* a vast storehouse of materials on both ethics and ascetics, and in his tract *On the Priesthood*, a stirring praise of the sacerdotal dignity. *PG.* xlviii-lxiv reproduces B. de Montfaucon's edition, Paris, 1718-38, except for the *Homilies on St. Matthew* for which the text edited by Field, Cambridge, 1839, is given. J. A. Nairn, (Cambridge Patristic Texts) 1906, has brought out a separate edition of the tract *On the Priesthood*. Eng. tr. of the *Homilies* iv-vii, ix, xi-xii, xiv-xv, xxvii-xxviii, Oxford, 1842-52; in *NPNF*. 1st Series ix-xiv, New York, 1903-1906. *On the Priesthood* tr. B. H. Cowpers, Lond. 1866; W. R. W. Stephens in *NPNF*. New-York, 1903; P. Boyle, C. M., New York : Benziger, 1903; T. A. Moxon *(Early Church Classics)* London : S. P. C. K. 1907. Selections by Mary A. Allies : *Leaves from Chrysostom*, London : Burns and Oates, 1889. cf. A. Puech, *St. John Chrysostom* (tr.) 2d. edn. London : Washbourne, 1917.

St. **Cyril of Alexandria**, († 444), *Book of Treasures on the Holy and Consubstantial Trinity*, his chief work on the subject, studies the relations of the soul to the Trinity. *PG.* lxxv reprints Canon J. Aubert's ed. Paris, 1638, with Latin version by B. Vulcain, Basle, 1676. Cardinal Pitra has edited fragments of the work in *Analecta Sacra and Classica*, Paris, 1888. While St. Cyril's works have received a great deal of attention on the part of modern scholars (cf. Bardenhewer-Shahan : *Patrology*, p. 367-368) this book has not been the object of recent study, nor has it been translated into English.

Pseudo-Dionysius Areopagita, (c. 500), *On the Divine Names, Ecclesiastical Hierarchy, Mystical Theology*, has influenced considerably later writers on the subject. The best complete edition of his works is that of B. Cordier, S. J., Antwerp, 1634, often reprinted. It is reproduced from the Venice edition of 1755-56 in *PG.* iii-iv. It is based on only some of the numerous Greek mss. and makes no account of the Syriac, Armenian, and Arabic versions. A great deal remains to do for the criticism of the text. A separate edition of the Greek of the *Ecclesiastical Hierarchy* was issued by J. Parker, London, 1899. J. Parker's translation of the works of Dionysius, London, 1897, is trustworthy. cf. A. B. Sharpe : *Mysticism, its true Nature and Values*, London : Sands and Co., St. Louis : Herder, 1910.

St. **John Climacus**, († 649), *Ladder to Paradise*. *PG.* lxxxviii. 632-1164, reprints the *editio princeps* of the famous work by M. Rader, Paris, 1633. A more recent edition of the Greek is that of Sophronios Eremites, Constantinople, 1883. John the Scholastic or the Sinaite owes his surname Climacus to his book (Klimax) which contains a summary of ascetical and mystical theology. This work gained as much popularity in the East as Cassian's *Institutes* in the West, and remained for centuries a classic on the subject of spiritual life.

St. **Maximus Confessor**, (580-662), also known as the Theologian, or Maximus of Constantinople, developed the teaching of Pseudo-Dionysius on contemplation, but threw greater light on the part played in spiritual life by the sacred humanity of the Savior, our leader and model. His *Scholia on Dionysius* are reprinted in *PG.*, iv, from the Venice edition of the works of the Pseudo-Areopagite. His *Treatise on Asceticism*, *PG.* xc. 912-956, in the form of a dialogue between an abbot and a young monk, and his *Mystagogia*, *PG.* xci. 657-717, a series of considerations on the symbolism of the Church and her liturgy, are reprinted from the edition of Fr. Combefis, O. P., Paris, 1675. The doctrine of St. Maximus is discussed by H. Weser : *S. Maximi Confessoris præcepta de Incarnatione Dei et deificatione hominis*, Berlin, 1869; A. Preuss : *Ad Maximi Conf. de Deo hominisque deificatione adnotationes*, Schneeberg, 1894; E. Michaud : *St. Maxime le Confesseur et l'apocatastase*, in *Revue internationale de Théologie*, 1902, pp. 257-272.

The writers of the 8th and 9th centuries need not be mentioned. They contribute no element of importance to our subject.

II — THE MIDDLE AGES.

We shall indicate only the most noted writers of the principal schools of mysticism.

I. THE BENEDICTINE SCHOOL : —

In the Abbey of Bec, in Normandy : **St. Anselm,** (b. 1033, Archbishop of Canterbury 1089, d. 1109), one of the most attractive writers of the Middle Ages. His *Meditations* and *Prayers* are full of unction and doctrine, *Liber Meditationum et Orationum*, *PL.* clviii. 709-820, a reprint of the Venice, 1744, edition of St. Anselm's works by the Maurist G. Gerberon, first issued Paris, 1675, the best as yet. *Orationes*, *PL.* clviii. 855-1016. *Cur Deus homo.*, an important treatise replete with solid considerations on Christ's atonement, *PL.* clviii. 359-432, or the separate edition by A. F. Fritzsche, Zürich : Schultes, 1894. Eng. tr. *Meditations* and *Prayers* with pref. by Card. Manning, London, 1872. *Cur Deus Homo?* tr. by Prout, London, 1887; S. N. Deane, with introd. and bibliography, Chicago, 1903.

In the Abbey of Citeaux : **St. Bernard** of Clairvaux, (1090-1153), whose lofty piety and practical knowledge have deeply influenced the Middle Ages : *Sermones de tempore, de sanctis, de diversis, in Cantica Canticorum; De consideratione; Tr. de gradibus et humilitatis et superbiæ; Lib. de diligendo Deo*, ed. J. Mabillon, Paris, 1667, 1690, 1719. The 3d ed. is reprinted in *PL.* clxxxii-iv, and for the *Sermones de tempore, de sanctis, de diversis* in P. L. Janauchek : *Xenia Bernardina*, vol. i-ii, with variants from additional mss., and a bibliography of St. Bernard to the year 1890, vol. iii-iv, Vienna : Hölder, 1892. Selections from the *Sermones in Cantica Canticorum* ed. with notes by B. Blaxland; New York : Gorham. *De diligendo Deo* ed. with tr. and notes by E. G. Gardner; New York : Dutton, 1916; the same ed. W. W. Williams and *De gradibus et humilitatis et superbiæ* ed. B. E. W. Mills (Cambridge Patristic Texts) 1926. Eng. tr. S. J. Eales : *Life and Works of St. Bernard*, from the ed. of Mabillon, 4 vols. London, 1888-97 (contains letters and sermons only); *Sermons on the Canticle of Canticles*, tr. by a priest of Mount Melleray, 2 vols., Dublin : Browne and Nolan, 1920; *Sermons for Seasons and Principal Festivals of the Year*, id., 3 vols., ib. 1921-23-25. *De consideratione* tr, introd. and notes by G. Lewis, Oxford, 1908; by a Priest of Mount Melleray, Dublin : Browne and Nolan, 1921, St. Louis : Herder; *De diligendo Deo* tr. M. C. and M. Patmore, London : Paul, 1881; W. H. Van Allen, New York : Young, 1910. *Vitis Mystica : the True Vine* (tr.), London : Washbourne, 1884. *The Virgin Mother* (tr.), London, 1886. Cf. E. C. Butler : *Western Mysticism*, New York : Dutton, 1923; A. J. Luddy : *Life and Teaching of St. Bernard*, Dublin : M. H. Gill and Son, 1927. *Sermons on Advent and Christmas*, New York : Benziger; *Some Letters* selected by F. A. Gasquet, St. Louis : Herder, 1904.

In the Monastery of Rupertsberg, near Bingen : **St. Hildegarde**, Abbess, (1098-1179), whose voluminous works are in need of further criticism. Her revelations entitled *Scivias* (scire vias Domini vel lucis) first ed. by Lefèvre d'Etaples, Paris, 1513 are reprinted in *PL.* cxcvii. 383-738 from the edition of Cologne, 1628. Her *Liber divinorum operum simplicis hominis* first edited by J. Mansi (in Baluze : Miscell. ii. 337) Lucca, 1761 reprinted in *PL.* cxcvii. 739-1058, is a contemplation of all nature in the light of faith. Her *Liber vitæ meritorum*, first edited by Card. Pitra in *Analecta Sacra*, viii, Monte Cassino, 1882, is a picturesque description of Christian life.   cf. F. M. Steele : *Life and Visions of St. Hildegarde*, St. Louis, 1915.

In the Monastery of Hefta (or Helpede) near Eisleben, Saxony : **St. Gertrude** the Great, (1250-1302-1311), a simple nun, not to be confused with the Abbess Gertrude von Hackeborn, *The Herald of Divine Love.* The German original of the work is lost. There remains its Latin version first printed by the Carthusian Johann von Lansperg, Cologne, 1536. The best edition of the *Legatus divinæ pietatis* is that of the Benedictines of Solesmes in *Revelationes Gertrudianæ et Mechtildianæ*, Paris, 1875-77. Eng. tr. *Life and Revelations of St. Gertrude*, London : Burns and Oates, 1892, New York : Benziger; The characteristic of St. Gertrude's mysticism is devotion to the Sacred Heart. cf. Dom Gilbert Dolan : *St. Gertrude*, London : Sands and Co., St. Louis : Herder, 1913; *Love of the Sacred Heart illustrated by St. Gertrude*, New York : Benziger, 1921; *Exercises of St. Gertrude*, same publisher; L. J. M. Cros, S. J.; *The Heart of St. Gertrude*, same publisher.

St. Mechtilde (Matilda von Heckeborn-Wippra), a sister of the Abbess Gertrude von Hackeborn, and the teacher of St. Gertrude the Great, († 1298), *Book of Spiritual Grace*, shows the same concept of spiritual life and the same devotion to the Sacred Heart as her disciple, who took down, unknown to her at first, the revelations consigned in this book. The original German, *Das Buch geistlicher Gnade*, was first printed at Leipzig, 1503, and a Latin version of it at Würzburg, 1510 with the title *Speculum spiritualis gratiæ*. A critical edition of this version is found in the *Revelationes Gertrudianæ et Mechtildianæ*, already mentioned. cf. *Life of St. Mechtilde*, St. Louis : Herder, 1900.

St. Mechtilde (Matilda von Magdeburg) at first a Beguine in her native town, later a nun at Hefta, where she died in 1280, wrote down her revelations in Low German. They were translated into High German, then into Latin as *Sororis Mechtildis lux divinitatis fluens in corda veritatis*, and are found in the *Revelationes Gertrudianæ et Mechtildianæ*. The *Divine Light flowing into hearts without guile* is marked by the same characteristics as the revelations of the preceding saints. cf. *Love of the Sacred Heart* illustrated by St. Mechtilde with a foreword by the Lord Bishop of Salford, London : Burns and Oates, New York : Benziger, 1912; A. Kemp-Welch : *Six Mediæval Women*, London : Macmillan, 1913.

In the Monastery of Vadstena, Sweden, the mother house of the Order of Saint Savior or Brigittines founded by her, **St. Bridget**, (1302-1373), whose *Revelations* describe with great realism the life and particularly the passion of Christ. These revelations translated freely from the Swedish into Latin were first printed at Lübeck, 1492, from the official mss. preserved at Vadstena. The Roman edition of 1628 is considered the best. Heuser has published an abridged edition, *Revelationes selectæ*, Cologne, 1851. cf. F. G. Partridge : *Life of St. Bridget of Sweden*, London : Burns and Oates, 1888; F. M. Steele : *St. Bridget of Sweden*, New York : Benziger, 1910.

In the Monastery of Cassel, Palatinate, Germany : **John** of Cassel, 1410, *De adhærendo Deo, De lumine increato.* cf. Dom J. Huyben in *Vie Spirituelle*, Nov. 1922, p. 22 ss. Jan. 1923, p. 80 ss.

2. THE SCHOOL OF ST. VICTOR. This school of mysticism which developed among the Augustinian Canons of the Abbey of St. Victor near Paris made most correct use of Platonism. Its main representatives are :

Hugh of St. Victor, (1097-1141), the most influential theologian of the 12th century, who describes the progressive steps of the soul in the way to contemplation in his chief work *De sacramentis christianæ fidei*, on the mysteries of the Christian faith. Among his other spiritual treatises must be mentioned. :

De vanitate mundi, Soliloquium de arrha animæ, De laude caritatis, De amore sponsi ad sponsam, De meditando, etc. The Rouen, 1648, edition of his works is considerably better than the *editio princeps,* Paris, 1518, but is hardly satisfactory. cf. Haureau : *Hugues de St. Victor : nouvel examen de l'édition de ses œuvres,* Paris, 1859. The *Praise of Love* has been tr. by J. Mc Sorley, New York : Paulist Press; the *Explanation of the Rule of St. Augustine,* by A. Smith, St. Louis : Herder, 1911.

Richard of St. Victor, († 1173), *Benjamin minor, seu de animi præparatione ad contemplationem, Benjamin major, seu de gratia contemplationis, Expositio in Cantica Canticorum, PL.* cxcvi, are print of the best edition of his works by J. Bertelin, Rouen, 1650. cf. Von Hügel : *The Mystical element in Religion,* London, 1909.

Adam of St. Victor, the most important liturgical poet of the Middle Ages, († 1177), *Sequentiæ, PL.* cxcvi. 1421-1534, a reprint of L. Gauthier's ed., Paris, 1858. Eng. tr. D. S. Wrangham : *The Liturgical Poetry of Adam of St. Victor,* 3 vols., London, 1881. Julian : *Dict. of Hymnology,* New York, 1892.

3.—The DOMINICAN SCHOOL unites liturgical prayer and contemplation with the ministry of preaching, according to the maxim of its founder, " Contemplari et contemplata aliis tradere " [1].

St. Dominic, (1170-1221), the founder of the Dominican Order patterned his *Constitutions* after those of the Premonstratensian Canons. *Life of St. Dominic* by T. Alemany, New York : O'Shea, n. d. ; A. T. Drane, New York : Longmans, 1892 : B. Jarret London : Burns and Oates, New York : Benziger, 1924. J. Guiraud (Eng. tr.) London-New York, 1901 and 1925; Jordan of Saxony (his first biographer, new translation) Columbus, O., Aquinas College, 1926.

Albertus Magnus (Blessed Albert the Great, 1206-1280), for a time bishop of Ratisbon, no less zealous for piety than for scientific and theological studies, has left many writings touching upon spiritual life, *Commentarii in Dionysium Areopagitam, In quatuor libros sententiarum, Summa theologiæ, De sacrificio missæ.* His works were edited by P. Jammy, O. P., Lyons 1651, and A. Borgnet, Paris, 1890-99. Cf. P. de Loë, O. P., *De vita et scriptis B. Alberti Magni* in *Analecta Bollandiana* xix (1900) 257-316 xxi (1902) 301-371; J. Sighart (Eng. tr. by T. A. Dixon) : *Albert the Great, his life and scholastic labors,* London, 1876; Dougherty : *Albertus Magnus* in *Cath. World* xxxvii (1883) p. 197 ff; Hewit : *Albertus Magnus vindicated* in *Cath. World* xiii (1871) p. 712 ff. *The Paradise of the Soul : a Treatise on Virtues Suitable for Mental Prayer,* by Blessed Albert the Great, edited by Raymond Devas, O. P., London : Burns Oates and Washbourne [2].

St. Thomas Aquinas, the Angelic Doctor, (1225-1274), has treated excellently all the important questions of asceticism and mysticism in various parts of his works, but more especially in his *Summa theologica, Expositio omnium epistolarum D. Pauli, In Canticum Canticorum, In Evangelia, De perfectione vitæ spiritualis opusc.* etc. and *Officium de Corpore Christi,* which he prepared in 1254 for Pope Urban IV. Among the many editions of his works the Leonine edition, begun in Rome under the patronage of Pope Leo XIII in 1882 and

---

[1] See *Vie spirituelle* for Aug. 1921 ; the whole number is devoted to the ascetical and mystical teaching of the Dominican order. P. MANDONNET : *St. Dominique, l'idee, l'homme et l'œuvre,* 1921. Also, *Analecta Sacri Ordinis Prædicatorum,* Rome, 3 volumes in-folio, a review published by wish of the Master General of the Order.

[2] The little treatises, *On union with God* (De adhærendo Deo), and *The Paradise of the Soul* (Paradisus animæ), published under his name, (St. Louis : Herder), are not his, but works of the 14th or 15th centuries.

continued under the Master General of the Dominicans is no doubt the best, although somewhat unwieldy on account of its size. The texts relating to ascetical and mystical theology have been excerpted from St. Thomas' works and arranged in a logical order by Th. de Valgornera : *Mystica theologia D. Thomæ*, Barcelona, 1665, Turin, 1889 and 1911. For an account of St. Thomas see D. J. Kennedy in *Cath. Encycl.* xiv (select bibliography pp. 675-676); R. B. Vaughan, O. S. B., *Life and Labors of St. Thomas of Aquin*, London, 1872; Cavanaugh : *Life of St. Thomas Aquinas*, London, 1890; Conway : *St. Thomas Aquinas*, London-New York, 1911; A. Whitacre : *St. Thomas Aquinas*, St. Louis, 1925. Eng. tr. *The Summa theologica* by the Dominicans of the English Province in 21 vols. and Index, London-New York, 1911-25. Under the title " *Aquinas Ethicus* " Jos. Rickaby, S. J., transl. the 2nd part of it in 3 vols. London-New York, 1892. A *Compendium de Summa theologica* was published in English by B. Bonjoannes, revised by W. Lescher, New York : Benziger, 1908. Of the minor works of the great Doctor the following are translated : *Apology for Religious Orders*, New York : Benziger, 1902; *On the Lords's Prayer, On the Commandments* (both by H. A. Rawes) New York : Benziger ;. *Religious State, Episcopate and Priestly Office* (by J. Proctor) St. Louis : Herder, 1902; *On Prayer and Contemplative Life* (by H. Pope) New York : Benziger, 1914. Selections translated and adapted : *Devout Commentary on the Epistle to the Ephesians, drawn chiefly from the works of St. Thomas Aquinas*, by A. A. H. Wilberforce, St. Louis : Herder, 1902; *The Bread of Life, or St. Thomas Aquinas on the adorable Sacrament of the Altar arranged as meditations* by H. A. Rawes, New York : Benziger; *Jesus Christ, the Word Incarnate, gathered from St. Thomas Aquinas* by R. Fredt, transl. from the Ital. by F. J. Sullivan, St. Louis : Herder, 1904; *New Things and Old in Thomas Aquinas* transl. with introd. by H. C. Neill, New York : Dutton, 1909.

St. Vincent Ferrer, (1346-1419), *De vita spirituali*, a true masterpiece, a great favorite with St. Vincent de Paul. This little treatise was first printed at Magdeburg in 1493; it is found in the edition of the complete works of our Saint, Valencia, 1591, and in appendix to his *Sermons*, Augsburg, 1729. Separate editions, Mechlin, 1888; Paris, 1899 with French tr. by Rousset, O. P.; A. Pradel : *St. Vincent Ferrer, his Life, Spiritual Teaching, and Practical Devotion* (tr. from the French) London, 1875; Mary H. Allies, *Three Catholic Reformers of the 15th Century*, London, 1879; S. M. Hogan, *St. Vincent Ferrer*, London-New York : Longmans, 1911.

St. Catherine of Siena, (1347-1380), *The Dialogue*, exalts particularly the goodness of God who has created us, sanctifies us, and shows us his mercy even in the punishments He sends. Best edition of Complete Works G. Gigli, Siena, 1707-26, of the *Letters* N. Tomasso, Florence, 1880. Eng. tr. *The Dialogue* by A. Thorold, London : Paul, 1898 and 1907; the *Letters* with a brief introduction to each in V. D. Scudder, *St. Catherine of Siena as seen in her Letters*, London : Dent, New York : Dutton, 1905. *Life* by Bl. Raymond of Capua, her confessor, tr. from the French, St. Louis : Herder, New York : Kenedy; A. T. Drane, London-New York : Longmans, 1880, 4th ed. 1914; A. T. Pierson, New York : Funk and Wagnalls, 1898; M. Roberts, New-York : Putnam; E. L. Aymé, New York : Benziger; F. A. Forbes, St. Louis : Herder 1914; C. M. Anthony ed. by B. Jarrett, O. P., St. Louis : Herder; Edmund G. Gardner, London : Dent, 1907, New York : Dutton, 1908 (the most elaborate and critical Bibliography).

4.—THE FRANCISCAN SCHOOL, faithful to the spirit of its founder, is marked by a preference for affective spirituality, love of the Cross, and absolute poverty. For a more detailed bibliography of the Franciscan School see V. Mills, O. F. M., *Bibliography of Franciscan Ascetical Writers in Franciscan Educational Conference*, Washington, 1926, pp. 248-332.

St. Francis of Assisi, (1181-1226), *Opuscula*, ed. crit., Quarracchi (near Florence) 1904. Eng. tr. P. Robinson, O. F. M., *The Writings of St. Francis of Assisi newly translated*, Philadelphia : Dolphin Press, 1906, St. Louis : Herder. Oldest and weightiest sources for the Life of St. Francis : the two

Vitæ of Thomas of Celano (written 1228-9 and 1246-7) ed. Rosendale Lond. :
Dent, New-York : Dutton, 1904, E. d'Alençon, Rome, 1906, tr. A. C. Ferrer
Howell, London : Methuen, New-York : Dutton, 1908; *The Speculum perfec-
tionis of Leo of Assisi* (written 1227), ed. Sabatier; Paris, 1898, tr. S. Evans,
London, 1890, Countess de la Warr, ib. 1902, R. Steele (in *Temple Classics*)
ib. 1903, New-York : Dutton: the *Chronicon* of Jordan of Giano (written about
1262) ed. Böhmer, Paris, 1908; the *Legenda trium sociorum* (Leo, Rufinus,
and Angelus, written not later than 1270) ed. Faloci, Foligno, 1898, tr. Salter,
London, 1902; the *Sacrum commercium* (anonymous of the year 1227) ed.
E. d'Alençon, Rome, 1900, tr. M. Carmichael, Lond. 1901; the *Legendæ duæ*
by St. Bonaventure (written after 1260) ed. Quarracchi, 1898 tr. Salter *(Temple
Classics)* London : Dent, New-York : Dutton, 1904. The autobiography of
Salimbene (1221-1388) throws much light on St. Francis' times and indirectly
on his life and the first developments of his work. It was translated under the
title, *From Francis to Dante*, London : Nutt, 1906, 2d ed. 1907. Modern
lives by Catholic writers : L. Le Monnier (tr. from the French) London : Paul;
New-York : Benziger, 1894; J. Jörgensen (tr. from the Danish) London and
New-York : Longmans, 1912; Fr. Cuthbert, O. S. F. C., New edition,
London and New-York : Longmans 1921; Gilbert K. Chesterton, New-York :
Dutton, 1924. Cf. also J. Herkless : *Francis and Dominic and the Mendicant
Orders*, New-York : Scribners, 1901; Fr. Cuthbert : *St. Francis and Poverty*,
New-York : Benziger, 1910; id. *The Romanticism of St. Francis*, London-
New-York : Longmans, 1915; 2d edition 1924; D. H. S. Nicholson : *The
Mysticism of St. Francis*, Boston : Small Maynard and Co. 1923. A. Linne-
weber, O. F. M., *Asceticism and Mysticism of St. Francis of Assisi* (*Fran-
ciscan Educational Conference*, Washington, 1926, pp. 37-96); H. Felder :
The Ideals of St. Francis of Assisi (tr.), New-York : Benziger, 1926. For a
short bibliography of St. Francis cf. P. Robinson : *A Short Introduction to
Franciscan Literature*, New-York, 1907 and id. Art. *Francis of Assisi* in
Cath. Encycl. The spirit of St. Francis is well illustrated by the exquisite
compilation known as the *Little Flowers of St. Francis of Assisi*, Lat. original
ed. Sabatier; Paris, 1902, Italian version considered the best by Cesare, Verona,
1822, often reprinted and translated into other languages; there are several
Eng. tr. of the same v. g., T. A. Arnold, New-York : Stokes, 1926, T. Okey,
New-York : Dutton, 1919, the first English translalion (by Lady Georgina
Fullerton, published 1864) rev. with introduction by D. Devas, New-York :
Benziger, 1927 etc.

St. Bonaventure, (1221-1274), has devoted a comparatively small part of
his writings to mystical or ascetical theology. The many editions of his complete works are superseded by the critical edition of the Friars Minor,
Quarracchi, 1881-1902. His ascetical treatises are gathered in vol. viii. Among
them must be mentioned *Soliloquium, Lignum vitæ, Vitis mystica,* a work on
the Passion, *De perfectione vitæ,* a treatise on religious perfection, but especially *De triplici via,* the shortest and most complete summary of his mysticism, and doubtless the first systematic exposition of the famous distinction
between the three ways of the spiritual life: the purgative way, the illuminative
way, and the unitive way. This excellent work in also known as *Stimulus
amoris,* or *Incendium amoris.* His *Breviloquium,* one of the best expositions
of dogmatics, and his *Itinerarium mentis ad Deum,* a tract on theodicy, contain
also suggestive references to mystical theology. They are found, the former in
vol. v, and the latter in vol. vii of the Quarracchi edition. *The Soul's
Progress to God* is available in English in *Journal of Speculative Philosophy*
xxxi (1887). Other works in Eng. trns. *Stimulus divini amoris* tr. B. Lewis,
edited by Phillipson, New-York: Benziger, 1927; *De perfectione vitæ,* tr.
L. Costelloe edit. by Fr. Wilfrid, St. Louis: Herder, 1923; *Franciscan view
of the Spiritual and Religious Life,* being three treatises of Bl. Bonaventure tr.
by P. D. Devas, New-York: Benziger, 1920. On the *Life and Writings of
St. Bonaventure* see Ignatius Jeiler in vol. x of the Quarracchi edition. Also,
L. C. Skey, *Life of St. Bonaventure,* London, 1889, New-York: Benziger;
L. Costelloe, *St. Bonaventure,* London-New-York: Longmans, 1911, and
St. Louis: Herder; D. Dobbins, O. M. Cap. : *Franciscan Mysticism;*

A Critical Examination of the Mystical Theology of the Seraphic Doctor, New-York: Joseph F. Wagner, 1927.

The *Meditationes vitæ Christi*, for a long time attributed to St. Bonaventure, is a mystical biography of Christ, introducing many pious reflections in the narrative drawn from the Gospels and also from personal revelations. Its author was certainly a Franciscan of the 13th century and probably an Italian. It was done into English by N. Love in the 15th century. This translation has been edited by L. F. Powell, *Mirrour of the blessed lyfe of Jesus Christ*, Oxford: Clarendon Press, 1908; *Life of Our Lord Jesus Christ*, by St. Bonaventure, New-York: Benziger.

Bl. Angela of Foligno, (1248-1309), the Umbrian penitent and mystical writer sets forth specially God's transcendence and Christ's sufferings in the *Book of Visions and Instructions*, which she dictated to her Franciscan confessor Fr. Arnold. The *editio princeps* of this work, known as *The Theology of the Cross*, Paris, 1598, remains the chief source for her life and teaching. It was reprinted at Cologne, 1601, *B. Angelæ de Fulgineo Visionum et instructionum liber*, and was reedited by Bollandus in *Acta SS.* I. Jan. 186-234. The work is available in English as *Book of Visions and Instruction* tr. Cruikshank, Derby, 1872 and New-York: Benziger, 1903, or *Book of Divine Consolation* tr. Steegmann, London, Duffield, 1909, and Oxford: Clarendon Press. 1922.

St. Catherine of Bologna, (1413-1463), Abbess of the Poor Clares of Bologna, an experienced master of the spiritual combat, has left in her *Treatise on the Seven Spiritual Weapons*, written in Italian in 1438, and translated into Latin by her first biographer Dionysius Paleotti, profound considerations on the ways of overcoming temptations. Her *Life* written by Paleotti appeared in 1502 and a fuller *Life* by Christopher Mansuetti was published in 1595. A Latin translation of both is included in the *Acta SS.* March II, 35-89. Leo: *Lives of the Saints and Blessed of the Three Orders of St. Francis*, Taunton, 1885, I, 394-437.

5. — THE GERMAN SCHOOL OF MYSTICS is indebted for its theology to the theories of pseudo-Dionysius and to Neoplatonism. Cf. J. B. Dalgairns: *The German Mystics of the Fourteenth Century*, London, 1850.

John Eckhart, O. P., († 1327), generally known as Meister Eckhart, may be considered as its founder. His last years were clouded by the accusation of heresy brought against him by the Archbishop of Cologne. Two years after his death 28 propositions drawn from his writings were condemned by Pope John XXII, March 27, 1329 (cf. Denziger's *Enchir.*, nos. 501-529). This has interfered with the preservation of his works, and renders it difficult now to form a correct estimate of his teaching. His *Sermons* in German were edited by Kachelouen at Leipzig in 1498, and at Basel in 1521 and 1522 by A. Petri. A more complete edition is that of Franz Pfeiffer in *Deutche Mystiker der 14 Jahrhunderts*, Stuttgart, 1857, but it is far from exhaustive. Additional material has been brought to light by Franz Jostes (*Collectanea Friburgensis*, ix, Freiburg, 1895), Sievers (*Z. f. d. A.* xv. 73sqq. 156sqq. 172sqq.), Berlinger (*Alemannia*, iii. 15sqq.), and Bech (*Germania*, viii. 223sqq. x. 391sqq.). His Latin works bore the title *Opus tripartitum*. Portions of them have been recovered at Erfurt and edited by H. Denifle, *Meister Eckharts lateinische Schriften* in *A. f. L. u. K. G. d. M.*, ii (1886) 417-615 and Supplement 616-640. Cf. R. A. Vaughan: *Hours with the Mystics*, 8th ed., London, n. d. Eckhart's best known disciples were John Tauler and Bl. Henry Suso.

John Tauler, O. P., († 1361), one of the greatest preachers and mystics of the Middle Ages, often called *Doctor sublimis* or *Doctor illuminatus* has left *Sermons* which rank among the finest monuments in the German language. Of the three early editions, Leipzig, 1498, Bazel, 1521, Cologne, 1543, the 2d and the 3d contain much that is spurious. The 3rd edition was translated or rather paraphrased into Latin by L. Surius, Cologne, 1548, whose work was translated into various modern languages, including a German retranslation, Cologne, 1660. The best edition of the original German is that of F. Vetter,

Berlin, 1910, largely based upon the Engelbert manuscript, which represents substancially the collection as revised by Tauler himself. There are available in English: A. W. Hutton: *The Inner Way, 36 Sermons for Festivals by John Tauler*, London, 1911; *History and Life of John Tauler, with 25 Sermons* tr. by S. Winkworth, New-York, 1907; *Conferences and Sermons of John Tauler*, first complete trn. by V. Rev. W. Elliott, Washington, 1911. Tauler's *Opera Omnia* edited by L. Surius, Cologne, 1603, contain additional works which are doubtfully genuine, or certainly spurious. The *Medulla animæ* and the *Institutiones divinæ* were compiled in part from his genuine writings. Though not his work, they fairly represent his doctrine. The *Exercitia super vita et passione Christi*, in English, *Meditations on the Life and Passion of Our Lord Jesus Christ*, tr. from the French by A. P. G. Cruicshank, with preface by B. Wilberforce, new edition, New-York: Benziger, 1925, though current under his name are almost certainly not his work.

Blessed Henry Suso (Sus, Suse, or Seuse), also called *Amandus*, a name adopted in his writings, († 1366). His works were edited by F. Fabri, Ausburg, 1482, and A. Sorge, in 1512; L. Surius edited them in a Latin translation at Cologne in 1555. Modern editions of the original German are those of H. Denifle, Münich, 1880 and H. E. Bihlmeyer, Stuttgart, 1907. His chief work is *Das Büchlein der ewigen Weisheit*, composed probably in 1328, and translated into Latin, with some additions, by Suso himself under the title *Horologium Sapientiæ*. It is accessible in English in the translation made by C. H. McKenna, O. P., *The Little Book of Eternal Wisdom*, New-York: Benziger, 1889. Denifle calls this Book the most beautiful fruit of German mysticism, and places it next to the *Homilies* of St. Bernard and the *Following of Christ*. It was one of the favorite books of meditation in the Middle Ages. Cf. also *The Life of Bl. Henry Suso written by himself*, tr. from the German by T. F. Know, London, 1865.

Blessed John Ruysbroeck (Jan van Ruusbroec) [1], one of the greatest mystics, surnamed *Doctor Extaticus*, (1293-1381). Despite the precision with which he was able to express the profoundest thoughts, his language is frequently obscure, through digressions, repetitions, and subtle divisions [2]. His works were translated into Latin by his disciples, and published by the Carthusian L. Surius at Cologne in 1552. The best Latin edition is that of Cologne 1609. The best edition of the original Flemish is that of J. B. David: *Werken van Jan van Ruusbroec*, 6 vols., Ghent: Annoot and Braekman, 1858-69. He was a prolific writer. Twelve of his treatises have come down to us. The most important are: *The Mirror of Eternal Salvation* or *The Blessed Sacrament, The Book of the Enclosures, The Seven degrees of the Ladder of Spiritual Love, The Kingdom of the Lovers of God, The Adornment of the Spiritual Marriage.* Are available in English: *Reflections from the Mirror of a Mystic: being gleanings from the works of Ruysbroeck*, tr. E. Baillie, London, 1905, New-York: Benziger, 1906; *The Adornment of the Spiritual Marriage, The Sparkling Stone, The Book of Supreme Truth*, tr. from the Flemish by Dom A. C. Wynschenk, ed. with an introduction and notes by Evelyn Underhill, New-York: Dutton, 1916; *Love's Gradatory* tr. with preface by Mother St. Jerome, New-York: Benziger, 1915; *The Kingdom of the Lovers of God*, now tr. for the first time from the Lat. of L. Surius, with an introd. by T. A. Hyde, New-York: Dutton, 1919. Ruysbroek's life written by Henry Pomerius is edited in *Anal. Boll.* iv (1885) pp. 263 sqq. Cf. also V. Scully: *Short Account of the Life and Writings of the Blessed John Ruys-*

---

[1] Though belonging to the Low Countries, Ruysbroeck must be added to the list of German mystics. His writings show markedly the influence of Meister Eckhart. He was strongly encouraged in his work by Tauler and Suso, who were his friends, and his writings have contributed not a little to further the teaching of the German School.

[2] His doctrine is explained by G. J. Waffelaert, S. T. D., Bishop of Bruges, in The Union of the Loving Soul with God, or Guide to Perfection, according to the teaching of Blessed Ruysbroeck, Tr. from the Flemish by R. Hornaert, Paris, Lille, Bruges, 1916.

broeck, London, 1910; id. *Mediæval Mystic*, New-York: Benziger, 1911; E. Underhill: *Ruysbroeck*, London-New-York: Macmillan, 1915: Wautier d'Aygalliers: *Ruysbroeck the Admirable*, authorized trn. New-York: Dutton, 1925.

6. — THE FLEMISH SCHOOL is closely connected with the German School, but leaves aside pure speculation to concentrate on practical mysticism. Mysticism in the Low Countries is chiefly represented by the Brethren of the Common Life and the Canons Regular of Windesheim. Among them we may mention:

Gerard Groot (Geert de Groote), (1340-1384), called Gerardus Magnus, the founder of the Brethren of the Common Life. His activity was predominantly pastoral. The complete list of his writings, some still unpublished, is given by Bonet-Maury: *Gerard de Groote*, Paris, 1878, p. 91 sqq., and A. Anger in *Mémoires... publiés par l'Académie Royale de Belgique*, xlvi (Brussels, 1892) pp. 266 sqq. His life written by Thomas a Kempis, in *Founders of the New devotion*, tr. J. C. Arthur, London and St. Louis, Herder, 1905.

Florentius Radewyns (Florens Radewijns, (1350-1400), the head of the community of the Brethren of the Common Life after the death of Groote, left but few writings, which were collected by his disciples, Gerard de Zütphen and Thomas à Kempis. His principal work is *Tractatulus devotus de extirpatione vitiorum et de acquisitione verarum virtutum*, ed. H. Nolte, Freiburg, 1862. His life by A Kempis in *Founders of the new devotion*, London and St. Louis: Herder, 1905.

Gerard of Zutphen (G. Zerbolt van Zütphen), (1367-1398), also a member of the community of the Brethren of the Common Life, left among other writings, some of disputed authorship, two works which established his fame, *De reformatione animæ* and *De spiritualibus ascensionibus*. His earliest life is by T. à Kempis: *Founders of the new devotion*, as above. A translation of the *De Ascensionibus* under the title, *Spiritual Ascent*, was issued by Benziger, New-York, 1908.

Gerlach Petersen (or Peters), (1378-1411), a scholar of Radewyns and a canon regular at Windesheim, presents great similarity to the doctrine of the *Imitation of Christ* in his various writings, the principal of which is the *Ignitum cum Deo soliloquium*, first edited Cologne 1616, and by Strange ib. 1849. Eng. trn. *The Fiery Soliloquy with God*, New-York: Benziger. The text of his *Breviloquium de accident. exterior.*, has been edited by W. Moll in *Kerkhistorisch Archief*, ii (Amsterdam, 1859) 179 sqq. An account of his activity is found in J. Busch: *Chronicon Wendeshemense*, ed. Grube, Halle, 1886, pp. 157 sqq. See also R. A. Vaughan: *Hours with the Mystics*, i, 356 sqq., London, 1879. *The Fiery Soliloquy with God*, by Rev. Master Gerlach Petersen of Deventer, London, Burns, Oates and Washbourne.

Thomas (Hemerken) a Kempis, (1379-1471) owes the surname à Kempis to his birthplace, Kempen, in the Rhine Province. After studying under the Brethren of the Common Life at Deventer, he became an Augustinian at Mount St. Agnes, Zwolle, near Amsterdam. His writings are all of a devotional character, and include tracts, meditations, sermons, letters, the *Life of St. Lydewine*, and biographies of Groot, Radewyns and nine other Brethren of the Common Life. The first edition of his works, Utrecht, 1475, included 15 different titles, but not the *Imitation of Christ*. The last and best edition of the *Opera omnia* is by M. J. Pohl, in 7 volumes, with an 8th volume containing a dissertation on the *Life and Writings* of the author, Freiburg: Herder, 1903-1922. Are accessible in English: *Alphabet of a scholar in the School of Christ; Garden of Roses and Valley of Lillies*, Baltimore: Murphy; *Golden Words*, New-York: Benziger; *The Little Follower of Jesus*, N.-Y.: Kenedy; *Lesser Imitation*, New-York: Benziger; *Meditations on the Incarnation of Christ*, tr. V. Scully, St. Louis: Herder, 1907; *Meditations on the Life of Christ*, tr. Wright and Kettlewell, New-York: Dutton; *Meditations on the Passion and Resurrection of Our Lord*, New-York: Benziger; *Prayers and Meditations on the Life of Christ*, tr. W. Duthoit, St. Louis: Herder, 1904; *Sermons to the Novices Regular*, tr. V. Scully, St. Louis: Herder, 1907; *True*

Wisdom, tr. F. Byrne, New-York: Benziger; *Acceptable Time, Daily Readings for Lent, Babe of Bethlehem, Daily Readings for Advent, Thoughts on Holy Week*, New-York: Paulist Press; *St. Lydwine of Schiedam*, New-York: Benziger, 1912; *Founders of the New Devotion: Lives of G. Groote, F. Radewein, and their Followers*, tr. J. P. Arthur, St. Louis: Herder, 1905; *Chronicle of the Canons Regular, of Mt. St. Agnes*, tr. J. P. Arthur, St. Louis: Herder, 1906. On the author see: S. Kettlewell: *Thomas à Kempis and the Brethren of the Common Life*, London, 1882, 2 vols., abridged edition 1885; Dom V. Scully: *Life of Thomas à Kempis*, London and New-York: Benziger, 1901; J. E. De Montmorency: *Thomas à Kempis*, New-York: Putnam, 1906.

The Imitation of Christ, first issued anonymously about 1418, is ascribed to Thomas à Kempis by a great number of critics, although it would appear that this authorship is not fully settled. For a sketch of the history of the fascinating controversy on the question see L. A. Wheatley: *Story of the Imitation of Christ*, London, 1891, and Pourrat, *op. cit.*, ii. 262sqq. and Kettlewell: *The Authorship of the Imitation of Christ*, London: Rivington, 1877.

John Mauburne (or **Mombaer**), Abbot of the Augustinian monastery of Livry, treats of the principal questions of ascetical theology, and in particular of the various methods of meditation, in his *Rosetum spirituale*, Spiritual Rosebush, first printed at Basel in 1491. Cf. L. E. Du Pin, *Bibliothèque des Auteurs ecclésiastiques du 15e siècle*, Paris, 1698, p. 581.

7. — THE CARTHUSIAN SCHOOL counts four main writers:

Ludolf of Saxony, or the Carthusian, († Apr. 13, 1378), is commended to posterity by his two principal works, while many of his other writings whether tracts or sermons are either lost or doubtful. His *Commentary on the Psalms*, first edited in 1491 and more recently by the Carthusians of Montreuil in 1891, develops particularly the spiritual sense. His *Life of Christ*, repeatedly edited since it was first printed at Strasburg and Cologne in 1474, and translated into various languages, is less a history than a series of meditations on the Gospel narrative, together with instructions on dogmatic or ascetical subjects related to it. It has been sometimes called *Summa Evangelica* and has been very popular in the past. Ludolph the Saxon: *Hours of the Passion* (tr.), London: Burns and Oates, 1887. On Ludolf cf. Dorean: *Ephemerides of the Carthusian Order*, iv. 384-393, Montreuil, 1900.

Dionysius (van Leeuwen) **the Carthusian**, the Ecstatic Doctor, (1402-1471), one of the most learned theologians of his time, is chiefly esteemed as an ascetical writer. His works include 187 titles in the catalogue issued by his first biographer, the Carthusian D. von Loher: *D. Dionysii Carthusiani, doctoris ecstatici, vita simul et operum ejus fidissimus catalogus*, Cologne, 1532. The same is responsible for the first edition of Dionysius' works, Cologne, 1530 and Paris, 1531. A more complete edition to be in 45 volumes, when finished, has been undertaken by the Carthusians of Montreuil in 1896, and is being continued at Tournai. Among Dionysius' ascetical works may be mentioned: *De arcta via salutis et de contemptu mundi, De gravitate et enormitate peccati, De conversione peccatoris, De remediis tentationum, De fonte lucis et semitis vitæ*, the most complete and solid treatise of spiritual life, often reprinted separately, and translated into various languages. This treatise deals also at the same time with the mystical conceptions of the author. The same must be said of the *De discretione spirituum*, a much neglected work, which was only printed in 1620 at Aschaffenburg. The principal treatises of Dionysius on mystical theology have been separately edited under the title, *Opuscula aliquot quæ ad theoriam mysticam egregie instituunt*, Cologne, 1534, reprinted at Montreuil in 1894. The most remarkable of these treatises is the *De contemplatione*, in which the author seems to have been the first to make a formal distinction between *active* or *ordinary* and *passive* or *extraordinary* contemplation. His *Commentaries on Pseudo-Dionysius Areopagita* has two separate editions at Cologne in 1536. They appeared also in one volume with his simplification of Boethius and his explanation of the *Ladder* of St. John Climacus, Cologne.

1540. His tract *De quatuor hominis novissimis* with its appendix *De particulari judicio* has been reedited more than 40 times, and particularly commended by the *Directorium* on the *Spiritual Exercises* of St. Ignatius, approved by the general assembly of the Jesuits in 1549. The chief source for the biography of Dionysius is his *Life* by Dietrich von Loher, reprinted with annotations by the Bollandists in *Act. SS.*, March, ii. 245-255.

John Lansperg (Johann Gerecht von Landsberg), a Carthusian famous for his devotion to the Sacred Heart, († 1539). His teaching paved the way for St. Margaret Mary and her mission. To him is due the first Latin edition of the *Revelations* of St. Gertrude, Cologne, 1536. A new revised edition of his works in Latin has been issued in 5 quarto volumes by the Carthusians of Notre Dame des Prés, Tournai, 1890. His chief work, *Alloquium Jesu Christi ad animam fidelem*, Louvain, 1572, was translated into English by Philip Howard, Earl of Arundel, who died in the Tower under Elisabeth. This translation reached its 4th edition, London, 1867. Cf. Dom Boutrain: *Lansperge le Chartreux et la dévotion au Sacré-Cœur*, Grenoble, 1878.

Laurentius Surius, (1522-1578), the hagiographer of the Carthusian school, translated into Latin many of the works of the German mystics. He is known chiefly by his *Vitæ Sanctorum*, 6 vols., Cologne, 1570-75, continued after his death by a Cologne Carthusian, and republished under the title *De probatis Sanctorum historiis*, Cologne, 1618. It was reprinted in 12 volumes at Turin in 1875. Surius followed in the footsteps of his older contemporary A. Lippomani, Bishop of Verona (1560), but greatly improved upon him. Although his historical sense is not unimpeacheable, the Bollandists have recognized Surius as the best predecessor of their work.

8. — INDEPENDENT FROM THE PRECEDING SCHOOLS are :

Peter d'Ailly, (1350-1420), Chancellor of the University of Paris and later Archbishop of Cambrai and Cardinal. His numerous works are as yet partly unpublished. His two tracts *De falsis prophetis* have been edited by Ellies Du Pin in the 1st volume of Gerson's *Opera omnia* (pp. 499-603) Antwerp, 1706. His mystical writings, *Tractatus and Sermones*, printed at Strassburg in 1490, at Mainz in 1574, and at Douai in 1634, are of great merit despite some blemishes coming from his leanings to Nominalism. His *Commentary on the Canticle of Canticles* gives further proof that he deserves an honorable mention in the history of mysticism. Cf. Hurter: *Nomenclator lit.*, iv. 601sqq., Innsbruck, 1899; L. Salembier: *Petrus de Alliaco*, Lille, 1886 (Bibliography).

John Gerson, (1363-1429), whose patronymic was Le Charlier, has adopted the name of his birthplace as his surname. A disciple of Peter d'Ailly at the College of Navarre, he became his successor in the chancellorship of the University of Paris. His works, first printed at Cologne in 1483 in four volumes, have been more completely edited by Ellies Du Pin in five volumes at Antwerp in 1706, thus far the best edition. In vol. iii are gathered most of his mystical or ascetical writings. The most important of his mystical treatises are : *De monte contemplationis*, *De theologia mystica speculativa et practica*, *De elucidatione scholastica mysticæ theologiæ*, and several smaller tracts as *De meditatione*, *De perfectione cordis*, *De simplicitate cordis*, *De directione cordis*, *Alphabetum divini amoris* etc. In vol. i are found treatises on: *De probatione spirituum*, *De examinatione doctrinarum*, and *De distinctione verarum visionum a falsis*, which also belong with mystical theology. Gerson reacted against the exaggerations of some mystical writers and emphasised the fact that the mystical process culminated not in an actual, but in a close moral union of the soul with God. His ascetical writings are full of unction as well as doctrine. Among them may be mentioned: *De vita spirituali animæ*, *De passionibus animæ*, *De oratione et suo valore*, *De tentationibus diaboli diversis*, *De conscientia scrupulosa*, *De oratione*, *De Sacramento Altaris*, *De exerciliis diversis devotorum simplicium*, etc. and written in French : *Dialogue spirituel*, *Discours sur la virginité*, *Considérations sur St. Joseph* and *Conférences spirituelles*. Gerson was one of the first promoters of the devotion to

St. Joseph, and one of the great leaders in the field of catechetics. His little tract *De parvulis ad Christum trahendis,* Eng. trn. *A Treatise on Bringing Children to Jesus Christ,* St. Louis: Herder, is justly famous. His *Ad Deum vadit* has been edited by D. H. Carnahan, *University of Illinois Studies in Lang. and Lit.* vol. 3, n. 1, 1917. Cf. also, Jourdain: *Doctrina Joannis Gersonii de theologia mystica,* Paris, 1838; Reynolds: *Early reprints for English readers: John Gerson,* London, 1880; L. Salembier: *The Great Schism of the West* (tr.) New-York: Benziger, 1907; id. *Gerson* in *Diction. de Théo. Cath.* vol. vi, Paris, 1920; J. L. Connolly: *John Gerson, Reformer and Mystic,* Louvain: Uystpruyst, London and St. Louis: Herder, 1928.

Walter Hilton, († 1396), an Augustinian monk at Thurgarton (Nottinghshire), who exercised great influence in England in the 15th century. His mystical system is in the main a simplification of that of Richard of St. Victor. The most famous of his works is the *Scala perfectionis* printed in London in 1494, 1517, 1659, Eng. trn. by Fr. Guy, O. S. B., London, 1869, reprinted by Fr. Dalgairn, London, 1870, *The Scale or Ladder of Perfection,* New-York: Benziger. *The Scale of Perfection modernized from the First Printed Edition with an Introduction* by Dom M. Noetinger, London: Burns, Oates and Washbourne, 1927. His *Letter to a devout man in temporal estate* first printed in London in 1506 is generally appended to the *Scala* in later edition's. His *Song of Angels,* first printed London, 1521, is properly mystical and deals with spiritual consolations. It is included in Gardner: *The Cell of Self-Knowledge,* London and New-York, 1909. A number of other works, most of them unpublished, are ascribed to Hilton, cf. list given by S. Autore in *Dict. de Théo. Cath.,* vi. 2480-81, Paris, 1920. On Hilton consult Horstman: *Richard Rolle of Hampole and his Followers,* London, 1895 and W. R. Inge: *Studies in English Mystics,* New-York: Dutton, 1906.

Juliana of Norwich, († 1442), probably a Benedictine nun, whose doctrine is clearly influenced by the teaching of W. Hilton recorded in her book, *Sixteen Revelations of Divine Love,* written about 1393, the mystical manifestations she had experienced some twenty years before on May the 8th or the 14th, 1373. Her book was first edited by S. Cressy, O. S. B., London, 1670. This was reprinted ib. 1845 and 1907. Other editions are by Collins, ib., 1877; G. Warrack, ib. 1901. 4th edn. New-York: Gorham, 1911; Tyrrell, London, 1902, new edn. New-York: Dutton, 1920. On the author see W. R. Inge, *op. cit.* Extracts from her writings in *Meditations on the Litany of the Sacred Heart of Jesus culled from the Writings of Juliana of Norwich* by F. A. Forbes, New-York : Benziger, 1921.

St. Lawrence Justinian, (1380-1456), Bishop and first Patriarch of Venice, noted as a zealous reformer of religious orders and distinguished by his practical piety. His ascetical writings include : *De compunctione et complanctu christianæ perfectionis, De vita solitaria, De contemptu mundi, De obedientia, De humilitate, De perfectionis gradibus, De incendio divini amoris, De regimine prælatorum* (a treatise on pastoral theology). They were first published in 1506 at Brescia. Their best edition is in the 2nd volume of his *Opera omnia,* 2 vols., Venice, 1751. His biography was written by his nephew, Bernardino Giustiniani, Venice, 1574. It is reprinted in *Act. SS.,* January, i. 501 sqq.

St. Catherine of Genoa (Caterina Fieschi Adorno), (1447-1510), whose mystical experiences are described in her life written by her confessor, Miratolli, first edited by Genuti at Florence in 1551. This life is as much a treatise on mysticism as a biography, and its editions usually include the works of the Saint, which are: *A Dialogue between the Soul and the Body; Self Love, The Mind and Humanity of Our Lord,* and *A Treatise on Purgatory.* They are translated from the original Italian in *Life and Doctrine of St. Catherine of Genoa,* London, 1858, New-York, 1874; *Life of St. Catherine of Genoa,* New-York : Christian Press, n. d. The *Treatise on Purgatory,* new edition, with preface by Cardinal Manning, London: Burns and Oates, New-York: Benziger, n. d. Consult further F. von Huegel: *The Mystical Element of Religion as Studied in St. Catherine of Genoa and her Friends,* London: Dent, New-York : Dutton, 1909, 2nd edn., 1923.

III. MODERN TIMES

The ancient schools continue to refine their doctrine, while under the influence of the Council of Trent and of the Counter-Reformation new-schools come into being and bring about a renewed spirituality. Hence one sometimes finds conflict in points of detail, but the doctrinal basis remains constant and rounds out through discussion.

Three ancient schools keep on developing : the Benedictine, the Dominican and the Franciscan.

1. The BENEDICTINE School holds to its tradition of affective and liturgical piety, adding to these certain refinements in doctrine.

Blosius (Louis de Blois) (1506-1566), Abbot of Liesse, published a great many spiritual tracts the chief of which is his *Institutio spiritualis*, a synthesis of asceticism and of mysticism containing the substance of his other works. Besides the edition of his complete works published at Antwerp (1632), there is also *Manuale vitæ spiritualis*, Freiburg : Herder, 1907; this ed. unfortunately lacks the *Institutio spiritualis*. Eng. tr. *Spiritual Works*, 6 vols., New-York : Benziger, 1926, include the following : *Book of Spiritual Instruction, Comfort for the Fainthearted, Mirror for Monks, Sanctification of the Faithful Soul, Paradise of the Faithful Soul*. Cfr. *Opera*, ed. A. de Winghe, 2 fol., Cologne, 1633.

Baker, D. A. (1575-1641) wrote several treatises which were condensed by S. Cressy in *Sancta Sophia; Holy Wisdom*, Cressy-Sweeney ed., London : Burns Oates and Washbourne, New-York : Benziger, n. d.; *Contemplative Prayer*, abgd. ed. of *Sancta Sophia*, Weld-Blundell, London : Washbourne, New-York : Benziger, c. 1908.

Bona, Giovanni Cardinal (1609-1674), general of the Feuillants. *Manuductio ad cælum*, Eng. tr. *A Guide to Eternity*, L'Estrange, London, 1900; *Principia et documenta vitæ christianæ; De sacrificio missæ*, Eng. tr. *Holy Sacrifice of the Mass*, Cummins, St. Louis : Herder, 1903; *De discretione spirituum; Horologium asceticum*, etc. Many eds. have been published, particularly at Venice, 1752-1764; cfr. extracts in *Opuscula ascetica selecta*, Freiburg : Herder, 1911.

Castaniza, John of, († 1598) : *De la perfección de la vida christiana; Institutionum divinæ pietatis libri quinque*.

Schram, Dominicus (1722-1797) : *Institutiones theologiæ mysticæ*, a didactic treatise of asceticism and of mysticism with excellent advice for spiritual directors; 2 vols., ed. Paris, 1868; *Little Manual of Direction for Priests*, Eng. tr. H. Collins, London, 1882.

Ullathorne, W. B., Bishop (1806-1889) : *The Endowments of Man*, London, 1880; *Groundwork of the Christian Virtues*, 1882; *Christian Patience*, 1886.

Guéranger, Dom P. (1805-1875) : restorer of the Benedictines in France, he rendered an inestimable service to souls by his *Année liturgique; The Liturgical Year*, Eng. tr. Shepherd, Dublin, 1870 sqq., Worcester, Eng., 1895-1903, in 15 vols.

Lehodey, Dom Vital, Abbot of Notre-Dame de Grâce : *Les Voies de l'oraison mentale*, 1908; Eng. tr. *Ways of Mental Prayer*, Dublin : Gill, 1924³; *Le saint abandon*, 1919; *Directoire spirituel à l'usage des Cisterciens réformés*, 1910. These works are characterized by clarity, precision and sureness of doctrine.

Abbess of Ste Cécile (C. J. Bruyère, Màdame Cecilia) : *Spiritual Life and Prayer* (tr.), London, 1905.

Marmion, Dom Columba, late Abbot of Maredsous, Belgium (1858-1923) : *Christ the Life of the Soul* (tr.), London : Sands, St. Louis : Herder, 1925²;

Christ in His Mysteries, London and St. Louis, 1924[2]; *Our Way and Our Life* (abgd. ed. of previous), St. Louis : Herder, 1927; *Christ the Ideal of the Monk.,* London and St. Louis, 1926.

Hedley, J. C., Bishop († 1915) : *The Holy Eucharist,* London, 1923; *A Retreat, 33 Discourses,* ib., 1894[10]; *Spiritual Retreat for Priests,* ib., Burns Oates and Washbourne, 1927[3]; *Spiritual Retreat for Religious,* ib., *Lex Levitarum* or *Preparation for the Cure of Souls,* New-York : Benziger, 1928[2]; *Christian Inheritance set forth in Sermons,* London, 1896; *Our Divine Saviour,* London, n. d., 7th ed.; *Light of Life,* London, 1899; *Spirit of Faith,* New-York, 1896.

Gasquet, F. Aidan Cardinal (1846-1929) : *Religio Religiosi,* New-York, 1923, on the purpose and end of the religious life; *Monastic Life in the Middle Ages,* ib., 1922.

Chautard, Dom J. B. : *L'Ame de tout apostolat,* 1915[5]; *The True Apostolate,* tr. Girardey, St. Louis; Herder, 1918; also another tr., *The Soul of the Apostolate,* tr. Moran, S. M., London and New-York, 1926.

Morin, Dom G. : *The Ideal of the Monastic Life found in the Apostolic Ages,* tr. Gunning, London.

Butler, Dom E. C. : *Western Mysticism,* New-York : Dutton, 1927[2]; *Benedictine Monachism,* London : Longmans, 1924[2].

Cabrol, Dom F. : *Liturgical Prayer,* tr. Benedictine nuns of Stanbrock, London : Burns Oates and Washbourne, 1922.

Louismet, Dom L. : *Mystical Knowledge of God,* London and New-York, 1917; *Mystical Life,* ib., 1916; *Mysticism True and False,* ib., 1919; *Divine Contemplation for All,* ib., 1920; *Mystical Initiation,* ib., 1923; *The Burning Bush, a treatise on Ecstatic Contemplation,* London, 1924.

Doyle, Dom F. C. : *The Teaching of St. Benedict,* 1887; *Principles of Religious Life,* London : Washbourne, 1890[2].

2. The DOMINICAN SCHOOL, deeply rooted in the teachings of St. Thomas, clearly and methodically explains and clarifies his doctrine on asceticism and contemplation.

Cajetan, Thomas (1469-1534), in his profound commentary on the *Summa.*

Louis of Granada (1504-1588), without attempting to write ascetical theology, treats with solidity and unction all the elements of Christian perfection. *The Sinner's Guide* (tr.), New-York, 1889.

Bartholomew of the Martyrs, Abp. of Braga (1514-1590) : *Compendium doctrinæ spiritualis,* first published at Lisbon, 1582; other eds. at Madrid, Paris, etc., the last appearing in Venice (1711) under the title *Compendium mysticæ doctrinæ* with additions made by Ildephonso Manrique; cfr. *Compendium spiritualis doctrinæ,* ed. Fessler, New-York : Benziger, 1864; Lady Herbert, *Dom Bartholomew of the Martyrs,* London, 1880.

John of St. Thomas (1589-1644) in his course of theology, which is partly a commentary on St. Thomas, treats in quite remarkable a manner of the gifts of the Holy Ghost.

Thomas of Vallgornera († 1665) : *Mystica theologia D. Thomæ,* latest ed. Turin, 1911. Here the complete teaching of St. Thomas on the three ways is gathered and classified.

Contenson, V. (1641-1674) : *Theologia mentis et cordis,* 2 vols., Cologne, 1722; at the end of each section the author draws certain ascetic conclusions or corollaries.

Massoulié, A. (1632-1706) : *Traité de l'Amour de Dieu; Traité de la véritable oraison; Méditations sur les trois voies.* The writer explains the doctrine of St. Thomas in refutation of the errors of the Quietists.

Piny, A. (1640-1709) : *L'Abandon à la volonté de Dieu; L'oraison du cœur; La clef du pur amour; La présence de Dieu; Le plus parfait,* and so on. The leading idea in these volumes is that perfection consists of conformity to God's will and of holy abandonment.

Rousseau, R. P. : *Avis sur les divers états d'oraison*, 1710; ed. Paris : Lethielleux, 1913.

Billuart, C. R. (1685-1757) : *Summa S. Thomæ hodiernis academiarum moribus accommodata*, 1746-1751.

Lacordaire, H. D. (1802-1861) : *Letters to Young Men*, London and New-York, 1903[2]; *Conferences*, London, 1851; *Jesus Christ*, 1869; *God*, 1870; *God and Man*, 1872 (3 last in 1 vol. Manchester : Robinson, London : Chapman, 1902[9]); see especially Chocarne, *Inner Life of Père Lacordaire* (tr.), London : Burns and Oates, 1923[11]; also, *Thoughts and Teachings*, New-York, 1904[2].

Meynard, A. M. : *Traité de la vie intérieure*, Clermont-Ferrand and Paris, 1884, 1899; an adaptation of the work of Thomas of Vallgornera.

Froget, B. : *The Indwelling of the Holy Spirit in the Souls of the Just*, Eng. tr. and adap. Raemers, New-York : Paulist Press, 1921; a very solid theological study.

Rousset, M. J., *Doctrine spirituelle*, Paris : Lethielleux, 1902; a treatise on the spiritual life and union with God according to Catholic tradition and the spirit of the saints.

Cormier, P., *Instructions des novices*, 1905; *Retraite ecclésiastique d'après l'Evangile et la vie des saints*, Rome, 1903.

Gardeil, P., *Les dons du S. Esprit dans les saints dominicains*, Paris : Lecoffre, 1903; in course of translation by Dominicans of Washington, D. C.; cfr. author's article on the same subject in *Dictionnaire de Théologie Catholique*; also *La structure de l'âme et l'expérience mystique*, 2 vols., Paris, 1927.

Hugueny, P. Et., *Psaumes et cantiques du bréviaire romain*, Brussels, 1921-1922.

Janvier, M. A., *Exposition de la morale catholique*, Paris, Lethielleux; the conferences given at Notre Dame of Paris in which Christian morality and asceticism are eloquently expounded.

Joret, R. P., *La contemplation mystique, d'après St. Thomas d'Aquin*, Lille, 1923.

Jarrett, Bede, *The Abiding Presence of the Holy Ghost in the Soul*, New-York : Catholic Library, 1918.

Raymond, V., *Spiritual Director and Physician*, Eng. tr. Smith, London : R. and T. Washbourne, 1917[2].

Naval, *Theologiæ asceticæ et mysticæ cursus*, Turin, Marietti, 1925[2].

Garrigou-Lagrange, R., *Perfection chrétienne et Contemplation selon St. Thomas d'Aquin et St. Jean de la Croix*, 2 vols., Paris, 1923[3].

Ridolfi, N., *A Short Method of Mental Prayer*, Eng. tr. Devas, London : Burns Oates and Washbourne, 1920.

Arintero, J., *Cuestiónes misticas*, Salamanca, 1920[2].

Francis Raphael, Mother, *Spirit of the Dominican Order*, London and Leamington : Art and Book C⁰., 1896.

Ollivier, M. J., *The Friendships of Jesus*, Eng. tr. Keogh, St. Louis : Herder, c. 1903.

Capes, F. M., *St. Catherine de Ricci, O. P.*, with treatise on the Mystical Life by Wilberforce, London, c. 1907.

See also two Dominican reviews, *La vie spirituelle* (1919 sqq.) and *La Vida sobrenatural* (1921 sqq.).

3. The FRANCISCAN SCHOOL maintains its characteristics : evangelical simplicity, poverty joyfully endured, devotion to the Child Jesus and to the suffering Christ.

Francis of Osuna (c. 1497-1540) : *Abecedario espiritual*, 1528 sqq., the third volume of which was for a long time St. Teresa's guide.

St. Peter of Alcantara, († 1562), a director of St. Teresa, wrote a tract on prayer which has been translated into many tongues. Eng. tr. *Treatise on Prayer and Meditation*, New-York : Benziger, 1926.

Alphonsus of Madrid, († c. 1529) : *Arte para servir a Dios*, Alcala, 1578.

John of Bonilla, († c. 1580) : *Tradado de la pay de l'alma*, Eng. tr. Collins, London, 1876; also included in St. Peter of Alcantara's *Treatise on Prayer and Meditation* (1926).

Matthias Bellintani of Salo, (1534-1611) : *Pratica dell' Orazione Mentale*, Brescia, 1573.

John of the Angels, (fl. 16th Cent.) : *Obras misticas*, new ed. Madrid, 1912-1917.

John Evangelist of Bois-le-Duc, (Balduke) (c. 1588-1635) : *The Kingdom of God in the Soul*, Eng. tr. Salvin (1657), ed. Nuns of Stanbrook, introd. Cuthbert, London : Sheed and Ward, 1930.

Joseph du Tremblay, (1577-1638), "l'Eminence grise"; *Introduction à la vie spirituelle par une facile méthode d'oraison*, ed. Le Mans, 1897, entitled *Méthode d'oraison*.

Mary of Agreda, (1602-1665) : *Divine Life of Blessed Virgin Mary*, abridgment of *Mystical City of God* (tr.), Philadelphia, 1872.

Yves of Paris, († 1685) : *Progrès de l'amour divin*, 1644; *Miséricordes de Dieu*, Paris, 1645.

Bernardine of Paris, († 1672) : *L'esprit de St. François*, ed. Paris, 1880.

Peter of Poitiers, († 1680) ; *Le jour mystique ou Eclaircissement de l'oraison et théologie mystique*, Paris, 1671.

Louis Francis Yves d'Argentan, (1615-1680) : *Conférences théologiques et spirituelles*, (three series), Paris, 1670-1674; *Les exercices du chrétien intérieur*, Paris, 1664.

Brancati de Laurea Laurentius, (1612-1693) : *De oratione Christiana*, Rome, 1675, a treatise on prayer and contemplation often cited by Benedict XIV. cfr. ed. by Carthusians of Montreuil-sur-mer, 1896.

Maes, Bonifacius, (1627-1706) : *Theologia mystica*, Ghent, 1668 (12 eds. since); *Franciscan Mysticism*, Eng. tr. Whelan, London : Sheed and Ward, c. 1929.

Thomas of Bergano, (1563-1631) : *Fuoco d'amore*, Augsburg, 1682.

Ambrose of Lombez, (1708-1778) : *Peace of the Soul*, (tr.), London, a classic for dealing with the scrupulous; also, *Traité de la joie de l'âme*, 1779; *Lettres spirituelles*, 1766.

Didacus a Matre Dei, († c. 1713) : *Ars mystica*, Salamanca, 1713.

Louis Chaix de Besse, (1831-1910) : *The Science of Prayer* (tr.), London : Burns Oates and Washbourne, New-York : Benziger, 1925; *La science du Pater*, 1904; *Eclaircissements sur les œuvres mystiques de St. Jean de la Croix*, Paris, 1893.

Adolphus Kestens, (1863-1925), of Denderwindeke : *Compendium theologiæ asceticæ ad vitam sacerdotalem et religiosam rite instituendam*, 2 vols. Hong-Kong, China, 1921. A very well documented work in the second volume of which one may find a rich bibliography on each question treated.

Devas, D., *A Franciscan View of the Spiritual Life*, New-York : Benziger, 1923; *Franciscan Essays*, 1924.

Cuthbert, Fr., *The Romanticism of St. Francis*, London : Longmans, 1924[2].

Vivès y Tuto, Joseph Galas, Cardinal (1854-1913) ; *Compendium theologiæ ascetico-mysticæ*, Barcelona, 1886, Rome, 1908[3]; quite serviceable as a text-book.

Dobbins, D., *Franciscan Mysticism*, New-York ; Wagner, 1927,

Mills, V., *A Bibliography of Franciscan Ascetical Writers* in *Franciscan Educational Conference Report*, vol. viii, n° 8, 1926, pp. 248-332 : very detailed, thoroughly scholarly, covering the complete field of Franciscan ascetical and mystical writing from the beginning to our own day.

Five of the new schools are especially noteworthy.

1.—The SCHOOL OF ST. IGNATIUS makes a specialty of *active, energetic* and *practical* spiritual life aiming at forming the will for personal sanctification and apostolic work.

St. Ignatius (1491, 1495-1556) : founder of the Society of Jesus; *Exercitia spiritualia*, new ed. Madrid, 1919. There are many English versions, for example those of Morris and of Joseph Rickaby. The *Exercises* comprise a method of procedure for *reforming* a soul and for *transforming* it to *conformity* with the divine model, Jesus Christ. " The work, " says Father Watrigant (*Etudes religieuses*, vol. cix, p. 134), " condenses a vast movement of spirit and of thought which had slowly been developed during the preceding centuries. It is the starting point of a flood of spiritual life that has since the sixteenth century been constantly rising, wave on wave, and it is likewise the point of convergence for diverse currents coursing through the Middle Ages and finding their beginnings in the earliest days of Christianity. "

Fully to understand the spirit of St. Ignatius, one should read the *Constitutions* and *Letters* (*Epistolæ*, 12 vols., M. H. S. J., 1904-1918). Cfr. also Thompson, F., *St. Ignatius Loyola*, New-York, 1909; Rose, S., *St. Ignatius Loyola and the Early Jesuits*. New-York, 1896[2]; Pise, C. C., *St. Ignatius, S. J.*, New-York, 1845; Mariani, F., *Life of St. Ignatius Loyola. Founder of the Jesuits*, Eng. tr. Faber, 2 vols., London, 1848; Joly, H., *St. Ignatius*, (tr.), London; Washbourne, 1899; Bartoli, D., *History of St. Ignatius of Loyola*, 2 vols., New-York, 1855; also, life by Pollen, 1922; Sedgwick, H. D., *Ignatius Loyola*, London and New-York : Macmillan, 1923; *Spiritual Exercises of St. Ignatius*, Eng. tr. fr. Spanish, ed. Lattey, St. Louis : Herder, 1928; *Spiritual Exercises tr. from the Autograph*, Eng. tr. Mullan, New-York, 1814; *Trans. and Commentary on Spiritual Exercises*, Rickaby, J., London : Burns and Oates, 1915; Bernhardt, W., *Die vier Zentralsideen des Exerzitiensbuches de hl. Ignatius*, Ratisbon : Habbel, c. 1928; Codina, A., *Los origenes de los Ejercicios de S. Ignacio de Loyola*, Barcelona, 1926; Watrigant, H., *La genèse des exercices de S. Ignace*, Amiens, 1897, and *La méditation fondamentale avant S. Ignace*, Enghien, 1907; Brou, A., *La spiritualité de S. Ignace*, Paris : Beauchesne, 1914, and *S. Ignace, Maître d'oraison*, Paris : Ed. Spes, 1925; *Spiritual Exercises of St. Ignatius of Loyola*, Eng. tr. with *Directorium* and Commentary, Longride (Anglican), London : R. Scott, 1919; Redman, J., *Soldier's Companion to the Spiritual Exercises*, London : Burns and Oates, c. 1882[2]; Curtis, J., *Way of Perfection in the Spiritual Exercises of St. Ignatius of Loyola*, Dublin : Gill, c. 1882; *Meditations on Life and Virtues of St. Ignatius of Loyola*, Eng. tr. M. A. W., London : Burns and Oates, New-York : Catholic Pub. Soc., c. 1888.

Lefevre, B. P. : *Memorial*, a detailed account of one year of his life (June, 1542-July, 1543). It has been called " one of the jewels of ascetical literature."

Alvarez de Paz (1560-1620) : *De vita spirituali ejusque perfectione*, 3 folio vols., Lyon, 1602-1612; a complete treatment of the spiritual life especially for religious; also, *Opera spiritualia*, ed. Vivès, 6 vols., Paris, 1875.

Suarez, F., (1548-1617) : *De religione*, in which one finds practically a complete treatise on spirituality, including such topics as prayer, mental prayer, vows and obedience to rules. Cfr. Humphrey, *The Religious State : Digest of the Doctrine of Suarez*, London : Burns and Oates, c. 1884.

Lessius, Ven. L., (1554--1623) : *De summo bono*, Eng. tr. Semple, *Virtues Awakened*, St. Louis : Herder, 1924; *De perfectionibus moribusque divinis; De divinis nominibus*, Eng. tr. *Names of God*, New-York : America Press, 1912.

Bellarmine, Bl. R. (1542-1621) : *De ascensione mentis in Deum per scalas creaturarum*, Eng. tr. *The Mind's Ascent to God*, Milwaukee : Morehouse, 1925; also, Eng. tr. and ed. Broderick, New-York : Benziger, 1929; *De æterna felicitate sanctorum ; De gemitu columbæ sive de bono lacrymarum ; De septem* *verbis a Christo in cruce prolatis; De arte bene moriendi.* Cfr. recent ed. *Opuscula ascetica,* New-York : Pustet, 1925; also, Broderick, J., *Life and Work of Bl. Robert Cardinal Bellarmine,* 2 vols., London, 1928.

Lancicius, N. : *Select Works,* Burns London : and Oates, 1884.

Caraffa, V.-Bouix, *School of Divine Love; or Elevation of the Soul to Goa* (tr.), Dublin : Gill, 1887.

Le Gaudier, († 1622) : *De perfectione vitæ spiritualis,* a complete treatise of the spiritual life, 3 vols., new ed. 1857.

Drexelius, J., (1581-1638) : *The Heliotropium : turning to Him,* ed. Bogner, New-York : Devin-Adair, 1924.

Alphonsus Rodriguez, († 1616) : *Exercicio de perfeción and virtudes religiosas,* 3 vols., Barcelona, 1613; *Practice of Christian Perfection,* Eng. tr. Jos. Rickaby, Chicago : Loyola Univ. Press, 1929. This is an excellent work which, leaving aside all theorizing, deals only with the actual practice of virtues; many eds. in various languages.

St. Alphonsus Rodriguez, († 1617) ; a Jesuit brother who was raised to very high contemplation. Two of his tracts have been recently published in French (Desclée, de Brouwer, Lille).

De la Puente, (De Ponte) († 1624) : many works, of which in English there is available *Meditations on the Mysteries of our Holy Faith,* New-York : Benziger, 1916. He was a spiritual director of St. Teresa of Avila, being himself a contemplative.

Binet, Stephen, (1569-1639) : *Les attraits tout-puissants de l'amour de Jésus-Christ; Le grand chef-d'œuvre de Dieu et les souveraines perfections de la Ste Vierge.*

Saint-Jure, J. B. de (1588-1657) : *Le livre des élus ou Jésus crucifié; L'homme spirituel; Treatise on the Knowledge and Love of Our Lord Jesus Christ,* Eng. tr. Sister of Mercy, 3 vols., New-York; *Union with Our Lord Jesus Christ in His Principal Mysteries* (tr.), New-York : Sadlier, 1876[3]. In some of his works Saint-Jure approaches the teachings of the French School of the seventeenth century.

Godinez, M. (Wading) (1591-1644) : *Praxis theologiæ mysticæ,* tr. de la Reguera into Latin, Paris : Lethielleux, 1920.

Nouet, J., (1605-1680) : *Conduite de l'homme d'oraison dans les voies de Dieu,* 1674; *Meditations on the Life of Our Lord for Every Day in the Year* (tr.), 2 vols., Dublin : Browne and Nolan, 1892; Baltimore; Lucas, 1855.

De la Colombière, Bl. C., (1641-1682); *Journal de ses retraites,* ed. Desclée, 1897; in this, see especially his *Grande retraite* in which there are indicated the graces and lights that God granted him during the retreat of 1674. In Eng., *Sufferings of Our Lord Jesus Christ* (tr.), London, 1876.

Bourdaloue, L., (1632-1704); *Sermons,* in which Christian morality and asceticism are developed with fullness and solidity; see also his *Retraite.* Cfr. *Œuvres complètes,* 4 vols., Paris, 1880[5]; also, *Spiritual Retreat for Pastors of Souls* (tr.), London, 1873; *A Spiritual Retreat,* Baltimore, n. d. ; *Sermons and Moral Discourses on the Important Duties of Christianity,* Eng. tr. Carroll, Dublin : Duffy, 1855[3].

Guilloré, F., (1615-1684) : *Maximes spirituelles; Les secrets de la vie spirituelle* (ed. 1922). Cfr. Eng. tr. *Self-Renunciation,* introd. Carter, New-York : Longmans, 1902[2].

Gallifet, J. : *Adorable Heart of Jesus,* mod. Eng. tr., New-York : 1899; *Devotion to the Blessed Virgin* (tr.), London : Burns and Oates, c. 1880.

Petit-Didier, († 1756) : *Exercitia spiritualia, tertio probationis anno a Patribus Societatis obeunda,* ed. Clermont, 1821; one of the best commentators on the *Spiritual Exercises.*

Bellecius, A., (1704-1752) : in Eng., *Solid Virtue* (tr.), New-York : Benziger, 1923; *Spiritual Exercises,* ibid., 1925.

Lallemant, L., († 1635) : his *La doctrine spirituelle* was published by Rigoleuc; it is a short, substantial work wherein the author shows how we may come to contemplation by frequent and affective recollection of God living in us, by purity of heart and by docility to the Holy Ghost. Eng. tr. *Spiritual Doctrine of Father Louis Lallemant*, ed. Faber, New-York : Sadlier, 1885. Cfr. especially Pottier, A., *Essai de théologie mystique comparée : Le P. L. Lallemant et les grands spirituels de son temps*, 3 vols. : I. *La vie et la doctrine etc.*, II. *L'école du P. Lallemant comparée avec les premiers représentants de l'école ignatienne française et avec St. François de Sales*, III. *La spiritualité bérullienne et les grands spirituels de la Compagnie de Jésus à l'âge d'or de l'ascéticisme français, 1500-1650* : Paris; Téqui, 1924-1929.

Surin, J., († 1665) : *Catéchisme spirituel; Les fondements de la vie spirituelle; La guide spirituelle*, and so on. In these Father Lallemant's teaching is developed.

Crasset, J. : *Meditations*, Eng. tr. Snow, 2 vols., London : R. Washbourne, 1888; also, *A Key to Meditation* (tr.), London : R. and T. Washbourne, New-York : Benziger, 1907; *Christian Considerations* (tr.), New-York, 1858; *Devout Meditations*, Eng. tr. Dorsey, New-York : O'Shea, 1906.

Huby, V. : *Retraite*, 1690, Eng. tr. *Spiritual Retreat*, Philadelphia, 1795; *Motifs d'aimer Dieu; Motifs d'aimer Jésus-Christ*. A critical ed. of his work is being prepared by Bainvel.

De Caussade, (1693-1751) : *Abandonment to Divine Providence* (tr.), St. Louis : Herder, 1921; *Progress in Prayer* (tr.), ibid., 1904; *Workings of Divine Will* (tr.), London : Burns and Oates, New-York : Sadlier, 1881.

Segneri, Paolo : *Manna of the Soul, Meditations for a Year* (tr.), 4 vols., London : Burns and Oates, 1879; *Practice of Interior Recollection with God* (tr.), Dublin : Gill, c. 1880; cfr. Moris, *Lights in Prayer of Ven. Fathers della Puente, Colombière and Segneri*, London : Burns and Oates, 1893.

Nepveu, (1639-1708): *Méthode facile d'oraison*, 3 vols, Paris, 1826; in Eng., *Like unto Him*, tr. Fairbanks, New-York : Wagner, 1923[3]; *Hidden Life*, London : Masters, c. 1869; *Higher Paths in Spiritual Life*, London : Richardson, 1851; *Spirit of Christianity*, New-York : Dunigan, 1859.

Pinamonti, J. P. (1632-1703): *Opere*, Venice, 1762; in Eng., *Art of Knowing Ourselves* (tr.), London : Burns and Oates, 1877; *Immaculate Heart of Mary*, Philadelphia : Messenger, 1890; *Mirror of Humility*, Manresa Press, 1923.

Scaramelli, G. B. (1687-1752): *Direttorio ascetico; Direttorio mistico*, the latter being among the most complete treatises on mysticism, though presenting the different forms of the same degree as *distinct degrees* of contemplation. *Directorium asceticum*, Eng. tr. and ed. Dublin : Kelly, 1869; London and New-York, 4 vols., 1902[5]; abgd. ed,, *Manual of Christian Perfection*, Msgr. Stockman ed., Los Angeles, 1921; cfr. also *Directorium mysticum in compendium*, ed. Voss, Louvain, 1881.

Grou, J. N. (1731-1803): *Spiritual Maxims* (tr.), London : Th. Baker, 1902; *Meditations on the love of God*, Eng. tr. Butler, St. Louis : Herder, 1929; *Manual for Interior Souls* (tr.), New-York : Benziger, 1927; *How to Pray* (tr.), London : Baker, New-York : Benziger, 1909; *Characters of Real Devotion*, Eng. tr. Clinton, Dublin, 1895; *Portraiture of True Devotion* (tr.), Baltimore, 1832. His teaching in analogous to that of Lallemant.

De Clorivière, P. : *Considérations sur l'exercice de la prière*, 1862, a brief explanation of ordinary and extraordinary prayer by the restorer of the Society of Jesus in France.

Ramière, H. (1821-1884): his work, *La divinisation du chrétien*, marks a return to the traditional doctrines supplying the basis of the spiritual life. Cfr. *Apostleship of Prayer*, (tr.), New-York : Apostleship of Prayer Press.

Boudreau, *Happiness of Heaven*, Baltimore : Murphy, 1871; *God, Our Father*, ibid., 1873.

Coleridge, H. J. (1822-1893) : a series of about 48 volumes on the Life of Our Lord, pub. London, Burns and Oates.

Humphrey, *The Divine Teacher,* London: Burns and Oates, 1882; *One Mediator,* ibid.; *Mary, Magnifying God.*

Morris, J., *Meditation: Instruction,* Roehampton: Manresa Press, 1889; *Journals of Retreat,* ed. Pollen, London: Burns and Oates, 1894.

Von Lehen, *Way of Interior Peace* (tr.), New-York: Benziger, c. 1889.

Rossetti, J. C., *De Spiritu Societatis Jesu,* Freiburg: Herder, 1888.

Clare, *The Science of the Spiritual Life,* New-York and London: Art and Book, 1898.

Vercruysse, B., *New Practical Meditations,* 2 vols., New-York, Benziger.

Chaignon, *The Mass Worthily Celebrated* (tr.), New-York: Benziger, 1897; *Sacerdotal Meditations* (tr.), New-York: Benziger, 1916.

Medaille, *Meditations on the Gospels,* London: Burns and Oates, 1891.

Olivaint, P., (1816-1871) : *Journal de ses retraites annuelles,* 1911 [8].

Valuy, B. : *Directorium spirituale, Guide for Priests in their Public and Private Life* (tr.), Dublin : Gill, 1907 [5].

Terrien, J. B., *La grâce et la gloire; La Mère de Dieu et la Mère des hommes.*

Gallwey, *The Watches of the Sacred Passion,* 2 vols., London: Herder, 1908.

Lucas, *In the Morning of Life,* London : Sands, 1904; *At Parting of Ways,* Herder, 1906.

De Maumigny, R., *Practice of Mental Prayer* (tr.), New-York: Kenedy, 1915.

Poulain, A., *Les grâces d'oraison,* a treatise of mystical theology (ed. Bainvel, 1922 [10]), Eng. tr. *Graces of Interior Prayer,* St. Louis : Herder, 1918.

De Smedt, Ch., *Notre vie surnaturelle: son principe, ses facultés, les conditions de sa pleine activité,* Brussels, 1913.

Eymieu, A., *Le gouvernement de soi-même,* Paris, 1911-1921.

Bainvel, J. V., *Devotion to the Sacred Heart* (tr.), New-York: Benziger, 1924; also *Le saint cœur de Marie,* 1918; *La vie intime du catholique,* 1916.

Meschler, M., *Three Fundamental Principles of the Spiritual Life,* St. Louis: Herder, 1912 [2]; *Life of Our Lord Jesus Christ, the Son of God, in Meditations,* Eng. tr. Sr. Margaret Mary, 2 vols., London and St. Louis: Herder, 1924 [5]; *Garden of Roses of Our Lady,* London : Burns Oates and Washbourne, c. 1907.

Donnelly, F. P., *Heart of the Gospel,* New-York : Apost. of Prayer, 1911; *Watching an Hour,* New-York : Kenedy, 1914; *Holy Our,* ibid., 1917; *Heart of Revelation;* etc.

Garesché, *Your Neighbor and You,* St. Louis : Queen's Work Press, 1912; *Your Soul's Salvation,* New-York : Benziger, 1918; etc.

Hull, E. R., *God, Man, Religion,* Bombay: Examiner, 1914; *Formation of Character,* London, Sands.

O'Rourke, *Under Sanctuary Lamp; Fountains of the Saviour; On Israel's Hills; Journeys with Our Lord,* and so on : New-York, Apost. of Prayer Press.

Russel, *At Home with God,* Longmans Green, 1912; *He is Calling Me,* London : Burns and Oates, 1912.

Semple, *Heaven open to Souls,* New-York: Benziger, 1916.

Longhaye, *An Eight Day Retreat,* Eng. tr. Wolferstan, London: Sands, 1928.

Plus, R., adapts the fundamental teachings of the French School of the seventeenth century. Of his works, the following are in Eng. tr. : *Christ in*

His Brethren, 1925; *How to Pray Always*, tr. Hernaman, 1926; *In Christ Jesus*, 1924²; *Living with God; Ideal of Perfection; How to Pray Well*, 1929; *God within Us; Folly of the Cross*. Cfr. also *La sainteté catholique*, in series *Bibliothèque Catholique de Sciences Religieuses*, Paris: Bloud and Gay, 1929; a series being published in English by Herder, St. Louis.

O'Rahilly A., *Father William Doyle, S. J.*, *Spiritual Study*, New-York and London: Longmans Green, 1925³.

Pesch, T., *Christian Philosophy of Life*, Eng. tr. McLaren, London: Sands, St. Louis: Herder, 1922.

Renouvier, F., *Conquest of Heaven: Perfect Charity and Contrition* (tr.), Baltimore, 1924.

Hill, O. A., *Charity and Our Three Vows*, St. Louis: Herder, 1925.

Charles, P., *Prayer for All Times*, Eng. tr. Monahan, 2 vols., New-York: Kenedy, London: Sands, 1925: 3 vols. in French.

Meyer, R. J., *The Science of the Saints*, 2 vols., St. Louis: Herder, I. 1923⁷, II. 1924⁴.

Moffatt, J. E., *Thy Kingdom Come*, New-York: Benziger, 1927; *The Sanity of Sanctity*, ib., 1929.

Maréchal, J., *Studies in the Psychology of Misticism*, Eng. tr. Thorold, New-York: Benziger, 1928.

Noldin, H., *Devotion to the Sacred Heart* (tr.), ed. Kent, New-York: Benziger, 1905.

Walsh, N., *Vetera et Nova*, Dublin: Gill, 1902.

De Heredia, C. M., *True Spiritualism*, New-York: Kenedy, 1924.

Pardow, *Life of Father Pardow*, New-York.

De Grandmaison, L., *Personal Religion*, Eng. tr. Thorold, London: Sheed and Ward, St. Louis: Herder, 1929.

Blount, *Leading Meditations of the Spiritual Exercises*, New-York: Benziger, London: Burns Oates and Washbourne, 1928.

Conroy, *Early Friends of Christ*, New-York: Benziger, 1925.

D'Arcy, M., *The Mass and Redemption*, London: Burns Oates and Washbourne, 1926.

Goodier, A., Abp., *Crown of Sorrow; Meaning of Life; Some Hints on Prayer; Charity of Christ;* Roehampton, Manresa Press. *Public Life of Our Lord Jesus Christ*, 2 vols., London: Burns Oates and Washbourne, 1930.

Le Buffe, F. P. *My Changeless Friend* (14 Series), New-York, Apost. of Prayer Press.

Husslein, J., *The Reign of Christ*, New-York: Kenedy, 1928; *The Mass of the Apostles*, ibid., 1930.

Scott, M. J., *God and Myself; Divine Counsellor*, New-York: Kenedy, 1922; *Holy Sacrifice of Mass*. ibid., 1928.

The America Press, New-York, prints many ascetical pamphlets for the various ecclesiastical seasons.

Since 1920 this school has under the editorship of J. de Guibert been publishing a quarterly magazine, *Revue d'ascétique et de mystique*, at Toulouse, France. Its purpose is to study the more important questions of asceticism and mysticism from the threefold point of view of history, doctrine and psychology.

2.—The CARMELITE SCHOOL, or the School of St. Teresa, insists that God is everything and man nothing. It urges complete detachment in order to come, God willing, to a state of contemplation and inculcates the practice of the apostolate by prayer, example and sacrifice.

St. Teresa (1515-1582) of Avila is model and teacher of the highest sanctity. The Church in the Missal invites us to study and to put into practice her spiritual doctrine " so we way be fed with the food of her heavenly teaching and grow in loving devotion towards Thee. " Her works furnish us with the richest source on mystical states as well as the most orderly and lifelike classification. Critical ed., *Obras de Sta Teresa, editadas y anotadas por el P. Silverio de St. Teresa*, 6 vols., Burgos, 1915; also, selections, 1 vol., 1922. Cfr. also *Letters of St. Teresa*, Eng. tr. Benedictines of Stanbrook, London: Th. Baker, 1919 sqq.; *Autobiography and Book of Foundations*, ed. Burke-Elliott, New-York: Columbus Press, 1911; *Spirit of St. Teresa,* tr. anon., London: Burns and Oates, 1885; Frassinetti, *St. Teresa's Pater Noster: Treatise on Prayer*, Eng. tr. Hutch, London: Burns and Oates, c. 1887; Hoornaert, R., *St. Teresa in Her Writings*, Eng. tr. Leonard, London: Sheed and Ward, 1930. See Maréchal, *Studies in the Psychology of Mysticism*, Eng. tr. Thorold, etc., ut supra.

St. John of the Cross (1543-1591): a disciple of St. Teresa. His four works make up a complete treatise on mysticism. Critical ed. Gerard, Toledo, Spain; Eng. tr. Lewis, ed. Zimmerman, London: Th. Baker, 1906 sqq : *The Ascent of Mount Carmel*, showing the steps to be taken to arrive at contemplation; *The Dark Night of the Soul*, describing the trials that go along with contemplation; *The Living Flame*, explaining its marvelous effects; *The Spiritual Canticle* in lyric style summarizing the teaching of the previous works. Cfr. Heriz, P.,*St. John of the Cross*, Washington, 1919; other works in English are *Precautions, Counsels and Maxims, Spiritual Letters, Poems*.

John of Jesus and Mary (1564-1615) : *Disciplina claustralis*, 4 folio vols. in which one may find various ascetical tracts, among them the *Via vitæ;* cfr. also *Theologia mystica*, ed. Freiburg: Herder, 1911; *De virorum ecclesiasticorum perfectione; Instruction of Novices*, Eng. tr. fr. Latin, New-York: Benziger, 1925,

Joseph of Jesus and Mary (1562-1626) : *Subida del alma a Dios*, Madrid, 1656, a treatise dealing with the soul's ascent towards God.

Bl. Mary of the Incarnation (Madame Acarie) (1599-1672), though she left no written work, may be understood from A. DUVAL'S : *La vie admirable de Mlle Acarie*, 1621, ed. 1893.

Ven. Anne of St Bartholomew : *Autobiography*, Eng. tr. Carmelite of St Louis : Herder, 1916.

Thomas of Jesus (1568-1627) : *De contemplatione divina libri VI*, ed. Cologne, 1684; *The Sufferings of Jesus* (tr.), 2 vols., London, 1869; also eds. Dublin and Philadelphia.

Nicholas of Jesus and Mary : called by Bossuet the most learned interpreter of St John of the Cross; *Phrasium mysticæ theologiæ Ven. P. Joannis a Cruce... elucidatio.*

Philip of the Trinity († 1671) : *Summa theologiae mysticæ*, 3 vols., ed. Brussels and Paris, 1874; a classic, clearly and methodically describing the three ways of perfection.

Anthony of the Holy Spirit († 1677) : *Directorium mysticum*, ed Paris, 1904. A manual like the preceding, but shorter and in one volume.

Honorius of St. Mary (1651-1729) : *Tradition des Pères et des auteurs ecclésiastiques sur la contemplation*, a work important in the history of this subject.

Joseph of the Holy Spirit : *Cursus theologiæ mystico-scholasticæ*, Seville, 1710-1740; med. ed. Bruges : Beyaert, c. 1923.

St. Teresa of the Child Jesus (1873-1897) : *Sœur Ste Thérèse of Lisieux : Autobiography*, Eng. tr. Taylor, New-York : Kenedy; London : Burns and Oates; also, Martin, G., *Little Way of Spiritual Childhood according to Bl. Thérèse*, New-York : Kenedy, 1923; Clarke, J. P., *Her Little Way : Bl. Thérèse of the Child Jesus*, New-York : Little Flower Book Shop, 1923; Laveille, Msgr., *St. Teresa of the Child Jesus*, Eng. tr. Fitzsimmons, London : Burns, Oates and Washbourne, 1928; Petitot, H., *St. Teresa of Lisieux*, Eng. tr., New-York : Benziger, 1927. A study by Trochu is soon to appear.

Aurelianus a Ssmo. Sacramento; *Cursus asceticus,* 3 vols., Ernakulam, India, 1917-1919.

Jerome of the Mother of God, *La tradition mystique du Carmel,* Bruges : Desclée, de Brouwer, 1929.

Fr. Alphonsus, *Practice of Mental Prayer and of Perfection,* 4 vols., Bruges, 1910.

Études carmélitaines, a quarterly founded in 1911, present editor Father Mary Joseph, publishes interesting articles on ascetical and mystical questions with a view to spread a right understanding of the teachings of St. Teresa and of St. John of the Cross.

3.—The SCHOOL OF ST. FRANCIS DE SALES (1567-1622) is chiefly concerned with the teachings of the founder himself. His great service was to show that devotion and even high sanctity are practicable *in every state of life.* A perfect gentleman and a devout humanist, an apostolic man and director, he knew how to make piety lovable without taking from it the spirit of sacrifice. The *Introduction to a Devout Life* is fundamentally a treatise on asceticism introducing souls to the purgative and illuminative ways; the *Treatise on the Love of God* raises them to the unitive way. In the latter work, contemplation is explained with the exact knowledge of a theologian and the psychology of a man who has gone through the experience. His Conferences directly address his own Visitandines, but do good to all. His many *Letters* apply the general principles explained in his books to each individual soul; one finds in them a delicately refined psychology, a quite exceptional tact, a good deal of frankness and of simplicity. Best French ed., *Œuvres,* Annecy.

In English, *Introduction to a Devout Life,* many eds., among them esp. Ross, New-York : Benziger, London : Burns Oates and Washbourne (Orchard Books), 1925; see also *Library of St. Francis de Sales,* 7 vols., 1908-1925. — *Treatise on the Love of God, Letters to Persons in Religion, Letters to Persons in the World. Catholic Controversy, Mystical Explanation of the Canticle of Canticles, Conferences.* Cfr. Saudreau, A., *Mystical Prayer according to St. Francis de Sales,* Eng. tr. Swinstead, London : Sheed and Ward; New-York : Benziger, 1930; Hamon, *Life of St Francis de Sales,* adapted by Burton, Eng. tr., New-York : Kenedy, 1926-1929; Sanders, E. K., *St Francis de Sales,* New-York : Macmillan, 1928; Bordeaux, H., *St. Francis de Sales,* (tr.) New-York Longmans, 1929; Stackpoole-Kenny, L. M., *St. Francis de Sales,* London, 1924; de Margerie, A., *St. Francis of Sales,* 6th imp., London, 1923; Sidney Lear, H. L., *St. Francis de Sales,* London, 1898; Marsollier, *Life of St. Francis of Sales, Bp. and Prince of Geneva,* (tr.), London, 1812; cfr. also Bremond, H., *Histoire littéraire, etc.,* (vols. 1 and 2), now in course of translation.

Camus, J. P., a friend of St Francis de Sales and a prolific writer : *Spirit of St Francis de Sales,* Eng. tr. J. S., London, 1925 (in *Library of St. Francis de Sales,* VII), New-York, Longmans.

St Jane Frances de Chantal (1472-1641) : *Sa vie et ses œuvres,* 7 vols., Paris, Plon, 1877-1893. In Eng., *Selected Letters of St. Jane Frances Fremiot de Chantal,* New-York : Kenedy, 1918; *Spirit of St. Jane Frances de Chantal,* New-York : Longmans, 1922; Sanders, E. K., *St. Chantal,* New-York : Macmillan, 1918; *The Spiritual Life, compiled from writings of St. Jane F. F. de Chantal,* St. Louis : Herder, 1928; *St. Jane F. de Chantal : Her Exhortations Conferences and Instructions,* rev. ed., Chicago : Loyola Univ. Press, 1929; Bougaud, Msgr. *St. Chantal and Foundation of the Visitation,* Eng. tr. Visitandine, 2 vols., 1895; Saudreau, A., *Mystical Prayer according to St Jane Chantal,* Eng. tr. Swinstead, London : Sheed and Ward; New-York : Benziger, 1930.

De Chaugy, Mère: *Mémoires sur la vie et les vertus de Ste Jeanne de Chantal,* Paris : Plon, 1893.

St. Margaret Mary Alacoque (1647-1693) : *Œuvres,* ed. Msgr. Gauthey, 3 vols., Paris : Poussielgue, 1914; Languet, J. J., *Life,* Eng. tr. Faber, 2 vols., London, 1850; Tickell, G., *Life,* New-York and London, 1869; Bougaud,

Msgr., *Life of St. Margaret Mary* (tr.) New-York : Benziger, 1920; Sr. Mary Philip, *Life*, St. Louis, 1919.

Tissot, *The Art of Profiting by our Faults*, Eng, tr. McMahon, New-York : Benziger, 1891 ; *The Interior Life*, Eng. tr. Mitchell, London : R. and T. Washbourne, New-York : Benziger, 1813.

Million, *Manrèze salésien :* meditations drawn from works of St. Francis.

Chaumont, II. (1838-1896) : a founder of three Salesian societies, this priest published or had published several tracts filled with the teaching of St Francis de Sales.

Giraud, S. M., *The Spirit of Sacrifice*, Eng. tr. Thurston, New-York : Benziger, 1905.

4.—The French School of the seventeenth century : its spiritual teaching flows from doctrines of faith, above all from the dogma of the Incarnation. Since we have been incorporated into Christ through baptism and have received the Holy Ghost who dwells in us, we must glorify God in union with the Incarnate Word living in us, reproduce His virtues, and vigorously fight against the contrary tendencies of the flesh, of the old Adam : " Let this mind be in you which was also in Christ Jesus... putting off the old man and putting on the new. "
The founder of the School was Cardinal de Bérulle. To it belong : the Fathers of the Oratory, St. Vincent de Paul, Father Olier and the Sulpicians, St. John Eudes and the Eudists, Bl. Grignion de Montfort, St. John Baptist de la Salle, Ven. F. M. Libermann and the Holy Ghost Fathers; de Renty, de Bernières, Boudon and Bishop Gay.

Càrdinàl de Bérulle (1575-1629) : founder of the Oratory in France *Œuvres complètes*, ed. Bourgoing, Paris, 1657[2]; also, Migne, Paris, 1856. His chief work is *Discours de l'Estat et des grandeurs de Jésus*, but for a full understanding of his teaching this must be supplemented by reading his smaller works. De Bérulle is the apostle of the Word Incarnate. For him to be a true Christian means to cling to Christ, to make Christ live in us by His virtues, to cut oneself off from creatures and from oneself. Cfr. Bremond, H., *Histoire littéraire*, etc., *Literary History of Religious Thought in France*, Eng. tr. Montgomery, London : S. P. C. K., (now in course of pub. and trans.); also, Pottier, ut supra, III. *La spiritualité bérullienne et les grands spirituels de la Compagnie de Jésus à l'âge d'or de l'ascéticisme français, 1500-1650*, Paris : Téqui, 1929; also, Sidney Lear, H. L., *Priestly Life in France*, London : Longmans, 1894.

De Condren, C. (1588-1641) : *Œuvres complètes* published after his death, first in 1668, later by Pin in 1857; see esp. his *L'idée du sacerdoce et du sacrifice* (Eng. tr. *Priesthood and Sacrifice*) and his letters. He completes de Bérulle's doctrine by his teaching on the priesthood and sacrifice : Jesus Christ, having become the unique adorer of the Father, by His self-abasement offers a sacrifice worthy of the Father; we share in this by abasing ourselves with Christ. Cfr. Sidney Lear, H. L., *Charles de Condren in Priestly Life in France.*

Bourgoing, F. (1585-1662) : *Vérités et excellences de Jésus-Christ... disposées en méditations*, ed. Ingold, Paris : Téqui, 1892[32].

St. Vincent de Paul (1576-1660) : founder of the Congregation of the Mission (Lazarists, Vincentians) and of the Sisters of Charity. Cfr. his *Correspondance, Entretiens, Documents*, ed. Coste, 1920 sqq. A disciple, but an original disciple, of de Bérulle, he in turn became a master whose prudence and sagacity really amount to genius. See Bougaud, Msgr., *History of St. Vincent de Paul*, Eng. tr. Brady, New-York, 1908; Boyle, P., *St. Vincent de Paul and the Vincentians*, London : R. and T. Washbourne, 1909; Lavedan, H., *Heroic Life of St. Vincent de Paul*, (tr.), New-York : Longmans, 1929; Leonard, J., *St. Vincent and Mental Prayer*, New-York : Benziger, 1925; Sanders, E. K., *Some Counsels of St. Vincent de Paul*, London and St. Louis : Herder, 1914; de Broglie, I., *St. Vincent de Paul*, Eng. tr.

Partridge, London : Burns and Oates, 1901 ; d'Agnel, A., *St. Vincent de Paul, maître d'oraison*, Paris : Téqui, 1929 ; *St. Vincent de Paul, directeur de conscience*, ibid., 1929.

J. J. Olier (1608-1657) : founder of the Society of St. Sulpice.   Abbé Bremond says that he alone gives us the teaching of the French School in the full extent of its principles and applications (*op. cit.*, vol. 3).   Besides many manuscripts, Father Olier has left the following : *Catéchisme chrétien pour la vie intérieure*, in which he shows how by practicing the crucifying virtues we may arrive at intimate and habitual union with Jesus; *Introduction à la vie et aux vertus chrétiennes*, explaining in detail the virtues that perfect this union all through the acts and circumstances of our life; *Traité des SS. Ordres*, written to make the young cleric ready to become a religious man by his transformation in Jesus Christ, high priest, sacrificer and victim; his *Lettres* complete this teaching, applying it to spiritual direction.   The *Pietas Seminarii S.-Sulpitii* gives a summary of all Sulpician devotions.   In Eng., *Catechism for an Interior Life*, Baltimore (out of print).

Blanlo, J. (1617-1657) : *The Childlike Spirit* (tr.), Baltimore, 1892, a participation in the spirit and grace of the Infant Jesus, Word Incarnate; another ed., *Sicut Parvuli*, tr. and ed. St. Louis : Herder, 1910.

Tronson, L. (1622-1700) : *Forma cleri*, 1727, 1770; *Particular Examens*, Eng. tr. by an Anglican, is a work sketched by Fathers Olier and de Poussé, and completed by Father Tronson; the latest ed. in French is by Branchereau. See also the treatises on obedience and humility : *Manuel du séminariste;* also, for complete works, Migne, 2 vols., 1857; *Conferences for Ecclesiastical Students and Religious*, Eng. tr. Clare, London : Burns and Oates, Dublin : Gill, 1878.

David, J. B. M. (1761-1841) : *The True Piety; A Spiritual Retreat of Eight Days;* ed. Spalding, Louisville, Kentucky, 1864.

Hamon, A. J. M. (1795-1874) : *Meditations* (tr.), 5 vols., New-York : Benziger, 1894[23].

Renaudet, G. (1794-1880) : *Month of Mary for use of Ecclesiastics* (tr.), Tournai : Desclée, 1911.

Bacuez, N. L. (1820-1892) : *Divine Office*, Eng. tr. Taunton, London : Burns and Oates, New-York : Cath. Pub. Soc., 1888; *Priestly Vocation and Tonsure*, (tr.), New-York : Cath. Lib. Associa., 1908; *Major Orders, Minor Orders*, Eng. tr. Nevins, London and St. Louis : Herder, 1913, 1912.

Ribet, M. J. : *La mystique divine distinguée des contrefaçons diaboliques et des analogies humaines*, 1879; *L'ascétique chrétienne*, 1902[3]; *Les vertus et les dons dans la vie chrétienne*, 1901.

Guibert, J. : *On Kindness* (tr.); *On Character; On Piety;* all in *Angelus Series*, London : Burns Oates and Wasbourne.

St. John Eudes, (1601-1680), a disciple of de Bérulle and de Condren, founder of the Congregation of Jesus and Mary (the Eudists) and of the Order of Notre Dame de Charité (Sisters of the Good Shepherd).   He perfectly assimilated the spiritual teaching of de Bérulle, clearly, popularly and practically expounded it, and wove the practice of the spiritual life into the devotion to the Hearts of Jesus and Mary, so much so that in the bull of beatification he is called the "father," the "teacher", and the "apostle" of the devotion to these sacred Hearts.   His work, redited in 12 vols., Paris, 1905; among them the chief are : *La vie et le royaume de Jésus dans les âmes chrétiennes:* here he explains that the Christian life is the life of Jesus in us and how we may do all our acts in Jesus and for Jesus; *Le contrat de l'homme avec Dieu par le saint baptême; Le Cœur admirable de la Mère de Dieu*, the 12th book of which deals with devotion to the Heart of Jesus — really the most important work of the Saint.   Also, *Le mémorial de la vie ecclésiastique; Règles et constitutions de la Congrégation de Jésus et de Marie* : these rules are made up of Scriptural texts logically grouped together, while the Constitutions consist of a practical commentary on the rules.   In Eng., *Reign of Jesus*, tr. and ed. Granger-Harding, London : R. and T. Washbourne, New-York :

Benziger, 1911; *Man's Contract with God in Baptism*, Eng. tr. Cullin, Philadelphia, 1859; O'Reilly, J., *Bl. Jean Eudes*, Halifax, 1909.

Lamballe, P. E., *La contemplation ou principes de théologie mystique*, 1912.

Bl. L. Grignion de Montfort (1673-1716) : founder of the Missionaries of the Company of Mary and the Daughters of Wisdom. Initiated into the spiritual doctrine of de Bérulle at the Seminary of St. Sulpice, he later wrote clear, popular and forceful treatises. Cfr. *Lettre circulaire aux amis de la croix*, Tours, Mame, many eds.; and in Eng., *True Devotion to the Blessed Virgin*, tr. Faber, London : Burns and Oates, New-York : Benziger, 1904[11]; *Secret of Mary*, (tr.), London : Burns Oates and Washbourne; Secular Priest, *Life of Blessed Louis Marie Grignion de Montfort*, 2 vols., London : Art and Book Co., 1892; *Life and Select Writings* (tr.), London : Richardson, 1870; Denis, G., *Reign of Jesus through Mary*, Eng. tr. Somers, London : Burns Oates and Washbourne.

St. John Baptist de la Salle (1651-1719) : founder of the Brothers of the Christian Schools (Christian Brothers). Being trained at St. Sulpice (Paris), he adapted the spiritual teachings of de Bérulle to his new institution. Cfr. in Eng., Thompson, F., *Life and Labours of St. John Baptist de la Salle*, London : Burns and Oates, St. Louis : Herder, 1911; F. C. N., *Life and Work of Ven. J. B. de la Salle*, New-York : Sadlier, 1878; Bro. Leo, *Story of St. John Baptist de la Salle*, New-York : Kenedy, 1921; Mrs Wilson, *Christian Brothers, their Origin and their Work*, London, 1883; Burke, P., *Thoughts of St. John Baptist de la Salle, etc.*, New-York : Sadlier, 1868; Bro. Agathon, *Virtues of a Good Master, etc.*, New-York : O'Shea, 1907; Anon., *Bl. de la Salle and his Educational Methods*, Chicago, Flanagan; Bro. Philip, *Meditation on the Passion of Our Lord Jesus Christ*, New-York : O'Shea, 1872; also, *Considerations for Christian Teachers*, Baltimore : Murphy, 1922.

Libermann, Ven. F. M., (1803-1852), founder of the Congregation of the Sacred Heart of Mary which was later joined to the Society of the Holy Ghost. He was trained at St. Sulpice and became an exponent of de Bérulle's spirituality in his treatises on prayer, especially on affective prayer, on the interior life and humility; cfr. his letters. Goepfert, P., *Life of Ven. Francis Mary Paul Libermann*, Dublin : Gill, 1880; Lee, G., *Life of Ven. F. Libermann*, St. Louis : Herder, 1911; *Spiritual Letters*, Eng. tr., Grunnenwald, vol. 1, Detroit : Bornmann, 1901; *Constitution of the Society of the Heart of Mary*, Winchester, 1890.

De Renty, († 1649) : his doctrine is given in the *Life*, by Saint-Jure, 1652; in Eng., *Life of Baron de Renty or Perfection in the World Exemplified* (tr.), London, 1873.

Gay, Bp. (1816-1892) : he received his training at St. Sulpice and wrote several works imbued with the teachings of Father Olier and those of St. Francis de Sales. In Eng., *Christian Life and Virtues considered in the Religious State*, tr. Burder, 3 vols., London : Burns and Oates, 1878; *Religious Life and Vows* (tr.), London, 1900[2].

Hogan, J. B. *Daily Thoughts*, Boston, 1899.

Grimal, J., S. M., *Priesthood and Sacrifice of Our Lord Jesus Christ*, Eng. tr. Keyes Philadelphia ; McVey, 1915; *Avec Jésus formant en nous son prêtre*, 2 vols., Paris and Lyon : Vitte, 1924.

Bruneau, J., *Our Priesthood*, St. Louis : Herder, 1930[2]; *Our Priestly Life*, Baltimore : Murphy, 1929.

F. P. H., *Meditation on the Passion and Eastertide*, Washington : Sulpician Seminary Press, 1928.

Farges, A., Msgr. *Mystical Phenomena* (tr.), London : Burns Oates and Washbourne, 1926; *Ordinary Ways of the Spiritual Life* (tr.), New-York : 1927. *Les écoles de spiritualité chrétienne*, Liége : Pensée Catholique, 1928.

5.—The SCHOOL OF ST. ALPHONSUS LIGUORI is notable for its practical and intense piety. Being based on the love of God and of Our Redeemer, it stresses prayer and mortification as *the* means for arriving at this love.

St. Alphonsus Liguori (1691-1787) : a most prolific writer. Besides his works on dogmatic and moral subject, he wrote on nearly every phase of the spiritual life; for Christian perfection in general see his *Complete Ascetical Works*, Eng. tr. Grimm, Cent. ed., 22 vols., New-York : Benziger, 1886-1892. St. Alphonsus' works are translated into French, German and English from the original Italian, the latest edition of which is that at Naples, 1840. Cfr. des Rotours, Angot, *St. Alphonsus Liguori* (tr.), New-York, 1916 ; Berthe, *Life of St. Alphonsus Liguori*, Eng. tr. Castle, 2 vols., St. Louis : Herder, 1906.

Desurmont, P. : *La charité sacerdotale*, 2 vols., Paris, 1899, 1901 ; *Le Credo et la Providence; La vie vraiment chrétienne*, and so on, Paris, 11, rue Servandoni.

Saint-Omer, P. : *Pratique de la Perfection d'après St. Alphonse*, Tournai, 1896 ; *St. Alphonsus' Prayer-Book : Selections*, Eng. tr. Ward, New-York : Benziger, 1890.

Dosda, J. : *L'union avec Dieu, ses commencements, ses progrès, sa perfection*, 1912.

Schrijvers, Jos. : *Les principes de la vie spirituelle*, Brussels, 1922; *Le don de soi; Le divin ami*, Tournai et Paris : Casterman, 1927, *Thoughts for a Retreat*.

Bouchage, F. : *Pratique des vertus; Introduction à la vie sacerdotale; Catéchisme ascétique et pastoral des jeunes clercs*, Paris : Beauchesne, 1916.

Bridgett, T. E. (1829-1899) : *History of the Holy Eucharist in Great Britain*, London : Burns and Oates, 1908.

Bronchain, *Meditations for Every Day*, Eng. tr. Girardey, 2 vols., St Louis : Herder, 1910.

Geiermann, *Private Retreat for Religious*, New-York : Benziger, 1909; and other works.

Girardey, F. : *Helps to a Spiritual Life*, trans. from German of J. Schneider, S. J., New-York : Benziger, 1903; *Meditations on Mysteries of Faith and Epistles and Gospels*, 2 vols., St Louis : Herder, 1906; *Conference Matter for Religious*, 2 vols., St Louis : Herder, 1914; *Prayer : Its Necessity, its Power, its Conditions*, St Louis : Herder, 1920.

Mueller, *Blessed Eucharist, our Greatest Treasure*, Baltimore : Kelly and Piet, 1868; *Prayer, Key of Salvation*, New-York : Pustet, 1909; *Catholic Priesthood*, 2 vols., New-York : Herder, Pustet, Benziger, 1885; and other books.

Coyle, J. B.; *Meditations and Readings from St. Alphonsus*, 6 vols., New-York : Herder, Dublin : Talbot, 1923-1929.

Miller, J. P., *Retreat Discourses and Meditations for Religious*, (J. P. Toussaint, author), St. Louis and London : Herder, 1929.

Stebbing, *The Redemptorists*, New-York : Benziger, 1924.

Warren, *Spirit of St. Alphonsus*, Boston : Mission Ch. Press, 1910; *Spirit of St. Francis de Sales*, ibid., 1910; *School of Christian Perfection*, ibid., 1912; *Characteristics from Works of St Alphonsus*, ibid., 1912.

6.—OUTSIDE THE PALE OF THESE SCHOOLS, there ought also to be mentioned :

Scupoli, L. (1530-1610) : *Spiritual Combat*, Eng. tr. fr. Italian, a work justly esteemed as one of the best treatises on the spiritual life by no less an authority than St Francis de Sales. Many eds., among them Baltimore : Murphy; London : Burns, Oates and Washbourne.

Marie de l'Incarnation, Ven. Mother (1599-1672) : *Autobiographie*, to be found in DOM CLAUDE'S *La vie de la V. M. Marie de l'Incarnation*, 1677, a work based on her letters and other writings; *Lettres de la V. M. Marie, etc.*, 1681 ; *Méditations et retraites*.

Bossuet, J. B. (1627-1704) : in addition to his polemical works against Quietism and his *Sermons* from which a treatise of ascetical theology might be drawn, he also published several tracts or opuscula of considerable worth : cfr. his *Instruction sur les états d'oraison*, containing the Christian principles on prayer, first ed. E. Levesque, Paris : Didot, 1897; also, *Les Élévations sur les mystères; Méditations sur l'évangile; Tr. de la concupiscence;* other small works on abandonment, prayer of simplicity, and so on, have recently been gathered in *Doctrine spirituelle de Bossuet,* Paris : Téqui, 1908.

Fisher, Bl. J. (1459-1535) : *Treatise of Prayer,* ed. O'Connor, London : Burns and Oates, 1887; and his other works. Cfr. Wilby, *Story of Bl. John Fisher,* 1929.

Fénelon, F., Abp. (1651-1715) : besides his *Maximes des Saints* and other writings in the Quietist controversy, he wrote numerous letters of direction. His works, on account of Quietist tendencies, should be read with caution. Cfr. summary of his spiritual teaching in Druon's *Doctrine spirituelle de Fénelon,* Paris : Lethielleux. In Eng., *Treatise on the Education of Daughters,* tr. Dibdin, Boston : Ewer, 1821; *Christian Counsels on Divers Matters pertaining to the Inner Life, and Spiritual Letters,* New-York : Dodd Mead, 1870; *Spiritual Progress, etc.* ed. Metcalf, ibid., 1853.

Courbon, *Familiar Instructions on Mental Prayer,* Eng. tr. E. F. B., New-York, 1871.

Benedict XIV (Prosper Lambertini) (1675-1758) : *De servorum Dei beatificatione et beatorum canonizatione,* Venice, 1788; *Heroic Virtue,* Eng. tr. F. W. Faber, 3 vols., London, 1850, 1852; See also *Canonisation of Saints* by Mackin, Dublin : Gill, New-York : Benziger, 1909.

Newman, J. H. Cardinal (1801-1890) : *Meditations and Devotions,* 1908; see also his *Sermons,* and his answer to Pusey regarding the cultus of the cultus of the Blessed Virgin. Cfr. *Works,* with Index by Rickaby, 40 vols., London and New-York : Longmans, 1874-1921.

Manning, H. E. Cardinal (1808-1892) : *Internal Mission of the Holy Ghost,* London : Burns Oates and Washbourne, 10th ed.; *Glories of the Sacred Heart,* London : Burns and Oates, 1876; *Eternal Priesthood,* Baltimore : Murphy; also, *Sin and Its Consequences; Love of Jesus for Penitent Sinners.*

Faber, F. W. (1814-1863) wrote very many ascetical works noteworthy for their unction and accurate psychology : *All for Jesus; The Blessed Sacrament; The Precious Blood; At the Foot of the Cross; Creature and Creator; Growth in Holiness,* Baltimore : Murphy, various eds.

Rosmini, Ant., *Maxims of Christian Perfection* (tr.), London : Burns and Oates, 1887.

Devine, A., C. P. : *Manual of Ascetical Theology,* London : R. and T. Washbourne, New-York : Benziger, 1902; *Manual of Mystical Theology,* ibid., 1903.

Gibbons, J. Cardinal (1834-1921): *Ambassador of Christ,* Baltimore : Murphy, freq. repr.

Beaudenom, L. (1840-1916) : *Spiritual Progress* (tr.), London : Burns Oates and Washbourne; *Path of Humility* (tr.), ibid., 1920.

Saudreau, A., *Degrees of the Spiritual Life* (tr.), 2 vols., New-York, 1907; *The Way that Leads to God,* Eng. tr. and ed. Smith-Camm, London : R. and T. Washbourne, New-York : Benziger, 1911; *Life of Union with God,* Eng. tr. Strickland, New-York : Benziger, 1927; *Mystical State,* Eng. tr. D. C. M., London, New-York : Benziger, 1925.

Lejeune, Msgr. *Introduction to Mystical Life,* Eng. tr. Levett, London : Burns Oates and Washbourne, 1924²; *Counsels of Perfection for Christian Mothers,* Eng. tr. Ryan, St Louis : Herder, 1913; also, *Holy Communion.*

Waffelaert, *Méditations théologiques,* Bruges and Paris : Lethielleux, 1919; *L'union de l'âme aimante avec Dieu; La colombe spirituelle, ou les trois voies du chemin de la perfection,* Desclée, 1919.

Gouraud, Msgr., *Directoire de vie sacerdotale.*

Challoner, Bp. R. (1691-1781) : many religious books, esp. meditations *Think Well On't, Garden of the Soul, Meditations for Every Day in the Year;*

cfr. work *Challoner's Meditations*, ed. Msgr. Virtue, London : Burns and Oates, New-York : Catholic Pub. Soc. 1879.

Hay, Bp. G. (1729-1811) : *Works*, ed. Strain, 5 vols., Edinburgh and London : Wm. Blackwood, Dublin : McGlashan and Gill, 1872 ; Boston : Noonan ; comprising *Sincere Christian, Devout Christian, Pious Christian*.

Wiseman, N. Cardinal (1802-1865) : *Daily Meditations*, Dublin : Duffy, c. 1869 ; *Meditations on the Incarnation, Meditations on the Passion*, 2 vols., London : Burns and Oates, New-York : Benziger, 1900.

Dalgairns, J. B. (1818-1876) : *Devotion to the Heart of Jesus*, London and Leamington : Art and Book Co., 1896 ; *On the Spiritual Life of First Six Centuries*, London : Richardson, c. 1867 ; *The Holy Communion : Its Philosophy, Theology, and Practice*, Dublin and London : Duffy, 1866² ; *Essay on Spiritual Life of Mediæval England* (pref. to Hilton's *Scale of Perfection*). London : Philip, 1871.

Lelong, Msgr., *Le saint prêtre*, being conferences on priestly virtues, 1901 ; *Le bon pasteur*, on the obligations of the pastoral cure, Paris : Téqui, 1893.

Landrieux, Msgr., *Sur les pas de S. Jean de la Croix dans le désert et dans la nuit ; Le divin Méconnu, ou les dons du Saint-Esprit.*

Mary Loyola, Mother : *Child of God, First Confession, Forgive Us Our Trespasses, First Confession Book for Little Ones, Simple Confession Book, First Communion, Soldier of Christ :* Burns Oates and Washbourne, London.

Chevrier, Ven. A., *Le prêtre selon l'évangile*, Lyon and Paris : Vitte, 1922.

Maturin, B. W. *Some Principles and Practices of the Spiritual Life*, New-York, Longmans ; *Self-Knowledge and Self-Discipline*, ibid., 1922 ; *Laws of the Spiritual Life*, ibid., 1924.

Stanton, A. J. F., *Catholic Mysticism*, London and Edinburgh : Sands, New-York : Benziger, 1929.

Tonna-Barthet, A., O. S. A., *The Christian Life, Compiled from the Works of St. Augustine*, Eng. tr. McGowan, New-York : Pustet, 1929.

Miriam Teresa, Sister, *Greater Perfection*, ed. Demjanovich, New-York : Kenedy, 1928.

Bellord, Bp. J., *Meditations on Christian Dogma*, 2 vols., London : C. T. S., 1906.

THE
SPIRITUAL
LIFE

INTRODUCTION [1]

It is the *perfection of the Christian life* that constitutes the proper object of ascetical and mystical Theology.

1. A God of all goodness vouchsafed to give us not only the natural life of the soul, but also a *supernatural life,* — the life of *grace.* This latter is a sharing of God's very life, as we have shown in our treatise *De gratia.* [2] Because this life was given us through the merits of Our Lord Jesus Christ, and because He is its most perfect exemplary cause, we call it rightly the *Christian life.*

All life must needs be perfected, and it is perfected by pursuing its end. *Absolute* perfection means the actual attainment of that end. This we shall attain only in Heaven. There, through the Beatific Vision and pure love, we shall possess God, and our life will have its complete development. Then we shall be like unto God, *because we shall see him as he is.*" [3]

Here on earth, however, the perfection we can reach is only *relative.* This we attain by ever striving after that intimate union with God that fits us for the Beatific Vision. The present treatise deals with this relative perfection. After an exposition of general principles on the *nature* of the Christian life, its *perfection,* the *obligation* of striving after it, and the general means of arriving thereat, we shall describe the *three ways, purgative, illuminative* and *unitive,* along which must go all generous souls thirsting for spiritual advancement.

2. First, however, some preliminary questions must be made clear in a short introduction.

In it we shall treat five questions :

I.   The *Nature* of Ascetical Theology ;

II.   Its *Sources;*

III. Its *Method;*

IV.   Its *Excellence* and *Necessity;*

V.   Its *Division.*

---

[1] TH. DE VALLGORNERA, O. P., *Mystica Theologia D. Thomæ,* t. I, q. I; E. DUBLANCHY, *Ascétique* in *Dict. de Théol.,* t. I, col. 2038-2046; HOGAN, *Clerical Studies,* ch. VI, art. 1; SCANNELL, *The Priest's Studies,* ch. VI.

[2] This treatise is found in our *Synopsis Theologiæ Dogmaticæ,* t. III.

[3] *I John,* III, 2 : " Similes ei erimus quoniam videbimus eum sicuti est ".

§ I. The Nature of Ascetical Theology

In order to show exactly what Ascetical Theology is, we shall explain : 1° The *chief names* given to it; 2° Its relation to the other theological sciences; 3° Its *relation*, both with *Dogma* and *Moral;* 4° The *distinction* between *Ascetical* and *Mystical* Theology.

I. Its Different names

3. Ascetical Theology goes by different names.

a) It is called the *science of the Saints*, and rightly so, because *it comes* to us *from the Saints*, who have taught it more by their life than by word of mouth. Moreover, ascetical theology is calculated *to make saints*, for it explains to us what sanctity is, and what the means are of arriving at it.

b) Some have called it *spiritual science*, because it forms spiritual men, that is to say, men of interior life, animated by God's own spirit.

c) Others have called it *the art of perfection*, for it is really a practical science, having for its goal to lead souls to Christian perfection. Again, they have called it *The Art of Arts*. And indeed, the highest art is that of perfecting the soul's noblest life, its supernatural life.

d) However, the name most commonly given to it to-day is that of Ascetical and Mystical Theology.

1) The word "*ascetical*" comes from the Greek ἄσκησις (exercise, effort) and means any arduous task connected with man's education, physical or moral. Christian perfection, then, implies those efforts that St. Paul himself compares to the training undergone by athletes with the purpose of obtaining the victory.[1] It was, therefore, natural to designate by the name of asceticism the efforts of the Christian soul struggling to acquire perfection. This is what *Clement of Alexandria* and *Origen* did, and, after them, a great number of the Fathers. It is not surprising, then, that this name of *asceticism* is given to the science that deals with the efforts necessary to the acquisition of Christian perfection.

2) Yet, during many centuries the name that prevailed in designating this science was that of *Mystical* Theology (μύστης, mysterious, secret, and especially a religious secret)

---

[1] *I Cor.*, IX, 24-27; *Ephes.*, VI, 11-16; *I Tim.*, IV, 7-8.

because it laid open the secrets of perfection. Later a time arrived when these two words were used in one and the same sense, but the usage that finally obtained was that of restricting the name *asceticism* to that part of the spiritual science that treats of the first degrees of perfection up to the threshold of contemplation, and the name of *mysticism* to that other part which deals with *infused* or *passive contemplation.*

Be that as it may, it follows from all these notions that the science we are dealing with, is indeed the science of Christian perfection. This fact allows us to give it a place in the general scheme of Theology.

II. Its Place in Theology

4. No one has made more clear the organic unity that holds all through the science of Theology than did St. Thomas. He divides his *Summa* into three parts. In the first, he treats of *God* as *the First principle.* He studies Him *in Himself*, in the Oneness of His nature, in the Trinity of His Persons, in the *works* of His creation preserved and governed by His Providence. In the second part, He deals with *God as the Last End.* Towards Him men must go by performing their actions for Him under the guidance of the law and the impulse of grace, by practising the theological and the moral virtues, and by fulfilling the duties peculiar to their state of life. The third part shows us the Incarnate Word making Himself *our way* whereby we may go to God, and instituting the Sacraments to communicate to us His grace unto life everlasting.

In this plan, ascetical and mystical theology belongs to the second part of the *Summa*, with dependence however on the other two parts.

5. Later theologians, without setting aside this organic unity of Theology, have divided it into three parts, *Dogmatic, Moral* and *Ascetical.*

a) *Dogma* teaches us what we must *believe* of God: His divine life, the share in it which He has willed to communicate to intelligent creatures, specially to man, the forfeiting of this divine life by original sin, its restoration by the Word-made-flesh, the action of that life on the regenerated soul, its diffusion through the Sacraments, and its completion in Heaven.

b) *Moral* theology shows us how we must respond to this love of God by cultivating the divine life He made us share. It shows us how we must shun sin, practise the virtues, and fulfil those duties of state to which we are stricly bound.

c) Yet, if we wish to perfect that life, desiring to go beyond what is of strict obligation, and wish to advance systematically in the practice of virtue, it is to *Ascetical* theology that we must turn.

III. ITS RELATIONS WITH MORAL AND DOGMATIC THEOLOGY

6. Ascetical theology is a part of the Christian Life. In truth, it is its most noble part, for its purpose is to make us perfect Christians. Although it has become a special, distinct part of Theology, it holds the closest relations both with Dogma and Moral.

1° *Its foundation in Dogma.* When describing the nature of the Christian life, it is from Dogma that we seek light. This life being actually a participation in God's life, we must soar up to the Blessed Trinity itself. There we must find its principle and source, see how it was bestowed on our first parents, lost through their fall, and given back by the Redeeming Christ.

There we must see its organism, its action in our soul, the mysterious channels through which it comes and grows, and how it is finally transformed into the Beatific Vision in Heaven.

All these questions are indeed treated in *Dogmatic* Theology. But if these truths are not set down once more in a short and clear synthesis, Asceticism will seem to be devoid of all foundation. We shall be demanding of souls costly sacrifices without being able to justify these demands by a description of what Almighty God has done for us. In truth, Dogma is fully what Cardinal Manning called it, the foutain-head of devotion.

7. 2° Ascetic Theology *also depends on Moral Theology and completes it.* The latter explains the precepts we must observe in order to possess and preserve the divine life. Ascetical Theology gives us in turn the means of perfecting it, and plainly presupposes the knowledge and the practice of those precepts. It would be indeed a vain and danger-ous illusion to neglect the precepts and, under the pretext of observing the counsels, to undertake the practice of the highest virtues without having learned to resist temptation and avoid sin.

8. 3° Withal, Ascetical Theology is truly a *branch* of Theology distinct from Dogma and Moral. It has its own proper object. It chooses from among the teachings of Our Lord, of the Church, and of the Saints, all that has reference to the *perfection* of the Christian life, and so coordinates all these elements as to constitute a real science. 1) Ascetical Theology *differs* from Dogma in this that, though grounded upon dogmatic truths, it actually directs these truths towards *practice*, making us understand, acquire a taste for, and live the life of Christian perfection. 2) It differs from Moral Theology, because, while it presents to our consideration the commandments of God and of the Church, which are the bases of all spiritual life, it insists also on the evangelical counsels, and on a higher degree of virtue than is strictly obligatory. Ascetical Theology, then, is truly *the science of Christian perfection.*

9. Hence its twofold character, at once *speculative* and *practical.* Without doubt, it contains a *speculative* doctrine, since it goes to Dogma when it explains the nature of the Christian life. Yet, it is above all *practical,* because it seeks out the means that must be taken to develop that life.

In the hands of a wise spiritual counsellor it becomes a *real art.* Here the art consists in applying the general principles with devotedness and tact to each individual soul. It is the noblest and the most difficult of all arts — *ars artium regimen animarum.* The principles and rules which we shall give will help to form good spiritual advisers.

IV. DIFFERENCE BETWEEN
ASCETICAL AND MYSTICAL THEOLOGY

10. What we have heretofore said of Ascetical Theology holds good also of Mystical Theology.

A) In order to make a distinction between them, we may thus define *Ascetical* Theology: that part of spiritual doctrine whose proper object is both the theory and the practice of Christian perfection, from its very beginnings up to the threshold of infused contemplation. We place the beginning of perfection in a sincere desire of advancing in the spiritual life; Ascetic Theology guides the soul from this beginning, through the *purgative* and *illuminative* ways, as far as *active* contemplation or the *simple unitive* way.

11. **B)** Mystical Theology is that part of spiritual doctrine whose proper object is both the theory and the practice *of the contemplative life*, which begins with what is called the first *night* of the senses, described by St John of the Cross, and the prayer of *quiet*, described by St. Theresa.

a) We thus avoid defining Ascetical Theology as the science of the *ordinary* ways of perfection, and Mystical Theology as the science of the *extraordinary* ways. Nowadays the word extraordinary is rather reserved to designate a special class of mystical phenomena such as ectasies and revelations which are special gifts *(charismata)* superadded to contemplation.

b) We do not distinguish here between acquired and infused contemplation so as not to become involved in controversy. Acquired contemplation being as a rule a preparation for infused contemplation, we shall treat it when speaking of the unitive way.

We purposely unite in this one treatise both Ascetical and Mystical Theology. 1) Surely there are *profound differences* between them. These we shall take care to point out later. There is, all the same, a certain *continuity* running through these two states, ascetic and mystic, which makes the one a sort of preparation for the other. *When He sees fit*, Almighty God makes use of the generous.dispositions of the ascetic soul and raises it to the mystic states. 2) One thing is certain, the study of Mystical Theology throws no little light upon Ascetic Theology and vice versa. This, because there is harmony in God's ways; the powerful action which He exercises over mystic souls being so striking, it renders more intelligible the milder influence He exerts over beginners. Thus the *passive trials*, described by St. John of the Cross, make us understand better the ordinary aridity that· is experienced in lower stages. Again, we understand better the mystic ways, when we see to what degree of docility and adaptability a soul can arrive that has for long years given itself up to the laborious practices of asceticism.

These two parts of one and the same science naturally throw light on one another and their union is profitable to both.

§ II. The Sources
of Ascetical and Mystical Theology

12. Since this spiritual science is one of the branches of Theology, it has the same sources as the others. We must give the first place to those that contain or interpret the data of revelation, that is, Holy Scripture and Tradition. Next in turn come the secondary sources, that is, all the knowledge that we acquire through *reason* enlightened by *faith* and *experience*. Our task is simply to point out the use we can make of them in Ascetic Theology.

I. HOLY SCRIPTURE

We do not find in Holy Scripture a scientific exposition of spiritual doctrine, yet, scattered here and there both in the Old and the New Testaments, we do find the richest data, in the form of *teachings, precepts, counsels, prayers* and *examples*.

13. 1° We find there the *speculative doctrines* concerning God, His nature and attributes, His immensity that pervades all things, His infinite wisdom, His goodness and justice, His mercy, His Providence exercised over all creatures and above all on behalf of men, in order to effect their salvation. We find likewise the doctrine concerning God's own life, the mysterious generation of the Word, the procession of the Holy Spirit — mutual bond of union between Father and Son. Lastly, we find God's works, in particular, those wrought for the welfare of man : man's share in the divine life, his restoration after the fall through the Incarnation and the Redemption, his sanctification through the Sacraments and the promise of everlasting joys.

It is obvious that such sublime teaching is a .powerful incentive to an increased love for God and to a greater desire for perfection.

14. 2° As to the *moral teaching*, made up of *precepts* and *counsels*, we find : The *Decalogue*, which is summed up in the love of God and the neighbour. Next, comes the high moral teaching of the *Prophets*, who ever proclaiming the goodness, the justice, and the love of God for His people, turn Israel away from sin, and especially from idolatrous practices, whilst at the same time they inculcate into the nation respect and love for God, justice, equity and goodness towards all, chiefly towards the weak and the oppressed. We have further the Sapiential Books, whose counsels, so full of wisdom, contain an anticipated exposition of the Christian virtues.

Towering above all else, however, stands the wonderful *teaching of Jesus*. His *Sermon on the Mount* is a condensed synthesis of asceticism. We find still higher doctrines in His discourses as recorded by *St. John* and commented upon by the same apostle in his Epistles. Finally, there is the spiritual theology of St. Paul, so rich in doctrinal ideas and in practical application. Even the bare summary which we shall give in an *Appendix* to this volume will show that the New Testament is already a code of perfection.

15. 3° We find also in Holy Writ *prayers* to nourish our love and our interior life. Are there any prayers more beautiful than those of the Psalter? The Church has deemed them so fit to proclaim God's praises and so apt to sanctify us, that She has incorporated them *into* her Liturgy, the Missal and the Breviary. Other prayers we also find here and there in the historical and sapiential books. But the prayer of prayers is the Lord's Prayer, the most beautiful, the most simple, and in spite of its brevity, the most complete that can be found. Added to this we have Our Lord's Sacerdotal Prayer, not to mention the doxologies contained in the Epistles of St. Paul and in the Apocalypse.

16. 4° Finally there are in Scripture *examples* that incite us to the practice of virtue : **a)** The Old Testament musters before us a whole series of patriarchs, prophets and other remarkable personages who were not indeed free from weaknesses, yet, whose virtues merited the praise of St. Paul, and are recounted at length by the Fathers, who propose them to us for imitation. Who would not admire the piety of Abel and Henoch, the steadfastness of Noe, who wrought good in the midst of a corrupt generation? Who would not pay homage to the faith and trust of Abraham, the chastity and prudence of Joseph, the courage, the wisdom and constancy of Moses, the fearless zeal, devotion and wisdom of David? Who would not admire the austerity of life in the Prophets, the heroic conduct of the Maccabees and countless other examples?

b) In the New Testament, it is of course Jesus Christ who appears as the ideal type of sanctity. Next, Mary and Joseph, His faithful imitators. Then, the Apostles, who imperfect as they were at first, gave themselves up so completely in body and soul to the preaching of the Gospel and to the practice of the Christian and Apostolic virtues, that their lives cry out to us, even louder than their words, " Be ye followers of me as I also am of Christ." [1]

---

[1] *I Cor.*, IV, 16.

If some of these holy ones had their faults, the manner in which they redeemed them adds greater worth to their example, for it shows us how we can, by penance, atone for our faults. [1]

II. TRADITION

17. Tradition completes Holy Writ. It hands down to us truths which are not contained in the latter. More, it interprets Scripture with authority. It is known to us by the *solemn* and *ordinary* teaching of the Church.

1° The *Solemn Teaching* consists chiefly in the definitions of Councils and Sovereign Pontiffs. It has but rarely concerned itself, it is true, with questions ascetical or mystical properly so-called; yet, it has often had to come to the fore in order to clear up and define those truths that form the bases of the science of perfection, to wit: God's life considered at its source; the elevation of man to a supernatural state; original sin and its consequences; the Redemption; grace communicated to regenerated man; merit, which increases in our souls the divine life; the sacraments, that impart grace; the Holy Sacrifice of the Mass in which the fruits of Redemption are applied. In the course of our study we shall have to make use of all these definitions.

18. 2° The *ordinary teaching* is exercised in two ways, *theoretically* and *practically*.

A) The *theoretical* teaching is given us first in a *negative* way, by the condemnation of the propositions of false mystics; secondly, in a *positive* manner, in the common doctrine of the Fathers and theologians or in the conclusions that follow from the lives of the Saints.

a) False mystics have at different times altered the true notion of Christian perfection. Such were the Encratists and the Montanists in the first centuries, the Fraticelli and the Beguines or Beghards [2] of the Middle-Ages, Molinos and the Quietists [3] in modern times. By condemning them, the Church has pointed out to us the rocks we must avoid and marked the course to which we must hold.

---

[1] In order to give an idea of the ascetical treasure contained in Holy Writ, we shall give, in the from of an *Appendix*, a synthetic summary of the spirituality of the Synoptics, St. Paul and St. John.

[2] DENZINGER, *Enchiridion*, 471-478; CATH. ENCYCL., *Beguines*.

[3] DENZINGER, *Enchiridion*, 1221-1288, 1327-1349; CATH. ENCYCL., *Molinos and Quietism.*

19. b) On the other hand, a *common doctrine* has gradually evolved from all those major questions that make up the living commentary of biblical teaching. This doctrine is found in the Fathers, the theologians and spiritual writers. In reading them we are impressed with their agreement on all vital points that have reference to the nature of perfection, the necessary means of arriving thereat, and the principal stages to be followed. Doubtless, there remain a few controverted points, but these concern secondary questions. Their very discussion simply brings into relief the moral unanimity that exists with regard to the rest. The tacit approval which the Church gives to this common teaching is for us a safe guarantee of truth

20. B) The *practical* teaching is to be found chiefly in the processes of the canonization of Saints, who have taught and practised the whole of these spiritual doctrines. We are all acquainted with the meticulous care exercised both in the revision of their writings and in the scrutiny of their virtues. It is easy to find out from the study of these documents just what principles of spirituality are the expression of the Church's mind with regard to the nature and the means of perfection. This can be clearly seen by perusing the learned work of Benedict XIV entitled : *De Servorum Dei Beatificatione et Canonizatione*, or some of the processes of Canonization, or even by reading biographies of the Saints, written according to the rules of sound criticism.

III. REASON ENLIGHTENED BY FAITH
AND EXPERIENCE

21. Human reason is a gift of God absolutely indispensable to man for the attainment of truth, whether natural or supernatural. It plays a very important rôle in the study of spirituality, just as it does in the study of the other ecclesiastical sciences. When it is question, however, of revealed truth, it needs to be guided and complemented by the *light of faith ;* and in the application of general principles to souls, it must look for help to *psychological experience.*

22. 1º Its first task is that of gathering, interpreting and setting in order the teachings of Scripture and Tradition. These are scattered through many books and need be put together if they are to form one consistent whole.

Besides, the sacred utterances were pronounced under diverse circumstances, elicited by particular questions, spoken to different hearers. In the same way, circumstances of time and place are often responsible for the texts of Tradition.

a) Therefore in order to grasp their meaning, we must needs place them in their proper setting, harmonize them with analogous teachings, and lastly, arrange them and interpret them in the light of the sum-total of Christian truths.

b) Once this first work is done, we may *draw conclusions* from these principles, show their legitimacy and their manifold applications to the thousand and one details of human life in its most varied situations.

c) Lastly, these principles and conclusions will be coördinated into one vast *synthesis* and thus will constitute a real science.

d) It is likewise the work of reason to *defend* ascetical doctrine against its detractors. Many attack it in the name of reason and science, seeing nothing but illusion in what embodies sublime reality. It is in the province of reason to make answer to such criticisms with the aid of philosophy and science.

23. 2º Spirituality is a science that is *lived*. It is important therefore *to show historically how it has been carried out in practice*. This requires the reading of the biographies of the Saints both ancient and modern, who lived in diverse countries and under different conditions. Thus we make sure of the way in which ascetical rules were interpreted when adapted to different epochs and peoples and to peculiar duties of state. More, since the members of the Church are not all holy, we must be thoroughly acquainted with the obstacles encountered in the practice of perfection and with the means employed to surmount them.

Psychological studies then are paramount, and to reading must be joined observation.

24. 3º It is further the task of reason enlightened by faith *to apply principles and general rules to each person in particular*. In this, account must be taken of the individual's temperament, character, sex and age, social standing, duties of state, as well as of the supernatural attractions of grace. One must also be mindful of the rules governing the *discernment of spirits*.

In order to fulfil this threefold rôle, it is not only necessary to possess a keen mind, but also a sound judgment
and great tact and discernment. One must add to this
the study of practical psychology, the study of temperaments, of nervous ailments and morbid conditions, which
exert such a great influence over mind and will. Then,
since it is question of a *supernatural* science, one must not
forget that the light of faith plays a predominant part,
and that it is the gifts of the Holy Ghost that bring this
science to its supreme perfection. This is true in particular
of the gift of *knowledge* which makes us rise even up to
God; of the gift of *understanding* which gives us a deeper
insight into the truths of faith; of the gift of *wisdom*
which enables us to discern and relish these truths; of the
gift of *counsel* that gives us skill to apply them to each
individual case.

Thus it is that the Saints, who allowed themselves to be
led by the Spirit of God, are the best fitted to understand
and the best to apply the principles of the spiritual life.

They have a sort of instinct for divine things, a kind of
second nature, that enables them to grasp them more
readily and to relish them more. " Thou hast hid these
things from the wise and prudent and hast revealed them
to little ones. " [1]

§ III. The Method to be followed [2]

What method must be followed in order to make the best
possible use of the sources we have just described? Ought
we to employ the *experimental*, also called the *descriptive*
method? the *deductive* one? or the combination of both?
What attitude should we adopt in the employment of these
methods? What aim should control their use?

25. 1° The *experimental* method, also called *descriptive*
and *psychological*, consists in the observation of ascetical or
mystical phenomena in oneself or in others, and in clas-
sifying these, in order to glean from them the characteristic marks peculiar to each state, as well as the virtues and
dispositions proper to them. This, without taking into
account the nature or cause of these facts, without any
further inquiry as to whether they have their origin in virtues, or proceed from the gifts of the Holy Ghost or from

[1] *Matth.*, XI, 25.
[2] R. GARRIGOU-LAGRANGE, O. P., *La Vie spirituelle*, 10 Oct. 1919, p. 11.

miraculous graces. This method, on its positive side, has many advantages, since facts must be well ascertained before we proceed to explain their nature and their cause.

26. **a)** But if this method were employed *to the exclusion* of the others, Ascetical Theology could not be made into a real science. This method does furnish the bases for a science, that is, facts and conclusions from these facts; it can even establish which are the practical means that ordinarily succeed the best. Yet, as long as one does not go on to the intimate nature and to the cause itself of these facts, one is dealing with psychology rather than with theology. Again, if one simply describes in detail the means of practising such or such a virtue, one does not sufficiently disclose the principle that motivates that virtue.

b) One would thus be exposed to form ill-founded opinions. For instance, if in studying comtemplation, one does not make a distinction between what is miraculous, like ecstasy or levitation, and that which constitutes the essential element of contemplation, to wit, a prolonged and loving regard of God under the influence of a special grace, then one can casily reach the conclusion that all contemplation is *miraculous*. This, however, is opposed to the common doctrine.

c) Many a controversy over the mystic states would amount to little, if to the descriptions of these states were joined the distinctions and accuracy, which the study of theology supplies. Thus a distinction between *acquired* and *infused* contemplation enables us to understand better some very real states of soul and to harmonize some opinions which at first sight appear to contradict one another. Again, there are numerous degrees in *passive* contemplation: some may be accounted for by the habitual use of the gifts of the Holy Ghost; in other cases, God intervenes in order to provoke ideas and to aid us in drawing to the most striking conclusions. Finally there are some that can be hardly explained by anything save infused knowledge. All these distinctions are the result of long and patient research in the fields of speculation and practice. In abiding by them we shall reduce to a minimum the differences that divide the various schools.

27. 2° The *doctrinal* or *deductive* method consists in studying the teaching of Holy Scripture, Tradition, and theology (especially the *Summa* of St. Thomas) concerning the spiritual life, and in drawing conclusions about its nature and perfection, about the obligation we have of making it the aim of our efforts, and about the means to be employed. In this method not enough stress is placed on psychological phenomena, on the temperament and character of individuals, on their special attractions, on the effects produced on individuals by certain particular means; nor is there a detailed study made of the mystic phenomena experienced and described by such persons as St. Theresa, St John of the Cross, St. Francis de Sales, etc. As we are liable to err in drawing conclusions, especially if we multiply them, it is simply wisdom to control our conclusions by facts. If, for instance, we discover that infused contemplation is rather rare, we shall then lay a few restrictions round the thesis sustained by some schools, namely, that all souls are called to the highest degrees of contemplation. [1]

28. 3° *Combination of both methods.*

A) Evidently, one must know how to harmonize both methods. This is in fact what most authors do, with this difference, that some lay more stress on *facts*, others on *principles*. [2]

We shall try to keep the golden mean without, however, making bold of success. **a**) The principles of mystical theology, drawn by the great masters from revealed truths, will help us to a better observation of the facts, to analyze the facts more thoroughly, to arrange them more systematically, and to interpret them more wisely. We must not forget the fact that, at least very often, the mystics describe their impressions without meaning to explain their nature. The principles spoken of will aid us also in seeking the cause of the facts, by taking into account truths already known, and to coördinate them into a real science.

b) *The study of the facts*, ascetical and mystical, will in turn correct whatever is too rigid and too absolute in purely dialectic conclusions. The truth is that there can be

---

[1] We rejoice therefore that two Reviews of different tendencies, *La Vie Spirituelle* and *la Revue d'Ascétique et de Mystique* have entered upon the course of making most careful and precise distinctions with regard to the call to contemplation : the *general* and *individual* call, the *proximate* and *remote*, the *efficacious* and *sufficient*. By narrowing down the sense of these words and studying the facts, the different schools come to understand one another better.

[2] Thus *Th. de Vallgornera* gives more prominence to the deductive method while P. Poulain, in the *Grâces d'oraison*, emphasizes the descriptive method.

no absolute opposition between the principles and the facts. Hence, if experience shows us that the number of mystics is quite limited, we cannot hasten to the conclusion that this is due solely to resistance to grace. [1] It is also well to keep in mind that in the process of canonization the Church ascertains genuine sanctity rather from the practice of heroic virtue than from the kind of contemplation. This goes to show that the degree of sanctity is not always and necessarily in proportion to the kind and degree of mental prayer.

29. B) *How can these two methods be combined?* **a)** It is necessary first of all to study *the deposit of revelation* as presented to us by Scripture and Tradition, including, of course, in the latter the ordinary teaching of the Church. From this deposit of truth we must determine by the *deductive* method what is Christian perfection and Christian life, what are its different degrees, what are the stages usually followed in order to reach contemplation, passing through mortification and the practice of the moral and theological virtues. Finally, from it we must also determine in what this contemplation consists, considering it either in its essential elements or in the extraordinary phenomena that at times accompany it.

30. **b)** This doctrinal study must be accompanied by methodical *observation :* 1) Souls must be examined with care; their qualities and their faults, their peculiar traits, their likes and dislikes, the movements of nature and of grace that take place within them. This phychological data will allow us to know better the means of perfection that are best suited to them; the virtues they stand in greatest need of and towards which they are drawn by grace; their correspondence with grace; the obstacles they encounter and the means most apt to insure success. 2) To widen the field of experience we must read attentively *the lives of the Saints*, especially those that, without hiding their defects, describe their tactics in combatting them, the means they availed themselves of to practise virtue, and lastly, how they rose from the ascetical to the mystical life, and under what influences. 3) It is also in the life *of the contemplatives* that we must study the different phenomena of contemplation, from its first faint glimmers to its full splendour. In them

---

[1] The full meaning of these remarks will be better understood when we come to the study of the contemporary discussions on contemplation.

we must study the *effects of sanctity* these graces work, the *trials* they had to undergo, the virtues they practised. All this will complete and, at times, correct the theoretical knowledge we may already possess.

31. **c)** With clear theological principles, with well-studied and well-classified mystic phenomena we can rise more easily to the *nature* of contemplation, its *causes*, its *species*, and distinguish what is normal from what is extraordinary in it.   1) We shall investigate how far the *gifts of the Holy Ghost* are formal principles of contemplation, and in what manner they must be cultivated so as to enter into the interior dispositions favorable to mystic life. 2) We shall examine whether the duly verified phenomena can all be accounted for by the *gifts of the Holy Ghost*, whether some of them postulate *infused species*, and how these work in the soul.   Again we may have to inquire further and see whether love alone produces these states of soul without any added knowledge.   3) Then we shall be able to see better the nature of the *passive state*, in what it consists, to what extent the soul remains active, and what part is of God and what of the soul in infused contemplation.   We shall be able to determine what is ordinary in this state and what is extraordinary and preternatural. Thus we shall be in a better position to study the problem of vocation to the mystical state and of the number of real comtemplatives.

Proceeding in this manner, we shall have a better hope of arriving at the truth, and at real practical conclusions for the direction of souls.   Such a study will prove as attractive as it is sanctifying.

32. 4° *What must be our attitude in following this method?*   Whatever the method employed, it is essential that we study these difficult problems with calmness, aiming at knowing the truth, not at making capital at all costs in behalf of a pet system.

a) Hence it is fundamental to seek out and place to the fore whatever is *certain* or *commonly admitted*, and to relegate to a second place whatever is disputed.   The direction souls must be given *does not depend on controverted questions*, but on commonly accepted doctrine.   All schools are unanimous in recognizing that charity and renouncement, love and sacrifice are indispensable to all souls and in all the ways of perfection, and that the harmonious combination of this twofold element depends largely upon the character of the person directed. It is admitted on all hands that no one can afford at any time to put out of his life the spirit of penance, even though it may take different forms according to the different degrees of perfection. In the same manner, it is agreed that, in order to arrive at the unitive way, one must exercise oneself more and more perfectly in the practice of both the moral and the theological virtues; that the gifts of the Holy Ghost, cultivated with care, endow the soul with a certain docility that renders it more submissive to the inspirations of grace, and, should God call it thither, prepares it for contemplation. No one questions the important fact that infused contemplation is essentially a *free gift of God;* that God bestows it upon whom He wills, and when He wills; that consequently it is not in anyone's power to place himself within the passive state, and that the indications of a proximate call to such a state are the ones described by St. John of the Cross. Likewise, all agree that once souls have reached contemplation, they must advance in perfect conformity with God's will, in a holy abandon and above all in humility.

33. b) It is our opinion that if we approach these problems in a *conciliatory manner*, looking for what tends to harmonise rather than for what would emphasize differences, we shall eventually not indeed eliminate these controversies, but shall certainly mitigate them and come to recognize the soul of truth contained in every system. This is the most we can do here and now. For the solution of certain difficult problems we must patiently await the light of the Beatific Vision.

§ IV. Excellence and Necessity of Ascetic Theology

The little we have said on the nature, sources, and method of Ascetical Theology will enable us now to survey briefly its *excellence* and its *necessity*.

I. EXCELLENCE OF ASCETICAL THEOLOGY

34. Its excellence comes from its object, which is one of the most exalted man can possibly study. It is in fact the divine life present and constantly fostered in the soul of man. If we analyse this notion we shall readily note how worthy of our attention this branch of theology is. [1]

1º First of all, we make a study of *God in His most intimate relations with the soul.* That is, we consider the Most Blessed Trinity dwelling and living in us, giving us a share in the divine life, collaborating in our good works and thus ever aiding us to develop that life; we see the same Triune God helping us to purify and beautify our soul by the practice of virtue, transforming it till it be ripe for the beatific vision. Can we imagine a like grandeur? We cannot think of anything more sublime than this transformation God works in souls in order to unite them to Himself and assimilate them perfectly.

2º We next study *the soul itself coöperating with God.* We see it weaning itself little by little from its faults and imperfections, nursing Christian virtues, making efforts to imitate the virtues of its Divine Model in spite of the obstacles it finds both within and without, fostering the gifts of the Holy Ghost, developing a marvellous responsiveness to the least touch of grace, and becoming each day more and more like its Father in Heaven. To-day, when *life* and the questions related thereto are considered the ones most worthy of our attention, we cannot overestimate the import of a science that treats of a supernatural life, of a participation in God's own life, that tells us its origin, its growth and its full development in eternity. Is it not the most noble object of study?

11. NECESSITY OF ASCETICAL THEOLOGY

To be the more precise in such a delicate matter, we shall explain : 1º Its *necessity* for the *priest;* 2º its *usefulness* for the faithful; 3º the *practical way* of studying it.

1º *Its necessity for the Priest.*

35. The priest is bound to sanctify himself and his brethren, and from this twofold view, he is obliged to study the science of the Saints.

---

[1] « The value of the science of Ascetic Theology is so obvious from its very definition that it need not be dwelt upon at any great length. The higher christian life is the noblest and greatest thing in the world. Its principles and its laws are of more importance to the Christian than all other philosophies and legislations, its methods more important to know than those by which fame is won and wealth accumulated. » HOGAN, *Clerical Studies*, p. 265.

A) We shall demonstrate with St. Thomas, later on, that the priest is not only obliged to strive after perfection, but that he must possess perfection in a higher degree even than the *simple religious*. Now, a knowledge of what the Christian life is and of the means of perfecting it is *normally* necessary to reach perfection, for *nil volitum quin praecognitum*.

a) Knowledge fires and stimulates desire. To know what sanctity is, its sublimity, its moral obligation, its wonderful effects on the soul, its fruitfulness, to know all this, we say, is to *desire* sanctity.

One cannot for any length of time behold a luscious fruit without conceiving the thought of tasting it. Desire, especially when vivid and sustained already constitutes an incipient act. It sets the will into motion and urges it on to the possession of the good the mind has apprehended. It gives it impulse and energy to obtain it; it sustains the effort required to seize upon it. This is all the more necessary when one considers how many are the obstacles that work counter to our spiritual advance.

b) To know in detail the various steps in the way to perfection, and to see the sustained efforts made by the Saints to triumph over difficulties and to advance steadily towards the desired goal, will stir up our courage, sustain our enthusiasm in the midst of the struggle and prevent us from becoming lax or tepid, especially if we recall the helps and consolations which God has prepared for souls of goodwill.

c) This study is of capital importance and all the more in our day : we actually live in an atmosphere of dissipation, of rationalism, of naturalism and sensualism. It envelopes even unawares a multitude of Christian souls, and finds its way into the sanctuary itself. It is idle to repeat, that the very best way to react against these fatal tendencies of our time is to live in close contact with Our Lord by a systematic study of the principles of the spiritual life — principles that are in direct opposition to the threefold concupiscence.

36. **B)** *For the sanctification of the souls entrusted to their care.* **a)** Even in the case of *sinners*, the priest must know Ascetical Theology to teach them how to avoid the occasions of sin, how to struggle against their passions, resist temptations and practise the virtues opposed to the vices they must avoid. No doubt Moral Theology suggests these things, but Ascetical Theology coördinates and develops them.

b) Besides, in almost every parish one finds *chosen souls* whom God calls to perfection. If they are well directed, they will by their prayers, their example, and the thousand means at their disposal, be a real help to the priest in his ministry. At all events a priest can train up such by choosing carefully from among the children attending Sunday school or sodalities. In order to succeed in this important task, the priest must of necessity be a good guide of souls. He must know thoroughly the rules given by the saints, which are contained in spiritual books. Without this, he will have neither the taste nor the ability required for this difficult art of guiding souls.

37. c) One more reason for the study of the ways of perfection lies in the guidance to be given *fervent souls.* These one meets with, at times, even in the most secluded country districts. In order to lead these souls to the prayer of simplicity and to ordinary contemplation one must, not to blunder and actually place obstacles in their way, know not only Ascetical but also Mystical Theology. On this point *St. Theresa* remarks : " For this, a spiritual director is very much needed — but he must be experienced... My opinion is, and will always be, that as long as it is possible, every Christian must consult *learned men* — the more learned the better. Those that walk in the ways of prayer have more need of such than the rest; and the more so, the more spiritual they are... I am thoroughly persuaded of this, that the devil will not seduce with his wiles the man of prayer who takes counsel with theologians, unless he wishes to deceive himself. According to my opinion, the devil is in mortal fear of a science that is both humble and virtuous; he knows full well that it will tear his mask and rout him. " [1] *St. John of the Cross* speaks in the same way : " Such masters of the spiritual life (who know not the mystic ways) fail to understand the souls engaged in this quiet and solitary contemplation... they make them take up again the ordinary ways of meditation, to exercise the memory, to perform interior acts in which such souls meet with nothing but dryness and distraction... Let this be well understood :

[1] *Life by Herself*, ch. 13. The whole passage to be read with others scattered through the works of the Saint.

Whoever errs through ignorance, when his ministry imposes on him the duty of acquiring knowledge that is indispensable, shall not escape punishment in proportion to the resultant evil. " [1]

Let no one say to himself: If I encounter such souls, I will abandon them to the guidance of the Holy Ghost. — The Holy Ghost will make answer that He has entrusted them to your care, and that you must coöperate with Him in guiding them. Without doubt, He can Himself guide them, but to preclude any fear of illusion, He wills that such inspirations be submitted to the approbation of a human counsellor.

2° Its usefulness for the Laity.

38. We say *usefulness* and not necessity, since lay folk can well entrust themselves to the guidance of a learned and experienced director and are not therefore absolutely bound to the study of Ascetical Theology.

Nevertheless the study of Ascetical Theology will be most useful to them for three good reasons : — **a**) In order to stimulate and sustain *the desire* of perfection as well as to give a definitive *knowledge* of the Christian life and of the means which enable us to perfect it. No one desires what one does not know, *ignoti nulla cupido*, whereas reading spiritual books creates or increases the sincere desire to put into practice what has been read. Many souls, as is well known, are ardently carried on to perfection by reading *The Following of Christ*, the *Spiritual Combat*, *The Introduction to a Devout Life* or the *Treatise on the Love of God*.

b) Even when one has a spiritual guide, the reading of a good Ascetical Theology *facilitates* and *completes* spiritual direction. One knows better what must be told in confession, what in direction. It makes one understand and retain better the advice of one's spiritual adviser because it may be found again in a work to which one can return and reread. It, in turn, relieves the spiritual director from entering into endless details. After giving some solid advice he can have the penitent himself read some treatise where he will find supplementary information. Thus he can shorten his direction without causing any loss to his penitent.

---

[1] *La vive flamme d'amour*, strophe III, v. 3, § 11, p. 308-311.

c) Finally, if a spiritual guide cannot be had or if spiritual advice can be had but at rare intervals, a treatise on the spiritual life will, in a way, *take the place* of spiritual direction.   There is no doubt, as we shall repeat later on, that spiritual direction constitutes the normal means in the training to perfection.   But if for some reason or other one is unable to find a good adviser, God provides for the lack; and one of the means He uses is precisely some such book as points out in a definite and systematic manner the way to perfection.

3° *The Way to study this Science.*

39.   Three things are needed to acquire the knowledge necessary for the direction of souls : a *Manual*, reading the *great masters*, and *practice*.

(**A**) *The Study of a Manual*.   The seminarian is indeed helped in acquainting himself with this difficult art by the spiritual conferences he listens to, the practice of spiritual direction, and above all by the gradual acquisition of virtue. To this, however, the study of a good Manual must be added.

1) The spiritual conferences are chiefly an exercise of piety, a series of instructions, of advice and exhortation concerning the spiritual life.   Rarely, however, do they treat *all the questions concerning the spiritual life* in a methodical and complete fashion.   2) At all events, seminarians will soon *forget* what they heard and will lack competent knowledge, unless they have a Manual to which they can relate the varied advice given them and which they can reread from time to time.   Rightly did Pius X say that one of the sciences young clerics should acquire at the Seminary is : " *The science of Christian piety and practice, called ascetical theology.*" [1]

40.   (B) *A deep study of the Spiritual Masters*, par-

---

[1] *Motu proprio*, 9 Sept. 1910, A. A. S., II, p. 668 — Pope BENEDICT XV has ordered that a chair of Ascetical Theology be established at the two great theological Schools of Rome.

In the meeting of the Seminary Department of the Educational Association at Cincinnati in 1908 the late Bishop Maes of Covington complained that our young men do not seem to be acquainted with the spiritual life and added : " If I were to put my finger on the great defect in the training of many Seminaries, I would point to the absence of a course of Ascetic Theology. "

In the meeting of the same Seminary Department at Milwaukee in 1924, the following resolution was passed :

" That ascetical theology should be systematically studied with a suitable text, and that the curriculum should be so ordered as to provide for such courses. "

ticularly those 'who have been *canonized* or those, who although not canonized, have *lived saintly lives.*

a) As a matter of fact, it is by coming into contact with these that the *heart* glows, that the *mind*, enlightened by faith, sees more clearly and relishes better the great principles of the spiritual life. It is at their touch that the will, sustained by grace, is drawn to the practice of the virtues so vividly described by those who have lived them in the highest degree. By the perusal of *the lives of the Saints* one will understand even better why and how one must imitate them. The irresistible influence of their examples will add new strengh to their teaching : " *Verba movent, exempla trahunt.* "

(b) This study, begun at the Seminary, ought to be *continued* and *perfected* in the *ministry*. The direction of souls will render it more practical. Just as a good physician is never through advancing in knowledge by practice and study, just so a good spiritual adviser will complement theory by actual contact with souls and by further studies, according to the needs of the souls entrusted to his care.

41. c) *The practice of Christian and Priestly virtues*, under the care of a wise director : To understand well the various stages of perfection, the best means is to go through them oneself, just as the best mountain-guide is the one that is familiar on first-hand information with the trails. Once one has been wisely guided, one is more competent to direct others for the simple reason that it is experience itself that shows us how to apply the rules to particular cases.

If these three elements are combined the study of Ascetical Theology will prove most fruitful both to self and to others.

42. Solution of some difficulties. A) A reproach often directed against Asceticism is that it produces a false conscience, by going so far beyond Moral Theology in its exactions, and by demanding of souls a perfection that is well-nigh beyond realization. This reproach would be indeed well grounded if Asceticism would not make a distinction between *commandment* and *counsel*, between souls called to high perfection and those not so called. This is not so, for while it does urge chosen souls toward heights that are out of the reach of ordinary Christians, it does not lose sight of the difference between commandment and counsel, between the conditions that are essential for salvation and those that are necessary to perfection. It keeps in view on the other hand, that the observance of certain counsels is indispensable to the keeping of the commandments.

43. **B**) Asceticism in also attacked on the ground that it fosters egotism since it puts personal sanctification above all else. But Our Lord Himself teaches us that our chief concern must be the salvation our souls : *" For what doth it profit a man, if he gain the whole world and suffer the loss of his own soul?"* [1] In this there is not the least egotism, for one of the essentials for salvation is love of the neighbor. This love is manifested by works both corporal and spiritual, and perfection precisely demands that we love our neighbor to the point of sacrifice as Christ loved us. Should this be *egotism*, we must acknowlegde that we have little to fear from it. We have only to read the lives of the Saints to see that they were the most unselfish and the most charitable of men.

C) The further objection is made that Asceticism, by impelling souls towards *contemplation*, turns them from a life of action. To state that contemplation is detrimental to an active life is to pass over historical facts. *" Real mystics, "* says *M. de Montmorand,* [2] an unbeliever, *"* are practical men of action not given to mere thought and theory. They possess the gift and the knack of organization as well as talent for administration showing themselves well equipped for the handling of affairs. The works instituted by them are both feasible and lasting. In the conception and conduct of their undertakings they have given proof of prudence and enterprise and full evidence of that exact appreciation of possibilities which characterizes common sense. In fact, good sense seemed to be their outstanding quality, — good sense undisturbed either by an unwholesome exaltation, or a disordered imagination, but rather, possessed of an uncommon and powerful keenness of judgment. "

Have we not seen in Church History that most of those Saints who have written on the spiritual life were at the same time men both of learning and action? Consider Clement of Alexandria, St. Basil, St. John Chrysostom, St. Ambrose and St. Augustine, St. Gregory, St. Anselm, St. Thomas and St. Bonaventure, Gerson, St. Theresa; St. Francis de Sales, St. Vincent de Paul, Cardinal de Bérulle, M. Acarie, and numberless others. Contemplation far from hampering action, enlightens and directs it.

There is therefore nothing worthier, or more important, or more useful than Ascetical Theology rightly understood.

§ V. Division of Mystical and Ascetical Theology

I. THE VARIOUS PLANS FOLLOWED BY AUTHORS

We shall first enumerate the various plans generally followed and then present the one which seems best suited to our purpose. Different points of view may be taken when making a logical division of the science of spirituality.

44. 1° Some look at it chiefly as a *practical* science. They leave aside all the speculative truths that form its

---

[1] *Matth.*, XVI, 26.
[2] M. DE MONTMORAND, *Psychologie des Mystiques*, 1920, p. 20-21.

basis and limit themselves to coördinate as methodically as possible the rules of Christian perfection. So did Cassian, in his *Conferences,* and St. John Climacus, in the *Mystic Ladder.* Rodriguez in modern times did the same in his *Practice of Christian Perfection.* The advantage this plan offers is it takes up at once the study of the practical means that lead to perfection. Its drawback is to leave out the *incentives* given by the consideration of what God and Jesus Christ have done and still do for us, and not to base the practice of virtue upon those *deep* and all-embracing convictions that are formed by reflecting on the truths of dogma.

45. 2° Likewise the most illustrious among the Fathers both Greek and Latin, to wit, St. Athanasius and St. Cyril, St. Augustine and St. Hilary have taken care to base their teachings regarding the spiritual life upon the truths of faith and to build on them the virtues, the nature and degrees of which they explained. The same is true of the great theologians of the Middle Ages, Richard of St. Victor, Blessed Albert the Great, St. Thomas and St. Bonaventure. This is exactly what was done by the French School of the XVII century, through such men as Bérulle, Condren, Olier, St. J. Eudes.¹ Its great merit lies in the fact that it makes for the enlightenment of the mind and the strengthening of convictions so as to render more easy to men the practice of those austere virtues it proposes. It is accused at times of being given too much to speculation while touching little on practice. To unite these two plans would be the ideal. Several have attempted it and with success.²

46. 3° Of those who strive to combine these two essential elements, some adopt the *ontological* order treating successively of the various virtues; others follow the *psychological* order of development of the said virtues throughout the course of the purgative, illuminative and unitive ways.

A) Among the former we find St. Thomas. In the *Summa* he treats successively of the theological and moral virtues, and of the gifts of the Holy Spirit which correspond to each virtue. He has been followed by the principal

---

¹ H. BREMOND, *Hist. litt. du sentiment religieux,* III, L'Ecole française, 1921.
² This has been very well done, among others, by St. Jean Eudes in his writings; by L. TRONSON in particular Examens, in which making use of the works of J. J. OLIER, he has aptly condensed the asceticism of the latter.

authors belonging to French School of the XVII century and by other writers. [1]

B) Among the latter are all those whose principal aim was to form directors of souls. They describe the progress of the soul 'through the three ways; at the head of their treatises they simply give a short introduction on the nature of the spiritual life. Such are Thomas of Vallgornera, O. P., *Mystica Theologia Divi Thomae,* Philip of the Blessed Trinity, O. C. D., *Summa theologiae mysticae,* Schram, O. S. B., *Institutiones theologiae mysticae,* Scaramelli, S. J., *Direttorio Ascetico,* and today, A. Saudreau, *The Degrees of the Spiritual Life,* Fr. Aurelianus a SS. Sacramento, O. C. D., *Cursus Asceticus.*

47. 4⁰ Others, like Alvarez de Paz, S. J. and P. Le Gaudier, S. J., have combined both methods: they treat at length, from the point of view of dogma, whatever appertains to the nature of the spiritual life and the chief means of perfection; then they make application of these general principles to the three ways. It seems to us that to attain the end we have in view, that is, *to form spiritual directors,* the last is the best plan to follow. No doubt, with such a scheme, one is bound to repeat and to parcel out, yet any division of the subject would necessarily offer like inconveniences. For these one can make up by proper references to subjects already dealt with or to be unfolded later on.

II. OUR PLAN.

48. We divide our Treatise of Ascetic Theology into two parts. The first is above all doctrinal. We entitle it *Principles.* In it we explain the *origin* and *nature* of the Christian life and its *perfection,* the *obligation* of striving after it and the *general means* of attaining it.

We designate the second part as *the Application of principles* to the different categories of souls. In it we follow the gradual rise of the soul that, desirous of perfection, goes successively through three ways, *purgative, illuminative,* and *unitive.* Although resting on dogma this latter part is chiefly *psychological.*

The first part is designed to *throw light* on our path by showing us the divine plan of sanctification. It should

---

[1] In our day by MGR.GAY, *De la vie et des vertus chrétiennes;* CH. DE SMET,S. J., *Notre vie surnaturelle.*

inspire us with courage in our efforts, for it reminds us of God's generosity toward us. It traces for us as in a foreground the great lines we are to follow in order to correspond to this bounty of God Almighty by the complete giving of self. The second part is meant to *guide* us in the detailed exposition of these successive stages, which, God helping, must be traversed to reach the goal. This plan, we hope, will unite the advantages of the various other divisions.

FIRST PART
𝔓rinciples

49. The aim of this first part is to call briefly to mind the principal dogmas upon which our spiritual life rests, to show the nature and perfection of this life, and the general means by which perfection is reached. Here we follow the *ontological* order, assigning to the second part the task of describing the *psychological* order normally followed by souls in the use they make of the various means of perfection.

DIVISION

C. I. *Origin* of the supernatural life : the raising of man to the supernatural state, his fall, and redemption.

C. II. *Nature* of the Christian life : God's part and the soul's part.

C. III. *Perfection* of this life : the love of God and of the neighbor carried to the point of sacrifice.

C. IV. Obligation for *laymen, religious* and *priests* to strive after this perfection.

C. V. *General means*, interior and exterior, of attaining perfection.

50. The reason for such a division is easily perceived.

The *first* chapter, by taking us back to the source itself of the supernatural life, helps us to a better grasp of its *nature* and *its excellence*.

The *second* chapter reveals the *nature* of the *Christian* life in regenerated man ; the part God takes therein by *giving Himself* to *us* through His Son; and by assisting us through the agency of the Blessed Virgin and the Saints. It likewise explains the *rôle* man plays in *giving* himself to God by a constant and generous coöperation with grace.

The *third* chapter shows that perfection in this life essentially consists in the love of God and of the neighbor for God's sake. It shows further, however, that this love here on earth cannot be exercised without generous sacrifices.

In the *fourth*, the obligation of tending to perfection is determined and the extent to which the faithful, religious, and priests are respectively bound.

A *fifth* chapter is devoted to specifying the general means that help us to advance in perfection, means common indeed to all, yet susceptible of degrees. These degrees will be treated in the second part when speaking of the three ways.

CHAPTER I.

Origin of the spiritual life

51. This chapter is intended to give us a better knowledge of the excellence of the supernatural life in as much as it is a free gift; and of the nobility as well as the weakness of man, upon whom it has been bestowed. To help us understand it better we shall see:

I. What the *natural* life of man is.

II. Man's *elevation* to the supernatural state.

III. His fall.

IV. His *restoration* by a Divine Redeemer.

ART. I. THE NATURAL LIFE OF MAN

52. Here we must describe man's condition as it would have been in the purely natural state, such as it is described by Philosophers. It is important to recall to mind, though briefly, what right reason teaches us on this point, because our spiritual life, while preserving and perfecting our natural life, is grafted on it. [1]

53. 1º Man is a mysterious compound of *body* and *soul*. In him *spirit* and *matter* closely unite to form but one nature and one person. Man is, so to speak, the nexus, the point of contact between spiritual and bodily substances — an abstract of all the marvels of creation. He is a little world gathering in itself all other worlds, *a microcosm*, showing forth the wisdom of God who united in this fashion two things so far apart.

This little world is full of life : according to St. Gregory, one finds there three sorts of life, *vegetative, animal* and

---

[1] Besides Philosophical Treatises, cf. CH. DE SMEDT, *Notre Vie surnaturelle*, 1912, Introduction p. 1-37; J. SCHRYVERS, *Les Principes de la Vie spirituelle*, 1922, p. 31.

intellectual. [1] Like *plants* man takes food, *grows*, and *reproduces* himself. Like *animals*, he is aware of sensible objects, towards which he is drawn by sensitive appetite, emotions and passions, and like animals he moves spontaneously from within. Like *angels*, though in a different manner and in a lesser degree, he knows intellectually suprasensible being and truth, while his will is freely drawn towards rational good.

54. 2° These three kinds of life are not superimposed one on the other, but they blend and arrange themselves in due relation in order to converge towards the same end — the perfection of the whole man. It is both a rational and a biological law that in a composite being life cannot subsist and develop save on condition of harmonizing and bringing its various elements under the control of the highest of them. The former must be mastered before they can be made to minister. In man, then, the lower faculties, vegetative and sensitive, must needs be subject to reason and will. This condition is essential. Whenever it fails, life languishes or vanishes. Whenever this subordination ceases altogether, disintegration of the elements sets in; this means decay of the system and, finally, death. [2]

55. 3° Life is, therefore, a struggle. Our lower faculties tend lustily toward pleasure, whilst the higher ones are drawn towards moral good. Often conflict goes on between these; what pleases us, is not always morally good, and, to establish order, reason must fight hostile tendencies and actually conquer. This is the *fight of the spirit* against *the flesh*, of the *will* against *passion*. This struggle is at times hard and painful. Just as in the springtime of the year the sap rises up within plants, so at times violent impulses towards pleasure rise in the sensitive part of our soul.

56. These impulses, nevertheless, are not *irresistible.* The will helped by the intellect exercises over these movements of passion a fourfold control. 1) The power of *foresight* which consists in *foreseeing* and *forestalling* a great many dangerous fancies, impressions and emotions, by a constant and intelligent vigilance. 2) The power of *inhibition* and *moderation*, by means of which we either check or at least allay the violent passions which arise in the soul.

[1] He says *(Homil. 29 in Evangelia) :* « Homo habet *vivere cum plantis, sentire cum animantibus, intelligere cum* angelis ».

[2] A. EYMIEU, *Le Gouvernement de soi-même,* t. III, *La Loi de la Vie,* book III, p. 128.

Thus we are able to prevent our eyes from lighting upon dangerous objects, our imagination from dwelling upon unwholesome pictures; should a fit of anger stir, we are able to stem it. 3) The power of *stimulation*, which through the will stirs and gives *impetus* to the movements of the passions. 4) The power of *direction*, which allows us to direct those movements towards good and thereby to divert them from evil.

57. Besides this inward strife, there may be other conflicts *between the soul and its Maker*. Although it is evident that our plain duty is that of entire submission to Our Sovereign Master, yet for this subjection we must pay the price. A lust for freedom and independence ever inclines us to swerve from Divine Authority. The cause lurks in our pride, which cannot be trampled upon, except by the humble admission of our unworthiness and our littleness in the face of those absolute rights the Creator has upon a creature. Thus it is that even in this purely natural state we would still have a fight to wage against the threefold concupiscence.

58. 4° If far from yielding to these evil inclinations we would have done our duty, we could have justly expect a reward. For our immortal soul, this reward would have consisted, first, in a deeper and a greater knowledge of God and of truth — a knowledge, of course, analytical and discursive; then, in a love, also purer and more enduring. If, on the contrary we would have voluntarily violated the law in grave matter and remained unrepentant, we should have failed of our end, meriting as punishment the privation of God and such torments as would fit the gravity of our faults.

This would have been our condition had we been constituted in a merely natural state. This state has not, as a matter of fact, ever existed, for according to St. Thomas, man was raised to the supernatural state at the very moment of creation, or immediately after, as St. Bonaventure says.

God in His infinite goodness, was not satisfied with conferring upon man natural gifts. He willed to elevate him to a higher state by granting him still others of a preternatural and supernatural character.

Art. II. the elevation of man to the supernatural state [1]

I. *Notion of the Supernatural*

59. Let us call to mind that Theology distinguishes between what is absolutely and what is relatively supernatural.

1° An *absolutely* supernatural gift is one which in its very essence *(quoad substantiam)* transcends nature altogether, so that it cannot be due to nor be merited by any creature whatsoever. It surpasses therefore not only all the active powers of nature, but even all its rights, all its exigencies.

Because it is given to a creature it is something *finite;* but since only what is divine can surpass the exigencies of all creation, it is also something *divine.* It is the communication of a divine thing, yet, it is shared in a finite way. We therefore keep clear of pantheism. Actually, there are only two instances of the *absolute*-supernatural : the *Incarnation* and *Sanctifying Grace.*

A) In the first instance, God, in the person of the Word, united Himself to man in such wise that the human nature of Jesus belonged absolutely to the Second Person of the Most Blessed Trinity. Thus Jesus is, on account of His human nature, true man, whilst as regards His person He is very God. This is a *substantial* union. It does not blend the two natures in one, but whilst preserving their integrity, unites them in one and the same person — that of the Eternal Word. It constitutes, then, a personal or *hypostatic* union. This is the absolute supernatural at its highest.

B) The other *absolute* supernatural — a lesser degree — is exemplified in *sanctifying grace.*

Grace does not change the person of man. It does not make him God. It does indeed modify his nature and powers, but only accidentally. He becomes similar to God — God-like, *divinae consors naturae,* — capable of possessing God directly through the Beatific Vision, and of contemplating Him face to face even as He beholds Himself when grace will finally be transformed into glory. Evidently this privilege of knowing and loving God as the

[1] St. Thomas, I, q. 93-102; J. Bainvel, S. J., *Nature et surnaturel;* Abbé de Broglie, *Confér. sur la vie surnaturelle,* t. II, p. 3-80; L. Labauche, *God ana Man.* vol. II, P. II, c. I-II; R. Garrigou-Lagrange, O. P., ch. II, art. II.

Father, Son and Holy Ghost know and love one another
surpasses all the exigencies of even the most perfect
creature, since it actually *makes* us share in God's intellectual life and in His nature.

60. 2° What is called' the *relative* supernatural, is in
itself something that would not be beyond the capacity or
the exigencies of all creatures, but simply beyond the
powers and actual needs of a certain particular nature, for
example, infused knowledge, which is beyond the capacity
of man but not of angels. If then it is granted to man, it
is supernatural *relatively*, that is with regard to man, but
not in itself, in its very substance, since it is natural to
angels; hence it is called also *preternatural.*

God gave man the supernatural in these two forms. In
fact, He bestowed upon our first parents *the gift of preternatural integrity*, which, whilst completing their nature,
fitted it for *grace* itself. The sum total of these two
endowments constitutes what is called *original justice.*

II. *Preternatural gifts conferred on Adam*

61. The *gift of integrity* perfect *nature* without raising
it to the level of the divine. This is, indeed, a *gratuitous*
gift, *preternatural*, above the wants and capacity of man,
yet not absolutely *supernatural*. This gift comprises three
great privileges, which without altering human nature in its
essence, gave man a perfection to which he had no title.
These are *infused knowledge, control of the passions* or the
absence of concupiscence, and *immortality of the body.*

62. A) Infused science. Our nature does not require
it, since it is the privilege of angels. Man left to his own
resources can acquire knowledge only gradually and painfully and in subjection to certain psychological laws. In
order to fit Adam for his rôle of first educator of the human
race God granted him infused knowledge of all the truths
he needed to know, and a facility for the acquisition of
experimental knowledge. In this sense man approached
the likeness of angels.

63. B) The control of the passions, that is, exemption
from the sway of concupiscence which renders so difficult
the practice of virtue. We have already remarked that,
owing to his very constitution, there takes place in man a
terrible struggle between the sincere desire for what is good,
on one side, and a reckless lust for pleasure and sensible

goods on the other, to say nothing of a marked proneness to pride. This is really what we call the threefold concupiscence. To counteract this natural drawback God endowed our first parents with a certain *control of the passions* which, without rendering them impeccable, made easy for them the practise of virtue. That *tyranny of concupiscence* that so vigorously pushes on to evil did not exist in Adam; there was simply a certain tendency toward pleasure but in due subordination to reason. Because his will was subject to God, his lower faculties were in turn subservient to reason and his body to his soul. This was order — perfect rectitude.

64. C) The immortality of the body. By nature man is subject to sickness and to death. In order that his soul could attend unencumbered to higher duties, a special disposition of Providence preserved him from this double infirmity. These three privileges were designed to fit man better for the reception and the use of a gift still more precious, a gift absolutely supernatural — *sanctifying grace.*

III. *The supernatural privileges conferred on Adam*

65. A) By nature man is the *servant* of God, His property. — In His infinite goodness God willed to incorporate us into His family. He made man His heir-apparent when He reserved for him a place in His kingdom. For this bounty man will never be able to thank God adequately.

In order that this adoption might not remain a mere formality, He gave him a share in His divine life. This communication of God's life to man is, indeed, a created quality but none the less real. It enables man here on earth to enjoy the light of faith (a light greater by far than that of reason), and in heaven, to possess God by the Beatific Vision and with a love corresponding to the clearness of that vision.

66. B) This was habitual grace. It perfected and deified, so to speak, the very substance of Adam's soul. To it were added the *infused virtues* and the *gifts of the Holy Ghost*, which in turn deified his faculties. Lastly, *actual grace* came to set in motion all this supernatural organism enabling man to elicit supernatural acts, — Godlike acts, meriting eternal life.

This grace is in substance the same as is granted to us by justification. We shall not explain it in detail now, but later when in the second chapter we speak of regenerated man.

All these prerogatives, with the exception of infused knowledge, were given to Adam, not as a personal gift, but as a family possession — a patrimony to be handed down to his heirs should he abide faithful to God.

ART. III. THE FALL AND ITS CONSEQUENCES [1]

I. *The fall*

67. In spite of these privileges man remained *free*, and in order to merit heaven he was put to a *test*. This test consisted in the fulfilment of the divine law. It consisted in particular in the carrying out of a *positive command* added to the natural law. Genesis expresses it in the form of a prohibition which forbade eating the fruit of the tree of *knowledge of good and evil*. Holy Writ narrates how the devil in the guise of a serpent came to tempt our first parents by raising a doubt in their minds as to the legitimacy of this ban. He tried to persuade them that if they ate the forbidden fruit, far from dying, they would become like gods, since they would know for themselves what was good and what evil, without need of recourse to the law of God : " *You shall be as Gods, knowing good and evil.* " [2] This was a temptation to pride, to revolt against God. Man fell and committed a formal act of *disobedience*, as St. Paul remarks, [3] but an act inspired by *pride* and soon followed by further delinquencies. It was a refusal to submit to God's authority, therefore, a grievous fault. The prohibition being an instrument to test the fidelity of the first man, this refusal amounted to a negation of God's wisdom and of His sovereign dominion. The violation was all the more grave since our first parents had full knowledge of God's liberality towards them, of His inalienable rights, of the importance of a precept carrying such a sanction, and since they were in no wise swept away by passion, having had ample time to weigh the frightful consequences of their act.

68. The question even suggests itself : how could they sin at all, since they were not under the sway of concupiscence. This we understand if we recall that no creature

---

[1] St. THOM., IIª IIæ q. 163-165; *de Malo*, q. 4; BAINVEL, *Nature et Surnaturel*, ch. VI-VII; A. DE BROGLIE, *op. cit.*, p. 133-134; L. LABAUCHE, *op. cit.*, Part II, ch. I-V; AD. TANQUEREY, *Syn. theol. dogm.* t. II, n. 882-886 ed. 1926.

[2] *Gen.*, III, 5.

[3] *Rom.*, V.

having a will of its own is impeccable. Free-will gives it the power of turning away from real good towards what is but apparent good. It implies the power of holding to the latter, preferring it to the former. This very choice is what constitutes sin. As St. Thomas says, impeccability can only be found where free will identifies itself with the moral law. This is God's privilege.

II. *The consequences of the fall*

69. Punishment followed quickly for our first parents and for their posterity.

A) The personal sanction visited upon them is described in Genesis. Here again God's goodness is to the fore. He could have on the spot punished them with death. His mercy halted Him. He merely left them shorn of those special privileges with which He had vested them, that is, stripped of the gifts of integrity and of habitual grace. He did not touch their nature or the prerogatives flowing therefrom. Doubtless, man's will is weakened compared with the strength it possessed when integrity was his. However, there is no conclusive evidence that it is actually feebler than it would have been in a purely natural state, at any rate it remains free in choosing good or evil. God even condescended to leave our first parents in possession of faith and hope and gave their forlorn souls the hopeful assurance of a redeemer, — their own offspring, who would one day vanquish the devil and reinstate fallen humanity. By His actual grace, at the same time, He invited them to repentance, and as soon as they repented, He granted them pardon of their sin.

70. **B)** But what will be the condition of their descendants? The answer is that mankind will be likewise deprived of *original justice*, that is to say, of *sanctifying grace* and the *gift of integrity*. Those endowments, free gifts in every sense, a patrimony, so to speak, were to be handed to his heirs should Adam prove faithful. This condition unfulfilled, man comes into the world deprived of original justice. When through penance our first parents regained grace, it was no longer as a heritage for their posterity, but solely as a personal possession, a grant to a private individual. To the new Adam, Christ Jesus, who would in time become the head of mankind, was reserved the expiation of our faults and the institution of a sacrament of *regeneration* to transmit to each of the baptized the grace forfeited in Paradise.

71. Thus it is that the children of Adam are born into this world without *original justice*, that is, without sanctifying grace and the gift of integrity. The lack of this grace is called *original sin*, sin only in the broad sense of the term, for it implies no guilty act on our part, but simply a fallen condition. It constitutes, considering the supernatural destiny to which we are called, a privation of a quality that should be ours, — a blemish, a moral taint that places us out of the pale of God's kingdom.

72. Moreover, on account of the forfeited *gift of integrity*, concupiscence rages in us and unless courageously withstood, it drags us into actual sin. With regard, then, to our primeval state we are as it were *withered* and *wounded*, subject to ignorance, prone to evil, weak against temptation.

Experience indeed shows that the force of concupiscence is not equally strong in all men. Each differs in temperament and character and therefore passions also vary in ardor and violence. Once the controlling check of original justice was lifted, explains St. Thomas, the passions regained full sway and prove more unruly in some, more subdued in others.

73. Must we go further and admit, with the Augustinian school, a positive, *intrinsic*, impairment of our *natural* energies and faculties? It is quite unnecessary. There is nothing to prove it. Should we admit, though, with some of the Thomists an *extrinsic* impairment of our powers? It consists, they say, in the fact that we have *more obstacles* to surmount, specially, the tyranny the devil wields over the vanquished, and the withdrawal of certain natural helps God would have granted us in a purely natural state. This is possible, nay, rather probable. But, in justice, we must add, that such hindrances find compensation in actual grace given us by God in virtue of the merits of His Son, and also in the protection accorded to us by His angels, particularly, our guardian angels.

74. Conclusion. This much we can safely say : owing to the Fall, man has lost the right balance he had as he came from the hands of God ; in comparison with his primeval state, he is now injured, *unbalanced*, as the actual plight of his faculties plainly shows.

A) This unbalanced condition becomes evident first of all with regard to our sensitive faculties. **a)** Our *exterior* *senses*, our eyes, for instance, eagerly light on what our curiosity craves, our ears are ever ready to catch every novelty, our flesh is alive to every sensation of pleasure, heedless the while of the moral law.   **b)** The same is true of our *interior senses*.   With each flight of fancy our imagination represents to us all sorts of images more or less sensual.   Our passions run headlong, oft times madly so, toward sensible or sensuous good, and utterly ignoring all moral good, endeavor to wrest compliance from the will.   True indeed, such tendencies are not irresistible, for our lower faculties remain, in a measure, under the control of the will, yet, their submission, once they revolt, demands much strategy and effort.

75.   B) The *intellectual* faculties, intellect and will, also have been injured by original sin.

There is no doubt that our intellect remains capable of knowing truth, and that with patient labor, even without the aid of revelation, it can obtain knowledge of certain fundamental truths in the natural order.   The failures, however, in this regard, are most humiliating.   The preoccupations of the present blind the mind to the realities of eternity. **a)** Instead of seeking God and the things that are God's, instead of rising spontaneously from the creature to the Creator, as it would have done in the primeval state, man's intellect gravitates earthward.   The study of creatures frequently absorbs it and prevents its ascent to their Maker. 1) Its power of attention, drawn by curiosity, centres round its own whims to the neglect of the realities that lead man to his end.   2) It *falls most readily into error*.   Innumerable prejudices to which we are victims and the passions that agitate our spirit drop a thick veil between our souls and the truth.   Alas! only too often we lose our bearings upon the most vital questions, on which the course and direction of our moral life depend.

b) Our will, instead of paying homage to God, has, on the contrary, the most daring and pretentious aspirations to *independence*.   It finds it bitter and painful to submit to God or to yield to His representatives on earth.   When the issue is to conquer those difficulties that oppose themselves to the realization of good, its efforts are weak and inconstant.   How frequently does it not allow sentiment and passion to carry it away!   Saint Paul describes such weakness in striking terms : " For the good which I will, I do not : but the evil which I will not, that I do.   For

I am delighted with the law of God, according to the inward man : but I see another law in my members, fighting against the law of my mind and captivating me in the law of sin that is in my members. Unhappy man that I am, who shall deliver me from the body of this death? The grace of God, by Jesus Christ Our Lord. " [1] On the testimony of the Apostle the remedy for this wretched condition is the *grace of redemption*.

ART. IV. REDEMPTION AND ITS EFFECTS [2]

76. Redemption is a wondrous work — God's masterpiece. By it, man disfigured by sin is *remade*. He is, in a sense, placed above his primordial state before the fall, so much so, that the Church in her liturgy does not hesitate to bless the fault that secured for us such a Redeemer as the God-man : " O happy fault, that merited such and so great a Redeemer ! "

I. *The nature of Redemption*

77. God who from all eternity had foreseen man's fall, willed likewise from all eternity to provide a Redeemer for men, in the person of His Son. He determined to become man so that becoming the head of mankind He could in full measure expiate our sin and give us back, together with grace, all our rights to heaven. Thus He drew good out of evil and harmonized the rights of *justice* with those of His *goodness*.

He was not indeed bound to demand full justice. He could have pardoned man and contented Himself with the meagre and imperfect reparation that the latter could have proffered. But He regarded it more worthy of His glory and more salutary for man to enable him to offer full reparation for his fault.

78. **A**) Full justice required an *adequate* reparation, *in proportion to the offense*, and offered by a *lawful representative* of mankind. God brought this about by the Incarnation and the Redemption.

a) The Son of God takes flesh and thus becomes the chief of humanity, the head of a mystical body whose members

[1] *Rom.*, VII, 19-25.
[2] St. THOM., III, q. 46-49; HUGON, O. P., *Le Mystère de la Rédemption;* BAINVEL, *op. cit.*, ch. VIII; J. RIVIÈRE, *The Atonement;* AD. TANQUEREY, *Synopsis theol. dogmat.*, t. II, n. 1124-1216; L. LABAUCHE, *God and Man*, vol. I. P. III.

we are. By this very fact, the Son can of right act and make atonement in our name.

b) This atonement is a satisfaction not only *equal* to the offense, but above it by far. If the moral value of any action proceeds first and foremost from the worth, the dignity of the person performing it, this reparation made by the God-Man has *a moral worth* that is *infinite*. A single act of the Son of God would have sufficed to make adequate reparation for all the sins of the human race. Now, as a matter of fact, Jesus, moved by the purest love, did make such acts of reparation without number. He filled the measure and crowned it with the greatest, the most sublime and heroic of actions, — the total immolation of self on Calvary. He has, indeed, made abundant and superabundant satisfactions : " *Where sin abounded, grace did more abound.* " [1]

c) The atonement is the same in kind as the offense. Adam's sin was *disobedience* and *pride*. Jesus makes reparation by *humble* obedience, inspired by *love*, — an obedience unto death, even the death of the cross. " *becoming obedient unto death, even to the death of the cross.* " [2]   Again, just as a woman was instrumental in Adam's fall, so a woman intervenes in man's redemption with her power of intercession and her merits. Although in a secondary rôle Mary, the Immaculate Virgin Mother of the Saviour, coöperates with Him in the work of reparation. " [3]

Thus God's *justice* is fully satisfied, and His *goodness* even more.

79.   B) Holy Scripture, in fact, attributes the work of our redemption to the infinite mercy of God and His exceeding great love for us. In the words of St. Paul : " *God, who is rich in mercy for his exceeding charity wherewith He loved us,..... hath quickened us together in Christ.* " [4] The three divine persons vie one with the other in this work, each moved by a love which, in truth, would seem to be excessive.

a) The Father has an only-begotten Son, equal to Him, whom He loves like another self, and by whom He is loved with the same infinite love. It is this very Son whom He gives and sacrifices for us that we may rise again to life

---

[1] *Rom.*, V, 5.
[2] *Philip.*, II, 1.
[3] Here it is question of the merit called *de congruo*, which we shall explain later on.
[4] *Ephes.*, II, 4.

from the death of sin : *"For God so loved the world, as to give His Only-Begotten Son : that whosoever believeth in Him may not perish, but may have life everlasting."* [1]   Could His generous love give more?   In giving us His Son, has He not given us all other things?   *" He that spared not even His own Son, but delivered Him for us all, how hath He not also, with Him given us all things."* [2]

80.   b) The Son joyously and generously accepted the mission entrusted to Him.   From the first instant of His Incarnation, He offered Himself to the Father as the victim that replaced all the sacrifices of the Old Law.   His entire life was a long sacrifice completed by His immolation on Calvary — a sacrifice born of the *love* He bore us : *" Christ also hath loved us and hath delivered Himself for us, an oblation and a sacrifice to God for an odour of sweetness."* [3]

81.   c) In order to finish His work He sent us the Holy Ghost.   This Divine Spirit, who is none other than the substantial love of the Father and the Son, was not satisfied with instilling grace into our souls together with the infused virtues, especially divine charity, but gave Himself to us in order that we might not only enjoy His presence and possess His gifts, but even His very person : *" The charity of God is poured forth in our hearts, by the Holy Ghost who is given to us."* [4]

Redemption is therefore, the masterpiece of divine love : this fact enables us to forecast its effects.

II. *The Effects of Redemption*

82.   Jesus did not stop short once He had offered reparation to God for our offense and reconciled us to Him. He merited for us all the graces lost to us by sin, and many more.

First of all, He gave us back all the *supernatural goods* we had lost by sin :

a) *Habitual grace* with all the infused virtues and the gifts of the Holy Ghost; then, to adapt Himself better to our human nature He instituted the *Sacraments*, sensible signs that confer grace upon us in every important circumstance of our life and thus furnish us with greater security and greater confidence.   **b)** He secured for us *actual graces* in a full measure, and according to the word of St. Paul,

---

[1] *John*, III, 16. — [2] *Rom.*, VIII, 32. — [3] *Ephes.*, V, 2. — [4] *Rom.*, V, 5.

we are justified in judging them even more abundant than those we should have received in the state of innocence : " *Where sin abounded, grace did more abound.* " [1]

83. **c)** It is true that the *gift of integrity* was not given back to us immediately, but it is given us *gradually*. The grace of regeneration leaves us still exposed to the attacks of the threefold concupiscence and subject to the burden of life's sufferings, but it gives us the needed strength to surmount them, rendering us more humble, more vigilant, more active in warding off and conquering temptation. Thus it grounds us in virtue and gives us the opportunity of increasing our merit. The example of Jesus, who so courageously carried His cross and ours, gives us new energy and sustains our efforts in the fight. The *actual graces*, which He has merited for us, and which He bestows with a lavishness truly divine make effort and victory easier. In proportion as we struggle under the leadership and protection of the Master, concupiscence weakens, our power of resistance grows, and a time comes when privileged souls are so grounded in virtue, that ever free as they remain to do evil, they never commit any fully deliberate venial sin. The final victory will come only with our entrance into heaven, but it will be all the more glorious having been bought at a greater price. Can we not also repeat : *O happy fault!*

84. **d)** To such interior helps our Lord has joined *external* ones, particularly that of the *Visible Church*, founded and designed by Him to enlighten our minds by her teaching, to stay our wills by the warrant of her laws and judgments, to sanctify our souls by sacraments, sacramentals and indulgences. In her we have an immense treasure-house of help for which we must thank God : *O felix culpa! O happy fault!*

85. **e)** Lastly, it is not certain that the Word of God would have taken flesh had the fall of our first parents not occurred. Now the Incarnation is such a priceless boon that it alone would suffice to explain and justify the cry of the Church : *O happy fault!*

Instead of having for the head of the race a man richly endowed, indeed, but liable to error and to sin, we have one who is none other than the Eternal Son of God. The head of mankind is the Word, clothed in our nature, true man as

---
[1] *Rom.*, V, 20.

well as true God. He is the *ideal mediator*, a mediator for worship as well as for redemption, who adores His Father not merely in His own name but in the name of the entire human race, nay more, in the name of the angels, for it is through Him that the heavenly hosts praise and glorify their Creator: " through Whom the angels praise. " [1]   He is the *perfect priest* who, while having free access to God on account of His divine nature, stoops down to His fellowmen, His brethren, to deal them kindness and indulgence the while He knows their weakness: " *Who can have compassion on them that are ignorant and that err : because He Himself also is encompassed with infirmity.* " [2]

With Him and through Him we can render to God the infinite homage to which He is entitled. With Him and through Him we can obtain all the graces we need both for ourselves and for others. When we adore, it is He that adores in us and through us; when we ask for help, it is He that supports our requests; and for this reason, whatsoever we shall ask of the Father in His name shall be graciously given us.

We must, therefore, rejoice in the possession of such a Redeemer, such a Mediator, and have a trust in Him that knows no limits.

CONCLUSION

86. This brief historical survey brings out most strikingly the supreme *worth* of the supernatural life and the *grandeur* and *weakness* of man on whom it is bestowed.

1º This life is, indeed, excellent since :

a) It is born of a *loving thought of God*, who has loved us from all eternity and has willed to unite us to Himself in the sweetest and closest intimacy : " *I have loved thee with an everlasting love, and therefore I have drawn thee to myself.* " [3]

b) It is a *real participation*, even if finite, *in the nature and in the life of God*, enabling us to know and to love God even as the Father, Son and Holy Ghost know and love one another : " partakers of the divine nature. " (See n. 106)

c) It has such worth in God's eyes that, to give it to us, the Father sacrifices His Only-Begotten Son, the Son makes a complete immolation of self, and the Holy Ghost comes to impart this life to our souls.

Indeed, it is the pearl of great price : " By whom he hath

---

[1] Preface of the Mass. — [2] *Hebr.*, V, 2. — [3] *Jer.*, XXXI, 3.

given us most great and precious promises, " [1] which we must hold dearer than all else and keep and cherish with jealous care : *its worth is that of God Himself!*

87. 2° Still, we carry this treasure in earthen vessels. If our first parents, endowed with the gift of integrity and enriched with all sorts of privileges, had the misfortune of forfeiting it both for themselves and their posterity, should we entertain no fear? We, who in spite of our spiritual regeneration, carry within us the threefold concupiscence?

No doubt, there are within us *generous* and *noble* impulses born of what is good in our nature. There are, besides, the supernatural forces which come to us through Christ's merits and through our incorporation into Him. However, we remain *weak* and *inconstant*, unless we lean upon Him who is our strength as well as our head. The secret of our power does not rest with us, but with God and Christ Jesus our Lord. The history of our First Parents and their lamentable fall shows us that the great evil in the world, the only evil, is *sin.* It shows us that we must be ever on our guard to repel at once and with all our might every attack that the enemy may make against us, be it from without or from within. We are nevertheless well protected and fully armed against his onslaughts, as our second chapter, dealing with the nature of the Christian life, will prove.

CHAPTER II

The Nature of the Christian Life

88. The supernatural life which, by virtue of the merits of Jesus Christ, is a participation in God's life, is often called *the life of God in us or the life of Jesus in us.* Such expressions are correct provided one takes care to explain them, so as to avoid anything savoring of pantheism. We have not a life *identical* with that of God or our Lord; we only have a life *similar* to theirs, a finite participation, yet most real.

We may define it thus : *a share in the divine life given us by the Holy Ghost who dwells in us, because of the merits of Jesus Christ; a life which we must protect against all destructive tendencies.*

---

[1] *II Petr.*, I, 4.

89. We see, then, that as regards our supernatural life God plays the principal rôle, we a secondary one. It is the Triune God that comes Himself to confer it upon us, for He alone can make us share in His own life. He communicates it to us in virtue of the merits of Christ (n. 78), who is the meritorious, exemplary and vital cause of our sanctification. It is perfectly true that *God lives in us*, that *Jesus lives in us*; yet, our spiritual life *is not identical* with that of God or of our Lord. It is distinct from but similar to the one and the other. *Our rôle* consists in making use of the divine gifts in order to live with God and for God, in order to live in union with Jesus and to imitate Him. But we cannot live this supernatural life without a continual struggle against the threefold concupiscence which still remains in us (n. 83). And moreover, since God has endowed us with a supernatural organism, it is our duty to make that life increase in us by meritorious acts and the fervent reception of the sacraments.

This is the meaning of the definition we have given, and this whole chapter is but its explanation and development. From it we shall draw practical conclusions concerning devotion to the Most Holy Trinity, devotion to and union with the Incarnate Word, and even concerning devotion to the Blessed Virgin and the Saints, since all these devotions flow from their relations with the Word of God-made-Flesh.

Although the action of God and that of the soul have parallel developments in the Christian life, we shall for the sake of clearness treat of them in two successive articles, one on the *rôle of God* and the other on the *rôle of man*.

God acts in us	1. By Himself	He dwells in us : hence devotion to the Blessed Trinity. He endows us with a supernatural organism.
	2. Through His Word Incarnate, who is primarily	Meritorious cause ⎱ Exemplary cause ⎰ of our life. Vital cause Hence devotion to the Incarnate Word.
	3. Through Mary who is secondarily	Meritorious cause ⎱ of our life. Exemplary cause ⎰ Distributive cause of grace. Hence devotion to Mary.
	4. Through the Saints and Angels	Living images of God : hence venerate them. Intercessors : Invoke them. Models : Imitate them.
We live and act for God	1. By fighting against	concupiscence. the world. the devil.
	2. By sanctifying our actions	Their threefold value. Conditions for merit. Way of rendering our acts more meritorious.
	3. By receiving the Sacraments worthily	Sacramental grace. Special ⎱ of Penance. grace ⎰ of the Eucharist.

ART. I. THE RÔLE OF GOD IN THE CHRISTIAN LIFE

God acts in us either directly, by *Himself,* or through the *Incarnate Word,* or through the mediation of the Blessed Virgin, the Angels and the Saints.

§ I. The Rôle of the Blessed Trinity

90. The first cause, the primary, efficient cause and the exemplary cause of the supernatural life in us is no other than the Blessed Trinity, or by appropriation, the

Holy Ghost. True, the life of grace is a work common to the Three Divine Persons, for it is a work *ad extra*, yet, because it is a work of love, it is attributed especially to the Holy Ghost.

Now the Most Adorable Trinity contributes to our sanctification in two ways : the Three Divine Persons come to *dwell* in our souls; there they create a supernatural organism which transforms and elevates them, thus enabling them to perform Godlike acts.

I. *The Indwelling of the Holy Ghost in the Soul* [1]

91. Since the Christian life is a participation in God's own life, it is evident that none but God Himself can confer it upon us. This He does by coming to dwell in our souls and by giving Himself wholly to us in order that we may first of all render Him our homage, enjoy His presence and allow ourselves to be led with docility to the practice of Christ's virtues and into the dispositions of His holy soul. [2] Theologians call this *uncreated grace*. Let us then examine first how the Three Divine Persons live in us, and next, what our attitude must be toward Them.

1° HOW THE THREE DIVINE PERSONS DWELL WITHIN US

92. God, says St. Thomas, [3] is in all creatures in a threefold manner : by His *power*, inasmuch as all creatures are subject to His dominion; by His *presence*, because He sees all, even the most secret thoughts of the soul, "*All things are naked and open to his eyes;*" [4] by His *essence*, since He acts everywhere and since everywhere He is the plenitude of being itself and the first cause of whatever is real in creation, giving continually to creatures not only life and movement, but their very being : "*In Him we live and move and are.*" [5]

Yet, His presence within us by *grace* is of a much higher and intimate nature. It is no longer the presence of the Creator and Preserver who sustains the beings He created;

---

[1] St. THOM., I, q. 43, a. 3; FROGET, *Indwelling of the H. Ghost;* R. PLUS, *God within Us;* MANNING, *Int. Mission,* I; DEVINE, *Ascet. Theol.,* p. 80; TANQUEREY, *Syn. Theol. Dog.,* III, 180-185.

[2] It is upon this truth that Father OLIER bases his spiritual system. See *Catechism for an Interior Life,* P. I, C. III : "Who deserves the name of Christian? He who is possessed by the Spirit of Jesus Christ... that makes us live both interiorly and exteriorly like Jesus Christ". — "He (the Holy Ghost) is there with the Father and the Son, and there infuses, as we have said, the same dispositions, the same sentiments and the same virtues of Jesus Christ".

[3] *Sum. theol.,* I, q. 8, a. 3.

[4] *Heb.,* IV, 13. — [5] *Acts,* XVII, 28.

it is the presence of the Most Holy Trinity revealed to us by faith. The *Father* comes to us and continues to beget His Word within us. With the Father we receive the *Son* equal in all things to the Father, His loving and substantial image, who never ceases to love His Father with the same infinite love wherewith the Father loves Him. Out of this mutual love proceeds the *Holy Spirit*, a person equal to the Father and the Son and a mutual bond between Father and Son. The Three are withal distinct one from the other. These wonders go on continually within the soul in the state of grace. The presence of the Three Divine Persons, at once *physical* and *moral*, establishes the *most intimate* and *most sanctifying* relations between God and the soul. Gathering all that is found here and there in the Scriptures, we can say that God through grace is present within us as a *father*, as a *friend*, as a *helper*, as a *sanctifier*, and that in this way He is truly the very source of our interior life, its *efficient* and *exemplary* cause.

93. A) By *nature* He is simply in us to give us natural endowments; by *grace* He gives Himself to us that we may enjoy His friendship and thus have a foretaste of the happiness of heaven. In the *order of nature* God is in us as the *Creator* and the *sovereign Master;* we are but His *servants*, His *property*. In the *order of grace* it is different; here He gives Himself to us as *our Father;* we are now His *adopted children;* an unspeakable privilege and the basis of our supernatural life. St. Paul and St. John repeat it again and again : " *For you have not received the spirit of bondage again in fear : but you have received the spirit of adoption of sons, whereby we cry Abba (Father). For the Spirit himself giveth testimony to our spirit that we are the sons of God.* " [1] God, therefore, adopts us as His children and in a way more thorough and more complete than men are adopted in law. By legal adoption men are, indeed, able to transmit to others their name and their possessions, but they cannot transmit to them their blood and their life. " Legal adoption, " says Cardinal Mercier, [2] " is a fiction. " The adopted child is considered by its foster parents just *as if it were* their child and receives from them the heritage to which their offspring would have had a right. Society recognizes this fiction and sanctions its effects. Withal, the object of such fiction is in no wise changed. But the grace of divine adoption is by no means a fiction... it is a

---

[1] *Rom.*, VIII, 15-16. — [2] *La Vie Intérieure*, ed. 1909, p. 405.

reality. God gives divine sonship to those who have faith
in His Word, as St. John says : " *He gave them power to be
made the sons of God, to them that believed in his name.*" [1]
This sonship is not such merely in name, but in very truth :
" *that we should be called and should be the sons of God.*" [2]
By it we come into the possession of the divine nature,
"*partakers of the divine nature.*" [3]

94. No doubt, this divine life in us is only a participation, a sharing, " *consortes,* " a similitude, an assimilation
which does not make us gods, but only *Godlike.* None
the less, it constitutes no fiction, but a *reality*, a *new life*,
a life not, indeed, equal but similar to God's and which, on
the testimony of Holy Writ, presupposes a new birth,
a regeneration : " *Unless a man be born again of water and the
Holy Ghost... by the laver of regeneration and renovation of
the Holy Ghost... he hath regenerated us unto a lively hope...
of his own will hath he begotten us by the word of truth.*" [4]
All these expressions show us that our adoption is not
merely nominal, but *true* and *real*, although distinct and
different from the sonship of the Word-made-Flesh. By it
we become heirs, by full right, to the kingdom of heaven
and coheirs of Him who is the eldest-born among our
brethren : "heirs indeed of God and joint heirs with Christ...
that he might be the firstborn amongst many brethren. " [5]
Is it not, therefore, most fitting to repeat the touching
words of St John : " *Behold what manner of charity the
Father hath bestowed upon us, that we should be called and
should be the sons of God!* " [6]

God has for us then the tenderness and devotedness of a
father. Does He not compare Himself to a *mother* that
can never forget the child of her womb? " *Can a woman
forget her infant, so as not to have pity on the son of her
womb? And if she should forget, yet will not I forget thee.*" [7]
He has most assuredly given proof of this, since in order to
save His fallen children He hesitated not to give and sacrifice His only-begotten Son : " *For God so loved the world,
as to give his only Begotten Son : that whosoever believeth in
him may not perish, but may have life everlasting.*" [8] The
same love prompts Him likewise to give Himself wholly,
and from now on, in a permanent manner to His children
by dwelling in their hearts : " *If any one love me, he will
keep my word, and my Father will love him, and we will*

[1] *John*, I, 12. — [2] *I John*, III, 1. — [3] *II Peter*, I, 4.
[4] *John*, III, 5; *Tit.*, III, 5; *I Peter*, I, 3; *James*, I, 18.
[5] *Rom.*, VIII, 17, 29. — [6] *I John*, III, 1. — [7] *Isa.*, XLIX, 15. — [8] *John*, III, 16.

come to him, and will make our abode with him." [1]   He lives
in us as a *most loving* and *most devoted Father.*

95. B) He gives Himself also as a *friend.* Friendship
adds to the relations between father and son a sort of
equality : *" amicitia æquales accipit aut facit. "* It adds
a kind of familiarity, a reciprocity whence flows the
sweetest intercourse. It is precisely such relations that
grace establishes between us and God. Of course, when
it is question of God on one side and man on the
other, there can be no real equality, but rather a certain
similarity sufficient to engender true intimacy. In fact,
God confides to us His secrets. He speaks to us not
only through His Church, but also interiorly through His
Spirit : *" He will teach you all things and bring all things to
your mind whatsoever I shall have said to you."* [2]   At the
Last Supper Jesus declared to His Apostles that from that
time on they would not be His servants, but His friends,
because He would no longer keep any secrets from them :
*" I will not now call you servants : for the servant knoweth
not what his lord doth. But I have called you friends : because
all things whatsoever I have heard of my Father, I have
made known to you."* [3]   A sweet familiarity will from now
on pervade their intercourse, the same that exists between
friends when they meet and speak heart to heart : *" Behold
that I stand at the gate and knock ; if any man shall hear my
voice and open to me the door, I will come into him and I will
sup with him ; and he with me."* [4]   What an unspeakable
familiarity is this! Never would man have dared dream of
it or aspire to it had not the Friend Divine taken the
initiative! This very intimacy has been and is an every-
day fact not only between Almighty God and His Saints,
but between Him and every man who by leading an interior
life consents to throw open the gates of his soul to the
Divine Guest. To this the author of the " Imitation " bears
witness when he describes the oft-repeated visits of the
Holy Spirit to interior souls, the sweet converse He holds
with them, the consolations and the caresses He imparts to
them, the peace He infuses, the astounding familiarity of
His dealings with them : *" Many are His visits to the man
of interior life, and sweet the conversation that He holdeth
with him ; plenteous His consolation, His peace and His
familiarity. "* [5]   The life of contemporary mystics, of
St. Theresa of the Child Jesus, of Elizabeth of the Blessed

---

[1] *John*, XIV, 23. — [2] *John*, XIV, 26. — [3] *John*, XV, 15.
[4] *Apoc.*, III, 20. — [5] *Imitation*, II, c. I, v. 1.

Trinity, of Gemma Galgani and of so many others, gives proof that the words of the Imitation are daily realized. There is no doubt that God does live in us as the most intimate of friends.

96. C) Nor is He idle there. He acts as our most powerful ally, our most efficient helper. Knowing but too well that of ourselves we can not foster the life He has engendered in us, He supplies for our deficiencies by working with us through actual grace. Are we in need of *light* to perceive the truths of faith which shall from now on guide our steps? The Father of Lights will be the one to enlighten our intellect pointing out clearly our last end and the means to reach it. He will suggest to us the godly thoughts that inspire godly actions. Again, do we want *strength* to give our life its orientation, to direct it towards its last end, the one great object of all our strivings, of all our efforts? The same God and Father will bring to us the supernatural help that gives the power to will and to do : " *for it is God who worketh in you both to will and to accomplish.* " [1] When it comes to combatting and controlling our passions or overcoming the temptations that at times assail us, once more it is none other than God who gives us the power to resist them and even to draw profit from them : " *God is faithful who will not suffer you to be tempted above that which you are able, but will make also with temptation issue, that you may be able to bear it.* " [2] If weary of well-doing and if discouraged we begin to falter, He draws close to sustain us and to secure our perseverance : " *He who hath begun a good work in you will perfect it unto the day of Christ Jesus.* " [3] No, we are never alone. Even when devoid of all consolations we think ourselves abandoned, God's grace is ever close at hand as long as we are willing to coöperate with it : " *And his grace in me hath not been void : but I have labored more abundantly than all they : yet not I, but the grace of God with me.* " [4] Leaning on this all-powerful Helper we become invincible : " *I can do all things in him who strengtheneth me.* " [5]

97. D) This divine Helper is at the same time our *Sanctifier.* Coming to live in our soul He transforms it into a *sacred temple* enriched with all manner of virtues : " *the temple*

[1] *Philipp.*, II. 13.
[2] *I Cor.*, X, 13.
[3] *Philipp.*, I, 6.
[4] *I Cor.*, XV, 10.
[5] *Philipp.*, IV, 13.

of God is holy, which you are. " [1]   The God that lives in us
is not merely the God of nature, but the Living God, the
Blessed Trinity, the infinite source of divine life, whose only
longing is to make us share in His holiness. Often this
indwelling of God in the soul is attributed or assigned to
the Holy Ghost by appropriation, since it is a work of love;
but being a work *ad extra* it is *common* to the Three Divine
Persons. This is why St. Paul calls us alike the temples of
God and the temples of the Holy Ghost : " *Know you not
that* you are the temple of God, and that the Spirit of God
dwelleth in you? " [2]

Our soul, therefore, is made the *temple* of the Living God,
a sanctuary reserved to the Most High, a Holy of Holies,
a throne of mercy where He is pleased to be lavish with
His heavenly favors and which He enriches with every
virtue. It follows that the presence within us of a Thrice
Holy God, as just described, cannot but *sanctify* us. The
Most Adorable Trinity living and acting within us must,
indeed, be the principle of our sanctification, the source of
our interior life. This holy presence constitutes likewise
its exemplary cause, for being sons of God by adoption we
are bound to imitate our Father. This we shall understand
better when we examine what our attitude should· be
towards these Three Divine Guests.

2º Our Duties towards the Most Holy Trinity Living within Us [3]

98. Possessing such a treasure as the Most Holy Trinity,
we ought to make it the object of frequent meditation —
" *to walk inwardly with God.* " Such a thought awakes in
us chiefly three sentiments : adoration, love and imitation.

99. A) The very first impulse of the heart is that of
adoration : " *Glorify and bear God in your body.* " [4] How
could we do otherwise than glorify, bless and thank that
Divine Guest who transforms our soul into a sanctuary?
From the time Mary received the Incarnate Word in her
virginal womb her life was but one perpetual act of adoration and thanksgiving : " *My soul doth magnify the Lord...
He who is mighty hath done great things to me, and holy is
his name.* " [5] Such are, even if lesser in degree and intensity,
the sentiments that lay hold of the Christian on becoming

---

[1] *I Cor.*, III, 17. — [2] *I Cor.*, III, 16.
[3] All these sentiments are wonderfully expressed in the beautiful morning prayer
composed by Father OLIER, cf. *Manual of Piety.*
[4] *I Cor.*, VI, 10. — [5] *Luke*, I, 46, 49.

aware of the Holy Ghost's presence within him. He understands that being God's dwelling he ought to offer himself constantly as a *sacrifice* of *praise* unto the glory of the Triune God. **a)** He begins his actions by making the Sign of the Cross, *in the name of the Father and of the Son and of the Holy Ghost*, and thus consecrates them all to the Three Divine Persons; he ends them by acknowledging that whatever good he has done must be attributed to Them : *Glory be to the Father and to the Son and to the Holy Ghost.* **b)** He loves to repeat the liturgical prayers that proclaim Their praises : the *Glòria in excelsis Deo*, which so well expresses all the religious sentiments towards the Most Holy Trinity, especially towards the Incarnate Word; the *Sanctus*, proclaiming the awful holiness of the Godhead; the *Te Deum*, the song of thanksgiving. **c)** This Divine Guest the Christian recognizes as his first beginning and last end. He realizes his inability to praise Him adequately and unites Himself to the Spirit of Jesus who alone can render to God that glory which by right is His : " *The Spirit also helpeth our infirmity : for, we know not what we should pray for as we ought; but the Spirit himself asketh for us with unspeakable groanings.* " [1]

100. **B)** After having adored God and proclaimed his own nothingness, the Christian gives vent to sentiments of the most confiding *love*. Infinite as He is, God nevertheless stoops down to us like a loving father toward his child, asking us to love Him and to give Him our heart : " *My son, give me thy heart.* " [2] He has a strict right to demand this love, yet He prefers to entreat us with the sweetness of affection so that our return may be, so to speak, more spontaneous, and our recourse to Him more confident and childlike. Could we refuse our trustful love to such thoughtful advances, to a solicitude so truly maternal?

Our love should be a *repentant* love, a love that expiates infidelities past and present; a *grateful* love that renders thanks to our great Benefactor, the devoted Co-worker who labors without stint and without rest. Above all, it should be the love of *friend for friend* holding sweet converse with the most faithful, the most generous of friends, whose part we should take, whose glory we should make known, whose name we should forever bless. This love then should not be a mere feeling, but a generous, daring love, forgetful of

---

[1] *Rom.*, VIII, 26. — [2] *Prov.*, XXIII, 26.

self to the point of sacrifice and the renunciation of our own wills, by a willing submission to the precepts and counsels of God.

101.   C) Such love will lead us to *imitate* the Most Adorable Trinity in the measure in which this is compatible with human weakness. Adopted children of an all-holy Father, living temples of the Holy Ghost, we can better appreciate the reason why we must be holy in body and soul. This was the lesson learned by the Apostle and repeated by him to his followers: " Know you not that you are the temple of God and that the Spirit of God dwelleth in you? But if any man violate the temple of God, him shall God destroy. For the temple of God is holy, which you are. " [1]   Experience is witness to the fact that with generous souls this is the most powerful motive to turn them away from sin and incite them to the practice of virtue. Temples wherein the thrice Holy One resides can never be too rich in beauty, too glorious in sanctity. It is remarkable that when our Lord wished to propose to us an ideal, a model of perfection, He pointed to God Himself: " Be ye perfect as your heavenly Father is perfect. " [2]   At first sight this ideal does seem too high. But when we recall that we are the adopted children of God and that He lives in us in order to impress upon us His image and to collaborate in our salvation, then we realize that a high rank imposes obligations, *noblesse oblige*, and that it is no more than our plain duty to approach ever nearer the divine perfections. It is chiefly in view of the fulfilment of the precept of *fraternal charity*, the love of our fellows, that Jesus Christ demands of us to keep before our eyes this perfect model, the indivisible oneness of the Three Divine Persons: " That they all may be one, as thou, Father in me and I in thee; that they also be one in us. " [3]   What a tender prayer! St. Paul echoes it later on begging his dear disciples not to forget that since they are but one body and but one spirit, and since they have but one Father who lives in all just souls, they should preserve the unity of spirit in the bond of peace. [4]

To sum up, we may say that the Christian life consists above all in an intimate, affectionate and sanctifying union with the Three Divine Persons who sustain us in the spirit of religion, love and sacrifice.

---

[1] *I Cor.*, III, 16-17. — [2] *Matth.*, V, 48. — [3] *John*, XVII, 21. — [4] *Eph.*, IV, 3-6.

II. *The Organism of the Christian Life* [1]

102.   The three Divine Persons inhabit the sanctuary of our soul, taking their delight in enriching it with supernatural gifts and in communicating to us a Godlike life, similar to theirs, called the life of grace.

All life, however, implies a threefold element : a *vital principle* that is, so to speak, the source of life itself; *faculties* which give the power to elicit vital acts; and lastly, the *acts* themselves which are but its development and which minister to its growth.   In the supernatural order, God living within us produces the same elements.   **a)** He first communicates to us *habitual grace* which plays the part of a *vital, supernatural principle.* [2]   This principle deifies, as it were, the very substance of the soul and makes it capable, though in a remote way, of enjoying the Beatific Vision and of performing the acts that lead to it.

103.   b) Out of this grace spring the *infused virtues* [3] and the *gifts of the Holy Ghost* which perfect our faculties and endow us with the immediate power of performing Godlike, supernatural, meritorious acts.

c) In order to stir these faculties into action, He gives us *actual graces* which enlighten our mind, strengthen our will, and aid us both to act supernaturally and to increase the measure of habitual grace that has been granted to us.

104.   Although this life of grace is entirely distinct from our natural life it is not merely superimposed on the latter; it *penetrates it through and through,* transforms it and makes it divine.   It assimilates whatever is good in our nature, our education and our habits.   It perfects and supernaturalizes all these various elements, directing them toward the last end, that is toward the possession of God through the Beatific Vision and its resultant love.

In virtue of the general principle explained above, n. 54, that inferior beings are subordinated to their superiors, [4] it is the part of the supernatural life to direct and control our

---

[1] St. Thom., Iª IIæ, q. 110; Alvarez de Paz, *De vita spirituali ejusque perfectione,* 1602, t. I, II, c. 1; Terrien, *La Grâce et la Gloire,* t. I, p. 75 sq.; Bellamy, *La vie surnaturelle.*

[2] " Gratia præsupponitur virtutibus infusis, sicut earum principium et finis. " *(Sum. theol.,* Iª IIæ, q. 110, a. 3).

[3] " Sicut ab essentia animæ effluunt ejus potentiæ, quæ sunt operum principia, ita etiam ab ipsa gratia effluunt virtutes in potentias animæ, per quas potentiæ moventur ad actum ". (Ibid., a. 4.)

[4] Eymieu, *op. cit.,* p. 150-151.

natural life. The former cannot develop nor endure unless it *reigns supreme* and keeps under its sway the acts of the mind, of the will and of the other faculties. This dominion in no way dwarfs or destroys our nature, but rather it elevates and completes it. We shall show this in the subsequent study of these three elements.

1° HABITUAL GRACE [1]

105. God out of His infinite goodness wills to lift us up to Himself in the measure that our weak nature allows, and for this purpose gives us a principle of supernatural life; a Godlike, vital principle, which is habitual grace. It is also called created grace [2] in contradistinction to uncreated grace, which is the indwelling itself of the Holy Ghost within us. Created grace makes us *like unto God* and unites us to Him in the closest manner : " *This deification consists, in so far as is possible, in a certain resemblance to God and union with Him.* " [3] These two points of view we shall explain presently by giving the *traditional definition* and by determining precisely the nature of the *union* that grace produces between God and the soul.

A) *Definition*

106. Sanctifying or habitual grace is commonly defined as a *supernatural quality inherent in the soul, which makes us partakers of the divine nature and of the divine life in a real and formal, but accidental manner.*

a) Grace is a *reality* of the supernatural order, but not a substance, for no created substance could be supernatural. It is but a *mode of being*, a *state of soul*, a *quality inherent* in the soul's substance that transforms it and raises it above all natural beings, even the most perfect. It is a *permanent* quality remaining in the soul as long as we do not forfeit it by mortal sin. " It is, " as Cardinal Mercier says, [4] on the authority of Bossuet, " a spiritual quality infused into our

---

[1] See St. THOM., I\a II\æ, q. 110; *Syn. Theol. Dog.*, III, n. 186-191 ; FROGET, *op. cit.*, IV\e P. ; TERRIEN, *La Grâce et la Gloire*, p. 75 ss. ; BELLAMY, *La vie surnaturelle*, 1895 ; SCHEEBEN, *The Glories of Divine Grace;* MANY, *La vraie vie*, 1922, p. 1-79

[2] This expression is not altogether exact, since grace within us is not a *substance*, but an *accident*, an accidental modification of the soul. But because it is something *finite* and can originate only in God, not being merited by us, this name of *created* or *con-created* is given to it, to show that it is derived from the power the soul as a created thing has of becoming whatever the Creator wills it to become.

[3] " Est autem hæc deificatio, Deo quædam, quoad fieri potest, assimilatio unioque ". Ps.-DIONYS, *De eccl. hierarchia*, c. I, n. 3, *P. G.*, III, 373.

[4] *La Vie intérieure*, p. 401.

souls by Jesus Christ, which penetrates our inmost being, instils itself into the very marrow of the soul and goes forth (through the virtues) to all its faculties. The soul that possesses it is made pure and pleasing in the eyes of God. He makes such a soul His sanctuary, His temple, His tabernacle, His paradise. "

107. b) This quality, according to the forceful expression of St. Peter, makes us "*partakers of the divine nature.*" [1] According to St. Paul, it causes us to enter into communion with the Holy Ghost, " *the communication of the Holy Ghost,* " [2] and St. John adds that it establishes a sort of fellowship between us and the Father and the Son : "*our fellowship... with the Father and with his Son Jesus Christ.*" [3] It does not make us the equals of God, but it changes us into *Godlike beings*, makes us like unto God. Nor does it give us the life of the Godhead itself which is incommunicable, but it imparts to us a life similar to God's. Our task is to explain this, so far as the human mind is able to comprehend it.

108. 1) God's own life consists in *direct self-contemplation* and love of Himself. No creature whatever, no matter how perfect, could of itself contemplate the essence of the Godhead, " who dwells in light inaccessible; " [4] but God, by a privilege, gratuitous in every sense of the word, calls man to contemplate this divine essence in heaven. As man is utterly incapable of this, God lifts him up, makes his intelligence transcend its natural capacities, and confers on him this power through the *light of glory*. Then, says St. John, we shall be like unto God because we shall see Him as He sees Himself, that is to say, exactly as He is in Himself : " *We shall be like him : because we shall see him as he is.* " [5] We shall see, adds St. Paul, no longer through the mirror of creatures, but face to face with luminous clearness : " *We see now through a glass in a dark manner : but then face to face.* " [6] Since we shall know and love God as He knows and loves Himself, we shall also share in God's own life, even if it be in a finite way. Theologians explain this by saying that the divine essence will come and unite itself with the soul's inmost being, so as to allow us to contemplate the Divinity directly, with the aid of no image or of any created intermediary.

---

[1] *II Peter*, I, 4. — [2] *II Cor.*, XIII, 13. — [3] *I John*, I, 3.
[4] *I Tim.*, VI, 16. — [5] *I John*, III, 2. — [6] *I Cor.*, XIII, 12-13.

109. 2) Habitual grace is already a preparation for the Beatific Vision and a foretaste, as it were, of that unspeakable boon; it is the bud that needs but to open to show forth the flower. Habitual grace and the Beatific Vision are, then, one in kind and one in nature.

A comparison, no matter how inadequate, will not be out of place. We can know an artist in three different ways : by studying his works, through friends, or by personal intercourse with him. The first is the kind of knowledge we get of God through His works, by the contemplation of His creatures. This is an inductive, imperfect knowledge; for though creation reveals His wisdom and His power, it tells us nothing of His personal, interior life. The knowledge we derive from faith illustrates the second manner in which we come to know God. On the authority of the sacred writers and, above all, on the testimony of the Son of God we believe what it has pleased Him to disclose to us, not only concerning His works and His attributes, but concerning His personal, interior life. Thus, we believe that from all eternity He begets the Word, His Son, that there exists a mutual love between Them, and that out of this reciprocal love proceeds the Holy Ghost. We do not, indeed, understand, nor do we in any way see, but we believe with invincible certainty. This faith makes us share in the knowledge that God has of Himself. But this is a veiled knowledge, rather obscure, though none the less real. Only eventually through the Beatific Vision shall we acquire direct knowledge of Him. Still, this second mode of knowledge, as can be readily seen, is at bottom of the same nature as the first, and assuredly far superior to mere rational or reasoned knowledge.

110. c) This participation in the divine life is *formal;* it is not simply virtual. Virtual participation means that we share a quality in a *different way* from that in which it is possessed by the principal where it is found. Thus, reason is simply a virtual participation in the divine intellect, because reason gives us a knowledge of truth, but vastly different from that knowledge of truth which God possesses. Mindful then of disparity and distinction, we can say that such is not the case between the Beatific Vision and faith. Both cause us to know God as He is, not in the same degree, it is true, but the knowledge acquired through either of them is the same in kind.

111. d) The participation we have in God's life is *accidental*, not *substantial*. It is thus distinct from the generation of the Word, who receives the whole substance of the Father. It is likewise distinct from the hypostatic union, which is a substantial union of the divine and human natures in the person of the Word. In our union with God we keep our personality, and therefore, this union is not substantial. This is the doctrine of St. Thomas : " Grace, being altogether above human nature, can neither be a substance nor the soul's substantial form. It can only be its accidental form. " [1]   Explaining his thought he adds that what exists in God substantially is given us accidentally, and makes us partake of the divine goodness.

With such restrictions we steer clear of pantheism and still conceive a very exalted idea of the nature of grace. It reveals itself to us as a *likeness of God* stamped by Him on our souls : " *Let us make man according to our image and likeness.* " [2]

112. In order to help us to understand this divine resemblance the Fathers have employed various comparisons. 1) Our soul, they say, is like to a living image of the Most Blessed Trinity, for the Holy Ghost Himself impresses His features on us as a seal does on molten wax, stamping and leaving there the divine likeness. [3]   They conclude that the soul in the state of grace possesses an entrancing beauty since the author of that image is none other than God Himself who is infinitely perfect : " Behold thy likeness, O man; see thy likeness beautiful, made by thy God, the Great Artist, the Master-Painter. " [4]   They rightly reason that, far from disfiguring or destroying such resemblance, we must perfect it more' and more.   At times they compare the soul to those transparent bodies that receiving the sun's rays become all aglow and reflect in turn a marvellous light all around. [5]

113. 2) To show further that this divine resemblance is not merely on the surface, they have recourse to the analogy of iron in the fire. As a bar of iron, they say, plunged into a glowing fire soon acquires the brightness, the heat and the pliancy of fire, so the soul in the fire of divine love is rid of impurities, burns, glows and becomes docile to God's inspirations.

114. 3) To express the idea that grace is a new life, the Fathers and spiritual writers liken it to a divine branch ingrafted into the wild stock of our nature, there combining with it to form a new, vital principle and, therefore, a life far superior in kind.   Yet, in the same way that the branch does not give its life to the stock in all its essence and particulars but only such or such of its vital properties, so sanctifying grace does not give to us God's entire essence but simply *something of His life*, which is for us a new life.

[1] *Sum. Theol.*, Iᵃ IIᵃᵉ, q. 110, a. 2. — [2] *Gen.* I, 26.
[3] *Homil. Paschal.*, X, 2, *P. G.*, LXXVII, 617.
[4] St. AMBROSE, *In Hexæm.*, l. VI, c. 8, *P. L.*, XIV, 260.
[5] St. BASIL, *De Spir. S.*, IX, 23, *P. G.*, XXXII, 109.

We share then in the life of the Godhead, but by no means possess It in Its fulness. This resemblance of the soul to the Divinity evidently prepares it for a most intimate union with the Most Holy Trinity that dwells in it.

B) *Union of God and the Soul*

115. From what we have said concerning the indwelling of the Most Blessed Trinity in the soul (n. 92) it follows that there is the closest and most sanctifying union between our souls and the Divine Guest. But is this all? Is there not something *physical* besides this moral union?

116. **a)** The comparisons the Fathers employ would seem to imply so.

1) A great many of them tell us that the union of God with the soul is like that of the soul and the body. There are in us two lives, says St. Augustine, the life of the body and the life of the soul; the life of the body is the soul, the life of the soul is God.[1] Evidently, these are only analogies; let us try to bring out the truth they contain.

The union of body and soul is a *substantial* union, so much so, that they form but one nature and only one person. The union between God and the soul is different. We retain always our own nature and our own personality and thus remain essentially distinct from the Godhead. However, just, as the soul gives the body its life, so God (without becoming the form of the soul, as the soul is of the body) gives the soul supernatural life, a life not equal to His, but *truly* and *formally* like unto His, producing a union that is *most real* between the soul and God. This implies a concrete reality which God communicates to us and which constitutes the bond of union between Him and us. Assuredly this new relation adds nothing to God, but it perfects the soul and makes it Godlike. Thus the Holy Ghost is not the formal cause, but the efficient and exemplary cause of our sanctification.

117. 2) The very same truth flows from the other comparison made by other authors.[2] They liken the union of the soul with God to the *hypostatic union*. Again, there is an essential difference. The hypostatic union is *substantial* and *personal*, for though the human and the divine natures

---

[1] " *Sicut vita corporis anima, sic vita animæ Deus.* " *(Enarrat. in psal.* 70, sermo 2, n. 3. P. L. XXXVI, 893.

[2] BELLAMY, *La Vie surnaturelle*, p. 184-191.

are absolutely different, yet, they constitute but one and the same person in Jesus Christ. The union of God with the soul through grace, on the contrary, leaves us our own personality, essentially distinct from that of God, and unites us to God in a merely *accidental* manner. " It is brought about in fact through the medium of sanctifying grace, an accident superadded to the soul's substance. Accidental union is the name given by the Scholastics to the union of an accident with a substance. " [1]

None the less it is true that the union of the soul and God is a union of *substance with substance*, [2] that man and God are in contact as closely as the incandescent iron is with the fire which permeates it, as closely as the glowing crystal is with the light that penetrates it. We can sum it up briefly in these few words : the hypostatic union makes a God-man, the union of grace makes deified men. In the same way as the actions of Christ are both divine and human, theandric actions, so those of the just man are Godlike, performed at once by God and by man. They are thus meritorious, worthy of eternal life, which is nothing else but direct union with Divinity. We can say with Father de Smedt [3] that " the hypostatic union is the type, the model, of our union with God by grace and that the latter is the most perfect imitation of the former that can be found among creatures. "

We conclude with this same writer that the union of God and the soul by grace is not a mere moral union, but rather one which contains a physical element and which justifies the name of physico-moral union : " The divine nature is truly and properly united to the substance of the soul by a special bond and in such a way that the soul really possesses the divine nature as if it were personally its own. As a consequence, the soul possesses a divine character, a divine perfection and a divine beauty which is infinitely superior to all possible natural perfection wherever found and in whatsoever creature, whether actually existing or capable of existing. [4]

---

[1] CARDINAL MERCIER, *La Vie intérieure*, ed. 1919, p. 392.

[2] This is perhaps the thought of Cardinal Mercier when he adds (*l. c.*) : " In a sense, however, this union is a *substantial* one. On the one hand, it takes place between substance and substance without the interference of any natural accident. On the other, it places the soul in direct contact with the divine substance; it places the latter within the immediate reach of the former after the manner of a gift which the soul has the power both to possess and enjoy. "

In this way are explained the expressions of the *Mystics* who with St. John of the Cross speak of the divine contact " that takes place *between the substance of the soul and the Divine substance* in the course of intimate and loving friendship. "

Father Poulain in " Graces of Interior Prayer, " C. VI, has gathered a great many texts from the *Contemplatives* on this point.

[3] *Notre Vie surnaturelle*, p. 51. — [4] *Op. cit.*, p. 49.

118. b) If we leave comparisons aside and look for the exact theological doctrine on the question, we arrive at precisely the same conclusion. 1) In heaven the Elect see God face to face without the aid of any intermediary. It is the divine essence itself that acts as the principle of knowledge or *species impressa* as it is called. [1] This means that there exists between God and the Elect a true and real union that can be called physical, since God can not be seen and possessed unless He be present to them by His essence, nor can He be loved unless He be actually united to their wills as the object of their love. But grace is nothing less than the beginning, the inception, the seed of glory. [2] Hence the union between the soul and God begun here on earth by grace is in fact of the same kind as that in heaven; it is real and, in a certain sense, physical, like the latter. The following is the conclusion of Father Froget in his beautiful work, " The Indwelling of the Holy Ghost. " Supported by numerous texts from St. Thomas he says : " God is then truly, physically and substantially present in the Christian in the state of grace; this is no mere presence, but a real possession with the initial enjoyment thereto attached. "

2) We draw the same conclusion from the *analysis of grace itself.* According to the teaching of the Angelic Doctor, based on the very texts of Holy Scripture we have quoted, habitual grace is given us in order that we may enjoy the possession not only of divine gifts but also of the Divine Persons. [3] But to enjoy anything whatever, adds a disciple of St. Bonaventure, the presence of the said thing or object is absolutely necessary, and therefore, in order to enjoy the Holy Spirit, His presence is necessary as well as the presence of the created gift which unites us to Him. [4] If the presence of the created gift is *real* and *physical,* should not that of the Holy Ghost be likewise real and physical?

Therefore, our deductions from Dogma as well as the comparisons employed by the Fathers authorize us to say that the union of the soul with God is not merely moral, nor on the other hand substantial, in the strict sense of the term,

---

[1] *In visione qua Deus per essentiam videbitur, ipsa divina essentia erit quasi forma intellectus quo intelliget.* St. THOMAS, *Sum. Theol.,* Suppl., q. 92, a. 1.

[2] " Gratia nihil est quam inchoatio gloriæ in nobis ". *Sum. theol.,* IIᵃ IIæ, q. 24, a. 3. — This is likewise the thought of Pope Leo XIII in his Encyclical, *Divinum illud munus:* " Hæc autem mira conjunctio, quæ suo nomine inhabitatio dicitur, conditione tantum statu ab ea discrepat qua cælites Deus beando complectitur ". CAVALLERA, *Thesaurus doctrinæ cathol.,* n. 546.

[3] " Per donum gratiæ gratum facientis perficitur creatura rationalis ad hoc quod libere non solum ipso dono creato utatur, sed ut ipsa divina persona fruatur. " St. THOMAS, *Sum. Theol.,* I, q. 43, a. 3.

[4] Ps. BONAVENTURE, *Compend. Theol. veritatis,* l. I, c. 9.

but that it is so real that it may be justly called a *physico-moral* union. However, it remains veiled and obscure; its growth is gradual, its effects are perceived more and more clearly in proportion as we make efforts to cultivate faith and the gifts of the Holy Ghost. Fervent souls who long for this divine union are ever possessed of an urgent desire to advance further each day in the practice of virtue and the use of these gifts.

2° THE VIRTUES AND THE GIFTS

A) *Existence and Nature*

119. In order to act and develop, the supernatural life ingrafted into our souls by habitual grace demands faculties likewise of a supernatural character. These the bounty and liberality of God have given us in the form of *infused virtues* and *gifts of the Holy Ghost*. As Leo XIII tells us: " The just man living the life of grace and acting through the virtues that fulfil the function of faculties, stands also in need of the seven gifts of the Holy Ghost. " [1]   In fact, it is only meet that our natural faculties which of themselves can produce but natural acts, should be perfected and deified by infused habits to place them on a supernatural plane and enable them to act supernaturally. Because God's liberality knows no bounds, He has granted us a twofold boon : first, the *virtues* which, directed by prudence, enable us to act supernaturally with the help of actual grace; then, the gifts making us so docile to the influence of the Holy Ghost that we are, so to speak, moved and directed by that divine Spirit, guided by a sort of divine instinct.   Here it must be noted that these gifts, conferred as they are together with the virtues and habitual grace, do not exert a frequent or an intensive action except in mortified souls who have by a prolonged practice of the moral and theological virtues acquired that supernatural docility and ease that render them completely obedient to the inspirations of the Holy Spirit.

120. The essential difference between the virtues and the gifts consists in their *different mode* of action within us. In the practice of *virtue* grace lets us act under the influence of prudence.   In the use of the *gifts*, once they have reached their full development, grace demands docility rather than activity.   We shall go deeper into this question when treat-

---

[1] " Homini justo vitam scilicet viventi divinæ gratiæ et per congruas virtutes tamquam facultates agenti, opus plane est septenis illis quæ proprie dicuntur Spiritus Sancti donis. " LEO XIII, *Encyc., Divinum illud munus.*   See the English translation in *The Great Encyclicals of Leo XIII*, p. 422-440.

ing of the unitive way. In the meantime, a comparison will help us to understand it : when a mother teaches her child to walk, she at times simply leads him supporting him at the same time so that he may not fall; at other times she takes him in her arms to help him over some hindrance in the way or to let him rest a while. The first instance illustrates the influence of the *virtues*, the latter that of the *gifts*.

From this it follows that normally the acts performed under the influence of the gifts are *more perfect* than those accomplished under the sole influence of the virtues precisely because in the former case the operation of the Holy Ghost is more active and also more fruitful.

B) *The Infused Virtues*

121. It is *certain* from the Council of Trent that at the very moment of justification we receive the infused virtues of faith, hope and charity.[1] The *common doctrine*, confirmed by the Catechism of the Council of Trent,[2] is that the moral virtues of prudence, justice, fortitude and temperance are likewise communicated to us at that same moment. We must remember that these virtues endow us, not with facility, but with a *supernatural, proximate power* of eliciting supernatural acts. In order to acquire that facility of action which acquired habits give, we need to perform repeated acts of such virtues.

Let us now see how these virtues *supernaturalize* our faculties.

a) Some of these virtues are *theological*, because their material object is God, their formal object some divine attribute. Faith, for instance, unites us to God, the Supreme Truth, and aids us to see all, to view all things by His divine light. Hope unites us to God, the source of our happiness, who is ever ready to pour forth upon us all His favors so that our transformation may be perfected, and to tender us His all-powerful help to enable us to elicit acts of absolute trust in Him. Charity takes us up to God, infinitely good in Himself. Under the influence of this love, we delight in the perfections of God even more than if they were our own; we desire to make them known and have them praised; we form with Him a holy friendship and a sweet intimacy. Thus we become more and more like unto Him.

---

[1] " In ipsa justificatione... hæc omnia simul infusa accipit homo, fidem, spem et caritatem. (*Trid.*, sess. VI, c. 7). — [2] P. ii, de Baptismo, n. 42.

122. **b)** These three *theological* virtues unite us directly to God; the *moral* virtues remove the obstacles to that union and thus prepare for and perpetuate it. The object proper of these moral virtues is a moral good distinct from God. Our actions are so regulated by them that, in spite of obstacles from within or without, they are kept in steady course towards God. Thus, *prudence* makes us choose those means best adapted to the pursuance of our supernatural end. *Justice*, by having us render to others what is due them, sanctifies our relations with them, so as to bring us close to God and to make us more like Him. *Fortitude* equips our soul for trials and struggles. It makes us endure suffering with patience and causes us to undertake with holy ardor and daring the most painful and laborious tasks for the glory of God. Lastly, since guilty pleasure would lead us astray, *temperance* controls our thirst for pleasure and brings it under subjection to the law of duty. All these virtues have their part to play either in removing obstacles or in supplying positive means to press onward towards God. [1]

C) *The Gifts of the Holy Ghost*

123. Here we shall not describe the gifts in detail, but simply show how they correspond to the virtues.

First, the gifts are in no way superior to the theological virtues. This becomes evident if we but think of divine charity. Their function, however, is that of *perfecting the exercise* of the virtues. By the gift of *understanding* we can penetrate farther into the truths of faith to discover the hidden treasures and discern the mysterious harmony therein contained. The gift of *knowledge* makes us look upon creatures from the point of view of their relation to their Maker. The gift of *fear*, by weaning us from the false goods of earth that might allure us into sin, fortifies the virtue of hope and intensifies the desire for the happiness of heaven. *Wisdom* makes us relish divine things thus increasing our love of God. The gift of *counsel* crowns the virtue of prudence by showing us in exceptional or difficult cases what it behooves us to do or not to do. *Piety* perfects the virtue of religion, making us recognize in God a Father whom we delight in glorifying by love. The gift of *fortitude* completes the virtue which bears the same name by urging us on to what is more heroic in endurance and in daring.

---

[1] In the second part of this work where we shall treat of the illuminative way, we shall explain these virtues in detail. The explanation of the gifts of the Holy Ghost we shall join to the treatment of the unitive way.

The gift of *fear*, besides rendering easy the practice of hope, perfects temperance by begetting in us a dread of the penalty and of the ills issuing from the illicit love of pleasure.

In this fashion the virtues and the gifts receive their harmonious development in our souls under the influence of actual grace, of which we must now briefly speak.

3° ACTUAL GRACE [1]

In the order of nature we can do nothing to bring power into action without the concurrence of God. The same is true in the supernatural order; without actual grace we cannot set our faculties into operation.

124. We shall explain: 1° the notion of actual grace, 2° its mode of action, 3° its necessity.

A) Notion. Actual grace is a supernatural, transient help given us by our Lord to enlighten our mind and strengthen our will in the performance of supernatural acts.

a) Its action on our spiritual faculties is *direct.* Now, grace acts on the mind and the will not simply to raise them to the supernatural order, but to set them in motion and cause them to elicit supernatural acts. For instance, *before* justification, that is, before the infusion into the soul of habitual grace, actual grace makes us see the malice and frightful consequences of sin in order to have us loathe it. *After* justification actual grace shows us by the light of faith God's infinite beauty and His loving kindness, in order to have us love Him with all our heart.

b) Besides these *interior* helps, there are others called *exterior* graces. These latter act directly on our *senses* and our *sensitive faculties.* They, therefore, indirectly reach the spiritual faculties, especially since they are often attended by real, interior helps. To this category of exterior graces belong, for instance, the reading of Holy Scripture or the perusal of some spiritual work, the hearing of a sermon or a piece of religious music, a pious conversation, etc. These do not of themselves strengthen the will, but they produce in us favorable *impressions* which by quickening the mind and rousing the will predispose them towards the supernatural good. Besides, God often gives in addition *inward promptings* which by enlightening the mind and giving strength to the will, move us on to amendment, conversion

---

[1] Cf. S. THOMAS, Iᵃ IIₐₑ, q. 109-113; TANQUEREY, *Syn. Theol. Dog.*, III, n. 122-123. Besides Latin works see WAFFELAERT, *Méditations théol.*, I, p. 606-650; DE BROGLIE, *Confér. sur la vie surnaturelle*, I, p. 249; LABAUCHE, *God and Man*, IIIᵉ P., C. 1; VAN DER MEERSCH, in the Dict. de théol.: "Grâce".

or advancement in the way of perfection. This is what we draw from the Book of the Acts where the Holy Ghost is spoken of as opening the heart of a woman named Lydia " to attend to those things which were said by Paul."[1] As for the rest, God who knows that it is through things sensible that we rise to things spiritual, adapts Himself to our weakness and makes use of the visible things of this world to bring us to the practice of virtue.

125. B) Its mode of action. a) Actual grace exerts its influence upon us both in a *moral* and a *physical* manner. In a *moral* way, by means of *persuasion* and *attraction*, just as a mother might in teaching her child to walk, call him to herself with a promise of something good. It influences us *physically*[2] by adding new forces to our faculties, too weak to act of themselves, as a mother not only coaxes her child to try to walk, but actually takes him by the arms and helps him to take a few steps. All schools admit that operating grace acts physically by producing in our souls indeliberate impulses. As to co-operating grace various schools of theology hold different opinions; these differences, however, have but little importance in practice. We shall not discuss them here since we do not wish to base the doctrine of the spiritual life upon questions that are matter for controversy.

b) From another point of view, grace either *goes before* the free assent of the will or *accompanies* it in the performance of an act. Thus, for example, the thought of making an act of love of God suggests itself to us without any effort on our part. This is a *preventing* grace, a good thought that God gives us. If we acquiesce in it and make an effort to perform the act of love, we then accomplish this through the help of a grace called *concomitant*. Another distinction analogous to this is the one between *operating* and *co-operating* grace : through the former God acts in us without us; through the latter God acts in and together with us, that is with the free co-operation of our will.

126. C) Its necessity.[3] The general principle is that actual grace is necessary for the performance of every *supernatural* act, since there must be a proportion between an effect and its cause.

---

[1] *Acts*, XVI, 14.
[2] This is at least the Thomist teaching thus summarized by Father Hugon, *Tract. Dog.*, II, p. 297 : " Gratia actualis... est etiam realitas supernaturalis nobis intrinseca, non quidem per modum qualitatis, sed per modum motionis transeuntis ".
[3] Cf. *Syn. Theol. Dog.*, III, n. 34-91. There we also examine how far grace is needed for the performance of natural acts.

a) Thus, when it is question of *conversion*, that is, of the passing from mortal sin to the state of grace, supernatural grace is needed to perform the preliminary acts of faith, hope, sorrow and love; nay, such a grace is needed even for that devout desire of believing which is the first step, the very starting point of faith. **b**) Our steadfastness in good, our *perseverance* unto the hour of death, is likewise the work of actual grace. In fact, in order to persevere one must resist *temptations* which assail even the justified soul so persistently and tenaciously at times, that without God's help one could not withstand their onslaught. This is why the Savior warns His Apostles immediately after the Last Supper to watch and pray, that is to say, to rely upon grace rather upon their efforts and good will, lest they fall victims to temptation. [1] Beside the resisting of temptations, perseverance also implies the accomplishment of one's duty. The constant and strenuous efforts we must put forth in order to fulfil it will not be made without the power of grace. He alone who has begun in us the good work of perfection can bring it to a happy close. [2] Only He who has called us unto His eternal glory can perfect and confirm and establish us. [3]

127. This holds true especially of *final perseverance*, a singular and priceless gift. [4] We cannot merit it strictly speaking. To die in the state of grace in spite of all the temptations that assail us at the last hour, to escape these by a sudden or tranquil death — falling asleep in the Lord — this is truly in the language of Councils the grace of graces. We cannot ask for it insistently enough. Prayer and faithful co-operation with grace can obtain it for us. [5]

c) We truly have to rely upon the divine favor. Think what this means, if one wishes not merely to persevere in grace, but to grow in holiness each day, to avoid deliberate venial faults and reduce as much as in our power lies even our faults of frailty. To pretend that we could for long escape all the faults that hinder our spiritual progress is to contradict the experience of the choicest souls, souls that sorrowed bitterly over their lapses; it would be to contradict St. John who declares that whoever imagines himself free from sin labors under a delusion; [6] in fine, it is to contradict the Council of Trent which condemns those who maintain that justified man can, without a special privi-

---

[1] *Matth.*, XXVI, 41. — [2] *Philip.*, I, 6. — [3] *I Peter*, V, 10.
[4] *Trid.*, sess. VI, Can. 16, 22, 23.
[5] S. AUGUST., *De dono persev.*, VI, 10, *P. L.* XLV, 999.
[6] *I Joan.*, I, 8.

lege from God, avoid all venial sin during the whole course
of his life. [1]

128. Actual grace is, therefore, needed even after justification. We obtain it of the divine mercy by prayer;
hence, the stress laid in Holy Writ upon the necessity of
prayer. We can also obtain it through our meritorious acts,
in other words, by our co-operation with grace; for the more
faithful we are in availing ourselves of the actual graces
received, the more will the Almighty be moved to grant us
new and greater ones.

CONCLUSIONS

129. 1o We must hold in greatest esteem the life of
grace, for it is a new life which unites and assimilates us to
God. It is a life much higher and richer than our own
natural life. As the life of the mind, our intellectual life, is
superior to vegetative or sensitive life, so the supernatural
life infinitely surpasses mere rational life. This latter in
fact is due to man the moment God determines to create
him, whilst the former is above the activities and the merit
of even the most perfect creature. What created being could
ever claim the right of becoming the adopted child of God?
Of being made the dwelling place of the Holy Ghost? Of
seeing, contemplating God face to face as He sees and contemplates Himself? The Christian life is, therefore, the
hidden treasure which we must hold dearer than all created
things.

130. 2o Once this treasure is ours, we must be ready to
sacrifice all things rather than run the risk of losing it.
This is the conclusion arrived at by Pope St. Leo:
" Understand, O Christian, what dignity is yours! Made a
partaker of the divine nature, do not by an unworthy life
return to your former wretchedness. " [2] No one should be
possessed of a greater *reverence for self* than the Christian,
not indeed on account of any merits of his own, but because
of that divine life in which he shares, because of the Holy
Ghost whose living temple he is. The holiness of this
temple must not be violated nor its beauty tarnished:
" Holiness becomes Thy house, O Lord, unto length of
days. " [3]

131. 3o Our plain duty is to make use of, to develop
this supernatural organism which constitutes our greatest

---

[1] Sess. VI, Cap. 23. — [2] *Sermones*, XXI, 3, *P. L.*, LIV, 195. — [3] *Ps.* XCII, 5.

possession. If on the one hand it has pleased the divine goodness to raise us to a superior rank, to endow us with virtues and gifts that perfect our natural powers; if at every moment God gives us His aid that we may live and act through those powers, it would be the blackest ingratitude to scorn and despise such gifts and to live a merely natural life without looking for fruits worthy of eternal glory. The more generous the giver, the more active and fruitful the co-operation expected. We shall understand this better still after we have studied the place of Christ in the life of the Christian.

§ II. Rôle of Jesus in the Christian Life [1]

132. The Three Divine Persons of the Most Blessed Trinity confer upon us that participation in the life of God described above. It is granted, however, because of the merits and satisfactions of Jesus Christ. On this account He plays a signal part in our supernatural life which is, therefore, called the *Christian life.*

According to the teaching of St. Paul, Jesus Christ is the head of regenerated humanity, just as Adam was the head of the human race; but, in a far more perfect manner. By His merits Christ regained for us our rights to grace and glory, and by His example He shows us how we are to live in order to sanctify ourselves and merit heaven. More than this, He is the *head* of a mystical body of which we are the members. Thus, He is the meritorious, exemplary, and vital cause of our sanctification.

I. *Jesus, the Meritorious Cause of our Spiritual Life*

133. When we say that Jesus Christ is the *meritorious cause* of our sanctification, we take the term in its broader sense as implying both satisfaction and merit. "Because of the exceeding great charity wherewith He loved us, by His holy passion on the cross, He merited for us justification and made satisfaction for us"[2]. *Logically,* satisfaction precedes merit. The offense done to God must first of all be atoned for to obtain the pardon of sin, before grace can be merited. In reality, however, all the free acts of our Savior

---

[1] St. Thom., III, qq. 8, 25, 26. 40, 46-49, 57 aud elsewhere; Bérulle, *Œuvres,* éd. 1657, p. 522-530; 665-669; 689; Olier, *Pensées choisies;* Prat, *Theology of St. Paul,* I, l. III, c. 1; l. IV, c. 3; II, l. III, IV; Marmion, *Christ, Life of the Soul;* Duperray, *Le Christ dans la vie chrétienne;* Plus, *In Christ Jesus.*
[2] Co. of Trent, sess. VI, c. 7.

were at once satisfactory and meritorious; all had an infinite moral value, as we said above, n. 78.   From this truth a few conclusions follow.

A) No sin is unpardonable provided that contrite and humbled we meekly ask for forgiveness. This is what we do in the tribunal of penance where the power of the Blood of Christ is applied to us by His minister. The same is effected in the Holy Sacrifice of the Mass. There Jesus offers Himself incessantly for us by the hands of His priests as a sacrifice of propitiation, which repairing the injury done to God by sin, inclines Him to forgive us and at the same time obtains for us graces which excite in our souls sentiments of sincere contrition. Christ thus obtains for us the full pardon of our sins and remission of the temporal punishment due to them. We may add that all the acts of our Christian life, when united to those of Jesus Christ, have a satisfactory value both for ourselves and for those for whom we offer them.

134. **B)** Christ likewise merited for us all the grace we need to attain our supernatural end and to develop in us the supernatural life : " Who hath blessed us with spiritual blessings in heavenly places, in Christ. " [1]   He merited for us the grace of conversion, the grace of steadfastness in good, the helps to resist temptation, the aids to profit by trial, the grace of comfort in the midst of tribulations, the grace of renewal of spirit and of final perseverance. He merited all things for us. We have the solemn word that anything we ask the Father in His name, that is, through His own merits, will be granted to us. [2]   Then in order to inspire us with greater confidence, He instituted the sacraments, visible signs, which confer His grace in all the important events of life and which give us a right to actual graces in time of need.

135. **C)** He has gone further still. In His desire to associate us with Himself in the work of our own sanctification, He has given us the power of satisfying and meriting, thus making us the secondary causes, the agents of our own sanctification. He has, as a matter of fact, made this co-operation a law and an essential condition of our spiritual life. If He has carried His cross, it is that we may follow Him bearing ours : " If any many will come after me, let him deny himself and take up his cross and

---

[1] *Eph.*, I, 3. — [2] *John*, XVI, 23.

follow me. " ¹   It was thus understood by the Apostles.
If we would share in His glory, says St. Paul, we must share
in His sufferings : " Yet so, if we suffer with him, that we
may be also glorified with him. " ²   St. Peter adds that if
Christ suffered for us it is that we may follow in His footsteps. ³   Moreover, self-sacrificing souls are urged, after the
manner of the Apostle of the Gentiles, to undergo suffering
joyfully in union with Christ for the sake of the Church, His
mystical body : " Who now rejoice in my sufferings for you
and fill up those things that are wanting of the sufferings
of Christ, in my flesh, for his body, which is the church. " ⁴
In this wise these souls share in the redeeming power of
Christ's passion and become secondary agents of the salvation of their brethren.   How true, how sublime, how consoling is this doctrine!   Compare it with the incredible
affirmation of certain Protestants who assert, that since
Christ suffered to the full for us, there remains for us only
to enjoy the fruits of His plentiful redemption without
drinking of His chalice.   They thus pretend to pay homage
to the fulness of Christ's merits.   Does not our Christ-given
power to merit show forth better the fulness of the redemption by Christ?   Does it not do more honor to Christ to
manifest the power of His satisfaction by enabling us to
join in His work of atonement and co-operate with Him
even though in a secondary manner?

II. *Jesus, the Exemplary Cause of our Spiritual Life*

136.   Jesus was not content to merit for us; He willed
to be the *exemplary cause*, the model of our supernatural life.

In order to develop a life that is no less than a participation in the life of God, we must strive as far as it
possible, to live a divine life.   Hence, the need we had of a
divine model.   As St. Augustine remarks, men whom we
see were too imperfect to serve us as a pattern and God, who
is holiness itself, was too far beyond our gaze.   Then, the
eternal Son of God, His living image, became man and
showed us by His example how man could here on earth
approach the perfection of God.   Son of God and son of
man, He lived a Godlike life and could say : " Who seeth
me seeth the Father. " ⁵   Having revealed the holiness of
God in His actions, He can present to us as practical the
imitation of the divine perfections : " Be you therefore

---

¹ *Matth.*, XVI, 24. — ² *Rom.*, VIII, 17. — ³ *I Peter*, II, 21.
⁴ *Coloss.*, I, 24. — ⁵ *John*, XIV, 9.

perfect as also your heavenly Father is perfect. "¹   Therefore, the Eternal Father proposes Him to us as our model.
At His haptism and His transfiguration He said : " This
is my beloved Son, in whom I am well pleased. "²   Because
He is well pleased in Him, the Eternal Father wills that
we imitate His only-begotten Son.   Thus with perfect
assurance our Lord tells us: " I am the way... no man
cometh to the Father but by me... learn of me because
I am meek and humble of heart...   I have given you an
example that as I have done to you so you do also. "³
At bottom the Gospel is no more than a relation of the
deeds and traits of our Lord's sacred person proposed
to us as a model for our imitation : " Jesus began to do
and to teach. "⁴   Christianity in turn is nothing more than
the imitation of Christ.   St. Paul gave this as the sum-
total of all our duties : " Be ye followers of me as I also
am of Christ. "⁵

137. **a)** The following are the qualities of the model
given us.   Jesus is a *perfect* model.   On the admitted
testimony of even those who do not believe in His divinity,
He is the highest type of virtue ever seen among men.   He
practised all virtues to the degree of heroism.   His motives
were the most perfect : religion towards God, love of His
fellow-men, utter self-effacement and horror of sin and its
approaches.⁶   And yet, this model is withal capable of
imitation; it is universal, magnetic, powerful.

138. **b)** All men *can imitate* Him.   Indeed, He willed
to bear all our weaknesses and miseries and even our temptations; He willed to be like us in all things, sin excepted.
" For we have not a high-priest who can not have compassion
on our infirmities : but one tempted in all things like we are,
without sin. "⁷   During thirty years He lived an ordinary
life, hidden and obscure; He was subject to Mary and
Joseph, working as an apprentice, a wage-earner, a toiler,
" the carpenter's son. "⁸   This has made Him the perfect
model for the great mass of men who have but lowly duties
to perform and who must work out their sanctification amid
humble occupations.   His public life was one of zeal.   This
He exercised, now by training His Apostles, His chosen ones,
now by evangelizing the multitudes.   He underwent hunger

---

¹ *Matth.*, V, 48. — ² *Matth.*, III, 17; XVII, 5.
³ *John*, XIV, 6; *Matth.*, XI, 29; *John*, XIII, 15. — ⁴ *Acts*, I, 1.
⁵ *I Cor.*, IV, 16; XI, 1; *Eph.*, V, 1.
⁶ This is very well explained by Father Olier, " Catechism for an Interior Life ',
Part I, C. I. — ⁷ *Heb.* IV, 15. — ⁸ *Matth.*, XIII, 55.

and fatigue, enjoyed the friendship of a few, and had to bear
the ingratitude and even the enmity of others. He had
His successes and reverses, His joys and His sorrows. In a
word, He passed through the vicissitudes of the man who
lives close to his friends and in daily contact with the people.
The sufferings of His passion have given us the example of
heroic patience in the midst of physical and moral torture,
endured not only without complaint but with a prayer for
His persecutors. And we must not reason that because He
was God He suffered less. He was also man, a man possessed of the most perfect, and therefore the most delicate
sensibility. So, He felt and felt more keenly, more vividly
than we ever could, the ingratitude of men, the defection of
His friends, the treason of Judas. He tasted weariness and
grief and terror to the full, so that He could not stay the
groaning of His heart, He could not halt the prayer that
if possible the bitter chalice might pass from Him. Lastly,
on the cross He let escape that woeful cry of utter dereliction,
torn from the recesses of His soul, and revealing abysmal
depths of interior sorrow : " My God, my God, why hast
thou forsaken me! " [1]

139. c) A universal model is also a *magnetic* one. Speaking of the manner of His death, He foretold that once He
be lifted up from the earth He would draw all things to
Himself : " And I, if I be lifted up from the earth, will
draw all things to myself. " [2] The prophecy has come
true. Gazing upon what Jesus has done and suffered for
them, generous souls are smitten with love for Him and for
His Cross. [3] In spite of the abhorrence of nature they
bravely carry their interior or exterior crosses to become
more like their Lord and Master, to give Him a proof of their
love by suffering with Him and for Him, to share more
richly in the fruits of His redemption, to join Him in working for the sanctification of men. This is revealed in the
lives of the Saints who seek after crosses more eagerly than
worldlings do after pleasure.

140. d) This attraction is all the stronger since He adds
thereto all the power of His grace. All the actions of Christ
before His death were meritorious; they merited for us the
grace of performing actions similar to His own. When we
observe His humility, His poverty, His mortification and

---

[1] *Matth.*, XXVII, 46; *Mk.*, XV, 34.
[2] *John*, XII, 32.
[3] This is the meaning of the prayer of the Apostle St. Andrew who, crucified for
His Master, lovingly greeted the Cross, saying : " O bona crux ".

all His other virtues, we are drawn to imitate Him, not merely by the persuasive force of His example, but by the impelling power, the efficaciousness of the graces which He merited for us by practising such virtues.

141. There are especially certain actions of our divine Savior that transcend all others. To these we must unite ourselves since they are the source of greater grace ; they are His *mysteries*. At His incarnation our Lord offered us all with Himself to the Eternal Father to consecrate us to Him. This mystery then merited for us the grace of self-renunciation and of union with God. The mystery of His crucifixion gained for us the grace of crucifying our flesh and its concupiscences. The mystery of His death obtained for us the grace of dying to sin and to the causes of sin. [1] The truth of this will be better realized by considering how Jesus is the head of a mystical body of which we are the members.

III. *Jesus the Head of a Mystical Body or the Source of our Spiritual Life* [2]

142. The doctrine of the mystical body is contained in substance in the words of our Lord : [3] " I am the vine and you the branches. " Here He asserts that we draw our life from Him as the branches do from the stalk. This comparison brings out the notion of our participation in the life of Christ. It is easy to pass thence to the conception of the mystical body in which Jesus, the Head, communicates His life to the members. St. Paul is most insistent on this teaching so fruitful in its consequences. A body must have a head, a soul and members. These three elements we shall now describe, following the doctrine of the Apostle.

143. 1º The head plays a threefold rôle in the human body : it is first of all its most prominent and *preëminent* part, its center of unity, holding together, controlling and directing all the members; it is the source of a vital influx, for life and movement proceed from it. This threefold function is exercised by Christ in the Church and in the souls of men. **a)** He is without question the most prominent and preëminent among men. As God-man He is the first-born of all creatures, the object of the divine complacency, the exemplar

---

[1] OLIER, *Catechism for an Interior Life*, P. I, C. XX-XXV.
[2] *Sum. Theol.*, III, q. 8; PRAT, *op. cit.*, I, ed. 1920, p. 358-369; DUPERRAY, *op. cit.*, C. I-II; MARMION, *Christ the Life of the Soul*, p. 79-92; PLUS, *op. cit.*
[3] *John*, XV, 5.

of all virtues, the meritorious cause, the source of our sanctification, who on account of His merits was exalted above His brethren and before whom every knee must bend in heaven and on earth.

b) He is the *center of unity* in the Church. Two things are essential to any complete organism : variety of organs and the functions they fulfil, and a single, common principle. Without these we should have a mass or a motley gathering of living beings with no tie to bind them together. After having given diversity of members to the Church by the establishment of a hierarchy, Jesus Christ still remains its center of unity; for it is He who as the invisible but real Head of the Church gives impetus and direction to its rulers.

c) He is likewise the *vital influx*, the principle of life that quickens all the members. Even as man He received grace in all its fulness to communicate it to us : " We saw him full of grace and truth... from whose fulness we have all received and grace for grace. " [1] He is in fact the meritorious cause of all the graces bestowed upon us by the Holy Ghost. The Council of Trent does not hesitate to affirm the reality of this influx, this vital action of Jesus upon the just : " For the same Christ... does infuse virtue into those that are justified... as the head unto the members. " [2]

144. 2° A living body must have not only a head but also a soul. The Holy Ghost is the soul of that mystical body whose head is Christ. This Holy Spirit infuses charity into the souls of men and also the graces Christ merited for us : " The charity of God is poured forth into our hearts by the Holy Ghost who is given to us. " [3] This is why He is called the Vivifier; " I believe in the Holy Ghost... the Vivifier ". This is what St. Augustine had in mind when he said that the Holy Ghost is to the body of the Church what the soul is to the human body : " What our soul is to the body, the Holy Ghost is to the body of Christ, which is the Church. " [4] These words have been adopted by Leo XIII in his encyclical on the Holy Ghost. This same Spirit dispenses the sundry spiritual gifts, the diversity of graces — charisms — " To one the word of wisdom, to another the word of knowledge, to another the working of miracles, to another prophecy, to another divers kinds of tongues... but all these things one and the same Spirit worketh, dividing to every one according as he will. " [5]

---

[1] *John*, I, 14, 16. — [2] Sess. VI, c. 8. — [3] *Rom.*, V, 5.
[4] Sermo 187, De Tempore. — [5] *Cor.*, XII, 6-11.

145. Nor can this twofold action of the Holy Ghost and of Christ work at variance. On the contrary, one completes the other. The Holy Ghost comes to us through Christ. When Jesus was on earth His holy soul possessed the Spirit in all its fulness, and by His actions and above all by His sufferings and death He merited for us the communication of this same Spirit. It is, therefore, because of Him that the Holy Ghost comes now to impart to us Christ's life and virtues and to make us like unto Him. Thus we see how on the one hand Jesus being man could alone be the head of a mystical body composed of men, since the head and the members must be one in nature; and we see on the other hand how as man He could not of Himself bestow the grace required for the life of His members. This the Holy Ghost does, but He does it in virtue of Christ's merits. Hence, we can say that this vital influx takes its origin in Christ in order to reach His members.

146. 3° Who are the members of this mystical body? All those who have been baptized. It is baptism that incorporates us into Christ. St. Paul says : " For in one Spirit were we all baptized unto one body." [1]   For this reason he adds that we have been baptized in Christ, that in baptism we put on Christ, [2] that is to say, we participate in the interior dispositions of Christ. This the Decree to the Armenians explains, saying that by baptism we become members of Christ and of the body of the Church. [3]   From this it follows that all the baptized are Christ's members, but in various degrees. The *just* are united to Him by habitual grace and the privileges that come with it; *sinners*, by faith and hope; the *blessed*, by the beatific vision. As regards *infidels*, they are not actually members of Christ's mystical body, although as long as they live upon earth they are called to become such. Only the *damned* are irrevocably excluded from this wonderful privilege.

147. 4° **The Consequences of this Doctrine. A)** This incorporation forms the basis of the doctrine of the communion of Saints. The just upon earth, the souls in purgatory and the blessed in heaven are all integral parts of Christ's mystical body. As such they all share in His life, come under His influence, and are obliged to love and help one another. St. Paul tells us : " If one member suffer anything,

---

[1] *I Cor.*, XII, 13.
[2] *Rom.*, VI, 3; *Gal.*, III, 25; *Rom.*. XIII, 17.
[3] **DENZINGER-BANN.**, n. 696.

all the members suffer with it; or if one member glory, all the members rejoice with it. " [1]

148. B) This is what makes all Christians brothers. From now on there is neither Jew nor Greek, neither freeman nor slave; we are all one in Christ Jesus. [2] We are all in closest fellowship so that what is profitable unto one is profitable unto all others. No matter how great the variety of gifts, or how great the diversity of offices, the whole body derives gain from whatever good there is in each member, and each member in turn shares in the common good of the body. This doctrine reveals to us the reasons why our Lord could say that whatever we do to the least of His little ones we do unto Him; [3] for the head is one with the members.

149. C) From St. Paul's teaching it follows that Christians are Christ's complement. God has in fact " made him head over all the Church, which is his body and the fulness of him who is filled all in all. " [4] The fact is that Jesus, Himself perfect, needs an increment in order to form His mystical body. From this point of view He is not sufficient unto Himself; in order to exercise all His vital functions He requires members. Father Olier concludes : " Let us yield our souls to the Spirit of Jesus Christ so that Jesus may have an increase in us. Whenever He finds apt followers, He expands, grows and diffuses Himself within their hearts, filling them with the same spiritual fragrance wherein He abounds. " [5] This is how we are able and are called to fulfil those things that are wanting of the sufferings of Christ, our Savior, for His body, which is the Church, [6] suffering even as He did, that His passion, so full in itself, be likewise fulfilled in His members through time and space. There is no doctrine more rich, more fruitful, than this doctrine of Christ's mystical body.

CONCLUSION : DEVOTION TO THE INCARNATE WORD [7]

150. From all that has been said concerning the rôle Jesus Christ plays in our spiritual life, it follows that in order to foster this life an intimate, affectionate and habitual union with Him is demanded of us, that is, devotion to the Incarnate Word. " He who abideth in me and I in him, the same beareth much fruit. " [8] The Church brings this

---

[1] *I Cor.*, XII, 26. — [2] *Rom.*, X, 12; *I Cor.* XII, 13. — [3] *Matth.*, XXV, 34-40.
[4] *Eph.*, I, 23. — [5] *Pensées*, p. 15-16. — [6] *Coloss.* I, 24.
[7] BÉRULLE (called the Apostle of the Incarnate Word), *Discours de l'Estat et des Grandeurs de Jésus.* — [8] *John*, XV, 5.

home to us when at the end of the Canon of the Mass she reminds us that through Him we receive all spiritual blessings, that through Him we are sanctified, quickened, blessed; that through Him, with Him and in Him is given to the Father Almighty in union with the Holy Ghost all honor and glory. A whole system of spiritual doctrine is here contained : having received from God all things through Christ, through the same Christ we must give God glory, through the same Christ we must ask further graces, with Christ and in Christ we must perform all our acts.

151. 1° Jesus is the only perfect adorer of His Father. In the words of Father Olier, He is the perfect worshipper of God, the only one that can offer Him infinite homage. It is clear, therefore, that in order to pay our debts to the Most Blessed Trinity, we can do nothing better than unite our every act of religion with the perfect worship of Jesus Christ. Nor is this difficult. Jesus being the head of a mystical body whose members we are, adores His Father not merely in His own name, but in the name of all those that are incorporated into Him. He puts into our hands, He places at our disposal the homages He pays to God Almighty; He allows us to make them our own and to offer them to the Blessed Trinity.

152. 2° With Him and in Him can we best make our petitions for new graces efficacious. He is the High-priest, "always living to make intercession for us." [1] Even when we have had the misfortune of offending God, He pleads for us and takes our part all the more eloquently as with His prayers He offers also the Blood He shed for our redemption. "If any man sin, we have an advocate with the Father, Jesus Christ the just." [2] More, He endows our prayers with such worth that if we pray in His name, that is, trusting to His infinite merits and uniting our poor prayers with His perfect prayers, we are certain of having our petitions granted. "Amen, amen, I say to you; if you ask the Father anything in my name, he will give it you." [3] The fact is that the value of His merits is imparted to His members, and God can not refuse anything to His Son. "He was heard for his reverence." [4]

153. 3° Lastly, it is in union with Jesus Christ that we must perform all our acts, by keeping, as Father Olier so aptly puts it, Jesus before our eyes, in our heart and in our

<hr>

[1] *Heb.*, VII, 25. — [2] *I John*, II, 1. — [3] *John*, XVI, 23. — [4] *Heb.*, V, 7.

hands. [1] Now, we keep Jesus before our eyes when we think of Him as the ideal, the model, we are to imitate; when like St. Vincent de Paul we ask ourselves : "What would Jesus Christ do were He in my place?" We keep Jesus in our heart by drawing into our soul the dispositions of His own heart, His purity of intention, His fervor, in order to perform our actions in the spirit in which He performed His. We have Jesus in our hands when we carry into action with generosity, determination and constancy the inspirations which He suggests to us. Then, our life is, indeed, transformed and we live Christ's own life. "I live, now not I, but Christ liveth in me." [2]

§ III. The Part of the Blessed Virgin, the Saints and the Angels in the Christian Life

154. Assuredly there is but one God and one principal mediator, Jesus Christ : "For there is one God : and one mediator of God and man, the man Christ Jesus." [3] However, it has pleased the Divine Wisdom as well as the Divine Goodness to grant us protectors, intercessors and models that are, or at least appear to be, closer still to us. Such are the Saints, members of Christ's mystical body, who having reproduced in their own lives the divine perfections and the virtues of Christ, are concerned in the welfare of their fellow-members, their brethren. By honoring them we honor none other than God Himself, since they reflect the divine perfections. In asking them to intercede for us before the Almighty, it is none other than God whom we really invoke. Lastly, since their own sanctity depends solely upon their imitation of the divine Model, upon the measure in which they themselves have reproduced His virtues, when we imitate them we do nothing else but imitate Jesus Christ Himself. Far from detracting, then, from the worship due to God and to the Incarnate Word, devotion to the Saints confirms it and carries it out in all its fulness. And since the Blessed Mother of Jesus occupies a unique place among the Saints, we shall first explain the place she holds in the Christian Life.

I. *The Part Mary Holds in the Christian Life.* [4]

155. 1° **Its foundation.** This rests upon the fact of Mary's intimate union with Jesus, in other words, upon the

---

[1] *Introd. à la vie et aux vertus chrét.*, c. IV, p. 47.
[2] *Gal.*, II, 20. — [3] *I Tim.*, II, 5.
[4] St. Thomas, *In Salut. Angel. Expositio;* Suarez, *De Mysteriis Christi*, disp.

dogma of her divine Motherhood. Corollaries deduced from this doctrine are her dignity and her office as the mother of men.

A) At the moment of the Incarnation Mary became the mother of Jesus, mother of the God-man, mother of God. If we consider the dialogue between Mary and the Angel, we discover that the Blessed Virgin is the mother of Jesus not simply inasmuch as He is a private individual, but inasmuch as He is the Savior and Redeemer of the world. " The Angel does not speak merely of the personal grandeur of Jesus. He tenders Mary a call to become the Mother of the Savior, of the expected Messiah, the Eternal King of regenerated mankind. The whole work of redemption hinges on Mary's "*fiat*". She is aware of what God proffers her; she accedes without restriction or condition to what God asks of her. Her "*fiat*" embraces the whole import of that divine invitation, it extends to the entire work of redemption." [1] The Fathers, following St. Irenaeus, remark that Mary is, therefore, the Mother of the Redeemer and that, being associated as such with His work of Redemption, she has in our spiritual restoration a part similar to that of Eve in our spiritual ruin.

Mary, the Mother of Jesus, has the most intimate relations with the Three Divine Persons. She is the *well-beloved Daughter of the Father* and His collaborator in the work of the Incarnation. She is the *Mother of the Son* with a real title to respect from Him, to His love and, upon earth, even to His obedience. By giving Him His body and blood, the instruments of our redemption, and by sharing in His mysteries, she was the secondary but true agent, the co-worker with her Son in effecting the sanctification and salvation of men. She is the *living temple*, the *privileged sanctuary* of the *Holy Ghost*, and, in an analogical sense, His Spouse; for with Him and under Him she has an active part in bringing forth souls to God.

156. B) At the Incarnation Mary became likewise the Mother of men. As we have already stated, n. 142, Jesus is

I-XXIII; BOSSUET, *Sermons sur la Ste Vierge;* TERRIEN, *La Mère de Dieu et la Mère des hommes,* III; GARRIGUET, *La Vierge Marie; Dict. d'Apol. (d'Alès),* "Marie"; HUGON, *Marie, pleine de grâce;* BAINVEL, *Marie, mère de grâce; Syn. Theol. dog.,* II, n. 1226-1263.
[1] BAINVEL, *op. cit.,* p. 73, 75. — The thesis can well be based on the words of the Angel: " Behold thou shalt conceive in thy womb and shalt bring forth a son : and thou shalt call his name Jesus (i. e. *Savior);* He shall be great and shall be called the Son of the Most High. And the Lord God shall give unto him the throne of David his father; and he shall reign in the house of Jacob forever. " *Luke,* I, 31, 32.

the head of regenerated mankind, the head of a mystical body whose members we are. As such did Mary conceive Him. She likewise conceived His members, all those who form part of Him, those who have been born again and those who are called to incorporation with Him. When she became the Mother of Jesus according to the flesh she became the mother of men according to the spirit. The scene on Calvary only confirms this truth. At the very moment that our redemption is to be completed by the death of the Savior, Jesus says to Mary: "Behold thy son!" Then to St. John himself He says: "Behold thy mother!" This, according to a tradition that goes back as far as Origen, was a declaration that all Christians are the spiritual children of Mary. This double title of Mother of God and Mother of men is the foundation of the office which Mary fills in our spiritual life.

157. 2° **Mary, a meritorious cause of grace.** We have seen, n. 133, that Jesus is in the strictest sense the chief meritorious cause of all the graces we receive. Mary, however, associated with Him in the work of our sanctification, merited these graces, not in the same manner as Christ, but secondarily and "de congruo,"[1] that is, under Christ and because of Him, in other words, because He conferred upon her the power of meriting for us.

She merited these graces first of all at the moment of the Incarnation when she uttered her "fiat"; for the Incarnation is already the beginning of Redemption. To co-operate then in the Incarnation is to co-operate in the Redemption and in all the graces resulting therefrom, and hence in our sanctification and salvation.

158. Besides, Mary whose will was ever in accord with God's will and with the will of her divine Son, associated herself during her whole life in the work of redemption. She brought up Jesus, she nourished and made ready the Victim of Calvary. Associated with Him in His joys as well as in His trials, in His lowly labors at the house of Nazareth as well as in His virtues, she also united herself to her Son with tender and generous compassion in His sufferings and death. At the foot of the Cross she again uttered her "fiat", acquiescing in the death of Him whom

---

[1] This expression has been ratified by Pope Pius X in his encyclical, "*Ad diem illum*", Feb. 2, 1904, wherein he declares that Mary has merited for us "*de congruo*" all the graces that Jesus had merited for us "*de condigno*".

her soul loved even more than herself while the cruel iron pierced her heart, fulfilling the prophecy of Simeon : " Thine own soul a sword shall pierce. " [1] For many of the Jews present on Calvary the death of Jesus was the execution of a criminal; for a few it was the murder of an innocent man; but for His Mother it was a sacrifice for the salvation of the world. She saw in the Cross an altar, in Her Son a priest, and in His blood the price of our redemption. She suffered in her soul what Jesus suffered in His body, and in union with Him she offered herself as a victim for our sins. What merits did not her perfect immolation gain!

Even after the ascension of Her Son into heaven she continued to acquire merits. The privation of the joy of His presence was a slow martyrdom. Though she ardently longed for the moment when she would be forever united to Him, yet, because it was God's will and for the sake of the infant Church, she lovingly accepted this ordeal and thus secured for us merits without number. Furthermore, her acts possessed the greater merit because born of a perfect purity of intention, " My soul doth magnify the Lord, " [2] because they were elicited with such fervor that they fully realized God'will : " Behold the handmaid of the Lord : be it done unto me according to thy word ; " [3] and lastly, because they were performed in a most intimate union with Jesus Christ, the very source of all merit.

No doubt, all these merits were first and foremost for herself, increasing her own treasure of grace and her titles to glory; but because of the part she took in the work of our redemption, she was also found worthy of meriting in our behalf; as St. Bernard says, she who was full of grace poured forth her overflow of grace upon us. [4]

159. 3° **Mary, an exemplary cause.** Next to Jesus, Mary is the most beautiful model offered for our imitation. The Holy Ghost who in virtue of her Son's merits lived in her, made her a living image of Christ. Never was she guilty of the least fault, never did she offer the least resistance to grace; on the contrary, she carried out her words to the letter : " Be it done to me according to thy word. " The Fathers, therefore, particularly St. Ambrose and Pope St. Liberius, represent her as the finished model of all virtues; " charitable and full of consideration for all who surrounded her, ever ready to serve them, never uttering a

---

[1] *Luke*, II, 35. — [2] *Luke*, I, 46. — [3] *Luke*, I, 48. — [4] *In Assumpt.*, sermo II, 2.

word or doing the least that could give pain, she was all-loving and beloved of all. " [1]

It will suffice to note the virtues mentioned in the Gospel: 1) Her deep *faith*. She unhesitatingly believed the marvels the Angel announced to her from God. For this faith she was praised by St. Elizabeth under the inspiration of the Holy Ghost: " Blessed art thou because thou hast believed. " [2] 2) Her *virginity* is revealed in her answer to the Angel: " How shall this be done for I know not man? " [3] 3) Her *humility* is evidenced by the confusion she experienced at hearing her praises on the lips of the Angel, and by her expressed determination of ever remaining the handmaid of the Lord at that very moment when she was proclaimed Mother of God. It further betrays itself in that ecstatic prayer, the Magnificat, as well as in her love of a hidden life, while as Mother of God she had a right to be honored above all creatures. 4) Her *interior recollection* whereby she pondered in silence all that concerned her divine Son : " But Mary kept all these words in her heart. " [4] 5) Her *love for God and men* which caused her to accept willingly all the trials of a long life, especially the immolation of her Son on Calvary and the painful separation from Him from the time of His ascension to the moment of her death.

160. This perfect model is also *wonderfully attractive*. First, Mary is a mere creature as we are, a sister, a mother whom we are drawn to imitate that we may show her our gratitude, our veneration and our love. Then, she is a model *easy* of imitation in this way that she sanctified herself in the ordinary, everyday life common to most of us, by fulfilling those lowly household duties of a young woman and a mother, leading a hidden, retired life both in joy and in sorrow, in the heights of exaltation and in the deepest humiliations. We are on firm ground when we imitate the Blessed Virgin. It is the best way of imitating Jesus and of obtaining Mary's all-powerful intercession.

161. 4° **Mary, universal mediatrix of grace.** Long ago St. Bernard formulated this doctrine in the well-known text : " It is God's will that we should receive all graces through Mary. " [5] It is important to determine the precise meaning of these words. It is certain that when Mary gave us Jesus, the Author and Meritorious Cause of grace,

---

[1] BAINVEL, *Le Saint Cœur de Marie*, p. 313. — [2] *Luke*, I, 45.
[3] *Luke*, I, 34. — [4] *Luke*, II, 19. — [5] *Sermo de aquæductu*, n. 7.

she thereby gave us all graces. But we can go further. According to a teaching which, as time goes on, is becoming unanimous, [1] men do not receive a single grace which does not come to them immediately through Mary, that is, through her intercession. It is question, therefore, of an immediate and universal mediation, subordinated, however, to that of Jesus.

162. In order to explain more exactly this doctrine we shall quote Father de la Broise : [2] " The actual disposition of the divine decrees ordains that any supernatural favor accorded to men be granted them by the common concord of three wills and in no other way. First of all, by the *will of God*, the Giver of all graces; then, by the *will of Christ*, the Mediator who by right of justice has merited and obtained grace; and lastly, by the *will of Mary*, a secondary mediator who through Jesus Christ has in all equity (de congruo) merited and acquired graces. " This mediation is *immediate* in the sense that for each grace granted to men Mary interposes the good offices of her past merits and of her actual intercession. This by no means implies that the recipient of a grace must of necessity demand it of Mary. She can intervene unasked in our behalf. Her mediation is also *universal*, that is, it covers all the graces given to men since the fall of Adam. However, it remains always subordinated to the mediation of Jesus; for if Mary can merit and obtain graces, it is solely through the mediation of her divine Son. Thus, Mary's mediation simply emphasizes the import and richness of Christ's own mediation.

This doctrine has been confirmed by an Office and Mass in honor of *Mary Mediatrix,* which Pope Benedict XV granted to the dioceses of Belgium and to all the dioceses of the Christian world that should request it. [3] The teaching is therefore safe and we can make practical use of it. It can not but inspire us with an immense confidence in Mary. [4]

---

[1] The proofs for this assertion will be found in Terrien, *op. cit.*, III.

[2] *Marie, mère de grâce*, p. 23-24.

[3] Cardinal Mercier by letter of January 23, 1921 makes the fact known to his flock in the following terms : "For years past the Belgian episcopate, the Faculty of Theology of the University of Louvain, all the Religious Orders of the nation, have been addressing their requests to the Sovereign Pontiff to have the title of the Blessed Virgin, " *Mediatrix of All Graces* ", authentically recognized. His Holiness, Benedict XV, has just granted to the churches of Belgium and to all those of the Christian world that will so request, a proper Office and Mass for the thirty-first day of May in honor of Mary Mediatrix. "

[4] On this subject see : BITTREMIEUX, *De Mediatione Mariæ;* O'CONNOR, *Our Lady Mediatrix of Graces;* HUSSLEIN, *All Graces through Mary;* and many articles in Catholic Reviews of recent years.

CONCLUSION : DEVOTION TO THE BLESSED VIRGIN

163. Since Mary plays such an important part in our spiritual life, we must entertain a great devotion to her. Devotion means *devotedness*, and devotedness means the gift of self. We shall be devoted to Mary, then, if we give ourselves entirely to her and through her to God. In so doing we simply imitate God who gives Himself and His Son to us through Mary. We shall give her our *intellect* by holding her in most profound reverence, our *will* by an absolute confidence in her, our *heart* by the gift of a tender and childlike love; in fine, our *whole being* by copying as far as possible all her virtues.

164. A) Profound veneration. Veneration for Mary has its foundation in her dignity as Mother of God and in the consequences of this dignity. We can never adequately honor and esteem the one whom the Word-made-Flesh reveres as His Mother, the well-beloved daughter whom the Eternal Father contemplates with loving eye, and whom the Holy Ghost regards as His chosen sanctuary. The *Father* wishing to associate her so intimately in the work of the Incarnation shows her the utmost respect; He sends her an Angel who hails her full of grace and who awaits her " Fiat ". The *Son* reveres, loves and obeys her as His Mother. The *Holy Ghost* comes and takes His delight in her. When, therefore, we venerate the Blessed Virgin we join with the Three Divine Persons in esteeming what They Themselves esteem.

No doubt, we must not exaggerate or indulge in any excess as regards this devotion to Mary. We must especially avoid anything that might suggest equality of Mary with Almighty God such as making her the source of grace. As long, however, as we see in her but a creature possessed of no grandeur, no holiness, no power save such as her Creator bestowed upon her, there can be no danger of sinning by excess. It is then God Himself whom we honor and venerate in her.

Our veneration for Mary must, moreover, surpass that which we give to the Angels and the Saints, for her dignity as Mother of God, her office of Mediatrix and her exalted holiness place her above all other creatures. Thus the devotion we accord her, although ever remaining what is technically called " cultus duliæ " (veneration), that is, the cult that we pay to created beings as distinct from the worship (adoration) which we pay to God alone (cultus latriæ), is nevertheless called by theologians " cultus hyper-duliæ " ·to show that it transcends the homage we pay to the Angels and the Saints.

165. B) Absolute confidence. This confidence is founded on two facts : the *power* and the *goodness* of Mary. **a)** Her power consists in an efficacious intercession with God, who will not turn a deaf ear to her whom He honors and loves above all creatures. And there is nothing more fitting than this. Mary gave to Jesus His very flesh, that human nature which made it possible for Him to acquire merit ; she co-operated with Him by her acts and sufferings in the work of redemption. Is it not, therefore, most fitting that she should have a share in the distribution of the fruits of redemption ? Jesus will, indeed, never refuse her requests, and we can say in all truth that Mary is all-powerful in her supplication, *omnipotentia supplex.* **b)** Her goodness is that of a mother who has for us, the members of Christ, the same affection she bears her own Son ; that of a mother who having brought us forth in pain and labor during the anguish of Calvary will measure her love for us only by the price of her sacrifice. Hence our trust, our confidence in her must be firm and universal.

1) It must be *firm* in spite of our miseries and our sins, for Mary is the Mother of mercy, whose business is not justice, but compassion, kindliness, condescension. Knowing as she does that we are ever exposed to the attacks of the world, the flesh and the devil, she takes pity on us who remain her children even when we have sinned. Thus, no sooner do we give the least intimation of good-will, of desire of returning to God, than she accords us a tender welcome ; nay, often her thougtfulness anticipates our prayer and obtains for us those very graces which produce in our souls the first desire of conversion. The Church, well aware of this, has instituted a feast for some dioceses under the title of the *Immaculate Heart of Mary, Refuge of Sinners*, a title at first strange to our ears, but fully justified in fact, for it is precisely because she is without blemish, because she has never been tainted with the least sin, that she overflows with compassion for her unfortunate children who, unlike her, have not been exempted from the bane of concupiscence.

2) Our confidence in Mary must also be *universal;* it must extend to all the graces we need for conversion, for spiritual growth, for final perseverance, for preservation amidst dangers, trials and difficulties. St. Bernard is never

weary of recommending this trust in the Mother of God : [1]
" When the storm of temptation arises, when you are midst
the reefs and shoals of tribulation, fix thy gaze upon the
Star of the Sea, call upon Mary.   If tossed by the rising
tide of pride and ambition, if lost upon the troubled waters
of scandal and contention, look then at the Star, invoke her
name.   Do the billows of anger, of avarice, of lust batter
against thy soul, cast thine eyes upon Mary.   Does the
greatness of thy crime fill thy soul with terror, does thy
wretched conscience beat thee down in shame and the fear
of judgment paralyze thy heart, then, when about to sink
to the depths of despondency, to plunge headlong into
despair, then think of Mary.   In perils and in sorrows and
in fears think of her, call upon her name.   Let her name be
ever on thy lips and the thought of her be ever in thy heart.
Follow her that the power of her intercession may attend
thee; imitate her, for in her footsteps thou canst not go
astray; call upon her and thou canst not despair; think of
her and thou canst not fail.   If she holds thee by the hand
how canst thou fall!   Under her protection thou shalst
know no fear; under her guidance thou shalt not falter;
under her patronage thou shalt surely reach the goal. "
Because we ever stand *in* need of grace to make progress
and to conquer our enemies we must time and again have
recourse to her who is so fittingly called *Our Lady of Perpetual Help and Mother of Divine Grace.*

166.   C) Our confidence in Mary must be accompanied
by *filial love*, a love like the child's, true, frank and tender.
Destined by the Almighty to be the Mother of His Son,
and therefore favored with whatever is lovable and endear-
ing, she is the most loving of mothers, thoughtful, kind
and devoted.   Was not her heart created expressly for the
one purpose of loving the God-man, her Son, and for loving
Him in the most perfect way?   Now, this very love she
had for her Son she bears also towards us who are His
living members, parts of His mystical body.   She reveals
this love in the mystery of the Visitation where she hastens
to bring to her cousin, Elizabeth, Him whom she holds in
her womb and whose very presence sanctifies the home of
Zachary.   Again, she shows her tender love for men at the
marriage-feast of Cana, where her delicate thoughtfulness
pleads with her Son to spare her hosts the shame of humiliation.   On Calvary she consents to sacrifice her dearest

---

[1] *Homil. II, de Laudibus Virg. Matris,* 17.

Possession for our salvation. In the Upper Room where the disciples prepare for the coming of the Holy Spirit, she intercedes in behalf of the Apostles to draw down upon them in a larger measure the precious gifts of the Holy Ghost.

167. The most lovable as well as the most loving of mothers, she should be also the *best loved mother*. This is one of her most glorious prerogatives. Wherever Jesus is known and loved, there Mary is also known and loved. Although aware of the vast difference between them, we love them both, but in different degrees. Jesus we love with the love that is due the Godhead; Mary we love under God as His Mother, with a tender, generous and devoted love.

We love her with a love of *complacency*, delighting in her greatness, her virtues and her privileges; meditating frequently on them, admiring them, rejoicing in them, and congratulating her on her exalted perfections. We love her with a love of *benevolence;* we sincerely long that she be better known and better loved; we pray that her influence over souls be widespread, and to our prayer we join the force of word and action. We love her with a *filial* love, with tenderness and without reserve, with all the abandon, with all the unreasoned, whole-hearted devotedness, with that sweet familiarity and respectful intimacy of a child with its mother. We strive to conform our wills in all things to the will of Mary and thereby to the will of God. In fact, this union of wills is the genuine mark of friendship.

168. D) *Imitation* of Mary is the most pleasing homage we can render her. In this way we proclaim by our deeds, by our life, and not merely by our words that we actually regard her as a perfect model for imitation. We have noted above (n. 159) how Mary, a living picture of her Son, is for us an example of all virtues. If to resemble her is to resemble Jesus, could we do better than to study her virtues, to ponder them and strive to imitate them in our own lives? There is no better way to accomplish this than to perform each of our actions *through Mary, with Mary and in Mary.* [1] *Through* Mary, asking through her intercession the graces we need in order to imitate her, going through her to Jesus. *With Mary*, that is to say, consid-

---

[1] This was the practice of Father Olier, popularized by Blessed Grignion de Montfort in " *True devotion to the Blessed Virgin*".

ering her as a *model* and *helper*, asking ourselves often
what Mary would do were she in our place, and humbly
begging her to help us to perform our actions according to
her will. *In Mary*, in entire dependence upon our good
Mother, taking her point of view, entering into her plans,
doing all things as she did them, for God's honor and
glory : " My soul doth magnify the Lord. "

169. These are the dispositions we must entertain in
offering up our prayers in honor of Mary : in reciting the
Hail Mary and the *Angelus* which bring back to mind the
scene of the Annunciation and recall her august title of
Mother of God; in saying the *Sub tuum præsidium*, an act
of confidence in her who shields us from harm, and the
O Domina mea, a full surrender into Mary's hands by which
we give her our entire being; in the recitation of the *Rosary*,
whereby we unite ourselves to her in her joyful, sorrowful
and glorious mysteries which render so easy the sanctification
of our joys and sorrows in union with her and with Jesus;
and lastly, in the recitation of the *Little Office of the Blessed
Virgin*, which will often remind those who are privileged to
say it of the grandeur, the holiness and the sanctifying
mission of this good Mother.

THE ACT OF ENTIRE CONSECRATION TO MARY [1]

170. Nature and extent of this act. This is an act
of devotion which in itself embodies all the others. As
explained by Blessed Grignion de Montfort it consists in the
entire gift of self to Jesus through Mary. It comprises two
elements : first, an *act* of consecration which is to be renewed
from time to time, and then an *habitual* attitude by which
we live and act in entire dependence on Mary. " The act
of consecration, " says Blessed Grignion de Montfort, " consists in giving oneself wholly to Mary and through her to
Jesus as her slave. " Let no one be shocked at the word,
" slave, " which today seems so repugnant to us, but which
has no such evil meaning as explained by this servant of
God. A mere servant, says he, receives his wages, is ever
free to quit his master's service. He gives his labor only,
not his person, not his rights, not his goods. A slave,
however, freely agrees to work without wages and, trusting to the master that gives him food and shelter, hands
himself over to him forever, with all that he is and has, in

[1] GRIGNION DE MONTFORT, *op. cit.;* A. LHOUMEAU, *La Vie spirituelle à l'école
du B. Grig. de Montfort*, 1920, p. 240-427.

order to live in entire dependence on the master in the spirit of love.

171. Carrying the application of the simile to things spiritual, the perfect servant of Mary gives himself over to her, and through her to Jesus :

a) *His body* with all its senses, keeping only the use thereof and pledging himself not to employ them except in accordance with the good pleasure of the Blessed Virgin or her Son. Moreover, he accepts beforehand the dispositions of Divine Providence as regards sickness and health, life and death.

b) *All wordly possessions*, using them solely in dependence on Mary, for her honor and the glory of God.

c) *His soul with all its faculties*, dedicating them under Mary's guidance to the service of God and the good of souls, and renouncing at the same time whatever might compromise his sanctification or imperil his salvation.

d) *All his interior and spiritual treasures*, his merits, the value of his satisfactory acts as well as the impetratory power his good actions may possess. All these are placed in the hands of Mary to the extent in which they can be given over to another. Let us explain this last point :

1) Our merits properly so called (i. e., de condigno) by which we procure for ourselves an increase of grace and glory cannot be given away. When, then, we make a gift of them to Mary it is not in order to apply them to others, but that she might hold them in trust for us and give them increase. It is quite otherwise with the merits called *de congruo*, which can be offered for others, and these we leave entirely to Mary's free disposition.

2) In the same manner we allow her [1] to dispose of and to apply freely the satisfactory value of our acts and the indulgences we may gain, since these can be given to others.

3) In virtue of our consecration to Mary we cede to her even the *impetratory* value of our acts, that is to say, of our prayers and our good actions, in so far as they are endowed with such efficacy.

172. Once we have made this act of consecration, we can no longer without her permission dispose of the goods we have made over to her. However, we *may* and at times we *should* beg her to favor according to her good pleasure

---

[1] St. THOMAS, *Supplement*, q. 13, a. 2.

those to whom we are bound by special ties and to whom we are under special obligation. The best way, therefore, of harmonizing our gift of self to Mary and our duties to others is to offer up to her all those who are near and dear to us: "I am all Thine, all mine are Thine." Thus the Blessed Virgin will draw on what we have given her, but more still on the treasury of her own merits and those of her Son in order to help those we have committed to her care. Our friends, therefore, will lose nothing.

173. Excellence of this act of consecration. It is an act of holy abandonment, of self-surrender, excellent in itself and containing, moreover, acts of the highest virtues : religion, humility and confiding love.

1) It is an act of *religion* toward God, the Word-made-Flesh, and Mary, the Mother of God. By it we acknowledge God's sovereign dominion and our own nothingness, and proclaim with heart and soul those rights over us which God has given Mary.

2) It is an act of *humility*, for by it we acknowledge our nothingness and our helplessness. We divest ourselves of everything that we have received from God and restore all to the Giver through the hands of her from whom, under Him and through Him, we have obtained every good gift.

3) It is an act of confiding *love*, for love consists in the gift of self; and to give oneself entirely and unreservedly presupposes absolute trust and living faith.

It may be said that this consecration if rightly made, and frequently and earnestly renewed, is even of greater worth than the *heroic act* by which we give up but the satisfactory value of our acts and the indulgences we may gain.

174. Fruits of this act of consecration. They come from its very nature. 1) By this act we *glorify God and Mary* in an unparalleled manner : we give ourselves to God forever, with all that we are and all that we have, without measure or stint, and we do so after the manner of Divine Wisdom, that is, returning to God in the very way He chose to come to us, and hence, in the way that is most pleasing to Him.

175. 2) We thereby also insure our *individual sanctification*. Mary cannot but minister unto the sanctification of those who, having disposed of their persons and goods in her behalf, are, so to say, her own property. She will most assuredly secure for us choice graces to safeguard our little

spiritual treasure, to make it grow and have it bring forth
fruit in season until the hour of death. She will help us
through her superabundant merits and satisfactions and
through her powerful intercession with God.

3) A third fruit of this consecration to Mary is the *sanctification of our neighbor*. This is true especially of the souls
entrusted to us. They are certain to gain by our gift. We
can be sure that when we leave the apportioning of our
merits to Mary's good-pleasure, everything will be done with
greater wisdom. She is by far more prudent than we are,
more thoughtful and more devoted. Consequently our
friends and relatives can only be the gainers.

176. It may be objected that by such an act we alienate
all our spiritual goods, above all, our satisfactions and the
indulgences and prayers that would be offered up for us,
thus rendering our purgatory all the longer. *In itself* this
is true; however, it resolves itself into a question of *trust*.
Do we rely more on Mary than on ourselves or our
friends? If we do, let us have no misgivings, for she
will care for our souls and further our interests far better
than we could ever do ourselves. If we do not, then
let us refrain from making this act of complete consecration for we might regret it before long. In any event
one should not make this act of consecration without reflection and advice.

II. *The Share of the Saints in the Christian Life*

177. By their powerful intercession and by their noble
example, the Saints in their blessed possession of God minister to our sanctification and help us to progress in the
practice of the Christian virtues. Hence, we should venerate, invoke and imitate them.

178. 1º We should *venerate* them. All the good they
possess is the work of God and His Divine Son. As mere
natural beings they are so many reflections of the divine
perfections. Their *supernatural* qualities are the work of
that divine grace which Jesus merited for them. Even their
meritorious acts, while being their own in the sense that
their free will co-operated with Almighty God, are none the
less the precious gift of the Divine Goodness who is ever
their first and efficacious cause : " Thou dost but crown
Thy gifts when Thou crownest our merits. " [1] When, there-

---

[1] " Coronando merita coronas et dona tua ". St. Augustine.

fore, we pay the Saints the homage of our veneration
it is God and His Son, Jesus, whom we really honor and
revere in them.

We venerate these Blessed Ones as: **a**) the living *sanc-
tuaries* of the *Triune God* who has deigned to dwell in
them, to adorn their souls with virtues and with gifts, to
prompt their faculties to action and cause them to elicit
meritorious acts, and to grant them at last the crowning
grace of perseverance to the end. **b**) We honor them as
the *adopted* and well-beloved children of the Father, who
surrounded by His paternal care knew how to respond to
His love and to grow more like Him in holiness and perfection. **c**) We hail them as the *brethren of Christ*, the faithful members of His mystical body, who drew from Him
their spiritual life and cultivated it in abiding love. **d**) We
revere them as *temples* of the Holy Ghost, as His docile
servants, who allowed His inspirations to be their guide
rather than blindly follow the bent of a corrupted nature.
Father Olier aptly expresses these thoughts : " You will be
able to adore with the most profound veneration this life of
God communicated to His Saints; you will honor Jesus
Christ who animates them all and who through His divine
Spirit makes them all one in Himself. It is Jesus Christ
Himself who proclaims in them the glory of God; it is He
who puts upon their lips their canticles of praise; it is He
through whom the sainted glorify God now and through all
eternity. " [1]

179. 2º We sould *invoke* the Saints in order to obtain
through their powerful intercession the graces we need.
True, the mediation of Jesus Christ alone is necessary and
all-sufficient in itself; however, because of the very fact that
the Saints are members of the risen Christ, their prayers are
united to His. Thus, the whole mystical body of the Savior
prays, and with its entreaties it does sweet violence to the
heart of God. When, therefore, we pray in union with the
Saints we join our petitions to those of Christ's mystical
body and thereby insure their efficacy. Moreover, the
Saints are glad to intercede in our behalf: " They love us
as brothers born of the same Father and they have compassion for us. Seeing our plight and remembering that it
once was theirs, they behold in us souls who like themselves
ought to contribute to Christ's glory. What joy must they
not experience in finding souls to join them in glorifying

---

[1] *Pensées choisies*, by G. LETOURNEAU, p. 181-182.

God! " [1] Their *goodness* and their *power* must inspire us with full confidence in them.

We are to invoke them especially on their feast-days. Thus we shall enter into the spirit of the liturgy of the Church, and share in the particular virtues practised by the different Saints.

180. 3° Lastly and above all, we should *imitate* the virtues of the Saints. Each one of them strove to reproduce the divine model and each one can address us in the words of St. Paul : " Be ye followers of me, as I also am of Christ. " [2] In most cases, however, the Saints have cultivated a special virtue which is, so to speak, their characteristic trait. Some have directed their efforts chiefly toward the cultivation of the spirit of faith, hope or charity; others have centered them round the spirit of sacrifice, humility or poverty; others, again, have excelled in the exercise of prudence, fortitude or chastity. We can beg of them their distinctive virtues with the assurance that they have a special power to obtain them for us.

181. This is the reason why we should be specially devoted to those Saints who lived in conditions similar to our own, who discharged the same duties that we must perform and who practised the virtues that we need most.

We should also have a special devotion to our *patron Saints*, seeing in the choice made of them on our behalf a providential arrangement. Still, if for special reasons the movements of grace draw us to some other Saints whose virtues correspond better to the needs of our souls, there can be no objection to our cultivating devotion to them.

182. Thus understood, devotion to the Saints is most useful to us. The example of men with the same passions as we have, who, tried by the same temptations, have won the victory with the help of the same graces that are accorded us, is a powerful incentive to make us ashamed of our faintheartedness and to strengthen in us the determination to put forth the efforts constantly required for the accomplishment of our resolutions. We thus naturally apply to ourselves the words of St. Augustine : " Canst thou not do what these have done? " [3]

---

[1] FATHER OLIER, *Pensées choisies*, p. 176.
[2] *I Cor.*, IV, 16.
[3] " Tu non poteris quod isti, quod istæ? " *Confessions*, VIII, c. 11.

III. *The Share of the Angels in the Christian Life*

The part of the Angels in the Christian life has its origin in the relations they have with God and with Jesus Christ.

183. 1° First of all, the Angels show forth God's greatness and perfection. " Each symbolizes individually some attribute or other of that infinite Being. In some we see His power, in others His love, in others His strength. Each is a reproduction of some beauty of the divine Original; each adores Him and glorifies Him in the perfection it portrays. " [1] It is God, then, whom we honor in the Angels. They are like mirrors reflecting the perfections of their infinite Creator. [2] Raised to the supernatural order, they share in the life of God; and victorious in trial, they enjoy the Beatific Vision : " Their angels in heaven always see the face of my Father who is in heaven. " [3]

184. 2° If we consider their relations with Jesus Christ, it may not appear absolutely certain that they hold their grace from Him; but this much does appear with certainty, that in heaven they unite themselves with Him, the Mediator of all religion, in order to adore, praise and glorify the Majesty of the Most High. It is their bliss to add in this wise a greater worth to their worship : " Through whom the Angels praise, the Dominations adore and the Powers hold in awe Thy Majesty. " [4] Hence, when we unite ourselves to Jesus Christ to adore God we join at the same time with the Angels and Saints in a heavenly harmony which renders the praise of the Godhead still more perfect. We can well make our own the words of Father Olier : " May all the Angelic Host, the mighty Powers that move the spheres of heaven, forever pour forth in Jesus Christ whatever be wanting to our song of praise. May they forever thank Thee, Lord, for all those gifts both of nature and of grace which from the goodness of Thy hand we all receive. " [5]

185. 3° From this twofold consideration it follows that they have at heart our sanctification. Since we share with them in the divine life, and since we are like them the religious of God in Christ Jesus, they long for our salvation that we may join them in glorifying God and in enjoying the Beatific Vision. **a)** Thus it is with joy that they accept those God-given missions to minister to our sanctification.

---

[1] OLIER, *Pensées choisies*, p. 158. — [2] *Ibid.*, p. 164. — [3] *Matth.*, XVIII, 10.
[4] *Preface*, Roman Missal. — [5] *Pensées choisies*, p. 169.

The Psalmist says that God has entrusted the just man to their care that they may guard him in his way : " For he hath given his Angels charge over thee to keep thee in all thy ways. " [1] St. Paul adds that the Angels are in God's service as servants to minister unto the welfare of the heirs of salvation : " Are they not all ministering spirits, sent to minister for them who shall receive the inheritance of salvation? " [2] In fact, they burn with the desire of rallying elect souls to fill the vacant thrones of fallen angels, and to glorify and adore the Almighty in their stead. Victors over demons, they ask but to shield us from the perfidious enemies of our souls. It is our part to ask their timely assistance in order to repel the assaults of Satan. **b)** They present our prayers to the Most High [3] by joining their own supplications to our requests. It is, therefore, to our advantage to call upon them, especially in the hour of trial, and above all, at the hour of death, that they may defend us from the attacks of our enemies and conduct our souls to Paradise. [4]

186. The Guardian Angels. Some among the Angels are commissioned with the care of individual souls : these are the Guardian Angels. This is the traditional doctrine of the Fathers, based upon scriptural texts and supported by solid reasons. It has been confirmed by the Church in the institution of a feast in honor of the Guardian Angels. The reasons that support this doctrine flow from our relationship to God, for we are His *children, members* of Jesus Christ and *temples* of the Holy Ghost. " Because we are His children, " says Father Olier, [5] " He appoints to us as tutors the princes of His realm, who hold it an honor to have us in their charge. Because we are His *members*, He wills that those very spirits that minister unto Him be also at our side to render us their services. Because we are His *temples* in which He Himself dwells, He wills that Angels hover about us as they do about our churches, so that bowed down in worship before Him they may offer a perpetual homage to His glory, supplying for our neglect and making reparation for our irreverence. " Father Olier goes on to say that God wishes to unite intimately through the agency of His Angels the Church Triumphant and the Church Militant : " He sends this mysterious host of Angels in order that they may by uniting themselves to us and bind-

---

[1] *Ps.* XC, 11-12. — [2] *Heb.*, I, 14. — [3] *Tob.*, XII, 12.
[4] That the Angels conduct our souls to heaven is a traditional doctrine, as is shown by DOM LECLERCQ, *Dict. d'Archéol.*, *Les Anges psychagogues*, I, col. 2121.
[5] *Pensées*, p. 171-172.

ing us to themselves form one body of the Church of heaven and the Church of earth."

187. Our Guardian Angel keeps us in constant touch with heaven. To derive full profit from his guardianship we can do no better than direct our thoughts frequently to our Guardian Angel, making him the object of our *veneration*, our *confidence* and our *love*. **a**) We *venerate* him by hailing him as one of those privileged beings who ever see the face of God and who are to us the representatives of our Heavenly Father. Therefore, we should do nothing that could displease or sadden our Angel; on the contrary, we must strive to give him proof of our respect by emulating his fidelity and loyalty in God's service. This is, indeed, the most touching way in which can attest our esteem for him. **b**) We show him our *confidence*, by bearing in mind the mighty protection he furnishes us and his unfailing goodness towards us, his God-given charges. Since he is a master in foiling the wiles of the devil, we should invoke him especially when we are assailed by this treacherous foe and in all dangerous occasions in which his foresight and his adroitness will be of great help. We should likewise call for his assistance when determining our vocation, for he better than any other will know the providential designs of God in our regard. Finally, in all important affairs with others it is well to address ourselves to their Guardian Angels that these persons may be well-disposed towards the mission we are about to discharge in their behalf. **c**) We manifest to our Guardian Angel our *love* by reflecting that he has ever been and is still our devoted friend, ever ready to render us services the extent and import of which we shall realize only in heaven. By faith, however, we can even now understand, though only imperfectly, something of his good offices toward us, and this suffices to call forth our gratitude and our love. When loneliness weighs heavily upon us, let us remember that we are not alone, that near us hovers a friend, devoted and generous, upon whom we can lean and with whom we can hold familiar converse. Let us bear in mind that honoring our Guardian Angel we honor God Himself whom our Angel represents here below, and let us often unite ourselves to him in order to give greater glory to God.

Summary

188. God, then, has a vast share in the work of our sanctification. He comes to dwell in our souls in order to give Himself to us and to sanctify us.   To impart to us the power to rise up to Him, He endows us with a supernatural organism composed of *habitual grace, the virtues and the gifts*.   Habitual grace penetrates the very substance of the soul, thus transforming it and making it Godlike.   The virtues and the gifts perfect our faculties and enable them with the help of actual grace to elicit supernatural acts that merit eternal life.

189.   God's love does not stop here.   He also sends His *Only-Begotten Son*, who, becoming one of us, becomes likewise the *perfect exemplar*, our guide in the practice of those virtues that lead to perfection and ultimately to heaven.   The Son of God *merits* for us the grace necessary to follow in His footsteps in spite of the difficulties that we find within ourselves and all about us.   In order to win us over to Himself He *incorporates* us into Himself, imparting to us through His Divine Spirit that life which is His in all its fulness.   Through this incorporation He gives to the least of our actions an immeasurable value, for, we being made one with Him, our actions share in the value of His own actions.   With Him, then, and through Him we can give adequate glory to God Almighty, obtain new graces, and become more and more like our Heavenly Father by reproducing in ourselves His divine perfections.

Mary, being the Mother of Jesus and His co-worker, though in a secondary manner, in the work of the Redemption, co-operates in the distribution of the graces Christ merited for us.   Through her we go to Him and through her we ask for grace.   We venerate and love her as a Mother and strive to imitate her virtues.

Lastly, Jesus, being the Head not only of mankind, but also of the Angels and the Saints, places at our service their powerful assistance as a protection against the attacks of the Evil One and as a safeguard against the weaknesses of our own nature.   Their example and their intercession are for us a tower of strength.

What more could God actually do for us?   If He has given Himself to us so prodigally, to what lengths should we not go to return His love? to what extent should we not be ready to spend ourselves to promote the growth of that divine life which He has so generously shared with us?

ART. II. THE SHARE OF MAN IN THE CHRISTIAN LIFE

190.   It is clear that, if God has done so much to have us share in His own life, we must in turn respond to His advances, gratefully accept His gift, cherish and foster it in our souls and thus prepare ourselves for that eternal bliss which will crown the efforts we shall have made on earth. This is for us a *duty of gratitude.* Indeed, the most telling way in which we can show our appreciation of a gift is to use it for the purpose for which it was given. Our *spiritual welfare* itself demands that we make such a return, for Almighty God will reward us according to our merits, and our glory in heaven will correspond to the degree of grace we shall have acquired by good works : " Every man shall receive his own reward, according to his labor. " [1] On the other hand, God owes it to Himself to punish with due severity those who wilfully scorn His divine gifts and abuse His grace. The Apostle tells us : " For the earth, that drinketh in the rain which cometh often upon it, and bringeth forth herbs meet for them by whom it is tilled, receiveth blessing from God. But that which bringeth forth thorns and briers, is reprobate, and very near unto a curse, whose end is to be burnt. " [2] God made us free beings and He respects our freedom; He will not sanctify us in spite of ourselves. But He never wearies of urging us to make the right use of the graces He has so liberally dispensed to us : " And we helping do exhort you that you receive not the grace of God in vain. " [3]

191. In order to correspond with this grace we must first of all practise the great devotions of which we have spoken in the preceding article : devotion to the Most Blessed Trinity, to the Incarnate Word, to the Blessed Virgin, the Saints and the Angels. Herein we shall find the most powerful *motives* for giving ourselves entirely to God, doing so in union with Jesus and under the protection of our mighty intercessors. In these devotions we shall also find *models* of *sanctity* to point out the way for us; nay more, we shall find *supernatural forces* that will enable us to realize more fully day by day the ideal of perfection proposed for our imitation.

In explaining these devotions we have followed the ontological order, arranging them according to their intrinsic excellence. In practice, however, it is seldom that we begin with devotion to the Most Blessed Trinity, but rather we generally begin with devotion to our Blessed Lord and our Blessed Lady and then gradually rise to the Holy Trinity itself.

---

[1] *I Cor.*, III, 8. — [2] *Hebr.*, VI, 7-8. — [3] *II Cor.*, VI, 1.

192.   But we must do more than this.   We must *make use of the supernatural organism* wherewith we are endowed, and develop it notwithstanding the obstacles to its growth encountered within our own selves and all about us.   1° First of all, since the *threefold concupiscence* is an ever-abiding foe, which spurred on by the world and the devil, inclines us perpetually towards evil, we must relentlessly combat it and its lusty allies.   2° We are to *multiply our merits*, since the supernatural organism of which we have spoken is given us for the purpose of producing Godlike acts, acts worthy of eternal life.   3° Because it has pleased Divine Goodness to institute *sacraments* productive of grace in proportion to our co-operation, we should approach them with the most perfect dispositions.   In this manner we shall preserve in us the life of grace; nay, we shall make it grow more and more.

§ I. The Fight against Our Spiritual Enemies

These enemies are *concupiscence, the world and the devil.* Concupiscence is the foe we carry within us.   The world and the devil are the foes from without that feed the fires of concupiscence and fan its flames.

I. *The Fight against Concupiscence* [1]

Saint John describes concupiscence in his well-known text : " For all that is in the world is the concupiscence of flesh and the concupiscence of the eyes and the pride of life." [2]

1° THE CONCUPISCENCE OF THE FLESH

193.   The *concupiscence of the flesh* is the *inordinate love of sensual pleasures.*

A) The evil of concupiscence.   Pleasure in itself is not evil.   God allows it when directed toward a higher end, that is, toward moral good.   If He has attached pleasure to certain good acts, it is in order to facilitate their accomplishment and to draw us on to the fulfilment of duty. The moderate enjoyment of pleasure, if referred to its end — moral and supernatural good — is not an evil.   In fact, it is a good act, for it tends towards a good end which is ultimately God Himself.   But to will pleasure without any reference to the end that makes it lawful, that is, to will

---

[1] Read the short, but admirable treatise of BOSSUET on *Concupiscence.*
[2] *I John.*, II, 16.

pleasure as an end in itself and as an ultimate end, is a moral disorder, for it is going counter to the wisdom of a God-established order. Such disorder leads to further evil, because when one's sole motive of action is pleasure, one is exposed to love pleasure to excess; one is no longer guided by an end which raises its barriers against that immoderate thirst for enjoyment which exists in all of us.

194.   Thus, God in His wisdom willed to attach a certain enjoyment to the act of eating, to offer us an incentive towards sustaining our bodily forces.   But, as *Bossuet* remarks, " Ungrateful and sensual men use this enjoyment rather to serve their own bodies than to serve Almighty God...   The pleasure of eating enslaves them, and instead of eating in order to live they live rather in order to eat. Even those who know how to curb their desires and who are guided in taking their meals by the needs of the body, are often deceived by pleasure and taken in by its allurement ; they soon go beyond due measure ; they gradually come to indulge their appetite and do not consider their needs satisfied, so long as food and drink gratify their palate. " [1] Hence, excesses in eating and drinking.   What shall we say of the still more dangerous pleasures of lust, " of that deep-rooted and unsightly sore of human nature, of that concupiscence that binds the soul to the body with ties at once so tender, so strong, so difficult to break ; of that lust which brings down upon the human race such frightful disorders? " [2]

195.   Sensual pleasure is all the more *dangerous* as the entire body is inclined to it.   Our sight is infected by it, for is it not through the eyes that one begins to drink in the poison of sensual love?   Our ears are a prey to the contagion ; a suggestive word, a lascivious song enkindles the fire, fans the flames of an impure love and excites our hidden tendencies to sensual joys.   The same is true of the other senses.   And what heightens the danger is that these sensual pleasures act as stimulants one to the other. Even those enjoyments which we fancy the most innocent, will, unless we are ever on the alert, lead on to guilty pleasures.   The body itself labors under a softening languor, a delicate and responsive sensitiveness that craves relaxation through the senses, quickens them and whets the keenness of their ardor.   Man so cherishes his body that he forgets his soul.   Over-solicitous for his health, he is led to

---

[1] *Tr. de la Concupiscence*, C. IV. — [2] *Ibid.*, C. V.

pamper the body at every turn.   All these sensual cravings
are but the branches of the same tree, the concupiscence of
the flesh. ¹

196.   B) The remedy for this great evil is found in the
mortification of the senses.   As St. Paul tells us, " They
that are Christ's have crucified their flesh, with the vices
and concupiscences. " ²   But to crucify the flesh, according
to Father Olier, " is to fetter, to smother all the impure and
inordinate desires we feel in our flesh. " ³   To crucify the
flesh is likewise to mortify our *exterior senses*, those channels
that put us in contact with things about us and stir within
us dangerous desires.   The motive, at bottom, giving rise
to the obligation of practising this mortification, is none
other than our *baptismal vow*.

197.   *Baptism*, by which we die to sin and are made one
body with Christ, obliges us to mortify in ourselves all
sensual pleasure.   " According to St. Paul, we are no longer
debtors to the flesh that we should live according to the
flesh, but we are bound to live according to the spirit.   If
we live by the spirit let us walk according to the spirit
which has written in our hearts the law of the Cross and
has given us the strength to carry it. " ⁴

The symbolism of baptism by immersion (the more
common way of administering baptism in Apostolic times
and in the early centuries) teaches us the truth of this
doctrine.   The catechumen is plunged into the water and
there he dies to sin and the causes of sin.   Coming out he
shares in a new life, the life of the Risen Christ.   This is
St. Paul's teaching : " We that are dead to sin, how shall we
live any longer therein?   Know you not that all we who
are baptized in Christ Jesus are baptized in His death?
For we are buried together with Him by baptism into
death : that as Christ is risen from the dead by the glory of
the Father, so we also may walk in the newness of life. " ⁵
Thus, the baptismal immersion represents death to sin and
to the concupiscence which leads to sin.   The coming out
of the baptismal waters typifies that newness of life through
which we are made sharers in the risen life of the Savior. ⁶

---

¹ In this paragraph we merely give a summary of the fifth chapter of Bossuet's
Treatise on Concupiscence.
² *Gal.*, V, 24.
³ *Cat. for an Int. Life*, Part. I, lesson 5. — ⁴ *Ibid.*, lesson 5.
⁵ *Rom.*, VI, 2-4.
⁶ " It does not alter the thought of the Apostle to express it in the following
theological language : The Sacraments are efficacious signs which produce *ex opere
operato* the effects wich they signify.   Now, baptism represents sacramentally the

Hence, our baptism obliges us to mortify the concupiscence that remains in us and to imitate our Lord who by the crucifixion of His flesh merited for us the grace of crucifying our own. The nails wherewith we crucify it are the various acts of mortification we perform.

This obligation of mortifying our love for pleasure so imposes itself upon us that our spiritual life and our salvation depend upon it. "For if you live according to the flesh, you shall die : but if by the spirit you mortify the deeds of the flesh, you shall live."[1]

198. In order to obtain a complete victory, it does not suffice to renounce *evil* pleasures (this we are strictly bound to do), but we must, in order to be on the safe side, sacrifice all *dangerous* ones, for these almost invariably lead us to sin : " He who loves danger shall perish in it."[2] Besides, we must deprive ourselves of some lawful pleasures in order to strengthen our wills against the lure of forbidden ones. In fact, whoever indulges without restraint in all lawful pleasures, is in proximate danger of falling into those that are sinful.

2° THE CONCUPISCENCE OF THE EYES
(CURIOSITY AND AVARICE)

199. A) The evil. The concupiscence of the eyes comprises two things : all unwholesome curiosity and inordinate love of the goods of this world.

a) The *curiosity* of which we speak consists in an excessive desire to see, to hear, to know what goes on in the world, the secret intrigues that are woven there ; not in order to derive any spiritual profit therefrom, but to indulge our craving for frivolous knowledge. Nor is this curiosity confined to present-day happenings ; it may cover the events of past centuries, as when we delve into the history of bygone days to seek not what will be a wholesome inspiration but what may please our fancy. A special object of this curiosity is the pseudo-science of divination whereby men make bold to peer into things hidden and into events to come, the knowledge of which God has reserved to Himself. This phase of curiosity " constitutes an aggression upon the rights of God Almighty and an attempt to wreck the confidence and trust wherewith man should abandon himself

---

death and the life of Christ. It follows that it causes in us a death, mystical in its essence, but real in its effects; a death to sin, to the flesh, to the old Adam; and a life in agreement with that of the Risen Christ ". (Cf. PRAT, *The Theology of St. Paul*, II, Book 5, C. 2).

[1] *Rom.*, VIII, 13. — [2] *Eccli.*, III, 27.

to his Providence."[1]   Furthermore, this curiosity extends
to true and useful science when men give themselves over
to its pursuit without moderation or to the detriment of
higher duties. Such is the case of those who read indiscriminately every kind of novel, play or poetry, "for all this
is nothing less than an excess, a morbid disposition of the
soul, the shrivelling up of the heart, a miserable bondage
allowing us no leisure to turn our thoughts upon ourselves,
and a source of error."[2]

200. b) The second form of the concupiscence of the
eyes is the inordinate love of money, regarded either as a
means for the acquisition of other goods such as honors or
pleasure, or considered as an object of attachment in itself,
an object which we delight to see and finger and in which
we find a certain sense of security for the future.   The
latter is avarice properly so-called.   Both expose us to the
commission of numberless sins, for cupidity is the prolific
source of all kinds of fraud and injustice.

201.   B) The remedy.   a) To combat *vain curiosity* we
must recall to mind that whatever is not eternal is not
worthy of winning and captivating the thought of immortal
beings such as we are.   "The fashion of this world passeth
away";[3] but one thing abideth, God and the possession of
God, which is heaven.   We must, therefore, heed only what
is eternal, "for whatever is not eternal is as nothing."   No
doubt, present-day events as well as those of the past may
and ought to engage our interest, yet only in so far as they
contribute to the glory of God and the salvation of men.
When God created this world and all that exists He had
but one end in view, to communicate His divine life to those
creatures He had endowed with intelligence — angels and
men — and to recruit His Elect.   All else is secondary and
should not be made the subject of our study, save as a
means of leading us to God.

202.   b) As regards *inordinate love* of *the goods* of this
world, we must bear in mind that wealth is not an end in
itself, but the means given by Providence to minister to our
needs.   God ever retains the supreme dominion over all
things, and we are but stewards who shall have to render
an account of the use we have made of our temporal possessions: "Give an account of thy stewardship."[4]   It is

---

[1] BOSSUET, *l. c.*, C. 8. — [2] BOSSUET, *l. c.*
[3] *I Cor.*, VII, 31. — [4] *Luke*, XVI, 2.

wise, then, to give a large portion of what is over and above
our needs in almsgiving and other good works. This is in
truth to enter into the designs of God who wills that the
rich be, so to speak, the treasurers of the poor; it is to make
in the bank of heaven a deposit which will be returned to
us with a hundredfold interest upon our entrance into eternity. " Lay up to yourselves treasures in heaven, where
neither the rust nor the moth doth consume, and where
thieves do not break through or steal. "[1] This is the way
to detach our hearts from earthly goods so as to raise them
to God; for as our Lord adds : " Where thy treasure is,
there is thy heart also. "[2] Let us then seek first the
kingdom of God, holiness, and all other things shall be
added unto us.

If we would be perfect we must go further and practise
evangelical poverty. " Blessed are the poor in spirit. "[3]
This may be achieved in three ways according to our
attractions and opportunities : 1) by selling all our goods
and giving the proceeds to the poor. " Sell what you
possess and give alms. "[4] 2) By having all things in
common, as is done in religious communities. 3) By
renouncing the right of using the capital which we retain,
refraining, for instance, from making any outlay not sanctioned by a prudent spiritual director.[5]

203. Whichever way is adopted, the heart must be
freed from its attachment to riches if it would take
its flight towards God. This is what Bossuet urges :
" Happy they who in the lowly seclusion of God's house
delight in the bareness of their narrow cells, in the beggarly
appointments that satisfy their wants in this earthly existence — a shadow of death — there to gaze solely upon
their weakness and the heavy, oppressing yoke of sin.
Happy those consecrated Virgins who no longer seek to
appear before the world and who would fain hide themselves
from their own eyes beneath the sacred veil that shrouds
their form ! Blessed that sweet restraint wherewith we
guard our eyes lest they light upon vain things, the while
we say with David : " Turn away mine eyes, that they may
not behold vanity. "[6] Happy those who, living in the world
according to their state of life, remain undefiled and unfet-
tered,... those who can say with Queen Esther : " Thou

---

[1] *Matth.*, VI, 20. — [2] *Matth.*, VI, 21. — [3] *Matth.*, V, 3.
[4] *Luke*, XII, 23, XVIII, 22, *Matth.*, XIX, 21.
[5] OLIER, *Introd.*, C. XI; *Chevrier, Le véritable disciple*, p. 248-267.
[6] *Ps.* CXIII, 37.

knowest, O Lord, how I scorn this emblem of pride (her crown); how I abhor the glory of the wicked and ungodly; how thy handmaid hath never rejoiced save in thee, O Lord God of Israel." [1]

3° THE PRIDE OF LIFE

204. A) The evil. " Pride, " says Bossuet, " is a profound depravity; it is the worship of self; man becomes his own god through excessive self-love. " [2] Forgetful that God is his first beginning and his last end, he overrates himself; he considers himself the sovereign lord and master of those qualities, real or imaginary, which he possesses, without referring them to God.   From this arises that spirit of *independence*, of self-sufficiency, that finally brings man to renounce allegiance to God and His representatives on earth.   Hence, also, that *egotism* which prompts him to do everything for self as though he were himself his last end; that vain *complacency* in his own excellence as though God were not its source; that conceit in his good works as though they were not above all the result of God's action on the soul.   Hence, again, the tendency to exaggerate the good qualities he possesses, and to attribute to himself others that he lacks.   Hence, too, the disposition to prefer self to others and at times, like the Pharisee, to despise others.

205.   This pride is accompanied *by vanity*, which seeks inordinately the esteem, the approbation, the praise of men.   It is called *vainglory*, for, as Bossuet points out, " if it be but an empty or undeserved applause, what an absurdity to delight in it! If it be genuine, why the further folly of rejoicing less at truth itself than at the tribute paid to it? " [3]   A paradox, indeed, that one should be more solicitous for the esteem of men than for virtue itself, that man should find cause for greater humiliation in a blunder committed in the sight of all than in a real fault committed in secret!   This failing once yielded to is not slow in bringing others in its wake.   It gives rise to *boasting*, to speaking of self and one's achievements; to *ostentation* which courts the public eye with finery and display; to *hypocrisy* which makes a show of virtue while careless about its practice.

206.   The *effects* of pride are deplorable.   This vice is the arch-enemy of perfection.   1) It robs God of the glory

---

[1] *Esth.*, XIV, 15-18. — [2] *L. c.*, C. X, XXIII.
[3] *Tr. de la Concupiscence*, C. XVII.

due Him and thereby deprives us of many graces and merits, since God can not allow Himself to be made an accomplice in our pride : "God resisteth the proud." [1]   2) It is the *source of many sins*, such as sins of *presumption* which are punished by lamentable falls and enslavement to shameful vices; sins of *discouragement* at seeing oneself fallen so low; sins of *dissimulation* because of the hardship of confessing certain sins; sins of *resistance* to *superiors*, of *envy* and *jealousy* towards the neighbor, etc.

207. B) The **remedy** consists : **a)** in *referring all to God*, recognizing that He is the author of all good and that, being the *first principle* of all our actions, He must be likewise their *last end.* This is what St. Paul means when he asks : "What hast thou that thou hast not received? And if thou hast received it, why dost thou glory, as if thou hadst not received it?" [2]   From this he concludes that all our actions must tend to the glory of God : "Therefore, whether you eat or drink, or whatsoever else you do, do all to the glory of God." [3]   In order to give these actions greater value, let us be mindful of doing them in the name and through the merits of our Lord Jesus Christ : "All whatsoever you do in word or in work, do all in the name of the Lord Jesus Christ, giving thanks to God and the Father by him." [4]

208. b) Since, however, our nature inclines us to self-seeking, we must, in order to react against this tendency, remember that *of ourselves* we are but nothingness and sin. No doubt, there are in us good qualities, natural and supernatural, which we are to hold in high regard and which we must cultivate; but coming as they do from God, is it not to Him that the glory is due? When an artist creates a masterpiece, it is he and not the canvass that is to be praised.

Of ourselves we are *mere nothingness.* "This is," says Father Olier, " what we have been from all eternity; the being wherewith God has clothed us is of His creation and not of ours; and whatsoever He has given us remains His own property by which He wills to be honored." [5]

Again, *of ourselves* we are but *sin* in the sense that by concupiscence we *tend to sin;* so much so that, according to St. Augustine, if we do not fall into certain sins we owe it to the grace of God. "To Thy grace it is due that some evil I left undone. For what might I not have done, seeing

[1] *James*, IV, 6. — [2] *I. Cor.*, IV, 7. — [3] *I. Cor.*, X, 31. — [4] *Colos.*, III, 17.
[5] *Cat. for an Int. Life*, Part I., lesson 15.

that I loved even fruitless misdoing. "¹   Father Olier thus
explains this doctrine : " This I can say about it : there is
no conceivable sin, no imperfection or disorder, no blight of
error, no confusion with which our flesh is not teeming.
Likewise, there is no fickleness, no folly, no stupidity of
which mortal flesh is not capable at any moment. "²   Assuredly, our nature is not totally corrupt, as Luther affirmed.
With God's concurrence, natural and supernatural, ³ it is
capable of some good, even of a great deal of good, as is
evident in the case of the Saints.   But since God is ever
the first and principal cause of this good, it is to Him that
thanks must be given.

209.   We conclude with *Bossuet :* " Trust not overmuch
in thyself, for this is the beginning of sin.   Covet not
the glory of men, for having received thy reward only torments shall await thee.   Glory not in thine own self, for
whatsoever of thy good works thou dost attribute to thyself,
thou takest away from God, its author, and thou placest
thyself in His stead.   Shake not off the yoke of God's law;
say not to thyself with the haughtiness of the proud : I shall
not serve; for if thou servest not unto justice, thou shalt be
the slave of sin and the child of death.   Say not : I am not
unclean, and reckon not that God has forgotten thy sins
because thou thyself rememberest them no more, for the
Lord shall rouse thee saying : See, look at thy paths in that
vale obscure. I have followed thee along thy ways.   I have
counted thy steps.   Resist not the counsel of the wise and
be not angry at correction ; for this is the consummation of
pride, to rebel against the truth itself when it reproves thee,
to kick against the goad. "⁴   If we follow this advice we
shall be stronger in our fight against the world, the second
of our spiritual enemies.

II. *The Fight against the World* ⁵

210.   The world we speak of here is not the total aggregate of men upon the earth, among whom are found both
choice souls and irreligious men; but the sum-total of those
who oppose Jesus Christ and are the slaves of the threefold
concupiscence. These are : 1) *unbelievers*, hostile to religion,

---

¹ *Confessions*, II, C. 7. — ² *Catechism*, P. I, lesson 17.
³ Theology teaches (*Syn. theol. dog.*, III. n. 72-91) that fallen man can do some
good in the natural order with the mere *natural concurrence* of God; but that in
order to observe the *whole* of the natural law and repulse *all* grievous temptations,
a *preternatural* or supernatural help is needed.
⁴ *Tr. de la Concup.*, C. XXXI.
⁵ Meyer, The World in Which We Live.

precisely because it condemns their pride, their love of pleasure, their lust for riches; 2) *the indifferent*, who do not want a religion that would stir them out of their apathy; 3) *hardened sinners*, who love sin because they love pleasure and are loath to part with it; 4) *worldlings*, who believe and even practise their religion, yet, combine with it the love of pleasure, of luxury and of ease, and who not unfrequently scandalize their neighbor by giving them occasion to say that religion has but little influence on morals. This is the world which Jesus cursed because of its scandals: " Woe to the world because of scandals! "[1]   Of this world St. John says: " The whole world is seated in wickedness. "[2]

211.   1º **The dangers of the world.**   The world which through visits, letters and worldly literature worms its way into the heart of Christian families, even into religious communities, constitutes a great obstacle to the attainment of salvation and perfection. It stirs up and feeds the fire of concupiscence; it seduces and terrorizes us.

212.   **A**) It **seduces** us with its maxims, with the show of its vanities and with its perverse examples.

a) It holds up *maxims* directly opposed to those of the Gospel. It actually extols the happiness of the wealthy, of the powerful, of the ruthless, of the upstart, of the ambitious, of all those who know how to enjoy life. On the lips of worldlings is ever the cry: " Let us crown ourselves with roses before they wither. "[3]   Must not youth have its day, must not each live his life to the full? Many others do this and Almighty God can not damn all mankind. One has to make a living, and were one to be scrupulous in business one could never become wealthy.

b) The world seduces us with the *show of its vanities and pleasures.* Most worldly gatherings cater to curiosity, to sensuality, and even to lust. Vice is made attractive by being concealed beneath the guise of what are called " innocent fashions and amusements, " but which are none the less fraught with danger. Such are, for instance, immodest dress and immodest dances, especially such as seem to have no other purpose than to occasion wanton looks and gestures. What must be said of most theatrical performances, of public entertainments, of the lewd literature that one encounters at every turn?

---

[1] *Matth.*, XVIII, 7. — [2] *I John*, V, 19. — [3] *Wisdom*, II, 8.

c) The world seduces us with its *evil examples.* At the sight of so many youths living solely for pleasure, of so many men and women who make light of their marriage-vows, of so many business-men who do not scruple to enrich themselves by questionable means, the temptation to follow suit is, indeed, very strong. Moreover, the world is so tolerant of human weaknesses that it actually seems to encourage them. A home-breaker is considered a sportsman; the financier, the business-man who amasses his wealth dishonestly is called a clever fellow ; the free-thinker is considered a broad-minded man who follows the light of his conscience. How many men are thus encouraged to lead a life of sin!

213. B) When the world fails to seduce us it attempts to **terrorize** us.

a) At times this takes the form of an actual, organized *persecution* against the faithful. Those that make public profession of their faith or send their children to the Catholic school are denied promotion in certain departments of business or of civic life.

b) At other times, the world turns timid souls from the discharge of their religious duties by mockery and jest. It refers to them as hypocrites and dupes believing still in antiquated dogmas. It holds up to ridicule parents whose daughters are modestly dressed, asking them if it is thus that they hope to make a match for them. Many souls are in this manner, in spite of the protests of conscience, driven to conform through human respect to fashions and customs that offend against Christian modesty.

c) Sometimes the world resorts to threats. Individuals are served notice that their religious affiliations disqualify them for certain positions, or they are made to understand that their prudishness will make them unwelcome guests at entertainments; or again, they are told that if their conscience stands in the way of business they must either do as every one else does — deceive the public and make more money — or be ready to lose their positions.

It is but too easy to let ourselves be won over or terrorized, for the world has its accomplice within our own hearts, in our natural desire for high places, for dignity and for wealth.

214. 2° **The remedy.** [1] To resist successfully this dangerous trend one must have the courage to look upon

---

[1] TRONSON. *Examens partic.,* XCIV-XCVI.

life from the point of view of eternity, and regard the world in the light of faith. Then the world will appear to us in its true colors, as the *enemy of Jesus Christ*, to be fought against with all our might in order that we may save our souls; it will appear to us as the *scene of action for our zeal* whither we must carry the maxims of the Gospel.

215. A) Since the world is the enemy of Jesus Christ, we must accept as our standard of life that which is opposed to the maxims and examples of the world. We must repeat to ourselves the dilemma proposed by St. Bernard : " Either Christ blunders, or the world is astray; but it is impossible for Divine Wisdom to blunder. " [1]   Since there exists a manifest opposition between Christ and the world, a choice on our part is absolutely necessary, for no one can serve two masters. But Jesus is infallible Wisdom itself. Hence, He has the words of eternal life, and it is the world that blunders. Our choice, therefore, will be quickly made, for as St. Paul says, " We have received not the spirit of this world, but the Spirit that is of God. " [2]   To wish to please the world, he adds, is to displease Jesus Christ : " If I yet pleased men, I should not be the servant of Jesus Christ. " [3]   St. James says : " Whosoever, therefore, will be the friend of this world, becometh an enemy of God. " [4]   Hence, the following practical resolutions.

a) Let us *read and reread the Gospel*, reflecting that it is the Eternal Truth that speaks to us, and praying its Divine Author to make us understand, relish and live its maxims. It is thus that we become true Christians and such is the price we must pay if we would become real disciples of Christ. Whenever we hear or read maxims that go counter to those of the Gospel let us courageously say to ourselves : This is *false*, since it is opposed to infallible Truth itself.

b) Let us likewise avoid *dangerous occasions* so numerous in this world. No doubt, those that live outside the cloister must of necessity mingle more or less in the world; yet, they must keep themselves free from its spirit by living in the world as those that were not of it; for Jesus asked His Father not to take His disciples out of the world, but to keep them from evil : " I pray not that thou shouldst take them out of the world, but that thou shouldst keep them from evil. " [5]   And St. Paul wants us to make use of this world as though we did not use it. [6]

---

[1] *Sermo III, de Nativitate*, n. 1. — [2] *I Cor.*, II, 12. — [3] *Gal.*, I, 10.
[4] *James*, IV, 4. — [5] *John*, XVII. 15. — [6] *I Cor.*, VII, 31.

c) This attitude towards the world is incumbent above all upon ecclesiastics. They should be able to say with St. Paul : " The world is crucified to me, and I to the world. " [1] The world, ruled as it is by concupiscence, can have no charms for us. Just as we are to it an object of repulsion, for by our character and even by our garb we stand as a condemnation of its vices; so the world in turn can not but inspire us with a like antipathy. Hence, we must dispense with social visits *purely worldly* in character, in which we should be out of place. No doubt, we shall have to make and receive such visits as courtesy, business, and above all, zeal for souls impose; but they shall be brief. We shall not forget what is said of our Lord after His resurrection, that He came among His disciples but rarely, and only in order to complete their training and to speak to them of the kingdom of God. [2]

216. B) We shall not, then, venture into the world except to exercise there our zeal either directly or indirectly, that is to say, to carry there the maxims and examples of the Gospel. a) We must not forget that we are " the light of the world. " [3] Without turning our conversation into a sort of sermon (which would be out of place) we shall judge everything, persons and things, by the light of the Gospel. Thus, instead of proclaiming the rich and the powerful the happy ones of this world, we shall note in all sincerity that there are sources of happiness other than those of wealth and success; that virtue does not go without its reward even in this world; that the pure joys of home and hearth are the sweetest; that the consciousness of duty done is a source of satisfaction and comfort to many unfortunate souls; that the peace of a good conscience is worth infinitely more than the intoxication of pleasure. A few examples will bring home these remarks. But it is chiefly by his *own example* that a priest is a source of edification in conversation. A profound impression is created upon those who listen to him if he is in every sense of the word a man among men, a Christian gentleman utterly devoted to the service of souls; if his whole bearing, as well as his words, reflects candor, good-fellowship, cheerfulness, charity, in a word, true sanctity. No one can help admiring those who live according to their convictions; and a religion which knows how to promote solid virtue is held in high regard. Let us, therefore, carry into practice the saying of

---

[1] *Gal.*, VI, 14. — [2] *Acts*, I, 3. — [3] *Matth.*, V, 14.

our Lord: "So let your light shine before men, that they may see your good works, and glorify your Father who is in heaven." [1]   The exercise of this apostolate is not limited to priests.   Men of conviction among the laity can practise it with real success, as persons are less on their guard against their influence.

217.   b) It is for such select souls and for priests to infuse into the more timid Christians the courage to fight the tyranny of human respect, of fashion and of legalized persecution.   The best means of effecting this is to band together into societies those influential laymen who have the courage of their convictions, and who fear neither to speak nor to act accordingly.   It is in this manner that the Saints brought about in their times the reformation of morals.   It is also in this manner that in our great centers of learning, the universities, solid groups have been formed that know how to make their religious practices respected and how to steady the weaker brethren.   On the day when such groups shall have been considerably multiplied not in cities alone but in the country-districts as well, the death-knell of human respect shall not be long in sounding, and true piety, if not universally practised, shall at least be held in real esteem.

218.   We must make *no compromise with the world.* We must make no concessions either to please it or to seek its esteem.   As St. Francis de Sales rightly says, "No matter what we do, the world shall ever war against us... Let us turn a deaf ear to this blind world; let it cry as long as it pleases, like an owl to disturb the birds of the day. Let us be constant in our designs and invariable in our resolutions.   Our perseverance will demonstrate whether we have in good earnest sacrificed ourselves to God and dedicated ourselves to a devout life." [2]

III. *The Fight against the Devil* [3]

219.   1º **The existence of and reasons for diabolical temptation.**   We have seen, n. 67, how the devil, jealous of the blessedness of our first parents, incited them to sin, and how well he succeeded.   Therefore, the Book of Wisdom declares that it was "by the envy of the devil that death

[1] *Matth.*, V, 16. — [2] *Introd. to a Dev. Life*, P. IV, C. 1.
[3] St. Thom., I, q. 114; St. Theresa, *Life by Herself*, C. XXX-XXXI; Ribet, *L'Ascétique chrét.*, C. XVI.

came into the world. " [1]   Ever since, he has not ceased
to attack the children of Adam or to lay snares for them.
And even though, since our Lord's advent into the world
and His triumph over Satan, the latter's power has been
greatly curbed, it is none the less true that we have to
battle not only against flesh and blood, but also against
the powers of darkness, against the spirits of evil.   This
is exactly what St. Paul teaches : " For our wrestling is
not against flesh and blood, but against the rulers of the
world of this darkness, against the spirits of wickedness. " [2]
St. Peter compares the devil to a roaring lion prowling
about, seeking to destroy us : " Your adversary, the devil,
as a roaring lion, goeth about seeking whom he may
devour. " [3]

220.   If divine Providence allows these attacks, it is in
virtue of the general principle that God governs men not
only directly, but also through the agency of secondary
causes, leaving to creatures a certain freedom of action.
On the other hand, He warns us to be on our guard, and
sends His Angels, particularly our Guardian Angels, to help
and protect us (n. 186 sq), to say nothing of the assistance
that He gives us directy, or through His Son.   By availing
ourselves of such helps we triumph over the enemy of our
salvation, grow in virtue and lay up to ourselves treasures
of merit in heaven.   These wonderful ways of Providence
show us all the more clearly the great importance we must
attach to the affair of our salvation and sanctification, an
affair in which both heaven and hell so concern themselves
that around the soul, at times within the soul itself, fierce
combats rage between the powers of heaven and those of
hell, — and it is the eternal life of the soul that is at stake.
In order to obtain the victory, let us see how the devil
proceeds.

221.   2⁰ **The devil's strategy.**   **A)** The Evil One can
not act *directly* on our higher faculties, the intellect and the
will.   God has kept these as a sanctuary for Himself, and
He alone can enter there and touch the mainspring of the
will without doing violence to it.   The devil, however, can
act directly on the body, on our exterior and interior
senses, and particularly on the imagination and the memory
as well as on the passions which reside in the sensitive
appetite.   Thus, the devil acts *indirectly* on the will, solicit-
ing its consent through the various movements of the sen-

---

[1] *Wisdom*, II, 24. — [2] *Eph.*, VI, 12. — [3] *I Peter*, V, 8-9.

sitive appetite. The will, however, as St. Thomas remarks, remains ever free to give or refuse consent. [1]

B) No matter how extensive the power of the devil over our faculties, there are nevertheless limits set to it by God Himself, who will not allow him to tempt us beyond our strength. " God is faithful, who will not suffer you to be tempted above that which you are able; but will make also with temptation issue. " [2] Whoever leans upon the Almighty in humble trust can be sure of victory.

222. C) We must not believe, says *St. Thomas*, [3] that all the temptations we experience are the works of the demon. Concupiscence stirred up by habits formed in the past and by imprudences committed in the present, is sufficient to account for a great number of them. " Every one is tempted by his own concupiscence, being drawn away and allured. " [4] On the other hand, it would be rash to assert, and contrary to the clear teaching of Scripture and Tradition, that there is no diabolical influence in any of our temptations. The envy the devil bears mankind and his desire to bring men into subjection adequately explain his intervention. [5]

How then will diabolical temptation be recognized? This is no easy matter, for our concupiscence itself may sufficiently account for the violence of temptation. It may be said, however, that when a temptation is sudden, violent, and protracted beyond measure, the devil is largely responsible for it. One can especially suspect his influence if the temptation casts the soul into deep and prolonged turmoil; if it excites a desire for the spectacular, for strange and conspicuous mortifications, and particularly if it induces a strong inclination to be silent about the whole affair with our spiritual director and to distrust our superiors. [6]

223. 3° **The remedies against diabolical temptation.** The Saints, and particularly St. Theresa, [7] point out the following remedies.

A) The first is humble and confident prayer to secure the help of God and His holy Angels. If God is for us who will be against us? [8] For, " who is like unto God? " Our prayer must be *humble*, for there is nothing that so quickly

---

[1] *Sum. theol.*, I, q. III, a. 2. — [2] *I Cor.*, X, 13.
[3] *Sum. theol.*, I, q. 114, a. 3. — [4] *James*, I, 14. — [5] *Sum. theol.*, I, q. 114, a. 1.
[6] See the rules for the discernment of spirits in the first and second weeks of the *Spiritual Exercises of St. Ignatius.*
[7] *Life by Herself*, C. XXX-XXXI. — [8] *Rom.*, VIII, 31.

puts to flight this rebellious spirit, who, having revolted through pride, never knew the virtue of humility.   To humble ourselves before God, to acknowledge our inability to conquer without His help, defeats the schemes of the prince of pride.   Our prayer must also be *full of confidence.* God's own glory is bound up with our triumph and we may, therefore, fully trust in the power of His grace.   It is likewise a good practice to invoke the intercession of St. Michael, who, having once obtained a signal victory over Satan, will gladly complete his triumph in us and through us in the day of our struggle.   He will have a powerful ally in our Guardian Angel provided we place our trust in him.   But above all, we must not forget to have recourse to the Blessed Virgin.   Her foot did crush the serpent's head and she is more terrible to the demon than a whole army in battle array.

224.   B) The second means consists in making use in all confidence of the *sacraments* and the *sacramentals.*   Confession being an act of humility routs the devil; the absolution which follows applies to us the merits of Jesus Christ and renders us invulnerable to the thrusts of the enemy. Holy Communion brings into our hearts Christ who triumphed over Satan and who now fills him with terror. Even the sacramentals, the sign of the Cross, or the prayers of the Liturgy, said in the spirit of faith in union with the Church, are a precious help. St. Theresa recommends in a special way the use of holy water, [1] perhaps because of the humiliation Satan must suffer at seeing himself baffled by such a simple device.

225.   C) The last means against diabolical temptation is an *utter contempt of the devil.*   It is once more St. Theresa who assures us of this.   " These cursed spirits torment me quite frequently, but they do not frighten me in the least, for I am convinced that they cannot stir except by God's leave.   Let this be known well, that every time we make them the object of our contempt, they lose their strength, and the soul acquires over them greater ascendancy.   They have no power except against cowardly souls who surrender their weapons.   Against such they do show their power. " [2]   It must be, indeed, a bitter humiliation to those proud spirits to be contemned by weaker beings such as men are.   As we have said, if we humbly lean on the strong arm of God, it is our right as well as

---

[1] *Life by Herself*, C. XXXI. — [2] *Ibid.*

our duty to despise them. "If God is for us who will be against us?" The evil spirits can bark; they cannot harm us unless through lack of prudence or through pride we put ourselves into their power. Thus it is that the fight that we must wage against the devil, the world and the flesh strengthens us in the supernatural life and enables us to make spiritual progress.

CONCLUSION

226. 1° We have just seen that the Christian life is a *warfare*, a harassing warfare that entails a lifelong and intricate manœuvering ending only with death, a warfare of supreme importance since it is our eternal life that is at stake. As St. Paul teaches, there are within us *two men :* **a**) the *regenerated* man, the new man, with tendencies which are noble, supernatural, divine. These the Holy Ghost produces in us through the merits of Christ and the intercession of the Blessed Virgin and the Saints. We strive to correspond to the higher tendencies by making use, under the influence of actual grace, of the supernatural organism wherewith God has endowed us. **b**) But there is also in us the *natural* or *carnal* man, the Old Adam, with all the evil inclinations which remain even after Baptism, with the threefold concupiscence inherited from our first parents. This concupiscence is stirred up and intensified by the world and the devil; it is an abiding tendency inclining us toward an inordinate love of sensual pleasure, of our own excellence, and of the goods of this world. These two men necessarily engage in conflict. The Old Adam, the *flesh*, seeks pleasure without regard to the moral law. The *spirit* in turn reminds the flesh that there are forbidden pleasures and dangerous pleasures which must be sacrificed to duty, that is to say, to the will of God. The flesh, however, is persistent in its desires; it must, therefore, with the help of grace be mortified and, if need be, crucified. The Christian, then, is a *soldier*, an *athlete*, who fights unto death for an immortal crown. [1]

227. 2° This warfare is *constant*, for in spite of all our efforts we can never fully divest ourselves of the *Old Adam*. We can but weaken him, bind him, while at the same time we fortify the New Man against his attacks. At the outset the fight is keener, more obstinate, and the counter-attacks of the enemy more numerous and more violent; but as we

---

[1] *II. Tim.*, II, 1-7. St. Paul describes the Christian's armor in *Eph.* VI, 10-18.

by earnest and persevering efforts gain one victory and then another, our enemy weakens, passions subside and, except for certain moments of trial willed by God to lead us to a higher degree of perfection, we enjoy a relative calm, a pledge and a foretaste of final victory. All success we owe to the grace of God. We must not forget that the grace given us is the grace for struggle and not the grace for peace; that we are warriors, athletes, ascetics; that like St. Paul we must fight on to the end if we would merit the crown. " I have fought the good fight : I have finished my course : I have kept the faith. As to the rest, there is laid up for me a crown of justice, which the Lord the just judge will render to me in that day." [1] This is the means of perfecting in us the Christian life and of acquiring many merits.

§ II. The growth of the spiritual life by merit [2]

228. We progress, indeed, by the fight we wage against our enemies, but more still by the meritorious acts which we perform day by day. Every good act freely done by a soul in the state of grace and with a supernatural intention, possesses a threefold value for our spiritual growth, inasmuch as it is *meritorious, satisfactory and impetratory.*

a) The *meritorious value* means an increase of sanctifying grace and a corresponding right to a higher degree of glory in heaven.

b) The *satisfactory value* contains a threefold element : 1) *propitiation,* by which with a contrite and humble heart we turn God, auspiciously towards us and incline Him to forgive our trespasses; 2) *expiation,* that is to say, the effacement of guilt by the infusion of grace; 3) *satisfaction,* which in view of the element of suffering accompanying our good works, cancels wholly or in part the punishment due to sin. This happy result is not merely the outcome of good works properly so-called, but also, as the Council of Trent teaches, of the willing acceptance of the ills and sufferings of this life. [3] What is more consoling than to be able to turn all manner of adversity into gain for the purification of the soul and closer union with God?

---

[1] *II Tim.*, IV, 7-8.
[2] St. Thom., I-II q. 114; Terrien, *La Grâce et la Gloire,* II, p. 15 foll; Labauche, *Man,* P. III, C. III; Hugon in *La vie spirituelle,* II (1920), p. 28, 273, 353; Tanquerey, *Syn. theol. dog.,* III, n. 210-235; Remler, *Supernatural Merit*; Wirth, *Divine Grace,* C. VIII; Scheeben, *Glories of Divine Grace.*
[3] Sess. XIV, De Sacramento pœnit., Cap. 9.

c) Lastly, these same acts, when they embody a request to the Divine Mercy for new graces, possess also an *impetratory value*. As St. Thomas justly remarks, we pray not only when we explicitly make a request to Almighty God, but whenever we turn our hearts to Him or direct any act of ours towards Him; so much so, indeed, that our life becomes a continual prayer when our activities are constantly directed towards God. " Man prays whenever he so acts in thought, word and deed as to tend towards God; hence, life is a constant prayer if wholly directed towards God." [1]   Is not this elevation of the heart to God a prayer? Is not this an effectual means of obtaining from Him for ourselves and for others whatever we desire?

For the end we have in view it will suffice to explain: 1) the *nature* of merit; 2) the conditions that *increase the merit* of our good works.

I. *Nature of Merit*

Two points must be made clear: 1º What we mean by merit; 2º What makes our actions meritorious.

1º What is Meant by Merit

229. A) Merit in general is a right to a reward. Hence, supernatural merit of which we speak here is a right to a supernatural reward, a right to a share in God's life, a right to grace and glory. Since, however, God is in no way obliged to make us share in His life, there must exist a promise on His part that confers upon us an actual title to such supernatural reward. Merit, then, may be defined: *a right to a supernatural reward arising both from a supernatural work done freely for God's sake, and from a divine promise to give such a reward.*

230. B) There are two kinds of merit: **a)** merit properly so called *(de condigno)* to which a recompense is due in justice, because there exists a sort of equality, a real proportion between the work and the reward. **b)** The other kind of merit, called *de congruo*, is not based upon strict justice; its claims are simply those of a certain fitness, since the reward outweighs by far the work done. The following example gives an approximate notion of this distinction. A soldier acquitting himself bravely on the battlefield has a strict right to his pay, but he can lay only a claim of fitness to a citation or a decoration.

---

[1] *In Rom.*, C. I, 9-10.

C) The Council of Trent teaches that the works of the justified man truly merit an increase of grace, eternal life, and, should he die in this state, the attainment of glory.

231. **D**) Let us recall briefly the general conditions for merit. **a**) A work to be meritorious must be *free*. If man acts through constraint or necessity, he is not actually responsible. **b**) The work must be *supernaturally good* in order to be in proportion with the reward. **c**) When it is question of merit properly so-called, the work must be performed in the *state of grace*, for it is this grace that causes Christ to dwell in our souls and makes us share in His merits. **d**) The work must be performed during our *life on earth*, for God has wisely decreed that after a period of trial wherein we can merit or demerit, we should reach the end where we shall forever remain fixed in the state in which we die. These are the conditions on the part of man. To them is added on the part of God the *promise* which gives us a real right to eternal life. As St. James says : " The just receive the crown of life which God hath promised to them that love Him. " [1]

2° WHAT MAKES OUR ACTS MERITORIOUS

232. At first sight it seems difficult to understand how very simple, ordinary and transitory acts can merit eternal life. This would be an insuperable difficulty if these acts were produced by us alone. But as a matter of fact they are the result of the co-operation of God and the human will. This explains their efficacy. God whilst crowning our merits, crowns His own gifts, for our merits are largely His work. To enable us to understand better the efficacy of our meritorious acts let us explain the share of God and the share of man.

A) God is the *first and principal* cause of our merits : " Not I, but the grace of God with me. " [2] In fact, it is God who has created our faculties; God who has perfected them, raised them to a supernatural state by the virtues and by the gifts of the Holy Ghost ; God who by His actual grace calls us to perform good works and assists us in doing them. He is, therefore, the first cause exciting the will to action and giving it new energies that enable it to act supernaturally.

233. **B**) Our free will, responding to God's solicitations, acts under the influence of grace and the virtues and thus

---

[1] *James*, I, 12. — [2] *I Cor.*, XV, 10.

becomes a *secondary*, but real and efficacious cause of our
meritorious acts, since it truly co-operates with God.
Without this free consent there can be no merit. In
heaven we can no longer merit, for there we cannot help
loving that God whom we clearly see to be Infinite Goodness and the Source of our beatitude. Besides, our co-
operation itself is supernatural. By habitual grace the very
substance of our being is deified; by the virtues and the
gifts of the Holy Ghost our faculties are likewise deified,
and by actual grace even our acts are made Godlike. Once
our actions are deified there exists a real proportion between
our works and grace, which latter is itself a Godlike life, as
well as between our acts and glory, which is the full development of that life. No doubt, the acts themselves are
transitory, while glory is eternal; yet, as in our natural
existence transient acts produce states of soul that endure,
it is but just that the same should hold good in the supernatural order, and that virtuous acts producing an abiding
disposition to love God be rewarded by a lasting recompense. Lastly, since our soul is immortal it is *fitting* that
such recompense should endure forever.

234. C) It might be objected that in spite of this
proportion between act and reward, God is in no manner
constrained to bestow a recompense so great and so
enduring as grace and glory. We fully grant this, and we
acknowledge that God in His infinite goodness rewards us
above our deserts. Hence, He would not be bound to have
us enjoy the Beatific Vision through all eternity had He not
promised it. But He has promised it by the very fact that
He has destined us for a supernatural end. His promise
recurs repeatedly in Holy Writ wherein eternal life is
represented as the reward *promised* to the just, and as a
crown of justice: " The crown which God hath promised to
them that love Him... a crown of justice which the just
judge shall render unto me. " [1] Therefore, the Council of
Trent declares that eternal life is at once a *grace* mercifully
promised by Jesus Christ, and a *recompense* which in virtue
of this promise is faithfully awarded to good works and to
merit. [2]

235. From the fact that merit is based on this promise
of God, we can infer that merit is something *personal*. It
is for *ourselves* and not for others that we merit grace and
life everlasting, for the divine promise goes no further. It

---

[1] *James*, I, 12; *II Tim.*, IV, 8. — [2] Sess. VI, Cap. 16.

is different with our Lord Jesus Christ, who having been made the moral head of the human race, has merited for each of His members, and this in the strict sense of the word. We can, indeed, merit for others, but by no title of justice, simply *de congruo*, that is, by a title of mere fitness. This fact is in itself most consoling, because this merit is joined to the one we gain for ourselves and thus it enables us to co-operate in the sanctification of our brethren whilst working at our own.

II. *Conditions for Increasing Merit*

236. These conditions evidently proceed from the different causes that concur in the production of meritorious acts, hence, from God and from ourselves. We can always count upon God's liberality, for He is always munificent in His gifts, and therefore, we must center our attention principally upon our dispositions. Let us see what can improve these dispositions either on the part of the one who merits or on the part of the meritorious act itself.

1º CONDITIONS ON THE PART OF THE ONE WHO MERITS

237. There are four principal conditions : the degree of habitual grace or charity, our union with our Lord, our purity of intention, our fervor.

a) *The degree of sanctifying grace.* To merit in the proper sense of the word, the state of grace is required. Hence, all things being equal, the more habitual grace we possess, the greater is our power for meriting. This, no doubt, is denied by some theologians on the ground that the amount of habitual grace does not always influence our acts so as to render them better, and that at times holy souls act negligently and imperfectly. But the doctrine we maintain is the common teaching, based on the following reasons.

1) The value of an act even in human affairs depends largely upon the *dignity* of the person that performs it, and upon the degree of *esteem* in which he is held by the rewarder. Now, what constitutes the dignity of the Christian and what makes him dear to the heart of God is the degree of grace, that is, of divine life to which he has been raised. This is why the Saints in heaven or the saints on earth have such great power of intercession. Hence, if we possess a higher degree of grace we are worth more in the eyes of God than those who have less; we please Him more,

and on this account our actions are nobler, more agreeable to God, and therefore, more meritorious.

2) Besides, this degree of grace will *ordinarily* exercise a happy influence on our acts. Living more fully a supernatural life, loving God more perfectly, we are led to improve the quality of our acts, to put into them more charity, to be more generous in our sacrifices. Now, every one grants that such dispositions increase our merits. Let no one say that at times the contrary happens. This is the exception, not the rule. We had that in mind when we said : all other things being equal.

How consoling is this doctrine! By multiplying our meritorious acts we daily increase our stock of grace. This store of grace enables us to put more love into our works and thus further the growth of our supernatural life : " He that is just, let him be justified still. " [1]

238. b) *Our degree of union with our Lord.* The source of our merit is Jesus Christ, the Author of our sanctification, the chief meritorious cause of all supernatural good, the Head of the mystical body whose members we are. The closer we are to the source, the more we receive of its fulness; the closer we approach to the Author of all Holiness, the more grace we receive; the closer we are to the Head, the more life and activity it imparts to us. Does not our Lord Himself tell us this in the beautiful allegory of the vine? " I am the vine and you the branches... he who abideth in me and I in him, the same beareth much fruit. " [2] We are united to Jesus as the branch is to the stem and, therefore, the closer our union, habitual and actual, with Him, the more we receive of His vital influence. This is why all fervent souls, all that wish to become fervent, have ever sought a more and more intimate union with our Lord. This is why the Church herself asks us to perform our actions through Him, with Him and in Him. *Through Him*, for : " No one cometh to the Father but by me; " [3] *with Him*, by acting in union with Him, since He consents to be our co-worker; *in Him*, in the virtue, in the power that is His very own, and above all, with His intentions. In the words of Father Faber : " To do our actions by Christ is to do them in dependence upon Him, as He did everything in dependence upon His Father and by the movements of His Spirit. To do our actions with Christ is to practise the same virtues as our Lord, to clothe

---

[1] *Apoc.*, XVII, 11. — [2] *John*, XV, 1-6. — [3] *John*, XIV, 6.

ourselves with the same dispositions, and to act from the same intentions, all according to the measure of the lowliness of our possibilities. To do our actions in Christ is to unite ours with His, and to offer them to God along with His, so that for the sake of His they may be accepted on high. " [1]

If we thus perform our actions in union with our Lord, He lives in us, inspires our thoughts, our desires and all our acts in such a way that we can say with St. Paul : " I live, now not I, but Christ liveth in me." [2] It is evident that acts performed under the influence of Christ's life-giving action and with the aid of His all-powerful coöperation, have a far greater value than those done by ourselves even with the help of ordinary grace and with only habitual union with Christ by sanctifying grace. In practice, then, we should unite ourselves frequently with our Lord, especially at the beginning of our actions ; we should make our own His perfect intentions, fully conscious of our inability to do anything good of ourselves and confident that He is able to overcome our weakness. Thus we strive to carry out the advice of St. Paul : " All whatsoever you do in word or in work, all things do ye in the name of the Lord Jesus Christ. " [3]

239. c) *Purity of intention* or perfection of the motive under which we act. For our actions to be meritorious it is enough, according to many theologians, that they be inspired by any supernatural motive : fear, hope or love. It is true that St. Thomas requires that our actions be at least virtually under the influence of charity through a preceding act of love the influence of which still endures. He adds, however, that this condition is fulfilled in all those that perform any lawful action whilst in the state of grace : " For those in the state of grace every act is meritorious or demeritorious. " [4] In fact, every good act springs from some virtue ; but all virtues converge into charity which is the Queen of virtues just as the will is the Queen of faculties. And charity ever active directs all our good acts towards God and gives life to all our virtues. If, however, we want our acts to be as meritorious as possible, we need a more perfect, a more actual intention. The intention is the principal element in our actions ; it is the *eye* that sheds its light upon them and directs them towards their end ; it

---

[1] *Growth in Holiness*, p. 467. — [2] *Gal.*, II, 20. — [3] *Colos.*, III, 17.
[4] *Quæs. disp.*, de Malo. q. 2, a. 5, ad 7. Hence, it appears that what St. Thomas calls *virtual* intention, modern theologians call *habitual*.

is the *soul* that animates them and gives them their worth in God's sight : " If thy eye be single, thy whole body shall be lightsome. " [1] Now, there are three elements that bestow special value upon our intentions.

240. 1) Since charity is the Queen and the soul of all virtues, every act inspired by it will have by far more merit than acts inspired by fear or by hope. It is important, then, that all our actions be done out of love of God and the neighbor. In this way even the most ordinary actions, like meals and recreations, become acts of charity and share in the merits of that virtue. To eat in order to restore our strength is lawful and, in a Christian, it is meritorious ; but to do this in order to work for God and for souls is to act from a motive of love which ennobles our action and bestows on it greater meritorious value.

241. 2) Since acts of virtue animated by charity lose none of their own value, it follows that an act done from more than one motive will thereby be more meritorious. Thus, an act of obedience to Superiors prompted both by respect for their authority and by the love of God whom we see in their persons, will possess the twofold merit of obedience and of charity. In this way one and the same act may have a threefold or a fourfold value; for instance, when I detest my sins because they offend God, I can also have the intention of practising penance and humility. Thus, I make this one act thrice meritorious. It is, there-fore, useful in performing our actions to propose to ourselves several supernatural motives. We must, however, avoid all excess and preoccupation in seeking to multiply intentions, for this would disturb the soul. The prudent way is to make use of the intentions that suggest themselves more or less spontaneously and to subordinate them to that of divine charity. In this manner we shall increase our merits without losing our peace of soul.

242. 3) Since our will is fickle, we must form and renew frequently our supernatural intention. Otherwise, it might come to pass that an action begun for God would be continued from curiosity, sensuality or self-love, and thus lose in part its worth. We say : in part, for since these secondary motives do not utterly destroy the first, the act does not cease to be supernatural and meritorious. When a steamer leaves Cherbourg for New York, it is not enough

---

[1] *Matth.*, VI, 22.

to direct it once and for all towards her destination. The tides, gales and ocean-currents tend now and again to change her course, and it is necessary that the pilot be constantly at the helm to keep her in her path. It is the same with the will. It is not enough to direct it towards God once for all or even once a day. Human passions and external influences will soon throw it out of course; we must, therefore, by explicit acts bring it back frequently in the direction of God and of charity. We should be careful to realize and to mean what we say when we recite the morning-offering: "I offer up to Thee, O my God, my thoughts, words, acts and sufferings of this day; grant that they may all tend to Thy glory and my salvation." We should renew this offering before every important action of the day. If we are faithful to this practice, God will gradually give us the facility to renew the offering even in the course of our actions, without depriving us of the requisite attention to do our work well.

243. d) *Fervor or intensity* of our actions. Even in the accomplishment of good works, it is possible for us to be careless and remiss; or, on the other hand, we may act with vigor, with all the energy at our command, making use of all the actual graces placed at our disposal. Evidently, the result in either case will be very different. If we act half-heartedly we acquire but little merit and at times become guilty of venial sins, which do not, however, entirely destroy our merit. If, on the contrary, we pray and labor and sacrifice ourselves whole-heartedly, each of our actions merits a goodly share of sanctifying grace. Without entering here into debatable questions, we can say with certainty that, since God renders a hundredfold for what is done for Him, a fervent soul acquires daily a great increase of grace and becomes perfect in a short time, according to the words of Wisdom: "Being made perfect in a short space, he fulfilled a long time." [1] What a mighty incentive to fervor! In truth, it is well worth the while to renew our efforts unceasingly and resolutely.

2° CONDITIONS ON THE PART OF THE ACT ITSELF

244. Subjective dispositions are not the only conditions that increase merit; there are also objective circumstances that contribute to render our actions more perfect. These are chiefly four:

---

[1] *Wisdom*, IV, 13.

a) *The excellence of the object* or of the act itself. There is a hierarchy among the virtues; the theological excel the moral. Hence, the acts of faith, hope and charity have greater worth than those of prudence, justice, temperance, etc. But, as we have said, the latter can, through the intention of the subject, become also acts of charity and thus share in the special worth that attaches to this virtue. In like manner acts of religion which of themselves have God's glory directly in view, are more perfect than those that look directly to our sanctification.

b) As regards certain actions, *quantity* may have some influence on merit. All other things being the same, a gift of a thousand dollars will be more meritorious than a gift of a hundred. But in this matter quantity is often a relative thing. The mite of the widow who deprives herself of much of her substance has a greater moral value than the princely gift of the rich man who simply gives a portion of his superfluous goods.

c) The *duration* of an act likewise may render it more meritorious. To pray or to suffer for an hour is worth more than to pray or to suffer for five minutes; for protracted prayer or suffering call forth more effort and more love.

245. d) The *difficulty* inherent to the performance of the act also increases merit, not precisely inasmuch as it is a difficulty, but inasmuch as it demands greater love and a more strenuous and sustained effort. For instance, to resist a violent temptation is more meritorious than to resist a light one; to practise meekness with a choleric temperament and in spite of frequent provocations from others is more difficult and more meritorious than to do so with a nature that is gentle and mild or when others are kind and considerate. We must not conclude, however, that the ease acquired by the repetition of virtuous acts necessarily diminishes our merit. Such facility, when used to sustain and to strengthen the supernatural effort, contributes to the intensity or fervor of the act, and in this way it rather increases our merit, as we have already explained above. Just as an efficient worker in the measure that he becomes proficient in his work avoids all waste of time, material and energy, and thus realizes larger gains with less labor, so the Christian who has learned to make better use of the means of sanctification saves time and effort, and thus with less trouble to himself gains greater merit. Because the Saints through the practice of virtue make acts of humility, obedience, religion, with greater facility, they are not therefore entitled to less merit; just the contrary, since they make acts of love of God with greater ease and frequency. Moreover, they continue their efforts to make sacrifices whenever necessary. In short, difficulty increases merit, not inasmuch it is an obstacle to be overcome but inasmuch as it calls for more energy and more love. [1]

We must add that these *objective* conditions have a real influence on merit only inasmuch as they are freely accepted by us, and thus react on our interior dispositions.

CONCLUSION

246. The logical conclusion of all this is the necessity of sanctifying all our actions, even the most ordinary. We have already said it : all our actions can become a source of merit if done with a supernatural end in view and in union with our Lord, who even in the workshop at Nazareth never ceased to merit for us. What progress can we not thus make in a single day! From the moment we awake until we retire at night the meritorious acts which we can perform, if we are recollected and generous, may be numbered by the hundreds. Indeed, there is a growth of the Godlike life of grace in our souls not only through every act of the day, but through every effort to make each action more perfect; through every effort to dispel distractions at prayer, to apply our minds to our tasks, to keep back an unkind word, to render a service to others. Likewise, every word inspired by charity, every good thought turned to good account, in short, all the movements of the soul directed by our free-will towards good are so many means of increasing merit.

247. It may be said in all truth that there is no means of sanctification more *efficacious*, more *practical*, than the supernaturalizing of our ordinary actions, — and this means is *within the reach of every one*. It is of itself sufficient to raise a soul within a short time to a high degree of holiness. Every act becomes a seed of grace and glory, since it gives us an increase of sanctifying grace and a right to a higher degree of heavenly bliss.

248. The *practical way* of thus converting our acts into merits is to recollect ourselves for a moment before we begin them, to renounce positively all evil or inordinate intentions, to unite ourselves to our Lord, our model and

---

[1] EYMIEU, *Le Gouvernement de soi-même*, I, Introd., p. 7-9.

our Mediator, with a keen sense of our own weakness, and to offer through Him every act for God's glory and the good of souls. Thus understood the oft-renewed offering of our actions to God is an act of self-renunciation, of humility, of love of our Lord, of love of God, of love of the neighbor. It is, indeed, a short-cut to perfection.[1]

§ III. Growth of the christian Life through the Sacraments [2]

249. We grow in grace and perfection not only by means of meritorious acts, but also by the reception of the *Sacraments*. Sensible signs instituted by our Lord Jesus Christ, they *symbolize* and *confer* grace. God, knowing how easily man is drawn to external things, willed in His infinite goodness to attach His grace to material objects and visible actions. It is a matter of faith that our sacraments *contain* the grace they symbolize and that they *confer* it on all those who place no obstacle in the way;[3] and this not solely in virtue of the recipient's dispositions, but *ex opere operato,* that is, in virtue of the sacramental rite itself. The sacraments are *instrumental causes* of grace, God ever being the *principal cause,* and our Lord the *meritorious cause.*

250. Besides habitual grace, each sacrament produces a special grace which is called *sacramental grace.* This does not differ specifically from sanctifying grace, but, according to St. Thomas and his school, it adds to it a special energy calculated to produce effects in harmony with the purpose of each sacrament. Be this as it may, all agree that it gives a right to *special graces* at the opportune moment for the more easy performance of those obligations which the reception of the various sacraments imposes. The Sacrament of Confirmation, for example, gives us the right to special actual graces of strength for combating human respect and for confessing our faith in the face of all.

There are four things we should dwell on : 1º *sacramental grace,* proper to each sacrament; 2º the *dispositions necessary*

---

[1] All spiritual writers recommend this practice in some form or other. See RODRIGUEZ, *Practice of Christian Perfection*, P. I, tr. 2, 3; OLIER, *Introd.*, C. XV; TRONSON, *Examens*, XXVI-XXIX ; FABER, *All for Jesus;* " Minting Money "; Growth in Holiness, p. 463-468.

[2] St. THOM., III, q. 60-62; SUAREZ, disp. VIII; DE BROGLIE, *Conf. sur la vie surnat.*, III; BELLEVUE, *De la grâce sacramentelle;* TANQUEREY, *Syn.*, III, n. 298-323; MARMION, *Christ the Life of the Soul,* p. 65 and foll

[3] *Council of Trent*, Sess. VII, Can. 6.

for the fruitful reception of the sacraments; 3° the *special dispositions* required for the sacrament of *Penance*; 4° those required for the reception of *Holy Communion*.

I. *Sacramental Grace*

The Sacraments confer special graces which correspond to the different stages of life.

251.   **a)** In *Baptism* a grace of spiritual regeneration is given by which we are purified from the stain of original sin, are born to the life of grace.   A *new man* is thus created within us, the regenerated man that lives the life of Christ.   According to the beautiful teaching of St. Paul, " We are buried together with Him (Christ) by baptism into death; that as Christ is risen from the dead, so we also may walk in newness of life. " [1]   Hence, the special or sacramental grace given us is: 1) a grace of *death to sin*, of *spiritual crucifixion* which enables us to oppose and to curb the evil tendencies of the Old Adam; 2) a grace of *regeneration* that makes us one with Christ, causes us to share in His life, renders us capable of living in harmony with His sentiments and examples and thus makes us perfect Christians.   Hence, the duty for us of combatting sin and its causes, of adhering to Jesus Christ and imitating His virtues.

252.   **b)** *Confirmation* makes of us soldiers of Christ. To the grace of Baptism it adds a special grace of *strength* that we may with generosity profess our faith in face of all enemies, in spite of human respect that keeps so many from the practice of their religious duties.   This is why the gifts of the Holy Ghost already given us in Baptism are conferred again in Confirmation, for the special purpose of enlightening our faith, of rendering it more vivid, more discerning, and of strengthening our will against sin. Hence, the duty of cultivating the gifts of the Holy Ghost, especially those that make for militant Christianity.

253.   **c)** The *Eucharist nourishes* our souls, which like our bodies need food for sustenance and strength.   None but a Divine Food can nourish a Divine Life.   The Body and Blood of Christ, His Soul and His Divinity transform us into other Christs, infusing into us His spirit, His sentiments and His virtues.   This will be developed further, (n. 283).

---

[1] *Romans*, VI, 3-6.

254. d) Should we have the misfortune of losing the life of grace by mortal sin, the Sacrament of *Penance washes away our sins* in the Blood of Jesus Christ poured upon us by absolution (cf. n. 262).

255. e) As death approaches we need to be fortified in the midst of the anxiety and the fear inspired by the memory of past sins, by our present failings, and by the thought of God's judgment. By the anointing of our senses with the Holy Oils the Sacrament of *Extreme Unction* infuses into our souls a grace of confort and spiritual solace that frees us from the remains of sin, revives our trust, and arms us against the last assaults of the enemy, making us share the sentiments of St. Paul who, after having fought the good fight, rejoiced at the thought of the crown prepared for him. It is important, then, to ask in good time for this Sacrament, that is, as soon as we become seriously ill, in order that we may receive all its effects, in particular, restoration to health should this be God's will. It amounts to cruelty on the part of those attending the sick to hide from them the seriousness of their condition and to put off to the last moment the reception of a sacrament from which flow such abundant consolations. These five sacraments suffice to sanctify the *individual.* There are two others instituted to sanctify man in his *relations to society*, Holy Orders and Matrimony. The former gives the Church worthy ministers, the latter sanctifies the family.

256. f) Holy Orders bestow upon the ministers of the Church not only the *marvellous powers* of *consecrating* the Body and Blood of Christ, administering the Sacraments and preaching the word of God, but also the *grace* of *exercising* these powers in a *holy manner.* This Sacrament gives them in particular an ardent love for the Blessed Eucharist and for the souls of men, together with a firm determination of spending and sacrificing themselves entirely. We shall speak later on of the high degree of sanctity at which God's ministers should aim.

257. g) In order to sanctify the family, the cradle of society, the Sacrament of Matrimony gives to husbands and wives the graces they so urgently need : the grace of an absolute and abiding fidelity so difficult to the human heart ; the grace of reverence for the sanctity of the marriage-bed ; the grace of devoted and steadfast consecration to the Christian education of their children.

258. At all the important stages of life, for every duty, individual or social, we receive through some Sacrament a wonderful grant of *sanctifying grace*. That such a grace may be turned to account, we receive likewise through each Sacrament a right to *actual graces* that urge us and help us to practice the virtues to which we are bound. It is our task then to correspond to these graces by bringing to the Sacraments the best possible dispositions.

II. *Necessary Dispositions for the Fruitful Reception of the Sacraments*

The amount of grace produced by the Sacraments depends both on God and on us.[1] Let us see how this grace can be increased.

259. **A)** No doubt, God is free in the distribution of His gifts. He may, therefore, grant more or less grace through the Sacraments, according to the designs of His Wisdom and His Goodness. But there are laws which God Himself has laid down and by which He wills to abide. Thus, He declares again and again that He cannot turn a deaf ear to prayer well said : " Ask and it shall be given you : seek and you shall find : knock, and it shall be opened to you. "[2] This holds good especially if our prayer is supported by the merits of Christ : " Amen, amen, I say to you : if you ask the Father anything in my name, He will give it to you. "[3] If, therefore, when we receive a Sacrament, we pray with humility and fervor and in union with our Lord for a greater measure of grace, we shall obtain it.

260. **B)** On our part two dispositions contribute to the reception of an increase of sacramental grace, namely, *holy desires* before approaching the Sacraments, and *fervor* in receiving them.

a) The *ardent desire* of receiving a Sacrament with all its fruits opens and dilates the soul. This is an application of the principle laid down by our Lord : " Blessed are they that hunger and thirst after justice : for they shall have their fill. "[4] Now, to hunger and thirst for the Holy Eucharist or for Absolution is to open wide our hearts to the divine communications. Then will God replenish our famished souls : " He hath filled the hungry with good things. "[5]

---

[1] Thus the Council of *Trent*, Sess. VI, Ch. 7 : " The Holy Spirit distributes to each according as He wills, and according to each one's disposition and cooperation. "

[2] *Matth.*, VII, 7. — [3] *John*, XVI, 23. — [4] *Matth.*, V, 6. — [5] *Luke*, I, 53.

Let us then be like Daniel, men of desire, and let us long after the fountains of living water, the Sacraments.

b) *Fervor* in the actual reception of the Sacraments will make the soul still more receptive; for fervor is that generous attitude of refusing Almighty God nothing, of allowing Him to act in all the fulness of His power and of co-operating with Him with all our energies. Such a disposition expands the soul, renders it more apt for the effusions of grace, more responsive to the action of the Holy Spirit. From this co-operation of God and the soul spring forth abundant fruits of sanctification.

261. We may add here that all the conditions rendering our actions more meritorious (cf. n. 237), perfect at the same time the dispositions we must bring to the reception of the Sacraments, and consequently increase the measure of grace conferred upon us. We shall understand this better when we apply this principle to the Sacraments of Penance and Eucharist.

III. *The Dispositions Required to Profit Well by the Sacrament of Penance* [1]

The Sacrament of Penance purifies our souls in the Blood of Jesus Christ, provided that we are well disposed, that our confession is sincere, and that our contrition is true and genuine.

1° CONFESSION

262. A) A word concerning grave sins. We speak but incidentally of the accusation of *grave faults*. This we have treated at length in our Moral Theology. [2] Should one that is tending toward perfection have the misfortune, in a moment of weakness, of committing any mortal sins, he should confess them clearly and sincerely, mentioning them at the very beginning of his confession and not half-concealing them midst a multitude of venial sins. He should state in all sincerity and humility the *number* and *species* of these sins, and the *causes* that brought them about, and ask

---

[1] Besides consulting treatises of Theology, see: BEAUDENOM, *Spiritual Progress;* ST. FRANCIS DE SALES, *Introduction to a Devout Life*, P. I, C. 19; P. II, C. 19; FABER, *Growth in Holiness*, C. XIX, XX; MANNING, *Sin and its Consequences, The Love of Jesus for Penitent Sinners;* TISSOT, *Profiting by Our Faults;* MOTHER MARY LOYOLA, *First Confession;* MARMION, *Christ the Life of the Soul*, P. I!, C. IV.

[2] *Syn. theol. moral.*, *De Pænitentia*, n. 242 and foll.

his confessor most earnestly for the *remedies* that will work a cure. He must, above all, have a *deep sorrow* for sin together with a *firm purpose* of avoiding in the future, not only these sins themselves, but also their *occasions* and *causes*.

Once these sins have been forgiven, he must keep within his soul *an abiding* and a *lively sense of sorrow*, and a sincere desire to *repair* the evil done, by an austere and mortified life, by an ardent and self-sacrificing love. An isolated fault immediately repaired, even though grave, is not for long an obstacle to our spiritual progress.

263.   B) Deliberate Venial Faults. [1] Venial faults are of two kinds : those that are deliberate, that is, committed with full knowledge that one is about to displease God and with a deliberate selfish preference for a created good to the divine will.   The others are such as are committed through *surprise, fickleness, frailty, lack of vigilance or courage*, and regretted on the spot, with the firm purpose of committing them no more.

Sins of the first category are a very serious obstacle to perfection, specially if the sins recur frequently and the heart is attached to them, for example, wilfully keeping petty *grudges*, habitually forming *rash judgments*, speaking *ill* of others, yielding to *the attraction* of inordinate, natural *affections*, stubbornly holding to one's own judgment, to one's own will.   These are cords that bind us to earth and prevent us from taking our flight toward God.   When one wilfully refuses Almighty God the sacrifice of one's tastes, of one's way, one can hardly expect of Him those choice graces which alone can lead to perfection.   Such faults should be corrected at any cost.   The better to achieve this task, we must take up successively the different *species* or categories of faults, for example, faults against charity, then those against humility, against the virtue of religion, etc. We must make a full avowal of them in confession, chiefly of those more humiliating to us, as well as of the *causes* that make us fall into such sins.   Lastly, we must make firm resolutions to avoid these causes entirely.   In this manner, each confession will be a step forward in the way of perfection.

264.   C) Sins of Frailty. Having once overcome deliberate faults, we set upon those proceeding from *frailty*, not indeed to avoid them altogether — this is impossible —

---

[1] Meyer, S. J., *The Science of the Saints*, Vol. I, C. XIII.

but gradually to diminish their number. Here again, we must have recourse to the same expedient of *dividing the task*. We may, no doubt, accuse all the venial sins we remember; but this we do rapidly and then we stress some particular faults; for instance, distractions in prayer, failings against purity of intention, lack of charity.

In the examination of conscience and in confession we shall not content ourselves with saying : "I have been distracted in my prayers" — which tells the confessor absolutely nothing — but we shall rather put things thus : "I have been distracted or careless during such or such a spiritual exercise, the reason being, that I failed to recollect myself properly before beginning it," or "because I had not the courage to repel at once and with determination the first vagaries of my mind," or again "because after having repelled distractions for a while I did not persevere and remain steadfast in the effort."

At other times we shall accuse ourselves of having been long distracted on account of an attachment to study or to a friend, or owing to some petty grievance.

The accusation of the causes of our sins will suggest the *remedy* and the *resolution* to be taken.

265. In order *to insure the effectiveness of the confession*, whether it be question of deliberate faults or not, we shall end the accusation by formulating *the resolution* for the coming week or fortnight of "combatting in earnest this source of distraction, that attachment, such preoccupation." In the next confession we shall be careful to render an account of our efforts, for instance : "I had taken such resolution, I kept it so many days, or kept it only in this regard, but I failed in this or that point."

Evidently, confession practiced in this manner, will not be a matter of routine but will on the contrary, mark a step forward. The grace of absolution will confirm the resolution taken and not only will it increase habitual grace within us, but it will also multiply our energies, causing us to avoid in the future a certain number of venial faults and to grow in virtue with a greater measure of success.

2° Contrition

266. In frequent confessions stress must be laid on *contrition* and on the *purpose of amendment* which necessarily goes with it. We must ask for it with earnestness and excite it in ourselves by the consideration of supernatural motives. These are always substantially the same, even if they vary with different souls and with the different faults accused. The general motives for contrition have their source in *God* and in the *soul*. We shall briefly indicate them.

267. A) *As regards God*, sin, no matter how trivial, is an offense against Him; it is resistance to His will; it constitutes an act of ingratitude toward the most loving and most lovable of fathers and benefactors — ingratitude that is all the more hurtful because we are His privileged friends. Hence God says to us: " For if my enemy had reviled me, I would have borne with it..., but thou a man of one mind, my guide, and my familiar, who didst take sweet meats together with me, in the house of God we walked with consent. "[1]   Let us lend a willing ear to His well-merited reproaches, and hide our face in shame and humiliation. Let us hearken also to the voice of Jesus, telling us that because of our transgressions His Chalice on the Mount of Olives was made more bitter and His agony more terrible. Then out of the depths of our misery let us humbly ask for pardon : " Have mercy on me, O God, according to Thy great mercy... Wash me yet more from my iniquity... "[2]

268. B) *As regards the soul*, venial sin does not indeed of itself lessen sanctifying grace, but it does affect the existing intimacy of the soul with God. What a loss this is! It brings to a standstill or, at least, it hampers our spiritual activity, clogging, as it were, the fine mechanism of the spiritual life. It weakens *the soul's power* for good by intensifying the love of pleasure. Above all, if it be deliberate, it *predisposes to mortal sin*, for in many matters, especially in what concerns purity, the line of demarcation between venial and mortal sin is so narrow, and the charm of forbidden pleasure so alluring, that the borders of mortal sin are easily crossed. Every sin committed means a yielding to and therefore a strengthening of some impulse of our lower nature; it means likewise a weakening of our wills and a lesser grant of grace. When this is repeated, it is easy to understand how the way is prepared for mortal sin.

When we ponder over these consequences of venial sin, it is not difficult to conceive a sincere regret for our negligences and a desire to avoid them in the future. [3]   In order

---

[1] *Ps.* LIV, 13-15.
[2] *Ps.* L. Meditation on this psalm is a splendid preparation for confession.
[3] BEAUDENOM, *op. cit.*, t. II, ch. II.

to have this good purpose take an actual, definite form, it is well to make it bear upon the means that should be taken to reduce the chances of subsequent falls, according to the method we have indicated above (N. 265).

269. In order to insure still further the presence of contrition, it is a good practice to accuse one of the more serious faults of the past for which we are surely sorry, especially a fault that is of the same species as the venial sins we deplore. Here we must be on our guard against two defects : *routine* and *negligence*. The first would make of this accusation a mere empty formula devoid of any real sentiment of sorrow; the other would render us unmindful of any actual regret for the venial sins presently accused.

The practice of confession carried out in this manner, the advice of the confessor, and above all, the *cleansing power of absolution* will be effectual means of disentangling ourselves from the meshes of sin and of advancing in virtue.

IV. *Dispositions Required to Profit Well by the Sacrament of the Eucharist* [1]

270. The Holy Eucharist is both a *sacrament* and a *sacrifice*. These two elements are most closely united; for the Sacrifice of the Mass makes present the Victim which we receive in Holy Communion. Communion is not, according to the common teaching, an *essential* part of the sacrifice; it is, however, an *integral* part since it is by virtue of communion that we partake in the sentiments of the victim and share in the fruits of the sacrifice.

The essential difference between the one and the other is that the sacrifice refers *directly to the glory of God* whilst the sacrament's *immediate end is the sanctification of our souls*. These two objects are but one in reality, for to know and love God is to glorify Him. Each, therefore, contributes to our spiritual progress.

1° THE SACRIFICE OF THE MASS AS A MEANS OF SANCTIFICATION [2]

271. A) Its Effects. a) The Sacrifice of the Mass first of all glorifies God and glorifies Him in a perfect manner,

---

[1] St. THOM., III, q. LXXIX; SUAREZ, disp. LXIII; DALGAIRNS, *Holy Communion;* HUGON, O. P., *La Sainte Eucharistie;* HEDLEY, *The Holy Eucharist.*

[2] Besides the works already cited, cf. BENEDICT XIV *De ss. Missæ Sacrificio;* BONA, *De Sacrificio Missæ;* LE GAUDIER, *op. cit.* P. I, sect. 10ª; GIHR, *The Holy Sacrifice of the Mass;* OLIER, *La Journée chrétienne,* Occupations intérieures pendant le saint sacrifice, p. 49-65; CHAIGNON, S. J., *The Holy Sacrifice;* BACUEZ,

for here Jesus Christ, through the ministry of the priest offers again to His Father all the acts of adoration, gratitude and love which He once offered on Calvary, — acts which have an infinite moral value. In offering Himself as victim, He proclaims in a manner most significant God's sovereign domain over all things — this is *adoration;* in giving Himself to God in acknowledgement of His benefices, Christ offers to Him a praise equal to His gifts — this is thanksgiving, and it constitutes the eucharistic worship. Nothing can prevent this effect from taking place, not even the unworthiness of the minister, [1] for the worth of the sacrifice does not depend essentially upon the one through whose ministry it is offered, but on the worth of the victim and on the dignity of the chief priest — no other than Jesus Christ Himself.

This is what the Council of Trent teaches in declaring that this unspotted offering cannot be stained by the unworthiness or malice of those who offer it; that in this divine sacrifice is contained and immolated, in an unbloody manner, the same Christ that offered Himself in a bloody manner upon the altar of the Cross. Hence, adds the Council, it is the same victim, the same sacrificing-priest who offers Himself now through the ministry of priests and who once offered Himself upon the Cross. There is no difference, save in the manner of offering. [2] Thus when we assist at Mass, and all the more when we celebrate Mass, we render unto God Almighty all the homage due to Him and that in a manner most perfect, since we make our own the homage of Jesus, Priest and Victim.

Let no one say that this has nothing to do with our sanctification. The truth is, that when we glorify God, He is moved with love toward us, and the more we attend to His glory the more He attends to our spiritual concerns. By fulfilling our duties to Him in union with the Victim on the altar, we do a signal work for our own sanctification.

272. b) The Divine Sacrifice has besides a *propitiatory* effect by the very virtue of its celebration (*ex opere operato,* as theologians say). It means that this Sacrifice, by offering to the Almighty the homage due to Him together with an

---

S. S., *Du divin sacrifice;* E. VANDEUR, O. S. B., *The Holy Mass Explained;* CARD. VAUGHAN, *The Mass ;* HEDLEY, *Retreat,* C. 24; *Retreat for Priests,* C. 13; *A Bishop and his Flock,* C. 10; DUNNEY, *The Mass;* MARMION, *Christ the Life of the Soul,* P. II, C. VII.
    [1] In other words, this effect is produced, *ex opere operato,* by the very virtue of the sacrifice.
    [2] Sess. XXII, cap. I-II.

adequate atonement for sin, inclines Him to bestow upon us, not sanctifying grace directly (this is the effect proper to the sacrament), but *actual grace*, which produces in us true repentance and contrition, thus securing for us the remission of even the greatest sins. [1]

At the same time the Sacrifice of the Mass is *satisfactory* in the sense that it remits *without fail* to repentant sinners at least part of the *temporal punishment* due to sin.   This is why the Holy Synod adds that Mass can be offered not only for the sins and satisfactions and needs of the living, but also for the relief of those that have died in the Lord without having sufficiently expiated their faults. [2]

We can easily see how this twofold effect of the Sacrifice, propitiatory and satisfactory, contributes to our progress in the Christian life.   The great obstacle to union with God is sin. By obtaining pardon for it and by causing its last vestiges to vanish, a closer and more intimate union with God is prepared : " *Blessed are the clean of heart : for they shall see God.* " [3]

How comforting to poor sinners thus to see the wall of separation crumble down! — a wall that had kept them from the enjoyment of divine life!

273.   c) Holy Mass produces also *ex opere operato* an *impetratory* effect and thus obtains for us all the graces we need for our sanctification.

Sacrifice is *prayer in action* and He Who with unspeakable groanings makes supplication for us at the altar is the same whose prayers are always heard : " He was heard because of His reverence. " [4]   Thus the Church, the authoritative interpreter of the divine mind, prays there unceasingly, in union with Jesus, Priest and Victim, " *through Jesus Christ Our Lord,* " for all the graces which her members need, for health of body and soul, " *for their longed-for salvation and well-being,* " [5] for their spiritual growth, asking for her faithful children, specially in the *Collect*, the particular grace proper to each feast.   Whoever enters into this stream of liturgical prayer with the required dispositions is sure to obtain for himself and others the most abundant graces.

It is clear, then, that all the effects of the Holy Sacrifice concur to our sanctification — this all the more effectively,

---

[1] This is the teaching of the Council of *Trent*, sess. XXII, c. II.
[2] *Loc. cit.* — [3] *Matth.*, V, 8. — [4] *Hebr.*, V, 7. — [5] Canon of Mass.

since we do not pray alone therein, but in union with the whole Church and above all in union with its invisible Head, Jesus Christ, Priest and Victim, Who, renewing the offering of Calvary, demands in virtue of His Blood and His supplications that His merits and His satisfactions be applied to us.

274. B) **Dispositions required to profit by the Holy Sacrifice.** [1] What dispositions should we have in order to profit by such a powerful means of sanctification? The fundamental and all-inclusive disposition is that of humble and trusting union whith the dispositions manifested by Christ on the Cross and renewed now on the Altar. We must strive to share His sentiments of religion and make them our own. In this way we can all carry out what the Pontifical demands of priests : " Realize what you do, and imitate the Victim you offer." And this is precisely what the Church through her Liturgy urges us to do. [2]

275. a) In the *Mass of the Catechumens* (as far as the Offertory, exclusive) she would have us form sentiments of penitence and contrition (the *Confiteor, Aufer a nobis, Oramus te, Kyrie eleison*); of adoration and gratitude (the *Gloria in excelsis*); of supplication (the *Collect*); and of sincere faith (the *Epistle, Gospel and Creed*).

b) The grand drama follows : 1) *The offering of the victim at the Offertory* for the salvation of the whole human race, " *For our salvation and that of the entire world"*; the offering of the Christian people together with the principal victim, " *We beg of Thee, O Lord, in humble spirit and with contrite hearts,* " followed by a prayer to the Most Holy Trinity to deign to bless and receive the offering of the entire mystical body of Christ. 2) The *Preface* heralds the great action itself. At the *Canon* wherein the *mystic immolation* of the victim is to be renewed, the Church summons us to join with the Angels and Saints, but chiefly the Incarnate Word, in thanking God Almighty, in proclaiming His Holiness, in imploring His help for the Church, for its visible head, its bishops and faithful children, and particularly those assisting at the Sacrifice and those to whom we are bound by closer ties of love.

---

[1] The fruits of the Mass, described above, are obtained in various degrees according to the inscrutable decrees of God, first by the celebrant, then by those for whom the Holy Sacrifice is offered, by those whom the priest remembers at the altar, and finally by all those who assist at Mass. We speak here only of these last.

[2] Cf. E. VANDEUR, O. S. B., *The Holy Mass; The Following of Christ*, Bk. IV, C. 8-9.

Then the priest, uniting in fellowship with the Blessed
Virgin, with the Holy Apostles, Martyrs, and all the Saints,
moves in spirit to the Last Supper, becomes one with the
Sovereign Priest, and with Him utters once more the words
Jesus spoke in the Cenacle. Obedient to His voice, the
Word-made-flesh descends upon the altar with His Body
and Blood, silently adoring and praying in His own name
and in ours. The Christian people bow in adoration of the
Divine Victim; they unite with our Lord's own sentiments,
His acts of adoration, His requests, and they strive to im-
molate themselves with Him by offering their own small
sacrifices " *through Him, and with Him and in Him.* "

c) The *Our Father* begins the preparation for *Communion*. Members of Christ's mystical body, we repeat the
prayer He Himself taught us. We thus offer with Him our
acts of religious homage and our entreaties, asking most of
all, for that eucharistic bread that will deliver us from all
evil, and will give us, together with the pardon of our sins,
peace of soul and abiding union with Christ : " *And never
permit that I be ever separated from Thee.* " Then, like the
Centurion, protesting their unworthiness and begging
humble pardon, the priest and the faithful eat the Body and
drink the Blood of Christ. Priest and people are thus united
most intimately to Jesus, to His inmost soul and through
Him to the very Godhead, to the Most Blessed Trinity.

The mystery of union is completed. We are but one
with Jesus, and since He is but one with the Father, the
sacerdotal prayer of the Saviour at the Last Supper is
realized : " *I in them, and thou in me : that they may be made
perfect in one.* " [1]

276. d) But one thing remains — to thank the Almighty
for such a stupendous gift. This is done at the Post-
communion and the prayers that follow. The blessing of
the priest bestows on us the affluent riches of the Triune
God. The last Gospel recalls to us the glory of the Incarnate Word, who has come once more to dwell among us,
whom we carry within us full of grace and truth, that we
may throughout the day draw life from life's Source, and
live a life like unto His.

It is evident that to assist at Mass or to celebrate it with
dispositions such as these is to sanctify ourselves and to
nurture in the best possible manner that spiritual life that is
within us.

---

[1] *John* XVII, 23.

2° HOLY COMMUNION AS A MEANS OF SANCTIFICATION [1]

277. A) Its Effects. The Holy Eucharist, as a *sacrament*, produces in us an increase of habitual grace, *ex opere operato*, by its own virtue. In fact, it has been instituted to be the *food* of our souls : " *My flesh is meat indeed, and my blood is drink indeed.* " [2] Its effects are, therefore, analogous to those of material food ; it maintains, increases, and repairs our spiritual forces, causing at the same time a joy that, if not always sensible, is nevertheless real. Jesus Himself, whole and entire, is our food ; His Body, His Blood, His Soul, His Divinity. He is united to us to transform us into Himself ; this union is at once *real* and *moral*, a *transforming* union, and by nature *permanent*.

Such is Christ's doctrine as found in St. John's Gospel and summarized by Father Lebreton : [3] " The union of Christ and the Christian as well as the life-giving transformation resulting therefrom are consummated in the Eucharist. Here there is no longer a question of adhering to Christ merely by faith, nor of being incorporated into Him through Baptism. This is a new union that is at once most real and most spiritual by which, it may be said, we are made not only one spirit but in a sense one flesh with Christ. " He that eateth my flesh and drinketh my blood, abideth in me and I in him. " [4]

" This union is so intimate that Our Lord does not hesitate to say : " As I live by the Father, so he that eateth me the same also shall live by me. " [5] No doubt, this is only an analogy ; yet if the analogy is to hold, we must see here not merely a moral union based on a community of sentiments, but a real physical union which implies the mingling of two lives or rather the sharing by the Christian in the very life of Christ. " This we shall try to explain.

278. a) This union is *real*. It is a matter of faith, according to the Council of Trent, that the Holy Eucharist contains truly, really, and substantially the Body and Blood of Jesus Christ, with His Soul and His Divinity — hence

---

[1] St. THOM., q. 79; TANQUEREY, *Syn. Thecl. Dogm.*, t. III, p. 619-628; DAL-GAIRNS, *Holy Communion*, p. 154 and foll.; H. MOUREAU, *Dict. de Théol. (Mangenot)*, under the word, *Communion;* P. HUGON, *La Sainte Eucharistie*, p. 240 and foll.; MARMION, *Christ the Life of the Soul*, *P.* II. *C.* VIII.; LEJEUNE, *Holy Communion;* HEDLEY, *The Holy Eucharist;* MOTHER LOYOLA, *Welcome; Spiritual Combat*, c. 53-57; *Introd. to a Devout Life*, *P.* II, *C.* XXI; THE FOLLOWING OF CHRIST, *B.* IV; *Approved Prayer-Books*.

[2] *John*, VI, 55.
[3] *Les Origines du dogme de la Trinité*, 1910, p. 403.
[4] *John*, VI, 57. — [5] *John*, VI, 58.

Christ whole and entire. [1]   Therefore, when we receive Holy
Communion we receive veiled under the sacred species the
real and physical Body and Blood of Christ, together with
His Soul and His Divinity.   We are, then, not only the
tabernacles but the ciboriums wherein Christ lives, where
the angels come and adore Him, and where we should join
the heavenly Spirits in adoration.   More, there exists
between Jesus and ourselves a union similar to that existing
between food and him who eats it — with this difference,
however, that it is Jesus that transforms us into Himself,
and not we who transform Him into our substance.   The
superior being is the one to assimilate the inferior. [2]   It is
a union that tends to subject our flesh more and more to the
spirit and to make it more chaste — a union that sows in
the flesh the seed of immortality : " He that eateth my flesh
and drinketh my blood hath everlasting life, and I will
raise him up in the last day. " [3]

279.   b) To this real union is added another union,
spiritual in its nature, most intimate in its character, most
transforming in its effects.   1) It is most *intimate*, most
sanctifying. The soul of Christ, in fact, unites with ours
to make us but *one heart and one mind with Him* — " *cor
unum et anima una.* " His *imagination* and His *memory*, so
righteous and so *holy*, unite themselves to our own imagination and our own memory to discipline them and turn them
toward God and the things of God, by bringing their activities to bear on the remembrance of His benefactions, on
His rapturous beauty, on His inexhaustible goodness.   His
intelligence, true light of the soul, enlightens our minds with
the radiance of faith ; it causes us to see and value all things
as God sees and values them.   It is then that we realize the
vanity of worldly goods and the folly of worldly standards ;
it is then that we relish the Gospel truths, so obscure before
because opposed to our natural instincts.   His *will* so
strong, so constant, so generous, comes to correct our weakness, our inconstancy, our egotism, by communicating to our
wills its own Divine energy, so that we can say with
St. Paul : " *I can do all things in Him who strengtheneth
me.* " [4]   We feel now that effort will become easy, that

---

[1] Sess. XIII, can. 1.
[2] This is the remark made by St. AUGUSTINE (*Confessions*, lib. VII, c. 10, n. 16,
P. L., XXXII, 742).   He puts these words on the lips of the Lord : " I am the
food of great souls, grow and you shall be able to eat of me ; but you shall not
change me into yourself like you do material food, it will be you that shall be
changed into me. "
[3] *John*, VI, 35. — [4] *Philip.*, IV, 13.

temptation will find us immovable, that steadfastness will no longer be above our strength, since we are not alone, but cling to Christ like the ivy to the oak, and thus *share* in His power.   His heart, aglow with love for God and for souls, comes to enkindle our own, so cold toward God, so tender toward creatures.   Like the disciples of Emmaus we say to ourselves : " *Was not our heart burning within us, whilst He spoke to us in the way?* " [1]   It is then that under the action of this divine fire we become conscious at times of a well-nigh irresistible impulse toward good, at others, of a sober yet firm *determination* to do all things, to undergo all sufferings for God and to refuse Him nothing.

280.   1) It is evident that a union such as this is truly *transforming*.   Little by little our thoughts, our ideas, our convictions, and our judgments undergo a change.   Instead of weighing the worth of things with the world's standards, we make the thoughts and the views of Jesus Christ our own ; we lovingly accept the maxims of the Gospel ; we continually ask ourselves the question : What would Jesus do if He were in my place? [2]

2) The same is true of our *desires*, of our *choices*.   Realizing that both *self* and the world are in the wrong, that the truth abides only in Jesus, the Eternal Wisdom, we no longer desire anything but what He desires, that is, God's glory, our own salvation and that of our brethren ; we will only what He wills, " *not my will, but thine be done;* " and even when this holy will nails us to the Cross, we accept it with all our heart, certain that it bids fair for our spiritual welfare and that of our fellows.

3) Our *heart* in like manner gradually frees itself from its more or less conscious egotism, from its lower natural affections and attachments, that it may love God and souls in God, more ardently, more generously, more passionately.   Now we love no longer divine consolations, be they ever so sweet, but God Himself ; no longer the comfort of finding ourselves midst those we love, hut rather the good we can do them.   We live now, but we live a more intense life,

---

[1] *Luke*, XXIV, 32.
[2] " We become one with Jesus.   That is, we have the same " will " as He has. What He loves, we love ; what He desires, we desire ; what He says ought to be done, we long to do and do ; His judgments are ours ; His behaviour under every kind of condition, under all circumstances of persons and occurrences, is the behaviour we are always striving to reproduce in our own life and action.   Thus, it is no exaggeration to say that in the Holy Communion, Jesus Christ gives us His own Heart, taking our heart away.   His Heart is the Heart of chartiy, of purity, of sacrifice. " BISHOP HEDLEY, *Retreat*, p. 279.

a life more supernatural, more divine than we did in the past. It is no longer *self*, the *old Adam*, that lives, thinks and acts, but Jesus Himself, His spirit, that lives within us and vivifies our own : " *I live, now not I, but Christ liveth in me.*" [1]

281. c) This *spiritual* union can be as *lasting* as we wish, as Our Lord Himself testifies : " *He that eateth my flesh and drinketh my blood, abideth in me and I in him.*" [2]   He desires to tarry with us eternally.   It rests with us, His grace helping, ever to remain united to Him.

How is this union maintained?   Some authors have thought with *Schram* [3] that Christ's soul folds itself, as it were, in the center of our own soul there to remain constantly. — This would be a miracle most extraordinary, for Christ's soul is ever united to His body and this latter disappears with the sacramental species.   We cannot, therefore, accept this opinion, since God does not multiply miracles without necessity.

If, however, His soul does depart from us together with His body, His *divinity* remains with us as long as we are in the state of grace.   More, His *sacred humanity* united to His divinity maintains with the soul a special union.   This can be explained theologically as follows : The Spirit of Jesus, in other words, *the Holy Ghost*, dwelling within *the human soul of Christ*, remains in us in virtue of the special relationship we have entered into with Jesus Christ by sacramental Communion, and produces therein interior dispositions similar to those of the Holy Soul of Christ. At the request of Jesus, Whose prayers for us are unceasing, the Holy Ghost grants us more abundant and more efficacious actual graces.   With a special care, He preserves us from temptations; He causes in us movements of grace, directs our soul and its faculties, speaks to our heart, strengthens our will, rekindles our love, and thus perpetuates within our soul the effects of sacramental Communion. To enjoy these privileges, however, one must evidently practice interior recollection, hearken attentively to the voice of God, and be ready to comply with His least desire. Thus Sacramental Communion is complemented by a *spiritual Communion* which renders its effects more lasting.

282.   d) This communion brings about *a special union with the Three Divine Persons of the Holy Trinity.* [4]   In virtue of the indwelling of each Divine Person within the

---

[1] *Galat.*, II, 20. — [2] *John*, VI, 56. — [3] *Instit. theol. Mysticæ*, § 153.
[4] Cfr. BERNADOT, *De l'Eucharistie à la Trinité*.

other — circumincession — the Eternal Word does not come alone into the soul; He comes with the Father forever generating His Son; He comes with the Holy Ghost forever proceeding from the mutual embrace of the Father and the Son : " If any one love me, my Father will love him and we will come to him and we will make our abode with him." [1] No doubt, the Three Divine Persons are already in us by grace, but at the moment of Communion they are present within us because of another, a special title : as we are then physically united to the Incarnate Word, the Three Divine Persons also are, through Him and by Him, united to us, and They love us now as They love the Word-made-Flesh, Whose members we are. Bearing Jesus in our hearts, with Him we bear the Father and the Holy Ghost. Holy Communion, then, is an anticipation of Heaven, and, if we are possessed of a lively faith, we shall realize the truth contained in the words of the Imitation, that " *to be with Jesus is a sweet paradise.*" [2]

283. B) Dispositions to profit well by the reception of the Eucharist. [3] Since the object of the Eucharist is to effect an intimate, transforming, and permanent union with Christ and God, whatever in our *preparation* and *thanksgiving* fosters that union will increase the effects of Holy Communion. **a)** The *preparation* will have the form of an *anticipated union* with Our Lord. We take for granted the union of the soul with God by sanctifying grace as already existing; without it, Communion would constitute a sacrilege. [4]

1) There is first the more perfect accomplishment of all our duties of state in union with Jesus and in order to please Him. This is the best means of drawing unto us Him Whose whole life was a continual act of filial obedience to the Father. " *For I do always the things that please Him.*" [5] This practice we explained in N. 229.

2) The second disposition should be a *sincere humility*, based, on the one hand, on the exalted sanctity of Jesus Christ and, on the other, upon our lowliness and our unworthiness : " *Lord, I am not worthy...*" This humility creates, so to speak, a void within the soul, emptying it of its

---

[1] *John*, XIV, 23. — [2] *The Imitation of Christ*, Bk. II, C. 8.

[3] **Mother M. Loyola**, *Welcome;* Lejeune, *Holy Communion; Approved Prayer-Books.*

[4] Hence, were one conscious of mortal sin, it would be imperative, first of all, to confess it with contrition and humility of heart, not being content with an act of contrition no matter how perfect. Cf. AD. TANQUEREY, *Syn. theol. Dogm.*, l. III, N. 652-654.

[5] *John*, VIII, 29.

egotism, its pride, its presumption. Now, the more we empty ourselves of self, the more ready we make the soul to let itself be inhabited and possessed by God.

3) To this humility must be added *an ardent desire* to be united to God in the Eucharist. Realizing our helplessness and our poverty, we should long for Him Who alone can give strength to our weakness, enrich us with His treasures and fill the void within our hearts. Such a desire will, by dilating the soul, throw it wide open to Him Who in turn desires to give Himself to us : " *With desire I have desired to eat this pasch with you.* " [1]

284. b) The best *thanksgiving* will be to prolong our union with Jesus.

1) It should begin by an act of silent *adoration*,[2] of self-abasement and *complete surrender* of ourselves to Him Who being God, gives Himself all to us : " *O Hidden God, devoutly I adore Thee... To Thee my heart I bow with bended knee.* " [3] In union with Mary, the most perfect adorer of Jesus Christ, we shall abase ourselves before the majesty of the Godhead to bless it, praise it, thank it, first, in the Word-made-Flesh, and then with Him and through Him, in the Most Blessed Trinity. " *My soul doth magnify the Lord... He Who is mighty hath done great things unto me, and holy is His name.* " [4] Nothing so enables Jesus to take complete possession of the soul, to penetrate its very depths, as this act of self-abasement. This is the manner in which we poor creatures can gives ourselves to Him Who is All. We shall give Him whatever of good is in us since all this good proceeds from Him and has never ceased to be His. We shall further offer Him our miseries that He may consume them with the fire of His love and place in their stead His perfect dispositions. What a wondrous exchange!

285. 2) Then take place sweet colloquies between the soul and the Divine Guest : " *Speak, Lord, for thy servant heareth... Give me understanding that I may know thy testimonies... Incline my heart unto the words of thy mouth...* " This is the acceptable time to listen attentively to Our Master and Our Friend, to speak to Him with

[1] *Luke* XXII, 15.
[2] Many, forgetting this first act, begin at once to ask for favors without considering the fact that our requests will be all the better received, if first of all, we render our homage to Him Who honors us with His presence.
[3] *Hymn of* St. Thomas. — [4] *Luke*, I, 46 and foll.

reverence, with candor, with love.   This is the moment in which Jesus instils into us His dispositions and His virtues. We must lay our soul open to the divine communications and not only receive them, but also relish them and assimilate them.   That this communion may not degenerate into a mere form, it will be good to vary, if not daily at least from time to time, the subject of our colloquies.   This can be done by choosing now one virtue and then another, or by the loving consideration of some Gospel-texts, begging Our Lord for help to understand and relish them, and for grace to live by them.

286.   3) One must not fail to thank God for the lights and the loving sentiments He has vouchsafed to us, to thank Him, too, for the very darkness and weariness of soul in which He has at times allowed us to remain.   Even these are profitable to us unto humility, unto the acknowledgment of our unworthiness to receive divine favors; profitable, because they enable us to adhere more frequently by will to Him Who even in the midst of our aridity, pours into us in a hidden and mysterious manner His life and His virtues. We ask Him to communicate to our souls His action and His life.   " *O Jesus living in Mary, come and live in thy servants.* " [1]   We beg Him to accept and transform the little good within us : " *Take, Lord, and accept my liberty.* " [2]

287.   4) We promise to make the *sacrifices required* to reform and transform our lives, especially in this or that particular point, and conscious of our weakness we beg earnestly for the courage of carrying this promise into effect. [3]   This point is of capital importance : each Communion should be received with this end in view, to advance in the practice of some particular virtue.

288.   5) This is likewise the moment *to pray* for all who are dear to us, for the vast interests of the Church, for the intentions of the Sovereign Pontiff, for bishops and priests. Let us have no fear of making our prayer too universal : this rather gives assurance that we shall be heard.

Finally, we conclude by asking Our Lord to vouchsafe us the grace of abiding in Him as He does in us, the grace of performing all our actions in union with Him, in a spirit of thanksgiving.   We entrust to the Blessed Virgin that same Jesus she guarded so well, in order that

---

[1] Prayer of *Father de Condren* completed by *Father Olier.*
[2] Prayer of *S. Ignatius* in the Contemplation on the love of God.
[3] On the spirit of a victim cf. L. CAPELLE, S. J., *Les âmes généreuses.*

she may aid us in making Him grow in our hearts. Thus
strengthened by prayer we pass on to action.

CONCLUSION

289. We have, then, at our disposal three great means
of sustaining and expanding that Christian life God has so
bountifully begotten within us — means of giving ourselves
as whole-heartedly to God as He has given Himself to us :

1) *Fighting* relentlessly and fearlessly against our
spiritual foes.   With the help of God and the aid of
all the heavenly protectors He has given us, certain
victory and the further strengthening of our spiritual life
are assured.

2) *Sanctifying* all *our actions*, even the most commonplace.   Through the oft-repeated offering of them to God,
we acquire numberless merits, add largely day by day to
our stock of grace, and strengthen our title to heaven, the
while we make reparation and atone for our faults.

3) The *sacraments*, received with right and fervent dispositions, add to our personal merits a rich bounty of grace
which proceeds from Christ's own merits.   Approaching so
frequently the sacrament of Penance and communicating
daily as we do, it is in our power, if we will, to become
saints.   Jesus Christ came and still comes to us to communicate with largess His life to us : " *I am come that they may
have life and may have it more abundantly.*" [1]

Our task is but to lay our souls open to receive this divine
life, to foster it and make it grow by our constant participation in the dispositions, the virtues, and the sacrifices of
Jesus Christ.   At last the moment will come when transformed into Him, having no other thoughts, no other sentiments, no other motives than His own, we shall be able to
repeat the words of S. Paul : " *I live, now not I, but Christ
liveth in me.*"

SUMMARY OF THE SECOND CHAPTER

290. At the close of this chapter, the most important
of this First Part, we can understand better the nature of
the Christian life.

1º It is a real *participation in God's life,* for God lives in
us and we in Him. He *lives in us* really — in the Unity of

---

[1] *John,* X, 10.

His nature and in the Trinity of His persons. Nor is He
inactive there. He creates in the soul a complete supernatural organism that enables it to live a life, not indeed equal,
but truly similar, to His, a Godlike life. More, it is He
Who gives it movement by His actual grace, He Who helps
us to make our acts meritorious, He Who rewards these
acts by a further infusion of habitual grace. *We* also *live
in Him* and for Him, for we are His co-workers. By the
aid of His grace, we freely accept the divine impulse,
co-operate with it and by it triumph over our enemies,
acquire merit, and prepare ourselves for the rich effusion of
grace given to us by the Sacraments. Withal, we must not
forget that even our free consent itself is the work of His
grace, and this is the reason why we refer to Him the merit
attached to our good works, living *unto* Him, just as we
live *by* Him and *in* Him.

291. 2° This life is also a *participation in the life of
Jesus*, for Christ lives in us and we live in Him. *He lives
in us* not only as the Father lives in us — as God, but He
also lives in us, as the God-man. He is, in fact, the *head of
a mystical body* whose members we are, and from Him it is
that we receive movement and life. He lives within us in a
still more mysterious manner, for through His merits and
prayers He causes the Holy Ghost to create within us dispositions like those which the same Divine Spirit produced in
His own soul. He lives in us really and physically at the
moment of Communion, and through His divine Spirit
communicates to us His sentiments and His virtues. *We
too live in Him.* We are incorporated into Him and we
freely receive His divine impulse. It is likewise by the free
action of our wills that we imitate His virtues, even though
our success comes from the grace He merited for us.
Lastly, it is freely that we adhere to Him *as* the branch to
the vine and open our souls to receive that divine life He
so liberally infuses into us. As we have all from Him, it is
by Him and *unto Him* that we live, only too glad to give
ourselves to Him as He gives Himself to us, our one regret
being that the manner of our giving *is* so imperfect.

292. 3° This life is, in a certain measure, also a
participation in Mary's life, or, as Father Olier says, a
participation in *the life of Jesus living in Mary*. Desiring
that His Holy Mother be a living image of Himself,
Jesus through His merits and prayers communicates
to her His divine Spirit, Who makes her share to a
preëminent degree in His dispositions and His virtues. It

is thus that He *lives in Mary*, and, since He wills that His Mother be also our Mother, He wills that she engender us in spirit. Giving us spiritual life (of course as a *secondary* cause), Mary not only makes us share in Jesus' life, but in her own as well. At the same time, then, that we participate in the life of Jesus, we participate in that of Mary — in other words, in the life of Jesus living in Mary. Such is the thought which the beautiful prayer of Father de Condren completed by Father Olier so well expresses : " *O Jesus, living in Mary, come and live in thy servants.* "

293. 4° Finally, this life is *a participation in the lives of the Saints of heaven and of those of earth.* As we have seen, the mystical body of Christ includes all those that have been incorporated into Him by Baptism and especially those enjoying the possession of grace and of heavenly glory. All the members of this mystical body share one common life, the life they receive from the Head, which is diffused in their souls by one and the same Spirit. We are then in all truth brethren, having our life from a common Father, a life spiritual, the plenitude whereof is in Christ Jesus, " *of whose fulness we have all received.* " Thus the Saints in heaven and those of earth have our spiritual welfare at heart and aid us in our struggle against the flesh, the world and the devil.

294. How consoling are these truths! Doubtless, the spiritual life here below is a warfare. Hell fights against us and finds allies in the world, and chiefly in our threefold concupiscence. But Heaven fights for us, and Heaven means not only the host of Angels and Saints, but Christ the victor over Satan, the Most Blessed Trinity living and reigning within the soul. We should, therefore, be full of confidence, being assured of victory, if only we distrust ourselves and rely upon God : " *I can do all things in Him Who strengtheneth me.* " [1]

---

[1] *Phil.*, IV, 13.

CHAPTER III.

The Perfection of the Christian Life

295. All life must perfect itself. This is true, above all, of the Christian life. It is by its very nature a *progressive* life, its completion being achieved only in Heaven. We must examine, then, in what *its perfection* consists, in order that we direct our steps more surely along its way. Since there exist erroneous conceptions and more or less incomplete ideas on this fundamental point, we shall begin by eliminating the *false notions* of Christian perfection, and then explain its *true nature.* [1]

I. False notions held by { Unbelievers
Worldlings
Devout Souls

II. The true notion { Consits in love
Presupposes sacrifice here on earth
Blends harmoniously this twofold element
Includes both the precepts and the counsels
Has degrees and limits

ART. I. FALSE NOTIONS CONCERNING PERFECTION.

These false notions are met with among unbelievers, worldlings, and even among devout souls.

296. 1° In the eyes of *unbelievers,* Christian perfection is no more than a *subjective phenomenon* without any corresponding reality.

A) Many of them study what they call mystical phenomena, only with malicious prejudices and without distinguishing the true from false mystics. Such are, *Max Nordau, J. H. Leuba, E. Murisier.* [2] According to them, the so-called perfection of the mystics is nothing more than a morbid phenomenon, a species of psycho-neurosis, a sort of exaltation based on religious feeling or even a special form of sexual love. This, they say, is shown by the terms spousals, spiritual marriage, kisses, embraces and divine caresses so frequently found in the writings of mystics.

---

[1] *Introd. to a Devout Life*, P. I, C. I-II; *Spiritual Combat*, C. I; FABER, *Growth in Holiness*, C. XXII-XXV; MEYER, *Science of the Saints*, Vol. I. C. XIX.

[2] MAX NORDAU, *Dégénérescence*, t. I, p. 115; J. H. LEUBA, *Psychological Study of Religion;* E. MURISIER, *Les maladies du sentiment religieux.*

It is evident that these authors, hardly acquainted with any but sensual love, have not the slightest conception of divine love; they are among those to whom the words of Our Lord can be aptly applied : " *Neither cast ye your pearls before swine.* " [1] No wonder then that other psychologists, such as *William James,* have pointed out that sexual instinct has nothing to do with sanctity ; that the true mystics have practiced heroic chastity, some having never experienced, or hardly so, the weaknesses of the flesh, others having overcome violent temptations by heroic means, for instance, throwing themselves among thorns. If they have, therefore, employed the language of human love, it is because every other falls short of terms to express the tenderness of divine love. [2] They have further shown by the whole tenor of their conduct, by the greatness of the works they have undertaken and brought to a successful end, that they were full of wisdom and poise and that at any rate we cannot but bless the neuroses that have given to the world an Aquinas and a Bonaventure, an Ignatius Loyola and a Xavier, a Teresa of Jesus and a John of the Cross, a Francis de Sales and a Jeanne de Chantal, a Vincent de Paul, a Mademoiselle Legras, a Berulle, an Olier, an Alphonsus Liguori, a Paul of the Cross.

297. B) Other unbelievers, such as William James and Maxime de Montmorand, [3] whilst doing justice to our mystics, yet doubt the objective reality of the phenomena they described. They acknowledge the marvelous effects caused in souls by the religious sentiment, an indomitable impulse toward good, an absolute devotedness to others. They recognize their supposed egotism to be in reality charity of the highest social character and productive of the most wholesome influence ; that their thirst for sufferings does not hinder them from enjoying unspeakable delights nor from radiating a measure of happiness to their surroundings. — Yet, they ask themselves the question : are not mystics the victims of auto-suggestion and hallucinations?

To this we answer that such salutary effects can only proceed from a proportionate cause ; that no real and lasting good can come from aught but what is true ; and that if Christian mystics have produced useful social works, it is because contemplation and the love of God, which have inspired such works, are not hallucinations but actual, living and working realities : " *By their fruits you shall know them.* " [4]

298. 2⁰ *Worldlings,* even when they have the faith, often entertain very false ideas concerning perfection or, as they call it, *devotion.*

A) Some look upon *devout* souls as hypocrites, who under the cover of religion, hide odious vices or political designs and ambitions, such as the desire to lord it over consciences and thus to control the world. This is the fallacy that identifies the thing with its *abuse.* The course of the present study will show us that frankness, honesty and humility are the true characteristics of piety.

---

[1] *Matth.,* VII, 6.
[2] W. JAMES, *The Varieties of Religious Experience,* p. 9-12.
[3] W. JAMES, *op. cit,;* M. DE MONTMORAND, *Psychologie des Mystiques,* 1920.
[4] *Matth.,* VII, 20.

299. **B)** Others see in piety a sort of *exaltation of feeling* and imagination, a kind of vehemence of emotion good at best for women and children, but unworthy of men who want to be guided by reason and will. And, yet, how many men whose names appear in the catalogue of the Saints, have been distinguished by proverbial good sense, an uncommon degree of intelligence, an energetic and persevering will! Here again a caricature is mistaken for the portrait.

300. **C)** Lastly, there are those who maintain that perfection is a Utopia beyond realization and hence fraught with danger; that it suffices to keep the Commandments without wasting time in punctilious practices or in the quest of extraordinary virtues.

The perusal of the lives of the Saints suffices to rectify such an erroneous view : perfection has been realized here on earth, and the practice of the counsels, far from working to the detriment of the precepts, simply renders their observance all the easier.

301. 3° Even among *devout souls* there are those who err as to the true nature of perfection, and who describe it, each according to the caprice of his own bias and fancy. [1]

A) Many, mistaking *devotions* for *devotion*, imagine perfection to consist in reciting a great number of prayers, in joining sundry religious societies, even if such practices entail the occasional neglect of their duties of state or of the charity due to the other members of the household. This is a substitution of non-essentials for the necessary, a sacrifice of the end to the means.

302. **B)** Others give themselves to *fastings and austerities* to the exhaustion of the body, and thus become unfit for the discharge of their duties of state and consider themselves dispensed therefore from the law of charity toward their neighbor. They dare not permit themselves any little dainties, yet they do not hesitate " to drench their lips with the life-blood of their fellow-men through calumny and slander. [2] " Here again one forgets the essentials of perfection and neglects the fundamental duty of charity in favor of practices good indeed but far less important. — The like mistake is made by those who *give generously to*

---

[1] Thus remarks St. FRANCIS DE SALES, *Introduction to a Devout Life*, Part. I, C. I, which should be read in its entirety.
[2] *Devout Life*, ib.

charity, but refuse to forgive their enemies, or those who, whilst forgiving them, think not of paying their debts.

303. C) Some, taking *spiritual consolations* for fervor, think they have arrived at perfection if they are filled with joy and can pray with ease, and they consider themselves lukewarm when they are seized by aridity and distractions. Such persons forget that what counts before God is the *generous*, oft-renewed *effort* despite apparent failures.

304. D) Others, taken up by a life of action and external activities, neglect the interior life to give themselves more entirely to works of zeal. They forget that the life and *soul of all zeal* is habitual prayer which draws down the grace of God and gives fruitfulness to action.

305. E) Others, having read mystical works or the lives of the Saints in which ectasies and visions are described, fancy perfection to consist in these extraordinary phenomena and strain their minds and imaginations to obtain them. They have never understood that such phenomena are, as the mystics themselves testify, but incidental; that they do not constitute the essence of sanctity and that it is foolhardy to covet them; that conformity to the will of God is by far the safer and more practical way.

Having thus cleared the ground, we shall be able to understand more easily in what perfection essentially consists.

ART. II. TRUE NOTION OF PERFECTION [1]

306. The State of the Question. 1° Any being is perfect (*perfectum*) in the natural order when it is finished, completed, hence, when it has attained its end : " *Each is said to be perfect in so far as it attains its own end, which is the highest perfection of anything.*" [2] This constitutes *absolute* perfection. However, there is also a *relative* and *progressive* perfection which consists in the approach toward that end by the development of all one's faculties and the carrying out in practice of all duties, in accordance with the dictates of the natural law as manifested by right reason.

---

[1] St. THOM., IIa IIæ, q. 184. a. 1-3; *Opuscul. de perfectione vitæ spiritualis,* ALVAREZ DE PAZ, *op. cit.*, l. III; LE GAUDIER, *op. cit.*, P. Iª; SCHRAM, *Instit. mysticæ*, § IX-XX; RIBET, *L'Ascétique chrétienne,* ch. IV-VI; IGHINA, *Cours de Théol. ascétique*, Introduction; GARRIGOU-LAGRANGE, dans la *Vie spirit.*, oct. et nov. 1920.

[2] *Sum. theol.*, IIª IIæ, q. 184, a. 1. *See also works referred to above, n. 295.*

307. 2° The *end of man*, even in the *natural* order, is
God : 1) Created *by Him*, we are of necessity created *for
Him* since He is the fulness of Being.   On the other hand,
to create for an imperfect end would be unworthy of
Him.   2) Besides, God being infinite perfection and thereby
the origin of all perfection, man is the more perfect as he
approaches closer to God and shares in His divine
perfections.   This is the reason why man cannot find in
creatures anything that can fully satisfy his legitimate
aspirations : " *The ultimate end of man is uncreated good,
that is to say, God, Who alone is capable, by His infinite
goodness, of satisfying completely the human will.* " [1] All
our actions then must be referred to God—to know, love
and serve Him and thereby glorify Him, this is the end of
life, the source of all perfection.

308. 3° In the *supernatural* order this is so all the more.
Raised by God to a state that surpasses all our needs and
all our capabilities, destined one day to contemplate Him
through the Beatific Vision, possessing Him even now
through grace, and endowed as we are with a supernatural
organism that we may unite with Him by the practice of
the Christian virtues, we cannot evidently perfect ourselves
unless we unceasingly draw closer to Him.   This, however,
we cannot effect except by uniting ourselves to Jesus — the
One indispensable way to go to the Father.   Hence, our
perfection will consist in living *for God in union with Jesus
Christ :* " *To live wholly unto God in Christ Jesus.* " [2]   This
we do when we practice the Christian virtues, theological
and moral.   The end of all these is to unite us to God more
or less directly by making us imitate our Lord Jesus Christ.

309. 4° Here the question arises whether there is among
these virtues any one which summarizes and embodies all
the others, thus constituting *the essence of perfection.*   Sum-
ming up the doctrine of Holy Writ and of the Fathers,
St. Thomas answers that perfection *essentially* consists in *the
love of God and of the neighbor* for God's sake : " *Essentially
the perfection of the Christian life consists in charity, first
and foremost in the love of God, then in the love of.neighbor.* " [3]
But in this life the love of God cannot be practiced without
renouncing inordinate self-love, that is, the threefold concu-

---

[1] St. THOM., I\ IIæ, q. III, a. 1. Cfr. TANQUEREY, *Synopsis Theol. moralis,*
Tr. de Ultimo fine, n. 2-18.
[2] FATHER OLIER, *Pietas Seminarii,* n. 1.
[3] *Sum, theol.,* IIa IIæ, q. 184, a. 3; Opusculum, *De perfectione vitæ spiritualis,*
cap. I, n. 56, 7.

piscence; therefore, in practice, sacrifice must be joined to love. This we are to explain by showing : 1) how the love of God and of the neighbor constitutes the essence of perfection; 2) why this love must go to the point of sacrifice; 3) how these two elements must be combined; 4) how perfection includes both precepts and counsels; 5) what are the degrees of perfection and how far perfection can be attained here on earth.

§ I. The Essence of Perfection consists in Charity

310. First of all we shall explain the *sense of this proposition.* The love of God and of neighbor here in question is *supernatural* by reason of its *object* as well as by reason of its *motive* and its *principle.*

The God we love is the God made known to us by revelation, the Triune God. We love Him because our faith shows Him to us *infinitely good* and *infinitely* loving. We love Him through *the will* perfected through the virtue of *charity* and aided by *actual grace.* This love then is not a mere sentiment. Man is indeed a composite being made up of body and soul and, doubtless, some feeling often enters into his affections even the noblest. At times, however, this sentiment which is wholly accidental, is utterly lacking. The essence of love itself is devotedness. It is a firm determination of the will to give itself up to God, and, if need be,to make the entire sacrifice of self to Him and His glory, preferring His good pleasure to that of self and others.

311. The same is to be said, with due proportion, of the love of neighbor. It is God Whom we love in him, a likeness, a reflection of God's perfections. The motive of this love is then the divine goodness as manifested, expressed and reflected in our neighbor. To speak more concretely, we see and love in our brethren a soul inhabited by the Holy Ghost, beautified by divine grace, redeemed at the price of Christ's blood. In loving him, we wish his supernatural perfection, his eternal salvation.

Thus there are not two distinct virtues of charity, the one towards God and the other towards the neighbor. There is but one, comprising at once God loved for His own sake, and the neighbor loved for God's sake.

With these notions in mind, we shall easily understand that perfection does really consist in this one virtue of charity. But what degree of charity is required for perfection? That the charity which necessarily accompanies the state of grace and which coëxists with the habit of venial sin and unmortified passions cannot be sufficient for perfection, every one will agree. On the other hand, charity causing us to love God as much as He deserves to be loved, or charity causing us to avoid all venial sins and imperfections, is not required, for as will be seen further (N. 344-348), such charity is not within our power here on earth. Charity required for perfection may then be defined : Charity so well established in the soul as to make us strive earnestly and constantly to avoid even the smallest sin and to do God's holy will in all things out of love for Him.

Proofs of the Thesis

312. 1° Let us see what **Holy Writ** tells us. **A)** Both in the Old and the New Testaments, the dominating principle wherein the whole law is summed up is the Great Commandment of love — the love of God and the love of neighbor. Thus when a certain lawyer asked our Lord what was to be done in order to gain everlasting life, the divine Master made the simple reply : "What saith the law?" And the lawyer without hesitation recalled the sacred text in Deuteronomy : "Thou shalt love the Lord thy God with thy whole heart and with thy whole soul and with all thy strength and with all thy mind: and thy neighbor as thyself." Our Lord approved it, saying: " This do: *and thou shalt live* " [1] He adds elsewhere that in this twofold precept of the love of God and of the neighbor are contained all the Law and the Prophets. [2] St. Paul declares the same when after having enumerated the principal precepts of the Decalogue he adds: "*Love therefore is the fulfilling of the Law.*" [3] Thus the love of God and of the neighbor is at one and the same time both the summary and the plenitude of the Law. Now Christian perfection cannot be anything else but the perfect and complete fulfilment of the Law, for the Law is the will of God, than which there can be nothing more perfect.

313. **B)** Another proof is the one drawn from St. Paul's doctrine on charity in the thirteenth chapter of the first *Epistle to the Corinthians.* There, in lyric language, he describes the excellence of love, its primacy over the

[1] *Luke.* X, 25-29; cfr. *Deut.* VI, 5-7.
[2] *Matth.*, XXII, 39-40. — [3] *Rom.*, XIII, 10.

charisms or freely given graces, and over the other theological virtues of faith and hope. He shows that it embodies
and possesses all virtues in the highest degree; so much so,
that love is itself the aggregate of all those virtues : " *Charity
is patient, is kind; charity envieth not, dealeth not perversely,
is not puffed up, is not ambitious, seeketh not her own, is not
provoked to anger, thinketh no evil.* "   He ends by affirming
that the charismata shall pass, but that charity abideth
eternally.   This means not only that love is the queen
and the soul of all the virtues, but that its worth is such
that it suffices to make man perfect by imparting to him all
the virtues.

314.   C) St. John, the Apostle of divine love, gives us
the fundamental reason for this doctrine.   God, says he,
is love.   This is, so to speak, what characterizes Him.   If
we, therefore, wish to be like unto Him, to be perfect like
Our Heavenly Father, we must love Him as He loves us,
" *because He hath first loved us.* " [1]   But since we cannot
love Him if we love not our neighbor, we are to love
our brethren even to the point of sacrifice : " *We also must
lay down our lives for the brethren.* "   " Dearly beloved, let
us love one another : for charity is of God.   And every one
that loveth is born of God and knoweth God.   He that
loveth not knoweth not God ; for God is charity... In this is
charity : not as though we had loved God, but because He
hath first loved us, and sent His Son to be a propitiation
for our sins.   My dearest, if God hath so loved us, we also
ought to love one another...   God is charity and he that
abideth in charity abideth in God, and God in him. " [2]   It
cannot be stated in clearer terms that all perfection consists
in the love of God and of the neighbor for God's sake.

315.   2° When we seek an answer to this question from
reason enlightened *by faith*, we arrive at the same conclusion, whether we consider the *nature of perfection* or the
nature of love.

A) We have said that the perfection of any being consists
in attaining its end or in approaching it as closely as possible (N. 306).   Now, man's end in the supernatural order
is the eternal possession of God through the Beatific Vision
and the love resulting therefrom.   Here upon earth we
approach the realization of this end by *living already
intimately united to the Most Blessed Trinity* dwelling in us,

---

[1] *John*, IV, 10.
[2] *I John*, IV, 7-16.   The whole Epistle should be read.

and to Jesus the indispensable Mediator with the Father. The more closely we are united to God, our last end and the source of our life, the more perfect we are.

316. Among the Christian virtues, the most unifying, the one which unites the whole soul to God is divine charity. The other virtues indeed *prepare* us for that union or initiate us into it, *but cannot effect it.* The moral virtues of prudence, fortitude, temperance, and justice do not unite us *directly* to God, but limit themselves to removing or reducing the obstacles that estrange us from Him, and to bringing us *closer* to Him through conformity to His order. Thus temperance by restraining the immoderate use of pleasure, weakens one of the most potent obstacles to the love of God; humility by putting off pride and self-love predisposes us to the practice of divine charity. Besides, these virtues, by making us observe order or right measure, subordinate the will to that of God. As to the *theological* virtues other than charity, they do indeed unite us to God, but in an incomplete fashion. *Faith* unites us to God, infallible Truth, and makes us see all things in the divine light, yet it is compatible with mortal sin which separates us from God. *Hope* raises us to God inasmuch as He is good to us and makes us desire the joys of Heaven, but it can exist along with grave faults that turn us away from our end.

317. Love alone unites us fully to God. It presupposes faith and hope, but it surpasses them. It lays hold of our *entire soul*, intellect, heart, will, activity, and delivers all unreservedly to God. It *excludes mortal sin*, God's enemy, and makes us enjoy the divine friendship : "*If any one love me... my Father will love him.*" [1] Now, friendship is the union, the blending of two souls into one : "*One heart and one soul... the same likes and dislikes,*" (*Cor unum et anima una : unum velle, unum nolle*). Thus our friendship with God is a perfect union of all our faculties with Him; a union of our mind that patterns our thoughts after those of God; a union of our *will* that causes us to embrace the divine *will* as our very own, a union of *heart* that prompts us to give ourselves to God as He has given Himself to us, "*My beloved to me and I to Him;*" [2] a union of *activities*, in virtue of which God places His divine power at the service of our weakness to enable us to carry out our good desires. Charity then unites us to God, our end, — to God,

---

[1] *John*, XIV, 23. — [2] *Cant.*, II, 16.

infinitely perfect, and thus constitutes the essential element of our perfection.

318.   B) If we inquire into the *nature of charity* we arrive at the same conclusion. St. Francis de Sales shows that *charity* includes all the virtues and even lends them a perfection all its own. [1]

a) *It comprises all the virtues.* Perfection evidently consists in the acquisition of virtues. If we possess all, not simply in an initial stage, but to a high degree, we are perfect. But whoever has the virtue of charity in the degree described in n. 311, has all other virtues and has them in all their perfection, without which it is impossible to know and love God's infinite loveliness; he has *hope*, which by inspiring trust leads to love; he has all the moral virtues, such as *prudence* without which charity could neither last nor grow, *fortitude* which triumphs over the obstacles impeding the practice of charity, *temperance* which curbs sensuality, that relentless enemy of divine love. Nay more, adds *St. Francis de Sales,* " the great Apostle does not simply say that charity bestows on us patience and kindness, and steadfastness and simplicity, but he says that charity is itself patient and kind, and steadfast, " because it embodies the perfection of all virtues.

319.   b) Charity, moreover, gives to other virtues a special *perfection* and worth. It is, according to St. Thomas, [2] the *form*, the soul, of all the virtues. " All the virtues when separated from charity fall very short of perfection, since they cannot in default of this virtue fulfil their own end, which is to render man happy. I do not say that, without it, they cannot be born and even develop; but they are dependent on charity for their perfection, for their completeness to draw therefrom the strength to will in God and to receive from His mercy the manna of true merit and of the sanctification of those hearts wherein they are found. Charity is among the virtues as the sun among the stars — it gives to all their brightness and their beauty. Faith, hope, fear, sorrow ordinarily precede charity into the soul, there to prepare its abode, but once love arrives they obey and minister to it like all other virtues; charity, by its presence, animates, beautifies and vivifies them all. " [3]   In other words, charity by directing our soul immediately toward

---

[1] *Treatise on the Love of God*, Book XI, C. 8.
[2] *Sum. theol.*, IIa IIæ, q. 23, a. 8.
[3] *St. Francis de Sales*, l. c., c. 9.

God, the supreme perfection and the last end, gives the selfsame direction and hence the same worth to all the other virtues under its sway. Thus an act of obedience or of humility, besides having its own proper value, derives from love a far greater worth, when done in order to *please God*. It becomes then an act of charity, an act of the most perfect of all virtues. Let us add that such an act becomes *easier* and more *attractive*. To obey and to undergo humiliation is a bitter thing to our proud nature, but this becomes easier once we are conscious that by the performance of such acts we actually practice the love of God and procure His glory.

Thus charity is not only the synthesis but the very soul of all virtues, it unites us to God in a manner more perfect and more direct than any of the others. Hence it is love that constitutes the very essence of perfection.

CONCLUSION

320. Since the essence of perfection consists in the love of God, it follows that the short-cut thereto is to love with a great love, with a generous heart, with intensity and above all with a pure and disinterested love. Now we truly love God not only when we give expression with our lips to an act of charity, but even each time we do His will or perform the least duty with the intention of pleasing Him. Each of our actions then, however commonplace, can be transformed into an act of love and become a help to our advancement in perfection. Our progress will be all the more real and rapid as our love becomes more intense and generous and our effort accordingly more *strenuous* and *steadfast*, for that which has value in the eyes of God is the will, the effort, apart from all sensible emotion.

Lastly, because the supernatural love of the neighbor is likewise an act of the love of God, all the services we render our brethren, while seeing in them reflections of the divine perfection, or, what is the same, seeing Jesus Christ in them, become acts of love that make us advance toward sanctity.

§ II. Love on Earth Requires Sacrifice

321. In Heaven we shall love without any need of self-immolation. Here on earth it is quite otherwise. In our present state of fallen nature, it is *impossible* for us to love God truly and effectively without sacrificing ourselves for Him.

This follows from what we have said above (n. 74-75) regarding the tendencies of fallen nature which remain in regenerated man. We cannot love God without fighting and curbing those tendencies. This is a struggle that begins with the dawn of reason and ends only with our last breath. Assuredly there are moments of respite when the struggle is not so intense, but even then, we cannot afford to rest upon our oars except at the risk of another sally on the part of the enemy. To this *Holy Writ bears witness.*

1º **Holy Writ** clearly states the absolute necessity of sacrifice and self-renunciation in order to love God and the neighbor.

322. A) *Our Lord* addresses the following invitation to all His disciples : " *If any man will come after me, let him deny himself and take up his cross and follow me.* " [1] In order to follow and to love Jesus, there is an indispensable condition, that of renouncing self, that is to say, renouncing the evil inclinations of our nature : selfishness, pride, ambition, sensuality, lust, inordinate love of ease and riches. There is the condition of carrying one's cross, of accepting the sufferings, the privations, the humiliations, the evil turns of fortune, labor, sickness, in a word, those crosses with which the hand of God's Providence puts us to the test, strengthens our virtue and makes easy the expiation of our faults. Then, and only then, can one be Christ's disciple and walk the way of love and perfection.

Our Lord confirms this lesson by *His example.* Having come from Heaven with the express purpose of showing us the way of perfection, He followed no other way than that of the Cross : " *Christ's whole life was a Cross and a martyrdom.* " [2] From Bethlehem to Calvary His life is a long series of privations and humiliations, of fatigue and apostolic labors, all crowned by the anguish and the tortures of His bitter Passion. It is the most eloquent commentary on His words : " *If any man will come after me.* " Were there a surer road, He would have shown it to us. But He knew there was no other and He followed it to draw us after Him. " *And I, if I be lifted up from the earth, will draw all things to myself.* " [3] Thus it was understood by the Apostles who

---

[1] *Matth.*, XVI, 24; cfr. *Luke*, IX, 23. — Read the commentary of *Blessed Grignion de Montfort* in his *Circular letter to the friends of the Cross.*
[2] *Imitation*, Book II, C. XII, n. 7. — [3] *John*, XII, 32.

repeat to us with St. Peter, that if Christ suffered for us it was that we might walk in his steps : " *Because Christ also suffered for us leaving you an example that you should follow His steps.* " [1]

323.   B) This is also the teaching of *St. Paul.* For him Christian perfection consists in divesting oneself of the old man to invest oneself with the new : " *Stripping yourselves of the old man with his deeds and putting on the new.* " [2]   Now the old Adam is but the sum-total of the evil tendencies we have inherited from the first man. It is that threefold concupiscence we are to fight and to muzzle by the practice of mortification. " *They that are Christ's,* " says he, " *have crucified their flesh with the vices and concupiscences.* " [3] This is the essential condition ; so much so that St. Paul himself feels obliged to punish his body : " *But I chastise my body and bring it into subjection, lest perhaps, when I have preached to others, I myself should become a castaway.* " [4]

324.   C) The Apostle of Love, *St. John,* is no less emphatic. He teaches that in order to love God we must keep the Commandments and fight the *threefold concupiscence* which holds the world under its sway. He adds that if one loves the world and the things that are in the world one cannot possess the love of God : " *If any man love the world, the charity of the Father is not in him.* " [5] But in order to hate the world and its allurements, it is clear that one must practice the spirit of sacrifice by foregoing dangerous and evil pleasures.

325.   2° This need of sacrifice is a consequence of *the condition of our fallen nature* as described in n. 74, and of the *threefold concupiscence,* n. 193. As a matter of fact, it is impossible to love God and the neighbor without sacrificing whatever goes counter to that love. The threefold concupiscence, as we have shown, does go counter to the love of God and of the neighbor ; hence, if we wish to advance in the way of charity, we must relentlessly fight against our bad tendencies.

326.   Let us consider a few instances. Our *exterior senses* eagerly tend toward whatever flatters them, thus putting at hazard our virtue. What is to be done to avoid this danger? Our Lord tells us very forcibly : " *If thy right eye scandalize thee, pluck it out and cast it from thee. For it*

---

[1] *I Peter,* II, 21. — [2] *Coloss.,* III, 9. — [3] *Galat.,* V, 24.
[4] *I Cor.,* IX, 27. — [5] *I John,* II, 15.

*is expedient for thee that one of thy members should perish,
rather than thy whole body be cast into hell.*" [1]   This means
that we must learn by mortification to deprive our eyes,
our ears, all our senses, of whatever constitutes for us an
occasion of sin.   Without this there is neither perfection
nor salvation.

The same holds true of our *interior senses*, particularly,
of our imagination and our memory.   Who does not know
from experience the risk we run, unless we repress their
vagaries from the outset?

Even our higher faculties, *intellect* and *will*, are liable to
go astray through curiosity, independence or pride.   What
efforts must be made, what combat sustained, in order to
place them under the yoke of Faith, in humble submission
to the will of God and to His representatives!

We must confess then, that if we want to love God and
our neighbor for God's sake, we must learn to mortify our
selfishness, our sensuality, our pride, our love for riches.
Thus sacrifice is the essential condition of loving God in
this life.

This seems to be the mind of St. Augustine when he
says : " Two loves have built two cities : the love of self
carried unto the contempt of God has built the city of this
earth; the love of God carried unto the contempt of self has
built the heavenly city. " [2]   In other words, we cannot truly
love God except through repression of our evil tendencies.

327.   The *conclusion* that necessarily follows is that, in
order to be perfect, we must not only multiply acts of love,
but also *acts of sacrifice*, for in this life love cannot be
without self-immolation.   Of course, it can be truly said of
all our good works that inasmuch as they detach us from
self and from creatures they are acts of sacrifice, and,
inasmuch as they unite us to God they are acts of love.
It remains for us to see how love and sacrifice can be
combined.

§ III. The Part of Love and the Part of Sacrifice in the Christian Life

328.   Since both love and sacrifice must have a part in
the Christian life, what shall be the rôle of each?   On this
subject there are points on which all agree, and there are
others on which a difference of opinion is manifest.   Practi-

[1] *Matth.*, V, 29.
[2] *De Civitate Dei*, XIV, 28.

cally, however, the present authors of the various schools arrive at conclusions that are nearly the same.

329. 1º All admit that objectively and in the order of *excellence*, love holds the first place. It is the *end* and the *essential element* of perfection, as we have proved in our first thesis, N. 312. It is love, then, that we must look to above all, it is love that we must seek without respite, it is love that calls for sacrifice and gives it its chief value. Hence, it is essential that even with beginners, the spiritual director should insist on the love of God; but he should make clear to them that while love renders sacrifice easier, it can never dispense with it.

330. 2º As regards the *chronological* order, all admit that both elements are inseparable and must be cultivated at one and the same time, nay more, that they must blend one with the other. This, because there is no true love here on earth without sacrifice, and because sacrifice made for God is one of the best signs of love.

The whole question resolves itself into this : Taking the chronological order, which of these two elements must be emphasized, love or sacrifice? Here we come upon two distinct schools and trends of thought.

331. **A)** *St. François de Sales,* resting upon the authority of many representatives of the Benedictine and the Dominican schools, and relying upon the resources which regenerated human nature has to offer, insists first on the love of God, in order the better to make us accept and practice sacrifice. But far from excluding the latter, he demands of Philothea much self-renunciation and self-sacrifice. If he does so with great caution and suavity of manner, it is to attain his purpose all the better. This becomes evident from the first chapter of the *Introduction to a Devout Life :* [1] " True devotion presupposes not a partial, but a thorough love of God... As devotion then consists in a certain excellent degree of charity, it not only makes us active and diligent *in the observance in God's commandments*, but it also excites us to the performance of every good work with an affectionate alacrity, even though it be not of precept but only of counsel. " But to keep the *commandments*, to follow the *counsels* and the inspirations of grace, is to practice mortification to a high degree. Besides, the Saint asks that Philothea begin by purifying herself not only from mortal

---

[1] *St. Francis de Sales,* Introduction to a Devout Life, C. I.

sins, but also from venial faults and from the affection for vain and dangerous things, as well as from evil tendencies. When he deals with the virtues, he does not forget their austere side; although he is ever concerned that all be pervaded by the love of God and that of the neighbor.

332. B) On the other side, we have the school of St. Ignatius and the French School of the Seventeenth Century. Without forgetting that the love of God is the end to be attained and that it must vivify all our acts, they place to the fore, especially for beginners, renouncement, the love of the Cross, the mortification of our passions, as the surest means of arriving at real effective love. The representatives of these schools seem to fear that unless this be insisted on at the beginning, many souls would fall victims to illusions, think themselves already far advanced in the love of God, whilst, in fact, their virtue is more sentimental and apparent than real. Hence those lamentable falls when grave temptations come or when spiritual dryness sets in. Besides, sacrifice courageously accepted for the love of God leads to a charity that is more generous and more constant, and the habitual practice of this charity gradually comes to complete the spiritual edifice.

333. Practical conclusion. Without any desire to settle this controversy, we shall simply propose some conclusions admitted by the most prudent of all schools.

A) There are two excesses to be avoided : **a)** that of wishing to lead souls prematurely into the so-called way of *love,* whilst failing to train them to the stern discipline of daily self-denial. It is in this way that illusions are fostered and at times the ground made ready for regrettable falls. How many souls experiencing those sensible consolations God dispenses to beginners, and thinking themselves well-grounded in virtue, expose themselves to occasions of sin and fall into grievous faults! A little more mortification, true humility, distrust of self, and a more determined fight against their passions, would have preserved them from such lapses.

b) The other excess is to speak constantly of renouncement and mortification without making it clear that these are but means of arriving at the love of God, or manifestations of that love. Thus some persons possessed of good will, but as yet of little courage are disheartened. They would take more heart and be filled with greater strength, if they were shown how such sacrifices become so much easier if done for the love of God : " *Where there is love, there is no labor.* "

334. B) Once these excesses are avoided, the spiritual director must know what path to point out to each penitent according to his character and the promptings of grace.

a) There are *affectionate* souls who have no taste for mortification until they have for some time practiced the love of God.   It is true that this love is ofttimes imperfect, more sentimental than generous and lasting.   However, if one takes advantage of these first flights to show that real love cannot endure without sacrifice, if one succeeds in inducing such souls to exercise themselves in some acts of penance for the love of God, in some acts of reparation, of mortification, such acts as are more indispensable to the avoidance of sin, then their will will be gradually strengthened, and the moment will come when they will understand that sacrifice and the love of God must go hand in hand.

b) On the other hand, if one has to deal with energetic characters, accustomed to act from a sense of duty, one may from the outset insist on renouncement as the *touchstone* of charity, and cause them to exercise themselves in penance, humility and mortification, while infusing into these austere virtues the motive of the love of God or zeal for souls.

Thus love and sacrifice will ever be united, and it will become evident that these two elements blend and perfect each other.

§ IV. Does Perfection consist in the Commandments or in the Counsels?

335. 1º **The State of the Question.** We have seen that perfection consists essentially in the love of God and of the neighbor carried unto sacrifice.   But the love of God and sacrifice include both *commandments* and *counsels;* commandments that oblige under pain of sin, *counsels* that *invite* us to do for God over and above what is demanded; failure in this case would not involve sin but wilful imperfection and resistance to grace.   It is this distinction of precept and counsel that Our Lord alluded to when He declared to the rich young man : " *If thou wilt enter into life, keep the commandments... If thou wilt be perfect, go sell what thou hast and give to the poor and thou shalt have a treasure in heaven.* " [1]   Thus, to observe the laws of justice

---

[1] *Matth.*, XIX, 17-21.

and charity in what concerns ownership suffices for entrance into heaven, but if one would be *perfect*, one must sell his possessions, give their price to the poor and so practice voluntary poverty.   St. Paul points out to us likewise that *virginity* is a *counsel* and not a commandment — that to marry is good, but that to be a virgin is better. [1]

336. 2º **The Solution.** Some authors have reached the conclusion that the Christian life consists in the *observance of the commandments*, and *perfection in that of the counsels*.   This explanation is a little too simple, and if wrongly understood, would end in fatal results.   In reality, *perfection* requires, in the first place, the *keeping of the commandments* and, in the second, *the observance of a certain number of counsels*.

This is the teaching of St. Thomas. [2]   After proving that perfection is nothing else *but* the love of God and of the neighbor, he concludes that, in practice, it consists *essentially in the commandments*, the chief of which is that of love; secondarily, *in the counsels* all of which are directed toward charity, for they remove the obstacles that hinder its practice.   We shall explain this doctrine.

337.   **A**) Perfection demands peremptorily and in the first place the *keeping of the commandments*.   It is important to impress this notion strongly upon certain persons, who, for example, in order to practice some devotions, forget their duties of state, or who under the pretext of almsgiving, defer indefinitely the payment of their debts; in a word, on all those who, aiming at a perfection of a higher order, neglect some precept of the Law of God.   It is evident that the infraction of a grave precept, like that of the payment of debts, destroys charity in us, and that the pretext of giving alms cannot justify this violation of the natural law.   In like manner, the wilful violation of a commandment in light matter is a venial sin which, though not destroying charity in us, impedes to a greater or lesser extent its exercise, offends Almighty God, and interferes with our intimacy with Him.   This is especially true of frequent deliberate venial sins which create in us attachments, and retard our advance towards perfection.   To be perfect, therefore, we must, above all, observe the commandments.

338.   **B**) To this, however, we must join the *observance of the counsels* — of a few at least — chiefly of those related

---

[1] *I Cor.*, VII, 25-40.
[2] *Sum. theol.*, II^a II^æ, q. 184, a. 3.

to our duties of state. **a)** Thus, religious, having bound themselves by vow to practice the three great evangelical counsels of poverty, chastity and obedience, cannot evidently sanctify themselves without fidelity to their vows.   Besides, this fidelity renders singularly easy the exercise of the love of God by detaching the soul from the chief obstacles which stand in the way of divine charity. *Poverty*, by uprooting disordered love for wealth, sets the heart free to reach out to God and heavenly things. *Chastity*, by spurning the pleasures of the flesh, even those the holy state of marriage would sanction, fosters an undivided love of God. *Obedience*, by fighting pride and the spirit of independence, subjects the will to that of God. This obedience is, in reality, a genuine act of love.

339. b)· Those who are not bound by vows must, in order to be *perfect*, observe the spirit of these vows, each according to his condition in life, the inspirations of grace, and the guidance of a prudent spiritual adviser.   Thus they will exercise themselves in *the spirit of poverty* by depriving themselves of many useless things, and so will spare money for almsgiving and for works of charity or zeal; in *the spirit of chastity*, even if they be married, by using with moderation or restraint the rights to the lawful pleasures of their state, and, above all, by scrupulously avoiding whatever is forbidden or dangerous; in *the spirit of obedience*, by submitting themselves with docility to their superiors in whom they will see the image of God, and by a like submission to the inspirations of grace, under the guidance of a wise spiritual director.

Hence to love God and the neighbor for God's sake, to know how to sacrifice oneself in order to fulfil the better this twofold commandment and the counsels related thereto, this is true perfection.

§ V. The different Degrees of Perfection

Perfection here on earth has degrees and limits. Hence two question : 1° What are the principal degrees of perfection? 2° What are its limits here on earth?

I. *The Different Degrees of Perfection* [1]

340.   The degrees by which one is raised to perfection are numerous.   The question here is not to enumerate all

---

[1] St. THOMAS, *Sum. theol.*, 2ª 2ᵃᵉ, q. 183, a. 4; *Catholic Encycl.*, *States*; *Cursus Asceticus*, I, p. 19-29.

of them, but only to note the chief stages. According to the common doctrine, explained by St. Thomas, there are three *principal stages* or, as they are commonly called, *three ways :* that of *beginners* — the purgative way, that of souls already *advanced* — the illuminative way, and that of the *perfect* — the unitive way.

341. **a**) The chief care of beginners is that of preserving charity. Their efforts, then, are directed toward the *avoidance of sin*, above all, *mortal* sin, and toward the conquest of evil inclinations, of the passions, and of all that could make them lose the love of God. [1] This is the *purgative way*, the end of which is the purification of the soul.

342. **b**) The chief concern of those already advanced, the *proficientes*, is progress in the *positive exercise of the virtues* and growth in charity. The heart, already purified, is all the more open to divine light and to the love of God. The soul wishes to follow Jesus and to imitate His virtues, and since by following Him one walks in the Light, this is called the *illuminative way*. [2] Here the soul strives to avoid not only mortal, but even venial sin.

343. **c**) Perfect souls have but one concern — *to cling to God* and *to take their delight in Him.* Ever seeking to unite themselves to God, they are in the *unitive way*. Sin fills them with horror, for they fear to displease God and to offend Him. The virtues that most attract them are the theological virtues, which unite them to God. Hence, the earth seems to them an exile, and, like St. Paul, they long to die to be joined to Christ. [3]

These are only brief indications. Later on we shall resume them again and develop them in the Second Part of this work. There we shall take the soul from the first stage, that of the purification, to the transforming union that prepares it for the Beatific Vision.

II. *The Limits of Perfection here on Earth*

344. When reading the lives of the Saints, and especially those of the great contemplatives, one marvels at the sublime heights to which a soul can rise that refuses nothing to God. There are, however, limits to our perfection here on earth. Beyond these we must not wish to go lest we fall back into a lower degree, or even lapse into sin.

---

[1] *Sum. theol.*, 2ª 2æ, q. 24, a. 9. — [2] *L. cit.* — [3] *L. cit.*

345. 1° It is certain that we cannot love God *as He deserves to be loved.* He is infinitely lovable, and, our hearts being finite, can never love Him, even in Heaven, except with a finite love. We can, therefore, always strive to love Him more. According to St. Bernard, the measure wherewith to love God is to love Him without measure. Let us not forget, however, that real love consists less in pious sentiments than in acts of the will, and that the best way to love God is to make the will conform to His. This we shall explain further on, when treating of conformity to the divine will.

346. 2° On earth one cannot love God uninterruptedly nor unfailingly. One can, no doubt, with the aid of choice graces granted to souls of good-will, avoid all *deliberate venial sin*, but not all faults of *frailty*. No one ever becomes impeccable, as the Church has declared on many occasions.

A) In the Middle Ages, the *Beghards* [1] pretended " that man is capable in this present life of reaching such a degree of perfection that he becomes altogether impeccable and can no more grow in grace. " They concluded from this that those who have attained this degree of perfection should neither fast nor pray, for in this state sensuality has been so completely subjected to the spirit and to reason, that a man may grant his body whatever he pleases; he is no longer obliged to observe the commandments of the Church nor to obey men, nor even to exercise himself in acts of the virtues, such things being only for the imperfect. These are dangerous doctrines leading to immorality. Once a person believes himself impeccable and no longer strives to practice virtue, he soon becomes a prey to the vilest passions. This happened to the Beghards, whom the Œcumenical Council of Vienne rightly condemned in 1311.

347. B) In the Seventeenth Century, *Molinos* [2] revived this error by teaching that " through acquired contemplation one arrives at such a degree of perfection that one no longer commits any sins, either mortal or venial. " He showed only too well, by his example, that with maxims that seem so exalted, one is greatly exposed to fall into scandalous disorders. He was justly condemned by Innocent XI on November 19, 1687. Upon reading the propositions he had dared maintain, one is horrified at the frightful

---

[1] DENZ.-BANN., n. 471-478. Cfr. P. POURRAT, *Christian Spirituality*, t. II; *Cath. Encyclop.*, BEGHARDS, Beguines. — [2] *Catholic Encyclop.*, MOLINOS.

consequences to which this pretension to impeccability could and did lead. [1]   Let us be more modest then and ever seek to correct our deliberate faults and to diminish the number of those of frailty.

348.   3° Contrary to what Fenelon maintained, [2] we cannot on earth love God with a *constant*, nor yet *habitual* love, which is at the same time perfectly pure and *disinterested*.   No matter to what degree of perfection we may attain, we are obliged from time to time to make acts of hope.   We, therefore, cannot remain altogether indifferent to our own salvation.   It is true that there have been Saints, who, in the midst of *passive trials*, have momentarily acquiesced to their reprobation, but on the supposition that it were so willed by God, whilst at the same time firmly declaring their unwillingness, were this the case, to desist from loving Him.   These are only suppositions that must be thrust aside since the fact is that God wills the salvation of all men.

From time to time, though, we can elicit acts of pure love with no thought of self whatever, and therefore without actually hoping or wishing for Heaven.   Such is the following act of love of St. Theresa : [3] " If I love Thee, Lord, it is not because of Heaven which Thou hast promised me.   If I fear to offend Thee, it is not because of Hell that threatens me.   What draws me unto Thee, Lord, is Thyself alone — it is the sight of Thee, nailed to the Cross, Thy body bruised' mid the pangs of death.   Thy love doth so hold my heart that were there no Heaven, I would love Thee still; were there no Hell, I would fear Thee yet. I need not thy gifts to make me love Thee, for although I should have no hope of all I do hope for, I would love Thee still with the selfsame love. "

349.   Ordinarily, our love of God is a *mixture of pure and interested love;* that is to say, we love God both for His own sake, because He is infinitely good, and also because He is the source of our happiness.   These two motives are not exclusive of each other, since it is the will of God that we find our happiness in loving and glorifying Him.   Let us not, therefore, be alarmed at this admixture of motives in our love of God.   Let us simply say to ourselves when thinking of Heaven, that our happiness will consist in the possession and the vision of God, in loving

[1] DENZ.-BANN., n. 1228-1288. — [2] DENZ.-BANN., n. 1327-1349.
[2] *The Bollandists, History of St. Theresa*, vol. II, c. 31.

and glorifying Him. Then even when we are influenced by the desire and the hope of Heaven, the predominant motive in our actions will truly be the love of God.

CONCLUSION

350. Behold, then, the whole of Christian perfection : — *love* and *sacrifice*. Who cannot, with God's grace, fulfil this twofold condition? Is it, indeed, so difficult to love Him Who is infinitely lovable and infinitely loving? The love that He asks of us is nothing extraordinary; it is the devotedness of love — the gift of oneself — consisting chiefly in conformity to the divine will. To want to love is to love. To keep the commandments for God's sake is to love. To pray is to love. To fulfil our duties of state in view of pleasing God, this is likewise to love. Nay more, to recreate ourselves, to take our meals with the like intention is to love. To serve our neighbor for God's sake is to love. Nothing then is easier, God's grace helping, than the constant excercise of divine love and through this, steady advance toward perfection.

351. As for *sacrifice*, doubtless it seems hard. But we are not asked to love it for its own sake. It is enough if we love it for God's sake, or, in other words if we realize that here on earth one cannot love God without renouncing whatever is an obstacle to His love. Then sacrifice becomes first tolerable and soon even lovable. Does not a mother, passing long, sleepness nights at the bedside of her son joyously undergo fatigue when she entertains the hope and, more especially, when she has the certainty of thereby saving his life? Now, when we accept for the sake of God the sacrifices He demands, we have not only the hope, but the certainty itself, of pleasing Him, of giving Him glory and of working out the salvation of our own souls. In this, have we not for our encouragement the example and the help of the God-Man? Has He not suffered as much as and even more than we ourselves suffer, for the glory of His Father and the salvation of our souls? Shall we, His disciples, incorporated into Him in Baptism, nourished with His Body and Blood, shall we hesitate when we are to suffer together with Him, for His love and for His intentions? Is it not true that in the Cross there is gain, especially for loving hearts? " In the Cross " says the author of the Imitation, [1] " is salvation; in the Cross is life; in the

---

[1] *Imitation*, Bk. II, C. 12, v. 2.

Cross is protection from enemies. In the Cross is infusion of heavenly sweetness. " We shall conclude with the
words of Saint Augustine : " There are no labors too great
for loving hearts. In fact, one finds pleasure therein, as
we observe in the case of the fisherman fishing, the hunter
at the chase, the merchant at the mart. For where there
is love, there is no labor, or if there be labor, it is a labor
of love. " [1]   Let us then hasten toward perfection by this
path of love and sacrifice.

CHAPTER IV.

The Duty of Tending to Perfection [2]

352.   Having already explained the *nature* of the Christian life and its *perfection*, we are now to examine whether
there is for us a real *obligation* to advance in it or whether
it suffices to keep it as we keep a treasure.   To answer
with greater exactness we shall examine this question with
regard to three categories of persons : 1° the laity; 2° the
religious; 3° the priests.

ART. I. THE DUTY INCUMBENT UPON ALL CHRISTIANS IN GENERAL TO TEND TOWARD PERFECTION

We shall explain : 1° The obligation itself.   2° The motives that make this duty more easy to perform.

§ I. The Obligation Itself

353.   In a matter so delicate as the one now under consideration, we cannot be too precise.   It is certain that one
must die in the state of grace in order to be saved, and that
this suffices.   It would appear then that for the *faithful* in
the world there is no other obligation than that of preserving
the state of grace.   However, the question is precisely
whether they can preserve the state of grace for a long time
without striving to grow in holiness.   To this, *authority* and
reason enlightened by *faith* answer that, in the state of
fallen nature, one cannot for long remain in the state of
grace without *striving* at the same time to make progress
in the spiritual life and to exercise oneself *from time to time*

---

[1] St. AUGUST., *De bono Viduitatis*, c. 21, *P. L.* XL, 448.
[2] ALVAREZ DE PAZ., *op. cit.*, lib. IV-V; LE GAUDIER, P. III, sect. I.,
sec. VII-X ; SCARAMELLI, *Guide Ascétique*, Traité I, art. II; RIBET, Ascétique,
ch. VII-IX ; IGHINA, *op. cit.*, Introd., XX-XXX. *Cursus Asceticus*, Vol. I, n. 15.

in the practice of some of the evangelical counsels. It is only in this restricted sense that we maintain the obligation of perfection for ordinary christians.

I. *The Argument from Authority*

354. 1º *Holy Writ* does not deal with this question *directly*. It does indeed furnish us with the distinction between precept and counsel (cf. n. 335), but it does not as a rule tell us which of the exhortations of Our Lord are obligatory and which are not. However, Holy Scripture lays so much stress upon the holiness that becomes a Christian, it proposes such an ideal of perfection, it proclaims so emphatically to all Christians the necessity of renouncement and of love — the essentials of perfection — that any impartial mind will draw the conclusion that in order to save our souls, we must, at least at times, do more than is strictly commanded and, therefore, strive after holiness.

355. **A)** It is evident that one who would merely aim at avoiding mortal sin would not be living according to the standard of moral conduct outlined in the Gospel. Our Lord proposes to us as the *ideal* of holiness the very perfection of Our Heavenly Father : " *Be ye therefore perfect, as also your heavenly Father is perfect.* " [1] Hence, *all* having *God for their Father* must approach this divine perfection — which evidently cannot be accomplished without progress. At bottom, the whole Sermon on the Mount is nothing but a commentary on and the development of this ideal. The path to follow is the path of renunciation, the path of imitation of Christ and of the love of God : " *If any man come to me, and hate not* " (that is to say does not renounce) " *his father and mother and wife and children and brethren and sisters, yea and his own life also, he cannot be my disciple.* " [2] We are bound, then, on certain occasions to choose God and His will rather than the love of parents, of wife, of children, of self, and to sacrifice all to follow Christ. This supposes *heroic* courage, which will be found wanting in the time of need, unless God in His mercy give a special grace and unless one be prepared by sacrifices that are not of strict obligation. True, this is a straight and narrow path and few there are that follow it, but Jesus Christ wills that we make *earnest efforts* to walk this path : " Strive to enter by the narrow gate. " [3] Does He not thereby ask us to strive after perfection?

---

[1] *Matth.*, V, 48. — [2] *Luke*, XIV, 26, 27; cfr. *Matth.*, X, 37, 38.
[3] *Luke*, XIII, 24; cfr. *Matth.*, VII, 13, 14.

356. B) The apostles speak the same language. St. Paul often reminds the faithful that they have been elected to be saints : " *That we should be holy and unspotted in His sight in charity.* " [1]   This cannot be accomplished without putting off the Old Adam and putting on the New, that is to say, without mortifying the tendencies of fallen nature and striving to reproduce the virtues of Christ. But St. Paul adds that this cannot be done without endeavoring to reach " *unto a perfect man, unto the measure of the age of the fulness of Christ.* " [2]   This means that being made into one body with Christ, we are His *complement* and that it is we who are to effect His completeness and the fulness of His growth by our own progress in the reproduction of His virtues. St. Peter likewise wants all his disciples to be saints, like Him Who has called them unto salvation : " *According to Him that hath called you, Who is holy, be you also in all manner of conversation holy.* " [3]   Could they be so, should they make no progress in the exercise of Christian virtues? St. John in the last chapter of the Apocalypse asks the just to cease not in the working of justice and invites the holy to become holier still : " *He that is just, let him be justified still ; and he that is holy, let him be sanctified still.* " [4]

357. C) The same doctrine follows from the nature of the Christian life. This life Our Lord and His disciples describe as a warfare, wherein watchfulness and prayer, mortification and positive exercise of the virtues are the necessary conditions for victory : " *Watch and pray that ye enter not into temptation.* " [5]   Having to struggle not only against flesh and blood, that is, the threefold concupiscence, but also against the evil spirits that excite our passions, we stand in need of arming ourselves spiritually and fighting fearlessly. But in a protracted struggle, if one remains always on the defensive, defeat is almost inevitable. Recourse, therefore, must be had to counter-attacks, to the positive practice of the virtues, watchfulness, mortification, and the spirit of faith and of trust. This is, in fact, the conclusion drawn by St. Paul after a description of the fight we are to sustain. He declares that we must be armed from head to foot after the fashion of the Roman soldier : " *Stand therefore, having your loins girt about with truth and having on the breast-plate of justice : and your feet shod with the preparation of the gospel of peace. In all things taking the shield of faith... and take unto you the helmet of*

---

[1] *Ephes.* I, 4. — [2] *Ephes.* IV, 13.   Read the entire passage, v. 10-16.
[3] *I Peter,* I, 15. — [4] *Apoc.,* XXII, 11. — [5] *Matth.,* XXVI, 41.

salvation and the sword of the Spirit... " [1]   In this way St. Paul shows us that we must do more than is strictly commanded in order to triumph over our enemies.

358.   2⁰ This doctrine is confirmed by *Tradition.*   When the Fathers wish to insist upon the necessity of perfection for all, they assert that we cannot remain stationary on the way that leads to God and to salvation, that we must advance or fall back : " *In the way to God, not to advance is to retreat.* "   Thus St. Augustine, noting that action is characteristic of charity, remarks that we must not halt on the way, precisely because to halt is to recede : " *He turns back who reverts whence he had once departed.* " [2] This principle is so evident that even Pelagius, his antagonist, admitted it.   St. Bernard, the last of the Fathers, explains this doctrine in a most telling way : " Dost thou wish to advance? — No. — Then dost thou wish to turn back? — By no means. — What, then, wishest thou ? — I wish to live in such a way as to remain where I have arrived... — This is impossible, for nothing in this world does remain in the same condition. " [3]   In another place he adds that : " Of necessity one must rise or else fall : if one tries to stop, one falls of a certainty. " [4]   No wonder then that Our Holy Father, Pius XI, in his Encyclical of January 26, 1923, on St. Francis de Sales, clearly states that all Christians without exception must tend toward sanctity. [5]

II. *The Argument from Reason*

The fundamental reason that obliges us to tend to perfection is the one given by the Fathers.

359.   1⁰ Life is movement, hence it is essentially progressive; no sooner does it cease to grow than it begins to decline.   The reason for this is that there are in all living beings disintegrating forces which, if not counteracted, end by causing disease and death.   The same holds true of our spiritual life.   Side by side with those tendencies that incline us toward good, there are other forces that incline us strongly toward evil.   The one effective means of combatting them is to strengthen within us the living forces of the love of God and the Christian virtues.   Then the evil forces abate.   If we stop trying to advance, our vices reawaken, gather strength, and assail us with added vigor and frequency; and unless we awake from our torpor, the moment

---

[1] *Ephes.*, VI, 14-17. — [2] *Sermon*, CLXIX, n. 18. — [3] *Epist.* CCLIV, n. 4.
[4] *Epist.*, XCI, n. 3. — [5] *Acta Apostolicæ Sedis*, XV, 50.

will come when from surrender to surrender we fall into mortal sin. [1] Such is, alas! the story of many a soul, and the experience of spiritual directors is witness to it.

A comparison will make us understand this. To work out our salvation we have to go counter to the current, more or less violent, of our own disordered passions bearing us on toward evil. So long as we make the effort to go against the current, we advance or at least we hold our own. The moment we stop we are carried along and driven seaward, there to meet the ocean storms, that is, grave temptations and perhaps lamentable falls.

360. 2° There are grave precepts that cannot at certain times be observed except by heroic acts. If we take into account psychological laws, we are not ordinarily capable of heroic acts, unless we have prepared for them in advance by sacrifice or, in other words, by the practice of mortification. A few examples will render this truth more concrete. Let us take, for instance, the precept of *chastity* and see the generous, at times heroic efforts required to keep it throughout life. Up to marriage (and many young men do not marry before their twenty-fifth or thirtieth year), this precept exacts *absolute continence* under the pain of mortal sin. Now, serious temptations make themselves felt in almost all of us at the age of puberty, at times even before. To resist them successfully, we must pray; we must avoid dangerous associations, readings, and shows; we must reproach ourselves with the slightest failings and profit by them in order to rise without delay and with added generosity, all this throughout a considerable part of life. Does not all this presuppose more than ordinary effort? Does it not demand at least some works of supererogation? Nor does marriage protect us against all grave temptations. There are periods when conjugal continence is imperative. To practice it, a heroic courage is required, a courage acquired only by habitual mortification of sensual pleasure and the unwearied practice of prayer.

361. Again, let us consider the laws of *justice* in financial, commercial and industrial transactions. Do we not at once think of the thousand and one ways there are of violating justice, of the difficulties of dealing with perfect honesty in an atmosphere where competition and greed cause prices to rise beyond just limits? We shall soon see that in order to remain simply honest, extraordinary efforts and self-denial are required. Will a man be ready for such

---

[1] This is the common teaching of theologians summarized by SUAREZ in *De Religione*, t. IV, l. I, c. 4, n. 12.

efforts if he has been accustomed to observe only the precepts that bind under pain of mortal sin? In order to shun this danger one must do at least a little more that is strictly commanded, so that the will, schooled by acts of generosity, may have the strength to resist temptations to commit acts of grave injustice.

On all sides this moral law is verified — in order not to fall into sin, we must stave off the danger by the performance of generous acts which are not directly prescribed by law. To strike the target we must aim above it; not to lose grace, we must fortify our will against temptation by works of supererogation; in other words, we must aim at some measure of perfection.

§ II. Motives that Make This Duty Easier

The numerous motives that may draw the faithful on to perfection can be reduced to three principal ones : 1º the welfare of our soul, 2º the glory of God, 3º the edification of the neighbor.

362. 1º *The welfare of our soul* means security of salvation, increase of merit, and joy of a good conscience.

A) The great work we are to accomplish here on earth, truly the one thing necessary, is *the salvation of our soul.* If we save our soul, even should we lose all the goods of earth : parents, friends, good name, wealth, all is saved; we shall find again in Heaven all we have lost, increased one hundredfold and that for all eternity. The most effective means, however, of securing our salvation is to aim at perfection, each one according to his state of life. The higher we aim, with due discretion and with constancy, the greater is the distance we put between ourselves and mortal sin, which alone can prevent our salvation. It is evident that when one sincerely strives to grow in perfection one thereby removes the occasions of sin, strengthens the will against surprises, so that when the moment of temptation arrives, the will, disciplined by effort toward perfection, accustomed to pray in order to obtain the grace of God, repels with horror the very thought of grave sin : " *Rather die than be defiled.* " On the other hand, those who allow themselves whatever falls short of grave sin, run the risk of falling the moment a prolonged and violent temptation presents itself; for, accustomed to yielding to pleasure in lesser things, there is reason to fear that carried away by passion they will end by falling, just as the man who constantly walks on

the edge of the abyss finally falls into it.   In order, then, to
make sure that we shall not offend God grievously, the best
means is to keep at a safe distance from evil by doing more
than is strictly commanded and by striving to advance
toward perfection; for the more we strive, with due prudence
and humility, the surer we are of our eternal salvation.

363.   B) In this way we likewise increase daily *habitual
grace* and acquire a title to a higher degree of glory in
heaven.   We have seen that every supernatural act done
for God by a soul in the state of grace results in an
increase of merit.   Whoever is unmindful of perfection
and is more or less remiss in the performance of his duty,
acquires but little merit, as we have said above, n. 243.   On
the contrary, he who tends to perfection and strives to make
progress, secures merit in large measure; he augments daily
his store of grace and glory; each of his efforts is rewarded
by additional grace here on earth and of happiness in
heaven : " *An eternal weight of glory.* " [1]

364.   C) If we desire to have *true happiness* on earth,
there is no better way than to cultivate piety (godliness)
which, as St. Paul says, " *is profitable to all things, having
promise of the life that now is and of that which is to come.*" [2]
Peace of soul, the joy of a good conscience, the happiness of
union with God, of growing in His love, of effecting a closer
intimacy with Christ, such are a few of the rewards which,
along with the comforting hope of life eternal, God dispenses
even now to His faithful servants in the midst of their
trials.

365.   2º *The Glory of God.*   There is nothing more
noble than to procure the glory of God, nothing more just
when we recall all that God has done and ever does for us.
Now, a perfect man gives more glory to God than a thousand ordinary souls.   For he multiplies day by day his acts
of love, of gratitude, of reparation ; he directs toward God
his whole life by the oft-renewed offering of ordinary
actions, thus giving glory to Him from morning until night.

366.   3º *The Edification of our Neighbor.*   There is
no better way to do good to others, to bring to God sinners
or unbelievers and to strengthen the wavering, than the
earnest effort to live a thoroughly Christian life.   Just as a
common-place life on the part of Christians invites the
critical and the unbelieving to scoff at Christianity, so true

---

[1] *II Cor.*, IV, 17. — [2] *II Tim.*, IV, 8.

sanctity calls forth their admiration for a religion that produces such effects : " *By their fruits you shall know them.* " [1] The best *apologetics* are those of example coupled with the fulfilment of all our social duties. This is likewise the best stimulus to careless Christians who would remain in their spiritual indolence if the earnest efforts of fervent souls did not stir them up.

This motive appeals today to many a soul. This is an age of proselytism, and lay people realize better than ever the necessity of defending and spreading the faith by word and example. It devolves upon priests to further this movement by creating round about them a choice body of resolute Christian men and women determined to become daily more and more faithful to all their duties, civic and social, and above all religious. These will be valuable co-workers, who going into places inacessible to the priest and the religious, will successfully second their efforts in the exercise of zeal.

ART. II. THE OBLIGATION INCUMBENT UPON RELIGIOUS OF TENDING TOWARD PERFECTION [2]

367. There are among Christians those who, wishing to give themselves all the more perfectly to God and to insure more effectively the welfare of their souls, enter the religious state. This state is according to the *Code of Canon Law*, [3] " a permanent manner of living in community wherein the faithful, in addition to those things that are of precept, engage themselves by vow to observe the evangelical counsels of obedience, chastity and poverty. "

All theologians agree that Religious are *bound to tend to perfection* in virtue of their state. The Code recalls this teaching when it declares that " each and every religious superior as well as subject is bound to tend toward the perfection of his state. " [4] This obligation is so grave that St. Alphonsus does not hesitate to say : " If a religious takes the firm resolution of not tending toward perfection or of

---

[1] *Matth.*, VII, 20.

[2] *Codex*, can. 487-672; St. THOM., IIa IIæ, q. 24, a. 9;q. 183, a. 1-4; p. 184-186; SUAREZ, *De Religione*, tr. VII; S. FRANCIS DE SALES, *Spiritual Conferences*, Letters to Persons in Religion; S. ALPHONSUS, *The Religious State*; VERMEERSCH, *De Religiosis;* VALUY, *Les Vertus Religieuses*, 1914; GAUTRELET, *Traité de l'état religieux;* J. P. MOTHON, *Traité sur l'état religieux*, 1923; GAY, *Religious Life and vows*; Card. GASQUET, *Religio Religiosi;* HEDLEY, *Retreat, Retreat for Religious;* BUTLER, *Benedictine Monachism;* SCOTT, *Convent Life;* BUCKLER, *Spiritual Perfection;* LORD, *Our Nuns;* GIRAUD-THURSTON, *The Spirit of Sacrifice in the Religious Life; Catholic Encyclop.*, *Religious Life.*

[3] Can. 487. — [4] Can. 593.

giving no thought whatever to it, he commits a mortal sin. " [1]
Such a religious would fail seriously in his duty of state,
which is precisely that of tending to perfection. On this
account the religious state is called a *state of perfection*, that
is to say, a permanent condition of life, officially recognized
as such by Canon Law, wherein one binds oneself to strive
after perfection. Hence, as St. Thomas teaches, it is not
necessary to have attained perfection before entering the
religious life, but one enters it precisely to acquire perfection. [2]

The obligation for religious of tending to perfection is
based chiefly on a twofold reason : 1° *their vows;* 2° *their
rules and constitutions.*

I. *The Obligation Based on the Vows*

368.   When one becomes a religious it is for the purpose
of giving, of consecrating oneself more perfectly to God.
This is the reason for the three vows. These vows impose
the obligation of performing acts of virtue which are not of
precept; and these acts are all the more perfect as the vows
add to their intrinsic worth the merit of the virtue of religion.
Moreover, these vows remove, at least in part, some of the
greatest obstacles to perfection. We shall understand this
better when we examine these vows in detail.

369.   1° By the vow of *poverty* we renounce *external
possessions* present or future. If the vow is *solemn,* we
renounce the very right to ownership, so that all acts of
ownership would be canonically void, as the Code has it,
Canon 579. If the vow is *simple,* we do not renounce the
right itself to ownership, but only the free exercise thereof;
consequently the use of this right depends upon the will of
Superiors and is confined within the limits set by them.

This vow is a help in overcoming one of the great obstacles to perfection, namely, the inordinate love of riches
and the cares inherent to the administration of temporal
goods. It is, therefore, a great means of spiritual progress.
Moreover, this vow imposes painful *sacrifices;* one has not
the security, the independence which the free use of one's
own goods confers. At times, one has to suffer certain
privations that community-life imposes : it is hard and
humiliating to be obliged to have recourse to a Superior for
everything one needs. Here we have acts of virtue imposed

---

[1] *Theol. moralis*, l. IV, n. 18.
[2] *Sum. Theol.*, IIa IIæ, q. 186, a. 1, ad 3.

by the vow of poverty which not only make us tend towards, but actually bring us nearer to perfection.

370. 2° The vow of *chastity* enables us to overcome a second obstacle to perfection, the concupiscence of the flesh, and frees us from the cares and worries of family-life. St. Paul calls attention to this when he says : " He that is without a wife is solicitous for the things that belong to the Lord : how he may please God. But he that is with a wife is solicitous for the things of the world : how he may please his wife. And he is divided. " [1] But the vow of chastity does not divest us of concupiscence; and the grace that is given to keep this vow is not meant to spare us pain and struggle. To observe life-long continence it is necessary to watch and pray, to mortify the exterior senses and curiosity, to check the sensitive appetite, to avoid idleness, to give the heart entirely to God by the practice of charity, to live in intimate and affectionate union with Our Lord, as we shall show when we speak of the virtue of chastity. Now, to do all this is evidently to tend to perfection. It is to renew constantly the effort to conquer self and control one of the most violent tendencies of fallen nature.

371. *Obedience* goes even further. It brings into submission not solely to God, but to Rules and to Superiors, that which we cling to most tenaciously, our own will. By this vow the Religious pledges himself to obey the commands of his lawful Superior in all that concerns the vows and constitutions. Here it is question of *formal commands*, and not of mere advice. Such a command is recognized by the formulas employed by the Superior, for instance, when he commands in the name of *holy obedience*, in the name of Our Lord, or when he uses any other equivalent expression making clear that he means to give a formal order. Of course this power of Superiors is limited. They are to command according to the rule, " not going beyond what is expressly or implicitly contained therein, that is, the constitutions, the statutes legally designed to ensure their observance, the penalties sanctioned to punish transgressions and prevent further infractions, and whatever relates to the fulfilment of the different duties and to an efficient and fair administration. [2]

In spite of these restrictions, it remains true that the vow

---

[1] *I Cor.*, VII, 32-33.
[2] VALUY, *Les Vertus Religieuses*, 19e éd. p. 106. To be valid in the external forum, the command must be given in writing or before two witnesses (Code, C. 24).

of obedience is one of those that come hardest to human nature, precisely because we are so much attached to our own will. To observe it we need humility, patience and meekness; we have to mortify that strong tendency of ours to criticise Superiors, to prefer our judgment to theirs, to follow our likes and at times our whims. To overcome these tendencies, to bend our will respectfully before that of Superiors and to see God in them is, without doubt, to tend to perfection, for it is to cultivate some of the most difficult virtues. Besides, since true obedience is the best proof of love, to practice it is to grow in the virtue of charity.

372. It is clear, then, that fidelity to the three vows entails not only the practice of the great virtues of poverty, chastity and obedience, but also of a great many others which are indispensable to their observance. To pledge oneself to keep them is certainly to oblige oneself to an uncommon degree of perfection.

II. *The Obligation Based on the Constitutions and the Rules*

373. Upon entering the religious state one assumes the obligation to observe the Constitutions and the Rules explained in the course of the novitiate, before profession. Now, no matter what Order or Congregation one may enter, there is not a single one that has not as its end the sanctification of its members and that does not determine, at times in great detail, the *virtues* they must practice and the *means* that facilitate their exercise. Hence, if one is sincere, one binds himself to keep at least in general those various rules, and by this very fact, to rise to a certain degree of perfection; for in keeping these rules, though it be only in a general way, one has plenty of opportunities to mortify oneself in things not of precept, and the effort one is forced to make in this direction is an effort toward perfection.

374. Here the question arises whether the infringement of the rules constitutes a *sin* or a mere imperfection. Many distinctions must be made to answer this question.

a) There are rules prescribing fidelity to those virtues that are of precept, or to the vows, and there are other rules determining the *means necessary* to the keeping of these virtues and vows, for instance, the rule of enclosure for cloistered communities. Such rules bind in conscience for the very reason that they simply *promulgate* an obligation flowing from the vows themselves, for when making these, one assumes the obligation of keeping them and taking the means necessary for their observance. These rules bind under the pain of sin, mortal or venial according to the importance of the matter. They are, therefore, *preceptive* and, in certain Congregations they are clearly noted as such, either directly or indirectly, by the infliction of a grave sanction which supposes a proportionate fault.

375. b) There are, on the other hand, rules which explicitly or implicitly are considered as being *simply directive*. 1) To break them without reason is no doubt an imperfection, but such infraction is not *in itself* even a venial sin, for there is no violation either of a law or of a command. 2) St. Thomas, however, justly remarks that one may sin grievously against the rule, if one violates it *out of contempt* (contempt of the rule itself or contempt of Superiors). [1] One may sin lightly if the violation in question is due to voluntary negligence, passion, anger, sensuality or any other sinful motive. In this case it is the motive that constitutes the fault. We may add with St. Alphonsus that the fault may be grave if the infractions are frequent and deliberate, either because of the resulting scandal, which gradually leads to an appreciable weakening of discipline, or because the delinquent exposes himself to expulsion from the community to the great detriment of his soul.

376. Superiors, therefore, are obliged in virtue of their office to enforce the rules with care. The Superior who would neglect to check transgressions of the rule, even slight ones, when they tend to become frequent, may be guilty of a grave fault, because he thereby encourages a gradual relaxation, which in a community constitutes a grave disorder. Such is the teaching of de Lugo, St. Liguori, Schram [2] and many other theologians.

But the true religious does not enter into these distinctions. He observes the rule as perfectly as he can, knowing this to be the best way of pleasing God : " *Who lives by rule lives unto God.*" In like manner, he is not satisfied with keeping to the letter of the vows, but rather he lives by their spirit in striving daily to approach perfection according to the word of St. John : " He that is holy, let him be sanctified still. " [3] Then, are fulfilled in him the words of St. Paul : " And whosoever shall follow this rule, *peace on them and mercy.* " [4]

---

[1] *Sum. theol.*, IIa IIæ, q. 186, a. 9, ad 1 et 3.
[2] SCHRAM, *Instit. Theol. Mysticæ*, § 655, Scholion.
[3] *Apoc.*, XXII, 11. — [4] *Galat.*, VI, 16.

ART. III. THE OBLIGATION INCUMBENT UPON PRIESTS OF TENDING TO PERFECTION [1]

377. Priests in virtue of their functions and of the mission which makes theirs the duty of sanctifying souls, are bound *to a higher interior holiness* than that of the simple religious not raised to the priesthood. This is the express teaching of *St. Thomas*, [2] confirmed by the most authoritative ecclesiastical pronouncements. The Councils, and particularly that of Trent, [3] the Supreme Pontiffs, and especially Leo XIII [4] and Pius X, [5] so insist upon the necessity of *holiness* in the priest, that to deny our thesis is to stand in open contradiction to authorities that cannot be gainsaid. Let it suffice to recall the fact that Pius X, upon the occasion of the fiftieth anniversary of his priesthood, issued a letter addressed to the Catholic clergy, wherein he shows the *necessity of holiness* in the priest, and enumerates one by one the *means* necessary to attain it, those very means, by the way, which are insisted on in our Seminaries. After describing *interior holiness (vitæ morumque sanctimonia)*, he declares that only this holiness makes us what our vocation requires us to be, " men who are crucified to the world, who have put on the new Adam, men whose thoughts are fixed on heavenly things and who strive by all possible means to lead others to heaven. "

378. The New Code has confirmed the views of Pius X by emphasizing more than the old legislation did the necessity of holiness in the priest and the means of exercising himself therein. It declares in no obscure words that

---

[1] Besides the authors already quoted, see ARVISENET, *Memoriale vitæ sacerdotalis;* MOLINA LE CHARTREUX, *L'instruction des prêtres*, 2e Traité ; OLIER, *Traité des SS. Ordres;* TRONSON, *Particular Examens;* DUBOIS, *Le saint Prêtre;* CAUSSETTE, *Manrèse du Prêtre;* GIBBONS, *The Ambassador of Christ;* GIRAUD, *Priest and Victim;* MANNING, *The Eternal Priesthood;* MGR. LELONG, *Le Prêtre;* CARD. MERCIER, *The Interior Life, Retreat to his Priests, Conferences to his Seminarians;* HEDLEY, *Lex Levitarum, Retreat for Priests;* CARD. VAUGHAN, *The Young Priest, Introduction to the Life of St. John B. de Rossi*; KEATINGE, *The Priest, His Character and Work;* MILLET-BYRNE, *Jesus Living in the Priest;* BRUNEAU, *Our Priesthood;* GRIMAL, *Priesthood and Sacrifice;* CARD. BOURNE, *Ecclesiastical Training ; The Teaching of St. Thomas on Priestly Perfection*, Cath. Educ. Assoc., 1924.

[2] " By Holy Orders a man is deputed to the most dignified ministry, to serve Christ in the Sacrament of the Altar. For this a greater interior sanctity is required than even the religious state demands. " IIa-IIæ, q. 184, a. 6, 8.

[3] Sess. XXII, de Reform. c. 1.

[4] Encyclical *Quod multum*, Aug. 22nd, 1886; Encyclical Letter *Depuis le jour*, Sept. 8, 1899.

[5] *Exhortatio ad clerum catholicum*, Aug. 4th, 1908. The entire letter should be read. See BRUNEAU, *Our Priesthood*, Appendix.

" clerics must lead an interior and exterior life holier than that of the laity and give these the good example of virtue and good works. " It adds that Bishops should see to it, " that all clerics receive frequently the Sacrament of Penance to be purified of their faults; that each day they apply themselves during a certain length of time to the exercise of mental prayer, visit the Most Blessed Sacrament, recite the beads in honor of the Blessed Mother of God, and make their examination of conscience. At least every three years diocesan priests must make a retreat. All clerics, but chiefly priests, are especially bound to respect and to obey their Bishop. " [1]

This doctrine, that the priest is obliged to tend to perfection, is proved : 1o by the authority of *Our Lord* and of *St. Paul*, 2o by the *Pontifical*, 3o by the very nature of the *priestly functions*.

I. *The Teaching of Our Lord and of St. Paul*

379. 1o *Our Lord* eloquently teaches the necessity of holiness in the priest by His examples as well as by His words.

A) *He gives* **the example.** He Who from the beginning was " *full of grace and truth* " has willed to submit Himself to the law of progress : " *Jesus advanced in wisdom and age and grace with God and men.* " [2] Nay, during thirty years He prepared for His public ministry by a hidden life and all that this implies : prayer, mortification, humility, obedience. Thirty years of the life of the Incarnate Word are summed up in these few words : " *He was subject to them.* " [3] To make His preaching of the Christian virtues more effective, He began by practicing them : " *Jesus began to do and to teach,* " [4] so that He could have proposed Himself as a model of all virtues, as He did of the virtues of humility and meekness : " *Learn of me, because I am meek and humble of heart.* " [5] At the close of His life He declared in all simplicity that He sanctifies and sacrifices Himself in order that His Apostles and His priests, their successors, be sanctified in all truth : " *And for them do I sanctify myself that they also may be sanctified in truth.* " [6] Now, the priest is the representative of Jesus Christ upon earth, another Christ : " *For Christ therefore we are ambassadors.* " [7] Hence, the priest, too, must be ever pursuing holiness of life.

---

[1] Can. 124-127. — [2] *Luke*, II, 52. — [3] *Luke*, II, 51. — [4] *Act.*, I, 1.
[5] *Matth.*, XI, 26. — [6] *John*, XVII, 19. — [7] *II Cor.*, V, 20.

380. B) What Our Lord teaches by His example, He teaches also by His word. The great work of the three years of His public life was *the training of the Twelve*. [1] In this He employed the most of His time; it was His habitual occupation. Preaching to the crowds was merely secondary and was to serve as a model of what the preaching of His disciples should be. From this are drawn the following conclusions : **a**) The sublime teachings on godliness, inward holiness, self-denial, the love of God and the neighbor, humility, meekness and all the other virtues so frequently inculcated in the Gospel, are meant, no doubt, for all Christians aspiring to perfection, but they are first of all addressed to the *Apostles* and their successors. For it is they who are commissioned to teach the people of God these great duties by their example even more than by their word. The *Pontifical* recalls this to the deacons : " *Take heed that ye show forth the living works of the Gospel unto whom you proclaim it by word of mouth.* " Every one agrees that these doctrines embody a *code of perfection* that is very high. Hence, it is a duty of state for priests to strive after holiness.

381. b) The exhortations to higher perfection that we find in so many places in the Gospel are most particularly addressed to the *Apostles* and to *priests :* " *You are the salt of the earth... You are the light of the world.* " [2] This *light* is not only *knowledge* but rather and chiefly the beacon-light of example, which enlightens and attracts even more than knowledge : " *So let your light shine before men that they may see your good works and glorify your Father who is in heaven.* " [3] It is likewise to priests that are addressed in a special manner the *counsels* regarding *poverty* and *chastity*, for in virtue of their vocation they are obliged to follow Christ more closely.

382. c) Lastly, there is a whole series of teachings that *directly and explicitly* are meant for the *Apostles* and their *successors :* the instructions He gave to the Twelve and to the Seventy-two when He sent them to preach in Judea, and the discourse He pronounced at the Last Supper. These utterances embody a code of priestly holiness so high as to imply the duty of tending to perfection. Priests must live a life of complete *detachment*, be poor in spirit, and poor in fact, being satisfied with what they need; they must

---

[1] DELBREL, S. J., *Jésus, Educateur des Apôtres*, ch. IV-VI.
[2] *Matth.*, V, 13 and 14. — [3] *Matth.*, V, 16.

exercise *zeal, charity,* absolute *devotedness, patience* and *humility* in the midst of persecutions, *courage* to confess Christ and preach His Gospel before all men and in spite of all men. They must be detached from the world and from their kin, learn to carry the Cross and live in total abnegation of self. [1]

383. At the *Last Supper* [2] He gives unto them that new commandment, to love one another as He has loved them, that is to say, unto the complete immolation of self. He counsels them to have faith, a live faith and an absolute confidence in the prayer that is offered in His name. He urges on them the love of God, which is made manifest by keeping His commandments; peace of soul in order to receive and relish the teachings of the Holy Spirit; an intimate and abiding union with Himself as the essential condition for their sanctification and the discharge of their ministry. He exhorts them to patience midst the persecutions of the world that shall hate them as it has hated their Master; to docility to the Holy Ghost, their Comforter in their tribulations; to steadfastness in the faith, to prayer in their trials. In a word, He recommends to them all those things which constitute the essential condition of what we call today the interior life or the life of perfection. He ends this discourse by that grand *sacerdotal prayer,* so full of tenderness, wherein He asks His Father to keep His chosen ones as He Himself has kept them during the course of His mortal life; to keep them from evil in the midst of the world which they must evangelize, and to *sanctify them in all truth.* He utters this prayer not only in behalf of His Apostles but for all those that through them would believe in Him, so that they may ever be one, even as the Three Divine Persons are one, that they may all be one with God and one with Christ : " *That the love wherewith thou hast loved me may be in them, and I in them.* " [3] This is a charter of perfection drawn up for us by Our High-Priest, Whose representatives on earth we are, Whose priesthood we share. It must be an inspiration for us to think that He prayed that we might live according to this standard.

384. 2° St. Paul, drawing his inspiration from this teaching of the Master, describes in his turn the apostolic virtues. Stating in the first place that priests are the dispensers of the mysteries of God, His ministers, the ambas-

---

[1] *Matth.*, X, XI; *Luke,* IX, X, etc.
[2] *John,* XIV-XVII. — [3] *John,* XVII, 27.

sadors of Christ, and the mediators between God and men, he then enumerates in the Pastoral Epistles the virtues wherewith deacons, priests and bishops must be adorned. For them, it is not enough to have once received the grace of ordination ; they must make it live vigorously lest it wane : " *I admonish thee that thou stir up the grace of God which is in thee by the imposition of my hands.*" [1] Deacons must be chaste and modest, sober, disinterested, discreet and faithful, knowing how to govern their houses with prudence and dignity. Even more perfect must priests and bishops be. [2] Their lives must be so pure as to be irreproachable. They must sedulously combat pride, anger, intemperance, avarice, and cultivate the virtues of humility, temperance, chastity, holiness, kindness, generosity, patience, meekness and above all godliness (which is profitable unto all things), faith and charity. [3] They must *be examples* of these virtues and must therefore practice them to a high degree : " *In all things show thyself an example of good works.*" [4] All these virtues presuppose a certain measure of perfection already acquired and a generous and constant effort to advance.

II. *The Teaching of the Pontifical*

385. It would be an easy task to show that the Fathers, commenting on the Epistles and Gospels, have unfolded these teachings and explained them in detail. We could even add that they have written *Letters* and entire *Treatises* upon the dignity and the holiness of the priesthood. [5] In order to be brief, however, we shall confine ourselves to the teaching of the Pontifical, which is the *Priestly Code*, as it were, of the New Law, embodying the summary of what the Catholic Church requires of her ministers. This simple exposition will show the high degree of perfection demanded of the Ordinands and still more of priests in the ministry. [6]

---

[1] *II Tim.*, I, 6.

[2] " For a bishop must be without crime, as the steward of God ; not proud, not subject to anger, not given to wine, no striker, not greedy of filthy lucre : but given to hospitality, gentle, sober, just, holy, continent : embracing that faithful word wich is according to doctrine, that he may be able to exhort in sound doctrine and to convince the gainsayers. " *Tit.*, I, 7-9.

[3] " *Pursue justice, godliness, faith, charity, patience, mildness.* " *I Tim.*, VI, 11.

[4] *Tit.*, II, 7.

[5] Most of these Treatises are to be found in a work entitled : " *Le Prêtre d'après les Pères* ", by RAYNAUD, 12 in-8º, Paris, 1843. See likewise the numerous texts in L. TRONSON's book, *Forma Cleri*.

[6] For the explanation of the Pontifical, cfr. OLIER, *op. cit.*, ; BACUEZ, *Major Orders, Minor Orders, Vocation and Tonsure;* GIRAUD, *op. cit.*, t. II; GONTIER, *Explication du Pontifical;* BRUNEAU, *Our Priesthood.*

386. 1º The Church demands of the *tonsured* cleric a *universal detachment* from whatever is an obstacle to the love of God, and an *intimate union with Our Lord*, that he may wage war against the tendencies of the Old Adam and may put on the dispositions of the New. The *Dominus pars*, which he should utter every day, reminds him that *God*, and *God alone*, is his portion, his inheritance, and that whatever cannot be referred to Him should be trodden under foot. The *Induat me* shows him that life is a warfare, a struggle against the evil inclinations of nature, an effort to cultivate the supernatural virtues implanted in our souls on the day of our Baptism. Thus, from the outset, it is the *love of God* that is given him as the *end* to be reached, and *sacrifice* as the *means* thereto, with the obligation of fostering these two dispositions in his soul, if he is to be promoted to higher ranks in the clergy.

387. 2º Minor Orders confer upon the cleric a *twofold power :* one over Christ's Eucharistic Body, the other over His mystical body, that is, over souls. Besides detachment, he is to have a *twofold love*, the love of Our Lord in the Blessed Sacrament and the *love of souls*. Both imply sacrifice.

As *porter*, he is separated from the occupations of the home and constituted the official custodian of the House of God. The *reader* rises above the interest of worldly studies to tarry in the consideration of the Sacred Text, to draw therefrom that doctrine which will work unto his own sanctification and that of others. The *exorcist* casts off sin and the remnants of sin, to evade all the more surely the power of Satan. The *acolyte* renounces *the pleasures of sense* to live in that state of purity which the service of the altar exacts. At the same time His love for God becomes stronger. He loves the God of the Eucharist, Whose guardian he is. He loves the Word, hidden beneath the sacred veil of Holy Writ. He loves Him at Whose commands the spirits of darkness tremble and obey. He loves the Victim of the Altar. This love blossoms forth in zeal : the cleric loves *souls*, whom with joyful heart he brings to God by word and example, whom he sanctifies by his participation in the Holy Sacrifice. Thus step by step he makes his way forward unto perfection.

388. 3º By his irrevocable consecration to God, the *subdeacon* immolates himself out of love for Him, a prelude to the Sacrifice he will one day offer upon the altar. He immolates his body by the vow of *chastity* and consecrates

his soul by dedicating it to the recitation of the divine office.
Chastity implies mortification of the interior and exterior
senses, of the mind, of the heart.   The duty of the Divine
Office supposes a spirit of recollection and of prayer, the
sustained effort for a life of union with God.   One cannot
be faithful in these two duties of chastity and of prayer
without *an ardent love of God*, which love alone can shelter
the heart from the allurements of sensual love and lay the
soul open to prayer and recollection.   *Sacrifice* and *love*,
then, is what the Church demands of the subdeacon, a sacrifice greater than any he had made up to the present; for the
efforts demanded at times by a life-long chastity are nothing
short of the heroic, and require an habitual spirit of watchfulness, humble mistrust of self, and mortification. [1]   Furthermore, it is a sacrifice which is *irrevocable* : "*But if you
receive this Order, you will no longer be at liberty to recede
from your resolution, but you will be obliged to serve God
perpetually, to serve Whom is to reign.*" [2]   That this sacrifice
be *possible* and *lasting* it must be made with a great deal of
love.   An intense love of God and love for souls alone can
shield us from profane love; it alone gives us the relish for
the sweetness of perpetual prayer, by directing our thoughts
and our affections toward Him Who alone can steady them.
Therefore, the Pontiff invokes upon the ordinand the seven
gifts of the Holy Ghost that he be made mighty unto
the fulfilment of the stern duties laid upon him by the
subdiaconate.

389.   4° Of *deacons*, who co-operate actively in the oblation of the Sacred Victim, who are "*co-ministers and co-ope-
rators of the Body and Blood of the Lord,*" the Pontifical
exacts even a more perfect purity : "*Be clean, undefiled,
pure, chaste.*"   Because they have the power to preach the
Gospel, they are asked to proclaim it even more by *example*
than by word : "*Take care that you may illustrate the
gospel, by your living works, to those to whom you announce
it with your lips.*"   Their life must be a living exemplifica-
tion of the Gospel and a constant imitation of the virtues of
the Master.   Thus, the Bishop praying that the Holy Spirit
may descend upon them with all His gifts, chiefly that of

---

[1] " Celibacy is an heroic virtue, and for heroic virtue we need high sanctity.
If I am asked what degree of perfection or holiness the Church demands of her
priests, it is enough for me to answer that she demands of them perfect chastity
and a life of celibacy.   This obligation is so heavy, its extent is so broad, that it
either presupposes or leads to a high degree of personal sanctity. " KEATINGE,
The Priest, His Character and Work, p. 101.
[2] *Pontifical*, ordination of Subdeacons.

fortitude, addresses to God this beautiful prayer : " *Let the practice of every virtue abound in them, mild authority, constant modesty, the purity of innocence, and the observance of spiritual discipline.* "   Is not this a petition in their behalf for the virtues that lead to sanctity?   In his final prayer, in fact, the Pontiff asks that they be adorned with all the virtues : " *Well-formed in all the virtues.* "

390.   5° The *Pontifical* demands even more of the priest. Because he offers the Holy Sacrifice of the Mass he must be both *priest* and *victim*.   This he shall be by the *immolation of his passions* : " *Bear in mind what you do.   Let your conduct be in conformity with the action you perform, so that celebrating the mystery of the Lord's death, you take heed to mortify your members from all vices and lusts.* "   He shall become such a victim by his constant renewal in the spirit of *holiness* : " *Renew in them, O God, the spirit of holiness.* " To attain this, the Law of God shall be the object of his thoughts by day and by night that he may teach it to others, that he may live by it himself and thus be an exemplar of all Christian virtues : " *That meditating on Thy law, day and night, they may believe what they read, teach what they believe and practice what they teach.   May they show forth in themselves justice, constancy, mercy, fortitude and all other virtues.* "   As he is to *be spent for souls*, he shall practice brotherly love in the form of devotedness : " *Receive the priestly vestment by which charity is signified;* " and, after the example of St. Paul, he shall spend himself entirely for the sake of souls : " *I most gladly will spend and be spent myself for your souls.* " [1]

391.   Thus it is that at each step toward the priesthood, the *Pontifical* demands a greater measure of virtue, of love and of sacrifice.   Coming finally to the priesthood, it requires *sanctity* in order, as St. Thomas [2] says, that the priest be made fit to offer worthily the august sacrifice and be enabled to sanctify the souls committed to his care.   The Ordinand is free to go on or not, but if he receives orders, he thereby evidently accepts the conditions so explicitly laid down by the Prelate, that is, the obligation of tending to perfection, an obligation which far from ceasing, becomes more urgent with the actual exercise of the sacred ministry.

---

[1] *II Cor.*, XII, 15.
[2] ST. THOMAS, *Suppl.*, q. 35, a. 1, ad 3. " For the worthy exercise of Holy Orders, ordinary virtue is not enough, but a high degree of sanctity is required. "

III. *The Nature of the Priestly Functions Demands Holiness of Life*

392. On the testimony of the Apostle St. Paul, the priest is the *mediator* between God and man, between heaven and earth. Chosen *from among men* to be their *representative*, he must be *acceptable* to God, called by Him so as to have a right to appear before Him, and to offer the homages of men and to obtain His favors : " *For every high priest taken from among men is ordained for men in the things that appertain to God, that he may offer up gifts and sacrifices for sin... Neither doth any man take the honour to himself, but he that is called by God, as Aaron was.* " [1] His functions can be reduced to two principal ones : he is the " *Religious of God,* " [2] charged with glorifying Him in the name of the whole Christian people ; he is also a Savior, a Sanctifier of souls, his mission being that of co-operating with Jesus Christ in the work of their sanctification and their salvation. He should be saintly on this twofold ground, [3] and should therefore ever tend toward perfection, since he will never fully attain to the plenitude of that holiness demanded by his office.

I° THE PRIEST, AS " THE RELIGIOUS OF GOD, "
SHOULD BE A SAINTLY MAN

393. In virtue of his mission, the priest must *glorify* God in the name of the Christian people. Truly, then, he is the *Religious of God*, and that by reason of the priesthood such as Our Lord instituted it. " *He is ordained for men in the things that appertain to God, that he may offer up gifts and sacrifices.* " It is above all through the Holy Sacrifice of the Mass and the recitation of the Divine Office that he acquits himself of this duty ; yet all his actions, even the most ordinary, may contribute thereto, if they be done with a view to please God. This mission cannot be fulfilled in a seemly manner except by a *priest* who is saintly or a least who is striving to become so.

394. **A)** What holiness is required in order to offer up the *Holy Sacrifice!* The priests of the Old Law had to be

---

[1] *Hebr.*, V, 1, 4.

[2] Religious in the sense that he is officially charged with fulfiling toward God the duties of religion, and not in the sense of a man entering a religious order and making the three vows.

[3] ST. THOMAS says : " Those who handle the divine mysteries obtain a regal dignity and must be perfected *in virtue.* " *(IV Sent.*, dist. 24, q. 2.)

holy, and this under pain of punishment, because they came near to God. (It is question here chiefly of legal holiness). *" The priests also that come to the Lord, let them be sanctified; lest He strike them. "* [1]   They were bound to be holy in order to offer worthily incense and the bread destined for the altar : *" For they offer the burnt offering of the Lord and the bread of their God : and therefore they shall be holy. "* [2]

How much holier should they be, how much greater interior holiness should they have who offer no longer shadows and figures, but the Great Sacrifice itself, the All-holy Victim!   All is holy in this Divine Sacrifice : *the Victim* and the chief *Offerer*, Jesus Himself, Who, says St. Paul, is *" holy, innocent, undefiled, separated from sinners, and made higher than the heavens. "* [3]   The *Church* in whose name the priest offers Holy Mass is likewise holy, whom Jesus hath sanctified with His Blood : *" Christ delivered Himself up for it... that it should be holy and without blemish. "* [4]   The *end* for which such offering is made is holy, to glorify God and bring forth in souls the fruits of holiness.   The *prayers* and *ceremonies* are holy, recalling the Sacrifice of Calvary and the effects it merited unto sanctification.   Above all is the *Communion* holy that unites us to the very source of all sanctity.

The priest, who as the representative of Jesus Christ and of the Church offers up this august Sacrifice, must of necessity be also clothed in holiness.   How could he worthily represent Christ, how could he be *another Christ*, if his life be but commonplace, void of any aspiration toward perfection?   Could he be the minister of the Church, the spotless Spouse of Christ, if his soul, attached to venial sin, is neglectful of spiritual progress?   Could he glorify God if his heart be void of love and sacrifice?   How could he sanctify souls if he lacked the earnest desire of sanctifying himself?

395.   How would he have the audacity to mount the altar uttering those prayers of the Mass which breathe the most pure sentiments of sorrow, faith, religion, love, self-denial, if his soul had no part in these?   How could he venture to offer himself with the Divine Victim, *" in a humble spirit and a contrite heart may we be received by Thee, O Lord, "* [5] if those sentiments were in contradiction with his life?   How can any man whose life is all human,

---

[1] *Exod.*, XIX, 22. — [2] *Levit.*, XXI, 6. — [3] *Hebr.*, VII, 26. — [4] *Ephes.*, V, 25-27.
[5] Prayer of the Offertory.

demand a share in the divinity of Jesus Christ? How could such a one make his own this protestation of innocence : " But as for me, I have walked in my innocence, " [1] if he make no effort to shake off the dust of a thousand and one deliberate venial sins? How dare he utter the *Sanctus* wherein God's awful holiness is proclaimed? How make bold to identify himself with Jesus Christ at the *Consecration*, with the Author of all holiness, if he strive not to sanctify himself with Him and through Him? Could he utter the Lord's prayer and not think that we must be perfect as Our Father in heaven is perfect? Could he repeat the *Agnus Dei* without a humble and contrite heart? What of those tender prayers before Communion : " *Make me always adhere to Thy commandments, and suffer me never to be separated from Thee.* " [2] And yet the heart far from God, far from Jesus! To unite himself daily in Communion with an All-holy God without a sincere desire of sharing in His holiness, without striving daily to become more and more like Him, would not this be a flagrant contradiction, a lack of loyalty, an abuse of grace and a lack of fidelity to the priestly vocation? Let priests meditate on and take to heart the Fifth Chapter of the Fourth Book of the Following of Christ : ON THE DIGNITY OF THE SACRAMENT AND OF THE PRIESTLY STATE. " *If thou hadst the purity of an angel, and the sanctity of St. John the Baptist, thou wouldst neither be worthy to receive nor to handle this Sacrament... Thou hast not lightened thy burden, but art now bound by a stricter bond of discipline, and art obliged to greater perfection of sanctity.* " [3]

396. B) What we have said of Holy Mass can be said in a certain sense also of the *Divine Office*. It is in the name of the *Church*, in union with *Jesus*, the great Religious of God, and for the whole Christian people, that seven times a day the priest appears before God to adore Him, to thank Him, and to obtain from Him the numberless graces souls need. If his prayer is but lip-service and not the tribute of his heart, will he not merit the reproach addressed by God to the Jews : " *This people honoreth me with their lips : but their heart is far from me.* " [4] And will grace be granted abundantly if he asks for it in so unworthy a manner?

---

[1] *Ps.* XXV. — [2] *Roman Missal*, Prayer before Communion.
[3] *Imitation*, Bk. IV, c. V, n. 1.
[4] *Matth.*, XV, 8; *Isaiah*, XXIX, 13.

397. Furthermore, in order that our ordinary actions be transformed into acts of worship pleasing to the Lord, they ought to be accomplished with dispositions inspired by *love* and by the spirit of sacrifice (cf. n. 309).

Whithersoever we turn, the selfsame conclusion imposes itself : as The Religious of God, the priest must aim at holiness of life.

2° THE PRIEST CANNOT BE SUCCESSFUL IN THE WORK OF SAVING SOULS UNLESS HE AIMS AT PERSONAL HOLINESS [1]

398. A) The priest's duty of state is to sanctify and to save souls. When Our Lord chose His Apostles it was in order to make them " fishers of men "; [2] in order that they should bring forth, in themselves and in others *abundant fruits of salvation :* " You have not chosen me : but I have chosen you, that you should go and should bring forth fruit; and your fruit should remain. " [3] For this must they preach the Gospel, administer the Sacraments, give good example and pray in all earnestness.

It is of faith that what converts and sanctifies souls is the *grace of God.* We ourselves are but *instruments* that God deigns to use, that bring forth fruit only in the measure wherein they are one with the principal cause. This is the doctrine of St. Paul : " I have planted; Apollo watered : but God gave the increase. Therefore neither he that planteth is anything, nor he that watereth : but God that giveth the increase. " [4] Now, it is certain that this grace is obtained in two ways, by *prayer* and by *merit.* In either case we obtain grace in proportion to our sanctity, to our fervor, to our degree of union with Our Lord (N. 237). If, then, our duty of state consists in the sanctification of souls, our first duty is to sanctify ourselves : " And for them do I sanctify myself, that they also may be sanctified in truth. " [5]

399. B) We arrive at the same conclusion if we consider the principal *means of zeal,* namely, preaching, example and prayer.

a) Preaching produces no salutary effects unless we speak in the name and in the power of God : " God as it were exhorting by us ". [6] This is what the fervent priest does. Before preaching *he prays* in order that grace may

---

[1] Read on this subject the excellent book of DOM CHAUTARD, *L'âme de tout apostolat.* Eng. Tr., *The soul of the Apostolate.*

[2] *Matth.*, IV, 19. — [3] *John*, XV, 16. — [4] *I Cor.*, III, 6-7.

[5] *John*, XVII, 19. — [6] *II Cor.*, V, 20.

inspire his words : He humbly asks Our Lord to be " in his heart and on his lips, " *Dominus sit in corde meo et in labiis meis.* Whilst preaching he seeks, not to please, but to instruct, to do good, to convince, to persuade; and because his heart is intimately united to that of Jesus, there is in him an emotion, a power of persuasion that moves his hearers. Because by *forgetting himself he attracts the Holy Spirit,* souls are moved by grace and either converted or sanctified. A lukewarm priest, on the contrary, preaches but with his lips and, because he seeks self, beats the air and often is but " sounding brass or a tinkling cymbal. " [1]

400. b) The priest cannot fulfil *his duty* [2] of giving good *example* to the faithful unless he concerns himself with his own spiritual progress. Then only can he repeat in all confidence the words of St. Paul : " Be ye followers of me as I also am of Christ. " [3] Witnesses of his piety, of his kindness, of his poverty and of his self-denial, the faithful realize that he *practises what he preaches,* that he is a *Saint;* they venerate him and are drawn to follow in his footsteps. The old saying is again verified, that " words touch the heart, but examples rule our lives. " A mediocre priest may be esteemed as an honest man who works at his craft like any other, yet his ministry will bear little or no fruit.

401. c) *Prayer* is and will ever remain the most effective means of exercising zeal. What a contrast is offered in this regard between the saintly priest and the commonplace priest? The former prays *habitually* and constantly, for his very actions, done for God, constitute a real prayer. He does nothing, he does not even give a word of counsel without acknowledging his helplessness and begging God to make up for it by His grace. God, " Who giveth grace to the humble, " [4] grants it to him in abundance and his ministry brings forth fruit. The imperfect priest prays little and prays poorly, and for this reason his ministry remains barren.

Therefore, whoever wishes to work successfully for souls, must make daily efforts to advance. Sanctity is *the soul of the true Apostolate.*

---

[1] *I Cor.*, XIII, 1. — [2] *Cod.*, Can. 124.
[3] *I Cor.*, IV, 16. — [4] *James*, IV, 6.

CONCLUSION

402. From all that has been said it is clear that before entering the priesthood one must be already possessed of a measure of sanctity; and that, once a priest, one must continually strive to attain to a higher degree.

1º To enter the priesthood one must needs have acquired already a certain measure of perfection. This is brought out by all the texts of the *Pontifical* cited above. Even of the mere cleric is required detachment from the world and from self, and attachment to Jesus Christ. If the Church prescribes *regular intervals* between ordinations, it is with a view that the young ecclesiastic may have the time of acquiring one by one the various virtues proper to the different orders. The *Pontifical* gives clear expression to this in the following words : [1] "*And thus let them advance from one Order to the other that as they grow in age, they may likewise grow in probity of life and in doctrine.*" Moreover, it demands *tried virtue :* "*Let tried virtue be to them in the stead of old age.*" [2] But such virtue is not acquired except by the painstaking fulfilment of the duties of state, by the unwearied exercise of the virtues which the Prelate points out in every ordination. This virtue should be so *solid* that it resembles that of men advanced in years *(senectus sit)*, who through long and arduous efforts have attained to the maturity and constancy becoming their age.

403. It is not any sort of virtue that is required for the right exercise of the sacred functions; it is a *superior* kind of virtue, says St. Thomas : "*For the worthy exercise of Holy Orders ordinary goodness does not suffice, superior virtue is required.*" [3] We have seen that the *Pontifical* requires of the Ordinands a solid and active faith, a great trust in God, a devoted love of God and of the neighbor, not to mention the moral virtues of prudence, justice, religion, humility, temperance, fortitude, constancy. The practice of these virtues must reach a high degree, since the Pontiff calls down upon the Ordinands the gifts of the Holy Ghost, which supplement the virtues and perfect their practice. Hence, it is not enough to be in the state of *beginners*, as yet exposed to relapse into serious faults. One must have undergone a purification from faults and inordinate attachements, be grounded in the

---

[1] De Ordinibus Conferendis. — [2] *Loc. cit.* — [3] *Supplem.*, q. 35, a. 1, ad 3.

exercise of those virtues that belong to the *illuminative* way, and have for goal a closer and closer union with Almighty God.

404.   2⁰ Once a man has become a *priest*, he must not stop, but rather go on daily from virtue to virtue.   This is the teaching of the Imitation : " *Thou hast not lightened thy burden, but art now bound by a stricter bond of discipline, and art obliged to greater perfection of sanctity.* " [1]   Not to advance is to fall back.   (N. 358, 359.)   Moreover, such is the extent of our obligation to follow in Christ's footsteps and to edify our neighbor, that despite all efforts, we still fall short of the ideal proposed to us by the Gospel and by the *Pontifical,* as we proved when we spoke of the priestly functions (N. 392 and foll.).   We must therefore say to ourselves each day that we have yet a great way to go before attaining the goal : " Thou hast yet a great way to go. " [2]

405.   This is all the more so, since we live in the midst of the world and its dangers, whilst religious are protected by their rules and all the helps of community life.   If they are obliged to tend constantly toward perfection, are we not under the same obligation, and even a greater one?   And if we have not for the protection of our virtue all the exterior helps that protect them, are we not bound to make up for these by greater interior strength?   This strength, it stands to reason, cannot be acquired but by an ever-renewed effort toward a better life; for the world wherein we must mingle forever tends to lower our ideal, and we must therefore raise it, again and again, by constantly stirring up the spirit of the priesthood.

What makes this spiritual progress a more pressing duty still is the fact that on the degree of our own sanctity depend the welfare and the sanctification of the souls entrusted to our care.   According to the ordinary laws of a supernatural Providence, the holier the priest, the greater the good wrought by him.   This we have shown (N. 398 and foll.).   Would it be in harmony with our mission as *sanctifiers of souls* to call a halt half-way or at the very outset on the road to perfection, when so many souls in imminent danger of being lost cry out on all sides, " Pass over... and help us. " [3]   A worthy priest has but one answer to this cry of distress.   It is Our Lord's own answer : " And

---

[1] Book IV, ch. 5. — [2] *III Kings*, XIX, 7. — [3] *Acts* XVI, 9.

for them do I sanctify myself, that they also may be sanctified in truth. " [1]

406. We shall not examine in this place the question of whether the priest, obliged as he is to an interior perfection greater than that of the religious who is not in Holy Orders, is or is not in the *state of perfection*. This is a question of Canon Law. It is commonly answered in the negative, for the priest's status, even if he be a pastor of souls, lacks that *stability* which is canonically required in order to constitute the *state of perfection*.

As regards the priest who is also a religious, he evidently has all the obligations imposed on him by his priesthood besides those imposed by his vows, finding in his rule additional helps to become holy. He must not forget, however, that his priesthood obliges him to a higher perfection than does his religious profession.

Thus the members of the clergy, secular and regular, far from falling into petty jealousies, should hold each other in mutual esteem and help each other, having but one and the same aim, to glorify God by gaining unto Him souls — as many as possible. They should find in the virtues and in the success of their brethren a stimulus to a noble emulation : " And let us consider one another, to provoke unto charity and to good works. " [2]

CHAPTER V.

General Means of Perfection

407. Once we have formed deep convictions concerning the obligation of tending to perfection, it remains but to seek and use the *means* that lead thereto. It is question here of the *general* means, common to all souls desirous of spiritual progress. In the *second part* we shall treat of the *special* means proper to the different stages of the spiritual life.

These means are *interior* or *exterior*. The former are dispositions or acts of the soul itself that gradually raise it toward God. The latter comprise besides these acts, *exterior* helps which aid the soul in this elevation. It is important to give first a brief survey of these means.

408. I. Among the *interior* means there are four that must be considered here : 1° *The desire of perfection* which

---

[1] *John*, XVII, 19. — [2] *Hebr.*, X, 24.

is the first step forward, giving us the impulse needed to overcome obstacles.

2° *The knowledge of God and of self.*   Since it is question of uniting the soul to God, the better these two terms are known, the easier will be the task of effecting such union : *May I know Thee, O Lord, that I may love Thee, may I know myself that I may despise myself!*

3° *Conformity to God's will.*   To surrender our will to that of God is the most genuine token of love and the most effective means of uniting ourselves to the source of all perfection.

4° *Prayer* viewed in its wider sense, as adoration and petition, mental or vocal, private or public, *any elevation of the soul to God.*   It unites all our interior faculties to God, our memory and imagination, our mind and will, and even our outward actions inasmuch as they are an expression of our spirit of prayer.

II.   The *exterior* means of perfection may likewise be reduced to four principal ones :

1° *Direction.*   Just as God has instituted a visible authority to govern His Church externally, so He has willed that souls be led by an experienced spiritual guide, who may help them to avoid danger, and further and direct their efforts.

2° *A rule of life*, which approved by such a director further extends his influence over souls.

3° *Conferences, exhortations, and spiritual reading.*   Well chosen, these put us in contact with the teachings and the example of the Saints and lead us to follow in their footsteps.

4° *The sanctification of our relations with others*, with parents, friends, or business-associates.   This enables us to direct toward God not merely our pious exercises, but all our actions and our duties of state.

I Interior Means	$\left\{\begin{array}{l} \text{Desire of Perfection} \\ \text{Knowledge of God and of Self} \\ \text{Conformity to the Divine Will} \\ \text{Prayer} \end{array}\right.$
II Exterior Means	$\left\{\begin{array}{l} \text{Direction} \\ \text{A Rule of Life} \\ \text{Spiritual Readings and Conferences} \\ \text{Sanctification of Social Relations} \end{array}\right.$

ART. I. INTERIOR MEANS OF PERFECTION

§ I. The Desire of Perfection [1]

409. The first step toward perfection is the sincere, ardent and constant desire to attain it. We shall examine, 1° its *nature*, 2° its *necessity* and *efficacy*, 3° its *qualities*, 4° the *means* of fostering it.

I. *The Nature of this Desire*

410. 1° Desire *in general* is a movement of the soul toward the *good* that is *absent*. It differs, therefore, from joy which is the satisfaction coming from the actual possession of a *good*. There are two kinds of desire : one is a feeling or passionate impulse toward a *sensible* good that is absent ; and the other, the *rational desire*, is an act of the will tending toward some spiritual good. At times this rational desire reacts upon our sensibility and is thus mixed whith feeling. In the supernatural order our good desires are influenced by divine grace, as we have said above.

411. 2° The desire of perfection, then, may be defined as *an act of the will, which, under the influence of grace, ever seeks after spiritual progress*. It may be at times accompanied by pious sentiments that intensify it, [2] but this element is not necessary.

412. 3° This desire is born of the combined action of God's *grace* and the human *will*. From all eternity God loves us, and by that very fact, desires to unite Himself to us : " I have loved thee with an everlasting love ; therefore have I drawn thee, taking pity on thee. " [3] His unfailing love follows us, pursues us, as if His own happiness were incomplete without us. Then, when our own soul illumined by faith looks into itself, it finds an immense void that nothing but the Infinity of a God itself can fill : " Thou hast made us unto Thyself, O God, and our heart finds no rest until it rests in Thee. " [4] Our soul, then, sighs after God, after His love, after perfection : " As the hart panteth after

---

[1] St. Fr. de Sales, *Devout Life*, P. I. C. I-III ; *The Love of God*, Bk. XII. c. 2-3 ; Alvarez de Paz, *De vitâ spirit.*, t. I, l. V ; Rodriguez, *Practice of Christian Perfection*, P. I, Tr. I, *On the Esteem of Perfection ;* Le Gaudier, *De perfect. vitæ spiritualis*, P. II, Sept. 1ª ; J. Arintero, *Du désir de la perfection*, *Vie spirituelle*, Fevr. 1920, p. 296 ; Scaramelli-Stockman, *Manual of Christ. Perfection* P. I, art. 2.

[2] See remark of St. Thomas, Iª IIæ, q. 30, a. 1, ad 1.

[3] *Jerem.*, XXXI, 3.

[4] St. August., *Confessions*, Bk. I, n. 1.

the fountains of water; so my soul panteth after Thee, O Lord... for Thee my soul hath thirsted. " [1]   Since on earth this longing will never be satisfied, for here this divine union can never be complete, it follows that if we place no obstacle in the way this desire will constantly grow.

413. 4° Unfortunately, obstacles abound that tend to stifle, or at least, to weaken this desire.   Such are the threefold concupiscence (which we have described above, n. 193), the fear of the difficulties to be overcome and of the continued efforts required for co-operation with grace and for spiritual progress.   Hence, we must thoroughly convince ourselves of the necessity of this desire and take the means to foster it.

II. *The Necessity and Efficacy of the Desire for Perfection*

414. 1° **Its Necessity.**   The desire for it is the *first step* toward perfection, the *indispensable* condition for attaining it.   The road to perfection is *arduous* and implies constant and energetic efforts, for as we have remarked, no one can make progress in the path of God's love without sacrifice, without struggling against the threefold concupiscence and against the law of least resistance.   No one ever enters upon any steep, rugged path unless he is possessed of an ardent desire of arriving at the goal; and were he to set out on such a path he would soon abandon it.   Likewise, no one starts on the way to perfection or perseveres in it unless sustained by a strong desire to reach the end.

A) Hence, everything in the Sacred Scriptures tends to inspire in us this desire.   The Gospels as well as the Epistles are a continual exhortation to perfection.   This we have shown in treating of the obligation of tending to perfection; the object of the texts that establish this obligation is to stimulate the desire of pressing forward.   What other purpose can they have?   They present to us as the ideal the imitation of the divine perfections; they propose to us Jesus Christ Himself as our model; they recount His virtues; they urge us to follow His example.   Does not all this inspire us with the desire of perfection?

415. B) The Church's Liturgy has the same aim.   By setting forth in the course of the liturgical year the various phases of Our Lord's life, it makes us give expression to the *most ardent longings* for the coming of Christ's kingdom in

---

[1] *Ps.* XLI, 2; LXII, 2.

the souls of men during the season of Advent; for His growth in our hearts, at Christmastide and the Epiphany; for penitential exercises, through the Lenten period, as a preparation for Easter graces; for an intimate union with God, through the Pascal time, and for the gifts of the Holy Ghost, from Whit-Sunday till the end of the cycle. Thus, all through the year the Sacred Liturgy, in one form or another, quickens our desire for spiritual growth.

416. **C)** The *experience* gained from reading the lives of the Saints or from the actual direction of souls shows us that without the oft-renewed desire for perfection, there is no progress in the spiritual life. *St. Teresa* [1] makes us well aware of this fact : " Let us not stifle our desires. This is highly important. Let us firmly believe that with the divine help and our own efforts we, too, can in the course of time obtain what so many Saints, aided by God, finally attained. Had they never conceived such desires, had they not little by little carried them into execution, they would never have risen so high... Oh! how important it is in the spiritual life to rouse oneself to great things!" The Saint herself offers us a striking example of this. As long as she was not determined to break all the bonds that interfered with her flight towards the heights of perfection, she painfully dragged along the way of mediocrity; from the day she resolved to give herself entirely to God, she advanced wondrously.

417. The *practise* of direction corroborates the teaching of the Saints. Generous souls possessed of a humble and persistent desire to advance in the way of perfection relish and employ the means we suggest to them. If, on the contrary, such desire is lacking, or exists but feebly, we readily observe that the most urgent exhortations produce but little effect. Spiritual nourishment, like food for the body, profits but those who hunger and thirst. God heaps His gifts upon those who crave them, but allots them with measured hand to those who do not prize them : " *He hath filled the hungry with good things; and the rich he hath sent empty away.*" [2]

418. 2° **Efficacy of the desire for perfection.** This desire is a real force that makes us grow in holiness.

a) *Psychology* demonstrates that an *idea* deeply impressed tends to elicit a corresponding *act*. This is the more true, when the thought is accompanied by the *desire*, for the

---

[1] *Life by Herself*, C, XIII. — [2] *Luke*, I, 53.

latter already constitutes an act of the will which sets our faculties in motion. Hence, to desire perfection is to tend towards it, and to tend towards perfection is to begin to attain it. To desire to love God is already to love Him, since God sees the heart and takes into account all our intentions. Hence, Pascal's profound words : " Thou wouldst not seek me, hadst thou not found me ". Now, to desire is to seek, and he who seeks finds : " *For every one that seeketh findeth.* " [1]

419. **b)** Furthermore, in the supernatural order, desire constitutes a prayer, an elevation of the soul towards God, a sort of spiritual communion which lifts our soul towards Him and draws Him to us. Now, God delights in granting our prayers, especially when their object is our sanctification, — the most ardent desire of His Heart : " *For this is the will of God, your sanctification.* " [2] Thus God, in the Old Testament, urges us to seek after, to pursue wisdom, that is to say, *virtue*, making the most wondrous promises to those that hearken to his voice, and granting wisdom to those that earnestly desire it : " *Wherefore I wished, and understanding was given me : and I called upon God, and the Spirit of wisdom came upon me.* " [3] In the Gospels, Our Lord invites us to quench in Him our spiritual thirst : " *If any man thirst, let him come to me and drink.* " [4] The more ardent our desires, the more abundant the graces we receive, for the Source of living water is inexhaustible.

420. **c)** Lastly, desire *dilates* the soul and so renders it more apt for the reception of divine communications. There is in God such a fulness of goodness and of graces, that the measure of His bounty is to a great extent in proportion to our capacity to receive. The more we expand our soul by earnest and ardent desires, the more capable it becomes of receiving of the fulness of God : " *I opened my mouth and drew unto myself the Spirit... Open thy mouth wide, and I will fill it.* " [5]

III. *The Qualities Which the Desire for Perfection Should Possess*

To attain such happy results, the desire for perfection must be *supernatural, predominant, persevering,* and *practical.*

---

[1] *Matth.*, VII, 8. — [2] *I Thess.*, IV, 3. — [3] *Wisdom*, VII, 7; cfr. *Prov.* I, 20-23.
[4] *John*, VII, 37. As *St. Thomas* remarks (I, q. 12, a. 6), desire renders the soul more fit — better disposed — for the reception of the desired object.
[5] *Ps.* CXVIII, 131; LXXX, 11.

421. 1º It must be supernatural in its *motive* as well as in its *principle*.

a) Supernatural in its *motive*, that is to say, based upon reasons furnished by faith, which reasons we have already explained : the nature and the excellence of the Christian life and of Christian perfection, the glory of God, the edification of the neighbor, the welfare of our soul, etc.

b) Supernatural in its *principle*, in the sense that it must be conceived under the influence of grace, which alone can impart to us the *light* that will make us understand and relish such motives, and the strength required to act in accordance with our convictions. Since grace is obtained through prayer, we must ask insistently of God that He increase in us this desire for perfection.

422. 2º It must be *predominant :* in other words, it must outdo in intensity any other desire. Since perfection is in reality the hidden treasure, that pearl of great price which must be bought at any cost, and since each degree of Christian perfection is attended by a corresponding degree of glory, of the Beatific Vision and of love, the same must be longed for and sought after in preference to any thing else whatsoever : " *Seek ye therefore first the kingdom of God and his justice.* " [1]

423. 3º It must be *persevering*. To seek perfection is a long and arduous work calling for constant progress. Hence the desire to do better must be renewed frequently. Our Lord tells us, therefore, not to look backwards over the distance traversed, or to cast complacent eyes upon the results of past efforts : " *No man putting his hand to the plough and looking back is fit for the kingdom of God.* " [2] On the contrary we must look ahead, as St. Paul tells us, to see the way we must yet travel and redouble our effort, like the runner who stretches forth his arm the better to reach hold of the goal : " *Forgetting the things that are behind, and stretching forth myself to those that are before, I press towards the mark, to the prize of the supernatural vocation.* " [3] St. Augustine lays great stress upon this same truth; he says that to halt is to fall back, to tarry in the contemplation of the way we have traveled is to lose our vigor. The motto of perfection is to go ever forward, to aim ever higher : " *Linger not*

---

[1] *Matth.*, VI, 33. — [2] *Luke*, IX, 62. — [3] *Philip.*, III, 13-14.

on the way, stray not from it... Always strive, always move, always advance. " [1].

We must not consider the good we have achieved but the good that is yet to be accomplished; we must not look to those who do less than ourselves, but to those who do better, to the fervent, to the Saints, and above them all to Jesus Himself, our True Model. Then, the more we progress the further we seem from the goal, just because we realize the better how lofty that goal is.

However, there must be an entire absence of anything like over-eagerness, impatience, and, above all, anything like presumption in our desires. Violent efforts are of short duration, and the presumptuous soon lose heart after the first failures. What really makes for our progress is a calm and oft-renewed desire based on convictions and on the omnipotence of grace.

424. 4° Then, desire becomes *practical* and *efficacious*, because it is directed not towards an ideal that is impossible to realize, but towards the *means* that lie within our reach. There are souls possessed of magnificent, but purely speculative ideals, souls who aspire to high perfection the while they neglect the means that lead thereto. Herein lurks a twofold danger : we may fancy we have attained perfection, simply because we dream of it, and thus fall into pride; or we may come to a standstill and fail. We must, instead, bear in mind the saying that he who wills the end wills also the means. We must recall that it is *fidelity in little things* that ensures fidelity in greater things, and that our desire for perfection should bear on our present duties, however trifling they may be, since the faithful accomplishment of these will guarantee fidelity in those of greater moment. " *He who is faithful in that which is least is faithful also in that which is greater.* " [2] To pretend to desire perfection and then relegate to the morrow the efforts that should accompany such desire, to wish to sanctify oneself through the performance of great actions and then take no heed of ordinary ones, is to labor under a double illusion, which reveals either a lack of sincerity or an ignorance of psychology. *High ideals* are, no doubt, required, but so also is their immediate and progressive *realization.*

---

[1] St. Augustine, Sermon 169, n.18.
[2] *Luke* XVI, 10.

IV. *Means to Stimulate this Desire for Perfection*

425. 1° Based upon supernatural convictions, the desire for perfection takes root and grows chiefly through *meditation* and *prayer*. It is necessary then first of all to *reflect* on the great truths we have explained in the foregoing chapters, on the greatness of this life which God Himself communicates to us, on the beauty and the wealth of a soul that cultivates it, on the delights which God has in store for it in heaven. It is necessary to meditate on the lives of those Saints who grew the more in holiness as their longing for perfection gained daily in constancy and ardor. That such meditation may be made more fruitful, we must join to it *prayer* which, drawing God's grace upon the soul, makes our convictions concerning the need of perfection deeper and more vital.

426. 2° There are certain favorable *circumstances*, in which the action of grace is more keenly felt. A wise spiritual director will know how to profit by them in order to awaken in his penitents the desire for perfection.

a) From the first dawn of reason, God invites the child to give himself to Him. How important it is that parents and confessors avail themselves of these divine solicitations to stimulate and direct the impulses of young hearts! This is true of the time of First Communion, of the moment when the signs of vocation first appear or a choice of life is to be made; of the time when one enters college, seminary, or novitiate; or of the time when one receives the sacrament of matrimony. On all these occasions, God grants special graces to which it is important to correspond with a generous heart.

427. **b)** The same is true of the time of *retreat*. The prolonged periods of recollection, the instructions, the readings and the examinations of conscience, and the prayers offered, above all, the more abundant graces then received, contribute to the strengthening of our convictions, to a better knowledge of our state of conscience, to the more sincere abhorrence of our faults and their causes, whilst new, more practical and more generous resolutions are suggested, giving us a new impetus toward perfection. Thus it has come to pass in recent years that more frequent *retreats* [1] have formed among the clergy and

---

[1] A. BOISSEL, *Retraites fermées, pratique et théorie.*

the faithful choice men whose one ambition is that of advancing in the spiritual life. Spiritual directors in seminaries, likewise, know the wonderful effects produced in their students by the general retreats and the retreats for ordination. Then it is that generous desires for a better life are conceived, renewed or intensified. We must, then, profit by these opportunities to answer God's appeal and begin or perfect the reformation of our life.

428. c) *Providential trials*, physical or moral, such as illness, death, moral suffering, evil turns of fortune are often accompanied by interior graces that urge us on to a more perfect life. Provided we take advantage of these ordeals to turn to God, they wean us from earthly things, purify our soul through suffering, inspire us with a yearning for Heaven and for perfection which is the way to Heaven.

429. d) Lastly, there are times when the Holy Spirit produces *interior movements* in the soul, inclining it towards a life of greater perfection. He enlightens us on the vanity of human things, on the happiness flowing from a more complete gift of self to God, and urges us to greater efforts. We must profit by these interior graces to hasten our progress.

430. 3° There are *Spiritual Exercises* which by their very nature tend to awaken in us the desire for perfection. These are :

a) *The particular examen*, which obliges us each day to study ourselves in regard to some one special point, not only in order to ascertain our failings or successes, but above all to renew our determination to advance in the practice of such or such a virtue. (N. 468.)

b) *The systematic practice of Confession* with a view to correct such or such a fault (n. 262).

c) The *monthly* and *annual retreats* that come to renew our desire of doing better.

CONCLUSION

431. In making use of these various means we shall continually or at least habitually keep our wills fixed on the end to be attained, spiritual progress. Then, upheld by God's grace, we shall more easily triumph over obstacles. No doubt, there will be slight failings now and then, but spurred on by the desire of advancing, we shall courageously resume our march, and our little setbacks, by exercising us in humility, will serve but to draw us nearer to God.

§ II. The Knowledge of God and the Knowledge of Self

432. Since perfection consists in the union of the soul with God, it becomes evident that in order to effect this union, we must be acquainted with its two terms, God and the soul. The knowledge of God will lead us directly to love : *May I know Thee, that I may love Thee.* The knowledge of self, by making us realize the worth of all the good wherewith God has endowed us, will awaken in us a corresponding sense of gratitude; while the sight of our miseries and our faults, by making us conceive a just contempt of self, will engender in us true humility : *May I know myself, in order that I may despise myself.* Divine love will be the result, for it is on the ruins of self-love that the love of God is built.

I. *The Knowledge of God* [1]

433. In order to love God it is necessary first of all to know Him. [2] The more profound our consideration of His perfections, the more ardent the love of our heart for Him; for, all is loveliness in Him. In Him is found the fulness of being, of beauty, of goodness and of love : *God is love.* This much is evident. It remains to determine : 1º What we must know of God in order to love Him, and 2º How to come to that affectionate knowledge of God.

1º WHAT WE MUST KNOW OF GOD

Concerning God, we must know whatever can render Him admirable and lovable. We must learn of His exis-

---

[1] FABER, *Creator and Creature, The Precious Blood, Bethlehem;* NEWMAN, *Grammar of Assent and other works* (See word God in Index to the Works of CARD. NEWMAN by RICKABY, S. J.); BELLORD, *Meditations on Dogma;* BRANCHEREAU, *Méditations,* vol. I, Méd. I-VI; HEDLEY, *Retreat,* IV-V; HOGAN, *Clerical Studies,* C. IV; A. I; SCOTT. S. J., *God and Myself;* BOSSUET, *De la connaissance de Dieu et de soi-même; Élévations sur les mystères; Méditations sur l'Évangile;* L. BAIL, *Théologie affective;* LESSIUS, *De perfectionibus moribusque divinis;* P. D'ARGENTAN, *Les Grandeurs de Dieu;* CONTENSON, *Theologia mentis et cordis;* BEAUDENOM, *Les Sources de la Piété;* SAUVÉ, *Dieu intime, Jésus intime, L'homme intime,* etc.; P. SAUDREAU, O. P., *Les divines paroles;* M. D'HERBIGNY, *La Théologie du révélé,* ch. VIII-XI; P. R. GARRIGOU-LAGRANGE, *Dieu, son existence, sa nature,* 1920.
[2] Contrary propositions *of* Molinos were condemned, DENZ.-BANN. **1226, 1329.**

tence, His nature, His attributes, His works, above all, His inner life and His *relations* with us. Nothing that concerns the Godhead is foreign to devotion; the most abstract truths themselves have an affective aspect which is a very great aid to our piety. Let us see this with the help of a few instances taken from philosophy and theology.

434. A) Philosophical Truths. [1] **a)** The metaphysical proofs of the existence of God seem abstract enough, and yet they are inexhaustible treasures of marvelous considerations leading to divine love : God, the Changeless *Prime Mover*, Pure Act, is the origin of all movement. Hence, we cannot move if not in Him and through Him. He must be, therefore, the first principle of all our actions. If He is our first principle, He shall be our last end : " *I am the beginning and the end.* " God is the *First Cause* of all beings, of whatever of good there is in us, of our faculties, of our acts. To Him alone, therefore, be all honor and glory! God is the *Neces-sary Being*, the Only Necessary Being. He is then the only good to be sought. All other things are contingent, accessory, transient, useful solely inasmuch as they lead us to this Only Necessary Being. God is *Infinite Perfection :* creatures are but the faint reflection of His beauty. He is then, *the Ideal* to pursue : " Be you therefore perfect, as also your heavenly Father is perfect. " [2] We must set no limits to our perfection : " I am infinite, " said Almighty God to St. Catherine of Sienna, " and I seek infinite works, that is, an infinite sense of love. " [3]

435. b) If we pass thence to the *divine nature*, even the little we know of it is sufficient to wean us from all created things and raise us up to God. He is the fulness of being : " *I am Who am.* " Hence, mine is but a borrowed existence, incapable of subsisting by itself, and I must acknowledge my utter dependence upon the Divine Being. This it was that God wished to teach St. Catherine of Sienna when He said to her : " Learn, my daughter, what you are and what I am... You are that which is not, and I am He Who is. " [4] What a lesson in humility! What a lesson in love!

436. c) We learn the same lesson from the consideration of the *divine attributes*. There is not one that if well meditated upon does not act as a stimulus to our love in one

---

[1] See especially JOYCE, *Natural Theology.*
[2] *Matth.*, V, 48; cfr. Commentary of IV Lateran Council. *(Denzinger*, 432).
[3] *Dialog.*, I, p. 40.
[4] *Vie*, by RAYMOND DE CAPOUE, trad. Cartier, t. I, p. 71.

form or another. The *simplicity of the Godhead* moves us to the practice of singleness of purpose or purity of intention, which causes us to tend directly to God, to the exclusion of every inordinate thought of self. His *immensity*, which encompasses and pervades our being, is the foundation of that practice so dear and so profitable to pious souls, the exercise of the presence of God. His *eternity* detaches us from all things that pass away with time, by recalling that whatever is not eternal is nothing. His *unchangeableness* aids us in the midst of human vicissitudes to maintain that peace of mind so necessary to a close and abiding union with Him. His *perpetual activity* spurs us on to action, preventing us from lapsing into indifference or into a sort of dangerous apathy or quietism. His *omnipotence*, ministering to His *unbounded wisdom* and His *merciful goodness*, inspire us with a filial trust that becomes a singular aid to prayer and to a holy abandonment of ourselves to Him. His *holiness* makes us hate sin and cherish that purity of heart which leads to a familiar union with Him : " Blessed are the clean of heart : for they shall see God. " The soundest foundation of our faith rests upon His *infallible truthfulness*. His *beauty*, His *goodness*, His *love*, captivate our heart, giving rise to outpourings of love and gratitude. Thus it is that saintly persons love to lose themselves in the contemplation of the divine attributes and by gazing adoringly upon God's perfections, to draw them in a measure into their own hearts.

437. **B**) Holy souls delight above all in the contemplation of **revealed truths,** all of which refer to the history of the *Divine Life :* its *source* in the Most Holy Trinity, its *first bestowal* by the creation and sanctification of man, its *restoration* through the Incarnation, its *actual diffusion* through the Church and the Sacraments, its final *consummation* in Heaven. Each of these mysteries enraptures and inflames souls with love for God, for Jesus Christ, for their brethren and for all things divine.

438. **a**) The *source* of divine life is the *Blessed Trinity.* God, the very plenitude of being and of love, eternally regards His Own Self. Out of this contemplation He brings forth His Word, the Word that is His Son, distinct from, yet in all things equal to Him, His own living and substantial image. He loves that Son and is in turn loved by Him; and from this mutual love proceeds the Holy Ghost, distinct from the Father and the Son yet equal in all things to Both. And this is the life wherein we share!

439.   b) Because He is infinitely good, God wills to communicate Himself to other beings. This He does by *creating* and above all by sanctifying men. By creation we are God's servants, which already constitutes a high honor. Indeed, what a cause for wonder, for gratitude, for love, that God should have thought of me from all eternity, that He should have chosen me out of billions of possible beings in order to bring me into existence and bestow upon me life and intelligence! But what shall I say of His calling me to share in His own divine life? Of His having adopted me as a child, having destined me for the clear vision of His essence and for His undivided love? Is not this the consummation of charity? Is not this a great motive-power urging us to love Him without measure or stint?

440.   c) Through the fault of our first parents we lost our right to this participation in the divine life, and of ourselves we had not the power to regain it. But behold! The Son of God sees our plight, becomes a *man* like ourselves and is thus constituted the Head of a mystical body whose members we are; He atones for our sins by His sorrowful Passion and His death on the Cross, reconciles us to God and makes that life He has drawn from the bosom of His Father flow once more into our souls. Can there be a stronger appeal to make us love the Word-made-Flesh, to urge us to unite ourselves to Him and through Him to the Father?

441.   d) To facilitate this union, Jesus remains among us. He abides with us through His Church, that transmits and explains His teachings; through His *Sacraments*, mysterious channels of grace, giving the life divine. He dwells among us, above all, in the Holy Eucharist wherein He at once perpetuates His Presence, His merciful action, and His Sacrifice : His *Sacrifice* through the Holy Oblation of the Mass, wherein in a mysterious manner He renews His immolation; His *merciful action*, through Holy Communion, wherein He comes to us with all the treasures of grace to perfect our souls and impart to them His own virtues; His *abiding Presence*, willingly imprisoned day and night within the Tabernacle, where we can visit Him, converse with Him, glorify with Him the Most Blessed Trinity, find health for all our spiritual miseries, and consolation in sorrow and discouragement : " Come to me all you that labour and are burdend : and I will refresh you. " [1]

---

[1] *Matth.*, XI, 28.

442.   e) This is but the dawn of the noonday light of eternity, wherein we shall see God face to face, as He sees Himself, and shall love Him with a perfect love.   In Him we shall behold and love whatever is good, whatever is noble.   We came from God by creation; we return to Him by glorification.   In glorifying Him we find perfect happiness.

Dogma is, then, the true source of real devotion.

2° MEANS OF ARRIVING AT THIS KNOWLEDGE OF GOD.

443.   Three principal means are at our disposal in order to acquire this affective knowledge of God : 1° the *devout study* of philosophy and theology; 2° *meditation* or mental *prayer;* 3° the habit of *seeing God* in all things.

A) *The Devout Study of Theology.* [1]   One may study philosophy and theology in two ways : *merely with the mind,* as one would study mathematics or any other secular science, or with *mind and heart.*   It is the latter that begets godliness.   When St. Thomas plunged into the depths of the great philosophical and theological questions, he studied them not as a Greek sage would, but as a disciple and lover of Christ.   According to his expression, theology treats of divine things and of acts inasmuch as they lead us to a perfect knowledge of God, in which eternal happiness consists. [2] This is why his piety was even more wonderful than his knowledge.   The same was true of *St. Bonaventure* and other great theologians.   Of course, the most of them have not gone into devout considerations concerning the great mysteries of our faith which they sought but to explain and prove, yet it is from these very truths that godliness springs. Whoever studies them in the *spirit of faith,* cannot but admire and love Him Whose grandeur and goodness theology reveals.   This holds especially if we know how to avail ourselves of the *gifts* of *knowledge* and of *understanding.*   The former lifts us up from creatures unto God, disclosing to us their relations with the Divinity; the latter

---

[1] The Church has condemned the assertion of Molinos that a theologian is not as well disposed for contemplation as an ignorant man (DENZ.-BANN., 1284). FATHER FABER writes : " Is not all doctrine practical?   Is it not the first use of dogmatic theology to be the basis of sanctity...?   He who separates dogmatics from ascetics seems to assert this proposition : The Knowledge of God and of Jesus Christ was not meant primarily to make us holy... " (FABER *Spiritual Conferences, Conf.* on Death, 3, p. 137).   (Theology) " is the best fuel of devotion, the best fuel of divine love...   If a science tells of God, yet does not make the listener's heart burn within him, it must follow either that the science is no true theology, or that the heart which listens is stupid and depraved.   In a simple and loving heart, theology burns like a sacred fire. " (FABER, *The Precious Blood,* c. 111). — [2] *Sum. theol.* I, q. 1, a. 4.

makes us penetrate to the very heart of revealed truths, to discern their marvelous harmony.

With the aid of these lights, the devout theologian will know how to rise from the contemplation of the most speculative truths to acts of adoration, of wonder, of gratitude and of love, which spring spontaneously from the study of Christian dogmas. These acts, far from paralyzing his intellectual activities, will but quicken and sharpen them; for one studies better, with more diligence and greater perseverance, whatever one loves. One discovers depths which the intellect alone could not sound, and draws inferences which broaden the field of theology, whilst nourishing piety.

444. B) *Meditation* must accompany study. We do not meditate sufficiently upon Christian dogmas, or we confine our consideration to their secondary aspects. We must not hesitate to take the very essence of these dogmas as the subject of our meditations. Then it is that the light of faith, under the influence of grace, reaches such heights and pierces such depths as the intellect alone could never discern. We find proof of this fact in the writings of unlettered persons, who having been raised to contemplation, have left us appreciations concerning God, Christ our Lord, His doctrines and Sacraments, that actually rival those of the most exalted theologians. And did not *St. Thomas* say that he had learned more from his Crucifix than from the works of Doctors? The reason for it is that God speaks more readily in the silent peacefulness of prayer; and that His Word, then better understood, enlightens the mind, enkindles the heart and sets the will in action. Then it is, likewise, that the Holy Spirit deigns to impart, over and above the gifts of knowledge and understanding, that of *wisdom*, which gives a relish for the truths of faith, causes us to love these truths and live by them, and thus establishes a very close union between God and the soul. This is well described by the author of the Imitation in the following words : " Happy is the soul that heareth the Lord speaking within her, and receiveth from His mouth the word of comfort." [1]

The repeated and affectionate remembrance of God is but the prolongation of the happy effects of our mental prayer. The frequent thought of God increases our love for Him, and this love deepens and refines our knowledge.

[1] *Imit.* Bk. III, c. 1.

445. **C)** Then it is that we acquire the habit of rising more easily from the creature to the Creator, and of seeing God in all His works, in *things, persons* and *events*. The basis of this practice is " *the divine exemplarism,* " taught by Plato, perfected by St. Augustine and St. Thomas, elucidated by the school of St. Victor, and taken up by the French school of the Seventeenth Century. [1] All beings have existed in the divine thought before their creation. God has begotten them in His mind before bringing them forth and He has willed that they reflect, in various degrees, His divine perfections. If, therefore, we regard created things, not only with the eyes of the body, but with the eyes of the soul, by the light of faith, we shall see there three things :

a) All creatures, according to their degree of perfection, are an image, a likeness of God; all proclaim God for their Maker and bid us join in praise of Him, since their own being, all their beauty and goodness, is but a created and finite participation in the divine essence.

b) *Intelligent creatures* in particular, raised as they are to the supernatural order, are images, living likenesses of God, sharing, though in a finite way, in His intellectual life. Since all the baptized are Christ's members, it is Christ that we must see in them : *Christ in all.*

c) All *events*, propitious or adverse, are designed in the mind of God to perfect the supernatural life wherewith He has endowed us, and to facilitate the recruitment of the elect; so much so, that we can profit by everything unto sanctification.

We must add, however, that in the order of time, souls go first to Jesus Christ. It is through Him that they go to the Father, and once they have reached God, they never cease to hold themselves in the closest bonds of union with Jesus.

CONCLUSION : THE EXERCISE OF THE PRESENCE OF GOD [2]

446. The affective knowledge of God leads us to the holy *exercise of the presence of God.* We shall now note

---

[1] See especially *La Journée Chrétienne* of FATHER OLIER where this doctrine is wonderfully applied.

[2] S. THOM., I, q. 8, a. 3; LESSIUS, *De perfectionibus moribusque divinis*, lib. II; RODRIGUEZ, *Practice of Christian Perfection*, Part I, Treatise VI; P. PINY, O. P., *La Présence de Dieu;* P. PLUS, S. J., *God in us, Living with God, In Christ Jesus;* S. FRANCIS DE SALES, *Introd. to a Devout Life*, P. II, c. II, XII, XIII; VAUBERT,

briefly the *foundation*, the *practice*, and the *advantages* of this exercise.

A) Its foundation is the doctrine of *God's omnipresence*. God is everywhere, not only by His all-contemplating vision and His all-pervading action, but likewise, by His substance. As St. *Paul* told the Athenians : " In Him we live, and move, and are. " [1]   This is true from both the natural and the supernatural point of view.   As *Creator*, after having given us our being and our life, He preserves us and quickens our faculties by His concurrence.   As *Father*, He begets us unto the supernatural life, which is a participation in His own, He co-operates with us as principal cause in its preservation and its growth, and He is thus intimately present in us, within the very center of our soul, yet without ceasing to be distinct from us.   As we have said above (n. 92), it is the Triune God that lives in us : the *Father*, Who loves us as His children, the *Son* Who deals with us as His brethren, and the *Holy Ghost* Who gives us both His gifts and Himself.

B) *The Practice of This Exercise.*   To find God, then, we need not seek Him in the heavens. **a**) We find Him close by *in the creatures* round about us.   It is there that we look for Him at the outset.   One and all suggest to us some divine perfection, but it is especially so of those creatures which, endowed with intellect, are the dwelling-places of the Living God (n. 92).   These constitute for us the steps, as it were, of a ladder by which we ascend to Him.   **b**) We know, moreover, that God is near those that confidently invoke Him : " The Lord is nigh unto all them that call upon Him, " [2] and our soul delights to call to Him now by ejaculatory prayers, now by long supplications. **c**) Above all we recall the fact that the Three Divine Persons dwell within us [3] and that our heart is a living tabernacle, a Heaven, wherein They give Themselves to us even now. It is enough, then, simply to recollect ourselves, to enter within the inner Sanctuary of our soul, as St. Catherine of Sienna calls it, and contemplate with the eyes of faith the Divine Guest Who deigns to abide there.   Then shall we live under His gaze, under His influence ; then shall we adore Him and co-operate with Him in the sanctification of our souls.

How to Walk before God; Spiritual Combat, c. 21-23; MATURIN, *Principles of the Spiritual Life,* p. 116-138; HAMON, *Medit.,* Vol. V, p. 95-125; CURSUS ASCETI-CUS, Vol. II, p. 308-317; HEDLEY, *Retreat for Priests,* II.
    [1] *Acts,* XVII, 28. — [2] *Ps.* CXLIV, 18. — [3] See C. I, a. I.

447. **C)** It is easy to see the *advantages* of this exercise for our sanctification.

a) It makes us *carefully avoid sin.* Who shall dare offend the majesty of God while realizing that God actually dwells within him, with His infinite *holiness* that cannot endure the least blemish, with His infinite *justice* obliging Him to punish the slightest fault, with His power to punish the guilty, above all with His *goodness*, forever seeking our love and our fidelity!

b) It *stimulates our zeal* for perfection. If a soldier fighting under the eyes of his commander is inspired to multiply his feats of valor, should we not be ready to undergo the most strenuous labors, to make the greatest efforts when conscious that not only does the eye of God watch us in our struggle, but that His victorious arm ever sustains us? Could we lag, when encouraged by the immortal Crown He holds out to us, and above all, by the greater love He bestows on us as a reward?

c) What great *trust* does not this thought inspire in us! Whatever may be our trials, our temptations, our weariness and our weakness, are we not assured of final victory, when we recall that He, Who is All-powerful, Whom nothing can resist, dwells within us and invests us with His power? Doubtless, we may sustain partial reverses and experience excruciating anguish, yet we are certain that, supported by Him, we shall conquer, and that even our crosses will but make us grow in God's love and multiply our merits.

d) Lastly, what a joy for us is the thought that He Who is the Joy of the Elect, and Whom we shall see one day face to face, is even now our portion, Whose presence and conversation we may enjoy all day long!

The knowledge and the habitual thought of God are, therefore, most sanctifying. The same is true of the knowledge of self.

II. *Self-knowledge* [1]

The knowledge of God leads us *directly* to love Him, since He is infinitely lovable. The knowledge of self helps us indirectly to love God by disclosing to us the absolute need we have of Him, in order to perfect the *qualities* with

---

[1] MATURIN, *Self-knowledge and Self-discipline;* RODRIGUEZ, *Christian Perfection,* P. I. tr. VII; S. FRANCIS DE SALES, *Introd. to a Devout Life,* P. II, X, XI, P. V, III-VII; MEYER, *Science of the Saints,* Vol. I, Lessons I, XIII-XVI; FABER, *Spiritual Conferences, Self-deceit;* CLARE, *The Science of the Spiritual Life;* SCARAMELLI-STOCKMAN, *Manual of Christian Perfection,* P. I, a. X.

which He has endowed us and to heal our deep miseries. We shall explain : 1° the *necessity* of self-knowledge, 2° its *object*, 3° the *means* of obtaining it.

1° THE NECESSITY OF SELF-KNOWLEDGE

A few words will convince us of this.

448. **A)** If we lack self-knowledge, it is morally impossible to perfect ourselves. The reason is that we then entertain *illusions* concerning our state, and, according to our character or our changing moods, we fall either into a *presumptuous optimism* that makes us believe we are already perfect, or into discouragement that causes us to exaggerate our faults. In either case, the result is almost identical — inaction, lack of sustained effort, carelessness. Besides, how can we correct faults with which we are not acquainted or of which we have at best but an imperfect knowledge? How undertake the cultivation of virtues, of qualities of which we have but a vague and confused notion?

449. **B)** An honest and accurate knowledge of ourselves on the contrary, is an incentive to perfection. The good qualities we discover move us to thank God and to show our gratitude by generous co-operation with His grace. Our *defects* and the realization of our helplessness show us how much we have yet to accomplish, and how important it is to lose no opportunity of advancing. Then we profit by all occasions to uproot or, at least, to weaken, mortify, overcome our vices and to foster and further the growth of our good qualities. Conscious of our weakness, we humbly beg of God the grace of advancing each day; and, upheld by trust in Him, we cling to the desire and the promise of success. This is what excites and steadies our efforts.

2° THE OBJECT OF SELF-KNOWLEDGE

450. General Remarks. That this knowledge be more profitable, it should extend to *all that is ours*, qualities and defects, natural and supernatural endowments, likes and dislikes, our personal history, our faults, our efforts, our progress; all this to be studied, not in a pessimistic frame of mind, but with due impartiality, with a right conscience enlightened by faith.

a) We should then candidly, without any sort of false humility, ascertain what are the good *qualities* that Almighty God has dealt out to us, not, indeed, to glory therein, but to thank the Giver and to cultivate His gifts. These are the talents He has entrusted to us and of which He will ask an account. The field to be explored, then, is vast indeed, comprising as it does all our *natural* and *supernatural* gifts : those things which we hold directly from God, and those we have received from our parents; those we owe to our Christian education and those that are the results of our own efforts sustained by grace.

451. b) We must, at the same time, face with courage the sight of our *miseries* and our faults. Drawn forth from nothing, thither forever we tend. We can neither subsist nor act, except by the ever-present concurrence of God. Drawn to evil by a threefold concupiscence (N. 193 and foll.), we have added new strength to our evil tendencies by our actual sins, and by the evil habits resulting from them. We must humbly acknowledge this fact and, without losing heart, set to work with the help of divine grace to heal these wounds by the practice of Christian virtue and thus approach the perfection of Our Heavenly Father.

452. Practical Applications. To guide ourselves in this study we may examine successively our *natural* and *supernatural* endowments, following a sort of *questionnaire* that will facilitate our task.

A) *Our Natural Gifts.* Regarding the **natural gifts,** we may ask ourselves, before God, what are our *outstanding tendencies.* In this we may adopt the following practical, if not strictly philosophical order. [1]

453. a) As regards the sensitive appetites. Is feeling predominant with us, or is it reason and will? There is within all of us this mixture of the higher and the lower, but not in the same proportion. Is our love a matter of sentiment rather than of devotedness and will? Do we control our exterior senses, or are we under their sway? What power do we hold over our imagination and our memory? Are not these faculties excessively flighty and often engaged in empty daydreaming? Are our passions properly directed and controlled? Is sensuality our ruling passion, or is it pride or vanity? Are we *apathetic*, soft, listless, sluggish? If we are slow by nature, do we, at least, persevere in our efforts?

454. b) As regards the mind. What sort of mind do we possess? Is it quick and clear but superficial, or slow but deep? Do we belong to the intellectual, reflective type, or do we belong to the class of practical men, who study in order to love and to act? How do we set about the work of cultivating our mind? Do we do so with earnestness

---

[1] In an Appendix will be found a brief study on character that will aid us in this study of self. Cf. DOSDA. *L'Union avec Dieu*, t. I, IIe p., ch. XXI.

or with unconcern; steadily, or by fits and starts? What results do we
obtain? What are our methods of study? Could we improve upon
them? Are our judgments *biased* by our feelings? Are we *obstinate*
in our opinions? Can we listen with an open mind to those who hold
views different from ours?

455. c) As regards the will. Is our will weak and inconstant,
or is it strong and persevering? What do we do to train it? The will
should *reign supreme* over the other faculties, but it cannot do so
unless we use great tact and make great efforts. What do we do to
assure the control of the will over our exterior and interior senses, over
the activities of our mind? What do we do to strengthen, to steady
the will? Have we strong convictions? Do we renew these frequently?
Do we strengthen our will power by fidelity in little things, and by the
small sacrifices of daily life?

456. d) As regards character. *Our character* is of capital
importance in what concerns our relations with the neighbor. A *good
disposition*, the gift of getting along with others, is a powerful asset to
zeal, and a *bad disposition* one of the greatest obstacles. A *man of
character* is one who, having the courage of his convictions, strives
resolutely and perseveringly to live up to them. A good character is
that harmonious combination of kindness and firmness, of meekness
and strength, of frankness and tact that elicits the esteem and the love
of those with whom it comes in contact. A *bad character* is one which
is lacking in frankness, in kindness, in tact or in firmness, or which, by
allowing egoism to hold sway, is rude in its manner and makes itself
repulsive, at times hateful to others. Here then, we have an important
element for study.

457. e) As regards habits. Habits result from a repetition of the
same acts, and they make the repetition of these acts easy and pleasant.
It is important to study such habits as we have already acquired, in
order to strengthen them, if they are good, to uproot them, if they are
bad. What we shall say in the second part of this treatise about the
capital sins and the virtues, will be of help to us in this inquiry.

458. B) Our supernatural gifts. Penetrated as our
faculties are by the supernatural, we would not gain a complete knowledge of ourselves if we did not take account
of the supernatural gifts God has imparted to us. These we
have described above (n. 119 and foll.). God's grace
however takes sundry forms in its way of working, [1] and it
is important that we study its special action upon our soul.

a) We must examine the *attraction* grace makes us feel
for such or such a virtue. Our sanctification, in fact,
depends on the docility wherewith we follow these motions
of grace.

1) There are *decisive moments* in life when God speaks
in clearer and more urgent tones. To hearken to His Voice
and follow His inspirations is of the utmost importance.

---

[1] *I Peter*, IV, 10.

2) We should ask ourselves whether there be among the attractions we feel, one that is predominant, stronger than the others, oft-recurring, drawing us toward a particular kind of life, toward a certain kind of prayer, toward some determined virtue. We shall thus find the *special way* wherein God wishes us to walk. It is important that we enter it, for it is there that we shall receive the fulness of grace.

459. b) Besides discovering our attractions, we must also take cognizance of the *resistance* we offer *to grace*, of our *failings*, of our *sins*, in order to regret them with all sincerity, make amends and avoid them in the future. This is a painful, humiliating study, especially if carried out honestly and minutely, but it is a most profitable one; for, on the one hand, it is a great aid in the practice of humility, and on the other, it throws us with perfect trust on the merciful love of God, Who alone has the power to heal our weaknesses.

3° THE MEANS OF OBTAINING SELF-KNOWLEDGE

460. Self-knowledge is *difficult* to attain. **a)** Attracted as we are by *outward things*, we hardly care to enter into ourselves to scrutinize that unseen miniature world ; we care even less, *proud* as we are, about discovering our faults.

b) Our *interior* acts are *extremely complex*. There is within us, as St. Paul says, the lower life of the flesh and the higher life of the spirit and often turbulent conflict ensues between them. In order to sift what proceeds from nature, what from grace, what is wilful, and what is not, a great deal of attention is required, a great deal of insight, of honesty, of courage, of perseverance. The light comes but gradually — a bit of knowledge leads to more, and this prepares the way for deeper insight.

461. Since it is through *examinations of conscience* that we come to know ourselves, we shall give, in order to facilitate this exercise, some *general rules*, offer a *method*, and suggest the *dispositions* with which these examinations should be made.

462. A) General Rules. a) In order to perform this examination well, we must first of all invoke the *light of the Holy Ghost*, Who " searcheth the reins and the hearts " of men, and beg Him to show us the inmost recesses of our soul by bestowing upon us the gift of knowledge, one of whose functions is to help us know ourselves and thus to lead us to God.

b) Next, we must bring before us the perfect Exemplar, *Jesus*, Whom we must resemble more and more every day, and we must adore and admire not only His exterior acts, but above all, His interior dispositions. By the light which the contrast between ourselves and our Divine Model will give, our faults and imperfections will be the more clearly discerned. Nor shall we be disheartened at the sight, for Jesus is also the Healer of souls Whose one anxiety is to dress our wounds and heal them. To make our confession to Him, so to speak, and humbly ask His forgiveness is an excellent practice.

463. c) Then comes the moment to enter into our inmost soul. From *outward* actions we pass on to the hidden causes from which they spring, our interior dispositions. Thus, if we have failed in charity, we shall ask ourselves whether it was through thoughtlessness, envy, jealousy, talkativeness, or from a desire to be witty.

Then to estimate the morality of the act, and to determine our responsibility, we must ask ourselves whether it was *actually* wilful, or wilful in *cause;* performed with *full* consciousness of its malice, or with only a half-advertence; with full consent of the will, or with a half-consent. At the outset, all this is rather obscure, but it gradually becomes clear.

To be even more impartial in our judgments, it is good to place ourselves in the presence of the Sovereign Judge, and to hear Him say to us, kindly, indeed, but with supreme authority : " *Render an account of thy stewardship.* " Then we shall endeavor to answer as frankly as on the last day we shall wish to have done.

464. At times, it is useful, especially for *beginners*, to make this examination in writing, so as to concentrate attention better and to be able to compare the results obtained each day and each week. Should anyone do so, however, care must be taken to avoid anything that savors of self-seeking, any studied elegance of style, and the danger of having such memoranda fall under the eyes of others. If we use a record with conventional signs, we must be on our guard against routine or shallowness. At all events, a time generally arrives when the better course is to discard such means and candidly examine ourselves under the eye of God immediately after the performance of the principal actions of the day, and make a general review of these in the evening.

465. In this, as in all else, we shall follow the counsel of a wise spiritual director, and ask him to help us to come to a better knowledge of ourselves. Experienced and impartial observer, he generally sees better than we do ourselves the depths of our conscience, and thus is more competent to judge the true character of our acts.

466.   B) Methods for the examination of conscience. Every one acknowledges that these have been greatly perfected by *St. Ignatius*.   In his *Spiritual Exercises*, he carefully differentiates between the *general* and the *particular* examination.   The former bears upon all the actions of the day, the latter upon one *special point*, a fault to be corrected, a virtue to be cultivated.   Both may, however, be made together.   In this case, one will limit the general examination to a summary glance over the day's actions in order to discover the chief faults, passing directly on to the particular examination which is far more important.

467.   a) The general examination, which every good Christian should make in order to know and to improve himself, comprises five points, says *St. Ignatius :* [1]

1) " The first point is to *return thanks to God* Our Lord for the benefits received. "   This is an excellent exercise, at once consoling and sanctifying, for it brings into relief our ingratitude, thus preparing the way for contrition, and at the same time it sustains our confidence in God. [2]

2) " The second is to ask grace to know the sins and cast them out. "   If we want to know ourselves it is in order to reform ourselves, but we accomplish neither without the helping grace of God.

3) " The third, to demand of the soul an account from the hour of rising to the present examen, taking hour by hour or period by period ; and first of thought, then of word, and afterwards of deed, in the same order that has been mentioned for the Particular Examen. "

4) " The fourth is to ask pardon of God Our Lord for the faults. "   In fact, we must not lose sight of this, that *sorrow* is the *principal* element of the examination and that this sorrow is mainly the work of grace.

5) " The fifth is to purpose amendment with His grace. " This resolution, to be practical, should bear upon the *means* of reform.   He who wills the end, wills also the means.

---

[1] *Spiritual Exercises*, Ist week.   The words within the quotation marks belong to St. Ignatius' own text ; translation is by Father RICKABY, S. J., *The Spiritual Exercises of St. Ignatius.*
[2] Here the *method of S. Sulpice* adds the adoration, that is to say all those acts by which we adore, praise, bless, love and express our gratitude to God ; we place ourselves then in the presence of Jesus Christ, our model and our Judge, as has been explained above, n. 462.

The recitation of the Our Father is a fitting conclusion for this examination, bringing before our eyes the glory of God which we must seek, and uniting us to Jesus Christ in our supplication for the pardon of our sins and for the grace of avoiding them in the future.

468. b) The particular examination, [1] in the judgment of St. Ignatius, is of greater moment than the general one, and of even more importance than meditation itself, because it enables us to run down, one by one, our defects and thus overcome them the more easily. Besides, if we examine ourselves thoroughly on some important virtue, we not only acquire that virtue, but all the others related thereto. Thus, whilst we advance in the practice of obedience, we perform at the same time acts of humility, of mortification, and we exercise ourselves in the spirit of faith. Likewise, to acquire the virtue of humility means that we are perfecting ourselves in the practice of obedience, of the love of God, of charity, since pride is the chief obstacle to the exercise of these virtues. There are, however, rules for the *choice of the subject* of examination, and for the manner of performing it

469. The choice of a subject. 1) In general we must attack our *predominant fault* by striving to practice the contrary virtue. This fault is, as a matter of fact, the great stumbling block, the great leader of the opposing forces. If it is conquered, the entire host is routed.

2) Once the subject is determined upon, we must attack first the *outward* manifestations of the particular fault so as to do away with whatever offends or scandalizes the neighbor. Thus, if charity be the subject chosen, we must begin by suppressing words and actions contrary to this virtue.

3) Then, we must without great delay pass to the subject of the *hidden cause of our faults*. This may be, for instance, feelings of envy, a desire to be brilliant in our conversation, etc...

4) It is important not to limit our efforts to this negative side, that is, to the struggle against faults, but we must carefully cultivate the *opposite virtue*. Here, to suppress means to replace.

5) Lastly, in order to make more certain of our progress, we should carefully divide the subject of our examinations

---

[1] MEYER, *Science of the Saints*, Vol. I, Lesson XIV.

in accordance with the different degress of a virtue, so as not to cover the whole field, but merely those acts that more exactly correspond to our individual needs.   Thus, as regards humility, one should practice, first, what may be called *self-effacement* or forgetfulness of self ; speaking but little, giving others the opportunity to speak by means of discreet questions, loving to be unnoticed, to lead a hidden life, etc...

470. The manner of performing the particular Examen. [1]

St. Ignatius tells us that this particular examen involves three periods of the day and two examinations of conscience.

The first time is that in the morning, as soon as the man rises, he ought to purpose to be carefully on his guard against that particular sin, or defect, of which he wishes to correct and amend himself.

The second, after dinner, the man ought to beg of God what he wants, to wit, the grace to remember how often he has fallen into that particular sin or defect, and to amend himself in future ; and thereupon let him make the first examen, taking account of his soul of that particular thing proposed, whereof he wishes to correct and amend himself, ranging through the time hour by hour, or period by period, beginning from the hour that he rose even to the hour and moment of the present examen ; and let him score on the top line of the figure as many dots as are the times that he has fallen into that particular sin or defect ; and afterwards let him purpose anew to amend himself until the next examen that he shall make.

The third time, after supper, the second examen shall be made also from hour to hour, beginning from the first examen until the present second examen ; and let him score on the second line of the same figure as many dots as shall answer to the times that he has fallen into that particular sin or defect.

471. HERE FOLLOW FOUR ADDITIONS FOR THE SPEEDIER REMOVAL OF THAT SIN OR DEFECT.

The first Addition is that, as often as the man falls into that sin or particular defect, he puts his hand to his breast, grieving that he has fallen, — which may be done even in presence of company without their noticing what he is doing.

The second, since the first line of the figure represents the first examen, and the second the second examen, let him observe at night whether there is any improvement from the first line to the second, that is, from the first examen to the second.

The third ; to compare the second day with the first, that is, the two examens of the second day with the other two of the day previous, and see whether from the one day to the other there has been improvement.

---

[1] From the translation of the Spiritual Exercices of S. Ignatius, by Father Joseph Rickaby, S. J.

The fourth Addition; to compare one week with another, and see whether there has been improvement in the present week upon the former.

We must observe that the first great ____ which follows signifies Sunday; the second smaller signifies Monday; the third Tuesday, and so of the rest.

472. This method may, at first sight, appear somewhat complex; in actual practice, it proves less so. Should one be unable to devote to it such a notable space of time as indicated above, one can condense the essential features of these acts within a shorter period, for instance, ten minutes at night. If one foresees that it cannot be performed in the evening, a part of the time given to visiting the Blessed Sacrament may be set apart for it.

473. C) The **Dispositions** that should attend this examination. That the examination of conscience, general or particular, may be effective in uniting us more closely to God, it must be accompanied by sentiments or dispositions that are, so to speak, its soul. We shall note the principal ones : *gratitude, sorrow, purpose of amendment*, and *prayer*.

a) First in order is a *lively sense of gratitude* toward God, Who all through the day has encompassed us about with His paternal Providence, protected us against temptation, and guarded us from innumerable sins. Without the aid of His grace, we should have fallen into many a fault. We should overflow with gratitude, thanking Him in a practical way — by putting His divine gifts to better use.

474. **b**) Such a sentiment will beget a *sincere sorrow*, all the more profound, as we have abused so many benefits received, offending so good and so merciful a Father. Out of this sorrow a sincere *humility* is born. Realizing from our own experience our frailty, our helplessness, our unworthiness, we accept with joy the *confusion* we feel at the sight of our repeated failures; we are happy to exalt the boundless mercies of a Father ever ready to forgive; and we rejoice that our misery serves to proclaim the infinite perfection of our God. These dispositions are not a passing mood; rather they abide with us through the spirit of penance, calling often to mind the thought of our faults : " *My sin is ever before me!* " [1]

475. **c**) The firm *determination to atone* for sin and *to reform* our lives will follow : *to atone* by acts of penance, which we take care to impose upon ourselves in order to deaden in us the love of pleasure, the source of our sins; *to reform* our lives by determining the *means* we shall employ, in order to lessen the number of our faults. Such determination must carefully exclude *presumption*, which by having us rely too much on our own will and our own strength, would deprive us of manifold graces and expose us to additional imprudences and further falls. On the other hand, our determination must rest *confidently* upon the omnipotence and the infinite goodness of God, ever willing to come to our aid when we acknowledge our weakness.

476. **d**) It is to implore this divine help that we conclude the examination with a *prayer*, all the more humble, all the more earnest, now that the sight of our sins has made us more distrustful of self. Realizing that of ourselves we are incapable of avoiding sin and still more incapable of rising up to God by the practice of virtue, we rely on

----

[1] *Ps.* L, 5.

the infinite merits of Jesus Christ, and cry out to God from
the depths of our wretchedness, to come unto us, to lift us
from the mire of our sins, and to raise us up to Himself.
It is through these dispositions rather than by a minute
scrutiny of our faults that our souls are gradually trans·
formed under the influence of grace.

CONCLUSION

477. In this way, then, the knowledge of God and of
self cannot but promote the intimate and affectionate union
between the soul and God. He is infinite perfection, and
we are absolute poverty. Hence, there is between the two
a certain contact. — He has all that we need, and we need
what He has. He stoops down to us to surround us with
His love and His favors, whilst we tend toward Him
as toward the One Being Who alone can supply for our
deficiencies, the One Who alone can make up for our
weakness. Our thirst for happiness and for love is quenched
only in Him, Who with His love satiates our heart and
all its longings, giving us at once both perfection and bliss.
Let us repeat these well-known words : " *May I know Thee,
O Lord, that I may love Thee; may I know myself, that
I may despise myself.* "

§ III. Conformity to the Divine Will [1]

478. The knowledge of God not only unites our mind
to that of God, but it also leads to love, because all in
God is lovable. By showing us the need we have of God,
the knowledge of self makes us ardently long for Him and
throws us into His arms. Conformity to the divine will,
however, unites us even more intimately and directly to
Him Who is the source of all perfection. In fact, it subordinates and unites our will to God, thus placing our ruling
faculty at the service of the Sovereign Master. It may be
said that our degree of perfection corresponds to the extent
to which we conform to the will of God. In order that
this be better understood we shall explain : 1º the *nature*
of this conformity, 2º its *sanctifying* power.

---

[1] P. DE CAUSSADE, *Abandonment to Divine Providence*, Part. I, l. I; LE GAU-
DIER *op. cit.*, p. III, sect. II; St. FR. DE SALES, *The Love of God*, Bks. VIII-IX;
DESURMONT, Œuvres, t. II, sur *La Providence*; MGR. GAY, *Christian Life and
Virtues*, XI, XIV; DOM V. LEHODEY, *Le Saint Abandon*, Iʳᵉ Partie; TISSOT, *The
Interior Life*, Part. II; DREXELIUS, *The Heliotropium or Conformity of the Human
will to the Divine*.

I. *Nature of Conformity to the Will of God*

479. By conformity to the divine will we understand the absolute and loving submission of our will to that of God, whether it be His " *signified will* " or His will of " *good pleasure.* "

As a matter of fact, God's will manifests itself to us under a twofold aspect : **a**) as the *moral norm* of our actions, clearly intimating what we must do in virtue of His *commandments* or His *counsels;* **b**) as the ruling principle that *governs* all things with wisdom, directing the course of events so as to make them work together unto His glory and the salvation of men, and made known to us by the providential events that take place in or about us.

The first is called the *signified* will of God, since it proclaims in clear terms what we must do. The second is called the *good pleasure* of God in the sense that God's will is here manifested by providential events to which we must submit. In practice, then, conformity to God's will means *doing God's will* and *submitting to God's will.*

We shall explain : 1° what is the *signified* will of God; 2° what is His will of *good pleasure;* 3° what degree of submission this latter includes.

1° THE SIGNIFIED WILL OF GOD OR OBEDIENCE TO GOD'S WILL

480. Conformity to God's *signified will* consists in willing all that God manifests to us of His intentions. Now, says St. Francis de Sales : " Christian doctrine clearly proposes unto us the truths which God wills that we should believe, the goods He will have us hope for, the pains He will have us dread, what He will have us love, the commandments He will have us observe and the counsels He desires us to follow. And this is called God's signified will, because He has signified and made manifest unto us that it is His will and intention that all this should be believed, hoped for, feared, loved and practiced. " [1]

This will of God, then, according to the holy Doctor [2] includes four things : the commandments of God and of the Church, the counsels, the inspirations of grace, and, for Religious, the Constitutions and the Rules.

481. **a**) God, being our Sovereign Lord, has the right to give us commands. Since He is infinitely wise and

---

[1] *Treatise of the Love of God*, Bk. VIII, c. 3, (Mackey's translation page 329).
[2] *Spiritual Conf.*, XV.

infinitely good, He commands nothing that is not conducive at once to His glory and our own happiness. We must, then, willingly and unquestioningly submit ourselves to His laws : the natural law, the positive divine law, ecclesiastical law, or a just civil law; for as St. Paul says, all lawful authority comes from God, and to obey Superiors within the limits of their authority is to obey God Himself, just as to resist them would be to offer resistance to Him : " *Let every soul be subject to higher powers. For there is no power but from God : and those that are, are ordained of God. Therefore he that resisteth the power resisteth the ordinance of God. And they that resist purchase to themselves damnation.* " [1] We do not inquire here in what cases disobedience to the various laws constitutes a grave or a light sin; this we have done in our treatise on *Moral Theology.* Suffice it to say that from the point of view of perfection, the more *faithful* and Christlike is our observance of law, the closer is our approach unto God, since law is the expression of His will. We may add that *duties of state* come within the category of commandments. They are, as it were, *particular precepts* incumbent upon us by reason of our special vocation and the special offices God has confided to us.

Sanctification, then, is impossible without the observance of the commandments and the fulfilment of the duties of our state. To neglect them under the pretext of performing works of supererogation is a dangerous illusion, a veritable aberration, for it is evident that commands take precedence over counsels.

482.   b) The observance of the *counsels* is of itself not *necessary for salvation,* nor does it fall under a direct and explicit command. But, as we have already said in speaking of the obligation of striving after perfection (n. 353), in order to remain in the state of grace, we must at times perform certain good works over and above the strict requirements of the law, that is to say, exercise ourselves in the practice of the counsels. This constitutes an indirect obligation based upon the principle that he who wills the end, wills also the means.

When it is question of perfection, however, we proved in n. 338, that one cannot sincerely and effectively seek it without observing some counsels, such as are in accord with our condition in life. Thus, a married person

---

[1] *Rom.*, XIII, 1-2.

may not carry out in practice those counsels which would go counter to the discharge of marital or parental duties. A priest in the ministry may not lead the life of a Carthusian. However, when we aim at perfection, we must be resolved to do more than that to which we are strictly bound. The more generous we are in giving ourselves over to the practice of the counsels compatible with the duties of our state, the closer we draw unto Our Lord, for such counsels are the expression of His designs upon us.

483. c) The same must be said of the inspirations of grace, when they are clear and are submitted to the control of our spiritual director. One may say that these are so many *particular counsels* addressed to individual souls.

No doubt, care must be taken to refer them in the main to the judgment of our spiritual director lest we should become an easy prey to illusion. Ardent, passionate souls readily persuade themselves that they hear the voice of God, when in truth it is the voice of their own passions suggesting such or such a dangerous practice. Punctilious or scrupulous souls would mistake for divine inspirations what is but the product of a feverish imagination, or even a diabolical suggestion, calculated to induce discouragement. Cassian relates many such instances in his Conferences on *Discretion,* [1] and experienced directors of souls know how the imagination does at times suggest practices morally impossible and directly at variance with the fulfilment of the duties of state, all colored by the appearance of divine inspiration. Such suggestions create trouble. If we yield to them, we make ourselves ridiculous; we waste and make others waste much valuable time. If we withstand them, we think we rebel against God, we yield to discouragement and end by surrendering to laxness. A certain control, then, is necessary and the rule to follow is this : if it be question of *customary* things generally done by fervent persons living under the same circumstances as we do, of things that do not trouble the soul, we may do them without hesitation and later on mention them to our director; but if it is question, on the contrary, of things *extraordinary,* even in the least degree, of things not usually done by devout souls, let us wait till we have consulted our spiritual adviser and, in the meantime, fulfil with all generosity our duties of state.

---

[1] Second Conference, c. 5-8.

484. With this limitation, it is evident that any one seeking perfection ought to lend a ready ear to the voice of the Holy Ghost speaking within his soul : " *I will hear what the Lord God will speak in me,* " [1] and he should without delay and without sparing himself comply with God's demands : " *Behold, I come to do thy will, O God.* " [2] This is nothing more than correspondence to grace, and it is precisely this willing and steadfast co-operation that makes us perfect : " *And we helping do exhort you that you receive not the grace of God in vain.* " [3] This is, in fact, the very characteristic of perfect souls, that they hearken to and carry out in practice these divine inspirations : " *I do always the things that please Him.* " [4]

485. **d**) As to those that live in communities, the more generously they obey their rules and constitutions, the more perfect they are. These rules are means of perfection which the Church has explicitly or implicitly approved and to the observance of which a Religious binds himself on entering the community. Undoubtedly, to fail through weakness in certain details of some rules does not of itself constitute a sin. However, often a more or less sinful motive enters into such wilful negligences, and the violation of rules, even when not sinful, certainly deprives us of a priceless opportunity for the acquisition of merit. It ever remains true that to observe one's rule is the safest means of accomplishing God's will and of living for Him : " *He who lives by rule, lives unto God.* " To fail wilfully in this matter, with no good reason for it, is an abuse of grace.

Thus it is that obedience to God's signified will is the normal way of attaining perfection.

2° CONFORMITY TO GOD'S WILL OF GOOD PLEASURE, OR SUBMISSION TO GOD'S WILL

486. This conformity consists in submitting oneself to all providential events willed or allowed by God for our own greater good, and chiefly for our sanctification.

a) It rests upon this basis, that nothing happens without God's order or permission, and that God, being infinite Perfection and infinite Goodness, cannot will or permit anything but for the good of the souls He has created, although this is not always apparent to our eyes. This is what Tobias said in the midst of his afflictions and the

---

[1] *Ps.* LXXXIV, 9. — [2] *Hebr.*, X, 9. — [3] *II Cor.*, VI, 1. — [4] *John.*, VIII, 29.

reproaches of his wife : " *Thou are just, O Lord... and all thy ways mercy and truth and judgment.* " [1]   This is what Wisdom proclaims : " *But thy Providence, O Father, governeth... She reacheth therefore from end to end mightily and ordereth all things sweetly.* " [2]   This is also what St. Paul teaches : " *To them that love God, all things work together unto good.* " [3]

But in order to understand this teaching we must take the point of view of faith and of eternity, of the glory of God and the salvation of men.   If we look only at the present life and its earthly happiness, we cannot understand the designs of God, Who has willed that we undergo trials here below in order to reward us in Heaven.   All things are subordinated to this end.   Present evils are but means of purifying our soul, of grounding it in virtue, and occasions of acquiring merits, all in view of God's glory, the ultimate end of all creation.

487.   **b)** It is our duty, then, to submit ourselves to God in all the events of life, happy or unhappy, midst public calamities or private ills, whether we are lashed by the hand of nature or gripped by that of want and suffering, in sorrows or in joys, in the unequal distribution of gifts natural and supernatural, in failure or success, in desolation or in consolation, in sickness or in health, in life or in death with its attendant suffering and uncertainties.   In the words of holy Job : " *If we have received good things at the hand of God, why should we not receive evil ?* " [4]   Commenting upon these words, St. Francis de Sales [5] cannot but admire their beauty : " O God!   How this word is great with love! He ponders, Theotimus, that it was from the hand of God that he had received the good, testifying that he had not so much loved goods because they were good, as because they came from the hand of the Lord; whence he concludes that he is lovingly to support adversities since they proceed from the hand of the same Lord, which is equally to be loved when it distributes afflictions and when it bestows consolations. "   And, indeed, it is affliction that enables us *to offer the more genuine proof of our love for God.*   To love Him when He lavishes His favors upon us is an easy task; but it is only a perfect love that accepts ills at His Hands, for they cannot be loved except for the sake of Him Who sends them.

[1] *Tob.*, III, 2. — [2] *Wisd.*, XIV, 3; VIII, 1. — [3] *Rom.*, VIII, 28.
[4] *Job.*, II, 10.
[5] *The Love of God*, Bk. IX, c. 2. (Mackey's translation, p. 370.)

488. The duty of submission under trial to the *good pleasure* of God is a duty of *justice* and *obedience,* for God is Our Supreme Lord and Master, Who wields all authority over us. It is a duty inspired by *wisdom,* since it would be folly to wish to elude the action of Providence, whilst in humble resignation we find our *peace.* It is a duty urged by our own *interest,* because God's will merely puts us to the test that we may be exercised in virtue and acquire merit. It is a duty imposed, above all, by *love,* which is the gift of self, even to immolation.

489. c) To *facilitate* this submission to the divine will for souls who are not as yet schooled in the love of the Cross, it is always good to offer them some means of assuaging their sufferings. We can point out two remedies, the one *negative,* the other *positive,* 1) The first is *not to aggravate* sufferings by employing false tactics. There are persons who occupy themselves in gathering together in their minds all their ills, past, present, and to come, until their weight seems insupportable. It is the contrary that we must do : "*Enough for the day is the evil thereof.*" [1] Instead of reopening past wounds, we must never give them a thought, unless it be to note the profit derived from them : increase of merit, growth in virtue, more strength to bear pain. Thus is suffering soothed, for ills only vex us when we heed them : slander, calumny, injuries hurt us only as long as we brood over them.

As to *the future,* it is irrational to let it prey upon the mind. True, it is the part of wisdom to foresee it and provide for it, in the measure that we are able, but to brood in advance over the ills that may befall us, to be saddened by them, is a loss of time and sheer waste of energy. Such ills may never come to pass; if they do come, then will be the time to bear them with the help of grace which will be given us for that purpose. Just now, we have not such grace and, left to our own forces, we shall surely succumb under the weight of a self-imposed burden. Is it not wiser to abandon ourselves into the arms of Our Heavenly Father, and to drive out relentlessly any wicked thought or evil fancy that would force upon our minds the ills of the future and of the past?

490. 2) The positive remedy consists in reflecting, when we suffer, upon the great advantages of suffering. Pain is a *teacher* and a source of merit. As a *teacher,* it is a source

---

[1] *Matth.,* VI, 34.

of *light*, a source of *power :* of light, for it reminds us that we are exiles on the way home and that we cannot entertain ourselves gathering the flowers of consolation, since our true bliss is in Heaven; of *power*, for while pleasure-seeking dulls activity, undermines courage, and leads to disgraceful surrenders, suffering, not indeed in itself, but by reason of the reaction it produces, tends to reinforce our energies, and develops in us manly virtues.

491. Suffering is also a *source of merit* for us and for others. Patiently borne for God's sake and in union with Jesus Christ, it merits for us an eternal recompense, a fact which St. Paul forever kept before the eyes of the early Christians : " *For I reckon that the sufferings of this time are not worthy to be compared with the glory to come that shall be revealed in us...* [1] *...that which is momentary and light of our tribulation worketh for us an eternal weight of glory.* " [2] For the benefit of generous souls he adds that in suffering with Jesus, they fulfil what is wanting to His passion and contribute with Him to the welfare of the Church : " *I fill up those things that are wanting of the sufferings of Christ, in my flesh, for His body, which is the Church.* " [3] This is a consequence of the doctrine of our incorporation into Christ (n. 142 and foll.). These thoughts, indeed, do not deliver us from pain, but they do lessen in no small measure its bitterness, by making us realize its fruitfulness.

Everything, then, invites us to conform our will to that of God, even in the midst of trials.

3° DEGREES OF CONFORMITY, OF SUBMISSION TO GOD'S WILL

492. *St. Bernard* distinguishes three degrees of this virtue, corresponding to the three stages of Christian perfection : " The *beginner*, moved by fear, *patiently* bears the Cross of Christ; the *one who has already made some progress* on the road to perfection, inspired by hope, carries it *cheerfully ;* the *perfect* soul, consumed by love, embraces it *ardently.* " [4]

A) *Beginners*, upheld by the *fear* of God, do not indeed love pain, but rather seek to escape it. However, they choose to suffer rather than to offend God and, though groaning under the weight of the Cross, they endure it in patience, they are resigned.

---

[1] *Rom.*, VIII, 18. — [2] *II Cor.*, IV, 17. — [3] *Coloss.*, I, 24.
[4] I Serm. S. Andreæ, 5.

B) Those *who have already made some progress*, are sustained by the hope and the desire of heavenly things, and, though they do not yet seek the Cross, they willingly carry it with a certain joy, knowing that each new pang represents an additional degree of glory : " *Going, they went and wept, casting their seeds. But coming, they shall come with joyfulness carrying their seed.* " [1]

C) The *perfect*, led by *love*, go further. To glorify the God they love, to become more like our Lord, they go forth to meet the Cross, they long for it and embrace it lovingly, not because it is in itself lovable, but because it offers them the means of proving their love for God and for Christ. Like the Apostles, they rejoice that they are counted worthy to suffer dishonor for the name of Jesus. Like St. Paul, they rejoice in their tribulations. [2]

This last degree is called *holy abandonment*, to which we shall return later when we speak of the love of God. [3]

II. *The Sanctifying Power of Conformity to the Will of God*

493. From what has already been said, we reach the evident conclusion that conformity to God's will cannot but sanctify us, since it makes our will one with God's and, by that very fact, unites all our other faculties to Him, Who is the source of all sanctity. The better to realize this, let us see how it *purifies* us, *reforms* us, and *make us like* unto Jesus Christ.

494. 1° This conformity to the divine Will *purifies* us. Already in the Old Dispensation God often said that He is ready to forgive all sins and to restore the soul to the stainless splendor of its pristine purity, if it but undergo a change of heart or will : " *Wash yourselves : be clean. Take away the evil of your devices from my eyes. Cease to do perversely. Learn to do well... If your sins be as scarlet, they shall be made white as snow.* " [4] Now, to conform our wills to that of God, is assuredly to cease to do evil, and to learn to do good. Is not this the meaning of that oft-repeated text : " *For* obedience *is better than sacrifices.* " [5] In the New Law, Our Lord declares from the very moment of His entry into the world that it is with obedience that

1 *Ps.* CXXV, 6-7.
2 *Following of Christ*, Bk. III, c. 17, Bk. II, c. XI-XII.
3 S. Fr. de Sales, *The Love of God*, Bk. IX, c. 15.
4 *Isaias*, 1, 16-18.
5 *I Kings*, XV, 22; cfr. *Osee*, VI, 6; *Matth.*, IX, 13; XII, 7.

He will replace all the sacrifices of the Ancient Law :
" Holocausts for sin did not please thee. Then said I :
Behold, I come... that I should do thy will, O God. " [1]
And, in truth, it is by obedience unto the immolation of
self that He has redeemed us : " He was made obedient
unto death, even the death of the Cross. " [2]   In the same
way, it is through obedience and through the acceptance of
God-ordained trials in union with Christ that we shall atone
for our sins and cleanse our soul.

495.   2º This conformity works out our *reformation*.
What has deformed us is the disordered love of pleasure,
to which through *malice* or through *weakness* we have
yielded.   Conformity to the divine will cures this malice
and weakness.

a) It cures our *malice*.   This malice is the result of our
attachment to creatures and, especially, of our attachment
to our own judgment and our own will.   Now, by conforming our will to that of God, we accept His judgments as
the standard of ours, His commandments and His counsels as the rule of our will.   Thus we wean ourselves
from creatures and from self and rid ourselves from such
attachments.

b) It cures our *weakness*, the source of so many failings.
Instead of relying on our own frail selves, we make through
obedience the Omnipotent God our support : He gives us
His own strength enabling us to overcome even the severest
temptations : " *I can do all things in Him Who strengtheneth
me.* " [3]   When we do His will, He takes His good pleasure
in doing our own by granting our petitions and helping
our weakness.

Thus freed from our malice and weakness, we no longer
sin deliberately against God and we gradually effect the
reformation of our lives.

496.   3º Through this conformity, we make our wills
one with Christ's.   **a)** The truest, the closest, the most far-
reaching union that can exist is that between two wills.
Through conformity to the divine will, we *unite* our will to
that of Jesus Christ Whose food was to do the will of His
Father. [4]   Like Jesus and with Jesus we desire but what
He wills and that all the day long.   This is the fusion of
two wills.   We are one with Him, we adopt His views, His

---

[1] *Hebr.*, X, 6-7. — [2] *Phil.*, II, 8. — [3] *Phil.*, IV, 13.
[4] *John*, IV, 34; VI, 38; VIII, 29.

sentiments, His choices : " *Let this mind be in you, which was also in Christ Jesus;* " [1] and soon we can make our own the word of St. Paul : " *I live, now not I, but Christ liveth in me.* " [2]

497. b) In submitting our will, we yield and unite to God all the other faculties which are under its sway; hence, we yield and unite unto Him our whole soul, which by degrees conforms itself to the will and wishes of the Master. Thereby the soul acquires one by one all the virtues of Our Lord. What we have said of charity, n. 318, can also be said of conformity to the divine will; that like charity it embodies all other virtues. In the words of St. Francis de Sales : " Abandonment is the virtue of virtues. It is the cream of love, the fragrance of humility, the merit, it seems to me, of patience and the fruit of perseverance." [3] Hence, Our Lord calls by the tender names of brother and sister and mother those who do the will of His Father : " *For whosoever shall do the will of my Father that is in heaven, he is my brother and sister and mother.* " [4] He repeatedly declares that the true test of love is doing God's will : " *If you love me, keep my commandments... not every one that saith to me, Lord, Lord, shall enter into the Kingdom of Heaven; but he that doth the will of my Father who is in Heaven, he shall enter into the kingdom of heaven.* " [5]

CONCLUSION.

498. Conformity to the divine will, then, is one of the most effective means of sanctification. Hence, we cannot but end with these words of St. Theresa : " The sole concern of him who has but entered into the way of prayer, — keep it in mind, it is very important — must be to strive courageously to conform his will to that of God... Herein lies, whole and entire, the highest perfection to which we can attain. The more perfect this accord is, the more do we receive from the Lord and the greater is our progress." [6] She adds that she herself had wished to live in this way of conformity without being raised to rapturous transports and ecstasies, so firm was her conviction that the path of conformity was all-sufficient to the most exalted perfection.

---

[1] *Philip.*, II, 5. — [2] *Galat.*, II, 20. — [3] Spiritual Conferences, XI.
[4] *Matth.*, XII, 50. — [5] *John*, XIV, 15; *Matth.*, VII, 21.
[6] *Interior Castle*, Second Mansion.

§ IV. Prayer [1]

499. Prayer embodies and completes all the preceding acts. It is itself a *desire for perfection*, since no one would sincerely pray who did not wish to become better. It presupposes some *knowledge of God* and *of self*, since it establishes relations between the two. It *conforms our will* to that of God, since any good prayer contains, explicitly or implicitly, an act of submission to Our Sovereign Master. Prayer, moreover, *perfects* all these acts, by bringing us in all humility before the Majesty of God, in order to adore Him, and to implore new graces that will enable us to grow in perfection. We shall, then, explain : 1º the *nature* of prayer; 2º its *efficacy* as a means of perfection; 3º the *way* in which our lives are transformed into a *habitual prayer*.

I. *The Nature of Prayer*

500. We use the word prayer here in the widest sense of the term, as an elevation of the soul to God. We shall explain : 1º The *notion* of prayer. 2º Its various *forms*. 3º The perfect prayer, *The Lord's Prayer*.

1º WHAT PRAYER IS

501. In the Fathers we find three definitions of prayer that complete one another. 1) In its broadest signification it is, says *St. John Damascene*, [2] *an elevation of the soul to God*. St. Augustine had stated before him that prayer is *the soul's affectionate quest of God*. [3] 2) In a narrower sense it has been defined as *the asking of seemly things from God*. [4] 3) To set forth the relations that prayer establishes between God and the soul, it has been represented as *a familiar conversation with God*. [5] All these aspects of prayer are true and, by uniting them, we may define prayer as *an elevation of our soul to God to offer Him our homage and ask His favors, in order to grow in holiness for His glory*. This definition we shall explain.

---

[1] St. THOM., IIª IIæ, q. 83-84; SUAREZ, *De Religione*, Tr. IV, lib. I, *De Oratione;* ALVAREZ DE PAZ, t. III, lib. I; St. ALPH. DE LIGUORI, *The Great Means of Prayer;* St. FRANCIS DE SALES, *Devout Life*, P. II; GROU, *How to Pray;* MESCHLER, *Three Fundamental Principles of the Spiritual Life*, P. I; *Spiritual Combat*, c. 44-52; HEDLEY, *Retreat*, XXI; *Retreat for Priests* IX, X; P. MONSABRÉ, *La Prière, Philosophie et Théologie de la prière;* P. RAMIERE, *L'Apostolat de la prière;* P. SERTILLANGES, *La Prière*, 1917. References to Works on Mental Prayer will be given in the Second Part of this Work.
[2] *De Fide Orthod.*, l. III, c. 24, *P. G.*, XCIV, 1090.
[3] *Serm.* IX, n. 3.
[4] S. JOHN DAMASCENE, ibidem.
[5] S. GREG. NYS., Orat. I, de Orat. Domini, *P. G.*, XLIV, 1124.

502. The term *elevation* is a metaphor indicating the effort we make to detach ourselves from creatures and from self in order to fix our thoughts on God Who not only surrounds us, but dwells in our inmost soul. As we are only too prone to let our faculties roam over a multitude of subjects, it requires an effort to snatch them away from these vain and alluring goods and center them on God. Such elevation is termed a *colloquy*, because prayer, whether it takes the form of worship or of petition, calls for an answer on the part of God and thus implies a sort of conversation with Him, even if it be of the briefest duration.

Our first act in this conversation, evidently, must be to render to God *religious homage*, just as we begin by saluting those persons with whom we hold converse. It is only after having acquitted ourselves of this fundamental duty that we may present our requests. Many forget it, and this is the reason why their petitions are less favorably answered. Even when we ask for the graces of sanctification and salvation, we must not lose sight of our principal purpose, *the glory of God.* Hence, the last words of our definition " *for His glory.* "

2° THE VARIOUS FORMS OF PRAYER

503. A) Considering the twofold end of prayer, we distinguish the prayer of worship, and the prayer of petition.

a) Prayer of Worship. This includes adoration, due to God as our Sovereign Master; thanksgiving, because God is likewise our Benefactor; and reparation, because we have offended Him.

1) The first sentiment that imposes itself when we raise our soul to God is that of *adoration*, that is to say, an acknowledgment of God's supreme dominion and of our absolute dependence. All creation adores God after its own manner, but inanimate nature lacks both an intellect to grasp Him, and a heart to love Him. It must be content to display before our gaze its own harmony, its activities, its beauty : " It cannot see — it reveals itself; it cannot adore — it brings us to our knees, loath to have us ignore the God it cannot apprehend... But man, a breath divine within a body of clay, possessed of reason and intelligence and capable of knowing God, both through his natural powers and through the agency of creation, is urged by his own self and by all creatures to bow before God in humble adoration. For this reason is man, himself a microcosm, placed in this world, that contemplating this universe and,

as it were, gathering it all up in himself, he may refer himself and all things to God alone. So much so, that man is made to contemplate the visible things of this creation, only in order that he may adore the Invisible Being Who brought them out of nothing by the omnipotence of His power. "[1] In other words, man is the *pontiff* of creation, upon whom it devolves to glorify God in his own name and in that of all creatures. This duty man fulfils by acknowledging "that God is perfection itself and hence incomprehensible; that God is Supreme; that God is Goodness... We are instinctively drawn to revere what is perfect,... to depend on that which is supreme,... to cling to what is good. "[2]

504. Thus it is that mystics delight to adore in creatures the power, the majesty, the beauty, the activity, the fecundity of God hidden in them : " My God, I adore Thee in all Thy creatures, Thou the real, the sole strength that bears this mighty world. Without Thee, nothing would be; nothing does subsist outside of Thee. I love Thee, O my God, and praise Thy Majesty shown forth in all creation. All that I behold, O God, but reveals to me the mystery of Thy beauty unknown to mortal eyes... I adore the splendour of Thy glory, the grandeur of Thy majesty that outshines the noon day sun a thousand times. I adore the fecundity of Thy power, more wonderful by far than that disclosed by the starry skies. "[3]

505. 2) Adoration is followed by *thanksgiving*. God is not merely Our Lord and Master but our great *Benefactor*, to Whom we owe all that we are, all that we have, whether in the order of nature or of grace. Therefore, He has a right to everlasting gratitude from us who forever receive new favors at His Hand. Hence, the Church daily calls upon us, just before the Canon of the Mass, to thank Almighty God for all His gifts, and chiefly for that which embodies all others, the Holy Eucharist : " *Let us give thanks to the Lord Our God. It is truly meet and just, right and salutary to offer thanks...* "[4] Hence, the Church also places on our lips formulas of thanksgiving : " We give Thee thanks for the greatness of Thy glory. "[5] In so doing, she but follows the example of Christ, Who often gave thanks to the Father; she but carries out the instruc-

---

[1] BOSSUET, *Sermon sur le culte de Dieu.* — [2] BOSSUET, l. cit.
[3] OLIER, *Journée chrét.*, II p.
[4] Preface of the Mass. — [5] *Gloria in excelsis Deo.*

tions of St. Paul, who invites us to give thanks to the Most High for all His blessings : *" In all things give thanks, for this is the will of God...* [1] *Thanks be to God for His unspeakable gift."* [2] Generous souls need not be reminded of this duty. They feel themselves impelled by the thought of the divine favors to give vent again and again to the gratitude that overflows their heart.

506. 3) In our present state of *fallen* nature, a third duty forces itself upon us — that of *expiation* and of *reparation.* We have but too often offended God's infinite majesty, using His gifts to offend Him. This constitutes an injustice requiring as full a reparation as we are able to offer. It consists of three principal acts : the humble *acknowledgment* of our faults; a sincere *sorrow* for them; the *courageous acceptance* of the trials God in His goodness may see fit to send us. If we desire to act with generosity, we shall add thereto the *offering of ourselves* as expiatory victims in union with the Victim of Golgotha. Then we may humbly beg and hope for pardon and ask for further graces.

507. b) The Prayer of Petition. Asking of God for what we need is itself homage rendered to Him, to His power, to His goodness, to the efficacious operation of His grace; it is an act of confidence that honors Him to Whom it is offered. [3] The reasons for prayer of petition are, on the one side, the love God bears His creatures, His children, and, on the other, the sore need we have of His help.

Inexhaustible source of all good, God longs to communicate it to souls : *goodness tends to communicate itself.* Being our Father, God desires nothing so much as to give us His life and increase it in our souls. The better to attain this purpose He sent to earth His Only-Begotten Son, Who came full of grace and truth purposely to fill us with His treasures. Nay more, He invites us to ask for His graces, and promises to grant them : *" Ask and you shall receive, seek and you shall find, knock and it shall be opened unto you. "* [4] We are, therefore, certain of pleasing God by presenting our requests to Him.

508. Besides, we stand in *sore need* of God's help. Whether in the order of nature or in the order of grace, we are poor, steeped in poverty. Depending of necessity upon

---

[1] *I Thess.*, V, 18. — [2] *II Cor.*, IX, 15.
[3] St. Thomas, IIa IIæ, q. 83, a. 3. — [4] *Matth.*, VII, 7.

God, even in the order of nature, we cannot so much as preserve the very existence He has given us; we are at the mercy of physical causes, themselves depending on God. In vain we may protest that we possess brain and sinews, and that we are well able with our strength and our energy to draw from the earth the things we need for our subsistence. That brain, those sinews, are sustained by God; they can work only with His concurrence. The earth flowers not, save when watered by the rain He sends; it produces nothing, save when quickened by the warmth of His glowing sun. And how many forces of destruction can wreck the fruit of man's work and man's care!

Our dependence upon God in the *supernatural* order is more absolute still. We need *light* to guide us, and who will give it to us if not the Father of lights? We need *courage* and *strength* to follow the light; who will give these except He Who is All-Powerful? What else then can we do but implore the help of Him Whose one desire is to succor us?

509. Let no one say that His omniscience is aware of all that is necessary and useful to us. St. Thomas answers that no doubt, out of pure liberality, God does bestow upon us innumerable benefits unasked, unsought, but that there are some which He will grant only at our request, and this for our own good, namely, that we should place our confidence in Him and come to acknowledge Him as the source and origin of all our goods. [1] When we pray, we cherish the hope of being heard and we are less exposed to forget God. As it is, we forget Him all too often; what would it be, if we should never feel the need of recurring to Him in our distress?

It is for very good reasons then that God demands of us prayer in the form of petition.

510. B) From the point of view of form, we can distinguish between *mental* and *vocal*, *private* and *public* prayer.

a) From the point of view of *expression*, prayer is *mental* or *vocal*, according as it takes place wholly within the soul, or is given outward expression.

1) Mental prayer is a silent intercourse of the soul with God. " I will *pray* with the spirit, I will *pray* also with the

---

[1] *Sum. theol.*, IIa IIæ, q. 83, a. 2, ad 3. — Cfr. MONSABRÉ, *La Prière*, 1906, p. 54-55.

understanding."[1] Every interior act of the mind or of the heart that tends to unite us to God, such as recollection, consideration, reasoning, self-examination, the loving thought of God, contemplation, a longing of the heart for God — all these may be called by the name of mental prayer.   All these acts, even our examination of conscience, the purpose of which is to make our soul less unworthy of Him Who dwells in it, raise us up to God.   All of these deepen our convictions, exercise us in virtue, and constitute our training for that heavenly life that is nothing else but an eternal, loving contemplation of the Godhead.   Mental prayer is likewise the very food and the soul of vocal prayer.[2].

511.   2) Vocal prayer finds expression in *word* and *act*. It is frequently mentioned in our Sacred Books, which call upon us to proclaim God's praises by word of mouth, with lip and tongue : " *I have cried to the Lord with my voice... O Lord, thou wilt open my lips : and my mouth shall declare thy praise.* "[3]   But why thus express our sentiments, since God reads them in the depths of our heart?   It is in order to honor Him not only with the soul, but also with the body, and, above all, with that *word* which He has given us to express our thought.   This is the teaching of St. Paul, who after showing that Jesus died for us outside the walls of Jerusalem, invites us to come out of ourselves and join our Mediator, in order to offer unto God a sacrifice of praise, the homage of our lips : " *By him, therefore, let us offer* the sacrifice of praise *always to God, that is to say*, the fruit of lips *confessing to His name.* "[4]   Vocal prayer, moreover, stimulates *devotion* by the very utterance of the words : " That man *may rouse himself by word of mouth* to devout prayer."[5]   Psychology, indeed, shows that gestures intensify the acts of the heart.   Finally, it works unto *the edification of our neighbor;* for, seeing or hearing others pray devoutly increases our own devotion.

512.   **b)** Vocal prayer may be *private* or *public,* according as it is offered in the name of an *individual* or of *society.* We have elsewhere proved that *society* as *such* owes God social homage, since it must acknowledge Him as its Sovereign Master and Benefactor.   This is why St. Paul

---

[1] *I Cor.*, XIV, 15.

[2] In the Second Part of this work we shall return to the subject of mental prayer indicating which kind is in harmony with each of the three Ways.

[3] *Ps.* III, 5; L, 17. — [4] *Hebr.*, XIII, 15.

[5] St. Thomas, *In Libr. Sentent.*, distinct. XV, q. 4, a. 4.

urged the early Christians to unite, not only with one heart, but with one voice in praising God with Jesus Christ : " *That with one mind and with one mouth, you may glorify God and the Father of our Lord Jesus Christ.* " [1]   Our Lord had already exhorted His disciples to come together in order to pray, promising to come to them and sponsor their requests : " *For where there are two or three gathered together in my name, there I am in the midst of them.* " [2]   If this is true of the gathering of one or two, how much truer is it when a multitude comes together to thank God in an official manner! St. Thomas says that the power of prayer is then irresistible : " *The prayers of the many cannot go unheeded, when they unite in one.* " [3]   Just as a father who would not yield to the request of a son is moved by the united requests of all his children, so Our Heavenly Father cannot resist the sweet violence of the united prayers of a great number of His children.

513. It is important, therefore, that Christians should often join in common prayer and worship. This is why the Church calls them on the Lord's Day and on holy days to assist at the great public prayer, the Holy Sacrifice of the Mass, and at other religious services.

514.   Since, however, the Church cannot gather her faithful children every day, and since nevertheless God deserves perennial praise, she commits to her *priests* and *religious* the discharge of this grand duty of public prayer. This they fulfil several times a day through the recitation of the *Divine Office,* which they perform, not in a private capacity, but in the name of the entire Church, and on behalf of all mankind.   Hence, it is important that they unite themselves to the perfect worship offered to God by the Incarnate Word, in order to give glory to God *through Him,* with Him, and in Him, and ask at the same time all the graces that the Christian people need.

3° THE LORD'S PRAYER

515.   Among all the prayers we recite, *private* or *public,* there is none so beautiful as that taught us by Our Lord Himself — the *Our Father.*

A) We find therein, first of all, an appropriate introduction which ushers us into God's presence and excites our confidence : *Our Father Who art in Heaven.* The very first

---

[1] *Rom.,* XV, 6. — [2] *Matth.,* XVIII, 20. — [3] *Commentar. in Matth.,* c. XVIII.

step in prayer is to draw nigh unto God. The word *Father*
places us at once before Him, Who is pre-eminently the
Father Who has adopted us as children. We face then the
God Who surrounds us with the same love wherewith He
loves His Son. And that Father is in Heaven; that is, He
is all-powerful, He is the source of all graces, hence we are
impelled to invoke Him with a filial trust that knows no
bounds, for we are His offspring; all brethren, because
children of the same God : *Our* Father.

516. B) The *object* of the prayer follows. We ask for
all we desire, and *in the order* in which we should desire
it : **a)** We place the *principal end* before all else — God's
glory : " Hallowed be Thy Name, " that is to say, may Thy
Name be known and proclaimed blessed. **b)** Then comes
the *secondary end* — the growth of God's kingdom within
us, which is the preparation for our entry into the Kingdom
of Heaven : " Thy Kingdom come. " **c)** Next, we ask for
the *essential means* for attaining this twofold end, that is,
conformity to the Divine Will : " Thy Will be done on
earth as it is in Heaven. "

We ask, after that, for the *secondary means*. — This
request constitutes the second part of the Our Father.
d) First, the *positive* means — our daily sustenance, food for
the body and food for the soul; we need one and the other,
if we are to subsist and grow : " Give us this day our daily
bread. " **e)** Lastly, we beg the *negative* means, which
comprise 1) the *remission of sin* — the only real evil, which
is forgiven us in the measure that we ourselves pardon
others : " Forgive us our trespasses as we forgive those who
trespass against us. " 2) *The removal of trials and temptations* to which we could fall victims : " Lead us not into
temptation. " 3) The *removal of physical evils*, of the
miseries of life so far as they constitute an obstacle to our
sanctification : " But deliver us from evil. Amen. "

A sublime prayer, since every word of it refers to God's
glory, and yet so simple that it is within the reach of
all ; for whilst glorifying God, we ask for all the things that
are most useful to us.

Hence, the Fathers and the Saints have taken delight in
commenting [1] on this prayer, and the Catechism of the
Council of Trent gives an extended and solid explanation
of it.

---

[1] Many of these commentaries are found in HURTER'S, *Opuscula Patrum selecta*,
t. II; cf *Sum. Theol.*, IIa IIæ, q. 83, a. 9; ST. THERESA, *The Way of Perfection;*
P. MONSABRÉ, *La Prière Divine, le Pater*.

II. *The Efficacy of Prayer for Sanctification*

517. The sanctifying power of prayer is such that the Saints never tired of saying that he lives well who prays well. Prayer produces three marvelous effects : 1) it *detaches* us from creatures, 2) it *unites* us entirely to God, 3) it gradually *transforms* us into God.

518. 1° *It detaches us from creatures* in so far as they are an obstacle to our union with God. This effect of prayer follows from its very nature as an elevation of the heart to God. In order to be raised up to God we must first loosen the bonds that fasten us to creatures. Drawn by these, and by the alluring pleasures they hold out to us, dominated moreover by selfishness, we cannot free ourselves except by breaking the shackles that fetter us to earth. Nothing works this happy deliverance more effectively than the elevation of the soul to God through prayer, for in order to think of Him and of His glory, in order to love Him, we are constrained to forget self and creatures with their deceitful allurements. Once we are nigh unto Him, united to Him in intimate converse, then His infinite perfections, His loving kindness, and the sight of His heavenly riches, complete the liberation of the soul : " *How wretched the earth when I gaze upon the heavens!* " We hate *mortal sin* more and more, for it would turn us away altogether from God. We detest *venial sin* because it would impede our ascent towards Him, and we deplore even *imperfections*, since they would cool our intimacy with Him. We are likewise schooled to a more vigorous strife against the disordered inclinations latent within our nature, because of the realization that they tend to make us wander away from God.

519. 2° Prayer moreover makes our union with God more complete and more perfect day by day.

A) More *complete*. Prayer lays hold of all our faculties, in order to unite them to God. **a)** It seizes the *higher* faculties of our soul: the mind, by absorbing it in the thought of divine things; the will, by directing it toward the Glory of God and the welfare of souls; the heart, by permitting it to pour out its love into a Heart ever open, loving, ever merciful, and enabling it to produce affections that cannot be but sanctifying. **b)** It seizes the *lower faculties* of the soul, by helping us to fasten upon God and Our Lord, our imagination, our memory, our emotions, and

even our passions in so far as they are capable of good.
c) It *even* takes possession of *our body*, helping us to mortify
our outward senses, which so often lead us astray, and to
regulate our exterior according to the dictates of modesty.

B) More *perfect.* Prayer, as just described, produces in
the soul acts of religion born of *faith*, sustained by *hope* and
vivified by *love :* "*Faith believes, hope and love pray, but
these could not exist without faith ; hence it is, that faith also
prays.* " [1]   Is there anything nobler, anything more sanctifying than these acts of the theological virtues?   Prayer,
likewise, presupposes the performance of acts of humility,
of obedience, of fortitude, of constancy, so that it is not
difficult to see that the holy exercise of prayer unites our
soul to God in a most perfect manner.

520.   3° No wonder, then, that through it, the soul is
gradually *transformed* into God.   Prayer causes, so to
speak, a mutual exchange between us and God : whilst we
offer Him our homages and our requests, He stoops down
to us and bestows upon us His graces.

A) The mere consideration of His divine perfections, the
mere fact of admiring them and taking in them a genuine
delight, draws them into us through the desire we thus feel
of sharing in them.   Little by little our soul feels, as it
were, all pervaded, possessed by that Simplicity, that Goodness, that Holiness, that Serenity which God would fain
communicate to us.

521.   B) Then God stoops down to hearken to our
prayers and to bestow upon us His graces in abundance.
The more we honor Him, the greater is His concern in
sanctifying a soul that seeks His glory.   We can ask a
great deal, provided we do so with humility and confidence.
He can refuse nothing to humble souls who care more for
His interests than for their own.   He gives them light to
show them the emptiness, the nothingness of human things;
He draws them to Himself by revealing Himself to them
as the Supreme Good, the origin of all good; He strengthens
and steadies their will that they may will nothing, love
nothing, but what is worthy.   We cannot but conclude
with St. Francis de Sales [2] : " If prayer be a colloquy, a
discourse or a conversation of the soul with God, by it then
we speak to God, and He again speaks to us; we aspire to

---

[1] St. Augustine, *Enchirid.*, VII.
[2] *The love of God*, Bk. VI. c. I. (Mackey's translation).

Him and breathe in Him, and He reciprocally inspires us and breathes upon us. " Happy exchange! It shall be altogether to our advantage, since its ultimate end is no other than the transformation of ourselves into God, by making us share in His thoughts and His perfections!

III. *How We Can Transform Our Actions Into Prayers*

522. Since prayer is such an effective means of sanctification, we should frequently and perseveringly make use of it. Our Lord said : " *We ought always to pray and not to faint.* " [1] St. Paul teaches the same doctrine both by word and example : " *Pray without ceasing... Making a remembrance of you in our prayers without ceasing.* " [2] How are we, however, to pray without ceasing, the while we discharge our duties of state? Is not this impossible? We shall see that it is simple, once we have learned to regulate our lives. To accomplish it, two things are required : 1º that we perform a certain number *of spiritual exercises* in harmony with our state of life; 2º that we *turn* our ordinary actions *into prayer.*

523. 1º *Spiritual Exercises.* In order to foster a life of prayer, first of all, a certain number of spiritual exercises re necessary, the extent and duration of which will vary in accordance with our duties of state. Here we shall speak of such as are proper to priests and religious, leaving to directors of souls the care of adapting this program to the laity.

Three different sets of spiritual exercises school the priestly soul to prayer : in the morning, meditation and Holy Mass present to us *the ideal* we are to pursue and aid us to realize it; throughout the day, the Divine Office, devout readings and some great Catholic devotions help to keep up in the soul the *habit of prayer;* in the evening the examination of conscience will cause us to *note* and *correct* our failures.

524. A) *The morning exercises* are sacred in character. Priests and religious can not dispense with them without giving up real concern for perfection. **a)** It is *meditation,* the loving thought of God, that, above all, recalls to mind *the ideal* we must ever keep before our eyes and *pursue* with all our strength. This ideal is no other than the one pictured for us by the Divine Master : " Be you,

---

[1] *Luke.* XVIII, 1. — [2] *I Thess.*, V, 17; I, 2.

therefore, perfect as also your Heavenly Father is perfect," [1]
So we must place ourselves in the *presence of God*, the
source and exemplar of all perfection; in the presence of
Our Lord Jesus Christ, Who has realized in the world this
ideal of perfection and has merited for us the grace of
imitating His virtues. After offering Him our homage, we
draw Him unto us by becoming one with Him in thought,
through the formation of deep-seated convictions regarding
the special virtue we want to practice; we then draw this
virtue from His heart into our own by earnest prayers that
obtain for us the grace of actually practicing it. Finally,
we humbly, but resolutely, co-operate with the grace
received by making the *generous resolve* of practicing the
said virtue during the course of the day. [2] **b)** Holy Mass
confirms us in this disposition by placing before our eyes,
in our hands, and at our disposal, the Sacred Victim we are
to imitate. Holy Communion causes His thoughts, His
sentiments, His interior dispositions, His graces and His
Divine Spirit to penetrate our own souls there to abide
the day long. We are priests, then, in order to act, and
our action vivified by His influence will be an unceasing
prayer.

525. **B)** That this be so, it is necessary that from time
to time there be exercises renewing and promoting our
union with God. **a)** This will be effected by the recitation
of the *Divine Office*, so aptly styled by St. Benedict *God's
Work*, wherein, in union with the perfect worship of God
by Jesus Christ, we shall glorify Him and implore His graces
for ourselves and for the entire Church. After the Holy
Sacrifice, this is the most important act of the day.
b) Another exercise fostering our union with God is the
reading of Holy Scripture and the lives of the Saints, the
perusal of which will once more place us in close contact
with God and His Saints. **c)** Lastly come what may be
called *the essential Catholic devotions* that nourish piety,
such as the visit to the Blessed Sacrament — a heart-to-
heart talk with Jesus — and the recitation of the beads,
through which we are privileged to hold familiar conversation with Mary and to consider devoutly the mysteries of
her life and her virtues.

526. **C)** At night, the two *examinations, general* and
particular, will take place. These we shall turn into a

---

[1] *Matth.*, V, 48.
[2] This we shall explain later when treating of the method of prayer.

humble and sincere confession to the Great High Priest, and into a means of seeing to what extent we have realized in the course of the day the ideal conceived in the morning. Alas! we shall ever find a discrepancy between our resolutions and their realization; but without any loss of heart, we shall retire to rest with a sense of trust in God, abandoning ourselves into His arms, determined to greater effort on the morrow.

Weekly, or at least fortnightly confession, together with the monthly retreat — a summary review of the month — will complete the work of our daily examination of conscience and be the occasion of a spiritual renewal.

527. 2⁰ This is the sum-total of spiritual exercises, that prevent us from losing sight of God's holy presence for any considerable time. What shall we do, however, to fill in the time between these various exercises and to transform all our actions into prayer? St. Paul answered this question when he wrote : " Whether you eat or drink, or whatsoever else you do, do all to the glory of God... All whatsoever you do in word or in work, all things do ye in the name of the Lord Jesus Christ. " [1] St. Augustine and St. Thomas tell us how this can be done; the former tells us to convert our life, our actions, our occupations, our meals, even our repose, into a hymn of praise unto God's glory : " *Let the harmony of thy life ever rise as a song, so that thou mayest never cease to praise... If thou wilt give praise, sing, then, not only with thy lips, but sweep the chords upon the psalter of good works; thou dost give praise when thou workest, when thou eatest and drinkest, when thou liest to rest, when thou sleepest; thou givest praise even if thou holdest thy peace.*" [2] The latter briefly expresses the same thought : " *Man prays so long as he directs his whole life toward God.* " [3]

It is love that directs our whole life towards God. The practical means of giving all our actions this direction, is to offer each of them to the Most Blessed Trinity in union with Jesus Christ living in us, and in accordance with His intentions (n. 248).

528. Father Olier shows the importance of performing our actions *in union with Jesus.* He explains first how the Son of God is within us in order to sanctify us. [4] " He dwells in us not only through His immensity, as the Word...

---

[1] *I Cor.*, X, 31, *Col.* III, 17. — [2] *In Psalm.* CXLVI, n. 2.
[3] *Comment. in Rom.*, c. I, lect. 5.
[4] *Catech. Int. Life*, Part. II, Lesson X. — Cfr. FATHER CHARLES, S. J. *Prayer for all Times.*

but also as the Christ, through His grace, in order to make us partakers of His unction and of His divine life. Jesus Christ is within us to sanctify both ourselves and our works and to fill all our faculties with His own Self. He wills to be the light of our mind, the fire of love in our hearts, the might and strength of all our faculties, in order that in Him we may have power to know and to fulfil the desires of God, His Father, whether it be to work for His honor or to suffer and endure all things unto His glory." Father Olier then explains how the actions we perform of ourselves and for ourselves are defective : " Because of our corrupted nature, our intentions and our thoughts tend toward sin and, should we decide to act of ourselves and follow the bent of our own sentiments, our works would be of sin."[1] His conclusion is, therefore, that we must renounce our own intentions so as to unite ourselves to those of Jesus : " You see thereby what great care you must take to renounce, upon undertaking any action, all your sentiments, all your wishes, all your own thoughts, all your desires, in order to enter, according to the word of St. Paul, into the sentiments and the intentions of Jesus Christ : *For let this mind be in you, which was also in Christ Jesus.*"[2]

When our actions endure for some time, it is useful to renew this offering by an affectionate gaze upon our Crucifix, or better, upon Jesus living within us, and to raise our soul to God through oft-repeated ejaculations.

In this manner our actions, even the most commonplace, will become a prayer, an elevation of the soul to God, and we shall thereby comply with the teaching of Jesus : " We ought always to pray and not to faint."[3]

529. Here then we have four interior means of perfection that tend at once to glorify God and perfect the soul. The desire to be perfect is, in fact, a first flight toward God, a first step toward holiness. The knowledge of God draws God down to us and helps us give ourselves to Him through love. The knowledge of self shows us the need we have of God and stimulates in us the desire of receiving Him in order to fill the void that exists within us. Conformity to His will transforms us into Him. Prayer lifts us up to Him while it draws unto us His perfections, making us share in them in order to render us like unto Him. All leads us to God, because all proceeds from Him.

---

[1] *Catech. of Int. Life*, P. II, Lesson VI.
[2] *Philip.*, II, 5. — [3] *Luke*, XVIII, 1.

ART. II. THE EXTERIOR MEANS OF PERFECTION

530. These means can be reduced to four principal ones : *spiritual direction* that provides safe guidance; a *rule of life*, which is the sequel and the complement of spiritual direction; *spiritual reading* and *devout exhortations*, which present to us the ideal to follow; the *sanctification of our social relations*, which enables us to supernaturalize our dealings with the neighbor.

§ I. Spiritual Direction [1]

Two points, chiefly, are to be elucidated : 1º The *moral necessity* of spiritual direction; 2º the *means* required to insure its success.

I. *Moral Necessity of Spiritual Direction*

Direction, although not absolutely necessary for the sanctification of souls, is one of the *normal means* of spiritual progress. *Authority*, and *reason* based on *experience*, demonstrate this.

1º PROOF FROM AUTHORITY

531. A) God, Who established His Church as a hierarchical society, has willed that souls be sanctified through submission to the Sovereign Pontiff and to the Bishops in things external, and to confessors in things internal. When Saul was converted, Our Lord, instead of directly manifesting to him His designs, sent him to Ananias to learn from this man's lips what he was to do. Cassian, St. Francis de Sales and Leo XIII argue from this fact to show the necessity of direction. "God," says Leo XIII, "in His infinite Providence has decreed that men for the most part should be saved by men; hence He has appointed that those whom He calls to a loftier degree of holines should be led thereto by men, 'in order that,' as Chrysostom says, 'we should be taught by God through men.' We have an illustrious example of this put before us in the very begin-

---

[1] CASSIANUS, *Collationes*, coll. II, c. 1-13; St. JOHN CLIMACUS, *L'Échelle du Paradis*, 4e Degré, n. 5-12; GODINEZ, *Praxis Theol. mysticæ*, lib. VIII, c. 1; SCHRAM, *Instit. theol. mysticæ*, P. II, cap. I, § 327-353; St. FR. DE SALES, *Introd. to a Devout Life*, Part I, ch. 4; TRONSON, *Traité de l'obéissance*, IIe Partie; FABER, *Growth in Holiness*, ch. XVIII; H. NOBLE, O. P., *Lacordaire apôtre et directeur des jeunes gens*, 1910; DESURMONT, *Charité sacerdotale*, § 183-225; *Catholic Encyclopedia, Direction*; F. VINCENT, S. *François de Sales, Directeur d'Ames*; ABBÉ D'AGNEL et Dr D'ESPINEY, *Direction de conscience*, 1922; V. RAYMOND, O. P., *Spiritual Director and Physician*, 1917.

ning of the Church, for although Saul, who was *breathing threatenings and slaughter*, heard the voice of Christ Himself, and asked from Him, *Lord, what wilt Thou have me to do?* he was nevertheless sent to Ananias at Damascus : *Arise and go into the city, and there it shall be told thee what thou must do.* This manner of acting has invariably obtained in the Church. All without exception who in the course of ages have been remarkable for science and holiness have taught this doctrine. Those who reject it, assuredly do so rashly and at their peril." [1]

532. B) Unable to quote all the authorities, we shall briefly review a few witnesses that can be considered representatives of ascetical theology. *Cassian*, who had spent long years among the monks of Palestine, of Syria, and of Egypt, has set down their teachings together with his own in two works. In the first, the *Book of Institutions*, he urgently exhorts the young cenobites to open their heart to the elder charged with the direction of their life; to disclose to him without false shame their most secret thoughts, and to submit themselves entirely to his decision as to what is good and what is evil. [2] He treats this point again in his *Conferences*, and, after showing the dangers to which those who do not seek counsel from their elders expose themselves, he affirms that the best means to overcome temptations even the most dangerous, is to disclose them to a wise counsellor. This he says on the authority of St. Anthony and the Abbot Serapion. [3]

What Cassian teaches to the Monks of the West, St. John Climacus instils into those of the East by his *Ladder of Paradise*. To *beginners* he says that those who wish to leave the land of Egypt for the Promised Land and subdue their disorderly passions, stand in need of another Moses to serve them as a guide. To those that are advanced he declares, that in order to follow Christ and enjoy the holy liberty of the children of God, one must humbly deliver the care of one's soul to a man that is the representative of the Divine Master; and that such a one must be chosen with care, because he must be obeyed in all simplicity, in spite of the shortcomings that may be detected in him; for the sole danger lies in following one's own judgment. [4]

---

[1] Apostolical Letter *Testem Benevolentiæ*, Jan. 22, 1899. From The Great Encyclical Letters of Leo XIII, P. 447.
[2] CASSIANUS, *De Cænobiorum institut.*, I, IV, c. 9; *P. L.* XLIX, 161.
[3] *Id. Collationes*, II, 2, 5, 7, 10-11; *P. L.* XLIX, 526, 529, 534, 537, 542.
[4] *Scala Paradisi*, Grad. I, IV; *P. G.* LXXXVIII, 636, 680-681.

533. For the period of the Middle Ages, two authorities will suffice. St. Bernard wants the novices to have a guide, a foster-father to enlighten them, direct them, console them, and encourage them. [1] To more advanced souls, like Ogier, the Canon Regular, he declares that whoever constitutes himself his own guide, becomes a disciple of a fool. He adds : " I know not what others think about themselves on this matter; for myself, I speak from experience and I hesitate not to say that I find it easier and safer to direct many others than I do to guide myself. " [2]   In the Fourteenth Century, the eloquent Dominican, St. Vincent Ferrer, stated that spiritual direction had ever been the practice of souls that wished to make progress, and he gave the following reason : " He who has an adviser whom he absolutely obeys in all things, will succeed much more easily and quickly than he could if left to himself, even if endowed with quick intellect and possessed of learned spiritual books. " [3]

534. It was not only in communities that this need of a spiritual guide was felt, but likewise in the world. The letters of St. Jerome, of St. Augustine, and of other Fathers, to widows, virgins, and other persons living in the world, are ample proof of it. [4] It is therefore with good reason that St. Alphonsus in explaining the *duties of a confessor* declares that one of the most important of these duties is that of *directing* devout souls. [5]

Besides, reason itself, enlightened by faith and by experience, shows us the necessity of a spiritual director in order to advance in the way of perfection.

2° PROOF FROM REASON BASED ON THE NATURE
OF SPIRITUAL PROGRESS

535.   A) Progress in holiness is a long and painful ascent over a steep path bordered by precipices. To venture thereon without an experienced guide is highly imprudent. It is extremely easy to deceive oneself as regards one's own condition. We are unable to gaze eye to eye upon ourselves, says St. Francis de Sales; we cannot be impartial judges in our own case, by reason of a certain complacency, " so veiled, so unsuspected that the keenest insight alone can discover its existence; those who suffer from it are not

---

[1] *De Diversis*, sermo VIII, 7. — [2] Epist., LXXXVII, 7.
[3] *De Vita Spirituali*, II Part, ch. I.
[4] See the instances given by FABER, *Growth in Holiness*, C. XVIII.
[5] *Praxis confessarii*, n. 121-127.

aware of it unless some one points it out to them. " [1]
Hence, he concludes that we need a spiritual physician to
make a sound diagnosis of our state of soul and to prescribe
the most effective remedies : " Why should we wish to
constitute ourselves directors of our own souls when we do
not undertake the management of our bodies. Have we
not noticed that physicians, when ill, call other physicians
to determine what remedies they require? " [2]

536. B) The better to understand this need, we have
but to explain briefly the chief dangers one encounters in
each of the three ways leading to perfection.

a) Beginners must be on their guard against relapses
and, in order to avoid them, they must undergo a long and
rigorous penance in proportion to the number and gravity
of their faults. Some of them, soon forgetting their past,
want to enter forthwith into the path of love. Such
presumption is frequently followed by a withdrawal of
sensible consolations, by discouragement and fresh falls.
Others give themselves without discretion to bodily mortifications, take therein a vain complacency, impair their
health, and then, under pretence of taking proper care of it,
fall into a state of relaxation. It is, therefore, important
that an experienced director hold the former to the spirit
and the practice of penance, and check the latter in their
impetuous ardor.

Another danger for beginners is *spiritual aridity*, following
the withdrawal of sensible consolations. In this state a
soul imagines itself abandoned by God, gives up its exercises
of piety, which now appear useless, and falls a prey to
lukewarmness. Who will be able to forestall this danger?
Only a wise spiritual director, who, during the season of
consolations, will give warning that these do not last forever,
and, at the time of aridity, will comfort this soul by explaining that there is nothing better than such trials for the
strengthening of virtue and the purifying of love.

537. b) In the *illuminative way*, a guide is still needed,
in order to discern which are the virtues especially suited
to this or that person in particular, as well as the means of
practicing these virtues, and the proper method of self-
examination. When a soul becomes a prey to that sense
of weariness experienced upon the discovery that the way
of perfection is longer and more arduous than imagined, it

[1] *Devout Life*, Part. III, c. 28.
[2] *Sermons recueillis*, pour la fête de N. D. des Neiges, t. IX, p. 95.

is hard to see what can prevent this feeling from degenerating into lukewarmness, if not the fatherly affection of a director who will be able to recognize the difficulty, obviate discouragement, console the penitent, urge him to new efforts and make him discern the fruits to be gained from such a trial courageously borne.

538. c) Direction becomes even more necessary in the *unitive way.* To enter herein, one must cultivate the gifts of the Holy Ghost by a generous and constant docility to the inspirations of grace. But to distinguish divine inspirations from those that proceed from nature, or from the Evil One, the counsel of a wise and disinterested adviser is ofttimes required. This is all the more necessary when one undergoes the first *passive trials,* when aridity, weariness, fear of God's judgments, besetting temptations, inability to reason in meditation, and contradictions from without burst all together upon a desolate soul and cast it into the greatest turmoil. It is evident that a pilot is indispensable to guide the disabled craft to safety. A spiritual director is equally necessary for one enjoying the delights of contemplation. This state presupposes so much discretion, humility, docility and, above all, so much prudence in harmonizing *passivity* with *activity,* that it becomes morally impossible not to go astray without the advice of an expert guide. This is why St. Theresa used to open her soul with such candor to her spiritual directors; this is why St. John of the Cross often insisted on the necessity of disclosing to him everything. "God," says he, "so desires that man place himself under the direction of another, that He absolutely does not want to see us give full assent to the supernatural truths He Himself imparts, before they have issued out of the mouth of man." [1]

539. To sum up what has been said, we can do no better than quote the words of Fr. Godinez : " Hardly ten in a thousand called by God to perfection heed the call; of a hundred called to contemplation, ninety-nine fail to respond. It must be acknowledged that one of the principal causes is the lack of spiritual directors. Under God, they are the pilots that conduct souls through this unknown ocean of the spiritual life. If no science, no art, how simple soever, can be learned well without a master, much less can any one learn this high wisdom of evangelical perfection, wherein such great mysteries are found. This is the reason

---

[1] *Sentences et avis spirituels,* n. 229, ed. *Hoornaert,* p. 372.

why I hold it morally impossible that a soul could without a miracle or without a master, go through what is highest and most arduous in the spiritual life, without running the risk of perishing."

540. It may be said, therefore, that the normal way to advance in the spiritual life is to follow the counsels of a wise spiritual adviser. As a matter of fact, fervent souls so understand it and seek direction in the tribunal of penance. When of late years a need was felt for a select body of truly devout and earnest Catholics, no better means of forming it was found than a strong direction given in Sodalities, vacation-camps and above all in regular retreats. Direction, then, is one of the normal means of spiritual progress.

II. *Rules to Insure the Success of Spiritual Direction*

That spiritual direction be profitable, 1° its *object* must be clearly determined; 2° the *co-operation* of both *director* and *penitent* must be assured.

1° OBJECT OF SPIRITUAL DIRECTION

541. A) General Principle. The *object* of spiritual direction consists in all that has a bearing upon the spiritual formation of souls. Confession limits itself to the accusation of faults; direction goes far beyond this. It reaches the *causes* of sin, deep-rooted inclinations, temperament, character, acquired habits, temptations, imprudences. This, in order to discover the right *remedies*, such as go to the very roots of the evil. In order to combat defects the better, direction in also concerned with virtues opposed to them, the virtues *common* to all Christians and those *special* to each particular class of persons. It includes the *means* most apt to foster the practice of these virtues : *spiritual exercises* such as mental prayer, the particular examination, devotion to the Most Blessed Sacrament, to the Sacred Heart, the Blessed Virgin, which supply us with spiritual arms to force our way onward in the practice of virtue. It deals with *vocation*, and, once this question is settled, with the duties peculiar to each state of life. Hence, it is clear that the field of direction is very wide.

542. B) Applications. a) In order to guide a person wisely, the spiritual director must be acquainted with the chief features of his *past life*, his habitual faults, his efforts to correct them, the results obtained, so that he sees clearly what is left to be done. He must, likewise, know his *present dispositions*, his likes and dislikes, the temptations he undergoes and the method employed to overcome them, the virtues he feels the greatest need of, and the means used to acquire them. The director must know all this in order to give proper advice.

b) Then it is that the director can more easily form a *plan of direction*, a *flexible* plan, adaptable to the actual condition of the penitent and calculated to foster his spiritual progress. It is impossible to lead all souls in the same way; a director must take them as they are, and lead them gradually through the various stages along the steep path of perfection. He must realize that some are more eager and more generous, others more calm, more slow, that all are not called to attain the same degree of perfection.

543. There is, however, a *progressive order* to be followed which gives a certain measure of unity to spiritual direction :

1) From the outset it is important that souls should be taught *to sanctify all their ordinary actions* by the practice of union with Our Lord (n. 248). This holds good for their whole life and the Director must insist on it again and again showing how such practice is grounded on the *spirit of faith* so indispensable in these days of rampant naturalism.

2) The *purification* of the soul, through the practice of *penance* and *mortification*, should never cease altogether; penitents should be often brought back to it, taking into account their state of mind, so as to vary the exercise of these virtues.

3) *Humility* is a fundamental virtue, which must be inculcated almost from the beginning, and penitents must be frequently reminded of it at all the stages of the spiritual life.

4) *Fraternal charity*, because so often violated, even by devout people, should be insisted upon in the examinations of conscience and in confession.

5) *Habitual union with Our Lord*, our model and co-worker, cannot be too frequently emphasized, for it is one of the most effective means of sanctification.

6) A thing to be cultivated with care, because so necessary in this our day, is manliness or *strength of character*, based upon strong convictions, and with it, honesty and loyalty which cannot be separated from it.

7) In an epoch of proselytism like ours, *zeal* is of paramount importance and a spiritual director should keep in view the formation of select souls who will be of help to the priest in the innumerable details connected with his ministry.

As for the rest, one has but to bear in mind what we shall say when explaining the three ways.

Direction will not produce any profitable results, unless both director and penitent work together in all earnestness.

1) Duties of the Spiritual Director

544. St. Francis de Sales [1] declares that a spiritual director must have three principal qualities : " He must be full of *charity*, of *knowledge* and of *prudence* : if he lacks one of these, there is danger. "

A) The *charity* wherewith he must be filled is a *supernatural* and *paternal* affection that makes him see in his penitents so many spiritual children confided to his care by God Himself so that he may cause Jesus Christ and His virtues to grow in them : " My little children of whom I am in labor again until Christ be formed in you. " [2]

a) Hence, he surrounds them all with the same thoughtfulness and care, making himself all things to all, in order to sanctify all ; spending his time, his efforts and himself to form in them the Christian virtues. In spite of himself, no doubt, he will at times feel drawn more to some than to others, but he will not allow his natural likes or dislikes to govern him, being careful to avoid sentimental affections that would tend to create attachments, at first innocent, then distracting and finally dangerous both to his good name and to his virtue. *Father Olier* rightly says that to wish to attach to oneself the hearts made to love God, constitutes a sort of treason : " Spiritual directors have been chosen by Our Lord to go forth to conquer kingdoms, that is to say, the hearts of men, which belong to Him, which He has bought by the shedding of His Blood, and in which He wants to establish His reign. What an ingratitude! What a fraud! What an outrage! What a betrayal! if instead of offering those hearts to Him as to their lawful sovereign, they constitute themselves their lords and masters. " [3] Such conduct would be equivalent to placing a well-nigh insurmountable obstacle in the way of one's own spiritual progress and in that of one's penitents, for God does not want a divided heart.

545. **b)** Kindness on the part of the spiritual director must not mean weakness. It must, on the contrary, be coupled with *firmness* and *frankness*. The director must have the courage to give sound, fatherly warnings, to point out to his penitents their defects, and *not allow himself to be directed by them*. There are persons very demure, yet very clever, who want to have a spiritual director, but on condition that he accommodate himself to their tastes and fancies. Such seek after approbation rather than guidance.

---

[1] *Introduction to a Devout Life*, P. I, C. IV. — [2] *Galat.*, IV, 19.
[3] *L'Esprit d'un directeur des âmes*, p. 60-61. Father OLIER often returns to this subject in this little work.

To be on guard against this abuse that might involve his own conscience, the spiritual director must not let himself be swayed by the schemes and manoeuvres of such penitents; he must remember that he represents Our Lord Himself, and resolutely render his decisions according to the rules of perfection and not according to the wishes of his penitents.

546. c) It is chiefly in directing women that one must be reserved and firm. A man of wide experience, Father Desurmont,[1] writes as follows on this subject :·" Let there be none of those affectionate words, none of those tender expressions, no private talks except those absolutely indispensable. Let there be nothing savoring of feeling, either in manner or gesture, nor the least shadow of familiarity. As to conversations, no more than is necessary; as to dealings outside of matters of conscience, only those that have a recognized serious purpose. As much as possible, let there be no direction outside the confessional, and no correspondence. They must not be made even to suspect that one is personally interested in them. Their mentality is so constituted that if they be led to think themselves the object of a particular regard or affection, almost without fail, they descend to a natural plane, be it through vanity or sentimentality. " The same author adds : " Generally speaking, it is best that they be not conscious of being directed at all. Woman has the defects of her qualities : she is instinctively pious, but she is likewise instinctively proud of her piety. The adornment of the soul affects her no less than that of the body. For her to know that one wishes to adorn her with virtues, ordinarily constitutes a danger. " One should, then, direct them without acquainting them with the fact, and give them counsels of perfection as if it were the common ordinary thing for the welfare of souls.

547. B) In the spiritual director, devotedness must be accompanied by the *knowledge* of ascetical theology so necessary to confessors, n. 36. He will, therefore, never tire of reading and re-reading spiritual authors, correcting his judgments by their standards, and comparing his own method with that of the Saints.

548. C) Above all, *prudence* and a *sound judgment* are needed in order to direct souls not according to one's own ideas, but according to the motions of grace, the temperament and character of the penitents, and their supernatural attractions. [2]

a) *Father Libermann* rightly remarks that the spiritual director is but an instrument in the hands of the Holy Ghost. [3] He should, therefore, first of all, apply himself to gain through discreet questions a knowledge of the action this Divine Spirit has upon the soul.

[1] *La Charité sacerdotale*, t. II, § 196.
[2] This is exactly what *St. Francis de Sales* practiced as shown by F. Vincent, *op. cit.*, p, 439-481.
[3] *La direction spirituelle*, d'après les écrits et les exemples du *Vén. Libermann*, 2e édit., p. 10-22.

" I consider it a capital point in spiritual direction, " he writes, " to discover the dispositions whereby a soul is animated..., to perceive how far you can urge it, to allow grace full scope, to distinguish true from false attractions, and prevent souls from going astray or running to excesses. " In another letter he adds : " The spiritual director having once ascertained God's action in a soul, has nothing else to do but to guide it that it may obey the promptings of grace... He must never attempt to inspire a soul with his personal tastes and individual attractions, nor lead it after his own way of acting, or his own peculiar point of view. A director that would thus act, would often turn souls from God's own guidance and oppose the action of divine grace in them. "

He adds, however, that this applies to souls who work earnestly to attain perfection. As to those that are *sluggish* and *lukewarm*, the initiative must be taken by the director, who will, by his exhortations, his counsels, his rebukes, and all the means which his zeal suggests, strive to stir them out of their spiritual torpor.

549. **b)** The *prudence* in question here is, therefore, a *supernatural prudence*, fortified by the *gift of counsel*, which a spiritual director should ever beg of the Holy Spirit. He will invoke Him especially in difficult cases, repeating in his heart the *Veni Sancte Spiritus* before rendering any important decision. Having consulted the Holy Ghost, he will listen with attention and childlike simplicity to the answer whispered to his soul, and communicate it to his penitent : " *As I hear, so I judge. And my judgment is just.* " [1] In this wise, a director will in truth become the instrument of the Holy Spirit — a joint instrument with God — and his ministry will be fruitful.

This care to take counsel with the Most High will not hinder the director from making use of all the means prudence will place at his command to acquire a thorough knowledge of his penitent. For this knowledge, he will not rely merely on the penitent's words; he will study his conduct, and without subscribing to all his judgments, will weigh these in accordance with the rules of prudence.

550. **c)** Let prudence guide the spiritual director not only in giving counsel, but in all *matters* connected with the practice of direction. I) He should devote no more time than is necessary to this duty of his ministry, important as it is. He should hold no protracted conversations, nor indulge in idle talk, nor ask indiscreet questions. He should limit himself to what is of real profit to souls. Brief advice to the point, the clear exposition of one of the means of perfection, will well occupy a penitent for a fortnight or a *month*. More, the director will strive so to lead souls that before long they may be, not indeed self-

---

[1] *John*, V, 30.

sufficient, but may rest satisfied with briefer spiritual direction, and be able to resolve their ordinary problems by means of the general principles imparted to them.

2) Although the spiritual direction of youths and men can be carried on anywhere, that of women demands greater reserve. Ordinarily, it should be given only in the confessional, and this briefly, without allowing them to go into useless details. We belong to all; time is limited and should not be wasted. We must, no doubt, be patient, giving each soul all the required time, but bearing in mind the while that there are other souls who also need our ministrations.

2) The Duties of Penitents

551. Penitents will see in their spiritual director the person of Our Lord Himself. If it is true that all authority comes from God, it is more so of the authority the priest exercises over consciences in the confessional. The power of binding and loosing, of opening and closing the gates of Heaven, of guiding souls in the paths of perfection, is a divine power and cannot reside outside of him who is the lawful representative, the ambassador of Christ. *" For Christ's therefore we are ambassadors, God as it were exhorting by us."* [1] This is the principle from which all duties toward a spiritual director flow — *respect, trust, docility*.

552. **A**) The director must be *respected* as the representative of God, clothed as he is with God's authority in what regards our most intimate and most sacred relations with God. Hence, if he has his shortcomings, let us not dwell on them, but simply regard his authority and his mission. A penitent will thus carefully avoid any *criticism* whereby the filial respect due his director is lost or lessened. He should likewise avoid excessive familiarity, hardly compatible with true respect. This respect will be tempered by an *affection* that is frank and genuine, but full of reverence, an affection of a child for his father, an affection that excludes the desire of being singularly loved, and the petty jealousies issuing from such desire. " In a word, this friendship should be strong and sweet, holy, all sacred, wholly divine and entirely spiritual. " [2]

553. **B**) A second duty toward the spiritual director is *filial trust* and *perfect openness of heart*. " Open your heart to him with all sincerity and fidelity, manifesting clearly the state of your conscience without fiction or dissimulation;

---

[1] *II Cor.*, V, 20.
[2] St. Francis de Sales, *Introduction to a Devout Life*, Part. I, C. IV.

by this means your good actions will be examined and approved, and your evil ones corrected and remedied... Place great confidence in him, but let it be united with a holy reverence, so that the reverence may not diminish the confidence, nor the confidence the reverence." [1] We are to open our heart to him, then, with full confidence, making known to him *our temptations* and *our weaknesses*, that he may help us conquer the former and heal the latter; we must submit to his approbation our desires and resolutions; we must tell him of the good we strive to accomplish, that he may help us to do even more; of our good purposes that he may examine them, and suggest the means of realizing them; in a word of whatever has a bearing on the spiritual welfare of our soul. The better he knows us, the more will he be able to counsel us wisely, to encourage, comfort and fortify us, in such wise, that after taking leave of him, we can repeat the words of the disciples at Emmaus : " Was not our heart burning within us, whilst he spoke...? " [2]

554. There are persons who, though willing enough to be thus perfectly open, through a sort of timidity or reserve do not know how to make known their state of soul. Let them speak of this to their spiritual director, who will help them with pertinent questions and, if need be, have them read some book or other that will enable them to come to a better knowledge of themselves and to analyze the state of their souls. Once the ice is broken, such intimate communications will be made with greater ease.

Others there are who, on the contrary, are liable to talk overmuch and to turn spiritual direction into pious prattle. These must remember that a priest's time is limited, that others wait their turn and may grow impatient of delay. They should, therefore, set a limit and leave less important matters for some future meeting.

555.   C) *Docility* in listening to and carrying out of a director's advice must accompany this frankness.   There is nothing less supernatural than to wish him to enter into our views, nothing more hurtful to the welfare of our soul, for then it is not the will of God we seek, but our own, with this aggravating circumstance, that we abuse a God-given means in order to attain our selfish purposes. Our only desire must be to know God's will through the agency of our spiritual director and not to extort his approval through more or less clever devices. One may deceive a spiritual director, but not Him Whom he represents.

Doubtless, it is our duty to make known to him our likes and our dislikes, and if we foresee serious difficulties in

---

[1] ST. FRANCIS DE SALES, *Introduction to a Devout Life*, P. I, C. IV.
[2] *Luke*, XXIV, 32.

carrying out his advice, we must candidly mention them to him. Once this has been done, we must submit to his decision, or if we think it unwise, seek another director. Strictly speaking, our spiritual director may be mistaken, but we make no mistake in obeying him, except, of course, were he to give counsel opposed to faith or morals. [1]

556. D) Only a grave reason and mature reflection should determine us to seek another spiritual guide. There should be in direction a certain continuity that cannot exist if changes be frequently made.

a) Some persons tired of listening to the same counsels, especially if these bear upon things disagreeable to nature, or led through *curiosity*, change confessors in order to see what the attitude of another will be. Others do the same through *inconstancy*, finding it impossible to hold for any length of time to the same practices. Others are inspired by *vanity*, wishing to go to one who enjoys a greater reputation, or who is more in vogue, or to one who will probably flatter them. Some change through a kind of *restlessness* that causes them to be ever dissatisfied with what they have and to dream of an imaginary perfection. Again, some do so, through an ill-regulated desire of opening their soul to *different confessors*, so as to engage their interest or to be reassured. Lastly, some change through a *false shame*, to hide from their regular confessor some humiliating weaknesses. Evidently, these motives are not sufficient, and one must learn to brush them aside, if one wishes to make consistent progress in the spiritual life.

557. b) On the other hand, we must remember the growing insistence wherewith the Church safeguards the *freedom* individuals must enjoy in the choice of a confessor; hence, if there be good reasons to have recourse to another, one must not hesitate to do so. What are the chief reasons? 1) If in spite of all our efforts we cannot have towards our director the respect, the confidence, and the openness above-mentioned, even if there be little or no grounds for such state of mind; [2] for in such a case, we could derive no profit from his counsels. 2) Should we have any grounded fears that our director would deter us from perfection, because of his too natural views, or because of a too strong and too sentimental affection he has shown on some occasions. 3) If we should detect in him a lack of the necessary knowledge, prudence or discretion.

---

[1] " This obedience to our director is a stumbling-block to many of us. I cannot think it would be so if we had a clear idea of it or, which is the same thing, an unexaggerated idea of it... A spiritual director is not a monastic superior... The superior's jurisdiction is universal, the director's only where we invite it or he asks it and we accord it... If we disobey a superior, we sin; it would require very peculiar and unusual circumstances to make disobedience to our director any sin at all. " FABER, *Growth in Holiness*, C, XVIII.

[2] P. LIBERMANN, *op. cit.*, p. 131.

Such cases are rare, it is true; but should they occur, we must remember that spiritual direction is productive of good only if there exist between director and penitent real co-operation and mutual trust.

§ II. A Rule of Life [1]

558. A rule of life extends the influence of the director, by imparting to the penitent principles and rules that will enable the latter to sanctify all his acts through obedience, and that will provide him with a norm of conduct at once sound and safe. We shall explain : 1º its *utility;* 2º its *qualities;* 3º the *manner* of keeping it.

I. *Utility of a Rule of Life*

Useful even to laymen who seek holiness in the world, a rule of life is of still greater importance to members of religious communities and to priests in the ministry. It is no less conducive to *personal* sanctification than to the sanctification of the neighbor.

559. 1º **Its utility as a means of personal sanctification.** In order to sanctify ourselves we must *make good use of our time, supernaturalize* our acts, and follow a certain program of *perfection.* Now, a rule of life wisely made with the help of our spiritual director secures for us this threefold advantage.

A) It enables us *to make a better use of our time.* Let us actually compare the life of a person that follows a rule with that of another that does not.

a) He that lives *without a rule* inevitably wastes a great deal of time : 1) He hesitates as to what is the best thing to do. Time is spent in deliberation, in weighing the reasons for and against, and, as in many cases there are no decisive reasons on either side, he is liable to remain inactive; then, natural inclinations gain the upper hand and he runs the risk of being led by curiosity, pleasure or vanity. 2) He *neglects* a certain number of duties, for having neither *foreseen* nor *determined* the acceptable time and place for their fulfilment, he no longer finds time to perform them all. 3) These negligences engender *inconstancy.* At times he makes vigorous efforts to steady himself,

---

[1] ST. FRANCIS DE SALES, *Introd. to A Devout Life*, Part. I, C. III; Part. III, C. XI; TRONSON, *Manuel du Séminariste;* ID., *Traité de l'obéissance*, IIIe Partie; RIBET, *L'Ascétique*, ch. XLI; KEATING, *The Priest, His Character and Work*, P. I, C. II; *The secret of Sanctity*, C. I.

while at other times he surrenders to his native indolence, and this, just because he has no fixed rule that would act as a corrective to the fickleness of his nature.

560. b) The man who holds to *a well-defined rule of life* saves considerable time : 1) He wastes no time in hesitation. He knows exactly what he is to do, and when he is to do it. Even if his schedule is not mathematically detailed, at least it sets off time-periods and lays down principles with regard to religious exercises, recreation, work, etc... 2) There is little or *nothing unforeseen*, for even should the unusual occur, he has already provided for it by determining beforehand exercises that may be shortened and the manner of making up for them. At all events, as soon as these exceptional circumstances cease to exist, he immediately comes back to his rule. 3) *Inconstancy* likewise vanishes. The rule urges him to do always what is prescribed, and that every day and at every hour of the day. Thus, habits are formed that, give continuity to his life and assure his perseverance; his days are full days, teeming with good works and merit.

561. B) A rule of life enables us to *supernaturalize* all our actions. **a)** They are performed through obedience, and this virtue adds its own special merit to that which is proper to every virtuous act. It is in this sense that the saying obtains, that he who lives by rule lives unto God; since it means the constant fulfilment of His holy will. Faithfulness to a rule has, besides, a decided *educative value*. Instead of caprice and disorder that run rampant in an ill-ordered life, duty and strength of will prevail, and as a consequence, order and system. The will submits to God, and our inferior faculties yield their obedience to the will. This is a gradual return to the state of original justice.

b) With a rule of life, it is easy to infuse *supernatural motives* into all our actions. The mere fact of conquering our tastes and whims puts order into our life and directs our actions towards God. Moreover, a good rule provides for a brief thought of God before every action of any importance, and for the forming of a supernatural intention. Thus each and every one of our actions is explicitly sanctified and becomes an act of love. What a great measure of merit can be thus gained each day!

562. C) A rule gives us a *program of sanctification*. **a)** What we have described already constitutes such a program, and by following it, we march on to perfection; it is none other than the highway of conformity to the Divine Will so extolled by God's Saints (n. 493-498).

b) Moreover, no rule of life is complete that does not single out the virtues best adapted to the individual penitent's condition in life and to his state of soul. Of course, this program will be subject now and then to change by reason of new needs that arise, but all this will be done in agreement with the spiritual director.

563. 2° A rule of life cannot but promote *the sanctification of the neighbor.* To sanctify others, we must join *prayer to action, make good use of the time* devoted to works of zeal, and give *good example.* This is exactly what is done by the man who is faithful to his rule.

A) In his well-regulated life he finds the practical means of combining prayer with action. Convinced that the soul of zeal is an interior life, he takes care that his rule devotes a certain portion of time to prayer, Holy Mass, thanksgiving, and all other exercises indispensable as spiritual food to the soul (n. 523).

This does not prevent him from devoting *a good measure of his time to works of zeal.* Having learned how to make a wise distribution of time (n. 560), he knows how to spare it whilst doing all things in an orderly and methodical manner. Fixed hours are devoted to the divers kinds of parochial work, like confessions and the administration of the Sacraments. The faithful, once they know these arrangements, readily abide by them, happy to know just when they may call on the priest in their various needs.

564. B) Furthermore, the faithful are edified by the example of *punctuality* and *regularity* which they observe in the priest. They cannot help thinking and repeating that he is a man of duty, ever faithful to the rules laid down by ecclesiastical authorities. When they listen to him urge from the pulpit or in the confessional obedience to the laws of God and of the Church, they feel drawn more by the force of his example than by his words, and they become in turn more faithful in their observance of the Commandments.

A priest that lives up to his rule sanctifies in this manner both himself and the neighbor. This is true also of those of the laity who devote themselves to works of zeal.

II. *Qualities of a Rule of Life*

That a rule be productive of these happy results, it must be devised with the help of our *spiritual director;* it must be at once *flexible* and *firm;* it must *grade one's duties* according to their relative importance.

565. 1º It must be devised with the help of our *spiritual director. Prudence* and obedience require this : **a)** *prudence,* because to draw up a practical rule of life, great discretion and experience are needed in order to see not only what may be good in itself, but also what is good for this particular individual; what is advisable in his case, what is beyond his strength, what is timely and what is not, considering his circumstances. Few, indeed, are those that can unaided settle all these things wisely. **b)** Besides, one of the advantages of a rule of life is to give us occasions to practice the virtue of obedience. This would never be the case if we were its sole framers and did not submit it to a lawful authority.

566. 2º The rule must be firm enough to sustain the will, yet *elastic* enough to be adaptable to the various circumstances arising in real life, which not unfrequently foil our calculations.

a) It will have the necessary *firmness* if it embodies all that is needed to fix, at least in principle, the time and the manner of performing our spiritual exercises, of fulfilling our duties of state, and of practicing the virtues proper to our condition in life.

567. **b)** It will possess the required *elasticity* if, once these points have been determined, it leaves a certain freedom of action as to changes of time, substitution of practices not essential in themselves by their equivalents, and if it makes allowance even for the shortening of exercises at the demand of charity or of some other duty, the more so if the religious exercises be completed at some later time.

This elasticity should especially apply, according to the wise remark of *Saint John Eudes,* [1] to forms of prayer and the manner of offering our actions to God : " I beg you to notice that the practice of all practices, the secret of secrets, the devotion of devotions, is not to attach oneself exclusively to any one particular practice or exercise of devotion. Take care, on the contrary, in all your exercises and all your actions to give yourself up to the Holy Spirit of Jesus with humility, confidence, and detachment from all things, so that, finding you detached from your own spirit and from your own devotion and dispositions He may have full power and liberty to act in you as He desires, to inspire you with such dispositions and sentiments of devotion as He shall judge well, and to lead you by the ways which are pleasing to Him. "

---

[1] *The Reign of Jesus,* p. 148.

568. 3º The rule must give *each duty its own relative importance* for there is a hierarchy in our duties : **a**) God must evidently hold the first place; then come the welfare of our soul and the sanctification of the neighbor. Assuredly there is no real conflict between these duties; on the contrary they will, if we desire it, blend most harmoniously; for to glorify God means simply to know and love Him. But to know and to love God is to sanctify oneself, and also to sanctify others by making them know and love Him. If, however, one should devote his entire time to works of zeal to the detriment of the great duty of prayer, he would evidently be neglecting the most efficacious means of zeal. It is likewise evident that should any one neglect his personal sanctification, he would very soon be lacking in genuine zeal for that of others. So, if we are careful first to give to God the portion of time that should be consecrated to Him and to reserve the necessary time for our essential spiritual exercises, the means of working out our own sanctification, then our works of zeal will most assuredly bear abundant fruit. Therefore, the first and the last moments of the day should be devoted to God and to our soul. Then we can safely give ourselves to works of zeal, stopping however from time to time to raise our mind and heart to God. Our whole life will thus be divided between prayer and works of zeal.

b) However, in urgent circumstances we must be guided by another principle : that the more necessary comes first. A case in point would be that of an urgent sick call; a priest leaves all else to attend to this. Still, while on the way he should strive to occupy his mind with holy thoughts, which will take the place of whatever spiritual exercise was then to be performed.

III. *The Manner of Keeping a Rule of Life*

569. That a rule be sanctifying, it must be observed *entirely* and *in a Christian manner.*

1º It must be observed **in its entirety,** that is to say, fully, in all its parts, and with punctuality. If we pick and choose among the various points of our rule, and this without reasonable cause, we shall carry out those that cost us less and omit those that are more difficult. We should thus lose the chief advantages to be derived from the exact observance of a rule, for even in the points we should observe, we would be in danger of acting from caprice or self-will. The rule, then, must be kept in its totality and to the letter, as far as possible. If for some grave reason this cannot be done, we must abide by the spirit of the rule and do all, that is, morally speaking, within our power.

570. There are two faults to be avoided here : *scrupulosity* and *laxity.* 1) Let there be *no scruples.* As long as there is a serious reason to dispense with a given point of the rule, to postpone it or to substitute an equivalent for it, let it be done without misgivings. Thus an urgent duty, a sick-call for instance, is sufficient to dispense from the visit to the Blessed Sacrament, should no time be left for it; one may easily supply for it by communing with Our Eucharistic Lord on the way. The same may be said of a mother's care of her children; it dispenses her from her regular communion, when it is impossible to harmonize this with the other duty. Spiritual communion, in that case, can take the place of sacramental communion.

2) Neither let there be *laxity.* A lack of mortification, the mere desire to prolong conversations without necessity, curiosity, etc., are not adequate reasons for deferring the performance of a given exercise, at the risk of omitting it altogether. Likewise, if the accomplishment of certain duties in the usual manner becomes impossible, we must strive to comply therewith in another way. Thus a priest who is obliged to take the Holy Viaticum during his time of meditation, will try to turn the fulfilment of this duty into an affective prayer, by offering his homages to the God of the Eucharist Who rests upon his heart.

571. Punctuality is an integral part of the observance of a rule of life. Not to begin an exercise at the prescribed moment, and that without a reason, already constitutes an act of resistance to grace, which admits of no delays; it is to run the risk of omitting or at least shortening this exercise from lack of time. If it is question of some public exercise of the ministry, a delay often means considerable inconvenience to the faithful; on the part of a teacher lack of punctuality sets before the students a bad example which they are but too prone to follow.

572. 2° The rule must be observed **in a Christian manner,** that is to say, with supernatural motives, in order to do the will of God, and thus give Him the most genuine proof of our love. This singleness of purpose is the *soul* of a rule; it gives to each of our actions its true worth, by transforming them all into acts of obedience and love. In order to practice this singleness of purpose, we must reflect a moment before acting, ask ourselves what our rule demands of us at the time, and then regulate our conduct thereby with the view of pleasing God : " *I do always the things that please Him.* " Thus the keeping of a rule will enable us to live constantly for God : " *He who lives by rule, lives unto God.* "

§ III. Spiritual Readings and Conferences [1]

573. Readings or conferences complete the spiritual direction of souls. A spiritual book is in reality a written direction. An exhortation is oral direction addressed to several. We shall explain : 1º their *utility ;* 2º the *dispositions* requisite to profit by them.

I. *The Utility of Spiritual Readings and Spiritual Conferences*

574. A) The Reading of Holy Scripture, especially of the New Testament, evidently holds the first place. [2]

a) Truly pious souls take their delight in the *Gospels.* 1) Therein they find Our Lord's *teachings* and *examples.* Nothing schools them better to a solid piety ; nothing draws them more powerfully to the imitation of the Divine Model.

Should we ever have understood the meaning of humility, of meekness, of the bearing of injuries, of virginal chastity, of fraternal charity unto the immolation of self, had we not read and pondered the example as well as the instructions of the Master concerning these virtues? True, pagan philosophers, especially the Stoics, had written beautiful pages upon some of these; yet how great is the contrast between their literary disquisitions and the persuasive call of the Master? Theirs, we feel, is the art of the rhetorician, and often the pride of the moralist, exalting himself above the masses : " *I loathe and shun the common herd.*" In Our Lord we behold perfect simplicity as He shrinks not from the lowly multitude, a perfect sincerity as He practices what He preaches and seeks not His personal glory, but the glory of Him that sent Him.

2) For devout souls, moreover, each utterance, each act of the Master holds a special grace that facilitates the practice of the virtues they set before us. In reading the Gospels, such souls worship the Divine Word ; and they beg Him to enlighten them to make them understand, relish, and live His teachings. This sort of reading is a meditation, a loving conversation with Jesus, and souls emerge from it determined more than ever to follow Him Who is the object of their admiration and their love.

b) The *Acts of the Apostles* and the *Epistles* likewise supply food for our piety. They are the teachings of Jesus lived by His disciples, explained, commented upon, and adapted to the needs of the faithful by those to whose care He entrusted the perpetuation of His work. There is nothing more tender or more stimulating than this first commentary on the Gospel.

---

[1] St. Bonaventure. *De modo studendi in S. Scriptura ;* Mabillon, *Des études monastiques,* IIe Part., ch. II, III, XVI; Le Gaudier, *op. cit.,* P. V, sect. I; Tronson, *Manuel,* IIe Part., Ent. I, XV, XVI; Ribet, *Ascétique,* ch. XLIV; D. Columba Marmion, *Le Christ idéal du moine,* p. 519-524; St. Francis de Sales, *Introd. to a Devout Life,* p. 11. C. 17; Faber, *Spiritual Conferences,* A Taste for Reading; Hedley, *Retreat,* c. XXX; A. Barry-O'Neill, *Priestly Practice,* VI. — [2] *The Following of Christ,* Book I, c. V.

575. c) In *The Old Testament :* 1) There are parts that should be in the hands of every one. Such are the Psalms. " *The Psalter*, " says Lacordaire, [1] " was our forefathers'manual of piety ; it was found on the table of the poor and it lay on the kneeling-bench of kings. Today, it is still in the hands of the priest a treasure whence he draws the inspiration that leads him to the altar, the Ark of Refuge wherewith he ventures into the perils of the world and into the desert land of meditation. " It is the most excellent of Prayer-books wherein we find in a language that always lives and never grows old, the most beautiful expressions of admiration, adoration, filial reverence, gratitude and love, together with the most ardent supplications, midst situations the most varied and trying : the appeals of the just to God when harassed by persecution, the bitter cry of the repentant sinner from a broken and humbled heart ; the note of hope for a merciful pardon and the promises of a better life. To read and reread them, to ponder them and to make their sentiments our own is surely a highly sanctifying occupation. [2]

2) The *Sapiential Books* may likewise be read with profit by pious souls. They will find therein besides the urgent calls of Uncreated Wisdom to a worthier life the exposition of the great virtues we are to practice in our relations to God, the neighbor, and ourselves.

3) As for the *Historical* and *Prophetical* Books, to read them to advantage a certain preparation is required. We must see in them above all God's providential action over the chosen people in order to keep them from falling into idolatry and to recall them again and again, despite their estrangement, to the worship of the true God, to the hope of a Deliverer, to the practice of justice, of equity, of charity, especially towards the poor and the oppressed. Having been thus initiated, we find in these books most inspiring pages. If the weaknesses of the servants of God are therein recorded together with their good works, it is to remind us of the frailty of human nature and of God's wonderful mercy, so full of forgiveness to penitent sinners.

576. B) Spiritual writers, if we choose the best, especially from among the Saints, are for us *masters* and *mentors.*

a) They are *masters*, who having learned and lived the science of the Saints, can impart to us an understanding of and a taste for the principles and the rules of perfection. They strengthen in us the conviction of our obligation to aim at sanctity ; they point out to us the means to be employed, showing the effectiveness of these in their own lives ; they exhort, encourage, and induce us to follow in their footsteps.

They are all the more helpful, since they are ever *available.* With the help of our spiritual director we can choose those best suited to our state of soul and hold

---

[1] *Letters to Young Men*, 2nd Letter.
[2] Numerous commentaries facilitate the understanding of the Psalms. Among the most recentare those of BOYLAN, C. FILLION, BARRY and HUGUENY, O. P., whose object is to give both the literal and spiritual sense in view of the devout recitation of the Divine Office.

converse with them *as long as we will*. We find excellent ones among them, adapted to the different states of soul and answering the needs of the moment. Our chief concern is to make a good choice and to read them with the earnest desire of profiting by them.

577. **b)** They are likewise most benevolent *mentors* who reveal to us our defects with great discretion and kindness. They do this by placing before us the *ideal* we are to follow, enabling us by the light of this *spiritual mirror* to recognize our good qualities and our defects, the stages we have reached and those we have yet to traverse in the pursuit of perfection. Thus we are easily led to self-examination and to generous resolutions.

No wonder, then, that the reading of spiritual books and of the lives of the Saints has brought about conversions such as those of Augustine and Ignatius Loyola, and led to the highest degrees of perfection souls that would have otherwise never risen above mediocrity.

578. **C) Spiritual Conferences** have a double advantage over the reading of spiritual books. **a)** Designed as they are for a special class of persons, they are better *adapted* to their peculiar needs. **b)** The *appeal* of the spoken word is stronger and, all things being equal, its *power* is greater than that of the writter word, better calculated to carry conviction to souls : the eye, the living voice, the gesture, bring out the import of the thought expressed. But that this be so, the speaker has to drink at the purest sources, be deeply convinced of what he says and beg God Almighty to bless and vivify his words. His hearers, likewise, must be possessed of the right dispositions.

II. *Requisite Dispositions in order to Profit by Spiritual Readings and Conferences* [1]

579. The real purpose of spiritual reading is to sustain in us the spirit of prayer. It is one of the forms of meditation, one of the ways of holding converse with God, with the writer or the speaker as interpreter.

580. 1º To draw real profit from these readings and conferences a great **spirit of faith** is required, making us see God Himself in the writer or speaker : " *God as it were exhorting by us.*" [2] This will be easy if the author or

---

[1] J. GAUDERON, *La Lecture Spirituelle d'après les principes de S. Jean Eudes, Vie spirit.*, juin 1921, p. 185-202. — [2] *II Cor.*, V, 20.

preacher is himself imbued with the teachings of the Gospel and can say in all truth that his doctrine is not his own, but that of Jesus Christ : " *My doctrine is not mine, but his that sent me.* " [1]

Let the pious reader or the devout hearer offer up to God a fervent prayer asking Our Lord to vouchsafe to speak to his heart through the Holy Ghost. Let him, moreover, be on his guard against *curiosity*, which seeks to learn novelties rather than to profit spiritually. He must beware of *vanity*, which prompts one to seek acquaintance with things spiritual in order to be able to speak about them and thus gain a reputation. He must beware of *censoriousness*, which prompts one to listen or read, not in order to gain profit, but to criticise the matter or the literary form of the discourses. His sole purpose must be his spiritual gain.

581. 2° A second requisite is **a sincere desire to sanctify oneself.** The fact is that we derive advantage from such readings and conferences in the measure in which we seek therein our own sanctification. Hence we must :

a) hunger and thirst for perfection, listening or reading with an *alert mind* that yearns after the word of God ; a mind that applies to itself, not to others, what it reads or hears, the better to assimilate it and carry it out in practice. We then find abundant food for the soul whatever may be the subject treated, for all things hold together in the spiritual life. What applies directly to beginners can be easily adapted to the more advanced ; what is said for the latter constitutes the ideal of the former, and what has a bearing on the future enables us to form resolutions in the present, thus preparing ourselves for the duties that will fall to us later on. Thus victory over future temptations is prepared by the vigilance we exercise here and now. We can always draw profit in the present from whatever we hear or read, especially, if we hearken to the *inward voice* that speaks to our inmost soul, if we have ears to hear : " *I will hear what the Lord God will speak in me.* " [2]

582. **b)** This is the reason why we should read *slowly*, as St. John Eudes advises : [3] " Stop to consider, ponder, and relish the truths that make the greater appeal to you, in order to fix them in your mind, therefrom to elicit acts and affections. " When this is realized, spiritual reading and conferences become a prayer ; little by little the thoughts

---

[1] *John*, VII, 16. — [2] *Ps.* LXXXIV, 9. — [2] *The Reign of Jesus*, P. II, § XV.

and sentiments we either read or hear penetrate the soul, and we form the desire and pray for the grace of putting them into practice.

583. 3° A third requirement is the earnest effort to begin **to practice** what is read or heard. This was St. Paul's recommendation to his readers : " Not the hearers of the law are just before God, but the doers of the law shall be justified." [1] St. Paul but comments here on the words of the Master Who in the parable of the Sower declares that they profit by the word of God " who in a good and perfect heart hearing the word, keep it and bring forth fruit in patience." [2]

We should, then, imitate St. Ephrem, of whom it is said : " *He reproduced in his life what he had read in the sacred pages.*" [3] Light is given to us for action, and our first act should be an effort to live according to the instruction received : " *Be ye doers of the word and not hearers only.*" [4]

§ IV. The Sanctification of Our Social Relations

584. Thus far we have spoken of the soul's relations with God, under the guidance of a spiritual director. It is clear, however, that our relations extend to many other persons as well, to our relatives, to our friends, and to those with whom we come in contact by reason of our position in life and of the share we take in works of zeal. All these relations can and should be sanctified and thus contribute to strengthen our spiritual life. In order to facilitate the sanctification of these relations, we shall explain the *general principles* that should govern them and we shall point out some of the principal applications.

I. *General Principles*

585. 1° In God's initial plan, creatures were designed to raise us up to God by reminding us that He is the Author and the *Exemplary Cause* of all things. Since the Fall, however, creatures so attract us that if we are not on our guard they will turn us away from God, or at least retard our progress towards Him. We must then react against this tendency, and by the spirit of faith and of sacrifice make use of persons and things as *means* to reach God.

586. 2° Among the relations we have with others, there are those that are willed by God, such as those born

---

[1] *Rom.*, II, 13. — [2] *Luc.*, VIII, 15. — [3] ENNODIUS, in ejus vita. — [4] *James*, I, 22.

of family-ties or imposed by our duties of state. These relations must be *maintained* and *supernaturalized*. One is not relieved from duties imposed by the natural law because one aspires to perfection; on the contrary, one is thereby obliged to fulfil them in a more perfect manner. These relations must, however, be supernaturalized by being directed toward our last end, God. The best way to accomplish this is to look upon those with whom we come in contact as the children of God, our brethren in Christ, respecting and loving them because they possess qualities which are the reflection of the divine perfections, and because they are destined to share in God's life and in His glory. In this way, it is God Whom we esteem and love in them.

587. 3° There are, on the other hand, relations which are *dangerous* or *bad*, which tend to lead us into sin either by stirring up within us the spirit of the world or by creating in us an inordinate attachment to creatures by reason of the sensible or sensuous pleasure we find in their company. It is our duty to flee from such occasions as far as we can, and, if it be impossible to avoid them, it is incumbent upon us to *remove them morally* (to make the danger remote) by fortifying our will against the disordered attachment to such persons. To act otherwise is to hazard our sanctification and our salvation, for " *he that loveth danger, shall perish in it.* " [1] The greater our desire for perfection, the more must we flee from dangerous occasions, as we shall explain later when speaking of faith, charity, and the other virtues.

588. 4° Lastly, there are relations which in themselves are neither good nor bad. They are merely *indifferent*. Such are visits, conversations, recreations. These may by reason of circumstance and motive be rendered useful or harmful. A soul striving after perfection will by *purity of intention* and by a spirit of *moderation* turn all such relations into good. First of all, we must seek those only which are truly *conducive* to the glory of God, the welfare of souls, or to the relaxation which health of body and mind requires. Then, in the enjoyment of these we must exercise prudence and reserve, and thus conform all our relations to the order willed by God. Hence, we must not indulge in long, idle conversations which constitute a loss of time and an occasion of fostering pride and lessening brotherly love, nor must we

---

[1] *Eccli.*, iii, 27.

give ourselves to protracted and violent amusements that
fatigue the body and depress the spirit. [1]   In short, let us
ever keep before us the standard laid down by St. Paul :
" *All whatsoever you do in word or in work, do all in the
name of the Lord Jesus Christ, giving thanks to God and the
Father by Him.*" [2]

II. *Sanctification of Family-Relations*

589.   Nature is not destroyed, but perfected by grace.
Family ties are God-given.   He has willed that men
increase and multiply through the sanctioned and indissoluble union of man and woman and that this bond be
further strengthened by their offspring.   Hence, the most
intimate and most tender relations between husband and
wife, parent and child.   These the sacramental grace of
marriage helps to supernaturalize.

1° THE CHRISTIAN CONCEPTION OF THE RELATIONS BETWEEN HUSBAND AND WIFE [3]

590.   By His presence at the marriage-feast of Cana,
and by raising Christian wedlock to the dignity of a
Sacrament, Our Lord taught husband and wife that their
union *can* be sanctified, and He merited for them that
grace.

A) Before marriage, a truly Christian love, a tender and
ardent love, pure and supernatural, has made their hearts
one, and prepared them to bear bravely the heavy burdens
of parenthood.   The flesh and the devil will no doubt
attempt to inject into this love a sensual element that might
threaten virtue.   However, the betrothed sustained by the
reception of the Sacraments, learn to control such influences
and to supernaturalize their mutual affection by realizing
that every worthy sentiment comes from God and should
be referred to Him.

591.   B) The sacramental grace of marriage, whilst
uniting their hearts in an indissoluble bond, refines and
purifies their love.   They will ever keep in mind the words
of St. Paul admonishing them that their union is the image
of the mysterious union between Christ and His Church.

---

[1] Concerning the sanctification of visits, conversations, recreations, journeys,
cf. TRONSON, *Particular Exam.* LXXVIII-XC.
[2] *Coloss.*, III, 17.
[3] ST. FRANCIS DE SALES, *Devout Life*, Part. III, C. XXXVIII, XXXIX;
GERRARD, *Marriage and Parenthood;* D'HULST-CONWAY, *The Christian Family,*
KANE S. J., *The Plain Gold Ring.*

" Let women be subject to their husbands, as to the Lord : because the husband is the head of the wife, as Christ is the head of the Church. He is the savior of his body. Therefore as the Church is subject to Christ : so also let the wives be to their husbands in all things. Husbands, love your wives, as Christ also loved the Church and delivered himself up for it : that He might sanctify it, cleansing it by the laver of water in the word of life : that He might present it to himself a glorious church, not having spot or wrinkle, or any such thing; but that it should be holy, and without blemish. So also ought men to love their wives as their own bodies... Nevertheless let everyone of you in particular love his wife as himself : and let the wife fear her husband. "[1] Hence, there should be between husband and wife a mutual respect and a mutual love that reproduce as far as possible the love of Christ for the Church. The wife must render *obedience* to the husband in all things lawful. The husband is bound to *cherish* and *protect* the wife. These are the duties outlined by the Apostle for the Christian husband and wife.

592. C) When. God blesses them with children, they receive these as a sacred trust from His hand, loving them not merely as their own offspring, but as *children of God, Christ's members, heirs-to-be of eternal glory.* They ever surround them with their devoted care and solicitude. They give them a Christian education, intent upon forming in them the very virtues of Christ. With this aim in view, they exercise the authority committed to them by God, with tact, thoughtfulness, strength and meekness. They do not lose sight of the fact that they are God's representatives, and they avoid that weakness which would spoil their children, that selfishness which would delight in children as in so many playthings and fail to inure them to labor and virtue. With God's help and the aid of carefully chosen teachers, they will help them to grow to the fulness of Christian manhood, thus exercising a sort of priesthood within the sacred precincts of the home. Thus, they will be counted worthy of the blessing of God Almighty and of the gratitude of their offspring.

2° DUTIES OF CHILDREN TOWARDS THEIR PARENTS

593. A) The grace that hallows the relations of Christian parents perfects, likewise, and supernaturalizes the duties of

---

[1] *Ephes.*, V, 22-33.

respect, love and *obedience* which children must render to them.

a) That grace makes us see in our parents the *representatives of God* and His authority. To them, under Him, we owe our life, its preservation, its guidance. Our *respect* for them, therefore, reaches *veneration.* We revere in them their participation in the Fatherhood of God, "*of whom all paternity in heaven and earth is named.*"[1] In them we pay homage to His authority, to His perfections, to God Himself.

b) Their attachment, their kindness, their solicitude are for us a reflection of the divine goodness, and our *filial love* in turn grows in intensity, rising to such perfect devotedness, that we are ready to sacrifice ourselves in their behalf and, if need be, lay down our lives to save them. Hence, we give them, to the full extent of our resources, all the temporal and spiritual *assistance* they need.

c) Seeing in them the representatives of the divine authority, we do not hesitate to render them *obedience* in all things, following the example of Our Lord, Who during thirty years of His life on earth was subject to Mary and to Joseph.[2] This obedience knows no other bounds than those set by God Himself : we must obey God rather than men, and hence, in what regards our soul and particularly in what pertains to our *vocation*, we must rather follow the advice of our confessor, after acquainting him with home conditions. In this again we but follow Our Lord's example, Who, to His Mother's question of why He had remained in Jerusalem, made answer : "*Did you not know that I must be about my Father's business?*"[3] Thus the rights and duties of each are safeguarded.

594. **B)** By entering the ranks of the clergy we quit the world and, in a sense, the family. This, in order to form part of the great ecclesiastical family and to consecrate ourselves henceforward, and before all else, to the glory of God, the good of souls and the welfare of the Church. The interior sentiments of respect and love for our parents are not suppressed; rather they are refined. Their outward expression, however, from now on is subordinated to our duties of state. We must not, in order to please our parents, do anything that would interfere with our ministry. Our first duty is to busy ourselves with the things of God.

---

[1] *Ephes.*, III, 15. — [2] *Luke*, II, 51. — [3] *Luke*, II, 49.

Hence, if their views, their words, their demands go counter to the claims of our service to souls, we shall sweetly and lovingly, yet firmly, make them understand that in what relates to our duties of state we are dependent on God and our ecclesiastical superiors. [1] We shall continue, however, to honor, to love, and to aid our parents to the full extent compatible with the duties of our office. These principles apply all the more to those who enter a religious order or congregation. [2]

III. *Sanctification of Friendship*

Friendship can become a means of sanctification or a serious obstacle to perfection accordingly as it is supernatural or merely natural and sentimental in character. We shall treat, then : 1º of *true* friendship, 2º of *false* friendship, 3º of that friendship wherein there is an *admixture of the supernal and the sentimental.*

1º TRUE FRIENDSHIP [3]

We shall explain its *nature* and its *value.*

595. A) Its Nature. a) Friendship being an interchange, a mutual communication between two persons, it receives its character chiefly from the variety of the communications themselves and from the diversity of the things communicated.   This is very well explained by St. Francis de Sales : [4] " The more exquisite the virtues are, which shall be the matter of your communications, the more perfect shall your friendship also be.   If this communication be in the sciences, the friendship is very commendable ; but still more so, if it be in the moral virtues : in prudence, discretion, fortitude and justice.   But should your reciprocal communications relate to charity, devotion and Christian perfection, good God, how precious will this friendship be!   It will be excellent, because it comes from God ; excellent, because it tends to God ; excellent, because its very bond is God ; excellent, because it shall last eternally in God.   Oh how good it is to love on earth as they love in heaven ; to learn to cherish each other in this world, as we shall do eternally in the next? "

---

[1] A. CHEVRIER, *Le Véritable Disciple*, 1922, p. 101-112.
[2] RODRIGUEZ, *Practice of Christian Perfection*, P. II, Treatise V.
[3] ST. FRANCIS DE SALES, *Devout Life*, Part. III, C. 17-22 ; RIBET, *Ascétique*, ch. XLIII, p. 437-441, 448-451 ; AD. A DENDERWINDEKE, *Comp. Theol. asceticæ*, 1921, n. 437-439 ; ROUZIC, *De l'Amitié;* MARCETTEAU, *The Young Seminarian's Manual*, p. 401-411.
[4] *Devout Life*, Part. III, C. **19.**

In general, then, true friendship is an intercourse between two souls with the purpose of procuring each other's good. It stays within the limits of *moral goodness* if the good mutually shared belongs to the natural order. *Supernatural* friendship, however, stands on a far superior plane. It is the intimate intercourse of two souls, who love each other in God and for God with a view of aiding each other to attain the perfection of that divine life which they possess. The ultimate end of this friendship is God's glory, the proximate end their own spiritual progress, and the bond of union between the two friends is Our Lord. This was the thought of the Blessed Ethelred : " We are two, you and I, and I trust a *third One is* with us, *Christ.*" Lacordaire thus renders this thought : " I can no longer love any one without reaching the soul behind the heart and having Jesus Christ as our common possession." [1]

596. b) Thus, supernatural friendship instead of being passionate, all-absorbing, exclusive after the manner of sentimental friendship, is marked by *calm reserve* and mutual *trust*. It is a *calm*, self-possessed affection precisely because it is rooted in the love of God and shares in His virtue. For the same reason it is *unwavering;* it grows, unlike the love that is founded on passions and which tends to grow cool. With it goes a *prudent reserve.* Instead of seeking familiarities and endearments like sentimental friendship, it is full of respect and reserve, for it seeks nothing but spiritual good. This reserve does not exclude *confidence.* Because there is mutual esteem and because one sees in the other a reflection of the divine perfections, there arises a strong mutual trust. This leads to an intimate intercourse since each longs to share in the spiritual qualities of the other, thus establishing an exchange of thoughts, of views, and a communication of holy desires for perfection. Because such friends desire each other's perfection they do not fear to point out their respective defects and to offer mutual help for their correction. This mutual confidence excludes all suspicion and uneasiness and does not allow the friendship to become all-absorbing or exclusive. One does not take it amiss that one's friend should have other friends, but one is rather glad of it for his sake and the sake of others.

597. B) The *value* of such friendship is evident. a) It has been praised by the Holy Ghost : " A faithful friend is a strong defence : and he that hath found him hath found

---

[1] P. Chocarne, *Vie de Lacordaire*, t. II, ch. XV.

a treasure... A faithful friend is the medicine of life and immortality. "[1] Our Lord Himself has given us an example in His friendship for St. John, who was known as " the disciple whom Jesus loved. "[2] St. Paul had friends to whom he was deeply attached ; he sorrowed at their absence ; meeting them again was his sweetest consolation ; and he was comfortless because, contrary to his expectation, he failed to find Titus : "*Because I found not Titus my brother.*"[3] He rejoiced upon finding him again : "*God comforted us by the coming of Titus... we did the more abundantly rejoice for the joy of Titus.*"[4] We see also the affection he had for Timothy, whose very presence did him so much good and helped him to do good unto others. Thus he called him his " fellow laborer, "[5] his " dearest son, "[6] his " brother, "[7] his " beloved son. "[8] Christian antiquity, likewise, furnishes us with illustrious examples, among which one of the best known is that of St. Basil and St. Gregory Nazianzen.[9]

598. b) True friendship has three important advantages, especially for the priest in the ministry.

1) A friend is a protection for virtue, *a strong defence* We must needs open our hearts to an intimate confidant. At times our spiritual director answers the purpose, but not always ; his friendship, *paternal* in nature, is not the fraternal intimacy we crave. We need *an equal* to whom we can speak with perfect freedom. If we do not find such a one, we are liable to be betrayed into indiscreet disclosures to persons unworthy of our trust, and such confidences have their dangers for those who make and for those who receive them.

2) A friend is also a *sympathetic counsellor* to whom we willingly bring our doubts and offer our difficulties in order that he may help us to reach a solution. He is likewise a *mentor*, prudent and devoted, who observing our ways and aware of what is said of us, will tell us the truth and save us from many an act of imprudence.

3) Lastly, a friend is a *comforter* who will listen with sympathy to the story of our sorrows, and who will find in his heart words of comfort and encouragement.

599. The question has been asked whether or not such friendships should be encouraged in *communities*. It may

---

[1] *Eccles.*, VI, 14-16. — [2] *John*, XIII, 23. — [3] *II Cor.*, II, 13. — [4] *II Cor.*, VII, 6, 13. [5] *Rom.*, XVI, 21. — [6] *I Cor.*, IV, 17. — [7] *II Cor.*, I, 1. — [8] *I Tim.*, I, 2. [9] ST. FRANCIS DE SALES, loc. cit., c. 19, refers to many others.

be feared that they will be detrimental to the affection which should unite all the members and that they will be the cause of jealousies.   Assuredly, care must be taken that such friendships do not interfere with the charity due to all, that they be supernatural and be kept within the limits set by Superiors.   With these provisions, friendship retains in communities all the advantages described above, since religious as well as others need the counsel, comfort and protection that a friend alone can give.   However, in communities more than elsewhere, all that savors of false friendship must be avoided with jealous care.

2° FALSE FRIENDSHIP

We shall speak of its *nature* and *dangers*, and of the *remedies* to be applied.

600. A) Its Nature. a) False friendship has for its foundation external or shallow qualities, and for its purpose the enjoyment of the sight and charms of its object.   Hence, fundamentally it is but a sort of masked egotism, since one loves the other because of the pleasure he finds in his company.   Undoubtedly, he is ready to be of service to him, but this again in view of the pleasure he experiences in drawing the other closer to himself.

b) St. Francis de Sales distinguishes three types of false friendships : *carnal* friendship in which one seeks voluptuous pleasure ; *sentimental* friendship, based mainly on the appeal outward qualities make to the emotions, "such as the pleasure to behold a beautiful person, to hear a sweet voice, to touch, and the like ; " [1] *foolish* friendship, which has no other foundation than those empty accomplishments styled by shallow minds virtues and perfections, such as graceful dancing, clever playing, delightful singing, fashionable dressing, smiling glances, a pleasing appearance, etc.

601. c) These various kinds of friendship generally begin with adolescence and are born of the instinctive need we feel of loving and being loved.   Often they are a kind of deviation of sexual love.   In the world such friendships arise between young men and women and go by the name of " fond-love. " [2]   In cloistered communities they exist between persons of the same sex and are styled particular friendships.   Such affections are at times kept up in mature life ; thus there are men who feel sentimental affection

---

[1] St Francis de Sales, loc. cit., C. 17. — [2] St Francis de Sales, loc. cit., C. 18.

toward boys because of their youthful and attractive appearance, their frankness and openness of character, and the charm and winsomeness of their manner.

602. d) The *characteristics* whereby sentimental friendships may be recognized are gathered from their *origin, development, effects.*

1) Their *origin* is *sudden* and *vehement* because they proceed from a natural and instinctive sense of sympathy. They rest upon exterior and showy qualities. They are attended by strong and, at times, passionate feelings.

2) Their *development* is fostered by conversations at times insignificant but affectionate, at others, fond and dangerous. In certain communities furtive glances take the place of familiar conversations.

3) These friendships are impetuous, all-absorbing and exclusive; the illusion that such affection will last forever is often brusquely destroyed by separation and the forming of new attachments.

603. B) The *dangers* of such friendships are apparent.

a) They constitute one of the greatest obstacles to spiritual progress. God Who does not want a divided heart begins by making interior reproaches to the soul and, if it hearkens not to His voice, He gradually withdraws, leaving the soul without light and inward consolations. In proportion as the attachments grow, the spirit of recollection is lost, peace of soul vanishes, as well as relish for spiritual exercises and love of work.

b) Hence a great *loss of time :* the absorbing thought of the friend hinders both mind and heart from devoting themselves to piety and to serious work.

c) All this ends in dissatisfaction and *discouragement;* sentimentality gains control over the will, which loses its strength and languishes.

d) It is at this point that dangers threatening purity arise. One would wish, indeed, not to trespass the bounds of propriety, yet fancying that friendship confers certain rights, one indulges in familiarities of a more and more questionable character. Now the descent is swift, and he who risks the danger will end by perishing in it.

604. C) The *remedies* against such friendships are :

a) To resist them in their beginnings. It is all the easier then, for the heart is not yet deeply attached. A few energetic efforts succeed, especially if one has the courage to mention the matter to one's director and to accuse oneself of the least failings in that regard. If one waits too long, the process of disentangling the heart will prove far more difficult. [1]

b) To root out these affections successfully, radical measures must be taken : " You must cut them, break them, tear them ; amuse not yourself in unravelling these criminal friendships ; you must tear and rend them asunder. " [2] So it is not enough to renounce intercourse with one to whom we are thus attached, but we must not even deliberately think of him ; and should it be impossible to avoid all association with him, we shall on these occasions show courtesy and charity, but never indulge in any confidences or bestow any special marks of affection.

c) The better to insure success, positive means must be used. Let one's activities be wholly devoted to the fulfilment of the duties of state, and when, in spite of all, the object of such affections presents itself unsought to the mind, this should be made the occasion of eliciting acts of love toward God : "*One is my beloved, One is my troth forever.*" We thereby profit by temptation itself to increase within us the love of Him Who alone is worthy to possess our hearts.

3° FRIENDSHIP AT ONCE SUPERNATURAL AND SENTIMENTAL

605. At times it happens that there is in our friendships a *mixture* of the *sentimental* with the morally good and the *supernatural.* One truly desires the supernatural good of a friend and at the same time craves the joy of his company and his words, sorrowing overmuch at his absence. This is well described by *St. Francis de Sales :* " They begin with virtuous love, with which, if not attended to with the utmost discretion, fond lovew ill begin to mingle itself, then sensual love, and afterwards carnal love ; yea, there is even danger in spiritual love, if we are not extremely on our guard ; though in this it is more difficult to be imposed upon because its purity and whiteness makes the spots and stains which Satan seeks to mingle with it more apparent and therefore when he takes this in hand he does it more subtilely, and endeavors to introduce impurities by almost insensible degrees. " [3]

606. Here again we must watch over the heart and take effective means so as not to be carried as it were insensibly down this dangerous grade.

---

[1] The following is Ovid's remark in *De Remediis Amoris :*

" *Principiis obsta, sero medicina paratur*
Cum mala per longas invaluere moras".

[2] *Devout Life*, loc. cit., C. XXI. — [3] *Devout Life*. loc. cit., C. XX.

a) If it is the *good* element that *predominates*, one may continue such a friendship whilst *purifying* it. For this, one must first of all forego what would foster sentiment, like frequent and affectionate conversations, familiarity, etc. From time to time one must deny oneself meetings otherwise in order, and be willing to shorten conversations that cease to be useful. In this way one gains control of sentiment and wards off danger.

b) If the element of *sentiment* predominates, one must for a considerable period of time renounce any special relations with the said friend beyond the strictly necessary, and when one must meet him one should abstain from speaking in terms of affection. Sentiment is thus allowed to cool; one waits for a renewal of relations until calm is restored to the soul. The renewed association then takes on a different character. Should it be otherwise, it must be severed forever.

c) In any case the results of our examination must be put to profit so that they may redound to a further strengthening of our love for Jesus Christ. We must protest that we want to love only in Him and for Him, and we should read frequently chapters VII and VIII of the second book of the Following of Christ. It is thus that temptations will become for us a source of victory.

IV. *Sanctification of Social and Business Relations* [1]

607. Professional relations are a means of sanctification or an obstacle to our spiritual progress, according to the view we take of our duties of state and the manner in which we discharge them. In reality the duties imposed by our calling are in themselves in harmony with the will of God. If we fulfil them with the intention of obeying God and of regulating our life according to the laws of prudence, justice and charity, they are an aid to our sanctification. [2] If, on the contrary, we have no other end in view than to secure position and wealth by the discharge of our professional duties in defiance of the laws of conscience, such relations become a source of sin and scandal.

A) A first duty then is *to accept* the profession to which God's Providence has led us as the expression of His will

---

[1] A. DESURMONT, *La sainteté dans les relations sociales, Œuvres*, t. XI, p. 272 and foll.; *Charité Sacerdotale*, t. II, § 205-213.

[2] BOURDALOUE in his second sermon *for the Feast of All Saints* shows how the Saints have sanctified their respective stations in life and profited by their condition to arrive at a high degree of perfection.

and to abide therein as long as we have no reasons justifying a change. It is part of the divine economy that there should be a diversity of arts, trades, and professions, and when we have found a place in any of them through a series of providential happenings, we may rightly believe that we are where God wills us to be. We make an exception when for prudent and lawful reasons we are convinced that it is our duty to effect a change, for whatever is in harmony with right reason lies within God's providential scheme. Therefore, whether we be employers or employees, industrialists or merchants, whether farmers or financiers, our duty is to carry on our activities so as to do the will of God, and conduct them according to the rules of justice, equity and charity. After this, nothing prevents us from sanctifying our actions by *directing* them *to the ultimate end,* a fact which does by no means exclude the *secondary end* we have in view, namely that of earning enough to provide for ourselves and those dependent upon us. As a matter of fact, Saints have sprung from each and every situation in life.

608. **B**) Our numberless activities and relations tend of themselves to fill our mind and thus to turn our thoughts from God. Hence, oft-renewed efforts are required on our part to offer to Him and so supernaturalize our ordinary actions. This we have noted above, n. 248.

609. **C**) Besides, since we move in a *rather dishonest* world, where regardless of the laws of justice man greedily vies with man for honor and for gain, it is important that we remind ourselves of the fact that we are to seek first the kingdom of God and His justice, and use for the attainment of our purposes only *legitimate means.* The best standard for judging what is permissible and what is not, is to observe the behavior of honorable Christian men of the same profession. There are *accepted ethics* in every profession. We cannot change them without incurring and causing others to suffer considerable damage.

Standards generally followed by good Christian men in the profession can be followed safely until by common agreement a change for the better can be effected without compromising lawful interests. [1] But we must never be led into imitating the practices and following the counsels of traders or producers who, *devoid of conscience,* mean to

---

[1] Thus, standard wages for the same kind of work in the same locality are determined by norms which an employer could not set aside without incurring such losses that would soon bring his business to a stand-still.

attain to wealth at any cost, even at the expense of justice. Their success does not justify us in employing similar, unlawful means. A Christian who would follow in their footsteps would be a stumbling block to others. We must seek first the kingdom of God and His justice, and all other things shall be added unto us. [1]

610. D) Thus understood and thus fulfilled, professional duties will prove a great aid to our spiritual progress, since they take up most of our time and most of our activity each day. Our Lord has shown us by His example that the most homely occupations, such as manual labor, can contribute to our personal sanctification and the spriritual welfare of our brethren. Therefore, if a laborer or a business man observes the rules of prudence, of justice, of fortitude, of temperance, of equity and of charity, numberless opportunities are offered to him daily for the practice of all the Christian virtues, the acquisition of all manner of merit, as well as for the edification of the neighbor. This is what has happened in the past, what is done today by fathers and mothers in the home, by employers and employees, by young and old, who by honesty in their work and in their dealings, elicit respect for the religion they profess and use their influence in the exercise of zeal.

V. *Sanctification of Works of Zeal*

611. That works of zeal may be for us a means of sanctification is not difficult to understand. However, there are those who find therein a cause of distraction, of spiritual loss, even an occasion of sin and a source of reprobation. Let us recall the words of a social worker to Dom Chautard : " It is my overeagerness that has brought on my fall. " [2] There are persons who allow themselves to become so absorbed by an active life, that they no longer find time for their most essential spiritual exercises. Hence, a moral break-down giving the *passions* a new lease of life and paving the way for lamentable surrenders. In every case where the interior life is lacking, little personal merit is acquired, whilst outward activities secure but meager results since God's grace cannot render fruitful a ministry from which prayer has all but disappeared, Outward works must needs be vivified by *the spirit of prayer.*

612. A) The first thing to remember is that *the means employed in the exercise of zeal differ in effectiveness and*

---

[1] *Matth.*, VI, 33. — [2] *The True Apostolate*, p. 67.

importance; there exists among them a hierarchy, the most effective being prayer and sacrifice. Example follows next in order, word and action holding the last place. The *example of Our Lord* is enough to convince us of this. His whole life was one of continual prayer and sacrifice. He began by practicing what He taught others, leading a hidden life for thirty years before He would give Himself to a public ministry of but three years' duration. Let us bear in mind the course taken by the Apostles, who committed to deacons the discharge of sundry works of charity, that they might give themselves more freely to prayer and the preaching of the Gospel : " *But we will give ourselves continually to prayer and to the ministry of the word.* " [1] Let the words of St. Paul resound in our ears : " *Neither he that planteth is anything, nor he that watereth : but God that giveth the increase.* " [2]

Prayer, then, will hold the first place in our life (n. 470). We shall make no surrender of the *essential* exercises of piety such as meditation, thanksgiving after Mass, the devout recitation of the Divine Office, examination of conscience, the explicit offering of our actions to God, fully persuaded that we thereby render greater service to souls than if we gave ourselves entirely to works of zeal. A shepherd of souls will be, as S. Bernard says, a *reservoir* not a *mere conduit*. The latter merely passes on what it receives, the former, being first filled, gives constantly of its overflow : " *If thou hast wisdom, thou shalt prove a fountain-spring and not a channel.* " [3]

613. B) *To aim at creating a chosen group* of devout souls without, however, neglecting the multitudes, will likewise help us to keep before our minds the absolute need of an interior life. We feel that we cannot succeed in this unless we are interior men. The study we make of the spiritual life, the advice we give to others, the virtuous practices we try to inculcate, will perforce lead us to a life of prayer and of sacrifice. But to attain our end, we must be generous enough to live by the advice we give to others. Then we need not fear laxity and lukewarmness. In fact, not a few priests have been brought to live an interior life, through their interest in leading chosen souls to strive after perfection.

614. C) In the doctrinal or moral instructions we give our flock, we must follow a definite plan enabling us to present the whole field of Christian truth and Christian virtue. The preparation of such instructions will nourish our piety, for what we preach to others that we shall aspire to practice.

[1] *Acts*, VI, 4. — [2] *I Cor.*, III, 7.
[3] St. BERNARDUS, *In Cantica*, sermo XVIII, 3.

615. D) Lastly, in the ordinary course of our parochial ministry, on the occasion of baptisms, marriages, funerals, sick-calls, visits of condolence and even social calls, we must ever remember that we are priests and apostles, that is to say, servants of souls. Therefore, after a few expressions of good will, we should not hesitate to raise minds and hearts towards God. Priestly conversation must always suggest the higher, the nobler things of life.

These are the various means whereby our interior life is preserved and strengthened. Our ministry vivified by grace yields fruit a hundred-fold : " *He that abideth in me and I in him, the same beareth much fruit.* " [1]

Thus, all our relations with our neighbor can and must be supernaturalized. All become then the occasion of further growth in virtue and of a development within us of that divine life of which we have received abundantly.

GENERAL SUMMARY

616. We have reached the end of the first part of our work, namely, *The Principles of the Supernal Life.* All we have said flows logically from the truths of our faith ; all can be reduced to unity : *God* is our *end, Jesus-Christ* is our *Mediator* and the Christian life is the *gift of God* to the soul and the gift of the soul to God.

1º It is *God's Gift to the Soul.* From all eternity the Most Holy Trinity has loved us and predestined us to that supernatural life which is a participation in the life of God. This Adorable Trinity living in our souls is both the *efficient* and the *exemplary* cause of that life, whilst the supernatural organism that enables us to elicit Godlike acts, is the work of the same Triune God.

The *Incarnate Word*, however, is the *meritorious* cause as well as the most perfect *model* of our supernatural life. Conformed to our weakness, He is man like unto us, without ceasing to be God. He is our friend, our brother, nay more, the Head of a mystic body whose members we are. Because Mary, associated as she is in the work of our Redemption, cannot be separated from her Son, she stands as the first stepping stone to Jesus, just as Jesus is the necessary Mediator with the Father. The Saints and Angels who form part of God's vast family aid us by their prayers and their example.

---

[1] *John*, XV, 5.

617.   2⁰ In order to correspond to God's loving kindness, we give ourselves entirely to Him, fostering that life so freely bestowed. We develop it by struggling against the concupiscence that remains in us; by eliciting supernatural acts which besides meriting an increase of divine life cause us to acquire good habits, that is, virtues; and by receiving the Sacraments, which add to our merits a sanctifying power that comes from God Himself.

The very essence of perfection is *the love of God unto the immolation of self*. To fight and annihilate within us the old Adam, that the new Adam, Jesus Christ, may live in us, is the task before us. In pursuing this work, that is, in making use of the means of perfection, we *tend constantly toward God through Jesus Christ*.

The desire for perfection is, fundamentally, but the generous answer of the soul to God's tender love. Such a desire brings us to the *knowledge* and the *love* of Him Who is all love, "God is love"; to a *knowledge of self*, that we may all the more forcibly feel the need we have of God and may entrust ourselves into His merciful arms. This love is shown by a *conformity*, to the full extent of our powers, to the will of God as manifested by His laws and His counsels, as made known by the events of life, propitious or adverse, all of which help us to love God the more. This love is, likewise, shown by *prayer* which becoming habitual constantly elevates the soul toward God. Even the *exterior* means lead us to God, for spiritual direction, a rule of life and spiritual reading are calculated to bring us into compliance with His will, whilst the relations by which we are brought into contact with others in whom we see a reflection of the divine perfections bring us to Him Who is the Source and Centre of all things. Since in the employment of all these means we constantly have before our eyes Jesus, our Model, our Co-worker, our Life, we are transformed into Him, into true *Christians*, for a true Christian is another Christ.

Thus is gradually realized the ideal of perfection outlined by Father Olier for his disciples at the beginning of the "Pietas Seminarii" : " *To live wholly unto God in Christ Jesus Our Lord, in such wise, that the Spirit of His Son may enter into our inmost soul,* " and that we, like St. Paul, may have a right to say : " I live, now not I : but Christ liveth in me. "

END OF THE FIRST PART

SECOND PART

The Three Ways

PRELIMINARY REMARKS[1]

618. The general principles explained in the *first part* of this work apply to all souls, and already constitute a body of *motives* and of *means* calculated to lead us to the highest form of perfection. But as we have stated above (n. 340-343) there is *a diversity of degrees* in the spiritual life — *different stages to traverse.* Hence, the importance *of adapting the general principles to the individual needs of souls*, taking account not only of their peculiar characters, their various attractions and their different callings, but also of the degree of perfection they have so far attained, in order that the spiritual director may guide them in the most suitable manner.

The *purpose* of this second part is to follow a soul in its gradual ascent from the moment it first conceives a sincere desire of advancing in the spiritual life, on to the loftiest heights of perfection — a long road indeed, but one wherein the soul tastes the sweetness of the choicest consolations!

Before entering upon the description of the *three ways* we shall explain : 1° the *basis* of this distinction, 2° the *practical way to employ* it wisely, 3° the importance of the study of the three ways.

I. BASIS OF THE DISTINCTION OF THE THREE WAYS

619. We make use of the expression, the *three ways*, to conform to traditional usage. We must note however that it is not question here of three *parallel* or *divergent* ways, but rather of three different *stages*, of *three marked degrees*, which souls who generously correspond to divine grace traverse in the spiritual life. Each way in turn has many *degrees* which spiritual directors must take into account, the

[1] S. THOM., IIa IIæ, q. 24, a. 9; q. 183, a. 4; THOM. DE VALLGORNERA, *Myst, theol.*, q. II, a. II; LE GAUDIER, *De Perf. vitæ spir.*, IIa Pars, sect. I, cap. I; SCARAMELLI, *Direttorio ascetico*, Traité II, Introd.; SCHRAM, *Instit. theol. myst.*, XXVI; SAUDREAU, *The Degrees of the Spiritual Life*, Preface; DESURMONT, *Charité Sacerdotale*, 138-140; *Cursus Asceticus*, Vol. I. Prolegomena.

most notable of which we shall indicate.   Likewise, there
are in the various *stages* many *forms* and *variations* dependent upon the character, the vocation, and the providential
mission of each soul. [1]   But, as we have said, following
St. Thomas, we way reduce these degrees to three, accordingly
as a soul *begins, advances* or reaches the *goal.* (n. 340-343)
This is the *general sense* in which we make a threefold division based upon authority and reason.

620.   1° This doctrine is based on the **authority** of
Scripture and *Tradition.*

A) No doubt, many texts could be found in the *Old
Testament* suggesting the triple distinction.

Thus Alvarez de Paz makes it rest upon the following passage, which
provided him with his division of the spiritual life : " *Turn away
from evil and do good: seek after peace and pursue it.* " [2]   *Turn away
from evil :* avoid sin; this is the purification of the soul or the *purgative* way. *Do good :* practice virtue; this is the *illuminative* way.   *Seek
after peace :* that peace which intimate union with God alone can give;
here we have the *unitive* way.   This interpretation of the text is
ingenious, but we must not see therein a conclusive proof.

621.   B) In the *New Testament :* **a)** Among others, one
could cite the following words of Our Lord which sum up
Christian spirituality as described in the Synoptics : " *If any
man will come after me, let him deny himself, and take up his
cross daily, and follow me.* " [3]   Self-denial, self-renouncement
— *let him deny himself* — behold the first degree.   The carrying of one's cross already presupposes the positive practice
of virtue, or the second degree.   *Follow me* is, in reality,
intimate union with Jesus, union with God, and, hence, the
unitive way.   Here, again, we have the basis for a real
distinction, but not a rigorous proof of the three stages.

622.   b) Neither does St. Paul explicitly make any such
distinction, yet he gives a description of three states of soul
which later on gave origin to this classification.

1) Recalling what athletes did in striving after a perishable crown,
he compares himself to them, for he also strives to run and struggle,
but instead of beating the air he buffets his body and brings it into
bondage lest he sin and be rejected : " *I therefore so run, not as at an
uncertainty : I so fight, not as one beating the air.   But I chastise my
body and bring it into subjection : lest perhaps when I have preached to
others, I myself should become a castaway.* " [4]   These are indeed, penitential exercises, practises of mortification inspired by a wholesome

---

[1] Thus in the *unitive* way two distinct *forms* are generally distinguished as we
shall later on explain : the *simple* unitive way, and that which is accompanied by
infused contemplation.

[2] *Ps.* XXXIII, 15. — [3] *Luke*, IX, 23. — [4] *I Cor.*, IX, 26-27.

fear in order to subject the flesh and purify the soul.   How often does he not remind Christians of the necessity of putting off the Old Adam and of crucifying their flesh with its vices and lusts?   This corresponds with what we call the purgative way.

2) Writing to the Philippians he declares that he has not yet reached perfection, but that he tries, following His Master, to attain it, and that without looking back he forges ahead toward the goal : " *Forgetting the things that are behind and stretching forth myself to those that are before, I press toward the mark, to the prize of the supernal vocation of God in Christ Jesus.* " [1] He adds that whoever would seek after perfection must do in like manner : " *Let us therefore as many as are perfect, be thus minded..... be ye followers of me, brethren.....* " [2]   And in another place : " *Be ye followers of me, as I also am of Christ.* " [3] These are the distinguishing marks of the *illuminative way*, wherein the principal duty is imitation of Our Lord Jesus Christ.

3) As to the *unitive way*, he describes its two forms, the *simple* unitive way by the constant effort to have Jesus live in him : " *I live, now not I, but Christ liveth in me;* " [4] and the *extraordinary* unitive way which is accompanied by ecstasies, visions, and revelations : " *I know a man in Christ : above fourteen years ago (whether in the body, I know not, or out of the body, I know not : God knoweth), such a one caught up to the third heaven.* " [5]

In St. Paul, then, as in the Gospels, we find that a true Christian must purify his soul, practice virtue, and strive after union with God, yet it is not clear that these constitute three *successive* stages of the spiritual life rather than three aspects of one process that goes on *simultaneously*.

623. Tradition gradually worked out this distinction, basing it at times upon the difference that exists between the three theological virtues, at others, upon the various degrees of love.

a) Clement of Alexandria is one of the first to employ the first of these methods.   To become a gnostic or a perfect man, many stages must be traversed : to shun evil through *fear*, and to mortify the passions ; then, under the influence of *hope*, to do good or practice virtues and lastly, to do good out of *love* for God. [6]   Cassian, from the same point of view, arrived at the differentiation of three degrees in the soul's ascent toward God : *fear*, peculiar to *slaves*, *hope*, fit for mercenaries working for a reward, and *love*, becoming the *children of God*. [7]

b) St. Augustine takes another point of view : perfection consisting in *love*, it is in the practice of this virtue that he discerns four degrees : *incipient* love, *growing* love, *full-grown* love, and perfect love. [8]   Since the last two degrees relate to the unitive way, his doctrine is, at bottom, the same as that of his predecessors. — St. Bernard also perceives three degrees in the love of God : after showing that the genesis of human love is love of self, he adds that man, realizing his own insufficiency, begins through faith to seek for God and to love Him on account of *His gifts;* this intercourse leads him then to love

---

[1] *Phil.*, III, 13-14. — [2] *Phil.*, III, 15-17. — [3] *I Cor.*, IV, 16. — [4] *Gal.*, II, 20. [5] *II Cor.*, XII, 2. — [6] *Stromata*, VI, 12. — [7] *Confer.*, XI, 6-8. [8] *De natura et gratia*, cap. LXX, n. 84.

Him both because of His benefits and *for His own sake;* finally, he comes to love God with an altogether *disinterested* love. [1] Lastly, St. Thomas, perfecting the teaching of St. Augustine, shows clearly the existence of three degrees in the virtue of love that correspond to the three ways or stages, n. 340-343.

624. 2º **Reason** shows the correctness of this division.

A) It is evident that before arriving at an intimate union with God, the soul must first of all be *purified* of its past faults and be strengthened against future ones.

Purity of heart is, on the authority of Our Lord, the first essential condition for seeing God, for seeing Him as He is in the next life, and also for seeing Him now imperfectly and obscurely but truly, and for uniting ourselves with Him : " *Blessed are the clean of heart for they shall see God.* " [2] But this purity of heart presupposes a cleansing from former faults by means of a sincere and rigorous expiation, an earnest and relentless fight againts sinful tendencies and the practice of prayer, meditation and such other spiritual exercises as are required for the strengthening of our will against temptation — in a word, all those means that tend to purify the soul and ground it in virtue. The sum-total of these means is what is called the *purgative way.*

625. **B)** Once the soul has been thus purified and reformed, it must be *adorned with Christian virtues*, virtues *of a positive character*, that will make it more like unto Christ. Its task then is to follow the Master step by step and gradually reproduce Christ's interior dispositions by the concurrent practice of both the *moral* and *theological* virtues. The former mold and strengthen the soul; the latter already initiate its union with God. Both are practiced simultaneously according to the needs of the moment and the attractions of grace. The better to attain this end, the soul perfects its own form of prayer, which becomes more and more *affective*, and strives to love and to imitate Jesus Christ. It thus advances toward the *illuminative* way, for to follow Jesus is to walk in the light : *He who followeth me, walketh not in darkness.*

626. **C)** A moment comes when the soul, purified from its faults, made strong and docile to the inspirations of the Holy Spirit, longs but for an *intimate union with God.* It seeks Him everywhere, even in the midst of the most absorbing occupations; it clings to Him and enjoys His

---

[1] *Epist.* XI, n. 8, *P. L.,* CLXXXII, 113-114. — [2] *Matth.,* V, 8.

presence. Mental prayer grows in *simplicity ;* it becomes a lingering, loving thought of God and of things divine, under the influence, latent or conscious, of the *gifts of the Holy Ghost.* This is the *unitive* way. [1]

Within these three great stages there are indeed many degrees and diversities of "*the manifold grace of God.*" [2] We shall describe a few. An acquaintance with the others may be obtained by studying the lives of the Saints.

II. THE PRACTICAL WAY TO EMPLOY THIS DISTINCTION WISELY

627. To make a right use of this distinction, great tact and intelligence are required : one must indeed study the principles explained here, but still more, study *each soul* in particular, with its characteristic traits, taking cognizance of the special action of the Holy Ghost upon it. In order to aid the spiritual director, a few remarks will not be amiss.

628. A) There can be nothing absolute or mathematical in the distinction of the three ways. a) A soul passes imperceptibly from one to the other, for there are no well-defined boundary lines dividing one sharply from the other. To decide, therefore, whether a soul is as yet within the limits of the purgative way, or has already crossed the borders of the illuminative way, is often impossible; for there is between the two a common ground, the exact bounds of which cannot be determined. b) Besides, the soul's progress is not always a sustained advance; it is a vital action, with its ebb and flow; at times the soul presses onward, at times it recedes; at others, it actually seems but to mark time making no apparent headway.

629. B) There is in each of the three ways a number of different degrees. a) Among *beginners*, there are those who have a heavy burden of sin to expiate; others there are who never lost their baptismal innocence. It is evident, all things being equal in other respects, that the former must undergo a longer course of penance than the latter. b) Be-

---

[1] *I Peter*, IV, 10.

[2] St. John of the Cross, and after him a number of authors, use a special terminology with regard to the three ways, a knowledge of which is important. He styles beginners those on the threshold of obscure contemplation or the "night of the senses"; he calls the advanced those already within the realm of passive contemplation; and the perfect, those that have passed through the "night of the senses" and the "night of the soul". Cfr. HOORNAERT, note on the *Dark Night*, t. III, des Œuvres spirituelles, (p. 5-6).

sides, there are differences arising from temperament, degree of earnestness and constancy.   There are souls that eagerly embrace penitential practices, whilst others, on the contrary, do so with reluctance; some are generous and would refuse Almighty God nothing; some respond to His advances only half-heartedly.   Undoubtedly, among such souls, all as yet in the purgative way, a marked difference will be in evidence ere long.   c) Nay, there is a considerable distance between those who have devoted but a few, short months to the purification of their souls, and those who have already consecrated *many years* to this task.   d) Likewise, and above all, account must be taken of *the action of grace*. Some souls seem to receive it in such an abundance that we can look to a swift advance toward the heights of perfection; others receive it in far smaller measures and their progress is slower.   A spiritual director must bear in mind that his action must be subordinated to that of the Holy Ghost, n. 548.

He must not imagine that there are such things as *moulds* into which all souls must be poured.   On the contrary, he must proceed on the assumption that each soul possesses peculiarities of which account must be taken, and that the outlines traced by spiritual writers must be elastic enough to be adapted to each case.

630.   C) In the direction of souls there is a twofold danger to avoid.   Some would, *by a forced march*, rush through the early stages, the sooner to arrive at divine love; others, on the contrary, but *mark time* and, through their own fault, tarry in the lower levels because of a lack of generosity or a lack of method.   A spiritual director must frequently remind the *former* that to love God is, indeed, an excellent thing, but that we do not attain to a pure and effective love, except trough self-abnegation and penance, (n. 321).   The *latter* he must encourage and advise, in order to stir them to action and aid them in perfecting their method of prayer or of self-examination.

631.   D) When spiritual writers speak of a particular *virtue* as being proper to this or that of the three ways, the statement is to be accepted with a great deal of caution. The truth is that all fundamental virtues belong to each of the three ways, varying only in degree.   Thus *beginners* must, assuredly, exercise themselves especially in the virtue of *penance*, but they cannot do so without the practice of the theological and cardinal virtues, though in a different way from that of the more advanced souls.   Beginners practice these virtues chiefly in order to purify their souls through self-denial. These same virtues must be practiced in the *illuminative* way, but to a different degree, in a more positive fashion, and with a view of resembling all the more the Divine Model. The same must be done in the *unitive* way, but to a higher degree still, as an earnest of love for God, and under the influence of the gifts of the Holy Ghost.

In like manner, the *perfect*, whilst exercising themselves above all in the practice of the love of God, do not give up the purification of their souls through penance and mortification ; but a purer and more intense love mellows their penitential practices, and gives them greater effectiveness.

632. E) A similar remark must be made with regard to the *different kinds of prayer*. Thus, discursive meditation is, generally speaking, suitable for beginners ; affective prayer, adapted to advanced souls ; and the prayer of simplicity and contemplation, proper to the unitive way. Yet, experience shows *the degree of prayer does not always correspond to the degree of virtue;* that owing to temperament, training or custom, some persons linger in the exercice of discursive meditation or affective prayer, who are the while intimately and habitually united to God ; and that others possessed of greater insight and more affectionate natures, readily practice the prayer of simplicity without having as yet attained that height of virtue which the unitive way demands.

It is important that from the outset we bear in mind these observations so as not to place the virtues in imaginary, air-tight compartments. In the exposition of each virtue, we shall accordingly note carefully the degrees that are in keeping with beginners, with advanced souls, and with those that have attained perfection.

III. Importance of the Study of the Three Ways

The foregoing remarks show how useful and how necessary is the intelligent study of the Three Ways.

633. 1º To *spiritual directors* this study is a real necessity. It is obvious, in fact, " that beginners and perfect souls are not to be guided by the same rules ",[1] for, as Father Grou[2] says, "the grace given to beginners is not that bestowed on souls already advanced, nor is the one

---

[1] *Articles d'Issy*, n. XXXIV. — [2] *Manual for Interior Souls.*

granted these the same as that received by those who have reached the heights of perfection. "

Thus, discursive meditation, necessary to beginners, would paralyze the efforts of more advanced souls. Likewise, with regard to the virtues, there is a manner of practicing them adapted to the purgative way, another to the illuminative, another to the unitive. A spiritual director who has not delved into these questions is liable to guide almost all souls after the same fashion and to counsel each according to what has answered his own purpose : because he finds affective, simplified prayer of great avail to himself, he will be led to prescribe the same method to all his penitents, unmindful of the fact that, as a rule, this is reached by gradual stages; if he finds in the habitual practice of the love of God all that he needs for his own sanctification, he will be inclined to recommend to all the ways of love, forgetting that fledglings are unable to fly to such heights ; should he have never been himself initiated into that form of prayer which consists in a lingering, loving thought of God, the prayer of simple regard, as it is called, he will blame those who exercise themselves therein, claiming that this is but spiritual sloth. The director, on the other hand, who has carefully studied the gradual ascent of earnest souls, will know how to give competent counsel and to impart effectual guidance adapted to the actual state of his penitents and calculated to produce the greatest measure of good in their souls.

634. 2º The faithful themselves will profit by the study of these various stages of the spiritual life. To be sure, they will be guided by the advice of their spiritual directors; yet, if through well-chosen readings they come to grasp — at least in the main — the differences that exist between the three ways, they will understand better the counsels given them and will turn them to greater profit.

We shall then take up successively the study of the *three ways*, bearing in mind, however, that there are no clean-cut divisions between them and that each admits many varieties and forms.

BOOK I

The Purification of the Soul
or the Purgative Way

INTRODUCTION [1]

635. The characteristic of the *purgative way*, or the *state of beginners*, is the *purifying of the soul* in view of attaining *to intimate union with God*.

We shall therefore explain 1º what is meant by *beginners*, and 2º the *end* these must strive to attain.

I. WHO ARE CALLED BEGINNERS?

636. 1º **Essential Characteristics.** In the spiritual life, *beginners* are those that habitually live in the state of grace and have a certain desire for perfection, but who have still attachments to venial sin and are exposed to fall now and then into grievous faults. We shall explain these three characteristics :

a) *Beginners live habitually in the state of grace :* hence, they generally struggle successfully against grave temptations. We therefore rule out of the class of beginners those that frequently commit mortal sin and do not avoid its occasions; who would no doubt wish to be converted, but lack the necessary firm and efficacious purpose. Such are not on the way to perfection. They are sinners, worldlings, who must first of all be helped to sever their attachment to mortal sin and to part with the occasions of sin. [2]

b) *They have a certain desire for perfection* or for progress, even if this desire be as yet feeble and imperfect. Thus we exclude from the category of beginners those wordlings — all too numerous — alas! whose highest purpose is to escape

---

[1] A. SAUDREAU, *The Degrees* of the Spiritual Life, the Purgative Way, I-II; SCHRYVERS, *Les principes*, IIᵉ Part., ch. II.

[2] No doubt, there are authors who with FR. MARCHETTI, (*Rev. d'Ascétique et de Mystique*, Jan. 1920, p. 36-47), are of the opinion that sinners must be included in the purgative way in order to convert them, yet he admits that in this he does not follow the common teaching. The conversion of sinners and the means to be suggested to them that they may persevere in the state of grace, belong rather to the province of *Moral* than of *Ascetic* theology. We may say, however, that the motives we shall soon propose as deterrents from mortal sin will be a confirmation of those given by Moral theology.

mortal sin, but who have no earnest desire of advancing
further.   As we have shown above, n. 414, the desire for
perfection is the first step on the way.

c) They have, however, *some attachment to deliberate venial
sin* and, therefore, they frequently fall.   This distinguishes
them from souls already advancing along the way of
perfection, who although they may from time to time commit
some wilful venial sins, yet earnestly strive to avoid them.
The existence of these attachments is due to the fact that
their passions are not as yet subdued; hence, they yield
to temptations of sensuality, pride, vanity, anger, envy,
jealousy, and uncharitableness in word and deed.   How
many persons called devout retain attachments of this
kind, which cause them to commit deliberate, venial sins
which expose them to fall from time to time into grievous
faults!

637. 2° **Different Categories.**   There are *different
categories* of beginners : —

a) *Innocents souls* desiring to grow in the spiritual life —
children, young men and young women who, not content
with the mere avoidance of mortal sin, wish to do something
more for God and want to become perfect.   The number
of these would be greater were priests active in arousing
this desire for perfection in Sunday school, at the meetings
of Sodalities and parochial organizations. (cf. 409-430.)

b) *Converts* from sin, who after having transgressed
grievously, return to God with all sincerity and who, in
order to withdraw further from the brink of the abyss, want
to press forward in the ways of perfection.   Here again
we may say that these would be far more numerous if
confessors would take heed to remind their penitents that in
order not to fall back they must advance, and that the
safest means of avoiding mortal sins is to tend to perfection.
(cf. 354-361).

c) The *lukewarm*, those who after having given themselves
once to God and having advanced in the way of perfection
have fallen into a state of remissness and tepidity.   These,
even if they had once reached the illuminative way, need to
return to the austere practices of the purgative way and
begin once more the work of perfection.   To aid their
efforts, one must carefully put them on their guard against
the dangers of carelessness and lukewarmness and teach
them to combat their causes, which are generally frivolity
or fickleness, listlessness and a sort of sluggishness.

638. 3° **Two classes of beginners.** Some show *greater generosity*, others *less*. Hence the two classes into which they are divided by St. Teresa.

a) In the first mansion or the Castle of the Soul, she gives a description of those souls that have good desires, are faithful to recite some prayers, but who are taken up with the world and have their minds filled with a thousand and one things which absorb their thought. The while they retain these many attachments, they strive from time to time to free themselves from them. Through such efforts they gain an entrance into the first and lower halls of the *Castle :* with them, however, enter a multitude of mischievous animals (their own passions) which hinder them from gazing at the beauty of the castle and abiding peacefully therein. To have entered this mansion, although it is the lowest, is already a singular good-fortune ; nevertheless the machinations and subterfuges employed by the devil in order to prevent such souls from advancing are ruthless. The world, likewise, wherein they are yet immersed, allures them with its pleasures and honors ; hence, they are easily conquered, even though they want to avoid sin and do perform good works. [1] In other words, these souls strive *to harmonize piety and worldliness*. Their faith is not sufficiently enlightened, their will is not strong enough, not generous enough to determine them to renounce not merely sin, but sundry dangerous occasions ; they have little realized the need of frequent prayer, of rigorous penance, or mortification ; still, they want not only to work out their salvation, but also to grow in the love of God by making some sacrifices.

639. b) The other class of beginners is described by the Saint in her *second mansion*. They are souls already *initiated in the practice of mental prayer*, who understand the necessity of sacrifice as a means of perfection, but who through lack of courage retreat at times to the first mansion, exposing themselves once more to the occasions of sin. They love as yet the pleasures of the world and its allurements, and occasionally fall into some grave fault ; but hearkening to God's call to penance, presently rise again. In spite of the appeals made to them by the world and the devil, they meditate on the emptiness of the world's false goods and on death that shall soon take these away. They grow apace in the love of Him from Whom they receive so many proofs of love ; they realize that apart from Him they shall find neither peace nor safety, and wish to avoid the wanderings of the Prodigal. This, then, is a state of struggle in which such souls have much to suffer from the manifold temptations that assail them, but wherein also God deigns to comfort and fortify them. By acting in conformity with God's holy will, which is the great means of perfection, they will finally emerge from the mansions wherein creep such venomous creatures, and they will pass to the other mansions beyond the reach of their poisonous sting. [2]

640. We shall not treat separately of these two classes, because the means to be suggested to each are practically the same. Let the spiritual director however bear this division in mind when giving advice. Let him draw the attention of souls of the first class to the consequences

---

[1] *Interior Castle*, First Mansion.
[2] *Interior Castle*, Second Mansion.

of sin, the necessity of avoiding its occasions, and awaken
in them a longing for prayer, penance and mortification.
Souls of the second class he will advise to give more time
to meditation, and to take the offensive against the capital
vices, those deep-seated tendencies which are the source of
all our sins.

II. THE END TO PURSUE

641. We have stated (n. 309) that perfection consists
essentially in *union with God through love*. But because
God is holiness itself, we cannot be united to Him unless
we are *clean of heart* — a state implying a twofold condition :
atonement for the past and *detachment from sin and the
occasions of sin for the future*.

The first task, then, of beginners is **purification of the
soul.**

We may add that the union of the soul with God will be
the more intimate as the soul grows in purity and detachment. The purification is more or less perfect according
to the *motives* that inspire it and according to the *effects*
produced by it.

A) The purification remains *imperfect*, if it is inspired
chiefly by motives of *fear* and *hope* — fear of hell, and hope
of heaven and heavenly gifts. The results of such a purification are incomplete. The soul, indeed, renounces mortal
sin, which would deprive it of heaven, but it does not
renounce venial fauts, even deliberate ones, since these do
not deprive it of its eternal welfare.

B) There is, then, a more perfect purification, which,
though not excluding fear and hope, has for its ruling
motive the love of God, the desire to please Him and hence
to avoid whatever would constitute even a slight offence.
Here is verified the word of the Savior to the sinful woman :
" Many sins are forgiven her because she hath loved
much. " [1]

It is at this second purification that souls should aim; still,
the spiritual director must remember that for many a beginner it is not possible to rise thereto at the outset, and whilst
speaking to such of the love of God, he will not forget to
offer them the motives of hope and of fear which make
a stronger impression.

---

[1] *Luke*, VII, 47.

DIVISION OF THE FIRST BOOK

642. Once we know the end, we must determine the **means** necessary for its attainment. Fundamentally, they may be reduced to two : **prayer,** through which grace is obtained, and **mortification** through which we correspond to grace. Mortification assumes different names according to the point of view from which we consider it. It is called *penance* when it prompts us to atone for our past faults; *mortification properly so called*, when it sets upon the love of pleasure in order to reduce the number of faults in the present and obviate their recurrence in the future; it is called *warfare against the capital sins*, when it combats those deep-rooted tendencies that incline us toward sin, and *warfare against temptation*, when practiced by way of resistance to the onslaughts of our spiritual enemies. Hence the five following chapters :

Chapter I. — The **Prayer** of Beginners

Chapter II. — **Penance,** to atone for the past

Chapter III. — **Mortification,** to safeguard the future

Chapter IV. — **Warfare** against the **capital sins**

Chapter V. — The **Warfare** against **temptation**

All these means clearly presuppose the practice in some degree of the *theological* and the *moral* virtues. No one can pray, no one can do penance and mortify himself, without a firm belief in revealed truth, without the expectation of a heavenly reward, without love of God, without the exercise of prudence, justice, fortitude and temperance. We shall speak of these virtues when we treat of the *illuminative way* wherein they attain their full development.

CHAPTER I

The Prayer of Beginners [1]

643. We have already explained (n. 499-521) the *nature* and the *efficacy* of prayer. After beginners have been reminded of these notions, they must : 1º be instructed as to the *necessity* and the *conditions* of prayer; 2º they must be gradually introduced to the practice of such *spiritual exercises* as befit them; 3º they must be taught *mental prayer*.

Article I. — Prayer in general $\begin{cases} \text{Necessity of Prayer} \\ \text{Conditions of Prayer} \end{cases}$

Article II. — Principal Spiritual Exercises

Article III. — Mental Prayer $\begin{cases} \text{General Notions} \\ \text{Advantages and Neces-} \\ \text{sity} \\ \text{The Mental Prayer of} \\ \text{Beginners} \\ \text{The Principal Methods} \end{cases}$

ARTICLE I. NECESSITY AND CONDITIONS OF PRAYER

§ I. Necessity of Prayer

644. What we have said regarding the twofold end of prayer, *worship* and *petition* (n. 503-509), shows us clearly its necessity. It is evident that as creatures and as Christians we are bound to glorify God through adoration, thanksgiving and love; that as sinners we must offer Him reparation (n. 506). Here it is question of prayer chiefly as *petition*, and of its absolute necessity as a means of salvation and perfection.

645. The necessity of prayer is based on the *necessity of actual grace*. It is a truth of faith that without such grace we are utterly incapable of obtaining salvation and, still more of attaining perfection (n. 126). Of ourselves, no

---

[1] ST. THOM., IIa IIæ, q. 83 and his Commentators; SUAREZ, *De Religione*, Tr. IV, lib. I, *De Oratione;* ALVAREZ DE PAZ, t. III, lib. I; TH. DE VALLGORNERA, q. II, disp. V; *Summa theol. mysticæ*, Ia Pars, Tract. I, discursus III; L. DE GRA-NADA, *Traité de l'Oraison et de la Méditation;* St. ALPHONSUS DE LIGUORI, *Prayer;* P. MONSABRÉ, *La Prière;* P. RAMIÈRE, *L'Apostolat de la prière;* ST. FRANCIS DE SALES, *Devout Life*, Part II; *Spiritual Combat*, C. 44-52; RODRIGUEZ, *Christian Perfection*, I, Treat. 5; GROU, *How to Pray;* MESCHLER, *Three Fundamental Principles of the Spiritual Life*, I; HEDLEY, *Retreat*, XXI.

matter how we use our freedom, we can do nothing positive that would prepare us for conversion to God, nor can we persevere for any length of time, much less until death : " *Without me you can do nothing.... Not that we are suffi-cient to think anything of ourselves, as of ourselves.... For it is God who worketh in you, both to will and to accomplish.* " [1]

Now, barring the first grace, which is gratuitously given us since it is itself the principle of prayer, it remains ever true that prayer is the *normal*, the *efficacious*, and the *uni-versal* means through which God wills that we obtain all actual graces.   This is the reason why Our Lord insists so frequently upon the necessity of prayer : " Ask, and it shall be given you : seek, and you shall find ; knock and it shall be opened to you.   For every one that asketh, receiv-eth : and he that seeketh, findeth : and to him that knocketh, it shall be opened. " [2]   Almost all commentators add that it is as if He said : " Unless you ask, you shall not receive ; unless you seek, you shall not find. "   On this necessity of prayer Our Lord constantly insists, especially when it is question of resisting temptation : " Watch ye and pray that you enter not into temptation : the spirit indeed is willing but the flesh is weak. " [3]   St. Thomas asserts that confidence not based on prayer is presumption, for God, Who is not in justice bound to grant us His grace, has not pledged Himself to give it except through prayer.   God, assuredly, does know our spiritual needs without our exposing them to Him, yet He wills that prayer be the spring that sets in motion His loving mercy, so that we may acknowledge Him as the Author of the gifts He bestows on us. [4]

646.   This is likewise the way in which tradition has understood the teaching of Our Lord.   The Council of Trent, making its own the teaching of St. Augustine, tells us that God does not command the impossible, for He commands us to do what we can and to ask His help for what we cannot do, His grace helping us to ask for it. [5] This manifestly implies that there are thing which without prayer are impossible.   Such is the conclusion the Roman Catechism draws : " Prayer is the *indispensable* instrument given us by God in order to obtain what we desire : there are things, in fact, impossible to obtain without the aid of prayer. " [6]

---

[1] *John*, XV, 5 ; *II Cor.*, III, 5 ; *Phil.*, II, 13.
[2] *Matth.*, VII, 7-8. — [3] *Matth.*, XXVI, 41.
[4] *Sum. theol.*, IIa IIæ, q. 83, a. 1, ad 3.
[5] Sess. VI, ch. II. — [6] *Catech. Trident.*, P. VI, c. I, n. 3.

647. Advice to the spiritual Director. This truth must be emphasized with beginners. Many, unknown to themselves, are saturated with Pelagianism or Semi-pelagianism, and imagine that by sheer strength of will they can accomplish all things. Soon, however, experience brings them to the realization that their best resolves often fall short despite their efforts. The spiritual director should at such times remind them that it is only through grace and through prayer that they can succeed. This personal experience will go far to strengthen their convictions on the necessity of prayer.

§ II. Essential Conditions of Prayer

648. Having already proved the necessity of *actual grace* for all the acts bearing on salvation (n. 126), we must infer its necessity for prayer. St. Paul clearly states this necessity : " Likewise, the Spirit also helpeth our infirmity. For, we know not *what we should pray for as we ought : but the Spirit himself asketh for us with unspeakable groanings.*" [1] We may add that this grace is offered to all, even to sinners; hence, all are able to pray.

Although the *state of grace* is not necessary in order to pray, it increases the value of prayer, since it makes us the friends of God and the living members of Jesus Christ.

We shall now inquire into the requisite conditions of prayer 1° on the part of the *object* of prayer, and 2° on the part of the one who prays.

I. *Conditions on the Part of the Object*

649. The most important condition regarding the object of prayer is to ask for those things only which lead unto life everlasting : for *supernatural graces* in the first place, and then, for *temporal goods*, in the measure in which they are conducive to salvation. This rule was laid down by Our Lord Himself : " *Seek ye therefore first the kingdom of God and his justice : and all these things shall be added unto you.*" [2] We have said (n. 307-308), that man's happiness as well as his perfection consists in the possession of God, and as a consequence in the possession of the means necessary to that end. We must, then, ask for nothing that is not in harmony with it.

1° *Temporal goods in themselves* are far too inferior, too inadequate to satisfy our heart's aspirations, and bring us

---

[1] *Rom.*, VIII, 26. — [2] *Matth.*, VI, 33.

true happiness; they cannot, therefore, be the chief object of our prayers. However, since in order to live and to secure our salvation we need some temporal goods, we are allowed to ask for our daily bread, the bread for the body as well as for the soul, subordinating the former to the latter. It happens at times that this or that particular good, wealth for instance — desirable in our estimation — would prove a danger to our salvation. Hence, we may not ask for such, except in subordination to the goods that are eternal.

650. 2° Even when it is question of such or such *particular grace*, we must not ask for it, except in conformity with the will of God. God in His infinite Wisdom knows better than we do what is suitable for each soul in accordance with its condition and degree of perfection. As St. Francis de Sales rightly remarks, we must desire our salvation after God's own way, and hence we must desire such graces as He dispenses to us and cling to them with a firm purpose, for our will must harmonize with His. [1] When it is question of particular graces, like one or other form of prayer, such and such consolations or trials, etc... we must not make any unqualified request, but rather refer all to the good pleasure of God. [2] God dispenses His graces, giving consolation or aridity, peace or struggle, according to the designs of His Wisdom and the needs of our soul. We have, therefore, but to leave in His Hands the choice of the graces which will prove most beneficial to us. True, we are permitted to express a wish, but in humble submission to the will of Our Heavenly Father. He will always answer our prayer if we ask as we should. If at times He gives us, in place of what we ask, something greater and better, far from complaining we should bless and thank Him. [3]

II. *Conditions on the Part of the Subject*

The most essential conditions to ensure the efficacy of our prayers are : *humility, confidence* and *attention*, or at least the earnest effort to be attentive.

---

[1] *The Love of God*, Book VIII, ch. IV.

[2] The reason why our petitions are not answered, says BOURDALOUE, is because we make use of prayer " in order to ask for whimsical, needless graces — graces according to our taste and fancy... We pray and ask for the grace of penance, the grace of sanctification — graces for the future, not for the present — graces that would do away with all difficulties, that would leave no room for effort, leave no obstacles to overcome — miraculous graces that would carry us as they did St. Paul, not those that would merely help us to walk.... graces which would alter the whole order of Providence, and revolutionize the whole scheme of salvation. " Lent. Sermon on prayer for Thursday of the 1st Week.

[3] In " *Le Saint Abandon*," P. III, of DOM V. LEHODEY, most apt details are given on the subject.

651. 1º The need of **humility** flows from the very nature of prayer. Since grace is a free gift of God to which we have no right whatever, we are as St. Augustine says, but beggars in relation to God, and we must implore of His mercy what we cannot demand as a right. It was thus that Abraham prayed, considering himself but dust and ashes in presence of the Divine Majesty : " I will speak to my Lord, whereas I am dust and ashes. "[1]   Thus did Daniel pray when he asked for the deliverance of the Jewish people, relying not on his merits and virtues, but on God's over-flowing mercies : " *It is not for our justifications that we present our prayers before thy face, but for the multitude of thy tender mercies.* "[2]   Thus prayed the publican, who was also heard : " O God, be merciful to me a sinner, "[3] whilst the proud Pharisee saw his prayer rejected. Jesus Himself gives us the reason : " *Every one that exalteth himself shall be humbled : and he that humbleth himself shall be exalted.* "[4] His Disciples understood this well. St. James insists that : " *God resisteth the proud and giveth grace to the humble.*"[5] This is mere justice : the proud man attributes to himself the efficacy of his prayer, whilst the humble man attributes it to God. Now, can we expect that God will hear us to the detriment of His own glory, in order to flatter our vain complacency? The humble soul, on the contrary, sincerely acknowledges that all it has is from God, and hence God in hearkening to his prayer procures His own glory as well as the welfare of him who prays.

652. 2º Humility in turn begets **confidence,** a confidence based, not upon our merits but upon the *goodness of God* and upon the *merits of Jesus Christ.*

a) Faith teaches us that God is *merciful* and that because He is merciful, He turns to us with greater love the more we acknowledge our miseries, for misery appeals to mercy. To call upon Him with confidence is in reality to honor Him, to proclaim Him as the source of all gifts, and as desiring nothing so much as to bestow them upon us. In the Scriptures He affirms again and again that He hearkens to those who hope in Him : " *Because he hoped in me I will deliver him.... He shall cry to me and I will hear him.* "[6]. Our Lord invites us to pray with confidence, and in order to inspire us to do so He resorts not only to the most

---

[1] *Gen.,* XVIII, 27. — [2] *Dan.,* IX, 18. — [3] *Luke,* XVIII, 13.
[4] *Luke,* XVIII, 14. — [5] *James,* IV, 6.
[6] *Ps.* XC, 14-15.   Those who recite the Divine Office know that the predominant sentiment expressed by the Psalms is that of trust in God.

pressing exhortations, but to the most touching parables.
After having affirmed that he who asks receives, He adds :
" What man is there among you, of whom if his son shall
ask bread, will he reach him a stone ?..... If you then being
evil, know how to give good gifts to your children : how
much more will your Father who is in heaven give good things
to them that ask him. " [1] At the Last Supper He comes
back to the same thought : " Amen, amen, I say to you....
whatsoever you shall ask the Father in my name, that will
I do : that the Father may be glorified in the Son. If you
shall ask me anything in my name, that I will do [2].... In
that day you shall ask in my name; and I say not to you,
that I will ask the Father for you. For the Father himself
loveth you, because you have loved me. " [3] To lack
a whole-hearted trust in prayer would amount to mistrusting
God and His promises, to underrating the merits of Jesus
Christ and His all-powerful mediation.

653. b) It is true that God at times appears to turn
a deaf ear to our prayer. This He does in order that we may
more fully fathom the depths of our wretchedness and realize
better the value of grace. But on the other hand, He shows
us in His treatment of the Canaanean woman, that even
when He seems to repel us, He is well-pleased at the sweet
insistence of our repeated requests. Behold, a woman of
Canaan comes and asks Jesus to deliver her daughter,
vexed with a devil. But the Master answers her not a word.
She beseeches the Disciples and cries after them, so that
they come and ask the Lord to send her away. Christ
turns to the woman and answers that He was not sent but
to the children of the house of Israel. Undaunted, the
poor woman worships Him, saying : " Lord, help me. "
Jesus replies, with seeming harshness, that it is not meet to
take the children's bread and cast it to the dogs. — " Yea,
Lord, " she says, " for the whelps also eat of the crumbs
that fall from the table of their masters. " — Conquered by
such a humble, unfaltering trust, Jesus grants her request :
" And her daughter was cured from that hour. " [4] Could the
Lord do more to make us understand that no matter what
ill success seems to attend our prayers, we can be sure that
they will be answered if we persevere in humble confidence.

654. 3° To this persevering confidence we must join
attention, or at least the serious effort to realize and to

---

[1] *Matth.*, VII, 7-11. — [2] *John*, XIV, 12, 13, 14.
[3] *John*, XVI, 26-27. — [4] *Matth.*, XV, 24-28.

mean what we say to God. *Involuntary distractions* do not constitute an obstacle to prayer as long as we strive to overcome them or reduce their number, for by these very efforts our soul keeps on its course toward God. They constitute indeed a loss though not a sin, but this loss may be made good in a measure by our efforts to pray attentively. On the contrary, *voluntary* distractions, those we freely and deliberately entertain, or which we but faintly repel, or the causes of which we are unwilling to suppress, are venial sins, since they constitute a lack of due respect towards God. Prayer is an audience which our Creator is kind enough to grant us; a conversation we hold with Our Heavenly Father, wherein we beg Him to vouchsafe to hearken to our words and heed our request : "*Give ear, O Lord to my words.... Hearken to the voice of my prayer.*" [1] Through voluntary distractions we do no less than refuse to make a serious effort to understand what we say and to be attentive to the divine voice; and this, at the very moment we ask the Almighty to hear us and to speak to us! Do we not deserve the reproach Our Lord cast upon the Pharisees : "*This people honoreth me with their lips : but their heart is far·from me?*" [2] Does this not constitute a glaring inconsistency as well as a lack of religion?

655. We must, then, *strive seriously* to repel *promptly* and *firmly* the distractions that present themselves to our mind; we must readily humble ourselves when they occur and unite again our prayer with the perfect prayer of·Jesus. We must, likewise, reduce the number of such distractions by a vigorous fight against their causes : habitual dissipation of mind, the habit of day-dreaming, the preoccupations and attachments that absorb the mind and the heart. We must also accustom ourselves little by little to recall frequently to mind God's presence, by offering up to Him our actions, as well as ardent ejaculatory prayers. Once we have taken these means, there is no cause for worry concerning such involuntary distractions as run through our minds or disturb our imagination. These are but trials, not faults, and once we have learned to profit by them, they but increase our merits and the value of our prayers.

656. The attention we can bring to bear upon our prayers may be of a threefold kind. 1) When we apply ourselves to the correct pronunciation of the words we give *verbal* attention which presupposes an effort to think of

---

what we say.   2) If we try to understand the *meaning of the words,* our attention is called *literal* or *intellectual*.   3) Should the soul, disregarding the literal meaning, rise toward God to worship Him, bless Him, unite itself to Him, or to enter into the spirit of the mystery it considers, attention becomes *spiritual* or *mystical.*   This last is hardly adapted to beginners, but rather to advanced souls.   The first two should be recommended to those who begin to relish prayer.

ART. II. THE EXERCISES OF PIETY OF BEGINNERS

657.   Prayer is one of the great means of salvation. Hence, the spiritual director should gradually initiate beginners into the practice of such spiritual exercises as form the framework of an earnest Christian life, taking account of their age, their vocation, the duties of their state, their character, supernatural attractions, and the progress they have made.

658.   1º The **objective** in view is to train souls gradually in the habitual practice of prayer in such a way that their whole life becomes in a measure a life of prayer (n. 522). It is evident that much time and prolonged efforts are required to approach this ideal, which is not within the reach of beginners, but which the spiritual director must know for the better guidance of his penitents.

659.   2º Besides morning and night prayers, which good Christians do not fail to say, the following are the chief spiritual exercises that render our lives a constant prayer :

A) The morning *meditation,* of which we shall soon treat, Holy Mass and Communion show us the ideal we are to pursue, and help us realize it (n. 524).   There are persons, however, who are prevented by their duties of state from assisting daily at the Holy Sacrifice.   They should make up for this by a spiritual communion to be made either at the end of meditation or even whilst engaged in manual labor.   At all events, they must be taught how to profit from attendance at Holy Mass and the reception of Holy Communion.   The Director does this by adapting to their capacity what we have said in n. 271-289.   They must also be taught to follow intelligently the liturgical services of Sundays and Holy days.   The sacred Liturgy well understood is one of the great helps to perfection.

660.   **B**) Besides the oft-renewed offering of their actions to God, they must be advised to recite during the course of the day some ejaculatory prayers, to do some devout reading suited to their state of soul on such fundamental truths as the end of man, sin, mortification, confession, and the examinations of conscience, adding thereto the lives of Saints who were noted for the practice of the virtue of penance. Such reading will be a light to the mind, a stimulus to the will, and a great help to mental prayer. The recitation of some decades of the *beads*, with meditation upon the mysteries of the Rosary, will be productive of an increased devotion to the Blessed Virgin and will strengthen the habit of union with Our Lord. A visit to the Blessed Sacrament, varying in duration according to their occupations, will reanimate within them the spirit of piety. For these visits they may use with profit the *Following of Christ*, especially the Fourth Book, and *Visits to the Blessed Sacrament* by St. Alphonsus Liguori.

661. **C)** In the evening, a serious *examination of conscience*, followed by the *particular examen*, will help beginners to note their failings, to foresee the remedies and to muster the strength of will needed to renew their purpose of amendment, thus preventing them from falling into indifference or lukewarmness. Here one must recall what we have said anent the examinations of conscience (460-476), and regarding confession (n. 262-269), and remember that the examination of beginners must bear chiefly upon deliberate venial sins. Such watchfulness is the best means of avoiding mortal sin and of repairing any grave sin committed in an unguarded moment.

662. 3° **Advice to the spiritual director.** **A)** The director should see to it that his penitents do not burden themselves with *too many* spiritual exercises that might hinder the fulfilment of their duties of state or be detrimental to true devotion. Less prayers and more attention is preferable. Our Lord Himself gives us this advice : " And when you are praying, speak not much, as the heathens. For they think that in their much speaking they may be heard. Be not you therefore like them : for your Father knoweth what is needful for you, before you ask him. " [1] After speaking these words He taught His Disciples that short and all-embracing prayer which embodies all our possible requests, the Our Father (n. 515-516). There are beginners who readily imagine that they grow in piety as they multiply their vocal prayers. A great

---

[1] *Matth.*, VI, 7-8.

service will be rendered them by recalling this teaching of the Master, and by showing them that a short attentive prayer is of greater worth than one lasting twice as long, and filled with more or less wilful distractions. To help them fix their attention, the spiritual director should remind them that a few seconds spent in placing themselves in the presence of God and in uniting themselves with Our Lord will do much to make their prayers truly effective.

663. B) To help them avoid the routine that is liable to creep into the repetition of the same formulas of vocal prayer, it is well to give them a *method*, at once easy and simple, of holding their attention. For instance, in the recitation of the Rosary they may meditate on the Mysteries with the twofold purpose in view of honoring the Blessed Virgin and of drawing unto themselves the particular virtue corresponding to each Mystery. This practice will be found very profitable; it will make the recitation of the Rosary a short meditation. But in this case it is well to recall that, generally speaking, we cannot at the same time pay attention both to the literal sense of the *Hail Mary* and to the meaning of the Mystery and that therefore either one suffices.

Art. III. The Mental Prayer of Beginners [1]

We shall explain : 1º Some *general notions* concerning meditation; 2º Its *advantages* and *necessity ;* 3º The *distinguishing characteristics* of meditation — the mental prayer of beginners; 4º The chief *methods* of meditation.

§ I. General Notions

664. 1º **Definition and Essential Elements of Mental prayer.** We have said (n. 510,) that there are two kinds of prayer : *vocal* prayer, expressed by word or by gesture, and *mental* prayer which takes place wholly within the soul.

---

[1] JOAN. MAUBURNUS, *Rosetum exercitiorum spiritualium et sacrarum meditationum;* GARCIA DE CISNEROS, *Exercitatorio de la vida espiritual;* ST. IGNATIUS, *Spiritual Exercises;* and *Commentators;* also la *Bibliothèque des Exercices de St. Ignace,* published under the direction of FATHER WATRIGANT; RODRIGUEZ, *Practice of Christian Perfection,* V. Treatise, On Prayer; L. DE GRANADA, *Traité de l'oraison et de la méditation;* A. MASSOULIÉ, *Traité de la véritable oraison;* ST. PETER OF ALCANTARA, *La oración y meditación ;* ST. FRANCIS DE SALES *Devout Life,* Part I, ch. I-IX; BRANCATI DE LAUREA, *De oratione christiand;* CRASSET, *A Key to Meditation;* SCARAMELLI, *op. cit.,* I. Treatise, art. 5; COURBON, *Familiar Instructions on Mental and Affective Prayer ;* V. LIBERMANN, *Ecrits spirit.,* p. 82-147; FABER, *Growth in Holiness,* ch. XV; R. DE MAUMIGNY, *Pratique de l'oraison mentale,* t. I; DOM LEHODEY, *The Ways of Mental Prayer,* P. I and II; LETOURNEAU, *La Méthode d'oraison mentale de S.-Sulpice;* CLARE, S. J., *Science of the Spiritual Life.*

The latter is defined as *a silent elevation and application of our mind and heart to God in order to offer Him our homages and to promote His glory by our advancement in virtue.*

It comprises five elements : 1) The *religious duties* rendered to God, or to Our Lord Jesus Christ, or to the Saints; 2) *considerations* bearing upon God and our personal relations with Him, in order to deepen and strengthen our convictions; 3) examination of conscience, in order to determine how we stand in relation to the subject of meditation; 4) *prayer* of petition by which we ask of God the graces necessary for exercising ourselves more perfectly in this or that particular virtue; 5) *resolutions* to do better in the future. These various acts need not follow in the order just described, nor must they all, of necessity, have a place in every meditation. Moreover, mental prayer must *be prolonged* over a notable period of time to deserve the name of meditation and to be distinguished from mere ejaculatory prayers.

As souls advance in perfection and acquire convictions which are easily renewed, they gradually devote less time to considerations and examinations, and give more to affections and petitions. These in turn become more and more simple, and at times mental prayer consists in a simple and loving gaze upon God. — This we shall explain later.

665. The **Origin** of Mental Prayer. We must carefully distinguish between *mental prayer in itself* and *methodical* mental prayer.

A) Meditation, or mental prayer, has always been practiced in one form or another. The books of the Prophets, the Psalms, the Sapiential Books are all full of meditations to nourish the devotion of the Chosen People. Our Lord, by insisting on the worship of God in spirit and truth, by spending whole nights in prayer, by the long prayer He offered at Gethsemane and upon Calvary, prepared the way for those saintly souls who through all ages to come would withdraw to the inner sanctuary of their hearts, therein to pray in secret to their God. Meditation or mental prayer, even in its highest forms, such as contemplation, is explicitly treated in the writings of Cassian and St. John Climacus, not to speak of the works of the Fathers. It may be said that St. Bernard's treatise *De Consideratione* is in reality a treatise on the necessity of reflection and of meditation. The School of St. Victor lays emphasis on meditation in order to arrive at contemplation, [1] and we know how strongly St. Thomas recommended it as a means of growing in the love of God and of giving ourselves to Him. [2]

---

[1] Cfr. HUGH OF S. VICTOR, *De modo dicendi et meditandi; De Meditando seu meditandi artificio,* P. L. CLXXVI, 877-880; 993-998.

[2] *Sum. theol.,* IIa IIæ, q. 82, a. 3.

666. B) Meditation as a methodical prayer dates from the XV Century. We find it explained in the *Rosetum* of John Mauburnus [1] and in the Benedictine writers of the same epoch. St. Ignatius in the *Spiritual Exercises* gives several methods of meditating, at once precise and varied. St. Theresa gives by far the best description of the different kinds of mental prayer. Her disciples have sketched the rules of systematic meditation. [2] St. Francis de Sales does not fail to trace a method of mental prayer for Philothea, and the French School of the XVII Century soon had its own method, perfected by Father Olier and Father Tronson, called today the method of St. Sulpice.

667. Meditation and Mental Prayer. The terms meditation and mental prayer are often interchanged. When differentiated, the former is applied to that form of mental prayer wherein considerations and reasonings predominate and which, owing to this, is called *discursive meditation.* The latter name is chiefly applied to those forms of mental prayer wherein pious affections or acts of the will are predominant. Discursive meditation itself, however, already contains affections, and affective prayer is ordinarily preceded or accompanied by some considerations, excepting the case when the soul is seized by the light of contemplation.

668. The kind of prayer generally suited to beginners is *discursive* meditation. They need it in order to acquire convictions or to strengthen them. There are, however, some souls who from the outset give considerable place to affections. But all must be taught that the best part of mental prayer lies in the acts of the will.

§ II. The Advantages and the Necessity of Mental Prayer

I. *The Advantages*

669. Meditation, as we have described it, is most helpful for the attainment of salvation and perfection.

1º It detaches us from sin and its causes. — When we sin, it is through *thoughtlessness* and *lack of will-power.* This twofold defect, however, is corrected by meditation.

a) It *enlightens* us as to the *malice of sin* and its fearful consequences, by showing it to us in the light of God, of eternity, and of what Jesus Christ did in order to atone for it. " It is meditation, " says Fr. Crasset, [3] " that leads us in spirit into the hallowed solitudes wherein we find God

---

[1] H. WATRIGANT, *La Méditation méthodique, Rev. d'Ascétique et de Myst.*, Jan. 1923, p. 13-29.
[2] V. P. JEAN DE JÉSUS MARIE, *Instruction des novices*, 3e Partie, chap. II, § 2.
[3] *Instructions sur l'Oraison*, Méthode d'oraison, ch. I, p. 253-254. Read the whole passage — *Engl. Transl.* A Key to meditation, p. 85-95.

alone — in peace, in calm, in silence, in recollection. The same it is that in spirit makes us descend to hell, therein to see our place; that brings us before the grave to see our last abode; that takes us up to Heaven to see our throne of glory; that carries us to the Valley of Josaphat to see Our Judge; to Bethlehem to see Our Savior; to Mount Thabor to see Our Love and to Calvary to see Our Model. " Meditation, likewise, detaches us from the *world* and its *false pleasures*. In reminds us of the instability of wordly goods, the anxiety they bring, the void, the ennui in which they plunge the soul. It forearms us against a false and corrupt world and makes us realize that God alone can constitute our bliss. Above all it detaches us from our pride and from our sensuality, by placing us before God Who is the fulness of being, and before our nothingness; by making us understand that sensual pleasure reduces us to the level of the brute, whilst godly joys ennoble us and make us soar unto God.

b) Meditation strengthens our will, not merely by providing us with strong convictions, as we have just said, but also by gradually healing our languor, our cowardice, and our fickleness. God's grace alone, our own efforts helping, can cure such infirmities. Now, meditation makes us ask for this grace all the more insistently, as it brings home to us through reflection our helplessness; whilst the acts of sorrow, of contrition that we perform, the firm purpose of amendment we conceive during meditation, together with the resolutions we take, already constitute an active co-operation with grace.

670. 2⁰ Meditation makes us also *practice all the great Christian virtues.* 1) It enlightens our *faith* by bringing before our eyes the eternal truths; it sustains our *hope* by giving us access to God to obtain His help; it enkindless our *love* by exposing to our view the beauty and the goodness of God. 2) It makes us prudent by supplying us with considerations to be taken into account before we act; it makes us *just* by having us conform our will to that of God; it renders us *strong* by making us share in God's own power; and temperate by cooling the ardor of our passions. There is no Christian virtue which we cannot acquire by daily meditation. Through it we hold fast to the truth, and truth, freeing us from our vices, makes us practice virtue : " *You shall know the truth : and the truth shall make you free.* " ¹

---

¹ *John*, VIII, 32.

671. 3° Meditation therefore *initiates* our *union* with God, nay more, our *transformation* into Him. It is, in fact, a conversation with God which from day to day becomes more intimate, more tender, and longer, since it continues the day long, even in the midst of our activities, n. 522. By virtue of daily intercourse with the Author of all perfection, we drink of His fulness, and are permeated by it, like the sponge by the water. We are transformed like the iron in the furnace that kindles, softens, and assumes the properties of living fire.

II. *The Necessity of Mental Prayer*

672. 1° **For the Laity. A)** Systematic meditation is a highly effective means of sanctification; however, *it is not necessary for the salvation of most Christians.* What is necessary is prayer by which we render homage to God and obtain grace. Evidently, this cannot be done without attention on the part of the mind and desire on the part of the heart. No doubt, to prayer must be joined the consideration of the great Christian truths and of the great Christian duties, together with self-examination. But we accomplish all these without the practice of systematic meditation, by simply listening to the religious instruction given in Church, by pious reading, and by the examination of conscience.

673. B) Meditation, however, is most *useful* and most *profitable* to all for salvation and perfection; to beginners, as well as to more advanced souls. It may be even said that it is the most *effective means of assuring one's salvation (n. 669).* This is the teaching of St. Alphonsus, who gives the following reason, that whilst habitually practicing the other exercises of piety, like the Rosary, the Little Office of the Blessed Virgin, fasting, etc.... one may, unfortunately, still continue to live in mortal sin, whilst the habitual practice of mental prayer cannot suffer one to remain long in such a state. One either relinquishes mental prayer or relinquishes sin. [1] How could we day by day go into the presence of God, the source of all holiness, while conscious of mortal sin, and not determine, with the help of grace, to break with sin and to seek in the Tribunal of Penance that pardon the supreme need of which we recognize? But, if we have no appointed time and no practical method for the consideration of the great religious truths, we allow ourselves

---

[1] *Praxis Confessarii*, n. 122.

to be carried away by dissipation of mind and the example of the world, until we lapse into sin and live in sin.

674.   2° The Moral Necessity of Mental Prayer for Diocesan Priests.   We do not speak here of those *Regulars,* who in the devout and prolonged recitation of the Divine Office, in their readings and in the prayers they offer may find the equivalent of mental prayer.   Nevertheless, we call attention to the fact that even in the Orders where the Office is recited in choir, the rule prescribes at least a half-hour of mental prayer, because meditation is the soul of all vocal prayers and insures their fervent recitation.   It should also be said that religious congregations dating from the XVI century insist even more upon mental prayer, and that the New Code directs superiors to see that all religious, unless they have a legitimate excuse, devote a certain amount of time each day to this exercise. [1]

But speaking of *diocesan priests,* absorbed in the activities of the ministry, we say that *the habitual exercise of mental prayer at an appointed time is morally necessary to their perseverance and to their sanctification.*   Their duties are many and heavy, and they are at times subjected to serious temptations, even while exercising their ministry.   Now, in order to resist these temptations and to fulfil all their duties with fidelity and in a supernatural way, they need deep convictions and choice graces, which as every one must admit are obtained through daily meditation.

675.   A) Nor let it be urged that the offering of the Holy Sacrifice and the recitation of the Divine Office replace mental prayer.   It is true that the Mass and the Breviary, attentively and devoutly said, are effective means of perseverance and progress in the spiritual life; yet, experience shows that priests absorbed in their ministerial work do not, as a matter of fact, acquit themselves well of these important duties, unless they develop in daily meditation the spirit of prayer and of interior recollection.   If a priest disregards this holy exercise, how can he, encompassed and pressed by labors, find the time to recollect himself and renew his sense of the supernatural?   If he fails in this, distracting thoughts invade his soul, even whilst he is engaged in the holiest occupations; his convictions weaken, his energy dwindles, his negligences and his failings grow, and lukewarmness ensues.   Should a serious, persistent, and

---

[1] *Can.* 595.

besetting temptation make its appearance, the strong convictions needed to repel the enemy are no longer clear to his mind, and he runs the risk of falling. [1] " If I meditate, " says Dom Chautard, " I am as it were clothed in steel armor, and *impervious* to the shafts of the enemy. Without mental prayer, I shall surely be their target. " The devout, learned and prudent Father Desurmont, one of the most experienced retreat-masters for priests, declares that " for the priest in the world, it is either meditation or a very great risk of damnation. " Cardinal Lavigerie writes in the same strain : " For an apostolic laborer, there is no alternative between holiness, if not acquired, at least desired and pursued (especially through daily meditation) and progressive perversion. " [2]

676. **B)** For the priest, it does not suffice to avoid sin. In order to fulfil the duties of *glorifying* God and *saving* souls he must be habitually united to Jesus Christ the Great High Priest, through Whom alone he can give glory to God and save men. Yet, how can the priest unite himself to Christ in the midst of the occupations and preoccupations of his ministry, if he does not set apart sufficient time to think leisurely and lovingly on that Divine Model, to draw unto himself through prayer His spirit, His dispositions, and His grace? Through this union the priest's energies are multiplied, his confidence increased, the fruitfulness of his ministry assured, for it is not he who speaks, but Jesus Who speaks through his lips : " *God as it were exhorting by us* " ; [3] it is not he who acts; he is but an instrument in God's hands. Because he strives to imitate the virtues of our Lord, his example wins souls even more than his words. If he gives up meditation, he loses the spirit of recollection and of prayer and he is but " sounding brass and a tinkling cymbal. " [4]

677. Hence, Pope Pius X, of holy memory, has proclaimed in clear terms the necessity of meditation for the priest : " *It is of the first importance that a certain time should be allotted every day for medi-*

---

[1] Let us ponder the following words of a priest reproduced by DOM CHAUTARD : " It is my overeagerness that has brought on my fall! My excessive devotion to the active life and my love for the same filled me with great joy at my success, and this together with the deceits of Satan led me to be so absorbed in laboring for others, as to neglect my own spiritual wants, prayer and meditation; and then when temptation came, I yielded in the weakness caused me by my lack of spiritual nourishment. " *The True Apostolate*, p. 67. All that this excellent writer says about the need of an interior life, applies to mental prayer which is one of the most effective means to foster this life.

[2] *L'âme de tout apostolat*, p. 179-180. Engl. Transl. *The True Apostolate*, p. 143-144.

[3] *II Cor.*, V, 20. — [4] *I Cor.*, XIII, 1.

tation on the things of eternity.   No priest can omit this without being guilty of serious negligence, to the detriment of his soul." [1]   The New Code bids Bishops to see that priests devote each day a certain time to the exercise of mental prayer, [2] and that students in seminaries do likewise. [3]   Are not such prescriptions equivalent to a proclamation of the moral necessity of meditation for ecclesiastics?

To advise priests absorbed in the parochial ministry to omit meditation so as to say their Mass and Office more devoutly is nothing less than a total ignorance of psychology.   Experience shows that, when mental prayer is absent, the devout recitation of the Office becomes well-nigh impossible ; it is said at odd moments with many attendant interruptions, and with the mind filled with the thoughts of other things.   It is, in fact, the morning meditation that guarantees the devout celebration of the Holy Sacrifice and that enables a priest to recollect himself before beginning his Office and to make its recitation a real prayer.

678.   What we say of the priest, can be said also to a certain extent of those *devoted men* and *women* who dedicate part of their time to works of zeal.   If they want their apostolate to be fruitful, it must be vivified by the spirit of recollection and by prayer.   Let it not be urged that the time consecrated to this exercise is taken from works of zeal.   It would be to approach closely to the error of Pelagius to imagine that action is more necessary than grace and prayer, whereas in reality works of zeal are all the more fruitful, as they are inspired by a life of greater interior recollection, which is in turn nourished by mental prayer.

§ III. General Characteristics of the Meditation of Beginners

We have already said that the mental prayer of beginners is chiefly a *discursive* prayer, wherein, though the affections have their place, reasoning predominates.   We now explain : 1º the ordinary *subjects* of their meditation, and 2º the *obstacles* they meet.

I. *The Subjects upon which Beginners Meditate*

679.   They must, in general, meditate upon whatever is calculated to inspire them with a *growing horror* for sin, upon the *causes* of their own faults, upon *mortification* that removes such causes, upon the principal *duties of their state*, upon *fidelity* to grace and its *abuse*, upon *Jesus Christ, a model for penitent sinners.*

680.   1º In order to acquire a *growing horror for sin*, they must meditate : **a)** on the *end* of man and of the Christian, and hence upon

---

[1] *Exhortation to the Clergy,* Aug. 4, 1908. — [2] *Can.* 125, 2º. — [3] *Can.* 1367, 1º.

the *creation* of man, his *elevation* to the supernatural state, his fall and his redemption (n. 59-87) ; upon the *rights of God* as Creator, Sanctifier, and Redeemer; upon such of the divine attributes as would inspire them with a horror for sin, for instance, God's *immensity*, whereby He is present to all creatures and especially to the soul in the state of grace; upon His *holiness* whereby He is bound to hate sin; upon His *justice* which punishes it; upon His *mercy* that moves Him to forgive it. All these truths tend to make us flee from sin, the one obstacle to the attainment of our end, the one enemy of God, the destroyer of that supernatural life given to us by God as the great proof of His love for us, and restored to us by the Redeemer at the price of His Blood.

b) Upon *sin :* its origin, punishment, malice, and frightful consequences, n. 711-735; upon the *causes* leading to sin : the world, the flesh, and the devil, n. 193-227.

c) Upon the means of *expiating and preventing* sin : penance, n. 705, and the mortification of our different faculties, of our evil tendencies, and chiefly of the seven capital vices. From our meditations on these points we shall draw the conclusion that there is no safety as long as we have not uprooted or at least controlled all these disordered inclinations.

681. 2° Beginners must also choose for the subject of meditation all the *positive duties of the Christian :* 1) *General* duties of religion toward God, of charity toward the neighbor, of mistrust of self on account of our helplessness and wretchedness. What will impress beginners most will be the external acts of these virtues; but this will be a preparation for the more perfect practice of the same virtues in the illuminative way. — 2) *Particular* duties, according to age, condition, sex, state of life. The fulfilment of these duties will prove to be the best kind of penance.

682. 3° Since *grace* plays an all-important *rôle* in the Christian life, beginners must be gradually instructed in this doctrine. The spiritual director, then, will explain to them in a familiar and easy way the doctrine of the indwelling of the Holy Ghost in our souls, of our incorporation into Christ, of habitual grace, of the virtues and of the seven gifts. At first, no doubt, they will grasp but the mere elements of these great truths, but even the little they will understand will not fail to exert a powerful influence on their spiritual formation and their spiritual progress. It is when we think of what God has done and incessantly does for us, that we are prompted to further generosity in His service. We should not forget that St. Paul and St. John preached these truths to pagan neophytes who were but beginners in the spiritual life.

683. 4° Then it will be easy and practical to propose *Jesus* as the *model for true penitents :* Jesus condemning Himself to a life of poverty, of obedience and of toil that He might be unto us an example; Jesus, doing penance for us in the desert, in the Garden of Gethsemane, in His cruel passion; Jesus dying for us upon the Cross. This series of meditations, presented to us by the Church in the yearly cycle of the liturgy, will have the advantage of making us practice penance in union with Jesus with greater generosity, with a greater love, and hence with greater efficacy.

II. *The Obstacles Encountered by Beginners*

The special difficulties encountered by beginners in meditation arise from their *inexperience*, their *lack of generosity*, and chiefly from the many *distractions* to which they are subject.

684. **A**) On account of their *inexperience* they are liable to turn their mental prayer into a sort of philosophical or theological *thesis*, or into a kind of *sermon* to themselves. This is not, indeed, a complete loss of time, since even this kind of meditation makes them give thought to the great truths of religion and strengthens their convictions. They would, however, derive greater profit if they proceeded in a more *practical* and in a more *supernatural* way.

This a spiritual director must teach them. He should point out to them : **a**) that considerations, if they are to bear practical fruit, must be made more personal, be applied to themselves and be followed by an examination in order to see to what extent the truths on which they meditate influence their lives, and what must be done in order to live by these truths during the course of the day ; **b**) that the most important part of meditation is found in the acts of the will : acts of adoration, thanksgiving and love toward God ; acts of humility, of sorrow, of firm purpose of amendment ; acts of petition to obtain the grace of correcting their faults ; and finally, firm and frequently repeated resolutions of doing better throughout the day.

685. **B**) Their *lack of generosity* exposes them to *discouragement* when they are no longer upheld by the sensible consolations God graciously bestowed on them at the outset in order to draw them unto Himself. Obstacles and the first spells of aridity dishearten them, and thinking themselves abandoned by God, they drift into carelessness. Hence, they must be made to see that what God asks is *effort* and *not success*, that perseverance in prayer, despite difficulties, is so much the richer in merit, and that God having proved Himself so generous towards them, to turn back when effort is required, would be an act of cowardice. These directions should be tempered by the mildness with which they are given and by paternal words of comfort.

686. **C**) The greatest obstacle, however, comes from *distractions*. Since in the first stages of the spiritual life, our imagination, our feelings and our attachments are far from being mastered, worldly and ofttimes dangerous fancies, useless thoughts and the divers emotional movements of the heart invade the soul at the very time of meditation. The help of the spiritual director is here of capital importance.

a) He should first of all remind them of the distinction between *wilful*[1] distractions and those that are not, bidding his penitents to concern themselves merely with the former in order to diminish their number. To succeed in this: 1) they must repel such distractions *promptly, vigorously* and *persistently, as soon as they become aware of them.* Even if these distractions are many and grievous, they are not culpable unless they are voluntary; the effort made to repel them is a meritorious act. Should they recur a hundred times and be a hundred times repulsed, the meditation will be excellent and worth far more than one made with fewer distractions but with little effort.

687. 2) They must humbly acknowlege their weakness, explicitly unite themselves to Our Lord, and offer to God His worship and His prayers. If need be, a book may be used, the better to fix the attention.

b) It is not enough to drive off distractions. In order to reduce their number, we must *attack their causes.* Many of them proceed from a lack of preparation or from an habitual dissipation of mind. 1) Beginners thus troubled with distractions should, therefore, be urged to prepare their meditation more carefully on the night before, not by merely reading the points, but by trying to see how the subject of the meditation is of practical advantage to them personally, and by thinking about it before falling asleep, instead of letting their mind become a prey to useless or unwholesome reveries. 2) Above all, beginners must be taught the means of controlling the imagination and the memory. In proportion as the soul grows in the practice of habitual recollection and detachment, distractions become less numerous.

§ VI. The Principal Methods of Mental Prayer

688. Since mental prayer is a difficult art, the Saints have ever been eager to offer counsel on the means of succeeding therein. One finds excellent advice in Cassian,

---

[1] Distractions are voluntary *in themselves* when they are deliberately willed, or when, aware that our mind wanders, we do nothing to prevent its vagaries. They are voluntary in *their cause,* when we foresee that such or such all-absorbing reading or occupation will be a source of distractions, and none the less we indulge in it.

St. John Climacus and other spiritual writers. It was not, however, until the XV Century that *methods* properly so called were elaborated, which have since guided souls in the ways of mental prayer.

Because at first sight these methods appear rather *intricate*, it is well, before introducing beginners to their use, to prepare them by what may be called *meditative reading*. They should be told to read some devout works, like the First Book of the *Following of Christ*, the *Spiritual Combat* or some work containing brief, solid meditations; and they should be taught to follow up this reading by asking themselves the following questions : 1º Am I thoroughly convinced that what I have just read is useful and necessary to the welfare of my soul? How can I strengthen this conviction? 2º Have I up to the present exercised myself in such an important practice? 3º What must I do today in order to improve? If an earnest prayer is added asking for the grace that one may carry out the resolutions taken, all the essential elements of a real meditation will be contained in such reading.

I. *Points Common to all Methods of Mental Prayer*

We find in all the various methods certain common traits which are manifestly the most essential; hence, attention must be called to them.

689. 1º There is always a *remote*, a *proximate*, and an *immediate* **preparation.**

a) The *remote* preparation is nothing more than the effort to make our daily life harmonize with prayer. It comprises three things : 1) the mortification of the senses and of the passions; 2) habitual recollection; 3) humility. These are, in fact, excellent dispositions for a good meditation. At the beginning they are imperfect; still, they suffice to enable us to meditate with some profit, and later on they will become more and more perfect in proportion as progress is made in mental prayer.

b) The *proximate* or, as others call it, the less remote preparation, includes three principal acts : 1) to select the subject of meditation on the preceding evening; 2) to revolve it in our mind in the morning upon awakening, and to excite in our heart corresponding sentiments; 3) to approach meditation with earnestness, confidence, and humility, desiring to give glory to God and to improve our life. In this way the soul is placed in the best dispositions to enter into conversation with God.

c) The *immediate* preparation, which is in reality the beginning of meditation itself, consists in placing ourselves in the presence of God Who is present everywhere especially within our heart, in acknowledging ourselves unworthy and incapable of meditating, and in imploring the aid of the Holy Ghost that He supply our insufficiency.

690. 2° Within the **body of the meditation,** the different methods likewise contain more or less explicitly the same fundamental acts:

a) Acts of worship rendering to the Majesty of God the *religious homage* due to Him.

b) *Considerations,* to convince ourselves of the necessity or the great importance of the virtue we want to acquire, so that we may all the more earnestly pray for the grace of practicing it, and firmly determine to make efforts necessary to co-operate with grace.

c) *Self-examinations,* to see our failings in this regard and survey the progress yet to be made.

d) *Prayers* or *petitions,* asking for the grace of growing in the said virtue and of using the means conducive thereto.

e) *Resolutions,* whereby we determine from that very moment to practice that virtue.

691. 3° The **conclusion,** which brings the meditation to a close, includes : 1) an *act of thanskgiving* for the favors received ; 2) a *review* of the manner in which we have made our meditation with the view to improve thereon the following day ; 3) a final *prayer* asking the blessing of Our Heavenly Father ; 4) the selection of some impressive thought or some telling maxim, which will during the day recall to our mind the ruling idea of our meditation.

The different methods are reduced to two principal types called respectively the method of *St. Ignatius* and the method of *St. Sulpice.*

II. *The Method of St. Ignatius* [1]

692. In the *Spiritual Exercises* St. Ignatius presents several methods of mental prayer, according to the subjects

[1] *Spiritual Exercises,* Ist Week, Ist Exercise ; (Translation by Father Rickaby, S. J.); See CLARE, S. J. *The Science of the Spiritual Life;* CRASSET, *A Key to Meditation;* FABER, *Growth in Holiness,* C. XV.

meditated upon and the results desired.   The one best adapted to beginners is the one called *the exercise of the three faculties*, so named because it consists in the exercise of the memory, the understanding and the will, the three chief faculties of the soul.   It is explained in the First Week of the Exercises in connection with the meditation on sin.

693.   1° The Beginning of the Meditation.   It begins

by a *preparatory prayer* in which we beg of God that our intentions and all our actions be solely directed to the service and honor of the Divine Majesty.

Two preludes follow : a) *the first*, which is the *composition of place*, has for its purpose to center the imagination and fasten the attention upon the subject of the meditation, the more easily to banish distractions.   1) If the object *falls under the senses*, for instance if it is one of the mysteries of Our Lord, it is presented to the mind as vividly as possible, not like an event having taken place in the distant past, but as if one were actually witnessing the facts and taking part in them. 2) If the object does not fall under the senses, e. g. sin, " the *composition of place* will consist in picturing and considering my soul imprisoned in this mortal body, and myself, that is, my body and my soul, in this vale of tears, exiled, as it were, midst animals devoid of reason " ; in other words, one considers sin in some of its effects in order to conceive a horror for it.

b) The *second prelude* consists in asking God what we want and desire, for example, shame and confusion at the sight of our sins.   As can be seen, the practical purpose of the meditation — the resolution — is clearly pointed out from the very outset : *In all things look to the end.*

694.   2° The Body of the Meditation.   This consists

in the application of the three faculties of the soul, the *memory*, the *understanding*, and the *will*, to each point of the meditation.   *Each* faculty is *in turn* applied to *each* point, unless one point furnishes adequate matter for the meditation.   It is not necessary in every meditation to make all the acts ; it is good to dwell upon the affections and sentiments which the subject suggests.

a) The exercise of the *memory* is performed by recalling the first point of the meditation, not in detail, but as a whole ; thus, says St. Ignatius : " This exercise of the memory as regards the sin of the Angels consists in calling to mind how they were created in a state of innocence ; how they refused to employ their freedom in rendering their Creator and Master the homage and obedience due to Him ; how pride, taking possession of them, they passed from the state of grace to a state of reprobation, and were cast from Heaven into Hell. "

b) The exercise of *the understanding* consists in reflecting in detail upon the same subject.   St. Ignatius proceeds no further, but Father Roothaan supplements his teaching by explaining that the office of the *understanding* is to make reflections upon the truths the memory has proposed, to make application thereof to the soul and the soul's needs, to draw therefrom practical conclusions, to weigh the motives for resolutions, to consider how we have heretofore conformed our conduct to the truths upon which we meditate, and how we must conduct ourselves with regard to them in the future.

c) The *will* has two duties to fulfil : to conceive *devout affections* and to form *good resolutions.* 1) The *affections,* indeed, must find a place in all parts of the meditation, at least they must occur very frequently, since it is these that make the meditation a real prayer ; but it is chiefly toward the end of the meditation that they are to be multiplied. One must not be concerned about the manner of expressing them ; the simpler the manner, the better they are. When some good sentiment spontaneously lays hold of us, it is well to entertain it as long as we can and until our devotion is satisfied. 2) The resolutions should be *practical,* designed to improve our life, and therefore *particular,* accommodated to our *present condition,* and capable of being carried out that very day ; they must be based upon *solid* motives. They must be humble and therefore accompanied by prayers to obtain the grace of carrying them into execution.

695. 3° **The Conclusion.** This comprises three things : a *summary view* of the various resolutions already taken ; devout *colloquies* with God the Father, Our Lord, the Blessed Virgin or some Saint ; and lastly, the review of the meditation, or the examination upon the way we have made it, in order to note its imperfections and to seek a remedy for them.

To give a clearer understanding of the method, we add the following synoptic table of the *preludes*, of the *body of the prayer*, and of the *conclusion*.

I. Preludes
- 1° A rapid recall of the truth to be considered
- 2° The *composition of place* through the imagination
- 3° The petition for a special grace in harmony with the subject

II. Body of the Meditation. Exercise of :

1° The *Memory* by
- A representation of the subject as a whole together with the chief circumstances

2° The *Understanding* by asking :
- 1° What should I consider in this subject?
- 2° What practical conclusions should I draw from it?
- 3° What are my motives in drawing these conclusions?
- 4° How have I heretofore lived up to this?
- 5° What must I do in the future the better to conform my life thereto?
- 6° What obstacles must I remove?
- 7° What means must I employ?

3° The *Will* by
- 1° Affections produced during the entire course of the meditation, especially at the end
- 2° Resolutions taken at the end of each point : practical, personal, sound, humble, full of trust

III. Conclusion

1° Colloquies : with God, Jesus Christ, the Blessed Virgin, the Saints

2° Review
- 1° How have I made this meditation?
- 2° Wherein and why have I failed, or succeeded?
- 3° What practical conclusions have I drawn? What requests have I made? What resolutions have I formed? What lights have I received?
- 4° Choice of a thought as a reminder of the meditation.

696. Advantages of this method. As may be readily observed, this method is highly *psychological* and highly *practical.* **a)** It lays hold of all the faculties, the imagination included ; applies them one after the other to the subject of meditation, and thus introduces an element of *variety* that makes it possible to consider a truth under its different aspects, to revolve it in our mind so as to assimilate it, to form convictions, and above all to draw therefrom practical conclusions for the present day.

b) Whilst this method lays emplasis upon *the important part played by the will*, which acts only after lengthy consideration of the motives, it does not minimize the *role of grace*, since one begs for it from the very outset, and again in the colloquies at the conclusion.

c) It is most suitable to *beginners*, for it states precisely, to the minutest details, what must be done from the preparation to the conclusion and thus prevents the faculties from wandering. Besides, it does not presuppose a deep knowledge of dogma, but only the contents of the Catechism, and hence adapts itself easily to the laity.

d) When *simplified,* this method is just as well suited to the *most advanced* souls; in fact, if one limits it to the main outline traced by St. Ignatius, it can be easily transformed into an *affective* prayer, which allows a wide scope to the inspirations of grace. The important thing is to know how to make an intelligent use of it under the wise guidance of an experienced spiritual director.

e) It has at times been criticized on the score that it does not give due prominance to Our Lord Jesus Christ. True, in the exercise of the three faculties Our Lord's place is but incidental; but St. Ignatius has given us other methods, in particular, that of the contemplation of Mysteries and the application of the senses wherein Our Lord becomes the central object of the meditation. [1]

There is nothing to hinder beginners from employing one or the other. The objection, therefore, has no foundation if the Ignatian methods are thouroughly followed.

III. *The Method of St. Sulpice* [2]

697. A) Origin. This method, coming after several others, has been influenced by them as to the details; but its underlying idea and broad lines originated with Cardinal de Bérulle, Father de Condren, and Father Olier, whilst the supplementary details are the work of Father Tronson.

a) The *underlying thought* is that of union with the Incarnate Word in order to render through Him the religious homage due to God and to reproduce in ourselves the virtues of Jesus Christ.

b) The three *essential acts* are: 1) *Adoration*, wherein we consider one of the attributes or one of the perfections of God, or else some virtue of Our Lord as the model of that virtue we are to practice. Then we offer to God or to Our Lord, or to God through Our Lord,

---

[1] We shall explain these methods when we treat of the *illuminative* way.
[2] G. LETOURNEAU, *La Méthode d'oraison mentale du Sém. de S.-Sulpice,* Paris, 1903, especially p. 321-332; FABER, *Growth in Holiness,* C. XV.

our religious homage in the form of adoration, admiration, praise, thanksgiving, love, joy or compassion. By thus paying our duties to the Author of grace we render Him propitious to our prayers. 2) *Communion*, whereby through prayer, we draw unto ourselves the perfection or the virtue which we have adored and admired in God or in Jesus Christ. 3) *Co-operation*, wherein under the influence of grace we determine to practice that virtue by forming at least one resolution which we strive to put into practice that very day.

This is the broad outline found in Cardinal de Bérulle, Father de Condren and Father Olier. As found in these writers it is rather a method of affective prayer, cf. n. 994-997.

698. B) The additions of Father Tronson. It is evident that this meagre outline, sufficient to souls already advanced, would prove inadequate for *beginners*. This was readily perceived at the Seminary of St. Sulpice, and whilst preserving the spirit and the essential elements of the original method, Father Tronson added to the second point, the communion, the *considerations* and *self-examinations* so indispensable to those that begin to meditate. Thus, once convinced of the importance or necessity of a virtue and realizing their lack of it, they ask for it with more earnestness, humility and perseverance. In this method, then, *prayer* is stressed even for beginners as the chief element of meditation. Hence, the name given to the third point — *Co-operation* — to remind us that our good purposes are more the effect of grace than of our own volitions, but that on the other hand grace works nothing in us without our co-operation, and that all the day long we are to work with Jesus Christ in striving to reproduce that virtue which has been the subject of our meditation.

699. C) A Summary of the Method. The following table will give an adequate idea of the method. We omit the *remote* preparation which is the same as the one explained in n. 689.

I. Preparation	**Proximate** or **Less Remote**	1° To choose the subject of the meditation the night before and determine what we are to consider in Our Lord; to foresee in particular, the considerations and requests we are to make and the resolutions we are to take.
		2° To remain henceforth in great recollection and keep in our mind the subject of the meditation whilst going to sleep.
		3° Upon rising in the morning, to avail ourselves of the first free time to make our meditation.
	Immediate	1° To place ourselves in the presence of God, present everywhere and especially in our heart.
		2° To humble ourselves before God at the sight of our sins. Contrition. Recitation of the *Confiteor*. Act of union with Our Lord.
		3° To acknowledge ourselves incapable of praying as we ought. Invocation of the Holy Ghost: recitation of the *Veni, Sancte Spiritus*.

II. Body of the Meditation

Ist point, Adoration: Jesus before our Eyes

1° To consider the subject of our meditations in God, in Our Lord, or in one of the Saints : **His sentiments, words, actions.**

2° To offer our homage: **adoration, admiration, praise, thanksgiving, love, joy,** or **compassion.**

2nd point, Communion: Jesus in our heart

1° To **convince** ourselves of the necessity or importance of the virtue through motives of faith, through reasoning or through a detailed examination.

2° To **reflect** on our conduct with **sorrow** for the past, **confusion** for the present, and **desire** for the future.

3° To **beseech** God to grant us the virtue upon which we are meditating. (It is chiefly through this prayer that we participate in the virtues of Our Lord). — To beg also of God whatever else we need, to pray for the needs of the Church, and of all those for whom we are bound to pray.

3rd point, Co-operation: Jesus in our hands

1° To form a resolution : particular, present, efficacious, humble.

2° To renew the resolution relative to our particular examination.

III. Conclusion

1° To thank God for the many graces He has bestowed upon us during the course of our meditation.

2° To beg His pardon for our faults and negligences during this holy exercise.

3° To beseech Him to bless our resolutions, the present day, our life, our death.

4° To select some striking thought that impressed us during our meditation in order to remember it during the day and thus recall our resolutions.

5° To place ourselves and the fruit of our meditation in the hands of the Blessed Virgin.

Sub tuum præsidium

700. D) Characteristics of this method. a) The method is based upon the doctrine of our *incorporation into Christ* (n. 142-149), and upon the resultant obligation of reproducing in ourselves His interior dispositions and His virtues. To succeed therein we must, as Father Olier puts it, have *Jesus before our eyes*, in order to gaze upon Him as our model and offer Him our homage — adoration; we must have Him *in our heart*, drawing unto us through prayer His sentiments and His virtues — communion; we must have Him *in our hands*, sharing with Him in the work of repro-

ducing His virtues — co-operation.   An intimate union
with Jesus, then, is the soul of this method.

b) It places the duty *of religion* (reverence and love
towards God) before that of petition.   God comes first!
The God it places before us is not an abstract, philosophical
concept, but a concrete, personal God, the living God of the
Gospels, the Most Blessed Trinity living in us.

c) In asserting the need both of grace and of our co-
operation, *it lays the emphasis upon grace* and hence upon
prayer, whilst at the same time it demands the energetic
and persevering effort of the will, of specific, pertinent,
oft-renewed resolutions on the keeping of which we examine
ourselves at the end of the day.

701.   d) It is a method of affective prayer supported by
considerations.   It begins with religious sentiments in the
first point; the *considerations* in the second are designed to
elicit from the heart acts of faith in the supernatural truths
on which we meditate, acts of hope in the Divine mercy,
acts of love towards God's infinite goodness; the *self-examinations* are accompanied by sorrow for the past, confusion
for the present, and a firm purpose of amendment for the
future; the aim of all these acts being to prepare a humble,
confident and persevering *prayer*.   In order to prolong this
petition, the method furnishes various motives, explained at
length, and further suggests a prayer for the whole Church
and for certain souls in particular.   The resolutions are to
be made with distrust of self, absolute confidence in Jesus
Christ, and accompanied by a prayer that we may be
enabled to put them into effect.   Lastly, the conclusion is
but a series of acts of gratitude, of humility and further
petitions.   Thus we avoid giving a too philosophical turn to
our reasoning and to our considerations, and prepare the
way for affective prayer and for prayer of simplicity; for
the method tells us that it is not necessary always to
perform all these acts, or in the order prescribed, but that
we should rather abandon ourselves to the affections that
God excites in us, and repeat frequently those to which we
feel particularity attracted by the Holy Ghost.   No doubt,
beginners as a rule give more time to reasoning than to
other acts, yet they are constantly reminded by the method
that affections are preferable, and thus they gradually give
to them a larger place in their meditation.

e) This method is especially suited to *priests and seminarians*.   It continually reminds them that being other
Christs by virtue of their character and their powers, they

should be so likewise in their dispositions and virtues, and that all their perfection consists in causing Jesus to live and to grow in their souls.

702.	These two methods, then, have their respective excellence according to the special object they have in view. The same may be said of all the other methods, which more or less approach one of these two types. [1] It is well that there are many of them, so that each one may with the advice of his director choose, according to his own super-natural attractions, the method that suits him best.

As Father Poulain [2] says, these methods are like the numerous rules of rhetoric and logic; beginners must be taught these, but once they have been so schooled in them that they possess their spirit and their elements, they need but follow the broad lines of the method, and then, without ceasing to be active, they give greater heed to the move-ments of the Holy Ghost.

CONCLUSION : THE EFFICACY OF PRAYER FOR THE
PURIFICATION OF THE SOUL

703.	From what we have just said, we may easily infer how helpful and how necessary mental prayer is for the purification of the soul.	**a)** In the prayer of *worship*, we offer God the homage due to Him : we admire, praise and bless His infinite perfections — His holiness, His justice, His goodness, His loving mercy. He in turn lovingly stoops down to forgive us, to inspire us with a deep horror of sin which offends Him, and to protect us against fresh faults. **b)** In *meditation*, we form, under the influence of divine light and of our own reflections, strong convictions on the malice of sin, on its frightful consequences in this life and in the life to come, on the means of expiating it and avoiding it in the future. Our heart is then filled with sentiments of shame, of humiliation, of love of God, of hatred of sin, together with purpose of amendment, and thus our faults are washed away more and more in penitential tears and in the Blood of Christ. Our will is fortified against the slightest surren-ders, and we embrace generously the practice of penance

---

[1] We make special mention of the method of St. Francis de Sales, *Devout Life*, II Part. ch. II-VII; of that of the Discalced Carmelites, *Instruction des Novices* by V. P. J. de Jésus-Marie, III Part. ch. II; Aurelianus a SS. Sacramento, *Cursus Asceticus* Vol. I, disput. III, sect. I; of that of the Reformed Cistercians, *Directoire Spirituel* by Dom Lehodey, 1910, sect. V, ch. IV; of that of the Dominicans *Instruction des Novices*, by Fr. Cormier.

[2] *Etudes*, 20 mars 1898, p. 782, note 2.

and self-denial. **c)** In the prayer of *petition*, supported by the infinite merits of Christ, we are the recipients of abundant graces to practice humility, penance, trust and love; these graces complete the cleansing of our soul, strengthen it against temptation, and ground it in virtue, chiefly in the virtues of penance and *mortification*, which complete the work of prayer.

704. Advice to spiritual directors. Mental prayer cannot be too strongly urged upon those who want to advance in the way of perfection. Spiritual directors should instruct them in its practice as early as possible. They should, likewise, have their penitents give an account of the difficulties they encounter in this exercise, in order to help them to overcome them, to show them how they can improve their method of meditation, and above all how they may avail themselves of this exercise to correct their faults, practice the contrary virtues, and gradually acquire the spirit of prayer, which, along with penance, will effect the transformation of their souls.

CHAPTER II

Penance

We shall briefly state the *necessity* and the *notion* of penance; then we shall explain: 1° The *motives* that should prompt us to *hate* and *avoid* sin; 2° the *motives* and the *means* of atoning for sin.

Necessity and Notion of Penance.

Art. I. — Hatred of sin $\begin{cases} \text{mortal} \\ \text{venial} \end{cases}$

Art. II. — Atonement for sin $\begin{cases} \text{motives} \\ \text{means} \end{cases}$

THE NECESSITY AND NOTION OF PENANCE [1]

705. Penance is, after prayer, the most effective means for *cleansing the soul of past faults* and even for guarding it against future ones.

---

[1] St. THOM. III, q. 85; SUAREZ, *De Pænitentiâ*, disp. I et VII; BILLUART, *De Pænit.*, disp. II; AD. TANQUEREY, *Synop. Theol. Mor.*, t. I, n. 3-14; BOSSUET, *Serm. sur la nécessité de la pénitence*, édit. Lebarcq, 1897, t. IV, 596, t. V, 419; BOURDALOUE, *Carême, pour le Lundi de la deuxième Semaine;* NEWMAN, *Disc. to Mixed Congregations*, Neglect of Divine Calls; FABER, *Growth in Holiness,*

1° When Our Lord is about to begin His public ministry, He has His Precursor proclaim the necessity of penance : "*Do penance : for the kingdom of heaven is at hand.*" [1] He Himself declares He has come to call sinners to repentance: "*I came not to call the just, but sinners to penance.*" [2] This virtue is so necessary, that unless we do penance we shall perish : "*But except you do penance, you shall all* likewise perish.*" [3] So well was this doctrine understood by the Apostles, that from the very first they insisted on the necessity of penance as a condition preparatory to Baptism : "*Do penance : and be baptized every one of you.*" [4] For the sinner penance is an act of justice; for having offended God and violated God's rights, he is bound to make reparation for the outrage. This he does through penance.

706. 2° Penance is *defined as a supernatural virtue, allied to justice, which inclines the sinner to detest his sin because it is an offence against God, and to form the firm resolve of avoiding sin in the future, and of atoning for it.*

Hence, it includes four chief acts, the origin and inter-relation of which may be readily perceived. 1) In the light of reason and of faith, we see that sin is an evil, the greatest evil, in truth the only evil, and this because it offends God and deprives us of the most precious gifts. This evil we *hate* with our whole soul : " I have hated iniquity. " 2) Moreover, conscious that this evil is ours since we have sinned, and that, even once forgiven, its traces remain in our soul, we conceive a lively *sorrow*, a sorrow that weighs upon and crushes the soul, a sincere *contrition*, a deep sense of humiliation. 3) To avoid in the future this heinous evil we form the *firm resolve* or the *firm purpose* of avoiding it, by carefully shunning dangerous occasions and by fortifying our will against the allurements of sinful pleasures. 4) Lastly, realizing that sin constitutes an act of *injustice*, we determine to *atone* for it, to *expiate* it by sentiments and works of penance.

ART. I. MOTIVES FOR HATING AND AVOIDING SIN [5]

Before explaining these motives, [6] we shall explain what mortal sin is and what venial sin is.

C. XIX and XX; TISSOT, *Profiting by Our Faults;* MANNING, *Sin and Its Consequences, The Love of Jesus for Penitent Sinners;* HEDLEY, *Retreat,* C. VII; MEYER, *Science of the Saints,* C. XIII; ST. FRANCIS DE SALES, *Devout Life,* P. I, C. V-VIII.
[1] *Matth.,* III, 2; — [2] *Luke,* V, 32; — [3] *Luke,* XIII, 5. — [4] *Acts,* II, 38.
[5] ST. THOMAS, Iᵃ IIæ, q. 85-89; SUAREZ, *De Peccatis,* disp. I-III; disp. VII-VIII; PHILIP. A S. TRINITATE, *Sum. theol. mysticæ,* Iᵃ P., tr. II, discursus I ; ANTON. A SPIRITU S., *Directorium mysticum,* disp. I, sect. III; TH. DE VALLGORNERA, *Mystica theol.,* q. II, disp. I, a. III-IV; ALVAREZ DE PAZ, T. II, P. I, De Abjectione peccatorum; BOURDALOUE, *Carême* mercredi de la 5ᵉ sem., sur l'état du péché et l'état de grâce; TRONSON, *Ex. Part.,* CLXX-CLXXX; MANNING, *Sin and its Consequences;* MGR. D'HULST, *Carême 1892; Retraite;* P. JANVIER, *Carême 1903,* 1ᵉ Conf.; *Carême 1908,* entirely. — *See other references,* no. 705.
[6] We develop the treatment of these motives somewhat at length, in order that the reader may be able to *meditate* on them. Once a lively horror of sin is conceived progress in the spiritual life is assured.

707. Notion and Species of Sin. Sin is a *wilful trans-gression of the law of God.* Hence, it is an act of *disobedience* to God, an *offence* against Him; for it is the choice of our own will in preference to His, and thereby a violation of the sovereign right God has to our submission.

708. a) Mortal Sin. When, with full advertence and with full consent we transgress in grave matter a law that is important, necessary to the attainment of our end, the sin is *mortal,* because it deprives us of habitual grace which is the supernatural life of the soul (n. 105). This is why St. Thomas defines mortal sin as "*an act whereby we turn away from God, our last end, willingly attaching ourselves in an inordinate manner to some created good.*" By the loss of habitual grace, which unites us to God, we turn away from Him.

709. b) Venial Sin. When the law we violate is not necessary to the attainment of our end, or when we violate such a law, but in a slight matter, or if the law is grave in itself, but we transgress it either without full advertence or without full consent, the sin is but *venial* and does not deprive us of the state of grace. Our soul still remains in union with God, since we want to do His will in all things necessary, to abide in His friendship and attain our end. Still, venial sin is truly a violation of God's law, constituting an offence against the majesty of the Law-giver.

§ I. Mortal Sin [1]

710. If we would pass sound judgment on grave sin, we must consider: 1º What it is *in the sight of God;* 2º What it is *in itself;* 3º What are its *baneful* effects. If through meditation we realize thoroughly these teachings of faith we shall conceive an invincible hatred of sin.

I. *What Mortal Sin is in the Sight of God*

To form an idea of what mortal sin is in God's eyes, let us see how He *punishes* it and how He *condemns* it in Holy Writ.

711. 1º **How God punishes mortal sin. A)** *In the rebel angels.* These committed but a single sin, an interior sin, a sin of pride; and God, their Creator and Father, God, Who loved them, not only as the work of His hands, but as

---

[1] ST. IGNATIUS, *Spiritual Exercises,* 1st Week, 1st Exercise; See also his numerous commentators.

His adopted children, punished their rebellion by casting them into Hell, where through all eternity they will remain separated from God and deprived of all bliss. And withal, God is just and punishes no one beyond his deserts; He is merciful even in His punishments, and tempers the rigors of His justice with His goodness. Sin, then, must be something abominable to merit such a terrible sanction.

712. B) *In our first parents.* They had been endowed with all manner of gifts, natural, preternatural and supernatural, n. 52-66; but having likewise committed a sin of disobedience and pride, they were directly despoiled, along with the life of grace, of all the free gifts that had been bestowed upon them; were banished from Paradise and left to bequeath their posterity that dismal heritage of original sin, the sad consequences of which actually weigh upon us all (n. 69-75). Still, God bore our first parents the love of a father and allowed them the joy of intimacy with Him. If an all-just and all-merciful God visited such a severe punishment upon them and their posterity, it is because sin is a frightful evil, an evil which we can never sufficiently detest.

713. C) *In the person of His Son.* In order not to let man perish forever and in order to safeguard the rights both of justice and of mercy, the Eternal Father sends His Son into the world, makes Him the Head of the human race and lays upon Him the charge of atoning for and expiating sin in our stead. And what is the price of this redemption? Three and thirty years of humiliation and pain, ending in the unspeakable torture of body and mind at Gethsemane, before the Sanhedrim, in the Pretorium, upon Calvary! If we would learn what sin is, let us follow the Savior of the world, step by step, from the Stable to the Cross, through that *hidden* life of obscurity, of submission, of poverty, of toil; through His *apostolic* life of fatigues and failures, midst the ill-will and persecutions He was made to endure; through His *suffering* life, wherein He underwent such anguish of body and soul from friend and foe, so that He could well be called *the Man of Sorrows.* If we would know what sin is, let us face this truth: " *He was wounded for our iniquities: He was bruised for our sins.* " [1] Then we shall not be at a loss to understand that sin is the greatest of evils.

714. 2° **How God condemns sin.** Holy Scripture describes sin as the most odious and the most criminal thing in existence.

a) It is an act of *disobedience* to God, a transgression of His orders, which is justly punished with the utmost severity, as we witness in our

---

[1] *Isaias,* LIII, 5.

first parents. [1] In the people of Israel, God's chosen portion, this disobedience is regarded as a revolt, a rebellion. [2] **b)** It is an act of *ingratitude* toward our greatest Benefactor, an unnatural lack of filial piety toward the most loving of fathers : " *I have brought up children and exalted them : but they have despised me.* " [3] **c)** It is unfaithfulness, a species of *adultery*, since God is the spouse of our souls and rightly demands inviolable fidelity : " *But thou hast prostituted thyself to many lovers.* " [4] **d)** It is an *injustice*, since by sin we openly violate the rights God has over us : " *Whosoever committeth sin committeth also iniquity.   And sin is iniquity.* " [5]

II. *Mortal Sin in Itself*

Mortal sin is an evil, the only real evil, since all other evils are but its consequences or its punishment.

715.   1º **In relation to God,** mortal sin is a crime *against the majesty of the Godhead;* it is an assault upon all of God's attributes, but chiefly an attempt against Him as our *first beginning*, our *last end*, our *Father*, and our *benefactor*.

A) God, the *first cause* of our being is our Maker, from Whom we hold all we are and all we have; He is thereby our Supreme Lord and Master to Whom we owe an absolute obedience.   By mortal sin we disobey Him; we affront Him by preferring our own will to His, by preferring a creature to the Creator !   Nay more — we *revolt* against Him, since by the fact of creation, we are subject to Him as we can be to no earthly power.   **a)** This rebellion is all the *more grave*, since this Master is infinitely wise and infinitely good, and commands nothing that is not conducive to our own happiness as well as to His glory ; whilst our will is weak, frail, liable to error.   In spite of this, we prefer it to that of God !   **b)** This defiance is all the *more inexcusable*, since we know well what we do; for from the days of our childhood, we have been taught by Christian parents and have a clear and precise knowledge of God's rights over us and of the malice of sin.   **c)** And why do we thus betray Our Lord and Master?   We do so for a vile pleasure that debases us, from a stupid pride whereby we arrogate unto ourselves glory that belongs to God alone, for paltry interests, for a transient gain, to which we sacrifice a good that is eternal.

716.   **B)** God is also our *last end*.   He created us, and created us for Himself alone.   He could not have done

---

[1] *Gen.*, II, 17; III, 11-19. — [2] *Jeremias*, II, 4-8. — [3] *Isaias*, I, 2.
[4] *Jeremias*, III, 1. — [5] *I John*, III, 4.

otherwise, for He is the Supreme Good, and outside Himself we could neither realize our perfection nor find our bliss. Besides, having come forth from God, we should and we must return to Him; being the work of His hand, we are His own and we must revere, praise, serve, and glorify Him; [1] being the object of His love we should love Him with our whole soul — and it is in the love of Him and in the worship of Him, that we find our perfection and our happiness. Hence, He nas a *strict right* that our whole life with all its thoughts, all its longings, all its acts be directed unto Him, unto His glory.

By mortal sin, however, we turn away from God in order to take our delight in some created thing; we do Him an injury when we choose one of His creatures, or rather our own selfish satisfaction in preference to Him, for at bottom, it is not so much the creature which we seek as the pleasure we find therein. This is flagrant *injustice*, since it constitutes an attempt to strip the Almighty of His supreme rights over us, of that outward glory we are bound to promote; it is a sort of *idolatry*, the setting up in the heart's sanctuary of an idol over agaithst the One True God; it is *scorning* the fountain of living water, which alone can quench the soul's thirst, to go, as Jeremias vigorously puts it, after the slimy waters that reek within abandoned wells: " For my people have done two evils: *They have forsaken me the fountain of living water, and have digged to themselves cisterns, broken cisterns, that can hold no water.* " [2]

717. **C)** God is to us also a Father, Who has adopted us as His children and Who bestows on us the thoughtful care of a parent (n. 94); He heaps upon us His choicest favors, endowing us with a supernatural organism, in order that we may live a life like unto His; He showers upon us abundant actual graces that we may make good use of His gifts, and thus by good works increase our spiritual life. Now, by mortal sin we scornfully fling aside those gifts, nay we fling them back at the Giver, our Benefactor, our Father; we spurn His grace at the very moment He overwhelms us with His bounty. Is not this *ingratitude?* Ingratitude all the more culpable because we have received so much, ingratitude that cries out for vengeance!

---

[1] This is the thought developed by St. IGNATIUS at the outset of the *Spiritual Exercises*, beginning with these words : " *Man was created to this end, that he glorify and worship the Lord his God, and that by serving Him he attain salvation.* '
[2] *Jeremias*, II, 13.

718.   2⁰ In relation to **Jesus Christ,** our Redeemer, mortal sin is a sort of *deicide.*   **a)** It is sin that has caused the sufferings and death of the Savior : " *Christ suffered for us...* ¹ *And washed us from our sins in his own blood.* " ² That this thought make an impression upon us, we must think of the personal share we have had in Christ's bitter Passion.   It is I who betrayed my Master with a kiss, and at times, for even less than the thirty pieces of silver.   It is I who caused violent hands to be laid upon Him, and a sentence of death to be passed on Him.   I was with the rabble that cried out : " Not this man, but Barabbas... Crucify him. " ³   I was with the soldiers, lashing Him through my self-indulgence, crowning His head with thorns through my interior sins of pride and sensuality, laying the heavy beam upon His shoulders and nailing Him to the Cross.   As Father Olier so well explains it, " our niggard-liness crucified His all-embracing charity, our ill temper His meekness, our intolerance His patience, our pride His humility.   Thus our vices rack and strangle, and quarter the Christ that lives in us. " ⁴   What hatred should we bear a sin that has so cruelly fastened Our Savior to the Cross!

b) Of course, we can no longer visit fresh tortures upon Him, since He can suffer no more, but our present faults do offer Him fresh insults; for when we wilfully commit them, we scorn His love and favors; as far as we are concerned, we render void the Blood He shed in such profusion; we hold back from Him that love, that gratitude, that obedience to which He is entitled.   What is this, if not repaying love with black ingratitude, and thereby calling down upon our heads a dreadful punishment?

III. *The Effects of Mortal Sin*

God has given the law a sanction; He has made happiness the reward of virtue and suffering the wages of sin.   Seeing then the effects of sin in this life and in the next, we can in a measure judge of its guilt.

719.   1⁰ To realize the dire effects of mortal sin in **this life,** let us remember what a soul in the state of grace is.   It is the dwelling-place and the delight of the Most Blessed Trinity.   The Three Divine Persons adorn it with divine graces, divine virtues, divine gifts.   Under the influence of actual grace, the good acts such a soul performs

---

¹ *I Peter*, II, 21. — ² *Apoc.*, I, 5. — ³ *John*, XVIII, 40, XIX, 6.
⁴ *Cat. for an Int. Life*, P. I, lesson II.

merit eternal life. Such a soul possesses the holy liberty of the children of God, shares in His power and virtue, and enjoys, especially at certain times, a happiness which is a foretaste of celestial bliss. And what does mortal sin do?

a) It *expels God from our soul*, and because the possession of God is already the beginning of heavenly joy, the loss of Him is, at it were, a prelude to eternal loss; for the loss of God is likewise the loss of all the goods of which He is the source.

b) Losing God we lose *sanctifying grace*, whereby our soul lived a life similar to that of the Godhead; hence, mortal sin is a sort of *spiritual suicide*. Together with sanctifying grace we lose that glorious galaxy of *virtues* and *gifts* that go with it. If in His infinite mercy God leaves us in possession of Faith and Hope, these virtues are no longer vivified by Love and now abide with us merely to infuse a wholesome fear and inspire us with an earnest desire of atoning and doing penance. In the meantime they show us the sad plight of our soul and excite the pangs of remorse.

720. c) The merits we have earned in the past with so much effort are likewise lost by mortal sin; we can only regain them by penance. Moreover, whilst we remain in the state of mortal sin, we can acquire no merits for heaven. What a waste of the supernatural!

d) To all this we must add the *tyrannical* yoke of *servitude* the sinner must from now on bear. Instead of " the liberty of the children of God, "[1] behold him now in the slavery... of sin, of evil passions now unloosed by the loss of grace, of habits soon formed after repeated falls — falls so difficult to avoid! " *Whosoever committeth sin is the servant of sin.* "[2] Little by little the moral strengh of the soul is sapped, actual graces become rarer, discouragement and at times despair ensue. This poor soul is lost unless God in His exceeding great mercy comes with His grace and rescues it from the abyss.

721. 2° If unfortunately the sinner remains obdurate to the end in his resistance to grace, then follows hell with all its horrors. A) First there is the well-deserved pain of loss. Grace had ever pursued the culprit, but he willingly died in his sin, that is he willingly died without God, and since his soul's dispositions can no longer change, he remains forever separated from Him. As long as he lived on earth absorbed in business or pleasure, he gave no time, no thought to the horror of his plight. But now there is neither business nor

---

[1] *Rom.*, VIII, 21. — [2] *John*, VIII, 34; *II Peter*, II, 19.

pleasure, and he faces constantly the harrowing reality. By the very constitution of his nature, by the cravings of his mind and of his heart, by the urge of his entire being, he is now uncontrollably driven towards Him, Who is his first beginning and last end, his one principle of perfection and only source of bliss; drawn towards that loving Father, so worthy of love, Who had adopted him as His offspring; toward the Redeemer of his soul, Who had so loved him as to die upon the Cross for him. Yet, a ruthless force beyond his power, the force of sin, his own sin, hopelessly thrusts him back upon himself. Death has forever stayed his spirit, irretrievably fixed his dispositions. Having rejected God the very moment death overtook him, he remains estranged from Him forever. Happiness and perfection are everlastingly beyond his quest; he remains attached to his sin and through sin to all that defiles and all that degrades : " *Depart from me, ye cursed.*"

722. **B)** To this pain of loss, by far the most terrible, is added the pain of *sense.* The body, a partner in sin, will share the torment of the soul ; the everlasting despair which will torture the reprobate soul, will produce in the body an unquenchable thirst that nothing can assuage. Besides, the damned will be tormented by a *real fire* different indeed from our material fire, but the instrument of divine justice to punish the flesh and the senses. In fact, it is but just that wherein a man sins, therein also he be punished :" *By what things a man sinneth, by the some also he is tormented;* " [1] and since the evildoer willed to take inordinate delight in creatures these will prove the instruments of torture. This fire enkindled and applied by a knowing hand will torture its victims with that same measure of intensity with which they once entered into their wicked delights.

723. **C)** There will be no end of this double woe, and this everlastingness is what fills the measure of the punishment of the lost; for if a slight discomfort by its persistence becomes well nigh unbearable, what shall we say of those pangs, of themselves so racking, which outlast millions of ages only to begin afresh!

And withal, God is just, God is good even in the sanction He is bound to inflict upon the damned. Mortal sin, then, must be an abomination to be thus punished! It must be the one real evil, the only evil. Hence, *better to die than be defiled* by a single mortal sin.

---

[1] *Wisdom,* XI, 17.

§ II. Deliberate Venial Sin

From the point of view of perfection there is a great difference between venial faults *of surprise* and those committed with full deliberation, with full consent of the will.

724. Faults of surprise. The Saints themselves at times commit such by allowing themselves to be momentarily betrayed though thoughtlessness or weakness of will into some carelessness in prayer, into imprudences, rash judgments, words against charity, or little lies to cover up a fault. No doubt, these faults are to be deplored, and fervent souls do deplore them sincerely; however, such faults are not an obstacle to perfection. Almighty God, Who knows our weakness, readily condones them. Besides, almost invariably fervent souls make amends on the spot through acts of contrition, of humility, of love — acts that endure longer and are more voluntary than are their sins of frailty.

All we have to do as regards these faults is to lessen their number and ward off discouragement. **a)** We diminish their number through *vigilance*, by striving to reach and suppress their causes. This we do without anxiety or overeagerness, relying more on the grace of God than on our efforts. We must, above all, endeavor to destroy all attachment to venial sin; for as St. Francis de Sales remarks, [1] " if the heart clings thereto devotion loses for us its sweetness, and all devotion vanishes. "

725. b) We must carefully avoid *discouragement*, the vexation of those who " are angry for having been angry, and vexed to see themselves vexed. " [2] Such feelings proceed from self-love; one is cast down and troubled at seeing oneself so imperfect. To escape this defect, we must look upon our faults with the same eye of tolerance with which we behold those of others; indeed, we must detest our faults and our failings, but with a calm hatred, highly conscious of our own weakness and misery, and firmly determined to make them an occasion of giving glory to God by bringing more love and more fidelity to the fulfilment of our present duties.

It is otherwise with deliberate venial sins, which are a very great hindrance to our spiritual progress, and which must be vigorously combatted.

---

[1] *Devout Life*, Bk. I, C. XXII. — [2] *Devout Life*, Part III, C. IX.

I. *The Malice of Deliberate Venial Sin*

726. Deliberate venial sin is a moral evil. In reality, it is, mortal sin excepted, the greatest evil. It does not actually turn us from our end, but it checks our progress, robs us of time beyond price, and constitutes an *offence against God.* It is in this that its malice consists.

727. It is *an act of disobedience to God,* in a slight matter it is true, but willed after reflection. Regarded in the light of faith, it is something truly hateful, since it challenges the infinite majesty of God.

A) It is a wrong, an indignity offered to God; for placing God and His glory over against our whims, our pleasure, and our vanity, we dare to choose the latter. What an outrage! A will infinitely wise and righteous sacrificed to our own, the slave of error and caprice! " It is, " says St. Theresa, [1] " as if we said : ' Lord, I know full well this action displeases you, yet I shall do it none the less. I am not unaware that your eyes see it, I know perfectly well you do not want it, but I will rather follow my bent and fancy than your will. Can this be of little consequence? As for myself, no matter how slight the fault might be in itself, I find on the contrary that it is grave and very grave. ' "

728.   B) Hence, there results through our own fault, a *diminution of God's external glory;* for we have been created in order that by a perfect and loving obedience to His law we may procure His glory. Now, by refusing to obey, even in slight matter, we withhold from Him a measure of that glory; instead of proclaiming with Mary our readiness to exalt Him in all our acts, " My soul doth magnify the Lord ", we positively refuse to glorify Him in this or that particular.

C) This, of itself, is an act of *ingratitude.* Loaded by God with numberless favors, raised to friendship with Him, and knowing that in return He claims our love and gratitude, we begrudge Him a small sacrifice. Instead of striving to please Him, we dare to displease Him. Hence, inevitably, a certain coolness in God's friendship towards us. God loves us without stint and asks us in return that we love Him with all our soul : " *Thou shalt love the Lord thy God with thy whole heart, and with thy whole soul, and with*

---

[1] *Way of Perfection,* ch. XLI.

thy whole mind. " [1]   Now, we do not make the entire gift of ourselves to Him, we hold something back, and the while we want to keep His friendship, we are niggardly with ours, offering Him but a divided heart.   This is evidently inconsiderate; it shows a lack of generosity, a smallness that cannot but alter our intimate relations with God.

II. *The Effects of Deliberate Venial Sin*

729. 1º **In this life.** Frequent deliberate venial sin deprives the soul *of many graces,* gradually *lessens its fervor,* and *predisposes it to mortal sin.*

A) Venial sin does not, indeed, take from the soul sanctifying grace or divine love, but it deprives it of the new graces, the increase of divine love and of the corresponding degree of glory that it could have acquired and that God meant to give.   Is not this an enormous loss, the loss of a treasure worth far more than the entire world?

730. B) It causes a *diminution of fervor,* that is to say, a waning of that generosity whereby we give ourselves without reserve to God.   This generosity presupposes a *high ideal* and an *unrelenting effort* to pursue it; but these two dispositions are incompatible with habitual venial sin.

a) Nothing so *lowers our ideal* as attachement to sin : instead of being ever ready to serve God in all things and to aspire to the highest, we purposely halt half-way along the road to relish some forbidden pleasure. We thus waste precious moments, turning away our gaze from the lofty peaks to linger and gather a few flowers that are soon to wither. We feel then the weariness of the way, and heights of perfection that God wants us to reach seem far too remote and too forbidding. We say to ourselves that it is not necessary to aim so high; that we can obtain our salvation on more reasonable terms; and the ideal which once shone before our eyes no longer moves us. We say to ourselves that after all this little self-complacency, these trifling sensual gratifications, these sentimental friendships, these uncharitable words are unavoidable. b) This lowering of our ideals necessarily paralyzes effort towards perfection. Before, we marched joyously on, sustained by the hope of reaching the goal ; now, we begin to feel the heat and the burden of the day, and when we want to resume our ascent, our attachment to venial sin holds us back. Even as the bird held by cords to the ground tries in vain to take its flight and falls back bruised, so our souls, held by ties we will not break, fall very soon, harmed in some degree by the fruitless attempt to rise. At times, indeed, it seems as if we were to regain our strength, but alas! other ties hold us and we lack the steady purpose that would tear them asunder. Hence, there ensues a cooling of charity that becomes alarming.

---

[1] *Matth.*, XXII, 37.

731. **C)** The *great danger* that confronts us then is that of *gradually drifting into mortal sin.* Our tendencies toward forbidden pleasure gather strength, our will becomes weaker and God's graces are reduced. Then a moment comes when any surrender may be feared.

a) *Our tendencies toward forbidden pleasures gather strength;* the more we yield to this treacherous and insatiable enemy, the more it demands.

Today sloth makes us shorten our meditation by a few brief minutes; tomorrow it demands twice as many. Today sensuality but asks for some slight gratifications; tomorrow it becomes bold and asks for more. Where shall we stop on this downward grade? We try to reassure ourselves by saying that such faults are only venial, but alas, step by step they come nearer and nearer to grievous sins; imprudences recur and stir the imagination and the senses more deeply than before. This is the fire that lies smouldering beneath the ashes and which may at any given moment be the source of threatening flames; this is the reptile that we warm in our bosom and which makes ready to bite and poison us. — The danger is all the more imminent since familiarity has partly dispelled our fear; we let fall one after the other the barriers that guarded the stronghold of the heart and an hour comes when with added fury in the assault, the enemy gains entry into the citadel of the soul.

732. **b)** This is the more to be dreaded, as God's *graces* are as a rule *reduced* in proportion to our infidelities. 1) It is the law of Divine Providence that graces are given us according to our own dispositions and our own co-operation. This is the sense of the Gospel words : " *For he that hath, to him shall be given, and he shall abound : but to him that hath not, from him shall be taken away that also which he hath.* [1] " By our attachment to venial sin we offer resistance to grace, we hamper its action in our soul and therefore receive it in smaller measure. If, then, even with a greater abundance of grace we failed to make a stand against the disordered tendencies of our nature, shall we succeed in restraining them now with less grace and less strength? 2) Besides, a soul lacking recollection and generosity hardly feels the promptings of the graces it receives; these are soon stifled by the turmoil of awakening passions. 3) Lastly, grace cannot sanctify us except through the sacrifices it demands of us, whilst the habits of pleasure we have acquired by our attachment to venial faults render such sacrifices all the more difficult.

773. We can, therefore, conclude with Father Lallemant : [2] " The multiplication of venial sins is the destruction of souls, causing the

---

[1] *Matth.*, XIII, 12. — [2] *Spiritual Doctrine*, Principle III, c. II, art. II.

diminution of those divine lights and inspirations, those interior consolations, that fervor and courage, which are needed to resist the
assaults of the enemy. Hence follow blindness, weakness, frequent
falls, an acquired habit of insensibility of heart; because, when once
an affection to these faults is contracted, we sin without feeling that
we are sinning. "

734. 2° The effects of venial sin in the *next world* [1]
show us how much we should dread it. It is in order to
to expiate venial sin that many souls spend a long time
in purgatory.

A) There they endure the most unbearable of sufferings,
the *privation of the vision of God*. This torture, it is true,
will not last forever, differing in this from the pains of
hell; nevertheless, for a time measured by the number and
seriousness of their faults, these souls who love God and
who, now removed from the pleasures and distractions of
earth, think of Him constantly and long to see His face,
are prevented from seeing and possessing Him, and therefore suffer indescribable anguish. They now realize that
outside of God there is no solace and no bliss; and still
before them looms, like insurmountable barriers, that host of
venial sins they have not as yet sufficiently expiated. They
are, moreover, so alive to the necessity of the purity required
to contemplate the Almighty face to face, that their very
shame would not allow them to appear before Him as they
are, nor would they ever consent to enter Heaven as long
as there remains upon them the least stain of venial sin. [2]
They find themselves, therefore, in a state of *torture* the
more excruciating as they realize that it is fully deserved.

735. B) Moreover, according to the teaching of St. Thomas, a subtle fire hinders their activity and makes them
experience physical sufferings whereby they may expiate
the guilty pleasures to which they gave consent. This trial,
no doubt, they most willingly accept as they realize the
need of it in order to effect their union with God.

" Seeing, " says St. Catherine of Genoa, [3] " that purgatory is designed
to cleanse them of their stains, souls throw themselves into it, deeming
it an unspeakable token of mercy that they are offered a place wherein
they can rid themselves of what prevents their union with God. "

---

[1] We do not speak of the *temporal* punishments of venial sin. Holy Writ
repeatedly makes mention of them. When it is question, however, of determining
whether a particular punishment is the chastisement for a venial sin, one is
reduced to conjectures.

[2] " If the soul could discover another purgatory still more terrible than that
which it endures, urged on by its love for God, it would eagerly plunge into it, the
more speedily to be freed of all that separates it from the Sovereign Good. "
(St. Catherine of Genoa, *Purgatory*, c. IX.) — [3] *Op. cit.*, c. VIII.

Such willing acceptance, however, does not do away with their great sufferings: " This resignation of the souls in purgatory does not relieve them of one whit of their torments; far from it, love pent up causes their woe, and their woe increases in proportion to that perfection of love of which God has made them capable. " [1]

And yet, God is not only just but merciful as well! He bears those souls a love that is real, tender, fatherly; He longs to give Himself to them for all eternity. If He does not do so, it is because there can be no possible fellowship between His infinite holiness and the least venial sin. Therefore, we can never hate venial sin too much, we can never undergo enough in order to avoid it, we can never endure enough to repair it.

ART. II. MOTIVES AND MEANS FOR EXPIATING SIN

I. *Motives of Penance*

Three principal reasons oblige us to do penance for our sins. The first is a motive arising from a duty of justice toward God; the second, a duty consequent upon our *incorporation* into Christ; the last is a duty imposed by *charity* to *ourselves* and to our *neighbor*.

1° A DUTY OF JUSTICE TOWARD GOD

736. Sin is a real *injustice*, since it deprives God of a portion of that eternal glory which is His due. Sin, then, requires a *reparation* which consists in rendering God, to the extent in which we are able, that honor and that glory of which, through our fault, we have defrauded Him. The offence, inasmuch as it is offered to the Infinite Being, is in this respect at least infinite and can never be adequately repaired. Therefore, our expiation of sin must extend over the full span of our life; and this obligation is the more far reaching, as we have been the recipients of more favors and have been guilty of graver and more numerous faults.

Bossuet remarks on this point: [2] " Have we not good reason to fear that God's goodness so foully outraged be turned into implacable wrath? If His just punishment of the Gentiles was so severe, will not His anger be more dreadful towards us? Does not a father feel more keenly the faithlessness of his children than the wickedness of his servants? " We must then, he adds, take sides with God against ourselves: " Thus if we side with divine justice as against ourselves, we oblige divine mercy to take sides with us against divine justice. The more we regret the plight wherein we have fallen, the sooner we

---

[1] *Op. cit.,* ch. XII. Read entire treatise.
[2] *Premier Panégyrique de S. Fr. de Paul.*

shall regain the good we have lost. God's loving kindness will accept the sacrifice of the broken heart we offer Him as satisfaction for our crimes; and looking not to the inadequate reparation we offer, this good Father will but regard the good will of the offerers." Besides, we can make our penance more effective by uniting it to the atonement of Christ.

2° A Duty Consequent upon our Incorporation into Christ

737. Through Baptism we have been incorporated into Christ (n. 143), and since we share His life we are to share His sentiments. Although impeccable, Jesus has taken upon Himself, as the head of a mystical body, the burden of our sins and, so to speak, assumed responsibility for them: "*And the Lord hath laid on him the iniquity of us all.*" [1] Behold the reason for His life of suffering from the moment of His conception to His death on Calvary. Knowing that the holocausts of the Ancient Law could not propitiate the Father, He gives Himself as an *offering* in the place of all victims. All His acts constitute an immolation through obedience, and after a lifelong martyrdom, He dies on the Cross, the victim of obedience and of love : "*He was made obedient unto death, even the death of the Cross.*" And He wills that His members, in orders to be cleansed from their sins, be with Him victims of expiation : "He willed to become a victim that He might become the Savior of mankind. But since His mystical body is one, if the head be immolated, the members likewise become living victims." [2] It is evident that if Jesus, being innocent, atoned for our sins through His passion and death, we the guilty must share in His sacrifice, in proportion to our guilt.

738. To move us to comply with this duty, the atoning Christ comes through His Divine Spirit, to live within us with all His sentiments of victim.

"Thus in reading the Psalms" says Father Olier, [3] "we must honor that spirit of penance that was David's and revere in silent adoration the interior dispositions of Christ's Spirit, the fountain-head of penance, as diffused in David's soul. Humbly, insistently, ardently and perseveringly we must ask the Holy Ghost to give us this spirit of penance, trusting that He will grant our request." We may not be *aware* of the operations of the Holy Spirit, for He often works in an imperceptible manner; but if we invoke Him with humility, He will hear us and infuse into our hearts the dispositions of the Heart of Jesus towards sin, and thus enable us in union with Him to detest and

---

[1] *Isaias* LIII, VI. — [2] Bossuet, *Premier Sermon pour la Purification.*
[3] *Introduction*, ch. VII.

expiate our sins. Then our penance will become more efficacious since it is no longer we alone who atone, but Christ atoning in us and with us. "All exterior penance," says Father Olier, [1] "that has not its source in the Spirit of Jesus Christ, is not true and genuine penance. One may inflict upon oneself rigors, even the most harsh, but if these proceed not from the atoning Christ within us, they cannot be acts of Christian penance. It is through Christ alone that we can do penance. He initiated it here on earth in His own person and He continues it in us, infusing into our soul sentiments of abasement, of confusion, of sorrow, of detestation of self and of fortitude, to fulfil in us the sufferings and the measure of that satisfaction which God the Father wills to receive from Jesus Christ in our flesh." This union with Jesus, then, does not exempt us from the exercise of the spirit of penance nor from the works thereof; its effect is that of conferring upon them a greater worth.

3° A DUTY OF CHARITY

Penance is a duty of *charity* both to ourselves and to our neighbor.

739. A) A duty to ourselves. Sin leaves in the soul baneful consequences against which it is necessary to react. **a)** Even when the *guilt* or fault has been remitted, there generally remains a temporal punishment varying according to the gravity and number of our sins, and according to the fervor of our contrition at the moment of our return to God. This punishment must be undergone either in this life or in the next. By far the most advantageous course is to make satisfaction in this life. The sooner and the more perfectly we acquit ourselves of this debt, the better fitted our soul becomes for union with God. Moreover, expiation on earth is easier, since this is the acceptable time for mercy; it is more fruitful, since the acts wherewith we make satisfaction are also meritorious, a source of grace and greater glory (n. 209). Therefore, personal interest and love for our own soul are best served by a prompt and whole-hearted penance.

b) Moreover, by the fact that sin intensifies in us the disordered love of pleasure and weakens our will, it bequeathes to us a pernicious facility to commit fresh faults. Nothing so well rectifies this disorder as the virtue of penance. By having us bear with fortitude the afflictions sent by Providence, by inflaming our desire for privations and austerities compatible with our health, it gradually weakens within us the love of pleasure, and inspires us with a fear of sin which exacts such amends. By inuring us to the exercise of such acts of virtue as are opposed to our evil habits, it helps us to correct them and thus gives us

---

[1] *Op. cit.*, c. VIII.

greater security for the future. [1]   Hence, to do penance is charity towards ourselves.

740. **B)** Penance is also an act of charity toward the neighbor. **a)** In virtue of our incorporation into Christ we are all brethren, all members of the same body of Christ (n. 148). Since our works of satisfaction can contribute to the welfare of others, will not our charity prompt us to do penance not only for ourselves, but likewise, in behalf of our brethren? Is not this the best means of obtaining their conversion or, if they have turned to God, their perseverance? Is not this the best service we could possibly render them, a benefit worth infinitely more than all the temporal goods we could confer upon them? Thus, to atone for our neighbor's faults is but to carry out the will of God, Who having adopted us as His children, commands us to love our neighbor as we love ourselves.

741. **b)** This duty of reparation devolves more particularly upon *priests.* For them it is a duty to offer sacrifices not only for themselves but for the souls committed to their charge, " *First for his own sins, and then for the people's.* " [2]   We do find, however, outside the priestly state *generous souls,* who, in the cloister or in the world, feel drawn to offer themselves as expiatory victims for the sins of others. A high calling that associates them with Christ's redeeming work! A call they should fearlessly answer, taking counsel from a wise spiritual director as to the appropriate works of reparation to which they should devote themselves. [3]

742. Let us say in conclusion that the *spirit of penance* is not a duty imposed merely upon beginners and only for a short period of time. Once we have understood what sin is, what an infinite offence it gives to God, we are obliged to do penance *all through life,* since a whole lifetime is but too short to make reparation for an infinite offence. Hence, we must never cease to do penance.

This point is so important that Father Faber, after giving much thought to the reason why so many souls make but little progress, came to the conclusion that the cause was " the want of *abiding sorrow* for sin. " [4]   To this the example of the Saints bears witness; they never ceased expiating the faults, at times very slight, into which they had formerly lapsed. God's attitude toward the souls whom He wants

---

[1] This is the teaching of the Council of Trent (Session XIV, C. VIII).

[2] *Hebr.*, VII, 27.

[3] P. PLUS, *The Ideal of Reparation,* Book III; L. CAPELLE, *Les Ames Généreuses.*

[4] This he explains at length in *Growth in Holiness,* C. XIX, and he adds : "Just as all worship breaks down, if it is not based on the feelings due from a creature to his Creator... just as all penances come to nought which do not rest on Christ... so in like manner all holiness has lost its principle of growth if it is separated from abiding sorrow for sin. For the principle of growth is not only love, but *forgiven love.*"

to raise to contemplation likewise confirms it; after they have striven for a long time to purify themselves through active exercises of penance, God sends them, in order to complete their purification, those *passive trials* which we shall describe in the unitive way; for only perfectly pure or perfectly purified hearts can attain to the sweetness of the divine union: " Blessed are the clean of heart because they shall see God! "

II. *The Practice of Penance*

The more perfectly to practice penance, we must unite ourselves to the atoning Christ, and ask Him to dwell within us with His dispositions of *victim* (n. 738); then, we must enter into His *sentiments* and join in His *acts* of penance.

SENTIMENTS OF PENANCE

743. These sentiments are most aptly expressed in the Psalms and particularly in the *Miserere*.

a) First comes *abiding* and *sorrowful remembrance* of our sins: " My sin is always before me. " [1]   No doubt, it is not expedient to recall them to mind in detail; this might stir the imagination and be a source of new temptations. Yet, we must always bear in mind that we have sinned and above all we must entertain a sense of *sorrow* and *humiliation*.

We have offended God in His sight: " *I have done evil before thee,* " [2] before that God Who is holiness itself, and Who hates iniquity, before that God Who is all love and Whom we have outraged by dishonoring His gifts. Nothing is left to us but to appeal frequently to His mercy and implore His forgiveness: " *Have mercy on me, O God, according to thy great mercy.* " [3]   Indeed, we cherish the hope of having been pardoned; still, longing for a more complete forgiveness, we humbly beg God to cleanse us even more in the Blood of His Son: " *Wash me yet more from my iniquity, and cleanse me from my sin.* " [4]   To effect a more intimate union with Him, we want our sins wiped out and their traces removed; we want our spirit and our heart renewed, and we want the joy of a good conscience restored to us. [5]

744.   b) This sorrowful remembrance is accompanied by an abiding sense of shame: " *Shame hath covered my face.* " [6]   We stand in confusion before God like Christ Who bore before His Father the infamy of our sins, especially at Gethsemane and on Calvary.   We carry our shame before men, seeing ourselves as criminals in the assembly of the Saints.   We bear the opprobrium in our own hearts, and unable to stand the reproach, to suffer the disgrace, we

---

[1] *Ps.* L. — [2] *Ps.* L, 6. — [3] *Ps.* L, 3. — [4] *Ps.* L, 4. — [5] *Ps.* L, 10-14.
[6] *Ps.* LXVIII, 8.

utter the sincere cry of the Prodigal: "Father I have sinned against heaven and before thee;" [1] we repeat with the publican: "O God, be merciful to me a sinner." [2]

745. c) Of this a *wholesome fear* of sin is born, a horror for all the occasions that might lead us into it; for despite our good will we ever remain exposed to temptation and liable to fall.

Hence, a great distrust of self follows, whilst from our hearts we are prompted to repeat the prayer of St. Philip Neri, "My God, beware of Philip; otherwise he will betray Thee," or the concluding petition of the Our Father, "Lead us not into temptation." This distrust makes us *foresee* the dangerous occasions that might bring a fall and the positive means that will ensure our perseverance; it keeps us *on our guard* against the least imprudence. Such diffidence, however, harbors no *faint-heartedness*. The more we are conscious of our weakness, the more we place our confidence in God, convinced that through the power of His grace we shall conquer.

III. *Works of Penance*

746. No matter how painful these *works* may be, they will seem of light account if we keep constantly in mind this thought: I am a *fugitive from hell*, a *fugitive from purgatory*, and, were it not for the mercy of God, I would be there now, undergoing the well-merited punishment of my faults; therefore, I can consider nothing as humiliating me overmuch or grieving me above measure.

The chief works of penance we must perform are:

747. 1⁰ The *submissive, willing*, and *joyful* acceptance of all the crosses Providence may see fit to send us. The Council of Trent teaches us that it is a great token of God's love for us that He deigns to accept as satisfaction for our sins [3] the patient endurance wherewith we suffer the temporal ills He visits upon us. Therefore, should we have any physical or moral trials to undergo, arising from the uncontrolled forces of nature or from reverses of fortune, from failure or from humiliation, let us, instead of breaking into bitter complaint as our tendencies would suggest, accept all such suffering in a spirit of gentle resignation, persuaded that they are the just wages of sin, and that patience in adversity is one of the best means of atoning for it. This acceptance, a mere resignation at first, will gradually grow into a manful, nay, a joyous endurance of ordeals, as we see our woes thereby assuaged and made fruitful. We should be glad thus to shorten our purgatory,

---

Luke, XV, 18. — [2] *Luke*, XVIII, 13. — [3] *Sess.* XIV, C. IX.

to become more like Our Crucified Master and to glorify the
God we have outraged. Then patience will bear all its
fruits and cleanse our soul because it will be a work of
love : " *Many sins are* forgiven her, because she hath
loved much. " [1]

748. 2⁰ To patience we shall add the faithful discharge
of our *duties of state* in a spirit of penance and reparation.
The most acceptable sacrifice we can offer God is obedience:
" *Obedience is better than sacrifices.* " [2]   Now, the duties of
our state are the manifest expression of God's will in our
regard.   To fulfil them as perfectly as we can is to offer
God the most perfect sacrifice within our giving, a perpetual
holocaust, since this duty rests upon us from morning until
night.   This is assuredly true for such as live in community:
faithful obedience to their rule, general or particular, and the
courageous accomplishment of the orders or directions of
their superiors multiply their acts of obedience, of sacrifice
and of love, and enable them to repeat with St. John
Berchmans: " *My greatest penance is community life.* "   Such
perfect discharge of the duties of state is likewise the best
means of doing penance for persons in the world.   Fathers
and mothers who loyally observe all their obligations as
husbands and wives and as parents have many occasions
of offering God sacrifices that will work unto the purification
of their souls.   The one thing necessary is that they acquit
themselves resolutely of their duties in a Christian manner,
for God's sake, and in a spirit of expiation and penance.

749. 3⁰ There are other works of penance recommended
in Holy Writ, such as *fasting* and *almsgiving.*

A) Fasting was, in the Old Dispensation, one of the great
means of making atonement; it was called "to afflict the
soul;" [3] but to be acceptable it had to be accompanied by
sentiments of sorrow for sin and mercy towards others. [4]
Under the New Law, fasting is an earnest of grief and
of penance.   The Apostles do not fast as long as the
Bridegroom is with them, but they will fast when He is
gone. [5]   Our Lord, wishing to expiate our sins, fasted forty
days and forty nights, and taught His Apostles that certain
evil spirits cannot be cast out except by prayer and fasting. [6]
True to His teachings, the Church has established the Lenten
Fast, that of the Vigils and of the Ember Days to offer
her children the opportunity of making expiation for their

---

[1] *Luke*, VII, 47. — [2] *I Kings*, XV, 22. — [3] *Leveticus*, XVI, 29, 32; XXIII, 27, 32.
[4] *Isa.*, LVIII, 3-7. — [5] *Matth.*, IX, 14-15. — [6] *Matth.*, XVII, 20.

faults. Many a sin takes its rise directly or indirectly in the craving for pleasure, in excess in eating and drinking, and nothing is so effective in making atonement as mortification in eating, reaching as it does the very root of the evil by mortifying the craving for sensual pleasure. This is why the Saints have made a practice of fasting even outside the seasons appointed by the Church. Generous Christian souls imitate them and, if they cannot keep the strict fast, forego some food at each meal in order thus to curb their sensuality.

750. B) *Almsgiving* is both a work of mercy and a privation; from this double title it derives great power of atoning for our sins : "*Redeem thou thy sins with alms.*" [1] When we deprive ourselves of some good to give it to Jesus Christ in the person of the poor, God does not allow Himself to be outdone in liberality, and He willingly remits part of the punishment due to our sins. The more generous we are, each according to his means, and the more perfect our intention in almsgiving, the more fully are our spiritual debts cancelled. What we say of almsgiving with regard to the things that minister to the body holds true even more of spiritual almsgiving, which is calculated to promote the welfare of souls and thereby the glory of God. Thus it is one of the penitential acts the Psalmist promises to perform in reparation for his sin : "*I will teach the unjust thy ways : and the wicked shall be converted to thee.*" [2]

4° Lastly, there come the *voluntary privations* and the acts of *mortification* we impose upon ourselves in expiation for our faults, particularly those that reach the heart of the evil, by punishing the faculties that have had part in our sins. This we shall treat in the following chapter on mortification. The priest after absolving the penitent sums up in striking words the means by which we can atone fully for our sins and cleanse our souls from the remains of forgiven sins : " May whatever good you do and whatever ill you bear be to you unto the remission of sins... "

---

[1] *Dan.*, IV, 24. — [2] *Ps.* L, 15.

CHAPTER III

Mortification [1]

751. Like penance, mortification has a part in the cleansing from *past faults*, but its chief purpose is to safe-guard us against sin in the *present* and in the *future*, by weakening in us the love of pleasure, the source of our sins. We shall, therefore, explain the *nature*, the *necessity* and the *practice* of mortification.

Nature $\left\{\begin{array}{l}\text{Various names}\\\text{Definition}\end{array}\right.$

Necessity $\left\{\begin{array}{l}\text{For salvation}\\\text{For perfection}\end{array}\right.$

Practice $\left\{\begin{array}{l}\text{General Principles}\\\text{Mortification of the exterior senses}\\\text{Mortification of the interior senses}\\\text{Mortification of the passions}\\\text{Mortification of the higher faculties}\end{array}\right.$

Art. I. The Nature of Mortification

After explaining the *scriptural* and the *modern* terms whereby mortification is designated, we shall give its *definition*.

752. I. Scriptural terms used to designate mortification. In Holy Writ we find seven principal expressions that describe mortification in its different aspects.

1º The word *renouncement :* "*Every one of you that doth not renounce all that he possesseth cannot be my disciple.*" [2] This presents mortification as a giving up of external goods in order to follow Christ as the Apostles did : "*Leaving all things they followed him.*" [3]

---

[1] St. Thomas, whose principal texts are quoted by Th. de Vallgornera, *op. cit.*, q. II, disp. II-IV; Philip. a S. Trinitate, *op. cit.*, Iª P., Tr. II, disc. I-IV; Alvarez de Paz, t. II, lib. II, *De mortificatione;* Scaramelli, *Guide ascétique*, Tr. II, a. 1-6; Rodriguez, *Practice of Christian Perfection*, Part II, Tr. 1 and II: Tronson, *Exam. part.*, CXXIX-CLXIX; Mgr Gay, *Christian Life and Virtues*, Tr. VII; Meynard, *Tr. de la vie intérieure*, l. I, ch. II-IV; A. Chevrier, *Le Véritable disciple*, IIe P., p. 119-323; St. Francis de Sales, *Devout Life*, Part. III, C. 23-28, 34; Meyer, *Science of the Saints*, C. 5-7; Maturin, *Self-Knowledge and Self-Discipline;* Meschler, *Three Fundamental Principles of the Spiritual Life*, P. II.

[2] *Luke*, XIV, 33. — [3] *Luke*, V, 11.

2° Mortification is likewise an act of *abnegation* or *self-renunciation :* " *If any man will come after me, let him deny himself.*" [1]

3° But mortification also has a positive aspect : it is an act that maims and cripples the inordinate inclinations of nature : " *Mortify therefore your members* [2]... *But if by the Spirit you mortify the deeds of the flesh, you shall live.*" [3]

4° Nay more, mortification is a *crucifixion* of the flesh and its lusts, whereby we attach, as it were, our faculties to the law of the Gospel by devoting them to prayer and labor : " *They that are Christ's have crucified their flesh, with the vices and concupiscences...*" [4]

5° This crucifixion, if it persists, produces a sort of *death* and *burial* whereby we seem to die completely to self and to be buried with Christ, to live with Him a new life : " *For you are dead : and your life is hid with Christ in God...* [5] *For we are buried together with him by baptism into death.*" [6]

6° To indicate this death, St. Paul makes use of another expression. Since in Baptism a new life is given us, supernatural life, the while our own natural life subsists with the threefold concupiscence, the Apostle, calling the latter the old man and the former regenerated man, declares that we must *put off the old man* and *put on the new :* " *Stripping yourselves of the old man... and putting on the new.*" [7]

7° And since this is not done without a struggle, he says that life is a fight : " *I have fought the good fight*", [8] and that Christians are the athletes who *chastise* their body and bring it into subjection.

From all these and similar phrases it follows that mortification comprises a twofold element : one *negative* — detachment, renunciation, despoilment; the other *positive* — the struggle against the evil tendencies of nature, the effort to curb and deaden them, a crucifixion, a death of the old man and his lusts, in order to live Christ's own life.

753. II. Modern expressions designating mortification. Today milder expressions are preferred which indicate rather the *object* to be attained than the *effort* to be undergone. It is said, for instance, that we must *reform ourselves, exercise self-control, train the will, practice self-discipline, turn our soul towards God.* These expressions

---

[1] *Luke,* IX, 23. — [2] *Coloss.,* III, 5. — [3] *Rom.,* VIII, 13. — [4] *Galat.,* V, 24.
[5] *Coloss.,* III, 3. — [6] *Rom.,* VI, 4. — [7] *Coloss.,* III, 9-10. — [8] *II Tim.,* IV, 7.

are exact, provided it is kept in mind that we cannot work out our reform nor master ourselves except by fighting against and mortifying the inordinate tendencies of our nature; that the training of the will is not accomplished without thwarting and curbing our lower faculties; that we cannot direct the course of our life towards God but by detaching ourselves from creatures and stripping ourselves of our vices. In other words, the two aspects of mortification must be duly combined, as is done in Holy Writ : the end to be attained must be kept in view in order to give us courage, but we should not lose sight of the effort necessary to the attainment of this end.

754. III. **Definition.** Mortification, then, may be defined as *the struggle against our evil inclinations in order to subject them to the will, and the will to God.* It is not so much a virtue as an ensemble of virtues — the first degree of all the virtues — which consists in overcoming the obstacles that stand in the way so as to restore to our faculties their lost balance and reestablish among them their right order. Thus it is easily seen that mortification is not an end in itself, but a means to an end. We mortify ourselves only to live a higher life; we despoil ourselves of external goods only the better to lay hold of spiritual goods; we renounce self but to possess God; we struggle but to obtain peace; we die to ourselves but to live the life of Christ, the life of God. Hence, the end of mortification is union with God.

ART. II. THE NECESSITY OF MORTIFICATION

We may consider this necessity from a twofold point of view, that of *salvation* and that of *perfection*.

I. *The Necessity of Mortification for Salvation*

There is a kind of mortification which is *necessary for salvation* in this sense, that if we fail to practice it, we run the risk of falling into mortal sin.

755. 1º Our Lord speaks of it in a very clear way concerning faults against chastity : " Whosoever shall look on a woman *to lust after her* hath already committed adultery with her in his heart. " [1] There are looks, then, that are gravely sinful, such as are prompted by evil desire. In this case mortification of the eyes is imperative under pain

---

[1] *Matth.*, V, 28.

of mortal sin. Our Lord says so in no uncertain language : " And if thy right eye scandalize thee, pluck it out and cast it from thee. For it is expedient for thee that one of thy members should perish, rather than thy whole body be cast into hell." [1]   It is not question here of putting out one's eyes, but of turning them away from such sights as are a cause of sin. St. Paul gives us the reason for these serious injunctions : " For if you live according to the flesh, you shall die; but if by the Spirit you mortify the deeds of the flesh, you shall live." [2]

As we have said, (n. 193-227) the threefold concupiscence that remains with us, spurred on by the world and the devil, often inclines us to evil and endangers our salvation, unless we take heed to mortify it. Hence, the absolute necessity of waging a constant warfare against our evil tendencies; of fleeing from the *proximate occasions* of sin, that is, from such things or such persons as, given our past experience, are to us a serious and a probable danger of sin ; of renouncing thereby a great many pleasures towards which our nature draws us. [3] There are then certain practices of mortification which are imperative; without them we should fall into mortal sin.

756. 2⁰ Other practices of mortification there are which the *Church* prescribes in order to determine the general obligation so often repeated in the Gospel. Such are : abstinence from flesh-meats on Fridays, the *fast* of Lent, the Ember Days and the Vigils. These laws bind under pain of grievous sin all those who are not legitimately excused. Here we must make a remark that is of importance. There are persons who for good reasons are dispensed from these positive laws; but they are not thereby exempt from the natural, divine law of mortification, and hence must comply with it in some form or other. Should they fail in this, they will ere long experience the rebellion of the flesh.

757. 3⁰ Besides these practices of mortification enjoined by divine and by ecclesiastical law, there are others which, when temptations grow more severe, individuals must undertake with the advice of their spiritual director. What these mortifications are shall be indicated in n. 767 and following.

---

[1] *Matth.*, V, 29. — [2] *Rom.*, VIII, 13.
[3] We treated more at length of these occasions of sin in our *Synopsis Theologiæ moralis*, De Pænitentiâ, n. 524-536.

II. *Necessity of Mortification for Perfection*

758. This necessity follows from what we have said of the nature of perfection, which consists in the love of God unto *sacrifice* and the *immolation of self* (n. 321-327). This is so true, that, according to the Imitation, the measure of our spiritual growth depends upon the measure of violence we do to ourselves : *In proportion as thou dost violence to thyself the greater progress wilt thou make.* [1] It will suffice, then, to recall briefly a few of the motives that may aid the will in the discharge of this duty; they are drawn from the point of view of our relation to *God,* to *Jesus Christ,* and from that of our *personal sanctification.* [2]

1° MORTIFICATION IS NECESSARY FOR OUR UNION WITH GOD

759. **A**) We cannot attain to union with God without mortification, without detaching ourselves from the *inordinate love of creatures.*

St. John of the Cross says : "A soul will become like unto the creature to which it cleaves; as the attachment grows, the identification asserts itself; for love establishes the equal adjustment of the lover to the thing beloved... Therefore, he who loves a creature stoops down to its level — nay, even lower, since love is not content with equality, but descends to slavery. This is why a soul under subjection to anything apart from God becomes incapable of entering into that pure union with Him and of being assimilated to Him, for the utter nothingness of the creature is farther from the sovereignty of the Creator than darkness is from light." Now, the unmortified soul soon clings to creatures in an inordinate way; for since the Fall, the soul of man feels itself drawn to them, captivated by their charms, and delights in them as if they were ends in themselves, instead of making them stepping stones unto God. To break this charm, to escape this snare, it is absolutely necessary that we *detach* ourselves from whatever is not God, or at least, from whatever cannot be looked upon as a means leading us to Him. This is why Father Olier, in comparing the condition of Christians to that of Adam in the state of innocence, sees a vast difference between the two : "Adam sought God, served Him, and adored Him in His creatures; Christians, on the contrary, are forced to seek God through faith, to serve Him and adore Him in the inaccessible heights of His own Being and of His holiness." [3] For this we have the grace of baptism.

760. **B**) By Baptism a real contract is concluded between God and ourselves. **a**) God on His part cleanses us from the stain of original sin, adopts us as His children, and admits us to share in His life, engaging Himself to bestow

---

[1] *The Following of Christ,* Bk. I, C. 25.
[2] These motives are similar to those we explained with regard to penance, n. 736 and foll. Penance is in reality but mortification that repairs past faults.
[3] *Cat. for an Int. Life,* P. I, Lesson IV.

upon us all the graces necessary to the preservation and development of that life. We know the liberality wherewith He has fulfilled His promises. **b)** On our part, we bind ourselves to live like true children of God, to strive to become perfect as Our Heavenly Father is perfect. This, however, we can do only if we practice mortification; for, on the one side, the Holy Ghost, given us in Baptism, "urges us to embrace contempt, poverty, suffering; and, on the other, our flesh longs for honor, pleasure, riches." [1] Within us, therefore, rages a conflict, an incessant struggle; nor can we be faithful to God unless we renounce the *inordinate* love of honor, pleasure, and riches. Thus in the rite of Baptism, the priest marks us with two Crosses, one upon the heart to stamp thereon the love of the Cross, the other upon our shoulders to give us the strength to carry it. We should be untrue to our baptismal vows, if we did not carry our cross by waging war against the lust for honor through humility, against the lust for pleasure through mortification, against the lust for riches through poverty.

2° MORTIFICATION NECESSARY FOR OUR CONFORMITY TO CHRIST

761. A) Through Baptism we have been incorporated into Christ, we have become His members, and as such, it is from Him we are to receive life, and motion, and inspiration, and thereby be made *conformable* to Him. But the Imitation tells us that " *The whole life of Christ was a cross and a martyrdom.* " [2] Ours, then, cannot be a life of pleasure and honors, but it must be a life of mortification. This is what our divine Head clearly tells us : " *If any man will come after me, let him deny himself and take up his cross and follow me.* " [3] If there is any one who must follow Jesus, it is he who seeks after perfection. But how can a lover of pleasure, of honors, of riches follow Jesus? How can one follow Christ, if one is unwilling to carry his cross daily — the cross that God Himself has chosen for him and sent to him? How can such a one follow Him Who from His very entry into the world embraced the Cross, Who throughout His entire life sighed for sufferings and humiliations, Who was wedded to poverty at the Crib and Whom poverty followed unto Calvary? " *It is shameful,* " says St. Ber-

---

[1] OLIER, *Cat. for an Int. Life*, Part I, Lesson VII.

[2] *Following of Christ*, Bk. II, C. XII, v. 7.

[3] *Luke* IX, 23. Read the beautiful commentary on this text in the Circular Letter to the Friends of the Cross by the Blessed L. GRIGNION DE MONTFORT.

nard, [1] "*that we appear as delicate members, shrinking at the least smart of pain, under a Head that is crowned with thorns.*" Therefore, if we wish to become like unto Jesus Christ and reflect His perfection, we must like Him carry our Cross.

762. **B)** If we *aspire to a life of apostolic service,* we find therein a new motive for the crucifixion of our flesh. It is through the Cross that Jesus saved the world; it is likewise through the Cross that we shall co-operate with Him in the salvation of our brethren; and the fruitfulness of our zeal will grow in proportion as we share in the Savior's sufferings. This was what compelled St. Paul to fill up in his flesh that which was wanting of the passion of His Master in order to obtain graces for the Church. [2] This is the motive that in the past sustained and even now sustains so many souls who consent to be victims, that God may be glorified and that souls may be saved. No doubt, suffering is hard to bear, but when we look upon Jesus walking before us with His Cross borne for our own salvation and that of our brethren; when we contemplate His agony; when we see Him unjustly condemned, scourged, tormented with a crown of thorns; when we hearken to the jeers, the insults, the calumnies He silently endured — how dare we complain! "*Ye have not yet resisted unto the shedding of blood.*" [3] If we prize at their worth our souls and the souls of our brethren, can we make so much of a few fleeting pangs of suffering endured for the sake of a glory that will have no end, endured in union with Our Lord and Master, as our share in His work of saving souls for whom He shed the last drop of His Blood?

These motives, high as they are, are entered into by some generous souls from the very moment of their turning to God. By proposing such motives to them, a spiritual director will further their purification and sanctification.

3° MORTIFICATION NECESSARY FOR OUR OWN SANCTIFICATION

763. **A)** We must secure our *perseverance* in good, and mortification offers without doubt one of the best means we have to keep free from sin. What causes us to surrender to temptation is the love of pleasure or *the horror of hardship, the hardship of the struggle.* Mortification combats this twofold tendency, which is really but one; for by having

---

[1] *Sermo V in festo omnium Sanctorum,* n. 9.
[2] *Coloss.,* I, 24. — [3] *Heb.,* XII, 4.

us break with some few legitimate pleasures, it arms our will against those that are unlawful, thus giving us an easier victory over sensuality and the love of self; "*inveighing against sensuality and self-love*", as St. Ignatius puts it. If, on the contrary, we yield to pleasure, allowing ourselves all lawful joys, how shall we be able to resist when our sensuality, hankering after new delights, dangerous or wrong, feels itself as if overpowered by the force of habit? The bias is so strong, that where our sensuous nature is concerned, it is easy to fall into the abyss, by a sort of vertigo. Even when it is question of pride, the downward plunge is far more rapid than we think : we lie about a trifle to cover up a fault, to escape humiliation; and then when we approach the tribunal of penance we run the risk of failing in sincerity through the dread of a mortifying avowal. Our safety demands, therefore, a warfare against self-love as well as against sensuality and greed.

764.   B) To avoid sin is not sufficient; we must *grow* in perfection. Here again, what is the great stumbling-block, if not the love of pleasure and a dread of the cross? How many would wish to be better than they are, to aim at perfection, were it not that they shrink from the effort required, from the trials sent by God to His best friends? Such persons must be frequently reminded of what St. Paul said time and again to the first Christians, that is to say, that life is a struggle; that we should blush for shame if we show less courage than those who strive for an earthly reward and who in order to assure victory deprive themselves of sundry pleasures, willingly submitting to a stern and arduous discipline : "*And they indeed that they may receive a corruptible crown : but we an incorruptible one.*" [1] Do we dread pain? Let us ponder the terrible sufferings of Purgatory (n. 734) which will be our lot for years should we persist in living heedless of mortification and ready to indulge in all those things that delight us. How much wiser are the children of this world! Many a one undergoes hard labor and at times endures harsh treatment that he may earn a living and secure decent comfort in his declining years; and we would be loath to impose a hardship on ourselves for the sake of an eternal abode in the Kingdom of Heaven! Is this rational?

We must, then, realise that there is no perfection, no possible attainment of virtue without the practice of morti-

---

[1] *I Cor.*, IX, 25.

fication.   How can we be chaste without deadening that
sensuality that urges us so strongly toward evil and dangerous pleasures?   How can we be temperate unless we curb
our greediness?   How practice poverty, nay justice, if we
do not combat our greed?   How be humble, meek, kind, if
we exercise no control over the passions of pride, anger,
envy, jealousy, that lurk in the recesses of every human
heart?   There is not one virtue which, in our fallen condition, we can practice for any length of time without effort,
without a struggle and, hence, without the practice of mortification.   We can, therefore, say with Father Tronson
that "just as a lack of mortification is the cause of all our
vices, mortification is the foundation and the source of all
our virtues." [1]

765.   C) We can go further and add that mortification, notwithstanding the privations and sufferings it
imposes, is even here on earth rich in goods of the highest
order.   The mortified Christian is as a rule more truly
happy than the worldling who abandons himself to every
pleasure.   This is what Our Lord Himself teaches when
He says : "*Every one that hath left house or brethren...
shall receive an hundredfold and shall possess life everlasting.*" [2]   St. Paul speaks the same language.   After having
spoken of modesty, that is, of moderation in all things, he
adds : "*And the peace of God, which surpasseth all understanding, keep your hearts and minds in Christ Jesus.*" [3]
Of this he was himself the living example.   In truth he
had much to suffer.   He recounts at length not only his
own inner conflict, but also the terrible ordeals he had to
undergo for the preaching of the Gospel.   He adds however: "*I exceedingly* abound with joy in all our tribulation." [4]

And so it was with all the Saints.   Undoubtedly, they had to endure
long and painful trials; but the martyrs mid their tortures gave testimony that "*they had never been so happy.*"   Reading the lives of the
Saints we meet two striking facts : the dreadful ordeals they sustained,
the mortifications they willingly embraced; and then their patience,
their joy, their peace in these sufferings.   They came to love the cross,
to lose all fear thereof, nay, to sigh after it, to count as lost the day
wherein they had but little to suffer.   This is a psychological phenomenon which puzzles the wordly, but which is a comfort to men of
good-will.   No doubt, one could not ask of beginners such love of the
cross; but one can, showing them the example of the Saints, make
them understand that the love of God soothes the pain of mortification,

---

[1] *Examens part.*, 1er Ex. de la Mortification.
[2] *Matth.*, XIX, 29; *Mark*, X, 29-30, where it is said : "*An hundred times as
much, now in this* time."
[3] *Philip.*, IV, 7. — [4] *II Cor.*, VII, 4.

and, if they consent to enter whole-heartedly into the practice of offer·
ing small sacrifices within their strength, that they will come themselves
to love the cross, to long for it and to find in it true spiritual comfort.

766. The author of the Imitation expresses this in a text which
briefly sums up the advantages of mortification : " *In the cross is salvation: in the Cross is life; in the Cross is protection from enemies.
In the Cross is infusion of heavenly sweetness; in the Cross is strength
of mind; in the Cross is joy of spirit. In the Cross is height of virtue;
in the Cross is perfection of sanctity.*" [1] The love of the Cross is but the
love of God unto the immolation of self. And this love, as we have
said, is the embodiment of all the virtues, the very essence of perfection
and therefore the strongest defence against our spiritual enemies, the
fountain-spring of consolation, the best means of growing in the spiritual life and of assuring our salvation.

ART. III. THE PRACTICE OF MORTIFICATION [2]

767. Principles. 1º Mortification must include the
whole man, body and soul; for each of our faculties unless
well-disciplined may be the cause of sin. It is true,
indeed, that the will alone sins, but it has for accomplices
and instruments our body with its exterior senses and our
soul with all its faculties. Hence, it is the whole man that
must be disciplined, that is, mortified.

768. 2º Mortification is the enemy of pleasure. True,
pleasure *of itself* is not an evil; rather, it is a good when
subordinated to its God-given end. God has willed to
attach a certain pleasure to the fulfilment of duty in order
to facilitate its accomplishment. Thus, we find a certain
enjoyment in eating and drinking, in our work, and in other
duties. In the divine plan, therefore, *pleasure is not an end,
but the means to an end.* Hence, the enjoyment of pleasure
in view of a more perfect acquittal of duty is not proscribed;
it is rather in accordance with the order established by God.
But to seek pleasure as an end in itself without any relation
to duty, is at least dangerous, since it exposes one to slip
from lawful to unlawful pleasure. To enjoy pleasure to the
exclusion of duty is a sin more or less serious, because it is
a violation of the order established by God. Mortification,

---

[1] *The Following of Christ*, Bk. II, c. 12.
[2] Since mortification is defined as the struggle against our evil inclinations, it
must be practiced first of all in resisting temptations. This aspect of mortification
will be treated in nos 900 and following. It is next practiced in overcoming our
evil inclinations, our vices. This will be seen in nos 818 and following. Here we
speak only of the mortification of our faculties, or rather of their inordinate tendencies.
It must be noted that the word mortification is not used in exactly the same
sense when we speak of the mortification of our sins and vices as when we speak
of the mortification of our faculties. In the former case it means *destroying, putting to death;* in the latter it means *correcting, training, disciplining.*

therefore, consists in foregoing *evil* pleasures, pleasures contrary to God's providential plan, or to His Law, or to the law of the Church; in renouncing dangerous pleasures, so as not to run the risk of sin; in abstaining from *certain licit pleasures*, so as to insure the dominion of the will over our sensuous nature. With this same end in view we not only forego some pleasures, but likewise impose upon ourselves some positive practices of mortification; for it is a matter of experience that nothing is so effective in breaking down the lure to pleasure as the voluntary undertaking of some additional labor, the shouldering of some additional burden.

769. 3° Mortification, however, must be practiced with *prudence* and *discretion*. It must be properly fitted to the *physical* and *moral* strength of each, and must be in keeping with the accomplishment of one's duties of state. 1) We must spare our *physical* strength, for according to St. Francis de Sales, "We are exposed to great temptations both when the body is overfed and when it is too enfeebled."[1] In the latter case one becomes an easy prey to neurasthenia, which subsequently demands a letting down that may prove dangerous. 2) We must take into account our *moral* strength, that is to say, we must refrain from imposing upon ourselves from the outset excessive privations which we could not long sustain, and the giving up of which may lead us to laxness. 3) Above all, our mortifications must be such as would be compatible with the duties of our state, for the latter are obligatory and take precedence over practices of supererogation. Thus it would be wrong for a mother to practice such austerities as would prevent her from fulfilling her duties towards her husband and her children.

770. 4° There is a hierarchy in the practices of mortification. Those that mortify our *interior* faculties have a greater worth than those that mortify our *exterior* senses, because the former attack more directly the root of the evil; yet we must not lose sight of the fact that the latter aid in a great measure the exercise of the former. Whoever would attempt to mortify the imagination without mortifying the eyes will hardly succeed, for the very reason that these furnish our fancy with sensible images whereon it thrives. To jeer at the austerities of former Christian days is a baneful error of *modern times*. As a matter of

---

[1] *Devout Life*, Part III, c. XXIII.

fact the Saints of all ages, those that have been beatified in these latter days as well as those of old, have severely chastised their bodies and their exterior senses, well aware that man's whole being must be brought into subjection, that in the state of fallen nature, man's whole being must be crucified if he is to belong wholly to God. We shall therefore examine in succession the entire range of mortifications beginning with those that are *exterior* in character, finally arriving at those of a more *interior* nature. This is the logical order; in actual practice we must learn how to combine them, and make proper use of them.

§ I. The Mortification of the Body and the Exterior Senses

771. 1º **Its motives.** **a)** Our Lord recommended to His disciples the moderate practice of fasting and of abstinence, the mortification of sight and of touch. St. Paul was so alive to the necessity of mortifying the flesh that he punished it severely in order to escape sin and final reprobation : " *But I chastise my body and bring it into subjection : lest perhaps, when I have preached to others, I myself should become a castaway.* " [1] The Church herself prescribes for the faithful certain days of fast and of abstinence.

b) Why this? No doubt the body, well held in check, is a profitable servant, nay, an indispensable one, whose strength must be preserved to place it at the soul's service. But in the state of fallen nature, the body seeks after the joys of the flesh regardless of what is licit or illicit; it has a special tendency towards forbidden pleasures, and at times rebels against the higher faculties when these stand in the way. This enemy is so much the more dangerous, because it is ever with us, at table, in our room, abroad; and because it often meets with abbettors ready to excite its sensuality and lust. The senses are but so many openings for forbidden pleasure. We are obliged therefore to keep an ever-watchful guard over our body, to overpower it and bring it into subjection. If we fail in this it will betray us.

772. 2º **The Modesty of the Body.** If we wish to mortify the body, we must begin by a faithful observance of the prescriptions of modesty and good deportment. Here we find an extensive field for mortification. The rule we must follow is the principle of St. Paul : " *Know*

---

[1] *I Cor.*, IX, 27.

*you not that your bodies are the members of Christ... that
your members are the temple of the Holy Ghost?"* [1]

A) We must, then, hold our body in reverence, as a holy
temple, as a member of Christ. Let there be nothing about
us savoring of those fads, more or less indecent, designed
to excite the unwholesome curiosity of lust. Let our dress
be in harmony with our condition in life, plain and modest,
ever becoming, ever decent.

The wisest recommendations on this subject are those of St. Francis
de Sales : " Be neat, Philothea ; let nothing be negligent about you ;...
but at the same time, avoid all affectation, vanity, curiosity, or levity in
your dress. Keep yourself always, as much as possible, on the side of
plainness and modesty, which, doubt not, is the greatest ornament of
beauty, and the best excuse for the want of it... Women who are
vain, are esteemed to be very weak in their chastity ; at least, if they
are chaste, it is not to be discovered amid so many toys and fopperies..." [2]
S. Louis briefly says, " that one should dress in accordance to one's
condition in life, so that the wise and the good might not say : ' you
are too fastidious, ' nor the young remark, ' you are too negligent. ' "

As regards religious and priests, they have rules that
prescribe the form and quality of their dress, and they
should conform to those directions. It is needless to say
that worldliness and affectation would be out of place in
them and could not but shock worldlings themselves.

773. **B**) Good deportment likewise furnishes everyone
with ample opportunity for the practice of mortification, an
excellent way of mortifying the flesh without endangering
our health or attracting undue attention, and of gaining
a wonderful control over the body. Examples of good
deportment are : the avoidance of anything like lack of
poise or of any bodily pose that smacks of primness or
softness; an erect, easy and natural carriage of the body;
holding the same even posture for a considerable space
of time; not to lounge when sitting or lean when kneeling;
to avoid all brusqueness of movement or manner and
ill-regulated gestures.

774. **C**) There are other positive means of mortification which
penitent souls inspired by generosity delight to employ in order to
subdue their bodies, to temper the importunities of the flesh and give
vent to their holy desires. The more customary ones are small iron
bracelets clasped to the arms, chains worn about the loins, hairshirts,
or a few strokes of the discipline when this last can be done without
attracting any notice. [3] As to all such practices one must faithfully

---

[1] *I Cor.*, VI, 15, 19. — [2] *Devout Life*, Part III, c. XXV.
[3] To resume the practices of corporal mortification is one of the most effective
means of regaining lost joy of spirit and fervor of soul : "Let us go back to our
bodily mortifications. Let us bruise our flesh and draw a little of our blood, and

follow the advice of one's spiritual director, shun whatever tends to evince any singularity or to flatter vanity not to speak of whatever would be against the rules of hygiene and personal cleanliness. The spiritual director should not give his sanction to any of these extraordinary practices except with the greatest discretion, only for a time, and on trial. Should it come to his notice that any inconveniences arise therefrom, he must bring them to a halt.

775. 3° **Modesty of the Eyes. A)** There are looks which are *grievously sinful,* that offend not only against modesty, but against chastity itself; from such we must evidently abstain. [1]   Others there are which are *dangerous;* for instance, to fasten our eyes on persons or things which would of themselves be apt to bring on temptations. Thus Holy Scripture warns us : " Gaze not upon a maiden : lest her beauty be a stumbling-block to thee. " [2]   Today, when indecency in dress, exhibitions of the stage and of certain types of drawing-room entertainment create so many dangers, what great care must we not exercise so as not to expose ourselves to sin!

776. B) The earnest Christian who wants to save his soul at all costs goes even further so as to make the danger more remote. He mortifies the sense of sight by repressing idle, curious glances and by duly controlling his eyes in all simplicity without any show of affectation. He takes the opportunity whenever offered of directing his looks towards those things that tend to raise his heart towards God and the Saints, such as holy pictures, statues, churches and crosses.

777. 4° **Mortification of the Ear and the Tongue. A)** The mortification of these senses demands that we speak no word nor lend a willing ear to utterances that hurt brotherly love, purity, humility and the other Christian virtues; for, says St. Paul, " Evil communications corrupt good manners. " [3]   How many souls have been turned from their godly ways by giving ear to impure conversations or to words against their neighbor. Obscene words induce a morbid curiosity, excite the passions, kindle desire, and incite to sin; whilst unkind words stir up strife and divisions even in the home, give rise to suspicion, enmity and rancor. We must, therefore, watch over the least of

---

we shall be happy as the day is long. If the Saints are such gay spirits, and monks and nuns such unaccountably cheerful creatures, it is simply because their bodies, like St. Paul's, are chastised and kept under with an unflinching sharpness and a vigorous discretion. " (FABER, *The Blessed Sacrament*, Book II, Section VII).

[1] *Matth.*, V, 28. — [2] *Eccli.*, IX, 5. — [3] *I Cor.*, XV, 33.

our words and we must know how to close our ears to whatever may sully purity, hurt charity or disturb peace.

778. B) The better to succeed in this, we shall at times mortify our *curiosity*, refraining from asking questions that would satisfy it, or repressing that itch for gossip that draws us into idle conversations not altogether devoid of danger : "*In the multitude of words there shall not want sin.*" [1]

C) Since negative means do not suffice. We should take care to direct our conversation to subjects not merely harmless, but good, elevating and edifying, without however growing burdensome to others by too serious remarks that do not naturally suggest themselves.

779. 5° The Mortification of our other senses. What we have said with regard to sight, hearing and speech, is applicable to the other senses as well. We shall return to the sense of taste when we speak of gluttony, and to the sense of touch when we treat of chastity. As to the sense of smell, suffice it to say that the immoderate use of perfumes is often but a pretext for satisfying sensuality, and at times a ruse to excite lust. Earnest Christians should use them with moderation ; clerics and religious should never use them.

§ II. Mortification of the Interior Senses

The two interior senses to be mortified are the *imagination* and the *memory*, which generally act in accord, memory-activities being accompanied by sense-images.

780. 1° Principle. These are two valuable faculties, which not only furnish the mind with the necessary material whereon to work, but enable it to explain the truth with the aid of images and facts in such a manner as to make it easier to grasp, and render it more vital and more interesting. The bare, colorless and cold statement of truth would not engage the interest of most men. It is not question, then, of atrophying these faculties, but of schooling them, of subjecting their activity to the control of reason and will. Otherwise, left to themselves, they literally crowd the soul with a host of memories and images that distract the spirit, waste its energies, cause it to lose priceless time while at prayer and work, and constitute the source of a thousand temptations against purity, charity, humility and other virtues. Hence, of necessity they must be disciplined and made to minister to the higher faculties of the soul.

---

[1] *Proverbs*, X, 19.

781. 2° **Rules to be followed. A)** In order to check the wanderings of the memory and the imagination, we must, first of all, strive to expel from the outset, that is, from the very moment we are aware of them, all *dangerous* fancies and recollections; for such, by conjuring up some crisis of the past, or by carrying us along midst the seductive allurements of the present, or on to those of the future, would constitute for us a source of temptation. Furthermore, since frequent day-dreaming by a kind of psychological necessity leads us into dangerous musings, we should take heed to provide against idle thoughts, by mortifying ourselves as regards useless fancies, which constitute a waste of time and pave the way to others of an even more perilous nature. *Mortifying idle thoughts*, the Saints tell us, *is dealing death to evil ones.*

782. B) The best means to attain this end is to apply ourselves whole-heartedly to the performance of the duties of the moment, to our work, to our studies, to our ordinary occupations. Besides, this is likewise the best means of doing well what we are about, by making all our activities converge towards the production of the one action : " *Do well whatever you do.* " Let young men remember that in order to succeed either in studies or in their profession, they must give more play to the mind and the will than to the lower faculties. Thus, whilst making provision for the future, they should avoid all dangerous flights of the imagination.

783. C) Lastly, the memory and the imagination will prove most helpful if they are employed to nourish our piety, by searching in the Scriptures, in the Liturgy, and in spiritual writers the choicest texts, the most beautiful similes, the richest imagery, and if the imagination is used to enter into God's presence, to picture in their details the mysteries of Our Lord and the Blessed Virgin. Thus, far from stunting this faculty, we shall fill it with devout representations which will displace dangerous fancies and enable us the better to grasp and present to our hearers the beauty of the Gospel-scenes.

§ III. The Mortification of the Passions [1]

784. The passions in the *philosophical* sense of the term are not necessarily nor wholly evil. They are active

---

[1] St. Thom., Ia IIæ, q. 22-48; Suarez, disp. III; Sénault, *De l'usage des passions;* Descuret, *La médecine des passions;* Belouino, *Des passions;* Th. Ribot,

forces, often impetuous, that may be used for good as well as for evil, provided we learn to control them and direct them towards a high purpose. In popular parlance, however, and with certain spiritual writers, the word is used to designate *evil* passions. We shall, then — 1° recall the principal *psychological notions* concerning the passions; 2° indicate their *good* and their *bad effects;* 3° give rules for their *right use.*

I. *The Psychology of the Passions*

Here we but recall briefly what is explained at length in Psychology.

785. 1° Notion. Passions are *vehement movements of the sensitive appetite toward sensible good, reacting more or less strongly on the bodily organism.*

a) At the bottom of passion, therefore, there is a certain knowledge, at least a sense-knowledge, of a good hoped for or already possessed, or of an evil opposed to the said good. From this knowledge spring the movements of the sensitive appetite.

b) These movements are *vehement* and thus differ from affective conditions, pleasant or unpleasant, which are calm, peaceful, and free from the eagerness and the violence found in passion.

c) It is precisely because they are *vehement* and act strongly upon the sensitive appetite that they have their *reaction upon the physical organism.* This is due to the close union that exists between body and soul. Thus, anger causes blood to rush to the brain and strains the nerves; fear causes us to turn pale; love dilates the heart and fear contracts it. These physiological effects do not reach the same degree in all subjects; they depend upon the individual temperament and the intensity of passion itself, as well as upon the measure of control acquired over self.

786. Passions differ from sentiments, which are movements of the will, and which presuppose, therefore, an intellectual knowledge; although they are strong, they lack the violence of passions. Thus there is a passion of love and a sentiment of love, a passionate fear and an intellectual fear. We may add that in man, a rational animal, the passions and the sentiments almost invariably blend in varying proportions, and that is is through the will aided by grace that we transform the most ardent passions into lofty sentiments by bringing the former under the sway of the latter.

787. 2° Their Number. Eleven are generally enumerated, all of which proceed from love, as Bossuet [1] lucidly

---

La psychologie des sentiments; La logique des sentiments; PAYOT, *The Education of the Will; Cursus Asceticus,* I, P. 157-236; MEYER, *The Science of the Saints,* II-IV; MESCHLER, *Three Fundamental Principles of the Spiritual Life,* P. II, C. X-XV; P. JANVIER, *Carême 1905;* H. D. NOBLE, *L'éducation des passions.*
[1] *De la connaissance de Dieu et de soi-même,* C. I, n. 6.

shows : " Our other passions refer but to love, love which embodies or stimulates them. "

1) *Love* is a yearning for union with a person or thing that pleases us ; we thereby crave possession of it.

2) *Hatred* is an eagerness to rid ourselves of what displeases us ; it is born of love in the sense that we hate that which militates against what we love. We hate disease only because we love health ; we hate no one, except those who place an obstacle to our possessing what we love.

3) *Desire* is a quest for an absent good and proceeds from the fact that we love that good.

4) *Aversion* (or flight) makes us shun or repel *approaching* evil.

5) *Joy* is the satisfaction arising from a *present good.*

6) *Sadness*, on the other hand, makes us grieve over and shrink from a *present evil*

7) *Courage* (daring) makes us strive after union with the object loved, the acquisition of which is difficult.

8) *Fear* prompts us to shrink from an evil difficult to avoid.

9) *Hope* eagerly bears us toward the thing loved, the acquisition of which is possible, though difficult.

10) *Despair* arises in the soul when the acquisition of the object loved seems *impossible.*

11) *Anger* violently repels what hurts us, and incites the desire of revenge.

The first six passions which take rise in what is called the *concupiscible appetite*, are generally known to modern psychologist as *pleasure-passions;* the other five, proceeding from what is termed the *irascible appetite*, go by the name of *aggressive passions.*

II. *The Effects of the Passions*

788. The *Stoics* assumed that the passions were radically evil and must be annihilated. The *Epicureans* deified the passions and loudly proclaimed the necessity of obeying them ; modern Epicureans reëcho their cry in saying that *life must be lived.* Christianity shuns these two extremes. Nothing, it holds, that God has bestowed on our nature is evil. Our Lord Himself had well-ordered passions. He loved not only with His will, but with His heart ; He wept over dead Lazarus and over faithless Jerusalem ; He let Himself be roused to righteous indignation ; He felt fear, underwent sadness and weariness ; yet He knew how to keep these passions under the control of the will and subordinate them to God. When, on the contrary, passions are ill-ordered they are productive of the most harmful results. Hence, they must be mortified and disciplined.

789. The Effects of ill-ordered Passions. Passions are said to be *ill-ordered* when directed towards some sensible good which is forbidden, or even towards a good which is lawful, but is pursued with too much eagerness and without any reference to God. Such ill-regulated passions have the following effects :

a) They produce *blindness of soul,* for heedless of reason, they move headlong toward their object, led on by attraction or by pleasure. This constitutes a disturbing factor which tends to unbalance our judgment and becloud right reason. The sensitive appetite is by nature blind; and should the soul allow itself to be guided by it, it will likewise become blind. The soul then, instead of being guided by duty, allows itself to be fascinated by the pleasure of the moment; it is as if a cloud stood between it and the truth. Blinded by the passions, the soul no longer sees clearly the will of God, the duty to be fulfilled; it is no longer competent to form a sane judgment.

790. b) Ill-ordered passions *weary* and *torture* the soul.

1) The passions, says St. John of the Cross,[1] "are as impatient little children that can never be pleased, that ask their mother now for this, now for that, and are never satisfied. A miser tires of digging in vain for a treasure; likewise the soul wearies of seeking what its appetites demand. If one of these appetites is satisfied, others arise and wear us out, because they cannot all be satisfied... Appetites afflict the soul, enervate it and trouble it as the wind agitates the sea."

2) Hence, a suffering all the more intense, the more ardent the passions, for they torture the soul until they are satisfied, and just as the appetite for food is whetted by eating, so the passions ever crave for more. If conscience offers resistance, they lose patience, they fret, they importune the will to yield to their ever-recurring desires. This is an unspeakable torture.

791. c) Ill-ordered passions also *weaken the will.* Drawn hither and thither by these rebellious passions, the will is forced to scatter its efforts in every direction and by so doing to lessen its strength. Every concession it makes to the passions increases their demands and diminishes its own energies. Like the useless, rapacious, parasitic shoots that sprout round the trunk of a tree, uncontrolled appetites

---

[1] *The Ascent of Carmel,* Bk. I, C. VI; See chapters VI-XII of the same book, wherein the Saint explains in a wonderful way the hurtful effects of the appetites, that is, of the passions. We but briefly sum up his thought.

grow and sap the strength of the soul. A time comes when the weakened soul becomes the prey of laxness and lukewarmness and is ready to make any surrender.

792. **d)** Ill-ordered passions, lastly, *blemish the soul.* When the soul, yielding to the passions, joins itself to creatures it lowers itself to their level. Instead of being the faithful image of God it takes on the likeness of the things to which it clings; specks of dust, blots of grime sully its beauty and impede a perfect union with God.

"I do not hesitate to affirm," says St. John of the Cross, [1] "that one single disordered passion, even if it lead not to mortal sin, is enough to cause the soul such a state of darkness, ugliness and uncleanness, that it becomes incapable of intimate union with God so long as it remains a slave of this passion. What then shall we say of the soul that is marred by the ugliness of all its passions, that is a prey to all its appetites? At what infinite distance will it not be from divine purity? Neither words nor arguments can make us understand the divers stains which all these appetites create in the soul. Each one of them in its own way places its share of filth and ugliness in the soul."

793. **Conclusion.** If we wish, then, to attain to union with God, we must repress all inordinate movements of the passions, even the most trifling; for perfect union with God presupposes that there be nothing in us contrary to the divine will, no wilful attachment to creatures or to self. The moment we deliberately allow any passion to lead us astray, this perfect union no longer exists. This is especially true of habitual attachments. These paralyze the will even if they be in themselves trivial. St. John of the Cross [2] says that "it makes little difference whether a bird be tied by a thin thread or a heavy cord; it cannot fly until either be broken."

794. **Advantages of well-ordered passions.** Passions are helpful when they are well-ordered, that is, when they are directed towards good, when they are controlled and made subservient to the will of God. They are live, powerful forces that stir our mind and will to action and thus render them signal help.

a) They act upon the mind by stimulating our ambition to work, our desire to know the truth. When we are passionately interested in any object, we are on the alert to know all about it; our minds grasp the truth more readily; the impression made upon our memory is more lasting. An inventor, for instance, burning with love for his country

---

[1] *Ascent of Carmel*, Bk. I, C. XI. — [2] *Ascent of Carmel*, Bk. I, C. XI.

works with greater zest, perseverance and insight because of the very fact that he wants to serve his country. In like manner a student inspired by the high purpose of putting his knowledge at the service of his countrymen makes greater efforts and obtains greater results. But above all, he who passionately loves Jesus Christ, will study the Gospel with greater zeal, understand it better and relish it more; the words of the Master are for him so many oracles that shed upon his soul a glowing light.

795. b) Well-ordered passions, likewise, exert their influence upon the *will*, grouping and multiplying its energies. Whatever is done out of love, is done more thoroughly, more whole-heartedly, pursued more perseveringly and attended by greater success. What does not a loving mother do to save her child? What acts of heroism does not patriotism inspire? A Saint in whom love for God and for souls is a passion balks at no effort, at no sacrifice, at no humiliation if he can but save his brethren. Undoubtedly, it is the will which dictates such acts of zeal, but it is a will inspired, stimulated, and sustained by a hallowed passion. When both the sensitive and intellectual appetites, that is to say, when the heart and the will join forces and work along the same lines, the attendant results are evidently of far greater import and much more lasting. Hence, the importance of knowing how to put the passions to good use.

III. *The Good Use of the Passions*

After recalling the psychological principles that will make our task easier, we shall show how evil passions are resisted, how passions are directed towards good, and how they are controlled.

1° PSYCHOLOGICAL PRINCIPLES TO BE APPLIED [1]

796. To attain mastery over the passions, we must first of all, count on the grace of God and, therefore, on prayer and the Sacraments; but we must also employ the *sound tactics* furnished by psychology.

a) Every idea tends to evoke a corresponding act, especially if the idea is attended by live emotions and associated with strong convictions.

Thus the thought of sensual pleasure, vividly depicted by the imagination, provokes a sensual desire, often a sensual act. On the other

---

[1] EYMIEU, *Le gouvernement de soi-même*, t. I, 3ᵉ Principe.

hand, the thought of noble deeds and their happy results excites the desire of performing such acts. This is especially true of the idea that does not remain cold, colorless, abstract, but, accompanied by sensitive images, becomes concrete, real and thereby captivating. It is in this sense that we can say that thought is *power*, a dynamic force, the beginning of action. If then, we are, to master our ill-ordered passions, we must cautiously banish every thought, every fancy that presents evil pleasure in an attractive guise; and, if we want to foster well-ordered passions or good sentiments, we must welcome the thoughts and the images that picture the beautiful side of duty, of virtue, and we must make these as vivid and as concrete as possible.

797. b) The influence of an idea abides as long as that idea is not obliterated and supplanted by a stronger one. Thus sensual desire continues to make itself felt so long as it is not driven out by some nobler thought which takes possession of the soul. Hence, if we would be rid of such desires we must through some reading or engaging study apply ourselves to an entirely different or to an absolutely contrary trend of thought; and should we wish to strengthen some good desire, we must dwell on it and think of such things as will tend to feed it.

c) The influence of an idea grows by being associated with correlative ones that enrich and broaden it. Thus the thought and the desire of saving our soul grow more intense and more active if associated with the idea of working for the salvation of our brethren. The life of St. Francis Xavier is a striking example of this.

798. d) Lastly, an idea attains its maximum power, when it becomes *habitual, absorbing*, a sort of *fixed idea*, the motive-power of action. This is exemplified in the sphere of the natural by the single-mindedness of those who hold but one purpose in view, for instance, that of bringing about some particular discovery; in the realm of the supernatural it is illustrated by those who are deeply impressed by some Gospel-truth which becomes the ruling principle of their life, for example: " Sell what thou hast and give to the poor. What doth it profit a man if he gain the whole world and suffer the loss of his own soul? For to me, to live is Christ. "

We must, therefore, aim at burying deep into our souls some *directing thoughts*, and then embody them in a maxim that makes them real and keeps them ever before our mind, such as : " *My God and my all! To the greater glory of God! God alone suffices! He who possesses Jesus, possesses all things! To be with Jesus is a sweet paradise!* " With a motto of this kind, we shall more easily triumph over ill-ordered passions and make a right use of well-ordered ones.

2° How to Wage War against Ill-Ordered Passions

799. As soon as we are aware of any ill-ordered movement of the soul, we must have recourse to every natural and supernatural means to stay and curb it.

a) From the outset, we should with the help of grace avail ourselves of the power of inhibition wielded by the will to thwart such motion.

We should avoid *exterior* acts and gestures which would but stimulate or intensify passion. Thus, if we feel roused to anger, we should avoid excited gestures, and words, holding our peace until calm is restored; if it be question of a too ardent attachment to some person, we should avoid any meeting, any conversation with that person, and above all we should refrain from showing, even in an indirect way, the affection we feel. In this wise, passion gradually subsides.

800. **b)** If it be question of some *pleasure*-passion one must strive to forget the object of that passion.

In order to accomplish this : 1) one must apply the mind and the imagination to any wholesome activity apt to divert attention from the object of passion; one must seek to engage all the powers of the mind on some absorbing subject of study, on the solution of some question or problem, or find distraction in play, social intercourse, conversation, walks, etc... 2) Then, when calm ensues one should have recourse to such moral considerations as may strengthen the will against the allurement of pleasure : considerations of the *natural* order, such as the untoward consequences, for the present and the future, with which a dangerous attachment, a too sentimental friendship may be fraught (n. 603); but above all, one should appeal to *supernatural* considerations, for instance, that it is impossible to advance in the way of perfection so long as we cling to such attachments, that these are but chains we forge for ourselves, that we thereby risk our salvation, that through our fault scandal may be given, etc.

If it be some *aggressive* passion with which we have to deal, anger for example, we must first of all, through instant flight, allow the passion time to cool ; then we can take the offensive, face the difficulty, convince ourselves through rational considerations and chiefly through motives of faith that it is unworthy of man, unworthy of a Christian to yield himself a willing prey to anger or to hatred ; that serenity, self-control is the highest, the noblest course to follow, the one most consistent with the Gospel.

801. **c)** Lastly, *positive acts directly opposed* to the harassing passion must be elicited.

If we experience dislike for any one we must act as if we wished to gain his good graces, strive to serve him, be amiable towards him and above all pray for him. Nothing so empties the heart of all bitterness as an earnest prayer offered for an enemy. If, on the contrary, we feel a too ardent affection for any one we shall avoid his company or, if this be impossible, treat him with that cold formality, that sort of courteous indifference wherewith we treat the rank and file of human beings. These contrary acts finally succeed in weakening passion.

3° THE DIRECTION OF PASSIONS TOWARDS GOOD

802. We have said that the passions are not in themselves evil; all can without exception be turned to good.

a) *Love* and *joy* can be directed towards pure and lawful family-affection, towards good and supernatural friendship, but chiefly towards Our Lord, Who is the most tender, the most generous, the most devoted of friends. This, then, is what matters most, that we center our hearts on Him by reading, meditation, and by actually carrying out in our lives the teachings contained in the two chapters of the Following of Christ, " *On the love of Jesus above all things,* " and " *On familiar friendship with Jesus*", two chapters which have proved a potent source of inspiration to many souls.

b) *Hatred* and *aversion* can be turned against sin, against vice, and against whatever leads to them, in order that we may loathe them and fly from them : " *I have hated iniquity.* " [1]

c) *Desire* is transformed into lawful ambition; into the natural ambition of doing honor to one's family, one's country, and into the supernatural ambition of becoming a saint, an apostle.

d) *Sadness,* instead of degenerating into melancholy, becomes a sweet resignation under trials, which are for the Christian soul a seed of glory; or it is changed into tender compassion for the suffering Christ, loaded down with insults; or it is turned towards afflicted souls.

e) *Hope* becomes a Christian virtue of unfailing trust in God and multiplies our energies for good.

f) *Despair* takes the form of a rightful mistrust of self, based upon our own insufficiency and our sins, but tempered by trust in God.

g) *Fear* is no longer that sense of depression which weakens the soul; but in the Christian it is a source of power. The Christian fears sin, he fears hell; but this righteous fear inspires him with courage in the struggle against evil. He fears God above all, he dreads to offend his Maker and treads under foot human respect.

h) *Anger* instead of causing us to lose self-control, is but a just and holy indignation that strengthens us against evil.

i) *Boldness* becomes *prowess* in the face of obstacles and dangers; the greater the difficulty we encounter, the more eager we are to make efforts to overcome it.

803. To attain these happy results, there is nothing like *meditation,* accompanied by devout affections and generous resolutions. Thereby, we conceive an *ideal,* and form deep-seated *convictions* that help us daily to approach that ideal. The purpose in view is to evoke and nurture in the soul such *thoughts* and *feelings* as are in harmony with the virtues we want to practice, and to remove images and impressions allied to the vices we want to shun. These

---

[1] *Ps.* CXVIII, 163.

results cannot be better realized than by the practice of daily meditation after the manner noted in no. 679 and following. In this intimate converse with God, infinite Truth and infinite Goodness, virtue becomes every day more attractive and vice more loathsome, whilst the will strengthened by convictions draws the passions towards good instead of allowing itself to be drawn by these towards evil.

4° How to Moderate the Passions

804. a) Even when the passions are directed towards good, one must know how to temper them, that is to say, one must know how to make them obey the dictates of reason and the control of the will, both reason and will being guided in turn by the light of faith and by grace. Without this restraining influence, the passions would at times run to *excess*, for they are by nature too impetuous.

Thus, the desire to pray fervently may become a strain; love for Jesus may manifest itself in forced emotions which wear out both body and soul; untimely zeal results in overstrain, indignation degenerates into anger, and joy into dissipation of mind. We are particulary exposed to such excesses in this age in which the feverish activity of our fellow-men readily becomes contagious. Even when these vehement impulses are directed towards good, they weary both mind and body and cannot, in any event, be of lasting duration, for *violence is shortlived*, whereas it is sustained effort that best secures spiritual progress.

805. b) We must, therefore, submit our activity to the control of a wise director, and follow the dictates of Christian prudence.

1) In the training of our desires and of our passions there must be a certain *habitual* moderation, a kind of calm tranquillity, and we must avoid being constantly under a strain. We have a long journey ahead and it is important that we save our strength, since our poor human machine cannot be forever under pressure without danger of collapse.

2) Before a great expenditure of effort, prudence demands that we enforce a certain rest, that we put a certain curb upon our ambitions, even the most legitimate, and upon our zeal, even the most ardent and the purest. Our Lord Himself gave us the example in this. From time to time He invited His disciples to rest: "*Come apart into a desert place and rest a little.*"[1]

Thus directed and tempered, the passions, far from constituting an obstacle to perfection, will be effective means of daily growth in holiness.

---

[1] *Mark.*, VI, 31.

§ IV. The Discipline of the Higher Faculties

The higher faculties, the *intellect* and the *will*, which make man what he is, need likewise to be disciplined, for they also have been affected by original sin, n. 75.

I. *The Discipline of the Intellect* [1]

806. We have been endowed with understanding, that we may know truth, and above all that we may know God and things divine. It is God Who is the true light of the mind. He illumines us with a twofold light, that of *reason* and that of *faith*. In our present state, we cannot come to the fulness of truth, without the joint help of these two lights. To scorn either of them is to blindfold our eyes. The discipline of the intellect is all the more important, since it is the intellect that enlightens the will and enables it to direct its course towards good. It is the intellect which, under the name of *conscience*, is the guide of our moral and our supernatural life. That it may rightly fulfil its office, its defects must be corrected. The chief of these are ignorance, curiosity, hastiness, pride and obstinacy.

807. 1º **Ignorance** is overcome by a constant and systematic application to study, above all, to the study of whatever refers to our last end, and to the means of attaining it. It would be irrational to concern ourselves with all sciences and neglect the science of salvation.

Indeed, each one must study those branches of human knowledge that relate to his duties of state; but the foremost duty being that of knowing God in order to love Him, to neglect this would be inexcusable. Yet, how many Christians there are, who, though well versed in some branch or other of learning, have but a very imperfect acquaintance with Christian truths, Christian doctrines, Christian morals, and Christian asceticism!

808. 2º **Curiosity** is a disease of the mind, which is one of the causes of religious ignorance, for it leads us to seek too eagerly the knowledge of things that delight us rather than of things that are profitable to us, and thus to lose precious time.

In order to overcome curiosity we must : 1) study before all else, not what is pleasing, but what is profitable, especially what is necessary. " *What is more necessary comes first* ", said St. Bernard, and we must not be occupied with the rest except by way of recreation. Hence, books that feed the imagination rather than the mind should be read

---

[1] *Cursus Asceticus*, I. P., 94-102. MATURIN, *Self-Knowledge and Self-Discipline*, P. 141-179; PAYOT, *The Education of the Will*, Bk. II, C. I, III.

sparingly; such are, for the most part, novels, newspapers and reviews of a worldly character. 2) In reading, we must avoid any undue eagerness, the desire to *rush through* a volume. It is especially when we read serious works that it is important to go slowly, the better to understand and to relish what we read (n. 582). 3) This will be all the easier, if we study, not from curiosity, not merely for the sake of knowledge, but from a supernatural motive, to improve ourselves and to enlighten others : " *That they edify others, and this is charity... that they be edified themselves, and this is prudence.*" [1] For, as St. Augustine tells us, knowledge should be put to the service of love : " *Let knowledge be used in order to erect the structure of charity.*" [2] This holds true even in the study of things spiritual. Some there are who seek in the pursuit of such studies satisfaction for their curiosity and their pride rather than the purification of their heart and the practice of mortification. [3]

809.   3° Pride is to be avoided, that pride of intellect which is more dangerous and more difficult to overcome than the pride of will, as Scupoli [4] says.

This is the pride that renders faith and obedience to superiors difficult. One wants to be self-sufficient; the more confidence one has in one's own judgment the more reluctantly does one accept the teachings of faith, or the more readily does one submit these to criticism and to personal interpretation. In like manner, one so trusts to one's own wisdom, that it is with repugnance that others are consulted, especially superiors. Hence, regrettable mistakes occur. Hence comes also obstinacy of judgment, resulting in the final and sweeping condemnation of such opinions as differ from our own. Herein lies one of the most common causes of strife between Christian and Christian, at times even between Catholic writers. St. Augustine calls those who cause unfortunate dissensions, destructive of peace and of the bond of charity, " *Dividers of unity, enemies of peace, without charity, puffed up with vanity, well pleased with themselves and great in their own eyes.*" [5]

810.   To heal this intellectual pride : 1) we must first of all submit ourselves with childlike docility to the teachings of faith. We are undoubtedly allowed to seek that understanding of our dogmas which is obtained by a patient and laborious quest with the aid of the Fathers and Doctors of the Church, especially St. Augustine and St. Thomas; but as the Vatican Council [6] says, this must be done with piety and with discretion, following the maxim of St. Anselm : " *Faith, seeking understanding.* "   Thus we avoid that hypercritical attitude that attenuates and minimizes our dogmas under pretense of explaining them. We submit our judgment not only to the truths of faith but to the directions of the Holy See. With regard to such questions

[1] S. BERNARD, *In Cant.*, sermon XXXVI, n. 3.
[2] *Epist.*, LV, C. 22, n. 39, *P. L.*, XXXIII, 223.
[3] SCUPOLI, *Spiritual Combat*, C. IX. — [4] *Loc. cit.* — [5] *Sermo III* Paschæ, n. 4.
[6] DENZING., n. 1796.

as are open to discussion, we give others the same freedom as we claim for ourselves and refrain from taking an attitude of contempt for the opinions of others. Thus, minds are at peace.

2) In the discussions we hold with others, we must seek, not the satisfaction of our pride and the triumph of our ideas, but the truth. It seldom happens that there is not in the contrary opinions a kernel of truth that has so far escaped our notice. The best means of drawing close to the truth, as well as of observing the laws of humility and charity, is to listen attentively and without prejudice to the reasons adduced by our opponents and to admit whatever is true in their remarks.

To sum up, in order to discipline the mind we must study what is most necessary and pursue this study with method, with perseverance and with supernatural motives, that is to say, with the desire to know and to love the truth and to live by it.

II. *The Training of the Will*

811. 1° **Necessity.** The will is in man the governing faculty. Being free, the will imparts its freedom, not only to the acts it performs itself, but to those acts it *bids* the other faculties perform; it gives them their merit or their demerit. The discipline of the will means the discipline of the entire man, and a well-disciplined will is one that is strong enough to *govern* the lower faculties and docile enough to *submit* itself to God. These are the two functions of the will.

Both are difficult. Ofttimes the lower faculties rebel against the will and submit only when one has learned to add tact to firmness; for the will does not exercise an *absolute* power over our sense faculties, but a kind of moral influence, a power of persuasion that leads them to compliance (n. 56).

Hence, it is only with difficulty and through oft-renewed efforts that we succeed in bringing the sense faculties and the passions under the sway of the will. Likewise, it is not easy to yield full submission of the will to God, because we aspire to a certain independence, and because God's will, in order to sanctify us, often demands sacrifices from which we naturally shrink. We often prefer our own tastes, our own whims, to the holy will of God. Here again, mortification becomes a necessity.

812. 2° **Practical means.** In order to effect the right education of the will, we must render it *supple* enough to obey God in all things and *strong* enough to control the body and the sensitive appetites. To attain this end, *obstacles must be removed* and *positive means* employed.

A) The chief **obstacles** are : a) *from within :* 1) *lack of reflection :* we do not reflect before acting and follow the impulse of the moment, passion, routine, caprice. We must take thought before acting and ask ourselves what God demands of us. 2) *Over-eagerness*, which, producing too great a strain, depletes the energies of body and soul to no purpose, and often causes us to stray in the direction of evil. We need self-possession and self-restraint even in doing good, so that we may start up a lasting fire rather than a darting flame. 3) *Indifference*, indecision, sloth, lack of moral stamina, which paralyze or atrophy our will-power. We must, then, strengthen our convictions and build up our energies. 4) The *fear of failure*, or lack of confidence, an attitude which notably weakens our power. We must, therefore, remind ourselves that, with God's help, we are sure of attaining good results.

813. **b)** To these interior obstacles are added others coming *from without :* 1) *human respect*, which makes us slaves of other men and causes us to stand in fear of their criticisms or their mockery. This is combatted by realizing that what matters is not man's judgment, always liable to error, but the ever-wise and infallible judgment of God ; 2) *bad example*, which draws us all the more easily as it is in accord with the tendency of our nature. We must remember that the only model we are to imitate is Jesus Christ, Our Master and Our Head (n. 136 and foll.), and that the ways of the Christian must go counter to the ways of the world (n. 214).

814. **B)** The **positive means** consist in a harmonious combination of the work of the *mind*, the *will* and *grace*.

a) It is the province of the *mind* to furnish those deep-seated *convictions* that are at once a guide and a stimulus to the will.

These convictions are those calculated to determine the will in the choice of what is in conformity with the will of God. They are thus summed up : God is my one end and Jesus Christ is the way which I must take to reach Him ; I must, then, do all things for God, in union with Jesus Christ. Only one obstacle sin, can come in the way of the attainment of my end. I must, then, flee from sin and should I have the misfortune of falling into it I must immediately atone for it. Only one means is necessary and suffices to avoid sin, always to do the will of God. I must, then, ever strive to know His will and conform my conduct to it. In order to succeed in this, I shall frequently repeat the words of St. Paul at the moment of his conversion : " *Lord, what wilt thou have me to do ?* " [1] In the evening, in my examination of conscience, I shall reproach myself for the least failing.

815. **b)** Such convictions exert a powerful influence upon the will, which, in turn, must act with *decision, firmness,*

---

[1] *Acts*, IX, 6.

and *constancy.* 1) *Decision* is necessary. Once we have reflected and prayed, according to the importance of the action we are about to perform, we must make an immediate decision, in spite of the amount of hesitation we may feel. Life is too short to lose time in such long deliberations. We take sides with what seems to be more in accordance with the divine will, and God Who sees our good dispositions will bless our action. 2) We must be *firm* in this decision. It is not enough to say: *I should like,* I wish; these are but *yearnings.* We must say: *I will,* and I will *at all costs,* and then set ourselves to the task without waiting for the morrow or for some grand opportunity. It is firmness in small things that secures fidelity in the greater. 3) This firmness, however, *is not synonymous with violence;* it is *calm,* for it must endure; and in order to give it *constancy,* we must often renew our efforts without ever allowing ourselves to be discouraged by failure; we are never vanquished except when we give up. In spite of a few failures, in spite even of a few wounds, we must consider ourselves the victors, because supported by God's grace, we are in reality invincible. If we have the misfortune of falling, we rise immediately. For the Divine Healer of souls there is no incurable wound, no incurable illness.

816. c) In the last analysis it is upon the grace of God that we must learn to rely. If we beg for it with humility and confidence, it will never be refused to us, and with it we are invincible. We must, then, often renew, especially before every important action, our convictions regarding the absolute necessity of grace; we must ask for it with insistence, in union with Our Lord so as to make its bestowal more certain. We must remind ourselves that Jesus Christ is not only our *model* but our *co-worker,* and lean confidently upon Him, assured that in Him we are powerful to undertake and to bring to completion all things pertaining to salvation: "*I can do all things in Him who strengtheneth me.*"[1] Then, our will is strong, since it shares in the very strength of God: "*The Lord is my strength;*"[2] it is free, for true liberty does not consist in yielding to our passions, but in securing the triumph of reason and will over instinct and sensuality.

817. Conclusion. Thus will be accomplished the purpose we have assigned to mortification — to bring our

---

[1] *Phil.,* IV, 13. — [2] *Ps.* CXVII, 14.

senses and our lower faculties under subjection to the will
and the will to God.

CHAPTER IV

The Struggle against the Capital Sins [1]

818. At bottom this struggle is but a species of mortification.

In order to complete the purification of the soul and
prevent it from relapsing into sin, we must set upon the
source of the evil in us, which is the threefold concupiscence.
The general characteristics of this we have already described
in numbers 193-209; but being the root of the seven *capital
sins*, these evil inclinations must be known and attacked.
They are tendencies rather than sins; however, they are
called *sins*, because they lead to sins; they are termed
captital, because they are the fountain-head or source of
other sins.

These tendencies can be referred to the threefold concupiscence in this way : from pride are born *vain-glory*,
envy, and *anger;* from the *concupiscence of the flesh* issue
gluttony, *lust*, and *sloth;* lastly, the concupiscence of the
eyes is one with *avarice* or the inordinate love of riches.

819.   The struggle against the seven capital sins has always had
a prominent place in Christian spirituality.   Cassian treats of it at
length in his *Conferences* and in his *Institutes;* [2] he enumerates eight
instead of seven, because he distinguishes pride from vain-glory.
St. Gregory the Great [3] clearly distinguishes the seven capital sins,
all of which he traces to pride.   St. Thomas also traces them all to
pride and shows how they can be logically classified, if account is
taken of the *special ends* towards which man is drawn.   The will may
be drawn towards an object by a twofold motion, the search for some
apparent good, or flight from an apparent evil.   The apparent **good**
sought by the will may be : 1) *praise* or *honor*, a *spiritual* good, pursued
in an inordinate manner by persons who are vain ; 2) the preservation

---

[1] Cassian, *De cœnobiorum institutis*, l. V, c. I, *P. L.*, XLIX, 202 and foll.;
Collationes, coll. V, c. X, ibid., 621 and foll.; St. John Climacus, *Scala Para-
disi*, XXII, *P. G.*, LXXXVIII, 948 and foll.; St. Gregory the Great, *Moral.*,
l. XXXI, c. XLV, *P. L.*, LXXVI, 620 and foll.; St. Thomas, I-II, q. 84, a. 3-4;
De Malo, q. 8, a. 1; St. Bonaventure, *In II. Sent.*, dist. XLII, dub. III;
Noel Alexandre, *De Peccatis* (Theol. cursus *Migne*, XI, 707-1168); Alvarez
de Paz, t. II, Lib. I, P. 2, De extinctione vitiorum; Phil. de la Ste Trinité,
P. I, Tr. II, disc. II and III, De vitiorum eradicatione et passionum mortificatione;
Card. Bona, *Manuductio ad cælum*, cap. III-IX; Alibert, *Physiologie des Pas-
sions*, 1827; Descuret, *La Médecine des Passions*, Paris, 1860; Paulhan,.
Les Caractères, Paris, 1902; Laumonier, *La Thérapeutique des péchés capitaux*,
Paris, Alcan, 1922.

[2] *De cœnobiorum institutis*, Lib. V, C. I; *Collat.*, col. V, c. X.

[3] *Moral.*, C. XXXI, c. 45, *P. L.*, LXXVI, 620-622.

of self or of the race, *corporal* goods, sought after excessively by *gluttonous* and *impure persons* respectively; 3) *external* things, loved to excess by such as are *avaricious*.   The apparent **evil** from which we flee may consist : 1) in the effort required for the attainment of good, which effort the *slothful* evade; 2) in the prospect of lost prestige, which both the *jealous* and the *irritable* dread, though in different ways.   Thus, the differentiation of the seven capital sins is based on the seven special ends which the sinner has in view.

We shall follow that division which shows the connection between the capital vices and our threefold concupiscence.

ART. I. PRIDE AND THE VICES RELATED THERETO [1]

§ I. Pride

820.   Pride is a *deviation* of that legitimate sentiment which prompts us to prize what is good in us, and to seek the esteem of others in the measure in which this is useful. There is no doubt that we *can* and that we *must* prize the good which God has given us, acknowledging that He is its first principle and last end.   This is a sentiment that honors God and makes for self-respect.   We may also desire that others see and appreciate the good that is in us and that they give glory to God for it, just as we ourselves must in turn recognize and appreciate their good qualities. This mutual regard fosters good relations among men.

However, these two tendencies may either go astray, or go beyond due limits.   At times we forget that God is the source of these gifts, and *we attribute them to ourselves.* This constitutes a disorder, for it denies, at least implicitly, that God is our first principle.   In like manner we are tempted to act for self, or to gain the esteem of others, instead of acting for God, and of referring to Him all the honor.   This is again a disorder, for it denies, at least in the same implicit manner, that God is our last end.   Such is the twofold disorder found in this vice.   We can, then, define pride as *an inordinate love of self, which causes us to consider ourselves, explicitly or implicitly, as our first beginning and last end.*   It is a species of idolatry, for we make gods of ourselves, as Bossuet remarks (n. 204). The better to combat pride, we shall expose :   1° the *principal forms* it takes, 2° the *faults* it engenders, 3° its *malice*, 4° the *remedies* to be applied.

---

[1] ST. THOMAS, II[a] II[æ], q. 162, q. 132; *de Malo*, q. 8-9; BOSSUET, *Tr. de la Concupiscence*, c. 10-23; *Sermon sur l'Ambition;* BOURDALOUE, *Carême*, Serm. pour le mercredi de la 2ᵉ sem.; ALIBERT, *op. cit.*, t. I, p. 23-57; DESCURET, *op. cit.*, t. II, p. 191-240; PAULHAN, *Les Caractères*, p. 167; BEAUDENOM, *The Path of Humility;* THOMAS, *L'Education des sentiments*, Paris, Alcan, 1904, p. 113-124, 133-148; LAUMONIER, *op. cit.*, C. VII.

I. *The Principal Forms of Pride.*

821. 1° The first form of pride is to regard oneself, explicitly or implicitly, as one's own *first principle.*

A) There are but few who go as far as to consider themselves *explicitly* as their own first principle.

a) This is the sin of atheists, who wilfully deny God, because they want no master, " *No God, no Master.* " Of such the Psalmist speaks when he says : " *The fool hath said in his heart : there is no God.* " [1]
b) This was, *equivalently*, the sin of *Lucifer*, who, desiring to be a *rule unto himself*, refused to submit to God ; the sin of our first parents, who wishing to be like God wanted to know of themselves what is good and what is evil ; the sin of *heretics*, who like Luther refused to acknowledge the authority of the Church established by God ; the sin of *rationalists*, who in their pride of intellect refuse to submit their reason to faith. This is also the sin of *certain intellectuals*, who, too proud to accept the traditional interpretation of dogmas, attenuate and deform them to make them conform to their own views.

822. **B)** A greater number fall into this fault *implicitly* by acting as if the *natural* and *supernatural* gifts which God has freely bestowed upon them were in every sense their own. True, they recognize in theory that God is their first principle, but in practice they esteem themselves beyond measure, as if they were the source of the qualities they possess.

a) Some there are who *delight* in their qualities and their worth as if these were due solely to themselves. " The soul, " says Bossuet, " seeing its own beauty, has delighted in itself and has become absorbed in the contemplation of its own excellence. It has failed for an instant to refer all it has to God ; it has forgotten its own dependence ; it has first centered upon self and then surrendered to it. But in seeking to free himself from God and the laws of justice, man has become the slave of his sin. " [2]

823. b) Graver still is the pride of those who, after the manner of the Stoics, attribute to themselves the *virtues they practice;* the pride of those who imagine that the free gifts of God are the *wages due their own merits*, or that their good works are more their own than God's, Who in reality is their principal cause ; the pride of those who look complacently upon such good works, as if these were wholly their own. [3]

824. **C)** By the same principle we *exaggerate our personal qualities.*

a) We close our eyes to our defects, we look at our good qualities through magnifying glasses, as it were, and we end by attributing to ourselves qualities we do not possess or, at least, qualities which have only the appearance of virtue. Thus, we give alms for show and we believe ourselves charitable when we are simply proud ; we fancy we

---

[1] *Ps.* XIII, 1. — [2] *Tr. on Concupiscence*, C. XI.
[3] Ibid., C. XXIII ; OLIER, *Introd.*, C. VII.

are saints because we enjoy sensible consolations, or because we have given expression to beautiful thoughts, or taken good resolutions, whilst in reality we have not advanced beyond the first few steps on the way to perfection.   Others pride themselves on being broad-minded because they make little of small practices, wishing to sanctify themselves by doing great things.   b) From this there is but one step to *an unjust preference of self to others.*   We examine their defects with a miscroscope, and we are scarcely conscious of our own; we see the mote in the neighbor's eye, but not the beam in our own.   At times we come, like the Pharisee, to despise our brethren;[1] at other times, without going that far, we unjustly lower them in our estimation, and we believe ourselves above, whilst in reality we are below them.   It is by the selfsame principle that we seek to lord it over our brethren and have our superiorty over them recognized.   c) In relation to *Superiors,* this pride takes the form of censure and fault-finding, prompting us to scrutinize minutely ^ll their acts, all their moves; we want to pass judgment on all things, to control all things.   Thus we render obedience far more difficult for ourselves; we find it hard to submit to the authority and the decisions of superiors; to ask their permission becomes a hardship; we aspire to independence, that is, to be ourselves our own first principle.

825.   2° The second form of pride consists in considering ourselves, explicitly or implicitly, as *our last end,* by performing our actions without referring them to God, and by desiring to be praised for them as if they were exclusively our work.   This fault proceeds from the first, for whoever looks upon himself as his own first principle wills also to be his own last end.   Here we must recall the distinctions already made.

A) Hardly any one *explicitly* considers himself as his own last end, except an atheist or an unbeliever.

B) Yet, many behave in practice as if they shared in this error. a) They want to be praised, to be complimented upon their good works, as if they were themselves the principal authors, and as if they were responsible only to themselves.   Instead of referring all to God, they expect congratulations for success, as if all the honor were due to them.   b) They are prompted by *egotism,* they act for their own ends, caring little for the glory of God, and still less for the welfare of their neighbor.   They even go so far as to take for granted that others must organize their lives to please and to serve them; thus they make themselves the *center,* and so to speak, the end toward which others are to gravitate.   What else is this if not the unconscious usurpation of the rights of God?   c) There are devout persons who, without going so far seek self in piety : they complain of God when He does not flood them with consolations; they pine with grief when in the midst of dryness, and thus form the false idea that the aim of piety is the enjoyment of consolations, forgetting that the glory of God must be the supreme end of all our actions, above all, of prayer and spiritual exercises.

826.   We must, then, acknowledge the fact that pride, under one form or the other, is a very common fault, even

---

[1] *Luke* XVIII, 9-14.

among those who follow the path of perfection, a fault that stays with us through all the stages of the spiritual life and disappears only when we die. Beginners are hardly aware of it because their study of self does not reach deep enough. Their attention must be drawn to this point; the more common forms of this fault must be indicated to them, so that they may make these the subject of their particular examination.

II. *Defects Born of Pride*

The chief ones are *presumption, ambition*, and *vain-glory*.

827. 1º *Presumption* consists in an inordinate desire and hope whereby we want to do things which are beyond our strength. It proceeds from too high an opinion of ourselves, of our natural faculties, of our knowledge, of our strength, of our virtues.

a) From the *intellectual* point of view we think ourselves capable of approaching and solving the most difficult questions, or at least of undertaking studies which are beyond the reach of our talents. We easily persuade ourselves that we abound in judgment and wisdom, and instead of learning how to doubt, we settle with finality the most controverted questions. **b)** From the *moral* point of view we fancy that we are possessed of sufficient light to be our own guides, and that it is hardly profitable to consult a spiritual director. We convince ourselves that in spite of past faults we need fear no relapses, and we imprudently walk into occasions of sin, and then we fall. From this come discouragement and vexation that often result in fresh falls. **c)** From the *spiritual* point of view, we have but little relish for hidden and mortifying virtues, preferring those that are more brilliant : instead of building upon the sound foundation of humility, we dream about greatness of soul, about strength of character, about a magnanimous spirit, about apostolic zeal, and about the imaginary successes we lay in store for the future. The first serious temptations, however, make us aware that the will is still weak and wavering. At times we make little of the ordinary ways of prayer, and of what are called the little exercises of piety, aspiring to extraordinary graces while we are still only at the beginning of the spiritual life.

828. 2º This *presumption*, added to pride, begets *ambition*, that is to say, *the inordinate love of honors, of dignities, of authority over others*. Because we presume overmuch on our strength, and because we consider ourselves superior to others, we want to dominate them, to rule them and impose upon them our ideas.

This disorder, says St. Thomas, [1] may show itself in three ways : 1) One seeks for undeserved honors, honors which are above one; 2) one seeks them for oneself, for

---

[1] *Sum. theol.*, IIa, IIæ, q. 131, a. 1.

one's own glory, and not for the glory of God; 3) one takes delight in honors for their own sake, without making them redound to the good of others, contrary to the order established by God Who requires superiors to procure the welfare of those under them.

This ambition invades every sphere of life : 1) the *political* realm, where men aspire to rule others, and that ofttimes at the price of so many meannesses, so many compromises, so many questionable practices, in order to secure the votes of constituents; 2) the *intellectual* domain, wherein men seek stubbornly to impose their ideas on others, even with regard to questions open to free discussion; 3) *civil* life, where men *vie* for the first places, [1] high office, and the plaudits of the crowd; 4) even the *ecclesiastical* state is not exempt, for as Bossuet [2] remarks, " How many safeguards have not been found necessary, even in ecclesiastical and religious elections, in order to curb ambition, to prevent factions, intrigues, underhand dealings, and the most criminal pledges and practices, simoniacal contracts, and other such irregularities too common in these matters? We cannot boast that these safeguards have uprooted such abuses; they have hardly done more than to conceal or to restrain them in part. " And, as St. Gregory [3] notes, are there not those, even in the ranks of the clergy, who want to be called doctors, and eagerly seek the first places and the praise of men? " They seek to appear learned, they long to excel others, and, as Truth bears witness, they crave the first salutations in public, the first places at table, the highest seats in councils. "

This fault, then, in more general than one would at first sight believe, and is closely allied with vanity.

829. 3° *Vanity is an inordinate love for the esteem of others.* It differs from pride, which is pleasure taken in one's own excellence; it generally springs from pride. When one has conceived too high an esteem for oneself one naturally desires the approbation of others.

830. A) The Malice of Vanity. We may rightfully desire the esteem of others, if we wish that our qualities, natural or supernatural, be acknowledged in order that God be glorified and that our influence for good be extended. Such a desire is not sinful, for it is in order that what is good should be esteemed, provided we acknowledge God as the author of that good and that He alone must be given the praise for it. [4] The most that can be said against such desires is that it is dangerous to center our thoughts upon them, because we run the risk of seeking the esteem of others for selfish purposes.

---

[1] It is not solely among the learned and the wealthy that this defect is found, Bossuet speaks *(Tr. on Concupiscence,* C. XVI) of the country-folk who peevishly contend for the more honorable places in the churches, going so far as to say that they will cease to attend divine services unless their wishes are given heed.
[2] *Tr. on Concupisc.,* C. XVI. — [3] *Pastoral;* P. I, C. I, *P. L.,* LXXVII, 14.
[4] Cf. St. Thomas, IIa IIæ, q. 132, a. 1.

The disorder, then, consists in wanting to be held in esteem *for one's own sake*, without referring this honor to God, Who has placed in us whatever good we possess; it may also consist in wanting to be esteemed *for the sake of vain things*, undeserving of praise; or it may consist in seeking the esteem of those *whose judgment is worthless*, of wordlings for instance, who hold in esteem only vain things.

No one has given a better description of this fault than St. Francis de Sales: "We call that glory *vain* which we assume to ourselves, either for what is not in us, or for what is in us, but belongs to us, but deserves not that we should glory in it. The nobility of our ancestors, the favor of great men, and popular honor, are things, not in us, but either in our progenitors, or in the esteem of other men. Some become proud and insolent, either by riding a good horse, wearing a feather in their hat, or by being dressed in a fine suit of clothes; but who does not see the folly of this? for if there be any glory in such things, the glory belongs to the horse, the bird, and the tailor... Others value themselves for a well-trimmed beard, for curled locks, or soft hands; or because they can dance, sing or play; but are not these effeminate men, who seek to raise their reputation by so frivolous and foolish things? Others, for a little learning, would be honored and respected by the whole world, as if every one ought to become their pupil, and account them his masters. These are called pedants. Others strut like peacocks, contemplating their beauty and think themselves admired by every one. All this is extremely vain, foolish, and impertinent; and the glory which is raised on so weak foundations is justly esteemed vain and frivolous. "[1]

831. B) Faults that spring from vanity. Vanity produces many *faults* which are but its outward manifestation. The principal ones are *boasting, ostentation* and *hypocrisy*.

1) *Boasting* is the habit of speaking of self or of those things that can redound to our advantage with a view to gaining the esteem of others. There are those who speak of themselves, of their family, of their success with a candor that amuses their hearers; others cleverly turn the trend of conversation to a subject wherein they can display their knowledge; others timidly speak of their defects, harboring the secret hope that these will be excused and their good qualities thereby made more apparent.[2]

2) *Ostentation* consists in drawing to self the attention of others by a certain way of acting, by pompous display, and by singularity.

3) *Hypocrisy* takes on the outward appearance of virtue to cover very real vices.

III. *The Malice of Pride*

To form a right idea of this malice we may consider pride *in itself* and in its *effects*.

---

[1] *Devout Life*, III, C. IV.
[2] *Spirit of St. Francis de Sales*, c. XIX.

832.   1⁰ **In itself: A)** *Pride properly so called*, that pride which consciously and wilfully usurps, even if implicitly, the rights of God, is a grievous sin, nay it is the gravest of sins, says St. Thomas, [1] because it is a refusal to submit to God's sovereign will.

a) To want to be *independent*, to refuse obedience to God or to His lawful representatives, in a serious matter, constitutes a mortal sin, since one thereby revolts against God, our rightful Sovereign.

b) To attribute to oneself what evidently comes from God, and especially the gifts of grace, constitutes likewise a grievous fault, for this is to deny implicitly that God is the first principle of whatever good is in us.   Some are guilty of this, for example, those who say that they have "made themselves what they are."

c) One sins gravely, again, when one wants to act *for oneself to the exclusion of God*, for this is to deny God His right to be our last end.

833.   **B)** *Mitigated* pride, which indeed acknowledges God as the first principle or last end but does not render Him all that is due to Him, and implicitly robs Him of a part of His glory, is without doubt a *venial* fault.   Such is the fault of those who glory in their good qualities or their virtues, as if they were convinced that all is theirs in their own right.   It is also the fault of the presumptuous, of the vain, of the ambitious, who, however, do nothing against a divine or a human law in serious matter.   At all events, such sins can become mortal if they lead to acts that are grievously reprehensible.   Thus, vanity, which in itself is but a venial fault, becomes a grievous one when it causes us to contract debts which we are unable to pay, or when it seeks to stir in others an inordinate love.   Pride, then, must be examined also in its results.

834.   2⁰ In its **effects: A)** Unrestrained pride produces at times *disastrous effects*.   How many wars have been started through the pride of rulers and sometimes through the pride of nations themselves! [2]   Without going that far, how many family discussions, how many personal hatreds are not due to this vice?   The Fathers rightly teach that it is the root of all other vices and that it vitiates many a virtuous act, since it causes men to perform them from selfish motives. [3]

835.   **B)** Taking the point of view *of perfection*, the one with which we are concerned, we can say that pride is the archenemy of perfection because it creates in the soul

---

[1] *Sum. theol.*, IIᵃ IIᵃᵉ, q. 162, c. 5-6.
[2] St. CHRYSOSTOM, *in Ep. II ad. Thess.*, C. I, homil. I, n. 2. *P. G.*, 471.
[3] St. GREGORY, *Moral.*, l. XXXIV, c. 33, n. 48, *P. L.*, LXXVI, 744.

a *barren waste* and is the *source of numerous sins.*   **a**) It
deprives us of many graces and much merit:

1) It deprives us of many *graces,* because God Who is
bountiful with His grace to the humble, withholds it from
the proud: " *God resisteth the proud and giveth grace to the
humble.*" [1]   Let us weigh well these words: God resisteth the
proud, " Because ", says Father Olier, [2] " the proud man,
challenging God to His face, is resisted by the Almighty in
his insolent and horrible pretensions; and, since God wills
to remain what He is, He lays low and destroys such as
rise up against Him. "

2) It deprives us of much *merit.*   One of the essential
conditions for meriting is purity of intention.   But the
proud man acts *for self* or in order to please men, instead
of acting for God, and thus deserves the reproach addressed
to the Pharisees, who paraded their good works before men
and who for this reason could expect no recompense from
God: " *Take heed that you do not your justice before men to
be seen by them: otherwise you shall not have reward of your
Father who is in heaven....   Amen, I say to you, they have
received their reward.*" [3]

836.   b) Pride is likewise a *source of many faults :*
1) Personal faults: through *presumption* one exposes oneself
to danger and falls; through *pride* one fails to ask earnestly
for the graces one needs and likewise falls; then come
discouragement and the temptation to conceal sins in confession.   2) Faults against the neighbor: through pride one
is unwilling to yield, even when in the wrong; one is caustic
in speech; one indulges in harsh and heated discussions
which bring dissension and discord; hence, acrimonious
words, even unjust ones, against one's rivals in order to
belittle them; hence, bitter criticism against Superiors and
refusal to obey their orders.

837.   c) Finally, pride is a *source of unhappiness* to those
habitually given to it.   Because we want to excel in all
things and lord it over others, we have neither peace nor
contentment, for we know no rest as long as we have not
succeeded in vanquishing our antagonists and, since this is
never fully accomplished, we are troubled, ill at ease
and unhappy.

---

[1] *James,* IV, 6. — [2] *Introduction,* c. VI. — [3] *Matt.,* VI, 1-2.

IV. *The Remedies against Pride*

838. We have already said (n. 207) that the great remedy against pride is the acknowledgment of the fact that God is the Author of all good, and that therefore to Him alone belongs all honor and glory. *Of ourselves* we are but *nothingness* and *sin,* and hence merit nothing but *forgetfulness* and *contempt* (n. 208).

839. 1° **We are but nothingness.** Beginners must form this conviction through meditation by pondering leisurely the following thoughts: I am nothing, I can do nothing, I am worth nothing.

A) I am nothing. — True, it has pleased the divine goodness to choose me out of millions of possible beings, to give me my existence, to endow me with life, with a spiritual and immortal soul, and for this I am bound to thank Him daily. Yet, **a)** *I came from nothing,* and by the very force of my being *I tend towards nothingness,* whereto I should surely return were it not for the abiding action of my Maker which sustains me. My being, then, is not mine, but is wholly God's, and it is to Him that I must render homage.

b) This being God has given me is a living reality, a great boon for which I shall never be able to return Him due thanks. Yet, wondrous as this being of mine is, side by side with the God-head it is as mere nothingness: " *And my substance is as nothing before thee,* " [1] for it is so imperfect. 1) This being is a *contingent being,* which could well cease to exist without detracting anything from the world's perfection. 2) It is a *borrowed being,* given to me on the explicit condition of remaining under the sway of God's supreme dominion. 3) It is a *frail* being, unable to subsist of itself, a being that ever needs the unceasing sustaining power of its Maker. Such being is, therefore, essentially *dependent* upon God, and has no other reason for its existence than that of giving glory to its Creator. To forget this dependence, to act as if our good qualities were absolutely our own and to boast of them, is an error hard to conceive; it is madness and injustice.

840. What we say of man considered in the order of nature is even truer of him in *the order of grace,* whereby we share in the life of God, wherefrom issue all our worth

---

[1] *Ps.* XXXVIII, 6.

and all our grandeur, that grace which is essentially a free gift of God and of Jesus Christ, which we cannot for long keep without the help of God, and wherein we cannot grow without His supernatural concurrence (n. 126-128). For this especially we must say: "Thanks be to God for His unspeakable gift."[1]   What ingratitude and injustice to attribute to self the least part of that gift essentially divine!   "*What hast thou that thou hast not received? And if thou hast received, why dost thou glory, as if thou hadst not received it?*"[2]

841. B) Of myself I can do nothing.   True, I have received from God wondrous powers that enable me to know and love truth and goodness.   These faculties have been perfected by the supernatural virtues and the gifts of the Holy Ghost.   These gifts of nature and of grace blending so harmoniously and complementing one another so perfectly surpass all wonder.   Yet, *of myself*, of my own accord, *I can do nothing* to set them in motion to work out their perfection.   I can do nothing in the *natural* order without the concurrence of God; I can do nothing in the supernatural order without actual grace, not even conceive a good thought unto salvation, nor a desire supernaturally good.   Knowing this, could I take pride in those natural and supernatural powers as if they were entirely my own? Here again there would be ingratitude and madness and injustice.

842. C) I am worth nothing.   In truth, if I consider what God has placed within me, what He works in me through His grace, I am worth a great deal, I am beyond price: "*For you are bought with a great price*"[3].... *You are worth what God is worth.*"   I am worth the price which was paid for me, and the price paid for me was the blood of God Himself!   Does the glory of my redemption and of my sanctification belong to me or to the Almighty? There can be no uncertain answer to such question.   But still, urges my vanquished self-love, I have something that is my own, something that invests me with greatness, my free co-operation with God's concurrence and His grace. Indeed, we have therein our share, yet *not the principal* share.   That free consent is the mere exercise of faculties freely bestowed on us by God, and at the very moment we give it, God is working within us as its principal cause: "*For it is God who worketh in you, both to will and to*

---

[1] *II Cor.*, IX, 15. — [2] *I Cor.*, IV, 7. — [3] *I Cor.*, VI, 20.

accomplish. " [1] Besides, for the one time that we agree to follow the impulse of grace, how many times are there when we resist grace or co-operate only half-heartedly? Truly, there is nothing wherein we should glory; rather there is cause for humiliation.

When a great artist creates a masterpiece, it is to him that we attribute it and not to the third or fourth rate artists who have been his collaborators. With far greater reason must we give to God the credit for our merits as their first and principal cause, since God, as the Church says with St. Augustine, but " *crowns His own gifts when He crowns our merits.* "

Therefore, from whatever point of view we see ourselves, whether we consider the great worth of the gifts wherewith we have been endowed, or the great value of our merits themselves, we find no cause for boasting, but cause for paying tribute to God and for thanking Him from our inmost heart. Moreover, we find that we have to beg His pardon for the bad use we have made of His gifts.

843. 2° **I am a sinner,** and as such I merit *contempt*, all the contempt which it may please God to heap upon me. To convince ourselves of this, it suffices to recall what we have said about *mortal* and *venial* sin.

A) If I have committed but a single mortal sin, I have merited eternal humiliation, since I have merited hell. True, I entertain the hope that God has pardoned me, yet it remains none the less true that I have criminally assailed the majesty of God, that I have attempted a species of deicide, perpetrated a sort of spiritual suicide (n. 719), and that in order to atone to the Divine Majesty for that offence, I must be ready to accept, nay, even to wish for every possible humiliation, every slander, every calumny, every injury, every insult. All this is far below the just deserts of him who has offended a single time the infinite majesty of God. And if I have offended against it a great many times, what must be my resignation, nay, my joy, when the occasion offers to expiate my sins by enduring a shame that lasts but for a short time!

844. **B)** We have all committed *venial sins* and, no doubt, *deliberate* ones, thus making a willing choice in favor of our own wills and our own pleasure as against the will and the glory of the Almighty. This, we have said, (n. 715) constitutes an affront to the Divine Majesty, an offence meriting such abject humiliations, that, should we spend the whole of our lives in the exercise of humility, we should never be able of ourselves to give back to God the glory that we have unjustly taken from Him. If this way of speaking seems to us an exaggeration, let us recall the tears and the austerities which the Saints, who had been guilty of but venial faults, thought always insufficient for the cleansing of their [souls and inadequate to repair the outrages offered to the majesty of God. These Saints saw this in a clearer light than we do, and if we think otherwise it is because we are blinded by our pride.

As *sinners*, therefore, far from seeking the esteem of others, we must despise ourselves and accept all the humiliations that God may see fit to send us.

§ II. Envy [1]

845. Envy is at once a *passion* and one of the *capital sins*. As a passion it consists in a sort of deep sadness experienced in the sensitive part of our nature because of the good we see in others. This sensitive impression is accompanied by a contraction of the heart, slowing the activity of this organ and producing a feeling of anguish.

Here we are mainly concerned with envy inasmuch as it is a capital sin, and we shall explain: 1° its *nature*, 2° its *malice*, 3° its *remedies*.

846. 1° **The Nature of Envy. A)** Envy is *a tendency to be saddened by another's good as if that good constituted an affront to our own superiority.* Often it coincides with a desire of seeing the neighbor deprived of the particular good that offends us.

This vice proceeds *from pride*, which can bear neither superior nor rival. When we are persuaded of our own superiority, we are saddened to see others better gifted than we are or, with no greater gifts than ours, succeeding better than we do. The object of envy is chiefly some brilliant quality; yet, with men of a serious turn of mind envy bears also upon solid qualities and even upon virtue.

This fault manifests itself in the pain we experience upon hearing the praises of others, and in the subsequent attempt we make to depreciate this good opinion by criticizing those that are thus commended.

---

[1] ST. CYPRIAN, *De zelo et livore, P. L.*, IV, 637-652; ST. GREGORY, *Moral.*, l. V, c. 46, *P. L.*, LXXV, 727-730; ST. THOMAS, II-II, q. 36; *De Malo*, q. 10; ALIBERT, *op. cit.*, t. I, p. 331-340; DESCURET, t. II, p. 241-274; LAUMONIER, *op. cit.*, C. V.

847. B) *Envy* is often confounded with jealousy. They differ, however, in that the latter consists in an excessive love of our own good accompanied by the fear lest we be deprived of it by others.   A student holding the first place in class, upon noting the progress made by a classmate, becomes jealous of him because he fears the latter may take away his rank.   If we enjoy the affection of a friend and we fear this affection may be alienated by a rival friend, we become jealous of him.   A man who has a large clientele, fearing lest it be reduced by a competitor, may likewise become jealous.   Hence arises the jealousy at times abounding among professionals, among writers, and sometimes even among priests.   The difference between envy and jealousy, to put it briefly, is this: *we are envious of another's good, and jealous* of our own.

C) There is also a difference between *envy* and *emulation*.   The latter is a praiseworthy sentiment, urging us to imitate, to equal, and, if possible, to surpass the good qualities of others, but always by means that are fair.

848.   2⁰ **Malice of Envy.**   We can make a study of this malice *in itself* and in its *effects*.

A) *In itself*, envy is by nature a *mortal sin*, because it is directly opposed to the virtue of charity which requires us to rejoice in the good fortune of others.   The more important the good we envy, the graver is our sin.   Thus, says St. Thomas, [1] to make envy bear upon the spiritual goods of the neighbor, to be saddened at his spiritual progress or his apostolic success is a very grave sin.   This is true only when these envious impulses are *fully consented to;* however, often they are mere emotional impressions, or at most, feelings in which there is but little reflection and will.   These latter constitute only a venial fault.

849.   **B)** In its *effects* envy is at times very culpable :

a) It stirs within us sentiments of *hatred :* we run the risk of conceiving a hatred for those whom we envy or of whom we feel jealous and, as a result, of speaking ill of them, of blackening their character, of calumniating them, of wishing them evil.

b) It tends to sow discord, not only between strangers, but between related families, and even among members of the same family.   We need only to recall the history of Joseph and his brothers.   These dissensions may go very far towards creating enmities and scandals.   At times envy divides the Catholics of a given region to the great detriment of the Church.

c) It urges men on to *the immoderate quest for riches and*

---

[1] *Sum. Theol.*, IIᵃ IIæ, q. 36, a. 4, ad 2.

for honors: in order to surpass those whom we envy, we indulge in overtaxing work, take steps of a more or less questionable nature, by which we sin against loyalty and even against *justice.*

d) It *disturbs our peace of soul:* we know no peace nor tranquillity as long as we do not succeed in eclipsing, in subjugating our rivals, and since this happens but seldom, we live in perpetual anguish.

850. 3° **The Remedies For Envy.** They are *negative* or *positive.*

A) The negative means consist: **a)** in scorning the very first intimations of envy and of jealousy that arise in the heart, in crushing such sentiments as something vile, as one would crush a viper; **b)** in *distracting* the *mind,* by occupying ourselves with any other thing, and when calm returns by constantly bearing in mind that the good qualities of our neighbor do not lessen ours, but are a stimulus to imitation.

851. B) Among the *positive* means, two are especially important.

a) The first is drawn from the fact of our incorporation into Christ: we are all brethren, members of a mystical body the head of which is Christ; the good qualities and the attainments of one member redound to all the others. Instead, then, of being saddened at the superiority of our brethren we must rejoice, according to the teaching of St. Paul, [1] since their superiority contributes to the common good and to our own particular welfare. If it be the virtues of another that we envy, " instead of bearing them envy and jealousy on account of those virtues, as occurs often through the suggestion of the evil one and of self-love, you should unite to the Holy Spirit of Jesus Christ in the Blessed Sacrament, honoring in Him the source of those virtues, and begging of Him the grace to share and partake therein. You will see how useful and how profitable such practice is to you. " [2]

852. b) The second means consists in cultivating that noble and Christian sentiment of *emulation,* which prompts us to imitate and even surpass the virtues of our neighbor, with the help of God's grace.

---

[1] *Rom.,* XII, 15, 16.
[2] OLIER, *Cat. for Int Life,* II, Lesson XIII.

In order that emulation be good and remain free from envy, it must be: 1) *right in its object*, that is to say, it must bear not on the successes, but the virtues of others, and this in order to imitate them. 2) It must be *worthy in its motives*, seeking not to vanquish others, humiliate them, bring them under subjection, but to make us better, in order that God may receive greater honor and the Church greater prestige.   3) It must be *fair in the means* it employs to attain its ends; not intrigue, not subterfuge nor any other unlawful proceeding; but effort, labor, the right use of the divine gifts.

Thus understood, emulation is an effective remedy against envy, since it works harm to no one and is at the same time an excellent stimulus.   For to consider as models the best among our brethren in order to follow in their steps or to go even further than they do, is in reality to acknowledge our own imperfections and to seek to remedy them by profiting by the example of those around us.   It is to imitate St. Paul, who invited his disciples to be imitators of himself as he was of Christ; [1] it is to follow the same Apostle's advice to the Christians: "Let us consider one another to provoke unto charity and to good works;" [2] it is to enter into the spirit of the Church, which, in proposing to us the Saints for our imitation, provokes us to a high and hallowed emulation.   Thus, what would have been envy, proves to be an occasion for the cultivation of virtue.

§ III. Anger [3]

The vice of anger is a perversion of that instinctive feeling that prompts us, upon attack, to resist force with force.   We shall speak of: 1° its *nature*, 2° its *malice*, 3° its *remedies*.

I. *The nature of Anger*

853.   There is a *passion of anger* and *a sentiment of anger*.

1° Anger considered as a *passion* is a violent need of reaction caused by physical or moral suffering or annoyance. This vexation excites a violent emotion which arouses our energies to overcome the difficulty.   We are then prone to vent our anger upon persons, animals and things.

There are two principal forms of anger: the *red rage* of the strong, and the *white rage* of the weak.   In the first kind of anger the heart throbs violently and pushes the blood to the surface; breathing becomes rapid, the face reddens, the neck swells, the veins expand

---

[1] *I Cor.*, XI, 1. — [2] *Hebr.*, X, 24.
[3] St. Gregory. *Moral.*, l. V, c. 45, *P. L.*, LXXV, 727-730; St. Thom., IIa IIæ. q. 158; *De Malo*, q. 12; Descuret, *op. cit.*, t. II, 1-57; Thomas, *op. cit.*, ch. IX, p. 94-103; Laumonier, *op. cit.*, ch. VI.

under the skin, the hair stands on end, the eyes sparkle and bulge out of their sockets, the nostrils widen and speech becomes raucous and halting, the muscles gather strength, the whole bodily frame is set for the onslaught and an irresistible motion strikes, breaks, or violently brushes aside the obstacle. White rage causes the heart to contract; breathing becomes difficult, the face assumes a death-like pallor, a cold sweat oozes from the brow, the jaws clench, and the person keeps an ominous silence. However, such pent up agitation ends by bursting forth into a rage and finds an outlet in the discharge of violent blows.

854. 2⁰ Anger as a *sentiment* consists in a vehement desire to repel and punish an aggressor.

A) There is a lawful sentiment of anger, a righteous indignation, which is the ardent, but rational desire to visit upon the guilty a just retribution. Thus it was that Our Lord was roused to anger against the money-changers whose traffic defiled His Father's house, [1] whilst on the other hand Heli, the high-priest, was severely reproved for not having curbed the shameful conduct of his sons.

That anger be legitimate, it must be: **a)** *just* as to its *object*, seeking to punish only those that deserve punishment, and only in the measure in which they have merited it; **b)** *tempered* by moderation in its *execution*, going no further than the offence demands and adhering to the requirements of justice; **c)** *animated* by *motives* of *charity*, not degenerating into sentiments of hatred, but aiming solely at the restoration of order and the amendment of the guilty. If any of these conditions are lacking, there is moral guilt. Lawful anger belongs chiefly to those in authority, like parents and superiors, yet it is at times the right and the duty of those in the ranks to resort to it in order to defend their common interests and prevent the ascendancy of the wicked, for there are men whom kindness fails to move and whom the fear of punishment alone can touch.

855. B) Anger as a capital vice is a violent and inordinate desire of punishing others, regardless of the three conditions we have noted. Often anger is accompanied by *hatred*, which seeks not merely to repel aggression but to take revenge. Such a sentiment is more deliberate, more lasting, and has, therefore, more serious consequences.

856. 3⁰ There are *degrees* of intensity in anger: **a)** at first, it consists in a mere impulse of *impatience;* the least annoyance, the least failure elicits a show of *temper*. **b)** This is followed by *agitation* which produces undue irritation and which manifests dissatisfaction by uncontrolled gestures. **c)** At times anger reaches the stage of *violence*, culminating not only in words but even in *blows*. **d)** It can develop into *fury*, which is temporary insanity: in this stage one is no longer master of self; one breaks forth into incoherent speech and into such wild gesticulation that it would seem real insanity. **e)** Lastly, anger at times degenerates into implacable *hatred*, breathing vengeance, and

[1] *John*, II, 13-17.

going so far as to desire death to the adversary. It is important to discern these degrees of anger in order to estimate its malice.

II. *The Malice of Anger*

It may be considered in *itself* and in its *effects*.

857. 1° In order to determine the exact malice of anger considered **in itself** we must make important distinctions: —

A) When anger simply consists in a *transient impulse of passion*, it is of itself a *venial sin*, because it exceeds proper measure, but it is only a venial sin because, as we presuppose, there is no violation of the great virtues of justice or charity.   However, there are instances when anger is so intense that self-control is lost and grave insult is offered to the neighbor.   If these impulses, even though born of passion, are deliberate and wilful they constitute a grievous fault; but often this is not the case.

858. **B)** Anger that goes as far as *hatred* and rancor, when deliberate and wilful, is of itself a *mortal sin*, for it grievously violates charity and often justice.   It is in this sense that Our Lord says : " But I say to you that whosoever is angry with his brother shall be in danger of the judgment. And whosoever shall say to his brother, Raca, shall be in danger of the council.   And whosoever shall say, Thou fool, shall be in danger of hell fire. " [1] Still, if this impulse of hatred is not fully deliberate, the fault will only be venial.

859. 2° The *effects* of anger when not repressed are at times terrible.

A) Seneca has described them in expressive words.   He attributes to anger treasons, murders, poisonings, divisions in families, dissensions and civil wars with all their horrible aftermath. [2]   Even when anger does not reach such extremes, it is the source of a great number of faults, because it disturbs the peace of families and gives rise to fearful enmities.

860. **B)** From the point of view of *perfection*, it is, St. Gregory [3] tells us, a great obstacle to spiritual progress, for if it is not curbed it makes us lose : 1) *good judgment,* mental poise; 2) *gentleness* which is the charm of social relations; 3) the sense of *justice,* for passion blinds us to the rights of others ; 4) the *spirit of recollection,* so indispensable to an intimate union with God, to peace of soul, to a ready compliance with the inspirations of grace.

---

[1] *Matth.*, V, 22. — [2] *De ira*, l. I, n. 2. — [3] *Moral.*, l. c., *P. L.*, LXXV, 724.

III. *Remedies against Anger*

These must attack the *passion* of anger and the sentiment of *hatred* which it at times engenders.

861. 1° We must make use of every means at our disposal in order to overcome the *passion* of anger.

A) Physical *hygiene* offers some means that combine to prevent or to soothe the anger, such as correct diet, lukewarm baths, abstention from stimulants and particularly from intoxicants. Such hygienic measures have importance in this matter because of the close union that exists between body and soul. However, account must be taken of temperament and health, and therefore prudence demands the advice of a physician. [1]

862. B) Withal, *moral* hygiene is even better. **a)** A good preventive of anger is to acquire the habit of reflecting before acting so as not to allow ourselves to be swept away by the first assaults of passion. This is uphill work, but most effective. **b)** When despite all, this passion has taken our heart by surprise, " it is better to drive it away speedily than enter into a parley; for, if we give it ever so little leisure, it will become mistress of the place, like the serpent, who easily draws in his whole body where he can once get in his head.... You must at the first alarm, speedily muster your forces; not violently, not tumultuously, but mildly, and yet seriously. " [2] Otherwise, whilst trying to repress anger with impetuosity we should but add to our perturbation. **c)** The better to check anger, it is useful to divert the mind, that is to say, to turn our thoughts to anything except the one thing liable to excite it. Therefore, we must banish all thought of past injuries, all suspicion, etc. **d)** " We must invoke the assistance of God when we find ourselves excited to wrath, in imitation of the Apostles when they were tossed by the wind and the storm upon the waters; for He will command our passions to cease, and a great calm shall ensue. " [3]

863. 2° When anger gives rise to sentiments of *hatred*, of *rancor*, or of *vengeance*, we can uproot these only by charity based on the love of God. At such times we must remind ourselves that we are all children of the same heavenly Father, all incorporated into the same Christ, all called to the same eternal happiness, and that these great

---

[1] Cf. DESCURET, *La Médecine des Passions;* J. LAUMONIER, *La thérapeutique...* p. 167-174.
[2] ST. FR. DE SALES, Introd. to a *Devout Life*, P. III, C. VIII.
[3] ST. FR. DE SALES, loc. cit.

truths exclude every sentiment of hatred. Therefore: **a**) we should recall the words of the *Lord's Prayer:* " Forgive us our trespasses as we forgive those who trespass against us, " and since we crave divine pardon, we should more willingly pardon our enemies. **b**) We should not lose sight of the example of Our Lord, still calling Judas His friend in the very moment of his treason, praying on the Cross for His executioners, and we should ask Him to give us the strength we need to forgive and forget. **c**) We should avoid all thoughts of injuries received and of what relates to them. Perfect souls pray for the conversion of those who have hurt them, and in this prayer they find a wonderful balm for the wounds of their souls.

Such are the chief means given us to triumph over the first three capital sins, pride, envy and anger. We now turn to consider the faults that have their source in sensuality: *gluttony*, *lust*, and *sloth*.

ART. II. SINS THAT PROCEED FROM SENSUALITY

§ I. Gluttony [1]

Gluttony is the abuse of that legitimate pleasure God has attached to eating and drinking, which are necessary means of self-preservation. We shall explain: 1º its *nature*, 2º its *malice*, and 3º the *remedies* against it.

864. 1º The **Nature** of Gluttony. Gluttony is an inordinate love of the pleasures of the table. The disorder lies in pursuing this satisfaction *for its own sake*, in considering it, either explicitly or implicitly, as an end in itself, as do those " whose God is their belly; " [2] or in pursuing the said delight *to excess*, at times even to the detriment of health, by disregarding the rules of sobriety.

865. Theologians point out four different ways in which we may violate these rules.

1) Eating when there is no need, eating between meals, and for no other reason than that of indulging our greed.

2) Seeking delicacies or daintily prepared meats, the more to enjoy their relish.

3) Going beyond either appetite or need, gorging oneself with food or drink with danger to health.

4) Eating with avidity, with greed, after the manner of certain animals. This fashion of eating is considered ill-mannered by the world.

---

[1] ST. THOMAS, IIa IIæ, q. 148; *de Malo*, q. 14; JAUGEY, *De quatuor virtut. cardin.*, 1876, p. 569-579; LAUMONIER, *op. cit.*, ch. II.
[2] *Philip*, III, 19.

866. 2° The **Malice** of gluttony comes from the fact that it makes the soul a slave to the body, it brutalizes man, weakens his intellectual and moral life, and insensibly paves the way to voluptuous pleasure, which at bottom is one in kind with it. To determine the malice of gluttony we must make a distinction.

A) Gluttony is a *grievous* fault: **a)** when it goes to such lengths that for a notable space of time it incapacitates us for the fulfilment of our duties of state or for the compliance with divine or ecclesiastical laws, for example, when it injures our health, when it is the cause of useless expenditures which endanger the interests of our home, when it makes us violate the laws of fast or abstinence. **b)** It is also a grave fault when it is the *cause* of other grievous faults.

By way of example: " Excess in eating and drinking " says Father Janvier [1], " paves the way to *unchastity*, the offspring of gluttony, the lust of the eyes and ears demanding to be fed with unwholesome shows and licentious songs ; the lust of the imagination and the memory, which search in the past for impressions apt to enkindle the fire of concupiscence ; the lust of the mind, which, going astray, fastens itself upon unlawful objects ; the lust of the heart, which longs after carnal affections ; the lust of the will, which surrenders to be a slave to sense.... *Intemperance at the table* leads to *intemperance in speech.* How many are the faults committed by the tongue in the course of those sumptuous and protracted feasts ! How many *improprieties....!* How many *indiscretions!* We betray secrets we had pledged ourselves to keep, professional secrets, sacred trusts, and we deliver to evil tongues the good name of husband, wife and mother, the honor of a family, and perhaps the future welfare of a nation. How many faults against *justice* and against *charity* are not thus committed ! Back-biting, calumny, and slander reveal themselves with dismal frankness in their most indefensible forms.... How many *imprudences* are committed ! We become entangled in situations in which we cannot remain without outrage to all the laws of morality. "

867. **B)** Gluttony is a *venial fault* when one yields to the pleasure of eating and drinking in an immoderate manner, yet without falling into grave excess, and without exposing oneself to violate a grave precept. Thus it would be venially sinful to eat or drink more than is proper in order to show one's appreciation of a fine repast, or in order to please a friend.

868. **C)** From the point of view of *perfection*, gluttony constitutes a serious obstacle : 1) It fosters a spirit of immortification, which weakens the will, whilst it develops a love for sensual pleasure predisposing the soul to dange-

[1] *Carême*, 1921, Retraite pascale, Excès de table.

rous surrenders. 2) It becomes the source of many faults, by exciting excessive mirth which leads to dissipation, garrulousness, jokes of a doubtful character, to lack of restraint and of propriety, and thus lays the soul bare to the attacks of the evil one. Hence, it is important that we should combat this vice.

869. 3° **Remedies.** Our guiding principle in the struggle against gluttony is that pleasure *is not an end* but a *means*, and that therefore it must be subjected to right reason enlightened by faith, (n. 193). Faith, however, tells us that the pleasure of eating and drinking must be sanctified by *purity of intention, moderation* and *mortification*.

1) First of all, we must take our repasts with a *right* and *supernatural intention*, not like the animal that merely seeks its pleasure, not like the philosopher who goes not beyond a naturally good intention, but as Christians the better to work for God's glory; in a spirit of *gratitude* towards God, Who in His goodness deigns to give us our daily bread; in a spirit of *humility*, saying, like St. Vincent de Paul, that we do not deserve the bread we eat; in a spirit of *love*, placing our renewed strength at the service of God and of souls. Thereby we comply with the advice of St. Paul to the first Christians, an advice recalled in many communities at the beginning of meals: " *Whether you eat or drink... do all to the glory of God.*" [1]

870. 2) This purity of intention will make us observe the rules of *sobriety*, for wanting to take our food in order to acquire the strength needed for the fulfilment of our duties of state, we shall avoid all excess that might compromise our health. Health-experts tell us that " sobriety (or frugality) is the essential condition of physical and moral vigor. Since we eat to live, we must eat sanely in order to live sanely. Hence, we must not exceed in food or in drink.... We must leave the table with a wholesome sensation of sprightliness and vigor, and with our appetite not completely satiated, thus avoiding the heaviness that comes from an excess of rich fare. " [2]

We must, however, note that the measure is not the same for all. Some need, in order to escape tuberculosis, a more abundant diet; others, on the contrary, to escape arterio sclerosis, must check their appetite. With regard, then, to the quantity of food one must abide by the advice of a competent physician.

---

[1] *I Cor.*, X, 31.
[2] E. CAUSTIER, *La Vie et la Santé*, p. 115.

871. The Christian must add to sobriety *certain practices of mortification.* **A)** Since it is easy to overstep the mark and to yield too much to sensuality, we must at times forego certain foods we relish, and which, though useful, are not necessary. We thereby acquire a certain ascendency over sensuality, we free the spirit from slavery to the senses, and give it more leisure for prayer and study, and we avoid many dangerous temptations.

B) An excellent practice is that of accustoming oneself to take no meal without some element of mortification. Such privations have the advantage of strengthening the will without injury to health, and are for this reason generally preferable to greater mortifications which we perform but rarely. Generous souls add a motive of charity, setting aside a part of their food for the poor and therefore for Christ living in them. St. Vincent Ferrer[1] points out that what we thus set aside must not be waste-matter, but some choice morsel, no matter how small. Another good practice is the habit of eating a little of something we dislike.

872. **C)** Among the most beneficial practices of mortification, we place those that relate to *intoxicating beverages.*
Let us recall the principles that bear on this matter:

a) *in itself* the moderate use of alcoholic drinks is not sinful.

b) To abstain from them in a spirit of mortification, or for the sake of good example, is assuredly most praiseworthy. There are priests and laymen belonging to social organizations who forego entirely the use of liquor, the more easily to deter others from its abuse.

c) There are cases when such abstinence is morally necessary to avoid excess. 1) When through heredity one has a certain inclination towards intoxicants; for in this case the mere use can develop an almost irresistible propensity, just as but a spark is needed to set inflammable matter afire. 2) When one has had the misfortune of contracting the inveterate habit of drinking to excess; then the only effective remedy will consist in total abstinence.

§ II. Lust[2]

873. 1º **The Nature of Lust.** Just as God has willed to attach sense-pleasure to the nutritive functions in order

---

[1] *La Vie Spirituelle*, IIe Part., ch. III.
[2] St. Thom., IIa IIæ, q. 153-154; S. Alphonsus, l. III, n. 412-485; Capelman. *Medicina pastoralis;* Antonelli, *Medicina pastoralis*, Romæ, 1905; Surbled, *Vie*

to help man's self-preservation, so He has attached a *special* pleasure to the acts whereby the propagation of the human species is secured.

This pleasure is permissible to married people, provided they use it for the purpose for which marriage was instituted; outside of this it is strictly forbidden.   In spite of this prohibition, there is in us an unfortunate tendency, more or less violent, especially from the age of puberty or adolescence, to indulge in this pleasure even out of lawful wedlock.   This is the tendency that is called *lust* and which is condemned by the sixth and ninth commandments:

" *Thou shalt not commit adultery.* "
" *Thou shalt not covet thy neighbor's wife.* "

It is not merely *exterior* actions that are prohibited, but also *interior acts*, fancies, thoughts, desires.   And this rightly so, for if one deliberately dwells upon impure imaginations or thoughts, upon evil desires, the senses become excited, whilst an organic disturbance is produced, which is too often but the prelude to actions against purity.   Therefore, if we wish to avoid such acts, we must fight against dangerous thoughts and fancies.

874. 2° **Gravity of faults against purity.   A)** When one seeks and *directly* wills the evil pleasure, there is always *mortal* sin, for to endanger the preservation and propagation of the human race is a grave disorder.   Now, were the principle to be admitted that one may seek voluptuous pleasure in thoughts, in words, or in actions otherwise than in the right use of marriage, it would be impossible to restrain this passion, the demands of which increase with the satisfactions accorded, and soon the purpose of the Creator would be frustrated.   This is what experience shows : there are but too many young people who render themselves incapable of transmitting life, because they have abused their bodies.   Hence, as regards evil pleasure directly willed, there is no lightness of matter.

B) There are cases in which this pleasure is not directly sought; it may follow from certain actions otherwise good or at least indifferent.   If one does not consent to this pleasure, and has, besides, a reason sufficient to justify the performance of the action, there is no guilt and no cause

de jeune homme, Paris, 1900; *Vie de jeune fille,* Paris, 1903; FONSSAGRIVES, *Conseils aux parents et aux maîtres sur l'éducation de la pureté;* MARTINDALE, S. J., *The Difficult Commandment;* GUIBERT, *Purity;* FOERSTER, *Marriage and the Sex Problem;* CATTERER-KRUS-VAN DER DONCKT, *Educating to Purity;* Mgr. DUBOURG, *Sixième et neuvième commandements; Après la vingtième année.*

for alarm. If, on the other hand the actions that give rise to such sensations are neither necessary, nor really useful, like dangerous readings, shows, conversations, lewd dancing, then it is evident that to perform such actions is a sin of imprudence, more or less grave, in proportion to the gravity of the disorder thus produced and of the danger of consent to the evil pleasure.

875. **C**) From the point of view of *perfection*, there is, next to pride, no greater obstacle to spiritual growth than the vice of impurity. **a**) When it is question of solitary acts or of faults committed with others, it is not long before *tyrannical habits* are formed which thwart every impulse towards perfection, and incline the will towards debasing pleasures. Relish for prayer disappears, as does love for austere virtue, while noble and unselfish aspirations vanish. **b**) The soul becomes a prey to *selfishness*. The love once borne to parents and friends gradually dies out; there is but the desire which becomes a real obsession to indulge at any cost in evil pleasures. **c**) The balance of the faculties is destroyed: it is the body, it is lust that takes command; the will becomes the slave of this shameful passion and soon rebels against God, Who forbids and punishes these unholy pleasures.

d) The sad effects of this surrender of the will are soon apparent: the mind becomes dull and weak because the vital forces are used up by the senses: taste for serious studies is lost; the imagination gravitates towards lower things; the heart gradually withers, hardens, and is attracted only by degrading pleasures. **e**) In some cases the physical frame itself is deeply affected: the nervous system, over-excited by such abuses, becomes irritated, weakened, and " incapable of fulfilling its mission of regulation and defence; " [1] the various bodily organs function but imperfectly; nutrition is improperly accomplished, strength is undermined and the danger of consumption threatens.

Evidently, a soul that has thus lost its balance, no longer thinks of perfection. It recedes from it daily, considering itself fortunate if it can gain control over itself at least in time to insure its salvation!

876. 3° **The Remedies.** To withstand so dangerous a passion, we need *deep convictions, protection against dangerous occasions, mortification* and *prayer*.

A) *Deep convictions* bearing at once upon the *necessity* of combatting this vice and upon the *possibility* of succeeding in the struggle.

---

[1] LAUMONIER, *op. cit.*, p. 111.

a) What we have said about the gravity of the sin of lust shows how necessary it is to avoid it in order not to run the risk of everlasting punishment. To this we may add two motives furnished by St. Paul:[1] 1) We are the living temples of the Holy Trinity, temples hallowed by the presence of an all-holy God, and by a participation in the divine life (97, 106). Nothing so defiles this temple as the vice of impurity which desecrates both the body and the soul of the Christian. 2) We are the members of Jesus Christ, into Whom we have been incorporated by Baptism. We must, therefore, honor our body even as Christ's own body. And we would profane it by acts contrary to purity! Would not this be a sort of sacrilege? And to think that we would perpetrate it just to relish a vulgar pleasure which lowers us to the level of the brute!

877. **b)** Many say that continence is impossible. So thought St. Augustine before his conversion, but once converted to God and sustained by the example of the Saints and the grace of the Sacraments, he realized that all things are possible once we know how to pray and how to fight. The truth is that of ourselves we are so weak and the evil at times so alluring, that we would finally yield; but as long as we lean upon divine grace and make earnest efforts, we emerge victorious from the severest temptations. Let no one assert that continence in youth is detrimental to health. Honorable and notable physicians have refuted this in the resolutions of the Brussels International Congress:[2] "Young men must, above all, be taught that chastity and continence are not only not harmful, but even commendable from a purely medical and hygienic point of view." As a matter of fact, there is no known disease resulting from the practice of continence, whilst many are found to originate in the opposite vice.

878. B) Avoidance of the occasions. That chastity is preserved chiefly by fleeing dangerous occasions is an axiom with spiritual writers. When we realize our frailty, we do not run useless risks. As long as such occasions are not *necessary* they must be carefully avoided : "*He that loveth the danger shall perish in it.*"[3] When it is question of readings, visits, meetings, dangerous entertainments from which we can exempt ourselves without any considerable inconvenience, there is no reason for hesitation; instead of looking for these we must flee from them as we would from a dangerous reptile. When these occasions *cannot be avoided*, then we must strengthen the will by interior dispositions that make the danger more remote. Thus St. Francis

---

[1] *I Cor.*, III, 16; VI, 15-20.
[2] IIe Congrès de la Conf. internationale, 1902. Examine many other testimonials in *Le problème de la chasteté au point de vue scientifique* by F. ESCLANDE, 1919, p. 122-136.
[3] *Eccli.* III, 27.

de Sales declares that if dances cannot be avoided they should at least be indulged in with modesty, self-respect, and good intentions. [1] How much more necessary is this today, when so many indecent dances are in vogue!

879. C) There are, however, occasions that cannot be avoided.   They are those we daily encounter, whether in ourselves or in our surroundings, and which we can overcome only by mortification.   We have already said in what this virtue consists, and how it is to be practiced, n. 754-815. We can but recall a few points connected more directly with the virtue of chastity.

a) The *eyes* should be especially guarded, for imprudent glances enkindle desires and these in turn entice the will.   This is why Our Lord declares that "*whosoever shall look on a woman to lust after her hath already committed adultery with her in his heart;*" [2] and He adds that if our right eye is to us an occasion of scandal it must be plucked out, [3] that is to say, forcefully withdrawn from the object that scandalizes us.   This modesty of the eyes becomes more imperative than ever today, since one is more liable to meet almost everywhere with persons and things apt to be a source of temptation.

b) The sense of *touch* is fraught with even more danger, for it provokes sensual impressions which easily tend towards illicit pleasure. Hence, one must abstain from such bodily contact or caresses as cannot but excite the passions.

c) As regards the *imagination* and the memory, let one follow the rules laid down in n. 781.   As to the will, the task is to strengthen this faculty by a virile education according to the principles explained in n. 811-816.

880. d) The *heart* also must be mortified by struggling against whatever may be sentimental or dangerous in the domain of friendship (n. 600-604).   Of course, a time comes when those looking forward to married life first fall in love. This love is lawful, but it must ever remain chaste and supernatural.   Even engaged persons, then, should avoid all signs of affection that are not according to the rules of propriety and should bear in mind that their love, to be blessed by God, must be pure.

With regard to those who are as yet too young to think of marriage, they must be on their guard against that sentimental and sensual affection, which, whilst enervating the heart, prepares for dangerous surrenders.   One cannot play with fire and not be scorched.   Besides, if one expects that the heart pledged in marriage be pure, must one not offer a heart equally pure?

---

[1] *Introd. to A Devout Life*, III P., C. XXXIII.
[2] *Matth.*, V, 28. — [3] *Matth.*, V, 29.

881. e) Lastly, one of the most profitable forms of mortification is a constant and earnest application to the fulfilment of our *duties of state.* Idleness is an evil counsellor; work, on the contrary, by engaging the whole of our activity keeps our imagination, our mind, and our heart away from dangerous objects. We shall speak of this again in n. 887.

882. D) Prayer. a) The Council of Trent tells us that God does not command the impossible, but that He requires us to do what in our power lies and to pray in order to obtain the grace of accomplishing that which, of ourselves, we are incapable of performing. [1] This injunction holds particularly in matters of chastity, with regard to which most persons, even those in the holy state of marriage, encounter special difficulties. To overcome these, frequent prayer and the consideration of the great truths of religion are necessary. Such oft-repeated elevations of the soul towards God gradually wean us away from sensual pleasures and make us rise to joys that are pure and holy.

b) To prayer must be joined the *frequent reception of the Sacraments.* 1) When we *approach frequently the tribunal of penance,* making a frank avowal of faults and imprudences against purity, the grace of absolution, together with the counsels we receive, strengthen the will against temptation. 2) This grace is further increased through *frequent Communion.* The intimate union with Him Who is the God of all holiness cools the fires of concupiscence, awakens the soul to the reality of spiritual goods, and thus withdraws it from attachments to degrading pleasures. It was through frequent Confession and Communion that St. Philip Neri reclaimed youths addicted to the vice of impurity, and even to this day there is no more efficacious remedy either to preserve or to strengthen this virtue. If so many young men and young women escape contagion from vice, it is due to the fact that they find in religious practices an antidote to the temptations that surround them. No doubt, the use of these means of defence requires courage, earnestness and repeated effort, but with prayer, the Sacraments, and a determined will we can surmount all obstacles.

---

[1] Sess. VI, De Justificatione, C. XI.

§ III. Sloth [1]

883. Sloth is connected with sensuality, for it proceeds from love of pleasure, inasmuch as it inclines us to avoid effort and hardship. There is in all of us a tendency to follow the line of least resistance, which paralyzes or lessens our activity. We shall explain: 1° the *nature* of sloth; 2° its *malice;* 3° its *remedies.*

884. 1° **Nature of sloth. A)** Sloth is an inclination to idleness or at least to aimlessness, to apathy in action. At times this is a *morbid disposition* due to poor condition of health. More frequently it is a *disease of the will*, which fears effort and recoils from it. The slothful want to escape all exertion, whatever might interfere with their comfort or involve fatigue. Like the real parasite, they live on others to whatever extent they can. Tractable and submissive as long as no one interferes with them, they become surly and peevish when one would rouse them from their inaction.

B) There are various degress of sloth. **a)** The *indolent* man takes up his task reluctantly, and indifferently ; what he does, he does badly. **b)** The sluggard does not absolutely refuse to work, but he delays and postpones indefinitely the accepted task. **c)** The truly lazy man wants to do nothing that proves irksome and shows a distinct aversion to all real work, whether physical or mental.

C) When sloth bears upon spiritual exercises it is called *spiritual sloth.* This consists in a species of dislike for things spiritual, which tends to make us negligent in the performance of our exercises of piety, causes us to shorten them or to omit them altogether for vain excuses. This is the foster-parent of lukewarmness, of which we shall speak when treating of the *illuminative way.*

885. 2° **Malice of sloth. A)** To understand the malice of sloth we have to remember that man was made to labor. When God created our first parents, he placed them in a garden of delights, " *to dress it and to keep it.* " [2] This is because man, unlike God, is not a perfect being, having many faculties which must act in order to be perfected. Hence, it is a *necessity* of man's *nature* that he should labor to cultivate his powers, to provide for his physical and spiritual wants and thus tend towards his goal. The law of work, therefore, is antecedent to original sin. But because man sinned, work has become for him not merely a law of nature, but also a *punishment*, in the sense that work has become

---

[1] St. Thom., IIª IIæ, q. 35; *de Malo*, q. 11; Noel Alexandre, *op. cit.*, p. 1148-1170; Melchior Cano, *Victoire sur soi-même*, ch. X; Faber, *Growth in Holiness*, XIV; Laumonier, *op. cit.*, ch. III; Vuillermet, *Soyez des hommes*, Paris, 1908, XI, p. 185. — [2] *Gen.*, II, 15.

burdensome and a means of repairing sin; it is in the sweat of our brow that we must eat our bread, the food of the mind as well as that of the body. [1]

The slothful man fails in this twofold obligation imposed both by natural and positive law; he *sins* more or less grievously according to the gravity of the duties he neglects. **a**) When he goes so far as to neglect the *religious* duties necessary to his salvation or sanctification, there is *grievous* fault, and so also when he wilfully neglects, in matters of importance, any of his *duties of state.* **b**) As long as this torpor causes him to fail in civil or religious duties of lesser moment, the sin is but venial. However, the downward grade is slippery, and if we do not struggle against sloth it soon becomes more dangerous, more baneful and more reprehensible.

886. **B**) Because of its baneful *consequences,* spiritual sloth constitutes one of the most serious obstacles to *perfection.*

a) It makes life more or less *barren.* One can well apply to the soul what the Scripture says of the field of the slothful man:

> " I passed by the field of the slothful man,
> and by the vineyard of the foolish man:
> And behold it was filled with nettles, and
> thorns had covered the face thereof, and
> the stone wall was broken down.......
> Thou wilt sleep a little, said I,
> Thou wilt slumber a little;
> Thou wilt fold thy hands a little to rest:
> And poverty shall come to thee as a runner:
> And beggary as an armed man. " [2]

Indeed, this is what one finds in the soul of the slothful man: instead of virtues, vices thrive there, and the walls which mortification had raised to protect virtue, crumble little by little, and open a breach for the enemy, sin, to enter in.

887. **b**) *Temptations* soon become more importunate and more besetting:" For idleness hath taught much evil. " [3] It was idleness and pride that brought Sodom low : " Behold this was the iniquity of Sodom thy sister, pride, fulness of bread and abundance and the idleness of her and of her daughters. " [4] Man's heart and man's mind cannot for long remain inactive; unless they be engaged by study

---

[1] *Gen.,* III, 19. — [2] *Prov.,* XXIV, 30-34.
[3] *Ecclus.,* XXXIII, 29. — [4] *Ezech.* XVI, 49.

or other work, they are soon filled with a host of fancies, thoughts, desires and emotions. In the state of fallen nature, what has full sway within us when we do not react against it, is the threefold concupiscence. Sensual, ambitious, proud, egotistical, selfish thoughts then gain the upper hand and expose us to sin. [1]

888. C) Our **eternal salvation** therefore and not merely our perfection is here at stake; for besides the actual faults into which idleness causes us to fall, the mere fact of failing to fulfil important duties incumbent upon us, is sufficient cause for reprobation. We have been created to serve God and to fulfil our duties of state. We are laborers sent by God to work in His vineyard; but an employer does not ask his employees simply to abstain from doing harm; he wants them to work. Therefore, if without doing anything positive against the divine law, we fold our arms instead of working, will not the Master upbraid our slothfulness? "Why stand ye all the day idle?" [2] The barren tree, by the mere fact that it bears no fruit, deserves to be cut down and thrown into the flames: "*Every tree therefore that doth not yield good fruit, shall be cut down and cast into the fire.*" [3]

889. Remedies. A) To reclaim the slothful it is necessary first of all to form in them strong *convictions* concerning the necessity of work; to make them understand that both the rich and the poor come under this law, and that its infringement may involve eternal damnation. This is the lesson given us by Our Lord in the parable of the barren fig-tree: for three years the owner came seeking fruit from it, and finding none, he ordered it to be cut down: "*Cut it down therefore. Why cumbereth it the ground?*" [4]

Let no one say: I am rich, I need not work. If you are not obliged to work for yourself, you must do it for others. God, your Lord and Master commands you; if He has given you strength, brains, a good mind, resources, it is in order that you may employ them for His glory and the welfare of your brethren. And, indeed, the opportunities are not lacking: how many poor need aid, how many ignorant need instruction, how many broken hearts are there to be comforted, what openings are offered for the carrying out of projects that would give work and daily bread to those who have neither! And, does not the rearing of a large family entail labor and toil if the future of the children is to be safeguarded? Let us keep in mind the universal law of Christian fellowship whereby the toil of each is the service of all; whilst sloth is detrimental to the common weal and to our individual welfare.

---

[1] MELCHIOR CANO, *La Victoire sur soi-même*, ch. X.
[2] *Matth.*, XX, 6. — [3] *Matth.*, III, 10. — [4] *Luke*, XIII, 7.

890. B) Besides having convictions, it is necessary to make a *sustained and intelligent effort* in accordance with the rules laid down, n. 812, for the training of the will. Since the slothful instinctively shrink from effort, they must be shown that in point of fact there is no creature more wretched than the idle man; not knowing how to employ, or as he himself says, how to kill time, he is a burden to himself, all things bore him, and he becomes wearied of life itself. Is it not preferable to exert ourselves, to become useful, and secure some real contentment by striving to make those around us happy?

Among the slothful there are those that do expend a certain amount of activity at play, sport, and worldly gatherings. These must be reminded of the serious side of life and of the duty incumbent upon them of making themselves useful in order that they may turn their activities into worthier fields of action, and conceive a horror of being mere parasites. Christian marriage with its attendant obligations frequently proves an excellent remedy for sloth. Parents realize the necessity of working for their offspring and the inadvisability of entrusting to strangers the care of their interests.

What one must constantly bear in mind is the *end of life :* we are here below in order to attain, through work and virtue, a place in heaven. God is ever addressing to us these words : " *Why stand you here all the day idle?..... Go you also into my vineyard.*" [1]

ART. III. AVARICE [2]

Avarice is related to the *concupiscence of the eyes*, of which we have spoken in n. 199. We shall explain : 1º its *nature*, 2º its *malice*, 3º its *remedies*.

891. 1º **Nature of Avarice.** Avarice is *the inordinate love of earthly goods*. To point out wherein the *disorder* lies, we must first recall the end for which God has given man temporal goods.

A) God's purpose is twofold : our own personal benefit and that of our brethren.

a) Earthly goods are given us to minister to our temporal needs of body and soul, to preserve our life and the life of those dependent upon us, and to procure the means of cultivating our mind and developing our other faculties.

---

[1] *Matth.*, XX, 6, 7.
[2] St. THOMAS, IIa IIæ, q. 118; *de Malo*, q. 113; MELCHIOR CANO, *op. cit.*, ch. XII-XIII; MASSILLON, *Discours synodaux*, De l'avarice des prêtres; MONSA-BRÉ, *Retraites pascales*, 1892-1894 : Les idoles, la richesse; LAUMONIER, *op. cit.*, ch. VIII.

Among these goods: 1) some are *necessary* for the present or the future: it is our duty to acquire them through honest work; 2) others are *useful* in order that we may gradually increase our resources, safeguard our welfare or that of others, contribute to the common good by promoting the arts or sciences. It is not at all forbidden to desire these for a good purpose, so long as we give a due share to the poor and to good works.

b) These goods are also given us that we may aid those of our brethren who are in need. We are, therefore, in a measure *God's stewards*, and should use our superfluous goods for the relief of the poor.

892. **B)** Now we can more easily show wherein lies the **disorder** in the love of earthly goods.

a) At times it lies in the *intention :* we desire wealth for its own sake, as an end in itself, or for other purposes which we ourselves set up as our ultimate end, for instance, to seek pleasures or honors. If we stop there and do not see in riches means to higher ends, then we are guilty of a sort of *idolatry;* we worship the golden calf; we live but for money.

b) The *disorder* further manifests itself in the *manner of seeking* riches: we pursue them with eagerness, by all kinds of means, regardless of the rights of others, to the detriment of our health or that of our employees, by hazardous speculation at the risk of losing all our savings.

c) The disorder likewise shows itself in the *way we use money :* 1) we spend it reluctantly and in a niggardly manner, because we wish to accumulate it in order to feel more secure, or to wield the influence that comes with riches. 2) We give little or nothing to the poor and to good works. To *increase our capital* becomes the supreme end of life. 3) Some reach the point where they love their money as an idol, they love to hoard it, to feel it: this is the classical type known as the miser.

893. **C)** Avarice is not generally a vice of youth, which as yet thoughtless and improvident, does not dream of hoarding money. There are, however, exceptions found among young people who are by character gloomy, worrisome, crafty. But it is rather in middle life or old age that this fault shows itself, for it is then that the fear of *want* develops, based sometimes upon the thought of sickness or accidents that might incapacitate for work. Bachelors and spinsters are particularly exposed to avarice, because they have no offspring to care for them in their old age.

894. **D)** Modern civilization has developed another form of this insatiable love of riches, plutocracy, the hankering thirst for becoming millionaires or multi-millionaires, not in order to safeguard one's future or that of one's family, but to attain the power and control which money gives. Vast sums at one's command secure a vast influence, a power ofttimes more effective than that of governments.   Iron-, steel-, oil-magnates, money-kings, rule sovereigns as well as peoples.   This reign of gold often degenerates into intolerable tyranny.

895.   2⁰ The Malice of Avarice.   A) Avarice is a sign of *mistrust in God*, Who has promised to watch over us with the care of a father, and not to allow us to lack the things we need, provided we trust in Him.   He would have us consider " the birds of the air that sow not nor do they reap, nor gather into barns, and the lilies of the field that labor not, neither do they spin. " [1]   This is not to encourage us to sloth, but to calm our anxieties and urge us to place our confidence in our Heavenly Father. [2]   But the avaricious man instead of putting his trust in God, puts it in the abundance of his riches, and insults God by distrusting Him : " *Behold the man that made not God his helper : But trusted in the abundance of his riches and prevailed in his vanity.* " [3]   This lack of confidence in God is accompanied by too great a confidence in self and personal efforts ; man wants to be his own *providence* and thus he falls into a species of idolatry making money his god.   Now, no man can serve two masters, God and Wealth : " *You cannot serve God and mammon.* " [4]

This sin is *of itself grave* for the reasons just adduced.   It is likewise grave when it causes one to infringe upon important rights of others through the employment of fraudulent means to obtain and retain wealth ; to sin against *charity* by omitting necessary almsgiving, or to fail against *religion*, by allowing oneself to become so absorbed in business that one disregards religious duties.   It constitutes but a venial sin when it does not cause one to fail in any of the great Christian virtues, duties to God included.

896.   B) With regard to *perfection*, the inordinate love of riches is a very serious obstacle.

a) It is a passion that tends to *supplant God in the human heart*.   That heart which is God's temple is crowded with all sorts of desires bent upon the things of earth, filled with all sorts of anxieties and distracting preoccupations.   Yet, to effect our union with God, we must empty our heart of all creatures, of all worldly cares ; for God wants " the whole soul, the whole heart, the whole time, the whole activity of his wretched creatures. " [5]   We must, above all, empty the heart of all pride ; but attachment to riches develops pride, since we place greater confidence in our riches than in our God.

---

[1] *Matth.*, VI, 26-28. — [2] *Matth.*, VII, 24-34. — [3] *Ps.* LI, 9. — [4] *Matth.*, VI, 24.
[5] OLIER, *Introd. aux vertus*, c. II.

To fasten our heart on riches is to hinder the love of God, for *where our heart is there is also our treasure.* [1] To detach the heart from riches is to lay it open to God. A soul despoiled of riches has God for its possessions; *its wealth is the wealth* of God Himself.

b) Avarice also leads to lack of mortification and to sensuality, for when we have money and love it, we either wish to enjoy the pleasures that money can procure, or if we forego these pleasures, our heart clings to the money itself. In either case money becomes an idol that makes us turn away from God.

897. 3° **Remedies of Avarice.** **A)** The great remedy is the profound conviction, resting upon reason and faith, that wealth is not an end, but a *means* given us by Providence to provide for our needs and those of our brethren; that God ever remains the Sovereign Master of all; that we are in truth but administrators who must one day render an account to the Sovereign Judge. Riches moreover are goods that *pass away* with time, goods we cannot take along with us into the next world. If we are wise, we shall lay up treasures not for this world but for eternity. " Lay not up to yourselves treasures on earth : where the rust and moth consume and where thieves break through and steal. But lay up to yourselves treasures in heaven where neither the rust nor the moth doth consume, and where thieves do not break through nor steal. " [2]

B) The most effective way of detaching ourselves from riches is to *invest our wealth in the bank of heaven* by giving generously to the poor and to good works. A gift to the poor is a loan to God ; it yields a hundredfold even in this world, in the joys which come to us from giving happiness to those around us. But above all, it yields a hundredfold for heaven, where Christ, considering as given to Himself what we have bestowed upon the least of His children, will take care to give us imperishable goods in exchange for those we sacrificed for Him. The truly *wise*, therefore, are those who exchange the treasures of this earth for those of glory. To seek God and holiness is the sum-total of Christian prudence: " *Seek ye therefore first the kingdom of God and His justice : and all these things shall be added unto you.* " [3]

898. **C)** Perfect souls go further : they sell all to give to the poor, or they renounce all ownership by the religious vow of poverty, or they retain their capital but use the

[1] *Matth.*, VI, 21. — [2] *Matth.*, VI, 19-20. — [3] *Matth.*, VI, 33.

income only according to the advice of a wise spiritual director, and thus while they remain in the state in which God's providence has placed them, they live in the practice of detachment of mind and heart.

CONCLUSION

899. Thus the struggle against the seven capital sins uproots the inordinate tendencies of the threefold concupiscence. No doubt, there will always remain in us some of those tendencies to try our patience and to remind us of our weakness, but they will prove less dangerous, and, aided by God's grace, we shall overcome them more easily. In spite of our efforts temptations will arise in the soul but it will be to give us occasions of gaining new victories.

CHAPTER V

The Struggle against Temptation

900. Notwithstanding the efforts we put forth to eradicate vice, we must expect temptations. We have spiritual foes, the world, the flesh, and the devil, n. 193-227, which cease not to lay snares for us. It is necessary, therefore, to treat here of *temptation in general* and of *the chief temptations of beginners.*

ART. I. TEMPTATION IN GENERAL [1]

901. Temptation is a *solicitation to evil on the part of our spiritual foes.* We shall explain: 1º The *providential purposes* of temptation. 2º The *psychology* of temptation. 3º The *attitude* we must take towards temptation.

I. *The Providential Purposes of Temptation*

902. God Himself does not tempt us directly : " Let no man, when he is tempted, say that he is tempted by God. For God is not a tempter of evils : and he tempteth no man. " [1] But He allows us to be tempted by our spiritual enemies, at the same time giving us the graces necessary to

---

[1] RODRIGUEZ, *Prat. de la perfect.*, IIe Part., 3e Tr.; ST. FRANCIS DE SALES, *Devout Life*, P. IV, C. III-X; SCARAMELLI, *Guide ascét.*, t. II, art. X; SCHRAM, *Instit. theol, myst.*, § CXXXVII-CXLIX; MEYER, S. J., *Science of the Saints*, IV; FABER, *Growth in Holiness*, XVI; DE LEHEN, *The Way of Interior Peace*, P. III, C. IV; P. DE SMEDT, *Notre vie surnat.*, IIIe P., ch. III; RIBET, *L'Ascétique*, ch. X; MGR. GAY, *Vie et vertus chrét.*, t. I, tr. VIII; DOM LEHODEY, *Le saint Abandon*, p. 332-343; BRUNETEAU, *Les Tentations du jeune homme*, 1912.

[2] *James*, I, 13.

resist : " God is faithful, who will not suffer you to be tempted above that which you are able : but will make also with temptation issue, that you may be able to bear it." [1] And this for excellent reasons of His own.

1º He wants *to make us merit heaven.* Undoubtedly He could have bestowed upon us eternal life as a pure gift, but in His wisdom He has willed that we merit it as a *reward.* He even wills that the recompense be in proportion to the merit and hence in proportion to the obstacle overcome. Temptation, which imperils our frail virtue, is certainly one of the most trying hardships; to struggle courageously against it is one of the most meritorious acts we can perform; and once we have triumphed with God's grace, we can repeat with St. Paul, [2] that we have fought the good fight, and that it only remains for us to receive the crown of justice which God has prepared for us. The more we have done in order to merit that crown, the greater shall be our honor and our joy.

903. 2º Temptation is likewise a *means of purification.* 1) It reminds us that through lack of vigilance and of effort in the past we have fallen, and it becomes thus an occasion for new acts of contrition, shame, and humiliation, which make for the purification of the soul. 2) It obliges us at the same time to put forth earnest and sustained efforts lest we fall; it makes us atone for our negligences and for our surrenders by the performance of contrary acts which further purify the soul. This is why when God wants to purify a soul more perfectly in order to raise it to contemplation, He allows it to undergo horrible temptations, as we shall see when treating of the unitive way.

904. 3º Lastly, temptation is an *instrument of spiritual progress.* **a)** It is like a stripe of the lash that awakens us at the moment we would lull ourselves to sleep and relax. It makes us realize the necessity of forging ahead, of not halting midway, but of ever aiming higher, the more surely to remove the danger.

b) It is *a school of humility,* of distrust of self. When tempted we realize more fully our weakness, our powerlessness; we feel more keenly the need of grace, and we pray with greater earnestness. We see all the better the necessity of mortifying in us the love of pleasure, the source of our temptations, and we embrace more eagerly the little

---

[1] *I Cor.,* X, 13. — [2] *II Tim.,* IV, 7.

crosses of every day in order to weaken the power of concupiscence.

c) It is a *school of love of God;* for to insure our power of resistance, we throw ourselves into God's arms there to seek for strength and shelter; we are more grateful to Him for His unfailing grace; we act towards Him as children of a most loving Father to Whom we have recourse in all our trials.

Hence, temptation possesses manifold advantages and it is on this account that God allows His friends to be tempted : " Because thou wast acceptable to God, it was necessary that temptation should prove you. " [1]

II. *The Psychology of Temptation*

We shall describe : 1° The *frequency* of temptation. 2° The *divers phases* of temptation.   3° The *signs* and *degrees* of *consent*.

905. 1° **The Frequency of Temptation.**   The frequency as well as the violence of temptations vary greatly. Some persons are often and violently tempted; others are tempted but rarely and without being deeply stirred.   There are many causes that account for such diversity :

a) First of all, there are *temperament* and *character*. Some persons are extremely passionate and at the same time weak of will; often tempted, they are upset by temptation.   Others are well-balanced and energetic; seldom tempted, they keep their peace in the midst of temptation.

b) *Education* accounts for other differences : there are souls who have been reared in the fear and love of God, in the habitual fulfilment of stern duty, and who have almost invariably received none but good example.   Others have been brought up in the love of pleasure, in the dread of any kind of suffering, and have seen too many examples of worldliness and sensuality.   It is evident that the latter will be more violently tempted than the former.

c) God's *providential designs* must also be taken into account. There are souls whom He destines for a holy calling and whose purity He shelters with a jealous care.   There are others whom He likewise destines to sanctity, but whom He would have pass through severe tests in order to ground them in virtue.   Lastly, others there are whom He does not destine to such a high vocation, and who will be more or less frequently tempted, but never beyond their strength.

906. 2° **The Three Phases of Temptation.**   According to the traditional doctrine, as expounded by St. Augustine, there are three different phases in temptation : suggestion, pleasure and consent.

---

[1] *Tobias*, XII, 13.

a) *Suggestion* consists in the proposal of some evil. Our imagination or our mind represent to us in a more or less vivid manner the attraction of the forbidden fruit; at times this representation is most alluring, holds its ground tenaciously and becomes a sort of obsession. No matter how dangerous such a suggestion may be, it does not constitute a sin, provided that we have not provoked it ourselves, and do not consent to it. There is sin only when the will yields consent.

b) *Pleasure* follows the suggestion. Instinctively our lower tendencies are drawn towards the suggested evil and a certain pleasure is experienced. " Many a time it happens, " says St. Francis de Sales [1] " that the inferior part of the soul takes pleasure in the temptation, without there having been consent, nay against the soul's superior part. This is the warfare which the Apostle St. Paul describes when he says his flesh wars against his spirit. " This pleasure does not, as long as the will refuses to consent to it, constitute a sin; yet it is a danger, since the will finds itself thus solicited to yield consent. The question then is: will it yield or not?

c) If the will witholds acquiescence, combats the temptation, and repels it, it has scored a success and performed a highly meritorious act. If, on the contrary, the will delights in the pleasure, *willingly* enjoys it and consents to it, the sin is committed.

907. 3° **Signs of Consent.** The better to explain this important point, let us see what are the signs of lack of consent, imperfect consent, and perfect consent.

a) We may judge *that there has been no consent*, if in spite of the suggestion and the instinctive pleasure accompanying it, we experience disgust, chagrin at seeing ourselves thus tempted; if we struggle so as not to be overcome; if we hold the proposed evil in horror; [2] especially if we turn to God in prayer.

b) We may be *culpably* accountable for the temptation in its cause, when we perform an action which we could avoid, foreseeing that it will be to us a source of temptation : " If

---

[1] *Devout Life*, Part IV, C. III.
[2] St. Francis de Sales tells (*Devout Life*, Part IV, C. IV.) how St. Catherine of Sienna, having been violently tempted against chastity, was asked by Our Lord : " Tell me, did those filthy thoughts in your heart give you joy or sorrow, regret or delight? " She answered : " Extreme regret and sorrow. " Thereupon Our Lord comforted her by adding that her sorrows were of great merit and of great profit.

I know," says St. Francis de Sales [1] " that some certain conversation leads me to temptation and to a fall, and I do voluntarily indulge therein, I am, doubtless, culpable of all the temptations that shall arise." Yet, one is guilty only to the extent of one's prevision, and if this is but vague and indistinct, the guilt is lessened in proportion.

908. **c)** One may consider consent to be imperfect :

1) When one does not repulse the temptation *as soon* as its dangerous character is perceived. [2] There is then a fault against prudence, which without being grave puts us in the danger of consenting to the temptation.

2) When one momentarily *hesitates*. One would fain relish somewhat the forbidden pleasure, but one is loath to offend God, that is, after a moment's hesitation, one repels the temptation. Here again there is a venial fault of imprudence.

3) If temptation is resisted in a *half-hearted way*. One does resist, but in a feeble, indolent manner, a half-resistance which implies a half-consent, hence a venial fault.

909. **d)** Consent is *full and entire*, when the will, weakened by first concessions, lets itself be drawn to taste willingly the sinful pleasure, despite the protests of conscience, which recognizes the evil. In such case, if the matter be grievous, the sin is mortal; it is a sin of thought or " morose delectation," as theologians call it. If to the thought is added desire, the fault is graver still. Lastly, if from desire one passes on to the *act*, or at least to the quest and pursuit of means adapted to the execution of one's designs, then there is a sin of *action*.

910. In the different cases we have explained, doubts arise at times regarding the consent or half-consent given. Then we must make a distinction between the *delicate* and the *lax* conscience; when it is question of the former, one may rule out consent, for the person is not in the habit of yielding consent, and if he had consented in this particular case he would know it. When it is question of the latter, the presumption is that the person has given full consent, for if he had not, his soul would not be troubled.

---

[1] *Devout Life*, P. IV, C. VI.
[2] " We are sometimes surprised by certain symptoms of pleasure which immediately follow the temptation, before we are well aware of it. This at most can only be a light venial sin; but it becomes greater, if after we have perceived the evil which has befallen us, we stop some time, through negligence, to determine whether we shall admit or reject that delectation. " (*Devout Life*, P. IV, C. VI).

III. *Our Attitude Towards Temptation*

There are three main things to be done, if we are to overcome temptations and make them redound to our profit : 1° we must *forestall* temptation; 2° *fight* it strenuously; 3° *thank* God after *victory* or *rise up* after a *fall*.

911. 1° Forestall temptation. We know the proverb that says : *One ounce of prevention is worth a pound of cure;* this is but what Christian wisdom teaches. When Our Lord took the three Apostles into Gethsemane, He said to them : " *Watch ye : and pray that ye enter not into temptation.* " [1] Watchfulness and prayer are the two great means of forestalling temptation.

912.   A) *To watch* means to put a sentry, as it were, about the soul, lest it be taken by surprise. It is so easy to fall in an unguarded moment! This watchfulness implies two main dispositions: *distrust of self* and *trust in God.*

a) We must avoid that proud *presumption* that thrusts us into *the midst of dangers*, under the pretence that we are possessed of sufficient strength to triumph over them. This was the sin of St. Peter, who at the moment Christ was prophesying the desertion of the Apostles exclaimed : " Although all shall be scandalized in thee, yet not I. " [2] Let us, on the contrary, be mindful of the words of St. Paul : " *Wherefore, he that thinketh himself to stand, let him take heed lest he fall,* " [3] for if the spirit be willing, the flesh is weak, and safety lies only in the humble mistrust of self.

b) But, we must likewise avoid those *vain terrors* which only increase the danger. It is indeed true that of ourselves we are weak, but we are invincible in Him Who strengthens us : " And God is faithful, who will not suffer you to be tempted above that which you are able : but will make also with temptation issue, that you may be able to bear it. " [4]

c) This proper mistrust of self makes us *shun all dangerous occasions*, this or that association, such or such amusement, etc.... which we know by experience expose us to fall. It declares war against *idleness*, one of the most dangerous of occasions, n. 885, as well as against that *habitual indolence* which relaxes all the springs of the will, and

---

[1] *Matth.*, XXVI, 41. — [2] *Mark*, XIV, 29.
[3] *I Cor.*, X, 12. — [4] *II Cor.*, X, 13.

prepares it for every kind of surrender. [1]   This mistrust holds in horror those empty day dreams, which people the soul with a host of living phantoms that become threatening ere long.   In a word, such mistrust leads to the practice of mortification, under the forms pointed out in nos. 767-817, the compliance with our duties of state, the leading of an interior life, and the exercise of zeal.   In such an intense spiritual life there is but little room left for temptation.

d) Vigilance should center round the soul's weak point, since the onslaughts generally proceed from that side.   In order to fortify this weak spot, we make use of the *particular examination*, which concentrates our attention during an appreciable length of time upon this defect, or rather upon the contrary virtue. (n. 468.)

913.   B) To watchfulness we must join *prayer*, which, placing God on our side, renders us invincible.   God is concerned in our success, for it is He Whom the devil assails in us, it is His work which he would wreck in us.   We may, therefore, call upon the Almighty with a holy assurance, certain that He wants to help us.   Any kind of prayer vocal or mental, private or public, prayer of adoration or prayer of petition, is good against temptation.   One may, especially in times of calm, pray for help in the moment of temptation.   When this moment does arrive, one has but to raise the heart to God in order to resist more successfully.

914.   2º Resisting Temptation.   This resistance will vary according to the nature of the temptations.   Some of these recur frequently, but are less serious ; these must be treated with scorn, as St. Francis de Sales [2] so well explains :

"As to these smaller temptations of vanity, suspicion, impatience, jealousy, envy, fond love, and such like trash, which like flies and gnats continually hover about us, and sometimes sting us on the legs, the hands or the face ; as it is impossible to be altogether freed from them, the best defence that we can make is not to give ourselves much trouble about them ; for although they may tease us, yet they can never hurt us, so long as we continue firmly resolved to serve God earnestly. Despise then these petty attacks, without so much as thinking of what

---

[1] This softness is well described by MGR. GAY, *Christian Life and Virtues*, Tr. VIII.   "Such a soul sleeps and hence it is exposed to the enemy's blows.   The slothful, indolent, remiss, pusillanimous soul which all sacrifice fills with terror, which all real work lays low, no matter how teeming it may be with desires, remains barren in good resolves and even more so in good deeds.   That soul that spares itself in all things, yields to well-nigh all its propensities and lets itself be carried along with the stream. "

[2] *Devout Life*, P. IV, C. IX.

they suggest. Let them buzz and hover here and there around you; pay no more attention to them than you would to flies. "

Here we concern ourselves chiefly with *serious* temptations. These must be fought *promptly, energetically, perseveringly*, and *humbly*.

A) *Promptly*, without parleying with the enemy, without any hesitation. At the outset the temptation is repelled easily enough, for it has not yet gained a foothold in the soul; if we wait until it has gained entry, the repulse will prove far more difficult. Hence, let there be no debate. Let us associate the idea of illicit pleasure with all that is repelling, with the serpent, with a traitor that wishes to ensnare us, and let us remember the word of Holy Writ: "*Flee from sins as from the face of a serpent: for if thou comest near them they will take hold of thee.*" [1] We effect this flight by prayer and by turning our minds to something else.

915. **B)** *Energetically*, not indolently and with regret, for this would be like inviting the temptation to return, but with determination and vigor, showing the horror in which such a proposal is held: "*Go behind me, Satan.*" [2] There are, however, different tactics to be employed, according to the kind of temptations that assail us: if it is question of those temptations to *alluring pleasures*, we must turn away from them and take to flight by concentrating our attention on any other matter calculated to engage our faculties. Direct resistance in such instances generally increases the danger. If it be question of temptations of *aversion* towards duty, of antipathy, hatred, human respect, the better course often lies in facing the difficulty squarely and honestly, and in having recourse to the principles of Christian faith in order to overcome it.

916. **C)** *Perseveringly*, for at times after having been routed, temptation returns with renewed obstinacy, and the devil brings with him from the desert seven other spirits worse than himself. [3] Equal tenacity, and not less, must be matched against this persistence of the enemies of our soul; he that fights unto the end, overcomes. To be all the more assured of victory we should make the temptation known to our spiritual director.

This is the advice given by the Saints, especially St. Ignatius and St. Francis de Sales: "For you must observe," says the latter, "that

---

[1] *Ecclus.*, XXI, 2. — [2] *Mk.*, VIII, 33. — [3] *Matth.*, XII, 45.

the first condition that the enemy of salvation makes with a soul which he desires to seduce, is to keep silence; as those who intend to seduce maids or married women, at the very first forbid them to communicate their proposals to their parents or husbands; whereas God requires, when he sends inspirations, that we should make them known to our superiors and directors." [1]   In truth, it seems as if a special grace were attached to this openness of heart. A temptation disclosed is a temptation half-vanquished.

917. D) *Humbly.* Humility attracts grace, and grace gives us the victory. The devil who sinned by pride, flees before a sincere act of humility; and the threefold concupiscence, that holds its power from pride, is easily overcome when by humility we have, so to speak, laid its head low.

918.   3° **After temptation** we must be on our guard against examining too closely whether we consented or not; such an imprudent course might bring about a recurrence of the temptation and create a new danger. Besides, it is easy to see from the testimony of our conscience, without any probing search, whether we came out victorious.

A) If we have had the good fortune of overcoming, let us thank God with our whole heart, God Who gave us the victory. This is a duty of gratitude, and the best means of obtaining new graces at the opportune moment. Woe to the ungrateful who, attributing to themselves the victorious issue, do not think of returning thanks to God! They will ere long be made to know from experience their own weakness.

919. B) If, on the contrary, we have had the misfortune of *succumbing,* let us not lose heart. Let us remember the welcome accorded the Prodigal Son, and let us, even as he did, cast ourselves at the feet of God's representative, with the same heartfelt plea: " Father, I have sinned against heaven and before thee: I am not worthy to be called thy son." [2]   And God, still richer in His mercies than the father in the parable, will give us the kiss of peace and restore us to His friendship.

In order, however, to prevent new falls, the repentant sinner will take the occasion of his fault to humble himself sincerely before God, to acknowledge his incapacity to do any good, to place his trust in God, to be all the more cautious, and return to the practice of penance. A fault thus repaired will not constitute a serious obstacle to perfection. [3] Those who act thus, "rise," as St. Augustine rightly

[1] *Devout Life*, P. IV, C. VII. — [2] *Luke*, XV, 21.
[3] Cf. TISSOT, *Profiting by Our Faults.*

remarks, " from a fall to be more humble, more prudent, more earnest. " [1]

ART. II. THE CHIEF TEMPTATIONS OF BEGINNERS

Beginners are subject to all kinds of temptations, springing from the sources we have indicated. There are some, however, that seem to be peculiar to them : 1° *illusions*, proceeding from consolations and from aridity ; 2° *inconstancy;* 3° *over-eagerness ;* 4° at times, *scruples.*

§ I. Illusions of Beginners with regard to Consolations [2]

920. God generally bestows sensible consolations on beginners in order to draw them to His service; He then deprives them of these in order to test and to strengthen their virtue. There are some persons who because they enjoy many consolations think they have already attained to a certain degree of sanctity; if the consolations happen to vanish and spiritual dryness or aridity takes their place they think themselves lost. It is, therefore, important in order that they may forestall both presumption and discouragement, that the true doctrine concerning consolations and aridity be explained to them.

I. *Consolations*

921. 1° **Nature and Origin of Consolations. a)** *Sensible* consolations are *tender emotions that affect our sensibility and cause us to experience a feeling of spiritual joy.* The heart expands and throbs with more energy, the circulation of the blood is accelerated, the features beam, and at times tears of joy flow. Sensible consolations differ from the *spiritual* consolations generally granted to more advanced souls: the latter are consolations of a higher order, acting upon the *intellect* by enlightening it, and upon the *will* by drawing it to prayer and to the practice of virtue. However, these two kinds of consolations often intermingle, and what we are about to say can in some measure be applied to both.

b) These consolations may proceed from three sources :

---

[1] *De corrept. et gratiâ*, cap. I.
[2] ST. FRANCIS DE SALES, *Devout Life*, P. IV, C. XII-XV; F. GUILLORÉ, *Les secrets de la vie spirituelle;* FABER, *Growth in Holiness*, XXIII; DOM LEHODEY, *Le Saint Abandon, The Ways of Mental Prayer*, P. II, C. VI; DE SMEDT, *Notre vie surnaturelle.*

1) From God, Who acts towards us as a mother towards her child and attracts us to Himself by means of the sweetness He makes us find in serving Him, in order to wean us away more easily from the false pleasures of the world.

2) From the devil, who acting upon the nervous system, upon the imagination and upon the feelings, is able to produce certain sensible emotions which he will later use to urge us on to ill-considered austerities, to vanity and to presumption soon to be followed by discouragement.

3) From our *nature*. There are imaginative, emotional, sanguine temperaments, which, while they apply themselves to piety, naturally find therein food for their emotions.

922. 2º **Advantages of consolations.** Consolations, assuredly, have their advantages:

a) They *facilitate the knowledge of God:* the imagination helped by grace, delights in representing the lovableness of God, and the heart rejoices in it. Then one loves to pray, to meditate at length, and the soul realizes better the goodness of God.

b) Consolations contribute to the strengthening of the will, which, finding the lower faculties to be no longer hindrances, but valuable helps, detaches itself all the more easily from creatures; it loves God more ardently, forms more vigorous resolutions, and keeps these more easily because of the aid obtained through prayer. Loving God with a sensible affection, the will courageously endures the little sacrifices of every-day life, and even undertakes on its own initiative certain mortifications.

c) Consolations help us to form *habits* of recollection, of prayer, of obedience, of love of God, which remain in some measure even after the consolations themselves have disappeared.

923. 3º **Dangers.** Withal, these consolations have also their dangers:

a) They excite a sort of *spiritual greed*, which makes us cling rather to the consolations of God than to the God of consolations, so much so that when spiritual comforts vanish, spiritual exercises and duties of state are neglected. Even whilst we enjoy these consolations, our devotion is far from being solid, for while we shed tears over Our Lord's sufferings, we refuse to sacrifice for Him this or that sentimental friendship or to undergo for His

sake such or such privation. But solid virtue exists only
when our love for God is carried as far as sacrifice, n. 321.
" There are many souls who experience these tendernesses
and consolations, and who, nevertheless, are very vicious,
and consequently, have not a true love of God, much less
true devotion. " [1]

b) These consolations often foster *pride* under one form
or the other. 1) *Vain self-complacency;* for when we enjoy
consolations, and prayer becomes easy, we readily believe
ourselves to be saints, whilst in truth we are but novices in
the ways of perfection. 2) *Vanity:* we wish to speak of
these consolations to others in order to make known our
worth; and in such cases God often withdraws them for
a notable period of time. 3) *Presumption :* we think ourselves invincible and at times expose ourselves to danger,
or at least, we begin to relax, when we ought to redouble
our efforts and forge ahead.

924. 4° **Our Attitude towards Consolations.** In
order to profit by divine consolations and escape the
pitfalls we have pointed out, the following rules are to be
observed :

a) We may wish for such comforts conditionally with
the intention of using them in order to love God and to
fulfil His holy will. Thus the Church has us ask for the
grace of consolation in the *Collect* of Pentecost : " That
we may ever enjoy His consolation. " Consolations are
a gift of God the purpose of which is to aid us in the work
of our sanctification. We must, therefore, hold them dear,
and we may well ask for them provided we submit ourselves
to the holy will of God.

b) When such consolations have been granted us, let us
receive them with *gratitude* and with *humility*, acknowledging ourselves unworthy of them and attributing all the
merit to God. If He does vouchsafe to deal with us as
with little children, let us bless Him for it; but let us also
recognize that we are as yet far from perfect, since we stand
in need of the milk of children : " *Who need milk and not
solid food.* " [2] Above all, let us not boast of them, for this
would be the surest and quickest way of losing them.

c) Having received them with a humble heart, let us
employ them with the utmost care according to the pur-

---

[1] St. Francis de Sales, *Devout Life*, Part IV, C. XIII.
[2] *I Cor.*, III, 2.

poses of the Giver. He gives them to us, says St. Francis de Sales, " to make us sweet towards every one and excite us to love Him. The mother gives little presents to her child to induce him to embrace her; let us then embrace our blessed Savior Who grants us favors. But to embrace Him is to obey Him, to keep His commandments, do His will, and follow His desires with a tender obedience and humility. " [1]

d) Lastly, we must realize that these consolations will not last forever, and we must humbly beg of God the grace to serve Him in dryness of soul, when it will so please Him. In the meantime, instead of trying to prolong these consolations by our own mental efforts, we must moderate them and cling steadfastly to the God of all consolations.

II. *Aridity*

In order to strengthen us in virtue, God visits us from time to time with aridity. We shall explain: 1º the *nature* of aridity; 2º its *providential purpose;* 3º our *attitude* towards it.

925. 1º **Nature of Aridity.** Aridity is a *privation* of those *sensible and spiritual consolations* which make prayer and the practice of virtue easy. In spite of oft-renewed efforts one no longer relishes prayer; one even experiences a sense of weariness; one finds prayer irksome and the time given to it endless; faith and trust seem dormant; once alert and joyous, one lives now in a sort of torpor and acts only by *sheer force of will.* This is, indeed, a most painful condition, but one not devoid of advantages.

926. 2º **Providential purpose of Aridity.** a) When God sees fit to visit us with aridity, it is in order to *detach* us from all created things, even from the happiness derived from devotion, that we may learn to love God *for His sake* alone.

b) He wants likewise to *humble* us, by showing us that consolations are not our right, but entirely free gifts.

c) God thereby also effects a further purification of the soul from past faults, present attachments and all manner of self-seeking. When we have to serve God without any relish, on principle and by sheer will-power, we suffer keenly, and our suffering becomes an act of expiation and atonement.

---

[1] *Devout Life,* Part IV, C. XIII.

d) Lastly, God thus *strengthens* us in virtue, for in order to persevere in prayer and in well-doing the will must be energetically and steadily exercised, and it is by such exercise that we are grounded in virtue.

927. 3° **Our Attitude towards Aridity. a)** Since dryness at times proceeds from our faults, we must first of all carefully search ourselves, yet without over-anxiety, in order to see if we are not the responsible cause 1) by reason of our tendencies, more or less consented to, towards self-complacency and pride; 2) by a sort of spiritual sloth, or, on the other hand, by an untimely and excessive straining of the mind; 3) by seeking after human consolations, after personal attachments that are too sentimental, after worldly pleasures; for God will not have a divided heart; 4) by a want of frankness towards our spiritual director: "For, since you try to deceive the Holy Ghost" says St. Francis de Sales, " it is no wonder that He withholds from you His consolations." ¹ Once the cause of aridity is discovered one must with due humility strive to remove it.

928. If we are not responsible for this aridity, it is important that we should draw profit from the ordeal. 1) The great means is to convince ourselves that it is more meritorious to serve God in the absence of attraction and warm emotions than in the midst of many consolations; that in order to love God it is enough *to will* to love Him, and besides, that the most perfect act of love consists in having our will conform to that of God. 2) In order to render such an act still more meritorious we can do no better than to unite ourselves to Jesus, Who in the Garden of Gethsemane consented to experience sadness and weariness of soul out of love for us, and to repeat after Him: " Not my will, but thine be done." ² 3) Above all, we must never lose heart, nor subtract anything from our exercises of piety, from our efforts, from our good resolutions; but rather imitate Our Lord, Who " being in an agony, prayed the longer." ³

929. Advice for the spiritual Director. In order that penitents may thoroughly understand these practical lessons regarding consolations and aridity, spiritual directors should frequently insist on them, for penitents are often persuaded that they are better off when things go according

---

¹ *Devout Life*, Part IV, C. XIV.
² *Luke*, XXII, 42. — ³ *Id.* XXII, 43.

to their wishes than when they go against the grain. Gradually, however, they are enlightened, and once they have learnt not to exalt themselves in their own eyes in time of consolation and not to be discouraged during periods of dryness, they make progress more rapidly and more steadily.

§ II. Inconstancy of Beginners

930. 1º **The Evil.** When a soul gives itself to God and begins to advance in the spiritual life, it is sustained by divine grace, by the attractiveness of the novelty and by a certain urge towards virtue, which removes many an obstacle. A moment arrives, however, when God's grace is given in a less sensible manner, when the soul grows weary of essaying again the self-same efforts, which seem to be thwarted by the self-same difficulties. It is then that the soul is liable to relax and falter.

This tendency to inconstancy and tepidity shows itself 1) in our *spiritual exercises*, which we now perform with less attention, which we shorten or omit; 2) in the *practice of virtue:* we entered full-heartedly into the ways of penance and mortification, but now we find this hard and irksome and we relax our efforts; 3) in the *habitual sanctification of* our actions: we had been accustomed to renew frequently the offering of our actions, in order to insure the purity of our intention; now we find this practice fatiguing, we neglect it with the result that soon many of our actions are inspired by routine, curiosity, vanity, sensuality. It is impossible to make progress with dispositions such as these, for we arrive nowhere without a sustained effort.

931. 2º **The Remedy.** **A)** We must realize that the work of perfection is a work of long endurance, demanding much steadiness of purpose, and that only those succeed who despite partial setbacks return again and again with fresh energies to the task. This is just what men do to succeed in business, and this is what must be done by anyone who wants to advance in holiness. Each morning we must ask again the question whether we cannot do *more*, and especially whether we can not do *better* for God; and every evening we must examine to see if we have carried out, at least in part, our program for the day.

B) Nothing insures constancy so well as the particular examination, n. 468. By concentrating our attention upon one objective, one virtue, and by rendering to our confessor an account of the progress made, we are certain to advance, even though we may not be aware of the fact.

What we have said regarding the training of the will, n. 812, is likewise a very apt means to overcome inconstancy.

§ III. Over–Eagerness of Beginners

Not a few beginners, full of good will, apply themselves too eagerly and too anxiously to the work of their perfection and end by fatiguing and exhausting themselves in futile efforts.

932. 1° **The Causes.** **a)** The chief cause of this defect is the *substitution of one's own activity for that of God.* Instead of reflecting before acting, of asking light from the Holy Ghost and following it, such beginners thrust themselves headlong into action. Instead of taking counsel with their spiritual director, they act first, and afterwards confront him with the accomplished fact. Hence, numerous .imprudences and many wasted efforts.

b) Often presumption enters into the case. They would like to emerge hastily from the discipline of penance and promptly arrive at the desired union with God. But alas! many an unforeseen obstacle appears; they then lose heart, retrace their steps and at times fall into grievous faults.

c) At other times, it is *curiosity* which predominates. They seek continually new means of perfection, try them a while and soon discard them before giving them a chance to produce their effects. They continually plan new projects of reform for themselves and for others and forget to carry them out. The net result of such over-exertion is the loss of interior recollection; it is excitement and trouble without any solid gain.

933. 2° **The Remedies.** **a)** The chief remedies are submission to and *entire dependence upon the action of God,* mature reflection before acting, prayer to obtain divine light, consultation with and docility towards a spiritual director. Just as in the workings of nature it is not violent force that yields the best results, but rather well controlled energy, so in the spiritual life it is not feverish efforts that make for progress, but calm and well-directed ones.

b) But if beginners are to submit themselves to the action of God, they must combat the causes that produce such over-eagerness; they must fight 1) a natural vivacity of character that inclines to hasty decisions; 2) a presumption that arises from too high an esteem of self; 3) curiosity that is forever in search of novelties. They should, therefore, direct their attacks successively against these defects by means of the particular examination, and then God will take once more His rightful place in their souls and lead them calmly and sweetly along the paths of perfection.

§ IV. Scruples[1]

934. Scruples are a disease, physical and moral, which produces a sort of derangement of conscience, and causes one to harbor vain fears of having offended God. This disease is not restricted to beginners; still, it is found in them as well as in the more advanced souls. Hence, we must say a word about them and explain: 1° the *nature*, 2° the *object*, 3° the *disadvantages* and *advantages* of scruples, and 4° the *remedies* against them.

I. *Nature of Scruples*

935. The term scruple (from the Latin *scrupulus*, pebble) was employed for ages past to designate a weight under which only the most sensitive scales would tilt. In the moral sense, it stands for some trifle which only the most delicate conscience would notice. Hence, this word has come to be commonly used to designate *the anxiety about having offended God which certain souls feel for little or no reason.* The better to know the nature of scruples we shall explain their *origin* and *degrees*, as well as the *distinction* between a scrupulous and a delicate conscience.

936. 1° **Origin.** Scruples arise sometimes from *purely natural* causes and sometimes they are due to *supernatural* intervention.

a) From a *natural* point of view, scruples are often a *physical* and *moral* disease. 1) The *physical* ailment which brings about this disorder is a sort of *nervous depression*, which hinders a well-balanced decision on moral questions and tends to produce without solid reasons the *obsessing idea* that one has sinned. 2) There are also moral causes which produce the same effect, such as a *meticulous* mind, a mind that loses itself amid the most trifling details, that wants to reach absolute certitude in all things; a *beclouded* mind, that represents God not as a just judge, but as

---

[1] St. IGNAT., *Exercit. spirit.*, Regulæ de scrupulis ; ALVAREZ DE PAZ, t. II, lib. I, Part. III, cap. XII, § V; SCARAMELLI, *Guide ascétique*, tr. II, art. XI; SCHRAM, *Inst. theol. mysticæ*, t. I, § 73-83; St. ALPHONSUS, *Theol. moralis*, tr. I. De conscientiâ, n. 10-19; LOMBEZ. *Interior Peace*, P. II, C. VII; FABER, *Growth in Holiness*, XVII; DUBOIS. *L'Ange conducteur des âmes scrupuleuses;* DE LEHEN, *The Way of Interior Peace*, P. IV; RAYMOND, *Spiritual Director and Physician*, P. II; A. EYMIEU, *Le gouv. de soi-même*, t. II, L'obsession et le scrupule; DOM LEHODEY, *Le saint Abandon*, p. 407-414.

a merciless one; a mind that confuses feeling with consent in human acts, and imagines, that because the imagination has been for long alive to vivid impressions, sin has been committed; an *obstinate* mind, that prefers its own judgment to that of the confessor for the very reason that it lets itself be led by impressions rather than by reason.

When these two causes, physical and moral, are present, the evil is more deeply rooted and the cure is more difficult.

937. **b)** Scruples can also arise from a *preternatural intervention* on the part of *God* or of the *devil*.

1) God allows us to be thus obsessed either as a punishment, chiefly of our pride, of our inclinations to vain complacency, or as a *trial*, to make us expiate our past faults, to detach us from spiritual consolations, and bring us to a higher degree of sanctity. This is the case especially with the souls whom He wants to fit for contemplation, as we shall explain when treating of the unitive way.

2) The devil also at times injects his activity into the morbid predisposition of our nervous system in order to create a turmoil in our souls. He persuades us that we are in the state of mortal sin in order to hinder us from receiving Holy Communion, or to hamper us in the discharge of our duties of state; above all, he strives to deceive us as to the gravity of some act or other in order to make us sin, because of a false conscience, even when there is no matter for sin and much less for grievous sin.

938. 2° **Degrees.** Evidently there are many degrees in scruples. **a)** At the outset it is simply question of a *meticulous* conscience, extremely fearful, which sees sin where sin does not exist; **b)** then it is a matter of transient scruples which one submits to the judgment of one's spiritual director, accepting forthwith his decision; **c)** lastly, it is a case of scruples *properly so called*, tenacious and obstinate.

939. 3° **Distinction between a Scrupulous and a Delicate Conscience.**

a) Their genesis or starting-point is not the same. The delicate conscience loves God ardently and, in order to please Him, wants to avoid the least fault, the slightest wilful imperfection. The scrupulous conscience is led on by a certain egotism which causes an inordinate eagerness for absolute certainty of one's state of grace.

b) The *delicate* conscience, possessed of a horror of sin and knowing its own feebleness, has a *rational*, yet quiet fear of displeasing God; the scrupulous conscience harbors vain fears of sinning in every circumstance.

c) The *tender* conscience knows how to *discriminate* between *mortal* and *venial sin*, and, in case of doubt, abides by the judgment of the spiritual director; the scrupulous conscience peevishly questions the decisions of the spiritual director and submits to them only with difficulty.

Whilst scruples are a real evil to be carefully avoided, there is nothing more precious than a delicate conscience.

II. *The Subject-matter of Scruples*

940. 1° Sometimes scruples are *universal*, bearing on all subjects. Before an action, they magnify beyond all proportion the dangers that may be encountered in this or that circumstance; after an action, they fill the soul with groundless anxieties and easily convince it of having sinned gravely.

941. 2° More often scruples bear upon a number of *particular subjects :*

a) *Past confessions:* even after having made several general confessions, one is not satisfied, one fears lest all has not been accused, or lest sorrow has been defective, and one wants always to begin all over again. **b**) *Evil thoughts:* the imagination is filled with dangerous or obscene thoughts, and since these make a certain impression, one fears one has given consent, nay one is sure of having consented, although one was quite displeased at them. **c**) *Blasphemous thoughts :* because such ideas cross the mind, one is persuaded of having acquiesced in spite of the horror one experiences. **d**) The virtue of *charity :* one has for instance, listened to conversations against the neighbor without protesting; one has, through human respect, neglected the duty of fraternal correction, one has scandalized the neighbor by indiscreet talk, or one has failed, upon witnessing a crowd congregate, to ascertain whether an accident had occurred where the ministrations of a priest might have been needed to give absolution to the dying; in all this, grievous sins are seen. **e**) The correct pronunciation and enunciation of the words of Consecration, the integral recitation of the Divine Office, etc....

III. *Disadvantages and Advantages of Scruples*

942. 1° When one has the misfortune of allowing oneself to be governed by scruples, baneful effects follow for body and soul : —

a) Scruples gradually induce a *weakening* and a certain *unbalancing* of the nervous system. Fears and continual anguish exercise a depressing action on bodily health; they may even become a real *obsession* and bring about a species of monomania, bordering on insanity.

b) Scruples *becloud* the mind and *distort* the judgment: little by little one loses the ability to discern between what is sin and what is not sin, what is grievous and what slight; and the soul becomes much like a ship without a rudder.

c) *Loss of true devotion* is often the sequel. The strain of living in anxiety and vexation turns one into a terrible egotist, for whom everybody becomes an object of mistrust, even God, Whom one deems too severe. Complaints arise that He leaves one in that wretched state. Evidently, the heart is incapable then of any genuine devotion.

d) Finally, come *faults* and even *grave falls.* 1) The scrupulous spend their strength in useless efforts over trifles, and retain but little energy to meet important issues, for the attention cannot be directed to bear with equal intensity upon the entire line of battle. Hence, surprises, faults, and at times even grievous sins. 2) Besides, they instinctively seek relief for their sorrows; but finding no solace in piety, they seek it elsewhere, in reading and in associations that are dangerous. This is sometimes the occasion of lamentable falls which throw them into a deep state of dejection.

943. 2° On the other hand, if we know how *to accept scruples* as a *trial,* and to correct them gradually with the help of a wise spiritual director we derive from them priceless advantages.

a) They serve *to purify the soul.* By being intent on avoiding the least sin and the least wilful imperfection, we acquire a great purity of heart.

b) They lead us to the actual exercise of *humility* and *obedience* by obliging us to refer our doubts in all simplicity to our spiritual director, and to follow his counsel with entire submission not only of will, but of judgment.

c) They contribute to increase the *purity of our intentions* by detaching us from spiritual comforts and by having us cling solely to God for Whom our love increases the more He puts us to the test.

IV. *Remedies against Scruples*

944. Scruples must be attacked before they take deep root in the soul. Now the great remedy and indeed the only remedy is **obedience,** full and absolute obedience to

an enlightened spiritual director. The light of conscience
has become dim and we must seek enlightenment elsewhere.
A scrupulous person is exactly like a ship without rudder
or compass. The spiritual director, therefore, must *win his
confidence* and must know how to wield authority over him
if he is to effect a cure.

945. 1° Before all else, it is necessary to gain his confidence; for we do not easily obey those whom we do not
trust. This, however, is not always easily accomplished.
True, the scrupulous soul instinctively feels the need of
a guide, but some scrupulous persons do not dare abandon
themselves entirely to the said guide; they want to consult,
indeed, but also to discuss the reasons. Now, one must not
enter into any discussion with the scrupulous, but speak to
them with authority, telling them categorically what they
must do.

To inspire this confidence the spiritual director must merit
it both by his *competence* and his *devotedness*.

a) He will allow the penitent to speak first, limiting
himself to a few remarks here and there to show that he
has thoroughly understood. After that he will put a few
questions to the penitent, to which the latter will answer yes
or no, and thus the director will himself conduct the methodical examination of the penitent's conscience. Then he
will add: I understand your case, you suffer in this or that
manner. To see that he has been well understood is already
a great comfort to the penitent, and at times suffices to win
his confidence.

b) *Devotedness* must be joined to competence. The
spiritual director should therefore show himself patient,
listening quietly to the lengthy explanations of the penitent, at least at the beginning. He must be *kind*, taking an
interest in that soul and expressing the desire and the hope
of curing it. He must be *gentle*, refraining from taking
a tone of severity or harshness, even when he is obliged to
use the language of authority. Nothing wins confidence
better than this union of kindness and firmness.

946. 2° Once the spiritual director has gained the
confidence of his penitent, he must exercise his authority
and exact **obedience,** saying: If you want to be cured you
must obey blindly; in obeying you are always safe, even if
your spiritual director be mistaken, for God demands of
you only one thing just now, and that is obedience. This
is so true that if you think that you cannot obey me, you

must seek another spiritual director. Blind obedience alone can cure you, and it will certainly do so.

a) In giving his orders the spiritual director must be direct, clear and precise, avoiding any equivocation; he must be *positive*, speaking categorically, never conditionally; for instance, he will not say: If that disturbs your peace, do not do it; rather he will say: Do this, avoid that, spurn such temptation.

b) Generally *no reasons must be given for the decisions*, especially at the beginning. Later on when the scrupulous penitent is capable of understanding them, and of feeling their weight, the director should briefly state these reasons in order to form his conscience little by little. But *there must be no discussion* of the decision itself. If there be any obstacles to prevent its immediate execution, they are to be taken into account, but the decision stands.

c) The spiritual director must not *reverse his judgments*. Before giving a decision he considers it fully, and gives no orders that he cannot insist upon; but once an order has been given, it must not be revoked so long as there is no new fact requiring a change.

d) To ascertain if the order has been clearly understood, penitents should be asked to *restate* it, and then it but remains to have them *carry it out*. This is difficult; but they must be plainly told that they must report on it, and that if they have failed to follow the advice given, they will not be listened to until they have complied. There will be ample opportunity, therefore, to repeat the same injunction many times. This is to be done without losing patience, but with increasing firmness, and in the end the scrupulous persons will yield obedience.

947. 3º When the moment arrives, the spiritual director must inculcate the **general principle** that will enable scrupulous penitents to disregard all doubts and if need be, he will have them put this principle in writing in this or a similar form: *I am in conscience bound* to take only *evidence* into account, that is to say, a certitude that excludes all doubt, a certitude as clear as the one that tells me that *two and two make four*. I cannot, therefore, commit a sin either mortal or venial, unless I am absolutely certain that the action I am to perform is forbidden under pain of mortal or venial sin, and that *fully aware* of this fact, I *will* nevertheless to do it just the same. I will, therefore, pay no attention whatsoever to probabilities, no matter how strong they may be, I will hold myself bound solely by clear-cut and positive evidence. Barring such, there is no sin. When the penitent proceeds to accuse himself of having committed a venial or a mortal sin, the confessor must ask: Can you affirm under oath that before acting you saw clearly that this action was a sin and that seeing this you gave full consent? Such a question will give precision to the general principle laid down and will make it better understood.

948. 4° Lastly, this general **principle must be applied** to the specific difficulties that arise.

a) With regard to a *general confession*, after allowing it *once*, the confessor should permit no repetition except when there is *certainty* on these two points: 1) a mortal sin was *committed*, and 2) this sin has *never been accused* in any valid confession. As for the rest, after a certain lapse of time the spiritual director should declare that the past must not be touched upon under any circumstances and that, should some sin have been omitted, it has been already pardoned along with the others.

b) With regard to *interior sins*, thoughts and desires, the following rule should be given: *during the crisis*, divert your attention by thinking of any other thing; *after the crisis*, do not examine yourself to see if you have sinned or not (this would bring back the temptation), but pursue the even tenor of your way by devoting yourself to your duties of state, and receive Holy Communion as long as there is no evidence that you have given full consent (n. 909).

949. c) *Communion* is often a torture to the scrupulous. They fear lest they be not in the state of grace or be not fasting. Now, 1) the *fear* lest they be not in the state of grace proves that they are not certain of that fact; hence, they should after a sincere act of contrition approach the Sacrament of the Altar; this contrition together with Holy Communion will put them in the state of grace if they are not in it. 2) The Eucharistic fast must not prevent the scrupulous from receiving Holy Communion unless they are *absolutely* certain of having broken it.

d) *Confession* for the scrupulous is a still greater torture, and therefore, it must be simplified for them. They should be told: 1) You are not bound to accuse any except mortal sins. 2) As to *venial* faults, make mention only of those that happen to come to your mind during your short examination of conscience, which should not exceed five minutes. 3) With regard to *contrition*, devote a little longer time to ask it of God and to excite yourself to it, and then you will have it. Should the penitent answer: " I do not *feel* sorry, " the confessor should reply that sorrow to be real need not be felt, since it is an act of the will which has nothing to do with feeling. In certain cases, when scruples are very intense, one must go further and prescribe to the penitent that he limit himself to this generic accusation: " I accuse myself of all the sins committed since my last confession and of all those of my past life, especially against this or that virtue. "

950. 5⁰ **Replying to Difficulties.** Sometimes a penitent will say to his confessor: You take me for scrupulous, whereas I am not. The confessor will answer: It is not for you but for your confessor to decide that. Are you absolutely sure that you are not scrupulous? Are you calm and at peace after making your confessions? Are you not troubled with such doubts and worries as most persons never experience? You are, therefore, not in a normal state; you are affected with some physical and moral disturbance, and therefore, need special treatment. Obey without argument, and you will be cured; otherwise your trouble will only be aggravated.

By this and other like means one finally succeeds, with God's grace, in curing this distressing malady of scruples.

Appendix: The Discernment of Spirits [1]

951. The different kinds of spirits that act in us. In the preceding pages we have spoken many times of *diverse interior promptings* that urge us to good or to evil. The importance of recognizing the *source* of these *promptings* is evident.

In theory they may proceed from six different causes:

a) from *ourselves:* from the spirit which urges us towards good, from the flesh that urges us towards evil.

b) from the *world*, in so far as, through our senses, it exercises its influence over our interior faculties to draw them towards evil (n. 212).

c) from the *good angels*, who inspire in us good thoughts.

d) from the *demons*, who act upon our interior and exterior senses to prompt us to evil.

e) from *God*, Who alone can penetrate into the inmost recesses of the soul and Who never urges us but to what in good.

---

[1] St. Thom., Ia IIæ, q. 80, a. 4; *De Imitatione Christi*, l. III, c. 54, De diversis motibus naturæ et gratiæ; S. Ignatius, *Exercit. spirit.*, Regulæ aliquot, etc.; Scaramelli, *Du discernement des esprits*, trad. Brassevin, Paris, 1910; Card. Bona, *De discretione spirituum;* Ribet, *L'Ascétique*, ch. XL; Mgr A. Chollet, *Discernement des esprits*, Dict. de Théol., t. IV, 1375-1415, avec une abondante bibliographie; Clare, *The Science of the Spiritual Life*, 41-47.

952. In practice it suffices to know whether these promptings arise from a *good* or from an *evil principle:* from a good principle, God, the good angels or the spirit aided by grace; from an evil principle, the devil, the world or the flesh. The rules by which we can distinguish the one from the other are called rules for the *discernment of spirits.* St. Paul laid the foundations of these rules by distinguishing within man the flesh and the spirit, and outside of man, the Spirit of God that leads us to good, and the fallen angels that solicit us to evil. Since then, spiritual writers like Cassian, St. Bernard, St. Thomas, the author of the Imitation and St. Ignatius, have drawn up rules to ascertain the divers promptings of nature and of grace.

953. Rules of St. Ignatius which apply especially **to beginners.**

The first two rules refer to the different attitudes which the good and the evil spirits take with regard to *sinners* and to fervent souls.

1° *First rule.* To *sinners* who do not put any curb on their passions, the devil proposes pleasures and delights in order to hold them fast and immerse them deeper in vice; the good spirit, on the contrary, stirs their conscience with uneasiness and remorse in order to make them emerge from their sad plight.

Second rule. When it is question of souls that have *sincerely returned to God,* the devil excites in them sadness, torments of conscience, and creates and all manner of difficulties in order to make them lose heart and halt their advance. The good spirit, on the contrary, inspires them with courage, energy and good thoughts to make them grow in virtue. By the fruits then will the tree be judged; whatever hinders progress comes from the evil one, whatever promotes it proceeds from God.

954. 2° *Third rule.* This rule deals with *spiritual consolations.* These proceed from the good spirit: 1) when they arouse fervor, first a spark, then a flame, lastly a glowing fire of divine love; 2) when they cause tears that are a true expression of interior compunction or of love for Our Lord; 3) when they increase faith, hope and charity, and bring quiet and peace to the soul.

955. 3° The following rules (4 th — 9 th) have reference to *spiritual desolation:* 1) Desolation here means either spiritual darkness or the inclination of the will towards the lower things, the things of earth, which render the soul sad, tepid, and sluggish. 2) In time of desolation we must not, in spite of the suggestions of the evil spirit, make any change whatever as to the good resolutions we have previously formed, but we must remain steadfast abiding by our former decisions. 3) Further, we must take advantage of desolation to grow in fervor, giving more time to prayer, examination of conscience and exercises of penance. 4) We must rely on divine help, which, though not felt, is none the less actually given us to aid our faculties in doing good. 5) We must be patient and await the return of consolation. We must say to ourselves that desolation may be a punishment for our *lukewarmness;* a *trial,* God wanting us to realize just what we are able to do when deprived of consolation; a *lesson,* God wanting to show us that of ourselves we are incapable of securing consolations, and thus to cure us of our pride.

956. 4° The *eleventh* rule returns to the subject of *consolations* to warn us that we need muster courage if we are to acquit ourselves well during the time of desolation, and to remind us that we must humble ourselves at the sight of how little we can do when bereft of sensible comfort, and of how much we can do in spiritual distress if we lean upon God.

957. 5° The *last three rules* (12 th — 14 th) explain and expose the ruses employed by the devil to seduce us: **a)** He acts like a mischievous woman, weak in the face of resistance, but fiery and cruel to those who yield; hence, the duty of vigorous resistance. **b)** He acts like a seducer, imposing silence upon the victim he allures to evil; hence, the best means of foiling him is to disclose all to the spiritual director. **c)** He follows the tactics of a commander, who attacks a garrison at its weakest point; hence, it is important that we watch that weak point in our examinations of conscience.

SUMMARY OF THE FIRST BOOK

The end at which beginners aim is the *purification of the soul*, so that unhampered by the remains and the occasions of sin they may effect their union with God.

958. To attain this end, they have recourse to **prayer.** By offering God their religious homage, they move Him to pardon all their past offences. By invoking Him with confidence in union with the Incarnate Word, they obtain the grace of contrition and firm purpose of amendment which further cleanse their souls and preserve them from future falls. The attainment of these ends is the better ensured through the practice of *meditation.* The solid convictions which we acquire by long and serious reflection, the self-examinations which show us more clearly our miseries and our needs, the ardent prayers that spring then from the recesses of our heart, the good resolutions we form and which we strive to carry out, all this purifies the soul, inspires it with a horror for sin and its occasions, and strengthens it against temptation and makes it more generous in the practice of penance.

959. Having a clearer conception of the offence offered God by sin and of the strict obligation of making atonement for it, the soul enters resolutely into the ways of penance. In union with Jesus, Who deigned to atone for us, the penitent harbors in his heart a sense of shame, of sorrow, of humiliation, and his sin is always a reproach before his face. With such sentiments, he yields himself to the hardships of **penance,** generously accepts the providential crosses which God sends him, undergoes some voluntary privations, practices almsgiving and thus atones for the past.

In order to avoid sin in the future, he practices **mortification,** disciplining his interior and exterior senses, the mind, the will, in a word, all his faculties to bring them into subjection to God and to do nothing but in accordance with His holy will.

No doubt, evil tendencies, the *seven capital vices*, still lurk deep within the soul; — but aided by divine grace, the soul undertakes to uproot them or at least to weaken them, and a time comes when it gains sufficient control over them.

Temptations, at times terrible, arise from the soul's lower depths stirred by the devil and the world, but the soul, leaning upon Him Who has overcome the world and the flesh, will fight from the outset and as long as necessary against these assaults of the enemy. With God's grace these attacks will in most cases but give occasion to fresh victories. Should an unfortunate fall occur, the soul, humbled but trustful, will forthwith throw itself into the merciful arms of God to beg His forgiveness. A fall thus atoned for will not constitute an obstacle to spiritual progress.

960. We must, however, add that the active purifications we have described in this first book do not suffice to render a soul perfectly pure. Therefore, this work of purification will continue through the illuminative way by means of the *positive exercise of the* moral and the theological *virtues*. It will not be thoroughly effected until the *passive purifications*, so well described by St. John of the Cross, supervene in the unitive way. These bestow on the soul the *perfect purity of heart* normally necessary to contemplation. Of them we shall treat in the third book.

BOOK II

The Illuminative Way

or

The State of Souls More Advanced in the Spiritual Life

---

961. Once the soul is purified from past faults by a long and arduous penance, in keeping with the number and gravity of those faults, once it has been grounded in virtue through the practice of meditation, of mortification, and resistance to the disordered inclinations and to temptations, then it enters into the **illuminative way.** This stage of the spiritual life is thus named because the great aim of the soul is now the imitation, the *Following of Christ,* by the *positive exercise of the Christian virtues;* Jesus is the Light of the World, and whosoever follows Him walks not in darkness: " *He that followeth me walketh not in darkness, but shall have the light of life.* " [1]

INTRODUCTION [2]

Before describing the virtues to be practiced by souls in the illuminative way, there are three questions that must be answered : 1° Which are the souls that belong in the illuminative way? 2° What is the *program* such souls are to follow? 3° What difference is there between *devout* and *fervent* souls walking along this way?

I. *Which are the souls that belong in the illuminative way?*

962. St. Theresa thus describes the inhabitants of the *third mansion,* [3] that is to say, the souls that are more advanced in the spiritual life: " They have an intense desire of not offending the Divine Majesty : they avoid even venial sins ; they love penitence ; they have their hours of recol-

---

[1] *John,* VIII, 12.
[2] PHIL. A SS. TRINITATE, *Sum. Theol. myst.,* P. II; LE GAUDIER, *De perfect. vitæ spir.,* P. IIᵃ, sect. IIᵃ ; SCHRAM, *Instit myst.,* § CIII ; A. SAUDREAU, *The Degrees of the Spiritual Life,* Vol. I, *The Illuminative Way,* p. 128-35; *Cursus Asceticus,* Vol. II.
[3] *Interior Castle,* Third Mansion, C. I.

lection; they employ their time usefully; they perform works of charity toward the neighbor.   Everything about them is in perfect order: their words, their clothes, their homes. "

From this description we can draw the following conclusions.

963.   1º Since the illuminative way consists in the imitation of Our Lord, in order to enter therein we must fulfil the three following conditions which enable us to follow the Divine Master through the positive practice of those virtues of which He has given us the example.

A) We must have already acquired *purity of heart* in some measure, in order to aspire without rashness to that habitual union with Our Lord which the imitation of His virtues implies.   So long as the soul remains exposed to fall from time to time into *mortal* sin, it must above all else avoid energetically the occasions of sin, combat the evil tendencies of nature and resist temptations.   It is only after these obstacles have been overcome that the soul concerns itself with the positive side of virtue.   The soul must likewise hold in abhorrence deliberate venial sin and stri e to avoid it.

B) In the second place, we must have *mortified our passions*.   To follow Our Lord it is necessary to renounce not merely mortal sin but *deliberate venial* sin as well, especially such as we often commit and to which we are attached.   It is by a determined fight against the passions and the capital sins that we gain that self-control which enables us to practice the positive side of virtue and thus to gradually come nearer to the Divine Model.   Then, indeed we can lead a well-regulated life, have moments in which to recollect ourselves and devote our time to the fulfilment of our duties of state.

964.   **C)** Lastly, it is necessary that through meditation we should have formed *profound convictions* on all the great truths, so that in our meditations we can give more time to devout affections and petitions, for it is by these that we attract to our heart Our Lord's virtues, and that we are able to practice them without too much difficulty.

The souls, then, that are progressing in the life of perfection are recognized by these two principal signs: 1) They experience great difficulty in making their mental prayer in a purely *discursive* fashion; the Holy Ghost inspires them to give less time to considerations and more to affections and petitions. 2) They are habitually possessed with a longing to be united to Our Lord, to know Him, love Him and imitate Him.

965. 2° From what we have just said, we can see the principal differences between the purgative and the illuminative way.

A) In both we find effort and struggle; but *beginners* struggle against sin and its causes, whilst the *souls in progress* struggle to *adorn* themselves with Christ's virtues. However, there is no opposition between these two ways; rather one leads into the other. By detaching oneself from sin and its causes in the purgative way, one already exercises oneself in the practice of the virtues, although in their lowest degree, which is predominantly negative. On the other hand, the positive virtues one practices in the illuminative way, perfect the detachment from self and from creatures. In the first instance it is the negative, in the second, the positive side that is emphasized. The one completes the other. By entering on the illuminative way one does not cease to practice penance and mortification, but one practices them with the view of becoming more like Our Lord.

B) The *means* used in the two ways remain substantially the same, but vary in the manner in which they are employed: meditation, which in the purgative way is *discursive,* becomes *affective* in the illuminative way; thought which heretofore centered in God, now converges round the Person of Our Lord, to know, love and imitate Him. He becomes the real *center* of life.

II. *Program to be followed in the Illuminative Way*

966. This program follows from what has been heretofore said.

1° The direct **object** in view is *so to assimilate ourselves to Our Lord* that He *becomes the center of our lives.*

A) We make Him the **center** of **our thoughts.** We love to study His life and His mysteries. The Gospel presents to us new charms: we read it slowly and affectionately; the least details of Our Savior's life, especially His virtues have a deep interest for us. We find in the Gospel an inexhaustible source of subjects for meditation. We love to ponder over the words of our Lord, to analyze them and to apply them to ourselves. When we wish to practice some virtue, it is *in Jesus* that we study it first of all, recalling His teachings and His examples, and finding there the great motive for reproducing in ourselves His own dispositions and virtues. It is on Him that we focus our thoughts during Holy Mass and Holy Communion: the liturgical prayers become for us an excellent means of studying Our Saviour. Lastly, by *devout readings* we strive to gain a deeper knowledge of His doctrines, especially of His spiritual teachings. It is Jesus *we seek* in books, "*Jesum quærens in libris.*"

967. B) This knowledge leads to **love,** and Jesus becomes **the center of our affections. a)** How could any one, day after day, contemplate Him Who is the perfection of beauty and goodness itself, and not feel drawn to love Him! "Since I have known Jesus Christ," said Lacordaire, "nothing has seemed to me beautiful enough that I should look upon it with desire."[1] If the Apostles on Mt. Thabor were ravished at the sight of the Lord's transfigured humanity and cried out in wonder and love: "*It is good for us to be here*",[2] our rapture must be still greater as we gaze on the resplendent comeliness of the Risen Christ.

b) How can we help loving Him if we often ponder the earnest proofs of love He has given and continues to give us, the Incarnation, the Redemption, the Holy Eucharist? St. Thomas has marvelously grouped within a single strophe the great things the Saviour has done for us:

> *Se nascens dedit socium,*
> *Convescens in edulium,*
> *Se moriens in pretium,*
> *Se regnans dat in præmium.*[3]

His birth made Him our fellow, our friend, our brother, and He never departs from us. By instituting the Holy Eucharist He becomes our food and drink, replenishing our souls with His Body, His Blood, and His Divinity. Dying on the Cross He paid the price of our ransom, set us free from the slavery of sin, restored to us our supernatural life, and gave us the greatest proof of love that friend can give to friend. In heaven, at

---

[1] CHOCARNE, *Vie du P. Lacordaire*, t. II, 119.
[2] *Matth.*, XVII, 4.
[3] Hymn of Lauds:

> "Born man, He makes Himself our kin,
> He gives His Body at the board,
> He dies and is the price of sin,
> He reigns and is our sweet reward. "

(Translation from **Donohue's** "*Early Christian Hymns.*")

last, He gives Himself as a reward, to be possessed for all eternity; henceforth His glory and our happiness are one. For all this we shall never be able to thank Him nor to love Him enough.

968. C) But love leads to **imitation.** By the very fact that we prize the qualities of a friend, that we are drawn to him by those qualities, we want to reproduce them in ourselves, so as to be but one with him in heart and soul; for we feel that our union will not be strong and deep unless we share in the thoughts and feelings and actions of our friend. We copy instinctively the one whom we love. And thus it is that Jesus becomes **the center of our actions,** of our whole existence. When we *pray*, we draw unto ourselves Our Lord with His spirit of religion to glorify the Father and effectively beg for the graces that we need. When we *labor*, we unite ourselves to the Divine Artisan of Nazareth, to work as He did, for the glory of God and the salvation of souls. When we want to *acquire some virtue*, we draw to ourselves the perfect model of that virtue, Jesus, and with Him we strive to practice it. Even our *recreations* are taken in union with Him and in His spirit, with a view to labor later on for the great interests of God and of His Church.

969. 2° To attain this end, however, **means** must be employed; these are, besides vocal prayers and *affective mental prayer*, a sustained effort to practice those Christian virtues which acquaint us better with Christ, increase our love for Him and enable us to follow closer in His footsteps, that is to say, the *theological* and the *moral* virtues. We aim at *solid* virtue, based not on emotions but on *deep-rooted convictions.*

A) We practice these virtues along parallel lines: we cannot exercise ourselves in the practice of the moral virtues without practicing the theological virtues, and vice versa. Thus we cannot cultivate *Christian prudence* without being guided by the light of faith, sustained by hope, and stimulated by the love of God; in like manner, *faith* and *hope* presuppose prudence, fortitude and temperance, and so it is with the other virtues.

However, there are some virtues that harmonize better than others with one or other of the degrees of the illuminative way. Thus, those who have but entered into this way, concentrate their efforts on the exercise of some of the *moral* virtues, the need of which they feel more keenly in order to triumph over pride or sensuality. Later on, when these vices have been brought under control, such persons devote themselves more especially to the practice of the *theological* virtues, which unite us more directly to God.

970. **B)** The better to understand this teaching, we must briefly note here the difference between these two kinds of virtues.

a) The *theological* virtues have God Himself as their *direct object* and some divine attribute as their motive. Thus, by Faith I believe in God, relying on His divine authority; by charity, I love Him because of His infinite goodness. On this very account these virtues *unite us directly to God;* faith makes us share in His thought, charity in His love.

b) The *direct object* of moral virtues is some *created good,* and their *motive* some moral good. Thus the object of justice is the rendering unto each one what is due him, and the motive of this virtue is honesty. These virtues *prepare* for our union with God by removing obstacles, and they even initiate that union; for instance, by being just I become one with God, Who is justice itself. However, it is the *theological* virtues that directly constitute and perfect our union with God.

971. **C)** From this it follows that if we study the virtues in the order of their *excellence,* we must begin with the *theological* virtues; but if we follow, as we do here, the *psychological* order, which proceeds from the less to the more perfect, then we must begin with the study of the *moral* virtues, without however losing sight of the aforesaid remark concerning the parallel development of all Christian virtues.

III. *Two Classes of Souls in the Illuminative Way*

In the illuminative way there are many classes of souls, two of which are of special interest : *devout* souls and *fervent* souls.

972. 1° Devout souls are those possessed of good-will, of ambition to do good, and who strive by serious efforts to avoid deliberate faults. But as yet, they are vain and presumptuous. Little inured to self-denial, they lack energy, steadiness of purpose, especially in the face of trials. Hence the frequent vacillation in their conduct : ready to suffer when trials are far of, they lack patience when facing pain and desolation; quick to form generous resolves, they carry them out but imperfectly in practice, especially if unforeseen obstacles arise.   Therefore, their advance is slow, and they stand in need of cultivating the virtues of fortitude, of constancy and of humility.

973.   2° *Fervent* souls are more humble and more generous.   Distrustful of self and confident in God, and already habituated to the practice of Christian self-denial, they are more energetic and more constant.   However, their abnegation is neither absolute nor universal.   They long for perfection, but their virtue has not yet been solidified by trial.   When consolation and spiritual joy come, they welcome them and rest complacently in them.   They have not as yet the love of the cross.   The firm resolutions they take in the morning, they carry out but partially during the day, because they lack constancy.   They have so far advanced in the love of God that they actually renounce what is dangerous, but they bestow their affections, at times overmuch, upon what God allows them to love : their parents, their friends, the consolations they find in their exercises of piety.   They have still to detach themselves more perfectly from whatever hinders their union with God.

We shall not treat separately of these two classes of souls.   The spiritual director will choose from among the virtues we describe the ones best suited to each individual.

DIVISION OF THE SECOND BOOK

974.   The *aim* of souls in the illuminative way being that of *making Jesus the very center of their lives,* 1° they must give themselves to the practice of *affective prayer,* in order to draw from it the knowledge, the love, and the imitation of their divine Model.   2° They must practice in a special though not exclusive manner, those moral virtues which, by removing the obstacles to union with God, initiate this union with Him, the Exemplar of all perfection. 3° Then the theological virtues which they practiced in the purgative way side by side with the moral virtues, develop in them and become the great motive power in their life. 4° But, since the warfare is far from being over, they must foresee and make ready for new onslaughts of the enemy. [1] Hence this second book comprises four chapters.

---

[1] We shall, therefore, not treat here, in the illuminative way, of the *passive purification of the senses,* nor of the prayer of quiet.   These are the beginnings of

---

CHAPTER I

Affective Prayer [1]

975.   Souls in the illuminative way continue in the
practice of the same spiritual exercises as beginners (n. 657),
but by increasing their number and by prolonging them,
they approach the state of *habitual prayer,* already described
in n. 522, which finds its perfect realization only in the unitive way.   They apply themselves particularly to the
practice of *affective prayer,* which little by little takes the
place of discursive meditation.   We shall explain : 1º the
nature of affective prayer; 2º its *advantages;* 3º its *difficulties;* 4º its *method.*

ART. I. NATURE OF AFFECTIVE PRAYER

976.   1º **Definition.**   Affective prayer, as the term
indicates, is that form of prayer in which *devout affections*
predominate, that is, those various *acts of the will* whereby
we express to God our love and our desire of glorifying
Him.   In this kind of prayer the heart is engaged to a greater
extent than the mind.

Beginners, as we have said (n. 668), need to acquire
convictions ; therefore they insist upon reasoning and give
but little time to affections.   But in proportion as these
convictions grow and take root in the soul, less time is

---

infused contemplation and therefore belong to the unitive way.   However, we beg
to call the reader's attention to the fact that some writers of note hold that the first
passive purification and the prayer of quiet belong to the illuminative way.
Cf. GARRIGOU-LAGRANGE, *Perfect. Chrét. et contemplation,* t. I, p. VIII.

[1] THOMAS DE VALLGORNERA, Q. II, disput. VI; RODRIGUEZ, *Christian Per-
fection,* P. I, Treat. V; CRASSET, *A Key to Meditation;* COURBON, *Familiar
Instructions on Mental Prayer;* LALLEMANT, *Spiritual Doctrine, Seventh
Principle;* GROU, *How to Pray;* POULAIN *Graces of Interior Prayer,* C. II;
LEHODEY, *The Ways of Mental Prayer,* P. II, C. VIII; SAUDREAU, *The Degress
of the Spiritual Life,* Vol. I, P. 249-274; R. DE MAUMIGNY, *Practice of Mental
Prayer,* I, P. III.

required to renew them and greater play is allowed to the affections. Smitten with love for God and charmed by the beauty of virtue, we rise with greater ease in loving aspirations towards the Author of all good in order to worship Him, to praise Him, to thank Him, to love Him; towards Our Lord Jesus Christ, our Saviour, Exemplar, Master, Friend, and Brother, in order to offer Him the tenderest sentiments of love; towards the Most Blessed Virgin, the Mother of God and our Mother, the dispenser of God's gifts, in order to express to her our filial, trustful and unselfish love (n. 166).

Other sentiments arise spontaneously in the soul: sentiments of shame, of confusion and humiliation at the sight of our miseries; ardent desires to become better, and confident petitions to obtain the necessary grace; zeal for God's glory which makes us pray for the great interests of the Church and the welfare of souls.

977. 2° **Transition from discursive meditation to affective prayer.** One does not attain suddenly to this kind of prayer. There is a period of transition when to a greater or lesser extent considerations and affections intermingle. There follows another period in which considerations still take place, but in the form of a colloquy after this fashion: " Help me, O my God, to realize how necessary is this virtue. " Some brief moments are then given to reflection, and the colloquy continues: " I thank Thee, O my God, for Thy divine lights. Vouchsafe to burn into my soul these truths, in order that they may affect my life more deeply... Help me, I beseech Thee, to see how short I fall of this virtue... what I must do to practice it better... this very day. " At last, a time arrives when reasoning all but ceases, or at least, it is so rapidly done that the greater part of prayer is passed in devout colloquies. Still, at times one feels the need of returning for a few moments to considerations so as to keep the mind sufficiently occupied. In all this one must follow the motions of grace under the guidance of a spiritual director.

978. 3° **Signs that warrant this change. A)** It is important that we recognize the signs which tell us when to relinquish discursive for affective prayer. To do so *prematurely* would be imprudent, for if the soul is not yet sufficiently advanced to entertain these affections, it will fall into distractions or aridity. On the other hand, it would be a loss to make the change too late, for according to all spiritual writers, affective prayer is more fruitful than discursive prayer, since it is chiefly by acts of the will that we give glory to God and attract virtue to ourselves.

B) These signs are as follows: 1) When despite good-will one finds it difficult to pursue considerations or to draw profit from them, and at the same time one is inclined towards affections in prayer. 2) When convictions are so firmly rooted in the soul that it takes but a moment to recall them. 3) When the heart, detached from sin, easily tends towards God or towards Our Lord. However, since no one is a fair judge in his own case, these signs are to be submitted to the judgment of the spiritual director.

979. 4° **Means of fostering affections in prayer. A)** These devout affections are multiplied and prolonged chiefly through the exercise of the virtue of *charity*, for they spring from a heart where the love of God reigns supreme. It is such a heart that moves us to *admire* the *divine perfections.* Aglow with faith, it makes visible to our eyes the infinite beauty, the goodness, and the loving mercy of God; a sense of awe and of wonder arises spontaneously and in turn gives birth to *gratitude, praise,* and *delight* in God. The more the soul loves God, the more are these various acts prolonged. The same is true of love towards Our Lord Jesus Christ. When we pass in review His many favors to us (n. 967), the sufferings He has endured for us, the love He shows us now in the Holy Eucharist, we are easily drawn on to sentiments of admiration, adoration, gratefulness, pity, love, and we feel constrained to praise and bless One Who loves us so much.

980. B) To nurture this love, souls in the illuminative way should be advised to meditate frequently on the great truths that recall to us what God has done and ceaselessly does for us: —

a) The indwelling of the Three Divine Persons in our soul and Their paternal action in our regard (n. 92-130).

b) Our incorporation into Christ and the part He plays in the Christian life (n. 132-153). His life, His mysteries and, above all, His cruel Passion, His love in the Eucharist.

c) The share of the Blessed Virgin, the Angels and the Saints in the Christian life (n. 154-189). Herein we find an excellent means of lending variety to the affections by addressing ourselves now to our Mother in Heaven, now to the Holy Angels, especially to our Guardian Angel, now to the Saints, and in particular to those that inspire in us greater devotion.

d) Such vocal prayers as the *Our Father*, the *Hail Mary*, the *Hymns of St. Thomas to the Blessed Sacrament*, etc... which abound in sentiments of love, gratitude, conformity to God's will.

e) The fundamental virtues: religion towards God, obedience to superiors, humility, fortitude, temperance, and, above all, the three theological virtues. These virtues are to be considered now not in the abstract but as *exemplified by Our Lord.* It is in order to resemble Him and to show Him our love that we strive to practice them.

f) We must nevertheless continue to meditate on penance, mortification, sin, and the last things, but in a manner different from that of beginners. We should consider Our Lord as a perfect model of penance and of mortification, loaded down with the burden of our transgressions and atoning for them through a long martyrdom, and we should strive to draw to ourselves these virtues. Should we meditate on death, heaven, and hell, it will be to detach ourselves from created things in order to unite ourselves to Jesus and thereby secure the grace of a happy death and a bright throne in heaven, close to Jesus.

ART. II. ADVANTAGES OF AFFECTIVE PRAYER

These flow from the very nature of this prayer.

981. 1º The principal advantage is a *closer and more abiding union with God.* Because this prayer multiplies affective acts, it produces an increase of love for God. Thus the affections are at once *effect* and *cause.* They spring from our love of God and at the same time perfect that love, since virtues grow by the repetition of the same acts. For the same reason they give us a better knowledge of the divine perfections. For, as St. Bonaventure [1] points out, " the best way to arrive at a knowledge of God is to taste the sweetness of His love; this is a far better way, worthier, and more gratifying than the way of intellectual research. " Just as we form a better appreciation of the fine quality of a tree by tasting the fruit it produces, so we realize all the better the worth of the divine attributes, once we experience the charming tenderness of God's love. This knowledge in turn increases our charity, our earnestness, and urges us on to the perfect exercise of all virtues.

982. 2º Because affective prayer increases our love for God, it perfects all the virtues that flow from charity : **a)** *conformity to God's will,* for we delight in doing the will of those we love; **b)** *desire to procure the glory of God* and the salvation of souls, for if we love we cannot but praise and seek praise for the object of our affections; **c)** *love of silence* and recollection, for we want to be alone with Him Whom we love, in order to think the oftener of Him and to tell Him again of our love; **d)** *desire of frequent Communion,* for we want to possess as perfectly as we can the object of

---

[1] *Sent.* l. III, dist. 35, a. 1, q. 2.

our love, to welcome Him joyfully into our hearts and joyfully abide with Him all the day long; e) *the spirit of sacrifice*, for we know that we cannot be one with the Crucified and through Him with God, except inasmuch as we deny ourselves and sacrifice our ease in order to carry our cross without faltering and to accept all the trials that Providence sends us.

983. 3º In affective prayer we often find *spiritual consolation.* There is no purer, no sweeter joy than that found in the companionship of a friend, and Jesus being the tenderest and most generous of friends, we relish in His presence a taste of Heaven's joys : *To be with Jesus is a sweet paradise.* True, side by side with these joys there are at times trials, such as aridity, but we accept these with a sweet resignation and we tell God again and again that in spite of all we wish to love and serve Him. The thought that we suffer for God's sake alleviates our sufferings and becomes a source of consolation.

We may add that affective prayer is not as difficult as discursive prayer. In the latter, fatigue follows quickly upon the effort of reasoning, whilst if we let our heart produce sentiments of love, of gratitude, of praise, the soul experiences a sweet rest, and is thus enabled to conserve its energies for action.

984. 4º Lastly, affective prayer becomes more and more simple as we lessen the number and the variety of affections and intensify a certain few of them, and it thus leads us on gradually to the *prayer of simplicity.* This already constitutes acquired contemplation, and it prepares for infused contemplation the souls that are called to it. Of this we shall speak when treating of the *unitive way.*

ART. III. THE DISADVANTAGES AND THE DANGERS OF AFFECTIVE PRAYER

The best things in this world are not free from disadvantages and dangers. This holds true of affective prayer unless it be practiced with discretion. We shall now point out its dangers and disadvantages together with the proper remedies.

985. 1º The first danger is *mental strain*, leading to fatigue and exhaustion. Some persons, anxious to lend intensity to their affective acts, strain their minds and hearts, and violently bestir themselves to produce acts of love in which nature plays a greater part than grace. Such efforts wear out their nervous system and cause the blood to rush to the brain; a sort of slow fever consumes their strength and they are soon exhausted. Physiological disorders even may ensue, and sensations more or less sensual may join with devout affections.

986. This is a *serious defect* which must be *corrected* at the very outset by consulting a wise director and following his advice. Now, the remedy consists in the profound conviction that true love of God is centered in the *will* rather than in the feelings; that the generosity of that love does not consist in vehement [1] emotional transports, but in a calm and determined purpose of refusing nothing to Almighty God. Let us bear in mind that love is an act of the will. No doubt, it does react on the feelings and excite more or less lively emotions, yet these do not constitute the essence of true devotion; they are but accidental manifestations thereof which must remain subject to the will and must be regulated by it. In the absence of this control, the emotions gain the ascendency, (which means disorder) and instead of fostering solid piety, they make it degenerate into sentimental, at times into sensual love, for all violent emotions are fundamentally of the same kind, and the passage from one to the other is easy. We must therefore strive to spiritualize our affections, to moderate them and press them into the service of the will. Then we shall enjoy a peace that lies above and beyond all feeling, " The peace of God which surpasseth all understanding. " [2]

987. 2⁰ The second danger of affective prayer is *pride* and *presumption*. Because one is possessed of good and noble sentiments, of holy desires, of fine projects for spiritual progress; because one experiences sensible fervor, and in such moments scorns the pleasures and goods and vanities of this world, one becomes easily persuaded that one is far more advanced in the spiritual life than one really is, and one may even wonder whether one has not all but reached the heights of perfection and contemplation. At times, one may even hold one's breath at prayer awaiting some divine communication. These sentiments show, on

---

[1] No doubt, there are Saints who have at times experienced transports of love, which manifested themselves by sensible phenomena; these however were not produced by the Saints themselves, but by the grace of God. To wish to stir up violent emotions in oneself by way of imitation of the Saints would amount to presumption. — [2] *Phil.*, IV, 7.

the contrary, that one is still far removed from such exalted heights; for, the saints and the truly fervent distrust themselves, ever regard themselves as the worst, and readily believe that others are better than themselves. Therefore, one must return to the practice of humility and self-distrust, taking into consideration what we shall say subsequently regarding this virtue. Besides, when these sentiments of pride develop, God frequently takes it upon Himself to bring back such souls to a right sense of their unworthiness and their insufficiency, by depriving them of consolations and of choice graces. Then they realize that they are as yet far removed from the desired goal.

988. 3° There are some who make their entire devotion consist in a *quest after spiritual consolations*, whilst they neglect their duties of state and the practice of the ordinary virtues. Provided they are able to make what they consider beautiful meditations, they imagine themselves to be perfect. This is a gross delusion. There is no perfection without conformity to the divine will; and it is God's will that besides keeping the commandments we should faithfully discharge our duties of state, practice the homely virtues of modesty, kindness, graciousness, amiability, as well as the greater ones. To believe that one is a saint because one loves prayer and especially the comforts of prayer, is to forget that he alone is perfect who does the will of God : " Not every one that saith to me, Lord, Lord, shall enter into the Kingdom of heaven : but he that doth the will of my Father. " [1]

Once we know how to remove these obstacles and dangers by using the means indicated, affective prayer becomes highly conducive to our spiritual progress as well as to the exercise of apostolic zeal.

Art. IV. Methods of Affective Prayer

These methods are reduced to two types : the method of *St. Ignatius* and that of *St. Sulpice*.

I. *The Methods of St. Ignatius* [2]

Among the methods of St. Ignatius there are three related to affective prayer : 1° *Contemplation.* 2° *The Application of the Senses.* 3° *Meditated vocal prayer.*

---

[1] *Matth.*, VII, 21.
[2] St. Ignatius, *Spiritual Exercises*, 2nd week; R. de Maumigny, *Practice of Mental Prayer*, I, P. V.

1° St. Ignatius' Method of Contemplation

989. It is not question here of *infused* contemplation nor even of *acquired* contemplation, but of a *method of affective prayer.* To contemplate any given thing is not merely to glance at it, but to *linger* on it with *pleasure*, to look at it with *wonder* and *love*, much as a mother gazes upon her child. The object of this contemplation may be the mysteries of Our Lord or the divine attributes.

When we meditate upon some mystery : 1) we contemplate the *persons* who take part in it, for instance, the Most Blessed Trinity, Our Lord, the Blessed Virgin, the Saints; 2) we *listen to their words*, see to whom they are addressed, and search their meaning; 3) *we consider* the nature and circumstances *of their actions.*

All these lead us to offer our homage to God, to Jesus Christ, to Our Lady and to the Saints, and thus to know and to love better our Blessed Saviour.

990. That this contemplation may be fruitful, we look upon the mystery in question, not as a past event, but as one *actually taking place* before our eyes. Moreover, we do not simply witness the mystery, but *actively share* in it, for example, by making our own the sentiments that animated the Blessed Virgin at the moment of Our Lord's birth. Besides, we seek to attain some *practical result*, for example, a more intimate knowledge of Jesus, a more unselfish love for Him.

We can easily see how a subject thus considered readily admits of all sentiments of admiration, adoration, gratitude, love towards God, as well as of self-reproach, unworthiness, sorrow at the sight of our sins, in a word, of every kind of prayer which we can offer for ourselves and for others.

In order that these manifold affections may not alter our peace of soul, we must not forget the wise remark of St. Ignatius [1] : " If I experience in this or that point of meditation such sentiments as I wanted to excite in my soul, I shall stop and tarry there, without concerning myself with proceeding further, until my soul has had its fill ; for it is not an abundance of knowledge that lays hold on the soul and satisfies it, but the inward relish of the truths it meditates. "

2° The Application of the Senses

991. This is the name given to a very simple and very devout way of meditating. It consists in the *imaginative* or *spiritual* exercise of our senses upon some mystery of Our Lord's life, in order that the soul may attain to a fuller realization of all the circumstances attending the said mystery, and that the heart may be moved to stir up pious sentiments and to make good resolutions.

---

[1] *Spiritual Exercises*, 2nd annot., 4th addit.; R. DE MAUMIGNY, *Practice of Mental Prayer*, I, P. V.

The following is an example taken from the mystery of the Nativity.

1) *Application of the sense of sight:* I see the tiny Babe laid in the manger, the straw whereon He rests, the swaddling clothes wherewith He is wrapped. I see His little hands trembling with cold, His eyes glistening with tears. This Infant is my God! I adore Him with lively sentiments of faith. I see the Blessed Virgin, a picture of meekness and heavenly beauty! I see her taking the Child Jesus in her arms, covering Him tenderly, pressing Him to her heart and laying Him upon the straw. That Babe is her Son and her God! I wonder and pray. Then I think of Holy Communion, in which I receive the self-same Jesus. Do I have Mary's faith, Mary's love?

2) *Application of the sense of hearing:* I hear the cries of the Divine Infant. I hear the sobs that suffering wrings from Him. He is cold, He suffers, chiefly because of the hard-heartedness of men. I listen to the words His heart speaks to the heart of His Mother. I hearken to the answer She makes, an answer full of faith, of adoration, of humility, of love. I join in her sentiments.

3) *Application of the sense of smell:* I breathe the aroma of the virtues the lowly manger holds, the fragrance of Christ Jesus, and I beg my Savior to grant me that spiritual sense that will enable me to breathe in the perfume of His humility.

4) *Application of the sense of taste:* I relish the delight of being nigh to Jesus, Mary and Joseph, the delight of loving them, and the better to enjoy this delight I silently rest close to my Savior.

5) *Application of the sense of touch:* With loving reverence I feel that straw whereon my Savior lies, I press it to my lips with love; and by the leave of the Divine Child, I kiss His sacred feet. [1]

One ends by holding a devout colloquy with Jesus and with His Blessed Mother, asking the grace of loving this Divine Savior with a more generous love.

992. As to meditation on the *divine attributes*, it is made by considering each of them with sentiments of adoration, of praise, and of love, in order to arrive at the complete surrender of self to God. [2]

3° VOCAL PRAYER MEDITATED

993. This method of meditating consists in a leisurely consideration of any vocal prayer, such as the *Our Father*, the *Hail Mary*, the *Hail Holy Queen* etc., in order to ponder and relish the meaning of each word.

Thus, with the Lord's Prayer, we consider the first word and say, for instance : O my God, Thou the Eternal, the Almighty Creator of all things, Thou hast adopted me as Thy child, Thou art my *Father*. Thou art so, because at Baptism Thou hast vouchsafed to have me share in that divine life which is Thine, because each day Thou dost foster it in my soul. Thou art so, because Thou lovest me with a love

---

[1] St. Ignatius dares not go this far. Other Saints have done so, and if grace prompts us we may imitate them.
[2] See the last contemplation of St. Ignatius, *Spiritual Exercises,* IV Week.

surpassing that of any earthly father or mother for a child, because Thou dost encompass me with a solicitude truly paternal.[1]

We dwell upon this one word as long as we find therein new depths of meaning and draw therefrom fresh sentiments that yield some light, strength or consolation. If we find in one word or two sufficient matter for all the time of our prayer, we do not proceed further, but we relish these words, draw from them some practical conclusion, and pray to be enabled to carry it out.

These methods are three simple and easy ways of making affective prayer.

II. *The Method of St. Sulpice*

We have already noted, n. 701, that this method is particularly adapted to affective prayer. Souls in the illuminative way may make profitable use of it if only they bear in mind the following remarks:

994. 1º The first point, *the adoration*, which was rather brief for beginners, is now prolonged more and more, and at times may take up over one-half of the time of meditation. The soul, seized by love for God, admires, adores, praises, blesses, thanks now the Three Divine Persons, now each of Them in particular, now Our Blessed Lord, the perfect model of the virtue we wish to make our own. According to circumstances, the soul likewise offers here its reverent, grateful, and loving homages to the Blessed Virgin and to the Saints, and whilst so doing it feels itself drawn to imitate their virtues.

995. 2º The second point, the *communion*, likewise becomes almost completely affective. The few considerations made are rather brief, and they are made in the form of a colloquy with God or with Our Lord, thus: " Help me, O my God, to establish this truth more firmly in my soul... " These colloquies are accompanied or followed by outpourings of gratitude for the lights received, and by ardent desires of practicing the virtue upon which we meditate. On turning to examine ourselves with regard to this virtue, we do so under the gaze of Jesus and by comparison with this Divine Model. The result is a clearer realization, by far, of our defects and of our misery which are brought out by the *contrast* between *Him* and *us*. Then sentiments of humiliation and shame are more deeply felt, our confidence in God increases because we find ourselves before the Divine Healer of souls, and instinctively the heart utters

---

[1] A. DURAND, *op. cit.*, p. 458-459; R. DE MAUMIGNY, *l. c.*, C. VI.

the cry: "Lord, behold him whom Thou lovest is sick." [1]
Earnest petitions are then made for the grace of practicing
some particular virtue, petitions in behalf of others, petitions for the universal Church, petitions full of confidence,
because being incorporated into Christ, we know our
prayers have His support.

996. 3° The third point, the *co-operation*, assumes a
more affective character : the resolution that we form is
submitted to Jesus for approval, and the desire which
prompts us to carry it out in practice is that of becoming
even more thoroughly one with Christ. For the realization
of this good purpose we rely on His collaboration, while
distrusting ourselves. We associate this resolution with a
spiritual bouquet, a loving aspiration which we repeat often
during the course of the day, and which helps us not only
to put our resolution into practice, but also to remind us of
Him Who inspired it.

997. There are times, however, when the soul affected by *aridity*,
cannot, save with great difficulty, produce such affections. Then, in
sweet abandonment to the will of God, it reaffirms its determination to
love Him, to remain loyal to Him, to abide in His presence and in His
service, no matter what it may cost; it humbly avows its own unworthiness, its own powerlessness, makes its will one with Christ's, offers
with Him the homages He renders to God and joins thereto its own
suffering at not being able to do more to honor the Divine Majesty.
These acts of the will are even richer in merit than devout affections.

Such are the principal methods of affective prayer. Let
each one choose the method best adapted to himself, and,
under the influence of divine grace, take from it what
actually answers to his needs and supernatural attractions.
In this manner the soul will advance in the practice
of virtue.

---

[1] *John*, XI, 3.

CHAPTER II

The Moral Virtues [1]

Before proceeding to describe them singly, we must briefly recall the theological notions concerning the *infused virtues*.

PRELIMINARY NOTIONS CONCERNING THE INFUSED VIRTUES

First we shall speak of the *infused virtues in general*, and then of the *moral virtues in particular*.

I. *The Infused Virtues in General* [2]

998. There are *natural* virtues, that is to say, there are good habits, acquired through the frequent repetition of acts, that render easy the performance of morally good actions. Thus, pagans and unbelievers can with the help of God's natural concurrence acquire and gradually perfect the moral virtues of prudence, justice, fortitude and temperance. We do not treat here of these natural virtues, but of the *supernatural* or *infused* virtues as they exist in the Christian soul.

999. Raised to the supernatural state, and having no other destiny than the Beatific Vision, we must tend thereto through acts performed under the influence of supernatural principles and of supernatural motives, for there must be a proportion between the end and the acts that lead to it. And so, the virtues which the world calls natural, must be practiced by us in a supernatural manner. As Father Garrigou-Lagrange [3], following St. Thomas, rightly says : " The Christian moral virtues are *infused and because of their formal object*, are essentially distinct from the highest of acquired moral virtues described by the greatest philoso-

---

[1] St. Thomas, Ia IIæ, q. 55-67; IIa IIæ, q. 48-170; Suarez, *Disput. metaphsy.*, XLIV; *de Passionibus et habitibus, De fide* etc.; Joannes a S. Thoma, *Cursus theol., Tr. de Passionibus, habitibus et virtutibus*, etc.; Alvarez de Paz, t. II, lib. III, de adeptione virtutum; Phil. a SS. Trinit., P. II, tr. II, dis. I, II; J. J. Olier, *Introd. à la vie et aux vertus chrét.;* Ribet, *Les vertus et les dons;* P. de Smedt, *Notre vie surnaturelle*, t. II; St. Francis of Sales, *Devout Life, passim;* Gay, *Christian Life and Virtues.*

[2] St. Thomas, Ia IIæ, q. 62-63; Suarez, *De passionibus et habitibus*, diss. III; J. a St. Thoma, *op. cit.*, disp. XVI; L. Billot, *De virt. infusis;* P. Janvier, *Carême* 1906; P. Garrigou-Lagrange, *Perfect. chrét. et contemplation*, p. 62-75.

[3] *Op. cit.*, p. 64.

phers... There is an infinite difference between Aristotelian temperance with reason as its only rule, and Christian temperance with the superadded rule of divine faith and supernatural prudence. "

We have already shown in nos. 121-122, how these virtues are communicated to us by the Holy Ghost dwelling in us; now we have but to describe : 1° their *nature,* 2° their *growth,* 3° their *decline,* 4° the bond of union existing among them.

1° THE NATURE OF THE INFUSED VIRTUES

1000. A) The infused virtues are *principles of action which God ingrafts in us, that they may perform in the soul the function of supernatural faculties and may thus enable us to perform meritorious acts.*

There exists an essential difference between the infused and the acquired virtues from the threefold point of view of *origin, mode of operation,* and *purpose.*

a) As regards *origin,* the natural virtues are acquired by the repetition of the same acts, whilst the supernatural virtues proceed from God, Who implants them in the soul together with habitual grace.

b) From the point of view of *operation,* the natural virtues, because they are acquired through the repetition of the same acts, give us a facility for producing the like acts readily and with a sense of pleasure ; the supernatural virtues, placed by God in the soul, simply give us the *power* to produce meritorious acts, together with a certain *tendency* towards the production of these acts; facility will come with frequent repetition.

c) With regard to their *purpose,* the natural virtues seek natural righteousness and direct us towards the Creator, the God of Nature ; the infused virtues pursue supernatural good and lead us to the God of Revelation, the Triune God, made known to us by faith. Hence, the motives inspiring the latter must be supernatural; they all refer to our friendship with God. I practice prudence, justice, temperance and fortitude, in order to be one with God.

1001. It follows that acts of supernatural virtue are possessed of a far higher perfection than acts of acquired virtue [1]. Christian temperance, for instance, leads us not merely to the moderation needed to maintain man's dignity, but to positive practices of mortification whereby we become more like Our Savior; Christian humility not only makes us avoid the excesses of pride and of anger incompatible with right reason, but it causes us to embrace humiliation, which renders us more like Our Divine Exemplar.

---

[1] *Sum. theol.,* IIa IIæ, q. 63, a. 4; H. NOBLE, *Vie spirituelle,* Nov. 1921 p. 103-104.

There is therefore an essential difference between acquired and infused virtues; for their *principle* and their *motive* differ.

1002. B) We have said that facility in the exercise of the infused virtues is acquired by the repetition of the same acts and lends readiness, ease and pleasure to action. Three main causes concur in producing this happy result:

a) Habit *lessens the obstacles* or the resistance offered by our lower nature, and thus, with the same amount of effort, better results are obtained. b) Habit likewise renders our faculties, more pliant, makes them quicker to respond to the motives that lead us to good and more skilful in the attainment of the good perceived; we even experience a certain satisfaction in the exercise of faculties so well trained, much as a musician does in playing upon a delicate instrument. c) Lastly, actual grace, bestowed upon us in proportion to our faithful correspondence, likewise gives us a singular facility to perform our task and to love it.

We may note in passing that this facility once acquired is not immediately lost when by mortal sin we lose the infused virtue; but being the result of oft-repeated acts, it still remains for a time, in virtue of the psychological laws governing acquired habits.

2°· THE GROWTH OF INFUSED VIRTUES

1003. A) The infused virtues are susceptible of growth in the soul and do, as a matter of fact, grow there with the increase of habitual grace, whence they flow. This growth is God-given, since He alone can give us an increase of divine life and of the elements that constitute it. Now, God causes this increase when we receive the *Sacraments*, perform *good works*, or recite our *prayers*.

a) Because of their very institution, the *Sacraments* cause within us an increase of habitual grace, and thereby of the infused virtues that go with grace, in proportion to our dispositions, nos. 259-261.

b) Our good works, also, merit not only glory, but an increase of habitual grace and thereby an increase of the infused virtues. This increase depends in a large measure upon the fervor of our dispositions, no. 237.

c) Prayer, besides its meritorious value, has an *impetratory* power; it obtains an increase of grace and of virtue in proportion to the fervor with which we pray. It is important, then, that we unite our prayers to those of the Church and that with her we ask for an increase of faith, hope, and charity.

B) According to St. Thomas, this increase is effected not by an accession of degree or of quantity, but by a *more perfect and more effective possession* of the virtue. It is in this manner that virtues take deeper root in the soul and become more solid and more active.

3° THE DECLINE AND LOSS OF THE VIRTUES

Any activity that is given up or is brought into play but seldom, tends to decline or even to be lost entirely.

1004. A) The Weakening of the Virtues. In reality, the infused virtues cannot be decreased, any more than can sanctifying grace, on which they depend. *Venial* sin cannot diminish them, just as it cannot decrease habitual grace itself. But venial sin, especially when frequent and fully deliberate, does *hinder* considerably the *exercise* of these virtues, by lessening the *facility* acquired through previous acts. This facility is the result of earnestness and perseverance in effort; but deliberate venial faults chill our ardor, and partly paralyze our activity, no. 730. Thus, venial sins against the virtue of temperance, though they do not detract from that infused virtue *itself*, gradually lessen the facility once acquired for mortifying sensuality. Besides, abuse of grace causes a reduction of the number of actual graces which help in the exercise of the virtues, and on this account the practice of virtue lacks vigor. Lastly, as we have stated, (no. 731) deliberate venial faults pave the way for grave ones and thereby for the loss of the virtues.

1005. B) The Loss of the Virtues. We can state as a principle that the infused virtues are lost by any act that destroys their *formal object*, their *motive*. In fact, virtue is thereby torn out by the roots.

a) Thus, *charity* is forfeited by *any* mortal sin, for such sin destroys the formal object or basis of that virtue, since mortal sin is directly opposed to God's infinite goodness.

b) The *infused moral virtues* also are lost through any mortal sin. They are bound to charity in such wise, that they come and go with it. However, the facility that had been acquired to perform acts of prudence, of justice etc., remains for a time after the infused virtues have been lost, due to the persevering character of acquired habits.

c) As to the virtues of faith and hope, these abide in the soul, even when grace has been lost by mortal sin, unless it be a sin directly opposed to either of these virtues. This is so because other sins do not destroy in the soul the foundations of faith or of hope; besides God in His infinite mercy wills that these two virtues stay with us as a last anchor of salvation. As long as we believe and as long as we hope conversion remains relatively easy.

4° THE BOND OF UNION EXISTING AMONG THE VIRTUES

1006. It is often said that all virtues are *correlated*. This demands explanation.

A) First of all, *charity* rightly conceived and rightly practiced comprises all the virtues; not only faith and hope (which is evident), but even the moral virtues, as we have explained, following St. Paul, in no. 318 : "*Charity is patient, is kind, etc.*" This is true in the sense that he who loves God and the neighbor for God's sake, is ready to practice one and all the virtues the moment conscience makes him aware of his obligation. As a matter of fact one cannot truly love God above all things, and not want to observe His commandments and even some of the counsels. Besides, the proper function of charity is that of directing all our acts towards God, our last end, and hence of controlling the acts of all the Christian virtues. One may say that a growth in charity is attended by a positive growth in the other virtues as well.

However, whilst the love of God inclines the will towards acts of the moral virtues and facilitates their practice, it does not immediately and necessarily bestow the perfection of all these virtues, for instance, of prudence, of humility, of obedience, of chastity. A sincerely converted sinner, for example, who had previously contracted evil habits, will not, though practicing charity in all earnestness, become at once perfectly prudent, perfectly chaste, or temperate. Time and effort will be required before he can discard old habits and form new ones.

1007. B) Since charity constitutes the form, the fulness of perfection of all the virtues, the latter are never perfect without it. Thus faith and hope which abide in the sinner's soul are indeed real virtues, but remain *incomplete*, that is to say, they lack that quality that directs them towards God as last end ; and so the acts of faith and of hope performed in the state of sin cannot merit heaven, even though they are supernatural and form a preparation for conversion.

1008. C) With regard to the *moral* virtues, if one possesses them in their perfection, that is to say, *animated by charity* and in a somewhat high degree, they are truly correlated in this sense that we cannot be in possession of one without possessing the others. Thus, all virtues in order to be perfect, require the virtue of prudence. Prudence itself cannot be practiced perfectly without the concurrence of fortitude, of justice, and of temperance. A weak character prone to injustice and to intemperance will in many circumstances fail in prudence. Justice, likewise, cannot be practiced in all its perfection without strength of soul and temperance. Fortitude in turn must be tempered by prudence and justice, and it would not long survive without the virtue of temperance.[1]

---

[1] Cf. St Augustine, Letter 167 to Jerome *P. L.* XXXIII, 735.

When however the moral virtues exist but in a low degree, the presence of one does not necessarily entail the practice of the others. Thus there are persons who are modest without being humble and others who are humble without being merciful, or merciful without being just. [1]

II. *The Moral Virtues*

We shall give a brief account of their *nature*, their *number*, and of the *character common* to all.

1009. 1° *Their Nature.* These virtues are called moral for a twofold reason: **a)** to distinguish them from the *purely intellectual* virtues, which perfect the intellect with no reference to the moral life, such as science, art, etc.; **b)** to differentiate them also from the theological virtues, which do indeed regulate our *moral life,* but which, as we have already said, have God *directly for their object,* while the moral virtues pursue directly a supernatural, created good, for example, the mastery of our passions. Withal, we must bear in mind that the supernatural, moral virtues themselves constitute a participation in the life of God and fit us for the Beatific Vision. Furthermore, according as these virtues become more and more perfect, and especially when they are complemented by the gifts of the Holy Ghost, they merge with the theological virtues in such wise as to become, as it were, permeated by these, until they are but the various manifestations of the charity that animates them.

1010. 2° *Their Number.* The moral virtues considered in their divers ramifications are very numerous, but all can be reduced to the four *cardinal* virtues (so called from the word *cardines,* hinges) since they are, so to speak, four hinges upon which all the other virtues depend.

These four virtues, in fact, meet all the soul's needs and perfect all its moral faculties.

1011. A) They *meet all the needs of the soul.*

a) First of all, we must make a choice of all the means necessary or useful to the attainment of our supernatural end: this falls within the scope of the virtue of *prudence.*

b) We must likewise *respect the rights of others:* this comes within the sphere of *justice.*

c) In order to defend, without fear or violence, both *ourselves and our possessions* from the dangers that threaten us, we stand in need of the virtue of *fortitude.*

---

[1] ST. GREGORY, *Moral.* l. XXII, c. I.

d) If we would use the goods of this world and its plea-sures without exceeding the proper *measure*, we need the vir-tue of *temperance*. Thus, *justice* regulates our relations with the neighbor, *fortitude* and *temperance* determine our duties to ourselves and *prudence* directs the other three virtues.

1012. B) They *perfect all the moral faculties.* The intellect is controlled by prudence, the will by justice, the irascible appetite by fortitude, and the concupiscible appetite by temperance. We must however call attention to the fact that inasmuch as both the irascible and concupiscible appetites receive their morality solely through the *will,* the virtues of fortitude and temperance reside in this superior faculty as well as in the lower faculties that are directed in their function by the will.

1013. C) Lastly, we may add that each of these virtues can be considered as a genus containing *integral, subjective* and *potential* parts.

a) The *integral* parts are complements so useful or necessary to the practice of virtue, that the virtue would not be perfect were these elements lacking. Thus, patience and constancy are integral parts of fortitude.

b) The *subjective* (or inherent) parts are, so to speak, different species subordinated to the principal virtue. Thus, sobriety and chastity are subjective parts of temperance.

c) The *potential* (or accessory) parts have a certain similarity to the principal virtue, but do not in every respect fulfil all the conditions found in it. Thus, the virtue of *religion* is an accessory part of the virtue of justice, because it tends to render to God the worship *due* to Him, but it can do so only inadequately, both as regards the perfection of the manner in which that worship should be rendered, and the extent in which it should be offered. *Obedience* likewise renders to superiors the submission due to them, but here again there exists no strict right, absolutely speaking, nor the relation of equal to equal.

Our task will be easier, and that of our readers also, if we do not enter into an enumeration of all these divisions and subdivisions. We shall select the principal virtues and we shall lay stress only upon their most essential elements from the twofold point of view of theory and practice.

1014. 3° *The Character Common to All Moral Virtues.* **a)** All the moral virtues strive to keep the *golden mean : in medio stat virtus.* They must follow the *rule* of right reason enlightened by faith. This rule may be broken either by excess or defect, and so, moral virtue consists in avoiding these two extremes.

b) The theological virtues as such do not consist in holding this middle course, since, as St. Bernard says, the measure wherewith to love God is to love Him without measure. However, considered in their relation to us, the theological virtues must likewise take cognizance of the golden mean, in other words, they must be controlled by prudence, which tells us what are the circumstances in which we can and must practice these virtues. It is prudence, for instance, which shows us what we must believe and what we must not believe, as well as how to avoid both presumption and despair.

DIVISION OF THE SECOND CHAPTER

1015. In this second chapter we shall treat of the four *cardinal* virtues and of the *principal* virtues related to them.

I. Prudence
II. Justice $\begin{cases} \text{Religion} \\ \text{Obedience} \end{cases}$
III. Fortitude
IV. Temperance $\begin{cases} \text{Chastity} \\ \text{Humility} \\ \text{Meekness} \end{cases}$

ART. I. THE VIRTUE OF PRUDENCE [1]

We shall explain: 1º its *nature;* 2º its *necessity;* 3º the *means* of progressing in this virtue.

I. *The Nature of Prudence*

The better to understand prudence, we shall give its *definition*, its *constituents elements* and its different *species*.

1016. 1º **Definition.** Prudence is a supernatural, moral virtue which inclines our intellect to choose in every instance the best means for attaining our aims, by subordinating them to our ultimate end.

Hence, it is not the *prudence of the flesh,* nor *merely human* prudence, but *Christian* prudence.

A) It is not the **prudence of the flesh,** such as makes one skilful in discovering the means whereby a bad end is to be attained, in satisfying one's passions, in obtaining wealth, in gaining honors. This kind of prudence has been condemned by St. Paul, because it is inimical to God, at odds with His law, and because it militates against man, whom it leads to eternal destruction. [2]

It is not **merely human** prudence, such as seeks out the means best adapted to attain a natural end, without referring them to the last end. Such is the prudence of the masters of industry, of merchants, artists, laborers, who seek gain or fame, unconcerned about God and eternity.

---

[1] CASSIAN, *Conferences*, II; ST. JOHN CLIMACUS, *Scala*, XXVI; ST. THOMAS, IIa IIæ, q. 47-56; CH. DE SMEDT, *Notre vie surnaturelle*, t. II. p. 1-33; P. JANVIER, *Carême 1917.* — [2] *Rom.*, VIII, 6-8.

These persons must be reminded that it profits us nothing to gain the whole world if one suffers the loss of one's soul. [1]

1017. B) It is **christian** prudence which, based upon the principles of Christian faith, refers all things to the supernatural end, that is to say, to God known and loved upon earth and possessed in heaven. Of course, prudence is not directly concerned with this end, which is proposed to it by faith, but it keeps it ever in view in order to discover by its light the means best adapted to direct all our actions. Prudence therefore concerns itself with all the details of our life. It regulates our *thoughts* to prevent them from straying away from God. It regulates our *motives* to keep them aloof from whatever may affect their *singleness of purpose.* It regulates our *affections*, our *sentiments* and our *choices*, so as to center them on God. It regulates even our exterior actions and the execution of our good resolves so as to refer them to our ultimate end. [2]

1018. C) This virtue **resides,** strictly speaking, in the **intellect,** since it judges and determines what in each particular circumstance is most suitable to the attainment of our end. It is an *applied science* which joins to the knowledge of principles the knowledge of the actual realities in the midst of which we are to live our lives. [3] The *will* however intervenes to command the intellect to engage in the consideration of the motives and of the reasons that will enable it to make an enlightened choice, and again to command the employment of the means thus chosen.

1019. D) The **rule** of Christian prudence is not reason alone, but reason enlightened by faith. Its noblest expression is found in the *Sermon on the Mount,* in which Our Lord completes and perfects the Old Law, by ridding it of the false interpretations of the Jewish doctors. Supernatural prudence, then, draws its light and inspiration from the Gospel maxims, which are directly opposed to those of the world. In the application of these maxims to the actions of every-day life, it draws inspiration from the examples of the Saints, who lived according to the Gospel, and from the teachings of the Church, our infallible guide. Thus, we are sure of not going astray.

Besides, the means employed by Christian prudence are not merely *right* means; they are *supernatural* means :

---

[1] *Matth.*, XVI, 26.

[2] " That prudence is at once true and perfect, which rightly counsels, judges, and commands in view of the end and aim of all human life. " (ST. THOMAS, IIa IIæ, q. 47, a. 73).

[3] " Hence the prudent man must know both the universal rational principles and the particular objects of action. " (ST. THOMAS, IIa IIæ, q. 47, a. 3).

prayer and the sacraments, which by multiplying our power for good cause us to attain far better results.

This will become still more apparent when we consider the *constituent elements* of this virtue.

1020. 2° **Its Constituent Elements.** To act prudently three conditions are particularly necessary : mature *deliberation*, a wise *choice*, and right *execution*.

A) First of all, a *mature deliberation* is required in order to discover the means most apt to the attainment of the end in view, a deliberation which must be in keeping with the import of the decision to be taken. This requires *personal* reflection and wise *consultation*.

1021. **a**) We must consider the past, the present, and the future.

1) The *remembrance of the past* will prove to be of great advantage : human nature remains essentially the same throughout the ages. We must therefore consult history to see how others have solved the problems that now confront us. The experiments whereby they attempted a solution will throw light upon our inexperience and will save us many a blunder. By observing what succeeded and what failed, we shall know better the dangers to be avoided and the means to be taken. We must likewise probe into our *personal experience*. From our early youth we have encountered at one time or another similar difficulties. We must examine what brought them to a happy issue and what proved a cause of failure and then determine resolutely not to expose ourselves to the same dangers and not to fall before the same temptations.

2) We must furthermore take account of the present, of the different conditions in which we live. Times differ and so do men. Youthful tastes are not those of maturer years. We must therefore know how to interpret *intelligently* past experiences in applying them to present issues.

3) Lastly, it is no less the part of prudence to look into the *future*. Before taking a decision, it is useful to foresee as far as can be done the consequences of our acts both to ourselves and to others. By recalling the past and foreseeing the future we can best plan our present course of action.

We may illustrate all that has been said by applying it to a particular virtue, chastity. History will tell us what the Saints did in order to remain pure in the midst of the world's dangers ; our own experience will recall our past temptations, the means used to resist them and our success or failure. From this we can conclude with a high degree of probability what will be the future result of such or such proceeding, of this or that reading, of such or such association.

1022. **b**) Reflection does not suffice; we must know how to *take counsel* with wise and competent men. A word, the remark of a friend, of a relative, even of an inferior, at times opens our eyes and reveals to us a side of things we had forgotten or overlooked.   Two heads are better than one, and enlightenment results from discussion.   This is especially true of consultation with our spiritual director; for knowing us and being a disinterested party, he sees better than we do what is good for our soul's welfare.   We should, then, seek with *docility* and care the advice of some judicious and experienced person.   This will in no way hinder us from exercising our own *powers of discernment*, by which we are to judge what is well-founded, both in the advice given and in our personal observations.

We must not forget to have recourse to the best of counsellors, the Father of Lights.   The confident invocation of the Holy Spirit will often prove more profitable to us than repeated deliberations.

1023.   B) Once we have deliberated, we must judge wisely, that is to say, we must *determine* which among the suggested means are really the most effectual.   In order to succeed in this: **a)** we must carefully rid ourselves of prejudice, passion and impressions, which would bias the judgment, and we must resolutely set our face towards eternity, so as to form an estimate of all things from the point of view of faith.   **b)** We must not rest content with a superficial examination of the reasons which incline us to this or that course, but we must probe into them carefully weighing the reasons for and against.   **c)** Lastly, we must decide *resolutely*, without allowing ourselves to be drawn hither or thither by excessive hesitation.   Once we have deliberated according to the relative importance of the question at hand, and have taken the course that seems best, Almighty God will not reproach us for the line of conduct adopted, since we did all in our power to know His holy will.   We can then count on His grace to carry out our resolutions.

1024.   C) We must not *delay* the execution of the plan we have adopted.   This makes foresight, discretion and caution necessary.

a) It requires *foresight*.   To foresee means to count in advance the effort necessary to attain our aims, the obstacles to be encountered and the means of overcoming them, in order to measure our efforts by the end in view.

b) It requires *discretion*.   We must open our eyes and view persons and things from every angle in order to derive therefrom the greatest possible advantage.   We must consider all the circumstances in order to adapt ourselves to them.   We must study events in order to profit by them if they be favorable, to prevent their consequences if they be adverse.

c) It requires *caution: " See, therefore, how you walk circum-spectly."*[1] Even when we have tried to foresee all, things do not always happen as we foresaw them, for ours is a limited wisdom and liable to err. Therefore, we must do in our moral life as we do in business, store up reserves and surround ourselves with safeguards. Our spiritual foes renew the offensive, as we have already explained in no. 900. Then we need to have recourse to our reserve force, to prayer, to the sacraments, to the advice of a spiritual director. Thus, we shall not be the victims of unforeseen circumstances, we shall not lose heart, and, with the help of God's grace, we shall bring to a successful issue the plans we had wisely laid.

1025. 3° The **different species** of prudence. Prudence varies in accordance with the diversity of the objects upon which it is exercised. It is *individual* when it regulates personal conduct ; this is the prudence of which we have spoken. It is *social* when its object is the welfare of society ; and since we distinguish three different kinds of societies, the family, the state, and the army, we distinguish likewise three kinds of prudence : *domestic* prudence, which regulates the relations of man and wife and of parents and children ; *civic* prudence, which pursues the common weal and good government ; *military* prudence, which is concerned with the direction of armies. Here we shall not go into details. The general principles we have explained suffice for our purpose. It is for Christian parents, for statesmen and military leaders, to look more deeply into the application of these principles to their respective situations.

II. *Necessity of Prudence*

Prudence is no less necessary for the control of our own *personal* conduct than it is for that *of others.*

1026. 1° For our own **personal conduct.** It is prudence that enables us *to avoid sin* and to practice *virtue.* **A)** In order to avoid sin, we repeat, we must know its *causes* and *occasions*, seek the *remedies* and apply the treatment. This is what prudence effects, as we can gather from the study of its constituent elements. From the consideration of past experience and the actual condition of the soul, prudence sees what is or will prove to be in the future a cause or an occasion of sin. And so, it suggests the best means to remove or moderate these causes, and the tactics that will best help us to overcome temptations and even to profit by them. Without such prudence how many sins would be committed! How many are actually committed because of the lack of prudence!

1027. B) Prudence is likewise necessary in order *to practice virtue* and to facilitate our union with God. The virtues are rightly compared to a chariot that conducts us to God and prudence to the driver who chooses the way.

[1] *Ephes.*, V, 15.

It is, so to speak, the soul's eye, which sees the road and the obstacles to be avoided.

1) Prudence is necessary for the exercise of all the virtues : of the *moral* virtues, which must keep to the golden mean and avoid extremes; of the theological virtues, which must be practiced in season and by such means as are in keeping with the various circumstances of our life. Thus, it is the part of prudence to scan the *dangers* that imperil faith and discover the means to remove them; to seek how faith can be strengthened and made more practical; to see how *trust in God* and *fear* of His judgments must go hand in hand, how both presumption and despair must be avoided, how all our actions can be animated by charity without hindering the discharge of our duties of state. What prudence is required in the practice of fraternal charity!

2) Prudence is even more necessary for the practice of certain *seemingly contradictory* virtues : justice and goodness, meekness and fortitude, a holy austerity of life and the right care of health, devotedness to our neighbor and chastity, the practice of an interior life and compliance with social duties.

1028. 2° When it is question of **works of zeal** in the ministry prudence is likewise necessary.

a) In the *pulpit*, prudence suggests what must be said and what must be left unsaid; it suggests the manner in which the thought must be expressed in order not to antagonize the hearers, in order to adapt the Word of God to their intelligence, to persuade, move and convert them. It is still more needful, perhaps, in teaching catechism, for it is question then of forming the minds and hearts of children, of making an impression for life on their souls.

b) In the *confessional* it is prudence that makes the confessor a keen and upright judge in discerning guilt, in putting clear and precise questions to penitents, according to their respective age, condition and circumstances. Prudence makes the confessor a *teacher* who knows how to instruct without giving scandal, when to leave souls in good faith and when to enlighten them. Prudence again makes of him a *physician* who can tactfully probe into the causes of the soul's ailments and prescribe the needed remedies. And it is prudence that invests him with the character of a *father*, so devoted as to inspire confidence, yet so reserved as to secure reverence.

c) Much tact is also needed to reconcile the wishes of parishioners with divine and liturgical ordinances in what relates to Baptisms, First Communions, Marriages, Last Rites, Funerals, etc., just as great discretion is demanded upon the occasion of sick-calls and other professional visits.

d) Great prudence is likewise required in the *administration of tem poralities*, with reference to stole fees, church dues and church funds, so as not to give offence or scandal to the faithful, or to compromise the reputation for perfect detachment which a priest must enjoy.

III. *Means of Progressing in this Virtue*

1029. One *means* is *general* and applicable to all the virtues, moral or theological : prayer, through which we draw unto ourselves Jesus Christ and His virtues. We mention this once and for all. We shall speak only of the means that are proper to each particular virtue.

1030. 1° **A general means,** one that governs all the others and which applies to all souls, is that of *referring all our judgments* and all our decisions to the *ultimate, supernatural end.* This is the advice offered by St. Ignatius at the outset of the *Spiritual Exercises* in his fundamental meditation.

a) We must note however that this principle will not be understood in the same manner by all. Beginners considering man's final end will emphasize *salvation;* perfect souls, *God's glory.* The latter mode of understanding this general principle is in itself the better way, but not all will be able thus to understand and relish it.

b) To give this principle a concrete form, it may be embodied in some maxim or other that presents it vividly to our minds, for instance: " *What does this matter for eternity?—Whatever is not eternal is of no account.—What does it profit a man, if he gain the whole world and suffer the loss of his soul?* "
In *practice*, the way to lay in our souls the foundation of Christian prudence, is to realize the full meaning of these maxims, to reflect upon them over and over again until we become familiar with them and habitually live by them.

1031. 2° Provided with this principle, **beginners** strive to *rid themselves of the faults* opposed to Christian prudence. [1]

a) They combat vigorously the *prudence* of *the flesh,* which seeks with avidity the means of satisfying the three-fold concupiscence; this they do by mortifying their love for pleasure, by remembering that the false joys of this world are often followed by bitter regrets and are as nothing compared to eternal happiness.

b) They carefully avoid *trickery, deceit, fraud,* even in the pursuance of honorable ends, well realizing that honesty is the best policy, that the end does not justify the means, and that according to the Gospel, the simplicity of the dove must be joined to the wisdom of the serpent. This is all the more necessary, since devout lay people, priests and

---

[1] Not to return repeatedly to the same virtues, we shall indicate here the degree of each corresponding to the different stages of Christian perfection.

religious are at times reproached with these defects, though unjustly in most instances. Perfect integrity and evangelical candor are therefore to be assiduously cultivated.

1032. c) They strive to hold in check those two disturbing elements of judment, *prejudice* and *passion: prejudices* that cause us to make decisions under the influence of flimsy and preconceived notions which are liable to prove groundless or unreasonable; *passions* of pride, sensuality, over-anxiety for the goods of this world, which unbalance men and cause them to choose not the best, but what is more agreeable or useful from the point of view of earthly interests. To free themselves from these perturbing influences, they call to mind the Gospel maxim: " *Seek ye first the kingdom of God and His justice.* " [1] They therefore avoid making decisions under the pressure of strong passion, delaying a choice until calm reigns in the soul. Should action be urgent, they place themselves, at least for a moment, in the presence of God, to beg His light and to follow it faithfully.

d) In order to resist *flightiness of mind*, hastiness of judgment or listlessness, they accustom themselves *never to act without previous reflection*, without accounting to themselves for the *motives* that prompt them to act, without looking into the consequences, good or bad, of their actions; all this, from the point of view of eternity. This reflection should be measured by the importance of the decision to be made, and in things of graver moment a judicious and experienced person should be consulted. Thus, the habit of deciding nothing, of doing nothing that is not referred to God is gradually acquired.

e) Lastly, to escape the bane of *indecision*, that is, extreme hesitation in making a choice, beginners take good care to remove the causes of this spiritual malady (a complicated and confused mind, a lack of initiative, etc.) by having a clear-sighted spiritual director devise fixed rules of action, whereby they will decide promptly and firmly in ordinary cases, and in greater difficulties have recourse to the director himself.

1033. 3° **Souls advancing** in the way of perfection grow in this virtue of prudence in three different ways :

a) By the study of Our Lord's *actions* and *words* as set forth in the Gospel, in order to find in them a rule of con-

---

[1] *Matth.*, VI, 33.

duct and to attract to themselves · through prayer and imitation the dispositions of that Divine Model. 1) Thus, they will contemplate His prudence, as manifested in His *hidden* life. For thirty years He practiced those virtues, the exercise of which is so hard for us, humility, obedience, poverty, knowing full well that without such an object lesson we should never learn to practice these necessary virtues. No less an object of admiration is His prudence as exemplified in His *public life*. He withstands Satan, so as to baffle his designs and confound him with replies that admit of no retort. He unfolds His teaching gradually according to circumstances, disclosing only by degrees His dignity as Messias and as Son of God. He makes use of familiar comparisons the better to make His thought understood; He employs parables to veil or reveal the same, as the occasion demands. He skilfully unmasks His adversaries and meets their cunning with disconcerting questions. He trains His Apostles step by step, suffering their defects and adapting His teachings to what they can actually bear : " *But you cannot bear them now.* " [1] He knows, withal, how to tell them unpleasant, but plain truths, as when He announces to them His Passion, in order to prepare them for the scandal of the Cross. In the very midst of that painful ordeal, He answers judges and underlings alike with the same unruffled calm, and He knows when to remain silent. In a word, He knows in all things, how to harmonize the highest form of prudence with firmness and devotedness to duty.

2) As regards His teachings, these are summed up in the following words : " *Seek ye therefore first the kingdom of God and His justice...* " [2] " *Be ye therefore wise as serpents and simple as doves...* " [3] " *Watch and pray.* " [4]

The chief means of growing in this virtue is the prayerful consideration of these examples and the ardent petition to Our Savior to make us share in His prudence.

1034. b) The constituent elements of this virtue must then be fostered, namely, common-sense, a habit of reflection, readiness to consult others, determination, foresight and caution.

1035. c) Lastly, efforts must be made to adorn prudence with those qualities of which St. James speaks. After distinguishing true from false wisdom he adds : " But

---

[1] *John*, XVI, 12. — [2] *Matth.*, VI, 33. — [3] *Matth.*, X, 16. — [4] *Mark*, XIII, 33.

the wisdom that is from above, first indeed is *chaste*, then *peaceable, modest, easy to be persuaded*, consenting to the good, *full of mercy* and good fruits, *without judging, without dissimulation.*" [1]

Chaste : on its guard to keep that purity of body and soul that unites us to God, and, which therefore unites us to the Eternal Wisdom Itself.

Peaceable : maintaining the soul's peace, the calm, the sense of proportion, the poise that enables one to make a judicious choice.

Modest : meek towards others, and by that very fact, *easy to be persuaded*, open to conviction, amenable to reason, thus precluding exasperation, which terminates in strife.

Full of mercy and good fruits : abounding in mercy towards the unfortunate, eager to do them good, since one of the characteristics of Christian wisdom is to lay up treasures in heaven.

Without judging, *without dissimulation :* that is, without partiality, duplicity or hypocrisy, which trouble the soul and the faculty of judgment.

1036. 4° In what concerns the exercise of this virtue by the *perfect*, suffice it to say that they practice it to a high degree, under the action of the gift of Counsel, as we shall explain when treating of the *unitive way*.

ART. II. THE VIRTUE OF JUSTICE [2]

After briefly recalling the theological doctrine on *justice*, we shall treat of the virtues of *religion* and *obedience*, which form parts of this virtue.

§ I. Justice Properly so Called

We shall explain : 1° its *nature*, and 2° the principal rules to be followed in its *exercise*.

I. *Nature of Justice*

1037. 1° **Definition.** The word *justice* often stands in Holy Writ for the sum-total of Christian virtues. Thus, Our Lord proclaims blessed those *who hunger and thirst after justice*, [3] that is, after holiness. However, in the strict sense in which we employ the term here, it designates that *moral, supernatural virtue, which inclines the will to render unto others at all times what is strictly their due.*

---

[1] *James*, III, 13-18.
[2] ST. THOM., IIa IIæ, q. 56-122; DOM. SOTO, *De justitiâ et jure;* LESSIUS, *De justitiâ;* AD. TANQUEREY, *Synopsis theol. moralis*, t. III, De virtute justitiæ; P. JANVIER, *Carême*, 1918. — [3] *Matth.*, V, 6.

This virtue resides in the will and regulates those *duties which we are strictly bound to discharge towards the neighbor.* It is distinguished from the theological virtue of charity which bids us regard others as brothers in Christ and inclines us to render them services not otherwise enjoined by strict justice.

1038. 2º **Excellence** of this virtue. Through justice, order and peace reign in the lives of individuals as well as in society at large.   In that it respects each one's rights, it makes for honesty in the affairs of men, it restrains deceit, it protects the rights of the helpless and the lowly, it checks the rapacity and injustice of the powerful, and thus it establishes social order. [1]   Without justice we should have anarchy, warfare between rival interests, oppression of the weak by the strong, the triumph of evil.

If such is the preëminence of *natural* justice, how much more excellent must Christian justice be, which is a participation in the very justice of God.   The Holy Ghost in communicating it to us, makes it enter into the inmost recesses of the soul and renders it resolute and inaccessible to corruption, inspiring us at the same time with such regard for the rights of others, that we not only loathe injustice, properly so called, but stand in horror of the least unfairness.

1039. 3º The **principal kinds** of justice.   They are chiefly two : *social* justice, which bids us render to society what we owe to it, and *individual* justice whereby we render to individuals what is their due.

a) The first is called *legal* justice, because it is based on the exact observance of laws; it obliges us to acknowledge the great benefits which we derive from *society*, by accepting our share of the lawful burdens it imposes upon us, and by rendering to it the services it expects of us.   Since the commonweal takes precedence over individual welfare, there are instances when citizens must sacrifice part of their goods, of their freedom, and even risk their lives in defence of the country.   But *society* likewise has *duties* to discharge towards its members.   It must effect the distribution of social advantages and social burdens, not according to the moods and whims of favor, but according to the capacity of each citizen and in keeping with the rules of equity. To all, society owes the full protection and aid needed for safeguarding the essential rights and interests of every citizen.   Favoritism towards some and persecution of others are abuses opposed to *distributive justice*, which society must observe towards its subjects.

---

[1] " When I speak of justice, I speak of the sacred bond that preserves human society, the indispensable curb to license... If justice prevails, good faith is found in treaties, truth in transactions, order in government, the earth is at peace, and heaven itself sheds over us its beneficent light and radiates down to us its blessed influence. "   BOSSUET, *Sermon on Justice.*

1040. b) The second kind of justice, called individual justice, regulates the rights and duties of individuals towards one another. It respects all rights, not only the right of *ownership*, but the right to *bodily or spiritual* goods, to life, liberty, honor and *reputation*.

We cannot in this place enter into all the details which we have explained in our course of Moral Theology.[1] It will suffice for our present purpose to recall the principal rules by which we must be guided in the practice of this virtue.

II. *Principal Rules Governing the Practice of Justice*

1041. 1° **Principle.** It is evident that devout laymen, religious and priests are obliged to practice the virtue of justice more perfectly and more scrupulously than the rank and file of persons in the world. Their duty is to set the good example in matters of honesty as well as in all other virtues. To act otherwise would be to set a *stumbling-block* for the neighbor, and furnish our enemies with a pretext to denounce religion. It would constitute an *obstacle to spiritual progress*, for an All-just God cannot have for intimate friends those who glaringly violate His formal commands regarding justice.

1042. 2° **Applications** of the Principle. **A**) One must, first of all, respect the right of *ownership* in what relates to *temporal goods.*

a) Hence, one must scrupulously shun petty thefts, which often and easily lead to graver forms of injustice. This principle should be instilled into children so that they will instinctively recoil with horror from the slightest infraction of justice. All the more must one avoid such thefts as are committed by dealers and manufacturers, who habitually defraud both as to the *quality* and the *quantity* of their goods, under the pretext that their competitors do likewise; who sell at too high a price, or buy at a ridiculously low one, taking advantage of the simplicity of those with whom they deal. One must keep clear of *wild speculations*, of those questionable transactions in which one's fortune is risked along with that of others with the hope of making huge profits.

b) One must carefully avoid contracting *debts*, when one is not sure of being able to pay them, and one must make it a point of honor to pay at the earliest possible moment those that have already been contracted.

c) We should treat a borrowed object with still greater care than if it were our own property, without ever forgetting to return it in due time. Much unconscious injustice is committed by those who neglect these precautions.

---

[1] *Synopsis Theologiæ Moralis*, t. III, De Virtute Justitiæ.

d) Any damage *voluntarily* caused must be repaired. If *involuntary*, one is not strictly bound to make restitution, yet those who aim at perfection will do so according to their means.

e) Should one be the recipient of *trust-funds* to be devoted to good works, one must take all the legal safeguards required, so that in case of death these funds may be applied according to the intentions of the donors. This holds especially in the case of priests who receive Mass stipends or alms. They must not only keep their accounts up to date, but must also provide a legatee or executor in the person of a priest who will attend to such Mass intentions and other obligations.

1043. **B)** Respect for the *good-name* and the *honor* of the neighbor is no less essential.

a) *Rash judgments* must be avoided. To censure others on mere appearances or for reasons more or less trivial, without knowing fully their motives, is nothing less than to arrogate to oneself divine rights, the rights of Him Who alone is the Supreme Judge of the living and the dead; it is an act of injustice against the neighbor, who is thus condemned without a hearing, without the knowledge of the unseen determining motives of his actions, and oftener than not, under the influence of prejudice or passion. Both justice and charity demand not only that we abstain from judging the actions of others, but that we interpret them in the best possible light.

b) Graver reasons bid one refrain from *slander*, which makes known to others the faults or the *secret* defects of the neighbor. These defects are real, but as long as they are not generally known, one has no right to reveal them. By speaking of them, one grieves the neighbor; and the dearer he holds his reputation, the more he is grieved. One lowers him in the estimation of his fellows, and one undermines his prestige, the good standing he needs in order to conduct his affairs and exercise his rightful influence. Thus, one may cause at times a damage that is well-nigh irreparable.

It is of no avail to argue that the person whose faults are thus made known has no right to his good name. This right remains as long as his faults are not public; and after all, one must not forget the Savior's word : " He that is without sin among you, let him first cast a stone. "[1] The Saints are extremely merciful; they seek in every possible way to safeguard the reputation of their fellow-men. We cannot do better than follow in their footsteps.

c) Thereby we shall more safely avoid indulging in *calumny*, which by false imputations charges to our neighbor faults he has never committed. This kind of injustice is all the more serious since it is often born of malice or of jealousy. The evils that follow in its wake are numberless. Such talk is, alas, all too welcome, and making the rounds from mouth to mouth, ruins the reputation and the prestige of its victims, and at times causes them considerable harm even in temporal matters.

1044. There exists, therefore, a strict *obligation of repairing slanders and calumnies*. No doubt, this is difficult, for it is painful to recant, and besides, the retractation, no matter how sincere, but covers up the injustice committed.

---

[1] *John.*, VIII, 7.

A lie, even when retracted, often leaves ineffaceable traces. This, of course, is no reason for not repairing the injustice committed; on the contrary, the greater the harm done, the more earnestly and persistently must one work at undoing it. The difficulty of such reparation ought to restrain us from whatever could, either proximately or remotely, expose us to a fall so grave.

This is the reason why those who tend to perfection cultivate not only the virtue of justice, but also that of charity, which by causing us to see God in our neighbor, makes us avoid whatever may sadden him. We shall return to this later on.

§ II. The Virtue of Religion [1]

1045. This virtue is related to *justice*, because it makes us render to God the worship that is *due* Him; but, since we are unable to offer to God the *infinite* homage to which He is entitled, our religion does not comply with all the requisite conditions of the virtue of justice, and thus it does not, properly speaking, constitute an act of this virtue, though it is closely related to it. We shall explain · 1° the *nature*, 2° the *necessity* and 3° the *practice* of religion.

I. *Nature of the Virtue of Religion*

1046. Religion is *a moral, supernatural virtue that inclines the will to render to God the worship due Him by reason of His infinite excellence and of His sovereign dominion over us.*

a) This is a special virtue, distinct from the three theological virtues, which have God Himself for their immediate object; the object proper to the virtue of religion is the *worship* of God, whether interior or exterior. However, it presupposes the virtue of *faith*, which enlightens us as to God's rights. When religion has attained its perfection, it is *animated* by charity and becomes but the expression and the manifestation of the three theological virtues.

b) Its *formal object* or motive is the acknowledgment of the infinite excellence of God, the first beginning and last end, the perfect Being, on Whom all things depend and towards Whom all things must gravitate.

---

[1] ST. THOMAS, IIa IIæ, q. 84; SUAREZ, *De virtute et statu religionis*, t. I, l. II; BOUQUILLON, *De virtute religionis;* J. J. OLIER, *Introd. à la vie et aux vertus*, ch. I; MGR D'HULST, Carême 1893, Conf. I; CH. DE SMEDT, *op. cit.*, p. 35-104; RIBET, *Les vertus*, ch. XXI.

c) The *acts* to which religion inclines us are *interior* and *exterior*.

1047. By the *interior* acts we subject to God our soul, with its faculties, chiefly the intellect and the will. 1) The first and the most important of these acts is that of *adoration*, in which we *abase* our whole being before Him Who is the fulness of being and the source of all the good that is found in creatures. It is accompanied or followed by the reverent admiration experienced at the sight of His infinite perfections. 2) Since He is the author of all the good we possess, we offer Him our *gratitude*. 3) Remembering that we are sinners, we enter into sentiments of *penitence*, to atone for the offences committed against His infinite majesty. 4) Because we stand in continual need of His help to do good and attain our end, we address to Him our *prayers* or requests, thus acknowledging Him as the source of all good.

1048. These interior sentiments are manifested by *exterior* acts, which have all the more worth as the interior acts they express are more perfect. 1) The *foremost* among these acts is, without question, that of *sacrifice*, which is an exterior and *social act, whereby the priest offers God, in the name of the Church, an immolated victim in order to acknowledge His supreme dominion, to repair the offence offered to His majesty, and to enter into communion with Him.* In the New Law there is but one sacrifice, that of the Mass, which, renewing the sacrifice of Calvary, offers to God an infinite homage and obtains for men all the graces they need. We have already pointed out, in nos. 271-276, the effects of the Mass and the requisite dispositions to profit by it. 2) To this principal act are added the *public* prayers offered in the name of the Church by her representatives : the Divine Office, Benediction of the Blessed Sacrament, *private* vocal prayers; oaths and vows prudently taken in God's honor and accompanied by all the conditions explained in the treatises of Moral Theology, supernatural exterior acts, done for the glory of God, which, according to the expression of St. Peter, are " *spiritual sacrifices, acceptable to God.* " [1]

We can conclude from this that religion is the most excellent among the moral virtues; for, by causing us to offer up divine worship, it brings us closer to God than do the other moral virtues.

---

[1] *I. Peter*, II, 5.

II. *Necessity of the Virtue of Religion*

To proceed methodically we shall show : 1° that *all crea-tures* must give glory to God; 2° that *for man*, this is a special duty ; 3° that it is so, above all, for the *priest*.

1049. 1° *All creatures must glorify God.* If every work must reflect credit on the doer, far higher must be the way in which the creature must proclaim the glory of its Maker! Man does not create things; he can but fashion them. This over, he has done with them. Now, God has not only formed his creatures, but He has drawn them *out of noth-ing;* He has not merely left the mark of His genius upon them, but also the reflection of His own perfections. More-over, He *preserves* them, lending them His *concurrence* and His *grace*, so that they are utterly dependent upon Him. They must, therefore, more than the works of man's crea-tion, declare the greatness of their Author. Inanimate creatures do this after their own fashion; by revealing their beauty and harmony, they invite us to glorify God : " The heavens shew forth the glory of God. [1] He made us, and not we ourselves." [2] This homage, however honors God but very imperfectly, since it is not free.

1050. 2° It is to man, then, that the duty falls of *consciously* giving glory to God, of lending his heart and his voice to inanimate creation to render Him a free and ratio-nal homage. To man, therefore, the king of creation, it belongs to contemplate these wonders, to refer them to God, and thus to become creation's own *high-priest.* Man must praise God, above all, in his own name; for endowed with a higher perfection than irrational beings, created to the image and likeness of God, sharing in His life, man's life should be one of perpetual admiration, perpetual praise, worship, thanksgiving, and love towards His Creator and Sanctifier. This St. Paul declares to us : " For of Him and by Him, and in Him, are all things : to Him be glory forever! [3] For whether we live, we live unto the Lord : or whether we die, we die unto the Lord." [4] Reminding his disciples that our body as well as our sôul is the temple of the Holy Ghost, he adds : " *Glorify and bear God in your body.*" [5]

1051. 3° This duty is particularly laid *upon priests.* Unfortunately the majority of men, absorbed in business or

[1] *Ps.* XVIII, 2. — [2] *Ps.* XCIX. 3. — [3] *Rom.*, XI, 36.
[4] *Id.* XIV, 8. — [5] *I. Cor.*, VII, 20.

pleasure, devote but little time to the worship of God. It was necessary, therefore, that from among them some special representatives acceptable to God be chosen, that they might, not only in their own name, but in the name of society, render God the religious duties to which He has a right. This is the rôle of the *priest*. He is chosen by God from among his fellows to be a mediator between earth and heaven, charged with glorifying God, with offering Him the homages of all creatures and with drawing down upon the earth God's graces and blessings. This is his duty of state, his profession, a real duty of justice, as St. Paul explains : [1] *" For every high priest taken from among men is ordained for men in the things that appertain to God, that he may offer up gifts and sacrifices for sins. "* For this reason, the Church has confided to him two great means of exercising the virtue of religion, the Divine Office and Holy Mass. This twofold duty he must discharge with great fervor, for by glorifying God, he at the same time renders this Divine Majesty propitious to our supplications. In this way, the priest procures his own personal sanctification and that of the souls entrusted to his care (nos. 393-401). His prayers are all the more effective, since it is the Church, since it is Jesus Who prays with him and in him, and the prayer of Christ is always heard : *" He was heard for his reverence. "* [2]

III. *The Practice of the Virtue of Religion*

1052. For the right practice of this virtue, we must cultivate true *devotion,* that is to say, *an habitual attitude of the will, wich causes us to lend ourselves readily and generously to whatever appertains to the service of God.* This disposition is in reality but a manifestation of love for God, and it is in this way that religion is related to charity.

1053. 1º **Beginners** practice this virtue : **a)** by the observance of the laws of God and of the Church regarding prayer, the sanctification of the Lord's Day and holydays of obligation ; **b)** by avoiding dissipation, interior or exterior, which is a source of many distractions during prayer. This is effected by being on guard against the pressing host of worldly amusements and empty day-dreams ; **c)** by inward recollection before prayer in order to make it with greater attention, and by practicing the holy exercise of the presence of God (n. 446).

---

[1] *Hebr.*, V, 1. — [2] *Hebr.*, V, 7.

1054. 2° Those **advancing** in the way of perfection strive to enter into *the spirit of religion* in union with Jesus, the supreme Worshipper of the Father, Who, in His life, as well as in His death, glorified God in an infinite manner (n. 151).

a) This spirit of religion comprises two main dispositions, *reverence* and *love*. The *former* is a profound sentiment of respect mingled with awe whereby we acknowledge God as our Creator and Sovereign Master and rejoice in proclaiming our utter dependence upon Him. The *latter* is directed towards God, to the most lovable and loving Father, Who has deigned to adopt us as His children and forever surrounds us with His paternal tenderness. From these two sentiments all the others proceed; namely, admiration gratitude, praise.

1055. b) It is from the *Sacred Heart of Jesus* that we seek to draw these sentiments of religion. This Divine Mediator lived only to glorify His Father : " *I have glorified thee on the earth.* " [1]   He died to carry out His Father's will, proclaiming by His death that nothing is worthy of life and being before the face of God. After His death He continues to glorify His Father, not only in the Eucharist where He unceasingly adores the Holy Trinity, but also in our hearts where, through His Divine Spirit, He produces religious dispositions like unto His own. He lives in the soul of every Christian, but especially in the soul of every priest, and through His priests He procures glory to Him, to Whom alone is due adoration and reverence. Through ardent desire, then, we must draw Him unto us and give ourselves to Him, that He may carry out the practice of the virtue of religion in us, with us, and through us.

" He comes to us then, " says Father Olier [2] " and abides upon the earth as a sacrifice of praise in the hands of His priests, that He may impart to us His spirit of victim, have us join in the praise He offers, and make us inwardly share in His sentiments of worship. He diffuses Himself within us, He infuses Himself into us, He envelopes our soul and replenishes it with the intimate dispositions of His spirit of religion, so that His soul and ours form but one, animated by the same spirit of reverence, of love, of praise, of interior and exterior sacrifice of all things unto the glory of His Father. "

1056. c) We must not forget, however, that Jesus requires *our co-operation*. Since He comes in order to make us share with Him in His condition and in His sentiments of victim, we must needs live with Him and in Him in the

---

[1] *St. John*, XVII, 4. — [2] *Introd. à la vie et aux vertus*, ch. I.

spirit of sacrifice, crucifying the ill-regulated tendencies of disordered nature, and yielding a ready obedience to the inspirations of grace. Then will all our actions be pleasing to God, then will they be so many sacrificial offerings, so many acts of religion, praising and glorifying God, our Creator and Father. We thereby proclaim the supremacy of God and the nothingness of the creature, since we sacrifice every part of our being, offer every one of our actions to the honor and glory of our Sovereign Master.

d) This we do more particularly in those acts of religion properly so called, like assistance at Holy Mass, the recitation of liturgical prayers or other prayers, as explained in numbers 274, 284, 523.

N. B.—*Perfect souls* practice this virtue under the influence of the *gift of piety*, of which we shall treat further on.

§ III. The Virtue of Obedience [1]

This virtue is allied to justice, since obedience is a homage, an act of submission due to Superiors; but it differs from justice inasmuch as it implies an inequality between superiors and subjects. We shall explain : 1º the *nature* and *foundation* of obedience; 2º its *degrees;* 3º its *qualities;* 4º its *excellence.*

I. *Nature and Foundation of Obedience*

1057. 1º **Definition.** Obedience is a *supernatural, moral virtue which inclines us to submit our will to that of our lawful superiors, in so far as they are the representatives of God.* These last words are the ones that need to be explained first, since they are the foundation of Christian obedience.

1058. 2º **The foundation of this virtue.** Obedience rests upon God's sovereign domain and upon the absolute submission creatures owe Him.

A) First of all, it is evident that we must obey God (n. 481).

1) We must be entirely dependent upon the holy will of God since we were created by Him : " All things serve Thee. " [2] As rational creatures, we are all the more obliged to this submission because we have

---

[1] St. John Climacus, *The Ladder of Paradise*, IV ; St. Thomas. IIa IIæ, q. 104-105 ; St. Francis of Sales, *Devout Life*, P. III, C. XI ; *Spiritual Conferences*, X-XI ; Rodriguez, *Christian Perfection*, P. III, Treat. V ; Gay, *Christian Life and Virtues*, Vol. II, Treat. XI.
[2] *Ps.* CXVIII, 91.

received more from Him; we have received in particular the gift of a free will, which we can best acknowledge by freely submitting it to the will of our Maker. 2) Being *children of God*, we must obey Our Heavenly Father as Jesus Himself did, Who having come into the world through obedience, through obedience went out from it: "He was made obedient unto death."[1] 3) *Redeemed* from the bondage of sin, we no longer belong to ourselves, but to Jesus Christ, Who gave His blood to make us His own : "And you are not your own, for you are bought with a great price."[2] We must, therefore, obey His laws.

1059. **B)** For the same reason we must yield obedience to **God's lawful representatives.** This point must be thoroughly understood. **a)** Because man is not self-sufficient for his physical, intellectual, and moral well-being, God willed that he live in society. Society, however, cannot endure without an *authority* which coördinates the efforts of its members towards the common good. Hence, it is God's will that in society there should be superiors commissioned to command, and subjects whose duty it is to obey. In order that this obedience might be more readily practiced, God has delegated His authority to legitimate superiors : "*For there is no power but from God.*"[3] This is so true that to render obedience to lawful superiors is to render obedience to God, and to disobey them is to provoke condemnation : "*Therefore he that resisteth the power, resisteth the ordinance of God. And they that resist, purchase to themselves damnation.*"[4] The duty of Superiors lies in exercising their authority. solely in the capacity of God's representatives in order to procure glory to God and to promote the general welfare of the community. Should they fail in this, they are responsible before God and their own superiors for such abuse of their authority. The duty of subjects is to obey God's representatives, to obey them as they obey God Himself: "*He that heareth you, heareth me; and he that despiseth you, despiseth me.*"[5] The reason for this is evident. Without such submission, there would be but chaos and disorder in each of the different parts of society to the detriment of all.

1060. **b)** But, *who are the lawful superiors?* The answer is, those who are placed by God at the head of the different kinds of societies.

1) In the *natural* order three different sorts of society may be discerned : *domestic* society or *the family*, at the head of which are parents, and especially the father; *civil* society, ruled by those who are the lawful holders of authority according to the different systems of

---

[1] *Phil.*, II, 8. — [2] *I Cor.*, VI, 20. — [3] *Rom.*, XIII, I.
[4] *Rom.*, XIII, 2. — [5] *Luke*, X, 16.

government accepted in the different nations of the world ; *professional* society, where we find employers and employees, whose respective rights and duties are determined by special, particular contracts. [1]

2) In the *supernatural* order, the hierarchical superiors are : the *Sovereign Pontiff*, whose authority is both supreme and immediate over the whole Church; *Bishops*, who have jurisdiction over their respective dioceses, and, under their authority, *pastors* and *curates*, each within the limits determined by the Code of Canon Law. Moreover, there are in the Church particular communities with constitutions and rules approved by the Sovereign Pontiff or by the Bishops, and having superiors appointed in accordance with their Constitutions or rules. Here, again, we find legitimate authority. Therefore, whoever joins a community binds himself to keep the rules and obey the Superiors who command within the limits defined by the rule.

1061. C) There are, then, **limits** set to the exercise of authority.

1) It is evident that it is neither obligatory nor permissible to obey a superior who would give a command manifestly opposed to divine or ecclesiastical laws. In this case we should have to repeat the words of St. Peter : [2] " *We ought to obey God, rather than men,* " words that proclaim and vindicate Christian liberty against all tyranny. [3] The same would hold true, if what is commanded is clearly beyond our powers, for *no one is held to do the impossible.* In case of *doubt*, however, since we are prone to illusions, we must act on the principle : in doubt *the presumption is in favor of the superior.*

2) If a superior should in commanding go beyond the limits of his authority, for instance, if a parent should oppose the duly considered vocation of his child, he would be exceeding his rights and the child would not be bound to obey. A similar case would be that of the Superior of a community who would give commands over and above

---

[1] See the Encyclical Letter of Pope LEO XIII, *Rerum novarum*, (Engl. transl. in The Great Encyclicals of LEO XIII, p. 209; AD. TANQUEREY, *De justitia*, wherein the Encyclical is commented upon).

[2] *Act.*, V, 29.

[3] This is the doctrine of ST. FRANCIS DE SALES : "Many have been greatly mistaken as to this condition of obedience, believing that it consisted in doing at random whatever should be commanded, even were it contrary to the Commandments of God and of Holy Church. In this they have been greatly mistaken, imagining a folly to lurk in this quality of blindness which is not there at all. In all that relates to the Commandments of God, just as Superiors have no power whatever to give any contrary command, so in such a case inferiors have no obligation to obey—indeed, if they did so they would sin. " Cf. *Spiritual Conferences of* ST. FRANCIS DE SALES, Conf. XI, p. 179. (Translation by Canon Mackey).

what the rules and constitutions permit, for these determine the limits of the authority of Superiors.

II. *The Degrees of Obedience*

1062. 1º **Beginners** apply themselves, first of all, to observe faithfully the Commandments of God and of the Church, and to conform to the orders of lawful superiors with diligence, punctuality, and in a supernatural spirit.

1063. 2º More **advanced** souls : **a)** carefully ponder the examples given by Jesus from the very first moment of His existence, when He pledged Himself to fulfil in all things the will of His Father, until the last instant of His life when He died a victim of obedience. They pray Him to come and live within them in that same spirit of obedience, and they strive to unite themselves to Him in submitting to their superiors, just as He was subject to Mary and to Joseph : "*He was subject to them.*" [1]

b) They submit their *wills* even in things that entail hardship and go against their preferences. They do so whole-heartedly, without complaint, even with joy at being able to imitate more perfectly their Divine Model. They avoid especially taking any steps that would lead the superior to conform to their desires, for, as St. Bernard remarks : "You need not flatter yourself with the idea that you are truly obedient, if, when you desire something, you strive either openly or covertly to have your spiritual father command it to you. In this you only deceive yourself, for it is not you that obey the superior, but the superior that obeys you." [2]

1064. 3º **Perfect** souls go even further. They submit their *judgment* to that of their superior, without even considering the reasons for his command.

St. Ignatius gives an excellent explanation of this degree of obedience. [3] "If, however, one wishes to make the perfect sacrifice of self, one must, after having submitted one's will to God, consecrate to Him one's *understanding* in such a way as not only to will what the superior wills, but to be of the same mind also, and to submit one's judgment to that of the superior to the extent that an already obedient will can sway the mind." Our judgment as well as our will can go astray in the things that touch us closely, and therefore, just as we conform our wills to that of the superior to prevent it, as it were, from losing its bearings : "so, lest our judgment go astray, we must likewise make it conform to that of the superior." The Saint adds, however, that "should another view come to our mind differing from that of the superior, and, if after having consulted the Lord in prayer, it seems to us that the same should be made known to him, we may well tell him. Still, lest our self-love and our own opinions deceive us, it is proper to take the precaution of maintaining a perfect evenness of mind both before and after disclosing our opinions, ever ready not only to under-

---

[1] *St. Luke*, II, 51. — [2] *Serm. de diversis*, XXXV, 4. — [3] Letter CXX.

take or to relinquish the purpose in question, but even to approve and acknowledge as the best course the one to be determined by the superior. " This is what is termed *blind* obedience which places us in the hands of superiors "after the manner of a *staff*... after the manner of a *corpse.*"[1] This obedience, however, if explained with the reservations of St. Ignatius and those we have noted above, is not unreasonable, since it is to God that we subordinate our will and our intellect.

III. *The Qualities of Obedience*

In order to be *perfect*, obedience must be *supernatural* in its motive, *universal* in its extent, and *entire* in its execution.

1065. 1º **Supernatural** in its motive, which means that we are to see God Himself, or Jesus Christ in the persons of our superiors, since they have no authority except from Him. Nothing can render obedience more easy, for who would refuse to obey God? This is what St. Paul recommends to servants : " Be obedient to them that are your lords according to the flesh, with fear and trembling, in the simplicity of your heart, as to Christ : *not serving to the eye, as it were pleasing men, but, as the servants of Christ doing the will of God from the heart* with a good will serving, as to the Lord, and not to men. "[2]

In the same tenor St. Ignatius wrote to his Religious of Portugal : " It is my ardent desire that you should carefully strive in all earnestness to see Our Lord Jesus Christ in your superiors, whosoever they may be, and, in their persons, reverently offer the Divine Majesty the honor due to Him... Let them not consider the person whom they obey but let them see in that person Jesus Christ, for Whose sake obedience is given. As a matter of fact, we are bound to obey a Superior not on account of his prudence, of his goodness or of any other personal qualities wherewith God may have endowed him, but because he is God's representative... Even if he should seem to lack in prudence and wisdom, this is no reason for failing in exact obedience, since in his capacity of superior, he represents a Person, Whose wisdom is infallible and Who will Himself provide for all those things in which His minister falls short, be it virtue or any other quality. "[3]

Nothing could contain greater wisdom than this principle; for, if to-day we obey our superior because his qualities please us, what shall we do to-morrow if we have another superior who seems to us to be devoid of such qualities? Besides, do we not forfeit the merit that should be ours, by subjecting ourselves to a man whom we esteem instead of submitting to God Himself? We must not, therefore, dwell upon the defects of our superiors, a thing that would render our obedience more difficult, nor yet

---

[1] St. Ignat., *Constit.*, VI, § I, rule 36.
[2] *Ephes.*, VI, 5-9. — [3] Letter CXX.

upon their personal qualities, a thing that would render it less meritorious, but we must consider God living and commanding in their persons.

1066. 2° **Universal** in its extent, in the sense that we are to comply with all the commands of a superior as long as he commands lawfully. St. Francis de Sales [1] says: "Obedience lovingly undertakes to do all that is commanded it with simplicity and without ever considering whether the command is good or bad, provided that the person who orders has authority to order, and that the command serves to unite our mind to God." He adds, however, that if a superior orders what is evidently against the law of God, it is one's duty not to submit. Such obedience, St. Thomas [2] says, would be injudicious: "Obedience in unlawful matters is injudicious."

Aside from this case, the truly obedient person does not go astray even when the superior is wrong and commands what is less good than what we ourselves would choose. Then as a matter of fact God, to Whom the submission is given and Who sees the heart, rewards this obedience by assuring success. St. Francis de Sales, [3] commenting upon the words, "*the obedient man shall speak of victory*", says: "The truly obedient man will come out the conqueror in all the difficulties into which he may be led by obedience, and with honor from all the roads he has traversed, however dangerous." In other words, a superior may err in commanding, but we make no mistake in obeying.

1067. 3° **Entire** in the execution, hence *prompt, without reservations, persevering* and even *cheerful.*

a) *Prompt;* for love, which is the prime mover of perfect obedience, makes us obey with readiness: "The obedient man loves the command, and as soon as he is aware of it, whether it be to his taste or not, embraces it, caresses it, and cherishes it tenderly." [4]

This is just what St. Bernard says: "The truly obedient man knows of no hesitation; he has a horror of procrastination; he ignores delays; he anticipates orders; his eyes are on the lookout, his ears on the alert, his tongue ready to speak the word, his hands ready to act, his feet ready to start; he is all intent on knowing the will of him who commands." [5]

b) Without *reservations;* for to make a choice, to obey in some things and disobey in others is to forfeit the merit of obedience; it is to show that we submit in what pleases us and, therefore, that our submission is not supernatural.

[1] *Spiritual Conferences*, XI, p. 179.
[2] St. Thom., IIa IIæ, q. 104, a. 3, ad 3.
[3] *Spirit. Conferences*, XI, p. 199. — [4] *Ibid.*, p. 186.
[5] *Sermo de diversis*, XLI, 7.—This should be read in its entirety.

Let us, then, remember what Our Lord says: "*One jot, or one tittle shall not pass of the law, till all be fulfilled.*" [1]

Perseverance is likewise required of us. This is one of the great merits of the virtue of obedience, "for to do a thing cheerfully which we are only commanded to do once, costs nothing; but when our superior says to us: You will do that always, and all through your life, there lies the virtue and there also the difficulty." [2]

c) *Cheerful,* "*for God loveth a cheerful giver.*" [3] In those things that entail hardship, obedience cannot be cheerful, unless it be animated by love. In fact, nothing is painful to him who loves, because he thinks not of the suffering undergone, but of the person for whose sake he suffers. Now, if we see Our Lord in the person of him who commands, how can we fail to love Him, how can we fail to offer with our whole heart the trifling sacrifice that He demands, Who died a victim of obedience for our sake! This is why we must always return to the general principle we have established, that is, to see God Himself in the person of our Superior.

IV. *The Excellence of Obedience*

1068. The excellence of obedience flows from all that we have said of this virtue. St. Thomas does not hesitate to say that, after the virtue of religion, it is the most perfect of all the moral virtues, for the reason that it unites us closer to God than any other virtue, inasmuch as obedience detaches us from our own will, which is the main obstacle to union with God. [4] Obedience is, besides, the mother and guardian of the other virtues, and transforms our ordinary actions into so many virtuous acts.

1069. 1° Obedience *unites* us to God and makes us habitually *share* in His life.

a) It subordinates our will directly to that of God and thereby all our other faculties, inasmuch as they are in turn subordinated to the will. This submission is all the more *meritorious* because it is *freely* made. Inanimate creatures obey God by an innate necessity of their nature, but man obeys by the free choice of his will. In so doing, man tenders His Sovereign Master the homage of what he holds most dear; he offers Him a pleasing sacrifice: "*Through obedience our wills are sacrificed.*" [5] Thus man enters *into communion with God*, since he has no longer any other will but God's will. He can make his own the words of Christ in His agony: "*Not my will, but thine be done.*" [6] This is a most meritorious and a most sanctifying union since it unites the best that is in us, our will, to that of God, ever good and ever holy.

---

[1] *Matth.*, V, 18. — [2] ST. FR. DE SALES, *Spiritual Conferences*, XI, p. 191.
[3] *II Cor.*, IX, 7. — [4] *Sum. Theol.*, IIª IIæ, q. 104, a. 3.
[5] ST. GREGORY, *Moral.*, l. XXV, c. 10. — [6] *Luke*, XXII, 42.

b) Since the will is the master-faculty in man, by uniting it to God, we unite to Him all the powers of our soul. Such a sacrifice is greater than the sacrifice of external goods made by the virtue of poverty, greater than the sacrifice of bodily pleasures entailed by the practice of chastity and of mortification. Obedience is, in all truth, the highest sacrifice we can make : "For obedience is better than sacrifices." [1]

c) Obedience likewise constitutes the most abiding and lasting union. Through Sacramental Communion we effect a temporary union with God, but through habitual obedience we establish in our soul a species of spiritual communion which is permanent, which causes us to abide in God as He abides in us, since we will what He wills and nothing but what He wills. This is, as a matter of fact, the most real, the most intimate, and the most effective of all unions— *unum velle unum nolle.*

1070. 2° Obedience is logically the *mother* and the *guardian* of all the virtues, as St. Augustine beautifully expresses it : "*In a rational creature, obedience is, as it were, the mother and guardian of all virtues.*" [2]

a) Obedience really becomes one with *charity*, for, as St. Thomas teaches, love effects primarily a union of wills. [3] And is not this the doctrine of St. John? After declaring that he who pretends to love God and keeps not His Commandments is a liar, the Apostle adds : "But he that keepeth His word, in him in very deed the charity of God is perfected; and by this we know that we are in Him." [4] And this is the teaching of the Divine Master Himself. He tells us that to keep His commandments is to love Him : "If you love me, keep my commandments." [5] True obedience, therefore, is in reality a genuine act of love.

1071. b) Obedience makes us practice the other virtues, inasmuch as they all fall under a precept or a counsel : "*All acts of virtue come under obedience, inasmuch as they are contained in a precept.*" [6]

Thus, obedience makes us practice penance and mortification, so frequently prescribed in the Gospels, as well as justice, religion, charity, and all the virtues embodied in the Decalogue. More, obedience likens us to the *martyrs*, who sacrificed their lives for God, as St. Ignatius[7] explains : "Through it, self-will and self-sufficiency are ever being immolated and laid as victims upon an altar, in such wise that instead of man's free-will there remains but the will of Jesus Christ Our Lord, made known to us by him who commands us. Nor is it merely the desire to live that is sacrificed by obedience, as happens in the case of martyrdom, but here all our desires are sacrificed at one and the same time." The same thought was expressed by St. Pacomius to a young monk longing for martyrdom : "It is far better to live in obedience and

¹ *I Kings,* XV, 22. — ² *De Civitate Dei,* l. XIV, c. 12.
³ *Sum. Theol.,* IIa IIæ, q. 104, a. 3. — ⁴ *I John,* II, 5. — ⁵ *John,* XIV, 15.
⁶ St. Thom., IIa IIæ, q. 104, a. 3, ad 2. — ⁷ Letter quoted above.

to die daily to self by mortifying our own desires, than to suffer martyrdom in imagination. He who mortifies himself, dies a martyr's death as far as need be; it is a far greater martyrdom to persevere in obedience all through life, than to die in a moment by a stroke of the sword." [1]

1072. **c)** Obedience offers us perfect *safety*. Left to ourselves, we would be wondering which would be the more perfect course to take, whereas obedience by determining what is our duty in every instance, points out to us the surest way of working out our sanctification. By doing what obedience prescribes, we realize to the fullest possible extent the one essential condition of perfection, that is, compliance with God's good pleasure: "*I do always the things that are pleasing to him.*" [2]

From this arises a sense of profound and abiding *peace: " There is great peace for them that love thy law, O Lord.*" [3] When we are desirous of doing only the will of God as manifested through superiors, we are not preoccupied about what is to be done nor about the means to be employed. All that we must do is to receive orders from him who holds God's place in our regard and to carry them out as best we can. Providence takes care of the rest, demanding of us, not success, but simply the effort to fulfil the orders given. Besides, we may rest assured of the final result. It is clear that if we do God's will, He will take care of doing ours, that is to say, of granting our requests and fostering our designs. Obedience, then, means peace on earth, and at the end of life's journey, it is obedience that opens for us the gates of Heaven. Lost through the disobedience of our First Parents and regained through the obedience of Jesus Christ, Heaven is reserved for those who allow themselves to be led by the human representatives of our Divine Savior. There is no Hell for the truly obedient: "*What else does God loathe or punish except self-will? Let self-will cease, and Hell shall be no more.*" [4]

1073. 3° Lastly, obedience *transforms* into virtues and merits the most commonplace occupations of life: meals, recreations, work. Whatever is done in the spirit of obedience shares in the merit of that virtue, is acceptable to God, and will be rewarded by Him. On the other hand, whatever is done in opposition to the will of superiors, no matter how praiseworthy in itself, is in reality an act of disobedience. The obedient man is therefore often likened to the traveller who goes aboard a ship that is in charge of an expert pilot. Each single day, even though he sleeps, he is steadily making for port, and, thus, without fatigue or preoccupation he reaches the desired goal, the haven of a blissful eternity.

---

[1] Quoted by St. Francis de Sales, *Spiritual Conferences*, p. 192.
[2] *John*, VIII, 29. — [3] *Ps.*, CXVIII, 165.
[4] St. Bernard, *Sermon III* for Eastertide, 3.

1074. We end with the following words addressed by God to St. Catherine of Sienna : [1] " How sweet and glorious is this virtue which in itself embodies all the others ! It has been conceived and begotten by charity. Upon it rests the foundation of divine faith... It is the very center of the soul, which no tempest can reach... Privation causes it no affliction, for obedience has taught it to desire nothing outside of Myself, Who am able, if I will it, to fulfil all its desires... O, Obedience ! thou dost accomplish the journey without fatigue, and reachest the haven of salvation without mishap ! Thou identifiest thyself with the Word, my Only-begotten Son. Thou sailest on the bark of the most hallowed Cross, ready to suffer all things rather than depart from obedience to the Word and infringe upon His teaching ! How great does thy long perseverance make thee ! So great that thou reachest from earth to heaven, since it is by thee and by thee alone that it can be laid open."

ART. III. THE VIRTUE OF FORTITUDE [2]

1075. Justice, complemented by religion and obedience, regulates our relations with others. Fortitude and temperance regulate our duties towards ourselves. We shall treat of fortitude by describing : 1º its *nature*, 2º the virtues *related* to it, 3º the *means* of practicing it.

§ I. Nature of the Virtue of Fortitude

We shall explain : 1º its definition; 2º its degrees.

I. *Definition*

1076. This virtue, called also strength of soul, strength of character, spiritual vigor, is *a supernatural, moral virtue that strengthens the soul in the pursuit of arduous moral good, without allowing it to be deterred by fear, even the fear of death.*

A) Its *object* is twofold, the repression of the feelings of *fear* which tend to paralyze our efforts towards good, and the control of the spirit of daring which, without such a check, would easily turn into temerity : " *And, therefore, the relations of fortitude to fear and to audacity consist in repressing the former and controlling the latter.*" [3]

1077. B) Its *action* is chiefly twofold : to *undertake* and to *endure* difficult things : " *Arduous tasks both to pursue and to sustain.*"

---

[1] *Dialogue.*
[2] ST. THOMAS, IIa IIæ, q. 123-140; his commentators, particularly *Cajetan* and *John of St. Thomas;* JANVIER, *Lenten Conferences* of 1920; RIBET, *Vertus,* ch. XXXVII-XLII; CH. DE SMEDT, *Notre vie surnat.*, t. II, p. 210-267.
[3] ST. THOM., IIa IIæ, q. 123, a. 3.

a) First of all, fortitude consists in *undertaking* and *carrying into execution difficult* enterprises. On the road to virtue and to perfection there lie innumerable obstacles, difficult to overcome and forever recurring. They must not only not be feared, but they must be faced with the courageous effort necessary to overcome them. This is the first act of this virtue.

This act implies : 1) *determination* to arrive quickly at the decision of doing one's duty no matter what the cost may be ; 2) *courage* and generosity in putting forth all the effort that the peculiar difficulties of the case may require ; 3) *steadfastness*, to prolong the effort to the end, in spite of the stubbornness and the repeated attacks of the enemy.

b) Furthermore, we must needs learn *to suffer* for God's sake the manifold and difficult trials which He sends us, to bear the sufferings, the illnesses, the mockeries, the calumnies of which we may be the victims.

This often proves even more wearisome than action. " *To bear is more difficult than to attack,* " [1] says St. Thomas, and for this he gives a threefold reason. First, because one who is on the defensive generally feels that his adversary is more powerful than himself, while he who takes the offensive comes on with a sense of superiority. Secondly, because the one who holds out in the face ef attack actually feels the difficulties, whereas he who takes the offensive can only foresee them. Now, an evil that is actually present inspires more fear than one we merely foresee. Thirdly, because to hold out under trials means unflinching perseverance for a notable time, for instance, in the case of a long and painful illness, or of violent and prolonged temptation ; whereas to undertake a difficult task often requires but a momentary effort.

II. *Degrees of the Virtue of Fortitude*

1078. 1° **Beginners** fight valiantly against the many fears that deter them from the fulfilment of duty :—

1) Fear of *effort* and fear of *risks*. They recall that man has even more priceless possessions than goods of fortune, health, good name and life itself. Such are the gifts of *grace* which are in themselves but the prelude of eternal bliss. They come therefore to the practical conclusion that one must unhesitatingly sacrifice the former to lay hold of the latter, which endure forever. They convince themselves of the fact that the only real evil is *sin*, and that, therefore, that evil must be avoided at all costs, even at the risk of suffering all the temporal ills that may befall them.

1079. 2) The fear of *criticism* or of ridicule, in other words, human respect, which leads them to neglect their

---

[1] *Sum. Theol.*, IIa IIæ, q. 123, a. 6, ad 1.

duty through fear of unfavorable comment, of the ridicule of which they may be the target, of the threats that may be hurled against them, of the injuries and injustices of which they may be the victims. Many a man dauntless on the battlefield cowers in the face of such sarcasm or such threats. Of what paramount importance it is to school the young in the contempt of human respect, to school them in that manliness that knows how to brave public opinion and follow convictions, without fear, without blush!

3) The fear of *displeasing friends.* This fear is at times more potent than that of incurring the vengeance of enemies. And yet, we must remember that it is better to please God than men; that those who would hinder us from doing our full duty are but false friends, and that if we were to please them we should forfeit the esteem and the friendship of Jesus Christ, Our Lord : "*If I yet pleased men, I should not be the servant of Christ.*" [1] With far greater reason must we avoid sacrificing duty to the craving for *vain popularity.* The plaudits of men die away. There is no approbation that is lasting, none that is truly worthy of us, save that of God, the infallible Judge. Let us then conclude with St. Paul that the only glory to be sought after is that which proceeds from loyalty to God and fidelity to duty : "*But he that glorieth, let him glory in the Lord. For not he who commendeth himself is approved : but he, whom God commendeth.*" [2]

1080. 2° Souls in the **illuminative way** exercise themselves in the practice of the positive side of the virtue of fortitude, by striving to imitate that strength of soul that Jesus Christ exemplified for us during His life.

1) This virtue appears in His *hidden life.* From the very first moment of His Incarnation, Our Lord offers Himself to His Father in the place of all the victims of the Old Law, by giving Himself for all mankind. He is aware that, in consequence, His life will be a protracted martyrdom, yet He freely chooses that martyrdom. That is why from His birth He eagerly seeks poverty, mortification and obedience; why He submits to persecution and exile; why during thirty years He hides Himself in the most complete obscurity, in order to merit for us the grace that would enable us to sanctify our most commonplace actions and to inspire us with a love of humility. Thus He teaches us the practice of the virtue of fortitude and courage amidst the thousand details of daily life.

2) This fortitude is likewise evident during the course of His *public* life : in the long fast which He undertakes before beginning His ministry; in His victorious struggle against Satan; in His preaching,

---

[1] *Galat.*, I, 10. — [2] *II Cor.*, X, 17-18.

where contrary to the preconceptions of the Jews, He announces the advent of a kingdom altogether spiritual, founded on humility, sacrifice, self-denial, as well as on the love of God. It is shown forth in the vigor wherewith He stigmatizes scandal and condemns the casuistry of the Doctors of the Law; in the jealous care wherewith He avoids popularity of a questionable character and eschews the royalty offered to Him; in the manner, at once sweet and forceful, with which he trains His Apostles, correcting their prejudices, their defects, and rebuking him whom he had chosen as the leader of the Twelve. It is shown again in the determination to return to Jerusalem, well knowing that He is to encounter suffering, humiliation and death. Thus He sets us the example of the calm and steady courage which we must have in all our relations with others.

3) Fortitude is manifested in His *Passion:* in the midst of that torturing agony, where, in spite of the absence of consolation and in spite of weariness of soul, He perseveres long in prayer: " *And being in agony, He prayed the longer;* " ¹ in the unruffled serenity He shows at the moment of His arrest; in the silence He maintains in the face of calumnies and the curiosity of Herod; in His dignified attitude before His judges; in the heroic patience which He exemplifies while in the midst of undeserved torments and the mockeries offered His sacred Person; in the calm resignation wherewith He commends His spirit into the hands of God, His Father, and gives up the ghost. ² He thereby teaches us *patience* amidst the severest trials.

As can be easily seen, there is here an ample field for imitation. The better to succeed in this we must beg Our Lord to deign come to dwell within us *in all the fulness of His power.* Besides, we must coöperate with Him in the actual exercise of this virtue, by practicing it, not only when some great issue demands it, but also in the thousand and one actions that make up the ordinary run of our life, remembering that the constant practice of these little virtues demands a higher degree of heroism than do brilliant deeds.

1081. 3⁰ **Perfect** souls cultivate not only the virtue, but likewise the gift of fortitude, as we shall explain in the unitive way. They maintain themselves in that generous attitude of immolating themselves for God, and of undergoing that slow, unbloody martyrdom, which consists in an ever-renewed effort to do all things for God and to suffer everything for His greater glory.

§ II. Virtues Allied to Fortitude

1082. There are four virtues connected with the virtue of fortitude. Two of them aid us in the accomplishment of things arduous: *magnanimity* and *munificence.* The other two help us to suffer in the right manner: *patience* and

---

₁ *Luke,* XXII, 43. — ² *Luke,* XXIII, 46.

constancy. St. Thomas holds these four to be *integral* and *potential* parts of the virtue of fortitude.

I. *Magnanimity*

1083. 1° Its **Nature.** Magnanimity, which is also called greatness of soul or nobility of character, is the noble and generous *disposition to undertake great things for God and for the neighbor.* It is not the same as ambition, which is essentially egotistical and goads us on to surpass others by wielding authority or receiving honors. The characteristic of magnanimity is disinterested service.

a) This virtue therefore presupposes a *noble soul*, possessed of high ideals and unselfish thoughts, a valiant spirit that does not hesitate to make its life accord with its convictions.

b) It is brought out not only by noble sentiments, but also by noble acts, and this in every sphere of action : in the army by brilliant exploits, in civil life by great reform movements, or great industrial, commercial, economic enterprises etc.; in the realm of the supernatural, by the pursuit of a high ideal of perfection, by generous efforts to conquer self and to rise ever higher, by striving to acquire solid virtue and to exercise zeal in its various forms. All this is done without fear of risking fortune, health, reputation and life itself.

1084. 2° The **contrary defect** is called *pusillanimity*, which, through an excessive fear of failure, makes one hesitate and remain inactive. Seeking to avoid blunders the pusillanimous fall into the greatest mistakes; they do nothing or almost nothing, and thus waste their lives. Evidently, it is better to risk making mistakes than to do nothing.

II. *Munificence or Magnificence*

1085. 1° Its **Nature.** Persons with a great soul and a big heart practice magnificence or munificence, *which inclines us to do great works*, and at the same time to undergo the *great expenses* that such works entail.

a) At times it is pride or ambition rather than virtue that inspires these undertakings. But when it is *the glory of God* or the *welfare of our fellow-men* which one has in view, one supernaturalizes that natural desire for grandeur, and, instead of forever saving and investing, one generously employs wealth for the furtherance of great undertakings such as works of art, public monuments, erection of churches, hospitals, schools, universities, in a word of all that promotes the common good. This virtue, then, makes one overcome the natural attachment one has for money and the thirst for further riches.

1086. **b)** This is an excellent virtue which must be urged upon the well-to-do by showing them that the best use they can make of the wealth Providence has entrusted to them is to imitate God's own liberality and His magnificence in all His works. There are Catholic institutions that languish because of lack of means. They offer an open field for the worthy employment of accumulated funds, and the best way of preparing for ourselves a glorious dwelling in Heaven. Then, there are numberless undertakings to initiate. Each new generation brings a host of new needs : churches to build, schools to found, a larger ministry to support; at times there are public calamities to relieve, at others new agencies of welfare to inaugurate for youth, for old age, etc. There is here a vast field, open to every activity and to every purse.

c) And there is no need of being rich in order to practice this virtue. St. Vincent de Paul was by no means rich, and yet, was there any other man who provided with such royal munificence for every misery of his day? Was there any who initiated such lasting and successful charitable enterprises? A noble soul always finds resources in public charity, and it seems as if Providence makes common cause with devoted service if one knows how to trust in God and to follow the dictates of prudence or the inspirations of the Holy Ghost.

1087. 2° The **contrary defects** are *miserliness* and *extravagance*.

a) *Miserliness* or stinginess paralyzes the impulses of the heart, knows not how to make adequate provision for important enterprises, and does nothing but what is cheap or small. **b)** Extravagance, on the contrary, impels one to make unnecessary expenditures, to be prodigal of money and at times to spend beyond one's means. This defect is also called *prodigality*. It is the part of prudence to hold a middle course between both extremes.

III. *Patience* [1]

1088. 1° Its **nature.** Patience is *a Christian virtue that makes us withstand with equanimity of soul, for the*

---

[1] St. Francis de Sales, *Devout Life*, Part III, C. III; Olier, *Introd.*, C. IX; Faber, *Growth in Holiness*, C. IX; D. V. Lehodey, *Le Saint Abandon*, Part III, C. III-V.

love of God, and in union with Jesus Christ, all physical and moral sufferings. We all have an ample share of suffering sufficient to make us saints, if we would only suffer courageously and from supernatural motives. Many, however, suffer complainingly, in bitterness of heart, at times even in a spirit of rebellion against Providence. Others, again, withstand suffering out of pride or ambition and thus forfeit the fruits of their endurance. The true motive that should inspire us is submission to the will of God (n. 487), and the hope of the eternal reward that will crown our patience (n. 491). Still, the most potent stimulus, is the thought of *Christ suffering* and *dying* for us. If He, innocence itself, bore so heroically so many tortures, physical and moral, in order to redeem us and sanctify us, is it not meet that we, who are guilty and who by our sins are the cause of His sufferings, should consent to suffer with Him and with His intentions, in order to coöperate with Him in the work of our purification and sanctification, and to partake in His glory by having shared in His sufferings? Noble and generous souls add to these motives the motive of zeal. They suffer to fulfil what is wanting of the sufferings of Christ and thus work for the redemption of souls (n. 149). Herein lies the secret source of that heroic patience of the Saints and of their love of the Cross.

1089. 2° The **degrees** of patience correspond to the three stages of the spiritual life.

a) At the *beginning*, suffering is accepted as coming from God; without murmur, without resentment, in hope of heavenly rewards. It is accepted in order to atone for faults and to purify the heart; in order to control ill-regulated tendencies, especially sadness and dejection. It is accepted in spite of our natural repugnance, and, if a prayer goes up that the chalice pass away, it is followed by an act of submission to the holy Will of God. [1]

1090. b) Patience, in its second degree, makes us eager to embrace suffering, in union with Jesus Christ, and in order to make us more like that Divine Model. Hence the soul is fond of following Him along the sorrowful road that He took from the Crib to the Cross; it contemplates Him, praises Him, and pours forth its love upon Him in all His sorrowful mysteries : at His entrance into this world when He " emptied Himself "; in His resignation

[1] *Matth.*, XXVI, 39.

within the lowly crib that was His cradle and wherein He suffered even more from the insensibility of men than from the cold and the elements; amidst the sufferings of His exile, the menial labors of His hidden life, the work, the fatigue, and the humiliations of His public life; but, above all, in the physical and moral tortures of His painful passion. Strengthened by the words of St. Peter, [1] *"Christ, therefore, having suffered in the flesh, be you also armed with the same thought,"* the soul takes new courage in the face of pain and sadness; side by side with Jesus, it tenderly stretches itself forth on the Cross, for love of Him: *" With Christ I am nailed to the cross."* [2] When suffering increases, a loving, compassionate glance upon the Crucified Christ brings the response from His lips: *" Blessed are they that mourn... blessed are they who suffer persecution for justice's sake."* [3] Then, the hope of sharing in His glory in the heavenly places renders more bearable the crucifixion undergone in union with Him: *" If we suffer with him, that we may be also glorified with him."* [4] Nay, the soul at times comes, like St. Paul, to the point where it rejoices in its miseries and tribulations, well knowing that to suffer with Christ means to comfort Him, that it means the completion of His passion, a more perfect love for Him here on earth, and a preparation for the further enjoyment of His love through all eternity: *" Gladly therefore will I glory in my infirmities, that the power of Christ may dwell in me..."* [5] *I exceedingly abound with joy in all our tribulation."* [6]

1091. c) This leads to the third degree of patience, the *desire* and the *love of suffering* for the sake of God Whom one wishes to glorify, and for the sake of souls, for whose sanctification one wants to labor. This is the degree proper to *perfect* souls and especially to apostolic souls, to religious, priests and devout men and women. Such was the disposition that animated Our Blessed Lord when He offered Himself as victim at His entrance into this world, and which He expressed in proclaiming His desire to suffer the baptism of His Passion: *" And I have a baptism wherewith I am to be baptized. And how am I straitened until it be accomplished."* [7]

Out of love for Him and in order to become more like unto Him, perfect souls enter into the same sentiments: " For ", in the words of St. Ignatius, " just as men of the world who are attached to the things of earth, love and seek with great eagerness honors, good name, and

---

[1] *I Peter*, IV, 1. — [2] *Galat.*, II, 19. — [3] *Matt.*, V, 5, 10-12. — [4] *Rom.*, VIII, 17.
[5] *II Cor.*, XII, 9. — [6] *II Cor.*, VII, 4. — [7] *Luke* XII, 50.

display among men... so those who march ahead in the ways of the spirit and who earnestly follow Jesus Christ love and ardently desire whatever is opposed to the spirit of the world... so that were it possible with no offence to God and scandal to the neighbor, they would want to suffer insults, slanders, and injuries, be reckoned as fools, though having given no occasion therefor, such is their intense desire to be likened in some way to Our Lord Jesus Christ... so that with the help of His grace we strive to imitate Him as far as we can, and to follow Him in all things, since He is the true way which leads men to life."[1]   Evidently, it is only love for God and for the Crucified Christ that can inspire a like love for the Cross and humiliations.

1092.   Must a soul go further, and offer itself to God as a victim and formally ask God for extraordinary sufferings, in order either to offer reparation to God, or to obtain some signal favor?   No doubt some of the Saints have done so and in our day there are still generous souls who are moved to do likewise.   However, generally speaking, such requests cannot be prudently counselled.   They may easily lead to illusions and are often the outcome of some ill-considered impulse of generosity which has its origin in presumption. "Such requests are made," says Father de Smedt, " in moments of emotional fervor, and once this is gone... one realizes one's weakness to accomplish the heroic acts of submission and resignation so energetically made in the imagination.   Therefrom issue violent temptations to discouragement and even to complaints against God's Providence...   It is a source of great annoyance and perplexity to the spiritual directors of such souls."[2]   Hence, we must not take it upon ourselves to ask for extraordinary sufferings or trials.   If one feels oneself drawn thereto, one must take counsel with a judicious director of souls and do nothing without his approval.

IV. *Constancy*

1093.   Constancy in effort *consists in struggling and suffering to the end, without yielding to weariness, discouragement, or indolence.*

1º Experience shows that after reiterated efforts one *wearies* of well-doing, one finds it irksome to be forever obliged to strain the will.   St. Thomas remarks : " *A special difficulty is attached to long persistence in a difficult task.* "[3]

---

[1] *Constitut. Soc. Jesu*, Exam. generale, cap. IV, n. 44.
[2] *Notre vie surnaturelle*, t. II, p. 260.—Father Capelle, who has made a special study of this particular matter *(Les Ames Généreuses*, 1920, 3e P., Ch. IV-VII) sums up his teaching in three propositions : 1) It is Our Lord Himself who selects such victims.   2) He warns them in advance of what they will have to undergo. 3) He asks their free consent.
[3] *Sum. Theol.*, IIa IIæ, q. 137, a. 1.

Yet, no virtue is solid that has not stood the test of time, that has not been strengthened by deeply rooted habits.

A sense of weariness often results in *discouragement* and *indolence.* The annoyance experienced at repeating efforts relaxes the energy of the will and produces a species of moral depression or discouragement; at this juncture, the love of pleasure and a sense of regret at being deprived of it gain the upper hand and one lets oneself be carried by the current of evil tendencies.

1094. 2° In order to react against this weakness, we must remember: 1) that perseverance is a gift of God (n. 127) obtained by prayer. Hence, we must ask insistently for it in union with Him Who persevered unto death, and through the intercession of Her Whom we rightly call *Virgin most faithful.*

2) We must, after that, renew our convictions as regards the shortness of life and the everlastingness of the reward that crowns our efforts. Having an eternal rest awaiting us we can well afford a measure of annoyance here on earth. If in spite of these considerations we still remain weak and hesitant, then we must beg insistently for that grace of perseverance the need of which we feel so keenly, by repeating the words of St. Augustine: " *Grant me O Lord what Thou commandest and then command whatever Thou wilt.* "

3) Finally, we must go back courageously to our task, supported by the all-powerful grace of God, and work on despite the apparently small measure of success that attends our efforts, remembering that it is effort and not success that God demands. Besides, we must not forget that we need a certain amount of relaxation, of rest, and of diversion: *Man cannot live long without some consolation.* Constancy does not therefore exclude due rest: " *Enjoy thy leisure that thou mayest the better perform thy labor.* " The important thing is that we take our rest in submission to God's will, according to rule and the advice of our spiritual director.

§ III. Means of Acquiring and Perfecting the Virtue of Fortitude

We refer the reader to what we have said in number 811 regarding the education of the will, adding here some few remarks more pertinent to the special subject now under discussion.

1095. 1° The secret of our strength lies in *distrust of self* and *absolute confidence in God.* Incapable as we are of any good in the supernatural order without the help of grace, we share in the very power of God and become invincible if we seek support in Jesus Christ: "*He that abideth in me, and I in him, the same beareth much fruit* [1]... *I can do all things in him who strengtheneth me.*" [2] This is why it is the *humble* who are strong, when the consciousness of their weakness is accompanied by trust in God. These two dispositions, then, must be cultivated in souls. If it is question of the proud and presumptuous, insistence must be laid upon distrust of self; when we have to deal with the timid and the pessimistic, confidence in God is to be emphasized, by explaining to them the consoling words of the Apostle: "*The weak things of the world hath God chosen, that he may confound the strong... and the things that are not, that he might bring to nought the things that are.*" [3]

1096. 2° To this twofold disposition of soul *deep convictions* must be joined, as well as the habit *of acting in accordance with such convictions.*

A) These convictions are those based upon the great truths, particularly, the end of man, the necessity of sacrificing all in order to attain this end, the horror that sin, the only obstacle to our end, must inspire in us, the necessity of submitting our will to the will of God in order to avoid sin and attain our end, etc. These convictions constitute the directing forces of our conduct and the motive-powers that infuse into us the courage required to triumph over obstacles.

B) This is the reason why it is so important to acquire the habit of acting from conviction. We are not so apt then to allow ourselves to be carried away by passing impulses, by the violent urge of passion, by routine, or personal interest; on the contrary, before acting, such questions as these will arise in the mind: "*What bearing has this on eternity?*" Does this action which I am about to perform bring me closer to God, nearer to the attainment of a blissful eternity? If we can answer in the affirmative we act; if not, we refrain. Thus directing all things to the final end, we live up to our convictions and we become strong.

1097. 3° The better to surmount obstacles it is well to *foresee* them, to look them squarely in the face, and to

---

[1] *John*, XV, 5. — [2] *Phil.*, IV, 13. — [3] *I Cor.*, I, 27-28.

muster courage to fight them. This, however, we do without magnifying the difficulties, counting upon the aid which God will not fail to grant us at the opportune moment. A difficulty foreseen is a difficulty half overcome.

1098. 4° Finally, we should bear in mind that nothing renders us so fearless as the love of God : " *For love is strong as death.* " If mother-love inspires a woman with courage and daring when it is question of defending her children, what cannot the love of God do if it be deep-rooted in the soul? Is it not love that has made martyrs, virgins, apostles and all the saints? When St. Paul describes the ordeals he underwent, the persecutions he suffered, the pains he endured, one cannot but wonder at the power that sustained his courage in the midst of so many adversities. He tells us himself it was love for Christ : " For the charity of Christ presseth us. " [1] This is why the Apostle is without apprehension for the future. " Who then shall separate us from the love of Christ? " [2] He enumerates the various tribulations that might befall him, and says : " Neither death, nor life, nor angels... nor things present, nor things to come, nor might... nor any other creature shall be able to separate us from the love of God which is in Christ Jesus Our Lord. " [3] What St. Paul said, every Christian also can say, provided he bears his God a loyal love ; and then He will share in the very power of the Almighty : " For Thou, O Lord, art my strength. " [4]

ART. IV. THE VIRTUE OF TEMPERANCE [5]

If fortitude is needed to restrain fear, temperance is no less necessary to control that allurement to pleasure which so easily turns us away from God.

1099. Temperance is a supernatural, moral virtue *that moderates the attraction towards sense-pleasure, especially the pleasures of the palate and the flesh, and keeps them within the proper limits of propriety.*

Its *object* is the moderation of all sense-pleasure, but particularly of that connected with the two great functions of organic life ; namely, the preservation of the individual by nourishment, and the preservation of the race by sexual

---

[1] *II Cor.*, V, 14. — [2] *Rom.*, VIII, 38-39. — [3] *Rom.*, VIII, 35. — [4] *Ps.* XLII, 2.
[5] ST. THOM., Iª IIæ, q. 141-170; SCARAMELLI, *Guide ascétique*, IIIe Traité, art. 4; RIBET, *Vertus*, ch. XLIII-XLVIII; CH. DE SMEDT, t. II, p. 268-342; P. JANVIER, *Carême*, 1921 et 1922. See references, Nos 751 and 864, under Mortification and Gluttony.

relations. Temperance causes us to make use of pleasure for an end which is worthy and at the same time supernatural. By that very fact it regulates the use of the said pleasures according to the dictates of reason and of faith. Precisely because pleasure is enticing and easily lures us beyond the proper limits, temperance leads us to mortify ourselves, even in some of the things that are permissible, in order to ensure the preponderance of reason over passion.

It is by the aid of these principles that we shall solve particular questions.

We have already dealt sufficiently with the rules to be followed in the regulation of the pleasure that accompanies the function of nutrition (n. 864). Now we shall treat of *chastity*, which moderates the pleasures attached to the propagation of the race. Then we shall speak of the two virtues allied to temperance; namely, *humility* and *meekness*.

§ I. Chastity [1]

1100. 1º **Notion.** The *aim* of chastity is to *check whatever is inordinate in voluptuous pleasures*. These pleasures have for their principal end the perpetuation of the race through the right use of marriage. They are lawful only between married persons, and then only when they further, or at least do not interfere with the primary end of marriage which is the procreation of children.

Chastity is rightly called the *angelic* virtue, because it likens us to the angels, who are pure by nature. It is an *austere* virtue, because we do not succeed in practicing it unless we subdue the body and the senses by mortification. It is a *frail* virtue, tarnished by the least wilful failing. On this account it is a *difficult* virtue, since it cannot be observed except by a generous and constant struggle against the most tyrannical of passions.

1101. 2º **Degrees.** 1) There are several degrees of chastity. The first one consists in carefully refraining from consent to any thought, fancy, feeling or action contrary to this virtue.

2) The second aims at ridding oneself *immediately* and *energetically* of every thought, image or impression that could soil the luster of chastity.

3) The third, which is seldom attained save after long efforts in the practice of the love of God, consists in acquir-

[1] CASSIAN, *Conferences*, XII; ST. JOHN CLIMACUS, *The Ladder of Paradise*, XV; ST. THOMAS, IIa IIae, Q. 151-156; RODRIGUEZ, *Christian Perfection*, P. III, Treat. IV; ST. FRANCIS OF SALES, *Devout Life*, P. III, C. XII-XIII; GAY, *Christian Life and Virtues*, Treat. X.—See references No. 873.

ing such a mastery over our senses and our thoughts that, when duty requires us to deal with questions relating to chastity, we do so with all the calm and composure that would attend the treatment of any other subject.

4) Finally, there are some who, by a special privilege, attain such a degree of chastity that they experience no inordinate feelings whatever, as is related of St. Thomas after his victorious issue from an extraordinary temptation.

1102. 3° **Kinds.** There are two kinds of chastity: *conjugal* chastity proper to persons living in lawful wedlock, and *continence* proper to the unmarried. After briefly treating of the first, we shall lay emphasis on the second, chiefly in so far as it applies to persons who lead a life of celibacy either in the religious or in the ecclesiastical state.

I. *Conjugal Chastity*

1103. 1° **Principle.** Married persons should never forget that, according to the teaching of St. Paul, Christian marriage is symbolical of the holy bond that exists between Christ and His Church: "Husbands, love your wives, as Christ also loved the Church and delivered himself for it, that He might sanctify it."[1] They must then love respect and sanctify each other (n. 591). The first effect of this love is an indissoluble union of hearts, and therefore an inviolable mutual fidelity.

1104. 2° **Mutual Fidelity.** a) Here we shall borrow the language of St. Francis de Sales[2] or give a summary of his thought.

"Preserve, then, O husbands! a tender, constant, and cordial love for your wives... If you desire that your wives should be faithful to you, give them a lesson by your example. How, says St. Gregory Nazianzen[3], can you exact purity of your wives, when you yourselves live in impurity?"—"But you, O wives, whose honor is inseparably joined with purity and modesty, be zealous to preserve this your glory, and suffer no kind of loose behavior to tarnish the whiteness of your reputation. Fear all kinds of assaults, how small soever they may be; never suffer any wanton address to approach you; for he that praises the ware which he cannot buy is strongly tempted to steal it, but if to your praise he adds the dispraise of your husband, he offers you a heinous injury; for it is evident that he not only desires to ruin you, but accounts you already half lost, since the bargain is half made with a second merchant when one is disgusted with the first."

---

[1] *Ephes.*, V, 25-26.
[2] *Devout Life*, Part. III, C. XXXVIII.
[3] *Orat.*, XXXVII, 7.

b) Nothing so well secures this mutual fidelity as the practice of *true devotion*, particularly of prayer in common.

" Thus, wives ought to wish that their husbands should be preserved with the sugar of devotion ; for a man without devotion is severe, harsh, and rough. And husbands ought to wish that their wives should be devout, because without devotion, a woman is very frail, and liable to obscure, and perhaps to lose, her virtue. "

c) " As to the rest, their mutual bearing with each other ought to be so great that they should never be both angry with each other at the same time, so that dissension or debate be never seen between them. " Therefore, if one be angry, let the other hold his peace, in order that peace may be restored the sooner. "

1105.   3° **Conjugal Duty.** They should reverence the holiness of the marriage-bed by the *purity of their intention* and the *seemliness* of their relations.

A) Their *intention* must be the same as that of the young Tobias when he took Sarah for wife ; " And now, Lord, thou knowest that not for fleshly lust do I take my sister to wife, but only for the love of posterity in which thy name may be blessed for ever and ever. "[1]   This is in fact the primary end of Christian marriage, to procreate children who are to be reared in the fear and love of God, to be trained to a pious and Christian life so as to become one day citizens of Heaven. The secondary end of marriage is mutual help to bear the sufferings of life, and to overcome passion by subordinating pleasure to duty.

1106.   **B**) They must, then, *faithfully* and *candidly* fulfil their marriage obligations. Whatever favors the transmission of life is not only licit, but praiseworthy. On the contrary, any act whatever whereby this primary end would be hindered constitutes a grave sin, since it is against the essential purpose of marriage. They should bear in mind the following observation of St. Paul :[2] " Defraud not one another, except, perhaps, by consent, for a time, that you may give yourselves to prayer : and return together again, lest Satan tempt you for your incontinency. "

C) Moderation is necessary in the use of the marriage right as it is in the taking of meals. It is even a hygienic measure, and propriety requires that continence be practiced at times. One does not succeed in this unless one has formed the habit of subordinating pleasure to reason, and unless one seeks in the frequent reception of the Sacraments a remedy for the too violent motions of concupiscence.

---

[1] *Tobias*, 9, VIII. — [2] *1 Cor.*, VII, 5.

However, let no one forget, that it is by no means impossible, and that through prayer one always obtains the grace of practicing virtue, even the most austere.

II. *Continence or Celibacy*

1107. Absolute continence is a duty of those who are not united in the bonds of lawful wedlock. Therefore, it must be practiced by all before marriage as well as by those who are widowed. [1] There is yet another class of chosen souls called to practice a life-long continence either in the religious state, or in the priesthood, or even in the world. It is well to give them special rules for the perfect preservation of purity.

Chastity is a frail and delicate virtue that cannot be preserved unless it be protected by other virtues. It is, as it were, a citadel that requires for its defence the raising of outward ramparts. These are four in number: 1° humility, which produces self-distrust and prompts to flight from dangerous occasions; 2° mortification, which by waging war against the love of pleasure, reaches the evil at its roots; 3° *devotion to the duties of state*, which protects one from the perils created by idleness; 4° *love for God*, which by filling the heart, prevents it from giving itself over to dangerous affections. Within these four ramparts the soul is not only able to repulse the onslaughts of the enemy, but also to grow in purity.

1° HUMILITY THE GUARDIAN OF CHASTITY

1108. This virtue produces in us principally three dispositions, which shelter us from many a danger: distrust of self and confidence in God, flight from dangerous occasions, sincerity in the Sacrament of Penance.

A) Distrust of self accompanied by *confidence in God*. Many a soul falls into impurity through pride and presumption. St. Paul calls attention to this fact with regard to the Pagan philosophers, who whilst glorying in their wisdom yielded to all manner of turpitude: "*For this cause, God delivered them up to shameful affections.*" [2]

Father Olier thus explains this fact: "God, Who cannot suffer pride in the soul, humbles it to the very depths; and, desiring to show the soul its weakness, and that it has no power of itself to resist evil and persevere in well doing... allows it to be tormented by those terrible

---

[1] See the excellent advice of St. Francis de Sales to widows, *Devout Life,* Part III, C. XL. — [2] *Rom.*, I, 26.

temptations, and at times even to fall, because such temptations are the most shameful and leave behind them the greater confusion." When, on the contrary one is firmly convinced that of oneself one cannot be chaste, one repeats the humble prayer which St. Philip Neri used to address to God: "My God, beware of Philip; otherwise he will betray Thee."

1109. **a)** This distrust must be *universal*. 1) It is necessary to those who have *sinned grievously*, for the temptation will return, and without the help of grace they will be exposed to a fresh fall. It is no less necessary to those who have *preserved their innocence*, for one day or another temptation will assail them, and will be all the more dangerous for them because of their inexperience. 2) This distrust must last to the very *end of life*. Solomon was no longer a youth when he let himself be caught by the love of women. It was old men that tempted the chaste Susanna. The evil spirit that assails us in mature life is all the more dangerous, because we thought him conquered. Experience shows that so long as there remains in us a spark of life, the smouldering fires of concupiscence may burst forth once more. 3) This diffidence is necessary for even the *holiest* souls. The evil one is more anxious to cause their fall than that of coarser souls, and he lays for them more treacherous snares. This is the warning of St. Jerome [1] in his letter to Eustochium, and elsewhere [2] he adds that it is vain to seek reassurance in the long years already lived in chastity, in holiness and in the pursuance of wisdom.

1110. **b)** Withal, this diffidence of self must be ever attended by a perfect *trust in God*. For God will never allow us to be tempted beyond our strength. He does not ask of us the impossible. He either gives us immediately the grace of resisting temptations or the grace of praying for the help necessary to overcome them. [3]

"One must, then," says Father Olier [4] "withdraw interiorly into Jesus Christ to find in Him the power of resistance to temptation... He wills that we be tried, so that, warned thereby of our weakness and of the need we have of His help, we may withdraw into Him to find in Him the strength which we lack." If the temptation becomes more

---

[1] *Epist.* XXII, ad Eustochium, *P. L.*, XXII, 396.

[2] *Epist.* LII, ad Nepotian. *P. L.* XXII, 531-532: "Trust not in your former chastity: you are not holier than David, nor can you be holier than Solomon. Always remember that a woman evicted the tenant of paradise from his possession."

[3] "For God does not enjoin the impossible; but when He commands, He bids us do what in our power lies and to pray for what lies beyond, the while He lends us the power to accomplish His command." (*Council of Trent*, Sess. VI, C. II, DENZ. 804.)

[4] *Introd.*, C. XII.

violent we must fall on our knees and lift our hands to Heaven to invoke the assistance of God.

When all these precautions have been taken one may infallibly count on God's help : " *And God is faithful, who will not suffer you to be tempted above that which you are able : but will make also with temptation issue, that you may be able to bear it.* " [1] We must not, then, have too much dread of temptation before it comes. That would be a way of bringing it on. Nor must we stand in dread of it when it actually assails us, since with reliance on God we are invincible.

1111. B) The Flight from Dangerous Occasions.
a) The mutual *attraction* that exists between the *sexes* creates dangers for those vowed to celibacy. Hence, useless meetings must be dispensed with, and when meetings are necessary, the danger must be made remote. [2] This is why the spiritual direction of women must be conducted exclusively in the confessional, as we have noted in n. 546. Two things we have to protect : our *virtue* and our *good name*. The one and the other make extreme reserve imperative.

b) Children of graceful appearance, of a joyful and affectionate nature, may likewise be a source of danger. One loves to look at them, to caress them, and, if one be not on guard one may be led to familiarities that perturb the senses. This disturbance is a warning given us by God, to make us understand that we must desist and that we have even proceeded too far. Let us recall to mind that those children have Guardian Angels who look upon the face of God; that they are the living temples of the Holy Trinity and members of Christ. Then we shall more easily treat them with a holy reverence while we show them real affection.

1112. c) In a general way, humility causes us to repress the *desire to please*, which prepares the way for many a fall. This desire, which proceeds both from vanity and from a natural longing for affection, is manifested by an exaggerated concern for our personal appearance, over-carefulness

---

[1] *I Cor.* VIII, 14.
[2] This was St. Jerome's advice to Nepotian : " A woman's foot should seldom if ever cross the threshold of your home... If in the course of your clerical duty you have to visit a widow or a virgin, never enter the house alone. Let your companions be persons, associates who will not disgrace you... You must not sit alone with a woman or see one without witnesses... Beware of all that gives occasion for suspicion; and to avoid scandal shun every act that may give colour to it. " *Letter* LII, 5, *P. L.*, XXII, 531-532.

in dress, an affected pose, tender language, caressing glances, the habit of complimenting others upon their exterior accomplishments. [1]   This manner of acting soon attracts notice, especially in a young ecclesiastic, in a priest, or a religious.   He soon jeopardizes his good name; and would that he stop before he likewise imperils his virtue!

1113.   C) Humility, finally, inspires us with that *candid frankness* toward our spiritual director which is so necessary to avoid the snares of the enemy.

St. Ignatius rightly says that "when the enemy of man wishes to lead a just soul into error by his tricks and ruses, he wants above all that such a soul listen to him and keep his words secret.   But should that soul confide all to an enlightened confessor, Satan is chagrined, because he knows that all his malice will become impotent the moment his attempts are detected and brought out into the light." [2]   It is especially in matters of chastity that this wise advice applies.   If we are faithful to disclose humbly and candidly our temptations to our spiritual director, we are warned in time of the dangers to which we are exposed, and we take the means suggested by him.   A temptation laid bare is a temptation already overcome.   If, on the contrary, trusting to our own lights we fail to seek advice, under the pretext that a temptation is not a sin, we fall easily into the snares of the great seducer of souls.

2° Mortification the Guardian of Chastity

We have already explained the necessity and the principal forms of mortification (n. 755-790). We shall recall here the points that bear more directly upon the present subject. Because the poison of impurity seeps through every opening, we must know how to mortify both our *exterior* and our *interior* senses, as well as the *affections of the heart.*

1114.   A) The body, we have said (n. 771 and foll.), must be disciplined, and if need be, chastised that it may remain subject to the soul : "*But I chastise my body and bring it into subjection : lest perhaps, when I have preached to others, I myself should become a castaway.*" [3]

From this principle arises the necessity of sobriety, at times of fasting, or of some other exterior forms of penance; also the need, at certain periods and especially in the spring of the year, of a less rich diet to abate the mounting surge of the blood and soothe the ardors

---

[1] St. Jerome well describes these oddities : "Such men think of nothing but their dress; they use perfumes freely, and see that there are no creases in their leather shoes.   Their curling hair shows the traces of tongs; their fingers glisten with rings; they walk on tiptoe across a wet road, not to splash their feet.   When you see men acting in this way, think of them rather as bridegrooms than as clergymen. " *Letter* XXII, 28.

[2] *Spiritual Exercises, Rules for the Discernment of Spirits*, XIII.

[3] *I Cor.*, IX, 27.

of concupiscence. Nothing is to be neglected that may ensure the dominion of the soul over the body. There should be no protracted hours of sleep, and as a general principle we must not remain in bed of mornings, once we are awake and are unable to fall asleep again.

Each of our bodily senses needs to be mortified.

1115. a) The just Job had made a pact with his eyes that they should not look upon such persons as could prove a source of temptation to him : " *I made a covenant with my eyes, that I would not so much as think upon a virgin.* " [1] The Book of Ecclesiasticus carefully recommends not to fasten our glances upon a maiden and to turn our eyes from a beautiful woman : " For many have perished by the beauty of a woman, and thereby lust is enkindled as a fire. " [2] All these counsels have a good psychological foundation. The eye acts as stimulus to the imagination, this enkindles the desire, and the latter solicits the will. If the will yields consent, sin enters into the soul.

1116. b) *Speech* and *hearing* are mortified by *reserve* in *conversation.* This reserve is not common even among Christian men and women. The reading of novels and the frequenting of theatres cause them to speak freely of many a subject that should be passed over in silence. Likewise, they want to keep informed about the scandals that occur in the world. At other times they chat pleasantly about things of a more or less risky nature. A sort of unwholesome curiosity finds delight in such pleasantries and reports, the imagination is fed on them and visualizes in detail the descriptions given, the senses react and often the will ends by taking culpable pleasure. And so it is that St. Paul rightly denounces evil associations as a source of corruption : " *Evil communications corrupt good manners.* " [3] The same Apostle says elsewhere : " Obscenity, or foolish talking, or scurrility, which is to no purpose... let it not so much as be named among you. " [4] Experience shows that sterling souls have been perverted through the unwholesome curiosity aroused by imprudent conversations.

1117. c) In the sense of *touch* there lurks a special danger (n. 879).

Father Perreyve understood this well when he wrote the following : [5] " More than ever, O Lord, I consecrate my hands to Thee. These

---

[1] *Job*, XXXI, 1.
[2] "Gaze not upon a maiden : lest her beauty be a stumbling block to thee... Turn away thy face from a woman dressed up; and gaze not about upon another's beauty. " *Ecclus. IX*, 5, 8, 9. — [3] *I Cor.*, XV, 33. — [4] *Ephes.*, V, 3 & 4.
[5] *Méditations sur les SS. Ordres*, p. 105.

hands are to receive priestly consecration within three days. On the morrow of the third day they will touch, hold, handle Thy Body and Thy Blood. I want to reverence these hands, honor them as hallowed instruments dedicated to Thy service and that of Thy altars..." When we recollect that in the morning we have held within our hands an All-holy God, we are more ready to abstain from whatever could soil their purity. Hence, deep reverence for our own person; hence reverence for others, treating all with the accepted marks of courtesy, but abstaining from any sentimental feeling or ill-ordered affection. To a priest who asked St. Vincent de Paul if it were expedient to feel the pulse of a dying woman, the Saint replied : "That practice must be carefully avoided, for the evil spirit might easily make use of it to tempt the living and even the dying. The devil, in this last moment uses any and every device to ensnare a soul... You should never touch eitheir girl or woman under any pretence whatever." [1]

1118. B) The *interior* senses are no less exposed to danger than are the exterior. Even when we modestly lower our eyes, importunate memories and obsessing images still pursue us. St. Jerome complained of this even in the solitude of the desert where, though parched by the burning sun and living in a bare cell, he would feel himself carried in fancy mid the pleasures of Rome. [2] He therefore urges *instant* riddance of such fancies : " *You must never let the suggestion of evil grow on you... Slay the enemy while he is small; and that you may not have a crop of tares, nip the evil in the bud.*" [3] The enemy must be strangled before his strength grows and the tares pulled up by the root before they sprout, otherwise the soul is invaded, obsessed by temptation, and the temple of God becomes the haunt of demons : " *Let not the temple of the Blessed Trinity become a place where demons shall dance and sirens make their dens.*" [4]

1119. In order to escape these dangerous fancies it is important not to indulge in the reading of such novels or attend such theatrical representations, where inhuman passions and chiefly that of love are presented in a vivid and realistic fashion. Such descriptions cannot but trouble the imagination and the senses. They persistently recur in our leisure moments, impart to temptation a more vivid and more alluring form, and at times extort consent. Now, St. Jerome remarks that virginity is forfeited not merely through exterior but also by interior acts : " *And so, virginity is lost even by thought.*" [5]

Furthermore, the Saints exhort us to mortify the imagination and useless *day-dreaming.* For, experience shows that these are frequently followed by dangerous sensual images, and that, therefore, if we wish to prevent the latter,

---

[1] MEYNARD, *Virtues and Spiritual Doctrine of St. Vincent de Paul*, C. XIX.
[2] "How often, when I was living in the desert, in the vast solitude which gives to hermits a wild dwelling-place, parched by a burning sun, how often did I *fancy myself among the pleasures of Rome!*" Letter, XXII, n. 7. — [3] *Ibid.*
[4] ST. JEROME, Letter, XXII, n. 6. — [5] *Letter quoted*, n. 5.

we must quickly banish the former. It is only by so doing that we gradually succeed in subjecting the imagination to the service of the will.

This is particularly necessary to the priest, who by the very reason of his ministry, is the recipient of confidences of a delicate nature. No doubt, he has the grace of state not to take any pleasure therein, but this on condition that upon leaving the confessional he does not voluntarily dwell upon what he has heard. Otherwise, his virtue would be put to a severe test, and God has not bound Himself to vouchsafe His help to imprudent souls that rush headlong into danger : " *He that loveth danger shall perish in it.* " [1]

1120. C) The *heart* needs to be mortified just as much as the imagination. It is one of the highest and noblest of faculties, but it is also a source of danger. By religious vow or by priestly ordination, we consecrate our heart to God and renounce the joys of family life. Still, the heart remains open to affection; and if it be true that we have special graces, they are graces for *the struggle*, and they demand of us great vigilance and great effort.

Besides the dangers common to all, the priest encounters in his ministry some peculiar to himself. He may become unconsciously attached to the persons to whom he does good, and they in turn may feel naturally moved to manifest their gratitude. Therefrom arise mutual affections; these are supernatural at first, but unless carefully controlled, they easily descend to the plane of natural, sentimental and absorbing attachments. Indeed, it is easy to deceive ourselves. " Oftentimes, " says St. Francis de Sales, " we imagine we love persons for God's sake, whilst in reality we love them for the sake of the pleasure we experience in their company. " A famous text, attributed to St. Augustine, shows us the successive degrees through which we pass from spiritual to carnal love : " *Spiritual love engenders affectionate love, affectionate love devoted love, devoted love tender love, and tender love carnal love.* "

1121. In order to escape such a misfortune, we must ask ourselves from time to time whether or not we see in ourselves any signs of friendship that is too natural and sentimental. [2] Father de Valuy [3] says that such a friendship exists : " If the presence of a person begins to captivate our eyes, or his agreeable disposition to thrill our heart; if we offer tender greetings, speak tender words, cast tender glances, make small gifts, exchange smiles more eloquent than words and permit liberties that little by little lead to familiarity; if we seek opportunities to meet alone, to prolong these meetings interminably and to renew them for no apparent reason ; if we speak little of divine things but a great deal of self and of mutual esteem ; if we praise, flatter or excuse each other ; if we complain bitterly of the warnings of superiors, of the obstacles they place in the way of our meetings and of the suspicions in which they seem to indulge ;... if we experience uneasiness and sadness at the absence of our friend; if we are distracted in prayer at the thought of him, and recommend him to God with extra-

---

[1] *Ecclesiasticus*, III, 27. — [2] cf. above, n°s 595-606—friendships, true and false.
[3] *Vertus religieuses*, pp. 73-74.

ordinary fervor; if we have his image deeply engraved on our mind, and are preoccupied with the thought of him day and night, anxiously wondering as to his whereabouts, as to the time of his return, and as to his affection for others; if we experience unwonted joy at his reappearance, undergo a species of martyrdom when again he must depart, and strive in a thousand and one ways to bring about a reunion. "

Let no one try to reassure himself by citing the piety of the persons to whom he thus attaches himself, for *the holier they are, the more they attract us.* Besides, such persons imagine that the affection they bear a priest holds no dangers whatever, and may, therefore, allow their affection to grow without fear. It is imperative, then, that the priest keep them at a distance by his own reserve.

3° APPLICATION TO STUDY AND TO DUTIES OF STATE

1122. One of the most profitable forms of mortification is the avoidance of idleness by an earnest application to ecclesiastical studies and to the faithful fulfilment of the duties of state. Thereby the dangers of idleness are removed : " *For idleness hath taught much evil.* " [1] For one demon that tempts a busy man there are a thousand evil spirits that tempt an idle one. What do we do, as a matter of fact, when we are not engaged in any useful task? We muse, day-dream, read light literature, indulge in protracted visits, hold conversations of a more or less dangerous nature, while our imagination teems with vain fancies, our heart drifts on towards sentimental affections and our soul, laid open to all sorts of temptations, finally yields to sin. On the contrary, when we become absorbed in study or the work of the ministry, our mind is filled with wholesome thoughts, [2] and our heart soars to worthy and pure affections. Our one absorbing thought is of souls, whilst the very multiplicity of occupations leaves no opportunity whatever for any inordinate friendships. If at any time temptation makes its appearance, the self-mastery acquired through assiduous work enables us to head it off far more quickly, for study and work make their wonted demands upon our attention, and we soon tear ourselves away from reveries to busy ourselves with the concrete realities that take up the greater part of our life.

1123. Hence, it is a great service to seminarians and priests to inspire them with a taste for study; to teach them how to avoid

---

[1] *Ecclesiasticus*, XXXIII, 29.

[2] " Love the knowledge of Scripture, and you will no longer love the sins of the flesh... Always have some work on hand, that the devil may find you busy. " ST. JEROME, Letter CXXV, n. 11.

idleness, even in holiday time, and how to turn to profit every moment of their life. When one can help them sketch a plan of study that they can follow in the ministry, or aid them in the preparation of some course of instructions, or interest them in some special question, one does them a signal service; for if they have no such program, they are liable to waste precious time, whilst with it, they bring to their task a greater enthusiasm and more perseverance.

4° ARDENT LOVE FOR JESUS AND HIS BLESSED MOTHER

1124. If work preserves the mind from dangerous thoughts, love for God shields the heart from sentimental affections, and thus spares us many a temptation. Man's heart is made for love. Priestly ordination or religious profession do not change this affective part of our nature, but they help us raise our affections to a supernatural plane. If we love God with our whole soul, if we love Jesus Christ above all things, we shall be less inclined to give our affections to creatures. St. John Climacus remarks: "He is truly virtuous upon whose spirit heavenly beauty is so engraved, that he deigns not to cast a look upon earthly beauty, and thus feels not the burning of that fire which consumes the hearts of other men." [1]

1125. But in order that love for Jesus may produce these effects, it must be intense, generous, and absorbing. Then it will bring us a threefold blessing: 1) It will so fill the mind and the heart that we no longer give a thought to human affections. If at times they make their way to our heart, we turn them aside, repeating these words of St. Agnes: "*I am espoused to Him Whom the Angels serve, at Whose beauty the very sun and moon stand in awe.*" It is easy to understand how all creatures vanish and lose their charm in the presence of Him Who is the fulness of beauty, of goodness and of power. 2) Should we unfortunately become entangled in any ill-ordered affections, Jesus Who cannot suffer strange gods in our heart, will reproach us severely and thus make us all the stronger for the fight against them. 3) Lastly, He will Himself protect with jealous care the hearts of those who give themselves to Him. He will come to our aid at the time of temptation and will strengthen us against the seductions of creatures.

This generous love for Jesus we draw from prayer, from the reception of Holy Communion, from silent adoration of the Blessed Sacrament, and we render it habitual and permanent through that intimate union with Our Lord which we described above, in number 153.

1126. To this we add a great devotion to Mary, the Virgin Undefiled. Her name breathes forth purity, and, it seems, no sooner do we confidently invoke Her, than temptation is put to flight. If we consecrate ourselves

---

[1] *Ladder of Paradise*, Degree XV, 7.

entirely to this Good Mother (n. 170-176), She will watch over us as Her very own, and help us to repel successfully the most harassing temptations. Let us, then, delight in the recitation of the prayer, *O Domina mea*, so powerful against impure suggestions, and the *Ave Maris Stella*, especially the following strophe:

> *Virgin of all virgins,*
> *Thee our queen we seek;*
> *Fire with love our bosoms,*
> *Make us chaste and meek.*

And if we are ever worsted in the struggle, we must not forget that the Immaculate Heart of Mary is also the sure refuge of sinners, that through the invocation of Her Name we shall find the grace of repentance, followed by the grace of absolution. Who could better ensure our perseverance than the Virgin most Faithful?

§ II. Humility [1]

This virtue could in some respects be connected with the virtue of justice, since it inclines us to mete out to ourselves what are our just deserts. However, it is generally related to the virtue of temperance, because it *moderates* the sense we have of our own worth. We shall explain: 1º its *nature;* 2º its various *degrees;* 3º its *excellence;* 4º the means *to practice* it.

I. *Nature of Humility*

1127. 1º Humility is a virtue that was unknown to the Pagans. For them humility connoted something vile, abject, servile or ignoble. It was not so with the Jews. Enlightened by faith, the best among them, conscious of their own nothingness and of their wretchedness, patiently accepted trials as a means of expiation. God, on His part stooped down to help them; He delighted in the prayer of the humble, and pardoned the contrite and humbled sinner. Therefore, when Our Lord came to preach humility and meekness, the Jews were able to understand Him. As for us, we understand Him even better, after reflecting on the examples of humility He has given us in His hidden life, during His public ministry, and in His passion, nay, gives us still in His Eucharistic life.

Humility may be defined as *a supernatural virtue, which, through the self-knowledge it imparts, inclines us to reckon*

---

[1] See references, Nº 818, under Pride.

ourselves at our true worth and to seek self-effacement and contempt. More succinctly, St. Bernard [1] defines it as "a virtue whereby man, through a true knowledge of himself, becomes despicable in his own eyes." This definition will be better understood after we have explained the basis of humility.

1128. The Basis of this virtue. Humility has a twofold basis: truth and justice. *Truth* causes us to know ourselves just as we are; justice inclines us to act upon that knowledge.

A) To attain self-knowledge, says St. Thomas, we must see what in us belongs to God, and what to ourselves. Now, whatever there is in us of good, comes from God and belongs to Him; whatever there is of evil, proceeds from ourselves: "*In man two things may be considered: what there is of God, and what there is of man. Of man there is whatever points to defect; but of God, all that makes for salvation and perfection.*" [2]

Justice, then, absolutely demands that we render to God, and to Him alone, all the honor and all the glory: "*To the king of ages, immortal, invisible, the only God, be honor and glory...* [3] *Benediction and glory, and wisdom, and thanksgiving, honor and power and strength, to our God.*" [4]

Undoubtedly, there is some good in us—our natural being and especially our supernatural privileges. Humility allows us to see and admire this good, but in such wise only that when we contemplate the gifts and graces of God in us, it is Him, and not ourselves that we admire, just as when we admire a work of art we give credit to the artist, not to the canvas.

1129. B) Besides, the fact of being sinners condemns us to humiliation. In a certain sense, of ourselves we are but *sin*, since born in sin, we keep within us concupiscence, which leads to sin.

a) Upon our entrance into the world, we are already tainted by *original sin*, from which only the mercy of God can cleanse us. **b)** How many *actual* sins have we not committed from the dawn of reason! If we have committed even one mortal sin, then on that score we deserve eternal humiliations. Even if we have fallen into but *venial* sins, we must remember that the least sin constitutes

---

[1] *De Gradibus humil.*, C. I, n. 2.
[2] II[a] II[æ], q. 161, a. 3. — [3] *I Tim.*, I, 17. — [4] *Apoc.*, VII, 12.

an offence against God, a wilful violation of His law, an act of rebellion whereby we prefer our will to His. A whole life-time of penance and humiliation would not suffice to atone for this. c) Furthermore, even after our regeneration, we still keep within ourselves strong tendencies to all kinds of sin, so much so that, according to St. Augustine, it is due to God's grace that we have not committed every sin in the world. [1]

In justice, then, we must love humiliations and accept all reproaches. If we are told that we are miserly, dishonest, proud, we must acknow-ledge it, since we have within us the inclination to each of these defects. Father Olier rightly comes to the conclusion that "in sick-ness, in persecution, in contempt, and any other affliction we must take God's part against ourselves and acknowledge that we justly deserve all that and more; that He has a perfect right to use every creature for our punishment, and that we must adore the great mercy He uses towards us, knowing full well that according to His justice we would fare far worse." [2]

Such is the twofold basis of humility. Being *nothing* of ourselves, we must love oblivion and self-effacement : *to be unknown, to be reckoned as nothing*. As sinners we deserve every kind of humiliation.

II. *The Various Degrees of Humility*

There are different classifications of the degrees of this virtue according to the various points of view taken. We shall note the principal ones, which can be reduced to three : that of *St. Benedict*, that of *St. Ignatius* and that of *Father Olier*.

1130. 1º **The Twelve Degrees of St. Benedict.** [3] Cas-sian discerned ten different degrees in the practice of humility. St. Benedict completed this division, adding two others. To understand this arrangement, we must know that St. Benedict conceived humility as " an habitual attitude of soul which regulates the entire range of a monk's relations with God, as a sinful creature and as an adopted son. " This concept is founded upon reverence towards the Almighty and comprises besides humility properly so-called, obedience, patience and modesty. Of these twelve degrees, seven refer to *interior* and five to *exterior* actions.

---

[1] " I realize that it is Thy grace that has prevented me from doing whatever evil I have not done; for what evil is there that I could not have done, being given that I could take pleasure in doing wrong just for the pleasure of doing it? And I confess to Thee, my God, that Thou hast pardoned all my sins, those which I freely committed, and those which because of Thy guidance I did not commit. " *(Confess.* II, C. 3, *P. L.* XXXII, 681).

[2] *Catech. for an Int. Life,* P. I, Lesson XVIII.

[3] BUTLER, *Benedictine Monachism,* p. 51.

1131. Among the *interior* acts he places:

1) The *fear of God* ever present to the mind and causing us to *keep the commandments.* This fear is, in the first place, fear of punishment, then reverential fear, which terminates in adoration: " *The fear of the Lord is holy, enduring forever and ever.* " [1]

2) *Obedience,* or the submission of our will to God's. For if we fear and reverence God, we shall do His will in all things. This obedience is, indeed, an act of humility, since it is the expression of our dependence upon God.

3) *Obedience to Superiors* out of love for God. It is more difficult to submit to Superiors than to God Himself. More faith is needed to see God in the person of one's Superiors; likewise a more perfect self-denial is needed because this obedience extends to many more things.

4) *Patient obedience* even in the most difficult things, bearing injuries without murmer, even and above all, when humiliation comes from Superiors. To succeed in this, one must consider the heavenly recompense awaiting us and the sufferings and humiliations of Jesus.

5) *The avowal of secret faults,* thoughts included, to the Superior, [2] apart from sacramental confession. This act of humility is a powerful check. The prospect of having to lay bare the most secret faults halts one on the brink of the abyss.

6) *The willing acceptance* of all *privations,* of *menial offices,* considering oneself unworthy of even such tasks.

7) To consider oneself in all sincerity as the lowest of men. This is a degree of humility rarely found. The Saints attain it by saying to themselves that if others had received as many graces as they, they would have made much better use of these divine gifts.

1132. These interior acts manifest themselves in *exterior* actions, the principal ones being:

8) *Avoidance of singularity:* to do nothing out of the ordinary, but to be satisfied with what is sanctioned by the common rule, the examples

---

[1] *Ps.* XVIII, 10.
[2] According to the Code of Canon Law (can. 530) religious Superiors can no longer in any way seek to induce their subjects to disclose to them their conscience; but the Code adds: "it is profitable for religious to approach their Superiors with filial confidence and manifest to them, if the Superiors be priests, their doubts and troubles of conscience."

of our seniors, and accepted customs. To wish to be singular is a sign of pride.

9) *Silence:* to know how to remain silent as long as conversation is not addressed to us, or as long as there is no good reason to speak. There is a great deal of vanity behind our readiness to talk.

10) *Moderation of laughter:* St. Benedict does not condemn laughter in so far as it is an expression of spiritual joy, but only laughter *of a vulgar kind*, uncouth laughter, sneering laughter, or the habitual disposition to laugh boisterously, and upon the least provocation, all of which shows little regard for God's presence and little humility.

11) *Reserve in speech:* when one speaks, it must be done quietly and humbly, with all the gravity and propriety of the wise man.

12) *Modesty of behavior:* to walk, sit, and hold oneself erect; to practice modesty of the eyes without affectation, to keep one's thoughts fixed on God, reflecting that one is not worthy of raising one's eyes to heaven: *Lord, I am not worthy, a sinful man, to raise my eyes to heaven.*

After explaining the various degrees of humility, St. Benedict adds that they lead to the love of God, that perfect love that excludes fear: " *Therefore, after having ascended all these degrees of humility, the monk soon reaches* the love of God, *that perfect love that casteth out fear.* " This, then, is the goal whither humility leads. The way is rough, but the heights to which it leads us are those of Divine Love.

1133. 2° **The Three Degrees of St. Ignatius.** Towards the end of the Second Week of the Exercises, before the Rules for Election, St. Ignatius proposes three degrees of humility, which are at bottom three degrees of self-abnegation.

1) The *first* degree consists "in perfect submission to the law of God, so that we should be ready to refuse the empire of the whole world, or even to sacrifice our lives, rather than transgress any precept which obliges us under pain of mortal sin." This degree is essential for every Christian who wants to remain in the state of grace.

2) The *second* is more perfect. " It consists in the indifference of the soul towards riches or poverty, honor or shame, health or sickness, provided the glory of God and the salvation of souls are equally secured; further, that no consideration of interest or temporal disgrace, not even the consideration of immediate death, should be capable of drawing us into deliberate venial sin. " This is a disposition already implying great perfection, and few souls attain it.

3) " The *third* is most perfect. It embodies the first two, and it goes further, preferring, for the sole love of Jesus Christ and from the wish to resemble Him the more,

poverty to riches, shame to honors, etc..., even though our salvation and the glory of God would be assured by either" This is the degree of perfect souls; it is the love of the Cross and the love of humiliation, in union with Christ and out of love for Him. When a soul has arrived thus far, it is already on the highroad to sanctity.

1134. 3° **The Three Degrees of Humility according to Father Olier.** After having explained in his "Catechism for an Interior Life" the necessity of humility and the way to combat pride, Father Olier in his Introduction to Christian Life and Virtues, goes on to explain the three degrees of interior humility proper to *fervent souls*.

a) The first degree is to *rejoice* in the knowledge of self, the knowledge of one's vileness, of one's nothingness, of one's defects, of one's sins. The mere knowledge of these miseries does not constitute humility; there are some who discover their faults, but who are saddened at the sight of them, and strive to find in themselves something good that will spare them the confusion they experience. This is an effect of pride. However, when one is pleased at the knowledge of one's wretchedness, when one loves one's own vile and abject condition one is truly humble.

If one has the misfortune of falling into sin, one must, of course, detest it, but at the same time be pleased at the humiliation. To rejoice in one's infirmities, one must remember that such a sentiment redounds to God's glory, by the very fact that one's littleness makes manifest God's greatness, and one's sins His holiness. In this way the soul acknowledges that it has no worth whatever, that of itself it is incapable of any good, and that all has its origin in God, that all depends on Him, and that all must be done through Him.

b) The second degree is that of *wanting to be known as vile*, as base, as being nothing but sin, and to be considered as such by all men. In fact, if knowing our misery and being pleased at it we should still wish to be esteemed by men, we should be *hypocrites*, wanting to seem better than we really are.

Alas! such is our tendency! Hence the chagrin we experience when our imperfections are discovered, the concern we have for the success of our undertakings, for gaining the esteem of men. To covet this esteem is to be a thief wishing to make his what belongs to the Sovereign Being. The humble soul, on the contrary, is unconcerned about the regard in which it is held. It is pained when praised, and would prefer a thousand injuries to a word of praise, since the former is based on truth, the latter on falsehood.

c) The third degree is to want not merely to be known as a vile thing, but *to be treated* as such, as a base and contemptible being; it is to accept joyfully all the scorn and all the humiliation possible; in a word, it is to want to be treated according to our deserts. And what contempt is not due to nothingness, and above all, to sin, which removes us from the One Who is our true good, God?

Thus, when God deigns to send us aridity of soul, interior desolations and reversals, we must take God's part against ourselves, and acknowledge that He is right in rebuking us and our works. Likewise, if we are ill-treated by our superiors, our equals, and even our inferiors, we must rejoice at this as being most just, most profitable to us and most in accord with the desires of Jesus Christ. We must not even aspire to a high place in Heaven from a *motive of pride.* Indeed, we must love God as much as He wishes to be loved, and be faithful so that we mary attain to the degree of glory and bliss that He prepares for us; but with regard to our place in Heaven we must leave that entirely in God's hands.

" Then we attain complete self-effacement, and God alone lives and reigns within us. "

1135. Conclusion. Each of these points of view concerning the degrees of humility as explained by St. Benedict, St. Ignatius, and Father Olier, has its foundation in fact. It is the duty of a spiritual director to advise the one which best harmonizes with his penitents state of soul.

III. *The Excellence of Humility*

To be able to understand the language of the Saints on this subject we must differentiate between humility *in itself,* and humility as the *foundation* of the other virtues.

1136. 1º Considered *in itself,* says St. Thomas, [1] humility is *inferior to the theological virtues,* which have God Himself as their direct object; it is even inferior to certain moral virtues; for instance, prudence, religion, and legal justice which refers to the common good; however, (with the possible exception of obedience) humility is superior to all the other moral virtues, because of its universal character, and because it subordinates us to the divine order in all things,

1137. 2º But, if we consider humility as being the *key* that *opens the treasures of grace* and as the *foundation* of all virtues, it is, as the Saints say, one of the most excellent of virtues.

A) It is the key that lays open the riches of grace : " *But to the humble He giveth grace.* " [2]   a) God knows that the humble soul does not take complacency in the graces He

---

[1] IIa IIæ, q. 161, a. 4. — [2] *I Peter,* V, 5.

bestows, that it is not puffed up with vanity because of them, but rather that it refers all the glory to Him. Almighty God can therefore pour upon that soul the abundance of His favors, since His own glory will be thereby increased. On the other hand, He sees Himself obliged to withdraw His grace from the proud — " God resisteth the proud, " [1] — since they would appropriate it to their own ends and would glory therein. This God cannot suffer : " *I will not give my glory to another.* " [2]

b) Besides, humility empties the soul of self-love and vain-glory, and thus creates there a vast capacity for grace, which God is ready to fill; for as St. Bernard says there is a close affinity between grace and humility: " *The virtue of humility is always found closely associated with Divine grace.* " [3]

1138. **B**) Humility is likewise the *foundation* of all the virtues. If not the mother of all, it is at least their foster-mother, and this from a twofold point of view : first in the sense that *without it* there is no solid virtue, and then that *with it* all other virtues grow in depth and perfection.

1) As pride is the great stumbling-block to *faith*, humility renders our faith more active, more ready, more firm, and even more enlightened : " *Thou hast hid these things from the wise and prudent and hast revealed them to little ones.* " [4] How much easier it is to subject the intellect to the authority of faith, if we are conscious of our dependence upon God! " *Bringing into captivity every understanding, unto the obedience of Christ.* " Faith in turn, [5] revealing to us the infinite perfection of God and our own nothingness, grounds us in humility.

2) The same occurs in the case of *hope*. The proud man trusts in himself and presumes overmuch in his own strength. He hardly thinks of imploring divine aid. The humble man, on the contrary, places all his hope in God, because he distrusts himself. Hope, in its turn, makes us more humble, because it shows us that the joys of heaven are so utterly beyond our powers that without the help of grace we could never attain them.

3) The enemy of the love of God, of *charity*, is the love of self. It is, then, by the "emptying of self" that the love of God grows, which in turn deepens humility, for we delight in effacing ourselves before Him Whom we love. Therefore, St. Augustine rightly said that there is nothing more sublime than charity, and that only the humble practice it : " *There is no higher road than that of charity, and none but the humble walk therein.* " [6] There is likewise no surer way to practice charity towards the neighbor than that of humility, which throws a veil over his defects and makes us sympathize with his infirmities, instead of becoming impatient with him.

---

[1] *I Peter*, V, 5. — [2] *Isaias*, XLII, 8. — [3] *Super Missus est*, Homil. IV, 9. [4] *Matth.*, XI, 25. — [5] *II Cor.*, X, 5. — [6] Enarrat. in Ps. CXLI, c. 7.

1139. 4) *Religion* is all the better practiced the clearer we perceive that all must be offered in holocaust and sacrificed to God.

5) *Prudence* demands humility. The humble are fond of reflecting and taking counsel before acting.

6) *Justice* cannot be practiced without humility, for the proud man exaggerates his own rights to the detriment of those of the neighbor.

7) Christian *fortitude*, proceeding as it does, not from self but from God, is not found except in those who, conscious of their weakness, find support in Him Who alone can strengthen them.

8) *Temperance* and *chastity*, as we have seen, presuppose humility.

9) *Meekness* and *patience* are never well practiced until we learn to accept humiliation.

And so, it can be said that without humility there is no solid and lasting virtue, and that, on the other hand, through humility, all virtues grow and take deeper root in the soul. We may well conclude with the words of St. Augustine : "*Dost thou wish to rise? Begin by descending. You plan a tower that shall pierce the clouds? Lay first the foundations on humility.*" [1] The loftier the building, the deeper must be its foundations.

IV. *The Practice of Humility*

1140. *Beginners*, as we have said (n. 838-844), wage war against pride; souls *advanced* in the spiritual life direct their efforts to the imitation of Our Lord's humility.

1141. 1° They strive to draw to themselves the humble dispositions of the soul of Christ. This is what St. Paul urges us to do : "*Let this mind be in you, which was also in Christ Jesus : Who being in the form of God, thought it not robbery to be equal with God, but emptied Himself...*" [2] We must, then, meditate frequently upon and strive to imitate the examples of humility given us by Our Lord in His *hidden* and *public* life, in His *Passion*, and in His *Eucharistic* life.

A) During His *hidden* life He practices humility chiefly under the form of self-effacement. **a)** He practices this self-effacement *before His birth* by hiding Himself for nine months in the virginal womb of Mary, where He conceals completely His Divine Attributes : "*He emptied himself;*" [3] by submitting Himself to Cæsar's edict : "*There went out a decree from Cæsar Augustus;*" [4] by suffering uncomplainingly the rude refusals His Mother had to face : "*There was no room for them in the inn;*" [5] above all, by being the object

---

[1] *Sermon 10 on the Words of the Lord.* — [2] *Phil.*, II, 5. — [3] *Ibid.*, 7.
[4] *Luke*, II, 1. — [5] *Ibid.*, 7.

of the ingratitude of men, who thought not of making ready a place for Him in their hearts : "*He came unto his own, and his own received him not.*" [1] **b**) He likewise practices self-effacement *at His birth* : He appears as a poor infant, bound in swaddling clothes, placed in a manger, and laid upon a bit of straw : "*You shall find the infant wrapped in swaddling clothes and laid in a manger.*" [2] And this little Child is the Son of God, coequal with the Father, Uncreated Wisdom!

c) He practices humility also in all the circumstances that *follow His birth :* like any ordinary child he is circumcised ; He is obliged to flee into Egypt to escape the persecuting hand of Herod, whom with but one word He could reduce to dust. **d**) His life at Nazareth is but continued self-effacement. Hidden away in a small Galilean village, He at first helps His Mother in her household duties, then becomes an apprentice, a workman, and spends thirty years in obedience to two human beings. He, the Lord of the world, "*was subject to them.*" [3] We can well understand the words of Bossuet : [4] "My God! I stand aghast once more! Come, ye proud ones, behold this spectacle! Jesus, a carpenter's son! Jesus, Himself a carpenter! Jesus, known only as a carpenter and as the son of a carpenter, and nothing more!"

1142. **B**) During the course of His public life Jesus does not cease to practice this forgetfulness of self to the extent compatible with His mission. He is, no doubt, obliged to proclaim both by word and deed that He is the Son of God; yet, He does so in a discreet, measured way, sufficiently clear to reach the minds of men of good will, but not with such evidence as to force assent. His humility appears in everything He does.

a) He surrounds Himself with Apostles, ignorant and uncouth, and therefore little esteemed, eleven fishermen and a publican. He shows a marked preference for those whom the world despises : the poor, sinners, the afflicted, little children, those disowned by the world. He lives by alms and has no place that He can call His home. **b**) His *teaching* is plain and simple, within the reach of all, and His similitudes like His parables are taken from ordinary, every-day life. He does not seek to excite the admiration of men, but to instruct them and to touch their hearts. **c**) His *miracles* are of *rare* occurrence, and when He does perform them He often charges His beneficiaries to speak of them to no man. There is no studied austerity in His life : He eats like every one else, He attends a wedding-feast at Cana, and some banquets to which He is invited. He shuns popularity; He does not hesitate when necessary to displease His disciples : "This is a hard saying," [5] and He takes to flight when the people would make Him king. **d**) If we look into the *innermost sentiments* of His soul, we see how He wishes to live in dependence upon God. [6] He speaks only to give expression to the doctrine of Him Who sent Him : "*I speak not*

---

[1] *John*, I, 11. — [2] *Luke*, II, 12. — [3] *Luke*, II, 51.
[4] *John*, VI, 61. — [5] *Élévations*, XXe Semaine, 8e Élév. — [6] *John*, VIII, 15-16.

of myself... " [1]   " *My doctrine is not mine, but his that sent me;* " [2]   He does nothing of Himself but only in deference to His Father: " *I cannot of myself do anything... But the Father who abideth in me, he doth the works.* " [3]   Thus it is not His own glory that He seeks, but that of the Father, and for this cause only He lives on earth : " *I seek not my own glory...* " [4]   " *I have glorified thee on the earth.* " [5]   Nay more, He, the Lord of Creation, becomes the servant of men : " *The Son of man is not come to be ministered unto, but to minister.* " [6]   In a word, oblivious of self, He continually immolates Himself for God and men.

1143.   **C**) This is all even more apparent in His *Passion* where He practices *abject* humility.

He, Holiness itself, wills to bear the weight of our iniquities and suffer the penalty, as if He were guilty : " *Him, who knew no sin, he hath made sin for us.* " [7]   **a**) Hence proceed that sorrow, that dejection, that weariness, which He feels at Gethsemane at seeing Himself loaded with our sins : " *And he began to fear and to be heavy... My soul is sorrowful even unto death.* " [8]

b) He bears the outrages heaped upon Him : betrayed by Judas, He has for him only friendly words : " *Friend, whereto art thou come?* " [9]   Deserted by His Apostles, He does not cease to love them. Arrested, bound like a common criminal, He heals Malchus wounded by the hand of Peter. Delivered to the rabble, He suffers their affronts in silence. Calumniated, He does not justify Himself, and utters not a word except to make answer to the abjuration of the high-priest in whom He respects the authority of God. He knows full well that His answer will bring upon Him the penalty of death, still He speaks the truth. Treated like a fool by Herod, He holds His peace; He speaks not a single word nor works a single miracle to vindicate His honor. The people to whom He had done so much good choose Barabbas instead of Him, and still Jesus ceases not to suffer for their conversion. Unjustly condemned by Pilate, He keeps silence, He lets Himself be scourged, crowned with thorns, vilified like a mock-king on the stage; He accepts without murmur the heavy cross that is laid upon His shoulders and allows Himself to be crucified without a word of complaint. Insulted and sneered at by His enemies, He prays for them and excuses them before His Father. Deprived of all heavenly comfort, deserted by His disciples, His dignity as man, His reputation, His honor, all set at naught, He suffers it seems every species of humiliation that the mind of man can conceive, and He can say with far greater truth than the Psalmist : " *I am a worm and no man : the reproach of men and the outcast of the people.* " [10]   It is for us sinners, it is in our stead, that He endures so heroically all those outrages without a murmur : " *Who, when He was reviled, did not revile : when he suffered, he threatened not, but delivered himself to him that judged him unjustly.* " [11]   How then can we, who are so full of guilt, ever complain, even should we be at times unjustly accused?

1144.   **D**) His Eucharistic life in the tabernacle reproduces these different examples of humility.

---

[1] *John*, XIV, 10. — [2] *John*, VII, 16. — [3] *John*, V, 30; XIV, 10.
[4] *John*, VIII, 50. — [5] *John*, XVII, 4. — [6] *Matth.*, XX, 28.
[7] *II Cor.*, V, 21. — [8] *Mark*, XIV, 33, 34. — [9] *Matth.*, XXVI, 50.
[10] *Ps.* XXI, 7. — [11] *I Peter*, II, 23.

a) Therein the Divinity of Jesus Christ is veiled to a greater extent than it was in the Crib and on Calvary : " *On the Cross was veiled Thy Godhead's splendor. Here Thy Manhood lieth hidden too.*" [1] And yet, from the recesses of the tabernacle, it is He Who is the first and principal cause of all the good done in the world, He the One that inspires, strengthens and comforts all apostles, martyrs and virgins. And He chooses to be hidden, *to be unknown, to be accounted as nothing.*

b) How many insults, how many affronts does He not receive in the Sacrament of His love, not only from unbelievers who refuse to acknowledge His Presence, from the impious who profane His Sacred Body, but also from Christians, who either out of weakness or shame make sacriligious communions, even from souls consecrated to His service who at times forget Him and leave Him alone in His tabernacle : " *Could you not watch one hour with me?* " [2] Instead of complaining He says to us incessantly : " *Come to me, all you that labor and are heavy burdened, and I will refresh you.*" [3]

Truly, we have here all the examples that we need to sustain and strengthen us in the practice of every form of the virtue of humility. And when we reflect further that at the same time Christ has also merited for us the grace of imitating these examples, how can we hesitate to follow Him?

1145. 2⁰ We shall now examine the manner in which we can, after Our Lord's example, *practice humility* towards *God*, towards our *neighbor* and with regard to ourselves.

A) Towards God, humility is manifested chiefly in three ways : **a)** By the spirit of *religion*, whereby we honor God as the plenitude of being and perfection. This we do by lovingly and joyfully acknowledging our nothingness and our sinfulness, glad to proclaim in this way the self-sufficiency that is God's and the perfection of His holiness. Thence spring those sentiments of adoration, of praise, of filial fear and filial love; thence comes the heart's cry : *Thou alone art holy, Thou alone art Lord, Thou alone art most high.* These sentiments issue forth from our hearts not only when we pray, but also when we contemplate God's work: His *natural* works wherein are mirrored the perfections of the Maker, His supernatural works wherein the eyes of faith perceive a real likeness, a participation in the Divine life.

1146. **b)** By a spirit of *thankfulness*, which sees in God the *source* of all the natural and supernatural gifts we contemplate in ourselves and in others. Then, like the Blessed Virgin, and in union with her, we glorify God for all the

---

[1] Hymn "*Adoro te*" of St. Thomas. — [2] *Matth.*, XXVI, 40. — [3] *Matth.*, XI, 28.

good He has bestowed upon us : " *My soul doth magnify the Lord... He that is mighty hath done great things to me, and holy is His name.*" [1] Thus, instead of priding ourselves upon such gifts, we refer to God all the honor that comes from them and acknowledge that we have often misused them.

1147. **c)** By a spirit of *dependence*, which makes us confess our inability to do any good of ourselves. Convinced of this fact, we never begin any action without first placing ourselves under the influence of the Holy Ghost, without imploring His grace, which alone can supply for our deficiency. This should be practiced especially by spiritual directors, who in the exercise of their ministry must not glory in the confidence which their penitents show them, but candidly avow their insufficiency, and consult the Almighty before dispensing any advice.

1148. **B)** As to the manner of practicing humility with regard to the *neighbor*, the principle that must guide us is the following : we must see in him all the good, natural and supernatural, which God has placed in him, and admire it without either envy or jealousy. On the other hand, we must throw a veil over his defects and overlook them, at least as long as it is not our duty to correct them.

In accordance with this principle : **a)** we rejoice at the virtues and successes of others, for all these redound to God's glory : " *So that by all means... Christ be preached.*" [2] Of course, we may wish to possess their virtues, but then we invoke the Holy Ghost that He may deign to give us a share therein, and thus a worthy emulation ensues : " *And let us consider one another, to provoke unto charity and to good works.*" [3]

b) If we see our neighbor commit some fault, instead of becoming indignant, we pray for his conversion, and frankly acknowledge that, were it not for God's grace, we should ourselves be guilty of greater sins (n. 1129).

1149. **c)** This is the attitude of mind that really enables us to consider ourselves *inferior to others :* " *In humility, let each esteem others better than themselves.*" [4] We may well reflect especially, if not exclusively, upon the good there is in others and the evil there is in ourselves.

The following is the advice of St. Vincent de Paul to his disciples : [5] " If, then, we study to know ourselves thoroughly, we shall find in all

[1] *Luke* I, 46, 49. — [2] *Phil.*, I, 18. — [3] *Hebrews*, X, 24. — [4] *Phil.* II, 3.
[5] MAYNARD, *Virtues and Spiritual Doctrine of St. Vincent de Paul*, p. 202, 203.

we think, in all we say, in all we do regarding either the substance or the circumstances, that we are fully and completely surrounded with cause for shame and confusion ; and if we do not flatter ourselves, we shall perceive that we are not only worse than other men, but even, in a certain sense, more wicked than the demons in hell. For, if these unfortunate spirits had had the graces that have been given to us, they would have made a thousand times better use of them. ”

One may ask how one can arrive at such a conclusion, since it does not always correspond objectively to the truth. Let us note, first of all, that this conviction is found in all the Saints, and, therefore, it must rest upon some solid foundation. The foundation is this : every man can and should *judge himself;* and when he knows himself intimately, he sees clearly that he is indeed guilty, and further, that there exist in him evil tendencies. From this he concludes that he must hold himself in contempt. Others, however, he should not and *cannot judge*, since he does not know their motives, which are essential elements for the appraisal of conduct. Neither does he know the measure of grace God has given to others, which grace, however, he must take into account in order to form a just appreciation of their actions. By judging self severely and not judging others, except leniently, one comes to the practical conclusion that one must assign to oneself a place below all others.

1150. C) In the practice of humility with regard to *ourselves,* the following principle will guide us : while recognizing all the good that is in us in order to give thanks to God for it, we must consider above all what is defective : our nothingness, our helplessness, our sinfulness, so as ever to keep alive within us a sense of humiliation and shame. With the help of this principle it becomes easier to practice humility, which must extend to the whole man, to *mind, heart and outward conduct.*

a) Humility of *mind* comprises chiefly four things :

1) A proper *distrust of self,* that prevents us from overrating our ability, and disposes us to feel humiliated at the ill-use we have made of the gifts of God. Such is the counsel of the Wise Man : “ *Seek not the things that are too high for thee, and search not into things above thy ability.* ” [1] This is what St. Paul recommended to the Christians of Rome : “ *By the grace that is given me, to all that are among you, not to be more wise than it behoveth to be wise, but to be wise unto sobriety and according as God hath divided to every one the measure of faith.* ” [2]

2) In the use we make of our talents, *we must not seek to make a display* or to be praised, but to be useful and to do good.

St. Vincent de Paul recommended this to his missionaries : [3] “ To do otherwise would be to preach self, not Jesus Christ. And he, who preaches for applause, for praise, for esteem, to have his name on everybody's tongue, what does he do? What does such a preacher do? He commits a sacrilege. Yes, a sacrilege! To make the word of God

[1] *Ecclesiasticus,* III, 22. — [2] *Romans,* XII, 3.
[3] MAYNARD, *Virtues and Doctrine,* p. 209.

and things divine the means of acquiring a reputation! Yes, it is a sacrilege!"

1151. 3) We must practice *intellectual docility*, not only by submitting to the official decisions of the Church, but by heartily accepting pontifical directions even when they have not the character of infallibility, reflecting that there is in them greater wisdom than in our own judgments.

4) This docility will prevent *obstinacy* in controverted questions. No doubt, it is our right to adopt whatever system appears to us as best founded, in questions where free discussion is in order, but is it not just and fair to allow the same freedom to others?

1152. b) *Humility of heart* requires that instead of wishing for and seeking glory or honors, we be satisfied with our situation and prefer a hidden life to an exalted position : *Love to be unknown and to be reputed as nothing.* This humbleness of heart goes even further; it hides whatever could cause us to be loved and esteemed and it wishes for the last place not only in rank but also in the esteem of men : "*Sit down in the lowest place.*"[1] Indeed, at times it goes so far as to make us wish that our memory perish from the earth.

Let us listen to St. Vincent de Paul :[2] "We should never turn or fix our eyes on what is good in us, but rather strive to know what is bad and defective; this is a great means of preserving humility. We ought not to dwell on the gift of converting souls nor on whatever other exterior talents we may have, for they are not ours; we are only the bearers of them, and even with these gifts we can lose our souls. For this reason, no one should flatter himself, nor take any complacency in himself, nor conceive any self-esteem because God works great things through him; he should rather humble himself and acknowledge that he is but a poor instrument which God deigns to employ."

1153. c) *External* humility should simply be the outward manifestation of our interior sentiments, still it may be said that exterior acts of humility react upon our interior dispositions to solidify and intensify them. Therefore, they must not be neglected. However, to them we must join real sentiments of humility, that is to say, the soul must be humbled together with the body.

1) Poor lodgings, plain clothes, even worn and patched, as long as they be clean, foster humility. Fine lodgings and expensive attire easily inspire sentiments contrary to this virtue.

2) A humble and unassuming posture, gait and behavior, devoid of affectation, help in the practice of humility;[3] humble occupations

---

[1] *Luke*, XIV, 10. — [2] MAYNARD, *Virtues and Doctrine*, p. 213.
[3] This is well explained by MGR. GAY in *Christian Life and Virtues*, Vol. I, On Humility, p. 370. "There is a habit of exterior humility in which the soul that

such as manual labor, mending one's clothes, etc., produce the same result.

3) The same may be said of the condescension, the marks of deference, the acts of courtesy shown to others.

4) In our *conversations*, humility prompts us to let others talk about what is of interest to them and to speak little ourselves. Above all, it prevents us from speaking of ourselves and of whatever concerns us. It takes a saint to speak ill of self and mean it ;[1] and to speak well of self is boasting. We must not, under the pretext of humility go to any extremes. St. Francis de Sales[2] says that "if some great servants of God have pretended to be fools, to render themselves more abject in the eyes of the world, we must admire, but not imitate them; for having had peculiar and extraordinary motives that induced them to this excess, no one ought thence to draw any consequence for himself."

Humility is, then, a most practical and sanctifying virtue; it extends to the whole man, and aids us in the practice of all the other virtues.

§ III. Meekness[3]

1154. Our Lord rightly associates meekness with humility, since the former cannot be practiced without the latter. We shall treat : 1º of its *nature*, 2º of its *excellence*, 3º of its *practice*.

I. *Nature of the Virtue of Meekness*

1155. 1º **Its Constituent Elements.** Meekness is a complex virtue which comprises three principal elements : a) a certain *self-mastery*, which forestalls and checks impulses of anger; from this point of view it is related to temperance; b) tolerance of the *failings of others*, which demands patience and, therefore, the virtue of fortitude; c) *forgiveness*

---

is truly humble always maintains the body. There is, exteriorly, a self-restraint, a reserve, a calm which gives to the whole physiognomy that charm which we express by the word "modesty". The look is modest, the voice is modest, the laugh is modest, and every movement is modest... Nothing is further from affectation than true modesty. St. Paul says : Let your modesty be known to all men, the Lord is nigh! There, in fact, is the secret of this ravishing and holy attitude. God is nigh to this soul, and this soul never forgets it : it lives in His Presence, and acts under His Eye, in the company of the good Angels. "

1 " We often confess ourselves to be nothing, nay, misery itself, and the refuse of the world; but we would be very sorry that any one should believe us, or tell others that we are really such miserable wretches. On the contrary, we pretend to retire, and hide ourselves, so that the world may run after us, and seek us out. We feign to wish ourselves considered as the last in the company, and sit down at the lowest end of the table; but it is with a view that we may be desired to pass to the upper end. True humility never makes a show of herself, nor uses many humble words. " (ST. FRANCIS DE SALES, *Devout Life*, III Part, C. V).

2 *Ibid.*

3 ST. JOHN CLIMACUS, *The Ladder of Paradise*, XXIV; ST. FRANCIS OF SALES, *Devout Life*, P. III, C. VIII-IX; OLIER, *Introduction*, C. X; CARD. BONA, *Manuductio*, C. XXXII; RIBET, *Ascétique*; VEN. A. CHEVRIER, *Le Véritable Disciple*, p. 345-354. — See references under Anger, Nº 853 and Fraternal Charity, Nº 1236.

of injuries, and *benevolence* towards all, even our enemies; in this respect it is inclusive of charity. From this we see that it is a combination of virtues, rather than a distinct virtue.

1156. 2° Meekness may be defined as *a supernatural, moral virtue, by which we prevent and restrain anger, bear with the neighbor in spite of his defects, and treat him with kindliness.*

Meekness is not that weakness of character which conceals deep resentment behind a suave demeanor. It is an interior virtue, existing both in the will and in the emotions, in order to make peace reign therein; but it is also outwardly manifested in word and gesture, by affability of manner. [1] It is exercised not only toward the neighbor, but also with regard to self and all beings animate or inanimate.

II. *Its Excellence*

Meekness is excellent both *in itself* and in its *effects*.

1157. 1° In itself, it is, as Father Olier [2] puts it, " the completeness of perfection in the Christian, for it presupposes in him absolute self-effacement and the death of all self-interest. "

Hence, he adds : " True meekness is hardly found outside those *innocent* souls within which Jesus Christ has continually dwelt from the moment of their regeneration. " *Penitent* souls rarely possess it in all its perfection, because few of them labor with sufficient energy and constancy to destroy the faults they have contracted. Thus Bossuet tells us that " the true mark of innocence whether preserved from the beginning or recovered, is meekness. " [3]

1158. 2° The great *benefit* meekness brings us is the reign of peace in the soul, peace with *God*, peace with the *neighbor*, peace with *ourselves*.

a) Peace with God, because it makes us accept all events, even the most adverse, with calm and serenity, as means of growing in virtue, and especially in the love of God : " And we know, " says St. Paul, " that *to them that love God, all things work together unto good.* " [4]

b) Peace with our *neighbor;* for, in preventing and repressing the impulses of anger, meekness makes us bear with

---

[1] St. Jerome gives an excellent description of this virtue in his *Commentary on Galatians*, V. 20 : " Meekness is a mild virtue, it is kindly, serene, gentle in speech, gracious in manner, it is a delicate blending of all the virtues. Kindness is akin to it, for, like meekness, it seeks to please; still it differs from the latter in that it is not as winsome and seems more rigid, for though equally prompt to accomplish good and render service, it lacks that charm, that gentleness that wins all hearts.
[2] *Introduction*, C. X. — [3] *Méditations sur l'Évangile*. — [4] *Romans*, VIII, 28.

our neighbor's faults and enables us to keep on good terms with others, or at least, to remain inwardly unruffled if others be provoked at us.

c) Peace with *ourselves.* If we happen to commit a fault, or make a blunder, we do not become impatient or lose our temper; but we reproach ourselves quietly and kindly, and learn by the experience to be more on our guard. Thus we avoid the mistake of those who, " being overcome by anger, are angry for having been angry, and vexed to see themselves vexed. " [1] Thus, we preserve our peace, which is one of the greatest blessings.

III. *The Practice of the Virtue of Meekness.*

1159. 1º Beginners exercise themselves in this virtue by fighting anger and the desire for revenge, as well as every impulse of passion stirring in the soul (n. 861-863).

1160. 2º Souls advanced in the way of perfection strive to attract to themselves the meekness of Jesus, which He teaches so admirably by word and example. [2]

A) Our Lord attaches such great importance to this virtue, that He had it announced by the prophets as one of the marks of the promised Messias, and had the fulfilment of this prophecy pointed out by the Evangelists. [3]

1161. **B)** He offers Himself as a *model* of that meekness and invites us to become His disciples, because He is meek and humble of heart. [4]

a) He fulfils perfectly the ideal of meekness described by the prophets. When He announces the Gospel, it is not with violence, animosity and bitterness, but with calm and serenity.

He utters no shouts, no useless cries, no angry words ; noise dies out and does no good. His manner is so mild that He does not break the bruised reed nor quench the smoking flax, that is, the spark of faith and love that still remain in the sinner's soul. To draw men to Himself, He is neither melancholy nor impetuous. He is kindness and meekness itself, and He invites those who labor and are heavily laden to come and seek repose in Him.

1162. **b)** Towards His *Apostles :* 1) His conduct is full of meekness : He bears with their faults, their ignorance, their rudeness; He proceeds tactfully with them, revealing

1 ST. FRANCIS DE SALES, *Devout Life*, Part III, C. IX.
2 P. CHEVRIER, *Le Disciple*, p. 345-354.
3 *Isaias*, XLII, 1-4; *Matth.*, XII, 17-21. — 4 *Matth.*, XI, 29.

to them the truth only by degrees and in the measure in which they can stand it, leaving to the Holy Ghost the care of finishing His work.

He defends them against the unjust accusations of the Pharisees who reproached them with not observing the fasts. He reprimands them when they fail in meekness towards the children that gather round about Him, and when they would wish to bring down fire from Heaven on a village of Samaria. When Peter strikes Malchus with the sword, He upraids him; but He forgives him his threefold denial and makes him atone for it with a threefold profession of love.

2) Furthermore, He *preaches* meekness to the apostolic workers: they must have the simplicity of the dove as well as the cunning of the serpent. They must be as lambs in the midst of wolves; they must not resist evil, but proffer the left cheek to him who strikes them on the right; they must yield their cloak rather than appear before the bar of justice, and they must pray for them that persecute them.

1163. c) He readily forgives *sinners*, even the most guilty, as soon as He sees in them the least indication of repentance.

It is with no small degree of delicacy that He elicits the avowals of the Samaritan woman and effects her conversion; that He pardons the adulteress and the penitent thief, for He is come to call, not the just, but sinners to repentance. Like the good shepherd, He goes in search of His stray sheep and brings it back to the fold upon His shoulders. He even gives His life for His sheep. If at times He speaks severelk to the Scribes and the Pharisees, it is precisely because they impose upon others unbearable burdens and thus hinder them from entering into the kingdom of God.

d) Even with His enemies He is meek: Judas after his sin of treason hears himself called by the sweet name of friend. Upon the Cross He prays for His executioners and asks His Father to take account of their ignorance and pardon them.

1164. C) *In order to imitate Our Lord* we must: **a)** avoid quarrels, harsh or hurtful words and actions, so as not to frighten away the timid. We must strive never to render evil for evil, to avoid all abruptness of manner, and never to speak while in an angry mood.

b) We must try to treat with due regard all those that approach us; to present to all a pleasant and affable mien, even if they be a cause of fatigue or boredom to us; to be especially kind to the poor, the afflicted, the sick, sinners, the timid, children; to soothe with a few kind words the sting which the reprimands we are called upon to administer may leave; to be ever ready to render service, at times to do even more than we are asked and, above all, to do so with good grace. We must, if need be, be ready to bear affronts, and to turn the left cheek to him who strikes us on the right.

1165. 3° Perfect souls strive to imitate the very meekness of God, as Father Olier [1] remarks: " He is meekness

---

[1] *Introduction*, C. X.

itself, and when He wishes to share it with a soul, He makes His abode therein in such a way that nothing of the flesh remains in it, but is all absorbed in God, in His being, His substance, His perfections, so that all that it does is done in meekness, and even when moved by zeal, it is always in a meek manner, because bitterness and harshness no longer have any part in it, just as they can have no part in God Himself."

1166. Conclusion. Not to be too long, we end here the explanation of the cardinal virtues. **a)** They *discipline, school* and perfect all our faculties by subjecting them to the dominion of reason and will. Thus, the original order that once prevailed in the soul, that is, the submission of the body to the soul, and the subjection of the lower faculties to the will, is gradually restored.

b) The cardinal virtues do even more : not only do they eliminate the obstacles which impede our union with God, but they *initiate* that union. For the *prudence* we acquire is a participation in God's wisdom, and our *justice* a participation in His justice; our *fortitude* proceeds from Him and unites us to Him; our *temperance* makes us share in the wondrous poise and harmony that exist in Him. When we yield *obedience* to our Superiors, it is He Whom we obey. *Chastity* is but a means of approaching the perfection of His purity. *Humility* creates a void in our soul solely that it may be filled with God, and our *meekness* is but a participation in the meekness of God.

Thus, our union with God, begun by the practice of the moral virtues, will be perfected by the theological virtues, the object of which is God Himself.

CHAPTER III

The Theological Virtues

1167. 1° St. Paul makes mention of the three theological virtues. He groups them together as three essential elements of the Christian life, and points out their superiority over the moral virtues. [1] Thus he urges the Thessalonians to put on the *breast-plate of faith* and *charity* and the *helmet of hope*, [2] and he praises in them the *work of faith*, the *labor of charity* and the *enduring of hope*. [3] As con-

---

[1] P. PRAT, *The Theology of St. Paul*, II.
[2] *I Thess.*, V, 8. — [3] *I Thess.*, I, 3.

trasted with the *charisms* (special gifts), which are of a transitory nature, faith, hope and charity are lasting. [1]

1168. 2° Their rôle is to *unite us to God* through Jesus Christ, in order to make us sharers in the Divine life. They are, then, at once *unifying* and *transforming* virtues.

a) Thus, *faith* unites us to God, *Infinite Truth*, and makes us enter into communion with the *divine mind*, since it makes us know God as He made Himself known through revelation. Thereby faith prepares us for the *Beatific Vision*.

b) *Hope* unites us to God, *Supreme Beatitude*, and makes us love Him for His *goodness to us*. By it we *firmly* and *trustfully* expect the happiness of Heaven, as well as the means necessary to attain it. Through it we prepare ourselves for the full enjoyment of celestial bliss.

c) *Charity* unites us to God, *Infinite Goodness*, and makes us love Him as infinitely *good and lovable in Himself*, and establishes a holy friendship between Himself and us, a friendship which makes us partake even now of His life, because we begin to love Him as He loves Himself.

Here on earth, charity always includes the other two theological virtues. It is, so to speak, their *soul*, their *vital principle* or *life;* so much so, that, devoid of charity, faith and hope remain imperfect, inert, dead. Thus, according to St. Paul, faith is not complete unless it bring forth love and action: "Faith that worketh by charity;" [2] nor is hope complete until it gives us a foretaste of heavenly bliss through the possession of sanctifying grace and charity.

ART. I. THE VIRTUE OF FAITH [3]

Three things must be explained: 1° the *nature* of faith; 2° its *sanctifying power;* 3° the *progressive growth* in the *practice* of this virtue.

I. *The Nature of Faith*

We briefly recall here what we have explained more at length in *Dogmatic and Moral Theology*.

---

[1] *I Cor.*, XIII. 13. — [2] *Galatians*, V, 6.

[3] ST. AUGUSTINUS, *Enchiridion de Fide, Spe et Caritate;* ST. THOMAS, II^a II^æ, q. I-XVI; JOANNES A S. THOMA, *De fide;* SUAREZ, *De fide;* J DE LUGO, *De virtute fidei divinæ;* SALMANTICENSES, *De fide;* SCARAMELLI, *Guide ascétique,* t. IV, art. 1; BILLOT, *De virtutibus infusis,* thesis IX-XXIV; GAY, *Christian Life and Virtues,* Vol. I, Treat. III; NEWMAN, *Discourses to Mixed Congregations,* X, XI; FINLAY, *Divine Faith;* BAINVEL, *Faith and the Act of Faith;* VAUGHAN, *Faith and Folly; Thoughts for All Times* P. III, C. VI, VII; McNABB, *On Faith,* McKENNA, *Theology of Faith;* HEDLEY, *The Spirit of Faith.*

1169. 1° **The meaning of faith in Holy Writ.** The word *faith* signifies, in the most instances, *an assent of the mind to truth*, which assent, however, is based upon *trust*. To believe any one, we must have confidence in him.

A) In the *Old* Testament, faith is presented as a necessary virtue, on which depends the salvation or the ruin of the nation : " Believe in the Lord your God, and you shall be secure." [1] " If you will not believe, you shall not continue." [2] This faith is an assent given to the word of God, but accompanied by trust, self-abandonment, and love.

B) In the *New* Testament, faith is so essential that to believe means to profess Christianity, and not to believe is not to be a Christian : " *He that believeth and is baptized shall be saved: but he that believeth not shall be condemned.*" [3] Faith means the acceptance of the Gospel preached by Jesus Christ and His Apostles ; therefore, it presupposes preaching : "*Faith, then cometh by hearing.*" [4] This faith, then, is not an intuition of the heart, nor a direct vision : "*We now see through a glass in a dark manner;*" [5] but it is the acceptance of divine testimony, free and enlightened, since man, on the one hand, can refuse belief, and on the other, he does not arrive at belief without reasons, without an intimate conviction that God has really spoken. [6] This faith is associated with hope and is perfected by charity : "*Faith that worketh by charity.*" [7]

1170. 2° **Definition.** Faith is *a theological virtue that inclines the mind, under the influence of the will and of grace, to yield a firm assent to revealed truths, because of the authority of God.*

A) Faith is before all else an act of the *intellect*, since it is question of knowing the truth. But, since this truth is not self-evident our assent cannot be effected without the action of the *will*, bidding the mind study the reasons for believing, and, when these are convincing, giving a further command to assent. Because it is question of a supernatural act, *grace* must intervene to enlighten the mind, and to aid the will. It is in this way that faith becomes a *free, supernatural* and *meritorious* act.

B) The *material object* or the subject-matter of our faith is the sum-total of revealed truths, both those that reason alone could not possibly discover, and those others which reason could come to know, but which faith makes better known.

All these truths refer to God and to Jesus Christ. They refer to *God* with regard to the Oneness of His Nature and His Trinity of Persons, our first beginning and our last end. They refer to *Jesus Christ*, Our Redeemer and Mediator, Who is none other than the Eternal Son of God made man in order to save us. Hence, these

---

[1] *II Paral.*, XX, 20. — [2] *Isaias*, VII, 9. — [3] *Mark*, XVI, 16. — [4] *Rom.*, X, 17. [5] *I Cor.*, XIII, 12. — [6] *Phil.*, III, 8-10; *I Peter.*, III, 15. — [7] *Galat.*, V, 6.

truths refer likewise to the work of Redemption and to whatever is
connected therewith. In other words, we believe what we shall one day
behold in the glory of Heaven : " *This is eternal life: that they may
know thee, the only true God, and Jesus Christ, whom thou hast sent.*[1]"

1171. **C**) The formal object or what is generally called
the *motive* of our faith is *divine authority* made known
through revelation and imparting to us some of the secrets
of God. Thus, faith is a virtue entirely supernatural, both
as to its object and its motive; it puts us in communion
with the divine thought.

D) Ofttimes revealed truth is authentically proposed to
us by the *Church* which Jesus Christ instituted as the official
interpreter of His teaching; this teaching is then termed a
doctrine *of Catholic faith.* If there has been no authentic
definition of the Church regarding revealed truth, the said
teaching is simply called a doctrine of *Divine faith.*

E) There is nothing more firm than the assent of faith.
Having full confidence in the Divine authority much more
than in our own lights, we believe revealed truth with our
whole soul. We do so with a far greater sense of security,
inasmuch as divine grace comes to facilitate and strengthen
our assent. And so it happens that the assent given by
faith to revealed truth is more prompt and more firm than
that given to natural truth.

II. *The Sanctifying Power of the Virtue of Faith*

1172. Faith thus understood cannot but have an important share in our sanctification. By bringing us into communion with divine thought it becomes the *foundation* of
our supernatural life and *unites* us *to God* in a most intimate way.

1173. 1° It is the **foundation** of our supernatural life.
We said that humility is looked upon as the foundation
of all the virtues, and we explained (n. 1138) in what
sense it is so regarded; but faith is itself the *foundation
of humility* (which, as we have said, was unknown to
Paganism) and therefore it is in a truer sense the foundation
of all the virtues.

The better to understand this fact, we have but to comment on the words of the Council of Trent stating that
"*faith is the beginning, the basis and the root of all justification,*"[2] and by that very fact, of sanctification.

---

[1] *John*, XVII, 3. — [2] *Sess.* VI, Cap. 8.

A) It is the *beginning* of justification, because it is the mysterious means used by God to initiate us into His life, to make us know Him as He knows Himself. On our part, it is the first supernatural disposition for justification, without which we can neither hope nor love. It is, so to speak, the taking possession of God and of divine things. In order to lay hold upon the supernatural and live by it we must first of all come to the knowledge of it : " *Nothing can be willed that is not foreknown.* " Now, we arrive at a knowledge of the supernatural through faith, a new light added to reason, which enables us to look into a new world, the supernatural world. It is like a telescope that enables us to discover far-off things invisible to the naked eye. Still, this is but an imperfect comparison, for a telescope is an outward instrument, whilst faith penetrates into the recesses of the mind and sharpens its power of perception as well as its field of vision.

1174. **B)** Faith is likewise the *foundation* of the spiritual life. This simile is intended to show that sanctity is like an edifice, vast and lofty, the basis of which is faith. Now, the deeper the foundations, the higher the edifice may rise without danger to its stability. Hence, it is important to strengthen the faith of devout souls, especially of seminarians and priests, so that upon this solid foundation may rise the temple of Christian perfection.

C) Lastly, faith is the *root* of sanctity. Roots seek in the soil for the chemicals necessary to nutrition and growth in a tree ; so, faith sinking its roots into the furthest recesses of the soul, and feeding there on divine truths, furnishes perfection with a rich, life-giving sap. Roots, if deep, lend solidity to the tree they sustain ; so the soul, imbedded in faith, withstands spiritual storms. Hence, deep faith is of capital importance in order to attain a high degree of perfection.

1175. 2° Faith *unites* us *to God*, and makes us share in His thought and in His life. This is God's own knowledge of Himself given in some measure to man. " By it, " says Mgr. Gay, " the light of God becomes our light; His wisdom our wisdom; His knowledge our knowledge; His Spirit our spirit; His life our life. " [1]

It unites our intellect directly to the Divine Wisdom; but, since the act of faith cannot be performed without the action of the will, this faculty also has a share in the results produced in our soul by faith. One may say, therefore, that faith is a source of *light* to the mind, a source of

---

[1] *Life and Virtues*, Vol. I, p. 156.

strength and *comfort* to the will, a source of *merit* to the entire soul.

1176. A) It is a light which illumines our intellect, and differentiates the Christian from the philosopher, as reason distinguishes a human being from an animal.   There is in us a threefold knowledge : *sense* knowledge, attained through the senses; *rational* knowledge, acquired through the intellect; and *spiritual* or *supernatural* knowledge, obtained through faith.   The last is by far superior to the other two.

a) It widens the scope of our knowledge of God and the things of God.   Reason tells us little of God's nature and of His inner life, whilst faith teaches us that He is a living God; that from all eternity He has begotten a Son, and that from the mutual love of the Father and the Son proceeds a Third Person, the Holy Ghost; that the Son became man for our salvation and that those who believe in Him become the adopted sons of God; that the Holy Ghost comes to dwell in our souls, to sanctify them and to endow them with a supernatural organism which enables us to perform acts that are Godlike and meritorious.   This is but a portion of what has been revealed to us.

b) It gives us a *deeper insight* into the truths already known by reason.   Thus the moral precepts of the Gospel are far more definite, far more perfect than those of mere natural ethics.

To be convinced of this we have but to read the *Sermon on the Mount.* From the very outset, Our Lord does not hesitate to proclaim blessed the poor, the meek, the persecuted ; He requires His disciples to love their enemies, to pray for them and to do good to them.   The holiness He preaches is not legal or exterior sanctity; it is an inward holiness, based on the love of God and of the neighbor.   To arouse our fervor, He proposes to us the most perfect ideal, God and His perfections, and since God seems far removed from us, He sends us His Son from Heaven to be made man, to live our own life, and thus to offer us a concrete example of the perfect life which we must lead on earth.   To impart to us the strength and constancy such an undertaking demands, He does not rest satisfied with going before us, but He comes Himself to dwell within us with all His graces and virtues.   We cannot, then, plead weakness.   He is Himself our strength, as well as our light.

1177. B) That our faith is a source of strength is well brought out in the Epistle to the Hebrews. [1]

Faith provides us with *deep convictions* which greatly strengthen our will : **a)** It shows us what God has done and what He incessantly does in our behalf, how He lives and acts in our soul to sanctify it,

---

[1] *Hebr.*, XI.

how Jesus incorporates us into Himself and makes us share in His own
life (n. 188-189); then, having our eyes directed towards the author
of our faith, Who preferred the Cross and humiliation to joy and
success, "*who having joy set before him, endured the cross, despising
the shame,*"[1] we feel ourselves strong enough to carry our cross courageously after Jesus.

b) Faith ever keeps before our eyes the *eternal reward*
that will be the rich fruit of the sufferings of a moment:
"*That which is at present momentary and light of our tribulation worketh for us above measure exceedingly an eternal
weight of glory.*"[2] Then, with St. Paul, we say: "*I reckon
that the sufferings of this time are not worthy to be compared
with the glory to come,*"[3] and like him we rejoice, even in
the midst of tribulations,[4] for each of these, if patiently
borne, will earn for us a further degree of God's vision and
of God's love.

c) If we are at times conscious of our weakness, faith
reminds us that, since God is Himself our strength and our
support, we have nothing to fear, even when the world and
the devil join forces against us: "*And this is the victory
which overcometh the world: Our faith.*"[5]

This is most evident in the wondrous change wrought by the Holy
Ghost in the Apostles. Armed at His coming with the power of God,
they, who up to this time, had been timid and slothful, go courageously
to meet all kinds of trials — scourgings, imprisonment, and death
itself — glad to undergo suffering in the name of Jesus: "*They went
forth rejoicing that they were accounted worthy to suffer reproach for
the name of Jesus.*"[6]

1178. **C)** Faith is likewise a *source of comfort*, not only
in the midst of tribulations and of humiliations, but also
when we have the misfortune of losing our dear ones. We
are not among those who sorrow without hope. We know
that death is but a sleep, to be soon followed by the resurrection, and that through death we merely exchange a
temporary dwelling for an everlasting mansion.

Our chief consolation is the doctrine of the *Communion of Saints*.
Whilst awaiting the day when we shall be reunited to those that have
departed this life, we are even now bound to them by the most intimate ties in Christ Jesus. We pray that their time of trial be shortened and their entrance into Heaven hastened; they in their turn, now
assured of their salvation, ardently pray that we may one day join
them.

1179. **D)** Finally, faith is a *source of manifold merit*:
a) The *act of faith* itself is *highly meritorious*, for it subjects
to divine authority the best that is in us, our intellect and

---

[1] *Hebr.*, XII, 2. — [2] *II Cor.*, IV, 17. — [3] *Rom.*, VIII, 18. — [4] *Rom.*, V, 3-5.
[5] *I John*, V, 4. — [6] *Acts* V., 41.

our will. This faith has all the more merit since in our times it is made the object of more numerous attacks, and since those who make open profession of their faith are, in certain countries, exposed to ridicule and persecution.

b) Furthermore, it is faith that *renders meritorious our other acts*, since they cannot become so without a supernatural motive and the help of grace (nn. 126, 239); but faith by directing the soul towards God and towards Jesus Christ enables us to act in all things with supernatural intentions. Likewise, by disclosing to us our own weakness and God's power, faith makes us pray ardently to obtain His grace.

III. *Practice of the Virtue of Faith*

1180. Since faith is at once a *gift of God* and a *free assent* of the mind to revealed truth, it is evident that in order to grow in faith, we must rely on *prayer* and our own *personal efforts*. Under this twofold influence, faith will become more enlightened, simple, strong and active.

We shall apply this principle to the various stages of the spiritual life.

1181. 1° **Beginners** should strive to strengthen their faith.

A) They *thank God* for this great gift, which is the foundation of all others, and with their whole soul they repeat the words of St. Paul : "Thanks be to God for his unspeakable gift"[1]. They thank Him all the more at the sight of so many unbelievers round about them. They pray therefore for the grace to preserve this gift in spite of all the dangers that beset it, and implore God's help for the conversion of unbelievers, heretics and apostates.

1182. **B**) With humble submission and with a firm conviction *they make acts of faith*, saying with the Apostles: "*Increase our faith*"[2]. Moreover, to prayer they add *study* or the *reading* of books calculated to enlighten and strengthen their faith. Much reading is done in our day, yet how few even among intelligent Christians read serious books on religion and spirituality! What a mistake! Men wish to know all things, save the one thing necessary.

1183. **C**) They *avoid* carefully whatever could trouble their faith: **a**) those *dangerous writings*, wherein the truths of faith are either attacked, ridiculed or called into question.

Most of the books that appear in our day, not only doctrinal works, but novels and plays as well, contain open or covert attacks against our

---

[1] *II Cor.*, IX, 15. — [2] *Luke*, XVII, 5.

faith. Unless we be on our guard, we are liable to drink in little by
little the poison of unbelief or, at least, to lose the purity of faith, and
a time may come when, shaken by hesitation and doubt, we no longer
know how to resist. In this matter we must respect the wise prescriptions of the Church, made known to us in her catalogue of bad or dangerous books, and not make light of them on the plea that we are
immune to the danger. In truth we are never immune. Balmes, one
of the great defenders of the Church, gifted with a keen mind and a
well-balanced judgment, and obliged as he was to read heretical books
in order to refute them, used to say to his friends: "You know how
deeply rooted within me are orthodox sentiments and doctrines. Not
withstanding, I never read a forbidden book without feeling the need
of going to the Bible, the Imitation, or Louis of Granada for strength
against unbelief. What will become of our foolish youth, which in its
inexperience dares read everything without the necessary safeguards?
The mere thought of it fills me with horror."[1] For the same good
reason no doubt we must avoid the conversations and discourses of
unbelievers.

b) Beginners likewise shun that *pride of intellect* which
seeks to bring all down to its own level and refuses to
accept what lies beyond its comprehension. They remember that there is above us all a Spirit whose infinite intelligence sees what our reason cannot understand, and that God
greatly honors us by the communication of His thought.
Once, therefore, we have ascertained that He has spoken,
there is but one rational attitude to take, to welcome gratefully this superadded knowledge. If we bow before the
authority of a man of genius, who deigns to impart to us
some of his knowledge, with what confidence should we not
bow before Infinite Wisdom Itself?

1184. **D**) With regard to *temptations* against faith, a distinction is to be made between those that remain *vague* and
those that definitely center around some particular object.

a) When they are *vague*, taking such form for instance
as: *Who knows if all that be true?* then we must quietly
drive them away.

1) We are in possession of truth, and we are sure of our title; this is
enough for us. 2) Besides, we have seen that our faith rests upon solid
grounds; again, this suffices, for we cannot be every day raising doubts
over things already proved. In the affairs of every-day life, we do not
stop when such doubts, such inane ideas, cross our mind, but we go
on, and certitude reasserts itself. 3) Lastly, others more intelligent
than ourselves believe these truths, and are persuaded that they are
well proved; therefore, I submit to their judgment which is far wiser
than that of those extremists who take a malicious delight in attracting
notice by undermining all the bases of certitude. To these common-
sense reasons we should add prayer : " I believe Lord, help thou my
unbelief."[2]

[1] A. DE BLANCHE-RAFFIN, *J. Balmes*, p. 44. — [2] *Mark*, IX, 23.

1185. b) If the *temptations* are *well-defined*, bearing or some particular doctrine, we hold firmly to our belief since we are in possession of the truth. But we seize the first opportunity to clear up the difficulty, either by personal study, if we have the intelligence and the documents required, or by consulting some learned man who may help us to solve the problem more easily. If we add prayer to this earnest and loyal research, a solution, as a rule, will not be long in coming.

However, we must remember that such a solution does not always do away with the difficulty. There are at times historical, critical, exegetical objections that can be cleared away only after long years of study. We must reflect, then, that once we have a good reason to hold something as true, wisdom demands that we continue to give it our assent even while the darkness lasts. The difficulty does not destroy the grounds of belief, it simply shows the deficiency of our minds. "Ten thousand difficulties do not make one doubt." [1]

1186. 2º **Advanced** souls practice not only faith, but the *spirit of faith:* " *The just man liveth by faith.*" [2]

A) They read the Gospel with loving attention, happy to follow Jesus step by step, to relish His maxims, to contemplate His examples in order to imitate them. Jesus becomes the center of their thoughts: they seek Him in their readings and in their labor, desiring to know Him better so that they may love Him more.

1187. **B**) They accustom themselves to see all things, to judge all things from the point of view of faith. 1) They see the Hand of the Creator in all *His works*, and they hear all creatures repeat the refrain : " *He made us, and not we ourselves.*" [3] Hence, it is God Whom they admire everywhere. 2) The *persons* that surround them are to them so many images of God, children of the same Heavenly Father, brethren in Christ Jesus. 3) Events, which at times are so baffling to unbelievers, are interpreted by them in the light of the great principle that all is ordained in behalf of the elect, and that good and evil are dispensed with a view to our salvation and perfection.

1188. **C**) Above all, they strive to *be led* in all things according to the principles of faith. 1) Their *judgments* are based upon the maxims of the Gospel, not upon those of the world; 2) their *words* are inspired by the Christian spirit, not by the spirit of the world, for they conform their words to their judgments and thus triumph over

---

[1] NEWMAN, *Apologia*, p. 239. — [2] *Rom.*, I, 17. — [3] *Ps.* XCIX, 3.

human respect; 3) their *actions* become more and more Christlike for they delight in considering Our Lord as their model, and thus escape being carried away by the examples of worldlings. In short, they live a life of faith.

1189. **D)** They strive, finally, to spread round about them *this faith* that is in them: 1) through their *prayers,* asking God to send apostolic workers to labor for the evangelization of infidels and heretics: "*Pray ye therefore the Lord of the harvest, that he may send forth laborers into his harvest;*" [1] 2) through their *example,* discharging so well their duties of state, that those who witness their life may feel drawn to imitate them; 3) through their *words,* declaring in all simplicity but without any human respect, that they find in their faith *power* to do good, and comfort in the midst of their trials; 4) through their *works,* doing their share by their generous offerings, their sacrifices, and their personal efforts for the moral and religious instruction and education of the neighbor.

3° **Perfect** souls, by cultivating the gifts of *knowledge* and *understanding,* perfect their faith still more, as we shall explain when treating of the *unitive way.*

Art. II. The Virtue of Hope [2]

We shall describe: 1° its *nature;* 2° its *sanctifying power;* 3° its *practice.*

I. *Nature of Hope*

1190. 1° **Different significations.** **A)** In the natural order, hope means two things: a *passion* and a *sentiment.*

a) Hope is one of the eleven passions (n. 787). It is, therefore, an *impulse of the sensitive appetite,* that tends towards some *absent good apprehended* by the senses, and which is attainable, but not without some difficulty. b) Hope is one of the worthiest *sentiments* of the human heart, which tends towards some absent *moral good,* despite the obstacles that stand in the way of its acquisition. This sentiment plays an important part in human life; it sustains men in their arduous undertakings: the laborer when he sows, the seafarer when he sails, traders and pliers of fortune when they embark on some enterprise.

B) There is also a *supernatural* hope that sustains the Christian midst the obstacles encountered in the attainment of salvation and perfection. The object of this hope is

---

[1] *Matth.,* IX, 38.
[2] St. Thomas, IIa IIæ, Q. XVII-XX; Suarez, *De Spe;* St. Francis of Sales, *The Love of God,* Book II, C. XV-XVII; Scaramelli-Stockman, *Christian Perfection,* P. IV, Art. II; Gay, *Christian Life and Virtues,* Vol. I, Treat. V; Faber, *Growth in Holiness,* II.

eternal life and the means of reaching it. Since this hope is founded upon the power and the goodness of God, it is firm and unshakable.

1191. 2° **Its essential elements.** If we analyze this virtue, we notice that it comprises three principal elements:

a) The *love* and *desire of supernatural good,* that is to say, of our supreme happiness, which is God.

The origin and development of this sentiment is as follows. The desire for happiness is universal. Now, faith shows us that God alone can constitute our happiness. We, therefore, love Him as the source of our happiness. This is an *interested* love, but it is *supernatural* since it has for object God as known to us through faith. Because this good is difficult to attain, we instinctively experience fear lest we fail to attain it, and to overcome this fear a second element intervenes, namely, the *well-founded expectation* of obtaining it.

b) Evidently, this expectation is not based upon our own strength which is insufficient of itself to attain such good, but it is based upon God, upon His *all-powerful help.* It is from Him that we expect all the necessary graces to obtain perfection in this life and salvation in the next.

c) But grace demands our *co-operation,* and hence there is a third element. This is an earnest *effort* to tend towards God and make use of the means of salvation placed at our disposal. This effort must be all the more determined and steadfast, the higher the object of our hope.

1192. 3° **Definition.** From what we have said, we may thus define hope: *a theological virtue that makes us desire God as our highest good, and expect with a firm confidence eternal bliss and the means of attaining it, because of God's goodness and power.*

A) The primary and essential **object** of our hope is God Himself, inasmuch as He constitutes our happiness; it is God eternally possessed by clear vision and undivided love. Our Lord said that eternal life is the knowledge, the vision of God and of Him Whom He sent: "*Now this is eternal life: That they may know thee, the only true God, and Jesus Christ Whom thou hast sent.*" [1] Besides, since we cannot attain this object without the help of grace, our hope is, likewise, directed towards all the supernatural aids needed in order to avoid sin, overcome temptation, and acquire Christian virtue; it even extends to temporal goods in the measure in which they are necessary or profitable to our perfection and salvation.

---

[1] *John,* XVII, 3.

1193. **B)** The motive of hope depends upon the point of view from which we consider hope itself. **a)** If we think, as Scotus did, that its principal act is the *desire* or *love* for God inasmuch as He is our happiness, the motive will be God's *goodness towards us*. **b)** If, with St. Thomas, we consider hope as consisting essentially in the *expectation* of a good difficult to attain, namely, the possession of God, then the motive will be the *assisting omnipotence* of God, which elevates our souls, snatches them from the hold of earthly goods and bears them towards Heaven. The *Divine promises* simply confirm the certainty of such help.

We may, then, say that the adequate motive of hope is both the goodness of God and His power.

II. *The Sanctifying Power of Hope*

Hope furthers our sanctification in three principal ways: 1° it *unites* us *to God;* 2° it imparts *efficacy to our prayers;* 3° it is a principle of *fruitful activity*.

1194. 1° It *unites us to God by detaching us from earthly goods*. We are drawn by *sense-pleasures*, the gratification of *pride*, the fascination of *wealth*, and lastly by the higher, *natural joys* of the mind and heart. Hope, based upon a lively faith, shows us that all these earthly joys lack two elements: *perfection* and *permanence*.

A) None of these goods is perfect enough to satisfy us. Having provided a short period of enjoyment, they soon produce satiety and weariness. Our heart is too great, its aspirations too vast and too high to be satisfied with material goods, which are but means of reaching a far nobler end. Neither do the natural goods of the mind and heart suffice us. Our intellect never rests satisfied but with the understanding of the First Cause, and our heart that seeks a perfect friend does not find him but in God. He alone possesses the plenitude of being, the perfection of beauty and of goodness, the fulness of power. He Who is perfectly self-sufficient is evidently sufficient for our happiness. The one important thing is to reach Him, and it is hope that shows Him to us stooping down in order to give Himself to us. Once we have understood this, our hearts break away from the things of earth to move towards Him, like the iron towards the magnet.

1195. **B)** Even if the goods of earth could satisfy us, they have their day and cease to be. We know this, and this thought casts its shadow upon our joy even when we possess these goods. God, on the contrary, abides forever, and death that severs us from all earthly things, merely unites us more perfectly to Him; and so despite the natural horror death inspires, we face it with confidence, because of the hope we harbor of being everlastingly united to Him Who alone can constitute our bliss.

1196. 2º It is hope also, that, united to humility, imparts *efficacy to our prayers* and thereby obtains for us all the graces of which we stand in need.

A) Nothing is more touching than the manner in which the Sacred Writers urge us to place our confidence in God. The Book of *Ecclesiasticus* sums up in these words the teaching of the Old Testament concerning hope: " My children, behold the generations of men : and know ye that *no one hath hoped in the Lord and hath been confounded. For who hath continued in his commandment and hath been forsaken? Or who hath called upon him, and he despised him? For God is compassionate and merciful, and will forgive sins in the day of tribulation.*" [1]

B) But it is chiefly in the New Testament that the efficacy of confidence is brought out.

Our Lord works His wonders in behalf of those who trust in Him. We have but to recall His attitude towards the centurion; [2] towards the paralytic who, unable to come near the Master, has himself let down through the roof [3]; towards the blind men of Jericho [4]; towards the Chanannean woman [5] who, thrice rebuked, reiterates her request; towards the sinful woman [6]; towards the leper who comes to thank Him. [7] Besides, how can we lack confidence when Christ Himself authoritatively asserts that all that we shall ask the Father in His name will be granted to us : " *Amen, amen, I say to you : if you ask the Father anything in my name, he will give it you.*" [8] Here lies the secret of our strength. When we pray in the Name of Jesus, that is to say when we trust in His merits and satisfactions, His Blood pleads more eloquently for us than do our own poor prayers.

C) Moreover, nothing *so honors God* as confidence. Thereby we proclaim His power and His goodness, whilst He, Who lets not His generosity be surpassed, responds to this confidence by a further effusion of graces. We may therefore conclude with the Council of Trent that *we must all place the most unhesitating confidence in the help of God.* [9]

1197. 3º Finally, hope is a *principle of fruitful activity.* a) It begets *holy desires,* particularly the desire to possess

[1] *Ecclus.*, II, 11-13. — [2] *Matth.*, 10, 13. — [3] *Matth.*, IX, 2.
[4] *Matth.*, IX, 29. — [5] *Matth.*, XV, 28. — [6] *Luke*, VII, 50.
[7] *Luke*, XVII, 19. — [8] *John*, XVI, 23. — [9] *Trent.*, sess. VI, C. 13.

God. This gives the soul the impulse, the motion, the necessary yearning to attain the coveted good, and it sustains our efforts until we have reached the goal.

b) It *increases our energies*, through the *prospect* of a reward that will be far in excess of our efforts. If people in the world labor with such earnestness to acquire perishable riches, if athletes submit to such arduous training, if they make desperate efforts in order to gain a corruptible crown, how much more should we not labor and endure for an eternal crown? " *And every one that striveth for the mastery refraineth himself from all things. And they indeed that they may receive a corruptible crown : but we an incorruptible one.*" [1]

1198. **c**) It infuses into us that courage, that endurance that gives us the assurance of success. Just as there is nothing so disheartening as to struggle without any hope of victory, so on the other hand, the *certainty of triumph* is a singular source of energy. Such certainty hope furnishes. Of ourselves we are weak, but we have powerful allies, God, Jesus Christ, the Most Blessed Virgin, and the Saints (n. 188-189).

Now, *if God is for us, who is against us?* [2] If Jesus, Who overcame the world and Satan, lives within us and communicates to us His Divine energy, are we not sure of triumphing with Him? If the Immaculate Virgin, who crushed the head of the serpent, sustains us by her powerful intercession, shall we lack the needed help? If God's friends, the Saints, pray in our behalf, will not these many supplications give us absolute security? And being assured of victory, are we to shrink from the few efforts required for gaining eternal possession of God?

III. *Gradual Progress in the Practice of Hope*

1199. 1º **General Principle.** To make progress in the practice of this virtue, we must strengthen its foundations and make it more *fruitful.*

A) To render our hope more *solid*, it is important that we meditate often on the motives on which it rests : the *power of God*, His goodness and the glorious promises He has made to us (n. 1193). Should these not be enough to strengthen our confidence, we have but to recall the words of St. Paul : [3] " *He that spared not even his own Son, but delivered Him up for us all, how hath he not also, with him, given us all things? Who shall accuse against the elect of*

---

[1] *I Cor.*, IX, 25. — [2] *Rom.*, VIII, 31. — [3] *Rom.*, VIII, 32-34.

God? God that justifieth. Who is he that shall condemn?
Christ Jesus that died. Yea that is risen also again; who is
at the right hand of God, who also maketh intercession for
us." Thus, on the part of God, our hope is absolutely
certain. However, on our part, we have reason to fear,
because we are far from being always faithful to correspond
perfectly to the grace of God. All our efforts, then, must
tend to render our hope more firm by making it more
fruitful.

1200. B) To gain this end, we have to collaborate with
God in the work of our sanctification : "*For we are God's*
coadjutors."¹ God by according us His grace, does not
mean to substitute His action for ours; He simply means
to supply for our insufficiency. Doubtless, He is the primary and the principal cause, but, far from suppressing our
activity, He wants to excite it and render it more effective.

St. Paul understood this well : "*But by the grace of God I am what*
I am. And his grace in me hath not been void: but I have labored
more abundantly than all they. Yet not I, but the grace of God with
me."² He urged others to do what he did himself: "*And we helping*
do exhort you that you receive not the grace of God in vain."³ It was
especially to his dear disciple Timothy that he addressed the following
urgent recommendation : "*Labor as a good soldier of Christ Jesus,*"⁴
because he was to labor not only for his own sanctification, but for that
of others. St. Peter employed the same language. He reminded his
disciples that although called to salvation, they were to render certain
that calling by the performance of good works : "*Wherefore, brethren,*
labour the more, that by good works you may make sure of your calling
and election."⁵

We must, therefore, be fully persuaded that in the work
of our sanctification all depends on God; still, we must act
as if all depended on ourselves. God never refuses us His
grace, and consequently, in actual practice all we have to
attend to is our own personal effort.

1201. 2° **Application** of the general principle to the
various degrees of the spiritual life. We can easily see
how the principle enuntiated above applies to the different
stages of the Christian life.

A) *Beginners* should be on their guard first of all against
the two excesses opposed to hope : *presumption* and *despair*.

a) .Presumption consists in expecting from God Heaven and the
graces necessary to reach it, without willing to take the means He has
ordained. One may presume on the Divine Goodness, by neglecting
God's commandments, persuading oneself that God is too good to

¹ *I Cor.*, III, 9. — ² *I Cor.*, XV, 10; *Phil.*, III, 13, 14.
³ *II Cor.*, VI, 1. — ⁴ *II Tim.*, II, 3. — ⁵ *II Peter*, I, 10.

sentence one to damnation. This is to forget that if God is good, He is likewise just and holy, and that He hates iniquity. [1] Again, one may through pride presume on one's own strength, rushing into the midst of dangers and occasions of sin, and forgetting that he that loves danger will perish in it. Our Lord promises us the victory, but on condition that we watch and pray: " *Watch ye: and pray that you enter not into temptation;*" [2] and St. Paul, who so trusted in God's grace, warns us to *work out our salvation in fear and trembling.* [3]

b) Others, on the contrary, are exposed to *discouragement* and, at times, to despair. Frequently tempted, and at times overcome in the struggle, or tortured by scruples, they lose heart; imagining they cannot reform, they come to despair of their salvation. This is a dangerous state of mind, against which we must be on our guard. We shall recall how St. Paul, tempted and realizing that of himself he could not stand fast, confidently abandoned himself to the grace of God: " *The grace of God, by Jesus Christ.*" [4] Following the example of the Apostle, we shall pray and we shall be delivered.

1202. **B)** After carefully avoiding these dangerous shoals, we must set ourselves to acquire *detachment from the goods of earth*, so that our thoughts and desires may frequently soar to Heaven. This St. Paul asks of us: " *Therefore, if you be risen with Christ, seek the things that are above, where Christ is sitting at the right hand of God. Mind the things that are above, not the things that are upon the earth.*" [5] Risen with Christ our leader, we must no longer seek and relish the things of earth, but rather those of Heaven where Jesus awaits us. Heaven is our true country, this earth but an exile. Heaven is our destiny, the true happiness we seek; this earth can yield us nothing but fleeting joys.

1203. 3° Those **advanced** in the way of perfection not only practice the virtue of hope, but entertain a *filial confidence* in God, relying on Jesus Who has become the center of their lives.

A) Incorporated into Christ, they await with *invincible trust* that Heaven where Jesus has prepared a home for them, [6] and where they already abide, through hope, in the Person of their Saviour: " *For we are saved by hope.*" [7] **a)** They await it, even in the midst of *adversities* and of the trials of this life, and with the Psalmist they say: " *I will fear no evils, for thou art with me.*" [8] Our Lord living within them comes to comfort them, saying as He did once to the Apostles: " *Peace be to you. It is I: fear not.*" [9]

1 *Ps.* CXVIII, 163. — 2 *Mark*, XIV, 38. — 3 *Phil.*, II, 12.
4 *Rom.*, VII, 24-25. — 5 *Col.*, III, 1-2. — 6 *John*, XIV, 2.
7 *Rom.*, VIII, 24. — 8 *Ps.* XXII, 4 — 9 *Luke*, XXIV, 36.

If *intrigues* and *persecution* come to trouble them, they recall what St. Vincent de Paul said to his disciples: " Even were the entire world to rise up to destroy us, it could do nothing but what is pleasing to God, in Whom we have placed our hope. "[1] If they suffer temporal losses, with the same Saint they say to themselves : "All that God does He does for the best ; and therefore we must hope that this loss, since it comes from God, will be profitable to us. "[2] If they have to face physical or moral sufferings, they look upon them as blessings from on high, destined to procure Heaven in exchange for a few fleeting pains.

1204. b) This confidence teaches them *to escape the clutches of pleasure and success*, more perilous still than the grip of suffering. "When life seems to smile upon our earthly hopes, it is hard to despise these flattering promises that seize upon our emotional nature; it is hard to steal away from the bonds of pleasure, to say to approaching bliss: you cannot satisfy my heart. "[3] But Christian souls remember that worldly joys are deceiving, that they hinder our flight towards God. In order to resist their attraction, they cling to the positive practices of mortification and seek for purer and holier joys in a more intimate friendship with Our Lord: " *To be with Jesus is a sweet paradise.* "[4]

c) If it be a sense of their *miseries* and *imperfections* that disturbs them, they reflect on these words of St. Vincent de Paul :

" You point out to me your miseries. Alas ! and who is there that is not full of them ! The only thing is to know them and to love the humiliation arising from them, as you do, without stopping save to lay the strong foundation of confidence in God ; for them the house is built upon a rock and when the storm comes it remains firm. "[5] Our miseries entitle us to Divine Mercy, when we humbly implore it, and they but fit us all the better for the reception of divine graces. St. Vincent adds that when God begins to do good to a person, He continues to do so to the end, unless that person makes himself unworthy. Thus, God's past mercies are a pledge of those to come.

1205. B) Hope makes us habitually live, in spirit, *in Heaven* and *for Heaven*. According to the beautiful prayer that the Church puts on our lips on Ascension Day, we must, even now, " *live in mind amid heavenly things.* "[6] This means that it is for Heaven that we must act and suffer, to heaven that we must turn our hearts and our desires : " *that amid the changing things of this world, our hearts may be fixed where true joy is found.* "[7] And, since

---

[1] MAYNARD, *Life and Doctrine*, p. 10. — [2] *Ibid.*, p. 9.
[3] MGR D'HULST, *Carême*, 1892, p. 201. — [4] *Imitation*, Bk. II, ch. 8.
[5] MAYNARD, *Life and Doctrine*, p. 10-11.
[6] Collect of the Mass for Feast of the Ascension.
[7] Id. for 4th Sunday after Easter.

the joys of Communion are a foretaste of Paradise, we shall, whilst waiting, seek therein the consolations our heart needs.

1206. **C)** This thought will make us pray often for the gift of *final perseverance*, the most precious of gifts. We cannot indeed merit it; but we can obtain it of the Divine Mercy. For this, we have but to join in those prayers in which the Church makes us ask for the grace of a happy death, for instance, the *Hail Mary*, which we so often recite and wherein we implore the special protection of the Blessed Virgin at the hour of death.

4° *Perfect* souls practice trust in God through *holy abandonment*. This we shall explain when speaking of the *unitive way*.

ART. III. THE VIRTUE OF CHARITY [1]

1207. The virtue of charity supernaturalizes and sanctifies the sentiment of love towards *God* and towards the *neighbor*. After a few preliminary remarks on the nature of love we shall speak: 1° of charity *towards God;* 2° of charity *towards the neighbor;* 3° of the *Sacred Heart of Jesus* as a *model* of both.

Preliminary Remarks

1208. 1° *Love in general* is an impulse, a tendency of the soul towards good. If the good towards which we are drawn is the kind which appeals to our sense-nature and which our imagination apprehends as agreeable, our love is *sensible* love. If the good is *moral* good acknowledged by our reason as worthy of esteem, our love is *rational* love. If the good is a *supernatural* good perceived by faith, our love is *Christian* love.

As we can see, love always presupposes knowledge; but, as we shall explain later on, love does not always correspond to that knowledge.

Whatever be the kind of love, four elements can be discerned in it: 1) a sort of sympathy felt for another person because of a certain harmony existing between him and ourselves. Now, this harmony does not imply that both are exactly alike, but rather that the one completes the other. 2) An *impulse* of the soul towards the beloved person, to draw close to him and enjoy his presence. 3) A certain union or communion of mind and heart to share in common the goods

---

[1] ST. BERNARD, *De diligendo Deo;* ST. THOMAS, IIa IIæ, Q. 23-44; SALMANTICENSES. Tr. XIX, *De caritate theologica;* ST. FRANCIS OF SALES, *The Love of God;* SCARAMELLI-STOCKMAN. *Manual of Christian Perfection*, P. IV, art. III; REGINALD BUCKLER, *Spiritual Perfection.* — See Nn. 306 sqq. *Notion of Christian Perfection.*

each possesses. 4) A sense of joy, of pleasure or of happiness experienced in possessing the object of our love.

1209.   2ᵒ *Christian love* is love that is supernaturalized
as to its *principle*, its *motive* and its *object*.

a) It is supernaturalized in its *principle* through the
infused virtue of charity that resides in the will.   This
virtue, set into action by actual grace, transforms naturally
good love and raises it to a higher level.

b) Then faith furnishes us with *a supernatural motive* to
sanctify our affections: it directs these, first, towards *God*,
by showing to us the Supreme, Infinite Good, which alone
can correspond to our rightful aspirations; then, towards
God's *creatures*, which it presents to us as *reflections of the
divine perfections*, so much so, that in loving them we love
God Himself.

c) The *object* of our love becomes supernaturalized in
this wise : the God we love is not God known merely by
reason, but the Living God known through faith, the
Father Who begets a Son from all eternity and adopts us
as His children; the Son, equal to the Father, Who by
taking flesh becomes our brother; the Holy Ghost, the
mutual Love of Father and Son, Who comes to diffuse
into our souls divine charity.   Men do not appear to us as
mere creatures of God, but they are seen in the light of
revelation as they truly are, the children of God, Our
Common Father, brethren in Christ Jesus, living temples
of the Holy Ghost.   All, then, is supernatural in Christian love.

According to St. Thomas [1], charity adds to love a certain perfection that proceeds from a high esteem for the
thing loved.   Hence, all charity is love, but not all love is
charity.

1210.   Charity may be thus **defined:** *a theological virtue
that causes us to love God above all things, for His own
sake, in the way in which He loves Himself, and to love the
neighbor for God's sake.*

This virtue, then, has a twofold object : *God* and the
neighbor.   These two objects, however, constitute but one,
since we love creatures only inasmuch as they are reflections
of the divine perfections, and therefore it is God Whom we
love in them.   We love the neighbor, adds St. Thomas [2],
because *God is in him* or, at least, *in order that God may be*

---

[1] *Sum. Theol.*, Iᵃ IIæ, q. 31, a. 3. — [2] *Qq. disp.* de Caritate, a. 4.

in him. This is why there is but one and the same virtue of charity.

§ I. The Love of God

We shall explain : 1° its *nature;* 2° its *sanctifying power;* 3° *how to advance in the practice of this virtue.*

I. *Its Nature*

1211. The first object of charity is God. Since He possesses the plenitude of being, the perfection of beauty and of goodness, He is infinitely lovable. It is God, considered in all the infinite reality of His perfections, and not some particular Divine attribute. The consideration of any given attribute, His mercy, for instance, readily leads us to the consideration of all His perfections; but it is not necessary to know them in detail. Simple souls love *Almighty* God as faith makes Him known to them, without analyzing His attributes.

To elucidate the notion of the love of God we shall explain the *precept* that imposes it upon us, the *motive* upon which it rests, and the different *degrees* through which we arrive at pure love.

1212. 1° **The Precept. A)** Already formulated in the Old Testament, it is reenacted by Our Lord in the New and proclaimed by Him as the sum-total of the Law and of the Prophets : " *Thou shalt love the Lord Thy God with thy whole heart, and with thy whole soul, and with all thy strength, and with all thy mind.* " [1] This is equivalent to saying that we must love God above all things and with all the faculties of our soul.

St. Francis de Sales explains this well : " Our love for Him should exceed all other affections, and reign over all the passions. He wishes that it should be the most sincere, that it should proceed from the heart and rule over its affections; He desires that we should consider it the most precious, the most valuable; He requires that it should fill the capacity of our souls; that it should be universal, extending to all our powers; that it should be elevated, and occupy the whole attention of the mind; and, in fine, that it should be generous and unalterable. " [2] The Saint ends with a magnificent effusion of love : " Yes, Lord, I belong to Thee alone : I live more in Thee than in myself, therefore, my love should be wholly centered in Thee : I should love Thee as the origin of my being, and as the term of my repose : I should love Thee more than myself, since I only exist in Thee. " [3]

1213. B) The precept of charity, then, is very extensive. *In itself* it has no limits, for *the measure of love of God is to*

---

[1] *Luke,* X, 27. — [2] *The love of God,* Bk. X, C. VI. — [3] *Ibid.,* C. X.

love Him without measure. Therefore, it obliges us *to tend unceasingly towards perfection*, (n. 353-361) and our charity must continue to grow until death. According to the doctrine of St. Thomas,[1] the *perfection* of charity is *commanded as an end* to be attained; hence we must *want* to attain it. Cajetan explains this by saying that "precisely because it is an *end*, it is enough in order not to fail in the precept, to be in a fit condition to attain this perfection some day, even though this be in eternity. Whoever possesses charity, even in the least degree, and thus advances towards Heaven, is in the way of perfect charity and thereby keeps the precept, which is necessary for salvation."

However, souls *aiming at perfection* are not content with this first degree; they climb ever higher, striving to love God not only with their whole soul, but with all their strength as well.

1214. 2º The **motive** of charity is not the good one has received from God or that which one expects to receive from Him; it is God's *infinite perfection*, at least as the *predominant* motive. Other motives may be joined with this, motives of wholesome fear, of hope, of gratitude, provided that the said motive be truly predominant. Consequently, love of self, in so far as it is *subordinated to the love of God*, is compatible with charity. Hence, when the Saints so harshly condemn self-love, it is the inordinate love of self they have in mind.

1215. A) The opinion of Bolgeni, however, cannot be admitted. He pretends that the only love of charity possible and obligatory is that which has for motive *God's goodness towards us*, since, as he asserts, we cannot love except what we perceive as meeting our needs and aspirations. The author in question mistakes what merely constitutes a *necessarily preexisting condition* for the real motive of charity. It is, indeed, true that love of itself presupposes that the object loved corresponds with our nature and our aspirations; yet, the *motive* for which we love God, is not precisely this harmony, but God's infinite perfection loved for itself.

Once more, St. Francis de Sales explains well this doctrine in the following lines: "If there could be an infinite good, with which we had no relation, no communication, and, consequently, no prospect of union (which is also impossible) we should still esteem it more than ourselves... This, properly speaking, is not to love, because love tends to union, which in this supposition is impossible. Still less could we be animated with love of charity for such an object, as this love is a real reciprocal friendship, terminating in union."[2]

---

[1] *Sum. theol.*, IIª IIæ, q. 184, a. 3; *Comment. of Cajetan* on this article; CARDINAL MERCIER, *Vie intérieure*, 1919, p. 98; P. GARRIGOU-LAGRANGE, *Perfection chrétienne*, t. I, p. 217-227.
[2] *Love of God*, Bk. X, C. X.

1216. B) We may ask ourselves whether the motive of *gratitude* suffices for perfect charity. Here there is room for distinction : if gratitude does not rise above the benefaction received to the Benefactor Himself, it does not suffice as a motive of charity, since it remains self-centered; but, if from the love of such benefaction we pass on to the love of the Benefactor, and if this love for Him is based on His infinite goodness, then this motive becomes one with that of charity.

As a matter of fact, gratitude easily leads to pure love, for it is a most worthy sentiment; and so, Holy Writ and the Saints often propose to us God's benefits as an incentive to the love of God. Thus, St. John, after saying that perfect love banishes fear, exhorts us to love God, "because God first hath loved us." [1] Many are the souls that have learned to love God with the purest love whilst pondering the love He has shown us from all eternity, and the love of Jesus for us in His Passion and in the Holy Eucharist.

If we desire a rule whereby to distinguish *pure* from *interested* love, we may put it thus : the former consists in loving God because He is *good* and in wishing *Him* well; the latter consists in loving God inasmuch as He is *good to us* and in desiring our own good.

1217. 3° As to the *degrees* of love, St. Bernard distinguishes four [2] : 1) First, man loves himself for his own sake, since he is flesh, and he cannot have any taste except for things in relation to himself. 2) Then, seeing that he is not able to subsist by himself, he begins to seek God by faith and to love Him as an indispensable aid; in this second degree man loves God, not as yet for God's sake, but for his own. 3) But soon, by approaching God, living close to Him, and realizing the need of His help, man gradually sees how sweet the Lord is, and begins to love Him for His own sake. 4) Finally, the last degree, attained by few in this life, consists in loving solely for God, and consequently, in loving God exclusively for His own sake.

If we leave aside the first degree, which is nothing but self-love, there remain three degrees of the love of God that correspond to the three stages of perfection which we have already explained in numbers 340, 624-626.

II. *The Sanctifying Power of the Love of God*

1218. 1° Charity is of itself the *most excellent* and the most *sanctifying* of all virtues. This we have already

---

[1] *I John,* IV, 19. — [2] *De diligendo Deo*, C. XV; *Epistola* XI, n. 8.

proved by showing that it is the very essence of perfection,
that is embodies all virtues, and that it imparts to them all
a singular perfection, by causing all their acts to converge
towards God loved above all (n. 310-319).

This is proclaimed by St. Paul in lyric language : " If I speak with
the tongues of men, and of angels, and have not charity, I am become
as sounding brass, or a tinkling cymbal. And if I should have prophecy and should know all mysteries, and all knowledge, and if I
should have all faith, so that I could remove mountains, and have not
charity, I am nothing. And if I should distribute all my goods to feed
the poor, and if I should deliver my body to be burned, and have not
charity, it profiteth me nothing.

Charity is patient, is kind : charity envieth not dealeth not perversely ; is not puffed up, is not ambitious, seeketh not her own, is not
provoked to anger, thinketh no evil : rejoiceth not in iniquity, but
rejoiceth with truth ; beareth all things, believeth all things, hopeth all
things, endureth all things.

Charity never falleth away… And now there remain faith, hope and
charity, these three, but the greatest of these is charity." [1]

1219. In its power to *unite* the soul to God and to
transform it, charity far excels all other virtues.

a) It unites to God the whole soul with all its faculties
and powers. It unites the *mind* to God through the esteem
conceived for ˙Him and the frequent thought of Him.
It unites the *will* by perfect submission to the Divine Will.
It unites the *heart* by the subordination of all our affections
to the Divine Love. It unites our *energies* by dedicating
them all to the service of God and of souls.

b) In thus uniting the whole soul to God, charity transforms it. Love takes us away from self, raises us up to
God, and inclines us to imitate Him, to reproduce in
ourselves the divine perfections. We desire, in truth, to
become like the one we love, because we consider him a
model worthy of imitation, and we wish, by becoming more
like him, to advance further in our intimacy with him.

1220. 2⁰ In its *effects*, charity contributes most effectively to *our sanctification*.

a) It establishes between the soul and God a certain
fellowship, *sympathy*, or affinity which causes us to *understand* and to *relish* better God and divine things. It is
this mutual sympathy that makes friends understand one
another, and become more and more intimately united.
Many a simple, untutored soul, seized by love for God,
relishes and lives the great Christian truths far better than
the learned. This is an effect of charity.

---

[1] *I Cor.*, XIII, 1-13.

1221. b) It *increases our energies* for good *a hundredfold* by communicating to us an indomitable strength to overcome obstacles and to perform the highest acts of virtue, "*for love is strong as death.*" [1]   How great is the strength a mother derives from love for her child!

Perhaps no one has described better the effects of divine love than the author of the Imitation. [2]   It lightens our sufferings and our burdens : "*For it carrieth a burden without being burdened, and maketh all else that is bitter, sweet and savoury.*" It lifts us unto God, because it is born of God : "*For love is born of God, and cannot rest but in God.*" It gives us wings to fly with joy unto the doing of the most perfect actions, unto the entire gift of self : "*The lover flieth, runneth, and rejoiceth... he giveth all for all;*" thus, it urges us to do great things and to aim at the highest perfection : "*The noble love of Jesus impelleth us to do great things, and exciteth us always to desire that which is the more perfect.*" It is ever watchful, uncomplaining of fatigue, untroubled by fear; rather, like a living flame it soars ever higher and passes securely through the midst of dangers : "*Love watcheth... When weary, it is not tired; when straitened, is not constrained; when frightened, is not disturbed; but, like a vivid flame... it mounteth upwards, and securely passeth through all.*"

1222. c) Charity, likewise, is productive of *great joy and expansion of soul;* for it is the initial possession of the Sovereign Good, *the beginning of eternal life in us*, and such possession fills our soul with joy : "*Giving true joy of heart.*" [3]

The *Imitation* goes on to say : "*Nothing sweeter than love... nothing more pleasant, nothing fuller or better in heaven or on earth.*" [4] The cause of such joy is that we begin to be more keenly aware of the presence of Jesus and of the presence of God within us : "*to be with Jesus is a sweet paradise.* [5] *When Thou art present, all things yield delight; but when Thou art absent, all things grow loathsome.*" [6]

1223. d) This joy is followed by a *profound peace.* Once we are convinced that God dwells within us and that He exercises a paternal action, a paternal solicitude over us, we abandon ourselves with sweet trust into His hands, we confide all our interests to His care, and thus we enjoy perfect peace and serenity : "*Thou makest a tranquil heart, great peace, and festive joy.*" [7] Now, there is no disposition more favorable for spiritual growth than inward peace : "*In silence and in solitude the devout soul maketh progress.*" [8]

Hence, from whatever point of view we consider charity, in itself or in its effects, it is of all the virtues the most potent to unite us with God and to sanctify us; it is, indeed, the bond of perfection.

---

[1] *Cant.*, VIII, 6. — [2] *Imitation*, Book III, C. V.
[3] Hymn for the feast of the Holy Name of Jesus.
[4] *Imit.*, Bk. III, C. V. — [5] *Imit.*, Bk. II, C. VIII. — [6] *Imit.*, Bk. III, C. XXXIV.
[7] *Imit.*, Bk. III, C. XXXIV. — [8] *Imit.*, Bk. I, C. XX.

III. *Progress in the Practice of Charity*

1224. General principle. Love being the gift of self, our love for God will be more perfect the more completely we give ourselves to Him, *without reserve and forever, with our whole soul, with our whole heart, with our whole strength.* Since on earth we cannot make the gift of self without self-sacrifice, our love will be more perfect the more unselfishly we practice this *spirit of self-sacrifice* for the love of God (n. 321).

1225. 1° **Beginners** practice the love of God by striving to *avoid sin*, especially mortal sin, and its causes.

a) They practice *repentant love* by bitterly regretting having offended God and having deprived Him of His due glory (n. 743-745).

This love has two effects : 1) it removes us further from sin and from creatures to which pleasure had made us cling ; 2) it reconciles us with God and unites us with Him, not only by removing sin, the great obstacle to divine union, but also by infusing into our heart those sentiments of contrition and humiliation which constitute the beginning of love, and which under the action of grace are often transformed into perfect love. "For," as St. Francis de Sales says, "perfect love wants God and needs Him ; penance seeks and finds Him ; perfect love possesses and holds Him fast." At all events, our sins are more perfectly remitted, the purer and the deeper is our love.

1226. b) They also practice, in its first degree, *the love of conformity with the divine will,* by obeying God's commandments and those of the Church, and manfully withstanding the trials that Providence sends them for the purification of their souls (n. 747).

c) Soon their love becomes a *grateful* love. Realizing that despite their sins, God continually showers upon them His blessings, and grants them such generous pardon, they evince a sincere sense of gratitude towards Him, praise His goodness, and strive to profit better by His graces. This is in itself a noble sentiment which constitutes an excellent preparation for pure love ; we easily rise from the benefaction received to the love of the Benefactor, and we desire His goodness to be recognized and praised the world over. This is perfect love, or charity.

1227. 2° Those **advancing** in the way of perfection practice the love of *complacency,* of *benevolence,* of *conformity to the will of God,* and thereby arrive at the love of *friendship.*

A) *The love of complacency* [1] is born of faith and reflection. **a)** Through faith we know and through meditation we realize

---

[1] St. Francis de Sales, *The Love of God,* Bk. V, C. I-V.

that God possesses the fulness of being, of perfection, of wisdom, of power, of goodness. Now, with but a little good-will, we cannot help taking complacency in such infinite perfection; we rejoice at seeing that our God is rich in goodness, we delight more in God's pleasure than in our own, and we show our joy by acts of admiration, approbation and praise.

b) Thereby we draw unto ourselves the perfections of the Godhead. God becomes *our* God; we live on the thought of His perfection, His goodness, His sweetness, His Divine life; for the heart feeds upon such things as it delights in. Thus we are enriched by the divine perfections, which we make our own by a loving complacency.

1228.   c) But in thus attracting to ourselves the divine perfections, we attract God Himself, and we give ourselves entirely to Him, as St. Francis de Sales [1] well explains:

"It follows that through this love of complacency we not only enjoy the perfections of God as if they were our own; but also, that since the divine perfections are infinitely above the powers and capacity of our mind and heart, we could not attract them into us to enjoy and possess them without being also possessed by them in turn. The love of complacency is then a reciprocal donation, in virtue of which we may truly assert that we belong to God, Who is also our possession." Thus, "the soul inflamed with the love of complacency exclaims from the midst of its repose and sacred silence: 'It suffices to my happiness to know that God is God; that His perfections are boundless, that His goodness is infinite. I am indifferent to life and death, since the object of all my love lives, and will live eternally, surrounded by the unfading splendor of endless glory.' Death cannot terrify a heart which breathes but to love, and which is aware that its sovereign good lives forever. It suffices to her to know, that He Whom she loves more than herself is overwhelmed with bliss: she lives more in the object of her predilection than in herself."

1229.   d) This love, when it contemplates the Suffering Christ turns into *compassion* and *sympathy*. A devout soul, beholding the depths of dejection and grief wherein the Divine Lover is plunged, cannot but share in the holy love that makes Him endure such afflictions. It was this love that caused the stigmata to be imprinted upon the flesh of St. Francis of Assisi, and the Sacred Wounds upon that of St. Catherine of Sienna. Complacency produced compassion, and compassion produced a wound like that of the Beloved.

1230.   B) From the love of complacency springs the love of *benevolence*, that is to say, an ardent desire of glo-

---

[1] *The Love of God*, Bk. V, C. III.

rifying the object of our love and of causing it to be glorified. This may be done in two ways in regard to God.

a) In what concerns His interior perfections, to which we can add nothing, we can give glory only in a hypothetical way, saying, for example : " If (assuming the impossible) I could procure Thee any good, I would unceasingly desire it, even at the cost of my life. If, being what Thou art, Thou couldst receive an increase of perfection, I would desire it with all my heart. "

1231. b) In what touches His *outward glory*, we desire unconditionally to increase it both in ourselves and in others, and with this end in view we desire to know and love Him better, in order that we may in turn make Him better known and better loved. That this love be not a merely speculative love, we strive to study in detail the beauties and the perfections of God, to praise them and cause them to be blest, sacrificing to this end studies and occupations which would naturally be more agreeable to us.

Filled, then, with esteem and admiration for God we long to have His Holy Name blessed, exalted, praised, honored, adored all over the earth. And as we are of ourselves incapable of doing this in a perfect manner, we call upon all creatures to praise and bless their Maker : *Let all the works of the Lord praise the Lord.* [1] We rise in spirit to Heaven there to join the Angelic choirs and the host of the Saints and sing in unison with them : " *Holy, Holy, Holy Lord...* " [2] We join the Blessed Virgin, who raised above the Angels, renders to God more glory than all other creatures, and we repeat with Her : " *My soul doth magnify the Lord.* " [3] We join ourselves especially to the Incarnate Word, the Great Worshiper of the Father, Who, being God and Man, offers the Most Blessed Trinity a praise that is infinite.

Lastly, we unite with God Himself, that is to say, with the Three Divine Persons, in their mutual praise and congratulation. " Then we exclaim : Glory be to the Father, and to the Son, and to the Holy Ghost ! And in order to prove that the object of this aspiration is not the accidental glory of created praise, but the essential, eternal glory which God has in Himself, by Himself, from Himself, and which is, in a word, nothing else than Himself, we add immediately : ' As it was in the beginning, is now and ever shall be, world without end,' wishing that God be ever glorified with that infinite eternal glory, which he possessed in Himself before the formation of creatures. " [4]

Religious and *Priests* realize that they are by virtue of their vows or of their priesthood specially bound to promote God's glory. Burning with the desire of glorifying Him, they never cease, even in the midst of their occupations, to bless and praise the Almighty, and they have but one end in view, one ambition, that of extending the Kingdom of God and of procuring the eternal praise of Him Whom they love as the only portion of their inheritance.

---

[1] *Dan.*, III, 57. — [2] *Apoc.*, IV, 8. — [3] *Luke*, I, 46.
[4] St. Francis de Sales, *The Love of God*, Bk. V, C. XII.

1232. C) The love of benevolence is manifested by the *love of conformity*. Nothing strengthens the reign of God in the soul more effectively than the accomplishment of His Holy Will: "*Thy Will be done on earth as it is in Heaven.*" Love is above all else a union, a fusion of two wills into one; and, since the Will of God is alone good and wise, it is evidently we who must conform our will to His: "*Not my will, but Thine be done.*" [1]

As we have explained in nos. 480-492, this conformity comprises obedience to the Commandments, the Counsels, the inspirations of grace, and the humble and loving submission to providential events whether fortunate or unfortunate : failure, humiliations, all sorts of trials sent to us for our sanctification and God's glory. Conformity in turn produces a *holy indifference* to whatever does not concern itself with God's service. Persuaded that God is everything and the creature nothing, we want but God, His love and His glory, and our will remains indifferent to all else. This indifference is not a stoical insensibility, for we continue to feel the attraction of those things that please us, but it is an indifference of mind and will. Neither does this indifference consist in *letting things take their course*, as the Quietists pretended. We are not indifferent to our salvation; on the contrary, we ardently desire it, but we desire it only in agreement with the Divine Will.

This holy abandon produces a *profound peace* of soul. We know that nothing can happen to us that will not be profitable unto our sanctification: "*To them that love God all things work together unto good.*" [2] Hence we joyfully embrace trials and the Cross, out of love for the Divine Crucified and in order to become more like unto Him.

Thus, perfect conformity to the Will of God, as Bossuet says, [3] "makes us find our rest whether in pain or in joy, according to the pleasure of Him Who is our good. It makes us rest, not in our satisfaction, but in that of God, ever praying Him to be well pleased and to do ever with us as He pleases."

1233. D) This conformity leads us to *friendship with God*. Friendship implies, besides benevolence, *reciprocity* or the mutual giving of self. Now this is well realized in charity.

This love is a true friendship, says St. Francis de Sales [4], "for it is known and acknowledged to exist on both sides; for God cannot be ignorant of our love for Him, since He Himself enkindles it in our hearts; nor can we have a doubt of His eternal predilection for us, since He has so frequently assured us of it... and He incessantly speaks to our hearts by the inspirations of His grace." The Saint adds: "The mutual love subsisting between God and His creature is not what is termed simple friendship; it is a friendship of benevolent preference, that is, a special love of God founded on our choice and our preference."

1234. This friendship consists in the gift of Himself, which God makes to us, and the gift of self which we make

---

[1] *Luke*, XXII, 42. — [2] *Rom.*, VIII, 28.
[3] *Elevations*, XIII, 7. — [4] *Love of God*, Bk. II, C. XXII.

to Him.   We must, therefore, see what is God's love for us in order to understand what must be our love for Him.

   a) His love for us is 1) *eternal:* " I have loved thee with an everlasting love ";[1] 2) it is *desinterested,* for being absolutely self-sufficient, He simply loves us for our good; 3) it is *generous,* for He gives Himself entirely, coming Himself to live lovingly in our soul (n. 92-97); 4) it is *prevenient,* for not only has He loved us first, but He solicits our love and begs for it as if He were in need of it: " *My delight is to be with the children of men... Son, give me thy heart.* "[2]   No one could ever dream of such delicate thoughtfulness.

   1235.   b) We must, therefore, correspond to this love with a love that is as perfect as possible: " *Who would not love Him Who loves us so much!* "[3]

   1) Our love must be *forever growing.*   Not having been capable of loving God from all eternity, and never being able to love Him as He deserves, we must at least love Him more each day, placing no limits to our affection for Him, refusing Him no sacrifice that He may demand, and ever seeking to please Him: " *I do always the things that please him.* "[4]   2) Our love must be *generous,* expressing itself in loving affections, frequent ejaculations and such simple acts of love as: " I love Thee with all my heart "; but it must also express itself by actions, chiefly by the entire gift of self.   God must be the center of our entire being: of our *intelligence,* by the frequent thought of Him; of our *will,* by a humble submission to His least desire; of our *sensitive nature,* by not allowing our heart to become entangled in affections that would only be an obstacle to God's love; of all our *actions,* by ever striving to please Him.   3) Our love must be *disinterested.*   We must love God far more than we love His gifts.   Hence we must love Him whether in desolation or consolation, protesting to Him again and again that we want to love Him and for His own sake.   It is in this way that in spite of our weakness we respond to His friendship.

§ II. The Love of the Neighbor[5]

After explaining the *nature* of this virtue and its *sanctifying power,* we shall indicate the *manner* of practicing it.

I. *Nature of Fraternal Charity*

   1236.   Fraternal charity is indeed a theological virtue, as we have said, provided that we love God Himself in our neighbor, or in other words, that we love the neighbor for God's sake.   Should we love the neighbor *solely for his*

---

   [1] *Jeremias,* XXXI, 3. — [2] *Prov.,* VIII, 31; XXIII, 26.
   [3] *Adeste fideles.* — [4] *John,* VIII, 29.
   [5] St. Francis of Sales, *Devout Life,* P. III, C. VII, XXVIII, XXIX, P. IV, C. VI; Rodriguez, *Christian Perfection,* Vol. I, Treat. IV; Scaramelli-Stockman, *Manual of Christian Perfection,* P. IV, Art. III; Valuy, *Fraternal Charity;* Reginald Buckler, *Spiritual Perfection,* Book II, C. II; Faber, *Spiritual Conferences, Kindness;* Guibert, *Kindness;* Schuyler, *The Charity of Christ;* Hedley, *Retreat, XXVI, A Bishop and His Flock, XXI-XXII; The Little Flower of Jesus,* C. X, XI.

own sake, or because of the services he may render us, this would not be charity.

A) Hence, it is God that we must see in the neighbor. He manifests Himself in men by *natural* gifts, which are a participation in His being and in His attributes, and by *supernatural* gifts, which are a participation in His nature and in His life (n. 445). Since the virtue of charity is supernatural, it is supernatural qualities that we must have in view as the motive of our love. Therefore, if we consider the neighbor's natural qualities, we must look on these with the eye of faith, that is, see them as supernaturalized by grace.

1237. B) The better to understand the *motive* of fraternal charity, we should analyze it by considering men in their relations with God. Then they will appear to us as *children* of God, *members of Jesus Christ, co-heirs* with us of the *Kingdom* of Heaven (nos. 93, 142-149).

Even if they be not in the state of grace or have not the faith, they are called to the possession of these supernatural gifts and it is our duty to contribute, at least by our prayers and our example, to the work of their conversion. This is a most powerful motive for loving them as brethren, and the differences that separate us from them dwindle into insignificance in comparison with all that binds us to them.

II. *The Sanctifying Power of Fraternal Charity*

1238. 1º Since the supernatural love of the neighbor is but another form of the love of God, we should repeat in this place all we have explained concerning the marvellous effects of the love of God.

Let it suffice to quote some texts of St. John: "*He that loveth his brother abideth in light; and there is no scandal in him. But he that hateth his brother is in darkness.*"[1] In the language of this Apostle, to abide in light means to abide in God, the source of all light, and to walk in darkness means to be in the state of sin. The same Apostle goes on to say: "*We know that we have passed from death to life, because we love the brethren... Whosoever hateth his brother is a murderer.*"[2] He concludes by saying: "*Dearly beloved, let us love one another: for charity is of God. And every one that loveth is born of God and knoweth God. He that loveth not, knoweth not God: for God is charity. If we love one another, God abideth in us: and His charity is perfected in us... God is charity: and he that abideth in charity, abideth in God, and God in him... If any man say: I love God, and hateth his brother: he is a liar. For he that loveth not his brother, whom he seeth, how can he love God, whom he seeth not? And this commandment we have from God, that he, who loveth God, love also his brother.*"[3] It would be impossible to express more clearly that to

---

[1] *I John*, II, 10-11. — [2] *I John*, III, 14-15. — [3] *I John*, IV, 7, 8, 12, 16, 20, 21.

love the neighbor is to love God, and that the love of the neighbor
confers on us all the privileges attached to the love of God.

1239. 2° Futhermore, Our Lord tells us that whatever
service is rendered to the least of His brethren, He considers
as rendered to Himself: " *Amen I say to you, as long as you
did it to one of these my least brethren, you did it to me.*" [1]
Now, Our Lord will not let Himself be outdone in generosity, and He will make return a hundredfold by giving all
manner of graces for the least service done to Him in the
person of His brethren.

How consoling is this thought to those who practice fraternal charity and perform the spiritual or corporal works of mercy; how much
more consoling to those whose entire life is devoted to works of charity or zeal! Every moment of the day they do some service to Jesus
Christ in the person of His brethren, and every moment of the day
Jesus likewise labors in their own souls to beautify and sanctify them.

III. *The Practice of Fraternal Charity*

1240. The **principle** that must always guide us is to
see God and Jesus Christ in our neighbor: [2] " *Christ in all,*"
and thus render our charity more *supernatural* in its motives
and its *means of action*, more *universal* in its scope, more
generous and more *active* in its exercise.

1241. 1° **Beginners** strive chiefly to *avoid* the *faults*
contrary to charity, and to *practice* those acts to which we
are bound by *precept*.

A) In order not to give pain to Jesus and the neighbor
they carefully avoid:

a) *Rash judgments*, slander and calumny, which are against justice
and charity, (n. 1043); **b**) natural *antipathies*, which when consented
to are often the cause of faults against charity; **c**) *bitter words*, words
of ridicule or contempt that cannot but engender or intensify enmities;
likewise, witticisms indulged in at the expense of the neighbor which
cause at times smarting wounds; **d**) *strife* and *discussions* born of
pride; **e**) *rivalries, discord, false reports*, which cannot but sow dissension among the members of the great Christian family.

1242. Nothing so effectively helps us to avoid all these faults
opposed to Christian charity, as the frequent consideration of the
touching words of St. Paul to the first Christians: "I therefore, a
prisoner in the Lord, beseech you that you walk worthy of the vocation

---

[1] *Matth.*, XXV, 40.
[2] ST. JOHN EUDES explains this very well in *The Kingdom of Christ Within Us*,
C. I, p. 29-30: " See your neighbor in God and God in him; that is, regard him as
one who has come forth from the heart and goodness of God, who is created to
return to Him one day, and to dwell within His bosom glorifying God for all
eternity; and in whom God will, in reality, be eternally glorified either by His
mercy or justice. "

in which you are called... supporting one another in charity, careful to keep the unity of the Spirit in the bond of peace. One body and one Spirit: as you are called in one hope of your calling. One Lord, one God and Father of all, who is above all, and through all, and in us all... Doing the truth in charity, we may in all things grow up in him who is the head, even Christ." [1] Elsewhere he writes: "If there be therefore any consolation in Christ... fulfil ye my joy: that you be of one mind, having the same charity, being of one accord, agreeing in sentiment. Let nothing be done through contention: neither by vain glory. But in humility, let each esteem others better than themselves: each one not considering the things that are his own, but those that are other men's." [2]

Who could remain unmoved by these exhortations of the Apostle? Forgetting the chains that bind him in his prison-cell, he is concerned with the thought of repressing the dissensions that disturb the Christian community; he reminds the Christians that since there are so many ties that unite them, they must put aside what divides them. After twenty centuries of Christianity this urgent appeal is not less pertinent today.

1243. But there is a fault against charity that must be especially avoided; it is scandal, that is, whatever could probably lead others to sin. We must carefully abstain from things, in themselves indifferent or lawful, but which, because of circumstances, may become to others an occasion of sin. This principle is enjoined by St. Paul regarding the meats offered to idols. Since idols are nothing, these meats are not *in themselves* forbidden; but, because many Christians believe that they are forbidden, the Apostle asks those who are more enlightened to take into account the scruples of their brethren: "And through thy knowledge shall the *weak* brother perish, for whom Christ hath died? Now when you sin thus against the brethren and wound their weak conscience, you sin against Christ. Wherefore, if meat scandalize my brother, I will never eat flesh, lest I should scandalize my brother." [3]

And today these words should still be the object of meditation. Christian men and women indulge in reading, shows and dances that are at least unbecoming, under the pretext that for them such things have no evil effects. This may be questioned, for alas! many who speak in this manner at times deceive themselves. Be this as it may, do they consider the scandal they give to those who witness their conduct and who take it as an excuse to indulge in pleasures still more dangerous?

1244. B) Beginners are not satisfied with avoiding these faults; they practice also *what the precept of charity*

---

[1] *Ephes.*, IV, 1-16. — [2] *Phil.*, II, 1-4. — [3] *I Cor.*, VIII, 13.

commands, particularly *bearing with the neighbor* and *forgiving injuries*.

a) They *bear with the neighbor despite his faults.*

Have we not ourselves faults that others must bear with? Besides, we are apt to exaggerate the faults of others, especially of those towards whom we feel a natural antipathy. Should we not, on the contrary, overlook their faults, and ask ourselves if it becomes us to notice the mote in the neighbor's eye when perhaps there is a beam in ours? Instead of condemning the faults of others, let us honestly ask ourselves if we have not like faults or perhaps worse ones. Let us think first of all of correcting ourselves: "*Physician, heal thyself.*"[1]

1245. **b)** Beginners have the further duty of *forgiving injuries* and of seeking reconciliation with their enemies, with those who have offended them or those whom they have offended. This duty is so imperative that Our Lord says: "If therefore thou offer thy gift at the altar, and there thou remember that thy brother hath anything against thee; leave there thy offering before the altar and go first to be reconciled to thy brother."[2]

According to Bossuet, the first gift we must offer God is a heart free from all resentment, of all enmity towards our brother. He adds that we must not even wait for the day on which we are to approach the altar, but that we must follow the advice of St. Paul: "Let not the sun go down upon your wrath;"[3] for "darkness will add to our resentment; our anger will return upon our awakening and become more bitter still."[4] We must not ask ourselves whether our adversary is more in the wrong than we are, whether it is for him to make the first advance. Let us, at the very first opportunity, clear up every misunderstanding by a frank explanation. If our enemy is the first to present his excuses, we must hasten to forgive: "For if you will forgive men their offences, your Heavenly Father will forgive you also your offences. But if you will not forgive men, neither will your Father forgive you your offences."[5] This is but justice, since we ask God to forgive our trespasses *as* we forgive those who trespass against us.

1246. 2° **Souls advancing** in the spiritual life strive to draw unto themselves the charitable dispositions of the Heart of Jesus.

A) They remember that the precept of charity is His precept, and that its observance will be the characteristic mark of Christians: "A *new commandment* I give unto you: that you love one another, *as I have loved you, that you also love one another.*"[6]

This commandment is *new*, says Bossuet,[7] "because Jesus Christ adds to the old this important feature of loving one another *as He has*

---

[1] *Luke*, IV, 23. — [2] *Matth.*, V, 23-24. — [3] *Ephes.*, IV, 26.
[4] *Méditat.*, XIVe jour. — [5] *Matth.*, VI, 14-15.
[6] *John*, XIII, 34. — [7] *Méditations*, La Cène, I Part., 75e jour.

loved us. His love reached out to us when we were not even thinking of Him. He came to us first. He is not disheartened by our infidelities, our ingratitudes: He loves us to make us holy, to make us happy; He loves us in a disinterested way, for He has no need of us, nor of our service." Charity is to be the distinctive sign of Christians: "By this shall all men know that you are my disciples, if you have love one for another."[1]

1247. **B)** They also try to imitate the examples of the Saviour.

a) His charity is *prevenient.* He loved us first, when we were His enemies: "*When as yet we were sinners.*"[2] He came to us sinners knowing that we were the sick who needed a physician. His preventing grace went to seek the Samaritan woman, the adulterous woman, the thief upon the cross, in order to convert them. It is to anticipate and heal our troubles that He gave us this tender invitation: "*Come to me, all you that labour and are burdened: and I will refresh you.*"[3]

We should imitate this divine thoughtfulness by taking the initiative with our brethren in order to discover and relieve their miseries, as do those who visit the poor to help them in their needs, and sinners, to lead them back gradually to the practice of virtue, and who do this without losing heart if at first they meet with resistance.

1248. **b)** Christ's charity is *compassionate.* When He beholds the multitudes that followed Him into the desert in danger of fainting from hunger, He multiplies the bread and the fishes to give them food. Above all, when He sees souls deprived of spiritual food, He takes pity at their plight, and desires that God be asked to send apostolic workers to their aid: "*Pray ye the Lord of the harvest that he send forth labourers into his harvest.*"[4] Leaving awhile the ninety nine faithful sheep, He goes after the lost one and brings it back upon His shoulders to the fold. No sooner does a sinner give signs of repentance than He hastens to forgive him. Full of compassion for the sick and the afflicted, He heals them in great numbers and often restores their souls to health by pardoning their sins.

Following Our Lord's example, we must harbor a great compassion for all the unfortunate and aid them according to our means. When our means are exhausted, let us at least show them kindness in word and deed. Let us, then, not be discouraged by the faults of the poor; and besides giving alms for the relief of the body, let us add some good word of advice that one day or other may bear fruit.

---

[1] *John,* XIII, 35. — [2] *Rom.* V, 8.
[3] *Matth.,* XI, 28. — [4] *Matth.,* IX, 38.

1249. **c**) Christ's charity is *generous*. Through love of us He consented to labor, and suffer, and die: "*He hath loved us and hath delivered Himself for us.*" [1]

Hence, we must be ever ready to render service to our brethren at the cost of real self-sacrifice, ready to care for them in illnesses, even if these be of a repelling nature, and to give them financial aid. This charity should be *whole-hearted* and *sympathetic;* for the manner of giving is worth more than the gift itself. It should likewise be *intelligent*, offering the poor not only a piece of bread, but if possible, the means of earning a livelihood. It should be *zealous*, doing good to souls by prayer and example and, upon occasion, by discreet and wise counsels. This duty of zeal is imposed especially upon priests, religious and devout persons. These must always remember that "*he who causeth a sinner to be converted from the error of his way shall save his soul from death and shall cover a multitude of sins.*" [2]

1250. 3° **Perfect** souls love the neighbor unto the *immolation of self*: "*In this we have known the charity of God, because he hath laid down his life for us: and we ought to lay down our lives for the brethren.*" [3]

a) This is what apostolic laborers do. Without shedding their blood for their brethren, they give their life-blood drop by drop, forever working for souls, immolating themselves in prayer, in study, even in the recreation they take. This is the ideal proposed by St. Paul: "I most gladly will spend and be spent myself for your souls: although loving you more, I be loved less." [4]

1251. **b**) This is what impelled holy priests to take the *vow of servitude* for souls: thereby they engaged themselves to consider the neighbor as a superior with the right to exact service, and they bound themselves to comply with all his legitimate wishes.

c) This charity is further shown by readiness to anticipate the least of our neighbor's wishes and to render him all possible service; at times also by the cordial acceptance of proffered service, for this is the means of making happy the one who offers it.

d) Lastly, it is manifested by a *special love for our enemies*, whom we consider as the executors of divine vengeance, and whom we revere as such, praying for them in a special way and doing them good on all occasions, according to the counsel of Our Lord: "Love your enemies: do good to them that hate you: and pray for them that persecute and calumniate you." [5] Thus we resemble Him "Who maketh His sun rise to upon the good and bad." [6]

§ III. The Sacred Heart of Jesus the Model and Source of Charity [7]

1252. 1° **Preliminary Remarks.** In concluding our study of charity, we cannot do better than to invite our

---

[1] *Ephes.*, V, 2. — [2] *St. James*, V, 20. — [3] *I John*, III, 16.
[4] *II Cor.*, XII, 15. — [5] *Matth.*, V, 44. — [6] *Matth.*, V, 45.
[7] St. John Eudes, *Le Cœur admirable de la T. S. Mère de Dieu*, l. IV et l. XII;

readers to seek in the Sacred Heart of Jesus the *source* and the *model* of *perfect charity*. In the Litanies officially approved by the Church we invoke the Sacred Heart as an "ardent furnace of charity" and as "full of goodness and love."

There are two essential elements in the devotion to the Sacred Heart: the one *sensible*, the heart of flesh hypostatically united to the person of the Word; the other *spiritual*, symbolized by the physical heart, which is nothing else but the love of the Incarnate Word for God and for men. Just as a symbol and the thing symbolized are but one, so these two elements are but one. Now, the love symbolized by the Heart of Jesus is, no doubt, His *human* love, but it is also His *divine* love, since in Jesus the divine and the human operations are indissolubly united. It is His love for *men*: "Behold the heart that has loved men so much"; but it is also His love for *God*, since, as we have shown, charity towards men flows from charity towards God, and draws from the latter its real motive.

We can, then, consider the Heart of Jesus as the most perfect Model of *love towards God* and of *love towards the neighbor*, and even as the *Model of all virtues*, for charity contains and perfects them all. Since Jesus, during the course of His mortal life, merited for us the grace of imitating His virtues, He is also the *meritorious cause*, the *source* of the graces that enable us to love God and our brethren and to practice all the other virtues.

1253. 2° **The Heart of Jesus as the Source and Model of love towards God.** Love is the complete gift of self. How perfect, then, must be the love of Jesus for His Father! From the first moment of the Incarnation He offers Himself and yields Himself as a victim in order to restore glory to God outraged by our sins.

At His birth, as well as on the day of His Presentation in the Temple, He renews this offering. During the years of His *hidden* life He shows His love for God by yielding obedience to Mary and to Joseph, in whom He sees the representatives of the Divine Authority. Who could tell of the acts of pure love that arose to the Most Blessed Trinity from the little house of Nazareth? In the course of His *public*

J. CROISET, *La dévotion au S. Cœur;* STE MARGUERITE-MARIE, *Œuvres,* éd. Gauthey; P. DE GALLIFET, *Excellence de la dévotion au S. Cœur;* DALGAIRNS, *Devotion to the Sacred Heart;* MANNING, *The Glories of the Sacred Heart;* J.-B. TERRIEN, *La dévotion au S. Cœur;* P. LE DORÉ, *Les Sacrés Cœurs et le V. J. Eudes; Le Sacré Cœur;* J. BAINVEL, *La dévotion au S. Cœur, doctrine, histoire;* L. GARRIGUET, *Le Sacré Cœur, exposé historique et dogmatique,* Cath. Encyclop., *Heart of Jesus;* NOLDIN, *Devot. to Sacred Heart of Jesus;* HUSSLEIN, *The Sacred Heart.*

life He seeks but the pleasure of His Father: "*I do always the things that please Him...*"[1]   "*I honor my Father.*"[2]   At the Last Supper He can declare that He has glorified His Father during His entire life: "*I have glorified Thee upon the earth.*"[3]   The following day He carries out His self-surrender even to self-immolation on Calvary: "*Made obedient unto death, even the death of the Cross.*"[4]   Who could ever number the interior acts of pure love that sprang incessantly from His Heart, and which made of His whole life a continual act of perfect charity?

1254.   Above all, who could give an idea of the perfection of that love?

"It is a love" says St. John Eudes,[5] "worthy of such a Father and of such a Son; it is a love that fits most perfectly the unspeakable perfections of the Beloved One; it is an infinitely loving Son that loves an infinitely lovable Father; it is God Who loves God... In a word the Divine Heart of Jesus, whether considered in its humanity or in its divinity, is infinitely more inflamed with love for His Father, and loves Him infinitely more at each single instant than all the Angels and Saints together could love Him throughout all eternity."

Now, this love of Jesus for His Father we can make our own, by uniting ourselves to the Sacred Heart of Jesus and by offering it to the Father, saying with Saint John Eudes: "My Saviour, I give myself to Thee in order to unite myself with the eternal, boundless, and infinite love which Thou bearest Thy Father. Adorable Father, I offer Thee all this eternal, boundless, infinite love of Thy Son Jesus as a love that is mine... I love Thee as Thy Son loves Thee."

1255.   3° **The Heart of Jesus The Source of Love for Men.**   We have seen (n. 1247) how Jesus loved men while on earth; it remains for us to point out here how He never ceases to love them now that He is in Heaven.

a) It is because He loves us that He sanctifies us through the *Sacraments:* these are, to borrow once more the thought of St. John Eudes, "so many inexhaustible fountains of grace and holiness which have their source in the boundless ocean of the Sacred Heart of Our Saviour; and all the graces that issue from the sacraments are so many flames of that divine furnace."[6]

1256.   **b)** It is in the *Eucharist* especially that He gives us the greatest proof of His love.

1) For nineteen centuries He has been with us night and day, like a father who is loath to leave His children, like a friend who finds his pleasure with his friends, like a devoted physician who constantly

---

[1] *John*, VIII, 29. — [2] *John*, VIII, 49. — [3] *John*, XVII, 4. — [4] *Philip.*, II, 8.
[5] *Le Cœur admirable*, l. XII, ch. II. — [6] *Ibid.*, Ch. VII.

remains by the bed-side of his patients. 2) He is ever active, adoring, praising and glorifying His Father for us, thanking Him for all the benefits He continually bestows upon us, loving Him in our stead, offering Him His Own merits and satisfactions to atone for our sins, and ever asking new graces in our behalf: "*Always living to make intercession for us.*"[1] 3) He never ceases to renew upon the altar the Sacrifice of Calvary; He does so thousands of times a day, wherever there is a priest to consecrate, and He does so out of love for us, in order to apply to each one of us the fruits of His Sacrifice (n. 271-273). And not content with immolating Himself, He gives Himself whole and entire to every communicant, to impart to each His graces, His dispositions and His virtues (n. 277-281).

This Divine Heart ardently longs to communicate to us His Own charity. "My Divine Heart," said He to St. Margaret Mary, "is possessed of such a passionate love for men and for you in particular, that unable to contain the flames of its burning charity, it must needs extend them through you, that it may be made known to them in order to enrich them with its priceless treasures."[2] It was then that Our Lord asked the Saint for her heart in order to unite it to His own and place in it a spark of His love. What Christ did in a miraculous manner for her, He does in an ordinary way for us in Holy Communion and every time that we unite our hearts to His; for He is come to earth to bring the sacred fire of charity, and His only desire is to enkindle it in our hearts: "I am come to cast fire on the earth. And what will I, but that it be kindled?"[3]

1257. 4° **The Heart of Jesus the Source and Model of All Virtues.** In Holy Writ the heart often signifies all the interior sentiments of man in contradistinction to his exterior acts: "Man seeth those things that appear; but the Lord beholdeth the heart."[4] The heart of Jesus, therefore, symbolizes not only love, but all the inward sentiments of His soul. It is thus that the great mystics of the Middle Ages, and, after them, St. John Eudes, understood the devotion to the Sacred Heart. The same may be said of St. Margaret Mary. No doubt she lays special stress, and rightly so, on the love wherewith this Divine Heart is filled; but in her various writings she shows us this Heart as the model of all virtues. Father de la Colombière, her confessor and interpreter, sums up her thoughts in an act of consecration, which is found at the end of the *Spiritual Retreats.*[5]

---

[1] *Hebr.*, VII, 25. — [2] *First of the Great Revelations.* — [3] *Luke*, XII, 49.
[4] *I. Kings*, XVI, 7.
[5] *Œuvres complètes*, Grenoble 1901, ch. VI, p. 124.

"This offering is made in order to honor this Divine Heart, seat of all virtues, source of all blessings, and the refuge of all holy souls. The principal virtues intended to be honored therein are: *in the first place*, the most ardent love for God His Father, together with the most profound respect and the deepest humility ever known; *secondly*, infinite patience in the midst of sufferings, the keenest of pains for the sins He had laid upon Himself, the trust of a tender son together with the shame of a great sinner; *thirdly*, a most lively compassion for our wretchedness, and in spite of all these emotions, an unalterable serenity, the result of the most perfect conformity to the Will of God, a serenity that could not be troubled by any event whatsoever."

Besides, since all virtues flow from charity and find therein their highest perfection (n. 318-319), the Heart of Jesus, being the source and model of Divine Charity, is at the same time the source and model of all virtues.

1258. In this the devotion to the Sacred Heart joins with the devotion to the *Interior Life of Jesus*, explained by Father Olier and practiced in the Seminaries of St. Sulpice. This interior life consists, says he, "in His interior dispositions and sentiments towards all things, for example: His sense of *religion towards God*, His *love towards the neighbor*, His *self-abnegation*, His *horror for sin*, His *condemnation of the world and its maxims*."[1]

Now, all these dispositions are found in the Sacred Heart of Jesus, and it is there that we must seek them. Father Olier wrote to a pious soul who delighted to withdraw within the Heart of Jesus: "Lose yourself a thousand times a day in His lovable Heart whither you feel yourself so strongly attracted... The Heart of the Son of God is the pearl of great price; it is His most precious gem; God's own treasury wherein He pours all His riches and where He dispenses all His graces... It is within that Sacred Heart, within that adorable Soul, that first are enacted all mysteries... See, then, to what Our Lord calls you by opening to you His Heart, and see how much you must profit by this grace, one of the greatest that you have obtained in your life. Let not creatures ever draw you out of that place of delights and may you be plunged therein for time and for eternity with all the holy spouses of Jesus."[2] In another place he said: "What a Heart is that of Jesus! What an ocean of love is contained therein, flooding the whole earth! O rich and overflowing source of all love! O inexhaustible depths of all religion! O Divine center of all hearts... O Jesus! allow me to worship, to adore the inmost recesses of Thy holy soul, to adore Thy *Heart which I have but to-day beheld*. I would picture it, but its ravishing beauty will not permit me. I beheld it as a Heaven radiant with light, full of love, of gratitude, and of praise. It breathed forth God, it showed forth His grandeur and magnificence."[3] For Father Olier, the Interior Life and the Heart of Jesus were but one and the same thing, that is, the center of all the dispositions of Christ's holy soul and of His virtues, the sanctuary of love and of worship, where God is glorified and whither fervent souls love to withdraw.

---

[1] *Cat. for an Int. Life*, P. I, Lesson I. — [2] *Lettres*, t. II, lettre 426.
[3] *Esprit de M. Olier*, t. I, 186-187, 193.

1259. Conclusion. That devotion to the Sacred Heart may be productive of these happy effects, it must consist of two essential acts: *love* and *atonement.*

1º Love is the first and the foremost of these duties, according to St. Margaret Mary as well as according to St. John Eudes.

Giving an account to Father Croiset of the second great apparition the former writes [1] : " He made me see that it was the great desire He had *of being loved by men*, and of withdrawing them from the road of perdition, that induced Him to conceive this plan of making His Heart known to men, with all the treasures of love, of mercy, of grace, of sanctification and of salvation, in order that those who wish to render and procure Him all the honor, glory, and love of which they are capable, might be abundantly and profusely enriched with the treasures of the Heart of God. " Another letter, to Sister de la Barge, ends thus: " Let us, then, love this, the only love of our souls, since He has loved us first and loves us still so ardently that He continually burns with love for us in the Blessed Sacrament. To become saints it suffices to love this Holy of Holies. What shall hinder us? We have hearts to love and a body to suffer... Only His Holy love can make us do His pleasure; only this perfect love can make us do it in His own way; and only this perfect love can make us do it in His own acceptable time. " [2]

1260. 2º The second of these essential acts is *atonement;* for the love of Jesus is outraged by the ingratitude of men, as He Himself declared in the third great apparition to St. Margaret Mary:—

" Behold this Heart which has so loved men that it has spared nothing, even to exhausting and consuming itself, in order to testify its love. In return, *I receive from the greater part only ingratitude*, by their irreverences and sacrileges, and by the coldness and contempt they have for Me in this Sacrament of love. " Then He asks her to atone for these ingratitudes by the ardor of her own love: " My daughter, I come into the heart I have given you in order that *through your fervor you may atone for the offences which I have received* from lukewarm and slothful hearts which dishonor me in the Blessed Sacrament. "

1261. These two acts are highly sanctifying. Love will, by uniting us intimately to the Sacred Heart of Jesus, make us share in His virtues, and give us the strength to practice them in spite of all obstacles. *Atonement* will further enkindle our fervor, by having us sympathize with the sufferings of Jesus, and will lead us, out of love for Him and in union with His Sufferings, to endure all the trials that it may please God to send us.

Thus understood, devotion to the Sacred Heart contains nothing that could savor of artificiality or sentimentality.

---

[1] *Lettres inédites*, IV, p. 142. — [2] Letter CVIII, t. II, p. 227.

It is rather the very spirit of Christianity, a happy blending of love and sacrifice, attended by the gradual development of the moral and the theological virtues. It is like a *summary* of the *Illuminative Way*, and an apt initiation into the Unitive Way.

CHAPTER IV

Counter-attacks of the Enemy

1262. Whilst we labor in the acquisition of the virtues, our spiritual foes are not idle. They return stealthily to take the offensive, either by causing in us a re-awakening, in a more subtle form, of the *seven capital sins*, or by leading us to *lukewarmness*.

ART. I. THE RE-AWAKENING OF THE CAPITAL SINS

1263. St. John of the Cross gives an excellent description of these capital sins as they exist in those whom he calls the *beginners*, that is to say, in those who are on the threshold of contemplation through the *night of the senses*. [1] We shall simply condense his psychological analysis.

I. *The Inclination to Pride*

1264. This inclination is manifested in six principal ways :

1) Whilst aiming at fervor and remaining faithful to their spiritual exercises, these beginners *take complacency in their works* and hold themselves in too high esteem. They presumptuously plan many projects and carry out scarcely any.

2) They *speak of the things of the spiritual* life rather to give lessons to others than to put these lessons into practice themselves, and harshly condemn those who do not approve of their type of spirituality.

3) Some of them cannot stand rivalry. If a rival happens to appear, they condemn him and belittle him.

4) They seek the good graces and the intimacy of their spiritual director, and if the latter does not approve of their ways, they look for another who will be more accommodating. The better to succeed in this, they tone down their faults, and if they happen to fall into a grave sin, they accuse it to another confessor and not to their regular director.

5) Should they commit a grievous sin, they get out of sorts with themselves and lose heart, peeved at not having reached sanctity as yet.

6) They love to attract notice by outward manifestations of their piety, and readily speak to others of their good works and their success.

---

[1] *Dark Night*, Bk. I, C. II-VII.

From pride springs **envy,** which betrays itself by displeasure at the sight of the spiritual good of others. They are pained at hearing others praised, saddened at their virtue, and, when the occasion presents itself, they do not fail to speak ill of them.

II. *Sensuality*

1265. A) **Spiritual Gluttony** manifests itself in two ways:

a) By an excessive craving for *consolations.* One seeks them even in the practice of austerities, in the *discipline* for instance, and one importunes one's director for permission to practice mortifications with the hope of thus obtaining consolations.

b) For the same reason, some persons make forced efforts during meditation or at the time of communion, in order to procure a feeling of devotion, or they wish to go frequently to confession with a view of finding some comfort in this exercise. Often these efforts and longings remain sterile, and then discouragement takes hold of these souls, who are more attached to consolations than to God Himself.

1266. B) **Spiritual Lust** appears especially under two forms: **a)** one seeks sentimental or sensual friendships, under the pretext of devotion, and one is loath to give them up, pretending that such relations are an aid to piety. **b)** At times, the sensible consolations experienced at prayer or Communion produce in persons of a tender and affectionate nature pleasures of another sort, which may prove to them a source of temptation or anxiety. [1]

1267. C) **Sloth** leads: **a)** to weariness in the performance of spiritual exercises when one does not find therein any relish, and prompts one either to shorten or omit them; **b)** to dejection of spirit, when one receives from a superior or spiritual director orders or advice which seem too difficult; one would prefer a more congenial sort of spirituality that does not interfere with one's ease or petty schemes.

---

[1] St. Theresa, writing to her brother Lorenzo de Cepeda, who complained of vexations of this kind, gave him this wise counsel: "As regards the distress of which you complain, in no instance must it be heeded. Although I be not able to speak from experience, since God has always preserved me from such passions, I understand what occurs. It is the very intensity of the soul's delight that produces such reaction in nature. With God's grace that shall pass away, if you will not be disturbed by it. " Letter 138, edition of *Vicente de la Fuente.*

III. *Spiritual Avarice*

1268. This avarice is thus described by St. John of the Cross:

a) "There are beginners who do not cease to cram their souls with spiritual counsels and precepts; they must possess and read numerous spiritual treatises on which they put all their time and have none left for the fulfilment of their first duty; namely, mortification and perfect interior detachment. **b**) Besides, they load themselves with holy pictures, rosaries, crucifixes and expensive and curious objects of devotion. Then they quit one thing for another, change and exchange, arrange and rearrange, and their final choice centers upon that which is singular or expensive." All this is clearly against the spirit of poverty, and it shows at the same time that one attaches undue importance to accidentals and neglects the essentials of true devotion.

1269. Conclusion. Evidently these imperfections are a great hindrance to spiritual progress. St. John of the Cross says that God, in order to correct them, introduces souls into the *Dark Night*, of which we shall soon speak. As to those souls who do not enter into this phase of the spiritual life, they must strive to disentangle themselves from these meshes by carrying out into practice what we have explained concerning consolations and dryness of soul, (n. 921-933) obedience, fortitude, temperance, humility and meekness (nos. 1057, 1076, 1127, 1154).

Art. II. Lukewarmness [1]

Unless we react against the aforesaid faults, it will not be long before we fall into lukewarmness, a most dangerous spiritual disease the *nature, dangers* and *remedies* of which we shall now explain.

I. *Nature of Lukewarmness*

1270. 1º **Notion.** Lukewarmness is a spiritual malady that may attack beginners or even perfect souls, but which manifests itself especially in the course of the *Illuminative Way*. It presupposes, in fact, that a soul has already reached a certain degree of fervor, and that it gradually allows itself to become lax.

Lukewarmness consists in a sort of *spiritual languor* which saps the energies of the will, inspires one with a horror for effort and thus leads to the decline of the Christian life. It is a kind of sluggishness, a species of

---

[1] BELLECIUS, *Solidæ virtutis impedimenta*, P. I, cap. II; BOURDALOUE, *Retreat*, 3rd Day, 1st Medit.; FABER, *Growth in Holiness*, C. XXV.

torpor which, though not death as yet, insensibly leads to it through a gradual weakening of our moral forces. One may compare it to those slow-working diseases, such as consumption, which little by little prey upon some vital organ.

1271. 2° **Its causes.** They are chiefly two: *a defective spiritual nourishment,* and *the entry into the soul of some noxious germ.*

A) To live and grow, our soul needs wholesome spiritual food. Now, the soul is nourished by the various spiritual exercises, that is, meditation, devout reading, prayer, examinations of conscience, the fulfilment of the duties of state, exercise in the practice of the virtues — all of which keep it in communion with God, the Source of spiritual life. Therefore, if these exercises are performed with negligence, with voluntary distractions, without efforts to react against routine or sluggishness, the soul is deprived of many graces, is poorly nourished, and becomes weak and incapable of practicing the virtues of the Christian life in face of even little difficulties.

We must note in passing that this condition is altogether different from that dryness or affliction of soul permitted by God to try us. In these, instead of welcoming distractions, one experiences pain and humiliation at having them, and one earnestly seeks to avoid them. The lukewarm man, on the contrary, lets himself be carried along by useless thoughts, takes pleasure in them, hardly makes any effort to be rid of them, and soon distractions well-nigh overrun his prayers.

Then, seeing how little profit he derives from his exercises of piety, he begins to shorten them, and in time suppresses them entirely. Thus, his examination of conscience, becoming wearisome, irksome, a mere matter of routine, ends by being omitted; he is no longer aware of his faults, of his defects, and he allows them to gain the upper hand. He no longer strives to grow in virtue, and soon his vices, his inordinate inclinations, tend to revive.

1272. **B)** The outcome of this spiritual apathy is the gradual weakening of the soul — a species of *spiritual anemia* — which paves the way for the entrance of some destructive germ, that is to say, one of the three concupiscences, or perhaps all of them at once.

a) The avenues of the soul being poorly guarded, the exterior and interior senses readily lay themselves open to the unwholesome suggestions of curiosity and sensuality, and frequent temptations arise only to be half-repulsed. At times the heart yields itself to the current of disturbing affections: one commits imprudences and courts danger; venial sins are multiplied and hardly regretted; one glides down a perilous grade, skirts the abyss, and is extremely fortunate to avoid a fall.

b) Besides, *pride,* never completely subdued, renews its onslaughts. One begins to indulge in self-complacency, to delight in exterior qualities, in outward successes. The better to exalt self, one makes comparisons with others still more lax than oneself, and despises as narrow and small-minded those who are more faithful to duty. This pride brings in its wake envy, jealousy, impatience, anger and harshness in the relations with others.

c) *Avarice* is rekindled in the heart. One feels the need of money to secure more pleasures, to make a greater impression; and to provide more of it one has recourse to questionable means, which border on injustice.

1273. Hence, *innumerable deliberate venial sins* are committed for which one feels scarcely any compunction, since the light of judgment and delicacy of conscience have been gradually weakened; one lives in habitual dissipation of mind, and performs the examination of conscience carelessly. Thus, horror for sin diminishes, God's graces become more rare, and the profit derived from them smaller. In a word, there is a weakening of the spiritual organism, which prepares the way to shameful surrenders.

1274. 3° **Its Degrees.** From what we have said it is evident that there are many degrees in lukewarmness. However, it is enough to distinguish *incipient* from *extreme* lukewarmness.

a) In the first instance, one as yet preserves horror for mortal sin, though committing imprudences that may lead thereto. One easily commits *deliberate venial sins*, notably, such as correspond to one's predominant fault. Besides, one brings little earnestness to the performance of spiritual exercises, and often performs them through mere routine.

b) By dint of allowing oneself to drift into such culpable negligences, one ceases to harbor the old instinctive horror for mortal sin. On the other hand, the love of pleasure so increases that one comes to regret the fact that such or such pleasure is forbidden under the pain of grave sin. One repels temptations but feebly, and a moment arrives when one asks, and not without reason, whether or not one is still in the state of grace. This is *extreme* lukewarmness.

II. *The Dangers of Lukewarmness*

1275. The special danger of this state consists in the *gradual weakening* of the soul's energies, a condition fraught with more danger than the commission of some isolated mortal sin. This is the sense in which Our Lord speaks to the lukewarm: "I know thy works, that thou are neither cold nor hot. I would thou wert cold or hot. But because thou art lukewarm and neither cold nor hot, I will begin to vomit thee out of my mouth. Because thou sayest: I am rich and made wealthy and have need of nothing: and knowest not that thou art wretched and miserable and poor and blind and naked."[1] It is just like the difference existing between *chronic* and *acute* diseases. The latter, once cured, leave no bad effects; the former, having slowly sapped the strength of the body, leave it for a long time in a state of great weakness. The succeeding paragraphs will show this in detail.

1276. 1° The first effect of lukewarmness is a kind of *blinding of conscience.* By dint of excusing and palliating faults, the judgment becomes warped, and sins in themselves grave come to be considered as slight. Thus a *lax conscience* is formed, which can no longer discern the gravity of the imprudences or the sins committed, which lacks the energy required to detest them, and which soon falls into culpable illusions: "There is a way which seemeth just to man: but the ends thereof lead to death."[2] One thinks himself rich, because one is proud, but in reality one is poor and miserable in the eyes of God.

1277. 2° Along with this comes the *gradual weakening of the will.*

a) By dint of making concessions to sensuality and to pride in small things, one ends by yielding to pleasure in things of greater moment; for all the elements of the spiritual life hold together. Holy Writ teaches us that "he that contemneth small things shall fall by little and little";[3] that "he that is faithful in that which is least, is faithful also in that which is greater; and that he that is unjust in that which is little is unjust also in that which is greater",[4] all of which means that the earnestness or carelessness with which we perform certain acts transfers itself to other actions.

b) Soon one reaches the point of *loathing effort.* The spring of the will being run down, one lets oneself go the way of natural desires, of indifference, of pleasure. In this there is great danger, and unless one reacts, grave faults are bound to ensue.

c) Indeed, in so acting, one abuses grace and offers frequent resistance to the inspirations of the Holy Ghost; one lends a readier ear to the voice of pleasure, and ends by sinning grievously.

1278. Such a fall is all the more *difficult to repair* since it occurs almost *insensibly.* One lets oneself *slide*, so to speak, to the depths of the abyss without any great shock. Then one tries to practice self-deception: one would convince oneself that the fault is only venial; that, if the matter be grave, there was no full consent; that it is a fault of surprise which cannot be mortally sinful.

---

[1] *Apoc.*, III, 15-17. — [2] *Prov.*, XIV, 12.
[3] *Ecclus.*, XIX, 1.
[4] *Luke*, XVI, 10. In the literal sense, the least things mean temporal goods and the greater things those of heaven.

In this manner a false conscience is formed and the regular confession continues to reveal only trivial matters; the confessor is deceived and thus may be begun a long series of sacrileges. When a ball falls from on high, it rebounds; when it *rolls* down to the bottom of the abyss, it stays there. And so it happens at times with lukewarm souls; they remain in the depths into which they have gradually and almost insensibly fallen.

III. *The Remedies for Lukewarmness*

1279. Our Lord has Himself pointed out the remedies: " I counsel thee to buy of me gold fire-tried, that thou mayest be made rich (the gold of charity and fervor of spirit); and mayest be clothed in white garments, and that the shame of thy nakedness may not appear (purity of conscience); and anoint thy eyes with eye-salve, that thou mayest see (frankness towards self and towards one's confessor). Such as I love, I rebuke and chastise. Be zealous therefore, and do penance. Behold, I stand at the gate, and knock. If any man shall hear my voice, and open to me the door, I will come in to him, and will sup with him, and he with me." [1] One must, therefore, never despair. Jesus is ever ready to give us His friendship, nay, His intimate friendship, if we be converted.

1280. To be converted: 1º one must needs *have frequent recourse to a wise confessor*, frankly open one's soul to him and sincerely beg his help to overcome tepidity. One must take and follow his counsels energetically and with constancy.

2º Under his guidance, one will return to the *fervent practice of the exercises of piety*, especially of those that secure the fulfilment of the others; namely, mental prayer, examination of conscience and the frequent renewal of the intention of doing all for God (n. 523-528). The fervor of which we here speak lies not in feeling, but in a generous will that strives to refuse God nothing.

3º One will also take up once more the practice of the *virtues* and the fulfilment of one's *duties of state* in all earnestness, making one's particular examination of conscience successively upon the chief points, and giving an account thereof in confession (nn. 265, 468-476).

By these means one will regain *fervor* and one will not forget that past faults demand an atonement through the spirit and the works of penance.

---

[1] *Apoc.*, III, 18-20.

APPENDIX: RULES CONCERNING THE DISCERNMENT
OF SPIRITS IN THE ILLUMINATIVE WAY

1281.   We have, following St. Ignatius, already outlined
the rules for the discernment of spirits with regard to
beginners (n. 953-957).   It will be useful to sum up in this
place the rules he gives for the *Illuminative Way*, that is,
for the Second Week of the Exercises.   They refer to two
principal points: 1° *spiritual consolations*, 2° *desires* and
projects for the future.

1282. 1° **Rules concerning Consolations. a)** The distinctive
work of the *good spirit* in a well-disposed soul is *true spiritual joy* and
peace.   The *evil spirit*, on the contrary, labors to destroy this joy by
means of sophistries, subtleties, and illusions.   He resembles an artful
lawyer defending a bad case.   This rule is based on the fact that God
is the Author of peace, whilst the devil casts trouble upon the soul in
order to discourage it.

b) God alone can infuse *true consolation without any antecedent
natural cause*, for He alone can penetrate into the inmost recesses of
the soul and draw it to Himself.   We say that such consolation has no
antecedent cause when nothing has intervened capable of producing it.
For instance, a soul is plunged in desolation, and lo! in an instant it
finds itself reassured, full of joy, of strength and of good-will.   This
was the case with St. Francis de Sales after violent scruples had
assailed him.

c) When consolation has been preceded by some cause, it may come
either from the good or the evil spirit.   It proceeds from the former,
if the said consolation enlightens and strengthens the soul to know
and to do good.   It proceeds from the latter, if it causes laxity, softness, love of pleasure or of honors, and presumption.   In other words,
the tree is judged by its fruits.

d) It is the part of the devil to transform himself into an angel of
light to enter at the outset into the pious desires of the soul, and to end
by suggesting his own designs.   Thus when he sees a soul given to the
practice of virtue, he first suggests sentiments in harmony with that
soul's good dispositions; after that, relying on the soul's self-love, he
suggests sentiments of vain complacency or of presumption, excessive
penances, so as to drive it to discouragement, or, on the contrary, less
strictness of life, under pretexts of health or study.   In this way he
succeeds in making the soul lower its standards little by little.

1283.   2° **Rules concerning desires or projects for the
future. a)** We must submit such inspirations to a strict examination,
considering if in their *inception*, in the course of their *formation*, and
in their final *unfolding*, they tend towards good; for if at any of these
stages there should enter anything of *evil*, anything of a nature to
distract us from God, anything less good than what we had previously
proposed; or again, if these desires disturb, trouble and weaken the
soul, this is a proof that they proceed from the enemy of our spiritual
progress and salvation.   The reason for this is, that for an action
to be good, there must not be in it anything contrary to the will of
God or to the spiritual welfare of the soul.   Hence, if in any of the

elements of an action some defect is noticed, it bears the mark of the evil spirit.

b) Once the intervention of the evil spirit is discovered, the best course is to go over the entire line of thought from the beginning and find out the way in which he entered into the soul to disturb it and lead it astray. This study will enable us to be on our guard against his manoeuvers in the future.

c) There is another rule deduced from the difference in the *mode of action* of the two spirits. The good spirit comes with sweetness upon the soul advancing in the way of perfection, like the morning dew penetrating a sponge; the evil one rushes in violently like a heavy rain beating on a rock.

d) Even when consolation comes from God, we must know how to distinguish between the moment itself of consolation and the time that follows. In the former, we act under the inspiration of grace; in the latter, we form resolutions and projects which are not directly inspired by God, and which must therefore be carefully scrutinized according to the preceding rules.

1284. 3º To these rules drawn up by St. Ignatius, a few others may be added, which flow from what we have said in this Second Book.

a) To aspire to a perfection inconsistent with our present duties, to practice showy *virtues*, to become singular, all this bears the mark of the *bad spirit;* for the good spirit inclines us indeed to the attainment of high perfection, but to such as is compatible with our duties of state and in keeping with a humble and hidden life.

b) *Contempt for little things* and the desire to be sanctified in a grand manner are not characteristic of the good spirit, which urges us to perfect fidelity to our duties of state and to homely virtues: "*One jot or tittle shall not pass of the law, till all be fulfilled.*" [1]

c) To reflect complacently upon self, to think one has done well, to desire to be held in esteem on account of one's piety and virtue, is also in opposition to the Christian spirit, whose first concern is to please God alone: "If yet I pleased men, I should not be the servant of Christ." [2] Hence, *false humility*, which blames self that self may be praised, and false meekness, which is in reality but the desire to please men, are contrary to the spirit of God.

d) To complain, to lose patience, to lose heart in the midst of trials and aridity of soul is a sign of the human spirit; the spirit of God leads, on the contrary, to the love of the Cross, to resignation, to a holy abandonment, and causes us to persevere in prayer amidst dryness and distraction.

SUMMARY OF THE SECOND BOOK

1285. 1º The **end** proposed in the *Illuminative Way* is the following of Christ by the imitation of His virtues. We advance by the light of His examples: "*He that followeth me walketh not in darkness, but shall have the light*

---

[1] *Matth.*, V, 18. — [2] *Gal.*, I, 10.

of life." [1] The ideal which we try to realize from day to day is that of *making Jesus the center of our thoughts, of our affections, of our entire life.*

For this reason our mental prayer becomes *affective* prayer, keeping Jesus continually before our *eyes* to adore Him, bringing Him into our *heart* to love Him and share in His dispositions, and holding Him in our *hands* to practice virtue in union with Him. The virtues which we practice are the *Theological* and the *Moral* Virtues; they go hand in hand and aid one another. Nevertheless, there are as it were two phases in the development of our spiritual life; in the one, the moral virtues are emphasized, and in the other, the theological.

1286. 2º The first requirement is that of training our faculties, of fitting them for union with God. This is effected by the *moral* virtues:

1) *Prudence* trains the mind to think before acting, to consult God and to take counsel with those who represent Him. Thus, prudence makes the mind *share in the wisdom of God.*

2) *Justice* bends our *will*, schooling it to respect God's rights and those of the neighbor by the practice of absolute honesty, religion and obedience to superiors. Thus we *take on something of God's justice.*

3) *Fortitude* disciplines our violent passions, moderates and restrains their excesses, and uses their energies in overcoming difficulties in the pursuit of supernatural good. It makes us practice *magnanimity*, *munificence*, *patience* and *constancy*, and thus gives us something of *God's own strength.*

4) To deaden and hold in check the *love of pleasure*, *temperance* helps us to mortify our gluttony through *sobriety*, to overcome lust through *chastity*, to subdue pride through *humility*, and anger through *meekness*.

1287. 3º Then follows the *second phase* of the Illuminative Way, the practice of the theological virtues, which unite us directly to God.

1) *Faith*, by its obscurity, submits the mind to God, and by its light unites it to Him, making it share in God's own knowledge.

2) *Hope*, like a powerful lever, raises the will, detaches it from the things of earth, directs its longings and ambitions heavenwards, and *unites us to God, the source of our bliss*, infinitely Powerful and infinitely Good, from Whom we confidently expect all the help we need to attain our supernatural end.

3) *Charity* lifts us higher still; it makes us love God for His Own sake, because He is infinitely Good in Himself, and makes us love our neighbor also for God's sake as a reflection of His own perfections. Therefore, *it unites the whole soul to God.*

---

[1] *John*, VIII, 12.

It is from the *Sacred Heart of Jesus* that we draw this twofold love. Intimately united with Our Lord, we overcome our selfishness, and, making His love and His dispositions our own, we live for God as He Himself did.

1288. 4º Doubtless, in the course of our progress in the spiritual life we are to expect *counter-attacks* on the part of our enemies. The *Seven Capital Vices* seek in a more subtle manner to reassert themselves, and, if we are not on our guard against them, they will cause us to fall into the state of lukewarmness. Vigilant souls however, relying on Jesus-Christ, repel these attacks, nay even turn them to profit, using them to strengthen their virtue, and thus prepare themselves for the *joys* and *trials* of the *Unitive Way*.

BOOK III

The Unitive Way

1289. Once we have purified our soul and adorned it by the practice of the virtues, we are ripe, so to speak, for habitual and intimate union with God, that is, for entrance into the *Unitive Way.*

PRELIMINARY REMARKS[1]

Before entering into the different questions in detail, we must briefly explain: 1° the *end* to be attained in the unitive way; 2° the *distinguishing* marks of this way; 3° the general notion of *contemplation,* which is one of its general characteristics; 4° the *order* to be followed in this third part.

I. *The End to be attained*

1290. This end is none other than habitual and intimate union with God, through Jesus Christ. It is very well expressed in these words of Father Olier at the beginning of his "Pietas Seminarii": "*The first and last aim of this Institution is to live supremely unto God, in Christ Jesus Our Lord, so that our inmost hearts may be penetrated with the interior dispositions of the Son of God, and each may be able to say what St. Paul truly said of himself: I live, now not I; but Christ liveth in me.*"[2]

To live altogether unto God, the Living God, the Most Blessed Trinity dwelling in us, to praise God, serve Him, revere Him and love Him, such is the aim of the perfect Christian; to live, not on the level of mediocrity, but to live *intensely,* with all the *fervor* that love imparts. Hence, we must aim at forgetting ourselves so as to think only of that God Who deigns to live within us, to love Him with our whole soul and to make all our thoughts, all our longings, all our actions converge towards Him. In this way will be realized what we ask in the office at *Prime:* "*Vouchsafe this day, Lord God of Heaven and Earth, to*

---

[1] PHIL. A SS. TRINITATE, *op. cit.,* IIIª P., Tr. I, dist. I; TH. DE VALGORNERA, *op. cit.,* Q. IV, Disp. I; SAUDREAU, *The Degrees of the Spiritual Life,* Vol. I; P. GARRIGOU-LAGRANGE, *op. cit.,* t. I, Introduction.
[2] *Galat.,* II, 20.

direct and sanctify, rule and govern our body and soul, our thoughts, words and actions in the keeping of Thy law and in the observance of Thy commandments."

1291.   Since we are of ourselves incapable of all this, we must unite ourselves intimately with Our Lord.   Made one with Him through Baptism, we are to render this union even closer by the frequent reception of the Sacraments, especially by the reception of Holy Communion. This communion is prolonged by habitual recollection in order that His *interior dispositions* may become ours and may inspire all our actions, and that we may thus be able to repeat and actually live the words of St. Paul: "I live, now not I; but Christ liveth in me."[1]   In order to obtain this happy result, Jesus sends us, through His merits and His intercession, His Holy Spirit, that same *Holy Spirit* Who produced in His soul the perfect dispositions wherewith it was animated.   By allowing this Divine Spirit to lead us, by being prompt and generous in obeying His inspirations, we come to think, speak and act as Jesus would were He in our place.   Then it is that Christ actually lives in us; with us and through us He glorifies God, sanctifies us, and helps us to sanctify our brethren. If therefore devotion to the Most Blessed Trinity becomes predominant in the unitive way, we do not for that reason cease to unite ourselves with the Incarnate Word through Whom we are to ascend to the Father: "*No man cometh to the Father, but by me.*"[2]

II. *The Characteristics of the Unitive Way*

All these characteristics are embodied in one, the need of simplifying all, of reducing all to unity, that is, of bringing all things to converge towards *intimate union with God through charity.*

1292.   1º The soul lives continually in the presence of God; it delights to contemplate Him living in the heart, "to walk inwardly with God."   In order to live thus, it carefully detaches itself from creatures, so as "to be held by no outward affection."   It is on this account that the soul seeks solitude and silence; it gradually builds in the heart a *sanctuary* where it finds God and converses with Him heart to heart.   Then there is established between the soul and God a sweet and loving intimacy.

[1] *Gal.*, II, 20. — [2] *John*, XIV, 6.

" Intimacy," says Monsignor Gay, [1] " is the consciousness, on the part of those who love, of mutual understanding and sympathy, a consciousness rich in light and feeling and joy and fruit. It is the sense and experience of their mutual attraction, of their fellowship and of their absolute accord, if not of their perfect similarity. It is a union that results in oneness... It is unbounded reliance and confidence in one another, it is a spontaneous candor which makes the heart transparent. Finally, it is as a consequence a mutual liberty, freely given, of contemplating one another and of looking into the very depths of the soul. " Now, it is such intimacy that God permits and even deigns to offer to those who lead an interior life, as the Author of the Imitation so well explains: " Many are His visits to the man of interior life, and sweet the conversation that He holdeth with him; plenteous His consolation, His peace, and His familiarity. " [2]

1293. 2º In this way *the love of God* becomes not only the principal virtue of the soul, but, one may say, its *only virtue*, in the sense that all the other virtues which it practices are for it but so many acts of love.

Thus, prudence becomes a loving consideration of things divine for the purpose of finding therein the standard of its judgments; justice becomes an imitation, as perfect as possible, of Divine righteousness; fortitude, the complete mastery of the passions; temperance, the utter forgetfulness of earthly pleasures, in order to make room for thoughts of Heaven. [3] Still more do the theological virtues now become an exercise of perfect love: faith is no longer limited to occasional acts, but becomes the spirit of faith, the life of faith animated by charity, " the *faith that works through charity;*" hope becomes filial confidence, a holy abandonment to God. At such heights, all the virtues are but one; they are so to speak but different forms of charity: " *Charity is patient, is kind*, etc...*"

1294. 3º A similar simplifying process takes place with regard to *prayer:* reasonings gradually disappear to make room for pious sentiments, which in turn become more simple, as we shall soon explain, until they become but a loving, lingering thought of God.

1295. 4º All this results in a *simplification* of our *whole life*. Whilst previously there were set hours of meditation and prayer, now *life is a perpetual prayer:* whether working, or recreating, whether alone or in the company of others, we continually rise towards God by conforming our will to His: " *I do always the things that please Him.*" [4]

---

1 *Élévations sur la vie... de N. S. J. C.*, 52e élév., t. I, p. 429.
2 *Imit.*, Bk. II, C. I, n. I.
3 ST. THOMAS explains this well in Ia IIæ, q. 61, a. 5: "There are some virtues of men who are on their way to and tending towards the Divine similitude; and these are called *perfecting* virtues... Thus, prudence sees nought else but the things of God; temperance knows no earthly desires; fortitude has no knowledge of passions; and justice, by imitating the Divine Mind, is united thereto by an everlasting covenant. Such are the virtues attributed to the Blessed, or, in this life, to some who are at the summit of perfection. "
4 *John*, VIII, 29.

This conformity is but an act of love and of abandonment into His Hands: prayers, ordinary actions, sufferings, humiliations, all are but so many means of manifesting our love for God: "*My God and my All.*"

1296. Conclusion. From what has been said, one can readily see which persons belong to the unitive way: they are those in whom the three following conditions are verified:

a) A *great purity of heart*, that is to say, not merely the expiation and reparation of past faults, but detachment from whatever may lead to sin, horror for all deliberate venial sins, and even for any wilful resistance to grace. This however does not imply exemption from certain venial faults of frailty, which are forthwith deeply regretted. This purification of the soul, begun in the purgative way and gradually perfected in the illuminative way by the positive practice of the virtues and the generous acceptance of providential crosses, is finally completed in the unitive way by *passive trials*, which we shall soon describe.

b) A *great mastery over self*, acquired by the mortification of the passions and the practice of the moral and theological virtues, which, by disciplining the faculties, subject them little by little to the will, and the will in turn to God. In this way the original order of things is to some extent restored, and the soul now in the full control, can give itself entirely to God.

c) A *constant need of thinking of God*, of conversing with Him and of performing every action with the view of pleasing Him. Real suffering is experienced at not being able to be constantly occupied with the thought of God, and, should the duties of state demand that attention be given to earthly cares, strenuous efforts are made to keep in mind His presence and to turn constantly towards Him: "*My eyes are ever towards the Lord.*" [1]

III. *General Notion of Contemplation* [2]

By dint of thinking of God, the soul lovingly fastens its gaze on Him. This is contemplation, which is one of the characteristic marks of this stage of the spiritual life.

---

[1] *Ps.* XXIV, 15.
[2] P. DE GUIBERT, R. A. M., avril 1922, *Trois définitions de théologie mystique*, p. 162-172; P. GARRIGOU-LAGRANGE, *Perf. et contemplation*, t. I, ch. IV, a. 2, p. 272-294; GABR. DE STE MARIE MADEL., *La contemplation acquise*, dans la *Vie*

1297. 1º **Natural Contemplation.** In general, to contemplate means to look admiringly at an object. There is a *natural contemplation*, which may be *sensitive, imaginative, or intellectual.*

1) It is *sensitive* when we linger with admiration on some beautiful scene, the vastness of the ocean, for example, or a range of mountains. 2) It is called *imaginative*, when we picture with admiration and affection some person or thing we love. 3) It is termed *intellectual* or *philosophic* when our mind dwells admiringly with one simple glance on some great philosophical synthesis, for instance, the absolutely simple and immutable Being, the beginning and end of all things.

1298. 2º **Supernatural Contemplation.** There is also a *supernatural* contemplation with which we are here concerned, the notion and species of which we shall now explain.

A) **Notion.** The term *contemplation* in its *proper signification* designates the act by which the mind simply looks upon some object, apart from the various emotional or imaginative elements which accompany this act. However, when the object of contemplation is beautiful and lovable, contemplation is attended by admiration and love. By *extension* of the term, we call contemplation a *prayer* characterized by the *predominance* of that simple intellectual gaze; hence, this act need not last as long as the meditation lasts, but it suffices that it recur frequently during the prayer and that it be accompanied by *affections*. In this way *contemplative prayer* differs from *discursive* or reasoned prayer (n. 667), since it excludes long reasonings; it differs, too, from *affective* prayer (n. 976), because it excludes the *multiplicity* of acts which characterize this latter. Contemplative prayer, then, may be defined as *a simple and affectionate gaze on God or things divine.* It is more briefly defined by St. Thomas as a *simple gaze on truth.* [1]

1299. B) **Species.** We can distinguish three kinds of contemplation : acquired, infused, and mixed contemplation. [2]

a) *Acquired* contemplation is, at bottom, nothing more than a simplified *affective* prayer, and may be defined as *contemplation in which the simplification of our intellectual and affective acts is the result of our own activity aided by grace.* Frequently even the Gifts of the Holy Ghost exert

---

spirit., sept. 1923, p. [277]; LEHODEY, *The Ways of Mental Prayer*, P. II, C. IX, P. III, C. I, IV; POULAIN, *Graces of Interior Prayer*, SAUDREAU, *The Degrees of the Spiritual Life*, Vol. II, Bk. V.

[1] *Summa theol.*, IIa IIæ, q. 180, a. 1 and 2.

[2] P. G. DE STE MADELEINE, *La contemplation acquise chez les Carmes, Vie spirit.*, Sept. 1923, (P. 277).

their hidden influence, especially the gifts of *knowledge*, of understanding and of wisdom, in order to help us fix our gaze lovingly on God, as we shall explain further on.

1300. b) Infused or passive contemplation is necessarily a free gift; we cannot obtain it by our efforts even with the help of ordinary grace. It is *a kind of contemplation in which the acts of the mind and of the will have become simplified under the influence of a special grace which takes hold of us and causes us to receive lights and affections which God produces in us with our consent.*

It is called *infused*, not because it proceeds from the infused virtues, since acquired contemplation likewise proceeds from them, but because it is not within our power to produce such acts, even with the aid of ordinary grace; and yet, it is not God *alone* that acts in us, but it is God acting in us with our consent, in the sense that we freely accept what He gives us. If our soul under the influence of operating grace is said to be *passive*, it is because it *receives* divine gifts, but it receives them freely, [1] as we shall explain later on. It is called *supernatural* by St. Theresa for a twofold reason: on the same ground that other acts are supernatural, and because God operates in us in a very special way.

1301. The third kind of contemplation is called *mixed* contemplation. We shall see later that *infused* contemplation is at times of *very short duration*. It may therefore happen that, in the course of the same prayer, the acts arising from our own initiative alternate with those produced by the special action of operating grace. This is exactly what occurs in the case of those who are being initiated into infused contemplation. Contemplation is then *mixed*, that is to say, it is alternately active and passive; however, this kind of contemplation is generally referred to infused contemplation of which it constitutes, so to speak, the first degree.

IV. *Division of the Fourth Book*

1302. In the unitive way two distinct [2] forms or phases may be distinguished:

1° *The simple or active unitive way,* characterized by *the cultivation of the gifts of the Holy Ghost,* especially the *active* gifts, and by the *simplification of prayer,* which

---

[1] One may say of contemplation what St. Thomas says of justification (Ia IIæ, q. III, a. 2, ad 3): "God does not justify us without our co-operation; because whilst we are justified, we freely conform to God's righteousness."

[2] This division is generally accepted today under one name or another. In a remarkable article in the *Vie spirituelle* for March 1923, p. 645, J. MARITAIN, whilst declaring the aim to be the same for all, namely, union with God through perfect charity and the gifts of the Holy Ghost, recognizes that there are in fact two ways, the way of those who are under the rule of the *active gifts* and who have

becomes the prayer of simplicity, called by many active contemplation.

2° The *passive* or *mystic unitive way*, characterized by *infused* contemplation, or contemplation *properly so-called*.

3° Moreover, contemplation is at times attended by *extraordinary phenomena* such as visions and revelations, to which are opposed the diabolical counterfeits of obsession and possession.

4° In matters of so difficult a nature, it is not surprising to find *varying opinions* or *controverted* questions. These we shall examine in a special chapter.

In the *conclusion* we shall point out what should be the attitude of the spiritual director toward contemplatives.

CHAPTER I

The Simple Unitive Way

1303. This Way is the state of fervent souls who habitually live in intimate union with God, without having so far received the gift of infused contemplation. Already accustomed to the practice of the moral and theological virtues, they strive to perfect these by the cultivation of the *gifts of the Holy Ghost*. Their mental prayer is *simplified* more and more, and becomes a *prayer of simplicity* or of *simple recollection* which goes by the name of *contemplation improperly so-called, acquired* or *active*. The existence of this state is shown by *experience*, by the distinction of the *two kinds of contemplation*, as well as by the difference between the *active* and the *contemplative* gifts.

1304. 1° First of all, *experience* shows that there are, both in the cloister and in the world, truly fervent souls,

---

only a contemplation in the loose sense of the word, and the way of the *contemplatives*, in whom the gifts of understanding and wisdom predominate. We shall come back later to this teaching.

living in habitual union with God, generously and perseveringly, and at times heroically practicing the Christian virtues, who nevertheless do not possess infused contemplation. These souls are docile to the Holy Ghost, habitually correspond to His inspirations, and from time to time are even the recipients of special inspirations, yet there is nothing that betrays either to themselves or to their spiritual director that they are in the passive state properly so-called. [1]

1305. 2° The same conclusion flows from the distinction between *acquired* contemplation and *infused* contemplation. Traces of this distinction are found even in the writings of St. Clement of Alexandria [2] and Richard of St. Victor, and since the end of the seventeenth century it has become *classical.* Such souls as continue to practice acquired contemplation during a notable period of their life are in the simple unitive way.

In order to avoid any misunderstanding we must state in this place that we do not say that there are two *diverging* ways; on the contrary, we admit that acquired contemplation is an excellent *preparation* for infused contemplation, whenever it shall please God to grant the latter. There are, however, numerous souls who do not receive it, although they remain intimately united to God. These remain therefore in the *simple unitive way* without any fault of their own. [3]

1306. 3° What confirms this is that among the gifts of the Holy Ghost, some are given chiefly for *action*, and others chiefly for *contemplation*. Now, it happens that certain souls, endowed with a more active temperament and otherwise absorbed by more numerous occupations, cultivate more especially the active gifts and are thus less fitted for contemplation properly so-called.

Father Noble [4] has this to say: "It is not midst the fatigue of labor, or the performance of tasks which are complicated and absorb our

---

[1] When one reads, for example, such biographies as those of Fathers Olivaint and Ginhac, of Mollevaut or de Courson, and so many others that have been published, one cannot help admiring their virtues, their union with God, their docility to the Holy Ghost, and yet, one cannot see where they practiced infused contemplation.

[2] DOM MÉNAGER, *La doctrine spirituelle de Clément d'Alexandrie, Vie spirituelle*, Jan. 1923, p. 424; See *Études carmélitaines*, 1920-1922, where there is a series of articles on acquired contemplation; our own article on *l'oraison de simplicité, Vie spirit.*, Dec. 1920, p. 167-174.

[3] This conclusion is admitted by Father GARRIGOU-LAGRANGE in answer to a letter of J. Maritain *(Perfection Chrét. et contemplation*, t. II, p. 75): "And so we have experienced no difficulty in recognizing it many a time; it may happen that even very generous souls, in default of certain conditions which do not depend on their will, would not arrive at the mystic way, except after a period of time longer in duration than that of average existence here below. This can be the result not only of an unfavorable environment, of a want of spiritual direction, but also of physical temperament. "

[4] *Rev. des Jeunes*, 25 Sept. 1923, p. 613. J. Maritain proves the same in the afore-mentioned article. He adds, it is true, that souls in which the active gifts

whole attention, that we can concentrate on our own thoughts and keep our eyes steadily fixed on spiritual and eternal realities. To be able to contemplate, one must not be harassed by persistent and fatiguing labors; at least one must be in a position to suspend them long enough to enable the heart and the mind to rise peacefully towards God."

These souls will not enjoy, at least habitually, infused contemplation; still, they will be intimately united with God and docile to the inspirations of the Holy Ghost. Such is the state which we call the *simple unitive way*.

Since it is characterized 1° by *the cultivation of the gifts of the Holy Ghost* and 2° by the *prayer of simplicity*, we shall treat successively of these two elements.

ART. I. THE GIFTS OF THE HOLY GHOST [1]

We shall treat: 1° of the gifts of the Holy Ghost *in general;* 2° of each of them *in particular;* 3° of the *share they have in contemplation;* 4° of the *fruits* and the *beatitudes* which correspond to the gifts.

§ I. The Gifts of the Holy Ghost in General

We shall explain: 1° their *nature;* 2° their *excellence;* 3° the manner of *cultivating* them; 4° how they may be *classified.*

1. *Nature of the Gifts of the Holy Ghost*

1307. We have spoken in no. 119 of how the Holy Ghost dwells in our soul and infuses, besides habitual grace, supernatural habits which perfect our faculties and enable them to perform supernatural acts under the impulse of actual grace. These habits are the *virtues* and the *gifts*. By bringing out the difference between these two kinds of habits we shall see more clearly in what the gifts consist.

---

predominate are in the *mystic state*, though they do not have infused contemplation. We think that to avoid misunderstandings it should be said they are in the *so-called* mystic state.

[1] ST. THOMAS, *In III Sent.*, dist. XXXIV-XXXV; Ia IIæ, q. 68; IIa IIæ, qq. 8, 9, 19, 45, 52, 121, 139; see commentators, especially JOHN OF ST. THOMAS, In Iam IIæ, q. 68; SUAREZ, *De gratia*, P. III, cap. VIII; DENYS LE CHARTREUX, *de Donis Spiritus S.;* J.-B. DE ST. JURE, *L'homme spirituel*, Ie Part., C. IV, Des sept dons; L. LALLEMANT, *Spiritual Doctrine*, 4th Principle, Docility to the Guidance of the Holy Spirit; MGR PERRIOT, *L'Ami du Clergé*, 1892, p. 389-393; FROGET, *The Indwelling of the Holy Ghost*, p. 378-424; CARD. BILLOT, *De virtutibus infusis* (1901), p. 162-190; GARDEIL, *Dons du S. Esprit, Dict. de Théol.*, t. IV, col. 1728-1781; D. JORET, *Les dons du S. Esprit, Vie spirituelle*, t. I, pp. 229, 383; P. GARRIGOU-LAGRANGE, *Perfect. et contemplation*, t. I, ch. IV, a. 5-6, p. 338-417; MGR LANDRIEUX, *Le divin méconnu*.

1308. 1° **Difference between the Gifts and the Virtues. A**) The fundamental difference does not come from their *material object* or field of action, since this is the same in both, but from the *different manner in which they act* in the soul.

St. Thomas [1] tells us that God may act in us in two ways: **a**) by accommodating Himself to the human mode of action. This is what He does in the case of the *virtues*. He helps us to reflect, to seek the best means to reach our end. In order to supernaturalize these operations He gives us actual graces, but *leaves us free to take the initiative* according to the dictates of prudence or of reason enlightened by faith. It is therefore we who act under the impulse of grace.

b) But, by means of the gifts, God acts in a supra-human way. He Himself takes the initiative. Before we have had the time to reflect and consult the dictates of prudence, He sends us *divine intuitions*, lights and inspirations which act in us, *without deliberation* on our part, but never without our consent. This grace, which sweetly invites and effectively obtains our consent, may be called *operating grace*. Under its influence we are rather passive than active; our activity consists chiefly in freely consenting to the operation of God, in allowing ourselves to be led by the Holy Ghost, and in promptly and generously following His inspirations.

1309. B) By the light of this fundamental principle, we understand better the **differences** existing between the *gifts* and the *virtues*:

a) The virtues incline us to act *in accordance with the nature of our faculties*: thus, with the help of the grace we receive, we inquire, reason and work as we do in actions of a purely natural order. The virtues are therefore energies that are primarily and directly *active*. The gifts on the contrary impart to us a *docility* and a *receptiveness* that enable us to *receive* and *follow* the motions of operating grace. This grace moves our faculties to act, without however taking away their liberty, so that the soul, as St. Thomas tells us, is more passive than active, "*is not the mover, but the thing moved.*" [2]

b) In the case of the virtues, we act according to the principles and rules of *supernatural prudence*. We are obliged to reflect, deliberate, take counsel, make choices, etc.

---

[1] In the *Book of Sentences* (III Sent., d. 34, q. 1, a. 1) he employs this expression: "The gifts are distinguished from the virtues by the fact that the virtues contribute to the performance of the act in a human way, but the gifts in a preterhuman way." In the *Summa* he uses a different expression: "By them (the gifts) man is disposed to become amenable to the Divine Inspiration" (Ia IIæ, q. 68, a. 1.) Cfr. J. DE GUIBERT, *Dons du S. Esprit et mode d'agir ultra-humain* in *Rev. d'Asc. et de Mystique*, Oct. 1922, p. 394. No doubt, there is here a shade of distinction; however, it remains true that under the influence of the gifts, once they have reached their full development, we are more passive than active.

[2] *Sum. theol.*, IIa IIæ, q. 52, a. 2.

Under the influence of the gifts, we let ourselves be led by a *divine inspiration* which suddenly and without any reflection on our part vigorously urges us to do such or such a thing.

c) Since the share of grace is far greater in the case of the gifts than in that of the virtues, the acts performed under the influence of the former are, all other circumstances being the same, *more perfect* than those performed under the action of the virtues. It is due to the gifts that the third degree of the virtues is practiced and heroic acts performed.

1310. **C)** Divers *comparisons* are employed to give a better understanding of this doctrine. **a)** To practice virtue is *to row*, to use the gifts is *to sail:* in this latter way one advances more rapidly and with less effort. **b)** The child who with his mother's help takes a few steps forward stands for the Christian who practices the virtues with the help of grace; whilst the child whom the mother takes in her arms to make him advance more rapidly stands for the Christian who makes use of the gifts by corresponding to operating grace. **c)** The artist who strikes the strings of a harp to produce harmonious sounds represents the Christian who practices the virtues; but, when the Holy Ghost comes Himself to touch the strings of the heart, the soul is then under the influence of the gifts. This is a comparison employed by the Fathers to picture the action of Jesus upon Mary's soul: "*A most melodious harp used by Jesus to delight the Eternal Father.*"

1311. 2° **Definition.** From what has so far been said, we can conclude that the gifts of the Holy Ghost are *supernatural habits which impart such docility to our faculties that they promptly comply with the inspirations of grace.* However, as we shall soon explain, this docility is at the outset but mere receptiveness which needs to be *cultivated* to attain its full development. Besides, it is never exercised, except when God bestows that actual grace which we call *operating* grace. On such occasions, the soul, whilst passive under the action of God, is most active in accomplishing His Will, and so, one may say that the gifts are at once "sources of suppleness and of energy, of docility and of power... which render the soul more passive under the Hand of God, and at the same time more active in His service and in the practice of good works." [1]

II. *Excellence of the Gifts*

This excellence will appear if we consider the gifts *in themselves* and in their relation to the *virtues*.

1312. 1° That these gifts are excellent *in themselves* is evident. The more united and the more docile we are to

---

the Holy Ghost, the source of all sanctity, the holier we are. Now, the gifts place us under the direct action of the Holy Ghost Who, living in our soul, enlightens our mind with His lights, points out clearly what we must do, enkindles our heart and strengthens our will to make us accomplish the good suggested. This union is therefore as close as it can be in this life.

The effects are likewise priceless. It is the gifts that cause us to practice the third or highest degree of the moral and the theological virtues, and the same gifts inspire the performance of heroic acts. It is through them that, when God so wills it, the soul is raised to contemplation, the suppleness and docility they produce being the *immediate disposition* required for the mystic state. This is, then, the shortest way to the highest perfection.

1313. 2° If we *compare* the gifts with the virtues, the former are, as St. Thomas [1] says, more perfect than the moral and the intellectual virtues. God is not the immediate object of these, whilst the gifts direct the virtues to a higher plane where, blending with charity, they unite us to God.

Thus, *prudence* perfected by the gift of *counsel* makes us share in the light of God; the gift of *fortitude* imparts to us, places at our disposal, God's very strength. The gifts however are not superior to the theological virtues, especially charity, for charity is the most perfect of all spiritual goods, the source whence the gifts flow. Nevertheless, it may be said that the gifts perfect the *exercise* of the theological virtues. Thus, the gift of understanding renders our faith more vivid and more discerning by disclosing the inner harmony that exists among our dogmas; and the gift of wisdom perfects the exercise of the virtue of charity by making us relish God and divine things. The gifts are therefore with regard to the theological virtues as means to an end, but they impart to the virtues a further perfection.

III. *Cultivation of the Gifts of the Holy Ghost*

1314. 1° **Gradual Development.** We receive the gifts of the Holy Ghost at the same time that we receive the state of grace. They are then merely *supernatural faculties*. When we come to the age of reason and our heart turns towards God, we begin, under the influence of actual grace, to use our whole supernatural organism, the gifts of the Holy Ghost included. It is indeed incredible that

---

[1] *Sum. theol.*, IIa IIae, q. 9, a. 3, ad 3. " The gifts are more perfect than the moral and intellectual virtues; they are not more perfect than the theological; but they are all rather related to the perfection of the theological virtues, as to an end. " Cfr. Ia IIae, q. 68, a. 8.

these gifts should remain unavailing and unavailable during a long period of our life. [1]

However, in order that they may attain their normal and complete development, we must have previously practised the moral virtues during a notable period of time, varying according to the providential designs of God and our co-operation with grace. It is, in fact, the moral virtues, as we have said, that little by little make the soul tractable and dispose it to enjoy that perfect docility required for the full exercise of the gifts. In the mean time, the latter grow as habits, together with habitual grace, and frequently, unknown to us, join their energies to those of the virtues to make us perform our supernatural acts.

There are even times when through His *operating* grace the Holy Ghost enkindles *temporarily* an unwonted fervor of soul which is a kind of passing contemplation. What fervent soul has not at times felt these sudden inspirations of grace when all it had to do was to receive the divine motion and follow it? It may have been while reading the Gospels or some devout book, on the occasion of some Communion or of a visit to the Blessed Sacrament, at the time of some retreat or when making a choice of a state in life, at the time of ordination or religious profession, that it seemed to us that the grace of God sweetly and strongly carried us along.

1315. 2° **Means for the Cultivation of the Gifts. A)** *The practice of the moral virtues is the first requisite condition* for the cultivation of the gifts. Such is the teaching of St. Thomas [2]: "*The moral and the intellectual virtues precede the gifts,* since man, through being well subordinate to his own reason, is disposed to be rightly subordinate to God." Indeed, to acquire that divine docility which the gifts confer, one must needs have previously conquered one's passions and vices and formed habits of prudence, of humility, of obedience, of meekness, of chastity. How can one discern, accept and follow with docility the inspirations of grace, when the soul is troubled by the prudence of the flesh, by pride, wilfulness, anger and lust! Before being led by divine impulses, one must needs have followed, first of all, the rules of Christian prudence; before obeying

---

[1] Some theologians, like Abbé Perriot *(Ami du Clergé,* 1892, p. 391), think that the gifts intervene in every meritorious work. Most theologians, without going that far, hold that they frequently exert their influence upon these acts without our being conscious of it.

[2] *Sum. theol.,* Iª IIæ, q. 68, a. 8, ad 2.

the motions of grace, one must needs have observed the commandments and triumphed over pride.

Cajetan,[1] the faithful commentator of St. Thomas rightly says: "Let spiritual directors note this and let them see to it that their disciples are, first of all, exercised in the active life before proposing to them the heights of contemplation. One must, in fact, tame one's passions by habits of meekness, of patience, etc., of liberality, of humility, etc., in order to be able, once the passions have been dominated, to rise to the contemplative life. In default of this previous exercise in asceticism, many who instead of walking rush along the ways of God, find themselves after having devoted a great part of their life to contemplation devoid of all the virtues, impatient, irritable, proud, if they are put to the least test. Such persons have neither had an active nor a contemplative life, nor the combination of the two, but have rather built upon sand, and would to God that this were a rare blunder!"

1316. B) The gifts are likewise cultivated by *combatting the spirit of the world*, which is diametrically opposed to the Spirit of God. This is what St. Paul asks of us: "*Now, we have received not the spirit of this world, but the Spirit that is of God... But the sensual man perceiveth not these things that are of the Spirit of God; for it is foolishness to him, and he cannot understand, because it is spiritually examined.*"[2] The better to combat this spirit of the world we must read and meditate upon the Gospel maxims and live according to them as perfectly as possible. Then indeed shall we be prepared to yield ourselves to the guidance of the Holy Ghost.

1317. C) Next come the *positive* and direct means which place us under the action of the Holy Ghost:

a) First of all, there is *interior recollection* or the habit of frequently thinking of God living not only near us but in us (n. 92). In this way one gradually comes to the point of never losing sight of God's presence, even in the midst of the most absorbing occupations. Often one withdraws into the inner shrine of the heart, there to meet the Holy Ghost and hearken to His voice: "*I will hear what the Lord God will speak in me.*"[3] Then one realizes what the author of the Imitation says: "*Happy is the soul which heareth the Lord speaking within her, and receiveth from His mouth the word of comfort.*"[4] The Holy Ghost speaks to the heart, and His words bring with them light, strength, and consolation.

---

[1] In IIam IIæ, q. 182, a. 1, § VII; cfr. JORET, *Vie Spir.*, 10 avril 1920, p. 45-49, and *La Contemplation Mystique*, 1923, p. 71.
[2] *I Cor.*, II, 12-14. — [3] *Ps.* LXXXIV, 9. — [4] *Imitation*, Bk. III, C. I.

1318. **b)** Since this Divine Spirit demands sacrifices, one must become accustomed to follow *promptly* and *generously* the least of His inspirations, whenever there is no doubt that it is He Who speaks: " *For I do always the things that please Him.* " [1] Otherwise, He would cease to speak, or at least He would speak much less frequently: " *To-day if you shall hear his voice, harden not your hearts: As in the provocation, according to the day of temptation in the wilderness: where your fathers tempted me...* " [2] If the sacrifices He demands seem difficult, let one not lose heart, but say with St. Augustine: " *Grant, O Lord, what Thou commandest, and command then what Thou wilt.* " What is important is never to resist deliberately His inspirations; for the more docile one is, the more will He be pleased to act on the soul.

1319. **c)** We must even go to meet Him, and in union with the Incarnate Word, Who promised to send us His Spirit, in union with Her who is the most perfect Temple and the Spouse of the Holy Ghost, confidently invoke Him as did the Apostles in the Upper Room where they were persevering in prayer " *with Mary, the mother of Jesus.* " [3]

The Church in her liturgy places at our disposal magnificent prayers for drawing unto ourselves the Spirit of God, such as the sequence, *Veni Sancte Spiritus*, the hymn, *Veni Creator Spiritus*, and other invocations found in the Pontifical for the ordinations of subdeacons, deacons, and priests. These prayers have no doubt a special efficacy, and their content is so full of beauty that we cannot recite them without being moved by pious emotions.

Another excellent practice is that of reciting before each one of our actions the antiphon, *Veni Sancte Spiritus*, and the adjoined prayer. In it we ask for Divine Charity, the source of the gifts, and the gift of wisdom, " *recta sapere,* " which, being the most perfect, contains all the others. This prayer, if recited with attention and fervor, cannot remain ineffectual.

IV. *Classification of the Gifts of the Holy Ghost*

1320. The prophet Isaias in announcing the coming of the Messias declares that " *the Spirit of the Lord shall rest upon him: the spirit of wisdom and of understanding, the spirit of counsel and of fortitude, the spirit of knowledge, and of godliness* "; [4] and since by Baptism we are incorporated into Christ, we share in these same gifts, which according to Tradition are seven in number.

They may be classified in various ways:

A) From the point of view of *perfection,* fear of the Lord is the least perfect, and wisdom the most perfect.

B) If we consider the *faculties* upon which they exercise their action, we may distinguish *intellectual* and *affective*

---

[1] *John*, VIII, 29. — [2] *Ps.* XCIV, 8; Hebr., III, 7-8. — [3] *Acts*, I, 14.
[4] *Isaias*, XI, 2-3.—The Hebrew text makes no mention of the gift of *piety*, but the Septuagint and the Vulgate do so, and Tradition, from the third century on, confirms the sevenfold number.

gifts. The former are those which enlighten the mind : knowledge, understanding, wisdom and counsel. The latter are those which strengthen the will : piety, strength and the fear of the Lord. Among the intellectual gifts there are chiefly three which produce infused contemplation : *knowlegde, understanding* and *wisdom.* The others are called *active* gifts.

C) If we examine the gifts in relation to the special virtues they perfect, the gift of *counsel* perfects the virtue of *prudence;* the gift of *piety* perfects the virtue of *religion* as related to the virtue of justice; the gift of *strength* perfects the virtue of *fortitude;* the gift of *fear* perfects the virtue of *temperance;* the gifts of *knowledge* and *understanding* perfect the virtue of *faith;* the gift of *fear* is connected with the virtue of *hope,* and the gift of *wisdom* with that of *charity.*

This is the division we follow, because it shows us better the nature of each gift, by placing it side by side with the corresponding virtue.

§ II. The Seven Gifts in Particular

I. *The Gift of Counsel*

1321. 1º **Nature. A)** The gift of counsel *perfects the virtue of prudence by making us judge promptly and rightly, as by a sort of supernatural intuition, what must be done, especially in difficult cases.* By the virtue of prudence we reflect, and we carefully seek out the best means of attaining a certain end, profiting by the lessons of the past and putting to advantage our present knowledge, in order to reach a wise decision. With the gift of counsel it is otherwise. The Holy Ghost speaks to our heart and in an instant makes us understand what we must do. Thus is fulfilled the promise made by Our Lord to His Apostles : " But when they shall deliver you up, *take no thought how or what to speak:* for it shall be given you in that hour what to speak. "[1] This is exactly what we see in the conduct of St. Peter after Pentecost. Arrested by order of the Sanhedrin and forbidden to Preach Jesus Christ any longer, he replies immediately : " *We ought to obey God, rather than men.* "[2]

Many Saints have enjoyed this gift of counsel. St. Antoninus had it to such a high degree that posterity bestowed on him the title of good counsellor, *Antoninus, the Counsellor;* for he was consulted not

---

[1] *Matth.,* X, 19. — [2] *Acts,* V, 29.

only by the simple faithful, but even by statesmen, particularly by Cosmo de Medici, who on several occasions chose him as his ambassador. We see this gift admirably exemplified in St. Catherine of Sienna, who, though very young and without having as yet pursued any studies, gave wise counsels to princes, Cardinals, and to the Sovereign Pontiff himself. We behold this gift also in St. Joan of Arc, who, unskilled in the art of war, planned a campaign that astonished the best generals of the time. She tells us whence she drew her wisdom: "You have held your council and I have held mine."

1322. **B)** The *proper object* of the gift of counsel is the right ordering of particular acts. The gifts of knowledge and understanding furnish us with the general principles, but the gift of counsel enables us to apply these to the thousand and one particular cases which present themselves. The light of the Holy Ghost then shows us what must be done at the time, at the place, and in the circumstances in which we are, and, if we are charged with the direction of others, what advice we must give to them.

1323. 2º **Necessity.** **A)** This gift is necessary *to all* in some of the more important and difficult situations, in which salvation or sanctification are concerned, for example, in matters of vocation, or in certain occasions of sin encountered even in the discharge of duty. Human reason being fallible and uncertain in its ways and able to proceed only slowly and with caution, it is of importance to receive in the decisive moments of our life the lights of this Divine Counsellor, Who with a single glance takes in all, and Who at the opportune moment makes us see with certainty what we must do in such or such difficult circumstances. [1] "With the gift of counsel," says Mgr. Landrieux, "the soul is able to discern the means; it sees its way; it goes along with assurance, be the way steep, deserted and forbidding... and it knows how to wait for the acceptable time." [2]

B) This gift is especially necessary to *superiors* and to *priests*, both for their own sanctification and for that of others. **a)** At times it is so difficult to know how to reconcile an interior life with one of zeal, or the affection due to souls with perfect chastity, or the simplicity of

---

[1] "Since, however, human reason is unable to grasp the singular and contingent things which may occurr, the result is that the *thoughts of mortal men are fearful, and our counsels uncertain* (Wis. IX, 14). Hence in the research of counsel, man requires to be directed by God, Who comprehends all things: and this is done through the gift of counsel, whereby man is directed as though counselled by God, just as in human affairs those who are unable to take counsel for themselves seek counsel from those who are wiser." (ST. THOM., IIa IIæ, q. 52, a. 1, ad 1).

[2] MGR LANDRIEUX, *op. cit.*, p. 163.—"The privation of this gift is for us a cause of very great evils," says Father ST. JURE. Part I, C. IV, § 7, "because without it there is confusion in our thoughts, blindness in our designs, hastiness in our resolutions, lack of reflection in our words, presumption in our actions."

the dove with the prudence of the serpent, that a special light from the Holy Ghost is none too much to show us what line of conduct to pursue. **b)** Likewise *Superiors* who must see that the rule is faithfully observed and retain at the same time the confidence and affection of their subjects, need great tact to combine due strictness and kindness, not to multiply orders and reprimands, and to have the rule observed through love rather than fear. **c)** *Spiritual directors* above all stand in need of special enlightenment in order to discern what suits their various penitents, to know their defects and select the best means to effect their reformation, to decide their vocations and to lead them to that degree of perfection or to that manner of life to which they are called.

1324. 3° **Means of cultivating this gift. A)** The cultivation of this gift requires, first of all, a deep sense of our weakness and frequent recourse to the Holy Ghost so that He may teach us His ways: " *Shew, O Lord, thy ways to me, and teach me thy paths.* " [1] He will not fail to come to enlighten us in one way or another, for He stoops down to the humble; and He will not fail us, especially if we take care to ask His help in the morning for the entire day, at the beginning of the principal actions of the day, and particularly in all difficult cases.

B) Further, we must accustom ourselves *to listen* to the voice of the Holy Ghost, to judge all things by His light without allowing ourselves to be influenced by human considerations, and to follow the least of His inspirations. Then, finding our soul open and docile, He will speak to the heart still more frequently. [2]

II. *The Gift of Piety*

1325. 1° **Nature.** This gift perfects the virtue of *religion*, which is a virtue related to that of *justice*, by *begetting in our hearts a filial affection for God and a tender devotion towards those persons and things consecrated to Him, in order to make us fulfil our religious duties with a holy joy.*

The *virtue* of religion is acquired only through effort, whilst the *gift of piety* is *communicated* to us by the Holy Ghost.

A) This gift makes us see in God not merely our Sovereign Master, but the best and most loving Father: " *You*

---

[1] *Ps.* XXIV, 4.
[2] This is why DONOSO CORTÈS asserted that it is the contemplatives who make the best counsellors: "Among the people whom I have observed closely, and I have observed many, the only ones in whom I have discerned an unruffled common sense, true sagacity, wondrous aptitude to offer practical and sound solutions to the most difficult problems... are those who have led a retired contemplative life. " (*Essai sur le catholicisme*, p. 200).

have received the Spirit of adoption of sons, whereby we cry Abba (Father)."[1] It fills the soul with confidence and love without endangering the reverence due to God.

It fosters in us a threefold sentiment: 1) *filial respect* towards God, which makes us adore Him with a holy joy as our most beloved Father. Then our spiritual exercises, instead of being an arduous task, become a need of the soul, a longing of the heart for God; 2) a *generous and tender love* that leads us to sacrifice self for God and God's glory, in order to please Him: "*I do always the things that please Him;*"[2] hence, it is not a selfish piety, which seeks consolations, nor an inert piety, which remains inactive when it should act, nor yet a sentimental piety, which but looks for emotional satisfaction and loses itself in idle dreams; but it is a virile piety, which expresses its love by complying with the Will of God; 3) an *affectionate obedience*, which sees in the commandments and in the counsels the wise and paternal expression of the Divine Will in our regard; hence results a holy abandonment into the hands of this loving Father, Who knows far better than we do what is good for us and Who tests us only to purify us and unite us to Himself: "*To them that love God all things work together unto good.*"[3]

1326. B) This same sentiment makes us love those *persons* and *things* which have a participation in the Divine Being and in His perfections.

1) Thus, we love and venerate the Blessed Virgin, because she is the Mother of God and our Mother (n. 155-156); and so we refer to her some of the veneration and some of the love we have for God, since of all creatures she best reflects His perfections. 2) We likewise love and revere in the Angels and Saints a reflection of the divine attributes. 3) Holy Writ is for us the Word of God, a letter from Our Heavenly Father, communicating to us His thoughts and His designs in our regard. 4) *Holy Church* is for us the *Spouse of Christ,* born of His Sacred Heart, perpetuating His mission upon earth, and invested with His own infallible authority; she is for us *a holy mother* who has brought us forth to the life of grace and nourished us with her sacraments. We are therefore interested in whatever concerns her, in her successes and her humiliations; we espouse all her interests and are glad to further them; we sorrow at her sorrows; in a word we bear her a *filial love.* To this we add a *sincere obedience*, well knowing that when we submit to her injunctions we yield obedience to God Himself: "*He that heareth you heareth me.*"[4] 5) The head of this Church, the Sovereign Pontiff, is for us the vice-regent, the visible representative of Jesus Christ upon earth. We therefore offer him the veneration and love we hold for the Invisible Head of the Church, and we delight in obeying him as if he were Christ Himself. 6) We entertain these same sentiments towards our *superiors* in whom we love to see Jesus Christ: "*I look upon my superior as upon the likeness of Christ;*" and if God confides subjects to our care, we have for them the same fatherly tenderness which God shows towards us.

1327. 2° **Necessity.** A) All Christians stand in need of this gift if they are to fulfil joyfully and readily their duties of religion towards God, of respectful obedience

---

[1] *Rom.,* VIII, 15. — [2] *John,* VIII, 29. — [3] *Rom.,* VIII, 28. — [4] *Luke,* X, 16.

towards their superiors, and of condescension towards their inferiors. Without it they will act towards God as towards a master, prayer will be a burden rather than a comfort, and God's providential trials will appear as severe or even unjust punishments. Under the influence of this gift, on the contrary, God appears to us as a Father; it is with child-like joy that we render Him our homages, and with a sweet resignation that we kiss the hand of Him Who strikes us only to cleanse us and unite us even more closely to Himself.

1328. **B)** This gift is even more necessary to priests, to religious and to all who strive to live a perfect life in the world. **a)** Without it, the numerous spiritual exercises which form so great a part of their life would soon become an intolerable burden; for no one can abide long in the thought of God, except he love Him. It is this very gift of piety which, united to charity, infuses into the soul those sentiments of filial tenderness towards God, that transforms our exercises of piety into sweet communion with Our Heavenly Father. Doubtless, aridity comes at times to disturb this intimate colloquy, but it is patiently, nay, joyfully accepted as coming from a Father Who hides Himself only to make His child seek Him; and since we entertain but one desire, to please Him, we are content to suffer for Him: " *When one loves, one labors not.* "

b) This gift is no less necessary in order to treat with kindness and love those persons who do not naturally appeal to us, to entertain for those whom God deigns to confide to our care a paternal tenderness, and to share the sentiments of St. Paul, who wanted to beget Jesus Christ Himself in the souls of his disciples: " *My little children, of whom I am in labour again, until Christ be formed in you.* " [1]

1329. 3° **Means of cultivating this gift.** **A)** The first means is frequent meditation upon the beautiful texts of Holy Scripture which portray the goodness, the paternal mercy of God towards men and particularly towards the just (n. 93-96). It is by the name of Father that He is pleased to be known and loved, especially under the New Dispensation. We must then have recourse to Him in all our difficulties, with all the eagerness and confidence of children. We shall thus perform our exercises of piety with love, seeking first and foremost the good pleasure of God and not our personal consolation.

B) The second means is that of *transforming our ordinary actions into acts of religion*, doing these actions in order to please Our Father Who is in Heaven (527). In this way our entire life becomes a prayer and consequently an act of filial piety towards God and of fraternal piety towards the neighbor. We fulfil perfectly the words of St. Paul: " *Exercise thyself unto godliness... for godliness is profitable to all things, having promise of the life that now is and of that which is to come.* " [2]

---

[1] *Galat.*, IV, 19. — [2] *I. Tim.*, IV, 7-8.

III. *The Gift of Fortitude*

1330. 1º **Nature.** *It is a gift which perfects the virtue of fortitude, by imparting to the will an impulse and an energy which enable it to do great things joyfully and fearlessly despite all obstacles.*

It differs from the virtue of fortitude in that it is not the outcome of our efforts, but of the action of the Holy Ghost, Who takes hold of the soul and gives it a singular dominion over the lower faculties and over exterior difficulties. The *virtue* of fortitude does not relieve us of a certain amount of hesitancy, of a certain apprehension with regard to obstacles or failures. The *gift* of fortitude brings with it determination, assurance, joy, the certain hope of success, and thus effects greater results. Thus, St. Stephen was said to be full of fortitude because he was full of the Holy Ghost: "*And Stephen, full of grace and fortitude... being full of the Holy Ghost...*" [1]

1331. To *act* and to *endure*, even midst difficulties of the most arduous nature, and at the price of heroic effort are the two acts to which the gift of fortitude leads us.

a) *To act*, that is to say, to undertake without hesitation or fear the most arduous tasks, for example, to practice perfect recollection in the midst of tireless activity, as did St. Vincent de Paul and St. Theresa; to remain humble when surrounded by honors, like St. Louis; to face dangers, weariness, labors, and death itself, as St. Francis Xavier did; to trample under foot human respect, to contemn honors, like St. John Chrysostom, who feared but one thing, sin. **b)** No less strength is required to *endure* long and painful maladies, as did St. Ledwina, or moral sufferings such as are endured by certain souls in the course of the passive trials; or to observe faithfully throughout life all the prescriptions of a rule. Martyrdom is considered the highest act of this gift, and rightly so, since we thereby surrender to God our most cherished possession, life; yet, to shed our blood drop by drop by spending ourselves completely for souls, as so many humble priests and devout laymen do, following the example of St. Paul, constitutes a martyrdom hardly less meritorious, and one which is within the reach of all.

1332. 2º **Its Necessity.** It would be useless to insist at length upon the necessity of this gift. We have already said (n. 360) that in many an instance we must do the heroic in order to preserve the state of grace, and it is precisely this gift of fortitude that enables us to perform in a spirit of generosity these difficult acts.

This gift is even more necessary in the discharge of duty imposed by certain professions or vocations in which health and even life itself are endangered. Such is the case with the physician, the soldier and the priest.

1333. 3º **Means of cultivating fortitude. A)** Since our strength is not from ourselves, but from God, we must

---

[1] *Acts*, VI, 8; VII, 55.

evidently look for it in Him, by humbly acknowledging our weakness. Providence makes use of the weakest instruments, provided they be conscious of their own weakness and rely upon Him Who alone is able to make them strong. Such is the meaning of the words of St. Paul· *"But the foolish things of the world hath God chosen, that he may confound the wise; and the weak things of the world hath God chosen, that he may confound the strong... that he might bring to nought things that are: that no flesh should glory in his sight."* [1] It is principally in the reception of the Holy Eucharist that we can seek from Jesus the strength we need in order to overcome all obstacles. St. Chrysostom speaks of the Christians returning from the Holy Table as having the strength of lions, since they share in the very power of Christ. [2]

1334. B) We must likewise carefully use the thousand and one circumstances wherein, by reason of the continuity of the effort, we can exercise ourselves in fortitude and in patience.

This is done by those who from morning to night submit joyfully to a rule, who strive to be attentive at their prayers, and recollected all day long, who keep silence when they feel inclined to speak, who avoid the sight of such objects as excite curiosity, who suffer without complaint the unseasonableness of the weather, who show kindness to those towards whom they feel a natural antipathy, who accept humbly and patiently the reproaches made to them, who accommodate themselves to the tastes, desires, and temperaments of others, who stand contradiction without irritation, in a word, who strive to vanquish their own petty passions and to conquer themselves. To do all this, not once in passing, but habitually, to do so not merely patiently, but joyfully — this is already heroic virtue, and when later on grave circumstances present themselves, heroic action will not prove too difficult: [3] for we shall then have the strength of the Holy Ghost Himself: *" You shall receive the power of the Holy Ghost coming upon you, and you shall be witnesses unto me."* [4]

---

[1] *I Cor.*, I, 27-29.

[2] " Let us return from that table as lions breathing fire, terrible to the devil. " *(In Joan.*, homil. LXI, 3).

[3] The following is the lesson given one day to Blessed Henry Suso by Divine Wisdom: "First of all, my servant must love self-abnegation and die entirely to self and to all creatures. This degree of perfection is rarely met with, but he who reaches it rises rapidly unto God... Is it surprising, then, that afflictions and crosses should not frighten such a one as they do those whose avowed desire is to avoid suffering? The Saints are not less sensitive to pain than are other men... But their souls are sheltered from harm, because they but seek after, they but love, the Cross... Their bodies suffer, but their souls are absorbed in God, and in such transport, they taste of an unspeakable sweetness... The love wherewith they are inspired allows them no longer to reckon pain as pain and affliction as affliction: they find in God but deep and unalterable peace. "

[4] *Acts*, I, 8.

IV. *The Gift of Fear*

1335. 1° **Nature.** It is not question here of that fear of God which, caused by the remembrance of our sins, disturbs, saddens and troubles us. Nor is it question of the fear of hell, which suffices to bring about a conversion, but not to achieve our sanctification. Here it is question of a *filial and reverential fear*, which causes us to dread every offence against God.

The gift of fear perfects the virtues of hope and temperance. It perfects the former by inspiring us with a fear of displeasing God and of being separated from Him. It perfects the latter by detaching us from the pleasures that could bring about that separation.

Hence, it may be defined as *a gift which inclines our will to a filial respect for God, removes us from sin, displeasing to Him, and gives us hope in the power of His help.*

1336. It comprises three principal acts: **a)** a vivid sense of God's greatness, and therefore extreme dread of the least sin that may offend His infinite Majesty. "Know you not," said Our Lord to St. Catherine of Sienna, "that all the sufferings a soul undergoes or could undergo in this life are not sufficient punishment for even the slightest fault. The offence done to Me, the Infinite Good, demands an infinite satisfaction. This is why I want you to know that all the sufferings of this life are not a punishment, but a correction."[1] The Saints understood this well: they reproached themselves bitterly for their slightest faults, and they never thought that they had done enough to atone for them. **b)** A lively *sorrow* for the least faults committed, because they have offended an Infinite God, Who is infinitely good. From this sorrow is born an ardent and earnest desire of atoning for sin by multiplying acts of sacrifice and of love.[2] **c)** *Vigilant care* in avoiding occasions of sin as one avoids a serpent: "*Flee from sin as from the face of a serpent;*"[3] and hence, a great concern to know at all times God's good pleasure in order to conform our conduct thereto. Acting in this wise, we evidently perfect the virtue of temperance by avoiding all forbidden pleasure, and that of hope by lifting up our eyes to God with filial trust.

1337. 2° **Its Necessity. A)** This gift is needed in order to avoid an excessive familiarity with God. Some are tempted to forget God's greatness and the infinite distance

---

[1] *Dialogue*, Bk. I, C. II.

[2] "What I want," God said to St. Catherine, "are the manifold works of manly endurance, effects of patience and the other interior virtues of the soul... I, the Infinite, am forever seeking infinite works, that is to say, an infinite sentiment of love. Hence, I require that works of penance and all other external practices be employed as means, and not occupy in the heart the principal place... It is the soul that conceives and begets virtue in truth, and it is through this interior virtue that finite works are united to the sentiment of charity; and then these works will be the object of my approval and delight. " (*Dialogue*, Bk. I, C. X.)

[3] *Ecclus.*, XXI, 2.

that separates us from Him, assuming towards Him and towards holy things an unbecoming familiarity, speaking to Him with too much boldness, and treating Him as an equal. No doubt, God Himself encourages certain souls to a sweet intimacy, to an astounding familiarity with Him; but it is for Him, not for us, to take the initiative. Besides, filial fear in no way excludes that tender familiarity that we witness in certain Saints. [1]

B) This gift is no less useful for preserving us in our relations with others especially our inferiors, from the haughty and proud manner that is more in accord with the pagan than with the Christian spirit. The reverential fear of God, Who is their Father as well as ours, will make us exercise our authority in a modest way, as befits those who hold authority not of themselves but of God.

1338. 3° **Means of Cultivating this Gift. A)** We must frequently meditate upon God's infinite grandeur, His attributes, His sovereignty, and reflect upon the nature of sin, which, no matter how slight, constitutes an offence against the infinite Majesty of God. We cannot help, then, conceiving a reverential fear of Our Sovereign Master, Whom we continually offend: "*Pierce thou my flesh with thy fear: for I am afraid of thy judgments;*" [2] and when we come into His presence, it is with a humbled and contrite heart.

B) In order to abide in this sentiment, it is well for us to perform with care our *examinations of conscience*, striving rather to stir up compunction in our hearts than to seek a detailed knowledge of our faults: "*A contrite and humbled heart, O God, thou wilt not despise.*" [3] To secure a greater purity of heart, it will be well to unite ourselves more and more with the Penitent Christ; for the more we share in His hatred for sin and in His humiliations, the fuller will be our pardon.

V. *The Gift of Knowledge*

1339. Remarks on the three intellectual Gifts. With the gift of knowledge we come to treat of the

---

[1] The following is the apposite remark of Father de Smedt (*Notre vie surnat.*, Vol. I): "When we harbor a high idea of another's superiority over us... we first approach him with a certain sense of timidity and even of anxiety; but if the said person, whom we consider far above ourselves, manifests great kindness, shows a genuine pleasure at seeing us, at speaking with us, at realizing our love for him... if he consents to live with us on terms of the most intimate familiarity, the respect with which his superiority inspires us is no hindrance to our conceiving an ardent affection for him... On the contrary, the loftier the idea we have of his superiority, the greater is our love, the deeper our gratitude, the keener our desire to show him our love and gratitude by tenderness and devotedness. Furthermore, when we see him at close range and enter into intimacy with him, we conceive an even higher appreciation of his qualities; our veneration for him grows, we feel overcome with gratitude and confusion at the esteem, the tenderness, the devotedness, and the thoughtfulness which he manifests to us."

[2] *Ps.* CXVII, 120. — [3] *Ps.* L, 19.

three *intellectual* gifts which bear more directly upon contemplation; the gift of *knowledge*, which makes us form a sound judgment of creatures in their relation to God; the gift of *understanding*, which discloses to us the intimate relations which exist among revealed truths; the gift of *wisdom* which makes us appreciate, prize and relish these truths. The three possess this in common, that they furnish us with *experimental* or *quasi-experimental* knowledge; for, they acquaint us with things divine, not through any process of reasoning, but by means of a higher light which makes us grasp them as though we had actual experience of them. This light communicated to us by the Holy Ghost is, no doubt, the light of faith, but it is now more active, more illuminating than it ordinarily is, and gives us a sort of intuition of these truths, similar to that which we have of first principles [1].

1340. 1º Its **Nature.** The knowledge of which we speak here is not *philosophical* knowledge acquired through the exercise of reasoning; nor is it *theological* knowledge, acquired by applying reason to the data furnished by faith; but it is the *science of the Saints*, whereby we rightly judge of creatures in their relation to God.

Hence, we may define the gift of science as *a gift which, by the illuminating action of the Holy Ghost, perfects the virtue of faith, and thereby gives us a knowledge of created things in their relations to God.*

Father Olier [2] tells us that God " is an Omnipresent and All-pervading Being. He manifests Himself in all external things. In the heavens as well as upon the earth He reveals something of what He is in Himself... Therefore, in all creatures, which are as it were sacraments, visible signs of the perfections of God, we must adore what they represent... This we should have done easily if the grace given to Adam had not been taken away from us..., but sin despoiled us of it, and it is restored through Jesus Christ to only those pure souls to whom faith reveals God's Majesty wherever it appears... This light of faith is properly called the science of the Saints. Without the instrumentality of the senses, without the aid of reason, it makes known to the soul the dependence of each creature upon God. This knowledge is acquired instantly and without labor. At a glance one discerns the cause of all things, and in each of these one finds food for prayer and for perpetual contemplation. "

1341. The *object* of this gift of knowledge is therefore created things, inasmuch as they *lead* us *to God*.

a) If we consider them in their *origin*, they tell us that

---

[1] D. JORET, *Les dons du S. Esprit*, dans *Vie spirit.*, Mars, 1920, p. 383-393.
[2] *Esprit de M. Olier*, t. II, p. 346.

they come from the Hands of God, their Creator and Preserver: "*He hath made us and not we ourselves.*" If we examine their nature we see therein a likeness or a reflection of God. Their *end* and purpose is to bring us to God; they are steps, as it were, by which to rise unto Him.

It is in this way that the Saints, particularly St. Francis of Assisi, looked upon created things. He looked upon all creatures as sharing a common relationship with the one and same Father of all, and each was to him a brother in the great family of the Heavenly Father — the Sun, the crystal waters, the flowers of the field, the birds of the air: "When he felt the immovable firmness and strength of the cliffs and rocks, he directly felt that God is strong and is to be trusted. The sight of a flower in the silence of the early morning, or of the mouth of a little bird confidently opened, revealed to him the pure beauty of God and His purity and the endless tenderness of the Creator. This feeling filled Francis with a constant joy in God, an uninterrupted tendency to thankfulness." [1]

b) This gift of knowledge likewise enables us to perceive quickly and rightly what concerns our own sanctification and the sanctification of others.

Thus it enlightens us as to the state of our soul, as to its secret motions, their source, their motives, and the effects that may result therefrom. It teaches us how to deal with others in view of their salvation. By it the preacher knows what he must say to his hearers in order to do them good; the spiritual director, how he must lead souls according to their particular spiritual needs and the attractions of grace, and this, in virtue of a light that enables him to see into the depths of the heart. This is the infused gift of discernment of spirits. Thus it was that some Saints, enlightened by Him Who searches the hearts and reins knew before the telling the most secret thoughts of their penitents.

1342. 2° Its **Usefulness.** It is evident that this gift is of great help to the faithful, but especially to priests and religious.

a) It *detaches* us *from creatures*, by showing us how empty and fleeting they are, how incapable of making us happy, nay how dangerous they are, since they tend to pervert us by alluring us, by enslaving us, by turning us away from God. Being detached from all these, we can more easily rise unto God Who alone can satisfy the longings of our heart, and we cry out with the Psalmist: "*Who will give me wings like a dove, and I will fly and be at rest? Lo, I have gone far off, flying away; and I abode in the wilderness.*" [2]

b) It helps us to make *a right use of creatures*, by prompting us to use them as so many means by which to rise as by a ladder to Almighty God. We instinctively long to enjoy creatures and we are tempted to make them our end; but under the influence of this gift we no longer see in them anything except what God has placed in them, and from this imperfect reflection of the Divine Beauty our mind turns

---

[1] J. JOERGENSEN, *St. Francis of Assisi*, p. 312. (tr. by Sloane). The same sentiments are to be found in the *Journée chrétienne* of Father Olier.
[2] *Ps.* LIV, 7-8.

to Infinite Beauty Itself, and with St. Augustine we say: "*Too late have I known Thee, Beauty ever old and ever new, too late have I loved Thee.*" [1]

1343. 3° **Means of Cultivating this Gift. a)** The great means is always to look upon creatures with the *eyes of faith.* Instead of tarrying in the contemplation of such fleeting shadows, must we not rather look beyond to the First Cause Who deigns to impress upon them a likeness of His perfections, and must we not cling to their Author and contemn all the rest? This is precisely what the Apostle St. Paul did, who, overcome by love for Christ, wrote: "*For whom I have suffered the loss of all things, and count them but as dung, that I may gain Christ.*" [2]

b) Animated by this spirit we shall know how to deprive ourselves of whatever is useless, and even of some things that are useful. We shall know, for instance, how to forego at times looking at beautiful objects, reading some interesting book, enjoying some delicious food, and the like, in order to make a sacrifice to God. In this manner we shall gradually detach ourselves from creatures, and see in them only that which can lead us to their Maker.

VI. *The Gift of Understanding*

1344. 1° Its **Nature.** The gift of understanding differs from that of knowledge in that the *object* of the former is by far more extensive. Its scope is not limited to created things; it extends to *all the revealed truths.* Furthermore, its insight is much deeper; it enables us to penetrate the inner meaning of revealed truths. It does not, of course, give us an understanding of mysteries, but it enables us to see that, despite their obscurity, they are *credible*, that they are in accord one with the other and with reason.

It may be defined as *a gift which, under the enlightening action of the Holy Ghost, gives us a deep insight into revealed truths, without however giving a comprehension of the mysteries themselves.*

1345. 2° Its **Effects.** This gift produces in us three principal effects:

A) It enables us to penetrate into the very core of revealed truths in six different ways, says St. Thomas: [3]

1) It discloses to us the *substance hidden beneath the accidents*, for example, Jesus Christ under the eucharistic species. This is what moved the peasant, of whom the Cure of Ars speaks, to say: "*I look at Him, and He looks at me.*"

---

[1] ST. AUGUSTINE, *Confessions*, Bk. X, C. 27.
[2] *Phil.*, III, 8. — [3] IIa IIæ, q. 8, a. I.

2) It explains to us the *meaning hidden beneath the words.* This is what Our Lord did in disclosing to the disciples on the way to Emmaus the meaning of the prophecies. The Holy Ghost often makes known to interior souls the depth of meaning contained in one or other passage of Holy Writ.

3) It makes manifest the mysterious signification of *sensible signs.* Thus, St. Paul shows us in Baptism by immersion the symbol of our death to sin, of our spiritual burial and our resurrection with Christ.

4) It makes us lay hold of the *spiritual realities* contained *beneath* the *outward appearances,* showing us the Creator of the world in the artisan of Nazareth.

5) By it we see the *effects contained in their cause,* for instance, in the Blood of Christ shed on Calvary we see the purification of our soul and our reconciliation with God; in the pierced side of Jesus we see the birth of the Church and the source of the Sacraments.

6) Lastly, by it we see the *cause in its effects,* for instance, the action of Providence in external events.

1346. **B)** This gift shows us the truths of faith under so full a light, that, though we do not comprehend their very nature, we are *confirmed in our belief.* This is what St. Thomas tells us: "We know that whatever be the outward appearances, they do not contradict the truth... we ought not to depart from matters of faith."[1] In a higher degree, this gift enables us to *contemplate* God, not indeed through a positive, immediate intuition of the Divine Essence, but by showing us *what God is not,* as we shall explain later.[2]

C) Finally it brings us to the knowledge of a *greater number* of truths, by aiding us to draw from revealed principles the theological conclusions therein contained. Thus, from the text, "*And the Word was made flesh and dwelt amongst us,*" nearly all our teaching concerning the Incarnate Word is deduced; and from the words, "*From whom was born Jesus Who is called the Christ,*" we draw all the teaching regarding the Blessed Virgin Mary.

This gift, so advantageous to all the faithful, is especially useful to priests and theologians, in order to gain an understanding of the revealed truths they are to explain to others.

1347. 3° **The Cultivation of the Gift of Understanding.** **A)** The main disposition required to obtain this gift is a *lively and simple faith* which humbly implores divine light, the better to lay hold of revealed truth: "*Give me understanding, and I will learn thy commandments.*"[3]

---

[1] IIa IIæ, q. 8, a. 2.

[2] "In this life, the (mind's) eye being cleansed by the gift of understanding, we can, so to speak, *see God...* The sight of God is twofold. One is perfect, whereby God's essence is seen: the other imperfect, whereby, though we see not what God is, yet we see what He is not... This second vision of God belongs to the gift of understanding in its state of inchoation, as possessed by wayfarers." (Ia IIæ, q. 69, a. 2, ad 3; IIa IIæ, q. 8, a. 7).

[3] *Ps.* CXVII, 73.

It was thus that St. Anselm was accustomed to act. He would make a lively act of faith before searching into the mysteries of our faith, in accordance with his maxim: "*Faith seeking reason;*" for it is through faith that we come to an understanding of supernatural truths.

B) Once this act of faith has been made, we should accustom ourselves to go to the very heart of the mystery, not in order to comprehend it, which is impossible, but in order to grasp its meaning, its bearing, its relation to reason. After studying a number of mysteries, we should compare them, one with the other, for such a comparison will often throw much light upon each one of them. The relations of the Word to the other two Persons of the Most Blessed Trinity, for instance, enable us to understand better the mystery of His union with a human nature and His work of redeeming mankind. The Incarnation and the Redemption, likewise, throw light upon the Divine Attributes and the relations existing between Father, Son and Holy Ghost. The better to grasp these truths however, we must love them, we must study them, even more with the heart than with the mind, and above all with a humble spirit. Our Lord Himself tells us this in the following beautiful prayer to His Father: "*I confess to thee, O Father, Lord of heaven and earth, because thou hast hid these things from the wise and prudent and hast revealed them to little ones.*"[1]

VII. *The Gift of Wisdom*[2]

We shall explain its *nature*, its *effects*, and the *means* of cultivating it.

1348. 1º Its **Nature.** Wisdom is a gift which perfects the virtue of charity, and which resides at once in the *intellect* and in the *will*, since it infuses *light* and *love* into the soul. Hence, it is rightly considered as the most perfect of all the gifts, the one which embodies all the others, just as charity embodies all the virtues.

A) St. Bernard calls this gift the *knowledge which relishes things divine.* The gift of wisdom therefore contains a twofold element: 1) a *light* which illumines the mind, and enables it to judge aright of God and of created things by relating them to their first principle and last end. It enables us to estimate things according to their highest causes and to gather them into one grand synthesis; 2) a *supernatural taste* which acts upon the will and enables it to relish divine things as by a sort of natural attraction.

A comparison may serve to set forth more clearly this twofold rôle of the gift of wisdom. It is like the sunbeam, a ray of *light* illuminating and delighting the eyes of the soul, and a ray of *heat* that warms the heart, inflames it with love, and fills it with joy.

1349. **B)** Wisdom, then, may be defined as *a gift which perfects the virtue of charity by enabling us to discern God*

---

[1] *Matth.*, XI, 25.
[2] St. Thomas, IIa IIæ, q. 45.

and divine things in their ultimate principles, and by giving us a relish for them.

It differs therefore from the gift of understanding, which enables us to know the divine truths in themselves and in their mutual relations, but not in their ultimate causes, and does not make us relish them directly; whilst wisdom makes us both love and relish them: *"Taste and see that the Lord is sweet."* [1]

It was this gift which enabled St. Paul to see at a glance the divine plan of Redemption, with the glory of God as its principal, final cause, the Incarnate Word as its meritorious and exemplary cause, the happiness of the elect as its final, secondary cause, and divine grace as its formal cause. It was this gift which brought forth from the depths of his soul this prayer of thanksgiving: *"Blessed be the God and Father of Our Lord Jesus Christ."* [2]

With the aid of this gift, St. John makes the whole of theology to converge in the mystery of the Divine Life, of which love is both the principle and the end : *"God is love."* By the assistance of this same gift, St. Thomas sums up his entire Summa in this one thought : God is at once the first principle whence all creatures proceed, the last end whither they return, and the way they must follow to reach Him. [3]

1350. 2° **Effects of the Gift of Wisdom.** Besides the increase of charity produced in the soul, this gift perfects all the other virtues.

a) It renders *faith unshakable* because of the quasi-experimental knowledge it gives us of the truths of revelation ; thus, after tasting for some time the joys of Holy Communion, how can we harbor doubts as to the Real Presence? b) It steadies our *hope;* having understood and relished the dogma of our incorporation into Christ, how can we fail in hope, since He Who is our Head is already in Heaven, and the Saints who reign with Him in the heavenly city are our own brethren? c) It enables us to practise the *moral* virtues in their highest degree; for when we have once tasted the joys of divine love, those of earth hold no relish for us; we love the Cross, mortification, effort, temperance, humility, meekness, because these are so many means of becoming more and more like the Beloved and of returning His love.

This, then, is the difference between the gift of *wisdom* and that of *understanding,* the latter is a view taken by the mind, while the former is an *experience undergone by the heart;* one is light, the other love, and so they unite and complete one another. Wisdom, withal, remains the more perfect gift; for the heart outranges the intellect, it sounds

---

[1] *Ps.* XXXIII, 9. — [2] *Eph.,* I, 3.

[3] Simple souls exercise the gift of wisdom after their own fashion by pondering at length some divine truth. Such was the poor woman who could never finish the recitation of the Our *Father;* "For nearly five years now," she said, "as soon as I speak the word *Father,* and think that He Who is in Heaven above is my Father, I begin to weep and so I remain all day long." (H. BREMOND, *Hist. littéraire,* t. II, p. 66).

greater depths, and grasps or divines what reason fails to reach. This is particularly the case with the Saints, in whom love often surpasses knowledge.

1351. 3° **Means of Cultivating this Gift. A)** Since wisdom is one of the most precious gifts, we must *long* for it ardently, *beg* for it insistently, and *pursue* it with untiring efforts.

This is the advice given us in the Book of *Wisdom*. The Sacred Author would have us espouse Wisdom, choose her as our lifelong companion, and he offers us a beautiful prayer to win her: "God of my fathers, and Lord of Mercy,... who by thy wisdom hast appointed man, that he should have dominion over the creature that was made by thee, that he should order the world according to equity and justice... give me wisdom that sitteth by thy throne, and cast me not off from among thy children: for I am thy servant and the son of thy handmaid, a weak man, and of short time, and falling short of the understanding of judgment and laws... Send her out of thy holy heaven, and from the throne of thy majesty, that she may be with me, and may labour with me, that I may know what is acceptable with thee. For she knoweth and understandeth all things, and shall lead me soberly in my works, and shall preserve me by her power. So shall my works be acceptable, and I shall govern thy people justly, and shall be worthy of the throne of my father." [1]

B) Since wisdom *refers all to God*, we should strive to see how all the truths we study proceed from Him as their *first principle*, and tend towards Him as their *last end*. We must, then, acquire the habit of referring all things to their principles, without losing ourselves in details; of reducing all things to unity, by making a particular synthesis of what we have studied, thus preparing the general synthesis of all our knowledge.

1352. **C)** Since this gift makes us *relish* divine things, we must seek to love and enjoy these things by recalling that all knowledge is vain that does not lead to love. And indeed, how can we help loving God, Who is Infinite Beauty and Infinite Goodness? "*Taste and see that the Lord is sweet.*" [2] How can we help loving divine things, in which we see a participation in God's beauty and God's goodness; we cannot love and enjoy God, and not love those things which share in His perfections.

§ III. Rôle of the Gifts in Prayer and Contemplation

From what has been said, it follows that the exercise of the gifts is of great help to us in prayer.

---

[1] *Wisdom*, IX, 1-12. — [2] *Ps.* XXXIII, 9.

1353. 1º From the moment we begin cultivating the gifts, and therefore, even before they have reached their full development, they add their light and their action to that of the virtues in order to facilitate prayer. Without introducing us into the passive or mystic state, they dispose the soul and render it more docile to the action of the Holy Ghost.

This is the common teaching of theologians. Father Meynard summarizes it thus. After noting the opinion of a few authors who thought that the gifts of the Holy Ghost are limited to the performance of heroic acts and have no part in the practice of ordinary virtue, he adds: "Their action extends as well to a multitude of circumstances in which the Will of God demands of us a certain readiness and docility, for example, when it is question of overcoming vice, of subduing the passions, of resisting the temptations of the flesh, the world and the devil. This is especially true if the weakness and the frailty of the person in question require more abundant and more effective help, and therefore a higher principle of activity. This view, which we believe to be the true one, is based upon the fact that the gifts do not produce results peculiar to themselves and distinct from those of the virtues, but simply come to facilitate the practice of the various virtues."[1] Now, if the gifts of the Holy Ghost exert an influence upon the exercise of the ordinary virtues, they also facilitate the exercise of prayer, which is an act of the virtue of religion and one of the most effective means of practicing the virtues.

These gifts, therefore, act in a *hidden manner*, so that it is not possible to distinguish their action from that of the virtues. At times, however, they act in a more evident way by imparting to us passing intuitions which move the soul more strongly than do reasonings, and by giving rise to impulses of love loftier than those we habitually experience.

1354. 2º These gifts aid us even more in *active contemplation*, which is a sort of *loving gaze* on truth. In fact, the proper function of the gifts of understanding and of wisdom even before their complete unfolding in the soul, is to facilitate this simple view of faith, by making our thought more penetrating and our love more ardent.[2] Without introducing us as yet into the mystic state, their action is already more frequent and more affective than in ordinary prayer; and this fact explains how our soul is able

---

[1] *Traité de la vie intérieure*, t. I, n. 246. He cites in support of his view *St. Antoninus, John of St. Thomas*, and *Suarez*. Such is also the teaching of GARRIGOU-LAGRANGE, *op. cit.*, t. I, p. 404; "We have always maintained that previous to entrance into the mystic state, the gifts exert their influence either frequently in a hidden way, or rarely in an open manner. " Cf. P. J. DE GUIBERT, R.A.M., Oct. 1923, p. 338.

[2] Such is the teaching of Father MEYNARD, t. I n. 126, 128, based on John of St. Thomas.

to dwell more at length and more affectionately upon one and the same truth.

1355. 3° But, it is above all in *infused contemplation* that the gifts play an important part. Having attained their complete development, they impart a wondrous docility to the soul, which fits it for the mystic or contemplative state.

A) Three of the gifts, knowledge, understanding, and wisdom, unite in a special manner in contemplation.

Let us explain: **a)** It is our higher faculties of intellect and will as perfected and transformed by the theological virtues and the gifts, and set in motion by actual operating grace, which are the principles that produce contemplation. The gifts are grafted on our faculties, and consequently, faculties and gifts act as one in the production of the same act. These faculties, thus transformed, constitute the *principles* which call forth contemplation, that is to say, they are the *proximate cause* whence flow, under the influence of an *operating* grace, the acts of contemplation. Thus, the intellect perfected by the virtue of faith is the principle which produces acts of faith.

b) All theologians recognize the gifts of *understanding* and *wisdom* as the principles which call forth contemplation, but some few do not attribute this function to the gift of knowledge. We believe with the majority of authors that there is no reason to exclude it, for contemplation at times takes creatures as its point of departure and then the gift of knowledge acts to enable us to see the image of God in creatures.

St. John of the Cross says that "God created all things and left in them some semblance of Himself, not only by creating them out of nothing, but also by endowing them with innumerable graces and qualities. He even increased their beauty by the admirable order and the unfailing dependence that unite them one to the other... Creatures have preserved a trace of the passage of God, that is to say, the imprint of His majesty, His power, His wisdom, and His other divine attributes." [1] Now, the proper function of the gift of knowledge is to raise us from the creature to the Creator, to show us God's beauty hidden beneath visible symbols.

1356. **B)** These three gifts support one another and either lend a united action, or act one after the other in the prayer of contemplation.

a) The gift of *knowledge* lifts us up from creatures unto God in order to unite us to Him: 1) It is accompanied by an *infused light* whereby we see clearly the nothingness of all that the world prizes, honors, riches, pleasures; the value of suffering and of humiliations as means of reaching God and of glorifying Him; the reflection of the divine perfections hidden in God's creatures.

---

[1] *A Spiritual Canticle*, V. Stanza.

2) This light is attended by a grace that acts upon the will in order to detach it from creatures and to aid it in using them solely as steps by which to attain God.

b) The gift of understanding gives us a still deeper insight by showing us the hidden harmony that exists between our soul and God, between revealed truths and our deepest aspirations, as well as the relations existing among those truths themselves; it centers our mind and our heart upon God's intimate life, upon His immanent operations, upon the mysteries of the Trinity, of the Incarnation, of grace, and makes us contemplate them in themselves and in their mutual relations. Indeed, it attaches us to these great truths in such a way that we find it difficult to turn our mind and heart from them. Ruysbroeck [1] compares it to the light of the sun, which by its radiance fills the air with pure light, illuminating every form and figure, and bringing out every shade of color. So, this gift permeates the intellect, producing therein a singleness of vision, through which rays of a singular clearness penetrate. Then we are indeed capable of receiving the knowledge of those sublime attributes of God, which are the source of all His works.

c) The gift of *wisdom*, by causing us to appraise all things according to their relation to God, and to relish things divine, centers our mind and heart more lovingly still on the object of our contemplation. Ruysbroeck thus describes the *savor* produced by this gift: "This savor is so intense that it seems to the soul that heaven and earth and all that they contain would dissolve and be absorbed in its unfathomable depths. These delights reach above and below (that is to say the higher and the lower faculties), within and without, and have encompassed and penetrated the entire domain of the soul. Thus, the mind contemplates the single principle whence all these delights flow. In virtue of this fact, enlightened reason begins to ponder, though it realizes full well that such incomprehensible delights must ever escape its knowledge; for the consideration of them is made by the aid of a created light, while its joys know no bounds. This is why reason fails in this consideration; but the intellect, which is transformed by this marvelous light, contemplates and finds the incomprehensible bliss of beatitude." [2]

1357. **C)** The other four gifts, though not playing such an important role in contemplation, have nevertheless a share in it, and that in two ways:

a) They fit us for it in that they themselves contribute to make our soul more responsive and more docile to the action of the Holy Ghost;
b) they co-operate in this work by arousing in our heart pious affections which sustain contemplation. Thus, the gift of *fear* stirs within us sentiments of compunction and of detachment from creatures; the gift of *piety*, sentiments of filial love; the gift of *fortitude*, sentiments of generosity and constancy; the gift of *counsel* enables us to apply both to ourselves and to others the lights we have received from the Holy Ghost.

It is therefore evident that each one of these gifts plays its own part in contemplation.

---

[1] IIe Livre, C. 66-68. — [2] *Royaume des amants*, C. XXXIII.

Note: The Five Spiritual Senses and the Gifts

1358. Some of the Fathers and theologians and many mystical writers speak of *five spiritual senses*,[1] analogous to the five *imaginative* senses of which we have already spoken in number 991.

St. Augustine describes them in this beautiful text: " What do I love, O my God, when I love Thee?... It is a kind of light that I love, and melody, and fragrance, and meat, and embracement of my inner man : where there shineth unto my soul what space cannot contain, and there soundeth what time beareth not away, and there smelleth what breathing disperseth not, and there tasteth what eating diminisheth not, and there clingeth what satiety divorceth not. This is what I love when I love my God. "[2]

What must we understand by these spiritual senses? It would seem that they are but functions or operations of the gifts of the Holy Ghost, notably of the gifts of *understanding* and of *wisdom*. Thus the spiritual senses of *sight* and of *hearing* refer to the gift of understanding, which makes us *see* God and things divine (n. 1341), and *hear* God speaking to our heart. The other three senses refer to the gift of *wisdom*, which causes us to *relish* God, to *breathe* the fragrance of His perfections, and to enter into *contact* with Him by a sort of spiritual embrace which is nothing else than an *experimental* love of God.

In this way one can harmonize the teaching of St. Augustine and St. Thomas, of Father Poulain and Father Garrigou-Lagrange concerning this matter.

§ IV. The Fruits of the Holy Ghost and the Beatitudes

With the gifts come the *Fruits* of the Holy Ghost and the *Beatitudes*, which correspond to and complete them, as well as the *charisms*, which have a certain relation to them (n. 1914).

I. *The Fruits of the Holy Ghost*

1359. When a soul corresponds faithfully to the actual graces which set in motion the virtues and the gifts, it performs acts of virtue, at first imperfectly and with difficulty, then more perfectly and with greater relish, so that the heart is filled with holy joy. These are the fruits of the Holy Ghost, and they may be defined as *acts of virtue*

---

[1] Father POULAIN, *Graces of Interior Prayer*, C. VI, cites many texts to prove this.
[2] *Confessions*, Bk. X, C. VI.

which *reach a certain degree of perfection and fill the soul with holy joy.*

St. Paul enumerates nine such fruits, charity, joy, peace, patience, benignity, goodness, faith, mildness, temperance.[1] It was not his mind to give a complete list, and St. Thomas rightly notes that this number is symbolic, and in reality designates all those acts of virtue wherein the soul finds spiritual consolation: "The fruits are any virtuous deeds in which one delights."[2]

1360. These fruits differ from the virtues and gifts in the same way as acts differ from the faculty which produces them. Moreover, the designation of fruit does not correspond to every act of virtue, but only to such as are attended by a certain spiritual sweetness. At the outset, acts of virtue often demand great effort and are at times distasteful to us. But once we have grown accustomed to the practice of virtue, we acquire facility and perform these acts without great difficulty, nay, rather with pleasure such as we take in the acts which we perform as the result of an acquired habit. It is then that we call them fruits.

It is therefore through the cultivation of the virtues and the gifts that the fruits are obtained; and through these the beatitudes, which are a prelude to eternal bliss.

II. *The Beatitudes*

1361. The beatitudes put the final touch to the divine work in us. Like the fruits, they are acts, but possessed of such perfection that they seem to flow from the gifts rather than from the virtues;[3] they are fruits, but fruits of such mature perfection that they already furnish us with a foretaste of heavenly happiness; hence, their name, beatitudes.

In the Sermon of the Mount, Our Lord reduces them to eight: poverty of spirit, meekness, tears, hunger and thirst for justice, mercy, purity of heart, and patience in the midst of persecution. One may say however that this number is also symbolic and is not meant to set a strict limit.

These beatitudes do not connote absolute and perfect bliss; they are rather effective means of reaching eternal happiness; for if one joyfully embraces poverty, meekness, purity, humiliation; if one has attained such mastery of self as to pray for one's enemies and to love the Cross, one is faithfully following the example of the Master and making great strides in the ways of perfection.

---

[1] *Galat.*, V, 22-23. The *Vulgate* enumerates twelve: "But the fruit of the Spirit is: charity, joy, peace, patience, benignity, goodness, mildness, faith, modesty, continence, chastity." Thus, it adds *longanimity, modesty* and continence, and puts chastity in place of temperance.

[2] *Sum. Theol.*, Ia IIæ, q. 70, a. 2.

[3] "Beatitudes are none but perfect works which, by reason of their perfection, are assigned to the gifts rather than to the virtues." (*Sum. theol.*, Ia IIæ, q. 70, a. 2.)

1362. Conclusion. Through the cultivation of the gifts of the Holy Ghost we are introduced into the unitive way. 1) They cause us *to practice all the virtues*, moral and theological, in their *highest degree*, and thus unite us to God, making us gradually grow like unto Him by the imitation of His divine perfections. 2) They impart to our soul that responsiveness, that *docility*, that enables the Holy Ghost to take possession of it and to act therein with perfect freedom. It is even under the hidden influence of these gifts, and at times under their *evident* influence, that the *prayer of simplicity* is made.

ART. II. THE PRAYER OF SIMPLICITY [1]

1363. The prayer of *simplicity*, called thus by Bossuet, was well known before him, and was given various names which it is well to recall.

- 1) St. Theresa calls it the *prayer of recollection*. This must be understood of *active* recollection in contradistinction to *passive* recollection, of which we shall speak in the second chapter. In this prayer the soul gathers its various faculties to concentrate them upon God, to listen to Him, and to love Him.

2) Many authors call this the *prayer of simple regard*, of the *simple presence of God*, of the *simple committal to God*, or of the *simple view of faith*, because the soul fixes its affectionate gaze on God, remains in His presence, yields itself to His action, and through a simple and unreasoned faith, gazes upon God and loves Him.

3) Bossuet calls it the prayer of *simplicity*, because it causes us to simplify all: the reasonings and affections of prayer, and even our whole life.

4) The *Carmelites*, and with them many authors since the seventeenth century, call it *acquired contemplation* to distinguish it from *infused* contemplation.

We shall explain: 1° the *nature* of this prayer; 2° its *advantages;* 3° *how to make* it; 4° its *relation to contemplation* properly so-called.

§ I. Nature of the Prayer of Simplicity

1364. Bossuet has given an excellent description of this kind of prayer:

" One must accustom oneself to nourish the soul by a simple, loving gaze on God and on Jesus Christ; to attain this result, one must gently

---

[1] BOSSUET, *Manière courte et facile pour faire l'oraison en foi, et de simple présence de Dieu;* THOMAS DE JÉSUS, *De contemplatione divinâ;* VEN. LIBERMANN, *Ecrits spirit., De l'oraison d'affection; Instruct. aux missionnaires,* C. V, art. II; POULAIN, *Graces of Interior Prayer,* C. II; LEHODEY, *The Ways of Mental Prayer,* p. II, C. VIII; TANQUEREY, *L'oraison de simplicité, Vie spirit.*, dec. 1920, p. 161-174; LALLEMANT, *Spiritual Doctrine,* 7th Principle; GROU, *How to Pray,*

free the soul from reasonings, from arguments and from the multitude
of affections, in order to keep it simple, respectful and attentive and
thus have it draw closer and closer to God, its first principle and its
last end... Meditation is excellent in its proper time, and highly
profitable at the outset of the spiritual life; but one must not linger
there, since the soul by its fidelity in mortifying and in recollecting
itself, ordinarily becomes the recipient of a purer and a more intimate
kind of prayer which one may call the prayer of *simplicity*, and which
consists in a simple view, regard, or loving thought on some divine
object, be it God Himself, or some of His mysteries, or any other
Christian truth. The soul puts aside reasoning and employs a gentle
contemplation that keeps it at peace, attentive and docile to the divine
operations and impressions which the Holy Ghost communicates;
it does little and receives much; its labour is sweet, yet very fruitful;
and since it approaches nearer to the source of all light, of all grace,
and of all virtue, it receives a still greater share in all these gifts."

This prayer, therefore, comprises two essential acts:
contemplation and love; to contemplate God or divine
objects in order to love them, and to love them, the better
to contemplate them. If we compare this kind of prayer
with *discursive* or *affective* meditation, we discover a threefold simplification which well justifies the expression
employed by Bossuet.

1365. 1º The first simplification consists in the *diminution* and then in the *suppression of reasoning*, which occupied
such a large place in the meditation of beginners. Obliged
to acquire profound convictions, and little accustomed to
making pious affections, beginners needed to reflect at
length upon the fundamental truths of religion and their
relation to the spiritual life, upon the nature and necessity
of the principal Christian virtues and the means of practising them, before their heart was able to bring forth sentiments of gratitude, love, contrition, humiliation and firm
purpose of amendment, and to send up long and ardent
petitions. **a)** But the moment comes when those convictions are so grounded in our soul that they form, so to
speak, part of our habitual state of mind, and but little
time is required to recall them. Then the pious affections
of which we have spoken spring forth readily and easily,
and prayer becomes *affective*.

1366. **b)** Later on, another simplification is effected:
the short space of time given to reflection is replaced by
an *intuitive intellectual gaze*. We thereby come to understand first principles without effort, as by an intuition.
After we have meditated for a long time upon the funda-

mental truths of the spiritual life, they become to us as certain and as clear as first principles, and at one glance we grasp them with ease and delight, without recourse to a detailed analysis. Thus, the idea of *father* applied to God, which at the outset required lengthy reflections before we could grasp its meaning, now appears to us at a glance so rich and so fruitful that we linger with it lovingly in order to relish its manifold elements.

c) It even happens at times that the soul rests content with but a *vague* vision of God or of divine things, which view however keeps it sweetly and affectionately in God's presence, and renders it more and more docile to the action of the Holy Ghost. Then, without multiplying the acts of the intellect or of the will, it abandons itself to God in order to receive His commands.

1367. 2° The *affections* undergo a similar simplification. At the outset they were manifold and varied and followed one another in quick succession : love, gratitude, joy, compassion, sorrow for sin, desire of amendment, petition for help, etc. **a)** But soon one and the same affection is prolonged during five or ten minutes: the idea of God Our Father, for example, excites in the heart an ardent love which, without expressing itself in a multiplicity of words, completely absorbs the soul for several minutes, penetrates it, and gives birth therein to dispositions of generosity. No doubt, this one idea will not suffice to occupy the entire time of prayer, and it will be necessary to pass on to other affections so as to avoid falling into distractions and into a sort of idle day-dreaming; still, each successive affection will last longer, and so there will be no need as before of multiplying their number.

1368. **b)** One of these affections will finally become predominant and recur continually to our mind and heart, while its object will become like a *fixed idea* towards which, no doubt, other ideas gravitate, but in small number and in subordination to the dominant affection. For some, it will be the thought of Our Lord's Passion, accompanied by the sentiments of love and sacrifice that it arouses : "*He loved me, and delivered himself for me.*" [1]   Others will make Jesus living in the Eucharist the center of their thoughts and affections, and they will continually repeat the words : "Devoutly I adore Thee, O my Hidden God." Others,

---

[1] *Galat.*, II, 20.

again, will be possessed by the idea of God abiding in their souls and they will think only of glorifying Him all the day long: "*We will come to him and will make our abode with him.*" — "*The temple of God is holy which you are.*" — "*Glorify and bear God in your body.*" [1]

This is explained very well by Father Massoulié: [2] "When the soul considers that not only is she privileged to be in the presence of God, but that it is her happiness to possess that presence within herself, such thought pierces her to the quick and causes her to enter into a deep state of recollection. She contemplates this God of love and of majesty, and the Three Divine Persons, Who deign to enter within her and dwell there as in Their temple. She beholds the Godhead with the keenest joy, she delights in the bliss of her possession, and she finds therein an unspeakable rest, seeing all her longings fulfilled in so far as they can be upon this earth; for what greater thing can the soul long and hope for than the possession of God?"

1369. 3° The process of simplification *soon* extends *to our whole life.* "The practice of this kind of prayer," says Bossuet, "must begin with our first conscious moment of the day, by an act of faith in God Who is everywhere, and in Jesus Christ Whose eyes are ever upon us, were we buried in the depths of the earth." It persists all the day long. While we devote ourselves to the performance of our ordinary actions, we unite ourselves to God, and contemplate and love Him. While engaged in liturgical and vocal prayer, we think rather of the presence of God living within us than of the particular meaning of the words, and we seek above all to show Him our love. The examinations of conscience are likewise simplified: a rapid glance shows us the faults we have committed, and we regret them immediately. Study and works of zeal are done in the spirit of prayer, under the eye of God, with the ardent wish of glorifying Him: "*To the greater glory of God.*" There are no actions, even the most commonplace, that are not permeated by the spirit of faith and of love and that do not thus become so many repeated sacrificial offerings to God: "*To offer up spiritual sacrifices, acceptable to God.*" [3]

§ II. Advantages of the Prayer of Simplicity

1370. The great advantage of this prayer is that it gives to our whole life a unity of purpose and makes it more and more like unto God's own life for the *greater glory of God* and for the *spiritual welfare of the soul.*

---

[1] *John*, XIV, 23; *I Cor.* III, 17; VI, 20.
[2] *Traité de la véritable oraison.* — [3] *I Peter*, II, 5.

1º *God is glorified* during the entire day.   This habitual and loving gaze of the soul on God makes Him better known and better loved than He would be in virtue of mere considerations: we forget self, and, with greater reason, creatures, or at least we see them only in their relation to God, under the influence of the gift of knowledge (n. 1341).   Life becomes a protracted act of the virtue of religion, an act of thanksgiving and of love, and we repeat with Mary: " *My soul doth magnify the Lord.* "

1371. 2º Thus, *our soul is sanctified.* **a**) By concentrating our attention upon one truth during a notable period of time, we gain a better knowledge of God, and since this contemplation is accompanied by love, we love Him more intensely and unite with Him in a more intimate way, thus drawing to ourselves the divine perfections and the virtues of Our Lord.

b) *Detachment* then becomes easier.   When we habitually think of God, creatures appear but as so many steps by which to reach the Creator.   Full of imperfections and misery, they have no value except in the measure in which they reflect the divine perfections and urge us to rise to the Source of all good.

c) *Humility* also becomes easier : by the divine light, we clearly see our nothingness and our sins, and we rejoice at being able, by the humble avowal of our faults, to give glory to Him Who alone is worthy of all honor and glory : " *To God alone honor and glory, unto me humiliation and shame.* "   Instead of preferring ourselves to others, we consider ourselves as the worst of sinners, ready to suffer out of love all kinds of trials and humiliations.

One may therefore say in all truth that the prayer of simplicity helps us in a singular manner to give glory to God and to sanctify our soul.

1372. Solution of Difficulties. a) At times an objection is made to this kind of prayer on the grounds that it fosters *idleness*.   St. Theresa thus makes answer : [1] " But to return to those who discourse with the understanding: these I would advise not to spend all their time in this exercise; for though it be very meritorious, yet as prayer is so sweet, they think there will be no Sunday nor any season wherein they will not be obliged to labor, and therefore they immediately suppose all that time is lost; whereas I think that loss is great gain.   But let them (as I have said) represent themselves to be in the presence of Christ; and without tiring the understanding, let them speak and regale themselves with Him, and not be fatiguing themselves in com-

---

[1] *Life of St. Teresa*, by Herself, C. XIII.

posing discourses, but only present their necessities, and acknowledge themselves unworthy to be allowed to appear in His presence. Some of these considerations may be used at one time and some at another, that so the soul may not grow tired of always feeding on the same food: they are also very sweet and profitable, if once we accustom ourselves to feed on them, for they bring with them great support for giving life to the soul, as well as much profit." In reality, the soul does not remain idle: it reasons no longer, but it gazes on God, loves and praises Him, and gives itself to Him, and if it remains silent for a moment, it is in order to listen to Him; if God ceases to speak, it takes at once to its own pious affections, and so is never idle.

1373. **b)** Others contend that to concentrate one's attention in this manner upon a fixed idea *fatigues the mind* and brings on mental strain. This would constitute a real danger were one to enter into this kind of prayer before being ready for it, and to persist in it by sheer force. But this is precisely what must be avoided, as Bossuet remarks:[1] "One must guard against *torturing the mind*, and against stirring up the emotions; one must rather take what presents itself to the gaze of the soul in all humility and simplicity, *with none of those violent efforts* which affect the imagination more than the will; one must allow oneself to be sweetly drawn to God and yield oneself to His Spirit." It is not question, then, of making violent efforts, but of gently following the attractions of grace. When one has exhausted the contents of one idea one must not force oneself to linger with it, but pass quietly to another. Then the prayer of simplicity instead of becoming a cause of fatigue, becomes a sweet haven of rest to the soul, which abandons itself to the action of the Holy Ghost.

§ III. How the Prayer of Simplicity is Made

1374. 1° **The Call to this Kind of Prayer.** In order that the prayer of simplicity become *habitual*, one must fulfil the conditions required for the *unitive* way indicated in number 1296. However, if it is question of practising it only from time to time, it suffices that one be attracted thereto by the grace of God.

One may reduce to two the *distinctive signs* of a divine call to this sort of prayer: **a)** A certain *dislike* for discursive prayer or for a multiplicity of affections, together with the *little profit* derived therefrom. We take it for granted that it is question of a *fervent* soul striving to meditate well, and not of a *lukewarm* soul resolved to live in mediocrity. **b)** A certain *attraction* for *simplifying prayer*, in order to fix one's gaze on God and remain in His presence, together with the profit drawn from this holy exercise.

In *practice*, when a spiritual director notices that an earnest person experiences great difficulty in making reasoned considerations or in producing manifold affections,

[1] *Opuscule de la meilleure manière de faire oraison*, t. VII, éd. Vivès, p. 501.

it is then time to explain to him the main lines to be
followed in this kind of prayer, to urge him to try it, and
to ask for a report.   If the results are good, the director
will advise him to continue the practice.

1375. 2º **The Prayer Itself.** Properly speaking there
is no such thing as a method for this kind of prayer, since
in it there is hardly anything to do but to *contemplate* and
to *love.*   Still, a few words of *advice* can be given to the
souls that are called thereto, in order to help them keep
themselves in the presence of God.   These counsels should
correspond to the character, the dispositions and the supernatural attractions of the different penitents.

a) Those who feel a need to *fix their senses* upon some
pious object, should be advised to direct their eyes to the
Crucifix, the tabernacle or some pious image apt to center
their thoughts on God.   As the Curé of Ars said, " we do
not need to say much in order to pray well. We know that
the Good Lord is there in the *tabernacle;* we open our
heart to Him; we delight to be in His Holy Presence.
This is the best form of prayer." [1]

b) Those possessed of a *lively imagination* may represent
to themselves some *Gospel scene,* not in detail as before, but
in a general way; for instance, Our Lord in the Garden of
Olives or upon Mount Calvary; then they may lovingly
contemplate Him suffering for us, and say to themselves:
" *He loved me and delivered Himself for me.*" [2]

1376. **c**) There are others who like to repeat slowly
some *text of Holy Writ* or some pious prayer, to ponder
over it and draw food from it.   This is recommended by
St. Ignatius in his *Second Manner of Praying* (n. 993);
and experience shows that many a soul is thereby initiated
into the prayer of simplicity.   Such persons should be
advised to make a collection of the most beautiful texts,
of those which have already impressed them [3] and to make

---

[1] *Life* by MONNIN, Bk. V, C. IV.
[2] *Galatians,* II, 20. — St. Teresa in her Life C. XIII, gives us an example of
this prayer; after inviting her Sisters to meditate upon the subject of Jesus scourged
at the pillar, she goes on to say: " But we should not weary ourselves with seeking
out these reasons, but only dwell upon them with a calm understanding. If possible we should employ ourselves in considering Who looks upon us; and we should
accompany Him and pray to Him, and humble ourselves before Him, and regale
ourselves with Him remembering that Our Lord deserved not to be there. Whenever we are able to do this, though it should be at the very commencement of
our prayer, we shall find great benefit from it..."
[3] Father ST. JURE has made such a collection entitled: *Le Maître Jésus-Christ
enseignant les hommes.* One may also find inspiration in "*Le Disciple*" by Father
CHEVRIER.

use of them in accordance with the attractions of the Holy Ghost.

1377. d) Persons of an affectionate nature should be advised to make *acts inspired by love for God* and to relish at length the thoughts called forth by such acts; such are, for instance, "I love Thee with my whole heart, O my God, because Thou art Goodness itself; God is charity, infinite beauty..." Or else they may address themselves to Jesus and think on all the titles He has to our love: "I love Thee, O Jesus, Who art all-lovable; Thou art my Lord, I wish to obey Thee; Thou art my Shepherd, I wish to follow Thee and be fed by Thee; Thou art my Teacher, I believe in Thee; Thou art my Redeemer, I bless Thee and cling to Thee; Thou art my Leader, I am one with Thee; Thou art my most faithful Friend, I love Thee above all things, and I want to love Thee forever more." They may also employ the old method of prayer bequeathed by Father Olier to his followers: *Jesus before our eyes:* "Let us stand in awe and reverence before the Divine, the Holy One of God, and after our heart has poured itself out in love, in praise, and in other acts of homage, let us for a time remain in silence before Him...;" *Jesus in our heart:* we shall implore the Spirit of Jesus to come to our soul that He may make us conformable to Himself, the Divine Model: "We shall yield ourselves to Him, in order to be possessed by Him and to be animated by His power; after this we shall still abide in silence before Him to allow His divine unction to permeate our whole being...;" *Jesus in our hands:* we shall desire "that His Divine Will be accomplished in us, His members, who must be subject to our Head, and who must perform no action except that which is received solely from Jesus Christ, our life and our all, Who, replenishing our soul with His Spirit, His power and His strength, must work in us and through us whatever He desires."[1]

1378. e) There are persons in whom the faculty of *will* is dominant and who can no longer engage in discursive reasonings. Moreover, finding themselves troubled by aridity and distractions, they succeed only with the greatest difficulty in drawing from their heart some devout affections. The simplified prayer that is proper for them is thus described by Father Piny:[2] "This prayer consists in *willing* to spend all the time of prayer in loving God and in loving

---

[1] *Introduction*, C. IV. — [2] *L'oraison du cœur*, C. I.

Him more than ourselves; in willing to pray God for the spirit of charity; in willing to remain abandoned to the Divine Will... It must be noted that love has this advantage over the acts of most other virtues and over the other ways of effecting a union with God, that if we *will* to love, we *do love,* that if by a real act of the will we choose to unite ourselves in love to the Will of Him Whom we love, or Whom we desire to love, we forthwith effect that union by this act of our will : love is in truth nothing else but an affective act of the will."

1379. f) In this kind of prayer we are exposed to *distractions* and to *aridity,* just as in affective prayer. We have but one course to follow : to humble ourselves, to offer to God the pain we experience, and to strive, in spite of all, to remain in God's presence, in perfect submission to His Will. Distractions may then prevent the mind from concentrating on God, but the *will* remains united to Him despite the wanderings of the imagination.

1380. 3° **The Preparation and the Conclusion. A)** The question has been raised as to whether the *subject of prayer* is to be prepared when one makes this prayer of simplicity. Generally, the answer must be in the *affirmative.* It is known that St. Francis de Sales advised St. Chantal to prepare her prayer : " I do not mean that once the preparation has been made one must not turn to this kind of prayer (of simple regard) if at the actual time for prayer one is attracted thereto. But to adopt the practice of making no preparation at all seems to me rather improper, for this would be to appear of a sudden before God without any thanks, without any offering, without any petition. All this may be done with profit, but I must confess to a certain repugnance at making it a rule." [1] This advice is very wise : the preparation of a subject will not prevent the Holy Ghost from suggesting another if He so pleases; but, if in His wisdom He should refuse to do so, we can then occupy ourselves with the subject we have prepared.

1381. **B)** This preparation includes the *resolution* which is taken at the end of prayer; it is assuredly better to determine upon one the evening before. It may be that the Holy Ghost will inspire another, or simply lead the soul to yield itself to God the whole day long ; still, the one already prepared will not be without fruit. We may add,

---

[1] Lettre du 11 mars 1610, t. XIV, p. 266.

however, that since the process of simplification extends to everything, often the best resolution will be one and the same, for instance that of living habitually in the presence of God, or of refusing Him nothing, or of doing all things out of love for Him. However, vague as these resolutions may seem to those who do not practice this kind of prayer, they are very definite to those whom God has led thereto, for God Himself will give them a practical turn through the inspirations He will frequently vouchsafe during the day.

§ IV. Relation of the Prayer of Simplicity to Infused Contemplation

To express accurately the common doctrine on this point, we shall show : 1° that in its beginnings the prayer of simplicity is in reality but *acquired* contemplation; 2° that it constitutes an excellent *preparation* for infused contemplation and at times leads up to it.

1382. 1° It is a form of contemplation. **a)** This was Bossuet's opinion. After describing this kind of prayer, he adds: "The soul then, leaving reasoning aside, resorts to a gentle *contemplation* which keeps it peaceful and attentive, and docile to the divine operations and impressions that the Holy Ghost communicates." The same conclusion follows from the very nature of this prayer when compared with contemplation, which is defined as a *simple intuition of truth* (n. 1298). Now, the prayer of simplicity, says Bossuet, "consists in a simple view, regard, or loving thought, directed towards some divine object." Therefore, it is rightly called contemplation.

b) It is, at least in the beginning, *acquired* and not infused contemplation, as long as it remains faint and intermittent; for it lasts but for some short moments, and then yields to other thoughts and affections. It is only little by little that the soul becomes accustomed to look at and to love God Himself by a simple view of faith for a notable period of time, much as the artist contemplates his master-piece the details and elements of which he had previously studied. It seems indeed that here there takes place an ordinary psychological process which evidently presupposes a live faith, and even the hidden action of the gifts of the Holy Ghost, but not a special intervention of God.

1383. 2° The prayer of simplicity *disposes* the soul for infused contemplation, for it induces a condition that renders the soul highly attentive to the motions of grace and *docile to the action of the Holy Ghost.* Therefore, whenever it will please Divine Goodness to *take* possession of it in order to produce a still deeper state of recollection, a simpler insight, a more intense love, then the soul enters into the second degree of the prayer of simplicity, such as Bossuet [1] described:

"Then we must not scatter our efforts in striving to produce other acts or different dispositions, but we must simply be mindful of the presence of God, remaining exposed to His divine gaze, continuing in this devout thought as long as Our Lord gives us such a grace; not hastening to do anything except what is done in us, since this is a prayer with God alone, a union which eminently contains all the other special dispositions and *prepares the soul for that passive state* wherein *God becomes the sole Master of our inner life* and *wherein He operates more particularly.* In this state, *the less the creature labors, the more powerfully does God act;* and since God's operation constitutes *a rest,* the soul becomes, in this kind of prayer, in a way like unto Him, and receives during it wonderful graces."

Note should be taken of the phrases we have italicized and which indicate so clearly the powerful, special action of God and the passivity of the soul. Here it is indeed question of *infused* contemplation; the prayer, begun with a certain amount of activity through a loving gaze on God, ends in repose or quietude where God acts more powerfully than does the soul.

1384. Thus there is a certain *continuity* between simplified, affective prayer, which one may acquire through a spirit of faith, and *quietude* or infused prayer, produced by the gifts of the Holy Ghost with the co-operation of the soul. There is an essential difference between the two, since the one is *acquired* and the other *infused;* but there is a bond of union, a link between them, that is, the prayer of simplicity, which begins by a simple view of faith and ends, *when it pleases God,* by the Holy Ghost's laying hold of the soul. No doubt, the Holy Spirit is not constrained, even when one has arrived at the prayer of simplicity, to transform this into infused prayer, which ever remains the gratuitous gift of God and to which we cannot rise of ourselves; still, the Holy Ghost does frequently effect that transformation, when He finds the soul well disposed; for He desires nothing so much as to unite to Himself in a more perfect way generous souls who will refuse Him nothing.

---

[1] *Opuscule,* No V.

CONCLUSION OF THE FIRST CHAPTER

1385. This first degree of the unitive way is already very high. 1) The soul, affectionately and habitually united to God, strives to practice the virtues in their highest form, with the aid of the gifts of the Holy Ghost, which act sometimes in a *hidden*, at other times in a more manifest way. The gifts that *predominate* in the soul are those which, due to temperament, occupations, and divine attractions, lead to action; but in acting, the soul remains united to God; it is for Him, with Him and under the action of His grace that it labors and suffers. 2) At the time of meditation its prayer is very *simple :* the soul looks through the eyes of faith at that God Who is its Father, Who dwells within it, Who works with it; and whilst contemplating Him, it loves Him. At times, this love manifests itself by generous aspirations; at other times by pure acts of the will, for the soul has its moments of aridity and trial, and then it can but say : My God, I love Thee, or at least I want to love Thee; I want to do Thy Will through love, whatever be the cost. 3) There are moments when the gifts of knowledge, of understanding, and of wisdom, which generally act only in a hidden way, manifest themselves as in a flash and place the soul for a moment in a state of sweet repose. It is a kind of *initiation into infused contemplation.*

CHAPTER II

Infused Contemplation [1]

After explaining the *general notions* concerning infused contemplation, we shall examine its *different degrees*.

ART. I. GENERAL NOTIONS
REGARDING INFUSED CONTEMPLATION

I. *Definition*

1386.   A) Earlier writers, not making any explicit distinction between acquired and infused contemplation, do not as a rule give the specific difference between the two. From different articles of St. Thomas on this subject one can draw the conclusion that contemplation is *a simple, intuitive gaze on God and divine things proceeding from love and tending thereto.* [2] St. Francis de Sales defines it thus : " *A loving, simple, and permanent attentiveness of the mind to divine things.*" [3]

B) Modern authors generally make the distinction between the two kinds of contemplation, and with Pope Benedict XIV they define or describe infused contemplation as : " a simple look of the mind attended by a gentle love

---

[1] ST. THOMAS, IIa IIæ, q. 180-182; St. BONAVENTURE, *De triplici viâ; Itinerarium mentis ad Deum;* H. SUSO, *The little Book of Eternal wisdom; Le livre de la vérité;* Bx F. RUISBROECK, *L'ornement des noces spirituelles;* GERSON, *La montagne de la contemplation; La théologie mystique spéculative et pratique;* DENIS THE CARTHUSIAN, *De Fonte Lucis et semitis vitæ; De contemplatione;* BLOSIUS (Louis de Blois), *A Book of Spiritual Instruction;* D. A. BAKER, *Sancta Sophia;* ST. TERESA, *Life by Herself; The Way of Perfection; The Interior Castle;* ST. JOHN OF THE CROSS, *The Ascent of Mount Carmel; The Dark Night of the Soul; Living Flame;* ST. FRANCIS DE SALES, *The Love of God,* Books VI-VII; ALVAREZ DE PAZ, *De Vita Spirituali,* T. III, Lib. V ; M. GODINEZ, *Praxis Theologiæ Mysticæ;* LALLEMANT, *Spiritual Doctrine,* Principle VII; SCARAMELLI, *Direttorio mistico;* RIBET, *La Mystique divine;* DE MAUMIGNY, *Practice of Mental Prayer;* POULAIN, *The Graces of Interior Prayer;* LEHODEY, *The Ways of Mental Prayer;* SAUDREAU, *The Degrees of the Spiritual Life,* Vol. II; MEYNARD, *Traité de la vie intérieure;* LAMBALLE, *Mystical Contemplation;* FARGES, *Mystical Phenomena;* JORET, *La contemplation mystique d'après saint Thomas;* GARRIGOU-LAGRANGE, *Perfect. chrét. et contemplation;* LEJEUNE, *An Introduction to the Mystical Life;* WILLIAMSON, *Supernatural Mysticism;* A. B. SHARPE *Mysticism, Its nature and value;* HOWLEY, *Psychology and Mystical Phenomena.*

[2] *Sum. theol.,* IIa IIæ, q. 180, a. 3, c. et ad 1; a. 7, c. et ad 1 : " Contemplation regards the simple act of gazing on the truth... It has its beginning in the appetite since it is through charity that one is urged to the contemplation of God. And since the end corresponds to the beginning, it follows that the term also and the end of the contemplative life has its being in the appetite, since one delights in seeing the object loved, and the very delight in the object seen arouses a yet greater love."

[3] *Love of God,* Bk. VI, C. 3.

for things divine, proceeding from God, Who in a special way moves the mind to know and the heart to love divine things, and Who through the gifts of the Holy Ghost — understanding and wisdom — co-operates in these acts by shedding a powerful light upon the mind and by inflaming the will with love. " This gives a very complete notion and points out clearly the share of God and of the Gifts of the Holy Ghost as well as the part our faculties play. Though God moves our mind to know and our heart to love, we co-operate freely with His divine motion.

We must note, however, that this definition only extends to *sweet* and not to arid contemplation. Hence, if one is looking for a definition that embraces both, one may say that it is a *simple, loving, protracted gaze on God and things divine, under the influence of the gifts of the Holy Ghost and of a special actual grace which takes possession of us and causes us to act in a passive rather than in an active manner.*

To understand this definition well, we must explain the share of God and that of man in contemplation.

II. *The Rôle of God in Contemplation*

God has the principal part, since He alone can take possession of us and put us in the passive state.

1387. 1º It is *God Who calls the soul to contemplation*, for according to all mystics contemplation is essentially a *gratuitous* gift. Such is the teaching of St. Theresa. Often she calls this prayer *supernatural.* In her second relation to Father Rodrigo Alvarez, she explains the term thus : " I call *supernatural* that which cannot be acquired either by industry or by effort, no matter what pains we take for the purpose. As to disposing oneself thereto, this indeed one can do, and this is no doubt a great thing. " [1] She further elucidates her thought by the following graceful comparison : " Our Lord is pleased to make the soul mount higher and higher towards Him ; then He catches this little dove and places it in a nest, there to repose. " [2]

Such is also the teaching of St. John of the Cross. He distinguishes two methods, one active and the other passive ; the latter, which is none other than contemplation, is " that in which the soul does nothing as *of itself*, neither does it make therein any efforts of its own ; but it is God Who works in it, giving special aids, and the soul is patient, freely consenting thereto. " [3] The Saint often returns to this distinction :

[1] Relation 54. — [2] *Life*, C. XVIII.
[3] *The Ascent of Mount Carmel*, Bk I, C. XIII, (Translation by David Lewis M. A. London, 1889).

" There is between the two states all the difference that exists between human and divine work, between natural and supernatural operation. Such souls do not act of themselves, but are under the action of the Holy Ghost; He is the principal agent, the guide, the mover in this state, and ceases not to watch over them, and lead them as so many instruments in His hands towards perfection through Faith and the Divine Law, through the spirit which God imparts to each one." [1] Now, if the initiative is all God's, if it is He Who moves souls, if He is the principal agent, and the soul but an instrument, it is clear that the soul cannot intrude itself into this state, nor merit it in the strict sense, that is, in justice, for we cannot merit in this way except what God has deigned to include within the scope of merit, namely, sanctifying grace and eternal glory.

The gratuity of this state is acknowledged even by that school which holds that all souls are called to contemplation. After saying that meditation is not beyond our efforts, Father Saudreau adds : " No one can of himself enter into mystic prayer ; no matter what efforts one may make, one will not attain it if one has not been raised to such a high state by divine favor." [2] Some indeed are of the opinion that one can merit it by a title of fitness, but such merit does not detract in the least from its essential gratuity.

1388. 2º Again, it is God Who *determines* the *moment* and the *manner*, as well as the *duration* of contemplation. He alone puts the soul into the passive or mystic state seizing its faculties in order to act in them and through them, but always with the free consent of the will. This constitutes a sort of *divine possession ;* and since God is the Sovereign Master of His Gifts, He intervenes when He wills and as He wills.

1389. 3º In contemplation God acts especially in what mystics call the *subtile point of the soul*, the *summit of the soul*, the *summit of the will* or *the inmost depth of the soul.* By this we must understand all that is loftiest in the intellect and the will; it is the intellect, not inasmuch· as it reasons, but inasmuch as it perceives truth by a simple glance, under the influence of the higher gifts of understanding and of wisdom; it is the will in its simplest act, which is that of loving and of relishing things divine.

The Venerable Louis de Blois [3] thinks that this center of the soul wherein contemplation takes place is far superior to the three controlling faculties, since it is the source of these faculties. " Therein," he adds, " the higher faculties themselves are but one thing ; therein reign perfect tranquility and perfect silence, for no image can ever reach there. It is in this center wherein the divine

---

[1] *The Living Flame*, III Stanza.
[2] *L'état mystique*, 2e éd., 1921, p. 19-20. — Father Janvier affirms the same doctrine (*Carême 1923*, Retraite, 2e Instr.) : " Infused contemplation is an eminent and singular grace which we do not obtain by our own efforts ; God grants it to *whom He pleases, when He pleases, and to the extent in which He pleases.* "
[3] *A Book of Spiritual Instruction.* London, 1900, c. XII.

image lies hidden, that we put on the divine likeness... O Peerless Center! the holy Temple whence the Lord never departs? O wondrous Recess! the dwelling-place of the Hallowed Trinity, and the source here below of eternal delights ! "

1390.   4° It is in this center of the soul that God produces at the same time *knowledge* and *love*.

a) He produces there a knowledge which though *obscure*, makes a vivid impression, because it is *experimental* or *quasi-experimental*. God may produce it in four different ways :

1) By *attracting our attention* to an idea already possessed, but which heretofore had not impressed us deeply. Thus we knew that God is love, but now divine light makes us understand and relish this thought so well that it penetrates our whole being and takes complete possession of us.

2) By *bringing together* in our mind two ideas which we have had and making us draw from them a forceful conclusion. Thus, from the thought that God is all and we are nothing, the Holy Spirit makes us understand that humility is for us an imperative duty : I am Who am, thou art what is not !

3) By producing within us what are called *infused impressions* which, because they proceed from God, represent divine things in a more perfect and more telling fashion; this is what occurs in some *visions* or *revelations*.

4) By granting to a soul a *transient vision of God* as He is in Himself, as was the case, according to St. Thomas, with Moses and St. Paul,[1] and, according to some of the Fathers, with the Blessed Virgin.[2] This, however, is a favor altogether exceptional, the actuality of which is doubted by grave theologians, who explain otherwise the texts of scripture adduced by St. Thomas.

1391.   **b**) God also produces in the soul an *ineffable love*. He enables it to understand by a sort of intuition, that He, and He alone, is the Supreme Good, and thus He attracts the soul to Himself in an irresistible way, like a magnet does, yet without doing violence to its free-will. The soul then moves towards God with all the ardor wherewith it moves towards happiness, yet freely, because its vision of God, though obscure, does not take away its freedom.

Then, according to the Venerable Louis de Blois, the soul goes out of itself in order to pass wholly into God and be lost in the abyss of

---

[1] *Sum. theol.*, II\a II\æ, q. 175, a. 3, ad 1.

[2] SUAREZ, in I\am, c. 30, n. 18 : " We should not be too quick to affirm or to extend such privileges. It may be piously believed that this favor was accorded the Most Blessed Virgin, and indeed, that if it was granted to any one, it was given to her above all. "

eternal love. "And there, dead to itself, it lives in God, knowing nothing, feeling nothing, save the love that inebriates it. It loses itself in the vastness of divine solitude and darkness; but to lose oneself here, is rather to find oneself, for the soul really divests itself of all that is human in order to clothe itself with God. It is all changed and transformed in God, just as iron in a fire assumes the aspect of fire and is changed into it. But the essence of the soul thus deified remains what it was, just as the incandescent iron ceases not to be iron. Heretofore there was but coldness in this soul, from now on it is all aflame; from darkness it has passed into the most radiant brightness; once insensible, it is now all tenderness... All consumed by the flame of divine love and wholly melted thereby, it passes into God by uniting itself to Him without any intermediary; it forms but one spirit with Him, just as gold and brass fuse to form one metal. Those that are thus ravished and lost in God reach different heights, for each one penetrates further into the divine depths in proportion as he turns towards God with greater sincerity, earnestness and love, and as he foregoes more completely in this quest all personal interest." [1]

III. *The Rôle of the Soul in Contemplation*

Moved by God's grace, the soul freely responds to the divine motion.

1392. 1° It lets itself be freely seized and moved by God, as a child lets itself be carried in its mother's arms. The soul is therefore both *passive* and *active* during contemplation.

a) It is *passive* in this sense, that it is powerless to act on its own initiative as it did previously; at the moment of contemplation it can no longer employ its faculties in a discursive way; it is dependent upon a higher principle which governs it, which fastens its gaze, its mind and its heart upon the object of contemplation, makes it love and relish that object, suggests what it must do and imparts to it a powerful impulse to enable it to act. However, in the first stages of contemplation there is not a complete powerlessness; the phenomenon of the *ligature of the faculties* is effected but gradually and does not exist *completely*, except in some of the higher stages of contemplation, particularly in ecstasy. Thus, in the state of quietude, vocal prayer and meditation fatigue the soul, but generally they are not beyond its powers; [2] in the state of perfect union, God suspends the exercise of the understanding, not indeed completely by preventing it from acting, but by preventing it from reasoning; He halts thoughts by centering them on a determined object; He causes speech to die away upon

---

[1] L. DE BLOIS, *A Book of Spiritual Instruction*, c. XII.
[2] ST. TERESA, *2nd Relation to Fr. Rodrigo; Way of Perfection*, C. XXXI.

the lips so that one cannot utter a single word without a painful effort. [1]

1393. b) Although the soul cannot reason as it did heretofore, it does *not* remain *idle*. Under the influence of the divine action, it *acts* by gazing on God and by loving Him, even if it be by acts that are at times but implicit. Nay, the soul exerts a greater activity than ever; for it receives an influx of spiritual energy which considerably increases its own. It feels itself transformed by a superior being which is, so to speak, its soul, and which lifts it up and carries it on towards God. This is the effect of *operating grace* to which the soul joyfully consents.

1394. 2° In this state God appears to the soul under a new aspect, as a *living reality*, grasped by a sort of *experimental* knowledge which human language cannot express. It is no longer by a process of induction or deduction that God is known, but by a simple intuition. However, this intuition is not as yet the clear vision of God; it remains obscure and is obtained by a sort of contact with God, Who causes us to feel His presence and relish His favors.

Perhaps no one has better described this experimental knowledge than St. Bernard:[2] " I confess, though I say it in my foolishness, that the **Word** has visited me, and even very often. But although He has frequently entered my soul, I have never at any time been sensible of the precise moment of His coming. I have felt that He was present. I remember that He has been with me; I have sometimes been able even to have a presentiment that He would come, but never to feel His coming, nor His departure... And thus I have learned the truth of the words I had read: In Him we live and move and have our being (*Acts*, XVII, 28); but blessed is the man in whom He is, who lives for Him, who is moved by Him. You will ask then, how, since the ways of His access are thus incapable of being traced, I could know that He was present. But He is living and full of energy, and as soon as He has entered into me He has quickened my sleeping soul; has aroused and softened and goaded my heart, which was in a state of torpor and hard as a stone. He has begun to pluck and destroy, to plant and to build, to water the dry places, to illuminate the gloomy spots, to throw open those which were shut close, to inflame with warmth those which were cold, as also to straighten its crooked paths and make its rough places smooth, so that my soul might bless the Lord, and all that is within me praise His Holy Name. Thus, then, the Bridegroom-Word, though He has several times entered into me, has never made His coming apparent to my sight, hearing or touch. It was not by His motions that He was recognized by me, nor could I tell by any of my senses that He had penetrated to the depths

[1] St. Teresa, *2nd Relation*, l. c.
[2] *Sermons on the Song of Songs*, Sermon LXXIV, n. 5-6. Translation by S. J. Eales, London, 1896.

of my being. It was as I have already said, only by the *revived activity of my heart* that I was enabled to recognize His Presence; and to know the power of His sacred Presence by the sudden departure of vices and the strong restraint put upon all carnal affections. From the discovery and conviction of my secret faults I have had good reason to admire the depth of His wisdom; His goodness and kindness have become known in the amendment, whatever it may amount to, of my life; while in the reformation and renewal of the spirit of my mind, that is, of my inward man, I have perceived, in a certain degree, the excellency of the Divine beauty." Thus the soul that contemplates the Word feels at once His Presence and His sanctifying power.

This is therefore an intermediate knowledge between ordinary faith and the Beatific Vision, but which in its last analysis belongs to faith and shares in its obscurity.

1395. 3° Often the soul's *love is greater than its knowledge* : this is *seraphic* contemplation, in contradistinction to *cherubic* contemplation in which knowledge predominates. The will attains its object in a manner different from that of the mind : the latter knows an object only according to the representation, the image, which it receives from that object; the will or the heart tends towards the *object* such as it is *in itself.* This is why we are able to love God as He is in Himself, although our mind here on earth does not understand His inner nature This very obscurity but causes a rekindling of our love for Him and makes us long ardently for His Presence. By an aspiration of the heart, the mystic, who cannot see God, rends the mystery that veils his own face and loves God in himself, in His infinite essence. [1] At all events some knowledge always precedes love; therefore, if certain of the mystics seem to deny this, it is because they emphasize what has particularly impressed them. But it still remains true, even in the mystic state, that no one can love what he in no wise knows.

1396. 4° In contemplation there is a *mixture of joy and sadness :* unspeakable joy in relishing the Presence of the Divine Host, sadness at not having complete possession of Him. At times it is joy that predominates, at others, it is sadness, according to the designs of God, the various phases of the mystic life and the different individual temperaments. Thus there are periods that are particularly *painful*, called *nights*, and others that are sweet or *pleasant.* Some minds, like that of St. John of the Cross and St. Jeanne Chantal, perceive and describe especially the trials of the mystic life;

---

[1] JOHN OF ST. THOMAS, in I^{am} II^æ, q. 68-70, disp. 18, n. 11-12; JORET, *Vie Spirituelle*, Sept. 1920, p. 455-456.

others, like St. Teresa and St. Francis de Sales, dwell more readily upon the joys and raptures of contemplation.

1397.   5° As the mystics admit, this contemplation is beyond the powers of human description.

"It cannot be discerned or described," says St. John of the Cross. [1] "Moreover, the soul has no wish to speak of it, and besides, it can discover no way or proper similitude by which to describe it, so as to make known a knowledge so high, a spiritual impression so delicate and infused. Yea, if it could have a wish to speak of it, and find terms to describe it, it would always remain secret still... The soul is like a man who sees an object for the first time, the like of which he has never seen before; he handles it and feels it, yet he cannot say what it is, or tell its name, do what he can, though it be at the same time an object cognizable by the senses. How much less then can that be described which does not enter by the senses?"

This impossibility of describing what one has experienced is explained on two grounds : on the one hand, the mind is plunged into *divine darkness* and perceives God but vaguely and obscurely, although it is very deeply impressed; on the other hand, the most striking phenomenon is that of an *intense love for God,* which one experiences but knows not how to describe.

1398.   **A)** Let us see first of all what is meant by the *divine darkness,* an expression borrowed from the Pseudo-Dionysius. [2]

"Delivered from the world of sense and the world of thought, the soul enters into the *mysterious darkness of a holy ignorance,* and dismissing all scientific knowledge, it loses itself in Him Who can neither be seen nor apprehended; it gives itself over completely to this Sovereign Object and belongs no longer to itself or to any other; it is united to the Unknown by the noblest part of its being in virtue of its renouncement of knowledge; finally, it draws forth from this utter ignorance a knowledge that the intellect would not be able to attain." To attain therefore to this contemplation, we must rise above sense knowledge, which evidently cannot perceive God, and even above *rational* knowledge, which knows God only by induction and abstraction. It is indeed solely through the subtile part of the intellect that we can perceive Him. On earth we cannot see Him directly; we can but reach Him through the method of *negation.*

St. Thomas explains this more clearly : "From negation to negation, the soul rises above the most excellent creatures and unites itself to God in what measure it can here below. For in our present existence, our mind can never see the Divine Essence, it can only know what It is not. Such union therefore as is possible here below between the mind

---

[1] *Dark Night of the Soul,* Bk. II, C. 17. Translation by David Lewis, London, 1891.
[2] *Mystical Theology,* C. I, § 3.

and God takes place when we come to know that God surpasses the noblest of creatures. " [1] The very notion of *being*, such as we conceive it, is too imperfect to be applied to God ; it is only after eliminating all specific being known by reason that our mind unites again with God. It is then that the mind finds itself in the *divine darkness*, and it is there that God dwells. [2]

If we ask ourselves how it is that such negative intuition can enlighten us as regards God, we can answer that we thereby learn not what God is, but what He is not ; that we thereby acquire a very exalted idea of Him, which produces in the superior part of the soul a profound impression of the divine transcendence and at the same time an ardent love for Him Whose grandeur and goodness nothing can express and Who alone can fill the soul. This contemplation, vague and affectionate, suffices under the influence of grace to cause implicit acts of faith, confidence, love and religion to well up in the soul, filling it completely, and generally producing in it a great sense of joy.

1399. B) The second element which renders a description of contemplation difficult is the ardent love which one experiences therein and which one knows not how to express.

" It is a canticle of love, " St. Bernard tells us, [3] " which the anointing of grace alone teaches, and experience alone makes the soul familiar with. Those who have had experience of it know it well ; let those who have not had that happiness earnestly desire, not to know it, but to experience it. It is not a cry from the mouth, but the gladness of the heart ; not the sounding of·the lips, but the impulse and emotion of joys within ; not a concert of words, but of wills moving in harmony. It is not heard without, nor does it make a sound in public. Only she who sings, and He in whose honour it is sung, that is, the Bridgegroom and the bride, hear the accents of that song. It is a nuptial song which is expressive of the chaste and sweet emotions of souls, the entire conformity of character, the blending of affections in mutual charity. But for the rest, this song is not to be sung or to be understood by a soul which is as yet a neophyte in virtue and but newly turned from the world. It belongs to the advanced and instructed soul which, by the progress in grace made by the power of God, has grown as far as to reach a perfect age, and, as it were, to have become marriageable through the merits it has acquired, and by its virtues to have become worthy of its Spouse. "

1400. 6o When contemplation is *arid* and *weak*, as in the first night of St. John of the Cross, *one is not conscious*

---

[1] *Comment. de div. nomin.*, c. XIII, lect. 3.
[2] ST. THOM., *I Sent.*, dist. 8, q. I, a. 1, ad 4.
[3] *Sermons on the Song of Songs*, Sermon I, n. 11-12.

of it; it is only later that, by examining the *effects* it has produced, one is able to establish the fact of its existence. When it is *sweet* it seems quite certain that one is not always conscious of it in its beginnings, because while it is still weak it is difficult to distinguish it from the prayer of simplicity, and because at times one passes from the one to the other without realizing it. However, once it has become intense, one is conscious of it. It may be said that all the various *supernatural* prayers described by St. Teresa are of this type, as we shall note when explaining the different phases of contemplation.

1401. Conclusion. From what we have said, it follows that the *essential element* of infused contemplation is passivity, as we heve described it, which means that the soul is led, acted upon, moved, directed by the Holy Ghost, and does not lead itself, move itself, or direct itself, though it preserves its freedom and its activity.

Therefore, it must not be said that the essential element of contemplation [1] is the consciousness of the presence of God or the *presence of God felt*, since at times this is lacking, particularly in the arid contemplation described by St. John of the Cross in the course of the *first night*. It is, however, one of its chief elements, since it reappears in all the degrees of contemplation described by St. Teresa, from the prayer of quiet to the transforming union.

§ II. Advantages of Contemplation

These advantages surpass even those of the prayer of simplicity, precisely because in contemplation the soul is more closely united to God and under the influence of a more efficacious grace.

1402. 1° *God thereby receives greater glory.* [2] **a)** By causing us to experience the infinite transcendence of God, infused contemplation abases our whole being before His majesty, causes us to praise and bless Him, not only at the time of mental prayer, but likewise the whole day long: once we have caught a glimpse of this divine grandeur, we are held spellbound in admiration and worship before it. This is so true that we are unable to contain ourselves, and

---

[1] Thus, FATHER POULAIN, *Graces of Interior Prayer*, C. V, while giving as the fundamental element of contemplation the presence of God felt, adds that in the lower degrees, the prayer of quiet, God makes His presence felt only in a rather obscure manner.

[2] ST. JOHN OF THE CROSS, *Living Flame*, Stan. III, v. 5 and 6.

we feel forced to invite all creatures to bless and thank God, as we shall see further on (n. 1444).

b) These homages are all the more pleasing to God, and honor Him all the more as they are directly inspired by the Holy Ghost : it is He Who adores in us, or rather, He Who causes us to adore with sentiments of great fervor and humility. He makes us adore God as He is in Himself, causing us to realize that this is a duty of our very condition, and that we are created solely in order to sing His praises. And in order to make us sing them with greater earnestness, He bestows upon us new favors and a great peace of soul.

1403. 2° *The soul is thereby made more holy.* Contemplation produces so much *light*, so much *love*, and so much *virtue* that it is rightly called a *royal road* to perfection

A) It enables us to know God in an ineffable and highly sanctifying way. "God now secretly and quietly infuses wisdom into the soul together with the loving knowledge of Himself, without many divers, distinct or separated acts, though He produces them sometimes in the soul, and that for some space of time. " [1] This knowledge is very sanctifying, because it enables us to know by *experience*, what we had previously learned through reading or personal reflection, and because it makes us see at a glance what we had analyzed by successive acts of the mind.

St. John of the Cross [2] gives an excellent explanation of this : " God in His one and simple essence is all the power and majesty of His attributes. He is omnipotent, wise, good, merciful, just, strong, loving ; He is all the other attributes and perfections of which we have no knowledge here below. He is all this. When the soul is in union with Him, and He is pleased to admit it to a special knowledge of Himself, it sees all these perfections and majesty together in Him... and as each one of these attributes is the very being of God, Who is the Father, the Son, and the Holy Ghost ; and as each attribute is God Himself ; and as God is infinite light, and infinite divine fire, it follows that each attribute gives light and burns as God Himself. " Now one can understand what St. Teresa [3] says : " When it is Our Lord who stops and suspends the understanding, He supplies it with matter to occupy itself, and ravish it with astonishment, so that without any reasoning it then understands more during the short space of a " *Credo* " than we ourselves could understand, with all possible study, during many years. "

Doubtless there are instances in which the light is not so clear but rather obscure and vague ; but even then it

[1] ST. JOHN OF THE CROSS, *Living Flame*, Stan. III, v. 3.
[2] *Living Flame*, Stan. III, v. I.
[3] *Life by Herself*, C. XII.

makes a deep impression on the soul as we explained in
number 1398,

1404. **B**) Contemplation produces, above all, a *very
ardent love*, which, according to St. John of the Cross, is
characterized by three special qualities : **a**) First of all, the
soul loves God, not of itself, but *through Him ;* this constitutes an excellent practice ; for it loves through the Holy
Ghost, as the Father and the Son love One Another.   This
the Son Himself declares through St. John : " *That the love
wherewith thou hast loved me may be in them, and I in
them.* " [1]

b) The second excellence is that of *loving God in God ;*
for, in this ardent union, the soul is absorbed by the love of
God, and God yields Himself with great readiness to the
soul.

c) The third quality of the supreme love is that in this
state the soul loves God *for what He is,* that is to say, it
loves Him not only because He shows Himself generous,
good, glorious, etc., but much more because He is essentially
generous and good etc.

We can add, with St. Francis de Sales, [2] that this love is all the more
ardent, because it is based upon experimental knowledge.   In the same
way that he who " with clear eyes feels and feels again the vivifying
splendour of the rising sun " loves that light far more than one born
blind who knows light but from hearsay, so he who enjoys God by
contemplation loves Him far better than the one who knows Him but
through study ; " for the actual experience of some good renders it more
lovable to us than all the speculative knowledge of it that we could
have. "   He goes on to say, that St. Catherine of Genoa loved God
more than the subtle theologian, Ocham ; the latter had more knowledge of God through science, the former through experience ; and this
experience carried her far ahead in seraphic love.

What increases this love still more is that it facilitates contemplation,
and that contemplation in turn deepens love : " For, love having
aroused our attention to contemplate, reciprocally this attention gives
birth to a greater and stronger love which finally attains its crowning
perfection when it enjoys the possession of the object loved... love
urges on the mind to the ever more attentive contemplation of the
beloved beauty, and the sight impels the heart to love it ever more
ardently. " [3]

1405. **C**) This love is attended by the practice of all the
moral virtues in their highest degree and, in particular, of
humility, of conformity to God's will, of holy abandonment,
and thereby of joy and peace of spirit even in the very
midst of the trials, terrible at times, which mystics undergo.

---

[1] *John*, XVII, 26. — [2] *Love of God*, Bk. VI, C. 3.
[3] *Love of God*, Bk. VI, C. 3.

This we shall see more in detail when analyzing the various degrees of contemplation, n. 1440 etc.

§ III. Proximate Call to Contemplation

1406.   We set aside for the time being the controverted question concerning the *general* and *remote* call of all the baptized to contemplation.   We wish to remain as far as possible on the *solid ground of facts* and to examine these two questions : 1º To whom does God generally grant the grace of contemplation?   2º What are the signs of a *proximate* and *individual* call to contemplation?

I. *To Whom does God Grant Contemplation?*

1407.   1º Contemplation being essentially a free gift (n. 1387), God grants it to whom He wills, when He wills, and in the way He wills.   Usually, however, He bestows it only upon souls well prepared for it.

By exception, God grants it at times in an extraordinary way to souls devoid of virtues, so as to snatch them from the power of the devil.

St. Teresa [1] affirms this : " God knows that He can attract certain souls to Himself by means of divine favours : He sees they are on the way to be lost, but He does not wish it to happen through any fault of His; therefore, though they are in a bad case and are lacking in goodness, He gives them consolations, delights, and tenderness of devotion which begin to excite their desires; He even sometimes raises them to contemplation, although but rarely, and for a very short time.   This is to prove whether such a grace will induce them to prepare themselves to enjoy His favours more often. "

1408.   2º There are *privileged souls* whom God calls to contemplation from their infancy, such as St. Rose of Lima, and in our own time, St. Teresa of the Child Jesus.   Others are brought to it later and make such rapid progress in it as would seem to be out of proportion to their virtues.

St. Teresa [2] recounts the following : " I remember one whom God in three days so enriched that were it not for the several years' experience together with her constant and growing improvement, I would think it impossible.   Another one I know who in three months reached contemplation ; and both of these were still young.   I have seen others receive this grace only after a long time...   No limits can be set to so great a Master, Who is so anxious to bestow His favours. "

1409.   3º But ordinarily God selects for contemplation those who have prepared themselves for it by detachment,

---

[1] *Way of Perfection*, C. XVI.
[2] *Concepts of Divine Love*, C. VI.

and the practice of the virtues and of mental prayer, especially affective prayer.

This is the teaching of St. Thomas, [1] who declares that one cannot arrive at contemplation except by mortifying the passions through the practice of the moral virtues (cfr. n. 1315).

St. John of the Cross is no less emphatic; he develops this teaching at length in the *Ascent of Carmel* and in the *Night of the Soul*, and shows that in order to reach contemplation, one must practice the most complete and universal self-abnegation. He adds that if contemplatives are so few, it is because there are few who are completely detached from self and creatures. " So act, " the Saint goes on to say, " that the soul may be established in pure, spiritual nakedness, and having become pure and simple it will be transformed into the simple and pure wisdom of God, which is the Son of God. " [2] St. Teresa returns to this again and again, recommending, above all, humility: " After having done what those in the preceding mansions do, practice humility, and again, humility! Thereby does the Lord suffer Himself to be overcome and to yield to all we desire of Him... My opinion is that when His Majesty bestows it, He gives it to such as are already taking leave of the things of the world. I do not say they do so in fact, for their condition prevents them, but they do so by desire. Then He calls them to concern themselves specially with interior things; hence, I believe that if we allow His Majesty full freedom of action, He will not limit Himself to this gift alone on behalf of one whom He has invited to higher things. " [3]

1410. 4° The main virtues to be practiced are: **a)** A great *purity of heart* and a complete detachment from all that can lead to sin and trouble the soul.

As examples of habitual imperfections which prevent a perfect union with God, St. John of the Cross cites: " much talking; certain attachments, which we never resolve to break with, such as to individuals, to a book or a cell, to a particular food, to certain society; the satisfaction of one's taste, science, news, and such things. " He then gives the reason why: " Does it make any difference whether a bird be held by a slender thread or by a rope, while the bird is bound and cannot fly till the cord that holds it is broken?... This is the state of a soul with particular attachments: it never can attain to the liberty of the divine union, whatever virtues it may possess. " [4]

1411. **b)** A *great purity of mind*, that is to say, the mortifying of curiosity, which troubles and disturbs the soul, distracts and scatters its attention in all directions. This is why those whose duties of state require them to read much and to study, must often mortify their curiosity, stop from time to time, and refer all their study to the love of God. This purity likewise demands that one be willing

---

[1] IIa IIæ q. 180, a. 2. — [2] *Ascent of Mount Carmel*, Bk. II, C. 13.
[3] *Interior Castle*, IV Mansion, C. II and III.
[4] *Ascent of Mount Carmel*, Bk. I, C. XI.

to abridge and, at the accepted time, relinquish reasoning in prayer, and simplify one's affections, so as to come, little by little, to a simple and loving gaze on God. On this point St. John of the Cross bitterly reproaches unskilled directors of souls who, being acquainted with discursive meditation only, want to oblige all their penitents to keep their faculties constantly in action. [1]

1412. c) A great *purity of intention* attained through mortification of the will and the practice of holy abandonment (nn. 480-497).

d) A *lively faith*, which makes us live in all things according to the maxims of the Gospel (n. 1188).

e) A *religious silence* which enables us to transform all our actions into so many prayers (n. 522-529).

f) Finally, and chiefly, an *ardent and generous love* which goes as far as self-immolation and the joyous acceptance of all trials (n. 1227-1235).

II. *Signs of a Proximate Call to Contemplation*

1413. When a soul is thus consciously or unconsciously disposed for contemplation, a time comes when God makes it understand that it must relinquish discursive meditation.

Now, St. John of the Cross [2] tells us there are three signs which indicate this moment.

1º " When one finds *one cannot meditate nor exert his imagination, nor derive any satisfaction from it, as he was wont to do* — when he finds dryness there, where he was accustomed to fix the senses and draw forth sweetness — then the time is come. But while he finds sweetness, and is able to meditate as usual, let him not cease therefrom, except when his soul is in peace, of which I shall speak when describing the third sign. " The cause for this dislike, the Saint goes on to say, is that the soul has already drawn from divine things well-nigh all the spiritual profit that discursive meditation can yield; it can no longer make such

---

[1] " A Spiritual director who, like a rough blacksmith, knows only the use of his hammer, and who, because all his knowledge is limited to the coarser work, will say '' Come, get rid of this, this is waste of time and idleness : arise and meditate, resume thine interior acts, ... everything else is delusion and folly... Such a director as this does not understand the degrees of prayer, nor the ways of the Spirit ... understands not that the soul has already attained to the life of the Spirit ... where God is Himself the agent in a special way, and is speaking in secret to the solitary soul. Directors of this kind bedaub the soul with the coarse ointments of particular knowledge and sensible sweetness to which they bring it back. " (*Living Flame*, Stan. III, V. 3). St. Teresa also complains of such directors, who force the faculties to work even on Sundays. (*Life by Herself*, C. XIII).

[2] *Ascent of Mount Carmel*, Bk. II, C. XI.

a prayer; the craving and the relish for it are gone; hence it needs a new method. [1]

1414. 2° "When he sees that he has no inclination to fix the imagination or the other senses on particular objects, exterior or interior. I do not mean when the imagination neither comes nor goes, — for it is disorderly even in the most complete self-recollection, — but only when the soul derives no pleasure from tying it down deliberately to other matters. "

This the Saint explains : "Such a soul betaking itself to prayer — like a man with water before him — drinks sweetly without effort, without the necessity of drawing it through the channel of previous reflections, forms and figures. And the moment such a soul places itself in the presence of God, it makes an act of knowledge, confused, loving, peaceful and tranquil, wherein it drinks in wisdom, love and sweetness. This is the reason why the soul is troubled and disgusted when compelled, in this state, to make meditations and to labour in particular acts of knowledge. Its condition, then, is like that of an infant at the breast, withdrawn from it while it was sucking it, and bidden to procure its nourishment by efforts of its own ; like one who loses a prize already in his power." [2]

1415. 3° "The third sign is the most certain of the three, namely, *when the soul delights to be alone, waiting lovingly on God, without any particular considerations,* in interior peace, quiet, and repose, when the acts and exercises of the understanding, memory, and will have ceased, at least discursively, that is, going from one subject to another, nothing remaining except that knowledge and attention, *general* and *loving*, of which I have spoken, without the particular perception of aught else." [3]

"This general knowledge of which I am speaking is at times so subtle and delicate — particularly when most pure, simple, perfect, spiritual, and interior — that the soul, withal, in the practice thereof, is *not observant* or *conscious of it.* This is the case when that knowledge is most pure, clear and simple, that is, when it enters into a soul most pure and detached from all other acts of knowledge and special perceptions, to which the understanding or the sense may cling. Such a soul, because freed from all those things which were actually and habitually objects of the understanding or of the sense, is not aware of them, because the accustomed objects of sense have failed it. This is the reason why this knowledge, when most pure, perfect, and simple, is the less perceived by the understanding, and is the most obscure. On the other hand, when this knowledge is less pure and simple, the more clear and the more important it seems to the understanding; because it is mixed up with, clothed in, or involved in, certain intelli-

---

[1] The explanations of each of these three signs are found in the fourteenth chapter of the *Ascent of Mount Carmel,* Book II.
[2] *Ascent of Mount Carmel,* Bk. II, C. XIV.
[3] *Ascent of Mount Carmel,* Bk. II, C. XIV.

gible forms, of which the understanding most easily takes cognizance, to its hurt. " [1]

The Saint explains this by the following comparison : " When the rays of the sun penetrate through a crevice into a dark room, and the air within is full of atoms and particles of dust, these are more palpable then, more visible to the eye ; and yet, those rays are then less pure, simple, and perfect, because mixed up with so much impurity : also, when they are most pure and most free from dust, the less are they cognizable by the material eye ; and the more pure they are, the less are they seen and considered. " [2] The same takes place in the case of spiritual light : the purer and more radiant it is, the less it is perceived, so much so that the soul believes it finds itself in darkness ; if on the contrary it be charged with some intelligible forms, it is more easily discerned, and the soul thinks itself better enlightened.

1416. We must note here with Saint John of the Cross that *these three signs must exist* at the same time before one can safely venture to abandon the state of meditation for the way of spiritual contemplation. And let us add with this Saint that it is profitable in the beginning of one's advancement to the ways of contemplation to return at times to discursive meditation. This will even become necessary if the soul finds itself unoccupied during the quiet of contemplation ; for meditation is imperative as long as the soul has not acquired the habit of contemplation. [3]

Conclusion : The Desire of Contemplacion

1417. It is permissible to desire infused contemplation, since it is an *excellent means of perfection*, but it must be done *humbly and conditionally*, with a *holy abandonment* to the will of God.

a) Since contemplation has so many advantages, n. 1402, it follows that one may desire it : " Contemplation is like a dew which makes virtues grow, which nourishes them, and from which they obtain their crowning perfection. " [4]

b) But this desire must be *humble*, it must be accompanied by the conviction that we are very unworthy of such a gift and by the desire of using it solely for the glory of God and the good of souls.

c) It must be *conditional*, subordinated in every way to the good pleasure of God. It must therefore be neither over-eager nor unpractical : one should remember that contemplation normally presupposes the practice of the moral and theological virtues, and that it would be presumption

---

[1] *Ascent of Mount Carmel*, Bk. II, C. XIV.
[2] *Ascent of Mount Carmel*, Bk. II, C. XIV.
[3] *Ascent of Mount Carmel*, Bk. II, C. XV.
[4] *Congrès carmélitain de Madrid*, theme VI.

to desire it before being schooled for a long time in these virtues. Besides, one must fully realize that if contemplation procures unspeakable joys, it is also attended by terrible trials which only strong souls can withstand, God's grace helping.

ART. II. THE DIFFERENT PHASES OF CONTEMPLATION

1418. Infused contemplation is not the same in all persons. God, Who is pleased to vary His gifts and to adapt them to the different temperaments and characters, does not confine His action within set forms; and so, when reading the mystics one finds very different forms of contemplation. [1] However, there seems to be a certain unity running through all this multiplicity which has enabled spiritual writers to classify the principal stages traversed by the mystics.

We shall not present here the different classifications adopted by the different authors. [2] They distinguish a greater or lesser number of degrees, according to their point of view, and at times they reckon as different degrees what in reality are but varying forms of the same state.

1419. Since all admit that St. Teresa and St. John of the Cross are the two great exponents of the mystic union, we shall keep to the divisions they give, and strive to combine them harmoniously. The various degrees are marked by a greater and greater hold of God on the soul. 1° When He takes possession of the subtle *point of the soul*, letting the lower faculties and the senses free to exercise their natural activity, we have the *prayer of quiet*. 2° When He seizes *all the interior faculties*, leaving merely the exterior senses to their own activity, we have the *full union*. 3° If He takes possession at the same time of the interior faculties and of the exterior senses, we have *ecstatic union* (spiritual espousals). 4° Lastly, once He extends His hold over all the internal and external faculties and this, no longer in a transitory manner, but in a *stable* and *per-*

---

[1] Cf. *Mère Suzanne-Marie de Riants de Villerey; Ami du Clergé*, 2 Août 1923.
[2] M. J. RIBET, *Mystique divine*, t. I, ch. X, enumerates the main classifications. Alvarez de Paz counts 15 : intuition of truth, interior concentration of the energies of the soul, silence, repose, union, hearing of God's word, spiritual sleep, ecstasy, rapture, bodily apparition, imaginative apparition, intellectual vision, divine darkness, manifestations of God, intuitive vision of God. Schram has a more complete and more obscure nomenclature. Scaramelli distinguishes twelve degrees : recollection, spiritual silence, quietude, inebriation of love, spiritual sleep, the anxieties and thirst of love, the divine touch, the simple mystic union, ecstasy, rapture, stable and perfect union. Father Philip of the Blessed Trinity numbers six : recollection, quietude, ordinary union, the divine impulse, rapture, spiritual marriage.

manent fashion, we have the *spiritual marriage.* Such are the four degrees of contemplation according to St. Teresa. St. John of the Cross adds to these the *nights* or *passive trials;* but the first night is but a species of quietude, *arid* and *crucifying;* the second night comprises the *sum-total of trials,* which precede the spiritual marriage, and which are found in the full union and in the ecstatic union.

Therefore, we shall treat of :

I   *Quietude* $\begin{cases} \text{arid} \\ \text{sweet} \end{cases}$

II *Full Union*

III *Ecstatic Union* $\begin{cases} \text{sweet} \\ \text{crucifying} \end{cases}$

IV *Transforming Union* or *Spiritual Marriage*

§ I. The Prayer of Quiet

This prayer generally begins in its *arid* form and terminates in its *sweet* form.

I. *Arid Quietude or the Night of the Senses.*

1420. We have said that a great purity of heart is required for contemplation. Now, even advanced souls are subject to many imperfections, and experience, though in a milder form, a reawakening of the seven capital sins (n. 1264). In order to purify them still more and to prepare them for a higher degree of contemplation, God sends them various trials which are called *passive* trials because it is God Himself who causes them and the soul has but to *accept* them *patiently.*

No one has described these trials better than St. John of the Cross does in the " Dark Night. " He calls them *night* because the divine action binds to some extent the sense-faculties in order to subject them to the mind, and prevents the mind in turn from reasoning, so that the latter finds itself in a kind of night : on the one hand, the mind can no longer exercise itself in discursive *reasoning* as it did before, and on the other, the light of contemplation it receives is so faint and so crucifying that the soul believes itself plunged into a night of darkness. The Saint distinguishes two nights : the first calculated above all to detach us from the things of *sense,* and therefore called the *night of the senses;* the second, to detach us from spiritual consolations and from all self-love.

1421. Here we speak only of the night of the senses.

" God establishes the soul in the dark night of sense, " says St. John of the Cross,[1] " that He may purify, prepare and subdue its lower

---

[1] *The Dark Night of the Soul,* Bk. I, C. XI.

nature, and unite it to the Spirit, by depriving it of light and causing it to cease from meditation. "

This is a complex state of soul and a baffling mixture of darkness and light, of aridity and intense though hidden love of God, of real weakness and latent energy, difficult to analyze without falling into apparent contradictions. St. John of the Cross himself should be read with the help we shall try to furnish. With this end in view, we shall explain : 1º the *constituent elements* of this spiritual night; 2º the *trials which attend* it; 3º its *advantages*.

1º Constituent Elements of this Ordeal

1422. A) The first and foremost of these elements is *infused contemplation*, which God begins to communicate to the soul in a secret, obscure manner as yet unknown to the soul, but which produces there a painful and agonizing impression. This, the Saint [1] says, is a " commencement of contemplation, dim and dry to the senses, which is, in general, secret und unknown to him who is admitted into it ;... it makes the soul long for solitude and quiet, without the power of reflecting distinctly, on anything or even desiring to do so. "

To help us understand this state of soul, the Saint further on [2] employs the following comparison which it will be well to keep in mind from now on : " The first action of material fire on fuel is to dry it, to expel from it all the water and all the moisture. It blackens it at once and soils it, and drying it by little and little, makes it light and consumes all its foulness and blackness which are contrary to itself. Finally, having heated and set on fire its outward surface, it transforms the whole into itself, and makes it beautiful as itself. The fuel under these conditions retains neither active nor passive qualities of its own, except bulk and weight, and assumes all the properties and acts of fire. It becomes dry, being dry it glows, and glowing, burns ; luminous, it gives light, and burns more quickly than before. All this is the property and effect of fire. It is in this way we have to reason about the divine fire of contemplative love which, before it unites with, and transforms the soul into itself, purges away all its contrary qualities. It expels its impurities, blackens it and obscures it, and thus its condition is apparently worse than it was before. For a while the divine purgation is removing all the evil and vicious humours, which, because so deeply rooted and settled in the soul, were neither seen nor felt, but now in order to their expulsion and annihilation, are rendered clearly visible in the dim light of the divine contemplation, the soul — though no worse in itself, nor in the sight of God — seeing at last what it never saw before, looks upon itself not only as unworthy of His regard, but even as a loathsome object, and that God does loath it. " [3]

---

[1] *Night*, Bk. I, C. IX. — [2] *Night*, Bk. II, C. X.

[3] Another comparison may further illustrate this state of soul : when we examine a glass of water with the naked eye, we see nothing in it to startle us ; but if we look at that same water through the microscope, we shudder at the sight of the living

1423. **B)** This kind of contemplation produces in the soul a *great aridity*, not only in the sense-faculties which are deprived of consolations, but also in the higher faculties which can no longer meditate in a discursive way as they did before. This is a painful situation : accustomed to the light, these faculties find themselves plunged into darkness ; formerly they knew how to reflect and to cause numerous affections to pour forth from the heart ; but now they have lost that facility, and prayer becomes most painful.

So it is, too, with the practice of the virtues : the efforts to grow in virtue once gladly made now appear arduous and forbidding.

1424. It is important to distinguish this purifying dryness from that caused by negligence and lukewarmness. St. John of the Cross [1] gives us three signs by which to make this distinction :

1) "The first is this : when we find no confort in the things of God, and none also in created things," whereas the lukewarm while they have no inclination towards the things of God, do feel drawn to earthly pleasures. " But still, inasmuch as this absence of pleasure in the things of heaven and of earth may proceed from bodily indisposition or a melancholy temperament, which frequently cause dissatisfaction with all things, the second test and condition become necessary."

2) " *The memory dwells ordinarily upon God* with a painful anxiety and carefulness ; the soul thinks it is not serving God, but going backwards, because it is no longer conscious of any sweetness in the things of God ; the peculiarity of lukewarmness is the want of earnestness in, and of interior solicitude for, the things of God." Likewise, when dryness comes from physical weakness, it produces nothing but disgust without the least sign of a desire of serving God such as accompanies purifying aridity, and which obscure contemplation infuses into the soul.

3) " The third sign we have for ascertaining whether this dryness be the purgation of sense, is *inability to meditate and to make reflections*, and to excite the imagination, as before, notwithstanding all the efforts we may make ; for God begins now to communicate Himself, no longer through the channel of sense as formerly, in consecutive reflections by which we arranged and divided our knowledge, but in pure spirit which admits not of successive reflections, and in the act of pure contemplation to which neither the interior nor exterior senses of our lower nature can ascend. " The Saint remarks however that this inability is not always continuous, and that at intervals one can return to ordinary meditation.

Let us also note that this inability generally refers only to things spiritual ; one is able to busy oneself with studies or business matters.

1425. **C)** To this aridity is added a *painful and persistent longing for a more intimate union with God.* At first this desire is not felt, but "the more it grows, the more the soul feels itself touched and inflamed with the love of God, without knowing or understanding how or whence that love comes, except that at times this burning so inflames it that it longs earnestly after God... Secret contemplation keeps the soul in this state of anxiety, until, in the course of time, having purged the sensual nature of man, in some degree, of its natural forces and affections by means of the aridities it occasions, it shall have kindled within it this divine love. But in the meantime, like a sick man in the hands of his physician, all it has to do, in the dark night and dry purgation of the desire, is to suffer, healing its many imperfections and practising many virtues that it may become meet for the divine love." [1]

The soul is now turned towards God and no longer desires creatures; but this turning to God is as yet vague and confused; it is like homesickness for God; the soul longs to be united to Him and to possess Him. If it has not so far experienced quietude in its sweet form, the attraction is indistinct, the longing undefined, the uneasiness indefinable; but if it has already experienced the mystic union, the desire to return to it is clear and well-defined. [2]

2° TRIALS WHICH ATTEND THE NIGHT OF THE SENSES

1426. Spiritual writers generally give a terrifying account of these trials, because they describe what transpires in the souls of the Saints, who, being called to a high degree of contemplation, have to bear very heavy crosses. There are however other souls called to a less exalted degree who are not so severely tried. It is well to know this, in order to reassure timid souls whom the fear of the cross might hinder from entering into this path. It must be remembered that God proportions His graces to the severity of the trials.

A) Besides that persistent dryness of which we have spoken, the soul also undergoes *terrible temptations* : 1) against *faith* : feeling nothing, it imagines that it believes nothing; 2) against *hope* : deprived of consolations, it believes itself abandoned, and is tempted to weariness and discouragement; 3) against *chastity* : "to some is sent the tool of Satan, the spirit of impurity to buffet them with horrible and violent temptations of the flesh, to trouble their minds with filthy thoughts, and their imaginations with representations of sin most vividly depicted; at

---

[1] *Night*, Bk. I, C. XI.
[2] LEHODEY, *The Ways of Mental Prayer*, P. III, C. III.

times, becomes an affliction more grievous than death;" [1]
4) against *patience :* amidst all this weariness, the soul is
tempted to complain of others or of self; blasphemous
thoughts present themselves to the imagination in such a
vivid manner that the tongue seems to utter them; 5) against
peace of soul : obsessed by a thousand scruples and perplex-
ities, the soul becomes so enmeshed in its own ideas that it
can follow no advice nor yield to any reasoning; this is a
source of the most intense pain.

1427. B) One likewise suffers from the actions of
others : 1) at times from the repeated and varied persecutions of unbelievers : " *All that will live godly in Christ
Jesus, shall suffer persecution;* " [2] 2) sometimes also from
superiors or *friends* who, not being able to understand such
a condition, are unfavorably impressed by one's failures and
persistent aridities; 3) at other times from the spiritual
director, who either mistakes this state of soul for lukewarmness, or is unable to relieve such distress.

C) *Evils from without* come sometimes to add to this
suffering from within : 1) one becomes a prey to strange
ailments which baffle physicians; 2) one *cannot succeed* as
one did before, on account of the helplessness in which one
finds oneself, or because one is absorbed in these interior
sufferings : one feels *stupid,* and others become aware of the
fact; 3) one undergoes at times *temporal* losses which bring
about a precarious situation. In a word, it seems as if
heaven and earth had joined against this poor soul.

In many cases these trials are natural and do not go
beyond what God sends fervent souls in order to procure
their perfection. But in other instances, these trials are really
mystic : they are recognized by their *suddenness,* by their
keenness, and by the good *effects* they produce in the soul.

3° ADVANTAGES OF THIS PURIFICATION

To be introduced into passive contemplation, even though
it is dark and painful, is already a great benefit; in
addition, there are others which St. John of the Cross calls
accessory advantages.

1428. 1° The *experimental knowledge of self* and one's
miseries : " The soul counts itself for nothing, having no
satisfaction in itself, because it sees of itself it does and can
do nothing. God then esteems more highly this diminished

---

[1] *Night,* Bk. I, C. XIV. — [2] *II Tim.,* III, 12.

satisfaction with self and the affliction it feels because it thinks it is not serving God, than He did all its former delights and all its good works, however great they may have been... The soul learns to commune with God with more respect and reverence, always necessary in converse with the Most High. Now, in its prosperous days of sweetness and consolation, the soul was less observant of reverence, for the favours it then received rendered the desire somewhat bold with God, and less reverent than it should have been. " [1] Thus, the virtue of religion gains by this purification.

1429. 2° The *knowledge of God* becomes purer and truer, and the *love* for Him more independent of feeling. The soul no longer seeks for consolations : it wants but to please God : " It is not presumptuous and self-satisfied, as perhaps it may have been in the day of its prosperity, but timid and diffident, without any self-satisfaction. Herein consists that holy fear by which virtues are preserved and grow. " [2]

1430. 3° The soul is thereby cured of the capital sins in their more refined form (cf. n. 1263).

a) The soul now practices humility, not only towards God, but also towards the neighbor : " Now, seeing itself so parched and miserable, it does not enter into its thoughts, even for a moment, to consider itself better than others... on the contrary, it acknowledges that others are better. Out of this grows the love of our neighbor, for it now esteems them, and no longer judges them as it used to do... Now, it sees nothing but its own misery, which it keeps so constantly before its eyes that it can look upon nothing else. " [3]

b) It practices *spiritual sobriety :* since it can no longer feed upon sensible consolations, it gradually detaches itself from them, as well as from all created things, in order to concern itself solely with eternal goods ; this is the beginning of spiritual peace which before was disturbed by consolations and attachments to creatures. In the midst of this peace, the soul exercises itself in fortitude, patience and longanimity, by persevering in practices which offer neither consolation nor attraction.

c) With regard to spiritual vices, such as envy, anger, sloth, the soul rids itself of them and acquires the contrary virtues : having become docile and humble under the influence of aridities and temptations, it becomes more tolerant with itself and with others ; charity displaces envy, because humility causes the soul to admire the qualities of others ; and the better it sees its own faults, the more it feels constrained to labor and exert itself in order to correct them.

1431. 4° Lastly, God seasons these aridities with a certain amount of *spiritual consolation.* When the soul

---

[1] *Night*, Bk. I, C. XII. — [2] *Night*, Bk. I, C. XIV. — [3] *Night*, Bk. I, C. XII.

least expects it, He gives it vivid intellectual lights and a pure love. These favors are far superior to anything previously experienced, and more sanctifying, although at the beginning they do not appear so, because this divine influence remains hidden.

To sum up, these aridities make the soul advance in the pure love of God : it no longer acts under the influence of consolations, and its only wish is to please God. No more the presumption and vain complacency of former days of sensible fervor; no longer those impetuous actions, those over-ardent and natural aspirations! Spiritual peace has already begun to reign in the heart. [1]

Conclusion : The Course to Follow in this Trial

1432. The spiritual director of souls who pass through this trial must show them the *greatest kindness* and devotedness; he must *enlighten* and comfort them by telling them frankly that this is a purifying ordeal, and that they will come out of it better, purer, humbler, better grounded in virtue and more pleasing to God.

a) The chief disposition which must be instilled into them is that of *holy abandonment* to God : they must kiss the Hand that strikes them, by acknowledging that they have indeed merited these trials; they must join Jesus in His agony and humbly repeat His words : " *My Father, if it be possible, let this chalice pass from me. Nevertheless, not as I will, but as thou wilt.* " [2]

b) In spite of dryness, they must persevere in prayer, in union with Our Lord, Who " *being in agony, prayed the longer.* " [3] The words of St. Teresa [4] should be kept in mind : " Whoever has begun mental prayer, I wish him not to give it up, whatever sins he may commit in the meantime, since this is the means by which he may recover himself again; but without it, he will find the work much more difficult. And let not the devil tempt him, as he did me, to leave it off through a motive of humility, " and, we might add, under pretext that it is useless.

1433. **c)** But there *must be no return to discursive meditation* once they have ascertained their inability to pray in that manner; they must keep their souls at rest, even though it may appear they are doing nothing, and they must be content with a loving and peaceful gaze on God.

---

[1] *Night*, Bk. II, C. XIII. — [2] *Matth.*, XXVI, 39.
[3] *Luke*, XXII, 43. — [4] *Life by Herself*, C. VIII.

" For if a man while sitting for his portrait cannot be still, but moves about, the painter will never depict his face, and even the work already done will be spoiled.   In the same way when the soul interiorly rests, every action and passion, or anxious consideration at that time will distract and disturb it ; " [1] and so when God wants to imprint His likeness upon their souls, and suspends the activity of their faculties, they have but to abide in peace, and through this peace the spirit of love will flare up and burn more brightly within them.   This state of repose is by no means one of inaction ; it is rather a different kind of occupation, which excludes sloth and languor.   They must therefore expel distractions, and if in order to do so they must return to considerations, let them not hesitate, provided they can accomplish this without violent efforts.

1434.   **d**) As to the *virtues*, it is evident that they must continue to cultivate them, particularly those that are proper to their state of life : humility, self-denial, patience, charity towards the neighbor, love of God through conformity to His holy will, and trustful prayer.   They must practice all these virtues in a spirit of holy abandonment into the hands of God ; and if they go about this courageously, this state of soul will prove a gold mine which will yield great profits.

e) The *duration* of this trial varies according to the designs of God, the degree of union to which He destines the soul, and the number of imperfections from which it must still be purified.   Spiritual writers tells us that this period may extend from two to fifteen years. [2]   But there are intervals of respite, during which the soul is at peace, enjoys God, and builds up strength for future combats ; hence, the need of *patience, confidence* and *holy abandonment.* This is, in summary, what the spiritual director must urge on these sorely tried souls.

II. *Sweet Quietude*

1435.   In treating this and the following states of soul, we shall make use, chiefly, of the Works of St. Teresa, who has described this prayer with a clarity of vision and a precision that have never been excelled.   She calls it by various names : the *Fourth Mansion* of the Interior Castle, [3]

---

[1] *Night*, Bk. I, C. XI.

[2] Cardinal BONA (*Via Compendii ad Deum*, C. 10, n. 6) says that St. Francis of Assisi spent two years in these purifying trials; St. Teresa eighteen; Blessed Claire of Montefalco fifteen ; St. Catherine of Bologna five; St. Magdalen of Pazzi five years at first and sixteen subsequently; the Venerable Balthassar Alvarez sixteen.   These figures embrace, no doubt, the duration of the two Nights, which are generally divided by a notable interval of sweet consolations.

[3] *The Interior Castle*, composed in the year 1577, at the Monastery of Toledo, five years before her death, at the request of Father Gratian and Father Velasquez, is the crown and synthesis of all her works.   In it she clearly and accurately de-

or the prayer of *Divine Delights*, because it is here that for the first time the presence of God is felt by a kind of spiritual delight; in her *Life* (C. XIV) she calls it the prayer of *quiet* and she explains it by the *second way of watering* the garden.   Other writers call it the prayer *of silence*, precisely because the soul then ceases to reason.

This prayer has, as it were, three distinct phases : 1° *passive recollection*, a preparation for it; 2° *quietude properly so called;* 3° the *sleep of the faculties*, which completes it and prepares for the full union of the faculties.

1° PASSIVE RECOLLECTION

1436. A) Nature.   This kind of recollection is called passive in order to distinguish it from *active* recollection, which is acquired through our own efforts aided by grace (n. 1317).   *Passive* recollection is not obtained " by means of the understanding labouring to consider God within itself, nor by the imagination representing Him within us, " [1] but by a direct action of divine grace upon our faculties.   On this account St. Teresa calls it the first supernatural prayer of which she had experience : " It is an inward recollection felt in the soul, seeming to it as though it possessed other senses analogous to the exterior ones.   The soul seems as if it would want to withdraw from the din of the latter; and thus sometimes it does draw them after itself; and one longs to close the eyes and neither hear nor see anything, nor be aware of anything but that which it does then, that is, to converse all alone with God.   In this state, the senses and faculties are not suspended; they remain in the soul's possession, but they so remain in order to be applied to God. " [2]

In another place she explains this by a graceful comparison : "Our faculties and senses had gone out (of the castle) to associate with

---

scribes the seven principal degrees of prayer corresponding to the seven stages of the spiritual life.   On the eve of the Feast of the Blessed Trinity, she was asking herself what would be the fundamental idea of this Treatise, when God deigned Himself to suggest it.   He showed her the soul in the state of grace as a magnificent crystal globe, having the shape of a castle with seven mansions, the seventh the center, in which God Himself dwells, radiant with a marvellous brightness by which all the mansions are illumined, each more brilliant as it stands closer to the center.   Outside the castle there are only darkness and uncleanness, and poisonous creatures which attack those who venture near.   The entrance to the castle is mental prayer, which makes us enter into ourselves and find God.   One leaves the castle through mortal sin, of which the Saint gives a terrifying description (I Mansion, C. II).   There are seven Mansions : the first two correspond to the purgative way; the third to the illuminative way; and with the fourth begins infused contemplation.

[1] ST. TERESA, *Interior Castle*, IV Mansion, C. 3.
[2] *Letter to Father Rodrigo Alvarez.*

strangers." Afterwards realizing their fault, they drew nigh again to the castle, though not yet resolved to enter. The Great King within the castle is willing in His mercy to call them back to Him : " Like a good shepherd (acts towards his sheep) He makes them know His voice by so sweet *a call*, that they themselves can scarcely hear it. This He does that they may not wander and be lost, but return to their mansion. This *call* of the Shepherd has such power, that they immediately abandon all those external things which deceived them, and hasten into the castle. Methinks I have never explained myself in the way I have now. "[1] St. Francis de Sales furnishes us with a no less telling comparison : " As when a loadstone is placed in the midst of several needles, they immediately turn towards the magnet and fix themselves firmly thereto, so something similar occurs when the Almighty favours us with His sensible presence : the faculties of the soul then direct all their strength and activity to the spot where it is most sensibly felt, in order that they may enjoy the company of their God, Who communicates such ineffable delights. "[2]

Passive recollection may therefore be defined as *a gentle and affectionate absorption of the mind and the heart in God, produced by a special grace of the Holy Ghost.*

1437. B) **Course To Follow During This Prayer.** This favor is ordinarily a prelude to the prayer of quiet; but it may be but *transitory*, as on certain occasions when one abounds in fervor, for instance at the time of receiving the religious habit, or of taking vows, or of receiving orders. From this fact two practical conclusions follow :

a) If God plunges us into this prayer of recollection, let us gently keep the understanding from reasoning, but without endeavoring to suspend it altogether :

" We should, without any violence or noise, keep the understanding from discoursing, but not suspend it, nor the imagination either; it is good for the soul to remember that it is in the presence of God, and who this God is. If what the understanding feels in itself absorbs it, well and good; but let it not try to understand what this is; for such a gift is bestowed on the will. Let the soul enjoy it without the interference of its own efforts, limiting itself to the utterance of some few words of love. "[3]

b) But if God does not speak to our heart, " if we perceive that this King has not heard us, nor pays any heed to us, we must stand there like dolts, " says St. Teresa. " For when the soul strives to bind its thoughts, it experiences a still greater aridity than before, and the very effort it makes to think of nothing makes the imagination more active. Besides, we must have but God's glory in view, not our consolations and personal tastes. When His Divine Majesty wishes the understanding to leave off discoursing,

---

[1] *Interior Castle*, IV Mansion, C. 3.
[2] *Love of God*, Bk. VI, C. 7. — [3] *Interior Castle*, Mansion IV, C. 3.

He employs it in another way, and gives it a light and knowledge so far above what we can arrive at, that He makes it to remain absorbed. " [1] Outside of this however our faculties are made for action.

2° QUIETUDE PROPERLY SO CALLED

We shall explain its *nature*, its *origin*, its *development*, its *various forms*, and the *course to follow during this prayer*.

1438. A) Nature. In this prayer the higher faculties of the soul, the intellect and the will, are seized by God and made to enjoy a very gentle repose and a very keen joy at His Presence; but the understanding, the memory and the imagination remain free and are at times a source of distractions.

a) St. Teresa explains in the following manner the *supernatural* character of this prayer, and the way in which the *will is seized by God*. [2] "This is something *supernatural, which we cannot acquire by all our diligence*, because it is a settling of the soul in peace; or rather, to speak more correctly, Our Lord leads her into peace, just as He did holy Simeon, for all the faculties are calmed. The soul understands, in a manner different from understanding by the exterior senses, that she is now placed near her God, and that in a very short time, she will become one with Him by union. This does not happen because she sees Him with the eyes of the body or of the soul,... but that she sees herself in the kingdom (at least, near the King Who is to give it to her), and the soul seems so impressed with such reverence that then she dare not ask anything...

Here the will is a captive, and if she feel any pain in this state, it is to see that she is to return to her former liberty... Nothing troubles them (those who are in this state) and it seems nothing can do so. In a word, while this continues, they are so inebriated and absorbed with the delight and satisfaction contained therein, that they remember not that there is anything more to desire; and they exclaim with St. Peter : *Lord let us make here three tabernacles.*" [3]

The Saint adds that, since the will alone is made captive, *the other two faculties may wander.* "The will must not heed them, but abide in the enjoyment of her pleasure and quiet; for if it seeks to recollect them, both she and they will roam. " [4] It is especially the imagination which strays at times and fatigues us by its deafening noise : " Let the mill-clapper go round and let us but heed the grinding of our own meal, not halting the action of our will and understanding. " [5]

1439. b) *The spiritual joy* produced in the state of quietude is quite *different from that experienced in active*

---

[1] *Interior Castle*, Mansion IV, C. 3.
[2] *Way of Perfection*, C. XXXI. The Saint speaks only of the will, because being the master-faculty, it is seized first and foremost, for contemplation is rather an act of love than of knowledge. However since the will acts only when enlightened by the intelligence, the latter likewise comes to some extent within the Divine grasp. — [3] *Way of Perfection*, C. XXXI.
[4] *Life by Herself*, C. XIV. — [5] *Interior Castle*, IV Mansion, C. I.

prayer. St. Teresa explains this difference by contrasting the *divine delights* produced by contemplation with the *joys* or consolations of active prayer. There is a twofold difference proceeding from the *source* and the *effects* of these prayers.

1) The *divine delights* come directly from the action of God, whilst the *joys* come from our activity aided by grace.

In order to make this clear, St. Teresa employs the comparison of the two cisterns supplied with water in different ways. In the one the water is brought from a distance through pipes, and rushes in with a noise; this resembles the consolations experienced in active prayer. The other cistern is fed by a spring rising from its depths and is filled noiselessly; this represents contemplation, or the water of consolation "which God causes to flow from our inmost soul, with great peace and calm and gentleness." [1]

2) Thus, the joys of contemplation are far superior to those of active prayer : "When this heavenly water begins to rise from the source... our whole interior seems to be enlarging and dilating, and producing certain delights which cannot be expressed. Neither can the soul understand what this is which is here given to her. A certain fragrance is diffused, as if (I may say so) some odoriferous perfumes were cast into a brasier, without any light being seen, or the place whence the odour comes..." [2] But the Saint adds that this is a very imperfect comparison. In her Life, [3] she states that such joys resemble those of heaven and that the soul loses all craving for the things of earth : "She sees clearly that even one moment of these pleasures cannot be purchased here below; and that no riches, nor dominions, nor honors, nor delights are capable of giving such happiness even for one instant, because this joy is real and we feel it satisfies us..."

The principal *cause* of this joy is the *presence of God felt :*

"God, for His greatness' sake, is pleased that this soul should now understand that His Divine Majesty is so close to her, that there is no need of sending any messenger to her; that she but needs to speak, herself, to Him, though not by word of mouth, since, being so near to her, He understands her even by the sole motion of her lips." [4] Of course, the Saint goes on to say that God is ever with us; but it is question here of a special presence : "This Divine Sovereign, our Master, wishes we should have understand that He knows us, and that we should feel the effects of His presence; that He particularly wishes to begin to work in our soul by giving her a great interior and exterior satisfaction." [5]

1440. c) This dilatation of the heart produces excellent *virtuous dispositions*, particularly a *fear of offending God* (which replaces the fear of hell), *love of penance and of crosses, humility, contempt for worldly joys :* —

1) "Neither is she distressed through the fear of hell; for though she feels greater fear now for having offended God, yet she is free from servile fear, and has a great confidence that she shall enjoy Him."

---

[1] *Interior Castle*, IV Mansion, C. 2. — [2] *Interior Castle*, IV Mansion, C. 2.
[3] *Life by Herself*, C. XIV. — [4] *Life by Herself*, C. XIV. — [5] *Ibid.*, l. c.

2) The fear she used to have of losing her health by doing penance has now ceased, and she thinks she can do all in God, as she has greater desires than ever of using austerities. The fear of afflictions, likewise, which she used to have, is now more moderate, because she has a more lively faith, for she knows that if she bears them for God's sake, His Majesty will give her grace to bear them with patience; nay sometimes she desires them, since she has a great desire to do something for God. 3) And as she now understands His greatness better, she accordingly esteems herself more vile. 4) Having, likewise, tried the delights of God, she finds those of the world but dung (in comparison); she separates herself from them by little and little, and for doing this she has more command over herself. In a word, she has improved in all virtues, and will not fail to go on increasing, unless she should relapse and offend God again, for then all is lost, however highly raised a soul may have been in virtue and contemplation. " [1]

1441. Definition. From this description one may conclude that quietude is a *supernatural state of prayer, not wholly passive, which is produced in the superior part of the soul and causes the latter to feel and relish God present within it.*

It is a *supernatural* state of prayer, that is to say, infused. In this we differ from some writers of the Carmelite School, who considering it as a prayer of transition, are of the opinion that it can be acquired in the same way as the prayer of simplicity.

With them we say that it is *not wholly passive*, since only the will (with the intellect) is seized, while the power of reasoning and of the imagination remain free to roam. As to the *divine delights* and the virtues which are the fruits of this prayer, we have sufficiently explained them in n. 1439.

1442. B) Origin and Growth of Quietude. a) Generally speaking, this form of prayer is granted to souls that are already accustomed to meditation for a notable period of time, and have passed through the *night* of the senses. Still, it is sometimes preceded by the latter, especially in the case of children or innocent souls who have no need of a special purification.

b) At first it is granted but at intervals, and in a rather faint and unconscious manner; it is of short duration, lasting, for instance, for the space of a *Hail Mary*, [2] as St. Teresa says. Later on it becomes more frequent and

---

[1] *Interior Castle*, IV Mansion, C. 3.
[2] St. John of the Cross remarks (*Ascent*, Bk. III, C. XIV) that the time passes so rapidly when one is in the state of contemplation that at times one mistakes its duration : what seems to have lasted but two or three minutes, may very well have lasted longer.

more prolonged, extending over a half-hour. But, since it does not always come suddenly nor stop abruptly, it may, from its first inception to its final cessation, endure for a full hour or even longer. Moreover, when it is *active* (n. 1445) and accompanied by spiritual inebriation, it may continue through an entire day or even two, without in any way interfering with the ordinary occupations.

c) As long as the purification of the soul is not completed, quietude may occur *alternately* in its *sweet* or in its arid form.

d) A time comes when quietude becomes *habitual :* then one enters into it from the moment one begins to pray. At times one is even seized by it unawares, even in the midst of the most common-place occupations. It also tends to become stronger and more conscious, and if the soul corresponds with grace, it develops into the full union and ecstasy. But if the soul is not faithful, it may fail and fall back into discursive meditation, or even suffer the loss of grace.

1443. C) Forms or Varieties of Quietude. There are three principal forms : *silent, praying, and active quietude.* [1]

a) In *silent* quietude, the soul contemplates God in the midst of a loving stillness, admiration so to speak stifling every utterance. The will immersed in God and burning with love for Him rests joyfully in Him through a union that is calm, tranquil and sweet.

Like a mother who feasts her eyes upon her child, the soul lovingly contemplates its God. " The soul, " says St. Teresa, [2] " is like the child that sucks, lying at his mother's breast ; and she, to please him, without moving his lips, forces the milk into his mouth. " So it is here ; for the will continues to love without any labor on the part of the understanding.

1444. b) At times the soul, unable to contain its love, pours itself forth in ardent prayer. This is *praying* quietude : now it gives vent to sweet colloquies, now it abandons itself to the effusions of its tenderness and calls upon all creatures to praise God : " She utters a thousand holy extravagances, always endeavoring to please Thee, who holdest her in this state. " [3]

In that state St. Teresa composed stanzas to describe her love and her suffering. Sometimes God responds to such outbursts of love with affectionate caresses, which produce a species of *spiritual inebriation.* According to St. Francis de Sales this heavenly intoxication " renders us more alive to spiritual things by alienating the corporal senses ; it does not reduce us to a level with brute creation, but renders us participators of the angelic, and even of the divine, nature ; it transports us out of ourselves to elevate us above ourselves. " [4]

---

[1] CASSIAN had already noted these varieties, *Conf.*, X, C. 24.
[2] *Way of Perfection*, C. XXXI.
[3] *Life by Herself*, C. XVI. — [4] *Love of God*, Bk. VI, C. VI.

1445. **c)** There are cases in which quietude becomes *active.* When the quietude is profound and prolonged, says St. Teresa, [1] (since the will alone is held captive), the other faculties are free to attend to things relating to God's service; and this they do with far greater energy. Then, while the soul is engaged in exterior works it continues to love God ardently : this is the union of action and contemplation, of the service of Martha and the love of Mary.

3° THE SLEEP OF THE FACULTIES

1446. This third phase of quietude is a still higher form of prayer which prepares for the full union of the interior faculties with God.

St. Teresa described it in the seventeenth chapter of her autobiography : " Now, I often have this kind of union whereof I am speaking ; and Almighty God is very often pleased to bestow this favor upon me in such a manner, that He makes my will and also my understanding recollected ; and then it no longer discourses, but is occupied in the enjoyment of God, as one who is looking on, and who sees so much, that he knows not which way to look... The memory remains free and so also seems to be the imagination : and when it sees itself alone one cannot conceive what a war it makes upon the will and the under standing, and how it endeavors to put everything in confusion. It makes me quite tired, so that I abhor it ; and often I have besough- Our Lord to deprive me entirely of it on these occasions, if it should continue to distract me... just like those importunate and restless little gnats which buzz about by night here and there. This comparison seems to me to be extremely proper ; for though these faculties have no strength to do harm, yet they trouble those who feel them. " As to the means of overcoming such wanderings, she notes but one : " To consider the memory no better than a madman, and to leave it alone with its madness, for God only can check its extravagances. " As one can see, this is a prayer of quiet, in which the understanding itself is seized by God, but in which the imagination continues to wander. It is a preparation for the full union.

THE COURSE TO FOLLOW DURING THE PRAYER OF QUIET

1447. The general disposition to be fostered in this state is that of *humble abandonment* into the hands of God from the very beginning to the end and throughout all the phases of this prayer.

a) One must not, then, make efforts to put oneself in this state by striving to suspend the functions of the faculties and even to hold one's breath : this would be wasted effort, since God alone can grant contemplation.

b) As soon as one is aware of the divine action, one must adapt oneself to it as perfectly as possible, giving up reflection and following the motions of grace with great docility.

---

[1] *Way of Perfection*, C. XXXI.

1) If we are called to the state of *loving silence*, let us contemplate and love uttering not a word, or at the most a few tender words, in order to rekindle the flame of love, but without making any violent efforts that might extinguish it.

2) If we are inclined to *make acts*, if our affections burst forth as from a spring, let us pray gently, without any noise of words, but with an ardent desire to be heard. "A few little straws... presented with humility, will be much more for the purpose, and will be of greater help in enkindling the fire of divine love, than great logs of wood — I mean by these those discourses that seem to us so learned, and which might extinguish that fire in the space of time required to recite the Creed."[1]   Above all, adds St. Francis de Sales,[2] we must avoid violent, immoderate outbursts which weary the heart and the nerves, as well as those disturbing reflections by which we try to discover whether the tranquility we enjoy is indeed tranquil.

3) If the understanding and the imagination *wander*, let us not be disturbed; let us not go in pursuit of them; let the will "remain in the enjoyment of the favor which has been granted it, as the busy bee remains in the depths of its cell.   If, instead, of entering into the hive, the bees were to go in pursuit of one another, how could any honey be made?"

§ II. The Prayer of Full Union

1448.   This prayer, which corresponds to the Fifth Mansion, is called *simple union* or *full union of the interior faculties*, because in it the soul is united to God, not only through the will, but also through all the interior faculties. It is therefore more perfect than the prayer of quiet.   We shall describe the *nature* and the *effects* of this prayer.

I. *Nature of the Prayer of Union*

1449.   1º Its essential characteristics are two : the *suspension of all the faculties*, and the *absolute certitude that God is present in the soul.*

"To return now to the proof which I said was certain.   You see that God makes this soul quite stupid, in order the better to imprint upon her true wisdom; hence, she neither sees nor heeds, nor understands, nor perceives all the time she is in this state, which is always short; and, indeed, it seems to her shorter than it is."[3]   In other words, not only the will, but the understanding, the imagination, and the memory are suspended in their functions.   St. Teresa goes on : "God so fixes Himself in the interior of this soul, that when she comes to herself, *she cannot but believe she was in God* and that God was in her.[4]   This truth in so deeply rooted in her, that though many years may pass away before God bestows the like favor upon her, she never forgets it or doubts it."[5]

---

[1] St. Teresa, *Life by Herself*, C. XV. — [2] *Love of God*, Bk. VI, C. X.
[3] *Interior Castle*, V Mansion, C. I; cf. *Life*, C. XVIII.
[4] St. Teresa gives the reason why, *Interior Castle*, V Mansion, C. I : "I dare venture to assert that His Divine Majesty is so joined and united with the essence of the soul, that the devil dare not approach... "
[5] *Interior Castle*, V Mansion, C. I.

1450.   2º From these two characteristics three others flow :

a) The *absence of distractions*, since the whole soul is entirely absorbed in God.

b) The *absence of fatigue :* personal effort is reduced to very little; to abandon oneself to the good pleasure of God suffices.   The Manna of Heaven falls upon the soul, which has but to enjoy it; and so this prayer, no matter how long it may endure, causes no injury to health. [1]

c) An extraordinary *abundance of joy.* " In this degree one feels nothing, one but enjoys, though yet without understanding what is enjoyed.   One knows, however, that a certain good is possessed in which all blessings are comprised.   All the senses are occupied with this joy in such a manner that they cannot apply themselves to anything else, either interiorly or exteriorly...." [2]   The Saint adds that a simple moment of such pure delights suffices to compensate for all earthly sufferings.

This prayer therefore *differs from quietude*, in which only the will is seized, and in which one wonders at times whether the soul has been really united to God.

We may define it as *a most intimate union of the soul with God, accompanied by the suspension of all the interior faculties, and of the certitude of God's presence within the soul.*

II. *Effects of the Prayer of Union*

1451.   1º The principal effect is a marvellous transformation of the soul which, according to St. Teresa, can be compared to the metamorphosis of the silk-worm.

"These little worms feed on mulberry leaves, till afterwards they become bigger and then on the boughs they go spinning silk with their little mouths, and making little cells very close, in which they are enclosed.   From this cell or bag, which contains a large but ugly worm that dies, there afterwards rises a white and very beautiful butterfly." [3] This is an image of the wondrous change that takes place in the soul through the prayer of union.   This soul, which before feared the Cross, now feels full of generosity, and is ready to make the most painful sacrifices for God's sake.

Here St. Teresa enters into some detail.   She describes the *ardent zeal* which spurs the soul on to glorify God, to

---

[1] "This prayer, however long it may last, produces no inconvenience, at least I feel none; nor do I remember when Our Lord bestowed this favor on me, however ill I might be, that I ever found myself worse : I was, on the other hand, much better. " *Life*, C. XVIII.
[2] *Life by Herself*, C. XVIII.
[3] *Interior Castle*, V Mansion, C. II.

make Him known and loved by all; the *detachment* from creatures, whereby the soul goes so far as to desire to quit this world where God is offended so often; the *perfect submission to the will of God*, whereby the soul offers no more resistance to grace than does soft wax to the seal impressed upon it; the *great charity towards the neighbor*, which is manifested by deeds, and which causes the soul to rejoice at the praises conferred upon others. [1]

1452. 2° This union is the prelude to another one more perfect still. It is like the first meeting with the betrothed, soon to be followed, if we correspond with grace, by the spiritual espousal and finally by the mystical marriage. St. Teresa urges those in this state to make progress in the way of detachment and love. Any halt would be followed by laxity and backsliding. [2]

§ III. Ecstatic Union (Spiritual Espousal)

This union presents itself in two forms: the *sweet* and the *bitter*.

I. *Sweet Ecstatic Union*

1453. The word ecstasy does not necessarily include the phenomenon of levitation, of which we shall speak in the following chapter; it refers simply to the *suspension of the activity of the exterior senses*. Ecstatic union is therefore more perfect than the two preceding ones, since it comprises, over and above the elements peculiar to the former, this suspension of the activity of the external senses. We shall describe: 1° its *nature;* 2° its *phases* or degrees; 3° its *effects*.

1° NATURE OF THE ECSTATIC UNION

1454. There are two elements which constitute this union: *the absorption of the soul in God* and *the suspension* of the activity of the senses. It is because the soul is wholly absorbed in God that the outward senses appear to be riveted on Him or on the object which He presents to them.

A) Two principal causes give rise to the *absorption in God*, as St. Francis de Sales so well explains: [3]

a) " Our admiration is excited when we discover a truth with which we were not previously acquainted, and did not expect to know. When beauty and goodness are joined to this truth, the admiration produced by the discovery is extremely pleasing... Thus, when it pleases God to enlighten the understanding of the devout soul, and to raise her to

---

[1] *Interior Castle*, V Mansion, C. II. — [2] *Ibid.*
[3] *Love of God*, Bk. VII, C. IV and V.

an extraordinary degree of contemplation, she sees the divine mysteries more clearly and perfectly than before, and discovers in them new beauties and attractions which fill her with admiration... When the subject of admiration is pleasing, the mind is closely attached thereto, not only on account of its great beauty, but also because of the fact that this great beauty has been newly discovered; it cannot be satiated with contemplating what it had never seen before, and finds so lovely. "

b) To admiration is joined *love :* " God touches the will by the attractions of His sweetness, and the will, inflamed with love, quickly forgets its terrestrial inclinations, to bound towards God and to be totally absorbed in Him, as a needle which has been touched with a loadstone seems to forget its natural insensibility to turn to the pole. The predominant features of this kind of rapture are not knowledge, sublime visions, admiration and speculative science, but affection, sensible consolation and enjoyment. "

1455. **c)** Moreover, admiration grows through love, and love through admiration :

" The understanding is sometimes replenished with admiration at the view of the happiness enjoyed by the will in its ecstasy ; and the will often receives a new degree of pleasure from witnessing the admiration of the understanding, so that these two powers mutually communicate their rapture. " [1]

It is not surprising that a soul thus given to the contemplation and the love of God, is at it were out of itself, ravished and borne towards Him. If one who lets himself be carried away by the passion of human love goes so far as to abandon all in order to yield himself to the object of his love, is there any cause for wonder if divine love, impressed upon a soul by God Himself, so absorbs it that it comes to forget all else in order to behold and to love Him alone?

1456. **B)** The suspension of the senses is the outcome of this absorption in God. It takes place *gradually* and does not reach the same degree in all.

a) In what regards the *exterior senses :*

1) At first, a more or less pronounced state of *insensibility* sets in together with a slowing down of the physical life, of breathing, and as a consequence of the natural body-heat : " One feels that natural warmth wanes, and that the body gradually cools, but with a gentleness and delight that are unspeakable. "

2) *A sort of immobility* ensues which causes the body to preserve the attitude in which it was when seized by the ecstasy; the eyes remain fixed upon some invisible object.

3) This condition, which should naturally weaken the body, rather imparts to it new energies. [2] True, at the moment of returning consciousness one feels a certain sense of fatigue, but this is followed by a recrudescence of vigor.

4) At times, the suspension of the senses is *complete;* at others, it remains *incomplete* and permits a narration of the revelations received, as can be seen in the life of St. Catherine of Siena.

---

[1] *Love of God*, Bk. VII, C. V.
[2] *Life by Herself*, C. XVIII and XX.

b) The *interior senses* are still more completely suspended than in the mystic union, of which we have already spoken.

1457. **c)** The question suggests itself as to whether free-will itself is not suspended. The common opinion based on such authorities as St. Thomas, Suarez, St. Teresa, Alvarez de Paz is that free-will remains, and that therefore the soul in ecstasy can merit. In fact, the soul freely *accepts* the spiritual favors that are then granted to it.

d) The *duration* of the ecstasy varies greatly. Complete ecstasy generally lasts but a few moments, at times a half-hour; but, since it is preceded and followed by moments of *incomplete* ecstasy, it may extend over several days if all its fluctuations are taken into account.

e) One comes out of the ecstasy by a reawakening, *spontaneous* or *provoked :* 1) in the first instance one experiences a kind of anguish, as if one were returning from another world, and then it is but gradually that the soul regains its control over the body.

2) In the second case, the reawakening is provoked by the *command of a superior :* if this command is vocal, it is always obeyed; if it is but *mental*, it is not always answered.

2° THE THREE PHASES OF ECSTATIC UNION

1458. There are three principal phases in ecstasy : *simple ecstasy, rapture,* and the *flight of the spirit.*

a) Simple ecstasy is a sort of *fainting-spell* which comes on gently and produces a sense of hurt at once painful and delightful. The Spouse of the soul makes it feel His presence, but only for a time. Now, the soul wants to have the joy of this divine presence continually and therefore suffers when deprived of it. Nevertheless, this enjoyment is always more delightful now than it was in the prayer of quiet.

Let us see what St. Teresa [1] has to say on this matter : " The soul feels herself to be most delightfully wounded, but she neither knows *how*, nor by whom. She knows well it is a favor which is to be prized, and she wishes well never to be healed : she complains in words of love, to her Spouse, and the words are external; she cannot do otherwise, knowing Him to be present but not willing to manifest Himself. This is a great but pleasant affliction... for it gives her more delight than the suspension of the Prayer of Quiet, which has no such affliction attached to it. "

It is already in this phase that the supernatural utterances and revelations occur of which we shall speak further on.

---

[1] *Interior Castle*, VI Mansion, C. II.

1459. b) *Rapture* takes hold of the soul with an *impetuosity* and a violence that are irresistible. It is as if one were carried on the wings of a powerful eagle, but whither one knows not. In spite of the pleasure experienced, natural weakness at first causes a sense of fear. "But this fear is mixed with an ardent and fresh love for Him Who shows such tender love to a worm that is nothing but corruption."[1] It is in the state of rapture that the spiritual espousal is concluded; and this is a precaution on the part of God; for were one to preserve the use of one's senses, one would perhaps die at seeing oneself so near to that Supreme Majesty.[2] Once the rapture is over, the will remains as it were *inebriated*, and can no longer occupy itself save with God; disgusted with the things of earth, it has an insatiable desire to do penance, so much so that it complains in the absence of suffering.[3]

1460. c) Rapture is followed by the *flight of the spirit*, which is so impetuous that it seems to sever the soul from the body, and resistance appears impossible.

"It seems to the soul," says St. Teresa, "that she has been altogether in another region quite different from this world in which we live, and there another light is shown to her very different from this here below; and though she should employ all her life long in trying to form an idea of this and other wonders, yet it would be impossible to understand them. She is in an instant taught so many things together, that should she spend many years in arranging them in her thoughts and imagination, she could not remember the one-thousandth of them."[4]

3° PRINCIPAL EFFECTS OF ECSTATIC UNION

1461. A) The one effect which includes all others is a great *holiness of life*, even to the point of heroism. So true is this that where such holiness does not exist the ecstasy itself is open to suspicion.

St. Francis de Sales[5] makes this statement: "A soul may be transported beyond herself in prayer; but if she be not habitually united to God, and elevated to the divinity by a life superior to nature and the senses: if her conduct does not visibly display that ecstasy of action and operation which is accomplished by a renunciation of worldly desires, of self-will, of the inclinations of corrupt nature, and the practice of interior virtues, as humility of heart, meekness, simplicity, a constant tender charity for our neighbor, raptures serve only to attract the admiration of men without rendering her more pleasing to God."

---

[1] *Life by Herself*, C. XX.
[2] *Interior Castle*, VI Mansion, C. IV. — [3] *Ibid.*
[4] *Interior Castle*, VI Mansion, C. V.
[5] *Love of God*, Bk. VII, C. VII.

1462. **B)** The *principal virtues* produced by the ecstatic union, are : 1) a *perfect detachment from creatures :* God, so to speak, makes the soul come to the highest ramparts of a fortress, from which it clearly sees the nothingness of things here below. So, from now on it does not want to have any will of its own; it would even wish to forego the possession of its free-will, were that possible. 2) An *immense sorrow for sins* committed : what pains it most is not the fear of hell, but that of offending God. 3) A *frequent and tender vision of Our Lord's Sacred Humanity* and of the Most Blessed Virgin. A wonderful companionship indeed, that of Jesus and Mary! Imaginative and intellectual visions become more numerous and complete the work of detaching the soul from creatures and of burying it in humility. 4) Lastly, a *marvelous patience* to withstand courageously the new passive trials which Almighty God sends, and which are called the *purification of love.*

Burning with the desire to see God, the soul feels as if it were pierced through and through by a *fiery dart*, and cries out in anguish at seeing itself separated from the sole Object of its love. This is the beginning of a veritable *martyrdom*, a martyrdom of soul and body, accompanied by an ardent desire to die so as never to be separated from the Well-Beloved, a martyrdom relieved at times by inebriating delights. We shall understand this better after studying the Second Night of St. John of the Cross, the *Night of the Spirit.*

II. *The Night of the Spirit*

1463. The First Night purified the soul to make it ready for the joys of quietude, of union and of ecstasy. But before entering into the still purer and more lasting joys of the spiritual marriage, there is need of a more profound and radical purification which generally takes place in the course of the ecstatic union. We shall explain : 1° the *reason* for such a purification; 2° the *severe trials* which attend it ; 3° the *blessed results* which follow from it.

1° REASON FOR THE NIGHT OF THE SPIRIT

1464. To be united to God in a manner so intimate and lasting as one is in the transforming union or spiritual marriage, one must necessarily be free from the last remaining imperfections. These imperfections, St. John of the Cross [1] tells us, are of two kinds, *habitual* and *actual.*

A) The former comprise two things : **a)** imperfect *affections* and *habits;* they are as it were roots, imbedded in the

---

[1] *Dark Night*, Bk. II, C. II.

depths of the soul, to which the purification of the senses could not reach; for instance, friendships a bit too ardent; these must be uprooted; **b**) a certain dullness of mind which makes one subject to distractions from within and to attractions from without. These frailties are incompatible with a perfect union of the soul with God.

B) *Actual* imperfections are also of two kinds : **a**) a certain pride, a vain self-complacency resulting from the abundance of spiritual consolations received. This attitude at times leads to illusions and makes one mistake false visions and prophecies for true ones; **b**) over-boldness towards God, causing one to lose that reverential fear of Him which is the safeguard of all virtue.

2° TRIALS OF THE NIGHT OF THE SPIRIT

1465. In order to purify and reform the soul, God leaves *the mind in darkness, the will in aridity, the memory in forgetfulness, and the affections immersed in pain and anguish.* This purification is wrought, says St. John of the Cross,[1] through the *light of infused contemplation*, a light *bright* in itself, but *dim* and *painful* to the soul on account of the latter's ignorance and impurity.

A) Sufferings of the Mind. a) The brilliant and pure light of contemplation dazes the mind's eye, too weak and too impure to behold it. Just as weak eyes are dazed by a clear, bright light, so the soul, still ailing, is tortured and paralyzed by the divine light, with the result that it seems that death itself would be a welcome deliverance.

b) This pain is intensified by the meeting of the *divine* and the *human* in the same soul : the *divine*, that is to say, *purifying contemplation*, invades the soul to renew it, to perfect it, to deify it; the *human*, that is to say, the soul itself with its faults, experiences the sense of annihilation, of spiritual death, through which it must pass in order to come to life again.

c) To this pain is added a keen realization of the soul's destitution and wretchedness. Its sensitive part immersed in aridity and its intellectual part in darkness, the soul has the agonizing impression of a man suspended in mid-air deprived of any support. At times it even sees hell yawning to swallow it forever. These are, of course, figurative expressions, but they give an idea of the effect of that light which shows on the one hand the greatness and the holiness of God, and on the other the nothingness and the misery of man.

1466. B) Sufferings of the Will are likewise beyond description : **a**) the soul sees itself deprived of all joy, and

---

[1] *Night*, Bk. II, C. V.

becomes convinced that this state is to last forever. Even the confessor is unable to give consolation.

b) In order to sustain the soul in this trial, God sends intervals of relief, during which it experiences a sweet peace in the enjoyment of divine love and familiarity. But such moments are followed by counter-attacks when the soul imagines itself to be no longer loved by God and to be *justly forsaken* by Him. This is the anguish of spiritual dereliction.

c) In this state, prayer is quite impossible; or if one does pray, it is amidst such aridity that it seems that God does not give ear. There are cases in which one cannot even attend to one's temporal interests, memory for such matters having gone completely. This is a *ligature of the faculties* as regards all natural actions.

To sum up in a word : this state is a sort of *hell* by reason of the torture experienced; it is a sort of *purgatory* by reason of the purification effected.

3° HAPPY RESULTS OF THE PURIFICATION OF THE SPIRIT.

1467. **A**) These results are thus summarized by St. John of the Cross : [1]

"This blessed night, though it darkens the mind, does so only to give it light in everything ; and though it humbles it and makes it miserable, it does so only to raise it up and set it free ; and though it impoverishes it and empties it of all its natural self and liking, it does so only to enable it to reach forward divinely to the possession and fruition of all things." To explain these effects, the Saint makes use of the comparison of a piece of green wood thrown into a fireplace, as mentioned in n. 1422.

1468. **B**) He then reduces them to four principal effects : **a**) An *ardent love for God.* From the very outset of this night, this love existed in the superior part of the soul, though unknown to itself ; a time comes however when God makes the soul aware of its love and then it is ready to dare all things in order to please Him.

b) A *piercing light :* at first this light revealed to the soul only its miseries and thus inflicted pain ; but once imperfections have been eliminated through sorrow, it reveals the riches to be gained and thus becomes a source of consolation.

c) A great *sense of security ;* for this light preserves the soul from pride, the great obstacle to salvation. It shows

[1] *Night,* Bk. II, C. IX.

it that it is God Himself Who leads it, and that the suffering He sends is more profitable than joy would be. Lastly,
this light places in the will the firm determination to do
nothing that might offend God, to neglect nothing that
redounds to His glory.

d) A *marvellous strength* to climb the *ten stepping-stones*
of divine love, which St. John of the Cross [1] is pleased to
describe, and upon which the soul must meditate in order
to conceive an idea of the wondrous ascents which lead up
to the *transforming union.*

§ IV. The Transforming Union
or Spiritual Marriage

1469. After so many purifications, the soul at last
reaches that calm and abiding union, called the *transforming union,* which seems to be the final goal of the mystic
union, the immediate preparation for the Beatific Vision.

We shall explain : 1º its *nature* and 2º its *effects.*

I. *Nature of the Transforming Union*

We shall call attention to : 1º its chief characteristics,
and, 2º the description of it given by St. Teresa.

1470. 1º **Its chief characteristics** are *intimacy, serenity, indissolubility.*

A) *Intimacy.* Because this union is still more intimate
than the others it is called *spiritual marriage.* Between
persons united in marriage there are no longer any secrets;
there is a blending of two lives. It is precisely such a union
that exists between the soul and God. In order to explain it,
St. Teresa [2] makes use of this comparison : " Here it is like
water descending from heaven into a river or spring, where
one is so mixed with the other that it cannot be discovered
which is the river-water and which the rain-water. "

B) *Serenity.* In this state there are no more ecstasies or
raptures, or at least very few; these have now disappeared
almost completely in order to make room for such peace
and quiet rest as are enjoyed by married persons who are
sure of each other's love.

C) *Indissolubility.* The other unions were but transitory;
the present one by its very nature is permanent, just as is
the bond of Christian marriage.

---

[1] *Night*, Bk. II, C. XIX-XX. — [2] *Interior Castle*, VII Mansion, C. II.

1471. Does this indissolubility imply impeccability? On this point St. John of the Cross and St. Teresa differ. The former is of the opinion that in this state the soul is confirmed in grace : " I believe that no soul ever attains to this state without being confirmed in grace... The Bride has entered ; that is, *passed* out of all temporal and natural things, out of all spiritual affections, ways and methods, having left on one side and forgotten all temptations, trials, sorrows, anxieties and cares. " [1]   St. Teresa is far from being so positive : [2] " Whenever I speak on this subject, and seem to mean that the soul is secure, my words must be understood thus, viz., as long as the Divine Majesty holds her in His Hand, and she does not offend Him. I know for certain that though she see herself in this state, and though it may continue some years, she does not, therefore, think herself secure. " It seems to us that St. Teresa's language is more in harmony with that of theology, which teaches that the grace of final perseverance cannot be merited ; in order to be assured of salvation therefore, one would need a special revelation bearing not only on the actual state of grace, but also on perseverance in this state until death. [3]

1472. 2º The *description* given by St. Teresa includes two apparitions, one of *Our Lord* and the other of the *Blessed Trinity.*

A) It is *Jesus* who introduces the soul into this last mansion by a twofold vision : one *imaginative*, the other *intellectual.*

a) In an imaginative vision which took place after Holy Communion, He appeared to the Saint [4] " in a figure of great splendour, beauty and majesty, just as He was after His resurrection. "

" He said to her that now was the time she should consider His affairs as hers, and that He would take care of hers... From henceforth you shall guard my honour, not only because I am your Creator, your King and your God, but yet because you are my true spouse. My honour is your honour and your honour mine ! " [5]

b) Then follows the *intellectual* vision : " That which God here communicates to the soul in an instant is so great a secret, and so sublime a grace, and what she feels such an excessive delight, that I know nothing to compare it to, except that Our Lord is pleased at that moment to manifest to her the glory which is in heaven ; and this He does in a more sublime way than by any vision or spiritual delight. More cannot be said (as far as can be understood) than that this soul becomes one with God. " [6]

---

[1] *Spiritual Canticle*, Stanza XXII.
[2] *Interior Castle*, VII Mansion, C. II.
[3] At times the spiritual marriage is celebrated with *special ceremonies*, exchange of rings, angelic hymns, etc. Following the example of St. Teresa we leave aside any description of these accessory details.
[4] *Interior Castle*, VII Mansion, C. II.
[5] Relation XXV. — [6] *Interior Castle*, VII Mansion, C. II.

1473. B) **The Vision of the Blessed Trinity.** Once the soul has been introduced into this mansion, the Three Persons of the Most Blessed Trinity manifest themselves to it in an intellectual vision, and they come directly upon it as in a cloud of extraordinary brightness. The Three Divine Persons manifest themselves as distinct, and by a wonderful communication of knowledge, the soul sees with absolute certitude that all Three Persons are but one substance, one power, one knowledge, one God.

" Hence, what we behold with faith, the soul here (as one may say) understands by sight, though this sight is not with the eyes of the body, because it is not an imaginative vision. All the Three Persons here communicate themselves to her, and speak to her, and make her understand those words mentioned in the Gospel, where Our Lord said that He, and the Father, and the Holy Ghost would come and dwell with the soul that loves Him and keeps His commandments! O my Lord! *What a different thing is the hearing and believing of these words from understanding in this way how true they are!* [1] Such a soul is every day more astonished, because these words never seem to depart from her; but she clearly sees (in the manner above mentioned) that they are in the deepest recesses of the soul (how it is, she cannot express, since she is not learned) and she perceives this divine company in herself. " [2]

II. *Effects of the Transforming Union*

1474. A union so profound and so intimate cannot but produce wondrous, sanctifying effects. These may be summed up in one word : *the soul is so transformed that it forgets self and thinks only of God and His glory.* Whence follow : 1° A *holy abandonment* into the hands of God in virtue of which the soul is supremely indifferent to all that is not God. In the ecstatic union it desired death as a means of uniting itself to its Beloved; now it is indifferent to life or death, so long as God be glorified : " All her thoughts and study will be how to please this Lord, and by what means she may be able to express the love she has for Him. For this object does she pray, hereunto does the spiritual marriage tend, from which good works always come. " [3]

1475. 2° *An insatiable thirst for suffering*, but devoid of anxiety and in perfect conformity with the will of God :

" If He wish them to suffer they are content; if not, they do not torment themselves about it, as they used to do at other times. These

---

[1] Note these expressions which point out the immense difference between the simple act of faith and the knowledge or conviction given by contemplation.
[2] *Interior Castle*, VII Mansion, C. I.
[3] *Interior Castle*, VII Mansion, C. IV.

souls feel likewise a great interior joy when they are persecuted, for then they enjoy more peace than I have ever before spoken of; and they do not feel the least hatred against their persecutors; nay, they conceive for them a particular affection. " ¹

1476. 3º *The absence of desire and of interior sufferings* : " The desires of these souls do not now run after consolations... They feel in themselves a desire of being always alone, or employed in things relating to the good of some soul. They have no aridities, nor internal troubles, but always have a memory and a tenderness for Our Lord, so that they would gladly do nothing but praise Him." ²

1477. 4º *The absence of raptures.* " The raptures cease in the manner I have mentioned, and there are no more ecstasies nor flights of the spirit : if they come at all, it is very seldom, and almost never in public. " ³ Hence, peace and *perfect serenity :* " In this Temple of God, for this mansion is His, He and the soul sweetly enjoy each other in the most profound silence. " ⁴

1478. 5º An *ardent,* yet discreet *zeal* for the *sanctification of souls.* It is not enough to abide in the enjoyment of this sweet repose; the soul must act, labor, suffer, become the slave of God and of the neighbor, strive to advance in virtue, especially in humility; for, not to advance is to go back. Perfection consists in taking the place of Mary and doing the work of Martha at one and the same time. One can work for the welfare of souls without leaving the cloister, and one can do good to those with whom one lives without aiming at reforming the entire world :

" A work so much nobler, as you are so much the more indebted to them. Do you think the gain small, that you have such great humility and mortification, and that you are the servant of all; and that you also have such great charity for *them,* and such love for Our Lord, that this fire inflames every one, and you are continually exciting them by the practice of your other virtues? Your gain will be exceedingly great, and your service highly pleasing to Our Lord. " ⁵

But above all, such works must be inspired *by love :* " Our Lord does not pay so much regard to the greatness of the works, as to the *love* whereby they are performed." ⁶

1479. In concluding, St. Teresa invites her Sisters to enter these Mansions, *if it please the Lord of the Castle to introduce them;* but she warns them not to wish to force their way.

---

¹ *Interior Castle,* VII Mansion, C. III.
² *Interior Castle,* VII Mansion, C. III.
³ *Interior Castle,* VII Mansion, C. III. — ⁴ *Ibid.*
⁵ *Interior Castle,* VII Mansion, C. IV. — ⁶ *Ibid.*

"I wish, then, to advise you not to use any violence, if you meet with some resistance, for you may thus displease Him so far as to cause you some trouble. He is a great lover of humility, and by considering yourselves unworthy even to enter .the "Third Mansion", you will the sooner obtain His good-will and favor to allow you afterwards to enter the fifth ; and you may serve Him there in such manner by often repairing thither, that He may at length admit you into that "Mansion" reserved for Himself." [1]

SUMMARY OF THE SECOND CHAPTER

1480. After the study of the four great phases of contemplation, with their alternating bitter trials and inebriating delights, it seems that the notion we gave of infused contemplation has been confirmed, that it is a *progressive taking hold of the soul by God, freely permitted by the soul itself.*

1º God gradually takes possession of the whole soul in contemplation. First, He seizes the will in the prayer of quiet; next, He lays hold of all the *interior faculties* in the prayer of full union; later He takes possession of both the *interior faculties and the exterior senses* in ecstasy; and finally in the spiritual marriage, He binds the *whole soul* to Himself in an abiding union.

Now, if God takes possession of the soul, it is to flood it with *light* and *love*, it is to make it share in His perfections. **a**) This *light* is at first weak and *painful* so long as the soul is not sufficiently purified; but it becomes stronger and more comforting, although always mixed with darkness, by reason of the feebleness of our own mind. It produces a profound impression, because it *comes from God*, and it gives the soul an *experimental* knowledge of God's infinite grandeur, goodness and beauty, and of the littleness, the nothingness and the miseries of creatures. **b**) The love infused into the soul in contemplation is ardent, generous, and burning with the desire of sacrificing all : one forgets self and one longs to be immolated for the Beloved.

1481. 2º The soul *freely consents* to this *divine possession* and joyously yields itself to God through the most profound *humility*, through the *love of the Cross* for the sake of God and of Jesus, and through *holy abandonment*. It is thus still more *purified* from its *imperfections; it is united to God* and so completely *transformed into Him*, that Our Lord's ardent desire, "*that they also may be one in us*" [2] is as fully realized as it possibly can be.

---

[1] *Interior Castle*, VII Mansion, C. IV. — [2] *John*, XVII, 21.

Such is true mysticism, and it is important to distinguish it from *false mysticism* or *quietism*.

APPENDIX : FALSE MYSTICISM OR QUIETISM

1482. Side by side with the true mystics, whose teachings we have just expounded, there have been *false mystics* who, under various names, have perverted the notion of the *passive state* and have fallen into doctrinal errors dangerous to good morals. Such were the doctrines of the Montanists and the Beghards.[1] But the most notorious of these errors was that of *Quietism*. It made its appearance under three different forms : 1° the *gross quietism of Molinos*, 2° the *mitigated* and *spiritualized quietism of Fénelon;* 3° *semi-quietist* tendencies.

1° THE QUIETISM OF MOLINOS [2]

1483. Born in Spain in 1640, Michael Molinos spent the greater part of his life in Rome, and it was there that he disseminated his errors in two works which met with great success : *The Spiritual Guide* and *The Prayer of Quiet.*
His fundamental error lay in the assertion that perfection consists in complete passivity of soul, in a continuous act of contemplation and of love whic , once made, dispenses with all other acts, even that of resistance to temptations. " *Let God Act,* " was his motto.

1484. The better to understand these errors in detail, we give the following parallel tables of the *Catholic teaching* and the *aberrations of Molinos.*

Catholic Teaching	Errors of Molinos
1) There exists a passive state of soul wherein God acts through His operating grace ; but one does not *ordinarily* arrive thereat, except after a long time spent in the practice of virtue and meditation.	There is but one way, the inner way, or the way of passive contemplation, which we can acquire ourselves with ordinary grace ; hence, we must enter as soon as possible into the passive way and thereby annihilate our passions.
2) The act of contemplation lasts but a short time, even though the state of soul resulting therefrom may last for several days.	The act of contemplation may last whole years, and even a whole lifetime, not excluding the hours of sleep, without being repeated.
3) Contemplation eminently embodies the acts of all the Christian virtues, but outside the period	Since contemplation is perpetual, it dispenses from all explicit acts of virtue, which are only for

[1] P. POURRAT, *Christian Spirituality*, I, p. 62-68 : II, p. 211-216; Cath. Encyc.. Beghards and Beguines.
[2] P. DUDON, *Le Quiétiste Espagnol Michel Molinos*, Paris, 1921; Cath. Encyc.,. Molinos, Mysticism, Quietism.

Catholic Teaching

of contemplation, it does not dispense one from making explicit acts of the virtues.

4) The *principal* object of contemplation is God Himself, but Jesus is its *secondary* object, and outside of the act of contemplation, one is not dispensed from thinking of Jesus Christ, the necessary mediator, nor from going to God through Him.

5) Holy abandonment is a virtue of high perfection; it must not, however, go as far as *indifference* concerning eternal salvation : on the contrary, one must desire it, hope for it and beg for it.

6) During interior trials the imagination and the sensitive appetite may be profoundly troubled, while the superior part of the soul enjoys a profound peace; the will, however, is ever bound to resist temptations.

Errors of Molinos

beginners, for instance, acts of faith, hope, religion and mortification, the acts connected with confession, etc.

To think of Jesus Christ and of His mysteries is an imperfection; it is necessary and sufficient to lose oneself in the divine essence : he who makes use of images or of ideas does not adore God in spirit and in truth.

In the state of contemplation one must be indifferent to all things, even to one's sanctification, to one's salvation, and one must relinquish hope, in order to make room for disinterested love.

One must not take the trouble to resist temptations; the most obscene fancies and the acts following upon them are not reprehensible, because they are the work of the devil. These are passive trials which the Saints themselves have undergone, and which one must carefully refrain from confessing. It is thus that one attains to perfect purity and to intimate union with God. [1]

This statement of the Catholic position obviates the need of refuting this error. The history of Quietism leads to the conclusion that when one wants to arrive at contemplation *too quickly*, and *through one's own efforts*, without having previously mortified one's passions and practiced the Christian virtues, one falls all the lower, the higher one pretends to go. *He who would play the angel becomes a beast.*

2° THE MITIGATED QUIETISM OF FÉNELON [2]

1485. In a less extreme form, and without the immoral consequences its author had deduced from it, the Quietism of Molinos was taken up by *Madame Guyon*, who, widowed at an early age, threw herself with ardor into the practice of an emotional and imaginative piety, which she styled the *way of pure love*. First, she won over to her ideas a Barnabite, Father Lacombe; later, to some extent, even

---

[1] In order to see how far Molinos goes, one has but to read the propositions taken from his books or from his statements and condemned by Innocent XI (Decree of August 28, and Constit., *Cælestis Pastor*, November 19, 1687) cf. DENZINGER, *Enchiridion*, n. 1221-1288.

[2] FÉNELON, *Maximes des Saints*, nouv. éd. par *A. Cherel*, 1911; GOSSELIN, *Œuvres de Fénelon*, t. IV; L. CROUSLÉ, *Bossuet et Fénelon*, 1894; HUVELIN, *Bossuet, Fénelon, le quiétisme;* A. LARGENT, *Fénelon*, (Dict. de Théol. t. V, col. 2138-2169); Cath. Encyc., Fénelon, Guyon.

Fénelon, who, in the *Explanation of the Maxims of the Saints regarding the Interior Life* (1697), formulated an *attenuated Quietism* in which he strove to demonstrate the doctrine of *pure love*, " pure charity without any admixture of selfish motives or self-interest. "

All the errors contained in this book can, according to Bossuet, be reduced to the four following propositions : 1) " There is in this life an habitual state of pure love, in which the desire for eternal salvation no longer has place. 2) In the final trials of the interior life, a soul can be convinced, with an *invincible* and *reasoned* conviction, that it has been justly rejected by God, and, under the influence of this conviction, offer to God an *absolute sacrifice* of its own eternal happiness. 3) In the state of pure love, the soul is indifferent to its own perfection and the practices of virtue. 4) Contemplative souls in certain states lose sight of Jesus Christ as the distinct, sensible and reasoned object of contemplation. "[1]

1486. No doubt this form of Quietism is far less dangerous than was that of Molinos. But the four propositions are false and could lead to baneful results.

1) It is false to say that there exists on this earth an *habitual state* of pure love *excluding hope;* for, as the Fifth Article of Issy[2] rightly states, "every Christian *in every state*, though not at every moment, is bound to express a desire and a prayer for his eternal salvation as something willed by God, Who wills that we desire it for His glory's sake. " It is true indeed that with perfect souls the desire for eternal happiness in often prompted by charity, and that there are *moments* when they do not think *explicitly* of their salvation.

2) The second proposition is no less false. No doubt, there are Saints who in the *lower part* of their soul experienced a *keen sense* of just reprobation; this was not, however, a reasoned conviction of the superior part of the soul. If some of them have made a *conditional* surrender of their salvation, this was not an absolute sacrifice.

3) Nor is it exact to say that the soul in the state of pure love is indifferent to its own perfection and to virtuous practices; on the contrary, St. Teresa does not cease to urge the thought of progress and the exercise of the fundamental virtues, even in the highest states of perfection.

4) Finally, it is false that in the *perfect states* one loses sight of Jesus Christ as the distinct object of contemplation. We have seen, in number 1472, that in the transforming union, St. Teresa had visions of the Sacred Humanity of Jesus Christ. What is true however, is that during certain *passing moments* one cannot explicitly think of Him.

3° SEMI-QUIETIST TENDENCIES[3]

1487. One meets at times in certain devout and otherwise excellent books, tendencies which are more or less quietistic, and which, were

---

[1] *Denzinger's Enchiridion* (1327-1349) contains Fénelon's propositions condemned by Innocent XII.

[2] These articles were redacted at the Seminary of Issy, as the result of the discussions conducted by Bossuet, Noailles, Bishop of Chalons, Fénelon, and Father Tronson, 1694-1695.

[3] P. JOSÉ, *Études relig.*, 20 déc. 1897, p. 804; MGR FARGES, *Mystical phenomena*.

they to be applied as rules for the spiritual direction of *ordinary* souls, would lead to abuses.

The main error of these writers is that of trying to instill into all persons alike, even into those who have made but *little progress* in the spiritual life, dispositions of passivity which belong only to the unitive way. They would have us take up more quickly the work of simplifying the spiritual life, forgetting that most souls cannot safely arrive at such simplification until they have passed through *discursive meditation, detailed* examinations of *conscience* and the practice of the *moral virtues*. Their error is one of excess; they would like to bring souls to perfection as quickly as possible by suppressing the intermediate stages and by suggesting from the outset the means which succeed with the most advanced souls.

1488. **a)** Thus, under the pretext of fostering disinterested love, they deprive *Christian hope* of the place it should occupy; they imagine that the desire of eternal happiness is but incidental and that God's glory is everything. In reality however the glory of God and our eternal happiness are intimately united; for by knowing and loving God we procure His glory, and this knowledge and love of God in turn constitute our happiness. Far from dissociating these two elements, we must keep them united and show how they complete one another, noting however, that if they are to be considered separately, the glory of God must come first.

b) The *passive* side of piety is likewise over-emphasized. It is said that we must *let God act in us, bear us in His arms*, without adding that God does not generally do so until we have practiced for a long time an active piety.

c) With regard to the *means of sanctification*, only such are proposed as belong ts the unitive way. *Methodical* and, as they call it, rule-bound meditation is severely criticized. *Specific* resolutions, they claim, destroy the unity of the spiritual life, and *detailed* examinations of *conscience* should be replaced by a rapid survey. They forget that beginners do not generally arrive at the prayer of simplicity except through discursive meditation; that general resolves to love God with all the heart must be particularized; that, in order to know their defects and correct them, beginners must enter into some details; that, as a matter of fact, they are but too prone to be satisfied with a superficial knowledge of self which will allow passions and defects to remain unchallenged.

In a word, these authors forget that there are many stages to be traversed before we can attain to the passive state and to union with God.

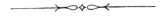

CHAPTER III
Extraordinary Mystical Phenomena

1489. In describing contemplation, we made no mention of the *extraordinary phenomena* such as visions, revelations, etc., which frequently accompany it, especially after the soul has reached the stage of ecstatic union. Since the devil apes divine works, *diabolical* phenomena are known to occur at times among the mystics, true or false. We shall speak first of the *divine* and then of the *diabolical* phenomena.

ARTICLE I. EXTRAORDINARY DIVINE PHENOMENA [1]

There are two kinds of such phenomena : those of the *intellectual*, and those of the *psycho-physiological* order.

§ I. Divine Intellectual Phenomena

These may be reduced to two main ones : **private revelations** and the **charisms.**

I. *Private Revelations*

We shall explain: 1º their *nature*; 2º the rules by which to distinguish the *true* from the *false*.

1º NATURE OF PRIVATE REVELATIONS

1490. A) Difference between Public and Private Revelations. Divine revelation in general is a supernatural manifestation by God of a hidden truth. When such a manifestation is made directly, *in behalf of the* whole *Church*, it is called *public* revelation; when it is made to private individuals for their own welfare or that of others, it is called *private* revelation. Here we speak only of the latter.

Private revelations have been made in every age: Holy Scripture and the processes of canonization furnish us with

---

[1] ST. TERESA, *Life*, C. XXV-XXX; *Interior Castle*, Mansion VI and elsewhere; ST. JOHN OF THE CROSS, Bk. I, C. XXI-XXX and eisewhere; ALVAREZ DE PAZ, *op. cit.*, t. III, lib. V, p. IV, *de discretione spirituum;* GODINEZ, *Praxis theol. myst.*, lib. X; BENEDICTUS XIV, *De beatificat.*, lib. IV, P. I; RIBET, *La Mystique divine*, t. II; POULAIN, *Graces of Interior Prayer*, C. XVII-XXI; GARRIGOU-LAGRANGE, *Perfect. et contemplation*, t. II, p. 536-562; Mgr. FARGES, *Mystical Phenomena.*

abundant examples. These revelations do not form a part of Catholic faith, which rests solely upon the deposit of truth contained in Scripture and Tradition, and which has been confided to the Church for interpretation. Hence, there is no obligation for the faithful to believe them. Even when the Church approves them she does not make them the object of Catholic faith, but as Benedict XIV states, she simply *permits* them to be published for the instruction and the edification of the faithful. The assent to be given them is not therefore an act of Catholic faith, but one of human faith, based upon the fact that these revelations are *probable* and *worthy of credence*[1]. Private revelations may not be published without ecclesiastical approbation[2].

Still, many theologians are of the opinion that the persons themselves to whom such revelations are made and those for whom they are destined may believe in them with real faith, provided they have had clear proof of their authenticity.

1491. B) The Manner in which Revelations are made. They are made in three different ways: through *visions, supernatural words,* and *divine touches.*

a) Visions are supernatural perceptions of some object naturally invisible to man. They are revelations only when they disclose hidden truths. They are of three kinds, *sensible, imaginative,* or purely *intellectual.*

1) *Sensible* or *corporeal* visions, also called apparitions, are those in which the senses perceive some real object that is naturally invisible to man. It is not necessary that the object be a real human body; it suffices that it be a sensible or luminous form.

The opinion of St. Thomas, which is generally held, is that after His Ascension, Our Lord rarely appeared in Person; He merely appeared in a visible form, but not in His real body. His apparitions in the Eucharist may be explained in two ways, says St. Thomas: either by a miraculous impression made on the sense of sight (which is the case when He manifests Himself to a single person) or by a form that is real and visible, but distinct from His own body; for, the Saint adds, the Body of Our Savior cannot be seen in its own proper form except in the one place which actually contains it.[3]

---

[1] *De Serv. Dei Beatif.*, l. II, c. 32, n. 11 : " Although an assent of Catholic faith may not and can not be given to revelations thus approved, still, an assent of *human faith*, made according to the rules of prudence, is due them; for according to these rules such revelations are probable and *worthy of pious credence.* ".

[2] Decrees of Urban VIII, March 13, 1625 and of Clement IX, May 23, 1668.

[3] *Sum. theol.*, III, q. 76, a. 8. The same conclusion is deduced from the testimony of St. Teresa, Relation XIII, where she says : " By some things which He told me, I understood that after He ascended into heaven He never descended on earth to converse with anyone, except in the Holy Sacrament. "

What has been said of Our Lord applies also to the Blessed Virgin. When she appeared at Lourdes for instance, Her body remained in heaven, and at the spot of the apparition there was but a sensible form which represented Her. This explains how she could appear now under one aspect, now under another.

1492. 2) *Imaginative* visions are those produced in the imagination by God or by the Angels, either during sleep or while one is awake. Thus an Angel appeared several times to St. Joseph in his sleep, and St. Teresa relates several imaginative visions she had of Our Lord while she was awake. [1] These visions are frequently accompanied by an intellectual vision which explains their meaning. [2] At times, one travels in vision through distant countries: such visions are for the most part imaginative.

1493. 3) Intellectual visions are those in which the mind perceives a spiritual truth without the aid of sensible impressions: such was St. Teresa's vision of the Holy Trinity, to which we referred in number 1473. These visions take place either through ideas *already* acquired, but which are coordinated or modified by God, or through *infused ideas* which represent divine things even better than do acquired ideas. Sometimes these visions are obscure and manifest only the presence of the object [3]; at other times they are clear, but last only for a moment: they are like intuitions which leave a deep impression. [4]

Some visions are at once sensible, imaginative and intellectual. Such was St. Paul's vision on the road to Damascus. He beheld with his eyes blinding light; he saw with his imagination the personal traits of Ananias; and his mind understood God's will.

1494. b) **Supernatural Words** are *manifestations* of *the divine thought conveyed* to the *exterior* or to the *interior* senses, or directly to the *intelligence*. They are called *auricular* when they come to the ear in the form of sound-waves, miraculously produced; *imaginative* when such manifestations are directed to the imagination; *intellectual* when addressed directly to the *intellect*. [5]

1495. c) **Divine touches** are spiritual sentiments full of sweetness, impressed upon the will by a kind of divine contact and accompanied by a vivid intellectual light.

---

[1] *Life by Herself*, C. XXVIII. — [2] *Ibid.*, C. XXIX.
[3] *Life by Herself*, C. XXVII. — [4] *Interior Castle*, VI Mansion, C. X.
[5] St. John of the Cross treats at length of these three different kinds of supernatural words, *successive*, *formal* and *substantial* (*Ascent of Carmel*), Bk. II, C. XXVI-XXIX.

We may distinguish two kinds of such touches : *ordinary* divine touches, and *substantial* divine touches ; the latter, though they affect but the will, make such a deep impression that they seem to take place within the very substance of the soul.

Hence the expressions of mystics describing their experiences as a contact of substance with substance. In reality these touches take place in the *superior part* of the will and the intellect, and according to St. Thomas, [1] it is the *faculties*, and not the substance, which receive these impressions.

1496.   C) Attitude to be taken towards these Extraordinary Graces. The great mystics are unanimous in teaching that one must neither desire nor ask for these *extraordinary* favors.   These are not necessary means to the divine union; nay, at times they are rather obstacles owing to our evil tendencies.   St. John of the Cross in particular points this out.   He asserts that the desire for revelations deprives faith of its purity, develops a dangerous curiosity which becomes a source of illusions, fills the mind with vain fancies, and often proves the want of humility and of submission to Our Lord, Who, through His public revelations has given all that is needed for salvation.

The Saint forcefully denounces imprudent directors who encourage the desire of visions : " They suffer their penitents to make much of their visions, which is the reason why they walk not according to the pure and perfect spirit of faith ; neither do they build up nor strengthen them in faith, while they attach so much importance to these visions. This kind of direction shows that they themselves consider visions matters of importance ; and their penitents, observing this, follow their example, dwelling upon these visions, not building themselves up in faith ; neither do they withdraw, nor detach themselves from them... The soul is no longer humble, but thinks itself to be something good, and that God makes much of it...   Some directors, when they see that their penitents have visions from God, bid them pray to Him to reveal to them such and such things concerning themselves or others, and the simple souls obey them... when in truth it is not pleasing to Him, and contrary to His will. " [2]

Since in this matter there is great danger of illusion, we must have some rules by which to discern the true from the false.

2° Rules for the Discernment of Revelations

1497.   In order to know true revelations and learn to recognize the human element that may enter into them, very precise rules must be drawn up concerning the *subjects*, the *object*, the *effects*, of revelations, and the *signs* which accompany them.

---

[1] St. Thom., Ia Iæ, q. 113, a. 8; *De Veritate*, q. 28, a. 3; cfr. Garrigou-Lagrange, *op. cit.*, t. II, p. 560.
[2] *Ascent of Carmel*, Bk. II, C. XVIII.

A) *Rules Concerning the Subjects of Revelations*

1498. God can no doubt make revelations to whomsoever He pleases, even to sinners; but *invariably*, He makes them only to persons who are not only fervent, but already raised to the *mystic state*. Moreover, even for the interpretation of true revelations, it is necessary to know the qualities and the defects of those who think themselves favored with revelations. Hence, we must study their *natural* and *supernatural* qualities.

a) **Natural Qualities :** 1) We must ascertain whether they are well-balanced or affected by *psycho-neurosis* or *hysteria;* for it is evident that in the latter case, there is ground for suspecting the alleged revelations, such temperaments being subject to hallucinations.

2) We must examine whether the persons in question are possessed of common sense, of sound judgment, or rather of a vivid imagination together with excessive emotionalism; whether they have received an education, and if so, from whom; whether their mind has been weakened by disease or long fasts.

3) We must see whether such persons are thoroughly sincere or whether they have the habit of exaggerating and of drawing on their imagination; whether they are self-possessed or passionate.

The mere verification of these particulars will not of itself prove the existence or non-existence of a revelation, but it will aid greatly in judging the value of the testimony profferred by those who claim to have received them.

1499. b) As to **supernatural qualities,** we must examine whether the persons concerned : 1) are endowed with *solid* and tried *virtue,* or merely with a more or less sensible fervor; 2) whether they are sincerely and deeply humble, or whether on the contrary, they delight in being noticed and in telling everybody about their spiritual favors; true humility is the *touchstone* of sanctity and the lack of it argues against a revelation; 3) whether they make the revelations known to their spiritual director instead of communicating them to other persons, and whether they readily follow his advice; 4) whether they have already passed through the *passive trials* and the first stages of contemplation; especially, whether they have *practiced the virtues in a heroic degree;* for God generally reserves these visions for perfect souls.

1500. The presence of these qualities does not prove the existence of a revelation, but simply renders more worthy of credence the word of those who claim to have received it; their absence does not disprove the fact of revelation, but makes it quite unlikely.

The information thus obtained will enable us to discover more easily the *lies* or the *illusions* of the alleged seers. There are some persons who, through pride or through the desire for recognition, voluntarily simulate ecstasies and visions. [1] There are others, more numerous, who, owing to a lively imagination are the victims of illusions, and mistake their own thoughts for visions or for interior words. [2]

B) *Rules Concerning the Object of Revelations*

1501. It is particularly to this point that our attention must be directed, for all revelations contrary to faith or morals must be absolutely rejected, according to the unanimous teaching of the Doctors of the Church based on these words of St. Paul : " *But though we, or an angel from heaven, preach a gospel to you besides that which we have preached to you, let him be anathema.* " [3] God cannot contradict Himself, nor can He reveal things opposed to what He teaches through His Church. From this fact follow a number of rules which we shall now recall.

a) We must consider as false every private revelation *in opposition to any truth of faith :* such are for example the alleged revelations of spiritualists which deny several of our dogmas, particularly eternal punishment. The same holds true if revelations are opposed to the unanimous teaching of the Fathers and Theologians, for this forms part of the ordinary teaching of the Church.

Any revelation pretending to solve a problem freely discussed among theologians must be suspected, for example, one claiming to settle the

---

[1] A notable instance was that of Magdalen of the Cross, a Franciscan Nun of Cordova, of the XVI Century, who after having given herself to the devil from her infancy, entered the convent at the age of seventeen and was three times Abbess of her monastery. Aided by the demon, she simulated all the mystical phenomena of ecstasy, levitation, stigmata, revelations and prophecies repeatedly fulfilled. Thinking herself at the point of death, she made a confession which she later retracted, was exorcised and moved to another convent of her order. See POULAIN, *Graces of Interior Prayer,* C. XXI, n. 36.

[2] St. Teresa in several places speaks of such persons. " It happens that some persons (and I know this to be true, for not three or four, but many persons have spoken with me on the subject) are of so weak an imagination that whatever they think upon, they say they see it clearly, as it indeed seems to them : they have also so vigorous an understanding, or whatever else it may be, for I know not, that they become quite certain of everything in their imagination. " (*Interior Castle,* VI Mansion, C. IX). — [3] *Galatians,* I, 8.

controversy between the Thomists and the Molinists. God is not wont to pronounce on such questions.

1502. b) We must likewise reject visions *opposed to morality or decency*, for instance, apparitions of nude human forms, vulgar and immodest language, detailed or meticulous descriptions of shameful vices which cannot but offend against modesty. God, Who makes revelations only for the good of souls, cannot, it is evident, be the author of such visions as lead by their very nature to vice.

For the same reason we must suspect such apparitions as lack dignity or proper reserve, above all, such as are ridiculous. This last characteristic is a mark of human or diabolical machination.

c) Nor are we, considering the laws of Providence and the miracles wich God is accustomed to work, to admit as coming from God commands impossible of realization, for God does not demand the impossible. [1]

C) *Rules concerning the Effects of Revelations*

1503. A tree is judged by its fruits; hence, we can judge revelations by the *effects* they produce in the soul.

a) According to St. Ignatius and St. Teresa, a divine vision causes at first a sense of wonderment and of fear, soon to be followed by *a sense of deep and lasting peace, of joy and of security.* The contrary is true with regard to diabolical visions; if at the outset they produce joy, they soon cause *uneasiness, sadness* and *discouragement.* It is thus that the devil brings about the downfall of souls.

1504. b) True revelations strengthen the soul in humility, obedience, patience and conformity to the divine will; *false* ones beget pride, presumption and disobedience.

St. Teresa[2] says: "This is a favor of Our Lord, which brings great *confusion* of oneself and *humility;* but, were it from the devil, the effect would be quite the opposite. Since, then, it clearly proves itself to be given by God... whoever receives it can in no way whatever imagine that it is a favor of his own, but that it comes from the hand of God... It is attended with immense gain and interior effects, which would not be, were melancholy the cause; much less could the devil effect so much good, nor would the soul enjoy such great peace, or *such continual desires of pleasing God, or such contempt for whatever does not conduce to unite us with Him.*"

---

[1] In the life of St. Catherine of Bologna it is related that the devil sometimes appeared to her in the form of the crucified Christ and demanded of her, under the appearance of perfection, the most impossible things, in order to drive her to despair. (*Vita altera*, cap. II, 10-13 in the *Bollandists* March 9).
[2] *Interior Castle*, VI Mansion, C. VIII.

1505. **c)** Here the question arises whether one may ask for *signs* in confirmation of private revelations. **a)** If the thing revealed is of *importance,* one may do so, but *humbly* and *conditionally;* for God is not bound to perform miracles in order to prove the truth of these visions. **b)** If signs are asked for, it is well to leave their choice to God. The parish priest of Lourdes requested Our Lady in apparition to make a sweetbrier to bloom in the midst of winter; the sign was not granted, but she did cause a miraculous spring to well forth which was destined to heal both body and soul. **c)** The careful verification of the requested miracle and its relation to the apparition affords a convincing proof.

D) *Rules for Discerning the True from the False in Revelations.*

1506. A revelation may be true in the main and yet contain some incidental errors. God does not multiply miracles without reason, and He does not right the prejudices or errors that they may lodge in the minds of the seers; He has in view their *spiritual welfare,* not their intellectual formation. We shall understand this better if we analyze the causes of error met with in some private revelations.

a) The first cause is the *uniting of human activity with supernatural action,* especially if the imagination and the mind are very active.

1) Thus, in private revelations we find the *errors of* the times in what relates to the *physical or historical sciences.* St. Frances of Rome asserts that she had beheld a heaven of crystal between the empyreal and the starry heavens and attributed the blueness of the sky to the starry heaven. Mary of Agreda thought she knew through revelation that this crystal heaven was divided into eleven parts at the moment of the Incarnation.[1]

2) At times we also meet with the prejudices and the systems of the spiritual directors of the seers. Relying upon her directors, St. Colletta thought she had seen in visions that St. Anne had been thrice married and was coming to visit her with her numerous family.[2] Sometimes Dominican and Franciscan Saints speak in their visions according to the systems peculiar to their Orders.

3) *Historical errors* also find their way into revelations: God is not wont to reveal the precise details of the life of Our Lord or of our Blessed Lady, when these have but little bearing on piety. Now, many seers, intertwining their own devout meditations with the revelations they receive, give details, numbers, dates, which contradict historical documents or other revelations. Thus, among the various accounts of the Passion, many little details related in visions, are either contradictory (for example, details regarding the number of strokes

---

[1] *The Mystic City,* Part II, n. 128; Part. I, n. 122.
[2] BOLLANDISTS, March 25th, p. 247.

Christ received in His flagellation) or in opposition to the best historical authorities.[1]

1507. b) A divine revelation may be wrongly interpreted. For example, St. Joan of Arc having asked of her "*voices*" whether she would be burnt, received the reply that she should trust in Our Lord, Who would assist her, and that she would be delivered through a great victory. In reality, her deliverance and victory were her martyrdom and her entrance into heaven. St. Norbert affirmed that he knew through revelation and with certainty that the Antichrist would come in his generation (XII Century). Questioned closely by St. Bernard, he said that at least he would not die before seeing a general persecution of the Church.[2] St. Vincent Ferrer announced the *Last Judgment* as *nigh*, and seemed to confirm this prediction by miracles.[3]

1508. c) A revelation may be unwittingly *altered* by the seer himself when he attemps to explain, or, still oftener, by those to whom he dictates his revelations.

St. Brigid realized herself that at times she retouched her revelations, the better to explain them;[4] these added explanations are not always free from errors. It is acknowledged today that the scribes who wrote the revelations of Mary of Agreda, of Catherine Emmerich, and of Marie Lataste modified them to an extent difficult to determine.[5]

For all these reasons, we can not be too prudent when examining private revelations.

CONCLUSION
OUR ATTITUDE TOWARDS PRIVATE REVELATIONS

1509. a) We cannot do better than to *imitate the judicious reserve of the Church and of the Saints*. The Church accepts no revelations except after long and careful investigation, and even then She does not force them on the faithful. Moreover, when it is question of inaugurating some feast or public undertaking, She waits long years before pronouncing, and decides only after the matter itself and its bearing on Dogma and Liturgy have been carefully considered.

Thus, Blessed Julienne of Liège, chosen by God to bring about the institution of the feast of Corpus Christi, did not submit her project

---

[1] BOLLANDISTS, January 13th, preface to the life of Blessed Veronica of Binasco; ST. ALPHONSUS LIGUORI, *Horologe of the Passion*.

[2] ST. BERNARD, *Letters*, No. LVI.

[3] Father FAGES, O. P., in the *Histoire de S. V. Ferrier*, explains that this was a conditional prophecy, like that of Jonas against Niniveh, and that the world was saved precisely on account of the many conversions the Saint brought about.

[4] *Supplementary Revelations*, C. XLIX.

[5] In the *Works of Marie Lataste* we find among her revelations passages translated from the Summa of St. Thomas.

to the theologians until twenty-two years after her first visions; fully sixteen years elapsed before the Bishop of Liege instituted the feast for his diocese, and it was six years after the death of Blessed Julienne herself that Pope Urban IV made it a feast of the entire Church. In like manner, the feast of the Sacred Heart was not approved until long after the revelations had been made to St. Margaret Mary, and then for reasons quite apart from these revelations.

In all this the Church has given us an example which we should follow.

1510. **b)** We must not therefore pronounce with *certitude* on the existence of a private revelation until we have had *convincing* proofs which are well summarized by Benedict XIV in his work on Canonizations. Generally, we must not rest satisfied with but one proof, and we should see whether the various proofs agree with and lend support to one another. The more numerous the proofs, the greater assurance we shall have.

1511. **c)** When a spiritual director is told by a penitent of his supposed revelations, he should carefully refrain from showing any *admiration*, for this would lead the seer at once to consider these visions as true, and perhaps to take pride in them. He must rather explain that such things are of far less importance than the practice of virtue, that one can easily be deceived in these matters and that one must therefore suspect, and at the beginning discount, such visions, rather than take stock in them.

This is the rule laid down by the Saints. St. Teresa [1] says: "Sometimes, and often, it may be only fancy, especially if the persons have a weak imagination, or are subject to great melancholy. No attention is, in my opinion, to be paid to these two kinds of persons... Such things are always to be feared until the spirit is understood. I consider it best to resist these "discourses" at first, because if they come from God they are a great help to advance us onwards; they also increase when they are thus tried. This is the case; but the soul should not be troubled too much, for truly she cannot do otherwise". St. John of the Cross is still more emphatic, pointing out the six main drawbacks of a too ready acceptance of such visions, he adds: "The devil rejoices greatly when a soul seeks after revelations and is ready to accept them; for such conduct furnishes him with many opportunities of insinuating delusions, and derogating from faith as much as he possibly can; for such a soul becomes rough and rude, and falls frequently into many temptations and unseemly habits." [2]

1512. **d)** However, the spiritual director should treat kindly those who think they have received revelations. He will thus succeed in gaining their confidence and he will obtain more easily the details which will enable him, after

---

[1] *Interior Castle*, VI Mansion, C. III.
[2] *Ascent of Carmel*, Bk. II, C. XI; The entire chapter should be read.

mature reflection, to pass judgment. Then, should he find the visions to be illusory, his decision will be more readily accepted.

This is the advice of St. John of the Cross, severe as he is with regard to visions: " But remember, though I say that these communications are to be set aside, and that confessors should be careful not to discuss them with their penitents, it is not right for spiritual directors to show themselves severe in the matter, or to betray any contempt or aversion ; lest their penitents should shrink within themselves, and be afraid to reveal their condition, and so fall into many inconveniences, which would be the case if the door were thus shut against them. " [1]

1513. e) If it be question of initiating some public enterprise, the director should carefully refrain from encouraging the venture without having previously well examined in the light of supernatural prudence the reasons *for* and *against.*

This is what the Saints did. St. Teresa, who was favored with so many revelations, did not want her directors to be guided in their decision solely by her visions. When Our Lord bade her to found the reformed monastery of Avila, she humbly submitted her plan to her director, and when the latter hesitated, she consulted St. Peter of Alcantara, St. Francis Borgia and St. Louis Bertrand. [2]

As to the seers themselves, they have but one rule to follow, to make their revelations known to some prudent director, and humbly follow his instructions. This is the surest way of not going astray.

II. *The Charisms.* [3]

1514. The revelations of which we have just spoken are accorded chiefly for the personal benefit of the recipient; the charisms are bestowed principally for the benefit of others. They are gratuitous gifts of an *extraordinary* and *transitory* nature, conferred directly *for the good of others*, though indirectly they may be made to minister to one's personal sanctification. St. Paul in the first Epistle to the Corinthians distinguishes nine charisms, all of which proceed from the same Spirit :

1515. 1) *The word of wisdom,* which enables us to draw from the truths of faith, as from principles, *conclusions* rich in dogmatic teaching.

2) *The word of knowledge,* which helps us to make use of human knowledge in order to explain the truths of faith.

3) *The gift of faith,* not the virtue of faith itself, but a special assurance capable of working wonders.

[1] *Ascent of Carmel,* Bk. II, C. XXIII.
[2] *Histoire de Ste Thérèse* par une Carmélite, ch. XII.
[3] PRAT, *Theology of St. Paul,* II; GARRIGOU-LAGRANGE, *op. cit.,* II, p. 536-53

4) *The grace of healing*, or the power over disease.

5) *The working of miracles*, which confirms divine revelation.

6) *The gift of prophecy*, or the power to teach in God's name, and, if need be, to confirm this teaching by prophecies.

7) *The dicerning of spirits*, or the infused gift of reading the secrets of hearts and discerning the good spirit from the evil one.

8) *Diverse kinds of tongues*, which for St. Paul means the power to pray with exalted feeling in strange tongues; according to theologians, it is the gift of speaking divers tongues.

9) *Interpretation of speeches*, or the power to interpret the aforesaid strange tongues. [1]

St. Paul and St. Thomas rightly remind us that all these charisms are far inferior to charity and to sanctifying grace.

§ II. Psycho-physiological Phenomena

1516. By this term we mean such phenomena as affect both soul and body, and which are more or less related to ecstasy. The principal phenomena of this kind are: 1° *levitation;* 2° *luminous rays;* 3° *fragrant odors;* 4° *prolonged fasting;* 5° *stigmatization.*

I. *Levitation*

1517. Levitation is a phenomenon whereby the body is raised above the ground and sustained in midair without any natural support. Sometimes the body rises to great heights; at other times it seems to glide rapidly over the ground.

We read of many facts of levitation in the lives of the Saints, both in the *Bollandists* and in the *Breviary;* for instance: St. Paul of the Cross, April 28th; St. Philip Neri, May 26th; St. Stephen of Hungary, September 2nd; St. Joseph Cupertino, September 18th; St. Peter of Alcantara, October 19th; St. Francis Xavier, December 3rd, etc... One of the most celebrated is St. Joseph of Cupertino. One day seeing some workmen at a loss to set a very heavy mission cross in place, he took his aërial flight, seized the cross, and planted it without effort in the place prepared for it.

This phenomenon is akin to that of an *extraordinary immobility*, which prevents one from being moved, even by a powerful force.

1518. Rationalists have attempted to explain this phenomenon by natural causes, for instance by air drawn deep into the lungs, by an unknown physical force, by the intervention of spirits, etc., which amounts to saying that they have no sufficient explanation to offer. How much

---

[1] St. Thomas in an interesting article (Iª IIæ, q. III, a. 4) summarizes these, divers graces and shows how useful they are to the preacher of the Word: 1) they give him a full knowledge of divine things; 2) they confirm his preaching by miracles; 3) they help him to preach the Word of God more effectively.

wiser Benedict XIV! He requires first of all that the fact be thoroughly verified so as to eliminate any chance of fraud. Then he states: 1) that a well-authenticated *levitation* cannot be explained on natural grounds; 2) that this phenomenon is not, however, beyond the power of angels or of demons, who can lift the body; 3) that with the Saints it is a sort of anticipation of a prerogative of glorified bodies [1].

II. *Luminous Rays.* [2]

1519. Ecstasy is at times accompanied by luminous phenomena: it may be a halo about the head, or a glow enveloping the whole body.

Here again we sum up the teaching of Benedict XIV. [3] The fact must first be thoroughly investigated in all its circumstances in order to ascertain whether the luminous effect can be ascribed to a natural cause.

In particular we should inquire: 1) whether the phenomenon takes place in full daylight or during the night, and if the latter be the case whether the light is more brilliant than any other light; 2) whether it is a mere spark, much like that produced by electricity, or whether the luminous phenomenon is prolonged over a considerable period of time, recurring again and again; 3) whether it is produced during the course of some religious act, an ecstasy, a sermon, a prayer; 4) whether there follow upon it effects of grace, lasting conversions, etc..., 5) whether the person, from whom this radiance proceeds is virtuous and holy.

It is only after a careful examination into all these details that we can pronounce upon the nature of the facts. If their supernatural character is ascertained, we have another anticipation of a prerogative of glorified bodies.

III. *Fragrant Odors*

1520. At times God permits the bodies of the Saints to give forth during their lifetime or after their death a fragrant odor, a symbol, so to speak, of the perfume of the virtues they have practised.

Thus, the stigmata of St. Francis of Assisi occasionally emitted a sweet perfume. When St. Teresa died, the water wherewith her body was washed retained a certain fragrance. During nine months a mysterious perfume rose from her grave, and when her body was exhumed, a sweet-smelling oil trickled from her limbs. [4] Many similar facts have been recorded.

---

[1] *De Beatificat.* Book III, C. XLIX.

[2] RIBET, *La Mystique*, IIe P., ch. XXIX; MGR FARGES, *op. cit.*, IIe Part. ch. III, a. 3.

[3] *De Beatificat.* Book IV, I Part., C. XXVI, n. 8-30.

[4] This miracle was carefully studied in the process of her canonization, and the examiners concluded that nothing in the natural order could explain it (BOLLANDISTS, Oct. 15th, t. LV, p. 368, n. 1132).

Pope Benedict XIV has indicated the procedure to be followed in verifying a miracle.   One must examine : 1) whether the odor is sweet and persistent; 2) whether anything near the body or in the earth can account for it; 3) whether miracles have been wrought by the use of the water or the oil coming from the body of the Saint .[1]

IV. *Prolonged Abstinence*

1521. There have been Saints, especially among those bearing the stigmata, who have lived many years without taking any other food than Holy Communion.

Dr. Imbert-Goubeyre [2] mentions some striking instances : " Blessed Angela of Foligno remained twelve years without taking any nourishment; St. Catherine of Siena, about eight years; Blessed Elizabeth of Rente, over fifteen years; St. Ledwina, twenty eight years; Blessed Catherine Racconigi, ten years... in our own time, Rosa Andriani, twenty eight years... and Louise Lateau, fourteen years. "

The Church is very exacting in the investigation concerning facts of this kind, and demands a strict surveillance of the person at all times, during a notable period, and by numerous witnesses well able to detect any fraud. [3]   The examiners must ascertain whether the abstinence is *absolute*, extending to drink as well as to food, whether it is *unbroken*, and whether the person concerned continues to attend to customary occupations.

We must mention here another phenomenon of a somewhat similar nature, that of protracted vigils.   St. Peter of Alcantara slept but one hour and a half a night for forty years; St. Catherine of Ricci slept but one hour a week.

V. *Stigmatization*

1522. 1º **Nature and Origin.**   This phenomenon consists in a kind of impression of Our Lord's Wounds made upon the feet, hands, side and brow.   These wounds appear spontaneously, from no exterior hurt, and periodically there is a flow of fresh blood.

The first person known to bear the stigmata was St. Francis of Assisi.   During a sublime ecstasy on Mount Alvernia on the seventeenth of September, 1222, he saw a Seraph presenting to him the image of Jesus Crucified and imprinting upon him the sacred stigmata.   A rich, red blood used to flow from these wounds, which remained with him until his death.   He tried to conceal the miracle, but was not wholly successful, and at his death, on the eleventh of

---

[1] *De Beatific.*, l. IV, P. I, C. XXXI, n. 19-28.
[2] *La Stigmatisation*, t. II, p. 183.
[3] BENEDICT XIV, *op. cit.*, l. IV, P. I, C. XXVII.

October, 1226, the prodigy became known. Since that time such cases have multiplied. Dr. Imbert counts three hundred and twenty, forty of which were those of men, and sixty-two of these persons have been canonized.

1523. It seems to be a well-established fact that stigmatization occurs only among those favored with *ecstasies,* and that it is preceded and attended by very *keen physical and moral sufferings* which thus render the subject conformable to the Suffering Christ. The absence of suffering would be an unfavorable sign, for the stigmata are but the symbol of union with Jesus Crucified and of participation in His martyrdom.

The existence of the stigmata has been proved by so many testimonies that unbelievers themselves generally admit the fact, but try to explain it by some natural means. They claim that it is possible to provoke in persons of an extremely sensitive nature bloody sweats resembling the stigmata, by causing in them an over-excitation of the imagination. As a matter of fact however, the few results they have obtained in this wise differ vastly from the phenomena observed in stigmatized Saints.

1524. 2° **Signs by Which to Discern Stigmata.** The better to discern stigmatization from the artificial phenomena provoked in some individuals, attention must be paid to all the circumstances which characterize true stigmatization.

1) The stigmata are localized in the very spots where Our Lord received the five wounds, a fact which is not true of the bloody sweat produced by hypnotism.

2) Generally, the wounds bleed afresh and the pains recur on the days or during the seasons which recall the Savior's Passion, such as Fridays or the feast days of Our Lord.

3) The wounds *do not become infected,* and the blood which flows from them is pure, whilst the slightest natural lesion in some other part of the body develops pus. The wounds *do not yield to the usual medical treatment,* and remain at times thirty or forty years.

4) The wounds bleed freely and produce a veritable *hemorrhage.* That this should occur at the moment when they first appear is quite conceivable, but that it should take place again and again is inexplicable. The extent of the hemorrhages remains likewise unexplained; the stigmata generally lie on the surface, removed from the great blood-vessels, yet the blood literally streams from them.

5) Lastly, and above all, the stigmata are not met with except in persons who *practise the most heroic virtues* and possess a special love for the cross.

A study of all these circumstances proves indeed that we are dealing here not with some ordinary, pathological case, but with a free, intelligent cause which exerts its influence in order to make these persons bearing the stigmata more like the Crucified Christ.

CONCLUSION : DIFFERENCE BETWEEN THESE SUPERNATURAL PHENOMENA AND MORBID CASES

1525. The phenomena connected with ecstasy have been so well established that unbelievers cannot deny them; they strive merely to liken them to certain *morbid phenomena* which are caused by psycho-neurosis, and particularly by *hysteria.* Some go so far as to maintain that they are simply a form of *mental derangement.* No doubt, the Saints are subject to illness just as other human beings are, but the question is whether in spite of their ailments they appear to be sane and well-balanced. On this point the differences between *mystical* and *psycho-neurotic* phenomena are so essential that no honest observer can fail to note them. [1] These differences are found : 1° in the *persons* themselves; 2° in the *diversity of the phenomena;* 3° in the *results.*

1526. 1° **Differences in the persons themselves.** If we compare those affected with *psycho-neurosis* with persons favored with ecstasies, we find that the former are unbalanced physically and mentally, whilst the latter are at least mentally sound.

A) The former lack *mental* and physical soundness.
We notice in them a decrease of intellectual and volitional power : consciousness is altered or temporarily suspended, attention is relaxed, intelligence deteriorates, memory disintegrates to such an extent that one is led to believe they have a double personality, and before long their mind is depleted save for a few fixed ideas the final result of which is monomania bordering on insanity. Their will likewise becomes weaker and weaker, their emotions gain control, and they become the playthings of their own whims or of some stronger will. This means a disintegration of personality and a lessening of intellectual and moral power. [2]

1527. **B)** It is very different with the *mystics.* Their mind develops, their will grows stronger, and they become capable of conceiving and realizing the greatest undertakings. We have seen how they acquire a new knowledge of God, of His attributes, of the dogmas of faith, of self.

---

[1] This difference is brought out by unbelievers such as M. DE MONTMORAND, *Psychologie des Mystiques*, 1920, although the latter attributes these phenomena to hallucination. For the refutation of these theories our readers are referred to A. HUC, *Nevrose et Mysticisme, Rev. de Philosophie (P. Peillaube)*, juil., août, 1912, pp. 5, 128; MGR. FARGES, *op. cit.*, p. 322-585.
[2] This is a summary of the characteristics noted by P. JANET, *L'Automatisme psychologique*, P. II, ch. III-IV.

Doubtless, they are unable to express all they see, but they sincerely declare that they learned more during a few moments of contemplation than by long and extensive readings. That they are right in their conviction is proved by the real progress made in the exercise of the most heroic virtues. We see that they become more humble, more charitable, more submissive to the Divine Will even in the midst of very intense suffering, and that they enjoy a sweet calm and peace which nothing can disturb. How utterly different all this from the spasms and the passionate commotions of hysteria!

1528. 2° **Differences in the phenomena.** Differences just as marked as the foregoing are likewise discernible in the *manner* in which the two kinds of phenomena occur.

A) Nothing is sadder and more heartrending than to witness the fits of hysteria.

1) The first stage of hysteria resembles a slight attack of epilepsy. It can be distinguished however from the latter by the *sensation of a lump rising in the throat.* In reality, there is a swelling of the throat which produces a feeling of suffocation accompanied by a sort of hissing sound perceptible to the ears. 2) The second stage is marked by uncontrolled gestures and contorsions of the entire body. 3) The third stage gives rise to attitudes of fright, of jealousy, of lust, according to the nature of the obsessing idea or image. 4) The fit ends in a paroxysm of tears or laughter. After the crisis has passed, the patient is left weary and exhausted, and suffers from various indispositions.

B) Note once more the difference between this and ecstasy. In the latter there are no convulsions, no violent spasms, but only the peace and the rapture of a soul intimately united with its God. So true is this that those who have witnessed a person in ecstasy, those for example who saw Blessed Bernadette during her visions at the Grotto of Lourdes, could not withhold their admiration. As St. Teresa remarks (n. 1456), the body, instead of becoming exhausted, gathers new energies during the time of ecstasy.

1529. 3° **Differences in the effects.** Here again hysteria differs widely from ecstasy.

A) With *hysterical* persons the disintegration of the faculties increases in proportion to the frequency of the crises. Dissimulation, lying, stupor, brutality and lewdness follow in the wake of this disease.

B) In the case of the *mystics*, on the contrary, there is a steady mental growth, an increase of the love of God and of devoted service to the neighbor. When they have the opportunity of engaging in some public enterprise, they give evidence of common sense, of an open and strong mind, of a determined will, and success crowns their efforts.

St. Teresa, in spite of the frequent opposition she encountered, founded sixteen convents for women and fourteen monasteries for men. St. Colletta established thirteen monasteries and restored discipline in a great number of others. Madame Acarie, who had been favored with ecstasies from her sixteenth year, was happily married for thirty years, reared a family of six children, restored her family's fortunes, which had been imperilled by her husband's imprudences, and after the latter's death, was instrumental in the establishment of the Carmelite Order in France. St. Catherine of Siena, who died at the age of thirty-two and who for a long time did not know how to read or write, played an important part in the stirring events of her times, and particularly in the return of the Popes of Avignon to Rome. A recent historian has called her a statesman, and a great statesman. [1]

It is evident then that the differences existing between the phenomena of hysteria and ecstasy are such that to attempt to place them in the same category is to violate all the canons of scientific investigation.

1530. 4° **Objection.** A final difficulty remains to be solved. There are those who with Ribot claim that ecstasy brings about a gradual narrowing of the field of consciousness to *one affective idea*, called by them *monomania*, since mystics think of nothing else but the intimate union with God. To answer this specious objection, we must distinguish between ideas and ideas. There is the case of an *obsessing idea* which little by little breaks down personality by unbalancing the judgment. Such is, for instance, the fixed idea of suicide. But there is also the case of a *healthy, constructive singleness of purpose*, of one main idea dominating all the others and making them bear on this one purpose, without however destroying the mind's equilibrium. Far from causing any disintegration of personality, such an idea gives strength and unity. It is just because great statesmen have such fixed ideas as these, provided always that the ideas be just ones, ideas on which they center all their plans, that they are able to accomplish great things.

This is exactly the case with the mystics. They have a dominant idea, a fixed idea of pursuing above all things their ultimate end, that is, intimate union with God, the Source of all bliss and all perfection, and they make all their other thoughts bear on this one idea, this one great purpose of life. And who can gainsay the justice of their cause? We are dealing here with a force that is in no way destructive; on the contrary, it is a power which coördinates thoughts and actions by directing them towards that one end which alone can give perfection and happiness. This is the reason why, even from a human point of view, the Saints are great doers, men of action imbued with common sense, energy and steadiness of purpose, men who conceive and carry out great enterprises. Even unbelievers them-

---

[1] Em. Gebhart, *Rev. hebdom.*, 16 mars, 1907.

selves have come to recognize this fact, as we pointed out before (n. 43).

Let us then be just, and acknowledge that mystics are not only saints, but men of character as well.

Art. II. Diabolical phenomena [1]

1531. The devil, jealous of God's influence on the souls of the Saints, strives to exercise his own dominion, or rather his tyranny, over men.   At times he, so to speak, besieges the soul *from without* by assailing it with horrible temptations; at other times, he *takes up his abode in the human body,* which he moves at will as if he were its master, in order thus to afflict the soul itself.   In the former case we have *obsession,* in the latter, *possession.*

There are two extreme views concerning the action of the devil.   There are those who attribute to him all the evils that befall mankind.   This is to forget that man is subject to morbid states which presuppose no diabolical intervention whatsoever, and has inordinate tendencies which proceed from the threefold concupiscence.   These causes suffice to explain many a temptation.   There are other persons who, forgetting what Holy Writ and Tradition tell us about the devil's influence, refuse to admit his intervention in any instance.   In order to keep to the golden mean, we must follow the rule of accepting as diabolical only such phenomena as point, because of their extraordinary nature or because of the sum-total of circumstances, to the action of the Evil One.

We shall treat first of *obsession,* and then of *possession.*

§ I. Obsession

1532.   I. Its Nature.   Obsession consists in a series of unusually violent and persistent temptations.   It is called *external* when the temptations affect the exterior senses by means of apparitions, and *internal* when they stir up sensations or emotions.   It is rare that obsession is purely external, for the devil acts upon the senses in order the more easily to disturb the soul.   However, there have been Saints who, though obsessed from without by all sorts of phantoms, preserved an unruffled peace of soul.

---

[1] Del Rio, *Disquisitiones magicæ,* 1600; Thyræus, *De locis infestis; De spirituum apparitionibus; De dæmoniacis,* 1699; Ribet, *Mystique divine,* t. III; Poulain, *Graces of Interior Prayer,* C. XXIV; Saudreau, *L'Etat mystique,* ch. XXII-XXIII.

1533. 1º The devil can act upon all the external senses :

a) Upon the sense of *sight*, by appearing sometimes under *repulsive* forms to frighten persons and turn them away from the practice of virtue, as he did to the Venerable Mother Agnes of Langeac [1] and to many others; at other times under *seductive* forms in order to lead them into sin, as he frequently did to St. Alphonsus Rodriguez. [2]

b) Upon the sense of *hearing*, by causing blasphemous or obscene words or songs to be heard, as is told in the Life of the Blessed Margaret of Cortona, [3] or by creating frightful noises, such as were experienced at times by St. Madeleine of Pazzi and the sainted Curé of Ars. [4]

c) Upon the sense of *touch*, and this in two ways : by blows and wounds, such as we read of in the Bulls of Canonization of St. Catherine of Siena, of St. Francis Xavier, and in the Life of St. Teresa; [5] or by embraces, the purpose of which is to tempt to sin, as St. Alphonsus Rodriguez relates of himself. [6]

Father Schram [7] remarks that there are cases in which these apparitions are pure hallucinations resulting from extreme nervous excitation. However, even in such cases they constitute formidable temptations.

1534. 2º The devil also acts upon the *interior* senses, the imagination and the memory, and upon the passions, in order to excite them. Distressing and besetting images flit through the imagination and remain there in spite of every effort to expel them. One appears to have become the prey to fits of anger, to the anguish of despair, to instinctive feelings of antipathy, or on the other hand, to a dangerous sentimentality which nothing seems to justify. No doubt, it is difficult at times to decide whether the case is one of real obsession, but when the temptations are at once sudden, violent, persistent and hard to account for by natural means, one may conclude that it is a special intervention on the part of the devil. In case of doubt, it will always be well to consult a Catholic physician, who can examine whether the phenomena are due to some morbid condition, and if they are, to prescribe the proper medical treatment.

1535. II. **Attitude of the spiritual Director.** He must unite enlightened *prudence* with paternal *kindness*.

a) Of course, he should not without serious evidence consider the case one of real obsession. Nevertheless,

---

[1] M. DE LANTAGES, *Vie de la Vén. M. Agnès* ed. Lucot, 1863, P. I, ch. X.
[2] *POULAIN*, op. cit., ch. XXIV, n. 94.
[3] *Bollandistes*, Feb. 22., t. VI, p. 340, n. 178.
[4] A. MONNIN, *The Curé of Ars*, III, C. II.
[5] *Vie* par une Carmélite, t. II, ch. XXVII.
[6] POULAIN, loc. cit. — [7] *Instit. theol. mysticæ*, 219.

whether there be obsession or not, he must be full of pity towards penitents who are assailed by violent and persistent temptations, and he must help them with judicious advice. He should remind them particularly of what we have said with regard to temptations, the manner of resisting them (n. 902-918), and the special remedies against diabolical temptation (n. 223-224).

b) If at the height of the temptation some disorder takes place but without any consent on the part of the will, he must remind them that where there is no consent, there is no sin. In case of doubt and when the person in question habitually avoids sin, he will decide that there has been no fault, at least no grave fault.

c) When dealing with *fervent* souls, the director may well ask himself whether these persistent temptations are not part of the *passive trials* which we described above (n. 1426), and if so, he must give them the advice suited to their state of soul.

1536. **d)** If it is morally certain or highly probable that there is diabolical obsession, the spiritual director may make use, *in private*, of the *exorcisms* contained in the *Roman Ritual* or of some shorter formulas. Should he determine to do so, he should not tell the penitent beforehand if he has reason to fear that it would only worry and excite him; it will suffice to say that he is going to recite over him some prayer approved by the Church. *Solemn exorcisms* may not be employed without the permission of the Ordinary, and then only with the precautions which we shall indicate when treating of possession.

§ II. Possession [1]

We shall explain: 1° its *nature*; 2° the *remedies* prescribed by the Roman *Ritual*.

I. *Nature of Possession*

1537. 1° **Its constituent elements.** Two elements constitute possession : the *presence* of the devil in the body of the possessed, and the *dominion* exercised by the devil over that body, and through it, over the soul. This latter point needs to be explained. The devil does not unite with the body in the same manner as the soul does, nor does he enter into the soul itself; it is only by acting upon the body in which he dwells that he can affect the soul. He can indeed act directly on the bodily members and cause them to perform all sorts of motions, and indirectly

---

[1] Besides the authors already mentioned, see MGR WAFFELAERT, in the *Dictionnaire d'Apologétique:* " *Possession.* "

he can move the faculties of the soul in so far as they depend for their operations upon the body.

We can distinguish two distinct states in possessed persons: the *crisis* and the period of *calm*. The crisis is like a violent attack in which the devil manifests his tyrannical sway by imparting to the body a feverish agitation which finds expression in contortions, outbursts of fury, and impious and blasphemous utterances. There upon the victims seem to lose all sense of what takes place within them, and they retain no memory of what they say or do, or rather, of what the devil does through them. It is only at the beginning of the crisis that they are aware of the invasion of the Evil One, and after that they apparently lose consciousness.

1538. There are however exceptions to this general rule. Father Surin, who himself became possessed while exorcising the Ursulines of Loudun, was conscious of all that took place within him. He describes how his soul was divided in twain, open on one side to diabolic influences, and on the other abandoned to God's action, and how he prayed while his body rolled over the ground. He says: " My state is such that there remain to me very few actions in which I am free. If I want to speak, my tongue rebels; during Holy Mass I am constrained to stop suddenly; at table I am unable to bring the food to my mouth; if I go to confession I forget my sins; I am aware of the devil within me as within his own house, going in and out as he pleases. "[1]

1539. During the intervals of quiet and calm there is nothing to disclose the presence of the evil spirit; it is as though he had departed. Sometimes however his presence manifests itself by a sort of chronic infirmity which baffles all the efforts of physicians.

Often enough *several* devils take possession of the same person. This fact would seem to indicate their relative weakness.

Generally it is sinners who fall victims to possession, but it is not always so, as may be seen from the case of Father Surin.

1540. 2° **The signs of possession.** Since there are nervous diseases, cases of monomania and of mental aberration, the symptoms of which resemble the manifestations of diabolical possession, it is important to know the signs whereby the latter can be distinguished from all such morbid phenomena.

According to the Roman Ritual [2] there are three principal signs by which possession may be recognized: " Speaking

---

[1] Lettre du 3 mai 1635 au P. d'Attichy.
[2] *De Exorcizandis Obsessis a Dæmonio.*

an unknown tongue or understanding it when spoken by another; making known distant and hidden things; exhibiting a strength out of all proportion with one's age and circumstances. These and other like signs, when they concur in great number, are the surest indications of possession." Just a word to explain these signs.

a) *The Use of Unknown Tongues.* To verify the fact, a thorough examination must be made to see whether the person in question has had in the past any opportunity of learning some words of the language used, whether he is uttering merely a few phrases learned by heart, or whether he really has a knowledge of a language hitherto unknown to him. [1]

b) *Making Known Hidden Things.* Here again a thorough inquiry must be made to see whether or not the knowledge can be explained by some natural means. If it be question, for instance, of things distant, one must make sure that the person had not been made aware of them by letter, telegram or some other purely natural means. If it be question of future events, one must wait for their occurrence and see whether they take place precisely as they were foretold. One must not therefore take account of those vague predictions announcing some great misfortune to be followed by some happy event or notable prosperity; if this were all that is required, one could rather easily establish a reputation as a prophet. Once the fact has been properly verified, one must ascertain according to the rules for the discernment of spirits whether this preternatural knowledge proceeds from the good or from the evil spirit, and if from the latter, whether from an evil spirit actually present in the possessed person.

c) *Exhibiting a Strength out of all Proportion with One's Age and Circumstances.* One must not forget that there are instances of over-excitation of the nervous system wherein one's energies are notably increased. We have already said that the phenomenon of *levitation* when correctly established is of a preternatural character. There are indeed cases which, all circumstances considered, can not be attributed to God or to His Angels, and must therefore be ascribed to the intervention of the devil.

1541. One might add here another sign pointing to the fact of possession to be found in the reactions produced by the use of exorcisms or of holy objects, especially if they are employed *without the knowledge* of the supposedly possessed persons. At times, the mere contact with a pious object or the recitation over them of the liturgical prayers drives them into a fury and provokes horrible blasphemies. However, this is not a sure sign of possession unless the experiment just described is made unknown to the patients, for if they realize what is about to be done, they may

---

[1] Cases of abnormal mental states have been recorded in which words or languages once heard or understood but later forgotten, were recalled; for instance, the priest's housekeeper who recited whole passages in Greek and Hebrew which she had heard the priest recite. The statement of the *Ritual* is therefore a judicious one: " Speaking an unknown tongue or understanding it when spoken by another. "

purposely work themselves into a state of frenzy, either because they have a horror of all things religious, or because they wish to deceive.

It is not easy therefore to recognize a case of real possession, and one cannot be too careful before making a decision.

1542.   3° Differences between possession and nervous diseases.   Experiments made upon persons affected with nervous troubles have shown a certain similarity between these morbid states and the *outward manifestations* of diabolical possession.   We should not be surprised at this. The devil can cause nervous disorders or other external phenomena similar to those of neuropathics.   This is one more reason for extreme care before passing judgment on alleged cases of possession.

It is worth noting that the similarity between nervous maladies and demoniacal possession does not go beyond the outward appearances, which of themselves are insufficient to prove the fact of possession.   No one has met with neuropathics who could speak unknown tongues or foretell the future with precision and certitude.   These are, as we stated before, the true signs of possession, and when all of these are absent, we may well consider the case one of simple psycho-neurosis.   If exorcists have at times been deceived, it is generally because they have departed from the rules laid down by the *Ritual*.   That such mistakes be avoided, one should have the case examined not only by priests, but also by Catholic physicians.

1543.   Father Debreyne, who had practised medicine before becoming a Trappist, tells of how he had to treat a community of women whose condition offered many points of resemblance to that of the Ursulines of Loudun.   He cured them in a short time by prescribing hygienic measures, particularly steady and varied manual labor. [1]

One must be especially skeptical when possession seems to become *epidemic*.   A real case of possession can induce in others witnessing it a nervous condition outwardly similar to that of possession.   The best way to obviate such contagion is to separate the persons thus stricken and to remove them from the environment in which they contracted their nervous malady.

II. *Remedies for Possession*

In general, the remedies consist in anything that can weaken the influence of the devil over man, purify his soul, and strengthen his will against diabolical assaults.   The *special* remedy is found in the exorcisms.

---

[1] *Essai de théol. morale*, ch. IV, revised edition by D$_r$ *Ferrand*, 1884.

1544. 1º **General remedies.** All the remedies pointed out (n. 223-224) for diabolical temptation are to be employed in dealing with possession.

A) One of the most efficacious of all is the *purification of the soul* by a worthy confession, particularly a general confession, which by humiliating and sanctifying the penitent puts to flight the proud and impure spirit. The *Ritual* counsels the addition of fasting, prayer and the reception of Holy Communion. ¹ The more pure and the more mortified one becomes, the weaker becomes the influence of the devil, and in Holy Communion one receives Him Who conquered Satan. It need hardly be said that Communion should not be given except in moments of calm.

B) The *Sacramentals* and *blessed objects* are also efficacious remedies because of the prayers said by the Church when blessing them. St. Teresa had great confidence in *holy water*, and rightly so, since the Church imparts to it the power of putting the devil to flight. ² But such objects are to be used in a spirit of faith, of humility and of confidence.

C) The Crucifix, the Sign of the Cross, and especially genuine relics of the True Cross are terrifying to the devil who was vanquished by the Cross : " That the one who conquered by a tree should himself be likewise conquered by the Tree." ³ For the same reason the Evil Spirit dreads the invocation of the Holy Name of Jesus, which, on the Master's Own promise, possesses a wondrous power for putting the devil to flight. ⁴

1545. 2º **Exorcisms.** The Church, having received from Christ the power of expelling devils, early instituted the Order of Exorcists, on whom She conferred the power of imposing hands on possessed persons, whether baptized or only preparing for baptism; and later She composed formulas of prayers to be employed by them in the exercise

---

¹ " The obsessed person should be urged, if he be mentally and physically able, to pray to God for help, to fast and to receive more frequently according to the advice of the confessor the Sacraments of Penance and the Holy Eucharist. " (*Rituale*, De exor. obsessis).

² " That thou mayest become water exorcised to put to flight every power of the enemy, and that thou mayest be able to eject and supplant this enemy himself together with his apostate angels... " (*Rit. rom.*, Ordo ad faciendam aquam benedictam).

³ Preface for the Feast of the Holy Cross.

⁴ *Mark*, XVI, 17. — St. Alphonsus Rodriguez was wont to make a large sign of the cross at the moment of the obsession and to command the tempter to bow down and adore Jesus, in virtue of that text of St. Paul: " That in the name of Jesus every knee should bow, of those that are in heaven, on earth, and under the earth. " (*Philip.*, II, 10). The Saint adds that this put the devil to flight.

of their office. Since this office is an extremely difficult one and presupposes much knowledge, virtue and tact, its solemn exercise has been *restricted* to priests expressly deputed for that purpose by the Ordinary. However, priests may perform private exorcisms, employing some prayers of the Church or other formulas. Even lay-persons may recite such prayers, but not in the name of the Church. [1]

1546. The Ritual prescribes the proceedure and gives to Exorcists a number of wise counsels. Once the fact of possession has been ascertained and one has been *delegated* to perform the exorcisms:

1) One should prepare for this function by a *humble and sincere confession*, so that the devil may not be able to accuse one of sin. Earnest prayer and fasting should form part of the preparation, for Christ has told us that there are devils who yield only to these means. [2]

2) The exorcisms should be performed in a church or a chapel, unless for weighty reasons another place is deemed preferable. In no case should the exorcist be alone with the person possessed. He should have serious and devout witnesses who are at the same time strong enough to control the patient during the moments of the crises. If the possessed person be a woman, the exorcist should secure the presence of matrons of tried prudence and virtue.

1547. 3) After the recitation of the prescribed prayers, the exorcist should proceed with the interrogations. He must do so *authoritatively*, limiting himself to such questions as are useful and recommended by the Ritual. He should ask about the number of the spirits present and about the time and the motives of their invasion. He should also bid them to declare when they will leave their victim and indicate the signs by which their departure is to be known, threatening to increase their torture in proportion to the resistance they continue to offer. With this end in view he should redouble those imprecations which seem to irritate the evil spirits most, such as invocations of the Holy Name of Jesus and of Mary, signs of the Cross, and aspersions with holy water. He should force the person possessed to genuflect before the Blessed Sacrament or the Crucifix, or to revere some holy relic. He should be careful to avoid useless words, idle questions, and above all, attempts at humor. Should the evil spirit or spirits give sarcastic or ridiculous answers or speak at random, he must with authority and dignity impose silence.

1548. 4) He must not allow the witnesses, who should be few in number, [3] to ask any questions; they should rather be asked to maintain silence and recollection, and to pray in union with Him Who puts the demons to flight.

---

[1] LEHMKUHL, *Theol. Moralis*, t. II, n. 574, edition of 1910.

[2] Mark, IX, 28.

[3] "The attendants, who should be few in number, must be warned not to ask the possessed person any questions, but rather to humbly and earnestly pray to God for him." (*Rit.*, loc. cit). Perhaps it was because of the violation of this rule that the exorcisms at Loudun had to be carried on for so long a time and not without some unfortunate happenings.

5) The exorcist must not, in spite of the authority he wields, try to consign the devil to any special place; he must be content to expel the evil spirit, leaving his fate and destiny to Divine Justice. He should continue the exorcisms for several hours and even for several days, according to the nature of the case, allowing intervals of rest, until the devil departs, or at least until the evil spirit declares he is ready to leave.

6) When the deliverance has been thoroughly proved, the exorcist should beg God to forbid the devil ever to reënter the body he has just left; he should thank Him and invite the person thus freed to glorify God and to avoid all sin in the future so as not to fall again under the power of the Evil One.

Conclusion

1549. These extraordinary phenomena, whether divine or diabolical, show on the one hand the mercy and the goodness of God towards His privileged friends, to whom He imparts, along with intense sufferings, such as in the case of stigmatization, the most signal favors as a foretaste of the glory He will one day bestow upon them in heaven; and on the other hand, the jealousy and the hatred of the devil, who seeks to exercise his tyranny over men by tempting them in a most extraordinary way, by persecuting them when they resist and spread the Kingdom of God, and by torturing some of his victims through taking possession of them.

Thus, there are in the world the two Cities, so well described by St. Augustine, the two Camps and the two Standards mentioned by St. Ignatius. True Christians can not hesitate; the more completely they give themselves to God, the more surely do they escape the empire of Satan. If God permits them to be tried, it is only for their greater good. Even in the midst of their sufferings they can say in all confidence : " If God be for us, who is against us? [1]... Who is like unto God? "

---

[1] *Rom.*, VIII, 31.

CHAPTER IV

Controverted Questions [1]

1550. So far we have explained the doctrine commonly held by all Schools of spirituality, and our readers have no doubt been able to recognize that this teaching fully suffices to lead and raise souls to the highest degrees of perfection. God does not make growth in holiness dependent upon the solution of controverted questions. Now, however, we can afford to touch briefly upon the main points under discussion. This we shall do as *impartially* as possible, aiming not at making divergent opinions appear identical (which cannot be done), but at showing that the differences among the more moderate exponents of the various Schools are not as great as they may at first sight seem to be.

1551. Causes of these divergences. 1) The first cause, no doubt, is to be found in the very *difficulty* and *obscurity* of the matters at issue. It is not an easy task to look into the secret designs of God concerning the *universal call* of all baptized persons to infused contemplation, or to determine the very *nature* of that mysterious act wherein God is the principal agent and wherein the soul is more passive than active, receiving light and love without forfeiting its freedom. It is not surprising then, that writers striving to understand these wonders do not always offer the same explanations.

2) Another cause of the existing differences is the diversity of *method employed.* As we have said (n. 28), all Schools strive to combine the two methods, the *experimental* and the *deductive;* but, whilst some employ chiefly the former, others rely more on the latter. Hence the differences in the conclusions reached: the former, impressed by the *small number of contemplatives*, will say that not all are called to contemplation; the latter, seeing that we all possess a *supernatural organism* adequate for the attainment of contemplation, will conclude that if there are not many contemplatives, it is because there are not many generous souls ready to make the sacrifices demanded by contemplation.

---

[1] SAUDREAU, *L'Etat mystique*, ch. IX, XI, XIV et appendices; POULAIN, *Graces of Interior Prayer;* MGR. LEJEUNE, art. *Contemplation* in *Dict. de Théol.;* MGR. FARGES, *Phénom. mystiques* et *Controv. de la Presse;* JORET, *La Contemplation mystique;* GARRIGOU-LAGRANGE, *Perfect. et contemplation.*

1552. 3) This divergence of opinion is further accentuated by temperament, education and actual occupation. Some persons are better fitted for contemplation than others, and when this natural aptitude is further developed by education and occupation, or by manner of life, one is naturally inclined to think that contemplation is the normal thing. There are others of a more active disposition, whose temperament and occupation are rather obstacles to contemplation, and who are therefore readily led to believe that contemplation is an extraordinary state.

4) Moreover, it must not be forgotten that the philosophical and theological systems which one may have adopted concerning knowledge and love, efficacious and sufficient grace, make their influence felt in mystical theology. If, for instance, one admits with the Thomists that grace is *intrinsically efficacious*, one is more inclined to consider the passive state a continuation of the active state, since even in the latter one acts under efficacious motions of grace.

We should not be astonished at these divergent opinions in matters of so delicate a nature; we are free to choose the system which in our judgment has the more solid foundation.

The poi ts of present-day discussion may be reduced to these three : 1° the *nature* of infused contemplation; 2° the *universal call* thereto; 3° the *normal time* at which it begins.

§ I. Controversy regarding the nature of contemplation

1553. All admit that *infused* or *mystic* contemplation is a free gift of God, Who places us in the passive state and gives us a knowledge and a love of Himself which we have but to accept. But in what does this knowledge consist? It is evidently not identical with the knowledge which comes from the light of faith, for everyone admits that it is an *experimental* or *quasi-experimental* knowledge (n. 1394). But does this knowledge come *directly* and *immediately*, that is, without any intermediary, or *indirectly* and *mediately*, that is, through acquired or infused ideas? Two answers have been given to this question.

1554. 1° **The theory of immediate knowledge.** This theory, which claims the authority of Pseudo-Dionysius, of the School of St. Victor, and the Flemish School of Mysticism, maintains that infused contemplation is a *perception* or an *intuition* or a *direct vision of God*, although *obscure* and *vague*. Being *direct*, it differs from the ordinary knowledge given by faith, and being *obscure*, it differs from the Beatific Vision. There are slight differences in the various expositions of this theory.

Father Poulain, basing his explanation upon the theory of the *spiritual senses*, thinks that the contemplative soul *feels* directly the presence of God. " During the union, when it is not too exalted, we are like a man placed beside one of his friends, in complete darkness and silence. He does not *see* him, therefore; he does not *hear* him; he only *feels* that he is there by the sense of touch, because he holds his hand in his own. And so he continues to think and to love him. " [1]

1555. *Father Marechal*, having ascertained that mystics affirm the existence of an intellectual intuition of Code and of the Indivisible Trinity during moments of exalted contemplation, is of the opinion " that in high contemplation a new element is involved, distinct in quality from normal activities and from ordinary grace... the active, not symbolic, presentation of God to the soul, with its corresponding psychology : *the direct intuition of God by the soul.* " [2] This, he adds, does not seem strange if one admits (as he previously explains) that the intuition of being is, so to speak, the center of perspective in human psychology.

This theory is completed by *Father Picard.* [3] After explaining that from a *natural* point of view the *direct*, but *vague* and *obscure apprehension* or *intuition* of God is not impossible once one has demonstrated by the traditional proofs the fact of His existence, he applies this theory to mystic contemplation. That same God, Whose living presence makes itself felt in the depths of the soul " sometimes takes possession of it by focusing its cognitive faculties upon Himself in silence, in wonder and in peace; at other times by seizing upon its will and its affections... When this seizure of the soul is felt rather by the cognitive faculties, we have the prayer of recollection; when by the volitional and emotional faculties, we have the prayer of quiet. " The author then goes on to show that in proportion as God tightens His hold, as He takes a more absolute, a more exclusive and a more extensive control, the soul advances to the higher degrees of contemplation.

Father Picard concludes by saying that this theory *differs* vastly from *Ontologism*, for it affirms that the *notion of being* has its origin in the perception of finite being ; that it is analogous, and can be applied to God only after a demonstration of His existence. He rejects the theory that we see on earth all things in the essence of God. It is, he says, our own finite and imperfect intellect with the sole aid of its own finite and imperfect ideas and acts which perceives all the truths of which it has any knowledge. Moreover, he speaks of an intuition which is essentially vague and obscure.

1556. 2° **The theory of mediate knowledge.** The opinion *commonly accepted* is that the knowledge of the contemplative, howsoever perfect it may be, is *mediate* and at the same time *vague* and *obscure*, although it is *quasi-experimental*. In the first degrees of contemplation God

---

[1] *Graces of Interior Prayer*, C. VI, n. 16.
[2] *La Mystique chrétienne*, in *Rev. de Philosophie*, 1912, t. XXX, p. 478.
[3] *La saisie immédiate de Dieu dans les états mystiques*, 1923.

contents Himself with projecting His light, the light of the
Gifts, upon the ideas already possessed, either by attracting
attention to an idea in a way that is calculated to make a
deep impression, or by making the mind draw from two
premises some striking conclusion (n. 1390). In the higher
states, as in the ecstatic union, God *infuses new ideas* which
represent divine truths much more clearly and impressively
than do naturally acquired concepts. It is now that the
soul is *enraptured* at perceiving truths which it had never
known before. And since the soul lives these truths and
really relishes them, it acquires of them a *quasi-experimental
knowledge.* This knowledge is still within the realms of
faith, but it is much more *vivid* and above all much more
affectionate than ordinary knowledge, from which it is distinguished by the fact that it is God-given, and that the soul
receiving it receives both knowledge and love, and has only
to consent to the divine action which produces in it these
priceless gifts.

1557. We adopt this view, which we have already
exposed in the second chapter of this book. It seems to
preserve better the essential difference between contemplation and the Beatific Vision, the former remaining *mediate*
and *obscure*, " as through a glass in a dark manner, " the
latter being *direct* and *clear.* However, we are careful to
refrain from making charges of Ontologism against those
who maintain as probable the opinion of a direct intuition,
so long as they stress its vague and obscure character and
reject the basic principle of Ontologism by asserting that
the intellect does not reach God except through creatures. [1]

It is true that many mystics make use of bold expressions which at
first sight seem to imply that they are in direct contact with the Divine
Substance and that they see God; still, when we examine the context,
we find that these words must be understood of the *effects* produced in
the soul by the divine action. [2] Through the gift of wisdom one is
made to relish the love, the joy, the spiritual peace which God infuses
into the soul : hence the name of *divine delights* given by St. Teresa
to the prayer of quiet. Through the *divine touches*, mystics seem to
feel the very substance of their soul moved, so deep is the impression
produced by divine love. But the descriptions they give us of these

---

[1] Such an accusation would be particularly unjust with regard to those who like
MGR. FARGES, *(Mystical Phenomena*, and, *Réponses aux Controverses)* admit that
from its very first stages contemplation is effected through *infused ideas*, and who
call it direct simply because the impressed idea is not that *which is seen*, nor even
that *wherein one sees*, but that whereby or through which the *thing itself is seen.*
This opinion is subject to criticism, but it is not open to charges of Ontologism.

[2] In order to appreciate better this manner of speaking, one should read the
passages gathered together by Father POULAIN, *Graces of Interior Prayer*, C. V-VI,
as well as the interpretations of these passages given first by himself, and then in
quite a different sense by Father SAUDREAU, *L'État mystique*, Appendice II.

impressions can all be referred to the different effects of an ardent and generous love. It may be said therefore that if they use expressions which appear too strong, it is due to the inadequacy of human language for describing the effects of grace produced in their soul.

§ II. Universal call to contemplation

1558. It is not question here of the *individual* and *proximate* call to infused contemplation of which we spoke in number 1406. On this point every one accepts the doctrine of Tauler and of St. John of the Cross. What is meant is the *remotely sufficient* and *general* call; in other words, we ask whether *all souls in the state of grace are remotely and sufficiently called to infused contemplation.* Once more we meet with two very different answers which flow, to a great extent at least, from the different views held concerning contemplation.

1559. 1º **A universal call,** remote and sufficient, is today admitted with slight variations by a great number of writers belonging to different Religious Orders, such as the Dominicans, [1] the Benedictines, [2] the Franciscans, [3] the Carmelites, [4] the Jesuits, [5] the Eudists, [6] as well as by a number of secular priests. [7] Various Reviews, notably *la Vie Spirituelle*, have been published in order to defend and propagate this opinion. Father Garrigou-Lagrange vigorously expounds it when he strives to prove that the mystical life is the *normal development* of the interior life and that consequently all souls in the state of grace are called thereto. We give a brief summary of his arguments.

a) The *fundamental principle of the mystic life* is the very same as that of the ordinary, interior life, that is, sanctifying grace or the grace of the virtues and the gifts. These gifts increase with charity, and, once they have attained their full development, they act in us according to their supra-human mode of action and put us in the *passive* or *mystic* state. Hence, the principle of the interior life contains in germ the mystic life, which is here below the flowering, as it were, of the spiritual life.

1560. b) The purification of the soul as it advances in the interior life is not completed except through the *passive trials*. Now, these

---

[1] *Fathers Arintero, Garrigou-Lagrange, Joret, Janvier,* etc.
[2] *Dom Louismet, Dom Huyben,* etc. — [3] *Father Ludovic de Besse.*
[4] *Father Theodore of St. Joseph, Essai sur l'oraison selon l'école carmélitaine,* 1923. — Note his restrictions contained on, p. 128.
[5] *L. Peeters, Vers l'union divine par les Exercices de S. Ignace,* 1924.
[6] *Father Lamballe, La Contemplation.*
[7] *Father Saudreau, L'Ami du Clergé,* etc.

purifications or trials are of a mystical nature. Hence, the interior life cannot attain its full development in any other way than through the mystic life.

c) The *end* of the interior life is the same as that of the mystic life, that is, a perfect disposition for the reception of the light of glory immediately after death. " Now, the perfect disposition for the reception of the beatific vision immediately after death can be none other than the *intense charity* of a soul thoroughly purified and possessed of an *ardent desire of seeing God*, such as we find in the mystic union, and particularly in the transforming union. The latter is therefore the highest development here below of the life of grace. " [1]

1561. 2⁰ **Theory of a special and restricted call.** The foregoing arguments do not appear convincing to all, and a great number of spiritual writers belonging to the Society of Jesus, such as Cardinal Billot, Fathers Maumigny, Poulain, Bainvel, J. de Guibert, and to the Discalced Carmelites, such as Father Mary Joseph of the Sacred Heart, and others outside these two Schools of thought, such as Mgr. Lejeune and Mgr. Farges, think that acquired contemplation is a *free gift which is not bestowed upon all*, and which moreover is *not necessary for the attainment of sanctity*. Their arguments are these: [2]

a) The theory of a universal call is indeed constructed along superb theological lines, but all of the structure is not equally solid. It has *not been proved*, for instance, " that the seven gifts correspond to seven *distinct infused habits* and not to seven kinds of graces for the reception of which the intellect and the will are prepared by a single habit. Moreover, even were this demonstrated, one would still need to prove that the gifts of wisdom and understanding can function perfectly only during contemplation and not during the reception of enlightening graces which do not necessarily include this particular form of prayer. Such demonstration has never been made. [3]

Nor has it been proved that the gifts *always* act in a supra-human way. Cardinal Billot [4] thinks that they act in two ways, now in an *ordinary manner*, accommodating themselves to our human mode of action, now in an *extraordinary* way by producing in us infused contemplation.

1562. b) No doubt, the *passive trials* seem to be the more *potent means of purifying the soul*, since they make the soul pass through a veritable purgatory; but in this vale of tears, where the occasions for

---

[1] GARRIGOU-LAGRANGE, *op. cit.*, p. 450.
[2] These arguments are expounded by P. R. DE MAUMIGNY, *Practice of mental Prayer*, t. II, P. V; MGR. FARGES, *Mystical Phenomena*, P. I, C. IV; *Controv. de la Presse*, C. IV; J. DE GUIBERT, *Rev. d'Asc. et de Mystique*, Janv. 1924, p. 25-32.
[3] J. DE GUIBERT, *loc. cit.*, p. 26.
[4] *De Virtutibus infusis*, th. VIII.

suffering and mortification are so numerous, is it not possible to effect this purification by a sweet resignation to the will of God and by positive acts of mortification performed under the inspiration of the Holy Ghost and the guidance of a prudent director? Has it been demonstrated that the graces of contemplation are the *only choice graces* of God? Every one admits that there are persons who have not yet been raised to infused contemplation and who are more perfect than others whom God has freely brought thereto precisely in order to make them become holy (n. 1407). And since they are more perfect, they are by that fact more thoroughly purified. It may well be therefore, that at the moment of death their purification is complete.

c) It is indeed true that the end of the interior life as well as that of the mystic life is to prepare for the beatific vision, and that the transforming union is for certain souls the best preparation for it. But is this the *only* preparation? There are persons continuing in discursive and affective prayer who are models of heroic virtue, who are outwardly, and in the estimation of those who know them well, just as virtuous as some contemplatives, or even more so. Has it been shown conclusively that the gifts of the Holy Ghost have no part in the thousand ejaculatory prayers offered up by many persons while performing their daily occupations? Has it been proved that the said gifts exert no influence on the constant and supernatural performance of professional duties, which by the very fact that they are so constant, require heroic courage? And yet, when one questions these persons, one finds no signs of contemplation properly so-called. Must we not then admit that God, Who knows how to adapt His graces to the character, training and circumstances of each individual, does not lead all souls by the same way, and that although He demands of all a perfect docility to the inspirations of the Holy Ghost, He makes use of different means to sanctify them?

1563. 3° While weighing the arguments advanced by both sides of the controversy, it seems to us that the two opinions are not so far apart as they may appear.

A) Let us first of all examine the points on which the moderate exponents of either view agree:

a) There have been and there are contemplatives of *every temperament* and of *every condition of life;* still, in point of fact, there are temperaments and modes of life which *lend themselves better* to infused contemplation. The reason for this is that contemplation is a *free gift* bestowed by God when and on whom He pleases (n. 1387), and that moreover God is wont to adapt His graces to the temperament and the duties of state of each individual.

b) Contemplation is not sanctity, but only one of the most effective means of attaining it. Sanctity really consists in charity, in intimate and habitual union with God. Now, although contemplation is *in itself* the *highway* to this union, it is *not the only way.* There are indeed persons who are not contemplatives " who are more advanced in virtue, in true charity, than others who have already received infused contemplation. " [1]

c) We have all received in Baptism a *supernatural organism* (habitual grace, the virtues and the gifts) which, when it attains its full development, leads *normally* to contemplation in the sense that it imparts that *docility* which permits God to put us in the passive state *when He pleases* and *in the way He pleases*. But as a matter of fact, there are souls who through no fault of theirs never attain to contemplation here below. [2]

1564. B) Despite agreement upon these important points, there remain *divergences* which proceed, in our opinion, from tendencies more or less favorable to the mystical state and from the more or less extraordinary character attributed to that state. We shall in all modesty offer our solution in two assertions: a) Infused contemplation considered *in itself* is a normal development of the Christian life. b) *In point of fact*, however, not all souls in the state of grace seem to be called to such contemplation inclusive of the transforming union.

a) Infused contemplation when considered independently of the extraordinary mystical phenomena which attend it, is not of a miraculous or of an abnormal nature; it is simply the resultant of two causes: the *cultivation* of our supernatural organism, especially of the gifts of the Holy Ghost (n. 1355), and of a *special grace* which of itself has nothing of the miraculous about it. We said that the infusion of *new ideas* is not necessary for the first degrees of contemplation (n. 1390). We might even assert with the Carmelite Congress of Madrid that *in itself* contemplation is the most perfect state of union between the soul and God that can be had in this life, the highest ideal and, as it were, the last stage of the Christian life in this world *for souls called to mystic union with God*, the ordinary way of sanctity and of habitual heroic virtue. [3] This seems indeed to be the traditional teaching as found in the mystic writers from Clement of Alexandria to St. Francis de Sales.

---

[1] GARRIGOU-LAGRANGE, *op. cit.*, t. II, p. [78].

[2] " This may proceed not only from an unfavorable environment, but from a want of direction, as well as from *natural temperament*. On this point it is well to recall with J. Maritain that, according to many Thomists, such as Bannez, John of St. Thomas, the Carmelites of Salamanca, the very temperament of the Elect is in a sense an effect of predestination. " GARRIGOU-LAGRANGE, *op. cit.*, t. II, p. [75].

[3] *Carmelite Congress*, 1923, Theme V. — The Congress avoided pronouncing on the question of the *universal call* to contemplation, because, no doubt, it looked upon this matter as doubtful.

1565. **b)** However, *it does not necessarily follow from these premises that all souls in the state of grace* are truly called, even in a remote way, to the *transforming union.* Just as in heaven there are different degrees of glory, " for star differeth from star in glory, " [1] so there are on earth different degrees of sanctity to which souls are called. Now, God, Who is ever free in the distribution of His gifts, and Who knows how to adapt His action to the temperament, education and manner of life of each individual, can raise souls by divers ways to the heights of holiness to which He destines them.

To those who by their more active character and their more absorbing occupations seem to be made for action, He gives graces especially suited to the exercise of the *active* gifts. Such persons live in intimate, habitual union with God; at times they even multiply their ejaculatory prayers beyond what seems possible to human power. Above all else they perform out of love for God, and with heroic constancy and docility to the inspirations of grace, the thousand and one little duties of daily life. Thus, they reach the degree of sanctity to which God destines them, and this without the help (at least habitual) of infused contemplation. They are in the simple unitive way, such as we have described it (n. 1303 and foll.).

No doubt, one might say that such persons are *exceptions* and that the *normal* way to sanctity is contemplation. [2] Still, when such exceptions are *numerous*, must one not take account of them in the problem of a remote call, since temperament and duties of state are elements which aid in deciding the question of vocation?

At bottom, the agreement of these authors is more real than the difference of language would seem to indicate. Some, viewing the matter in an *abstract* and *formal* way, admit numerous exceptions to the universal call while maintaining the principle of its universality; others, taking a more *practical* view, prefer to say simply that the call is not universal albeit that contemplation is the normal development of the Christian life.

1566. **c)** The solution we propose is, it seems, *based* on *traditional teaching.* 1) On the one hand, well-nigh all the spiritual writers, from Clement of Alexandria to St. Francis de Sales, speak of contemplation as the normal consummation of the spiritual life. [3] 2) On the other hand, rather few

---

[1] *I. Cor.*, XV, 41. — [2] GARRIGOU-LAGRANGE, *op. cit.*, t. II, p. (71-79).
[3] Abundant documents can be found in the following works : HONORÉ DE STE MARIE, *Tradition des Pères et des auteurs ecclésiastiques sur la contemplation,*

of them explicitly examine the question of a universal call to contemplation. Those that do so have in mind most of the time choice souls living in contemplative communities, or at least, very fervent souls. When, therefore, they assert that all or nearly all can arrive at the fountain of living waters (contemplation), it is for the members of their communities that they speak, and not for all souls in the state of grace. Besides, from the seventeenth century on, from which time greater precision of language began to prevail in these matters, a great number of writers require for infused contemplation a *special call*, and many positively assert that one can arrive at sanctity without contemplation. [1]

The two questions are therefore not to be confounded, for one can admit that contemplation is the normal development of the spiritual life without affirming that all souls in the state of grace are called to the transforming union.

1567. Let us add that the attainment of sanctity and the direction of the souls tending thereto do not depend upon the solution of such a difficult problem. By insisting upon the cultivation of the gifts of the Holy Ghost as well as upon perfect detachment from self and from creatures, by gradually leading souls to the prayer of simplicity, by teaching them to listen to the voice of God and to follow His inspirations, one places them in the way that leads to contemplation; the rest belongs to God, Who alone can lay hold of these souls, and, according to St. Teresa's graceful metaphor, *place them in the nest*, that is to say, in the contemplative repose.

1568. With most authors we think that infused contemplation belongs to the unitive way. Of course, there are *exceptional* cases in which God raises less perfect souls to contemplation, precisely with the intent of perfecting them more effectively (n. 1407). This is not however what He ordinarily does.

Still, there are writers of note, such as Father Garrigou-Lagrange, who refer the *purification of the senses* and the

---

SAUDREAU, *La vie d'union à Dieu*, Ed. 3. 1921; GARRIGOU-LAGRANGE, *op. cit.*, t. II, p. 662-740; POURRAT, *Christian Spirituality*. However, a critico-historical study of these documents from the special point of view of the *universal* call to contemplation is still wanting.

[1] This seems to be the solution of DOM V. LEHODEY, *Ways of Mental Prayer*, P. III, C. XIII; *Le saint Abandon*, P. III, ch. XIV; of MGR WAFFELAERT, R. A. M., janv. 1923, p. 31, and in his various works; of the *Carmelite School*, and of those writers who admit a state of *acquired* contemplation, no matter how brief. It is similar to the solution given by P. M. DE LA TAILLE, *L'oraison contemplative*, as well as to that proposed by M. J. MARITAIN, *Vie Spirituelle*, mars 1923, and appearing in the work of GARRIGOU-LAGRANGE, t. II, p. (58-71).

prayer of quiet to the illuminative way. They take their stand on the authority of St. John of the Cross, who in the Dark Night writes : " The night of sense is common, and the lot of many : these are the beginners... [1] The soul began to *set out* on the way of the spirit, the way of *proficients*, which is also called the *illuminative way*, or the way of *infused contemplation*, wherein God Himself teaches and refreshes the soul." [2] We have been for a long time acquainted with this text, but like H. Hoornaert, [3] who has translated the works of the great mystic, we find in it quite a different meaning. In his various works, St. John of the Cross speaks only of infused contemplation ; now, as regards this contemplation there are beginners, proficients and perfect souls : for him, the *beginners* are those who are about to enter into the *passive purification of the senses :* this is why he speaks of them from the very first chapter of the Dark Night. By the *proficients* he means those who have entered upon infused contemplation, *quietude* and *full union*. The *perfect* are those who have gone through the night of the spirit and are in the ecstatic or in the transforming union. This is an altogether different point of view.

1569. Furthermore, since we are writing a text-book, it is important to bring together and compare all that relates to the various kinds of contemplation, in order to bring out more clearly its nature and divers degrees. This is why we thought we should keep to the plan commonly followed. But we hasten to add that God, Whose ways are as *manifold* as they are *wonderful*, does not always follow the *logical lines* we strive to trace. It is therefore important that the spiritual director follow and not anticipate the motions of divine grace.

1570. Hence, we conclude with these words of *L'Ami du Clergé :* " What is so energetically discussed in theory does not prevent certitude regarding a goodly number of essential practical rules... In order to profit by the medicinal qualities of a plant, it is not absolutely necessary to know its history and nomenclature. The same may be said of contemplation : there is no agreement concerning its definition or its place in theological classifications... Without waiting for technical and theoretical conclusions, directors are quite able to distinguish the goal towards which generous and predestined souls turn their steps, and to help them reach it. " [4]

---

[1] *Dark Night*, Bk. I, C. VIII. — [2] *Ibid*., C. XIV.
[3] Note sur la *Nuit obscure*, p. 5-6. — [4] 8 dec. 1921, p. 697.

Conclusion of book iii: spiritual Direction
of contemplatives

In several places of this book we have laid down rules for the direction of contemplatives; however, it may be well to give a resume of them here and to point out what course the spiritual director should follow in order to *prepare* souls for contemplation, to *guide* them through its dangers, and to *lift them up* if they falter in the way.

1571. 1º It is the duty of the director, if he has in his care *generous* souls, to prepare them little by little for the unitive way and for contemplation. He must avoid two extremes : that of urging *indiscriminately* and too hastily all fervent souls to contemplation, and that of not being concerned at all about this matter.

1572. A) In order to avoid the first mistake, **a)** the spiritual director should remember that one cannot ordinarily aim at contemplation until one has for a long time exercised oneself in prayer and in the practice of the Christian virtues of purity of heart, detachment from self and from creatures, humility, obedience, conformity to the Will of God, the spirit of faith, of trust and of love.

He should call to mind the teaching of St. Bernard : [1] If among the monks there are any contemplatives, they are not the novices in virtue, who but erstwhile dead to sin, labour in tears and in the dread of judgment in order to heal their as yet fresh wounds. They are rather those who after a long co-operation with grace have made solid progress in virtue, who need no longer revolve again and again in their minds the sorrowful picture of their sins, but, on the contrary, find their delight in meditating day and night and in keeping the law of God.

b) Should the director notice that the desire of contemplation is *excessive* and even *presumptuous*, he must seek to restrain it, recalling that no one can force his way into contemplation, and that moreover the joys of prayer generally come only after bitter trials.

c) He must carefully guard against mistaking the *sensible consolations* of beginners, or even the *spiritual* ones of advanced souls for the *divine delights* (n. 1439), and he should wait, before passing judgment on the entrance of a soul into the passive state, for the three distinct signs which we indicated in numbers 1413-1416.

1573. B) In order to avoid the second error, he should remember that God, ever prodigal of His gifts, gives Himself generously to fervent and docile souls.

a) Without speaking explicitly about contemplation, he should exercise these good souls not only in virtue, but also

---

[1] *In Cantica* sermo LVII, n. 11. We have given a summary of his thought.

in devotion to the Holy Ghost. He should frequently speak to them of the indwelling of that Divine Spirit in the human soul, of the duty of thinking often of Him, of adoring Him, of obeying His inspirations, of cultivating His gifts.

b) He must teach them to make their prayer more and more affective, to prolong the acts of religion, of love, of self-offering, of self-abandonment to the Will of God, and to repeat these acts frequently during the course of the day by a simple elevation of the heart without in any way neglecting duties of state or the exercise of virtue. When he notices that they are inclined to remain in silence in the presence of God in order to listen to Him and to do His bidding, he must encourage them by extolling this practice as excellent and exceedingly fruitful.

1574. 2° Once the soul has entered into the mystic ways, the director will need the greatest prudence in order to be a faithful guide amidst the *aridities* and the *divine delights*.

A) He must lend his help during the *passive trials* so that the soul may be able to fight off discouragement and the other temptations of which we spoke in numbers 1432-1434.

B) In sweet contemplation, the soul may be exposed to *spiritual gluttony* and to *vain-complacency*.

a) In order to avoid the first of these defects, it is important ever to remember that we must love the God of consolations rather than the consolations of God, that consolations are only a *means* to unite us to Him, and that we must be ready to renounce them completely the moment it pleases God to withdraw them : *God alone sufficeth.*

b) Sometimes God Himself undertakes to curb the impulses of pride by vividly impressing upon the soul a sense of its nothingness and its miseries, and by showing clearly that His favors are *pure gifts* in which we can in no way glory. As long as souls have not been completely purified through the night of the spirit, they need, as St. Teresa says, to be exercised in humility and in conformity to the Will of God (n. 1447, 1474). Above all, they must be warned against the desire of visions, revelations and other extraordinary phenomena. We are *never* permitted to desire these, and the Saints went so far as to repel them by acts of humility (n. 1496).

1575. C) We must not forget that ecstasy is but an illusion if, to use the expression of St. Francis de Sales, it is unrelated to ecstatic manner of life, that is to say, to the practice of heroic virtue (n. 1461). It would be a serious mistake to neglect our duties of state in order to give more time to contemplation. Father Balthazar Alvarez, confessor to St. Teresa, distinctly declared that one must relinquish contemplation in order to fulfil one's duties or to minister to the neighbor's needs, and that God bestows upon him who thus learns to mortify himself more light and more love in one hour of prayer than He gives to others during several hours. [1]

1576. **D)** It would be a still greater mistake to imagine that contemplation confers the privilege of *impeccability*. History shows that false mystics, like the Beghards and the Quietists, who thought themselves impeccable, fell into the grossest vices. St. Teresa insists constantly upon the necessity of watchfulness in order to avoid sin, even after the highest degrees of contemplation have been reached, and St. Philip Neri was used to say : " My God, beware of Philip, or he will betray Thee. " Indeed we can not persevere for long without a special grace, and this grace is given to the humble who know how to distrust themselves and to place all their confidence in God.

1577. 3° We must therefore realize that contemplative souls can fall into sin. Such falls may come from several causes :

a) The soul may have been raised to contemplation before it had sufficiently mastered its passions. Instead of courageously keeping up the fight, it lulled itself to sleep in the sweetness of repose. Then violent temptations arose, and the soul, trusting overmuch in its own strength, fell a victim to sin. The means of restoration are *compunction of heart*, return to God with a contrite and humbled heart, and long and laborious penance. The greater the heights from which one has fallen, the more humble and constant must be the efforts to take up the long and arduous climb once more. It is the office of the director to drive home this truth with kindness but also with firmness.

b) There are contemplatives who fought valiantly and successfully to bring their evil tendencies into subjection. But imagining that the struggle was over, they relaxed their efforts and became less generous in fulfilling certain duties which they looked upon as less important. Indifference gradually set in and finally begot lukewarmness. Now, the director must check this downward movement by reminding them that the more generous God has been with them, the more they must increase their fervor, that the least negligence on the part of God's friends hurts to the quick Him Who bestows His favors so freely upon them. One should read St. Margaret Mary's autobiography in which she relates the severe reproaches Our Lord addressed to her in order to correct her smallest infidelities, her lack of respect and attention during the Office and during mental prayer, her lack of uprightness and purity of intention, her vain curiosity, her least failings in obedience, even when these latter were due to an attempt to increase her austerities. This reading should move the director to work energetically for the return of such souls to fervor.

1578. **c)** Other souls expected to find only sweetness and divine delights in contemplation, once the first passive trials were over. But in reality God continues to send them

---

[1] *Vie* by P. Dupont, ch. XIII, ch. XLI, 5ᵉ difficulté.

alternately desolation and consolation, so as to sanctify them all the more effectively. They give way to discouragement and thus lay themselves open to laxity and its consequences. The director should teach them to apply the great remedy, *love for the Cross.* Not that the Cross is in itself lovable, but because it renders us more conformable to Jesus Crucified.

The sainted Curé of Ars used to say : "The cross is the gift which God makes to His friends. The love of crosses must be asked for. Then they become sweet. I have tried it... O, I had plenty of crosses; I almost had more than I could bear! I began to ask for a love of crosses; then I became happy... Truly, there is no happiness except there." [1]

One word may sum up the duty of the spiritual director towards contemplatives : to study the works and the biographies of the mystics, and to beg for the gift of counsel, so as never to address these souls without having previously consulted the Holy Ghost.

EPILOGUE :
THE THREE WAYS AND THE LITURGICAL CYCLE [2]

1579. After taking a survey of the Three Ways, or the three stages, which lead to perfection, it will not be without profit to see how each year Holy Mother the Church invites us through her *liturgy* to start anew and to perfect the work of our sanctification with its three degrees of *purification, illumination and union with God.* The spiritual life is in truth a continuous·series of *new beginnings*, and the *liturgical cycle* comes each year to inspire us to new efforts.

Everything in the liturgy conters about the **Incarnate Word,** our Mediator and Redeemer, presented to us not only as a model for imitation, but also as the Head of a mystical body, Who comes to live in His members in order to enable them to practise the virtues of which He has given them the example. Each festival, each liturgical period recalls to us some one or other of the virtues of Jesus and brings to us the graces which He has merited and which enable us with His co-operation to reproduce these virtues in ourselves.

1580. The liturgical year, which corresponds to the four seasons of the year, also symbolizes the four main phases of

---

[1] MONNIN, *The Curé of Ars*, Bk. III, c. III.
[2] DOM. GUÉRANGER, *The Liturgical Year;* DOM LEDUC and DOM BAUDOT, *Catéchisme Liturgique;* DOM FESTUGIÈRE, *La Liturgie Catholique;* F. CAVALLERA, *Ascéticisme et Liturgie.*

the spiritual life. [1] *Advent* corresponds to the *purgative way; Christmastide* and *Epiphany* to the *illuminative way* wherein we follow Jesus by the imitation of His virtues; the period of *Septuagesima* and the season of *Lent* bring about a *second purification of the soul* more thorough than the first; *Paschal* time typifies the *unitive way*, the union with the Risen Christ, a union perfected by the Ascension and the Descent of the Holy Ghost. We add a brief explanation of this liturgical year.

1581. 1° **Advent**, which signifies a coming, is a preparation for the coming of the Savior, and as such is a period of *purification* and *penance*.

The Church invites us to meditate upon the threefold coming of Christ : His advent upon earth through the Incarnation, His entrance into the souls of men through grace, and His appearance at the end of time to judge all mankind. It is chiefly upon the first coming that the Church centers our attention : she recalls to us the longings of the Patriarchs and the Prophets, in order to make us long with them for the coming of the promised Redeemer and the establishment or strengthening of His Kingdom in our souls. This is, then, a time of *holy desires* and ardent supplications, a time when we ask God to pour down upon us the dew of grace, and above all, the Redeemer Himself : "Drop down dew, ye heavens, from above, and let the clouds rain the just!" This prayer takes on the character of still more earnest longing in the great antiphones, *O Emmanuel*, King of Glory, etc... which, by recalling the glorious titles given by the Prophets to the Messias and the chief characteristics of His mission, make us yearn for the coming of Him Who alone can relieve our misery.

1582. But Advent is also a season of *penance*. It is then that the Church reminds us of the Last Judgment for which we must make ready by the expiation of our sins : the preaching of St. John the Baptist invites us to do penance and thus to prepare the way for the Savior : "Prepare ye the way of the Lord, make straight his paths." [2] Formerly, Christians fasted three days a week, a practice still kept up by some Religious Orders, and if the Church no longer holds her children to this fast, she urges them to make up for it by other practices of mortification. In order to remind us of our duty of penance, she has her priests celebrate the Masses of Advent in violet vestments, the color of mourning.

These holy desires and penitential practices evidently tend to purify the soul and thus prepare it for the reign of Christ.

1583. 2° **Christmastide.** The Word appears in the weakness of our flesh, with the charms of childhood, but also with its helplessness. He invites us to open our hearts to Him that He may reign therein as our King and enable us

---

[1] Although but three ways are distinguished in the spiritual life, there is such a great difference between the *passive purifications* and *sweet contemplation*, that a division within the unitive way into two stages is quite justified.

[2] *Luke*, III, 4.

to share in His dispositions and His virtues. This is the beginning of the *illuminative way*. Purified of our faults and separated from sin and its causes, we unite ourselves more and more closely to Jesus in order to share in His abasement, in His virtues of *humility, obedience* and *poverty*, which He practised from the very first moment of His birth. He comes to redeem the world; but, who is there to welcome Him? None but a few shepherds and the three Wise Men from the East come to offer Him their homage. The Jews, His Chosen People, refuse to receive Him : " He came unto his own,and his own received him not." [1]   He is forced to flee into the land of Egypt. Returning, He buries Himself in a small Galilean village and there He remains for thirty years, growing in wisdom and knowledge as well as in age, performing the manual labor of a simple tradesman, and being in all things subject to Mary and Joseph. Such is the vision which the Liturgy brings before us during the season of Christmas and Epiphany in order to present us with the examples we are to imitate. At the same time, it invites us to *adore* profoundly the Infant-God Who abases Himself for us, and it bids us offer our *thanks* and our *love* to " Him Who has loved us so much."

1584.   3° But before we can taste the joys of divine union, a *new purification* more painful and far-reaching than the former is required. This purification is to take place during the seasons of **Septuagesima** and **Lent**.

Septuagesima is a prelude, as it were, to Lent. The Church, placing before us in the Bible-lessons of the Divine Office the fall of man and the sins which followed in its wake, the deluge which came as a punishment for these sins, and the holy lives of the Patriarchs which were to expiate them, urges us to consider in the bitterness of our soul all our personal sins, to detest them sincerely and to expiate them through a whole-hearted penance. The means which the Church proposes towards this end are : 1) *work*, or the faithful accomplishment of all our duties of state for the love of God : "Go you also into my vineyard; " [2] 2) *struggle against the passions :* in the Epistle of the Mass the Church compares us to athletes taking part in a race or a wrestling contest in order to win the prize, and she urges us to chastise our body even as these men do in order to bring it into subjection; 3) *voluntary acceptance of sufferings and trials*, our just punishment, together with a *humble prayer*

---

[1] *John*, I, 11. — [2] *Matth.*, XX, 4.

that we may profit thereby : " The sorrows of death encompassed me... and in my affliction I called upon the Lord. " [1]

1585. *Lent* offers us some additional means whereby to
purify our hearts still more and to triumph over temptation :
fasting, abstinence and almsgiving. We shall use these
means in *union with Jesus,* Who for forty days withdrew
into the desert, there to do penance in our stead, and Who
consented to be tempted in order to teach us how to overcome Satan. The Preface of the Mass will remind us that
fasting curbs our evil tendencies, elevates our heart to God
and obtains for us an increase of virtue and of merit.

The scene on Mount Thabor described in the Gospel for the Second
Sunday of Lent will show us that penance has its joys, once we have
learned to perform it in a spirit of prayer, and to raise up our eyes to
God in search of help : " My eyes are towards the Lord, for he shall
pluck my feet out of the snare. " [2] The Introit for the Fourth Sunday,
" Rejoice, O Jerusalem, " will sustain our courage by enabling us to
discern the joys of heaven, joys of which Holy Communion, symbolized
by the multiplication of the loaves, gives us a foretaste.

1586. On Passion Sunday the standard of the Cross is
raised : " Abroad the Royal Banners fly. " It is the Cross
alone that appears, for the image of the Savior is veiled as
a sign of mourning and sorrow, in order to remind us that
moments will come when we must suffer without consolations. But the Epistle of the day will bring us comfort by
showing us our High priest, Who by the shedding of His
blood enters into the Holy of Holies, and by telling us again
that the Cross, the symbol of death, has become a source of
life : " That whence came death, thence also life might
arise. " [3]

Palm Sunday, soon to be followed by the sorrowful
mysteries, will teach us how ephemeral are earthly triumphs,
and how the deepest humiliations follow close upon them.
Then out of the depths of a soul in anguish will rise the
cry : " My God, my God, look upon me : why hast thou
forsaken me? " [4] It is the cry of Jesus in the Garden of
Olives and on Calvary. It is the cry of the Christian soul
when visited by interior sufferings or exposed to calumny.
The Epistle however will bring us consolation by urging us
to make our own the interior sentiments of Jesus obedient
unto death, even the death of the Cross, but soon after
rewarded by such an exaltation that every knee bends before
Him. If therefore we share in His suffering, we shall

---

[1] *Introit*, Septuagesima Sunday. — [2] *Introit*, Third Sunday of Lent.
[3] *Preface* of the Cross. — [4] *Introit*, Palm Sunday.

likewise share in His victory : " Yet so if we suffer with him, that we may be also glorified with him." [1]

1587. 4º The Feast of the **Resurrection** and the season of **Easter** recall to us Christ's glorious *risen life*, the model of the *unitive* way. This life is heavenly rather than earthly. During the time of His ministry Our Lord dwelt constantly upon earth; He labored, conversed with men and exercised His apostolate. After His resurrection He lives more than ever apart from external things, appearing but rarely to His Apostles to give them His last instructions, and then He returns to His Father : " Appearing to them and speaking of the kingdom of God." [2]

This is the model for souls in the unitive way, henceforth seeking solitude in order to converse intimately with God. If their duties of state oblige them to deal with others, they do so with the hope of sanctifying them. They strive in all things to approach the ideal of Christ described by St. Paul : " Therefore, if you be risen with Christ, seek the things that are above, where Christ is sitting at the right hand of God. Mind the things that are above, not the things that are upon earth. For you are dead : and your life is hid with Christ in God." [3]

The *Ascension* symbolizes a still higher degree of union with God. Henceforth Jesus lives in heavenly places, at the right hand of the Father, making intercession for us without ceasing. His apostolate becomes only the more fruitful, because He sends His Holy Spirit, the Sanctifier, Who transforms the Apostles, and through them, millions of souls. In like manner contemplatives who in heart and mind already live in heaven, do not cease to pray and to sacrifice themselves for the salvation of their brethren, and thus their apostolate becomes all the more fruitful.

1588. *Pentecost* symbolizes the descent of the Holy Ghost upon individual souls in order to work in a more gradual and hidden manner the wondrous internal transformation which He wrought in the Apostles. The Mystery of the *Holy Trinity* comes to place before our eyes the grand object of our faith and of our religion, the efficient and exemplary cause of our sanctification. The feasts of *Corpus Christi* and of the *Sacred Heart* tell us once more that Our Lord, Who in the Holy Eucharist manifests the riches of His Sacred Heart, has a strict right to our adoration and our love, and that He is at the same time the great Worshipper of the Father through Whom and in Whom we can render due homage to the Most Adorable Trinity.

The various Sundays which follow upon Pentecost represent the full development of the work of the Holy Ghost, not only in the Church of God, but also in every Christian soul, and they invite us to produce under the action of this Holy Spirit abundant fruits of salvation, even

---

[1] *Romans*, VIII, 17. — [2] *Acts*, I, 3. — [3] *Coloss.*, III, 1-3.

until the day when we shall go to heaven to join with Him Who has gone before us to prepare a place for us.

1589. Within this liturgical cycle occur the *feasts of the Saints*. The examples of these persons, members of Christ like ourselves, who reproduced His virtues in spite of all kinds of temptations and obstacles, serve as a powerful stimulus. We hear them saying to us with St. Paul: " Be ye followers of me, as I also am of Christ; " [1] and while reading in the Breviary the story of their heroic virtues, we repeat to ourselves the words of St. Augustine: " Could you not also do what these men and women have done? "

It is above all from the feasts of Our Lady that we draw inspiration, from that Queen of the Angels and the Saints, from that Mother of the world's Savior, who is constantly associated with her Son in the Liturgy of the Church, the Son whom we cannot honor without at the same time honoring, loving and imitating His Blessed Mother.

Thus, sustained and helped by the Blessed Virgin and the Saints, and incorporated into the Word Made flesh, we draw nearer to God while we follow the liturgical cycle each succeeding year.

1590. But in order to profit well by the abundant means of sanctification which the Church offers us, we must draw unto ourselves the *interior dispositions of Jesus*. To accomplish this end we can avail ourselves of the beautiful and highly efficacious prayer, " *O Jesus Living in Mary.* " We cannot bring this compendium to a close in a more fitting manner than by giving a brief explanation of this prayer.

PRAYER : *TO JESUS LIVING IN MARY* [2]

O Jesu vivens in Maria	O Jesus living in Mary,
veni et vive in famulis tuis,	come and live in Thy servants,
in spiritu sanctitatis tuæ,	in the spirit of Thy holiness,
in plenitudine virtutis tuæ,	in the fulness of Thy power,
in perfectione viarum tuarum,	in the perfection of Thy ways,
in veritate virtutum tuarum,	in the truth of Thy virtues,
in communione mysteriorum tuo-rum ;	in the fellowship of Thy myste-ries,
dominare omni adversæ potestati,	rule Thou over every adverse power,
in Spiritu tuo ad gloriam Patris.	in Thy Spirit, for the glory of the Father.

---

[1] *I. Cor.*, IV, 16.

[2] This prayer, composed by FATHER DE CONDREN and completed by FATHER OLIER, is recited daily at the end of meditation in all Sulpician Seminaries. The VEN. FATHER LIBERMANN has written a pious commentary on it. cf. *Lettres*, t. II, p. 506-522.

The prayer is obviously made up of three parts of unequal length: the first part indicates the *person addressed;* the second, the *object* of the prayer; the third, the *final aim* of the prayer.

1591. 1° The **Person addressed** is *Jesus,* living in Mary, that is to say, the Incarnate Word, the God-Man, Who in the oneness of His Person possesses at once the divine and the human natures and Who is the *meritorious,* the *exemplary* and the *vital cause* of our sanctification (n. 132). We address ourselves to Him as *living in Mary.* For nine months He dwelt *physically* in her virginal womb : our prayer does not allude to this indwelling in Mary which ended with Our Savior's birth. He also lived in Mary *sacramentally* through Holy Communion, but this sacramental presence came to an end with Mary's last Communion on earth. He lived, and still lives in her *mystically,* as the Head of a mystical body of which all Christians are indeed members, but Mary the most exalted of all, since she occupies the place of honor in that body (n. 155-162). He lives in Mary through *His Divine Spirit,* that is to say, through the Holy Ghost, Whom He imparts to His Holy Mother in order that this Spirit may produce in her dispositions similar to those which He wrought in His own holy soul. By virtue of the merits and prayers of the Savior, the Holy Ghost comes then to sanctify and glorify Mary, to make her more and more like Jesus until she becomes the *most perfect living image of Christ.*

Father Olier [1] explains this well : " What Our Lord is to the Church, that He is preëminently to His Holy Mother. Thus He constitutes her interior and divine plenitude of grace, and as He sacrificed Himself more particularly for her than for the whole Church, He imparts to her God's life more abundantly than to the entire Church. This He does from a sense of gratitude, in return for the life which He received from her; for just as He promised to render to all His members a hundred-fold for what they give Him here on earth, so He wills to render to His Mother a hundredfold for that human life which He received from her love and devotion. This hundredfold is the Divine Life of infinite value... We must then regard Jesus as Our All, living in the Most Blessed Virgin in the plenitude of Divine Life, of that Life which He received from the Father, and of that other life which He acquired and merited for men through the mediation of His Mother. It is in her that we must see all the treasures of His riches, the glory of His beauty and the bliss of the Divine Life... There He dwells in all His fulness; there He works with all the power of His Divine Spirit; He is but one heart, one soul, one life with her." [2]

1592. Jesus lives *fully* in Mary in order to sanctify not only her, but through her, the other members of His mysti-

---

[1] Lettre CCCLXXXIII, t. II, p. 468, ed. 1885.
[2] OLIER, *Journée chrét.,* p. 395-396.

cal body. She is, as St. Bernard says, the aqueduct through which all the graces merited by her Son reach us : " He willed us to have all things through Mary. " It is therefore most pleasing to Jesus and most profitable to our soul that we address ourselves to Jesus living in Mary.

1593. 2º **The object of this prayer** is the *interior life* with all its constituent elements, which is nothing less than a participation in that life which Jesus communicates to His Mother and which we beg Him to deign to communicate to us as well.

A) Since Jesus living in Mary is the *source of this life*, we humbly beg Him to *come and live in us*, and we promise Him to submit in all docility to His influence: COME AND LIVE IN THY SERVANTS.

a) He comes to us as He comes to Mary, *through His Divine Spirit* through *habitual grace*. Every time sanctifying grace is increased, the Spirit of Jesus likewise grows in our soul, and consequently each time we perform a supernatural, meritorious act, this Divine Spirit comes to us and makes our soul still more like the soul of Jesus and that of Mary. What a powerful motive for multiplying and inten- sifying our meritorious actions by animating them with divine love!

b) He acts in us through *actual grace* which He merited for us and which He imparts to us through His Divine Spirit: " He worketh in us both to will and to accomplish. "[1] He becomes the mainspring of our interior movements, of our interior dispositions, so much so that our acts proceed only from Jesus communicating to us His Own Life, His sentiments, His affections, His desires. Then we can say with St. Paul : " I live, now not I, but Christ liveth in me. "[2]

c) That this be so, we must let ourselves be led by Him as *faithful servants* and we must co-operate with His grace. Like the humble Virgin we must say in all sincerity : " Behold the servant of the Lord, be it done unto me according to thy word. " Conscious of our misery and our helplessness, we must obey promptly the least inspira- tions of His grace. This means for us honorable servitude, for to serve Him is to reign. It means a service of love that subjects us to Him Who is indeed Our Master, but also Our Father, Our Friend, and Who commands nothing that is not profitable to our own soul. Let us then open our hearts to Christ Jesus and to His Divine Spirit that He may reign therein as He reigned in the heart of His Blessed Mother!

1594. **B**) Because Jesus is the *source of all holiness*, we ask Him to live and to act in us, in order that He may commu- nicate to us His Own sanctity : **In the spirit of thy holiness.**

There is in Him a twofold holiness : *substantial* holiness which flows from the hypostatic union, and *participated* holiness which is nothing else but created grace (n. 105). It is this latter holiness that we beg Him to communicate to us. It consists first of all in a *horror of sin* and in the severance from whatever may lead thereto, in a thorough

---

[1] *Philip.*, II, 13. — [2] *Galat.*, II, 20.

detachment from creatures and from all self-seeking; but it consists also in a participation in the Divine Life; in an *intimate union* with the Three Divine Persons; in a love for God which controls every other affection; in a word, in positive sanctity.

1595. Since we are unable to acquire such an exalted sanctity through our own efforts, we beg Him to come to us **in the fulness of his power.** Nay, since we fear lest we turn traitors to God, we pray with the Church that He "deign to subject to His sway our rebellious faculties."

It is an *efficacious grace* therefore that we beg for, which, while it respects our liberty, knows how to touch the secret springs of the will and to procure its free consent; a grace which is not rendered powerless by our instinctive repugnance or our irrational opposition, but which sweetly and firmly works in us to will and to accomplish.

1596. C) Since holiness cannot be attained without the *imitation of Our Divine Model*, we beg Him to make us walk **in the perfection of his ways,** that is to say, to make us able to imitate His conduct, His exterior and interior actions, in all their perfection. In other words, we ask to become living images of Jesus, other Christs, that like St. Paul we may be able to say to those who would learn of us: "Be ye followers of me, as I also am of Christ." So perfect is this ideal that, of ourselves, we can not realize it. But Jesus becomes our way: "I am the way," a shining and living way, a moving way, so to speak, which draws us in its wake: "And I, if I be lifted up from the earth, will draw all things to myself."[1] We shall willingly allow ourselves to be drawn by Thee, O Divine Model, and we shall strive to reproduce Thy virtues!

1597. D) Hence we add: **in the truth of thy virtues.** The virtues we ask for are real virtues. There are persons who, under a veneer of exterior righteousness, conceal a pagan pride and sensuality. External manners do not constitute holiness. What Jesus comes to bring us therefore are interior virtues, *crucifying* virtues: humility, poverty, mortification, perfect chastity of mind, heart and body; and *unifying* virtues: the spirit of faith, of confidence and of love. This is what makes the Christian and this is what transforms him into another Christ.

1598. E) Jesus practised all these virtues especially in His mysteries, and on this account we pray Him to make us partake in the grace of His mysteries: **in the fellowship of thy mysteries.** No doubt, all the principal actions of Our Lord are called mysteries, but more especially those

---

[1] *John.*, XII, 32.

six great mysteries described by Father Olier in his Christian Catechism : the Incarnation, which invites us to put off all self-love in order to consecrate ourselves entirely to the Father in union with Jesus : " Behold I come to do thy will, O God;" the Crucifixion, Death and Burial, which express so many degrees of that total immolation of self by which we crucify our disordered nature and seek to put off and bury our evil inclinations; the Resurrection and the Ascension, which are the symbols of a perfect detachment from creatures and of the altogether heavenly life which we desire to lead in order to reach heaven.

1599. F) We can not assuredly attain such perfection unless Jesus comes to vanquish our *powerful enemies*, the world, the flesh and the devil : **to rule over every adverse power.** These three enemies will never cease their bitter onslaughts, nor will they be completely annihilated as long as we live upon this earth. But Jesus, Who triumphed over them, can thwart them and subjugate them by giving us efficacious graces wherewith to resist their attacks. It is this for which we humbly pray.

3º Lastly, in order to obtain this grace more readily, we proclaim that with Him we have but *one end* in view, to procure the glory of the Father under the action of the Holy Ghost : **by thy spirit unto the glory of the Father.** Since He is come to earth to seek His Father's glory, " I glorify the Father, " we beg Him to fulfil His work in us and to impart to us His own interior holiness, so that with Him and through Him we may be enabled to give glory to that same Father, and that we may have Him glorified by those about us. Then shall we be truly members of His mystical body, true worshippers of God, and He will live and reign in our hearts for the greater glory of the Most Adorable Trinity.

This prayer therefore constitutes a synthesis of the spiritual life and a summary of our Compendium.

In bringing our work to a close, we cannot but bless, and invite our readers to bless with us, that God of love, that loving Father, Who in making us partakers of His Own Life, has filled us with all manner of blessings in His Son.

BLESSED BE THE GOD AND FATHER OF OUR LORD JESUS CHRIST, WHO HATH BLESSED US WITH SPIRITUAL BLESSINGS IN HEAVENLY PLACES, IN CHRIST.

THE END.

APPENDICES

I. *The spirituality of the New Testament* [1]

In order to help our readers to understand better and to systematize the spiritual treasures found in the New Testament, we shall give a short synthesis of the spirituality of the *Synoptics*, of *St. Paul* and of *St. John.*

1° THE SPIRITUALITY OF THE SYNOPTICS

The central idea of Christ's teaching as recorded by the Synoptics is that of the *Kingdom of God.* In order that we may see the spirituality implied in this idea, we shall explain the *nature* and the *constitution* of this kingdom together with the *conditions of admission.*

A) Its nature. The kingdom of God preached by Our Lord is not an earthly one, but, contrary to the prejudices of the Jews, a spiritual kingdom opposed to that of Satan and his rebel angels. **a)** It is presented under a threefold form : 1) At times it is the Kingdom of Heaven or the place reserved for the Elect : " Come, ye blessed of my Father, possess you the kingdom prepared for you from the foundation of the world. " [2] 2) At other times it is the *interior* kingdom as already established upon earth, that is to say, grace, friendship, sonship bestowed by God and received by men of good-will. 3) Lastly, it is the *external* kingdom which God establishes in order to perpetuate His work in the world. [3] **b)** These three forms constitute but one and the same kingdom ; for the visible Church was founded only to enable the interior kingdom to expand peacefully, and the latter is, so to speak, the sum-total of the conditions that open to us the kingdom of heaven.

B) Its constitution. This interior kingdom has a King, Who is none other than God Himself. [4] Now, this God is the *Father* of His subjects, not merely collectively as in the Old Dispensation, but of each individual in particular. His goodness is so great that it embraces even evil-doers [5] as long as they live upon earth ; still, His justice is visited upon hardened sinners, for they shall be cast into hell. [6]

This kingdom was established upon earth by Jesus Christ, the Son of God and the Son of man, Who is also our King by *right of birth,* since He is the Son, the natural heir, the one Who alone knows the Father even as the Father knows Himself ; Who is our King by *right of conquest,* since He came to save that which was lost, and since He shed His blood for the remission of our sins. [7] He is a King utterly devoted to His subjects, a King Who loves the lowly, the poor, the forsaken ; a King Who goes after the lost sheep to bring it back to the fold ; a King Who upon the Cross pardons His very executioners. [8]

---

[1] POURRAT, *Christian Spirituality,* P. I. — [2] *Matth.,* XXV, 34.
[3] TANQUEREY, *Synop. Theol. Fundam.,* n. 608-611, in which many texts are quoted in support of this assertion.
[4] *Matth.,* VI, 9-10 ; XXVI, 29.
[5] *Matth.,* V, 16, 45. — [6] *Matth.,* XXV, 41.
[7] *Matth.,* XI, 27 ; XIV, 33 ; XVI, 16 ; XX, 28 ; XXV, 31, 34, 40 ; *Luke,* X, 22 ; XIX, 10 ; XXII, 20 ; XXIII, 2, 3.
[8] *Matth.,* IX, 13, 36 ; X, 6 ; XVIII, 12-24 ; XIX, 14 ; *Mark,* II, 16 ; *Luke,* XI, 12, etc.

1*

But He is also the Judge of the living and the dead. On the Last Day He will separate the good from the bad; the just He will receive into His abiding kingdom, but the wicked He will condemn to the eternal fires of hell.[1] Hence, there is nothing in this world of greater value than this kingdom. This is indeed the pearl of great price, the hidden treasure to be obtained at any cost.

C) **Conditions of admission.** Admittance to the kingdom is gained through penance,[2] baptism, belief in the Gospel, and observance of the commandments.[3]

But the ideal proposed to the members of the kingdom is the imitation, as far as this is possible, of God's Own perfection. Since we have been made His children, we must strive to live up to our dignity and to model our conduct on the divine perfections : " Be you therefore perfect, as also your heavenly Father is perfect. "[4]

In order to reach so high an ideal, two essential conditions must be fulfilled. We must *renounce* self and creatures and thus detach ourselves from whatever constitutes an obstacle to union with God. Moreover, we must *love* God and give ourselves entirely to Him by imitating Our Lord : " If any man will come after me, let him deny himself and take up his cross and follow me. "[5]

a) **Renunciation** has its degrees. In every case it must exclude that disordered love of self and of creatures which constitutes sin, and it must above all rule out grievous sin, which is an absolute obstacle to the attainment of our destiny. So true is this, that should our right eye be a source of scandal to us, we must not hesitate to pluck it out : " And if thy right eye scandalize thee, pluck it out and cast it from thee. "[6] For those who would become *perfect*, renouncement must be still more absolute. It must embrace the practice of the evangelical counsels, *real* poverty, the giving up of family ties, and perfect chastity or continence.[7] Those who are unwilling or unable to carry their renouncement so far as this will content themselves with an *interior* renunciation of family ties and of worldly goods; they will live in the spirit of poverty and of interior detachment from whatever militates against the reign of God in their soul. They can even thus attain to a high degree of holiness.[8]

These manifold degrees of renunciation are grounded in the distinction between precepts and counsels : to enter into life it suffices for us to keep the commandments; but to be perfect one must sell one's goods and bestow them on the poor : " If thou wilt enter into life, keep the commandments... if thou wilt be perfect, go sell what thou hast and give to the poor. "[9]

Perfect renunciation goes as far as the *love of the Cross* : " Let him take up his cross. " One comes to love the cross, not indeed in and for itself, but because of the Crucified Christ Whom one would follow unto the end : " And follow me. " Nay more, one finally finds joy in the Cross : " Blessed are the poor in spirit... Blessed are the meek... Blessed are those who suffer persecution... Blessed are ye when they shall revile you. "[10]

---

[1] *Matth.*, XXV, 31-46.
[2] *Matth.*, IV, 17; *Mark*, I, 15; *Luke*, V, 32.
[3] *Mark*, XVI, 16; *Matth.*, XXVIII, 19-20.
[4] *Matth.*, V, 48. — [5] *Luke*, IX, 23. — [6] *Matth.*, V, 29.
[7] *Matth.*, XIX, 16-22; *Luke*, XIV, 25-27; *Matth.*, XIX, 11-12.
[8] *Matth.*, V, 1-12. — [9] *Matth.*, XIX, 16-22. — [10] *Matth.*, V, 3-12.

b) However, renunciation is only a means of attaining to the *love of God and the love of the neighbor* for God's sake. In truth, love sums up the whole law : " In these two commandments dependeth the whole law and the prophets. "[1] It is love that makes us yield ourselves to God with all our heart, with all our soul, with all our mind : " Thou shalt love the Lord thy God with thy whole heart and with thy whole soul and with thy whole mind... And the second is like to this : thou shalt love thy neighbor as thyself. "[2] This is the greatest of all the commandments, the one which embodies all perfection.

1) This love must be a *filial* love. It moves us to glorify first of all our Heavenly Father : " Our Father... hallowed be thy name, thy kingdom come. "[3] And in order that we give Him glory in a more perfect way, it prompts us to keep His commandments : " Thy will be done on earth as it is in heaven... Not everyone that saith to me, Lord, Lord, shall enter into the kingdom of heaven : but he that doth the will of my Father. "[4]

2) It must be a *confiding* love for the Heavenly Father cares for His children far more than He does for the birds of the air and the lilies of the field : " Are not you of much more value than they? For your Father knoweth that you have need of all these things. "[5] This confidence is shown by prayer, which, according to the promises of the Divine Mediator, obtains all that is properly asked for : " Ask, and it shall be given you : seek, and you shall find : knock, and it shall be opened to you. For every one that asketh, receiveth : and he that seeketh, findeth : and to him that knocketh, it shall be opened. "[6]

3) This love begets *love of the neighbor*. Since we are all children of the same Heavenly Father, we are all brethren : " For one is your master : and all you are brethren. "[7] In order to impart to this virtue the greatest possible motivating power, Our Lord declares that on the day of judgment He shall consider as done unto Himself every service rendered to the least of His brethren.[8] He identifies Himself with His members, and so in loving the neighbor, it is Christ Himself Whom we love. This love includes even our *enemies*, with whom we must patiently bear, for whom we must pray, and to whom we must do good.[9] It must therefore be accompanied by meekness and humility, even as was the love of Our Divine Model : " Learn of me because I am meek and humble of heart. "[10]

Renunciation and love, then, are the two essential conditions of admittance into the Kingdom of God and of attaining to perfection. We have seen elsewhere (n. 309 and foll.) how they include all the virtues.

2° THE SPIRITUALITY OF ST. PAUL[11]

By a different procedure St. Paul arrives at the same conclusions as the Synoptics. The central idea with him is not indeed the Kingdom, but the *saving plan of God* Who desires to save and to sanctify *all* men, Jews and Gentiles, through His Son, Jesus Christ, made the Head of the human race and into Whom we must all be incorporated :

---

[1] *Matth.*, XXII, 40. — [2] *Matth.*, XXII, 36-40. — [3] *Matth.*, VI, 9.
[4] *Matth.*, VII, 21. — [5] *Matth.*, VI, 26-33. — [6] *Matth.*, VII, 7-8.
[7] *Matth.*, XXIII, 8. — [8] *Matth.*, XXV, 40. — [9] *Matth.*, V, 44.
[10] *Matth.*, XI, 29.
[11] PRAT, *Theology of St. Paul;* POURRAT, *Christian Spirituality;* DUPERRAY, *Christ in the Christian Life.*

" Blessed be the God and Father of our Lord Jesus Christ, who hath blessed us with spiritual blessings in heavenly places, in Christ... in Whom we have redemption through his blood... and he hath subjected all things under his feet and hath made him head over all the church. "[1]

Thus, from all eternity God wills to sanctify us and to adopt us as His children. But an obstacle stands in the way — *sin, original sin*, committed by Adam, the first head of the human race and transmitted to his descendants together with concupiscence, that law of the flesh that holds us captive under the law of sin. God however takes pity on man. He sends him a Redeemer, a Savior, Who will be the new Head of the race and Who will reclaim us through His obedience unto death, even the death of the Cross. Jesus then will be the center of our lives ; " For to me, to live is Christ. "[2] His merits and His satisfactions are applied to us especially through *Baptism* and the *Holy Eucharist*. Baptism regenerates us, incorporates us into Christ and makes us new men, who under the guidance of the Holy Ghost must fight relentlessly against the flesh, the Old Adam. [3] The Holy Eucharist makes us share more abundantly in the death and in the life of Our Lord, in His inner sentiments and in His virtues. [4]

But in order to receive these Sacraments with profit, in order to foster the Divine Life which they impart, we must live a life of faith : " The just man liveth by faith. "[5] We must place all our confidence in God and in Our Lord, and we must above all practise that most excellent of all virtues, charity, which will indeed be one of our joys in heaven, [6] but which now in this valley of tears exacts the crucifixion of nature. [7]

All these ascetical practices are summed up in a formula recurring again and again in the writings of the Apostle : we must incorporate ourselves more and more into Christ Jesus and therefore put off the Old Man with all his tendencies to evil, and *put on the New Man with all His virtues* : " Stripping yourselves of the old man with his deeds, and putting on the new, him who is renewed unto knowledge, according to the image of him that created him. "[8]

A) First of all, *we must put off the Old Adam.* **a**) This Old Adam, which is also called the *flesh*, is our nature, not indeed as it is in itself, but as vitiated by the threefold concupiscence. Consequently, the works of the flesh are the sins man commits, not only those of sensuality and lust, but those also of pride in its various forms. [9]

b) We are under a *strict obligation* of mortifying or crucifying the flesh, an obligation based on two chief reasons : 1) The danger of consenting to sin and of being damned ; for the flesh, or concupiscence which has not been destroyed by Baptism, urges us on with violence to sin, and it will enslave us under the law of sin if we do not combat it relentlessly with the help of God's grace : " Who shall deliver me from the body of this death? The grace of God, by Jesus Christ our Lord. "[10] The second reason for mortification of the flesh is to be found in our *baptismal promises*.

We are dead to sin and have been buried with Jesus Christ through Baptism, and in order to live with Him of a new life, we pro-

---

[1] *Ephes.*, I, 3, 7, 22. The entire chapter should be read in order to obtain an idea of the basic notions of St. Paul's spirituality.
[2] *Phil.*, I, 21. — [3] *Rom.*, VI, 4 ; *Ephes.*, VI, 11-17.
[4] *I Cor.*, X, 14-22 ; XI, 17-22. — [5] *Rom.*, I, 17.
[6] *I Cor.*, XIII, 1-13. — [7] *Galat.*, V, 24. — [8] *Colos.*, III, 10.
[9] *Rom.* ,VIII, 1-16 ; *Galat.*, V, 16-25. — [10] *Rom.*, VII, 24-25.

mised to avoid sin and thereby to carry on a vigorous campaing against the *flesh* and the *devil.* [1] Life then, must be a combat, a struggle, the victor's reward being the crown of glory reserved unto us by the God of all justice and love. [2]

c) What sustains us in this struggle and what renders the victory relatively easy despite our weakness and our helplessness, is the grace of God merited by Jesus Christ. If we co-operate with it, we are sure of victory : "And God is faithful, who will not suffer you to be tempted above that which you are able : but will make also with temptation issue. [3] I can do all things in him who strengtheneth me. "

d) This mortification has two degrees : 1) There is the mortification necessary for the avoidance of mortal sin and reprobation : " I chastise my body and bring it into subjection : lest perhaps, when I have preached to others, I myself should become a castaway. " [4] 2) But there is also the mortification, which is profitable unto perfection, such as virginity, perfect humility, absolute disinterestedness. [5] From another point of view St. Paul distinguishes three degrees of mortification : *crucifixion* of the still recalcitrant flesh, then a species of *spiritual death*, and lastly, *burial.* [6]

B) By putting off the Old Adam we *incorporate* ourselves into Jesus Christ, we put on the *New Man.* This New Man is the Christian regenerated through Baptism, united to the Holy Ghost and incorporated into Christ, transforming himself under the influence of grace into Christ Jesus. In order to understand this doctrine thoroughly, it is necessary to explain the rôle of the Holy Ghost, of Christ, and of the soul itself in this new supernatural life.

a) The Holy Ghost, that is to say, the Most Blessed Trinity, dwells in the soul of the just and transforms it into a holy temple : " For the temple of God is holy, which you are. " [7] b) He operates in the soul, moves it by actual grace, gives it a filial trust in God the Father, and enables it to pray with singular efficacy : " God who worketh in you both to will and to accomplish... Whereby we cry : Abba (Father). The Spirit also helpeth our infirmity... Himself asketh for us with unspeakable groanings. " [8]

c) Christ is the Head of a mystical body whose members we are, and He imparts to us motion, direction and life. By *Baptism* we are incorporated into Him, and in *Holy Communion* we are associated with Him in His passion, which we commemorate, in His sacrifice, and in His risen life in which He makes us share while we await our entrance into heaven where we already dwell to some extent through hope : " For we are saved by hope. " [9] This communion is prolonged by a sort of spiritual communion whereby all through the day we make our own the thoughts and the affections of Our Lord : " For let this mind be in you which was also in Christ Jesus... And I live, now not I, but

---

[1] *Rom.*, VI, 1-23.
[2] *I Cor.*, II, 12; IX, 25; *Ephes.*, VI, 11-17; *II Tim.*, IV, 7; *I Tim.*, VI, 12.
[3] *I Cor.*, X, 13; *Phil.*, IV, 13. — [4] *I Cor.*, IX, 27.
[5] *I Cor.*, VII, 25-34; *Phil.*, II, 5-11; *I Tim.*, VI, 8.
[6] " They that are Christ's have crucified their flesh... For you are dead : and your life is hid with Christ in God... For we are buried together with him in baptism into death... " (*Galat.*, V, 24; *Colos.*, III, 3; *Rom.*, VI, 4). — The spiritual meaning of these texts is very well explained by Father Olier in his Christian Catechism, I, C. XXI-XXIII.
[7] *I Cor.*, III, 17. — [8] *Philip.*, II, 13. ; *Rom.*, VIII, 15, 26. — [9] *Rom.*; VIII, 24.

Christ liveth in me." [1] Thus, nothing can separate us from Him Who is our All : " Who then shall separate us from the love of Christ?" [2]

d) From this arises the duty of remaining closely united to Jesus, our Head, our Source of life, the perfect Model, whom we must constantly imitate until we be transformed into Him. 1) We must first of all imitate His *inner dispositions*, His *humility* and His *obedience :* " For let this mind be in you, which was also in Christ Jesus, who being in the form of God... emptied himself... becoming obedient unto death." [3] We must imitate His *charity* which prompted Him to sacrifice Himself for us : " Christ also hath loved us and hath delivered himself for us." [4] We must imitate His *exterior conduct* by practising modesty, bodily mortification, mortification of our vices and passions, in order thus to submit ourselves more completely to Jesus and His Holy Spirit : " Let your modesty be known to all men." [5]

This imitation of Christ admits of many degress. At first we are like children, thinking, speaking and acting as such. Then we begin to grow to perfect manhood, " unto a perfect man, unto the measure of the age of the fulness of Christ," [6] until we are completely transformed into Christ : " For to me, to live is Christ... But Christ liveth in me." [7] It is then that we can say to the faithful : " Be ye followers of me, as I also am of Christ." [8]

There is therefore no essential difference between the spirituality of St. Paul and that of the Synoptics. To put off the Old Adam is to practise renunciation, and to put on the New Man, the New Adam, is to unite oneself to Jesus Christ and through Him to God ; it is to love God and the neighbor.

3° THE SPIRITUALITY OF ST. JOHN

In the writings of St. John, the dominant idea is not that of the Kingdom, nor that of God's plan of sanctification for man. It is the *spiritual life*. He acquaints us with the *interior life of God*, of the *Incarnate Word*, of the *Christian soul.*

A) God is *life*, that is to say, light and love. He is a Father, and from all eternity He begets a Son, Who is none other than His Word. [9] Together with His Son, He is the source whence proceeds the Holy Ghost, the Spirit of truth and of love, Who completes the mission of the Incarnate Word by abiding with Christians until the end of time in order to enlighten and to strengthen them. [10]

B) God wills to communicate this life to men. Hence, He sends into the world His Own Son, Who by taking flesh becomes man, and by imparting to us His life makes us the adopted children of God. [11] Equal to the Father by nature, He openly proclaims His inferiority to Him as man and His utter dependence upon Him. He judges not, He speaks not, He acts not of Himself, but He conforms His judgments, His words and His actions to the good pleasure of the Father and thus manifests His love for Him. [12] He is obedient unto death in order to glorify His Father and to procure the salvation of men. [13]

1 *Philip.*, II, 5 ; *Galat.*, II, 20. — 2 *Rom.*, VIII, 35. — 3 *Phil.*, II, 5-11.
4 *Ephes.*, V, 2. — 5 *Phil.*, IV, 5. — 6 *Ephes.*, IV, 13.
7 *Phil.*, I, 21 ; *Galat.*, II, 20. — 8 *I Cor.*, IV, 16.
9 *John*, I, 1-5. — 10 *John*, XIV, 26 ; XV, 26 ; XVI, 7-15. — 11 *John*, I, 9-14.
12 *John*, V, 19, 30. — 13 *John*, X, 18.

With regard to us, He is : 1) the *light* that enlightens us and leads us unto life; [1] 2) the *Good Shepherd* Who feeds His sheep, protects them from the hungry wolf and lays down His life for them; [2] 3) the indispensable *Mediator* without Whom no one can go to the Father; [3] 4) the *Vine* whose branches we are, receiving from Him as we do our supernatural life. [4]

C) From Him, then, must flow our interior life, which consists in an intimate, affectionate union with Him, and through Him with God; [5] for He is the Way that leads to the Father. [6]

a) This union begins with *Baptism*, which gives us new birth, spiritual life, [7] which incorporates us into Christ, and enables us to bring forth fruit unto salvation. [8]

b) This union is strengthened by the reception of *Holy Communion*, which nourishes our soul with the Body and Blood of Christ, with His Divinity, with His whole Person, so that we live His very life, and live for Him even as He lives for His Father. [9]

c) This union is made abiding by a kind of *spiritual communion*, which causes Jesus to dwell in us and us in Him. [10] So close is this union, that Our Lord compares it with that existing between Himself and the Father : " I in them, and thou in me." [11]

D) This union enables us to share in the virtues of the Divine Master, above all in His *love for God* and *for men* carried to the point of *self-immolation*.

a) God loves us as His children. We love Him as Our Father. And because we love Him, we keep His commandments. [12] Thus, the Three Divine Persons come to dwell in our soul : " We will come to him and make our abode with him." [13] We must therefore love God because He is love — *God is charity* — and because He has loved us first, sacrificing even His Own Son for us. [14]

b) *Fraternal love* flows from the love of God. We must love our brethren not only as we love ourselves, but as Jesus has loved them. We must therefore be ready to sacrifice ourselves for them : " A new commandment I give unto you : That you love one another as I have loved you [15]... Because he hath laid down his life for us : and we ought to lay down our lives for the brethren." [16] In truth, we are all but one spiritual family whose father is God and whose savior is Jesus Christ. So close must our union be that it is likened to that existing between the Three Divine Persons : " That they may be one, as we also are one." [17] This virtue of the love of the neighbor is so necessary that to pretend to love God without loving the neighbor is a lie, [18] whereas fraternal charity is the surest guarantee of eternal life. [19]

St. John then, is the Apostle of *love*, the love he practised so well himself. But this love has its foundation in *faith*, particularly in belief in Christ, belief in His Divinity as well as in His Humanity. It presupposes the struggle against the threefold concupiscence, and hence, mortification. In this St. John agrees with the Synoptics and St. Paul, though he emphasizes *divine charity* more than they do.

---

[1] *John*, I, 9; VIII, 12. — [2] *John*, X, 11. — [3] *John*, XIV, 6.
[4] *John*, XV, 1-5. — [5] *John*, XV, 5-10. — [6] *John*, XIV, 6. — [7] *John*, III, 3.
[8] *John*, XV, 1-10. — [9] *John*, VI, 55-59. — [10] *John*, VI, 57. — [11] *John*, XVII, 23.
[12] *John*, XIV, 21. — [13] *John*, XIV, 23. — [14] *I John*., IV, 19.
[15] *John*, XIII, 34. — [16] *I John*, III, 16. — [17] *John*, XVII, 22.
[18] *I John*, IV, 20-21. — [19] *I John*, IV, 12-17.

According to the Synoptics, then, perfection consists in *renunciation;* according to St. Paul, in *incorporation into Christ,* which implies the putting off of the Old Adam and the putting on of the New; according to St. John, in *love* carried to the point of *sacrifice.* We have here fundamentally one and the same doctrine, but expressed in various terms and under different aspects, so that it can be easily adapted to the character and the training of each individual soul.

II. *The study of characters.* [1]

When speaking of self-knowledge, (n. 452) we said that a study of temperaments and characters would contribute greatly to our knowledge of self.

Frequently the two terms, temperament and character, are taken as synonymous. The distinction between them lies in this, that the former is the sum-total of those fundamental tendencies which flow from the *physiological* constitution of individuals, and the latter the sum-total of the *psychological* dispositions, based on temperament as modified by education and will-power, and made lasting by habit.

It will therefore prove more profitable to study characters than temperaments, for the important thing from the spiritual point of view is not so much physical temperament as the character of the soul. This fact was well understood in olden times, for in the description of various temperaments, the psychological rather than the physiological differences were stessed.

We shall limit ourselves here to the question of characters, and shall make use mainly of the admirable work of Father Malapert, *Les Eléments du Caractère,* simplifying, and at times correcting, his classifications. We shall give a brief explanation of the basis of our classification, and of the various characters that may be distinguished in relation to the three great activities of man.

1° BASIS OF OUR CLASSIFICATION OF CHARACTERS

A) When we wish to specify the principal tendencies which differentiate characters, the most reliable means is to study characters in relation to man's different activities. We shall not touch on the question of the purely *vegetative* activities of man, since they are of little importance from our point of view, and shall study the main characters in relation to *feeling,* to the *spiritual activities* of mind and will, and to *external activities.* A brief synoptic table will make clear our purpose.

---

[1] MALAPERT, *Les éléments du caractère et leurs lois de combinaison,* 1897; DEBREYNE-FERRAND, *La Théol. Morale et les sciences médic.,* Paris, 1884; p. 9-46; FOUILLÉE, *Tempérament et caractères,* 1895; PAULHAN, *Les Caractères,* 1902.

Characters in relation to	Feeling	Cold-blooded	Phlegmatic / Determined
		Hot-blooded	Emotional / Passionate
	Spiritual activities	of the Mind	Speculative or disinterested / Practical or interested
		of the Will	Masters of self / Masters of others
	External activities	Timid or reserved	
		Active	Restless / Men of action

B) Before we explain this classification, a few preliminary remarks are necessary :

a) The characters we are about to describe do not exist as so many pure types; rather, they possess characteristics of several types, and this in varying degrees. Thus, cold-blooded persons have not only the traits common to this type, but they experience also a certain amount of emotional activity. They are classified as cold-blooded, because this is their characteristic or *predominant* trait. The same is to be said of every other type; it is the predominance of one certain element which marks off the type from all others. Moreover, this predominant element admits of many degrees.

b) Again, each individual must be studied from the threefold point of view outlined above in the schematic chart. For instance, a cold-blooded person may be intellectual or volitional, just as an intellectual may be interested or disinterested in his pursuit of knowledge. One must therefore learn to take these different points of view into consideration before attempting to place a man in this or that category.

c) The characters we describe are not rigidly fixed types, but rather indications which may enable the spiritual director to observe and to understand better the peculiarities of each of his penitents. Final judgment must not be passed on a man's character after but a few conversations with him. Such snap judgments are generally faulty and must be revised. The process by which we really come to know a person's character must necessarily be slow, for it must be one of careful and studied observation of unnumbered actions and reactions.

d) Lastly, we must not forget to beg humbly, frequently and perseveringly for the lights of the Holy Ghost, for we need them in order to acquire a true knowledge of self and of others.

2° DIFFERENT TYPES OF CHARACTER IN RELATION TO FEELING.

Feeling is of course common to all human beings, but some persons have so little of it that they are called *cold-blooded*, while others, on the contrary, are called *hot-blooded*, precisely because in them feeling is so highly developed.

A) Cold-blooded persons have an abnormally low sensibility and little emotionalism. They have few desires, show little enthusiasm for anything, and are seldom aroused to passion. We can divide them into two classes : the phlegmatic and the determined.

a) The *phlegmatic* are slow and awkward in action. They are selfish, but not malicious, and so indifferent as to hardly feel the need of loving or of being loved. As a general rule, their judgment is sound, precisely because their passions lack intensity. They have little taste for active work, but when they must get down to it, they succeed best in those undertakings which demand patience rather than imagination and feeling.

As regards the *spiritual life*, they are not attracted to a high degree of virtue, but neither are they held back by violent passions. They are virtuous when not forced to contend against great temptations, but hardly know how to resist when dangerous occasions present themselves, or how to amend their lives when once they have fallen into habits of sin. They readily accept the spiritual advice given them, provided they are not asked to aim at a high degree of perfection, or urged onward too fast.

It is not among these that vocations to the priesthood or the religious life are to be sought. Such persons are fitted only for quiet professions which are not too exacting and which are compatible with the enjoyment of legitimate and moderate pleasure.

b) Persons who are cold-blooded but *determined* are indeed slow to action, but steady and methodical in their efforts. By dint of patient work they obtain notable results.

From the point of view of *intellect*, these persons possess little imagination or brilliancy, but they succeed in serious work which demands reflection, patience and methodical investigation.

From the *moral* point of view, they entertain no grand dreams, but they act from conviction, with steadiness of purpose, and are therefore capable of ttaining to a high degree of virtue. Hence, they offer excellent m..terial for the priesthood or the religious life once they have been imbued with profound convictions, love of duty for God's sake, and of the need of making constant and methodical efforts towards perfection. They proceed slowly, but surely : " Persistent labor overcomes all things. "

B) *Hot-blooded* natures, on the other hand, are characterized by a *predominance of feeling*. They sense keenly the need of loving and of being loved. In them it is the heart that rules. We may divide them into two classes : the *emotional* and the *passionate*.

a) Emotional persons are quick of movement; they have an engaging smile and a sprightly appearance. They love art in most of its forms. They are light-hearted and extremely changeable, giving themselves over readily to the most contrary emotions, and acting on the spur of the moment.

Gifted with a lively imagination and an ardent heart, they attain success in literary work, speak with great facility, and charm all with whom they come in contact.

From the *moral* point of view, they are easily drawn to sensual pleasure, to gluttony and to voluptuousness; but they quickly and sincerely repent of their faults, and just as quickly fall back into these same sins at the first opportunity. They have a good heart; they are quick to love and become very much attached to those who love them. They are frank and open in confession and spiritual direction, are readily convinced, and form good resolutions which they soon forget. It is by appealing to their heart that they are to be conquered and brought to God. If one succeeds in implanting in them an ardent love of Our Lord, one can turn them to good account. Through love they will make many sacrifices which at first seemed repugnant to their nature; through love they will pray, frequently receive Holy Communion, visit the Blessed Sacrament and practise works of zeal. But they must be taught to love God in dryness of soul and in suffering as well as in times of consolation. Little by little, under the influence of divine grace and of their own reflection, their emotions will yield to convictions, and while preserving all their former spirit, they will bring to their endeavors greater perseverance and constancy. If they can not acquire this energy and steadiness of purpose, they must not be encouraged to choose a state of life such as that of the priesthood, which requires a well-grounded and tried virtue.

b) *Passionate* natures are those in which deep and ardent passions hold sway. They may be reduced to three different types : the *melancholic*, the *sanguine* and the *choleric*.

1) Melancholic persons have a natural tendency to see the dark side of things, to dwell particularly on the difficulties and the unpleasant features of situations, and to exaggerate them. Hence, they are prone to sadness, to diffidence, to a kind of misanthropy. They suffer very much, and without intending it, make others suffer also.

Unless they seek consolation in God, Who alone can console them, and unless they dispel their gloomy thoughts, they fall an easy prey to weariness, discouragement and scrupulosity.

St. Teresa[1] maintained that persons who are highly predisposed to melancholy are not fit subjects for the religious life. Indeed, since melancholy implies a rather marked predominance of the imagination and the emotions over reason, it may after a time devolve into a sort of madness. At all events, in order to weaken such an unwholesome disposition, one must know how to treat such persons with great sympathy, but always with authority and firmness, not allowing them to follow their whims or act upon their suspicions. Since their judgment is not sufficiently clear, they must submit to the decisions of a spiritual director or some prudent friend.

2) *Sanguine* or *impulsive* persons are the ready prey of the first vivid impression that makes itself felt. They are expansive, volatile and spasmodic, passing quickly from gaiety to sadness, from hope to anxiety, from enthusiasm to discouragement. If contradicted or humiliated, they fly into a fit of passion and give vent to their spleen in violent words and gestures. In brief, they frequently lose their self-control and use harshly those about them.

In order to combat this defect, one must make constant and energetic use of the power of *inhibition*, check from the outset the first inordinate impulses, and reflect before acting; in a word, one must regain, little by little, control over self.

Unless a man succeeds in attaining mastery over nerves and emotions, he must not think of entering the priesthood, since violent anger; as St. Paul remarks, constitutes an insuperable impediment : " For a bishop must be without crime... not subject to anger... no striker." [2]

3) *Choleric* persons are those in whom passion is not only violent, as in sanguine natures, but also enduring. They are energetic, long-suffering and tenacious. Generally they are ambitious, and seek leadership and glory. They are destined to work a great deal of good

---

[1] *Foundations*, C. VII. — [2] *Titus*, I, 7.

or a great deal of harm. It all depends on whether they use their passions for their own selfish ends or for the glory of God and the good of souls. It is from their ranks that great conquerors and apostles come. Richly endowed as they are, one can make them render great service by keeping their eyes fixed on the glory of God and the conquest of souls, as was done for St. Francis Xavier by St. Ignatius of Loyola.

3° DIFFERENT TYPES OF CHARACTERS
IN RELATION TO THE SPIRITUAL FACULTIES OF MIND AND WILL

Those in whom the higher faculties of intellect and will predominate are naturally divided into two classes : the *intellectual* and the *wilful*, accordingly as it is the intellect or the will that has control.

A) The *intellectual* are those who are absorbed in the pursuit of knowledge. Among these however there are some of a *purely speculative* turn of mind, and others who are *less disinterested* and who are goaded on by *active hopes* and *practical ambitions*.

a) Those of the *purely speculative* type spend their lives in the construction of systems of thought. Such were, for example, Kant, Cuvier and Ampere. Some of them engage in thought for the sheer pleasure of thinking — art for art's sake — and thus fall into a dangerous form of *dilettantism* which may end in scepticism, as it did with Montaigne and Bayle.

b) The more *practical* and *ambitious* among the intellectuals are motivated by some *ardent passion*. There are those who while engaged in stirring up ideas within themselves also wish to stir up men, and consequently become passionately intent upon the triumph of some idea or some system of thought.

With either of these types, the purely speculative and disinterested, or the more practical and ambitious, we are dealing with men of great resources. The former however are liable to become too systematic, too abstract, and thus neglect the ordinary duties of life. The latter have need to place their knowledge and their activity at the service of God and truth, otherwise they may fall and cause others to fall into fearful excesses.

B) *Wilful* natures are endowed with a firm, tenacious, unbending will to which they subordinate all things. They divide into two groups : those who are *masters of self* and those who, being *men of action*, are *masters of others*.

a) The former bend their efforts especially on *mastering themselves*, and with this in view, on overcoming their passions. Hence, they strive with relentless energy to bring their feelings under control, and no one with a little power of observation can fail to notice the efforts they are making to hold themselves in check. This preoccupation creates in them a certain reserve, and at times even a certain rigidness accompanied by distrust of whatever might tend to make them lose their control over self. But once they have by dint of constant work gained complete victory, they become wonderfully even-tempered, and know how to harmonize firmness with gentleness.

From the *spiritual* point of view, their one great aim is to subject that strong and disciplined will to the will of God. Thus they acquire something of that perfect poise, that perfect subordination of faculties which man possessed in the state of original justice.

b) There is the other type of wilful characters which aims rather at *dominating others* than at mastering self. Persons of this type want to force their will on others and to rule over their equals. They keep their eyes constantly fixed on their objective; they do not allow obstacles to discourage them, and they never give up until they have had their way.

Such persons are evidently energetic and persevering and can be made to render great service. But they must master themselves before they attempt to master others; they must devote their energies to the service of God and the good of souls, and learn how to unite mildness with firmness in the exercise of their authority.

4° DIFFERENT TYPES OF CHARACTERS IN RELATION TO EXTERNAL ACTIVITIES

Here we meet with two types : the *timid* or reserved, and the *active*.

A) The *timid* are over-diffident, have little initiative, and seem paralyzed in their undertakings by the fear of failure. They succeed well only when given proper direction and when supported and encouraged by superiors or friends who can inspire them with confidence and help them to acquire a certain amount of assurance.

From the supernatural point of view, they must be drilled in the virtue of trust in God and reminded constantly that God makes use of even the poorest instruments, provided only that, conscious of their insufficiency, they seek support in Him Who alone can strengthen them : " The weak things of the world hath God chosen, that He may confound the strong [1]... · I can do all things in him who strengtheneth me. " [2]

B) The *active* have a natural penchant for action. They are enterprising, bold, courageous and energetic, and must of necessity find an outlet for their surplus energy. Among these latter, the *restless* expend their forces in feverish activity, the *men of action* in well-planned efforts.

a) The *restless* are so strongly attracted to activity in some form or other that they cannot remain quiet. They want to act at all costs, even before they have formulated or matured a plan of action. Forever in quest of new projects, they lack the time to accomplish any one of them. They rush about here and there, and never really settle down anywhere. They make a good deal of noise and accomplish rather little. They are at the service of everybody, but soon forget the promises they have made.

In order that they may benefit by their tremendous store of energy and their desire for activity, they must learn to reflect before acting, to allow their plans to ripen before putting them into execution, to seek competent counsel from those wiser and more experienced than themselves. Once the stage has been set, they must apply themselves to their task, and until this has been accomplished, to no other enterprise. Reflection and constancy are for them the essential conditions of success.

b) *Men of action* meditate a long time on their projects before putting them into execution. They weigh carefully the reasons for and against; they think not only of the means to be used, but also of

---

[1] *I Cor.*, I, 27. — [2] *Phil.*, IV, 13.

the obstacles to be encountered; they organize everything in the light of the end to be attained, no matter what may be the difficulties.

Such a disposition is a priceless asset to social workers and to priests, and should be cultivated by them. But in order that their well-planned undertakings be productive of good results, they must make sure, through prayer and the practice of the interior life, that they have God on their side. To be *Christian* men of action, they must become men of prayer. God and man, grace and human endeavor, will thus unite harmoniously in them unto the accomplishment of excellent results : " For we are God's coadjutors. " [1]

In concluding, let us bear in mind that in reality most characters are the product of the combination of many different types, and that it is by striving to acquire those qualities which one has not received as a heritage that one succeeds in overcoming natural defects, in acquiring proper balance and in producing the best results. The cold-blooded, for instance, should force themselves to acquire a little more of feeling ; the intellectual should cultivate will-power and action ; the wilful should reflect before acting, and employ gentleness in the exercise of their power. Through effort and the grace of God we can do much to perfect our temperament and develop a well-balanced character. This will become clear from the study of the Spiritual Ways.

---

[1] *I Cor.*, III, 9.

ALPHABETICAL INDEX [1]

Abandonment (holy), 492, 757, 1232, 1432, 1447, 1474.

Abnegation, see *self-denial, mortification*.

Abstinence, prolonged, 1521.

Acts : every good act is meritorious, satisfactory and impetratory, 228; meritorious acts, 228; see *merit*. — Necessity of sanctifying our acts, 246-248; see 561; how to transform our acts into prayers, 522-529.

Adam, his preternatural and supernatural gifts, 61-66; his fall and punishment, 67-76.

Adoption, divine, contrasted with human adoption, 93.

Adoration, the first act of prayer, 503-504; duty towards the Blessed Trinity dwelling in us, 99; an act of religion, 1047; the first point of meditation, 697.

Advent, a time of penance, 1581.

Affective prayer, 975-996.

Ambition, 828.

Angels : their office in the Christian life, 183-188; their relation to God, 183; to Jesus Christ, 184, to men, 185. — *Guardian angels* and our duties towards them, 186-187.

Apostleship and **Personal Holiness**, 611-615.

Apostolic zeal : a professional duty of priests, 398-401; a duty of charity for the faithful, 366; how to sanctify it, 611-615.

Apparitions, supernatural, 1491.

Aridity, see *dryness*.

Ascetical theology : its names, 3; its place in theology, 4; its relation to dogmatic and moral theology, 6; difference from mystical theology, 10-11; sources, 12-24; method, 25-33; excellence, 34; necessity for priests, 35-37; usefulness for the faithful, 38; how to study it, 39-41; objections made against it, 42-43; divisions, 44-48.

Attention, required in prayer, 654-656.

Attributes, divine, stimulate love for God, 436.

Avarice : its nature, 891-893; its malice, 895-896; remedies, 897-898.

Baptism, incorporates us into Christ, 146; regenerates us, 232, 251.

Beatitudes, 1361.

Beginners, in the way of perfection, 340-341, 636; various classes, 637-639; their spiritual exercises, 657-663; their meditation,, 668, 679-702; their practice of the various virtues, see virtues of *penance*, 705-750, *mortification*, 751-817, *religion*, 1053, *obedience*, 1062, *fortitude*, 1078-1079, *patience*, 1089, *humility*, 838-844, *meekness*, 861-863, *faith*, 1180, *hope*, 1201, *love of God*, 1225-1226, *love of neighbor*, 1241-1245.

Body, mystical, see *Jesus Christ*.

Call to **contemplation**, 1406-1416, 1558-1567.

Capital sins, see *sin*.

Character, good and bad, 456.

Charity, see *love*.

Chastity, vow of, 370; virtue of : notion and degrees, 1100-1107; means of practising it, 1108-1126.

Children, duty towards parents, 593.

Christ, see *Jesus Christ*.

Church, filial love for, 1326.

Communion, holy, a powerful means of sanctification, 277-280; dispositions for, 283-288. — Communion, the second point of mental prayer, 697-699, 995.

Concupiscence, struggle against the threefold concupiscence, 192-209; concupiscence of the *flesh* : its dangers and remedies, 193-198; of the *eyes*, 199-203; of the *mind* (pride), 204-209. — See also, 324-326, *mortification of passions, capital sins*.

Conferences, spiritual, 578.

Confession, dispositions for, 262-265.

Confirmation, 252.

Conformity to **God's will**, a means of perfection, 478. It means *doing* God's will as made known by precepts, counsels, inspirations of grace, rules, 479-485. — It means *submission* to God's will, 486-488; degrees of conformity, 492; how it sanctifies us, 493-498.

Consecration to **Mary**, 170-176.

---

[1] References are to the numbers not to pages.

15*

Redemption, work of justice and love, 77-81; effects of, 82-85.

Religion, virtue of, its nature and acts, 1046-1048; importance, 1049-1051; practice of, 1052-1056.

Religious, their obligation to strive after perfection, 367-373; duty to obey superiors and rules, 371, 374-376.

Resolutions, to be taken in meditation, 690, 694, 701.

Retreats, spiritual, foster desire for perfection, 427.

Revelations, private, their nature, 1490-1496; practical rules, 1497-1513.

Rule of life, its usefulness, 558-564; qualities, 565-568; how to observe it, 569. — Rules of Religious Orders, 373-376.

Sacraments, means of sanctification, 249-258; dispositions for fruitful reception, 259-261. — See *Confession, Communion,* etc.

Sacrifice, see *Mass.*

Saints, the, the reading of their Lives, 23, 30, 40; their place in the Christian life : veneration, invocation, imitation of, 177-182.

Sanctity, see *perfection.*

Scripture, Holy, a source of Ascetical and Mystical Theology, 13-17, 22; the Word of God, 1326; devout reading of, 574-576.

Scruples, their nature, degrees, subject-matter, good and bad effects, remedies, 934-950.

Self-Denial, see *mortification.*

Selfishness and Asceticism, 43.

Self-Sacrifice essential to perfection, 322-334.

Senses, mortification of, 771-783; application of senses a method of mental prayer, 991-992.

Sensuality, an obstacle to perfection; mortification of, 193-198.

Simplicity, prayer of, see *prayer.*

Sin, notion and kinds, 707-709. — Mortal sin, in the eyes of God, in itself, in its effects, 711-723. — Venial sin, of surprise and frailty, of deliberation; malice and effects, 724-735. — Confession of sins, 262-264; sorrow for sin, 266-269; reparation of, see *penance.* — Prevention of, see *mortification, sin, temptations.* — Capital sins, notion and number, 818-819; struggle against them, 820-898. — See *pride, envy,* etc. — Original sin, its consequences, 67-75.

Sloth, a capital vice, its nature, malice, remedies, 883-890.

Spiritual reading, 573-583.

Submission to God's will, 478-498.

Supernatural, notions and kinds; gifts of Adam, 59-66. — Supernatural life, see *life.*

Temperament and character, influences in contemplation, 1563.

Temperance, virtue of, 1099. — See *gluttony, mortification.*

Temptation, notion, purpose, frequency, three phases, how to deal with them, 900-919; their source : concupiscence, world, devil, 193-227. — Special temptations of beginners, 920-950; of souls in the illuminative way, 1262-1280; of souls in the unitive way, 1426.

Thanksgiving, after Holy Communion, 284-288; one of the acts of prayer, 522-529.

Theology, dogmatic, moral, ascetical, mystical; their relations, methods, 4-8, 25-34.

Tongue, mortification of, 777-778, 1116; sins of, 1043-1044.

Tradition, a source of Ascetical, Mystical Theology, 17-22.

Trials, a means of perfection, 428; passive trials, 1420-1434, 1463-1468.

Trinity, Blessed, indwelling in us; our duties to the Three Divine Persons, 90-101.

Understanding, Gift of, 1344-1347, 1356.

Union, of soul with Christ by Holy Communion, 277-282; of soul with God by grace, 90-118, 115-119; union perfected by prayer, 519-521; union with Christ by grace, 142-148; with God in the unitive way, 1290, 1448-1462, 1469-1479; practice of union with Our Lord, in meditation, 77, in doing penance, 737-738, 743-744; in practice of mortification, 761-762, by making Him the center of our lives, 966-968; in practice of the virtues : of religion, 1054-1056, of obedience, 1063, of patience, 1090, of humility, 1141-1144, of meekness, 1160-1164. — See *Sacred Heart,* and numbers 85, 150-153, 207, 238, 246-248, 273-274, 340, 514, 567.

Unitive way, see *ways.*

Vice, see capital sins under *sin.*

Virginity, see *chastity.*

Virtue, in general : natural and supernatural, acquired and infused, 998-1002; growth and decline, mutual

><>◇><

If you have enjoyed this book, consider making your next selection from among the following . . .

Prices subject to change.

Moments Divine—Before the Blessed Sacrament. *Reuter* 8.50
Miraculous Images of Our Lady. *Cruz* 20.00
Miraculous Images of Our Lord. *Cruz* 13.50
Raised from the Dead. *Fr. Hebert* 16.50
Love and Service of God, Infinite Love. *Mother Louise Margaret* 12.50
Life and Work of Mother Louise Margaret. *Fr. O'Connell* 12.50
Autobiography of St. Margaret Mary. 6.00
Thoughts and Sayings of St. Margaret Mary 5.00
The Voice of the Saints. *Comp. by Francis Johnston* 7.00
The 12 Steps to Holiness and Salvation. *St. Alphonsus* 7.50
The Rosary and the Crisis of Faith. *Cirrincione & Nelson* 2.00
Sin and Its Consequences. *Cardinal Manning* 7.00
Fourfold Sovereignty of God. *Cardinal Manning* 5.00
Dialogue of St. Catherine of Siena. *Transl. Algar Thorold* 10.00
Catholic Answer to Jehovah's Witnesses. *D'Angelo* 12.00
Twelve Promises of the Sacred Heart. (100 cards). 5.00
Life of St. Aloysius Gonzaga. *Fr. Meschler* 12.00
The Love of Mary. *D. Roberto* 8.00
Begone Satan. *Fr. Vogl* 3.00
The Prophets and Our Times. *Fr. R. G. Culleton* 13.50
St. Therese, The Little Flower. *John Beevers* 6.00
St. Joseph of Copertino. *Fr. Angelo Pastrovicchi* 6.00
Mary, The Second Eve. *Cardinal Newman* 3.00
Devotion to Infant Jesus of Prague. *Booklet* .... .75
Reign of Christ the King in Public & Private Life. *Davies* 1.25
The Wonder of Guadalupe. *Francis Johnston* 7.50
Apologetics. *Msgr. Paul Glenn* 10.00
Baltimore Catechism No. 1 .... 3.50
Baltimore Catechism No. 2 .... 4.50
Baltimore Catechism No. 3 .... 8.00
An Explanation of the Baltimore Catechism. *Fr. Kinkead* 16.50
Bethlehem. *Fr. Faber* 18.00
Bible History. *Schuster* 13.50
Blessed Eucharist. *Fr. Mueller* 9.00
Catholic Catechism. *Fr. Faerber* 7.00
The Devil. *Fr. Delaporte* 6.00
Dogmatic Theology for the Laity. *Fr. Premm* 20.00
Evidence of Satan in the Modern World. *Cristiani* 10.00
Fifteen Promises of Mary. (100 cards). 5.00
Life of Anne Catherine Emmerich. 2 vols. *Schmoeger* 37.50
Life of the Blessed Virgin Mary. *Emmerich* 16.50
Manual of Practical Devotion to St. Joseph. *Patrignani* 15.00
Prayer to St. Michael. (100 leaflets) 5.00
Prayerbook of Favorite Litanies. *Fr. Hebert* 10.00
Preparation for Death. (Abridged). *St. Alphonsus* 8.00
Purgatory Explained. *Schouppe* 13.50
Purgatory Explained. (pocket, unabr.). *Schouppe* 9.00
Fundamentals of Catholic Dogma. *Ludwig Ott* 21.00
Spiritual Conferences. *Tauler* 13.00
Trustful Surrender to Divine Providence. *Bl. Claude* 5.00
Wife, Mother and Mystic. *Bessieres* 8.00
The Agony of Jesus. *Padre Pio* 2.00

Prices subject to change.

Prices subject to change.

Prices subject to change.

Hail Holy Queen (from *Glories of Mary*). *St. Alphonsus* 8.00
Novena of Holy Communions. *Lovasik* 2.00
Brief Catechism for Adults. *Cogan*............................... 9.00
The Cath. Religion—Illus./Expl. for Child, Adult, Convert. *Burbach* 9.00
Eucharistic Miracles. *Joan Carroll Cruz*......................... 15.00
The Incorruptibles. *Joan Carroll Cruz* 13.50
Pope St. Pius X. *F. A. Forbes* 8.00
St. Alphonsus Liguori. *Frs. Miller and Aubin*....................... 16.50
Self-Abandonment to Divine Providence. *Fr. de Caussade, S.J.* 18.00
The Song of Songs—A Mystical Exposition. *Fr. Arintero, O.P.* 20.00
Prophecy for Today. *Edward Connor* 5.50
Saint Michael and the Angels. *Approved Sources* 7.00
Dolorous Passion of Our Lord. *Anne C. Emmerich*.................... 16.50
Modern Saints—Their Lives & Faces, Book I. *Ann Ball*................ 18.00
Modern Saints—Their Lives & Faces, Book II. *Ann Ball*............... 20.00
Our Lady of Fatima's Peace Plan from Heaven. *Booklet*................. .75
Divine Favors Granted to St. Joseph. *Père Binet*..................... 5.00
St. Joseph Cafasso—Priest of the Gallows. *St. John Bosco*............. 5.00
Catechism of the Council of Trent. *McHugh/Callan*.................. 24.00
The Foot of the Cross. *Fr. Faber.* 16.50
The Rosary in Action. *John Johnson* 9.00
Padre Pio—The Stigmatist. *Fr. Charles Carty* 15.00
Why Squander Illness? *Frs. Rumble & Carty*....................... 2.50
The Sacred Heart and the Priesthood. *de la Touche* 9.00
Fatima—The Great Sign. *Francis Johnston* 8.00
Heliotropium—Conformity of Human Will to Divine. *Drexelius* 13.00
Charity for the Suffering Souls. *Fr. John Nageleisen* 16.50
Devotion to the Sacred Heart of Jesus. *Verheylezoon* 15.00
Who Is Padre Pio? *Radio Replies Press* 2.00
Child's Bible History. *Knecht*.................................... 5.00
The Stigmata and Modern Science. *Fr. Charles Carty* 1.50
The Life of Christ. 4 Vols. H.B. *Anne C. Emmerich*.................. 60.00
St. Anthony—The Wonder Worker of Padua. *Stoddard*................. 5.00
The Precious Blood. *Fr. Faber* 13.50
The Holy Shroud & Four Visions. *Fr. O'Connell* 2.00
Clean Love in Courtship. *Fr. Lawrence Lovasik* 2.50
The Prophecies of St. Malachy. *Peter Bander.* 7.00
St. Martin de Porres. *Giuliana Cavallini* 12.50
The Secret of the Rosary. *St. Louis De Montfort*..................... 5.00
The History of Antichrist. *Rev. P. Huchede*......................... 4.00
St. Catherine of Siena. *Alice Curtayne* 13.50
Where We Got the Bible. *Fr. Henry Graham* 6.00
Hidden Treasure—Holy Mass. *St. Leonard*......................... 5.00
Imitation of the Sacred Heart of Jesus. *Fr. Arnoudt* 15.00
The Life & Glories of St. Joseph. *Edward Thompson*.................. 15.00
Père Lamy. *Biver.* 12.00
Humility of Heart. *Fr. Cajetan da Bergamo* 8.50
The Curé D'Ars. *Abbé Francis Trochu*............................. 21.50
Love, Peace and Joy. (St. Gertrude). *Prévot* 7.00

At your Bookdealer or direct from the Publisher.
Call Toll-Free 1-800-437-5876.

Prices subject to change.

ABOUT THE AUTHOR

Fr. Adolphe Tanquerey (1854-1932) is most familiar to American readers as the author of the classic *The Spiritual Life,* a work which he produced toward the end of his fruitful writing and teaching career.

Adolphe Tanquerey was born on May 1, 1854 at Blainville, France and was baptized the same day. His father died when Adolphe was very young, and the boy was raised by his devout mother. From the age of six he wanted to be a priest, missionary and martyr. He saw in the priesthood, with its consuming zeal and sacrifice, the work of works. He entered the seminary at age 18 and joined the Society of St. Sulpice, the Sulpicians. During these years his devotion to the Sacred Heart of Our Lord and to the Blessed Virgin Mary grew and deepened. The seminarian was sent to study in Rome and then was ordained at St. John Lateran on April 20, 1878. That same year he gained a twofold doctorate in Theology and Canon Law and was soon given a teaching assignment.

Fr. Tanquerey had an extraordinary talent for teaching. He influenced his students by his great supernatural spirit, his attractive good nature and the brilliant light he threw on questions of theology. His students loved him.

From 1887-1903 Fr. Tanquerey was assigned to the Sulpician seminary in Baltimore, Maryland, where he taught Dogmatic Theology and Moral Theology and for one year served as Vice Rector. Here too he was beloved by all. Students would corner him outside of class to continue the eager discussions they had begun during class time.

Fr. Tanquerey produced a number of famous theology works: *Synopsis Theologiae Dogmaticae* (3 vols.), *Synopsis Theologiae Moralis et Pastoralis,* and, with the help of two other priests, *Brevior Synopsis Dogmatica* and *Brevior Synopsis Moralis.*

The Spiritual Life is known in its original French as *Précis de Théologie Ascétique et Mystique.* This work was a dream toward which Fr. Tanquerey had worked for many years. Within a few years of its publication it had sold a hundred thousand copies to clergy and faithful—an extremely impressive number. The book was translated into several languages. After this, Fr. Tanquerey published *Les Dogmes, Générateurs de la Piété.*

From 1903 to 1915 Fr. Tanquerey served at the seminary of St. Sulpice, Paris. His last great ministry was that of Superior at the Sulpician seminary at Issy between 1915-1927 (with an interruption during World War I). He derived great consolation from the work of forming young Sulpicians. He especially loved to pass on to them the spirituality of Fr. Olier and "the French

School," which he considered "so apt for forming good priests and interior souls."

Fr. Tanquerey was a diligent worker who continued his intellectual labors to the end of his life. He skillfully revised and amplified each new edition of his works, and he knew how to cull out and make use of the truth contained in sociology and other secular disciplines. He utilized the positive method and the speculative method without raising between them an airtight partition. In *The Spiritual Life,* Fr. Tanquerey mined the works of the principal authors on the spiritual life, methodically organized their teaching, took care to be both doctrinal and practical, and tied everything in with the teaching of St. Paul and St. John, as presented in the French school.

In 1927 Fr. Tanquerey was allowed to resign as Superior at Issy and retire to the Sulpician seminary at Aix in order to devote more time to publishing. He published a series of brochures for the formation of advanced souls and made himself available to help priests and seminarians with their studies and as director of souls.

From that year, Fr. Tanquerey began to prepare more particularly for death (which he had repeatedly prepared for by a yearly retreat). He wrote: "To raise my courage I recall that Jesus, not having been able to suffer in His own person the infirmities of age, willed to endure them in the person of Christians, especially priests, members of His Mystical Body. Since those infirmities have touched me, and since they can only increase as time goes on, I will to accept them bravely, joyfully, wholeheartedly."

After about a week of serious illness, Fr. Tanquerey gave his soul to God on Sunday, February 21, 1932. At his request his body was buried in the cemetery of Aix, in the tomb of the diocesan priests. Many beautiful tributes from Bishops and priests were received by the Sulpicians at his passing. Cardinal Lepicier expressed the belief that Fr. Tanquerey had increased a hundredfold the talents that God had entrusted to him.

The Vicar General of Aix said, "For several years we have benefitted from the exquisite nourishment of a substantial teaching which, month by month, this *vir doctus, robustus, validus* [learned, strong, orthodox man] did not stop feeding us. . . ." Addressing Fr. Tanquerey in spirit as "O Venerable Old Man," the Vicar General expressed the desire of all who had known him: "May we one day find you again more alive than ever in God and in Christ, whom you have taught us to serve better."

The above is excerpted and summarized from the brief biography circulated in the Sulpician Society after Fr. Tanquerey's death. (P. Boisard, "Tanquerey, Adolph," in *American Necrology of the Society of St. Sulpice,* ed. Vincent M. Eaton, S.S., Baltimore, 1991, pp. 263-270.)